A Library
of Literary
Criticism

A Library of Literary Criticism

VOLUME 4

Sahgal
to
Ziyadah

MODERN WOMEN WRITERS

Compiled and edited by
LILLIAN S. ROBINSON

A Frederick Ungar Book
CONTINUUM · NEW YORK

1996
The Continuum Publishing Company
370 Lexington Avenue
New York, NY 10017

Printed in the United States of America

Library of Congress Cataloging-in-Publication Data

Modern women writers / compiled and edited by Lillian S. Robinson.
     p.   cm. — (A library of literary criticism)
  "A Frederick Ungar book."
  Includes bibliographical references and index.
  ISBN 0-8264-0823-0 (set). — ISBN 0-8264-0813-3 (v. 1). — ISBN
0-8264-0814-1 (v. 2). — ISBN 0-8264-0815-X (v. 3).—ISBN 0-8264-0920-2 (vol. 4)
   1. Literature—Women authors—History and criticism.
  2. Literature, Modern—20th century—History and criticism.
  3. Women authors—Biography. I. Robinson, Lillian S. II. Series.
PN471.M62 1996
809'.89287'0904—dc20   94-43197
                                            CIP

AUTHORS INCLUDED

Volume 4

Sahgal, Nayantara	India
Salisachs, Mercedes	Spain
Sanchez, Sonia	U.S. (African American)
al-Sammān, Ghāda	Syria
Sandel, Cora (Sara Fabricius)	Norway
Sandoz, Mari	U.S.
Sarraute, Nathalie	France
Sarton, May	U.S.
Sata Ineko	Japan
Sayers, Dorothy L.	Great Britain
Schoultz, Solveig von	Finland
Schreiner, Olive	South Africa
Schwarz-Bart, Simone	Guadeloupe
Sebbar, Leila	Algeria
Seghers, Anna	Germany
Seidel, Ina	Germany
Senior, Olive	Jamaica
Serao, Matilde	Italy
Sexton, Anne	U.S.
al-Shaykh, Hanan	Lebanon
Shange, Ntozake	U.S. (African American)
Shen Rong	China
Sidhwa, Bapsi	Pakistan
Silko, Leslie Marmon	U.S. (Native American)
Silva, Clara	Uruguay
Sinclair, May	Great Britain
Sitwell, Edith	Great Britain
Slesinger, Tess	U.S.
Smedley, Agnes	U.S.
Smith, Pauline	South Africa
Smith, Stevie	Great Britain

Södergran, Edith	Finland
Somers, Armonía	Uruguay
Somerville and Ross	Ireland
Sono Ayako	Japan
Sontag, Susan	U.S.
Soriano, Elena	Spain
Sow Fall, Aminata	Senegal
Spark, Muriel	Great Britain
Stafford, Jean	U.S.
Stark, Freya	Great Britain
Stead, Christina	Australia
Stein, Gertrude	U.S.
Stern, G. B.	Great Britain
Stockenström, Wilma	South Africa
Storni, Alfonsina	Argentina
Struck, Karin	Germany
Suckow, Ruth	U.S.
Swenson, May	U.S.
Szymborska, Wislawa	Poland
Tafdrup, Pia	Denmark
Taggard, Genevieve	U.S.
Tan, Amy	U.S. (Asian American)
Taylor, Elizabeth	Great Britain
Teasdale, Sara	U.S.
Teliha, Olena	Ukraine
Telles, Lygia Fagundes	Brazil
Terry, Megan	U.S.
Thirkell, Angela	Great Britain
Thomas, Audrey	Great Britain
Thorup, Kirsten	Denmark
Tikkanen, Marta	Finland
Tlali, Miriam	South Africa
Tolstaya, Tatiana	Russia
Traba, Marta	Argentina
Treadwell, Sophie	U.S.
Triolet, Elsa	Russia–France
Trotzig, Birgitta	Sweden
Tsushima Yuko	Japan

Tsvetaeva, Marina	Russia
Tūqān, Fadwā	Palestine
Tusquets, Esther	Spain
Ty-Casper, Linda	Philippines
Tyler, Anne	U.S.
Tynan, Katharine	Ireland
Ukrainka, Lesya	Ukraine
Under, Marie	Estonia
Undset, Sigrid	Norway
Uno Chiyo	Japan
Valenzuela, Luisa	Argentina
Vega, Ana Lydia	U.S. (Puerto Rican)
Vilalta, Maruxa	Mexico
Villanueva, Alma	U.S. (Mexican American)
Villemaire, Yolande	Canada
Vorse, Mary Heaton	U.S.
Voznesenskaya, Iulia (Julia)	Russia
Waciuma, Charity	Kenya
Waddington, Miriam	Canada
Wakoski, Diane	U.S.
Walker, Alice	U.S. (African American)
Walker, Kath (Noonuccal, Oodgeroo)	Australia
Walker, Margaret	U.S. (African American)
Wang Anyi	China
Warner, Sylvia Townsend	Great Britain
Warner-Vieyra, Myriam	Guadeloupe
Watson, Sheila	Canada
Webb, Mary	Great Britain
Webb, Phyllis	Canada
Weil, Simone	France
Weldon, Fay	Great Britain
Welty, Eudora	U.S.
West, Jessamyn	U.S.
West, Rebecca (Cicily Isabel Fairfield)	Great Britain

Wharton, Edith	U.S.
White, Antonia	Great Britain
Wickham, Anna	Great Britain
Wilder, Laura Ingalls	U.S.
Williams, Sherley Anne	U.S. (African American)
Wilson, Ethel	Canada
Wiseman, Adele	Canada
Wittig, Monique	France
Wohmann, Gabriele	Germany
Wolf, Christa	Germany
Woolf, Virginia	Great Britain
Wright, Judith	Australia
Wylie, Elinor	U.S.
Xiao Hong	China
Xi Xi	China–Hong Kong
Yamamoto, Hisaye	U.S. (Asian American)
Yang Jiang (Chiang)	China
Yezierska, Anzia	U.S.
Yosano Akiko	Japan
Young, Marguerite	U.S.
Yourcenar, Marguerite	France
Zamora, Bernice	U.S. (Mexican American)
Zardoya, Concha	Spain
Zelda (Zelda Shneúrson Mishowsky)	Israel
Zhang Jie	China
Zhang Kangkang	China
Zhang Xinxin	China
Zhu Lin	China
Ziyadah, Mayy	Lebanon–Egypt

SAHGAL, NAYANTARA (INDIA) 1927–

Why do women write so poorly on politics? With a few exceptions—Mary McCarthy and Simone de Beauvoir—there is hardly any good political comment by women writers.

When one turns to India, the picture is even more bleak and disappointing. Though we have a band of fairly distinguished Indo-English women writers, they seem to shy away from current political problems.

There is, however, one big exception—Nayantara Sahgal. She is undoubtedly the only woman writer in English in India who is also a political columnist, whose newspaper articles (mostly in the *Sunday Standard*) are characterized by their topicality, simplicity and, above all, boldness. She makes a point of keeping in touch with the latest controversy and her writing is often courageous in the best tradition of liberal journalism. . . .

Mrs. Sahgal is nothing if not political and each one of her novels has a political substratum. If one speaks of politics as her "primordial predilection," the central core of her being, it wouldn't be an exaggeration. Politics is all pervasive in all of her books, as if by some divine fiat, peeping all through, through each chink, every crevice.

Permissive in outlook, she stands for the new humanism and a new morality, according to which woman is not to be taken a mere toy, an object of lust and momentary pleasure, but man's equal and honored partner, in word and deed, as against the inhuman, traditional postures; "old, impossible ideas," taboos and prejudices which were getting obsolete must be cast aside like old, worn out and torn clothes. . . .

Women's lot in India is still a matter of tears. But one cannot weep every day. Mrs. Sahgal has chosen to pursue a more honorable course, that of fighting it out with fire and fervor. All can cry. But how many can fight? Whereas Kamala Markandya has talent and Anita Desai sparks of genius, N. Sahgal has both talent and genius, which she uses largely in the service of humanity, as its heirophant. . . .

With the publication and debut of her third regular work of fiction: *Storm in Chandigarh* (1969), Nayantara Sahgal has made her position safe and secure among the major Indo-English novelists. The earlier two novels: *A Time to Be Happy* and *This Time of Morning,* afford a delectable reading, but in this novel she has a thought, she has maturity, she has objectivity, and she has spunk. As a writer, she never ceases to be adult. The stamp of good and sophisticated living runs through her pages. What T. S. Eliot calls Blake's "terrifying honesty" is there in abundance in her. It is a tour de force—a novel spotlighting the fearsome jungle of man-woman relationships. She loves

Hinduism, would not want to be anything else but a Hindu; she is very proud of her blue-blooded Brahminic descent and yet she does never feel hesitant in laying bare the tyranny of race and hollowness of religion.

Mrs. Sahgal has a mature, refined, and lyrical style. This is no gimmicky, cleverly intellectual writing. She is at ease with her medium and has confidence and insight as a writer. *Storm in Chandigarh* can be read, without its "Indo-English" tag, as a good modern English novel.

Shayam M. Asnani. *Indian Literature.* 16, 1973, pp. 36–39, 49, 60

Nayantara Sahgal has been active on the literary scene both as a creative writer and a political columnist for more than two decades. Though she is not the only writer to combine journalism with creative writing, she is the only one to interrelate and strengthen the two by a common concern. She has the unique distinction of being the only political novelist on the Indo-English literary scene. Her work has a strong realistic base and reflects not only her personal values but also the changing values of a society exposed for the first time to both freedom and power. The struggle is not between the old and the new but between dedication and power. Understandably, Nayantara Sahgal stresses the need for morality in political life deriving her beliefs as she does from Gandhian values. She is, however, in no way limited by them or by any other political ideology. If one is required to define her views Nayantara Sahgal has the conscience of a liberal and the spirit of a nonconformist.

What I found rewarding in her writings is a genuine concern for human values and human beings. Her characters come alive as individuals sensitive to their surroundings; her ideas are consistent, yet not obtrusive in their impact on the reader. Her work is specially enjoyable and meaningful when viewed in its totality. For various reasons her work has been slow to win critical acclaim. Chief among these is a fragmented approach to her work when critics have been content to view her either as a journalist or as a writer of the ironic mode. The predominantly autobiographical note of her writings has also hindered an objective assessment. . . .

Her novels reveal a deep understanding of the Indian situation and while recognizing the near desperate condition of its masses persist in an almost idealistic belief in the human being. What she has achieved for Indo-English fiction is the success of the down-to-earth attitude as a narrative technique combined with a solid intellectual content. In her hands the political novel has come of age.

Jasbir Jain. *Nayantara Sahgal* (London: Arnold-Heinemann, 1978), pp. 9–10

The eight novels that Nayantara Sahgal has written so far revolve around dual themes: first, the political one, that India is passing through a transitional period and Indians must adjust themselves to the changing times; second, that the lack of communication between people, especially between husband and wife, results in unhappiness and prevents human fulfillment. The novelist herself makes it clear that each novel "more or less reflects the political era we are passing through." But along with the political themes, she also portrays the modern Indian woman's search for individual freedom and self-realization. She delineates both the political and personal motif in a subtle manner, highlighted by an intricate and polished writing style.

Liberal in her outlook, Sahgal believes in the new humanism and new morality, according to which a woman is not to be taken as "a sex object and glamor girl, fed on fake dreams of perpetual youth, lulled into a passive role that requires no individuality," but as a man's equal and honored partner. There is a happy blend of two sensibilities in her work—the sensibility of an artist and that of a humanist. As a humanist she stands for an unfettered freedom and "pleads for the new marital morality, based on mutual trust, consideration, generosity, and absence of pretense, selfishness and self-centeredness." . . . She is intensely moral in her artistic vision and has great respect for the affirmative values of life, suggesting in *A Time to Be Happy* that "The world is in need of a universal culture, universal language, if not in literal terms, at least in terms of thought and values."

Her first novel, *A Time to Be Happy,* is primarily concerned with the sociopolitical life of the turbulent period of Indian history just before the advent of Independence. It throws broad hints about the novelist's advocacy of women's individual freedom, which becomes the central motif in the later novels. . . .

Through Sahgal's eight novels there has been a visible progression in her vision. In the earlier work the female characters have vaguely craved freedom and attempted to shake off orthodox conventions and moribund tradition, whereas in the later novels the women have freed themselves from bondage and regained their identity. Moreover, their freedom is no longer restricted to the superficial aspects, such as matters of dress, eating habits, smoking, drinking, but has enlarged to encompass the whole individual.

Ramesh Chadha. In Robert L. Ross, ed.
*International Literature in English: Essays
on the Major Writers* (New York: Garland,
1991), pp. 261–62, 267–68

SALISACHS, MERCEDES (SPAIN) 1916–

The first book that Mercedes Salisachs wrote was not, properly speaking, a novel, although it comes close to one. In its first appearance, it was entitled *Fohen,* and in its new version is called *Adan Helicoptero* (Adam helicopter).

The author has revised the original version, which I am not familiar with, and I limit myself, in this discussion, to the definitive edition.

Adan Helicoptero is a novelistic fantasy, a pageant of fine imaginative writing that encapsulates precisely what we have defined as Salisachs's best qualities. A frame-story situates the writer in a place whence she contemplates the history of the earth in a global vision that conflates past, present, and future. . . .

The writer's sharpness and ingenuity reaches its highest moments here. Given that all the characters, from whatever period they may be, and their comments lead to a very up-to-date satire or, what is better anyway, into an ironic vivisection of feelings, topics, concerns, human needs that are timeless. Salisachs's cerebral nature runs around at its ease in this book, untrammeled by subjection to immediate facts. Reality is like clay that the writer manipulates freely, the way a potter kneads his vases. . . .

Her ability to "define" is demonstrated in those two different prints called *La escuela internacional femenina* and *La escuela internacional masculina* (International feminine and international masculine schools). Other novelists are better able to give immediate life to that immense arsenal of "realities" that she accumulates in these pages; but her strength lies in this theorizing.

There are uneven chapters in *Adan Helicoptero,* but the good ones predominate. *La bolsa de costumbres* seems like a vision rooted in Quevedo's *Sueños:* a picture that's alive, animated, intentional, very good. The conversation of Juana of Naples and Henry VIII is delightful and mordant. In the chapter "What Shakespeare Didn't Say," she insists on a theme that is congenial to her: matrimonial disillusionment born of habit and vulgarity. She imagines Romeo and Juliet finally married and fallen, like birds out of the nest, from their original romanticism.

Juan Luis Alborg. *Hora Actual de la Novela*
Española, II (Madrid: Taurus, 1962),
pp. 403–4

In the second volume of *Situations,* Sartre indicated the principal characteristic of bourgeois literature, the spirit of analysis. In this spirit, "the components must necessarily be reduced to an ordering of simple elements, which unalterably retain their essential properties." This spirit excludes the perception of collective realities. But, also according to Sartre, in our time the analytic spirit is on the defensive.

The twenty-fourth "Planeta" prize, awarded for last year, has been given to the twelfth novel by Mercedes Salisachs, a novelist already known and well thought of within the publishing world, where her work began appearing about twenty years ago. In 1956, she won the "City of Barcelona" Prize for a novel, with one of her first books, *Una mujer llega al pueblo* (A woman comes to town). The following year, she began publishing her books with the Planeta publishing house, whose prize she has won—after having been a finalist before—with her latest publication, the voluminous *La Gangrena* (Gangrene), which implies the culmination of her career. The work of Mercedes Salisachs, appreciated by the general audience, has been ignored by the critics.

In a sense, Mercedes Salisachs and the Planeta Prize were destined to meet one day. This award presupposes a certain commercial flavor; this is not a criticism, but a definition. . . .

The five hundred and some pages of *La Gangrena* proclaim the vices and the virtues of bourgeois narrative, the triumph and servitude of traditional narrative. Everything is in its place, prepared and carefully calculated to provoke the planned effect. It is a question of the life of a man, a winner, who, from a modest and poor background, climbs the social ladder to end up at its pinnacle. Around him, in small doses, we see rapidly revealed the life of the collectivity that surrounds him: the history of Spain for the last half century. Characters, settings belonging to the Catalan bourgeoisie—in Barcelona, for the most part—combine to form a panorama.

But there is more: this character is a morally culpable being. In a sense, the best moments of the novel are encountered in this moral examination. The moral—if not religious—preoccupation constitutes a constant in Mercedes Salisachs's narrative, and her best depth is rooted in it. But at no time do we descend to analytic literature. The vision of the collective episodes—above all of war—is the loosest in the book. Which, for the rest, is a worthy, honestly made book, worked out with minuteness and sincerity. A model of consumer literature.

Rafael Conte. Insula. 353, April, 1976, p. 5

[*Carretera intermedia*] was a finalist for the Premio Planeta. Set on the Riviera, it is the story of Bibiana, a homely woman of 40, who has just recovered from a nervous breakdown suffered after the tragic accidental death of her child and the subsequent abandonment by her husband. She was also abandoned by the man she loved, who, because of religious scruples, did not sexually consummate that love. Bibiana is a unique protagonist for the period in that she has a profession; she is a chemist; but, although her profession played some role in her past—her husband accused her of neglecting their child for her laboratory—it is not important in the action of the narrative. There is more concern with the depiction of her loveless marriage, of her earlier reluctance to embark on an affair, and on her awakening to sex at a mature age. . . .

[*El volumen de la ausencia,* (The volume of absence)] which was on the best-seller list in Spain late in 1983 and early in 1984, tells the story of a middle-aged woman who has just been told that she has a terminal illness. In a walk through the streets of Barcelona, she evokes memories of her past and plans how she will live to the fullest her few remaining months of life. The omniscient narrator alternates with the directly quoted thoughts of the protagonist. Many times external stimuli—las Ramblas, an avenue—stimulate the memories. This work is often considered one of the best by the author, especially in its psychological portrayal.

Carolyn L. Galerstein, ed. *Women Writers of Spain* (Westport, Connecticut: Greenwood Press, 1986), pp. 286, 288

Salisachs was five years (1948–53) in writing this novel [*Primera mañana, última mañana*; First morning, last morning] which covers "fifty years in Spanish life in all of its aspects: social, artistic, human," and she considers it her best work. Some 430 pages of small print, the novel is narrated from the viewpoint of a male artist, and constitutes (according to the cover blurb) "an implacable portrait of the Madrid aristocracy and Catalan upper class." . . .

Vendimia interrumpida (1960; Interrupted wine harvest) is a personal favorite of the novelist, who considers it her most authentic work. *La estación de las hojas amarillas* (1963; The season of yellow leaves) is a love story, set during the Civil War, but the war is of little importance: what matters is the intimate psychology of the characters, the description of a world of selfish passions in conflict with more generous impulses that do not manage to prevail. In a sense, the relegation of the war to the background may be seen as symbolic. *El declive y la cuesta* (1966; The slope and the hillside) takes as its point of departure the "good thief," Dimas (converted to Christianity upon the cross), but concentrates upon his mother, who questions the meaning of her life, devoted to service to someone who dies as he did. *La última aventura* (1967; The last adventure) is another psychological study, linked to social problems, the story of a man in quest of an impossible happiness. An egotistical and shortsighted dreamer, he abandons his wife for the sake of a hoped-for new love, foredoomed to failure. Also during this period Salisachs produced a sort of do-it-yourself manual, *El gran libro de la decoración* (1969; The great book of decorating.) It would be six years, however, between *La última aventura* and her next novel.

Adagio confidencial (1973; Concert of confidences), a neoromantic work, and one of her most successful best-sellers, reissued in paperback, examines the casual encounter between a man and a woman who have not seen each other for twenty years. The dialogue between the couple, mature adults who evoke a past they can never quite forget, takes place in a few hours in an airport lounge, and constitutes an analysis of their frustrated relationship, as well as a clarification of many vague or misunderstood points concerning their mutual circle of friends in former years.

La gangrena (1975; Gangrene), the most famous and successful of Salisachs's novels, presents the thoughts of narrator-protagonist Carlos Hondero, jailed as a suspect in the murder of his second wife, Serena. During some three days he remembers essentially his entire life, beginning with a childhood spent with his beautiful mother (of the ruined Madrid aristocracy) and her lover, "Uncle" Rodolfo (who pays for Carlos's studies). The novel's historical framework includes the abdication of Alfonso XIII (introducing the Second Republic), the beginning and end of the Civil War, and events of the 1960s and early 1970s, such as the election of Pope Paul VI and the diplomacy of Henry Kissinger. This historical background is interwoven with a social fabric formed by more than one hundred characters, intended to permit situating Carlos within his sociohistorical context. A combination of internal monologue and dialogue, the novel shifts continually between past (Carlos's remembering) and present (his reflections while in jail). . . .

Viaje a Sodoma (1977; Trip to Sodom) has as its protagonist a boy, Jacobo, the hapless victim of his parents' divorce, who goes to spend a time with his uncle, a bohemian painter who lives a dissolute existence in a picturesque village on the Costa Brava. . . .

In 1978 Salisachs published a short-story collection, *El proyecto* (The project), and a year later, another novel, *La presencia* (1979; Presence). Following very much the plan of *Adagio confidencial,* this novel portrays a man and woman who meet in a village of the Costa Brava, and during the course of a few hours, evoke crucial moments of their lives. United by a common tragedy but separated by insuperable incompatibility, they mentally reconstruct the circumstances that produced their definitive separation. . . .

La sinfonía de las moscas (1982; Symphony of the flies) is set in Barcelona in the 1950s, the time when it was actually written; the author withheld it, fearing it would be censored. Essentially, the novel deals with the hopes and expectations of change introduced in the life of the protagonist, Julio (almost sixty and employed in a publishing house), when he receives the news that he has won approximately two million pesetas in the lottery. . . .

Without having a feminist thesis, [*El volumen de la ausencia* (The volume of absence)] is a profoundly feminist text.

> Janet Pérez. *Contemporary Women Writers*
> *of Spain* (Boston: Twayne, 1988), pp. 105–10

AL-SAMMĀN, GHĀDA (SYRIA) 1942–

The collection *Your Eyes Are My Destiny* contains sixteen stories, of which fourteen have women as their main subject, while two have men. This shows clearly enough that the major subject of the collection is woman herself. Even so, that subject has a number of different aspects, in that the writer can deal with the problems of women in general or with problems of Arab women in particular vis-à-vis their social situation and inner feelings. . . .

The style the author uses suits the peculiarities of the characters very well. We cannot reasonably expect a character who is extremely excitable to speak in a slow or relaxed fashion. As anyone will perceive in real life, emotional people tend to speak in an abrupt way without using the normal connectors of the language. Ghāda al-Sammān realizes this fact, and deliberately omits connections between phrases and sentences at points in the story that portray rising excitement. In fact, she even hurls the sentences at you in a rough and frenzied fashion to a degree that you the reader have no time to take a breath while reading. . . . She makes very little use of dialogue (and then it is interior) because it would lessen the intensity of the situation and would not suit the nature of such emotional characters. . . .

Not all the stories in this collection are of the same level of excellence. Some of them are genuinely brilliant, others are mediocre, and one is a failure, namely "The Baby with Burning Cheeks." . . . Each incident in the story is a separate story, a complete subject in its own right; what we have is actually three stories in one. There is no real link between the events in the story . . . and the use of dialogue between the inner and outer selves of the character makes the story confused and disjointed and spoils the overall effect. . . .

In general, however, this collection succeeds in showing that its author has considerable talent and possesses a considerable command of the short-story genre. This emerges first in the appropriate use of character types and their reaction to events, in other words, in the understanding of "situation." Second, the author will begin with an idea or an event, and then, instead of making it develop naturally or simply continuing with it, we see her leaping forward to a second idea, then a third—leaps that are a particular feature of excitable imaginations. . . . Third, there is a subtle observation of emotions with all their variations, so that each character appears before our eyes as a living tableau.

Muhammad Haydar. Al-Ādāb. June, 1962,
pp. 31, 34

In a newspaper interview the author of this collection, *There Is No Sea at Beirut,* declares that she gave it this title because it conveys the ultimate sense of rejection, doubt, and anxiety and an insistence on the need to create new values that we can use as new bases for our society, values that cannot lose their authenticity or be hampered by apathy and inertia. . . .

The book itself certainly contains some excellent, even original, imagery, but it does not fit into the context; it is usually far more than is required. It frequently becomes a goal in itself. The style exhausts and dulls all the symbols and images, and makes them lose most of their significance. Rarely will you find a noun without one or even two adjectives. All this turns the pen into a bellows, while the experience of the book as a whole becomes a gaudy balloon being stretched to the point of bursting. Within all this there moves a single female organizing all the different versions of the experience. She lies, and knows it. She makes herself believe she is playing with her own values, and knows that too. She is convinced that she is being torn apart, and that delights her. She is forever on the move so that her illusion will not dissipate; all the while her eye is on the external world. When she falls into the abyss of her own psychological loneliness where the genuine experiences would begin, she leaps out to the external world once more, beating the drums for yet another tale of banishment. Her relationships with men are merely escapades of a pen filled with ink, set in a bourgeois atmosphere that shows not the slightest trace of rejection, doubt, anxiety, and so forth. In order to attract the reader's attention to these features, she sets up worlds, erects characters, injects events, sleeps with the language, and breaks the nerves of the very words themselves. . . .

Perhaps it is features such as these that have made *There Is No Sea at Beirut* such a successful collection. As an expression of the generation of rejection which is formulating the revolution in the Arab homeland at the moment, it is one hundred percent accurate and realistic. This is indeed a document that reveals with great clarity the revolutionary hot air filling the minds of our revolutionaries and all the ranting and raving with nothing of any worth beneath it.

Hānī al-Rāhib. Hiwār. 10, 1964, pp. 133–34

Ghāda al-Sammān's literary output is actually a product of the fascination the poetic person feels toward subjects involving the self and society, and also of her tremendous sense of sound and music in language. The primary feature of her writing is the headlong and boisterous outpouring of genuine feelings and sensibilities and the daring ideas that are poured onto the page, sometimes easily within the reader's grasp and own emotional outlook, at other times shrouded and remote. These ideas are packed full of metaphors and symbols, and also are evidence of an overflowing imagination. . . .

To Ghāda al-Sammān the story is a poetic vision, a psychological screen, a sociological "find," a collection of psychological and social tableaux. It is the poetic vision that validates the artistry of the narrative. The different hues of that artistry occur in its structure and shape, in its descriptions, its analyses or its style. . . .

Above all, her work contains no colloquial usage at all, not even in dialogue between representatives of various classes of people. . . .

This latest collection, *Night of Strangers,* undoubtedly represents new horizons in the cultural exploration of the Eastern personality, both male and female. She has, no doubt, drawn her inspiration from the occasions when she traveled abroad to get her higher education and came into direct contact with Western society. . . . Other stories go into detail about the questions of commitment and experiences with the homeland, the people, and friends. . . . Still others are bold exposés, on both the individual and social level, of matters relating to sex, love, contemporary life, family life, married life, and so on. Certainly, some of these subjects in which she explores society and states her views on commitment can be considered new in her output . . . while others can be found in her previous collections.

But what is new in her artistry and represents a big leap forward is the conscious and unconscious association of ideas, coupled with solitary conversation, overt interior monologue, and even at times a tendency to use the "absurd" style and symbolism.

'Adnān ibn Dhurayl. *Al-Ādāb*. March, 1967, p. 41

In her latest stories, Ghāda al-Sammān seems to be setting sail in the ship of her own personal feelings toward the further shores of revolutionary rejection, of commitment to the problems of the Arab homeland and the anxieties of the poor. . . . In so doing, she puts a distance between herself and the usual type of flashy slogans and the falsities of bourgeois society, and with persistent fidelity searches out her true Arab identity, and at the same time her real situation as a human being. She utterly rejects the usual and traditional in order to try out new experiences. She is genuinely authentic in her originality and her veracity. . . .

With all the skill of a great surgeon, Ghāda uses the scalpel that is the Arabic language to make incisions in the body of the Arab homeland. She is soon able to reveal where the malignant tumors are to be found; from the districts of Yemen to the streets of Vienna and even the cafes on Hamra Street in Beirut, we find ourselves afloat in the uncharted regions of the Arab soul. And this is not restricted to place alone. In five out of the six stories in *Leaving the Ancient Harbors,* the story is told from the viewpoint of a girl of bourgeois background and upbringing who continually rejects her situation and aspires to achieve selfhood without guile in a merciless world. But we always come to realize in the end that her fidelity is a societal one, and that the sole solution is a conscious freedom and a revolutionary rejection of all the factors that lead to frustration, despair, and defeat. Ghāda, then, begins with a woman but finishes with mankind; from the individual she moves to the homeland as a whole. This is a genuine "departure" for Ghāda al-Sammān in these new stories, as opposed to her earlier works, such as *Your Eyes Are My Destiny* and *There Is No Sea at Beirut*. This aspiration to undertake a new journey may have represented the furthest stage of the personal despair and exile to be sensed in *Night of Strangers*.

Riyād 'Ismat. *Al-Ma'rifa*. December, 1975, pp. 94–95

What distinguishes al-Sammān's writing is her obsession with identity and loss of self. Indeed, even before the [1967] war, she had written of identity fragmentation. In the first of her *Incomplete Works*, "Time of the Last Love," this fragmentation is limited to complete identification with another: the lover, whose voice comes out of her throat, whose cigarette smoke comes out of her lungs. Already there is the suggestion that the individual is no more than the sum of a number of points that only become a line, a thread of continuity, in retrospect . . . in a flashback? She is in constant anguish about her direction, for wherever she goes she is assailed by roads, cars and worlds whirling around her madly. Indeed it is as though she were on an LSD trip and her mind had entirely dissociated itself from the burden of her body. As she runs through life her disintegrating body is abandoned along the wayside only to take root in the asphalt and to sprout up as plants in the spring.

This early work is often obscure, sometimes brilliant but unfailingly violent and protesting. With the war has come concentration and perhaps direction. Protest, which, before the war, had been the main reason for writing, has changed into a challenge. The social protest that she had indulged in until well into the 70s has become an anachronism. The time for "flower-power" whining has passed, now is the time to shout and scream, to defy Death by living fully. And it is this call for life that distinguishes the works of all these writers. No longer is tomorrow dreaded as a dull repetition of today, no longer are we living in an Osborne-type hell. This hell is different and, for its difference, it is better. For now tomorrow is ever different, bringing the hope for some of peace and order, for others of danger and excitement.

Miriam Cooke. *Journal of Arabic Literature.*
13, 1982, pp. 127–28

In *Beirut '75,* al-Sammān deals with many of the issues discussed in her earlier works such as discrimination, the sexual oppression of women, the concept of honor in modern Arab society, injustice, political corruption, and tribal revenge. In this novel, however, she deals with these issues as they relate directly to the state of Lebanese society in general and that of Beirut in particular just before the Lebanese Civil War erupted. The novel may almost be described as prophetic, in that its characterization and setting lay bare the complex roots of the ongoing strife. It is to be noted that women's issues are not an overriding concern here, but are taken up by al-Sammān only to the extent that they impinge on the condition of society as a whole. . . .

Al-Sammān's novel is composed of contrasts from beginning to end. She contrasts dreams and reality, life and death, all of which she uses to foreshadow the events and destinies of the characters as they develop in the novel. The dreams of the characters are emblematic of different kinds of death, whether psychological, spiritual, or physical. Yasaminah, for instance, undergoes a dual death, at once psychological and spiritual, once she indulges in sexual gratification and neglects her poetic talents. And she is of course faced with physical death (murder) at the hands of her brother. While Yasaminah's dream becomes a reality, Farah struggles to realize his own. Once he transforms the dream into reality, however, he finds that he has lost his manhood.

In general terms, al-Sammān in *Beirut '75* deals with three distinct issues: politics, sex, and death. These three issues are interconnected throughout the novel, and she skillfully balances all three of them in her characterizations and settings for the action of the novel. We see, for example, how her political commentary is presented through glimpses of the social and sexual events in which the characters participate and her descriptions of the environment in which these take place. What is not clear, however, is whether she intends to commit herself to a specific political ideology; she allows us faint glimpses and insights, but there is no possibility of discerning the precise outlines of her creed.

Al-Sammān also makes the reader very much aware of time and place in her novel. Beirut is a wise choice as the focal point of the novel's intrigue. . . .

Perhaps, where al-Sammān is concerned, Beirut is the Arab world in miniature, a microcosmic arena in which Arab society wages civil war on itself; it would be less a city than a symbol of Arab division. Many things she says about Beirut suggest that this is the view she takes of it. But whether this is so or not, it must be admitted that she has done a masterly job of conjuring up a vision of a city that is nothing if not unique in the long annals of human civilization.

Al-Sammān is also very successful in her technique of writing. Narration, description, monologue, soliloquy: she demonstrates unquestionable competence in the handling of all of these. She is also impressively competent in her use of the complex "stream-of-consciousness" device, and in effect admits that she stands in debt to James Joyce and Virginia Woolf. Her choice of characters is, of itself, very significant, in that it tells us a very great deal about the kind of people who have shaped her opinions concerning Arab society. Finally, it is characteristic of her writing at this stage in her career that it is marked by a certain inconclusiveness in the unravelling of the plot, as if she meant to suggest that the fiction writer cannot hope to arrest time and must shape his intrigue accordingly.

> Hanan Awwad. *Arab Causes in the Fiction*
> *of Ghadah al-Samman, 1961–1975*
> (Sherbrooke, Quebec: Éditions Naaman,
> 1983), pp. 95, 108–9

In 1976, Ghāda al-Sammān published *Beirut Nightmares*. This novel chronicles seven days and 206 nightmares spent in a villa next to the Holiday Inn and Phoenicia Hotel during the Hotels Battle of October and November 1975. The protagonist is trapped with her cousin, her uncle and the cook.

Ghāda al-Sammān chose the journal format to give the illusion of fact recorded. But the hard edges of fact blur as fantasy intrudes. The journal is a pretext for fiction. The protagonist endures the helpless waiting, armed only with Mutanabbi's poetry and a fierce determination to survive. Desperate to leave the confinement and particularly her cousin's uncongenial company, she determines that if she sees anything at all move and survive, she will venture out. A dog. A shot. She is answered: the sniper will, must, shoot because killing is for him the only way he knows he is alive.

Negative self-awareness is then reflected in an almost psychedelic stream of consciousness: the bed; her aunt who had died in it (why not sleep in coffins from birth?); incessant shooting; the telephone. An acquaintance asks a trivial favor. Stunned, she hangs up. Outside, the Holiday Inn burns. . . .

Throughout the *Beirut Nightmares* that hurtle from dream to reality al-Sammān maintains a tight authorial control and vision, never allowing the narration to become an abstraction whose only impact is to convey numbness. The balance between a frightening present and its exaggerated possibilities is struck in such a way that the reader enters a fevered imagination, and does not reject as too much, as too implausible, the recounted horrors. There is no limit to what can be imagined, but there is a very definite limit to what can be tolerated in experience.

Beirut Nightmares is held together by an autistic perspective and the use of recurrence that zooms in with cinematographic clarity on people and details. It is an important device to give integrity to stream of consciousness, flashbacks, flights of fantasy, news briefs and descriptions of the dailiness, the lived reality of the war. . . .

In *Beirut Nightmares,* Ghāda al-Sammān exploits the journal format to measure the dailiness of the war. The difference between this journal and most others is that while the dailiness is recounted it is not divided into days but is a continuum linking events and moods. Although the war was the ultimate rupture, it had to be lived as normal. This journal demonstrates the mood of the new routine: under the most traumatic circumstances life went on; what was different was the proportion of the details and the individual's alienation from these enhanced details. . . .

Only discursive unity can give the protagonist of *Beirut Nightmares* the stability and the assurance that she, at least, is one; now even that has gone. The break up of the memory is essential to the break up of the self in disharmony with the present. Since writing is a process of creating not only a text, but also the world, the disintegration of words signals the ultimate disintegration. Again, it is the dot/circle paradigm that exemplifies loss. It is almost as if positive deconstruction must take place before reconstruction may be contemplated:

> I looked at my watch again. It really had no hands, nor even figures. It was just a small, white closed circle with a black dot in the middle. I felt as though I, like the black dot, was a prisoner of a mysterious desolate fate imprisoned by some circle or other.

The relationship of dot to circle is not dynamic but dead. In *Beirut Nightmares* the only unifying factor throughout moments of greatest fragmentation is the tenuous line of author/observer that weaves through the work. Yet the line is threatened when the perception of the self is altered and distorted.

The novel ends with the shooting of the dead lover. Having eliminated the obsession, she ceases to exist and her pen frenetically conjures up strange, disjointed stories. The whole is finally reduced to an indefinite series of impressions each fleetingly made concrete by some visual representation seen by the reader, not the protagonist.

In her book of poems entitled *To Catch a Fleeting Moment,* the need for love and individual worth in the anonymity imposed by a senseless war has become a consuming passion. The poems lament the loss of a love that allows for survival through, and not against, another. Once war is lived as norm, life becomes urgent. Life's shortest span becomes defined by war and death: each moment is the first and the last, the only moment that counts. Each moment screams to be filled, not with death but with life in love. Thus love can annihilate war, but it must annihilate it at each moment, in dreams, in seconds like bubbles that can be caught in an eternal evanescence: "Life is a bubble. Paint it before it bursts."

In *To Catch a Fleeting Moment,* the love that al-Sammān calls for is aggressive, making the loved one, or rather the one to be loved, into an insipid object outshone by her need to love him.

Miriam Cooke. *War's Other Voices: Women Writers on the Lebanese Civil War* (Cambridge: Cambridge University Press, 1988), pp. 43, 45–46

SANCHEZ, SONIA (UNITED STATES) 1935–

Sonia Sanchez (born . . . in Birmingham, Alabama) first came to public attention as one of Broadside Press's New Black Poets writing the militant, anti-white oppression, rhetorical poetry which was then in vogue. . . . She wrote this poetry well, being extremely good at capturing black dialect and devising her own notation to convey it. Like almost all of the New Black Poets, she also gave frequent public readings of her work (especially on the lecture circuit during that time when colleges and universities were being rocked by black student demands). Here, too, she excelled, doing hums, shouts, moans, rhythms, songs, etc. so enchantingly that even those persons who later walked out (in protest of her "obscenities") were momentarily seduced. All of this characterizes and parallels the Black Movement in poetry of the late 1960s and early 1970s. Sanchez and other young black women poets were fully a part of that movement.

However, at the same time, most of her poetry derived from a black female core, an aspect of themselves which many of these young women did not slight in their work. She writes of relationships between black men and women, of the problems and possibilities that lie in black children, and, most poignantly, of personal/black female selfhood and pain. . . .

Much of this personal poetry is written in standard English, proving (if it needed to be proven) that she could also "poet" in the mainstream tradition and manner. Perhaps the most impressive poem of this kind is her elegy for Malcolm X.

After the flaming heyday of militant poetry, most young black poets began to eschew "offing whitey" themes and started to address black people from an even more separatist position of "black togethery-ness," as Gwendolyn Brooks has dubbed it. They also turned to expressing more inwardly directed concerns. Sanchez had been developing along these lines throughout her career. For her, this direction culminated in her 1974 volume, *A Blues Book for Blue Black Magical Women*. . . .

The secrets she tells are autobiographically based ones about herself. However, they chronicle a history which she shares with black women of her time. Sanchez seems to reflect a realization of this fact in the way that she draws on epic and myth for the form and content of this, her most elaborately written and structured work. Part 2, especially, is pregnant with black female history. First, she invites the reader to "Come into Black geography," the geography of herself "born / musician to two / black braids." Then she invokes the earth mother to sing her history, to "tell me how i have become, became / this woman with razor blades between / her teeth." The succeeding sections follow this black girl from her birth, to childhood game playing, to aphasic trauma caused by her stepmother, to teenage grinding in New York City project basements, to love and young womanhood as "a proper painted / european Black faced american," to a crisis in racial identity and breakdown, to civil rights activism, to finally a womanhood of blackness. Here Sanchez reveals personal and collective history. . . .

Sanchez is undoubtedly one of the most under-appreciated poets writing today. Her pristine lyricism combined with her strong voice and black female themes make her special.

Gloria Hull. In Sandra M. Gilbert and Susan Gubar, eds. *Shakespeare's Sisters: Feminist Essays on Women Poets* (Bloomington: Indiana University Press, 1979), pp. 176–79

Sonia Sanchez respects the power of Black language. More than any other poet, she has been responsible for legitimatizing the use of urban Black English in written form. Her use of language is spontaneous and thoughtful. Unlike many poets of the sixties, her use of the so-called profane has been innovatively shocking and uncommonly apropos. Her language is culturally legitimate and genuinely reflects the hard bottom and complicated spectrum of the entire Black community. She has taken Black speech and put it in the context of world literature. This aspect of her work has often been overlooked. However, she, along with Baraka, Neal, Dumas, and a few others of the sixties poets, must be looked upon as a recorder and originator of an urban Black working language. Long before the discovery of Ntozake Shange, Sanchez set the tone and spaces of modern urban written Black poetry. In her early works, we can read and feel the rough city voices screaming full circle in all kinds of human settings.

Haki Madhubuti. In Mari Evans, ed. *Black Women Writers (1950–1980)* (New York: Anchor, 1984), p. 421

The title of Sonia Sanchez's first collection, *Homecoming,* marks with delicate irony the departure point of a journey whose direction and destination can now be considered. *I've Been a Woman,* her most recent book, invites such an appraisal, including as it does a retrospective of her earlier work as well as an articulation of a newly won sense of peace. . . .

The new poems in *I've Been a Woman* benefit from the sense of continuity and evolution conferred by the earlier work. The impact of the section entitled "Haikus/Tankas & Other Love Syllables" is immeasurably enhanced by *Love Poems,* for instance; the new poems, drawing on a relatively limited stock of images (water in various forms, trees, morning, sun, different smells), are an accumulation of moments that define love, age, sorrow, and pride in terms of action. Particular configurations recur: the rhythms of sex, the bent silhouettes of old age, the stillness of intense emotion. But taken together, these poems are like the spontaneous eruptions that punctuate, geyserlike, the flow of experience.

The other new poems in *I've Been a Woman* consist of a series of eulogies, collectively titled "Generations," in which Sanchez explicitly claims her place among those who speak of and for Black people. There is a schematic balance operating here: the individual poems respectively eulogize Sterling Brown (age), Gerald Penny (youth), Sanchez's father, and the idea and reality of mothers. The synthesis implied in this design is enacted in the poetry itself; the imagery and rhythms of the verse in this section convey an overwhelming sense of resolution and serenity.

David Williams. In Mari Evans, ed. *Black
Women Writers (1950–1980)* (New York:
Anchor, 1984), pp. 433, 446

It is appropriate when analyzing a work such as *Homegirls and Handgrenades* (1984) to wonder about what might have been the motivation for its subject matter and form. It might be declared by some that this is just another in a long line of Sonia Sanchez's books of poems. Her very first volume, *Homecoming* (1969), was an impressive display of staggered-lined poems with word-splitting diagonals. *We a BaddDDD People* (1970) and *It's a New Day* (1971) contained even more of the same stylistic devices. Part of Sanchez's early effort was to experiment with words in verse to create a new perspective on how blacks should perceive themselves within the context of a nation struggling to admit them into the fold of social equality. Although that task remains incomplete, one can nevertheless sense a development on the part of the poet as she advances her work to include the mystical *A Blues Book for Blue Black Magical Women* (1973) as well as *Love Poems* (1973) where there can be seen an attempt to reconcile all the various aspects of black culture for the benefit of progress. *I've Been a Woman* (1978) and *Under a Soprano Sky* (1987) are further examples of how the author has examined, in particular, the plight of black women as they strive toward freedom in a world not always conducive to that undertaking.

Nonetheless, it is in *Homegirls* where Sanchez delivers what Henry Louis Gates has characterized as "the revising text . . . written in the language of the tradition, employing its tropes, its rhetorical strategies, and its ostensible subject matter, the so-called Black Experience."

James Robert Saunders. MELUS. 15, 1988,
p. 73

Such brief works as "poem," "to all sisters," and "definition for blk/children" are also examples from *Home Coming* of a revolutionary didacticism meant to inspire mass audiences. It is easy to view such efforts as oversimplifications, but in truth, their sentiments, issues, tone, and language fit them out ideally as addresses to an enormously complex situation in which few people speak in abstract syllables or demand wit, ambiguity, and refined tension. If the reception accorded "to all sisters" is exemplary, such didactic poems reveal Ms. Sanchez's genius for the vernacular. They also reveal her commitment to one of the most familiar cultural performances in the Afro-American community—"running it down."

In such performances, the single speaker puts into forceful language the wisdom of the tribe, stripping away pretense and, in almost shamanistic ways, colloquially exorcising demons of racism, sexism, and intraracial dissension. "Telling it like it 't'is" describes the process admirably, or, as Ralph Ellison's respondent says in *Invisible Man:* "We with you, Brother. You pitch 'em we catch 'em!" . . .

If the notion of a black renaissance may be assumed to imply communal leadership and a response among black people themselves—a self-direction, selection, and empowerment that do not recreate bourgeois forms for private gain and white acknowledgment—then Sonia Sanchez and her audience clearly mark a new, postmodern, and dynamically sounding *renaissancism*.

There may well be more celebrated Afro-American women writers, but Sonia Sanchez helps bring an enduring spirit of *black* renaissancism to contemporary effectiveness. Her name is legion; it subsumes the world's dispossessed as referent. Nobody performs like Sonia Sanchez; nobody brings quintessential black cultural rights to the high note she achieves.

Houston A. Baker, Jr. In Henry Louis
Gates, Jr., ed. Reading Black, Reading
Feminist (New York: Meridian, 1990),
pp. 332, 345

In her eight volumes of poetry, which appeared between 1969 and 1987, Sanchez's voice is sometimes abrasive but never as profane as the conditions she knows must be eradicated; her tone ranges from gentle to derisive, yet the message is one of redeeming realism. Also undergirding her poetic expression is a deep concern for heritage; for the sovereignty of time with all its ramifications of birth, change, rebirth, and death; for the impress of the past and memories; and for nurture, nature, and God. Moreover, these themes reveal Sanchez's strong Southern imagination, one that was born in the impressionable times of her youth in Alabama, where the tensions of struggle were fed with mama's milk.

Homecoming (1969), Sanchez's first book of poems, is her pledge of allegiance to blackness, to black love, to black heroes, and to her own realization as a woman, an artist, and a revolutionary. The language and the typography are experimental; they are aberrations of standard middle-class Americanese and traditional Western literary forms. As such, they reflect her view of American society, which perceives blacks as aberrations and exploits them through commercialism, drugs, brutality, and institutionalized racism. In this book and the poetry that follows, the vernacular and the forms are clear indications of her fierce determination to redefine her art and rail against Western aesthetics. *Homecoming* also introduces us to a poet who is saturated with the sound and sense of black speech and black music, learned at the knees of Birmingham women discovering themselves full voiced and full spirited. The rhythm and color of black speech—the rapping, reeling, explosive syllables—are her domain, for she is steeped in the tradition of linguistic virtuosity that Stephen Henderson talks about in *Understanding the New Black Poetry*. Black music, especially the jazz sounds of John Coltrane, Ornette Coleman, and Pharoah Sanders, pulse, riff, and slide through her poetry.

In her second volume, *We a BadddDDD People* (1970), Sanchez is wielding a survival sword that rips away the enemy's disguise and shears through the facade of black ignorance and reactionism. Arranged in three groups, "Survival Poems," "Love/Songs/Chants," and "TCB/EN Poems," the poems extend the attack begun in *Homecoming* and tell black people how to survive in a country of death traps (drugs, suicide, sexual exploitation, psychological slaughter via the mass media) and televised assassination. Her message, however, is not one of unrelieved gloom, for it is rooted in optimism and faith: "know and love yourself." Like Sterling A. Brown's "Strong Men" and Margaret Walker's "For My People," "We A BadddDDD People," the title poem of the volume, is a praise song that celebrates black love, talent, courage, and continuity. . . .

A Blues Book for Blue Black Magical Women (1974) is a dramatic departure from the poetry of earlier volumes. The scope here is large and sweeping. The language is no longer the raw vernacular of *Homecoming,* though, as in *We A BadddDDD People,* it is possessed by the rhythms of the chants and rituals. At its most prosaic, it is laden with the doctrine of the Nation of Islam and ideologically correct images. At its best, it is intimate, luminous, and apocalyptic. Tucked inside *A Blues Book* is a striking spiritual odyssey that reveals the poet's growing awareness of the psychological and spiritual features of her face.

In 1978, Sanchez culled some of her best poetry from earlier volumes in *I've Been a Woman: New and Selected Poems.* To these she adds a collection of haiku and tankas that is dominated by the theme of love: the sensual love of a man, the love of old people and young, the love for a father and spiritual mothers. . . .

In *homegirls & handgrenades* (1984), Sanchez shows the further deepening of the poet's consciousness, for it is a sterling example of her going inside herself, inside the past, to pull out of her residual memory deeply personal experience. From the past, she draws images that explode the autobiographical into universal truths. The predominant genre in this volume is the sketch, much like those that stud Jean Toomer's *Cane*. . . .

Distinguishing much of her poetry is a prophetic voice that brings the weight of her experience to articulating the significant truths about liberation and love, self-actualization and being, spiritual growth and continuity, heroes, and the cycles of life. Her vision is original because it is both new (a fresh rearrangement of knowledge) and faithful to the "origins" of its inspiration. Therefore, it is not surprising that in her most recent volume of poetry, *Under a Soprano Sky* (1987), the mature voice of the poet is giving expression to the sources of her spiritual strength, establishing and reestablishing connections that recognize the family-hood of man/womankind, and singing, as another Lady did, of society's strange fruit sacrificed on the altars of political megalomania, economic greed, and social misunderstanding.

> Joanne Veal Gabbin. In Tonette Bond Inge,
> ed. *Southern Women Writers: The New
> Generation* (Tuscaloosa: University of
> Alabama Press, 1990), pp. 181–84

As a poet, Sonia Sanchez has evolved since her first book *Homecoming* published in 1969 during the heart of the Black Power Movement. Back then her poetics included a strident tropology that displayed a matriarchal protection of black people. Today, after publishing twelve books of poetry, including the acclaimed *Homegirls and Handgrenades* and *Under a Soprano Sky,* one can still discover poetic conventions developed during the Black Arts Movement. The purpose of this artistic movement involved challenging the Eurocentric hegemony in art by developing a new aesthetic that represented the ethos, pathos, and expression of African Americans. These neo-renaissance artists were inspired by the rhetorical eloquence and activism of Rev. Martin Luther King, Jr. and Malcolm X. From this era of intense political activism, artists such as Sonia Sanchez wrote poems illustrating a resistance to inequality best described in "Black Art" by Imamu Amiri Baraka (1969).

It is obvious that revolutionary fervor characterized some of Sanchez's work, but it is essential for understanding her poetics, as well as the neo-aesthetic of the sixties, to recognize that anarchy was not the goal. These poets considered themselves to be word soldiers for black people, defending their right to have equality, honor, and glory. In each of Sanchez's volumes of poetry, for example, one finds the artist handling themes that include love, harmony, race unification, myth, and history.

Regina B. Jennings. In Carol Aisha
Blackshire-Belay, ed. *Language and*
Literature in the African American
Imagination (Westport, Connecticut:
Greenwood Press, 1992), p. 119

Sanchez is perceived as a militant writer. Such a perception has as much to do with the themes she addresses in her poetry as the form she uses. Critics, however, tend to focus on her militant themes. Certainly it is understandable that critics focus on Sanchez's use of certain themes in her work, but her disruption of the haiku form is directly related to her fusion of function and ethos in poetry, and though she is consistently revolutionary, she is also a skilled artist. Ironically, because of the general perception of her as militant, Sanchez's use of the haiku puzzles some scholars who associate her militancy solely with free verse and rarely with haiku. . . .

Because of her tendency to focus on the human condition in her poetry, Sanchez is often associated with militancy. Two misconceptions account for this tendency: Sanchez's highly militant and often publicized free verse poetry, which employs tropes and themes associated with political struggle, and the conventional notion of haiku that influences both the poetry and critical community. . . .

In transforming haiku, Sonia Sanchez declares her own "linguistic manumission," refusing to be boxed in by its form. As she textualizes the form, forging her Afrocentric vision and Afrocentric structure within the discipline of the haiku form, she moves closer to a unique structure that carries her own signature.

Frenzella Elaine DeLancey. In Carol Aisha
Blackshire-Belay, ed. *Language and*
Literature in the African American
Imagination (Westport, Connecticut:
Greenwood Press, 1992), pp. 32–33, 35–36

SANDEL, CORA (pseud. SARA FABRICIUS) (NORWAY)
1880–1974

Tromso, Norway, is a little over two hundred miles north of the Arctic Circle. Isolated, sparsely populated, and all too often icebound, it is the kind of place that breeds resignation. The winter days are short, gray, and cold, the jagged coastal landscape inhospitable. The town itself, small and somewhat defensive about its location, cannot help but be oppressive. In these unpromising surroundings Cora Sandel spent her adolescence, and here she sets *Alberta and Jacob,* the first novel of her newly rediscovered trilogy. (Published in Norwegian in 1926–1939, the books were translated into English in the 1960s, but—inexplicably—drew little attention and soon were out of print.)

The stark setting of her childhood clearly had an enormous effect on Sandel, and has just as great a hold on her fictional counterpart. Young Alberta has a somewhat dogged streak, but even more than determination, what her rugged environment gives her is an ability to make do, at least temporarily, with very little.

She needs it. Even within her family, life is far from enviable. The Selmers are bound by narrow circumstances; bleak though life is in Tromso, they cannot afford the passage south. At fifteen Alberta is plucked from school so that the money can be spent on her brother's education. She passes her days dispiritedly doing the household chores and contriving ways to get warm; whenever she can, she steals steaming gulps of coffee from the pot on the stove and waters down what remains to avoid her mother's suspicion. Her mother, dreary as well as stingy, is given to sighing over Alberta's domestic incompetence and shortage of charm. Her father is as unhappy as his wife and consequently drinks, causing Alberta much worry and humiliation. Her parents, naturally, quarrel continually.

Out of this general wretchedness, however, emerges Alberta's remarkable sensibility. Predictably, she yearns to get away—from her family, from the creeping numbness of the townspeople, from north Norway. She doesn't know precisely what she's after; all she knows is that it's in the south. It's there, she thinks that "life was lived and events took place."

She does, in the course of the trilogy, make it there, but her early days in the north have two lingering effects. Never, it seems, can she get warm enough—never is there quite enough food or light or company to erase the chilly desolation of her childhood. And, having been brought up in a place that acknowledged to itself that life happened elsewhere, she never quite feels part of what's going on around her.

Her status as observer, however, is central to the nature of these books. There is little here in the way of plot, and what there is runs true to the form of novels about people who yearn for more and try to find it. Alberta leaves home, goes to Paris, meets artists and writers, has several difficult relationships with men, tries to make a living. Her experience has been described by some critics in feminist terms, but this is slightly misleading. She does struggle to define a life and a career for herself, but she doesn't think about her predicament politically. In one sense though, she is a feminist heroine: like many novels of the genre, these are concerned with the slow, incremental nature of their heroine's development and with her sense of being on the fringe of things. For all the vivid particularity of her prose, Alberta is an oddly detached viewer.

Her descriptions, though, are certainly vivid. Since much of what she describes—rotting fish, cruel husbands—is unpleasant, they are also sometimes hard going. A tolerance for unforgiving temperaments, as well as unforgiving landscapes, is required to read these books. But the same intensity of description provides some lovely details: the exact smell of boxwood on a crowded street in August; a narrow brook flowing "solitary and intricate among the meadows." Alberta survives on her capacity to see these things. Living alone in Paris, in a tiny room where mice drown in the washbasin, she tells herself, "It was already something of a feat not to be lying becalmed in quite the wrong place—and after all, this was life, life itself, irreplaceable." There is, at times, something grim about her tenacity, but there is something admirable too. Beneath her determined accuracy of description runs a stubborn refusal either to romanticize life or to give up on it.

Kathleen Kearns. *The New Republic.*
September 10, 1984, p. 41

In the English-speaking world Cora Sandel is best known for her Alberta trilogy. The books have rarely been out of print in their English translation and, in recent years, have been recognized as feminist classics. Sandel's semi-autobiographical story of a woman's long struggle to define herself as a writer has parallels with the work of many twentieth-century writers, but her particular emphasis on the difficult economics of being a woman, especially a mother, is comparatively rare. Like Jean Rhys, a writer to whom she bears some resemblance, Sandel was eminently gifted at dissecting the unequal power relations between men and women. Unlike Rhys's heroines, however, Alberta fights against her passivity and ultimately finds her freedom and herself.

In Norway and Sweden Cora Sandel is considered a major short story writer as well as a novelist. Her short fiction has long been recognized for its lyric intensity and stylistic economy and is often anthologized. More recently, Scandinavian women critics have been rediscovering the feminist content of her work, and she has been the subject of several books and numerous articles. . . .

Cora Sandel's views of marriage and male-female relationships are often bleak. Separated by personal and social misunderstandings as well as different values and needs, her men and women continue to seek each other blindly and hurtfully in such stories as "Thank You, Doctor," "The Child," and "The Flight to America." Sandel's struggle for custody of her son finds echoes in the latter two stories, as she records the loss children suffer when their parents are estranged. . . .

Cora Sandel was a writer who perfected each sentence and carefully shaped each story. As a fiction writer, I have been awed by her mastery of the craft and inspired in my own work. As well as a stylist, however, she was an instinctively radical story-teller who wrote with compassion and humor about the oppressed, the marginal and the simply lonely. An undercurrent of anger runs through much of her writing, an anger directed toward hypocrisy and injustice of any kind. At the same time Sandel's characters are never victims. Sometimes independent, sometimes trapped, never quite extinguished, they continue to struggle to keep their dignity and to win their freedom.

> Barbara Wilson. Introduction to Cora
> Sandel. *Cora Sandel: Selected Short Stories*
> (Seattle: Seal Press, 1985), pp. v–viii

Norwegian born Sandel (pseudonym of Sara Fabricius) is best known for the semi-autobiographical The Alberta Trilogy, published at the beginning of this century. In this current collection of shorter works written between the 1920s and 1972 [*The Silken Thread: Stories and Sketches*] the stories are intimate, economical recordings and observations of 20th century women, and Sandel's feminist orientation and eye for painterly detail, which invite comparison with Colette (whose books she translated into Norwegian), are evident. The theme of woman's imprisonment in the male-female relationship is explored with irony in "The Women in the Bath House," a picture of pathetic, pampered concubines; in "The Bracelet," where a "woman without a man" is humiliated; in "Avalanche," where silence between a husband and wife is fatally eloquent. Sandel's sketches of animals, particularly cats ("Puttycass"), exude a Colette-like sensuousness. Less successful, perhaps because of translation obstacles, is the poem "Today the Rose."

> Sybil Steinberg. *Publishers Weekly*. June 12,
> 1987, p. 71

[Sandel's] novels are already available in English. Now we can read some of her marvelous stories—poignant, lyric, told with grace, economy, wit. The earlier ones, published in the 1920's, are brief character sketches: Winesburg, Ohio, translated to Finnmark, Norway, but more impressionistic, more compressed—like the story about Katrine, the town's most wretched prostitute, heckled, snubbed, and by the narrator too, who finally thinks Katrine's face "breaks free of memory's chaos and looks at me. It torments me. It accuses me." In later stories, from the 30's and 40's, the characters range from "The Child Who Loved Roads"—the roads "where freedom had no boundaries"— to the parrot Papen, finally resigned to his cage. There's the child who "doesn't suspect that he constitutes the living chain of flesh and blood and nerves binding two incompatible people together, and that he will have to pay for it." And, most memorably, there's the Czechoslovak refugee in "To Lukas," writing to the husband torn from her, who she dreams is alive, for whom she wants to stay pretty, to whom she confesses her longing for a little warmth. Then she is entrapped by the fur coat she accepts from a benefactor (who will of course expect some return); she finally pleads that exiles, that slaves in ancient times, also "in the end took what life offered them." Barbara Wilson has done a magnificent service by selecting these stories and translating them into vibrant prose.

> Beverly Lyon Clark. *The New York Times*.
> February 23, 1986, p. 22

Sandel's major work is a trilogy of novels about her fictional alter ego, Alberte, the first volume of which was published when she was forty-six: *Alberte og Jakob* (1926; *Alberte and Jacob,* 1962). It tells the story of Alberte's childhood in her northern city above the polar circle. Through careful selection of sensuous detail Sandel vividly communicates Alberte's dread at the harsh climate, her family's near-poverty, and the awful respectability of the town's middle-class ladies with their "oil cloth sofas and porcelain dogs." As the first volume ends, Alberte half-heartedly attempts to commit suicide and then recovers her will to live. Volume two, *Alberte og friheten* (1931; *Alberte and Freedom,* 1963), relates the story of Alberte in Paris, where she ekes out a living by working as a model—lonely, almost morbidly sensitive, but with a toughness in her that ultimately saves her. The final volume, *Bare Alberte* (1939; *Alberte Alone,* 1966), chronicles Alberte's final, painful steps in becoming an artist. She returns to Norway and finally writes a novel very much like the Alberte trilogy.

Sandel's other books include the novels *Kranes konditori* (1945; *Krane's Sweetshop,* 1968) and *Kjøp ikke Dondi* (1958; *The Leech,* 1960), also the following collections of short stories: *En blå sofa* (1927; A blue sofa), *Carmen og Maja* (1932; Carmen and Maja), *Mange takk, doktor* (1935; Many thanks, Doctor), *Dyr jeg har kjent* (1945; Animals I have known), *Figurer på mørk bunn* (1949; Figures against a dark background), and *Vårt vanskelige liv* (1960; Our difficult life). In these works Sandel turns her attention to struggles similar to those in the Alberte books, to portraits of children, dreamers, trapped housewives, passionate and inept people who struggle to maintain themselves against the forces of small-mindedness and bigotry.

William Mishler. In Steven R. Serafin and
Walter D. Glanze, eds. *Encyclopedia of
World Literature in the 20th Century* (New
York: Continuum, 1993), p. 538

SANDOZ, MARI (UNITED STATES) 1896–1966

Gulla Slogum was a mean woman, even for the tough Nebraska frontier. When she got in trouble with the law because she was forcing her older sons to rustle cattle, she squeezed out of it by prostituting a pretty daughter to the sheriff. When her youngest son, Ward, fell in love with the daughter of a Polish settler, Mother Slogum fixed him up neatly: She went to the Pole, tried to buy the girl for her brothel, with the result that Ward was half killed the next time he came courting. When her daughter Annette sneaked off with a poor neighbor boy named René, Mother Slogum decided to teach both children a lesson, sent her brutal brother and two sons out to give René "a good scare." But even Mother Slogum was frightened when she heard they had castrated the boy.

In *Slogum House,* Mari Sandoz sets herself the gigantic task of making this unnatural mother humanly understandable, is kept from doing so by Gulla Slogum's many crimes, her lack of all familiar human characteristics except greed. An old-fashioned, 400-page chronicle, slow-moving despite its many melodramatic episodes, *Slogum House* is set against the same brutal Nebraska-pioneer background pictured in Mari Sandoz's *Old Jules,* which won the *Atlantic Monthly* five thousand dollar Nonfiction Prize in 1935. That unsparing biography of the author's father showed how he had been hardened by years of struggle against neighbors as mean as himself, quick-shooting cattlemen, sandstorms, dishonest politicians. It made hash of sentimental pioneer legends. But it presented a far kindlier version of life on the sod-house frontier than does *Slogum House,* which shows Gulla's successful villainy still ripening in her rotten old age. Overburdened with violence to a point that occasionally touches burlesque, *Slogum House* is nevertheless written with power, gives a clearer picture of the wild environment than of the people who fought to make it better or the ones, like Gulla, who tried to make it worse.

Time. November 29, 1937

The design on the jacket of Mari Sandoz's novel, *Capital City,* suggests a bursting bomb. While the book's materials are potentially explosive, I doubt that its final effect on the reader will be more than that of a mild concussion. For one thing, Miss Sandoz is too obviously out to shock: her very sentences show the strain. For another, though the journalistic value of *Capital City* is high, it is simply not a very good novel.

Miss Sandoz aims to pin down with the brass tacks of fact the picture of American Fascism that Sinclair Lewis drew so tellingly in *It Can't Happen Here.* In the not-so-imaginary Midwestern State of Kanewa is the not-so-imaginary capital city of Franklin. Things are going on today in Franklin and in a hundred Franklins throughout the land, if we are to trust Miss Sandoz's angry eye and pen. Gold Shirts, college-boy Storm Troopers, mysterious deaths of people with names like Greenspan, demagogues and new democratic leaders rising in opposition to the demagogues; the town's "best people" scared into violence by fear, desperate with the knowledge that they are not the men and women their pioneer forefathers were; the loose-enders, the intellectual outcasts uniting around social issues instead of aesthetic issues as in Carol Kennicott's day; newspapers, puzzlingly subsidized, with names like the *Christian Challenger,* printing open incitements to pogroms. In brief, not Fascism but the possible setup for Fascism.

That's what *Capital City* is about. All the material is real enough, perhaps even yanked out of newspaper files and yet *It Can't Happen Here,* which was based on a mere hypothesis, has greater solidity, as both art and propaganda, than Miss Sandoz's book. In *Capital City* the town itself has a certain vividness, but the characters have none. Also, there's too much of what one can only call scandal-mongering, even though Miss Sandoz is on the side of the angels. The author has plenty of hardbitten talent, as *Old Jules* and *Slogum House,* her previous books, testify, but I think *Capital City* makes very little use of them.

The message of *Capital City* is not one American citizens can lightly disregard. It seems too bad that it has not been clothed in more convincing form. Indignation alone does not make novels.

Clifton Fadiman. *The New Yorker.*
December 2, 1939, pp. 94, 96

In 1935, Mari Sandoz won the *Atlantic* nonfiction prize of five thousand dollars for her first book, *Old Jules,* the biography of her father. Reviewers praised its taut, vigorous style and unsquinting honesty. Bernard De Voto called it more than an "enthralling" story: "it is an experience in citizenship." The reviewer for the *New York Herald Tribune* felt that he had read "the history of all pioneering"; and Stephen Vincent Benet called it "the best and most honest of its kind since Hamlin Garland's *A Son of the Middle Border.*"

Yet some critics, despite their appreciation of its stylistic strength and forthrightness, were put off by the portrayal of Old Jules, as was the reviewer for *Books* who wrote, "The old man's virtues—his toughness, perseverance, and unexpected intellectual interests—didn't seem to us to compensate for his insensitiveness, even brutality, toward his family and neighbors. The hardships of pioneer life are no excuse. The man was just mean, and would have been mean anywhere. There was something appalling in him."

Two years later, in 1937, Sandoz published *Slogum House,* a novel set in the 1890s and first three decades of the twentieth century in the Nebraska Sandhills, the same territory and time period as in the biography. Again crediting the author with a style powerful enough to match the story, reviewers called this book "a brutal book written for strong stomachs," "a burning, searing narrative," a book "overburdened with violence to a point that occasionally touches burlesque." After recognizing that the novel was not "pretty," the critic for the *Boston Transcript* went on in its defense: "it may be attacked in some quarters as a sordid book. The arbiters who pronounced *Tobacco Road* obscene and edited the dialogue of *Dead End* probably will have a word to say about *Slogum House.* It is neither sordid nor obscene, however, because it is free of any gratuitous intention in these respects. Mari Sandoz has included nothing here which is not a necessary and legitimate part of her picture."

The violence that virtually every reviewer of *Slogum House* felt compelled to comment upon permeates every facet of the book. It is in the assaults that an uninviting land inflicts upon anything so audacious as to believe it can survive. It is in the wars between cattlemen and sheepmen, and between farmers and rangemen over whose way of exploiting the land and its resources shall prevail. But most consistently and vividly, the violence is spawned in

Slogum House and carried by the members of the Slogum family like a contagious disease across the Sandhills. . . .

Mari Sandoz saw many times over the use of violence to acquire power over other people, but she also saw a few people acquire another kind of power—people like her mother [Mary] who had to pull from within themselves the will and means to survive. Mary Sandoz lived many years after the death of her husband Jules, and in that time she came to own many acres of land and left to her children an inheritance far surpassing that which Old Jules had left. In Ruedy Slogum, Gulla's husband, Mari Sandoz created a character whose staying power equalled that of her mother. Gulla Slogum, always contemptuous of a husband she regarded as weak-willed, saw her dreams shattered by the Depression, her husband gone to his own house and land, and her children dead or fled as her control weakened. Finally, like a child as a result of a succession of strokes, she was carried to Ruedy, who, always sustaining an opposition that Gulla could not overcome, was described by a neighbor as "like the little cedar on a rock, its roots finally splitting it wide open."

In both her books, Sandoz vividly depicts, and thereby focuses the reader's attention on, the individual whose desire for domination carried with it a will for the violent pursuit of that desire. She shows the extent to which that will was responsible for both the cruelty and the strength in the pioneer character. But readers of *Old Jules* and *Slogum House* should not overlook Sandoz's portrayal of the "cedars on the rock"; for despite their vulnerability and their seeming acquiescence to dominant forces, they do prevail and, ultimately, inherit the earth.

Rosemary Whitaker. *Western American
Literature*. 16, 1981, pp. 217–18, 223–24

Mari Sandoz is recognized as a novelist, historian, and biographer, as well as an authority on the Indians of the Great Plains. Her work varies in quality, her novels usually considered least successful, and her histories, particularly her biographies, most trenchant. In the latter she has fused her skill as a writer, her mastery of historical research, and her empathy for her subjects to create works of unique and lasting value. . . .

Mari's interest, and the theme of all her books, was in the relationship of man and the land. "Why doesn't anyone who really understands the farmer's weaknesses, his strengths, his triumphs, and his problems—and appreciates the fierce affection that grows up in him for his not always friendly plot of soil—write of him?" she asked early in her career. In particular, she spoke poetically about the country of the Running Water, the Niobrara River, which would never accept the intruder unless he gave himself wholly to it; no one, she said, who had even been in that region could forget it. Her concern was not with the history of dates or wars, but with the history of man in his environment.

On her chosen landscape, the trans-Missouri basin, certain memorable men appeared from time to time, and it is their experiences she relates in her biographies and histories. Her subjects are significant because of their unique qualities as human beings, but also because in their individual lives they exhibit certain universal qualities. They respond and react to the force of events on the Great Plains, caught in a historical moment when one culture supersedes another. . . .

As a writer, she enjoyed working with both old and new forms. Allegory, one of the oldest and most didactic forms of storytelling, is recognizable in *Winter Thunder, Slogum House, Capital City,* and *The Tom-Walker.* Her nonfiction is less obviously allegorical, but the elements are there, stressing the author's belief in the absolute necessity of development through struggle, and, particularly in the Indian books, the loss the white civilization had inflicted upon itself because of its discrimination. She felt that the United States would always have on its conscience the sin of what it had done to the Indians, and for that reason would never be what it could have been. . . .

The re-creation of early settler life abounds in Plains literature, but Mari Sandoz's *Old Jules* is so unusual that it has few imitations. Her ability to fuse Jules's importance to the region with scenes from his domestic life, while involving herself, is rare. (The only biography I know that manages similar emotional material so unemotionally, achieving aesthetic distance, is Edmund Gosse's *Father and Son,* about life in the 1800s in England.) In 1935, *Old Jules* shocked people, not only because of the domestic scenes but because it showed the public a stark, unromantic view of the frontier.

Helen Winter Stauffer. *Mari Sandoz: Story
Catcher of the Plains* (Lincoln: University
of Nebraska Press, 1982), pp. 1–2, 5, 7–8

Stories are published because they tell an engaging tale in an engaging manner: that is, they succeed or fail ultimately as art. And it is as art that the best of Sandoz's stories succeed, a proposition I hope to demonstrate by [considering] one of Sandoz's very best stories, "The Smart Man." Published in 1959, this story was actually written much earlier, and its history suggests that Sandoz herself thought it one of her very best pieces. In a letter to Virginia Faulkner, Sandoz disclosed that "The Smart Man" dated "from the late 1920s" and was one of the two stories that she "didn't burn back in 1933 (when I tried to put all the writing business behind me, once and for all.)" Sandoz implied that she did not burn "The Smart Man" because it "was out" when she destroyed the others but added that she probably would not "have burned it anyway." I would suggest that Sandoz may very well have thought "The Smart Man" a story of exceptional merit, one worth saving. If she failed in her effort to "put all the writing business behind" her, "The Smart Man" would be a good piece to be known by. . . .

Sandoz resists an easy resolution of the tensions within her central figure: Emil Karr remains deeply torn by the demands of self and society, his sound heart and his regard for social opinion. Sandoz does, however, suggest a metaphoric resolution of the larger conflict between nature and society implicit in the story. When Emil first learns of [his wife] Noreen's pregnancy, he scratches the name of his son, YOUNG EMIL, into one of his fine Hubbard squashes. Later, when the squash has grown to full size and the letters have "spread in silvery gray over the darkening green," Emil enters it in a local fair, seeking again the blue ribbons that proclaim him a "smart man." The squash wins first prize, despite the judge's telling Emil that "marred vegetables" are usually disqualified. Thus Sandoz metaphorically suggests the power of nature to overcome human intrusion: the natural vitality of the squash, responding to Emil's own natural capacity for nurturing, is more than sufficient to overcome the scars he inflicts upon it in his search for social approval. The urge and urge of the world is ultimately irresistible. The metaphor applies to Emil's son as well. The child is "marred" by Emil's desire to make him an object of social approval, a further proof of his father's being a "smart man." But despite being "marred," young Emil will grow "into a strong wide-standing man," for he, like the squash, will respond to that quality in his father that is stronger finally than his need for social acceptance: his deep natural ability to nurture, to make things grow and live.

Fritz Oelschlager. South Dakota Review.
19:4, Winter, 1982, pp. 66, 74–75

Old Jules is one of the very few western histories to explore the pioneer West's dominant institution, marriage, and to imply that relations among women and men are a significant historical theme. Sandoz's award-winning book anticipates many of the conclusions of recent scholarship on pioneer women and, with its focus on violence against women, presents unique insights on the lives of western women.

    Old Jules can also help to illuminate the problems women scholars face as they reconstruct women's history. Feminist critics have been sorely confused about how to judge the lives of western women. Some search for literary and historical foremothers who defy the traditional roles of the nineteenth century's "women's sphere" to achieve in their lives the measure of freedom our cultural myths associate with the frontier; others acknowledge the truth in the stereotype of the reluctant woman pioneer, accepting that most women were confined within restrictive definitions of their character, often powerless, though perhaps creating order and meaning in their lives through connections to other women and to a woman's subculture. While Jules Sandoz found the freedom Frederick Jackson Turner described, the West did not offer Mary Sandoz, his wife, the same bargain. After exposing in *Old Jules* the violent and circumscribed lives of her mother and other plains women, Sandoz turns in her later histories to the classic masculine West and its themes, to what she calls "the romantic days." Interested in heroism, individualism, and power, which she sees as the natural subjects of history, Sandoz never again gives a woman a starring role in western history, though women sometimes are protagonists in her fiction. Sandoz's uncertainty about whether to identify with her father's or her mother's West, clearly separate worlds in *Old Jules,* and her struggles to assess the relative heroism of her pioneer parents' lives help elucidate central questions raised by contemporary feminists. . . .

Old Jules is valuable to students of women's history because it explores the power dynamics within the pioneer marriage and undercuts the myth of the heroic frontiersman, but also because it reveals the difficulties of writing about women while aspiring to male freedom and the importance, in [Carolyn] Heilbrun's words, of learning to aspire "*as women,* supporting other women, identifying with them, and imagining the achievement of women generally." Sandoz's confusion about her "emotional identity" as a woman scholar is one that all women share, though we may not realize it.

Melody Graulich. *Western American Literature.* 17, 1983, pp. 3–4

About the time that Sandoz was rewriting *Old Jules* and fashioning *Slogum House,* she became intrigued with the work and philosophy of Friedrich Nietzsche, and the will-to-power individual. In her letters she stated that, not only was Gulla Slogum a will-to-power figure, Old Jules was, as well. . . .

Sandoz believed and said frequently that there could not be a story without a conflict, and in book after book written by her, conflicts raged and were somehow resolved, for better or worse. The protagonist in *The Tom-Walker* returns from the Civil War minus one leg, to find his family wealthy as a result of war profiteering. He leaves Ohio and goes west to pioneer and tame the land. The generations that spring from him also sustain injuries in subsequent wars. Thus, three generations of a family swim against the current to struggle for social change, especially in the aftermath of war.

Cheyenne Autumn details the struggle of the epic 1500-mile flight of the Cheyenne Indian tribe in 1878 from their reservation in the Indian Territory of Oklahoma to their ancestral home on the Yellowstone River in Montana. This was a large-scale rebellion, ending in massacre and tragedy for most of the Indians, but a few finally made it.

Claire Mattern. *CEA Critic.* 49: 2–4, 1986–87, pp. 110–111

[In *Crazy Horse*], Sandoz experimented with a new idiom to help readers experience the mentality and viewpoint of the Plains Indians at a time when white settlers, hunters, and miners were coming west to replace the Indians' "savage" culture with their own "civilized" one. Young Crazy Horse is, like Huck [Finn] and Edna [Pontellier in *The Ana Kening*), coming to a new consciousness about his place in the universe, and his vision at the end of part 1 shows he will play a key role in his people's fate as they fight to ward off a culture whose view of ownership is foreign to the Sioux. Part 2 depicts the major battles of the 1860s over possession of the Yellowstone River Basin west of the Black Hills, a fertile area for the buffalo upon which the Indians rely for their whole livelihood. The buffalo is "the brother of the Indian" and an integral part of his religion. . . .

In part 3, in spite of huge odds, he emerges as a successful strategist against Crook on the Rosebud and Custer at the Little Big Horn. Now he marries Black Shawl, a good woman who serves him well at home as she provides him fresh horses on the battlefield. Later, after he comes into the white agency, Crazy Horse is given a white wife, who is also loyal, keeping him in contact with the larger white political world. But, faithful as these women are, they don't fulfill in Crazy Horse the special affection he has for [Black Buffalo Woman,] the woman he lost. For some critics, this love story is more imaginative than the epic history in the novel (Gannet), but through it Sandoz demonstrates, like Twain and [Kate] Chopin, the causal connection between possessiveness in the white culture and the deep human need for personal love and acceptance.

Thomas Matchie. *Journal of American Culture.* 11:4, Winter, 1988, pp. 9–10

SARRAUTE, NATHALIE (FRANCE) 1902–

Many writers, in passing, have brushed against the wall of inauthenticity, but I know of none who, quite deliberately, has made it the subject of a book: inauthenticity being anything but novelistic. Most novelists, on the contrary, try to persuade us that the world is made up of irreplaceable individuals, all exquisite, even the villains, all ardent, all different. Nathalie Sarraute shows us the wall of inauthenticity rising on every side. But what is behind this wall? As it happens, there's nothing, or rather almost nothing. Vague attempts to flee something whose lurking presence we sense dimly. *Authenticity,* that is, the real connection with others, with oneself and with death, is suggested at every turn, although remaining invisible. We feel it because we flee it. If we take a look, as the author invites us to do, at what goes on inside people, we glimpse a moiling of flabby, many-tentacled evasions: evasion through objects which peacefully reflect the universal and the permanent; evasion through daily occupations; evasion through pettiness. . . .

The best thing about Nathalie Sarraute is her stumbling, groping style, with its honesty and numerous misgivings, a style that approaches the object with reverent precautions, withdraws from it suddenly out of a sense of modesty, or through timidity before its complexity, then, when all is said and done, suddenly presents us with the drooling monster, almost without having touched it, through the magic of an image. Is this psychology? Perhaps Nathalie Sarraute, who is a great admirer of Dostoievsky, would like to have us believe that it is. For my part, I believe that by allowing us to sense an intangible authenticity, by showing us the constant coming and going from the particular to the general, by tenaciously depicting the reassuring, dreary world of the inauthentic, she has achieved a technique which makes it possible to attain, over and beyond the psychological, human reality in its very *existence.*

Jean-Paul Sartre. Preface to Nathalie
Sarraute. *Portrait of a Man Unknown* (New
York: George Braziller, 1958), pp. xi, xiv

Nathalie Sarraute does not offer a rational description of [the] interior universe whose swarming activity, instability and disconcerting logic many critics have already analyzed. She explores it with intelligence, with relentless lucidity and determination not to be fooled by the *trompe-l'oeil* of appearances; she also looks at it with an eye at times childish. Yet the task to which she has set herself and which gives her works both a new content and a personal style, is precisely to shun the temptation of making hasty clarifications, to avoid limiting herself to the exclusive use of rational analysis.

Anne Minor. *Yale French Studies.* Summer,
1959, pp. 96–97

In *The Era of Suspicion,* a brilliant essay on the novel, Mme. Sarraute staked out her domain: the hidden, emotional life of the depths in constant flux, with its subtle interchanges, its infinitesimal variations in pressure, which reveal, way beneath the rational social patterns of behavior, the watchful, hunted human hunter, peering like some small ferocious shell-fish fearfully out of his shell. What is most curious perhaps . . . is that she manages so intensely to suggest not the modes of a solitary individual life, but patterns emerging from a common human substance, that of the "species," organically a whole, our ultimate reality.

Germaine Brée, *The New York Times.*
November 1, 1959, pp. 4, 43

She insists that the reader spend his time with nerve-racking, irritating people whose problems are either banal or factitious. Yet Mme. Sarraute is not boring at all. The risk is run but failure is avoided. She is fascinating because, while she seems to be entirely concerned with little truths about small personalities, she has a firm grip on a very large truth—the accepted description of man as a "social animal" means not that he loves his fellows but only that he can't do without them.

The thoroughness with which Mme. Sarraute pursues this single theme, delineating the constant fluctuations of feeling in a small group in close emotional quarters is compelling. To some readers it may seem almost cruel.

Naomi Bliven. *The New Yorker.* March 26,
1960, p. 152

Few contemporary novelists have been so successful at portraying sensitive and frail beings at odds with a dark, hostile world in which perfidy and conventionality regularly triumph. Nathalie Sarraute, who has criticized Virginia Woolf, is not unlike her. She directs her microscope at the apparently insignificant and endows it with poetry and with tragic implications. She implicitly protests against all that is insincere in men and delves into a deeper authenticity, buried in our lower depths.

> Henri Peyre. *The New York Times.* May 15, 1960, p. 46

The center of Mme. Sarraute's nondescript universe is occupied neither by the author nor by a proxy hero. Through many eyes and more than one consciousness we encounter the characters, not in repose but as they gravitate toward or away from each other. . . . Mme. Sarraute does not lead her reader by the hand into the subconscious strata of her characters, but instead projects their self-awareness into the exterior world, where they may be observed. She does not pass judgement on their moral worth with intricate analyses of their actions. She does not break down personality to arrive at its comprehension; she aspires, instead, to its synthesis.

> Anna Balakian. *Saturday Review of Literature.* June 11, 1960, pp. 35–36

Steadily, at the rate of one novel every sixth year, Nathalie Sarraute has been forcing upon her readers a new awareness of their sub-surface selves. An inner world of gelatinous beings thus stands revealed under a pallid light; all anxiously groping for identical satisfactions, these pseudo-human creatures alternately experience pleasure and pain as tumor-like feelers either mingle with similar excrescences or become bruised by hostile reactions and are forced back into their own transparency and nakedness.

> Leon S. Roudiez. *Yale French Studies.* Spring–Summer, 1961, p. 90

For Madame Sarraute, the reader is the enemy; he is there to be ambushed, demoralized, ultimately brainwashed. But the reader . . . is sometimes tempted to resist his fate. He snarls and starts looking for a bolt-hole. If only, somehow, out of this faceless nightmare, he could create a sane, familiar world, he might perhaps escape. If he could see these monsters, suddenly as *characters* well-classified, related to a solid social setting, then he might climb above them, criticise them, drive them off. Facelessness and anonymity are the essential materials from which Madame Sarraute constructs her particular Inferno. But suppose the reader will not have this? Suppose in desperation he should restore faces to the flayed and bleeding heads, and thus, out of mere pronouns, start creating *people*? At once, of course, the hallucinatory power of the novel is lost.

That this *can* happen is the evident weakness of Nathalie Sarraute the novelist.

Richard N. Coe. *Time and Tide.*
March 29, 1962, n.p.

What is the point of this multiplication of realities? . . . When [the writer] comes to the literary marketplace bearing his jar of tiny and as yet uncatalogued marine specimens, are we to welcome him in the name of science? (The writer as marine biologist.) Of sport? (The writer as deep sea diver.) Why does he deserve an audience? How many fragments of reality will readers of novels tolerate? How many do they need?

It really is science, or better yet sport, that Sarraute has in mind. Hence her revulsion against the beautiful and the pleasurable as such. . . . Thus Sarraute summons the novel to take its belated place in the anti-hedonistic revolution that has already conquered painting and music—to renounce pleasure and beauty, because these are attached to "familiar appearances." It is a stern appeal and may find a willing audience.

Susan Sontag. *Partisan Review.* Summer,
1963, p. 267

It is hard not to sound like a Philistine in bringing opposition to Mme. Sarraute, because she walls her position around with all the traditional bricks of the avant-garde. She grabs off the right to be boring; she promises herself recognition by posterity; she speaks of art as though it were a vow of celibacy; she keeps distinguishing between the modern and the old-fashioned—the modern always being hers. . . . She would rather be right than true, and one way of seeming right is by making all others appear wrong—very irritating in someone posing all the time as a relativist who is conscious of the eclectic nature of our period.

Alfred Chester. *The American Scholar.*
Summer, 1963, p. 490

In *Martereau* the poetic element stands out from the work as a whole, from its structure. And the prominence of the poetic element has a very important meaning, because when a writer no longer adheres to the exterior contours of the event but rather, always moving toward the interior, seeks to seize the fleeting states of the soul and the subtlest ramifications of thoughts and sensations, then men and situations—"formless models, chaos in which a thousand possibilities collide"—open up and overflow. Except for Martereau, nobody in this novel has a name. They are "I," "he," "she." And all of them are alike to the point of being interchangeable.

Matter such as this cannot be imprisoned in a mold. At the most, it can be organized according to internal rules, that is, according to a rhythm. And that is what Nathalie Sarraute has done.

A creative order can be found in the admirable continuity with which inner space, the space of thought, is evoked. And it can be found even more in the repetitions. For in this space all sorts of things—a word someone has dropped, a situation staged for someone's benefit, a hat worn by a woman, for example—are temporarily eliminated, only to surface again, in spontaneous memories, while they continue to follow their own course. They take on another appearance because time has elapsed; they take on a second meaning, often terrifying; and later they often take on a third. . . .

This repetition is the source of the rhythm and of our impression of a kind of music: a music composed of banal and fragile substances, a music whose themes rise against the muffled sound of background noise, in variations that are always new, in harmonies that are always changing.

Gerda Zeltner. In Mimica Cranaki and Yvon
Belaval. Nathalie Sarraute (Paris:
Gallimard, 1965), pp. 231–32

Nathalie Sarraute no longer believes in human types; she refuses to describe individuals and characters. But she believes in the power, the necessity, and the approaching advent of a psychology that will be subtler, deeper, and truer, a psychology freed from characters. Although she wants to deprive the public of the "unforgettable characters" of the traditional novel, her reason is only that she fears seeing "easy vitality" preferred to the tremblings and the shimmerings of real psychological states.

Her pejorative use of the word "surface" as opposed to "depth" is in itself highly meaningful. Characters bother Sarraute because they represent the *surface of things*, whereas she dreams of plunging the reader into abysses "where nothing remains of these comfortable points of reference." . . .

The world risks being completely dissolved, being annihilated, by the operation on it she is contemplating. When a writer neglects the *surface of things* in favor of a *depth* that is always more distant, always more inaccessible, is the writer not forced to cease describing anything but shadows, reflections, and patches of fog? Since the world, unlike these depths, is hard, obstinate, and immediately present, would it not be more worthwhile to cling to this *surface* that has been so slandered, rather than to what it (supposedly) is hiding?

Dialogue will serve as our best, most precise example. In the spoken sentence there is a solid, huge, unquestionable *presence* that radically separates the spoken sentence from all thought, especially from those flashes of thought—barely formulated, drowned by their movement and their perpetual mutations—which Nathalie Sarraute eagerly provides for us.

Alain Robbe-Grillet. Critique. July, 1956,
pp. 700–701

According to Nathalie Sarraute in her *The Age of Suspicion,* the word "psychology" is one that no author today can hear mentioned in connection with himself *without lowering his eyes and blushing.* She herself makes the assertion without lowering her eyes or blushing, with the aplomb of one who is expressing a truth that has passed into the public domain. But it is the assurance of a writer loudly dissociating herself from that of which she knows she is an accomplice, if not indeed guilty herself.

"No author"? That is not at all exact, if only by virtue of the attention some of us still pay to psychology, a word we no longer need to put in quotation marks or underline, while at the same time we recoil from it somewhat with a kind of disdain. The orthodoxy that Mme. Sarraute wishes here to represent, however, finds in her a defender who is suspect. There are many among us who want to reintroduce psychology into the modern novel without, at the same time, having it lose any of its power. After some strange detours, Nathalie Sarraute herself finally concurs with this in *The Age of Suspicion,* which does not surprise us when we remember that she is the author of the most psychological stories possible, which are, nonetheless, new. I am thinking about those amazing books which pile up pages of psychological riches: *Tropisms, Portrait of a Man Unknown, Martereau, The Planetarium.* Whoever reads *The Age of Suspicion* without keeping the novels of Nathalie Sarraute in mind will not avoid the misconception of seeing an indictment in what is, for anyone who is not duped by appearances, a speech for the defense. . . .

Nathalie Sarraute . . . disdains psychology all the less in that she, more than any other novelist today, excels in this field. . . . This novelist always comes back to the same theme; what she says corresponds to what our experience has taught us, but as nobody has expressed it before her. I never tire of watching her clear away and cultivate the psychological domain which she has appropriated and where she reigns.

Claude Mauriac. *The New Literature*
(New York: George Braziller, 1959),
pp. 235–36, 242–43

A few words, harmless in appearance, that arise during a conversation between one speaker and another form the nucleus of a whole universe within which the very birth of language can be witnessed [in *The Planetarium*]. Only by taking into consideration the whole phenomenon of which the words are only some kind of residue can we possibly account with any accuracy for the effects of the words.

What I have just said about a few words arising between the two partners in a dialogue is just as true for an object that can change the milieu in which these conversations can occur; this object is like the stone thrown into a pool of water, transforming the entire surface of the water. The stone gives rise to circles that can clash with other circles, thus producing knots and whirlwinds whose existence would be unintelligible if we do not consider the play of influences.

Thus, Nathalie Sarraute's novel *The Planetarium* is, so to speak, encircled by the wave caused by the installation of a new door of natural oak in an old woman's apartment. Each of the events that populate the novel, no matter how minuscule they may seem at a first glance, gives rise to a circle or a sphere, and is inscribed on a trajectory that influences all the others.

Michel Butor. *Arts.* June 3–9, 1959, p. 2

Since they are writing at the same period, our own, what [Nathalie Sarraute and Alain Robbe-Grillet] tell us about reality is perhaps not—in spite of all that separates them—so very different.

The opposition between them resides more in what interests them, in what they are seeking, than in what they state. Sarraute is still—albeit in the most extended, most extreme form—a novelist of the period I have characterized as concerned with the disintegration of the character. The all-encompassing structures of the social world do not interest her very much; everywhere she is seeking authentically human, immediately lived experience: Robbe-Grillet is also seeking the human, but as an exteriorized form, as a reality that forms part of an all-encompassing structure.

Once this difference is made clear, their statements seem very close to one another. In seeking immediately lived experience, Sarraute states that this experience no longer exists in exteriorizations, which are all, almost without exception, inauthentic, distorted, and deformed. Thus, faced with this extreme disintegration of character, she limits the universe of her works to the only domain in which she can still find reality that seems essential to her (although naturally what she finds here is equally deformed and exasperating by the impossibility of exteriorization): that domain is feelings and human experiences prior to all expression, what she calls tropisms, subconversations, subcreations. In this sense, she seems to me (and I hope that she will not hold this against me) a writer expressing an essential aspect of contemporary reality in a form for which she undoubtedly creates a new modality, but a form which is still that of the writers concerned with the disappearance of character—Kafka, Musil, Joyce—to whom she very frequently refers. . . .

Robbe-Grillet expresses this same reality of contemporary society in an essentially new form.

Lucien Goldmann. *Pour une sociologie du roman* (Paris: Gallimard, 1964), pp. 195–97

In an author who has gone to such lengths to explain what she is doing, conspicuous elements she has not mentioned may be all the more noteworthy. First, there is the entirely negative character of [Sarraute's] discoveries, which Sartre found so striking. Nothing in either her method or subject matter explains the catastrophic nature of the inner life, the complete or almost complete absence of love, generosity, magnanimity, and the like in her work. Every word, if it is not meant to deceive, is a "weapon," all thoughts are "assembled like a large and powerful army behind its banners . . . about to roll forward." The imagery of warfare is all-pervasive. Even in Kafka, as she herself has noted—let alone in Dostoevsky or in Proust and Joyce, the earlier masters of the inner monologue—there are still these "moments of sincerity, these states of grace," which are absent from her own work. There is, second, and more surprisingly, the fact that she has never elaborated on her enormously effective use of the "they"—what "they say," the commonplace, the cliché, the merely idiomatic turn of the phrase—emphasized by many of her reviewers and admirers. "They" made their first appearance in *Portrait of a Man Unknown,* moved into the center of the plot in *The Planetarium,* and became the "hero" of *The Golden Fruits. . . .*

There is finally the "metamorphosis," the moment of truth, around which each novel is centered, as Greek tragedy is centered around the moment of recognition. This is what gives Nathalie Sarraute's writing a dramatic quality which is, I think, unique in contemporary fiction. (She probably borrowed the word from Kafka's famous story—in *Portrait of a Man Unknown* she even uses the original image: Father and Daughter confront each other like "two giant insects, two enormous dung beetles.") The metamorphosis occurs in the rare moments when "sub-conversation" and "sub-conversation" confront each other, that is, at the moment of descent from the daylight world of seeming down to "the bottom of a well" where naked, "clasped to each other," slipping and fighting in a nether world, as private and incommunicable as the world of dreams and nightmares, the characters meet in a murderous intimacy that will conceal nothing.

Hannah Arendt. *New York Review of Books.*
March 5, 1964, pp. 5–6

The picture [in Sarraute's novels] is not a happy one. But when has depth psychology ever been jovial? Has Sarraute shown herself to be more severe than La Rochefoucauld or Freud? She is, in fact, *less* despairing than La Rochefoucauld, who depends upon Jansenist theology. She is closer to Freud; his pessimism was similar to Schopenhauer's, but based on science, and it led to an optimistic technique or action.

At the very least, Sarraute teaches us that no one can really fool anyone else, because we all have the same essence. Of course, this has nothing to do with lies, to which everyone falls victim. It has to do with the insincerity we bring to social relationships, one person toward the other. The man who does not feel what another is truly thinking is not really looking at the other; he lets himself forget the other and gets lost in his own egocentricity. Thus—and here begins Sarraute's lesson in optimism—he refuses real communication.

The need to communicate can lead to hysteria and to debasement (as, according to Sarraute, Dostoevsky has shown). But the need to communicate can also be a manifestation of a passionate interest in others. Sarraute's novels take the form of dialogue, conversations, subconversations; her novels require partners; her characters never exist except in relation to someone else—all because the essence of man is, after all, a passionate interest in man. Evil is perhaps other people. But love, too, is other people.

Mimica Cranaki and Yvon Belaval. *Nathalie Sarraute* (Paris: Gallimard, 1965), pp. 130–31

There is a special fitness in [an] international reputation for a writer whose background has been to an unusual degree international. The child of Russian parents who met while university students in Geneva (Jewish students being just then unwelcome in Russian universities), she was born . . . in Russia, but as her parents were divorced when she was two she lived, sometimes with her mother (a writer of popular novels), sometimes with her father, in Switzerland, Paris, and Russia, speaking and reading French and Russian. From the age of eight she lived with her father, remarried by then and settled in Paris, so that her schooling was French, but from her stepmother's mother she learned German. English she learned early and took her degree in English at the Sorbonne, after which she began work for a B.A. in history at Oxford (1921–22). To her keen disappointment her father did not permit her to continue; one of her sharpest regrets was having to relinquish the captaincy of the punting team.

A year at the Faculty of Letters of Berlin University studying sociology was followed by law studies at the University of Paris and admission to the Bar. She had married a fellow law student and during the next twelve years she practiced law in a desultory fashion, thinking only, she says, of writing, and her three daughters were born. The variety of her studies, activities, and interests provides a rich and diverse background for her writing—a career embarked upon later than is usual even for novelists. Her mastery of four languages has relevance to her theory and practice of criticism and the novel. Of the modern writers who invoke as influences Proust, Dostoievsky, Joyce, and Kafka, few others can have read them all in the original.

Ruth Z. Temple. *Nathalie Sarraute* (New York: Columbia University Press, 1968), pp. 5–6

The action [in Sarraute's work] is simplified, conventional, classic—a Punch and Judy show, Keystone comedy, or Pearl White cliff-hanger—having to do with the seesawing of power in a human group, which can be as large as a mob or as small as a single integer. Some creature is being chased; he makes a narrow escape; they are after him again; he tries to hide, flattens himself against a wall, melts into a crowd, puts on a disguise; they catch him, tear off his false whiskers; he begs for mercy, uttering pathetic squeals. It is always the One and the Many, even and most emphatically when the delicate power-balance trembles and oscillates within a palpitating individual heart. In the outer world, alliances and ententes, protective networks, more or less durable, can be made, but within the individual heart there is a continuous division and multiplication. What counts statistically as one person is a turmoil of constant side-changing, treachery, surrender, appeasement; in that sanctum nobody can be safe even long enough to get his breath.

At the outset, Mme. Sarraute's reader, finding himself in this strange and unquiet territory, may be somewhat bewildered. He hears voices talking but cannot assign them to bodies with names, hair-color, eye-color, identifying marks. It is like listening to a conversation—or a quarrel—on the other side of the thin partition of a hotel room; you long to rush down and consult the register. But there is no register in this hotel; no telltale shoes are put out at night in the corridor, and the occupants of the room next to you keep changing just as you think you have them placed.

Mary McCarthy. New York Review of Books.
July 31, 1969, p. 4

[In 1946] I felt sorry for Nathalie Sarraute, though without letting it show. Writing tortured her, writing made her ill. Time fought its way onward, I was being crushed by that weight, by that flagstone, by that monument she carried every day on her shoulders once her fountain pen had been unscrewed. And yet the ardor in her eyes left me a hope. Two firebirds. She expressed her tragedy and her passion for literature by means of distant insinuations, enigmatic waverings, probing silences, questioning looks, and pauses that were pools of promises. She labored to explain, she labored before venturing to explain herself, she labored to get each detail right, she labored as she questioned everything she had just said, she advanced step by hard-won step across ruins and crumbling footholds, over black ice, over worm-eaten scaffoldings, over the shakiest of constructions, over condemned catwalks, over treacherous repairs, so that there was always the risk she might fall and never recover; she explained again that she didn't like Faulkner all that much, she was sorry, it was a pity, that's how it was, after all the last word has never been spoken, but really, she exploded, she didn't like him one bit. . . . Without dominating the conversation, she went back over the point she had been making, she went on musing, among her books, in the sheltered hollows of her reading; she continued to concentrate on the idea that we liked Faulkner and that she didn't. . . .

It stared one in the face: literature was her reason for living. I imagined a scientist in love with love, a scientist doing research on love, making experiments on love in a laboratory full of complicated apparatus. Nathalie Sarraute was like that. She did not research, she made her experiments on and with literature, which was what she loved most in the world. . . . We talked about Camus, abut Gide, about Kafka; she weighed their talent or their absence of talent with a thousand-kilogram weight which she lifted in slow motion.

Violette Leduc. Mad in Pursuit (New York:
Farrar, Straus & Giroux, 1971),
pp. 47–48, 79

Readers of Miss Sarraute's most successful novel to date, *The Golden Fruits*, will recall her astonishing feat in bringing to life a prize-winning writer through the thoughts and conversations of his friends and enemies. This is an infinitely difficult process because characters do not appear as such but only as figures mirrored in the minds of others. A casual comment, a fleeing thought, a twitching eyebrow—such are the mosaics out of which the personalities in a Sarraute novel are constructed.

In *Do You Hear Them?* she attempts to do for the world of art what she did for the world of letters in *The Golden Fruits*. As you would expect, no characters step forward to be introduced. Instead we are immediately confronted with a series of interior monologues in which tableaux are cumulatively created—a father who is an art collector and his children who cannot understand why he lavishes so much attention on inanimate objects like pre-Columbian figures or Cretan sculptures. So they laugh at him.

The narrative, if one can call it that, consists of a continuum of monologues or soliloquies in which the father's attitude to art is searchingly explored with obbligatos of sly, mischievous or derisive laughter from the children. Occasionally the author enters briefly and discreetly in the third person to illuminate a scene or relationship without, however, intruding on what she calls tropisms, or nuances of thought. Sarraute's aim is to build persons and situations out of a network of obliquely stated sentiments and observations.

Though the book is none too easy reading it is worth doing so for the rewarding final result. . . . Yes, this is one example of the new novel that works, but the book leaves you wondering whether the results so subtly sculptured have any greater impact than might have been achieved through traditional realism.

John Barkham. *New York Post.* February 26, 1973, p. 11

Once having appropriated to herself the tiny domain of tropisms, Sarraute has persevered in exploring it inch by inch, in all her works, novels and plays alike. By exposing these hidden, unbidden fragments of feeling that underlie human discourse and behavior, she has isolated a timeless quality common to all human beings, of whatever background, nationality, or social stratum. The critics who accuse her of depicting a "bourgeois" milieu or a middle-class mentality have failed—like many of her own characters—to transcend appearances, to discover the kernel of eternal truth concealed beneath a semblance of momentary circumstance.

From the initial observation of tropisms as they *exist* and as they precondition behavior in the restricted arena of the family, Nathalie Sarraute has expanded the terrain in which tropisms flourish to include every conceivable area of human relationships. But if she were merely repeating the evidence of the earlier books in a broader field, her works would be repetitious and, eventually, stagnant. It is because she has used the medium of tropisms as a lens through which to view fundamental issues of human concern that Sarraute's work has attained a panoramic dimension. Never deviating from the very particularized tropistic response, Sarraute manages to call into question problems of both individual and universal scope. From the dilemma of "knowing" another person, she progresses to the concept of "knowledge" about literature, art, and ideas; from everyday clichés of speech, she proceeds to the totalitarian possibilities inherent in the misuse of language generally; from a concern with standards of aesthetic judgment, she advances to the broader consideration of ethical values and conduct. Her earliest novels unmasked the dangers and conflicts menacing members of the same family; her latest works hint at the far more dangerous threat that collective ignorance, fearfulness, and intolerance pose to individual members of society. It is the recapitulation of certain universal themes—their unifying resonance from book to book—that welds the self-contained entities of the individual novels and plays into a cohesive *oeuvre*. It is the unlimited human implications of these evanescent impulses that turn the minuscule domain of tropisms into a microcosm of the world.

Gretchen R. Besser. *Nathalie Sarraute*
(Boston: Twayne, 1979), pp. 171–72

What has been taking place in Sarraute's work since *Les Fruits d'or* is so total a transformation of the substance of the novel that it is difficult to grasp it as such. As it has the volatility of spoken words, I will call the material with which she works—in order to establish a comparison with what linguists call "locution"—"interlocution." By this word, infrequently used in linguistics, I imply all that occurs between people when they speak. It includes the phenomenon, in its entirety, which goes beyond speech proper. And as the meaning of this word derives from *interrupt,* to *cut someone short,* that which does not designate a mere speech act, I extend it to any action linked to the use of speech: to accidents of discourse (pauses, excess, lack, tone, intonation) and to effects relating to it (tropisms, gestures).

In this perspective, Nathalie Sarraute's characters are interlocutors: More anonymous even than Kafka's K., they have the tenor of Plato's Georgias, Critons, Euthyphrons. Called forth by dialogue and the same philosophical necessity, they disappear like meteorites or like people we pass in the street, people who are neither more nor less real than characters of a novel and who are bedecked with a name to satisfy the needs of our inner fiction. But what matters here over and above those interlocutors who, for the reader, are ordinary characters, ordinary propositions, is Sarraute's philosophical matter, the locution and the interlocution, what she herself, with regard to the novel, calls "l'usage de la parole" [the use of speech]. Unlike the science of linguistics, which has but one anatomical point of view on language, the point of view of the novel does not have to impose limits on itself for it can collect, gather, in a single movement, causes, effects, and actors. With Sarraute, the novel creates phenomena in literature which as yet have no name, either in science or philosophy. . . .

Any social actor makes use of this weapon of commonplaces, whatever his situation, for it is the debased form of reciprocity that has founded the exchange contract. But the conflict due to the confrontation of the two modes of relation to language (locution and interlocution) remains, nevertheless, insurmountable, from whatever point of view.

The substance of Sarraute's novels envelops this double movement, this deadly embrace, with its violent, vehement, passionate words. That is what leads me to say that the paradise of the social contract exists only in literature, where the tropisms, by their violence, are able to counter any reduction of the "I" to a common denominator, to tear open the closely woven material of the commonplaces, and to continually prevent their organization into a system of compulsory meaning.

Monique Wittig. In Lois Oppenheim, ed.
Three Decades of the French New Novel
(Urbana: University of Illinois Press, 1986),
pp. 132, 139

Sarraute's enduring interest in "tropisms" as well as in the reader's experience of them has remained constant since her earliest work *Tropismes (Tropisms)*, 1939. The concept demonstrates the new territories she charted for writing, particularly women's writing. The best definition of tropisms, the driving force in Sarraute's work, was given by the novelist herself: "I thought they might be called 'tropisms,' after the biological term, because they are purely instinctive and are caused in us by other people or by the outer world and resemble the movements called tropisms by which living organisms expand or contract under certain influences, such as light, heat, and so on. These movements glide quickly round the border of our consciousness, they compose the small, rapid, and sometimes very complex dramas concealed beneath our actions, our gestures, the words we speak, our avowed and clear feelings." Sarraute felt the need to extend and change the novel so that it would convey this unexplored dimension of human psychic reality, these tropisms, or complex inner movements that underlie the most ordinary human interchanges. She wanted to convey what is barely felt, never verbalized, fleeting, never arrested, impersonal, common to all, and developing at different levels of awareness. Since these tropisms encompass experiences that can neither be formulated in thought nor captured in words, tropisms defy expression. They can no more be expressed in traditional forms than the new feminist perceptions because, Sarraute explains, "Scarcely does this formless thing, all timid and trembling, try to show its face than all powerful language, always ready to intervene so as to re-establish order—its own order—jumps on it and crushes it."

Lucille Frackman Becker. *Twentieth-Century
French Women Novelists* (Boston: Twayne,
1989), pp. 111–12

In her most recent book [*Tu ne t'aimes pas* (You don't like yourself)] the author/narrator asks how individuals perceive themselves. As she moves toward the truth about ourselves/our selves, someone tells her that he is proud to have found in himself two beings in all respects. As the narrator progresses from reason to subconscious impulses, he (or she) finds it more and more difficult to verbalize what he finds, because he can no longer see clearly; images are in flux and rapidly dissolve. He can no longer hear voices or distinguish anything, yet somehow new images appear and new words are found. Human beings consist not only of two opposites but of innumerable inner voices struggling endlessly for self-assertion. Sometimes, facing infinite shapes, voices, and figures in motion, the narrator asks himself questions in a voice addressed to nobody/no body but himself. He contemplates fleeting, barely perceptible impressions. Like clouds before a storm, these shadows of things dissolve, then recoalesce, only to dissolve once more. Unsure of himself, the first-person narrator speaks in his own name, as *je* or *moi*, two words that have a specific meaning in this context, as if they referred to two distinct identities; yet the narrator then states that it is as if he were murmuring something to himself.

Overwhelmed by the immensities of invisible beings on his inner stage, the narrator wonders whether all human beings are aware that each one of them is multitude and whether they love themselves. He discovers that there is somebody who loves himself, and this love unites all the invisible beings on his inner stage: "Un seul bloc serre, referme sur soi."

Anna Otten. World Literature Today. 64,
1990, p. 607

Sabine Raffy offers a model for one of the lessons to be found in Sarraute's novels when she speaks of "the constitutive journey" of the sarrautien subject from "the crystalization of the unconscious" to the construction of an "imaginary base" by which the subject establishes relations with the world and an ideology which gives meaning to the subject's existence. This construction makes it possible for the subject to enter "a social milieu which confers it a representative character." The descriptive style of *Portrait d'un inconnu* and *Martereau* allows the feminist reader to reconstruct representative gendered characters out of the narrators of these novels. If that reader identifies herself in relation to these "characters" she risks remaining stuck in Kristeva's first two generations, that is, identifying herself as "like" or as "not like" a male subject. In *Le Planétarium,* however, the reader is both witness to and actor in the process by which figures construct "imaginary" bases in order to interact. The tropistic representation of these constructions shakes loose the fixity of identity they imply. In *Entre la vie et la mort,* the central figure moves toward and away from the "representative character" conferred on him by his milieu. The reader's simultaneous role as witness and actor in this novel is itself brought under scrutiny by a style in which the recognizably gendered identity of the central figure which could exclude the reader is continually thrown into a nongendered space of creation. . . .

Although certain resonances in Sarraute's novels tempt the feminist reader away from what Sarraute wishes to create, "les réactions entre des consciences, peu importe lesquelles" [reactions between consciousness, it matters little which ones], the experience of finding those resonances delineates the surface, the mirror, of the reader's reading, of her history. In the works that follow, L'Usage de la parole, Enfance, and Tu ne t'aimes pas, words take over and become a kind of window or frame for exchange, much as they did in "disent. . ."; for as Sarraute explains to Benmussa, "C'est le mot [. . .] qui est intéressant ici, ce ne sont pas les consciences elles-mêmes" (It's the word (. . .) that is interesting here, not the consciousnesses themselves). For the feminist reader who is interested in a "de-dramatization of the 'fight to the death' between rival groups and thus between the sexes," the words are interesting as well. It is in the reading and writing of words that she encounters her own desire as she faces the socio-symbolic contract alone, able to look with irony at the constructs she carries within her, with recognition of the history she represents, and with compassion for any Other she may find out there.

Sarah Barbour. Nathalie Sarraute and the
Feminist Reader (Lewisburg, Pennsylvania:
Bucknell University Press, 1993), pp. 269, 277

SARTON, MAY (UNITED STATES) 1912–95

A good part of Miss Sarton's poems are love sonnets. . . . To achieve the high polish which these sonnets possess it has been necessary for the poet to employ a good many pre-fabricated emotions, just as the sonnet form itself lends a ready-made gloss to the verse. The result is that the whole performance inevitably calls up Millay et al., in their second April moods, and Miss Sarton's sonnets seem to stem from literary rather than personal emotions. . . . The finest piece of work in every way is a lyric in ten fluid parts, "She Shall Be Called Woman." This poem seems to me to reveal that secret access that women have into the core of their sensations and feelings. And it is certainly from that heightened consciousness that their best and unique work always comes. It is to be hoped that Miss Sarton's future writing will take its departure from this point.

Sherman Conrad. Poetry. July, 1937,
pp. 229–31

Only a poet and, perhaps, only a young poet could have written this beautiful and distinguished first novel (The Single Hound). In it May Sarton has created a little world of some half dozen people and she has given them rich, bountiful life, not only pregnant with meaning for this present instant of time in which she has placed them, but deeply rooted in that humanity which is ageless. . . . Here, as in her poems, May Sarton's aim is to arrive at what she calls "transparency." She has, also, in *The Single Hound* exemplified a way of life and enunciated a literary creed.

Jane Spence Southron. The New York
Times. March 20, 1938, p. 6

Done with something of the eighteenth-century care for the sedate, unemotional line, her poems suggest the even lawns and precise gardens of the time of Queen Anne and the first of the Georges, before the turbulence of the romantic movement rushed in from the left to bewilder and overturn a strictly ordered world. Nevertheless, there is at the same time more emotion beneath the surface of Miss Sarton's dignified verses than was common in eighteenth-century poetry. The result of this slightly paradoxical combination is interesting. Let one try to visualize a butterfly imprisoned within a cake of ice and one will have a fairly good parallel to the poems.

Percy Hutchison. The New York Times.
March 5, 1939, p. 5

May Sarton is an artist of remarkable powers. She is one of those rare poets who, in making use of simple combinations of words—and of the words of our common speech at that—has achieved a vocabulary and style as distinctly her own as any poet now writing. . . . She has drawn upon the whole stream of English literature to develop her subtle cadences and delicate, all-but-inaudible rhythms. . . . One wonders at the extreme simplicity of her statement (for such simplicity needs courage), and the more one wonders the more one is aware of the great gifts set forth. . . . Whatever life-images Miss Sarton chooses to turn into poetry become poetry. Her work is worth the admiring attention of everyone who considers himself a reader.

Martha Bacon. Saturday Review of
Literature. April 17, 1948, p. 50

I suspect that what has always been considered that admirable simplicity of May Sarton's poetry is something more than that. . . . She demonstrates a great range of feeling and subject, an unusual strength in describing what comes before her eyes and touches her heart. Whether she speaks of zinnias or swans or the irradiating light of Provence, she testifies to a deep experience of reality which far surpasses purely speculative philosophy. . . . Her words . . . are never deadened by artifice or prose. The ease with which images in her poetry transpose notions provides the notions or the abstractions with their own firmness and poetic vigor.

Wallace Fowlie. The New Republic.
December 14, 1953, p. 19

Hinged on irony, *Faithful Are the Wounds* swings open onto tragedy. The movement of the book is, in its classical climbing and clearing shape, toward light and truth. It has none of that intellectual wasp sting that such a subject might afford itself. It is a quiet and ever-deepening penetration into the roiled darknesses of uncommitted passion, of jelled fervors in the cold air of doubt; it touches that reserve that jails the modern conscience in its own dubious safety from which it can utter only the cry of "Why can't love help?". . . . Miss Sarton's method, even as that of her men and women who crave the light of day against self-inflicted darkness, is to turn to light what is shadowed, raise to the level of the common ground what is half-buried underground.

William Goyen. *The New York Times*.
March 13, 1955, p. 6

In her new novel, *Faithful Are the Wounds,* May Sarton moves from the world of purely personal relationships, brought to glowing life and examined in minute detail, to one of the most violently burning public questions of our day, democratic dissent in a time of national crisis. Yet the change is much less than the statement implies. . . . Once again the kaleidoscope of feeling is turning throughout and once again the reader feels himself constantly in the presence of a master of English fiction. There is a maturity here, a command, command of the language first of all, and of the situation, the character, the change and growth, that make one terribly impatient with much that the American novel is now bringing forth.

Frank Getlein. *Commonweal.* April 8, 1955,
p. 19

The Birth of a Grandfather is not a "woman's novel," a lending library favorite; it is much too precisely observed, truly told and serious minded. But it is limited to much the same material as these contrivances, the feminine world of family and home. What is worse, the delineation of its male characters is weakened by what may well be a conscientious scruple; a refusal (since one is not male) to try to see these characters in male terms, because such an effort would involve invention almost in the sense of falsification.

For a novelist as finely observant, as capable, as Miss Sarton, such scruples are nonsense.

Elizabeth Janeway. *The New York Times*.
September 8, 1957, p. 4

The author has long considered the difficulty of achieving personal harmony through human relationships. All her books, and much of her poetry, have shown preoccupation with the growth of personality, the ability or lack of it to communicate love, or, for that matter, to feel it in the first place, the acceptance of birth and death as cyclical parts of man's continuity. These are primary concerns, usually wrapped in the thunderclouds of Sturm and Drang. But Miss Sarton's style is quiet, her dialogue true and sure. She describes no scene "folkloristically" yet each has abundant authentic detail. And her situations, though low-keyed, are basic, alive with their own kind of tension, drama, and suspense.

Frances Keene. *Saturday Review of Literature.* September 14, 1957, p. 50

May Sarton's *In Time Like Air* is, to a poet at least, a book to carry in the pocket and reread with delight, the sort in which a second reading will disclose things undiscovered at first. What is the difference between this book and run-of-the-mill verse? It is partly a matter of personality, partly, perhaps, a matter of intellectual heritage, in no small degree a matter of the best kind of virtuosity. In Miss Sarton's writing there is passion, discretion, grief, joy, music and the intimation of delight. What gives her work its great distinction is its willingness to achieve its aims by simplicity when simplicity serves best and by elaboration when elaboration is proper. . . . Miss Sarton's extraordinary gift is her ability to make the actualities of physical existence and motion serve as the imaginative metaphor pointing to metaphysical reality.

Raymond Holden. *The New York Times.* December 22, 1957, p. 4

In *I Knew a Phoenix,* May Sarton, poet and novelist, recreates with a commingling of tenderness and reserve, the people who shaped her as she is. Autobiographical in the sense that in each of its chapters the book is concerned with either Miss Sarton's parents, her teachers, or her friends, it is not so much about herself as it is a mirror to refract the very special lights that lit her path to maturity. Because the kind and quality of her experience, rare at any time or in any country, is becoming rarer still in the political and commercial anonymity now threatening to engulf us, this modest story of a highly individual education has a nostalgic poignance all its own.

Virgilia Peterson. *New York Herald Tribune.* April 26, 1959, p. 3

"A small, accurate talent, exploited to the limit, let us be quite clear about *that!*" says F. Hilary Stevens, the seventy-year-old poet who is the heroine of poet May Sarton's latest book [*Mrs. Stevens Hears the Mermaids Singing*]. And perhaps Mrs. Stevens's definition of her own gift is the best description of her creator's as well. . . .

Miss Sarton's writing is sensitive to the point of fussiness, and totally without humor. The lack of this saving grace inevitably leads her into pitfalls of inadvertent hilarity. And there is something embarrassing about her probing of Art, as there is in the intimate obstetrical confidences of a comparative stranger. It is not that either subject is intrinsically embarrassing; but the acute self-consciousness often foundering in archness, the solemn conviction that here is revelation, make the listener uncomfortable.

Ruth L. Brown. *Saturday Review of Literature.* October 23, 1965, p. 68

The style [of *Mrs. Stevens Hears the Mermaids Singing*], unguarded by irony ("It was as if she and the boy were standing in a great cleared place"); the set-up situations (the interview forces Hilary to *express* her beliefs, the guidance she gives a young apprentice tempted by homosexuality forces her to *examine* her beliefs, the interviewers demonstrate male and female sensibilities); the stagey names (Sirenica, Mar, Adrian), conversations and directions (people "rush out of the house," their eyes "twinkle," they "utter" and "mutter" such things as "Drat the boy!" or "Trapped by life!") make this novel wholly vulnerable. And yet . . . and yet it is moving, it tells the truth, if not convincingly about art, which may require more astringent expression, then at least about love, with a kind of brave disregard for the critical eye. And the critical eye is finally blinded by an integrity that shines out of the book.

Mona Van Duyn. *Poetry*. February, 1967,

p. 333

May Sarton's *A Private Mythology* is remarkable for the savage brilliance of its poems about India, different in style from her previous work. She was offended by India; she was unprepared for it, and her response has the power of resentment and struggle. She was perhaps over-prepared for Greece and Japan; her poems about those countries have the quality of notes thought out in advance and carefully composed. . . .

Aside from the travel series, there is a resistant Lazarus, a first stanza to the Rilkean angels in the opening poem, country scenes of mowing and of pastoral Provence, and two important elegies, which have the wrathful commitment of her India poems: for a fiery child, and one of great power for a psychiatrist. Miss Sarton has moved to a new phase of sensibility with these elegies and the India poems. Considering the established range of abilities in this poet, this is a situation of the utmost promise.

Joseph Bennett. *The New York Times*.
November 13, 1966, p. 6

There are many brief evocations of an actual rural world [in *A Durable Fire*], but it is, every bit of it, so *used* and directed, that what is concrete in it melts and re-freezes as yet another impenetrable abstraction. So while this kind of poetry appears superficially to work by equivalencies of fact with emotion, nothing in the end has its own real life to begin from: it is all props on which, we are assured, great inner consequences lean. Looking for perceptions of observed nature, all I can find is how they are, one by one, turned immediately to the grasping uses of Human Nature. . . .

May Sarton's poems to her psychiatrist, so obviously intense in gratitude and love, stand as the absolute embodiment of the poet's failure to transform her life into (or should I say, in) poetry: they admit nothing actual—a reticence anyone deserves—but neither do they communicate any convincing reasons for their intensity; mean reality has been replaced by earnest pieties that describe "The Action of Therapy."

Rosellen Brown. Parnassus.
Spring–Summer, 1973, pp. 49–50

A dialogue of undiminished intensity has been carried on in Sarton's work for thirty-seven years. Its greatest daring, the source of its greatest moral energy, has been openness: to experience, pain, the perils of passion, loneliness, and truthtelling. This has inevitably been the dialogue of an isolated human being, a self-dialogue, recognizable certainly to housewives, desperate in loneliness and devoid of the solitude Sarton has created.

Sarton has not avoided the dangers inherent in such an openness and such a dialogue: the appearance of self-indulgence, self-pity. These dangers might as well be mentioned in their harshest form, together with her other sin: a certain laxity of style, a tendency to seize the first metaphor to hand, rather than search out the one, perfect phrase. In the intensity of her exploration, Sarton has not eschewed the assistance of the familiar metaphor, nor always observed the niceties of point of view.

Carolyn G. Heilbrun. Introduction to May
Sarton. Mrs. Stevens Hears the Mermaids
Singing (New York: Norton, 1974), p. xii

May Sarton has designed her Collected Poems with a lifelong process in view. Her aim has been to reveal the development of a career and of a person, because the whole of her career is greater than the sum of its stages, despite the brilliance of many individual achievements. She writes of the feminine condition, of art, love, landscape, travel, and the search for a lasting home, and of the inexplicable violence that can wreck even the mildest people. Her tone is often gently didactic. The largeness of her themes makes them worth returning to again and again; her didactic tone helps give her poetry its distinctiveness, for very few poets of this age seem willing to be purposeful about poetry's power to instruct.

Henry Taylor. The Hollins Critic.
June, 1974, p. 2

Often [Sarton] gives her work (and thus provides us conveniently with) unusually indicative titles: Kinds of Love (1970) or the poetic account of love, aging and her time in psychiatry, A Durable Fire (1972). Journal of a Solitude, in the same year, advances her conviction that it is not in relationships but in maintaining one's aloneness that a creative woman realizes herself. And The Small Room (1961), the book that appealed especially to academic women (I was one then) because it raised (but never tried to solve) the question of how it was possible to be productive, scholarly, creative and yet lead the life women were "destined" for.

As a longtime reader of hers I want to join the celebration because I admire the *nature* of her career—serene-seeming despite "the anguish of my life . . . its rages"; her declared traumas of bisexual love, breakdown, conflict; her increasing productivity (to my mind her book published last summer, *As We Are Now,* is one of her finest achievements), everything she has written entirely professional, solid yet sensitive. As a women I feel a closeness to her message, an alliance with her lifelong, solitary control.

Doris Grumbach. *The New Republic.*
June 8, 1974, p. 31

Sarton's work is filled with the longing to touch someone else, and the simultaneous distaste for the unsatisfactory nature of human relations. Art becomes her substitute for human experience, a way of talking about life, not living it. Even art is "ultimately" unsatisfactory. Not only do the critics fail to applaud one enough, or at the right time, or for the right reasons, but for the sterile, lonely, childless woman, the work of art itself is only a poor substitute. The childless woman, and particularly the homosexual woman, does not realize that children, like poems, are never what one thought they would be when one created them. . . .

Much of Sarton's work is conceived with the journey as a metaphor for life, and it is a mark of Sarton's new maturity that she faults the journey contained in *Crucial Conversations.* . . .

For most of her central characters, the pain of love, the price, is not worth the joy. As a result, it is hard to care what happens to her characters. All of them have a bloodless quality. They must choose between head and heart, but their heads are not screwed on very straight and their hearts seem shriveled. Sarton's women are like so many "modern" women—too easily distracted yet with just enough talent to make them fretful and dissatisfied with themselves and their lives with others. . . . Too concerned with the function of her art for herself, she never asks what the function of her art is for the reader. Sarton's journals, poems, and novels all suffer from this sense of finding one's own center, but never communicating "these gifts" to her audience. If art is her surrogate lover, it betrays, as does the lover, because of the excess of her great expectations. That excess is directly connected to her unwillingness or inability to be "engaged" with her characters, or to have them "engaged" with one another.

We close her books with a sense of promise undelivered. Despite the fact that Sarton herself is not enamored of the novel, *Crucial Conversations* is a step forward, though only a step. The lives of Reed, Poppy, and Philip, or, more accurately, their conversations about their lives, may mark the beginning of a new stage in Sarton's development, where she no longer mistakes the signposts for the journey, and moves forward in her explorations of and commitment to human relationships.

Nancy Yanes Hoffman. *Southwest Review.*
1977, pp. 259, 263, 266–67

Ostensibly a novel about dying, *A Reckoning* is actually about coming to terms with one's own life. May Sarton, a prolific writer of poetry, memoirs, and fiction, has published over thirty books in the last four decades. *A Reckoning* is her 16th novel and like much of her previous work, it reflects the inner life and passion of a woman, the private life revealed in all its intensity.

The heroine is a sixty-year-old widow, Laura Spelman, who is told abruptly on page one that she has inoperable lung cancer. In this moment of crisis, Laura experiences a sudden clarity of vision: unafraid of death, but not of dying, she wants to "do it well" her own way. Laura faces death gracefully but her impassioned plea is less for dying well than for living honestly. . . .

Drawing deeper into an inner world of illness and reminiscence, Laura willingly "lets go her identity as a person in the world" and becomes "a listener to music, a watcher of light on the walls." Miss Sarton handles this transition well; it allows her to see the world from only Laura's perspective. This is Miss Sarton more as poet than as novelist, a single voice she is obviously most comfortable with. . . .

Cancer and homosexuality are, admittedly, difficult subjects to write well about; until recently, they were, for different reasons, unmentionable as well. But this novel does not deal effectively with either; it is marred by Miss Sarton's style, which tends toward the ready cliché and occasionally teeters on the edge of sentimentality. Miss Sarton is best at evoking the private sensibility of one person. But in *A Reckoning,* where separate voices and the fabric of other lives are necessary to create a world outside the main character, this kind of interior singularity approaches solipsism.

Lore Dickstein. The New York Times.
November 12, 1978, p. 14

Sarton confronts . . . the inhumanity of American society toward the elderly and images the old as embattled, giving up their lives at the same time as they are fighting for them. The ideal of graceful aging yields to guerrilla warfare. In *As We Are Now,* Sarton's most powerful novel, a frail, single woman in her seventies struggles against the repressive structure of the nursing home and asserts the value of the total human being over the total institution. . . .

Sarton's portrayal of old age is a welcome departure from the Western literary tradition of gerontophobia—fear of aging and disgust for the elderly—particularly since over the centuries the most vicious satire of the elderly has been leveled at female characters. From Sarton's first novel *The Single Hound* (1938), whose heroine is an elderly Belgian poet, to *Kinds of Love* (1970), a passionate encomium to old age, her literary world has been populated with ideal portraits of aging characters and allusions to elderly persons—especially women, and often single women—whom she admires. Aging with grace and dignity has been a persistent, even obsessive theme in her work. . . .

The new complexity of Sarton's vision of old age is reflected in the quality of her writing. *As We Are Now* has a hardness to it that is lacking in her previous fiction, which is basically dominated by aphorism, not power or drama. . . . And Sarton has carried this new understanding of the tragedies of old age into her writing since then. As we have seen, Sarton's vision of old age in her earlier work is unrelievedly romantic. But her recent writing is more cautious and more cognizant of the real physical and mental disabilities of old age in general and of the vulnerability of elderly women in particular.

> Kathleen Woodward. In Janet Todd, ed.
> *Gender and Literary Voice* (New York:
> Holmes and Meier, 1980), pp. 109, 124

Seldom in our time has a novelist so consistently and courageously defended human freedom against the historic patterns of violence and degradation as has May Sarton. Hardly a form of violence, from physical to psychological, escapes her concern. Stalinism, Communism, Fascism, racism, Nazi-ism, censorship, conscription, laws denying freedom to homosexuals, intellectuals, women, loom large in her work. Since she knows only too well that the power of the sword and the war machine have failed to achieve the freedoms for which each war was presumably fought, she uses the power of her pen to make a series of convincing arguments for the rights of individuals against repressive institutions and laws which deny human freedom. Hers is a rage for justice, for political and social change, and for international peace.

Sarton is concerned lest in failing to challenge the history of past and present tyrannies we may be condemned to repeat them on an ever more deadly scale in a not too distant future. Political, social, and psychological violence symbolize the forces of darkness against which her heroes and heroines test their moral fiber. By their resistance, passive as it is at times, their personal acts of refusal to serve, like civil disobedience itself, is the price conscience pays for its victory in seeming defeat.

> Mary Bryan. In Constance Hunting, ed.
> *May Sarton: Woman and Poet* (Orono,
> Maine: National Poetry Foundation, 1982),
> p. 133

May Sarton is a secular writer, but she draws freely upon a Christian tradition which has long contemplated the psychology of spiritual growth, the power to accept or to enact a change in one's life for one's inherent moral betterment. In both the Christian tradition and May Sarton's novels, this self-examination essential for growth can never occur productively in an intellectual vacuum of self-adoration but only against an awareness of genuine virtue. Using the language of scripture and liturgy, Sarton attempts to identify that indefinable and indispensable quality of virtue within the particular experiences of the characters in her novels, and presses new meanings both from the traditional emblems of language and from the experiences themselves.

Sarton finds elements of virtue in nature imagery, particularly in her close study of the plants and birds of New England. She treats these natural objects with observant realism, introducing religious terminology only as a common body of images to expose the mind's pondering these things. In *Kinds of Love* (1970) Jane Tuttle receives a dead owl as a love offering from the troubled Nick Comstock: she examines the bird first scientifically, using a reference book to distinguish the Barred Owl from a Great Gray, then mythically—"'Athene's bird,' Jane murmured. 'You can see why the owl has haunted men'"—and at last religiously—"She laid a hand gently on the incredible softness of the head, as if to bless it." Repeatedly Sarton's characters discover virtue in natural objects by contemplating them with this wholly attentive, admiring respect for the things as they are. . . .

May Sarton also redefines the traditional Christian role of the ministry in her novels of the seventies. Not ordination but response to human need determines a man's role as a minister—or more often, a woman's role. The author makes grave demands of her clergy; they are not mere counselors or administrators but divine comforters, saviors, agents of God. In *As We Are Now* Caro Spenser, left to die in a rest home, imagines a temporary housekeeper, Anna Close, as a "heavenly nurse [who has] come to be with me." Anna comes when Caro is most desperate for the palpable reassurance of a physical human presence. . . .

Although all of Ms. Sarton's seventies' novels are studies of this effort toward intellectual and moral growth, *Crucial Conversations* is the most bitter in its denunciation of society as a stifler of spiritual development. . . .

Christian humility, particularly the tradition of womanly tact, gains a new definition through May Sarton's novels. As the author perceives a widening gap between Christian virtue and public morality, she begins to define anger as a necessary part of virtuous behavior. More and more insistently as these novels develop through the seventies their author demands that her characters turn their moral growth into decisive actions. The self-losing, self-discovering surrender to natural forces and to human affection in *Kinds of Love* (1970) turns to a rebellious insistence on one's own moral integrity by *Crucial Conversations* (1975). Sarton does not use the language of scripture and liturgy as a private code or as a general symbol for goodness but as a means to explore self-conscious psychological experience. She always tests the language in a dramatic situation. This is her art: her novels are not treatises on morals or abstract studies of virtue but a vital working out of the consequences of personal moral decisions in the conscious inquiring minds of their characters.

Gayle Gaskill. In Constance Hunting, ed.
May Sarton: Woman and Poet (Orono,
Maine: National Poetry Foundation, 1982),
pp. 157, 159, 162–63

As her journals, letters, essays, novels, and poetry make clear, Sarton's aesthetic philosophy emerges from a feminist ethos. Her statements about art and the artist are always couched in metaphors and images of relationship, communion, and community. Sarton differentiates between this philosophy of wholeness and a patriarchal concept of art characterized by fragmentation.

Male writers have described the artist as "priest, prophet, warrior, legislator, and emperor." Sarton's artist is most often a lover. In a 1983 interview, Sarton linked "art making" with lovemaking: "I feel more alive when I'm writing that I do at any other time—except when I'm making love." She goes on to explain that the two are parallel because during both you forget time, "nothing exists except the moment." There are, however, a number of other connections between love and art expressed in her work. At times she substitutes one concept for the other. For instance, we often say that love is the great healer; Sarton says the same of poetry in *Recovering*. She equates love and the writing process: "Tenderness is the grace of the heart, as style is the grace of the mind." She links love and work when she says that through both one forges identity: "How does one find one's identity? My answer would be through work and through love, and both imply giving rather than getting." She explains that she has made her style as "simple and plain as possible"; otherwise, style "makes a wall between writer and reader." Thirty-seven pages later, she says that "passionate love breaks down the walls" that are barriers preventing "two isolated human beings from being joined.". . .

May Sarton has been accused of not being feminist enough, yet her aesthetic philosophy, her vision of life as it is expressed for more than fifty years of writing fiction, poetry, and prose, is one that celebrates feeling, relationship, communion, and community. She recognizes that the woman artist is in a unique position to connect with others. She shares with us the values that have always united and empowered feminists. She teaches us that art, like love, requires "the subtle exchange of a life."

Susan Swartzlander. In Susan Swartzlander
and Marilyn R. Mumford, eds. *That Great
Sanity: Critical Essays on May Sarton* (Ann
Arbor: University of Michigan Press, 1992),
pp. 110, 118

May Sarton published *Mrs. Stevens Hears the Mermaids Singing* in 1965. The novel was, in many ways, ahead of its time. Lesbian protagonists were rare and provided a risk to their creator's career. The sexual revolution, the most recent wave of feminism, and the lesbian/gay rights movement were still quietly evolving. By virtue of publishing this novel, Sarton declared herself to be a lesbian feminist. Because she was firm, but quiet, in her positions, and because she preferred a life of solitude to visibility as a public figure, her contributions to the lesbian feminist movement have often been overlooked. It seems that we are finally beginning to rectify that error and include her in the lesbian feminist movement, where she belongs. . . .

The Education of Harriet Hatfield, published in 1989, also has an older lesbian as protagonist, and the novel lends insight to Sarton's presentation of women and lesbianism, and of the relationship between art and lesbianism. . . .

There are many similarities between *The Education of Harriet Hatfield* and *Mrs. Stevens Hears the Mermaids Singing*—and many differences. Both Hilary and Harriet find the primary love in their lives with women, although they are "nourished" by men and enjoy their companionship and support as well. Harriet Hatfield, like Hilary Stevens, is an older woman in search of self. Hilary lives with Sirenica, a white cat, and two turtles; Harriet has Patapouf, a Labrador retriever, for companionship. While Hilary lives by the ocean, on Cape Ann, Harriet has moved to Somerville, a "'working' community" outside of Boston. In many ways, their locations are as telling as any personal details: Hilary says that "Women do not thrive in cities," but Harriet certainly does. While Hilary is isolated in her home on Cape Ann, Harriet has broken through the insulation of nature, moving from her home and gardens to the city where she has extensive interaction with other people. Both women are older, in good health, still actively living their lives. Both women believe that age provides the security and wisdom to encourage truth. Harriet is, in many ways, an evolved Hilary. While Hilary creates art with her life, Harriet's creation of life is her art.

The meaning of "lesbianism" used in this essay is derived from both novels, since Sarton makes the meaning of a primary relationship between women clearer in her more contemporary book, and the use of the term *lesbian* is consistent with that found in *Mrs. Stevens* regarding female homosexuality. In *Mrs. Stevens,* Hilary tells Mar, "I loved my husband, but . . . others touched the poet as he did not." "Others," while perhaps inclusive of the male physician and male critic who nourished her, also indicates the women with whom Hilary fell in love, and the women who served as her muses. The double entendre of "touch" is suggestive both of the physical/ sexual relationship usually associated with lesbianism, and more important, of being touched emotionally, at the heart of self. In *Harriet Hatfield,* Harriet questions whether her friends have ever loved other women, focusing on love and the emotional aspect of the relationship. She does not ask if they have ever been sexually attracted to other women. It is, then, important to broaden the common definition of lesbianism when working with Sarton's novels, and to derive a fuller and more accurate understanding than suggested by the terms *sexual preference* or *sexual orientation.*

Hilary says that "woman's work" is "never to categorize, never to separate one thing from another—intellect, the senses, the imagination, . . . some total gathering together where the most realistic and the most mystical can be joined in a celebration of life itself. Woman's work is always toward wholeness." You can't separate the woman from her work. Lesbianism and art were interwoven in Hilary's life and in her writing, as they are interwoven in Sarton's: interwoven parts of wholeness.

K. Graehme Hall. In Susan Swartzlander
and Marilyn R. Mumford, eds. *That Great
Sanity: Critical Essays on May Sarton* (Ann
Arbor: University of Michigan Press, 1992),
pp. 167, 178–80, 185

SATA INEKO (JAPAN) ca. 1906–

Her first published story, "From a Caramel Factory" *(Kyarameru Kōjō kara),* is based on Ineko's first job in Tokyo—wrapping and boxing caramels—and her bitter disappointment at having to quit school. While the humiliating experience of young factory workers are convincingly described, the story does not make any overt political statement. It conveys not only the sadness and fear of the girl protagonist toward the unknown world of adults—including her father—but also the tension between victim and victimizer.

For the next several decades, Ineko continued to write fiction based on her own experiences as a woman, wife, mother and committed socialist. . . . She viewed her participation in socialist activities as an integral part of her activity as a writer. Ineko lived in a working-class neighborhood and became involved in the labor disputes of the textile industry. In 1931, she published a work about the strike at Tōyō Muslin; that same year she became the editor of *Working Women (Hataraku Fujin),* a Communist Party publication.

During the difficult time prior to the outbreak of World War II, Ineko was increasingly preoccupied with a more personal conflict, namely her identity as a wife and mother and as a writer. This theme is taken up in her novella, *Crimson (Kurenai),* written in 1936. Heavily autobiographical, the novella analyzes Ineko's own feelings, thoughts and actions during the dark years before the War and chronicles the corrosion of her marriage to Kubokawa. First serialized in *Women's Forum (Fujin Kōron)* in 1937, *Crimson* is considered to be one of Ineko's best works. . . .

The central issue of *Crimson* is a question Japanese women writers had never before asked: can the different roles, being a professional woman and a wife and mother, be happily combined? A conflict familiar to us in the post-women's liberation era, it was strikingly new to Ineko's generation. For women like Ineko, whose lovers and husbands were involved in the leftist movement, the gradual realization that the revolutionary theory of sexual equality was largely ignored in practice came with sorrow and a sharp sense of betrayal.

Ineko later wrote another novella, entitled *A Grey Afternoon* (*Haiiro no Gogo,* 1959), in which she again treats the theme of the discord experienced by an intellectual couple; it has a somewhat broader perspective than *Crimson,* involving the interactions of the protagonist's women friends. . . .

Ineko's writing was motivated by the urge to reflect on her own life and to discover a new understanding—a mode of writing that has been extremely popular among modern Japanese writers. Ineko's treatment of the mother-child relationship, for example, draws heavily on her own experiences both as a mother and a child. For a poor mother, children are "the light that eases the pain of life," Ineko once wrote, and her own children provided her with a great deal of strength during troubled times. But Ineko's harsh childhood allowed her no illusions about idealized parent-child relationships. In Ineko's fiction, children are given a right to see and judge the adult world according to their own capacities and limitations. Rather than using a child's perspective to give a fresh view of the adult world, as other writers did, Ineko included children in her work because she believed the life and world of a child were equally significant to that of an adult. Though she did not often write exclusively about children, her work shows an understanding of what it is like to be powerless, at the mercy of other people.

The year after World War II ended, Ineko started writing *My Map of Tokyo (Watashi no Tōkyō Chizu).* In this impressionistic work reminiscent of wood-cut prints, she recalls her past, tracing the memory of the places she knew as a child and a young woman. The history of both narrator and city come alive in a vivid tableau as the narrator reconfirms the connection between herself and the people around her. The work evokes a sense of nostalgia for what has been lost forever—the narrator's own innocence as well as that of the Japanese people—and an empathy with the nameless individuals who lived, as young Ineko had, in the many corners of Tokyo. Ineko's skills as a writer are at their best as she depicts the ordinary people—workers, housewives, daughters and rootless wanderers—who are trying to live their difficult lives as best as they can.

After completing *My Map of Tokyo,* Ineko continued writing for the next thirty years, producing about eighty books of fiction and essays by 1970. Now in her eighties, she remains active on the Japanese literary scene. A writer whose sympathy for the powerless and the poor helped to give them a voice in literature, Sata Ineko exemplifies the continuing dynamic of art and social commitment.

Yukiko Tanaka. *To Live and to Write*
(Seattle: Seal Press, 1987), pp. 163–65

Almost all of Sata's stories, whether autobiographical or not, represent a series of soundings in time and are influenced in their overall tone by the chronological and psychological distance between the surface moment (the present) and the depth (the past) and by the prevailing mood of the times in which the "sounding" is taken. Taken together, the two stories we have considered indicate the considerable range afforded by such developed artistry.

The sense of the interconnectedness of human lives, glimpsed briefly in "Kyarameru kōjō kara" in the context of the shared burden of the workers is made explicit in "Yuki no mau yado." In this story meaning and the synthesis of past and present are achieved through verbal exchange. Incidents long isolated within the individual consciousnesses of the protagonists remain emotionally undigested, until, once recounted, they become the subject of discourse and interpretation. So the past becomes open to the present and to revision, and the shared present expands backward into a past made communal. . . . It would seem that the past is never final, but continues to be accessible to present consciousness, a consciousness itself continually subject to revision in the course of time.

It has been Sata's project throughout fifty years of writing to examine experience in the contexts (social, political, and personal) of changing times. Her art evolves from the early stories which, although faithful to the personal dimension of human existence, nevertheless evidence an urgency in articulating the social crises of the era. From the mid-1930s onward through the early 1950s, she faced pressures on many levels. The proletarian movement, in which she had found a community of like-minded individuals and a sense of mission, had been dispersed. The forces of oppression within her own country had triumphed, and she allowed herself to be drawn into the support of a war effort that was diametrically opposed to her own most cherished beliefs. The complexities involved in the reexamination of the past had multiplied, but Sata remained committed to such discipline. Works from the middle of her career thus concern themselves both with personal defeat and compromise, and with the necessity of building the possibility for personal growth upon such unpromising ground. Inevitably, the stages of human life—childhood, youth, maturity, and old-age—are ever more clearly articulated in the works of her later years, and a sense of both the disintegrative and reintegrative force of duration becomes an ever-present motif within them.

Her artistic life is almost coterminous with the Showa era, and her corpus, by combining the broad social concerns of proletarian literature with the personal dimension of autobiographical fiction, has the unique quality of representing the tension and interplay between history and the individual consciousness. Sata's writing in the later decades of her career evinces a genuine recognition of an ability to reproduce the complex experiences of the life lived in a layered and shifting context. Her *zenshu* evokes some fifty years of change in a nation and in an individual from a perspective that the reader comes to trust, in part because of its own admitted waverings and uncertainties. Narrated [in a] voice that, in spite of a variation in tone and an extension of range over the course of years, remains recognizable and relatively unchanged, her works are ultimately deserving of . . . [respectful] assessment. . . . [S]he has made her own life the foundation of her work, and . . . she "clearly yet subtly reflects the constrictions of the society of her time along with the aspirations of human beings." From the force of duration itself her works gather strength and depth, and it is not the least significant aspect of her particular gift as a writer that she is able to render the effect of time upon the individual with astonishing clarity.

Victoria V. Vernon. *Daughters of the Moon: Wish, Will and Social Constraint in Fiction by Modern Japanese Women* (Berkeley, California: Institute of East Asian Studies, 1988), pp. 102–5

SAYERS, DOROTHY L. (GREAT BRITAIN) 1892–1957

There are certain writers who have made their success in a genre remote from playwriting and yet have displayed a dramatic flair which has perhaps surprised no one more than themselves. Dorothy Sayers is certainly an example, for she has been long established in the field of detective fiction where her careful confections concerning Lord Peter Wimsey have been relished by peer and peasant. Her first venture into the drama, in fact, was a pleasant, if rather mild, melodrama, *Busman's Honeymoon,* in which she portrayed her favorite hero with the collaborative efforts of M. St. Clare Byrne. A year later she revealed her true interest in the stage in her composition of *The Zeal of Thy House,* a poetic and religious drama written for production at Canterbury. This has high quality, sensitiveness of expression, and dramatic sweep. The same may be extended to *The Devil to Pay* (1939).

George Freedley. In Barrett H. Clark and George Freedley, eds. *A History of Modern Drama* (New York: Appleton-Century, 1947), p. 216

The first volume of Dorothy L. Sayers's version of *The Divine Comedy* shows her returning to her old love—medieval literature. She has produced the most rapidly moving and apparently effortless translation, with a valuable introduction and notes which with maps and diagrams (by C. W. Scott-Giles) help to make clear both story and allegory.

Geoffrey Bullough. *Year's Work in English Studies.* 1949, p. 15

What Dorothy Sayers is about in this slim collection of pamphlets and addresses [*Creed or Chaos?*] is a definition of Christianity as "a religion for adult minds." The adult mind, she feels, is what Christianity's attackers, and all too frequently its defenders, lack. . . .

Miss Sayers has no comforting illusions. She speaks out against tawdry church art, against Christian tolerance of mammon and ungraciousness toward publicans, but most of all against nominal Christians, "both lay and clerical." In her view every problem and every struggle is at base a question of theology. She sees the chief problem of theology (or rather *about* theology) today as the doctrine of Christ, the God-man.

Riley Hughes. *Saturday Review of Literature.* July 16, 1949, p. 15

Whether Mr. [C. S.] Lewis regards himself as a serious creative writer I do not know. Miss Sayers certainly so regards herself, and this not only on the basis of her religious plays, but also of her detective fiction which . . . she uses as the material of aesthetic theory, with insufficient attention (though in this field alone) to the other creative productions of mankind. She seems to be well versed in the *Divine Comedy;* and if she had chosen this work, let us say, instead of her own novel *Gaudy Night* as the material for her analysis of the creative process [in *Unpopular Essays*] such objectivity might have saved her from the great risk of confusing the introspective and the creative, which always besets the writer of projected fantasies. . . . There is no reason why Miss Sayers should not write detective fiction. There is a legitimate market for competent entertainment. But since there is no doubt that Miss Sayers at least takes her Wimsey phase rather too seriously, we have some ground for suspecting that the preference of both these writers for abstraction is significant. Their later theological development illuminates an incapacity or a dislike for analyzing and comprehending concrete individual human character, which was always characteristic of them.

Kathleen Nott. *The Emperor's Clothes* (Bloomington: Indiana University Press, 1954), pp. 254–56

It is now twenty years ago since Lord Peter Wimsey popped the question to Miss Harriet Vane bang under the Warden of New College's windows. *"'Placetne magistra?'—'Placet!'"* (how that dreadful scene sticks in the memory). . . .

Re-reading Miss Sayers again this week, I remembered how we loved it all at thirteen, and how sophisticated we felt on the train that took us back to the grim Warwickshire prep school. . . . Lord Peter struck it rich in the sexual imaginings of my generation. His *dicta* preceded the chivalrous infantilism of G.K.C. (the white nights of an adolescent flirting with Rome) by about one year. . . . all that is by the by. For, of course, we all enjoyed Miss Sayers's stories themselves egregiously, reveling in the Bradshawnmanship of *The Five Red Herrings,* the campanalogy and fen-flooding in *The Nine Tailors,* Puffet, the comic sweep in *Busman's Honeymoon*, the Duke's trial scene in the Lords, the Mitfordian splendors of Duke's Denver, the tramps and gigolos of *Have His Carcase.* I am afraid we even delighted in that dreadful capping of literary quotations.

In a sense, my generation grew up with Lord Peter. . . . As we aged, Lord Peter grew almost wholly serious. By *Gaudy Night* the only traits remaining from the old unregenerate bachelor Wimsey were his taste in port and his passion for incunabula.

John Raymond. *New Statesman and Nation.*
June 30, 1956, pp. 756, 758

Dorothy Sayers died in 1957; and as a period of disesteem normally follows hard on the death of writers and composers, this connection of twelve addresses [*The Poetry of Search and the Poetry of Statement*] is a timely reminder of her remarkable achievements. Having earned a world-wide fame as writer of detective stories, which often threw an entertaining and informative light on the milieu in which the ingenious plot was laid, she gained so great a success by her religious play, *A Man Born to be King,* that it outsold all her detective stories put together. Then she found yet a third and wholly absorbing outlet for her skills, and enthusiasm in the study and translation of Dante's *Commedia,* while her version of *The Song of Roland* bore witness to her early training as a medieval linguist. . . .

Half the addresses bear directly or indirectly on the *Commedia,* and in them, together with her two volumes of *Introductory Papers,* she has given the English student of Dante a stimulus and a guide not to be found elsewhere. Besides their interpretational value, they retain that fervor which made her lectures a spiritual tonic. . . .

Certainly her listeners enjoyed themselves, and readers of these "Essays of Statement" will have cause to wish they had been there, too.

(London) *Times Literary Supplement.*
September 13, 1963, p. 690

An interesting clue (and when writing about Miss Sayers, it is tempting to use the detective-story terms she herself employs so interestingly as critical tools) to the "problem" of a writer who is perhaps equally famous as a detective novelist, theologian, and scholar (and peripherally, as a writer of children's books) is furnished by a tantalizing statement in *The Mind of the Maker.* . . . The key phrase is "a hymn to the Master Maker," and the "youthful set of stanzas" contain the essential theme: man's striving to praise God, the "Master Maker," through his own earthly creations and the inevitable frustrations and disappointments which stem from his inability to reach perfection. And, as Miss Sayers states, this great theme runs, in a number of keys and modes, through all of her works, from the detective novels of the 1930s through the religious plays and Dante papers of the 1940s and 1950s.

Miss Sayers quite rightly points to *Gaudy Night* and *The Zeal of Thy House* as focal points of the fictional presentation of this theme, which is most fully and explicitly developed in *The Mind of the Maker. Gaudy Night* is perhaps the most complex of Miss Sayers's novels; indeed, as in a number of her other works, particularly *The Nine Tailors,* the "detective" element plays so minor a role in *Gaudy Night* that it demands the title "novel" rather than "detective story." *Gaudy Night* also marks the climax not only, as Miss Sayers says, of "a long development in detective fiction," but also of the courtship of Lord Peter Wimsey, Miss Sayers' detective-hero, and Miss Harriet Vane, whom Lord Peter had saved from the gallows in *Strong Poison.* And the courtship of Lord Peter is of great importance here, since it is by means of this "second" plot ("subplot" would here be too strong a term) that Miss Sayers introduces a series of variations upon the Creator theme and its implications in human affairs.

Charles Moorman. *The Precincts of Felicity:
The Augustinian City of the Oxford
Christians* (Gainesville: University of
Florida Press, 1966), pp. 113–15

Dorothy L. Sayers, the creator of Lord Peter Wimsey, has been dead eleven years, and there is many a detective story reader, including some who never read any detective stories but hers, who would, if they could, offer her resurrection on condition that she produce more Lord Peter novels. Over thirty years ago, alas, Lord Peter (having married, solved a most cunning and intricate crime, and wept out his horror at the murderer's execution in the arms of his new-wed wife), departed forever from the world of the detective novel.

True, he made one or two casual, short appearances—in the course of one of which his first baby was born—but with the coming of the war his creator finally succeeded in her earlier determination to marry Peter off and get rid of him. It is forty-five years since Lord Peter's first appearance, and all of the books about him are still in print in hard cover. Lord Peter's admirers continue to turn to his adventures more than three decades after his creator abandoned detective fiction to take up the mysteries of theology.

Dorothy Sayers was no fly-by-night writer of thrillers. Not only did she write superbly constructed detective plots, played out in witty comedies of manners; she was also a scholar of great erudition who had taken first honors in medieval literature at Oxford, and who was to become, after the disappearance of Lord Peter, one of the outstanding translators and interpreters of Dante, as well as a formidable Christian apologist. She has written what is widely accepted as the best history of the detective story and has managed, in addition, to draw the fire of such notable critics as Edmund Wilson, Q. D. Leavis and W. H. Auden, and the attention of everyone who has ever written about detective fiction. In Howard Haycraft's *The Art of the Mystery Story,* a collection of every notable essay on the detective story written prior to 1948, her name is mentioned more frequently than any save that of the fictional Sherlock Holmes. Indeed, Q. D. Leavis, with that lack of courtesy as marked in the Leavises as their astuteness, railed at her in *Scrutiny* with such vehemence as positively to affirm Miss Sayers's importance as a literary figure. Can Agatha Christie or Erle Stanley Gardner match that? Eleven years dead, Dorothy Sayers is yet a literary and social phenomenon to be grappled with.

So is Lord Peter. It is certainly arguable that no marriage in literary history has caused as much interest as Lord Peter's. If female readers complained that Peter was throwing himself away on Harriet Vane, there was a strong male faction who insisted, according to his creator, that Harriet was thrown away on Peter. As these two fell into each other's arms at the end of *Gaudy Night* and spent the subsequent hours, before Lord Peter rushed off on one of his assignments for the Foreign Office, kissing each other madly in a punt, Dorothy Sayers found herself with a best seller on her hands. Hers was a success that the years, as is not their usual fashion in the matter of detective novels, have steadily increased.

Carolyn G. Heilbrun. *The American Scholar.* Spring, 1968, p. 324

The reputation of Dorothy Leigh Sayers in the craft of detective fiction rests upon a number of achievements other than simply portraying characters. She put criticism of life into her stories. She worked to the model of Wilkie Collins, with the novel of manners in view. She knew how to use language. She successfully managed intrigue and suspense. She educated readers in a variety of subjects pertinent to plots and settings. She created enduring characters.

Sayers, of course, did not achieve equal distinction in her fiction. Few writers do. Sometimes—as in *Five Red Herrings* or *Have His Carcase*—intricacy of plot development may become oppressive. Some of the short stories are only puzzles. But at her best—for example, in *The Documents in the Case,* in *The Nine Tailors,* in *Gaudy Night*—she is superb on almost every count. The evidence in the last analysis chiefly lies in the constant reprinting of her works.

All of this, however, was receding. Events [in the late 1930s] were leading Sayers resolutely away from the golden age of stories of sleuths. For one thing, in *Gaudy Night* she had realized her ideal in detective fiction. In it, also, she had solved the problem of what to do with that "nuisance" Peter Wimsey. All that remained was what she accomplished in *Busman's Honeymoon*—he was married off. Moreover, the pattern of "The Long Week-end," as British society knew it between the wars, was drawing to a close. The social revolution impelled by political, psychological, and technological developments, in turn, forced upon many artists and writers a crisis of personal identity.

Ralph E. Hone. *Dorothy L. Sayers: A Literary Biography* (Kent, Ohio: Kent State University Press, 1979), pp. 81–82

In 1935 Dorothy Sayers published *Gaudy Night,* her penultimate Wimsey novel and a book that clearly marks a change in her attitude toward her responsibilities as a writer. *Gaudy Night,* like *The Documents in the Case,* has an important theme, viz., the duty of workers to be faithful to their work. Furthermore, there is a genuine development of the characters of the principals, Harriet Vane and Lord Peter, who during the course of the novel come to a new understanding of themselves and of one another and, in the end, become engaged. But what is most significant is that for the first time in Sayers's writings there is a clear indication that the humorous inanities of a person might, if looked at from the right angle, constitute a part of a comprehensive comic vision of the universe. That indication comes toward the end of Lord Peter's long courtship of Harriet. There, protesting that he had never wanted Harriet to sacrifice herself to him out of a sense of gratitude for favors received, he observes, "I have nothing much in the way of religion, or even morality, but I do recognize a code of behavior of sorts. I do know that the worst sin—perhaps the only sin—passion can commit, is to be joyless. It must lie down with laughter or make its bed in hell—there is no middle way."

This is a brief but basic statement of the whimsical vision. Even in this concise form it reveals a paradoxical pattern of integration based upon the recognition and laughing—or, alternatively, the creative—acceptance of reality. The vision rests on man's perception of unity in diversity. On the one hand, a duality really exists at one stage of development or from one point of view. Man encounters his body and, as an extension of his body, the world itself as in some sense "opposed" to him, i.e., to his conscious will. . . .

On the other hand, although this duality can never be completely abolished, a genuine unity may tenuously be established by one possessed of sufficient imagination to make creative use of the diversity of reality. A reconciliation is possible only by accepting reality and respecting its integrity, and then by living creatively within the limits of that reality. . . . Thus, even though there is a resolution to the paradox, to the human "problem," still the resolution, like everything human, can only be temporary at best.

> Robert Paul Dunn. In Margaret P. Hannay,
> ed. *As Her Whimsey Took Her: Critical
> Essays on the Work of Dorothy L. Sayers*
> (Kent, Ohio: Kent State University Press,
> 1979), pp. 204–5

Since the publication of *Christian Letters to a Post-Christian World* and of a new edition of *The Man Born to Be King,* Dorothy Sayers's noncyclical plays (*The Zeal of Thy House* [1937], *He That Should Come* [1938], *The Devil to Pay* [1939], *The Just Vengeance* [1946], and *The Emperor Constantine* [1951]) have become the least accessible of her works. This situation is particularly unfortunate, for while the essays collected in *Christian Letters to a Post-Christian World* adequately summarize the range of Sayers's thought, *The*

Man Born to Be King does not and cannot represent plays which differ as radically as do these five.

In fact, so marked are these differences that any thematic analysis of these plays seems doomed from the start. The subtle political intrigue and still more subtle theology that characterize *The Emperor Constantine* are absent from *He That Should Come*, a straightforward account of the birth of Christ. *The Zeal of Thy House* discusses the relationship of artists to their art in order to supply a supernatural interpretation of a piece of human history, while *The Devil to Pay,* Sayers's interpretation of the Faust story, furnishes a human interpretation of a supernatural legend. *The Just Vengeance* mixes the human (Samuel Johnson and George Fox), the supernatural (Gabriel and the Recording Angel of Lichfield), the historical (Cain's murder of Abel and Judas's betrayal of Jesus), and the imaginary (Adam's invention of the ax and God's healing of Samuel Johnson's dimmed vision) into an examination of atonement and redemption.

But beneath this very real diversity of content and method is a single intention. Commenting on the status of British Christianity, Sayers writes: "The brutal fact is that in this Christian country not one person in a hundred has the faintest notion what the Church teaches about God or man or society or the person of Jesus Christ." But Sayers manages to find some grounds for optimism: "Theologically, this country is at present in a state of utter chaos. . . . We are not happy in this condition and there are signs of a very great eagerness, especially among the younger people, to find a creed to which they can give wholehearted adherence." The purpose of the plays, then, is simply to present the truths of Christianity in such a way as to "drag out the Divine Drama from under the dreadful accumulation of slipshod thinking and trashy sentiment heaped upon it, and set it on an open stage to startle the world into some sort of vigorous reaction." The truths she emphasizes and the devices she uses to "startle" the theatergoer differ from play to play, but the plays are united by their author's desire to show the effects of the Timeless irrupting into time.

William Reynolds. In Margaret P. Hannay,
ed. *As Her Whimsey Took Her: Critical
Essays on the Work of Dorothy L. Sayers*
(Kent, Ohio: Kent State University Press,
1979), pp. 91–92

Dante's loneliness and exile echoed Sayers's own. She too was an outcast from her beloved city for much of her life—visiting Oxford only as a celebrated guest, not as a citizen. Like him, she reaped the bitter harvest of a changing world. The excitement of living in a new age of scientific progress and artistic experimentation was offset by the discomfort of uncertainty and stress. She, like Dante, turned to tradition as an anchor to balance change, experimenting with new forms while respecting the old. She, like him, tried to reconcile the new philosophy with the enduring faith, the theories with the life experience.

But she had a special struggle that the old Florentine could not share. She was a woman, trying to reconcile the traditional role of woman with the new sense of liberation. No other time in history has seen woman so torn by conflicting views of duty as our century. And Dorothy L. Sayers was at the cutting edge of the change—in the first class of Oxford women graduates, among the first women in the professional world, one of the first women playwrights and translators. At each step, she was judged first as a woman, then as an artist. She was never allowed to forget that she was "only" a woman. If she became occasionally overzealous in her struggle or strident in her tone, she certainly had justification. Yet she tried to maintain balance, to refrain from angry assertions about women's rights. Her intellectual integrity demanded that she be judged as an individual performing a job, not a woman proving she could do "man's" work. She was not just any woman; she was Dorothy L. Sayers. And this was not "man's" work; it was hers, assigned by God himself.

Because of her steady insistence on the vocation of the individual Christian, she never had the comradeship afforded by the women's movement to sustain her and lessen her loneliness. Hers was the solitary path of the exile from collective thought. The fiercely independent thinker pays the price, in any society. Sayers laughed at the way her world at one moment found her ridiculous and at another described her as courageous. She had not changed; the world had. She never shared her path for long with a congenial traveling companion, but then Bunyan's pilgrim also found himself frequently alone. Even Evangelist stayed with him only a short time.

Nancy M. Tischler. *Dorothy L. Sayers:
Pilgrim Soul* (Atlanta: John Knox Press,
1980), pp. 152–53

Readers remember the sounds and looks of Sayers's people. Besides her ability to create unusual situations that challenge us and to arrange them in unified designs that suggest more than they say, her loving skill with character portrayal leaves her people with us long after we have forgotten the intricacies of ciphers and timetables. Hers is a world of vital human beings who live in a realm of language.

"We've got to laugh or break our hearts in this damnable world," announcers an older, more somber Lord Peter in *Busman's Honeymoon*. Laughter, finally, characterizes the tone of Sayers's detective canon. As author of the Mustard Club adventures and the playful Detective Club round-robins, Sayers made a joyful noise unto the Lord. Her characters and their creator resemble the redeemed in Dante's *Divine Comedy:* "for them is the song, the shouting, the celestial dance, revolving like a mill-wheel, spinning like a top . . .—for them the laughter of the rejoicing universe, for them the Divine Comedy."

We rejoice in the universe that Sayers created in her detective fiction in celebration of creation itself. In the back of an antique shop in *Gaudy Night,* Peter and Harriet sing together—"tenor and alto twined themselves in a last companionable cadence." In the most exuberant scene in *Busman's Honeymoon,* Peter and Harriet sing, "Here we sit like BIRDS in the wilderness" with Mr. Puffett, Miss Twitterton, and Mr. Goodacre.

At the New Year's Eve service in *The Nine Tailors* another community joins in song. At first, the congregation seems lost in the large church of the Fen country. Then the people begin to sing. They are joined with each other and with the divine presence evident in the cherubim and seraphim that echo the human voices from high above. "My God!" exclaims Lord Peter. His expletive appropriately expresses the majesty of the hymn, "Let everything that hath breath praise the Lord." Celebration and praise of the glory of creation characterizes Sayers's works.

Sayers discovered, by reading about Cyrus the Persian in a children's book of Greek history and later in a context that marched him "clean out of Herodotus and slap into the Bible," that literature, history, and the Bible are all of a piece. Her artistry shows similar connections. Like the dove in Genesis, Lord Peter announces God's grace after the flood. The dons in *Gaudy Night* echo women of the Renaissance. Harriet and Peter bring the sexuality of John Donne's poetry to a modern audience by using Donne's language on their honeymoon. At the end of *Gaudy Night,* they revivify an ancient ritual and language by giving them a new context of love. They replay the old tales of Cinderella and Sleeping Beauty. They recall to us the Biblical story of Adam and Eve, and Milton's image at the end of *Paradise Lost,* where Adam and Eve leave the Garden hand in hand.

Sayers's art of synthesis and consistency shows us that by being true to her work, by serving its design, the artist once again releases the powers of the old truths and of imagination.

> Dawson Gaillard. *Dorothy L. Sayers* (New York: Frederick Ungar, 1981), pp. 102–3

Brian Garfield has argued that "the literature of crime and suspense can provoke images and questions of the most complex intellectual and emotional force; it can explore the most critical of ethical and behavioral dilemmas." Since for Dorothy L. Sayers the chief such problem was man's sinful nature, the only solution she could find acceptable would have to be based on the Christian dogma she wholeheartedly upheld. The villains of her first novels are swollen with the intellectual pride that successfully tempts them to put themselves above the laws that order human behavior—both society's and God's. But for the grace of God Sayers herself, with her formidable mind, might have fallen victim to that failing, but in the mid-1930s she began to scrutinize herself deeply, first in her attempts at autobiography and then by bringing Harriet Vane to life, the creative artist to Peter's performing one. She achieved artistic equilibrium by creating a new form of detective fiction, more concerned with the riddles of human values than with the thrill of the chase. *The Nine Tailors* throws the pride he took in his brilliant detection back in Wimsey's own face, making him pay for it in body and in spirit. *Gaudy Night* purges the pride that kept Peter and Harriet apart, at the same time laying the issue of intellectual pride to rest; so far as Sayers is concerned in this novel, the climax of her career as a detective novelist, work can only have value so long as it is anchored in truth. For dramatic purposes she let Wimsey trap one last killer in *Busman's Honeymoon,* and during the harrowing eve of the murderer's execution, she made Peter face the real sinner every believing Christian must confront at the end—*himself.* . . .

Sayers's detective stories arose as much from her response to the wickedness she encountered as a young woman as from her need to support herself, and her wartime plays and essays confirm her Christian stance, rather than revealing any change in her thinking about the steps she believed Britain and the West should take in the face of godless totalitarianism. When she turned so gladly to Dante in the last year of World War II, she was directly facing one of the world's noblest answers to the ultimate horror of the pit—mindless evil for evil's sake.

Mitzi Brunsdale. *Dorothy L. Sayers: Solving the Mystery of Wickedness* (Providence: Berg, 1990) pp. 205, 207

In the case of Dorothy L. Sayers, the evidence points to a serious, conscientious, multifaceted artist who was ever growing and testing herself. She once observed that such experimentation and variation is necessary, because it is fatal for a writer to do the same book over and over again ("Craft of Detective Fiction"). She herself demonstrated this capacity for change and growth, not only in the development of her fiction, but also in the numerus genres she employed throughout her writing life. Although I regret that she did not write more novels, I must respect the courage and conscience which made her explore other forms. And I am happy, for her sake, that she was able to venture into so many of the regions where her whimsy took her. Novelist, essayist, dramatist, scholar, critic, translator, poet—Dorothy L. Sayers may properly be awarded the title few have earned: woman of letters. . . .

The world she made is both timebound and universal, a paradox that has allowed it to survive the many changes in fashion and taste which have occurred since she first put pen to paper. A novelist at once popular and literary, a critic scholarly but never precious, Dorothy L. Sayers reminds us of the real functions of art and learning. Her impeccable craftsmanship and emphasis upon the timeless truth of human experience have secured a devoted audience spanning many cultures and generations. Wide appeal does not necessarily prove artistic merit, of course, but the common modern contempt for writers who have such appeal does not prove the opposite, either. And wide appeal over time does indeed suggest genuine merit.

Sayers mastered and redefined the art of detection, moving inevitably into an exploration of the mystery of human nature and finally into the infinite mysteries of meaning, the universe, and life itself. This thread of mystery, and of the human being's noble attempts to resolve it, runs throughout the fabric of her work. In all her guises, she is also a storyteller *par excellence,* breathing immortal life into fictional creatures, recreating Christ's life on earth, describing her own discovery of Dante, tracing the pattern of the universe. Reading Sayers is an exciting, invigorating experience because she is so full of life herself. It is, in fact, this sense of felt life, made present through luminous language, that captures our attention and makes an indelible impression.

Catherine Kenney. *The Remarkable Case of
Dorothy L. Sayers* (Kent, Ohio: Kent State
University Press, 1990), pp. 269–70

Although Dorothy Sayers left narrative to write more specifically theological material, the case can be made that her novels enabled her theology. The credibility and popularity she gained as a writer and a thinker through the Wimsey stories led her to write the play *Busman's Honeymoon.* The success of this play occasioned the invitation she received to write a play for the 1937 Canterbury Festival, for which she produced *The Zeal of Thy House.* It was in this play that she first began to expand her ideas on the creative nature of work, which led, of course, to *The Mind of the Maker.* Her theology, therefore, began with her narratives.

Sayers presented an analogy by which we might understand the spiritual nature of human creativity; she then left it up to each individual to understand how, and if, that analogy might be made intelligible in each person's own life. She was not prescriptive. "Critics are then free to relate it to whatever works their own imaginations can discover or . . . to render a fuller and more complete account of the creative act itself." I now wish to exercise this freedom to suggest some ways in which her work might give a clearer understanding of the theological significance of women's narrative voice. . . .

As women write their own experience they deny [male] definition [of them] and take unto themselves the power of self-creation. Men may listen if they choose, but the power of the word has overthrown the authority of patriarchal definitions. Women create, and in so doing they image forth the divine in the aspects of the feminine.

Elizabeth A. Say. *Evidence on Her Own
Behalf: Women's Narrative as Theological
Voice* (Savage, Maryland: Rowman &
Littlefield, 1990), pp. 99, 104

SCHOULTZ, SOLVEIG VON (FINLAND) 1907–

Considered the foremost contemporary Finland-Swedish woman author, Solveig von Schoultz has published eleven poetry and seven short story collections. Her themes focus on woman in her various changing relationships—with men, with other women, with herself in honest self-evaluation—and on the challenge to discover the healing integration of her intellect and her emotions. She has been widely praised for her style, which through the years has developed a sophisticated simplicity, capable of expressing the most subtle nuances of mood and thought in the dialogue of her characters.

> Ingrid Claréus, ed. *Scandinavian Women Writers: An Anthology from the 1880s to the 1980s* (Westport, Connecticut: Greenwood Press, 1989), p. 169

For all the recognition Solveig von Schoultz . . . has received in Finland and, to an extent, in Sweden, she has somehow never quite got her due. The range of her writing and the accuracy of its observations and style deserve much more than the literary historian's or the critic's routine accolade; her lyrics have become even tighter and more precise, and her novellas have a human range that should forbid any feminist attempt to praise (and diminish) her solely as a writer for and about members of her own gender. I had not realized, though, how skillful a penetrator she was of the world of infants and very small children: to my shame, I must confess that until now I had never read her 1942 classic about the first seven years, the "seven days," the heptameron, of the formation of a life. It has been reprinted by the Alba publishing house with a new introduction; the original subtitle, *Två barn skapar sin värld* (Two children create their world), has been omitted.

Since the book is a small one, it cannot—and does not intend to—give an annual account of how von Schoultz's daughters Uva and Barbara became persons of their own, ready at last to set out to school and to that slow estrangement from parents which is inevitable. Instead, *De sju dagarna* (Seven days) concentrates on the reactions of Uva, the elder by two years, to the new arrival—Uva's slow process of finding her way back into equilibrium after the loss of her position as the one and only apple of her parents' eye. By far the more placid of the pair, Barbara is, truth to tell, less fascinating to her mother than her problematical and imaginative sister.

Nothing very dramatic happens, really, in the book's first sections, "To Become Two" and "To Become a Human Being," where introductions are made and defiance and tantrums and games and funny sayings are described—nothing, of course, except the molding of first the one girl and then, with less detail, the other. The third part, "To Travel in War," tells about the little family's evacuation (the father, naturally, stayed behind) to Sweden during the Winter War; with its little outburst of justifiable patriotism, it is the portion that has aged. The finale consists of the seven tales, almost prose poems, about "days of creation," conversations on birth and death and God and angels and fairies and bombers (the so-called Continuation War of 1941–44 has begun) and happiness and fish and giants and teddy bears and, finally, the "workshop," the children's urge to create, in colored clay and crayons and cardboard and paste. Nothing cloying is in the text, nothing cute (even the reproduced baby talk manages to avoid this trap), no condescension on the mother's part toward the children, no knowing adult wink at the audience. Maybe the secret of the book's attraction lies in its sobriety (and, as always in von Schoultz, its remarkable refinement of language): the mother does not try to make her children seem exceptional, and heaven knows, she does not make herself out to be an exception.

Apart from the triangle of mother and daughters, two other human characters appear in *De sju dagarna:* Tata, the nursemaid with whom the mother has, admittedly, a secret rivalry; and the father, who is, understandably, very pale. Other fathers, reading the book, might want to know more about him; but in those days fathers were not supposed to be emotionally entwined in their offspring's lives, at least when the children were small. However, fathers too will be moved by *De sju dagarna* and wonder how much of their own children's early existence, and their own, they can recall. As Rilke said at the conclusion of his poem "Kindheit" (Childhood), about the receding impressions of those most important and most evanescent of our years, we can only guess whither they have gone: "Wohin? Wohin?" As everyone knows, the Nordic literatures have a particularly rich treasury of books about childhood, and Solveig von Schoultz, watching her daughters in a constant act of alert love, has contributed one of its masterpieces, a poignant masterpiece.

George C. Schoolfield. *World Literature Today.* 63, 1989, pp. 119–20

Schoultz claims that the line between a poem and a story is fluid, and her poems and short stories do have much in common in their themes and technique. In her poetry she creates "portraits of life," vignettes of human existence, caught in a fleeting, often dreamlike moment, as in "Tre systrar" (Three sisters), where through a technique of transparency she gives threefold depth to a single human gesture. Nature in Schoultz's work not only interacts with the author's mood, but suggests multiple metaphorical dimensions, as in "Siesta." Schoultz can be seen more as younger friend than as heir of the Finland-Swedish modernists. Her language, though unconventional and suggestive in a novel way, has found a simplicity and lucidity all its own. This language has undergone an increasingly strict condensation in Schoultz's short stories and corresponds to the frugality with which she pries open whole human destinies through seemingly insignificant everyday events. The collection *Somliga mornar* (1976; Some mornings) gives glimpses of complex human relationships: a mother thinking of her child while waiting for her lover, or an aging husband and wife, as cunning in their last power struggle as in their cautiously expressed tenderness for each other.

The measure of Schoultz's literary vitality is demonstrated by her capacity to recast the Finland-Swedish cultural heritage into contemporary themes through post-modernist literary forms of her own creation.

Margareta Neovius Deschner. In Virpi Zuck,
ed. *Dictionary of Scandinavian Literature*
(Westport, Connecticut: Greenwood Press,
1990), p. 547

Solveig von Schoultz (b. 1907) belongs to the second generation of the avant-garde school of Finland-Swedish writers, which during and after World War I began to experiment with free, unrhymed forms introducing European expressionism, surrealism, and imagism in Scandinavia. Having published over thirty books ranging from poetry collections to plays for television and having won numerous literary prizes, von Schoultz today is recognized as the grande dame of Finnish literature. [In *Snow and Summers*] Anne Born, a poet herself and an accomplished translator, has selected texts from collections that range from the poet's debut volume in 1940 to her latest work from 1989.

In a somewhat superfluous introduction another prolific Finland-Swedish writer, Bo Carpelan, briefly characterizes some of the collections from which the texts have been chosen, focusing—and thereby significantly limiting his scope—on the motif of the tree. The condensed, imagery-filled, poetic language of von Schoultz's verse speaks convincingly for itself and indeed evidences her undiminished artistic intensity. Taking their point of departure in concise observations of nature, her texts open up horizons of surprising and overwhelming beauty and depth of thought. No development in poetic skill is noticeable—and none was needed, for that matter. In her very first collection von Schoultz had already perfected her intense, poetic expression. Born's translation, in spite of several inaccuracies, reads well; particularly impressive is her ability to capture the ever-changing subtle rhythms of the original text. The handsome volume is marred only by very sloppy proofreading.

The companion volume of short stories *Heartwork* forms a most welcome supplement to our knowledge of von Schoultz, best known for her lyric works. Like *Snow and Summers,* it opens with a rather commonplace introduction by Carpelan that totally fails to acknowledge her superb handling of language in the poetic tradition of imagism. Thematically the stories focus on the interrelationship between humans and the sometimes unsuccessful efforts at establishing contact between marriage partners or between two generations. However, it is precisely von Schoultz's mastery of language that raises her stories above traditional psychological realism. It gives them an almost mystical quality, which is the hallmark of all Finland-Swedish modernists from the 1920s to the present. The seven texts are translated with a unique sense for poetic and psychological nuances and do perfect justice to these gems of prose.

Sven H. Rossel. *World Literature Today.* 64, 1990, p. 658

Solveig von Schoultz began her verse career in 1940 with *Min timme;* although she owes much of her reputation to her novellas, she has considered herself a lyricist before all else. The process of compression that critics have noted over the decades is even more evident in *Ett sätt att räkna tiden* (A way to reckon time): the poems are almost all short, with the exception of the finale (itself only thirty lines), which gives the book its name, a description of a descent into a cave where stalactites have formed: "in bunches the roof's heavy fruits hung, / and for millions of years dropped/ their wet lime, a way to reckon time."

The book is divided into four sections. The strength of the first lies in the portrait poems: Lars Wivallius, the Swedish adventurer and poet of the early seventeenth century, imprisoned at Kajana in northern Finland; Chopin and George Sand on their way to Mallorca (a voyage described more romantically by Sand in her memoirs); a scholar seated before a television set, who reckons time rather differently from the Olympic prizewinner he sees on the screen; a Lutheran pastor's widow of the distant past, who, according to custom, had to be wed by her husband's successor, even though she was worn out by childbearing; Madame Stravinsky walking in her husband's shadow; Beethoven waiting for his ne'er-do-well nephew. The section closes with a suite of five dream-poems, a subgenre in which von Schoultz has long excelled: "an angel / came aside me. An angel / lifted its broom / and hesitated, stood and lifted its broom / and hesitated still when the dream burst." (At this point in her career von Schoultz does not shrink from simplicities: the angels, on Judgment Day, have the task of sweeping "the condemned downward, the blessed upward.")

The second section contains poems about common concerns: primal hunger (a lynxlike animal caught "with its cruel and yellow eyes" in the headlight beams of a car); attachment to a childhood long gone (an old man puts his nose into the soft feathers of a fallen bird's nest and recalls "with a violent sense of loss / the years in the down"); and "happiness" (an ape mother with her child, swinging through the trees). . . .

Section three offers times, things, places: Whitsuntide, rotting tulips, kitchen utensils, old shoes, cluttered rooms at night, a meeting place to which a treasured friend no longer comes ("Did you ever ask me for permission to die?"), a November park, a hospital where a woman slowly dies. Finally, the fourth section moves abroad for its themes: sculptures on cathedral pillars in Autun, the "lady with the unicorn" in the tapestries of the Musée de Cluny, Anuradhapura (its Buddha "resting thirty meters long / with giant, calm feet"). Then there are mothers: Iranian mothers whose sons have become "martyrs" of war, birth on a refugee boat, a mother imprisoned, a leprous mother, the meeting between Mary and Anna—"still neither of them knows whom she bears, / and no one guesses the sword through the heart."

Every collection by Solveig von Schoultz has its poems that catch the eye and ear and hold the mind. One more poem in her latest volume should be mentioned, "Twilight": an old woman collects what a scythe has left behind, "her skirt is spacious, her pockets are full."

George C. Schoolfield. *World Literature Today.* 64, 1990, p. 323

SCHREINER, OLIVE (SOUTH AFRICA) 1855–1920

[Olive Schreiner] wrote many things and then destroyed them; she told me that, when *The Story of an African Farm* was finished, it seemed so bad to her, so far short of what she had meant, and she was so weary, that she nearly threw it into the dam on the farm the morning after she finished it. . . .

On one side she was a child; on another a woman; while those who think the "masculine mind" is a male prerogative would say she was a man; but usually her intellect was an impersonal one; she used to tell with mirth of a prominent man who described her as a "disembodied intellect." All this complexity made her personality baffling. It was a surprising experience, when the baby side was up, suddenly, in a flash, to be confronted with one of the most brilliant and powerful intellects in the world; or for a man, who might think it was the woman he was speaking to, to be knocked out by a "masculine" intellect, beside which his own must seem but a puny thing. . . .

On her great side she was very great indeed, elementally great in heart and brain; and she had flashes of insight, which, expressed in her great, simple language, stilled and awed. All suffering had her vehement sympathy, and all oppression, cruelty and injustice her relentless and uncompromising hostility. . . . Through all her philosophy ran the great idea of self-abnegation, renunciation, self-sacrifice. She was an almost defenseless person.

S. C. Cronwright-Schreiner. *The Life of Olive Schreiner* (London: T. Fisher Unwin, 1924). pp. 221, 239

One cannot legitimately complain because a writer leans toward the tragic. Hardy, Loti, Conrad, Olive Schreiner—her name does not seem little in such great company. In a chronological list, hers would come first. Indeed, it is possible that both Hardy and Conrad learned something from the great South African. The snobbery which condemns South African writings merely because they are South African had better take thought before denigrating Olive.

But it is not snobbish to object to the fact that whenever Olive Schreiner leaned toward the tragic she toppled over and wallowed in it. She gives us a close-up of the struttings or torments of this homuncule or that, only to snatch us away to would-be poetic heights of contemplation in which these antics dwindle to nothing against the gigantic African background. Then, when a Rabelaisian laugh seems called for, comes the unctuous flow of tears.

E. Davis. *South African Opinion.* January,
1947, p. 22

A careful study of Olive Schreiner's novels today does not reveal her, to the dispassionate critic, as the great novelist so many of her contemporaries claimed her to be. The faults of *The Story of an African Farm,* generally considered by her admirers as her masterpiece, have become obvious. Yet what is as clear from her writings as the Karoo sunlight she loved so passionately all her life long is that she is both poet and prophet, and a truly great South African.

Perhaps the main fault of *The Story of an African Farm* flows from the fact that Olive Schreiner is not basically a novelist but a poet, highly individual and subjective with all the passionately intense inner life characteristic of the poet's unique personality. In all her novels she is more lyrical than epic, she lacks balance and poise, objectivity, detachment not only from her own feelings but also from the characters she wishes to portray.

At times in *The Story of an African Farm* Olive Schreiner almost burns herself up with her fierce lyricism—the lyricism of her proud, rebellious spirit, of her fiery revolt against woman's lot in the man-made world of the nineteenth century, and of the sorrows and despairs of her lonely adolescence on the desolate Karoo farm where as a girl still in her teens she started writing her first novel. Then she is at loggerheads with the novelist, of whom it is demanded that he should see life straight and see it whole, with the result that the harmony and unity of her novel are seriously impaired.

This youthful lyricism has an even more harmful effect on her other three novels. (Not only was her first novel completed on that Karoo farm but also most if not all of *Undine* and large portions of *From Man to Man.*) Olive Schreiner had completed *The Story of an African Farm* before she was 23. Up to her death, more than forty years later, she had added only three novels, *Trooper Peter Halket of Mashonaland*—her impassioned defense of the black man against British Imperialism—*Undine* and *From Man to Man,* not one of them in any way superior to her first flawed but strangely moving book. With maturity, her many years spent in England and on the continent of Europe, the inspiration of her lifelong friendship with some of the best minds and most gifted writers of her time, all the wealth of experience and knowledge of life and men the years had brought, and her complete dedication to the writer's craft, Olive Schreiner gained nothing as a novelist: her first novel remained easily her best. Does this lack of any development in her art, her *métier,* not seem to corroborate my contention that she was not, intrinsically, a novelist?

Uys Krige. Introduction to Uys Krige, ed.
Olive Schreiner: A Selection (Cape Town:
Oxford University Press, 1968), pp. 1–2

[*The Story of an African Farm*] had had a hard birth, refused by one publisher after another. Not only was it about an Africa unfamiliar to England; but it had an unmarried mother whom the author refused to provide with a wedding ring. Then Chapman and Hall took it on the advice of George Meredith. Cuts and changes were suggested, and some made: it is said, with resentment. . . . It was not only Meredith who recognized the novel. An extraordinary assortment of the remarkable people of her time praised it. It was one of the best novels in the English language. It was greater than *The Pilgrim's Progress.* It had genius. It had splendor. For the rest of her life she was the famous author of this novel that she had written in her early twenties. And, until she died, people from every part of the world would come up to her and say that it had changed their lives. Some claim that it would have made no difference if she had never written another word. This is true, from the point of view of literature; but there were other sides to her.

Now I must write personally; but I would not, if I didn't know that nothing we can say about ourselves is personal. I read the novel when I was fourteen or so; understanding very well the isolation described in it; responding to her sense of Africa the magnificent—mine, and everyone's who knows Africa; realizing that this was one of the few rare books. For it is in that small number of novels, with *Moby Dick, Jude the Obscure, Wuthering Heights,* perhaps one or two others, which is on a frontier of the human mind. Also, this was the first "real" book I'd met with that had Africa for a setting. Here was the substance of truth, and not from England or Russia or France or America, necessitating all kinds of mental translations, switches, correspondences, but reflecting what I knew and could see. And the book became part of me, as the few rare books do. A decade or so later, meeting people who talked of books, they talked of this one, mentioning this or that character, or scene; and I discovered that while I held the strongest sense of the novel, I couldn't remember anything about it. Yet I had only to hear the title, or "Olive Schreiner," and my deepest sense was touched. . . .

The true novel wrestles on the edge of understanding, lying about on all sides desperately, for every sort of experience, pressing into use every flash of intuition or correspondence, trying to fuse together the crudest of materials, and the humblest, which the higher arts can't include. But, it is precisely here, where the writer fights with the raw, the intractable, that poetry is born. Poetry, that is, of the novel; appropriate to it. *The Story of an African Farm* is a poetic novel: and when one has done with "the plot" and the characters, that is what remains: an endeavor, a kind of hunger, that passionate desire for growth and understanding, which is the deepest pulse of human beings. . . .

It is the right time for this book to be republished. There is an atmosphere that is sympathetic to it, particularly among young people. It makes me very happy to introduce Olive Schreiner to a fresh generation of readers.

Doris Lessing. Afterword to Olive
Schreiner. *The Story of an African Farm*
(New York: Fawcett, 1968), pp. 273–75, 290

Olive Schreiner's constant battle with hope and despair, her ambivalence about her own worth, and her profound interest in women's rights and dignity make her a peculiarly contemporary writer, though she was born more than a hundred years ago. She is best known for her masterpiece, *The Story of an African Farm,* but all her work, even when it is flawed, continues to reverberate human experience in a constant intensity. . . .

Olive Schreiner . . . is both an example and an analyst of that modern neurosis—ambivalence to one's self. At many times in her life she acted in a saintly manner, and always her heroines exemplify infinite patience and generosity and compassion. At other times her heroines and she mock themselves and seek a punishment to suit the guilt they feel but for which no crime is recorded.

Martin Tucker. Introduction to Olive
Schreiner. *Undine* (New York: Johnson
Reprint, 1972), pp. v, xviii

Trooper Peter Halket of Mashonaland is a book built out of issues, and because these issues are unfortunately still on hand, it seems that it demands to be tackled in terms of those issues. [Olive Schreiner] meant the book as a moral challenge to the English world, and, if one has any respect for her at all, the challenge should be graciously accepted. . . .

The very fact that Schreiner's *Trooper Peter Halket of Mashonaland* is not a meticulously balanced construction of the realist sort . . . but a somewhat curiously thrown-together construction that relies on hugely magnified symbolic sections, on digressions and on wide arcs of elliptical cross-reference, that some of the tangents lead off into culs-de-sac; that layer upon layer of meaning can co-exist with far less chaos than one would suppose; the very fact that Schreiner is delighted to probe a bit here, then follow another track, double back, and doesn't mind roughening her stylistic surface with overlapping polemical interruptions and leaps of point of view—all these are indicative of the fact that she rejects the realist novel *because she rejects the morality which the realist novel encodes.* She does this, just as she rejects and pokes fun at the adventure novel, as has been shown, because she feels that its form reflected a falsehood. . . . What she does come up with goes a good deal of the way towards a resolution of her problems as a fiction writer. Its successor, although Mr. Mailer does not know it, is a book like *Armies of the Night,* which some seventy years later deals with history novelistically, and the novel as history. Its successors in terms of density of South African theme are Nadine Gordimer's *The Conservationist* and J. M. Coetzee's *Dusklands.*

For Schreiner, somewhat amazingly and even prophetically, is using techniques of documentary and fiction in amalgamation that have become normal to us in our new consciousness of media. She knows that the novel is not merely an abstract and inanimate conveyance of an artistic sensibility, but that it can carry news and information too.

Stephen Gray. *English in Africa.* September, 1975, pp. 23, 36–37

Olive Schreiner's *Woman and Labour* (1911) was called the Bible of the international woman's movement. It still retains its elemental prophetic power. And its outmoded anthropological and social darwinist trappings, its dream of matriarchal origins based in Bebel and Spencer, only add to its Old Testament hunger and thirst for justice and freedom. It expresses the need of the oppressed to see themselves as a chosen people. Women are for Olive Schreiner a lost tribe, keeping the memory of original sexual freedom alive in the slavery of centuries of diaspora. Like the Old Testament, *Woman and Labour* combines history and poetry. It curses the enemy, bewails woman's fate, urges her on with tales of the trials and tribulations of her forebears, sings her to sleep with a lullaby of revenge on her enemies and hope of peace after struggle, for her daughters. It is a text for "keeping the faith," that is, woman's faith in herself, and was meant to be chanted aloud in small groups of struggling, persecuted women, as the books of the Bible were read by persecuted Jews and Christians. And so it was. In Holloway Gaol and prisons throughout the British Isles, suffragettes "kept the faith" by whispering or shouting aloud Olive Schreiner's words of wisdom and courage. . . .

If *Woman and Labour* is her Old Testament, *Trooper Peter Halkett of Mashonaland* is her New Testament. Christ himself is one of Olive Schreiner's characters in his most endearing role as friend of the common man. But in the allegories of *Dreams* (1893) she wrote her prophetic books for womankind. *Dreams* is a feminist *Pilgrim's Progress.* In her hands, as in Bunyan's, the spiritual journey, the moral tale, is political as well as religious. The teller, the reader and the listener (for surely these allegories were meant to be spoken, sister to sisters) form a conspiracy. The wretchedness of their lives is to be redeemed by hope. The suffragettes in their cells found solace in *Dreams* and strength for their hunger strikes, courage for passive resistance. They repeated Olive Schreiner's words as nuns say their beads, alone and in groups, casting spells on doubt and despair with the power of the word. . . .

It is a mistake to read Olive Schreiner as sophisticated intellectuals do, dismissing her power because her prose lacks logic or her biology a scientific basis. Some books can best be judged by their readers, and *Dreams* is one of them.

The critics who are discomforted by Olive Schreiner's prose style have been taught that irony, not allegory, is the sharpest tool for shaping the literature of dissent. But irony is only the last resort of the defenseless intellectual, not the hapless black, woman or working class prophet. Irony is an upper-class weapon. It can utterly defeat its enemies by the assumption of mental superiority. . . .

Olive Schreiner's allegories never mock the common reader. Here it is the skilled reader who is confused and disturbed by the primitive outcry, the naked dream and wish, the language of scripture and the archetypal image.

> Jane Marcus. *Minnesota Review.* n.s. 12,
> Spring, 1979, pp. 58–60

Since Olive Schreiner was so widely acclaimed during her lifetime, it is curious that she is hardly known or studied today. Aside, perhaps, from some general familiarity with the novel, *The Story of an African Farm,* few scholars, reformers, or feminists have read her writing. Most of the studies on Schreiner's writing, moreover, focus almost exclusively on her fiction. There is at best a cursory glance at the main themes of *Woman and Labour,* a work which was regarded as "the Bible" of the Woman's Movement in the early twentieth century and which her most recent biographer declared was a "world-wide sensation" and "possibly the noblest contribution to the feminist movement." Literary critics continue to debate her stylistic shortcomings as a novelist, but rarely do they analyze her portraits of English or African society, her perceptions on the nature of men and women and their relationships, or her vision of human progress. While the undeniably heavy didacticism of her fiction and non-fiction easily offends the twentieth century reader, that is insufficient justification for scholarly inattention to the distinct merit of her social thought.

> Joyce Avrech Berkman. *Olive Schreiner:*
> *Feminism on the Frontier* (St. Alban's,
> Vermont: Eden Women's Press, 1979), p. 2

Twenty-eight years elapse between the publication of *African Farm* and *Woman and Labour.* This period, between 1883 and 1911, sees the emergence, especially in women's writing of the 1890s, of a concern with fantasy and utopia. In novels it takes the form of intricacies of plot involving cross-dressing and role reversal; in allegory with the visionary portrayal of the real world of the future. In this new world the divisions between men and women are overcome by recourse to idealization and retreat—this to a "far-away" place, perhaps uninhabited, perhaps a colony of "new" men and women. What we know historically, of course, is that women had begun to take a more active part in the public life of the time; it seems that a public discussion of "private" life—at least as it is reflected in the idealizing allegory of the period—remained elliptical, even fey. It was at this time that Olive Schreiner's imaginative writing was also at its most obscure, though its subject matter was real enough: the allegorical writing to which she turned in the late 1880s rehearsed over and over again the theme of sexual love, self-esteem, and the struggle for "love."

Between the writing of the early novels and her later feminist testament, she published only these allegories and a series of political essays. This was the long, unproductive period when she was unable to sustain her work beyond the length of a brief sketch or the urgency of journalism. She worked and reworked old manuscripts, carrying the unfinished sheets with her wherever she moved. Her writing was changing and experimental; she was now making a self-conscious attempt to find an appropriate literary form, but in her eyes, and those of others, she failed. . . .

She moved from themes of women's subjection and powerlessness to those of national oppression and the struggles of subject races and classes. She was an advocate first of the Boer cause against British imperialism, and then of the African people of South Africa subordinated in the interests of both Boer and Briton. Almost alone of her contemporaries she perceived the race conflicts during South Africa's industrial revolution in terms of a worldwide struggle between capital and labor. She was an outspoken critic and mentor of politicians in public life, but she cut a lonely, isolated figure, issuing prophetic warnings about the future of the country and retreating into a shy personal life.

The range and seeming incompatibility of her imaginative work and her political writing have placed her at continuing risk of being fragmented by admirers and detractors alike. In general, those interested in her novels have not been attentive to her politics.

Ruth First and Ann Scott. *Olive Schreiner*
(London: André Deutsch, 1980), pp. 16–17

The Story of an African Farm (1883) by the South African writer Olive Schreiner is a critique of three dominant narratives, a critique deliberately articulated, intellectually principled, and emotionally coherent. The Christian story and the teleological melodrama on which it depends features a battle between good and evil, which conventionally ends with the triumph, or at least the martyred justification, of right. This story about the revealed ruling purpose of the cosmos is run aground in the first part of *African Farm*. The second story, a *Bildungs* plot, centers in *African Farm* on Waldo Farber, who searches vainly for purpose, but stops and simply dies. The third story, centering here on Lyndall, combines various romantic thralldom and marriage plots in which fictional heroes and heroines have traditionally acted. Taken as a whole, the book marks the "end" of the consoling stories of the Christian, quest, and romance varieties. . . .

With the publication of *The Story of an African Farm* Olive Schreiner originated the critique of narrative characteristic of twentieth-century writing by women. As in her own allegory the body of her work became a bridge between nineteenth-and twentieth-century projects. Her accomplishment is to reject and dismantle tales of great cultural magnitude, making a whole *Story* of the critique of story, writing *finis* to three resonant narratives. She, with other women writers, "breaks the sentence" so that alternative and oppositional stories about women, men, and community can be constructed beyond the teleological formulations of quest and romance.

> Rachel Blau Du Plessis. *Writing Beyond the Ending: Narrative Strategies of Twentieth-Century Women Writers* (Bloomington: Indiana University Press, 1985), pp. 21, 30

Paradoxically, Schreiner's passion to cure the intellectual and social maladies of her time was her preeminent intellectual contribution to posterity as well as her key weakness. The strengths of her passion are prodigious. Surpassing her contemporaries she, like current poststructuralists, was bent upon exposing culture-bound binary oppositions, locating their roots in the errors of religion and science which reflected and upheld Victorian power relations in private and public spheres. Unlike present-day thinkers, who can marshal a plethora of twentieth-century scientific, historical, and philosophical evidence for their views on the cultural construction of gender, class, and race, Schreiner attacked widely held assumptions about human differences without such scholarly support. . . .

Her optimism was her lifeline. To sustain that optimism she could not bear the full weight of her unresolved conflicts. As early as postadolescence, she no longer suffered keenly the tension between her view of nature's caprice and malice and its sacred beauty; her dulling of this conflict is reflected in her self-styled mysticism and her failure to probe systematically the relation between altruistic and competitive forces in evolution. Within the context of her colonial birth as well, she resolved her conflicting national identity as both South African and English by asserting a global citizenship, idealizing her role as both an insider and an outsider in South African political life. Inadequately exploring this conflict, she overestimated her ability to convert English men and women to her anti–imperialism and to convert liberal white South Africans to her constitutional proposals. There is no doubt but that she and we benefitted from her optimism, whatever its cost, for it enabled the treatises and fiction that have inspired subsequent generations of critics of South African capitalism and racism.

> Joyce Avrech Berkman. *The Healing Imagination of Olive Schreiner: Beyond South African Colonialism* (Amherst: University of Massachusetts Press, 1989), pp. 231, 235

Ironically, of all late nineteenth-century women writers in English, Schreiner was one of the most public, one of the most exposed to the eyes of both the South Africans and the British, for her espousal of several prominent political causes: support for the Boers (Afrikaners) against the British in South Africa, opposition to the imperialism of Cecil Rhodes, support for the Blacks and Coloureds in South Africa, for the rights of women, and of Jews. These causes were her total preoccupation in the last 40 years of her life. Here, then, is a woman with a name for having written, first, three of the most personal novels ever published and then, after a break of nearly two decades, some of her age's most outspoken public tracts. The shift is a remarkable one, and one struggles to think of a male equivalent. The explanation would seem to be that Schreiner found the "indulgence" of self-representation an intolerable strain, and could only resolve the dilemma by putting fiction aside and taking up writing as a public service. This explanation seems to be borne out by her own words about the only new creative writing she did from the eighties onwards, the "dreams" or "allegories" that were published as *Dreams* (1890) and the pamphlet-sized *Dream Life and Real Life* (1893).

> Ruth Parkin-Gounelas. *Fictions of the*
> *Female Self: Charlotte Brontë, Olive*
> *Schreiner, Katherine Mansfield* (New York:
> St. Martin's, 1991), p. 93

Schreiner's connection of economic and sexual colonization is . . . negative. . . . for Schreiner the usurpation of the body, like the rape of the landscape, is essentially a seizing, despoiling, a trafficking in and taking away by force of that which is not rightfully one's own. The act of destroying or crushing land and body appears in Schreiner's autobiographical novel, *The Story of An African Farm* (1883), in her political novel, *Trooper Peter Halket of Mashonaland* (1897), and in her novel of ideas, *From Man to Man; or, Perhaps Only . . .* (1927), these narratives demonstrating her growing concern with the interlocked aspects of sexual and racial injustice in the personal and geopolitical spheres. In addition, these novels are significantly concerned with the meaning and limits of both real life and the artistic medium of words—a development of what the German poets and artists of the nineteenth century called romantic irony, wherein the limitations of art, language, and life are self-consciously played against each other. . . .

Schreiner's fictional output is not small, if one includes the stories, dreams, and allegories she wrote when she was unable to complete her longer imaginative works. Although her dreams and allegories are thematically related to the conflicts and imagery of her historically and politically textured fiction, they no longer are as widely read or known. In them, mentally or spiritually charged images of an inward vision replace fictional characterization and narrative. Some argue that the allegorical themes, self-consciously weighty, comprehensively broad, and flattened by omission of particular incident, lack the human interest that evokes attention or empathy. Their idealistic social and political schemes resonate with an impractical and dated Victorian visionary message that cries out for a less mystical, more realistic treatment. One century and several wars later, some readers reject evolution toward Utopia as a viable creed. However, it is important to note that when Schreiner responded *autobiographically* to the crisis of World War I, she produced a resonant, allegorically charged statement of hope for the future in "The Dawn of Civilization" (1921). Possibly one might argue that for Schreiner the allegorical turn was far from being a defect in her technical repertoire but was an artistic vehicle of great antiquity that provided her with an effective means of probing social issues in relation to her most intensely experienced personal moods. In this light, allegorical interiority freed Schreiner's voice in ways that a more dutiful realism never could.

> Gerald Monsman. *Olive Schreiner's Fiction:*
> *Landscape and Power* (New Brunswick,
> New Jersey: Rutgers University Press,
> 1991), pp. 4–5

SCHWARZ-BART, SIMONE (GUADELOUPE) 1938–

In Schwarz-Bart's novel, [*Pluie et vent sur Télumée Miracle* (Rain and wind on miracle worker Télumée; *The Bridge of Beyond*)] the matriarchal culture remains intact, although in the more global terms of the colonial conflict it is not only oppressed but emotionally one-sided because of its devaluation of the black man. . . .

It is my hypothesis that, in Schwarz-Bart's novel, the heroine Télumée's capacity to posit herself as a speaking subject stems from the ease with which she is able to insert herself into a female history. The novel opens with a section entitled *"Présentation des miens,"* which is, in fact, the narration of the matriarchal lineage into which Télumée is born and inscribed, in which she will participate, and which she must assume fully in order to perpetuate it. This retroflection is the precondition for reflection and introspection, and it is not without significance that these women are portrayed in terms of a geography as well as a biography. The lives of the women who preceded Télumée constitute mini-narratives which establish the woof upon which the warp of the heroine's own story will be woven. Each ancestor has her own texture, and at the same time is paradigmatic in the way she confronts problems; she leaves the threads of her answers, from which Télumée then weaves her own meanings. On a narrative level the heroine's life takes the shape of many repetitions.

The key to Télumée's ability to become the subject of her text is her relationship to her grandmother. The essence of this bond is its mirroring structure: first and foremost this bonding occurs by means of the *"regard,"* and its analogues, such as echo, reflection, or dream. And it is within the parameters of this possibility for reflection, in the perpetual and metaphysical senses of the word, that the girl comes to be and to know.

Ronnie Scharfman. *Yale French Studies.*
1981, pp. 88–90

To build bridges of understanding with the humblest and most deprived people in a society is a vital function for the writer.

In *The Bridge of Beyond* Simone Schwarz-Bart has responded to this challenge. She takes a character who could merely be seen and taken for granted, an old woman offering peanuts for sale by a country church. Her novel makes that women exist for us as a unique and irreplaceable person. For a writer who is herself highly sophisticated and much traveled, it is an achievement to have thought herself into the experience of an old peasant woman who has spent her life in a remote district of Guadeloupe, and to have found a style in which to tell the story from inside, as a first-person narrative. In Caribbean fiction we so often hear the voices of the emancipated young men, exiles and intellectuals. It has taken a woman author to give a hearing to the voice of the mothers and grandmothers.

The Bridge of Beyond is the title given to the English edition of a novel which first appeared in French in 1972 as *Pluie et vent sur Télumée Miracle.* A more literal translation would read: "Rain and Wind on Miracle-Woman Télumée." This identifies the book clearly as a tribute to an exceptional woman who withstands the adverse elements. It is useful to see the novel's origin in this way, as a positive act of paying homage. It commemorates Fanotte, a real person from Goyave, Simone Schwarz-Bart's village in Guadeloupe, who died in 1968. In such circumstances we expect an affectionately nostalgic portrait and a concern to bring out the positive values of the past. The attitudes and situations also reflect the earlier part of this century, not contemporary ideological debates.

Simone Schwarz-Bart has chosen very deliberately to focus on what is distinctive about a woman's experience. It is altogether appropriate that France's most important magazine for women, *Elle,* should have awarded this book its literary prize. The heroine belongs to a dynasty of Lougandor women. . . . From Minerva, her great-grandmother, freed from slavery (abolition finally came in 1848 for the French colonies), down to her adopted daughter, Sonore, we have a span of five generations of women harshly dealt with by life. Yet their sufferings only strengthen them, and their abundant faith in life is never lost. Even the best of their menfolk seem vulnerable in comparison, and most prove downright inadequate. In an accurate reflection of the sociology of the West Indian family, Schwarz-Bart shows fathers too often proving temporary, and failing in their role as providers and guides. It is the mothers, and in many cases the grandmothers, who are the mainstay of the family unit. The essential idea of *The Bridge of Beyond* is contained in the relationship between Télumée and her grandmother Toussine, whose skills and moral values she inherits in a triumphant example of continuity.

The English title, *The Bridge of Beyond,* emphasizes a significant aspect of Schwarz-Bart's image of woman, that is as a link with the unseen world and source of spiritual values.

Bridget Jones. Introduction to Simone
Schwarz-Bart. *The Bridge of Beyond*
(London: Heinemann, 1982), pp. iv–v

The life of . . . a black man and his attitude to women is the subject of Simone Schwarz-Bart's next novel *Ti Jean l'horizon* (1979). The main character is Ti Jean, a "child of nature" from Fond Zombi. At first he is happy and contented with his childhood sweetheart Egée, until one day she mysteriously disappears and at the same time the island is quite unaccountably cut off from the outside world. Ti Jean goes off to try to find the solution to these problems. His search takes him back in time to the Africa of the past, and leads by way of France to the Guadeloupe of the eighteenth century, when slavery still existed. During his travels he meets many women; in all of them he looks for his Egée, but in vain. Not until the end of the book, when the sun returns to his island and contact with the outside world has been restored, does he meet a girl "like she was, a black girl without airs or pretence, a pure nature in all her simplicity."

Simone Schwarz-Bart obviously sets great store by the background of her characters, the story of their ancestors and their ties with Africa. She distances herself from the "modern" period, as represented by urban society, and one may assume that she does so deliberately, as she writes all her books in Paris, where she has lived for many years.

Ineke Phaf. In Mineke Schipper, ed.
*Unheard Words: Women and Literature in
Africa, the Arab World, Asia, the
Caribbean, and Latin America* (London:
Allyson and Busby, 1985), p. 189

For Schwarz-Bart, the individual self can only be grasped through the mythical genealogy of many past selves. And those selves are all female. . . .

Misjudged as a "folk" narrative, [*Pluie et vent sur Télumée Miracle*] was immensely popular, obtained a literary prize and has been, somewhat hastily, translated into English *(The Bridge of Beyond).* It starts with a long, top-heavy first part criticized as unbalanced by some critics and entitled "Histoire des miens." This family history, which has mainly to do with female lineage, is the key to Schwarz-Bart's whole corpus. One names oneself by writing oneself and, in so doing, brings oneself to life.

There are two legitimate reasons for Télumée's self-birthing through a long line of female ancestors. First, sociologically, the absent male is a constant of Caribbean life. Second, her use of what I would call "the matriarchy principle" is a good example of how this writer makes factual sociology serve symbolic ends. The absence of Man at the center of the narrative space (the uterine circularity of the hut within the village within the island within the sea) give priority to the female fable within. *Télumée-Miracle* recounts, in a series of flashbacks, the lives of four women: the woman Télumée, her mother, her grandmother and the semi-mythical mother of them all, Minerva the slave who remembered. Each life follows a trajectory concentric to the others, a rise and fall pattern, until we are led to the last pages, the last moments of Télumée herself: destitute, alone but, thanks to the women's spiritual legacy, undefeated. Woman has thus no need for *Négritude,* no desire to go back to her roots, to search for the lost father. For she is her own genitrix. Therein lies the "miracle."

However, all is not well in the island queendom. Since Télumée, unlike her forebears, dies childless, her demise renders problematic the passing of matriarchal power down the chain of female figures. In fact we, the readers, are the only children left to her. Likewise, Schwartz-Bart has declared that she wrote *Télumée* to preserve the passing of a certain way of life for the future generations, the young people of Guadeloupe who are no longer in contact with "the old ways." A history that has to be retold is always suspect. When the chain is broken, oral history become written text. Or, maybe a fairy tale.

Such is her second novel, *Ti-Jean l'Horizon* (Little John the horizon), a story which draws on the well-known trickster figure of Caribbean legends, itself inspired by African legends.

Although it has been rightly pointed out that the female figures in *Ti-Jean* are weak and stereotyped as compared to the formidable matriarchs of the previous works, I prefer to focus on two key aspects of Ti-Jean himself, in their relationship to history. One, the fact that the character, in the folktales as well as in the novel, can change at will from a man into a woman and vice versa. In a bisexual nature, Ti-Jean embodies all of the human species. The other, a trajectory—both physical and spiritual—which takes him/her from the Caribbean back to Africa (the common enough slave-inspired belief of return after death), and, again, from Africa back to the Caribbean. Thus Schwarz-Bart bypasses the limitations of nation, or race, or sex-specific history to encompass all of us and all of it.

Clarisse Zimra. *Journal of Ethnic Studies.*
12:1, Spring, 1984, pp. 69–71

Critical discussions of this novel [*The Bridge of Beyond*] have stressed the way in which the narrator's life, like that of her female ancestors, falls into a recurrent pattern of ascent, ruin and subsequent renaissance, in seeming obedience to a cyclical view of man's progression through time. . . .

The story of Télumée and Medard, a microcosm of the larger structure of ascent and fall, renews the tree imagery of *The Bridge of Beyond* by contrasting Medard, the fallen manchineel, with Télumée, the *flamboyant,* trees which have earlier been proposed to the reader as antithetical symbols of ruin and salvation. This last cycle of the life of Télumée prepares the way for the conclusion of the book, where Télumée will finally become "like the tree called Resolute, on which it is said the whole globe and all its calamities could lean"—the "finest tree" of the forests, "the one that is cut down the most often" but that shares with the black race the strength "to be born again." The dignity of her new name, Télumée Miracle, not only completes the pattern begun by her grandmother, Queen Without a Name, but also redeems and honors the forgotten women of Guadeloupe who have dreamed and suffered in the past: "all the women lost before their time, broken, destroyed," at whose wakes the mourners tried in vain "to think of the name, the true name they had deserved to bear." Built upon the paradoxical "splendor of human uncertainty," *The Bridge of Beyond* promises salvation through individual courage, and celebrates the role of women in the Caribbean struggle for survival.

> Beverley Ormerod. *An Introduction to the*
> *French Caribbean Novel* (London:
> Heinemann, 1985), pp. 110, 130

In Schwarz-Bart's *Ti Jean,* the hero is at once an orphan (his mother's husband dies before he is born) and a divine son to Wademba (also known as "The Immortal"), the island's cultural protector. Wademba has overseen Guadeloupe's generations since the slave trade crossing, and upon his death he entrusts the protection of their cultural legacy to Ti Jean. Furthermore, he confers upon him a mission to return to Africa and to restore the links to the cultural homeland. In taking on this spiritual and cultural enterprise, Ti Jean "orphans himself." As Jesus renounced his worldly parents in order to embrace his spiritual family, Ti Jean leaves his home and his wife-girlfriend in order to regain the larger family ties between his Caribbean people and their African homeland. . . .

In *Pluie* the young protagonist's largest experience is with her grandmother, who is the ideal and future reflection of herself. Télumée comes to know the world, to reflect upon it, through her grandmother's political, social, historical, and psychological links with it.

The positive reflection of Télumée's soul is offset, however, by the numerous negative variants of non-reflecting surfaces found in her encounters with members of the white community. . . .

In *Pluie et vent,* Télumée, who triumphs over affliction (the "rain" and "wind" of the title), helps others in the community to endure and to overcome their own painful struggles. . . . [Similarly,] Ti Jean's return to his community inaugurates a transformation, a new era of hope and strength, and his marriage to Égee—who is likened to the damp, the sands, to the brilliance of flame itself—signifies a hierogamous union, a wedding between Guadeloupe and the cosmos itself.

> Josie P. Campbell. *Comparative Literature*
> *Studies.* 22, 1985, pp. 397, 405

The story of the central character, Télumée Miracle, is a fictional autobiogra-phy, inspired by an old Guadeloupean woman (Stéphanie Priccin) who had fascinated and intrigued the author during her childhood. From these child-hood memories, Schwarz-Bart has reproduced a collection of what she calls "des moment privilégiés" in the life of this remarkable woman. She recounts the story as a grand adventurous odyssey of the four women of the Lougandor family: Minèrve, the great-grandmother; Toussine, the grandmother (eventu-ally known as Reine Sans Nom [Nameless Queen]); Victoire, the mother, and finally Télumée.

From a broader perspective, however, the novel is more than a mere testimony to one woman and her three ancestors. Its more compelling mes-sage is found in the praise it offers to an entire generation of black Caribbean women: to their fortitude, their resilience, their dignity. Schwarz-Bart tells us: "Télumée Miracle est un hommage à une femme de Goyave. Ce n'est pas seulement sa vie, mais aussi le symbole de toute une génération de femmes connues, ici, à qui je dois d'être antillaise, de me sentir comme je me sens." [Télumée Miracle is an homage to a woman of Goyave. It is not only her life, but also the symbol of a whole generation of women I have known here, to whom I owe my sense of being an Antillean woman.]

This story comes from the pen of a writer whose previous works have all reflected a great pride in her homeland, Guadeloupe. It is noteworthy that *Pluie et vent sur Télumée Miracle* was the first novel undertaken by the author independently from her writer-husband, André Schwarz-Bart; for here, she emerges as a powerful novelist in her own right.

Karen Smiley Wallace. *French Review.* 59,
1986, p. 428

At first glance, Télumée Lougandor hardly seems to qualify as the heroine of a quest. We are told at the beginning of the book that the measure of her heart was always and remains linked to her island of Guadeloupe. Her life is resolutely grounded in the here and now, and the literal boundaries of her adventures are circumscribed by the rural villages in which she lives. The account of her life does not contain grandiose adventures, supernatural inter-cession, or any of the traditional thematic trappings of quest literature. Yet her story does offer a resolute and very poetic coming to terms with man and woman, self and community, material richness and spiritual treasure. This is, in short, a quest that moves full circle without ever leaving its point of departure. The basic truth, the language of identity, is there from the start, yet it takes Télumée a lifetime and us the fictive space of that lifetime in the text to grasp its full meaning. . . .

Simone Schwarz-Bart's novels, on the other hand, attempt to treat the predicament of the woman and West Indian society at the level of the individ-ual enduring life: self-esteem and self-worth are restored through a process of revalorizing of images and a heritage seen in negative terms by most *Antillais.* Schwarz-Bart reverses the connotations of the closed space and emphasizes only its positive, nurturing aspects. Her heroines' voyages are symbolic interior journeys.

Kitzie McKinney. French Review. 62, 1989,
p. 651

Simone Schwarz-Bart's novel *The Bridge of Beyond* is a celebration of life, manifest through a story told. The heroine, Télumée, has puzzled out a meaning for her life, and she shares it with us. It is the essential feature of Télumée's story that she tells it. In doing so she integrates the entire fabric of her life, by naming herself and each person in her life, and situating them all in time and place, on her island home of Guadeloupe. Throughout the text, and the life that the text embodies, words are a charged and living force, for good or ill, and silence can be tantamount to destruction or annihilation. Thus Télumée's story is a triumph simply because it exists as an ordered narrative. As a story told, it is a gift of life.

We can read this work as a story told for black women. The growing body of works by black women writers of the African diaspora, collectively, have strategic impact, for within these works our writers re/collect the separated fictions of our lives, in order to reclaim our stories and to re-write our histories. In doing this, they legitimize lives and world views which have hitherto been alienated and removed from narrative account, and become for us the manifestation of that voice re-found. Thus the reclamation of our voices through these texts has become a socio-political reality, a reality which is also placed as a vital theme *within* some of these works themselves. Simone Schwarz-Bart's *The Bridge of Beyond* is significant not simply because it is given to us, but because within that gift we are bequeathed the story of a woman who has learnt to give an account of her life, and who can acknowledge why that, in itself, is a gift worth possessing.

Abena P. A. Busia. In Carole Boyce Davies
and Elaine Savory Fido, eds. Out of the
Kumbla: Caribbean Women and Literature
(Trenton, New Jersey: Africa World Press,
1990), pp. 289–90

Simone Schwarz-Bart's play *Ton beau capitaine* (Your handsome captain) was inspired by the real-life circumstance of Haitian men who leave their native land in search of work. Set in 1985, it presents agricultural worker Wilnor Baptiste, who lives in Guadeloupe while his wife Marie-Ange remains behind in Haiti. During their years of separation they communicate by way of audio cassette. Wilnor's simultaneous absence from Haiti and presence in Guadeloupe are the subjects of this 1987 play. Consequently, patterns of isolation, separation, displacement, and exile are found throughout the text. . . .

The patterns of displacement, separation, isolation, and exile that characterize the fictional *Ton beau capitaine* are mirrored in the real-life struggles of contemporary migrant workers everywhere. The longing that Wilnor and Marie-Ange feel for each other is a desire for the *pays natal.* Wilnor and Marie-Ange's story can also be seen as a metaphor for the millions of people who were forcibly removed from Africa and brought to the Americas as slaves, victims all of circumstance.

Renée Laurier. *World Literature Today.* 64,
1990, pp. 57, 59

SEBBAR, LEILA (ALGERIA) 1941–

In *Fatima,* [*ou les algériennes au square* (1981; Fatima; or, the Algerian women in the park)], as in *L'amour, la fantasia* (Love, fantasia), oral narrative assumes importance. Like [Assia] Djebar's *porteuses de feu,* these women tell their tales, stories of their own lives and the lives of others, in their maternal language. For Maghrebian women in France the relationship between *écriture* and *kalaam,* between the written and the spoken word, is redefined. The French language enters the home as both a written and spoken language. Living in France and attending French schools, *Beur* children of the immigrant population loosen their hold on their mother's language and begin to favor French.

Sebbar's oral narrative, in contrast to Djebar's, is imagined; she has not transcribed actual conversations. Her purpose is different from Djebar's as well. Djebar attempts to preserve the heroic deeds for posterity and transmit exceptional moments; Sebbar uses oral narrative to mirror daily life. For Sebbar, orality attests to a strong sense of community and female bonding and at the same time expresses alienation and victimization. These women know that they are victims of poverty and of the patriarchy. If Djebar's *porteuses de feu* reveal the courage to fight, Sebbar's Fatima and her friends (like Faulkner's Dilsey in *The Sound and the Fury*) have the courage to endure.

Sebbar's ear is finely tuned to the ebb and flow of women's conversation in daily life. Their speech is sometimes lyrical, sometimes strident, sometimes hopeful, sometimes desperate. It becomes clear that Fatima and her friends are deeply attached to their children and loyal to their husbands. Dalila is witness to their struggle to gain control of their lives and to their encounter with obstacles: cramped quarters, illiteracy, unemployment, health problems. . . .

The French painter Eugène Delacroix provides Shérazade with a key to her past. In order to forge a new identity, she must come to terms with her dual legacy: Algerian patriarchy and European colonialism. Both deny women freedom of self-expression. This dual legacy is indeed apparent in Shérazade's dress: an Algerian scarf at her neck, a walkman plugged into her ears. It is also evident in her actions. Fleeing home—like Dalila, who leaves the maternal realm—Shérazade chooses the open road. At the end of the novel, she is no longer in Paris but has gone south, heading for Algeria. Escaping death in a car explosion and presumed dead by the French police, Shérazade is free and anonymous. She can forge a new identity and construct a new life.

It appears from this study that the children of the diaspora do indeed share the concerns and conflicts of Algerians at home. The weight of colonialism and traditional patriarchy are oppressive factors in both geographical settings. In addition, Djebar and Sebbar's heroines respond in similar fashion. They leave the home, maternal space, but carry with them echoes of women's voices, of whispers from the harem.

Mildred Mortimer. Research in African
Literatures. 19, 1988, pp. 307–8, 310

In five novels, in essays, stories, and articles, Sebbar has explored her existential condition, which she further articulates in *Lettres parisiens* (1986; Parisian letters), a correspondence intended for publication with Canadian author Nancy Huston, also living in Paris and writing in French: "I am a woman in exile, that is to say, always on the brink, living on the frontier, independent, standing apart, always on the edge, shifting from one side to the other, in permanent imbalance. . . . I write about silence, a blank memory, a history in pieces, a community dispersed, splintered, forever divided. I write of fragments, the void, a poor land, uncultivated, sterile—where you must dig deep and far to bring to light that which you would have forgotten forever."

Her first full-length novel, *Fatima*, treats her most favored character type, the illiterate immigrant mother who is "very protective and very attentive and very curious about everything. . . very alert and very often the head of the family." As in subsequent works, events in the story are far less important than the thoughts, memories, and conversations of the many characters who are linked in an almost seamless fashion—literally, without paragraph break or even punctuation. Recollections shared with female friends in the park portray the North African family in the housing project in the French suburbs, a family whose father is in a sanatorium and whose mother single-handedly raises her children, who no longer speak her language. . . .

The work which has received the greatest attention in Algeria—the tour of a stage adaptation is projected, although the books are not readily available—is *Parle mon fils parle à ta mère* (1984; Speak my son speak to your mother), an almost unbroken monologue by an immigrant mother addressing the runaway son who has suddenly returned home for a brief visit. To monosyllabic responses, she rambles on about the family, the ideal (Arab) wife for him, what she has heard on the radio, admonishments to remember his prayers. In her original presentation of the French spoken by an unschooled immigrant Arab, in a single eighty-four-page paragraph punctuated only by long dashes and ellipses, Sebbar has created a highly sympathetic and realistic character.

Sebbar's first full-length novel, *Shérazade* (1982), relates the picaresque adventures of a seventeen-year-old daughter of Algerian immigrants who flees the suburban housing project for Paris, possessed only of lots of nerve, green eyes, brown frizzy hair, and a Walkman. . . .

In keeping with her concern for the "Beur" population, Sebbar's most recent publication is the literary text for a photo album entitled *Génération métisse* (1988, Crossbreed generation), which deals with the current artistic contributions of this same group. Her numerous short stories deal principally with the second generation of North Africans in France. . . . She develops her stated love for the voices of women to a mythic degree in "La loi de retour" (1987), in which women harvesting olives begin to shout and continue shouting until they manage to draw everyone who hears their cry, even from very far away, back to them. The only man among them is the public scribe who records the poem they are shouting. Finally, the soldiers open fire, killing everyone but the scribe, who continues to write "what he understands of these words that came to him from the voices of women who shout no longer".

In the autobiographical essay "Si je parle la langue da ma mère" (1978) Sebbar painstakingly dissects her emotional refusal and final acceptance of her unpronounceable Arab name and her relation to the French language, her "mother tongue," her mode of communication passed on by the severe schoolmistress, her mother: "I'm called Leïla and I teach the language of my mother to those who speak it because they speak the language of their mothers. And I write in the tongue of my mother. To come back to myself. I was a good colonized subject. Like my father." With understated passion and wry humor, Leïla Sebbar gives voice to those who do not have access to the general public. Hers is a woman's voice; it speaks French, but it addresses concerns common throughout the world.

Nancy Du Plessis. World Literature Today.
63, 1989, pp. 415–17

Leila Sebbar, the noted Algerian novelist . . . has now brought out *La négresse à l'enfant* (The negress with a child), a collection of eight short stories, half of which have appeared previously in different magazines. What she emphasizes here is the cross-cultural world of the big city, with its subcultures of immigrant workers from France's former colonies. With light irony and pathos she portrays working women in particular, bewildered by languages not their own, by a technological environment they must manipulate but do not understand, and by the conflict between their indigenous values and beliefs and the mores of a capitalistic society. Often she paints a women's world: servants bringing their employers' washing to a laundromat, maids in domestic service, or a line of garment workers lunching outdoors behind a sheltered sidewalk. Women observers may wonder about some individual, different from themselves in color or language or habit, who passes before them and then inexplicably disappears.

The title story shows the peculiar bond between a black nanny and her white charge. The child senses the disparity between the worlds of the privileged and the poor, talks with her nanny of experiences they share in a world of which the parents know nothing, but, without being told, discloses none of this to her parents. Other selections treat such themes as the reluctance of a Middle Eastern laundress to take her own intimate apparel to a laundromat, where it might be glimpsed by a man; a Mauritian worker who "surprisingly" tempts a big-city official ("On dit qu'elle est très belle et que même la couleur de sa peau l'embellit, les femmes voudraient bien la voir pour savoir si c'est vrai"); and a museum guard who, while protecting a valuable painting, *La jeune fille au turban,* spends her time listening and hoping that a passing visitor might utter a word in her own language.

For the most part the stories are poignant. Their interest lies not in the action but in the interplay of cultures and traditions they depict. The half-light cast on those who inhabit the passing scene intrigues the reader. Sebbar neither laments nor prophesies. She skillfully creates vignettes wherein the First World and Third World exist together but do not blend with each other.

Charlotte H. Bruner. *World Literature*
Today. 65, 1991, pp. 347–48

The daughter of a French mother and an Algerian father, Sebbar re-creates the world of marginalized immigrants in order to lessen her own personal sense of exile. Having spent her formative years in colonial Algeria, she now resides in Paris. During the past decade, she has written seven novels that explore the world of the Beurs, the second generation of Maghrebian immigrants who live in the urban ghettos of France. Although not a Beur herself, Sebbar interprets their world. Her work carries the message that Beur culture today must redefine itself in terms of both its North African culture of origin and the European culture of domination in which it is embedded. Living in a francophone secular state that marginalizes the Arabic language as well as Islam, Beurs must appropriate a new space, positioning themselves apart from the dominant Western culture while at the same time forging links with it.

If the solution to Beurs' exile is to accept some elements of Eastern and Western culture while rejecting others, will they be able to do so successfully? Will they strike a balance between two conflicting worlds, or will they embrace one while abandoning the other, or will they assimilate bits and pieces of both superficially with little understanding of either? As children of immigrants, exiles for whom the ancestral homeland is often a cloudy memory, can they achieve the "contrapuntal awareness" which, in Said's view, compensates for the sense of loss? Grappling with these questions, Sebbar portrays adolescent Beurs who rebel against restrictions imposed on them by a transplanted Maghrebian patriarch and become *fugueurs,* adolescent runaways. Her protagonists pass through a nomadic phase in their search for empowerment, self-affirmation, and a new space situated at the intersection of Occidental and Oriental cultures.

> Mildred Mortimer. *Research in African*
> *Literatures.* 23, 1992, pp. 195–96

SEGHERS, ANNA (GERMANY) 1900–1983

Readers of *The Seventh Cross (Das siebte Kreuz)* will begin *Transit* with hope and finish it (if they can bear its vagaries that long) with a complete sense of let-down. Frau Seghers' first novel, despite its turgidity and its Teutonic tendency to moon, was good melodrama, lashed by the whips of evil older than history. Her second attempt in that direction has kept the turgidity of its predecessors and kindled its Teutonic mooniness to psychotic pitch. It has kept its shape of evil too—without its terror; its pattern of a doomed and dying Europe—without its heartbreak. To be blunt about it, *Transit* is one of the dullest failures this reviewer has encountered in a long, long time.

> William Du Bois. *The New York Times.*
> May 14, 1944, p. 7

Among the best-known exponents of . . . "socialist realism" is Anna Seghers, a prolific writer whose collected works run so far into eight volumes. She belongs to that hierarchy of Communist writers which includes the early Malraux, Aragon, Eluard, Brecht, Becher and Wolf. Like these she has devoted much of her work to an "Abrechnung" [accounting] with the inter-war years and has helped to drum out in work after work the collective guilt of the German people for the rise of Hitler. Her novels perform a literary autopsy on the corpse of the Weimar Republic, tracing the growth of the Nazi cancer back to the immediate post-war malaise. And if her work is not always free of that self-righteous undertone common to this school of novelists, it nevertheless rises at its highest level to a generous democratic humanism; at its lowest, as in some of the shorter novels, it degenerates into party bickerings and the abrasive combativeness of the political manifesto.

> R. C. Andrews. *German Life and Letters.*
> 1954–55, p. 121

Anna Seghers's novel *Die Toten bleiben jung* (The dead stay young), successfully exploits those artistic qualities that distinguish socialist from critical realism. The complex story structure and its fragmentation into several subplots reflect the author's intention to capture the destiny of the nation and all its classes. This is why Anna Seghers does not concentrate on the development of one social stratum as the representative and symbol of the nation as a whole. Her national approach is the polar opposite of Thomas Mann's, which finds its subject matter in the bourgeoisie. Anna Seghers presents the typical as the key to the life of the nation in its totality.

> Klaus Hermsdorf. *Weimarer Beiträge.* 1961,
> p. 295

The stories around all the characters with whom Anna Seghers is willing to be concerned are never written down for their own sake. Rather, the destinies described are "representatives" of something else. This implies that the themes treated in this writer's historically relevant and significant narrative style are related to one another and that repetitions of the same theme are unavoidable; for instance, the description of one and the same event through observers of diverging social attitudes. This imposes, in a sense, a cyclical form. Anna Seghers' typical working procedure, as it is here envisaged, is strikingly apparent in the link between the two narratives, "Die Hochzeit zu Haiti" (The wedding in Haiti) and "Wiedereinführung der Sklaverei in Guadeloupe" (Reintroduction of slavery in Guadeloupe), both of 1948, and the story "Das Licht auf dem Galgen" (The light on the gallows), published twelve years later in 1960, which serves to impart the definitive form of a triadic cycle to an epic complex that the author had obviously been regarding as fragmentary. . . .

It appears that the stories of Anna Seghers are arranged in accordance with definite artistic principles of epic and objective reporting. . . .Looked at superficially, many of these stories rather appear to be works of historiography. . . . The objectivity of the reporting, with the implied anonymity of both the narrator and the audience, approaches documentation and chronicle, though, to be sure, the individual story (seemingly in contrast to this narrative manner) maintains at all times and with emphatic insistence the narrator's right to artistic powers of imagination.

> Hans Mayer. *Die Neue Gesellschaft/*
> *Frankfurter Hefte.* 1962, pp. 765–66

Erzählungen (Stories), volume 1. . . . The artistic climax of the volume is the story "Der Ausflug der toten Mädchen" (The outing of the dead girls). It was written during the last years of the war and outranks by far anything written at the time in Germany. Here again Anna Seghers does not argue. There is no need for her to argue. That Hitler and his war destroyed the lives of so many former schoolmates in one way or another, that they drove the writer herself into exile, these are facts that need not be discussed and demonstrated. The memory of things lost is, in itself, enough of an accusation. The tormenting awareness of the loss of so many broken lives transmutes the memory of the school outing into a shining present: more real than Mexico, where the writer has made her home, more beautiful no doubt than it really was, gone forever yet never to be lost. Across the abyss of space and time Anna Seghers conjures up a world that once was hers.

Rudolf Hartung. *Neue Rundschau.* 1964, p. 501

There is something homespun about Anna Seghers's narrative style. The stories in her new collection, *Die Kraft der Schwachen* (The strength of the weak), could almost all be included in elementary-school readers and not only in those prepared for children in the German Democratic Republic. The theme here is one of central significance in all her works: seemingly weak and often insignificant individuals can muster great energy to achieve their goal when that goal is to do good for their fellow men. This, of course, is not meant to have metaphysical implications . . . the stress lies on the world of realities. The heroes in these stories are simple men and women representing the common people. In most cases they discover their own strength only when they suddenly find themselves confronted with a situation in which others who are in need or danger must be helped.

Eberhard Semrau. *Welt und Wort.* 1966, p. 308

Her outstanding book of the war and the one which became an international success is *The Seventh Cross.* In this novel Anna Seghers describes the flight of seven prisoners from the Westhofen concentration camp, shortly before the Second World War [, and] the varying reactions of the different people whom the escaped prisoners encounter during their flight. Thereby she is able to present a fascinating picture of German social conditions as a whole.

Theodore Huebener. *The Modern Language Journal.* 1966, p. 210

The scope of Anna Seghers's humanism reflects the communal experiences of socialist democracy. She starts out from the conviction that mankind does not owe its achievements to a chosen few; the power to change oneself and to change the world is inborn even in the least of men; and historical progress is the fruit of an infinite number of great and small deeds and acts of courage. At the same time we sense Anna Seghers's personal concern to draw the reader's attention to values and to human destinies that all too often remain unnoticed.

Her story "Der Führer" (The leader), together with the stories "Agathe Schweigert" and "Duell" (The duel), is a work that has an assured place in modern German narrative literature. The abundance of poetic resources on which Anna Seghers draws here, the sensuous radiance of her language, the integral completeness of the work from its rich dramatic opening to its savage conclusion are striking, especially in view of the extreme simplicity—a simplicity that at times impresses us as ascetic—which she maintains in most of her other tales. There is great power particularly in her descriptions of nature that put before our eyes the shapeless, wild, and threatening character of that archetypal mountain landscape, and which belong among the best she has ever created.

Friedrich Albert. *Sinn und Form.* 1966,
pp. 1043, 1049

In the German Democratic Republic Anna Seghers never found her way back to the dry and woodcutlike prose of her early works. . . .

In the collection of stories *Die Kraft der Schwachen*, which was published in 1966, only one of the nine stories takes place in the German Democratic Republic. . . . The almost arid plainness that once was the preeminent characteristic of the great prose of Anna Seghers has slipped into puling. The content has retained its seriousness, but the language has come to lag and sag and is now trivial. Suddenly the vocabulary of this storyteller consists of frenzies of color—red-gold, green-gold, dead-gray, dead-purple, gray-purple, gold-purple, greenish silver, "faded stars," an "immeasurable sky," and a sun "resplendent as though through a crystal"—that is the fabric of a once disciplined narrator who is now bent on snatching up emotions, political conclusions, and history instead of relying on concrete observation, instead of filtering out vision and understanding not from the abstract concept but from things touched, tasted, and seen. This naiveté goes so far that Anna Seghers of all people utilizes the harmless and legitimizing phrase, Hitler's "accession to power," as though what happened was merely that a man, having proved his qualifications, took over a position that was his due.

Fritz J. Raddatz. *Germanic Review.* 1968,
p. 51

Everything Anna Seghers wrote before 1945, however different in plot, sounds basically the same note—candid snapshots, ephemeral reflections of reality, personal episodes that at the same time are also political episodes. All these are captured by her and scattered about at random, full of genuine emotion but lacking depth and limited in what they have to say. In short, they lack the totality of society, a view of the world as a whole.

Jürgen Rühle. *Literature and Revolution.*
(New York: Praeger Publishers, Inc., 1969),
p. 202

The novel *The Revolt of the Fishermen* treats her basic theme, the struggle of the economically disadvantaged against oppression and social injustice. The setting is a fishing village in Brittany, but the action could take place anywhere at any time. *The Seventh Cross* was first published in English in the United States in 1942 and immediately became a best seller. It was not published in German until 1962. The plot involves the fate of seven men who escaped from a concentration camp in Germany shortly before the outbreak of World War II. *Transit*, also published in English in 1943, is basically an autobiographical novel, elaborating on the hopeless situation of refugees from the Nazis, waiting in Marseille for a boat to take them to the New World. The atmosphere is one of confusion and despair. After her return to Germany, Anna Seghers wrote *The Dead Stay Young,* which was revised and published in 1949. This novel presents a comprehensive picture of the political conditions in Germany from the end of the First World War through the Second World War. The lengthy novel *The Decision (Die Entscheidung)* 1959, shows how people of different backgrounds reach their decisions about living in a socialist society. *The Crossing (Die Überfahrt)* 1971, is another novel dealing with a young man of German descent who decides to return from South America to East Germany. Anna Seghers also published essays on such topics as peace, art in a socialist society, Russian literature, and the people of the Soviet Union as well as a number of short stories and legends. In her writings, socialism often seems more a matter of emotion than one of thought, and instinctive and mystical forces permeate political events.

Elizabeth Rutschli Herrmann and Edna
Huttenmaier Spitz. *German Women Writers
of the Twentieth Century* (Elmsford, New
York: Pergamon, 1978), p. 37

In an essay published in *Notizbuch* in 1980, Erika Haas reproached Anna Seghers, asserting that her "masculine view" kept this communist writer from making an authentic contribution to "feminine discourse." This critique obviously tossed onto the scrap-heap concepts like "realism" and "social reality" that were of central relevance to Anna Seghers. The question is not whether Seghers's representation of women corresponds in each instance to that particular social reality, but rather whether she succeeds in contributing something of value to the struggle to attain a specific feminine identity. Posed in this way, the question must be answered—admittedly with a touch of sadness at the betrayal of a "fellow" woman and Leftist—with an emphatic "no." . . .

Nowhere has Seghers depicted the problems of this struggle for emancipation of all oppressed subjects more convincingly and more completely than in her three *Caribbean Stories.* The failure of the Caribbean revolution did not succeed in transforming the emancipatory ideals of the French Revolution into a reality within the framework of Colonialism and the Bonapartist reaction. This failure serves as a warning and simultaneously sets an example of the need for a revolutionary strategy that is based on the historically and economically determined realities of a given society. Such a society does not lend itself to transformation into a classless utopia from one day to the next, but rather must confront the problems posed by uneven and sporadic development among groups and classes of the most varied composition.

John Milfull. In Manfred Jürgensen, ed.
*Frauenliteratur: Autorinnen, Perspektiven,
Konzepte* (Bern and Frankfurt: Lang, 1983),
pp. 46–47

After her story "The Haitian Marriage," written upon her return from exile (during which Anna Seghers had spent some time in Haiti), the author again [in *Drei Frauen aus Haiti,* (Three women from Haiti)] uses the Caribbean island as background for the theme of survival of an oppressed humanity. The three women of the slender volume are the heroines of three very short stories about three different periods in the story of Haiti. Each time invaders and oppressors endanger the life and liberty of the native population. After being discovered by Columbus, the Haitians are enslaved and taken to Spain. Liberated by the French Revolution, they are again made into slaves by Napoleon. In the twentieth century the bloody rule of the Duvaliers leads to the cruelest persecution.

In each story it is a woman who has the strength not only for her own survival but also for the salvation of humanity, which in turn preserves the hope for a better future. The last of the three stories is the most interesting one, since here Seghers projects her theme into the future. Her heroine survives the regime of Duvalier *fils,* since Bébé [Doc] Duvalier—who in real life still rules the island—dies of smallpox in her story. This idealistic utopianism, informing the entire book, along with Seghers's usual sparse language, avoiding all ornamentation and sentimentality, contributed to the immense success of the book in 1980, when it was the national best-seller of the GDR. Another homage to Anna Seghers in her eightieth year.

S. Bauschinger. *World Literature Today.* 55,
1981, p. 471

SEIDEL, INA (GERMANY) 1885–1974

There is no poetess that can be placed on a par with Ina Seidel, in either depth of feeling or power of expression, in the experience of her own womanhood and motherhood, particularly in their innermost relationship to the rule and rules of all-embracing nature, of mother earth. . . . in Ina Seidel the rare event has come to pass that an intense feeling of motherliness and an equally intense experience of motherhood can be given lyrical expression on a high plane through the presence of a strong power of poetic re-creation. . . . This does impose limits on Ina Seidel's lyrical range, but it also provides her work with coherence and intensity. The most beautiful flowers of her lyrical art have sprung from the interrelationship between a loving wife and nature, between a motherly woman and mother earth. . . .

Only rarely does she allow her poetic imagination to escape from the confines of bodily bonds into the vastness of metaphysical eternities. . . .That is the secret of the strong form of this lyrical poetry.

Hans Jaeger. *Germanic Review.* 1931,
pp. 268, 292–93

The hermetic secret of Ina Seidel's work is not her amazing mastery of a vast array of material or her patient depiction of valid characters; in short, it does not lie in the calm strength of her progressing step by step in the swinging rhythm of the harvesting scythe but rather in the vision that precedes all these acts, in the attitude precipitating them. It is the vision of the narrator beholding her material, her design, her edifice: a material whose root is the matrix, a design whose archetype is the rune, and an edifice whose ground plan is that of the temple. Yet, Ina Seidel's attitude does not persist in a cheap polarity that excuses the mind's endeavors with the realities of the blood and the blood's passion with the bent of the mind. Instead, she knows of the obligation inherent in the coexistence of these elements, in the fact that the spirit is an indwelling spirit, and in the redemptive powers of nature. Even in the darkest of her books, *Das Labyrinth,* the reader knows in the end that the Fates smile.

Elisabeth Langgässer. Neue Rundschau. II.
1933, pp. 846–47

Both her poetry and her prose give expression to an innate consciousness of belonging to the whole of existence, the temporal and the timeless, of being at once an entity and a part, of depending on all, and of the ultimate obligation of having all depend on the part. Nature's law . . . is the only right one, and its penalties for non-conformity are the most severe. A sense of freedom can be realized only through relationships which enable the individual to make the greatest possible contributions to Life, demanded and determined by his own endowment. The women of the books discussed here have shown to advantage over the men. . . . Ina Seidel . . . considers woman, as a mother, closer to Nature, more responsible for bringing about the necessary harmony of the world and better fitted to reconcile values. . . .

She speaks with the conviction of one who has found the center of existence, whose utterances are, at times, almost prophetic. . . .

Mary McKittrick. Monatshefte. 1938, p. 93

In any event, this novel, *Das unverwesliche Erbe* (The imperishable heritage), is immersed in the deepest past and yet touches us with the power of the immediate present.

Both the title and the motto (I Corinthians 15:20) identify the continuous thread to which the intent of the work is tied. The focus is represented by a Protestant-Catholic mixed marriage. The split in faiths, which rests heavily on the entire family, ought to be attenuated by the knowledge that there is after all a shared discipleship in Christ. So then, it is the author's insistence on the need—to use a modern word—for coexistence and a deeper revitalization of Protestantism that represent her didactic and, in a sense, propagandistic concern.

Das unverwesliche Erbe is, however, so warm-blooded a work that an interpretation quite different from that just presented may likewise seem

legitimate . . . the overall impression, in any event, is that of the rich resonance of a strong and warmly flowing language. Seen as a whole, it is fortunate
that the preacher Ina Seidel, however serious and wise and however honorable she may be, is outvoted and overpowered by the great poetess and
mature artist in her.

Gottfried Hafner. Welt und Wort. 1955,
pp. 56–57

Die Fahrt in den Abend (A journey into nightfall). On the occasion of her
seventieth birthday Ina Seidel presents us with a concise story that unmiti-
gatedly bears witness to the mastership distinguishing her great prose works.

The story is clearly counterpointed in the spirit of the old school at its
best. It is full of tangibles, of the frangrance and atmosphere of actualities
and physical existence. Driving a car and being driven in one have rarely
been described as alive (and yet as something transcending reality) as in this
story. . . . It is the way in which the imaginary breaks through the real without contrivance or discontinuity that imparts to the story its classical severity
of structure and simultaneously its "golden translucency."

Josef Mühlberger. Welt und Wort. 1955,
p. 370

Das Wunschkind (The wish child), this great novel of life and of time, represents, together with *Lennacker,* the center of gravity in the work and the
entire creative career of Ina Seidel. Here the ultimate essentials of the phenomenon, Ina Seidel, are most clearly manifest.

. . . It is the story of war and revolution as they are experienced by a
woman, not simply as a passive, suffering onlooker, but as an active, demanding participant and contributor. In the destiny of Cornelie we see the
female pendant of what happens to the male in times of war: the tension
between the sexes—between the share in life of man and the world of
woman—becomes excessively intense; their mutual relationship is no longer
based in their joint contribution to home and family but is only a spark linking
extreme poles. . . . Man and woman no longer share a directly linked destiny
but exert a fructifying influence on one another through oppositional
tension. . . .

. . . As the novel evolves, we are introduced time and again to individuals
who are able to look below the surface of reality, discerning the underlying
framework—if such a medical metaphor is permitted—of stromal tissue.

. . . They all enrich the novel by the dimension of depth that enables
the spirit to find in myth and symbol the highest and ultimate expression of
historical truths.

As we reread *Lennacker* today, we cannot but be taken aback as we note
how much was foreseen in this work, how much prophetic pleading there is
in it. It is not simply that the vision of burning cities and fleeing men, women,
and children looms up before our mind's eye with all the impact of its somber

power, that we meet with superstition and fanaticism in their most distorted forms, that we are made aware of the devilish nature of the forces determining the age; there is also the fact that here already the question is asked of "being and not being," the question as to whether fear and care are the only deciding features of our existence or whether there is, beyond them, a something that perfuses us with transcendental energies and imparts meaning and determination to every step we take.

Karl August Horst. *Ina Seidel* (Stuttgart:
Deutsche Verlagsanstalt, 1956), pp. 102, 104,
110, 138

Long neglected as a work having a significant place in the anti-Hitlerian literature of *innere Emigration,* Ina Seidel's novel *Lennacker* (1938) develops an existential dialectic of subjective decision and responsibility that is intended to draw its readers into a critical reflection directed against the totalitarian regime of the Third Reich. . . . Seidel's novel delineates a clear relationship involving (a) the necessity of the individual human, when confronted with a constellation of reality hostile to the absolute mandates of his conscience, to set himself in opposition to this reality by means of an irreducible ethical decision. This form of ethical responsibility, occurring as a free response on the part of the concrete individual existing in the spatiotemporal domain of ontic facticity, exhibits (b) an intimate relationship to a mystical form of transcendence, an epiphany which transports the individual *beyond* the ontic sphere of reality. The concept of history depicted in Seidel's novel involves a consistently articulated repetition of the dialectic encompassing the two elements indicated above. Moreover, the type of historical representation found in the work has a clear connection to other novels in the literature of *innere Emigration.* Herbert Wiesner points out that a common characteristic among many works in this movement lies in the transference of contemporary ethical and political problems into historical constellations far removed, in terms of their temporal situation, from the present. By this means, it is possible for an author to avoid any salient impression of hostility towards existing political reality. This technique thus enables a writer to conceal a critical, potentially subversive theme by couching it in a narrative recounting events lying deep within the past—events which have, ostensibly, little relevance for contemporary reality. . . .

The intrinsic nature of Seidel's existential dialectic involves a numinous Revelation which has exclusive power for guiding the authentic individual into performance of ethically "right" actions. This kind of mysticism amounts to an ethics that is purely contemplative—one that is clearly incapable of inspiring any form of political critique that goes beyond a philosophical resignation to the organized might of the status quo. The particular form of *innere Emigration* found in Ina Seidel's *Lennacker* reflects, in the end, a consummate example of what Georg Lukács perceives as a major reason why the majority of German intellectuals in the 1930s failed to establish an effective movement of resistance against Hitlerian fascism. This failure involves the tendency, prevalent in Seidel's novel, to escape full responsibility for making concrete ethical decisions by nullifying the realm of historical necessity in which such decisions are meaningful and real. . . . [I]n *Lennacker* this negation of objective historical reality lies, in particular, in the ontology that forms the basis of the ethical dialectic developed throughout the work.

Rodney Taylor. *Michigan Germanic Studies.*
16, 1990, pp. 68, 87

SENIOR, OLIVE (JAMAICA) 1943–

Short stories and poems by Olive Senior have been appearing in journals and anthologies in Jamaica and overseas for more than a decade. It was not however till December 1985 that the first complete volume reached the bookstands—a collection of poems, *Talking of Trees,* published by Calabash Press, Jamaica. A few months later (early 1986), a collection of short stories, *Summer Lightning and Other Stories,* now in its second printing, was published by Longman, U. K. . . .

Senior's short stories and poetry are the work of a creative talent of great sensitivity which expresses tremendous understanding of the human condition, particularly that of poor people both rural and urban. The attempt to slot her writing into a particular genre immediately gives one an uncomfortable feeling. For the work is knit together by a common landscape and a recurring concern for humanity. Both poetry and prose bring the country paths of Senior's childhood and the urban experiences of her young womanhood into focus. The themes of both concern the experiences of people in these environments who represent different points along a scale of social and financial privilege. . . .

But poverty in the prose fiction receives less harsh censure than religion and adult control. It is frequently accompanied by positive values of love and community feeling. It is rural poverty in close knit societies where people take care of each other and where the land provides at least subsistence. The starkness of real need is described in the poetry where urban poverty is treated. In the city the human spirit buckles under circumstances it cannot overcome and even friendship is useless. . . .

Other thematic interests in Senior's work include historical matters reflecting Senior's personal research into the history of the Jamaican people at home and in countries in which they have migrated, especially Panama. Of the poems reproduced here, "Nansi Tory" is concerned with the Afro-Jamaican, the man who did not return to Africa; "Searching for my Grandfather" is about the Jamaican who did not return from Panama. "The Arrival of the Snake-Woman" explores the Jamaican situation in which ex-African and ex-Asian strive to find a place in the post-colonial society.

The village is a microcosm of Jamaica. Senior gives a believable description of the integration of a post-emancipation immigrant into a rural village. Through the child's eye the author reveals early attitudes of the races to each other, the garbled versions of history available to the unlettered poor and the interplay of Afro-Caribbean religion and American evangelism. Without implying any evaluation, the author allows the haphazard pattern of Jamaican family life and of community living to become part of the reader's consciousness. . . .

Olive Senior is a talent not to be taken lightly. Few writers are able to combine social comment with such a deep understanding of human nature and such a linguistic facility. Her extensive research into aspects of Jamaican history and social context, and her fine eye for detail as she lives and moves around Jamaica, arm her with "facts" which she transforms into prose and poetry.

Velma Pollard. Callaloo. 11, 1988, pp. 540,
542–43, 545

From the very first time I had the good fortune to travel to the Caribbean, I have been moved by the musical quality of the West Indian speech. Despite the differences between, say, Bajan and Jamaican accents or, more subtly, Trinidadian and Tobagonian accents, the lilting, enthusiastic, and almost urgent sound patterns of West Indian speech continually intrigue and amaze me. (*Cote Ce Cote La* by Trinidad's John Mendes remains an outstanding, yet humorous "reference" to this phenomenon.)

Olive Senior, perhaps more than any writer I've encountered—Paule Marshall notwithstanding—captures this musical quality in all of its intriguing vigor. In this, her first collection of short stories, [*Summer Lightning and Other Stories*] she handily investigates and grapples with some of the most basic human emotions—love, faith, ambition, jealousy—using "regular" folks as her heroes.

Set in rural Jamaica, these stories turn the world slightly on its ear, but only so that we can get a different, more humorous perspective. With such great titles as "Love Orange," "Country of the One Eye God," "Real Old Time T'ing," "Do Angels Wear Brassieres?" and others, Ms. Senior's stories both educate and entertain.

Kuumba Kazi-Ferrouillet. Black Collegian.
March–April, 1989, p. 173

Olive Senior's first collection of short prose, *Summer Lightning,* brought her the Commonwealth Writers Prize in 1987. Her second, *Arrival of the Snake Woman and Other Stories,* offers seven new selections. The setting, as always, is the author's native island of Jamaica, where her protagonists—usually naïve, sensitive, and vulnerable children and women—meet with a real world of evil and ambition and, in the process, find their own way. The heroine of "The Tenantry of Birds," for example, is a young girl always under the domination of someone, first her mother and later her husband; ultimately she finds the courage and will to do as she pleases, freed from parental and marital bonds. The passage from childhood to girlhood is the subject of the tender story "The Two Grandmothers"; the rural ambience of the grandmothers' hut, so attractive to the young female protagonist during her early years, becomes so dull to her as she matures that she even leaves her grandmother sick in bed and instead hurries home to watch "Dallas."

The title story has a different heroine, an Indian girl who comes to a remote and devout mountain village, where her beauty, strange apparel, and jewelry provoke hostility among the locals, especially the village priest. Once settled in, however, she adopts the local customs and by story's end is the mother of eight and the richest, most respected woman in the community. This brave woman's struggle, her adaptation to her new surroundings, and her gradual appropriation of local customs and slow penetration into the milieu of country women are all viewed through the eyes of a young boy. The protagonists of "Tears of the Sea" and "See the Tiki-Tiki Scatter" are also children. In "Lily-Lily" the eponymous heroine is the beloved beauty of a respectable family who turns out to be the product of an incestuous union and the object of a stepfather's abuse.

The backdrop of all the stories is the mixed society of Jamaica, with its stark divisions among whites, blacks, and others. Senior's presentation of her characters' initial realization that they belong to a despised underclass is fine and sensitive, as when one pampered and conceited young girl is suddenly called a "dirty nigger" for the first time. It is on such shocks of real adult life that Senior—who is also a journalist *(Jamaica Journal),* poet *(Talking of Trees),* and reference-book author *(A to Z of Jamaican Heritage)*—builds her human dreams.

Nadežda Obradović. *World Literature Today.* 64, 1990, p. 514

Olive Senior writes out of a clear awareness of a conflicted life which is only by effort brought into any kind of control and clarity. She spoke recently of her childhood lived between two homes, a village, "darkskin" one and a "lightskin," middle-class environment, where she was alone and being groomed for status and advancement. In her recent volume, *Talking of Trees,* she uses as a superscription to a section of the book Brecht's statement, "What kind of period is it / when to talk of trees / is almost a crime / because it implies silence / about so many horrors?" and of course this is the source of the book's title as well. Similarly, she quotes Martin Carter "But what the leaves hear / is not what the roots ask." Her vision is often one of aloneness "Alone I will walk through the glass." In "Cockpit Country Dreams" she speaks of father and mother saying different things as "Portents of split future." There are two cultures here, the father's and the mother's:

> My father said: lines on paper
> cannot deny something that *is*.
> (My mother said: such a wasted life
> is his).

But in the end the poet makes sense of this division:

> Now my disorder of ancestry
> proves as stable as the many rivers
> flowing around me. Undocumented
> I drown in the other's history.

Poetry becomes the balancing point, the crossroads at which all directions have to meet. . . . Part of the solution to these tensions is the control which poetry gives. In "To the Madwoman in My Yard," the poet speaks with an exasperated understanding and sisterhood but in the end they are divided by the certainty in the poet that "Life Equals Control." . . .

Even Senior's use of line order suggests this constant attempt to control and order fragmentation: she experiments a good deal with various formations and these suggest a vigilant awareness of possible rearrangements of reality all the time.

Elaine Savory Fido. In Carole Boyce Davies
and Elaine Savory Fido, eds. *Out of the
Kumbla: Caribbean Women and Literature*
(Trenton, New Jersey: Africa World Press,
1990), pp. 33–35

The problems inherent in the literary expression of cultural identity come into particularly sharp focus in the twelve nations of the English-speaking Caribbean because the lingering pull of the old colonial power, Britain, is so forcefully augmented by the looming presence of the United States. To a certain extent, Caribbean writers have little choice but to define themselves within the "empowered" or "dominant" discourse of the West. They may adopt a different point of view (and often a political stance at least mildly critical of the West), but their linguistic medium, their genres, and even their audience tend to be primarily Western.

Senior succeeds, to a greater degree than most, in finding a voice that is, through the frequent use of Jamaican English and a shrewd reliance on the devices of oral storytelling, somewhat different from standard forms of European discourse. Although she has published only two volumes of short stories, she has already established herself as one of the more talented artists currently working in that genre and a major force in the development of a postcolonial West Indian literature. . . .

In several of the stories in her first book, *Summer Lightning*, a version of vernacular Jamaican speech—and one not so obviously "invented" as Reid's or Selvon's—is the norm rather than the deviation. . . .

Senior herself has offered the most succinct description of her fictional world. The stories of *Summer Lightning*, she says, focus on the Jamaica of her childhood and emphasize the problems and perspectives of poor rural children, while those in *Arrival of the Snake-Woman* are more expansive, involving characters "of different races and classes," rich and poor, in both rural and urban settings. But both collections are explorations of Jamaican experience and identity within a larger network of competing cultures. "I want people to know," she states, "that 'literature' can be created out of the fabric of our everyday lives, that our stories are as worth telling as those of Shakespeare—or the creators of *Dallas*." An awareness of that enveloping, sometimes corrosive larger culture is never very far in the background of Senior's stories precisely because the problematic relationship between the isolated, enclosed societies of the West Indies and the wider world is such a pervasive fact of Caribbean life.

Richard F. Patteson. *Ariel.* 24, 1993,
pp. 13–16

SERAO, MATILDE (ITALY) 1856–1927

A very different book [from *The Development of Palestine Exploration*] is that of an Italian lady, Matilde Serao, *In the Country of Jesus*, . . . which takes its place in the lighter literature of its subject. Here we find many unusual out-of-the-way things, seen by the keen eye of an experienced traveler, woven by a devout Catholic Italian mind into an attractive and charming narrative. At every point of interest—as, for example, at Bethel or in Galilee—the author has caught and recorded things that nine-tenths of the travelers and writers would never see or think of mentioning. Devoutness, too, is found everywhere, except where the author attempts a bout with a dragoman or a cunning impostor. Her picturesque narrative is illustrated by a few first-class half-tones of some of the choicest scenes on the journey. The evident enthusiasm of the writer enlivens the whole story, and makes the reader feel like engaging quarters on the next steamer to Jaffa, that he too may be stirred by the same sights and scenes.

Dial. October 1, 1906, p. 211

A reader of modern Italian literature will experience mixed feelings on finding that the privilege of appearing in an English dress has been conferred upon *Ella non rispose* (She does not reply) or *Souls Divided,* by Matilde Serao.

Matilde Serao's Neapolitan stories are unquestionably her best work. In these the local color is not a mere back-cloth, but the very marrow of their being, with the result that it is almost impossible to reproduce it adequately in a translation. But as a rule the moment the Italian novelist leaves his home—and the novel in Italy is bound to remain more or less regional, unless the war is going to break down the barriers that separate the various provinces far more thoroughly than seems likely at present—and sets himself to enlarge his canvas, some tricksy spirit has a way of compelling him to abjure his rough magic and sink to a place among the crowd of more ordinary mortals. Doubtless Matilde Serao's non-Neapolitan novels have a larger circulation abroad, possibly even in Italy, than her tales of her native city, since she never falls below the level of an accomplished feuilletoniste, but their success owes its impetus to the fame she acquired as a writer on Naples.

In her introduction to this volume she tells us that the letters she receives from all parts of the world—"Madam, how I wept with joy and sorry while reading your book"—mean far more to her than professional criticism, and "therefore I am waiting for the letter of that soul who shall have shed silent and solitary tears of human pity with me over the luckless love of Diana and Paolo." Nor do we imagine she waited in vain. There is a positive orgy of feeling in these passionate outpourings from the moment when Paolo Ruffo was seized with violent love for Diana Sforza on hearing her sing "Che far senza Euridice" in the villa of her English friend from his rooms in the Via Boncompagni in Rome. . . .

The fact that the whole story, except the epilogue, is related in Paolo's letters to Diana is bound to give it an air of unreality, since he is obliged to writer her a detailed description of her own wedding, as seen from the steps of the English Embassy, including the value of the jewels she was wearing and a description of her clothes that might do credit to a fashion paper. But the Southern passion of the letters, though it strikes one as a little strained in our colder Northern tongue, has a genuine ring about it, and the lady reader who falls under its spell will readily forgive such little improbabilities.

(London) *Times Literary Supplement.*
November 27, 1919, p. 689

Souls Divided . . . is probably a better novel than the translator has managed to project, yet even with this allowance its theme and substance tend toward emotional futility. The story of a "sudden, fantastical, and absurd love" is developed through a man's letters; but there is a lack of subtlety and stamina in the performance.

Dial. 68, March 1920, p. 399

Matilde Serao's early twentieth-century popular novel *La mano tagliata,* (The severed hand) presents an interesting case of how a single truncated body part can speak for larger issues in the text and address questions of the importance of materiality in the detective/mystery genre. The hand is used in a complicated way in the novel, both as a clue . . . and as a kind of relic. As a secular relic, it speaks to a racial and religious confrontation. As a clue, it leads back to a body and is also an agent of conversion, as several protagonists convert from Judaism to Catholicism. What is at stake in this drama of cultural hegemony is foregrounded by the use of the hand as an instrument of change. . . .

What is at stake here in this cultural, religious, and racial confrontation? It seems that there are two related agendas. The first, and most striking, is an attempt to reconstitute one religious and racial configuration and substitute it for another, that is to say, conversion: not in the simpler sense of the word, of leaving one religion for another, but in a much more extreme sense. Not only does the soul repent and the penitent embrace a new and different religious structure: this is achieved through a physical transfer of religious/ mythic construct. Maria loses her hand to a diabolical doctor of her own [Jewish] race. The hand is then found by a Christian who recognizes it for what it is, a Christian object of worship—albeit in a secular context. The events which the truncation sets in motion lead to her dying a most Christian death. The conversion is not attained by a change in the God or of the God to whom she prays, but by what happens to her flesh, both before and after death.

The second agenda is another configuration of the first. How can a physical body part become invested with so much religious and psychological meaning and still refuse to cross that thorny path into a clearly figural or symbolic use? It seems to be the nature of semiotic reconstitution which is at stake here. A trace remains physical, and through its materiality *will* lead to, and point to materially, the material construct which is its truest nature and expression. Mystery fiction keeps one foot in the grave, and this morbid interest is expressed through an insistence on material constructs of meaning.

Nancy Harrowitz. *Stanford Italian Review.*
6, 1987, pp. 191, 204

In Matilde Serao's *La mano tagliata,* the doctor in the novel is an evil hunchback with glacial green eyes and hypnotic powers, who uses his medical skills to set himself up as a Messiah figure.

Serao wrote another popular novel entitled *Il delitto di via Chiatamone,* (The crime on Via Chiatamone) the title of which was changed to *Temi il leone* (I fear the lion) and then back to the original title. This novel, first published in episodes in the newspaper *Il Giorno* of Naples in 1907, begins with the failed assassination attempt of a young woman, Teresa Gargiulo. The mystery is a genealogically motivated one, as we discover at the end of the novel. . . .

This Serao text is dominated by two major mysteries: who tried to kill Teresa and the motive behind it. We as readers have our suspicions, which are not confirmed until almost the end of the text when Teresa herself learns the truth from the lawyer. A smaller mystery also emerges and becomes tied into the larger ones: the meaning of the motto "Temi il leone," which is inscribed on the necklace Teresa wears. "Temi il leone," a mysterious, unexplained warning Teresa's mother used to say to her, refers to the Vargas family from which Teresa's father was estranged. The genealogical mystery in the novel is thus expanded and further complicated by a physical clue, the necklace that bears this warning. . . .

The itinerary of displaced and misplaced personal objects and even body parts furnish important clues to the nature of the epistemology of materiality and detection. The narrative of *Il delitto di via Chiatamone* links the notion of the orphan, the orphan's body, location in the city, and murder. The genealogical murder which the duke attempts is an interesting way of tying these issues together and of bringing out tensions between them. The orphaned state expresses the nature of the city, and the urban landscape seems to create (as well as destroy) orphans. The anonymity of the city is reflected in the creation of a person with no identity, a *trovatello,* someone who is found, unattached. In both novels the female and mother's body is inextricably linked to the notion that sex leads to death, and that being an orphan or unattached somehow marks the path of sex leading to death as a viable one, an escape form the genealogical dilemma.

Nancy Harrowitz. Stanford Italian Review.
9, 1990, pp. 55–56, 66

Critics of "La virtù di Checchina" [Checchina's virtue], the 1884 short story by Matilde Serao, have often taken as their starting point either the protagonist's relationship with the seductive marchese, her bourgeois husband or even her sulky maid. But her relationship with her elegant friend, Isolina, and the role this character plays in the narrative, have rarely been treated. This critical blindspot is perhaps a result of the traditional neglect of female friendships, both in society and in literature. Critical attention has traditionally focused on male-female relationships within a text and has avoided the ties of friendship and love between female characters. . . .

With "La virtù di Checchina," Serao undermines the traditional structure of nineteenth-century romances. . . .

Checchina's quest for love is, finally, a quest for self. Isolina's independent lifestyle provides the inspiration for this quest. Both women, however, fail to succeed in their endeavor. Isolina is deserted by her lover, and Checchina is defeated by her own inability to act. Their narratives do not end in death or marriage, but rather in a return to the limitations and desolation of their previous existence.

Laura A. Salsini. Romance Languages
Annual. 3, 1991, pp. 309, 312

It is hard to see why *The Conquest of Rome* has been included in this series [NYU Press Women's Classics] since it does not evince distinctively female concerns or attitudes. It is the story of a young politician who rises through drive and luck and falls through a passion for a virtuous married woman who will not gratify him sexually, and it is bogged down in details of the topography of Rome and of the Italian political scene in the 1880s. The central relationship is presented from a characteristically masculine point of view: that is, Angelica is blamed for being the object of the hero's self-destructive passion and for refusing to do what he wants. Although her husband sacrifices her to his political career and her would-be lover is selfish and unscrupulous, the two have a touching final scene together in which they declare their tender love for Angelica and agree that she is a "woman who knew not how to love."

Katherine M. Rogers. *Belles Lettres.*
8, Spring, 1993, p. 18

SEXTON, ANNE (UNITED STATES) 1928–74

To Bedlam and Part Way Back is a remarkable book . . ., in which we feel not only the poet's experience but also something of the morality behind recalling and recording it. There is more here than a case-history or a "cruel glass."

The experience itself, though involving a stay in an asylum, is simple, moving and universal. Miss Sexton describes the loss of a child, or rather the *estrangement* of a mother from her child. Hardly born, it reminds the mother unbearably of her own childhood, and continues to do so after the asylum. . . . With such a theme, developed not paradigmatically in the manner of Yeats, but directly in the manner of Lowell's life studies, did the poet have to exploit the more sensational aspect of her experience?

Geoffrey H. Hartman. *Kenyon Review.*
Autumn, 1960, p. 698

She tells stories. Her book [*To Bedlam and Part Way Back*] is full of undistinguished, unmythological people, in tensely dramatic situations which can be exploited only by an equally intense inward sympathy: a lonely empty-headed old woman, a speechless unwed mother, the author's own agonizing journey "part way back" from insanity and her complex relation to her dying mother and her unfamiliar child. Sexton's best work has qualities of the modern short story: the brutal tale like a forced confession, "better unsaid, grim or flat or predatory"; the compressed dramatic pattern of *hybris,* catastrophe, and recognition; the primitive irony of actual experience rather than the witty irony of meditation on it; the intense inward awareness of the teller; the concentration on a narrow circle of concrete persons and events; the forced brevity of narrative and lack of transition; the refusal to easily generalize.

When truth bursts from the tight surface of such poems with the violence of sudden discovery, it seems the result of actual struggle.

Neil Myers. *Minnesota Review*. Fall, 1960,
p. 99

The most memorable poems in Anne Sexton's new book [*All My Pretty Ones*] involve death and the response to death. The title of the volume is taken from the scene in *Macbeth* in which MacDuff, learning of the entire extinction of his family, cries out "All my pretty ones?" in a poignant exclamation of disbelief. How this relates to Mrs. Sexton is made explicit in the dedication to the very first poem, "The Truth the Dead Know": "For my mother, born March 1902, died March 1959, and my father, born February 1900, died June 1959." It is easy to understand how so much catastrophe coming so quickly can create crisis. Mrs. Sexton's book is a record of her crisis. . . . The sure attack, the fine use of sound, make it clear from the start that Mrs. Sexton is a lyricist of power. If one does not read carefully and accepts the hypnotic music of the lines, one can even think one is reading a conventional elegy. But of course the poem is no such thing. Earlier epochs would have found it immensely shocking. Not only does the mourner refuse to accompany the body to the grave, but she drives off to the cape "to cultivate myself where the sun gutters from the sky." We are in a post-Christian world where ceremonial has ceased to be important and death is something one seeks to dismiss from one's mind.

Cecil Hemley. *Hudson Review*. Winter,
1962–63, p. 613

Her manner, learned from Robert Lowell and W. D. Snodgrass, is at once confessional and understated. . . . A number of the new poems center on the deaths of Mrs. Sexton's parents, neither yet sixty, within a few months of one another. She evokes some of the same terror of the flesh that we feel in [Allen Ginsberg's] *Kaddish,* and as in that poem the emphasis (with love) is on parental weaknesses that were crucial in the poet's early unhappiness. A great difference is in the ultimately more clinical, self-analytical character of Mrs. Sexton's elegies (or anti-elegies) and other poems. Another is the exquisite lyric purity she achieves over and above her energetic self-pursuit and self-exposure.

M. L. Rosenthal. *The Reporter*. January 3,
1963, p. 48

Anne Sexton is, by any standards, a bold and impressive poet. At first glance, the unsuspecting reader may be jolted by the self-revelation that so plainly serves as the basic raw material of her art. . . . Undisguised revelation and examination—of her parents, her lovers, her friends; of the unbelievable torment of both mental and physical illness as she has had to endure them; of her struggles with a religious belief that eludes her but doesn't leave her; of the face of death as she has frequently seen it—comprise Mrs. Sexton's poetic cosmos. The eye the poet brings to bear on these contents of her life is mercilessly lucid; yet she can be compassionate toward others and is without self-pity. Her life, as must be clear by now, has been graced only slightly with what we ordinarily conceive as happiness; its occasional joys and moments of tenderness are wrung from the general pain of experience. Yet these pleasures and affections are the more precious because of the cost involved in obtaining them, and also because of the poet's strong love which brings them about in spite of the odds. Mrs. Sexton has further discovered an ability to introduce order into existence, to allow valued things to survive through the imaginative act that in the making of a poem can create its own patterns of justice, meaning, and love.

> Ralph J. Mills. *Contemporary American
> Poetry* (New York: Random House, 1965),
> pp. 218–19

The literary quality of Anne Sexton's new poems, in *Live or Die,* is impossible to judge, at least in the brief time given a reviewer; they raise the never-solved problem of what literature really is, where you draw the line between art and documentary. Certainly her book is one of the most moving I have read in a long time. It is the record of four years of emotional illness, the turns of fear and despair and suicidal depression, a heartbreaking account. The wonder is that she was able to write any poetry at all. What she has written is strong, clear, rather simple, never repressed and yet never out of hand. Some of the poems wander a little; they are unstructured, they start up, flag, then start again, or slip into references too private for us to understand. But I do not want to give the impression that they are jottings or notes, that they are merely documentary. They are poems. They are the work of a gifted, intelligent, woman almost in control of her material.

> Hayden Carruth. *Hudson Review.* Winter,
> 1966–67, p. 698

Anne Sexton's art is particularly notable for the way it picks up the rhythms of the kind of sensibility with which she is concerned. The examples I have so far given catch the note of the self reduced to almost infantile regression (what hostile critics have called 'baby-talk'), but the mature intelligence of the speaker is ultimately that of one no longer in the literal predicament presented by the poems.

> M. L. Rosenthal. *The New Poets* (Oxford,
> 1967), p. 134

In her third volume of poetry [*Live or Die*], Anne Sexton has fashioned a brilliantly unified book. Though thematically related to *All My Pretty Ones* and to her first book, *To Bedlam and Part Way Back, Live or Die* is more passionate in its intensity and more abundant in its desperate concentration on vision. . . . This is a crazily sane and beautifully controlled work. It is the Oedipal eye; its poems are honest, terrifying! And the voice is terrifying—the voice of the human being *seeing* the nightmare and the dream that is man.

Philip Legler. *Poetry*. May, 1967, pp. 125–27

Miss Sexton's is a poetry of the nerves and heart. She is never abstract, never permits herself to be distracted from her one true subject—herself and her emotions. It is remarkable that she never flinches from the task at hand, never attempts to use her art as a device for warding off final perception. Unlike a poet like Frederick Seidel, she is willing to make her connections explicit. Her poems lack that hurtling momentum which keeps diverse elements in a sort of perpetual disrelation in the work of Seidel. Miss Sexton is painfully direct, and she refuses to keep her meaning at a tolerable distance. *Live or Die* projects an anguish which is profoundly disturbing precisely because its sources are effable, because the pressure of fantasy has not been permitted to distort or mediate Miss Sexton's vision.

Robert Boyers. *Salmagundi*. Spring, 1967,
p. 62

Love Poems is not sentimental, not trivial, it is simply not believable. The poems have little to do with believable love, having none of love's privacy and therefore too frequently repelling the reader; they have as little to do with believable sexuality as an act of intercourse performed onstage for an audience. Because neither revulsion nor amusement is a fair response to a poet with this much talent, one must, for the sake of the poet and the poems, totally suppress the word "confessional" and substitute the word "fictional." Only then, when the "I" is a character separate from the author, does the woman become as innocent of exhibitionism as Molly Bloom in her soliloquy. One would not, even then, return and return to these poems as one does to other love poems of past and present, because their self-absorption is too great to allow an empathic entrance. . . . However, it is clear, I think, that it is from Miss Sexton's almost incredible feats of "indiscretion" in attitude and image, her grotesque, near-comic concentration on her every emotional and physical pore, and her delineation of femaleness, so fanatical that it makes one wonder, even after many years of being one, what a woman is, that her poems derive their originality and their power, as well as their limitations.

Mona Van Duyn. *Poetry*. March, 1970,
pp. 431–32

At a reading at the Guggenheim Museum, Anne Sexton—after three books of poems—finished one of her poems and said, "But it is not true." That hall feels cold and artificial. It was a beautiful woman standing there, in a beautiful dress. The expectation and the gossip around one was of confessional poetry. Now this is a curious genre, one taken to promise a new order of secret, and one finds secrets that everyone knows; taken to promise emergent men, emergent women, who may bring to speech the lives of these generations; too, one is often given disposable poems, made without the structural reinforcements, those lattices on which the crystal grows.

However, when Anne Sexton said, "But it is not true," a waver went through the audience. No, I cannot say that, I can speak only for myself. I thought, "It may very well be true." She had cut through the entire nonsense about confessional writing, and returned me to the poem.

The issue in most of Anne Sexton's poems has been survival, piece by piece of the body, step by step of poetic experience, and even more the life entire, sprung from our matrix of parental madness. It is these people, who have come this way, who have most usefulness for us, they are among our veterans, and we need them to look at their lives and at us.

Muriel Rukeyser. Parnassus. Fall–Winter,
1973, p. 215

Vital as her early volumes were, however, *The Death Notebooks* goes far beyond them in making luminous art out of the night thoughts that have haunted this poet for so long. The book's epigraph is a line from Hemingway's *A Moveable Feast*—"Look, you con man, make a living out of your death"— which succinctly summarizes the poet's goal, a goal both shrewdly ironic (at least she can write, and thus make a living out of her obsession) and ambitiously metaphysical (what is there to make a *living* from except death?). But if irony and shrewdness have always characterized Anne Sexton's work, the largeness of her metaphysical ambition is what is newly notable about *The Death Notebooks.* The seductions of suicide no longer concern her; the deaths of friends and relatives are secondary. Now, like John Donne, she is lying down in the inescapable coffin that is her own, "trying on," as she tells us, her "black necessary trousseau." In doing this, she has inevitably to define the death that is neither a handful of pills nor somebody else's funeral but, in a sense, a pre-condition of life itself.

Sandra M. Gilbert. The Nation. September
14, 1974, p. 215

If, as "The Double Image" and many of her early poems reveal, the cause of Sexton's madness and its accompanying desire for death has been her woman's situation, experience, identity, it is also true that the affirmation of life at which she arrives through the acts of her poems is founded in her womanhood. "Live," the final poem in her third book, *Live or Die,* helps her to locate the source of and reason for life in woman's situation, experience, identity. . . .

Being a poet causes Anne Sexton to understand herself as possessor of "the excitable gift," because the act of poetry unites understanding with experience; its vision is insight. Though her poetry begins as therapy for her personal salvation, because it is a public act it reaches out to others. Yet it is always rooted in her personal self, her private life, as is the sun. It does not, like much of the "confessional" poetry of men, abstract or generalize upon its own experiences, either explicitly or implicitly; nevertheless, it communicates to others and offers its gift. . . .

Sexton . . . tries to explain how this gift works. Commenting upon her explorations of self, of "that narrow diary of my mind," she finds their purpose to have been, not beauty, but "a certain sense of order there." If she had tried "to give [him] something else, / something outside of myself," he would not then know "that the worst of anyone / can be, finally, / an accident of hope." Generalizing, in other words, destroys the very meaning sought.

Suzanne Juhasz. *Naked and Fiery Forms:*
Modern American Poetry by Women,
A New Tradition (New York: Octagon
Books, 1976), pp. 124–25

To mourn the woman by telling less than the truth about the poet is to perform no service. She was, let it be said, a flawed poet who became more deeply flawed, as she made of her worst tricks a trade. I did not follow her career attentively. In a life filled with books to read and things to do, one may be excused for giving second place to a poetry that dwells irritably on the squalor of the everyday, without abatement or relief. Did no one acquaint this poet with [Matthew] Arnold's famous words?—that there are "situations, from the representation of which, though accurate, no poetical enjoyment can be derived? They are those in which the suffering finds no vent in action; in which a continuous state of mental distress is prolonged, unrelieved by incident, hope, or resistance; in which there is everything to be endured, nothing to be done. In such situations there is inevitably something morbid, in the description of them something monotonous. When they occur in actual life, they are painful, not tragic; the representation of them in poetry is painful also." The amused or wry tone of some of her poems was sheer ballast. She was sustained by a long argument, and a *private* one, which might well have been carried on in prose or in a diary, about whether life was worth its cost in suffering.

She decided not. And in her last book, together with much ballast, there is an evil spirit brooding, and something more hateful than bitterness. It is hatred. A lover is addressed as "Mr. Panzer-Man." He is the Nazi, she the Jew. Sylvia Plath had used the same analogy, in her celebrated attractive-repulsive poem, "Daddy." How far does it hold? Do fathers and lovers seek to exterminate women who are poets, is there a plan to wipe them out, are they hauled from their beds and beaten and killed? No, it is not sincere. Perhaps the subject ought to be dropped: it is too disgusting. Confessional poetry, we must see, has come to us historically in two kinds. There is the terrible secret (Baudelaire) and there is the beautiful secret (Wordsworth). The newer confessional poets touched neither of these bases. "I am desperate," they were saying. "Others are responsible. The world has done this to me. Look!" *Life Studies* inaugurated the reign of a personal and debased mode of the poetry of grievances; the author of that book [Robert Lowell] brought a few of his students with him; now they are gone, and his own poetry has grown indistinguishable from theirs.

David Bromwich. *Poetry*. December, 1976,
pp. 170–71

Of all the confessional poets, none has had quite Sexton's "courage to make a clean breast of it." Nor has any displayed quite her brilliance, her verve, her headlong metaphoric leaps. As with any body of work, some of the later poems display only ragged, intermittent control, as compared to "The Double Image," "The Operation," and "Some Foreign Letters," to choose three arbitrary examples. The later work takes more chances, crosses more boundaries between the rational and the surreal; and time after time it evokes in the reader that sought-after shiver of recognition.

Women poets in particular owe a debt to Anne Sexton, who broke new ground, shattered taboos, and endured a barrage of attacks along the way because of the flamboyance of her subject matter, which, twenty years later, seems far less daring. She wrote openly about menstruation, abortion, masturbation, incest, adultery, and drug addiction at a time when the proprieties embraced none of these as proper topics for poetry. Today, the remonstrances seem almost quaint. Anne delineated the problematic position of women— the neurotic reality of the time—though she was not able to cope in her own life with the personal trouble it created. If it is true that she attracted the worshipful attention of a cult group pruriently interested in her suicidal impulses, her psychotic breakdowns, her frequent hospitalizations, it must equally be acknowledged that her very frankness succored many who clung to her poems as to the Holy Grail. Time will sort out the dross among these poems and burnish the gold. Anne Sexton has earned her place in the canon.

Maxine Kumin, ed. Introduction to Anne
Sexton. *Complete Poems of Anne Sexton*
(Boston: Houghton Mifflin, 1981), p. xxxiv

Her poems tend, on the whole, to begin well, to repeat themselves, to sag in the middle, and to tail off. She had an instinct for reiteration; she wanted to say something five times instead of once. Her favorite figure of speech is anaphora, where many lines begin with the same phrase, a figure which causes, more often than not, diffuseness and spreading of effect rather than concentration of intensity. . . .

Sexton's poems read better as a diary than as poems. They then seem a rather slapdash journal stuck with brilliant phrases. Even the most formally arranged poems have, underneath their formal structure, no real or actual structure: they run on, they chatter, they moan, they repeat themselves, they deliquesce. Or, conversely (as in the famous "Her Kind") they stop without any particular reason—they could have been shorter, they could have been longer. If, as A. R. Ammons once said, a poem begins in contingency and ends in necessity, the trouble with Sexton's poems is that they lack that necessity—the conviction that they were meant to be just as they are, with just these words and no others, extending to just this length and no other, with each part pulling its weight. [Emily] Dickinson and [Elizabeth] Bishop often make us feel that necessity; Edna St. Vincent Millay—like Sexton a facile and prolific writer—does not. . . .

As Sexton passes into the anthologies, the more obviously "feminist" poems will no doubt be chosen, and there is no reason not to represent them. . . . But the evil eye (as Sexton put it) should be in the anthologies too. This "evil," unsympathetic, flat, malicious, gleeful, noticing eye is neither male nor female, but it is Sexton's most distinguishing characteristic. . . .

Sexton's chief flair [was] a knack for the flat, two-dimensional cartoon. Some of that shrewd caricature should make its way into the anthologies too.

Helen Vendler. The New Republic.
November 11, 1981, pp. 34–36

Anne Sexton's poetry tells stories that are immensely significant to mid-twentieth-century artistic and psychic life. Sexton understood her culture's malaise through her own, and her skill enabled her to deploy metaphorical structures at once synthetic and analytic. In other words, she assimilated the superficially opposing but deeply similar ways of thinking represented by poetry and psychoanalysis. Sexton explored the myths by and through which our culture lives and dies: the archetypal relationships among mothers and daughters, fathers and daughters, mothers and sons, gods and humans, men and women. She perceived, and consistently patterned in the images of her art, the paradoxes deeply rooted in human behavior and motivation. Her poetry presents multiplicity and simplicity, duality and unity, the sacred and the profane, in ways that insist on their similarities—even, at times, their identity. In less abstract terms, Sexton made explicit the intimacy of forces persistently treated as opposites by the society she lived in.

Diana Hume George. Oedipus Anne: The
Poetry of Anne Sexton (Urbana: University
of Illinois Press, 1987), p. xi

A close reading of the eight individual volumes from To Bedlam and Part Way Back (1960) to The Awful Rowing toward God (1975) produces a consistent awareness of progress—of process—which might be defined in two different ways. In secular terms, it is a progress from alienation in time to reconciliation with her moment in history; in theological terms, it is a pilgrimage to Grace. If the writing of poetry was, for Anne Sexton, a healing art, the cure seems to have directed the explicit, conscious statement of the poetry from youthful doubt, bewilderment and isolation to a middle-aged assurance of belonging in a universe filled with the praiseworthy manifestations of a Deity. The reader is invited to share this progress. (The posthumous volumes, 45 Mercy Street and Words for Dr. Y, scrupulously edited by her daughter, contain several strong poems, but are necessarily outside the *oeuvre,* and are given less attention here.)

In this pilgrimage, Anne Sexton's poetry does link itself to a great tradition—one not at all eccentric, amateur or isolated; that of the conversion narrative.

> Richard E. Morton. *Anne Sexton's Poetry of Redemption: The Chronology of a Pilgrimage* (Lewiston, New York: Edwin Mellen Press, 1988), p. 7

Sexton's *Complete Poems* is a compilation of the eight books she saw into print, plus an edited collection of work left in manuscript at the time of her death; Sexton's good friend Maxine Kumin supplies a valuable introduction. The early poetry (*To Bedlam and Part Way Back,* 1960; *All My Pretty Ones,* 1962) holds up very well. But as this volume shows, Anne Sexton made bolder exploration of her lifelong subject—her experiences of madness—in later work, beginning with the volume *Live or Die* (1966). Mining the realm of the unconscious as she had been taught by both psychotherapy and contemporary writing, after 1962 Sexton became increasingly preoccupied with the psychological and social consequences of inhabiting a female body. . . .

No matter what poetry she had on an evening's agenda, Sexton offered persona as a point of entry to her art. "I" in the poem is a disturbing, marginal female whose power is associated with disfigurement, sexuality, and magic. But at the end of each stanza, "I" is displaced from sufferer onto storyteller. With the lines "A woman like that . . . I have been her kind" Sexton conveys the terms on which she wishes to be understood: not victim, but witness and witch. . . .

Sexton's *Complete Poems* yields most when read as if it contained a narrative: an account of a woman cursed with a desire to die. . . .

Always in Sexton's poetry, stationed above her in a heavenly state of knowing, possessor of the wild card or the third eye, has been this inaccessible, controlling being. Whether parent, doctor, god, he is the forceful reminder of intolerable separation. And so *Complete Poems* loops back on itself with its last poem—the last Sexton oversaw into print. "The Rowing Endeth" is a closing poem without reconciliation, integration, transformation, or any other kind of healing in its hand.

But neither is it a suicide note, or in any other way valedictory. Sexton's *Complete Poems* ends not with a "last word" but with 141 pages of unpublished work in various stages of finish. An epigraph for the book might well have been, "This story ends with me still rowing" ("Rowing"). The mysterious curse of her mental illness, and the death wish at its core, could be lifted neither by medical nor by others means; but in becoming its storyteller Sexton achieved an emancipating relation to it. "This is madness / but a kind of hunger . . . Turn, my hungers!" In the leap from madness to metaphor Sexton fled solitary confinement again and again.

Diane Wood Middlebrook. *Parnassus*. 12,
1985, pp. 293–95, 312

AL-SHAYKH, HANAN (LEBANON) 1945–

[Hanan al-] Shaykh's controversial novel, *Zahra's Tale* (1980), tells the story of an unattractive girl who finds in the war emotional salvation.

It is interesting to note in Shaikh's case how the war has developed her art. Whereas in 1971 she had written a very self-conscious *I am Free Anā Hurra* novel entitled *The Devil's Mare,* out to prove how liberated the heroine is because of the success of her sexual aggressiveness, she now writes of a traumatised, pathetic but credible girl. After visiting an emigré uncle in Africa, Zahra returns to Beirut to find the capital embroiled in civil strife. Except for her compulsive attachment to her mother, Zahra has never been able to relate to others, and with the war she turns in on herself to live in a world of concrete comic-strip balloons, where the line between reality and illusion often blurs into nothing. This is not the unlikely metamorphosis of a shy teenager into a glamorous *femme fatale,* this is a rending tale of what the war does to a lonely, lost girl. . . .

The heroine revels in a brinksmanship that makes her whole being throb with self-awareness as fear pumps adrenaline through her benumbed brain. Indeed, the description of her actual death is less graphically presented than is the previous presentation of her apparent death. When she is actually dying the description dissolves in an abstraction of moods, longings and cryptic descriptions.

Miriam Cooke. *Journal of Arabic Literature.*
13, 1982, pp. 125, 128

Hanan Al-Shaykh's *Story of Žahra*, [is] a demanding but powerful realization of life from inside the head of a passive, disturbed, acne-ed, mistreated Lebanese Shi-ite girl (with brief excursions into the heads of Uncle Hesham exiled in Africa and of Majed, Zahra's short-lived bewildered husband). Zahra, too, is seen as more mad than she experiences herself to be. The novel (banned in some Arab countries) takes you gradually into Zahra's world until you are compelled to share Beirut's "formerly neutral streets . . . suddenly filled with a spirit of revenge and tension," the alarming presence of Brother Ahmad doped on dope and fighting, her own coming to sexual life in her bizarre affair with a rooftop sniper. While transmitting the sensations of being part of Beirut better than an infinitude of news reports, this imaginative inhabiting of a person formed by a particular and very troubled environment could not be further from documentary.

Gillian Wilce. *The New Statesman.*
April 25, 1986, p. 27

The tragedy of a homely young girl, Zahra, is written by Hanan al-Shaykh, who was born in Lebanon in 1945 and educated in Cairo. There she wrote her first novel, *Suicide of a Dead Man.* After returning to Beirut to work as a journalist, she wrote *The Story of Zahra,* which is banned in several Arab countries for its explicit sex and its politics. It is the first of the author's novels to be translated into English.

The chaos of Lebanon provides a terrifying, sad, noisy, and intrusive background against which the endless exploitation of Zahra is displayed. Exploited by her mother, who forces her to be present during her assignations as an excuse and a shield, Zahra, burdened by terrible pimples for which there seems to be no cure, seems also to be exploited by Nature. A married man takes full advantage of her feelings of insecurity and inferiority. After two abortions, she flees to an uncle in West Africa who is a forgotten and exiled hero of the *Parti Populaire Syrien.* Zahra enters an unhappy marriage with her cousin Majed and finally returns to Lebanon. There she falls in love with a sniper, with whom she has a few moments of happiness, before he kills her for carrying their child.

Al-Shaykh paints a pitiful picture of the treatment of women in a traditional society aggravated by war. *The Story of Zahra* weaves together the themes of culture/tradition and politics/history beautifully and is a worthy addition to the growing number of books about Lebanon's tragedy.

Jean-Louise Thacher. *Middle East Journal.*
42, 1988, p. 484

Her entire oeuvre has been produced outside Lebanon, yet she is considered one of the Beirut Decentrists. In addition to *The Suicide of a Dead Man,* her novels include *Faras al-Shaitan (Praying mantis,* 1971), *Hikayat Zahra (The Story of Zahra,* 1980, translated into English in 1986) and *Misk al-Ghazal* (The musk of the gazelles, 1988). She has also published a collection of short stories entitled *Wardat al-Sahra* (Desert rose, 1982).

[The short story] "A Girl Called Apple" was published in the *Wardat al-Sahra* collection. It tells of a Bedouin girl's resistance to tribal customs for the arrangement of marriage. She wants to marry and to have children, but she refuses to be commodified. Her rejection is total, it is also painful.

Margot Badran and Miriam Cooke. *Opening
the Gates: A Century of Arab Feminist
Writing* (London: Virago, 1990), p. 155

In the fiction of the Lebanese writer Hanan Al-Shaykh, only a portion of whose work has been translated into English, women play the major roles,

but only in the sense of plot and conflict. In some cases her female protagonists are more acted upon than active: the victims of an Islamic patriarchy
that treats them as second-class citizens, powerless both politically and economically. Bewildered and passive, they permit themselves to drift along from
event to event (and often from man to man) with little sense of fulfillment or
awareness that their situations might be altered. In other instances, when
they attempt to assert some kind of independent stance from male authority,
it is only with a sense of reluctance—not that this is their right, but simply
a matter of happenstance. It is impossible to think of her characters as committed feminists, though the mere fact that Hanan Al-Shaykh herself painstakingly describes the situations that entrench women within the
contemporary Islamic world implies that she herself identifies her role as that
of a reluctant spokesperson for change in women's lives. . . .

Perhaps the metaphor that best typifies the conflict between the male
and female worlds in Al-Shaykh's writing is the unknowable. Too many of
her male characters act as predators, stalking women because they know
little about them: sexually, emotionally, mentally. Others merely endure the
situation in which they find themselves, demonstrating little or no curiosity
about the opposite sex. . . .

Women of Sand and Myrrh [*Misk al-ghazál*], Al-Shaykh's fifth published
book and her second translated into English, would not seem so disturbing
were it not for the fact that four female characters dominate the narrative,
quadrupling the bleakness of *The Story of Zahra*. The setting is an Arab
country somewhere in the Gulf, most probably Saudi Arabia, where Al-
Shaykh lived for a time with her husband. The four women referred to in the
title of the English version represent differing perspectives and degrees of
entrapment within the patriarchal order, though often the confinement is
more figurative than literal. . . .

If Al-Shaykh's picture of life in an Islamic gulf state is accurate, it then
becomes a question of who is fooling whom. The activities of both the men
and the women in this novel are dominated by sex, liquor, and videos—not
the sand and the myrrh of the English title but rather what can be imported,
especially in the form of consumer goods. Air-conditioners, telephones, and
swimming pools (whatever money can buy)—all these material objects are
vehicles for escaping the traditional world. One is left with the impression of
a medieval society that has been transported into the modern world. When
all else fails, the government can resort to censorship and repression. . . .

Are all the incidents in *Women of Sand and Myrrh* a challenge to traditional Islam? When I asked Hanan Al-Shaykh that question, she responded:

> Of course not. I have never thought only of religion when I was
> writing [*Women of Sand and Myrrh*]. I knew that I wanted to
> open a curtain on a way of living which is part of the Middle
> East and yet different. This closed atmosphere attracted me and
> became juicy material for my imagination . . . for the unusual

daily life there which carries many social problems, tempted me to write about my feelings. That women are still oppressed, etc. . . . Even when I write [about] what appears to be Islamic behaviour, it is really more under the domain of social habits— which don't relate to the true teaching of Islamic societies.

Nevertheless, Al-Shaykh adds that her second novel ("The Praying Mantis," yet to be translated into English) shows "how a young girl who belongs to a pious religious family can suffer!!"

It seems proper to conclude that what Al-Shaykh means by her answer to my question—and what her fiction clearly demonstrates—is the condition of exploitation that women in certain areas of the Moslem world experience. I would call this exposé spontaneous feminism without the more familiar dogma of some of her Western counterparts. Without that rhetoric, her writing soars above the commonplace. Certainly it is only a matter of time before her dialogue with the Islamic patriarchy is no longer one-sided.

Charles R. Larson. *World Literature Today.*
65, 1991, pp. 14–17

Shaykh first came to international attention with the publication of *Hikāyat Zahrah (The Story of Zahrah)*. Lebanese critics condemned its overt expression of sexuality, unprecedented for a woman. Many tried to dismiss the novel as artless. But this ploy for the suppression of women's writings failed; in 1986, the novel was translated into French under the title *L'histoire de Zahra,* and the following year it came out in English. European accolades found their echo at home, so that when *Misk al-ghazāl* was published, its sensationalist language and subject matter were not universally attacked. Indeed, some Arab critics in the West hailed it as a great novel.

Whereas her earlier works are more autobiographical in nature, *Hikāyat Zahrah* conveys little if anything of the author's life. It tells the story of a pathetic middle-aged woman who finds in the Lebanese Civil War an opportunity to escape the oppression and physical exploitation that had until then been her lot. After a brief sojourn in Africa, where she had stayed with her lecherous uncle and had to marry one of his undesirable associates, she returns to a Beirut at war with itself. Chaos transforms her and gives her a courage she had never before experienced. She initiates an affair with a sniper, which culminates in a pregnancy that she wants, but which he ends by killing her.

Women of Sand and Myrrh is more sexually explicit in its language than *Hikāyat Zahrah* and more critical of social mores. Set primarily in an expatriate community in an anonymous desert country, *Misk al-ghazāl* tells the story of four women, each from her own perspective. Two of the women are Arabs from the country in question, one is Lebanese, and the fourth is American. Each woman is seeking to fulfill herself in a context that militates against women's self-assertion. Each woman chooses a different path that is ultimately self-destructive. The novel allows for few successful feminist options.

Although Shaykh has become known as a novelist, her short stories are powerful and well crafted. They criticize patriarchal notions of how Arab women should behave, but they also praise Arab cultures that adhere to a premodern way of life and to traditions that give women a measure of power to negotiate their own realities.

Miriam Cooke. In Steven R. Serafin and
Walker D. Glanze, eds. *Encyclopedia of
World Literature in the 20th Century* (New
York: Continuum, 1993), p. 553

SHANGE, NTOZAKE (UNITED STATES) 1948–

There are as many ways of looking at Ntozake Shange's *for colored girls who have considered suicide / when the rainbow is enuf* as there are hues in a rainbow. One can take it as an initiation piece, for instance, particularly with its heavily symbolic "Graduation Nite" and the girlhood perspectives of the mama's little baby/Sally Walker segment and in the voice of the eight-year-old narrator of "Toussaint." *colored girls* also might be seen as a black feminist statement in that it offers a black woman's perspective on issues made prominent by the women's movement. Still another approach is to view it as a literary coming-of-age of black womanhood in the form of a series of testimonies which, in Shange's words, "explore the realities of seven different kinds of women." Indeed, the choreopoem is so rich that it lends itself to multiple interpretations which vary according to one's perspective and experiences.

I would suggest, however, that the least appropriate responses are those exemplified by reviewers who said that black men will find themselves portrayed in *colored girls* "as brutal con men and amorous double-dealers," or that "The thematic emphasis is constantly directed at the stupid crudity and downright brutality of [black] men." Comments such as these are particularly misleading because they appear in reviews which contain generous praise for *colored girls,* thus suggesting that it is the condemnation of black men, which gives the book its merit. Too, such comments have the effect of diminishing the work to nothing more than a diatribe against black men, when, quite the contrary, Shange demonstrates a compassionate vision of black men— compassionate because though the work is not without anger, it has a certain integrity which could not exist if the author lacked a perceptive understanding of the crisis between black men and women. . . .

colored girls is certainly woman's art but it is also black art, or Third World art, as Shange probably would prefer to have it designated. As suggested, however, the primary focus of *colored girls* is on the quality of relationships between black women and their men. . . .

Black men and women have not communicated successfully. It might even be said that they have tried everything imaginable to avoid articulating their needs—extended families, promiscuity, no-strings-attached fatherhood, getting/staying high together, even the Black Power Movement in which black people were all sisters and brothers, which meant that everyone *naturally* had everyone else's welfare at heart and so there was no need to explain *anything*. Like the lady in purple, many black women find themselves saying, "i don't know any more tricks / i am really colored and really sad sometimes."

Shange has given us an exquisite and very personal view of the politics of black womanhood and black male-female relationships. Too few black writers are doing that—perhaps because the truth is really as painful as that depicted in *colored girls,* and in telling it one opens oneself to charges of dividing the race and exposing blacks to ridicule by reinforcing stereotypes. That allegation has been levied against *colored girls,* which is unfortunate because the only thing of which Ntozake Shange is guilty is a sincere, eloquent rendering of what she has come to understand about black love relationships. Critics cannot afford to insist that black writers forgo expressing such visions simply because they are painful, embarrassing, or potentially divisive. If that is true, maybe it is because blacks have been so preoccupied with political and economic survival that they no longer know, if they ever did, how to confront their own responsibility for what happens between black men and women. In that case, blacks really *do* have a great need for *colored girls* and similar works.

Sandra Hollin Flowers. *Black American Literature Forum.* 15, 1981, pp. 51–52, 54

In 1976 *for colored girls who have considered suicide / when the rainbow is enuf* exploded upon the stage and established Ntozake Shange as a major force in American theatre. Since that time, she has written at least five other plays, three of which were published in 1981 under the title *three pieces.* One of the most outstanding features of Shange's dramaturgy to date is a dialectic between the felt constrictions of the social order and the perceived limitlessness of the natural order. On the one hand, there is an awareness of social oppression and commitment to struggle; on the other, there is a desire to transcend or bypass, through music and dance, the limitations of social and human existence.

My purpose is to analyze one aspect of this dialectic, an element which Shange terms "combat breath," and to sketch broadly the dimensions of the opposing entity, which I am describing as a will to divinity. The contours, if not the purpose, of this fighting spirit are easily recognizable, while a discussion of the will to divinity, with its heavy allegiance to an African world view, could easily be the subject of a paper in and of itself. By focusing primarily on combat breath, I hope to explain the reason that Shange's plays not only startle and energize but also infuriate and disturb many of her audiences.

Shange borrows the term "combat breath" from Frantz Fanon. . . . Implicit in Shange's reference to Fanon is the understanding that the struggle for liberation involves the entire community, that liberation for women necessitates a concomitant liberation or redefinition of the position of men. . . .

Shange's combat breath resides in her preference for raising issues, suggesting directions, and daring audiences to write their own endings. *spell #7* forces both performers and audience members to acknowledge the terrible distortion of their lives. Both in its on-stage images, and its residual aftereffects, it is an arrogant challenge to all to reexamine so-called coping strategies.

Ntozake Shange practices combat breath at tremendous risk. Posing questions touching upon complex, vaguely defined issues may be dissatisfying to a public accustomed to finding in literature ordered, albeit idealized solutions to problems, a public which tends to value more the positing of answers which alleviate anxiety. Having created emotionally resonant pictures of distress without offering equally compelling projections of health, Shange runs the risk that her audiences, angered at having confused feelings exposed, will reject the reminder of their anguish and vilify her. . . .

It is important to note the major challenge Shange undertakes, for it is a risk similar to that involved in combat breath. The playwright depends on the spontaneity of the moment and the people on both sides of the footlights to carry a significant portion of her "message." Like the pastor of a Black church or the *mae dos santos* of a *candomble* house, she carefully structures her plays, utilizing the differing forces of language, music, dance, gesture, and other production elements in anticipation of the manifestation of a particular spirit. But inherent is the gamble that a sufficiently strong harmonizing force will appear to unify disparate elements, energize the audience/congregation and release it back into the world able to withstand challenges and courageous enough to attempt the merger of the sacred and the profane.

Sandra L. Richards. Black American
Literature Forum. 17, 1983, pp. 73, 76

Ntozake Shange's choreopoem, *for colored girls who have considered suicide / when the rainbow is enuf,* presents the paradox of the modern American city as a place where black women experience the trauma of urban life, yet find the strength to transcend the pain. The women depicted by Shange become physically and spiritually whole, thus free, through the psychic/psychological healing power that resides in the ancient, fundamentally religious act called "the laying on of hands." The believer "knows" that touch can heal if the one who touches is empowered by God; thus, touching stabilizes a person physically while freeing the troubled soul to soar spiritually.

Shange uses the physically and morally desolate cityscape as a backdrop before which to reveal her spiritual vision of female strength and survival.

In this respect, therefore, *colored girls* differs from the legion of literary works that depict the lives of urban Afro-Americans. She neither denies nor romanticizes urban black experiences: the choreopoem graphically describes the complex ways in which the rape victim is further victimized by the "authorities"; it reveals the loneliness and guilt of the woman who decides to have an abortion; it details the betrayal women continue to experience in their relationships with men.

While none of these problems is uniquely urban, they are exacerbated by the human estrangements that characterize city life. But Ntozake Shange does have a larger vision. One might think of this vision in terms of two concentric circles, with the outer circle temporarily more powerful than the other. The geographical and psychological "settings" represent one circle; the other is a fragile circle promising transcendence. The external circle is clearly discernible from the beginning; the internal is revealed slowly, growing in strength and intensity until *it* is the dominant one at the end. The second circle, at first a figurative one, becomes a visible, magic enclosure of women who, in joining hands, bless and heal one another while naming their own empowering female god.

> Carolyn Mitchell. In Susan Squier, ed.
> *Women Writers and the City* (Knoxville:
> University of Tennessee Press, 1984),
> pp. 230–31

Ntozake Shange's works defy generic classifications: just as her poems (published in *Nappy Edges* and *A Daughter's Geography*) are also performance pieces, her works for the theater defy the boundaries of drama and merge into the region of poetry. Her most famous work, *for colored girls wo have considered suicide / when the rainbow is enuf,* is subtitled "a choreopoem." Similarly, she has written *Betsey Brown* as a novel and then again (with Emily Mann) in play form, and her first work of fiction, *Sassafrass, Cypress & Indigo,* is as free with its narrative modes—including recipes, spells, letters— as Joyce was in *Ulysses.* Perhaps more so than any other practicing playwright, Shange has created a poetic voice that is uniquely her own—a voice which is deeply rooted in her experience of being female and black, but also one which, again, refuses and transcends categorization. Her works articulate the connection between the doubly "marginalized" social position of the black women and the need to invent and appropriate a language with which to articulate a self. . . .

Shange . . . makes the minstrel-masking into a ceremony of sorts in the opening scene of *spell #7,* and the resemblance of the giant minstrel face above the stage to an African voodoo mask is wholly intentional. At the same time, though, the blackface masks that the actors wear at the beginning of the play also invoke the *travesty* of a ceremony, for the masks represent the "parts" each must play (in the Western tradition) in order to get a job. . . .

Spell #7's ultimate vision may be more cynical than that of *for colored girls,* but its call for redefinitions is one which echoes throughout Shange's theater pieces. She invites a reconsideration of role-playing which suggests that in the process of acting out the various "masks" that blacks/women are *expected* to assume, one undergoes an experience of interior drama. Liberated through monologic language and by dance, song, etc., which release different, richer, more complex characters and experiences, the very nature of role-playing has been appropriated as a tool for "performing a self." She sees role-playing as a way simultaneously to give her characters an archetypal fluidity and to confront role-oriented stereotypes. On some level Shange's characters are always aware that they are speaking to an audience; perhaps this emphasis is an acknowledgment of the sense that women—as John Berger discusses in *Ways of Seeing*—are always the objects of vision and so are constantly watching themselves being watched. Rather than decentering the position of authorship in her plays by providing a sense that the characters are as if "self-created," though, Shange appears to share Michelene Wandor's view that deliberate attention to the author's role as "storyteller" provides a backbone, a controlling structure, for the play. Interwoven with this is a revision of spectacle as a vehicle for amusement; Shange's interpretation of "spectacle" insists upon questioning both the *mode* of performance which lures the audience's attention (as in the minstrel show at the beginning of *spell #7*) and the *subtext* of the spectacle itself. The monologue, then, is both an object for transformation and a means by which transformations can occur. Above all, Shange feels passionately that "we must move our theater into the drama of our lives." Her works attempt to speak, in the way that she says Layla's unconscious does in *boogie woogie landscapes,* of "unspeakable realities / for no self-respecting afro-american girl wd reveal so much of herself of her own will / there is too much anger to handle assuredly / too much pain to keep on truckin / less ya bury it."

Deborah R. Geis. In Enoch Brater, ed.
*Feminine Focus: The New Women
Playwrights* (New York: Oxford University
Press, 1989), pp. 210, 218, 223–24

This collection of prose and poetry [*Ridin' the Moon in Texas*] calls forth so many images that the reader will see him/herself in every page. It becomes an exposé of the reader's psyche. Now that's saying a lot for a slender volume that takes "old wine and puts it into new bottles." That is, Shange has employed the technique of using visual art as a takeoff for creating the substance of her verbal images. Thus, the book also contains color reproductions of exciting contemporary art in various media: painting, sculpture, and photography. . . .

Shange's book itself becomes an elaborate, extended metaphor. The title comes from a prose sketch (I will not call it a short story or even prose fiction, if we think of the word *fiction* in the generic sense of having plot

structure, situation, and dénouement) inspired by photographer Patricia Olli-
son Jerrols. This sketch consists entirely of dialogue with no identification
of speakers. It could easily have been a transcription of a back-of-the-corral
verbal exchange (overheard by the author) between black rodeo cowboys
talking about rodeos, horses, and women. However, Shange captures the
ambience of the moment so that the disconnected bits of dialogue weave their
own "tapestry" and take us into a world that few of us will ever know or
experience except vicariously. . . .

The sheer virtuosity of Shange's subject matter makes this book a significant leap into the world of what it means to be a writer, one capable of
deriving inspiration from every nuance of living and feeling, of absorbing life
as a source of material to be transformed into art.

The book rocks, it rolls; but it also soars ethereally, shifting gears with
dizzying speed. Breathless in its Joycean stream of consciousness, it just as
quickly plummets to mother earth, its choice of style being adapted to the
mood and subject.

Pinkie Gordon Lane. *Black American
Literature Forum.* 24, 1990, pp. 578–79

The poignancy in Shange's writing extends from her successful mingling of
languages. Poetry and music exist in the same spaces as dialogues and
dreams. Women's sharing of their most intimate and creative language with
each other is a significant feature of Shange's method. Part of this sharing is
clearly evident in the recipes and letters from Sassafrass's, Cypress's, and
Indigo's mother, but it is also an important dimension of the lesbian relationships in this novel. Some of the most generative and thickest language surrounds Shange's descriptions of the women's dance collective the Azure
Bosom.

Dense in color and texture, and full and resonant in shapes and forms,
this collective represents the deepest levels of the stylistic effort in *Sassafrass, Cypress & Indigo.* Here, the language is as full-bodied as the women's
gender dance, "a dance of women discovering themselves in the universe."
In the house Cypress shares with the dancers from the Azure Bosom, she
sees "herself everywhere . . . nothing different from her in essence; no thing
not woman." In this novel, Shange brings full circle the revelation of her
dramatic choreopoem *for colored girls.* . . . Here, the generational dimensions of womanself are explored as a variety of creative energies—Sassafrass's weaving and writing, Cypress's dance, and eventually Indigo's
personification of biological creativity. She becomes a midwife—a creatrix.
Because it is Indigo's vision that both opens and closes the story, she is
Shange's final coalescence of the extended imaginative dimensions of the
novel. Indigo represents the metaphorical bridge between African-American
women and their African ancestry. She is an elemental link, embodying the
qualities of air ("a moon in her mouth"), earth ("earth blood, filled up with
the Geechees long gone"), and water ("and the sea." It is not until Sassafras

wears white and sees a vision of her "Mother" (Shange capitalizes this word, giving it a resonance and depth that extends beyond her immediate biological mother) that she finds the spirit she shares with her sister Indigo. By this time in the story, Indigo has come to embody the midwifery talents of her mentor Aunt Haydee. We are told that her place in the ancestral tradition Haydee represents is appropriate because, more than having "an interest in folklore," Indigo "was the folks."

Karla F. C. Holloway. *Black American*
Literature Forum. 24, 1990, pp. 620–21

Identifying herself as "a poet first and a playwright second," Shange developed the choreopoem form as a new genre in American theater, a form rooted in an African tradition of movement, song, music, and emotional catharsis. As a black person, as a black woman, as a black feminist, as a black artist, and as a black female artist, Shange champions the women of color specifically and people of color generally as they move toward optimal self-consciousness, positive self-identity, and unlimited self-realization in an oppressive and blatantly sexist and racist modern society. A crusader for renewed race consciousness, preservation of the black race, and accurate documentation of the lives of people of color, Shange not only renounces the "redundancy of being sorry and colored at the same time in the modern world" but expounds on the "metaphysical dilemma of being alive and being a woman and being colored" *(for colored girls).*

Neal A. Lester. *Black American Literature*
Forum. 24, 1990, p. 718

for colored girls established Shange in 1976 as the "authentic" black woman's voice in American theater, a voice heeded on Broadway in part because her choreopoem addresses issues of gender to which many woman would relate, regardless of their ethnicity. In *spell #7,* first produced in 1979, Shange foregrounds racism rather than sexism, although the two forms of oppression are never separated. In a medley of poems, songs, and dialogue reminiscent of the nonrealist form employed in *for colored girls,* nine actors and would-be actors reenact with mockery, and sometimes despair, the stereotypes expected in their profession. This play never received the critical acclaim given to *for colored girls,* although in terms of text it is sharper, wittier, and more unforgiving of dominant culture. . . .

Spell #7 explores, more overtly than the earlier play, the effects of racism on the African American community and on heterosexual relations in that community. One of the funniest monologues in the script, describing "white girls," was cut from the New York production because it was considered offensive to white women. The monologue is offensive, but it is also wickedly funny, as it treats stereotypes about white women's frivolity, laziness, and sexual dysfunction, stereotypes that erase differences among white women. But watching an African American woman with a very short afro enact flinging her hair as she waters her house plants and picks unwanted clothes out of her closet to give to her black housekeeper is, if you are a white woman, at once discomforting and hilarious. If you had any doubts before, you realize that this play is not about you. You can learn from it, enjoy it, but it does not address you.

Catherine Wiley. Theatre Journal. 43, 1991,
pp. 382–83

Against the background of *Brown v. Board of Education* (1954) and the fledgling civil rights movement of the late 1950s, Betsey Brown (Raquel Herring), tries to find a place in her world for love, for poetry, and for politics. Jane (Pamela Isaacs), her mother, leaves the house at the beginning of the play to sort out her own conflicting feelings about "advancing the race" and protecting her children from racist attacks in their newly integrated schools. Carrie (Kecia Lewis-Evans) is hired as a housekeeper after Betsey's grandmother (Ann Duquesnay) pleads for help raising four kids. Carrie's version of mothering and Jane's are completely different; Jane taught her children poetry; Carrie teaches them how to praise the Lord and how to keep a man.

The politics of the play [which is based on Shange's eponymous novel] are refreshingly matter-of-fact: racism and sexism are abhorrent, neither is necessary, and neither is easily escaped. In the scenes with white people at the school, white face masks convey the stiffness and rigidity with which the white establishment greeted "progress." In her newly integrated school, Betsey gets into a heated contest with her white English teacher about American poets: the teacher says Wallace Stevens; Betsey says Paul Dunbar Nelson; the teacher says Emily Dickinson; Betsey replies with Phyllis Wheatley. Betsey's link to the black poetic tradition is her link to America and its history, the bond with her wandering mother, and the key to her own future as a writer. Betsey cannot afford to let the white teacher's ignorance restrict her access to these intimate and public poems.

Betsey's love for Jane is tested by Carrie's arrival. Initially Betsey cannot abide Carrie, and she mocks her singing and strutting with a fiercely pointed mimicry. Trying desperately to be bigger in every way than she actually is, Betsey confirms only the depth of her ambition to be different than she has been. The aspiration to be a poet in a world that resists rhyme requires both mad confidence and weariness with one's prosaic self. The achievement of *Betsey Brown* is that this insight becomes elegantly linked to the aspiration to create a social revolution; for revolution also requires a kind of mad confidence and a determined exhaustion with the status quo. When Betsey's mother's return calls for Carrie's departure, Betsey balks until Carrie reminds her that presence does not require physical proximity. The power of memory is the power of history and poetry, and memory's power comes from the desire not to be left by and not to leave those we love.

Peggy Phelan. Theatre Journal. 43, 1991,
pp. 383–84

Ntozake Shange strives to fill a void in the female literary canon. With novels such as *sassafrass, cypress and indigo* in 1982 and *Betsey Brown* in 1985, and her dramatic choreopoem *For Colored Girls Who Have Considered Suicide/When the Rainbow is Enuf* in 1977, she has joined the ranks of prominent black women who are giving a voice to their sisters. Through her works, the audience is exposed to the issues facing black women as they develop into adulthood. Issues of racism and sexism must be addressed in order for her characters to grow. Although each of her characters finds a definition of herself as a black woman, the paths taken are unique to the individual. Each woman fulfills herself with a particular interest from which she derives power, be that interest music, dancing, or weaving cloth. These women must also learn to relate to and separate themselves from the men in their lives. With strength of character, Shange's women imprint themselves permanently in our memories. Shange wrote in *sassafrass, cypress and indigo* that the novel is dedicated to "all women in struggle." Within that statement lies the power of her writing. Her works are about black women, but they are indeed for ALL women. She uses Ebonics in a manner that does not exclude any gender, class or culture. Rather it invites all readers to enjoy as well as understand and confront issues facing us. . . .

Ntozake Shange's first novel, *sassafrass, cypress and indigo,* is a paradox because somehow this shaman of a writer manages to integrate tradition with rebellion, chaos with peace, reality with fantasy, and poetry with life. Meanwhile music, art, and food become literature. The result is a lively/tranquil story that is painful/joyous and real magic.

Shange's novel *Betsy Brown* is about a black family, but it focuses primarily on the struggles of the oldest daughter, Betsey. By virtue of age, comparisons between Indigo and Betsey seem natural. They are also the only two children that Shange has devoted extensive attention to in her works to date. Both girls have an incredible ability to perceive situations and an uncanny grasp of life for their young age. However, Indigo is much more secure in her growth than Betsey, who must deal with constant family turmoil. As Shange says: "Indigo has a knowing sense of what's possible and who she can be. We discover with Betsey what her possibilities are, which is different, I think, from Indigo giving us permission to share what she already knows." . . .

From *Colored girls . . .* to *Betsey Brown* to *sassafrass, cypress, and indigo,* Shange has created journeys of self-discovery. She has woven tales that reach out to the "searching and yearning" that went on inside her in her own adolescence and extended these stories to touch the lives of all women of all colors. She says that women's novels are like breathing for her, and that seems to capture the essence of her works. The development of women as they struggle to find themselves is as much a part of life as breathing. It is impossible to simply read her works and walk away; they linger in the mind. Shange is "for colored girls who have considered suicide / but are movin to the ends of their own rainbows." Shange is for women. Shange is for anyone interested in a greater sense of self-awareness. She touches us all.

Geta LeSeur. In Carol Aisha Blackshire-Belay, ed. *Language and Literature in the African American Imagination* (Westport, Connecticut: Greenwood Press, 1992), pp. 167, 177, 179

SHEN RONG (CHINA) 1936–

Sensitive character sketches, passages of descriptive beauty and real-life suspenseful plots abound in seven stories *[At Middle Age]* that possess enduring appeal. In the title piece, a respected physician tries to balance career and family demands. After she falls sick, a cleverly constructed stream-of-consciousness narrative recounts the joys and sorrows of her life. A conflict between materialism and idealism emerges in "A Rose-colored Evening Meal," when an unhappy son visits his parents on a festive occasion and, instead of rejoicing, cynically contemplates their "petty bourgeois" possessions. Throughout the collection, the direction of characters' lives is intertwined with that of China's politics; the specter of the Cultural Revolution haunts the protagonists of "Ten Years Deducted." Overall, each story is not only crafted ingeniously but is suffused with a vitality that makes every word crackle. With her mastery of the form, Rong manages both to portray a society that remains mysterious to the West and to express the common humanity of contemporary Chinese individuals.

Penny Kaganoff. *Publishers Weekly.* October 7, 1988, p. 109

After a long struggle with her superiors that procured for her the time and resources to write, Shen Rong was able to take time off from her job as a school teacher and put her energy into literature. By the time her novella "At Middle Age" [Ren dao zhongnian] and the movie which followed gained her national fame, she herself was a middle-aged writer whose reputation was based on her ability to write realistic fiction that revolves around the issues of economic and social reform. However, although Shen Rong has avoided experimentation with various styles of literary modernism, she also has surpassed reform issues by investigating themes and motifs which may be incorporated into the issues of reform, yet deal with subjects that are not strictly related to reform itself. Included in these motifs are the characterization of an "ideal" woman and the problems she will encounter in Chinese society, and the definition of what literature and the writer are and should be within the context of a society undergoing reform.

Many of Shen's stories center on a "contradiction" which exists in the reform process and is manifested by an aspect of life presented as frightening in its ability to damage or destroy personal relationships, work, and individual peace of mind. These phenomena exist because reform has failed to reach or not yet reached the roots of the problem itself, or, in some cases, because the process of reform actually has produced the contradiction. . . .

If many of Shen's works indicate serious ambivalence about the role of the writer in Chinese society today, others show the writer as a super-perceptive, engaged observer of society. In her works which mock the creativity or social reputation of writers as reflectors of reality, the despondency of the characters speaks to the desire for a more active, engaged position for the writer. "Yang Yueyue and the Study of Sartre," published in 1983, shows a positive if hesitant portrayal of the writer in that role; "Scattered People," published in 1985, once again calls that definition into question. Clearly, Shen Rong is expressing her desire that the members of a profession which has been the butt of many political movements since 1949 take up a renewed, vigorous role within society; just as clearly, however, that role is fraught with problems and is not yet reality. Implicit in her argument is an acceptance of the methods of literary realism, which purports to reflect society in all of its colors without changing them. This stance corresponds with Shen's attempts to reflect problems associated with reform in society and the plight of women functioning within this society. In this regard, the position of the writer should be (yet still is not) secure. The position of the literary work, however, is subject to varying reception within society, and this again depends on the values and approaches of the reader. Although a writer or reader of realism will not accept the definition of the work as escapism, neither can she accept the definition of the work as necessarily indicative of any particular ideology or point of view.

Wendy Larson. In Michael S. Duke, ed.
*Modern Chinese Women Writers: Critical
Appraisals* (Armonk, New York: M. E.
Sharpe, 1989), pp. 174, 193

SIDHWA, BAPSI (PAKISTAN) 1938–

Bapsi Sidhwa's *The Crow Eaters* is an excellent novel, her first, a book about India which one can wholeheartedly enjoy rather than respectfully admire. The author is a born storyteller, an affectionate, shrewd observer of the Parsi family whose history is here related. She organizes her material well and writes with authority and flair.

"Faredoon Junglewalla, Freddy for short, was a strikingly handsome, dulcet-voiced adventurer." It is an opening paragraph to whet the reader's appetite and the subject is not one to disappoint his public. Freddy is first seen trundling towards Lahore in a bullock cart with his wife Putli, his baby daughter and his dreadful mother-in-law. He has some trouble with the rooster sharing the ride, a perverse bird who likes to cling to our hero's buttocks at the climax of love-making "like an experienced rodeo rider." In a matter of days Freddy finds an excuse for sacrificing this favorite and is soon eating chicken curry. That is the measure of the man. It is easy to credit his meteoric rise to fortune (aided by arson and insurance fraud); it is inevitable that his children are lesser figures, that Yazdi should renounce his inheritance in disgust, that Billy should become one of the richest misers in the continent. A Parsi Forsyte Saga? Who knows? Mrs. Sidhwa's fiction may develop in a number of directions but one thing is certain, she will be read.

Judy Cooke. The New Statesman.
September 19, 1980, p. 23

The Crow Eaters, Bapsi Sidhwa's first published novel, purports to be a succinct and satirical account of the success story told the youngsters in his later years by the Parsi Seth Faredoon Junglewalla himself, the central figure whose rise to fortune and social stardom we follow in the three hundred-odd pages strewn with matters "local" and much goodnatured humor and drollery. The speech is laconic, yet winsome, as the Junglewalla relates how he managed it. . . .

The Parsi background and focus give additional significance to this narrative, as very little is known generally of this isolationist sort of community in the subcontinent, particularly at a personal or imaginative level. As such, a recognition of the novel's particular landscape is to register time through a consciousness with which perhaps not many outsiders would be familiar. . . .

Bapsi Sidhwa writes from a deep historical consciousness. Her evocation of a part of Lahore life as lived in the first half of this century is convincing—and charming to me as a Lahorite myself. She herself grew up in Lahore and makes her home there; the first-hand knowledge of it certainly lends credence to the irony, as it arises out of a deep understanding of the place and people and their ways. She is looking at the whole, and the constituent parts, through the diminutive lens of insidious comicality as an outsider who knows better; as a member of the Parsi minority in Pakistan who knows her people's secrets, real strengths, and foibles. Her novel, beyond particular situation and character, aims at a sweep that encompasses a people and may well be better considered in that light.

What a wonderful relief from the quantities of underbelly, feline fiction that our magazines usually put out. The vigorous style of the book is a riding crop for any pair of "amorous buttocks" used to blushing at mild innuendo. To the small body of fiction written in this country, Bapsi Sidhwa has added her witty and piquant voice, and a loquaciousness that is endearing. The title of the book refers to the Parsis' "notorious ability to talk ceaselessly at the top of their voices like an assembly of crows." If this fiction is any evidence, it pleases.

Alamgir Hashmi. World Literature Written in
English. 20, 1981, pp. 373–74, 376

Sidhwa's first published novel, The Crow Eaters, introduced a robust, farcical style in the Pakistani novel. The Bride was written earlier but has only now been published. It narrates the story of Zaitoon, who lost her parents in the Indo-Pakistan riots in the summer of 1947 and was adopted by Lahore-bound Qasim, a Himalayan tribesman also fleeing the mountains after committing a crime and losing his wife and children to the fatalities inflicted by smallpox.

Zaitoon is so named by Qasim, after his own late daughter, and raised from the age of five in the city of Lahore as his adopted daughter. Against better counsel, he decides to marry her off at fifteen to a tribesman in the northern mountains, whence he himself originated. The city-bred young girl now must learn the ways of the tribesman's world outside the civilized, urban though decadent life of the plains, where she spent most of her years. The result is as expected. Sakhi is not the husband she wants; nor is she the wife he can endure. So she must escape the rugged hills, which she does, and find her way back, which we cannot know about. Honor, commitment, marriage and loyalty are at stake, and there is really no way either to quash or to salvage them in the painful predicament in which Zaitoon's circumstances have placed her.

Escape from the oppressive, no-go "civilization" is what Carol also decides upon. She appears midway through the book, apparently to highlight Zaitoon's dilemma and to judge it with the outsider's objective eye. Carol is American and married to a Pakistani engineer living in the northern mountains, extremely dissatisfied with her own life as much as with local mores, which she finds "too ancient" and "too different." She decides to go "home," thus mirroring Zaitoon's flight from the "different" North. The two story lines combine to produce a splendid tale examining sociocultural differences at a level far above that which is familiar in Pakistani Anglophone writing.

Alamgir Hashmi. World Literature Today.
58, 1984, pp. 667–68

Ice-Candy-Man is Bapsi Sidhwa's third novel, following The Crow Eaters (1978) and The Bride (1983). As in the first two, the mode of narration is realistic. The quality of this surface realism is a product of acute intelligence, integrity, and imagination, the same qualities which enabled her to portray the life of the Parsi community with unflattering verisimilitude in The Crow Eaters and to which the conflict between the male-dominant values of the tribesmen and the people of the cities owes its power in The Bride. In the new work, however, the emphasis is not on representing phenomenal reality faithfully. The novel is an imaginative response to the traumatic events of the Partition of India in 1947, and Sidhwa has used surrealistic techniques, somewhat like Salman Rushdie, to make it an adequate symbol for the effect of external events on human beings.

The logical narrative which can be abstracted from *Ice-Candy-Man* involves a love story. The voluptuous and much-wooed Ayah, a Hindu, is abducted by Muslim hoodlums and raped. Somehow she comes into the hands of her admirer, the Ice-Candy-Man, who makes her a dancing girl and marries her. She is discovered by the narrator Lenny's godmother, who arranges her rescue and sends her to India. Ice-Candy-Man "too, disappears across the Wagah border into India" in pursuit of her.

That story is of little significance in Sidhwa's sophisticated, symbolic novel, however. More important are the narrative techniques, for they contribute to the work's total effect. Foremost among them is the first-person, present-tense narration. Lenny, like Saleem Sinai in Rushdie's *Midnight's Children . . .* is—or was—a child when the events described take place, and the events are seen through her consciousness, the present tense providing immediacy and a certain simultaneity between past and present. By the end of both novels the narrator knows much about human perfidy, mainly through the impact of external events. Lenny learns of the perverse nature of amorous human passions from her experiences with her cousin Hamida, who woos her with a determination equaled only by the Ice-Candy-Man's pursuit of Ayah; religious passion's potential for breeding fanatical hatred and violence, as in the killing of the Hindus in Lahore and the Muslims in the Punjab of the Sikhs, is reflected in the story of Lenny's friend Ranna, a harrowing account of the human atrocities that can be perpetrated when all civilized restraints are removed through external events or political propaganda.

Without a word of protestation or preaching and without histrionics, Sidhwa has written one of the most powerful indictments of the riots which occurred during the Partition. Previously there was almost nothing in English on the subject except for several works by Khwaja Ahmad Abbas and a few short stories by H. K. Burki and Tabussum. There was of course much that was good in Urdu literature and other languages, but only Khushwant Singh's *Train to Pakistan* (1956) took up the theme of the Partition. Now there is *Ice-Candy-Man,* which shows the human personality under stress as a result of that cataclysmic event and depicts a society responding to it in the way societies do react: through sheer indifference, gossip, trivial and malicious activities, making love, and also killing, raping, and going insane. These last aspects of reality are often lost in novels and short stories in which the trivial, the absurd, the obscene is not juxtaposed with the tragic, the sublime, and the momentous. Sidhwa's novel manages to do just that, and to do so with great symbolic significance. I consider it among the best works of Pakistani fiction in English and one of the truly good novels of this century.

Tariq Rahman. *World Literature Today.* 62,
1988, pp. 732–33

A third of the way through Bapsi Sidhwa's new novel, which pretends to be a tale about independence, Mohandas Gandhi arrives in Lahore. The year is post-World War II, pre-Partition—say 1946. Lahore, then as now, is the intellectual center of Muslim literature, the site of a great university and the home of Urdu poets. Then it was in India, now it is in Pakistan.

It would be ridiculous to presume that the Mahatma would choose to visit the city that is the heart of Muslim culture at that specific time for anything less than a calculated, political expediency. However, in the hands of Sidhwa, Gandhi's visit to the city is portrayed thus: "I am puzzled why he's so famous—and suddenly his eyes turn to me. My brain, heart and stomach melt. He is the man who loves women. And lame children. And the untouchable sweeper—so he will love the untouchable sweeper's constipated girl-child best." Unfortunately, no untouchable sweeper's constipated girl-child materializes in this novel to help either the poor reader or poor Gandhijee along.

Rather, the book is peopled (for lack of a better description of how Sidhwa conceives of her characters) by a ragbag of sub-continental stereotypes. There are The Gurkha Soldier ("short and stocky like most of his race"), The Parsees ("prosperous, eating-drinking households"), the British Inspector General shouting, "You won't be able to blame everything on us for long, old chap!" and the Turbulent Unshaven Sikh who tries to take the Brit. Insp. Gen.'s eyes out with a fork at dinner, screaming, "Whyfore then you think we cannot do Home Rule?"

There are also Mother, Father and Electric-Aunt, whose names and roles (although not their dialogues) are blatantly derivative of the rambunctiousness of characters in *Midnight's Children*—but when Sidhwa sets a character with the potentially dramatic name "Slavesister" to talking, the words come out like this: "'After the Mountbatten plan to tear up the Punjab how can you . . .' mumbles Slavesister, shaking her head at the stove a looking martyred."

To which the other female in this scene answers, "If your mutilated body was discovered in the gutter then you'd know how it feels!" Again, no mutilated body in the gutter arrives to help the *reader* know just how the Mountbatten plan must have felt. . . .

Much of Sidhwa's trouble in telling this tale lies in her choice of narrative voice. She has chosen to address the most important issues of her country through the words of a seven-year-old girl, a polio victim called Lenny, who recites narrative action like this: "Ayah comes. And with her, like a lame limpet, come I." and, during the aforementioned visit by Gandhi to Lahore, Lenny tells the reader: "Gandhijee certainly is ahead of his times. He already knows the advantages of dieting."

As character fails, so does any sense of the politics of the time—so does any sense of place. The city of Lahore just cannot emerge from this imprecise and amateurish prose. "I am seeing more of Lahore, too," Lenny promises halfway through the book:

> Ayah and I roam on foot and by bus: from Emperor Jehangir's
> tomb at Shahdara to Shahjehan's Shalimar Gardens. From the

outskirts of the slaughter house to the banks of the Ravi in low flood. We amble through the tall pampas grass—purposefully purposeless—and sniffing the attar of roses, happen upon Masseur: his creamy bosky-silk shirt, his strong forearms and broad ankles stretched out on a dhurrie on the gray sand.

More about the banks of the Ravi and less about the creamy bosky-silk shirt and strong forearms would have helped the reader to make sense of what the fuss was all about. As it is, *Ice-Candy-Man* is a fuddled attempt to inflate a Mills and Boon plot into a novel about Partition and although Sidhwa's interest in the major issue cannot be faulted, hers is the dramatic failing of having chosen to write about events to which her imaginative power adds no new insight.

Marianne Wiggins. *The New Statesman.*
February 26, 1988, p. 41

Bapsi Sidhwa's *The Bride* and *Ice-Candy-Man* both portray history through the lens of female characters, and in so doing pose a challenge to the ideologies of Patriarchy and War.

Sidhwa's second published novel, *The Bride,* challenges the patriarchal culture and values of Indian-Pakistani society, for the heroine Zaitoon refuses to submit to the system and to accept the status quo. Thus, Sidhwa's ideological stance functions simultaneously as a strategy for challenging "the system" dominated by men and as a strategy of "liberation" for the female self that remains marginalized within that system. In contrast to the attitude of conservative paternalism, which is the hallmark of so many male writers of the subcontinent, such as Ahmed Ali, Sidhwa's attitude toward "the system" in place in post-Partition Muslim Pakistan is much more challenging. . . .

Sidhwa, contrary to writers like Ali, does not romanticize a system that makes a virtue of defending the honor of women—where a woman may be killed if she is suspected of even imaginary infidelities or of exhibiting the slightest desire for independence, as in Zaitoon's case. . . .

In *The Bride,* Sidhwa does not offer any radical solutions to the dilemma of being a woman in a patriarchal culture. Zaitoon survives but only to be taken up and protected by a man who hopefully loves her and will not treat her as cruelly as the comparatively uncivilized tribal husband did. Thus, Zaitoon, despite her heroism, must remain an object in a culture whose history continues to marginalize women. It is important to note, however, that Sidhwa's stance on the idealization of patriarchal culture and history is clearly one of challenge.

In her third novel, *Ice-Candy-Man,* Sidhwa still depicts women as little more than objects in history but moves away from seeing women solely as victims to describing them as emotional pillars of strength who can, through the power of compassion, effect good for others. In this world gone awry, where friend betrays friend, the women suffer the most; yet, ironically, only the women can offer any hope for the salvation of humanity.

Fawzia Afzhal Khan. In Robert L. Ross, ed.
*International Literature in English: Essays
on the Major Writers* (New York: Garland,
1991), pp. 272, 274

SILKO, LESLIE MARMON (UNITED STATES) 1948–

Leslie Marmon Silko's first novel, aptly entitled *Ceremony,* fits into [the story-telling] tradition. It is the story of Tayo, an American-Indian veteran of World War II, who has come back home in a state of shock. In the South Pacific he saw his half-brother die; he also witnessed the execution of many Japanese prisoners of war. To Tayo, the Japanese seemed very like his brother, and this similarity reminds us that the aboriginal population of the Americas is thought to have come originally from Asia. This global connection is also emphasized by recalling that the atom bomb dropped on Hiroshima was first tested in New Mexico following laboratory tests near Los Alamos, on land taken from the Cochiti Pueblo.

When Tayo comes home from the war, he is sent to the psychiatric ward of a Los Angeles veterans hospital. His treatment there accomplishes little because, as Tayo realizes, "medicine didn't work that way. . . . His sickness was only part of something larger, and his cure would be found only in something great and inclusive of everything." . . .

[The] novel is about Tayo's search for sanity. He goes to Gallup, a tough and dusty town near the Arizona border famed for its annual Inter-Tribal Ceremonial which brings Indians (and tourists) from all parts of the West. There Tayo meets a man who knows Indian medicine and who undertakes to exorcise the disturbing ghosts of Tayo's past. The ceremony involves sand paintings and prayer sticks and is therapeutic in that it forces Tayo to face reality and open himself to unconscious experiences, rather than withdraw from what he does not like or understand.

Leslie Silko's method of narration imitates the ceremony itself, for she shifts her story from one time and place to another until eventually everything is made clear. These shifts are not disruptive, however, for the story is always vivid and concrete. When Tayo stands on the bridge overlooking the shacks along the river bank where the prostitutes live, it is evident that he was once there as a child, himself the product of some hasty union, hiding furtively while his mother met a customer. The novel is full of dramatic encounters, barroom fights, drunken drives in pick-up trucks across the barren countryside, ugly meetings with white landowners.

For some years Leslie Silko has been working this material. A number of her short stories, published in a 1974 anthology, *The Man to Send Rainclouds,* showed that she was exceptionally gifted. *Ceremony* confirms that impression and establishes her without question as the most accomplished Indian writer of her generation. Her achievement lies partly in the way she has woven together the European tradition of the novel with American-Indian storytelling. She has used animal stories and legends to give a fabulous dimension to her novel. These are set aside from the prose narrative and look like curative and ceremonial chants that are recited in hogans. All of these devices reflect the theme of the novel, which is that the war has made all people one, "united by a circle of death that devoured people in cities twelve thousand miles away, victims who had never known these mesas, who had never seen the delicate colors of the rocks which boiled up their slaughter."

Leslie Silko has avoided the easy sentimentality of treating Indians as morally superior to whites; indeed, she has Old Betonie insist that the whites themselves have influenced the ceremonies, and that such changes are necessary in order to keep them alive. . . .

Leslie Silko is herself part-white, part-Indian. Her dual sensibility has given her the strength to blend two forms of narrative into a single work of art. It may also have given her the perspective, as a woman, to write so movingly about her male characters. Her novel is one of the most realized works of fiction devoted to Indian life that has been written in this country, and it is a splendid achievement.

Frank MacShane. *The New York Times.*
June 12, 1977, p. 15

The 1960s and 1970s produced works of imaginative literature that are truly remarkable in their harmonious blending of cultural affirmation and undoctrinaire but politically-revolutionary concepts.

An extraordinary example of this phenomenon is Leslie Silko's *Ceremony,* a 1978 novel by a woman who grew up on the Laguna Pueblo Reservation in New Mexico. In my judgment, this book represents not only a genuine advance in the evolution of Native American literature, but it is precisely the kind of work that those of us devoted to studying the culture of "internal colonialism" ought to point to as exemplary of what ought to inspire creative practice in the 1980s. The book has, of course, already been the subject of several essays that have emphasized its remarkable technical innovations and its cultural derivation from Native American oral tradition. . . .

Silko has in this area transcended all hitherto known thematic boundaries in Native American fiction. This is done through the startling perspective she brings to bear on the way in which capitalism objectively unites people of color through its domestic violence and international wars. . . .

Ceremony is a first novel and not without certain flaws and limitations. Silko may have to some degree sacrificed the psychological realism of some of her characters to the daring esthetic achievements of her fresh, dramatic language and her provocative flashbacks, juxtapositions, and transitions; a few of her characters may seem to be contrived to exhibit different modes of assimilation to or resistance against the dominant culture. Sometimes they are one-dimensional—either replete with self-hatred or else mystically sensual and bound to nature.

Nevertheless, I find Silko unequaled in the way she has used craft and imagination to provide a longer-range perspective for the kinds of sentiments expressed by rebellious youth of the 1960s and 1970s. I sense that she is trying to transfer the political themes of anti-imperialism and Third World solidarity characteristic of the Vietnam era back to the less-questioned World War II era, in order to suggest that similar mechanisms of racism and economic exploitation are involved in *all* wars waged by the United States. In summary, *Ceremony* is the culmination of what was best in the politico-cultural rebellion of the 1960s and 1970s. On the one hand, it offers profound testimony to the creative resources of the Native American cultural tradition. On the other hand, Silko's political intuition and insight surpass other writers who fail to see that American imperialism's crimes against people of color are not simply aberrations that can be reformed out of existence but that they inhere in the character of the social structure itself.

Alan Wald. *MELUS*. 8:1, 1981, pp. 23–24, 26

Conventionally, modern writers have toyed with a dichotomy between an objective and apparent reality and illusion, a false subjective reflection of that objective reality. Many modern and contemporary writers explore the place of illusion in our lives; some even conclude illusion, that subjective rendering of objective reality, is all that is human, all we can truly call our own. John Barth and more recent avant-garde fiction writers like [Ron] Sukenick and [Ishmael] Reed defy the notion that fiction is made of the illusionary end of the spectrum, i.e., this character did not exist, this action never happened. These writers claim their stories have a superior reality almost on a mythic scale where the so-called boundaries that separate the world of the story from the world of objective reality are eradicated. As Sukenick says, "This isn't a story, man; this is life." Leslie Silko as a contemporary writer and a Laguna brings a new perception to the effort to topple those boundaries, or rather an old one, older than American Literature. Her short fiction and her novel *Ceremony* are illuminated by the assumption that the story has a greater, truer reality than the objective reality of the world around us. In the story reality, the seeming simplicity and reality of objective actions are reinterpreted and woven into a larger scheme through which the actions take on a new and deeper meaning and their place in a mythic pattern emerges. The characters and the readers must believe as much as the author that the world exists in story which gives objective reality its meaning, or they are lost. Although the story may be stretched over eons, although it may move slowly and our understanding of it come only with great difficulty, we can understand it; we can enter into the story reality. Despite the hardships and the violent wrenchings of perspective required to do this, the attempt is necessary because it is only through entry into the story reality that each character is given his/her identity and perhaps ultimately so are we, the readers. . . .

However, when we put the book down, another important question can be asked. Has the reader understood the story? Has he entered the story reality? If the reader has, then he has an identity determined by the story either as a victim, a manipulator, or one of the aware people who must unite to defeat the destroyers. Let's hope we can all get the ending right.

It may be commonplace to say that Silko's work attempts to introduce dimensions of oral literature into written literature, and seeks a unification of the two in a new reality or a better explanation of the ordinary one, but her work at once stands out from modern fiction because of it and blends with it.

Jim Ruppert. Journal of Ethnic Studies. 9,
1981, pp. 53, 56

When Leslie Marmon Silko published *Ceremony* in 1977, the critical reaction was good. The book was praised in the *New York Review of Books* and in other established critical publications. But, something of even greater significance happened for those interested in Southwestern literature and American Indian literature. A novel came into existence that challenged readers, Indian and White, to expand and merge their cultural frameworks. The novel was, at once, grounded in Indian tradition and informed by contemporary American fiction. While remaining a popular novel taught in many classes, it continues to open up fresh insights into fiction and culture, for it is not only a novel that presents a philosophical and cultural viewpoint, but a novel that teaches us how to read it and how to understand its special narrative structures. Through its formal and stylistic elements, it fuses story and reality to define an identity for its protagonist and the reader.

Perhaps the most immediate way the reader sees its uniqueness is in its form. *Ceremony* merges what we would call poetry and prose. Silko says that ideally these sections should be heard, not read, so that they approximate the position of a listener before the storyteller. The stories or myths told in the poems are broken up and placed periodically throughout the text, so that the completion of the poem stories and the prose narrative converge at the end. It would seem that Silko wants us to hear a different voice in the poetry, while still forcing the reader to acknowledge a unity of purpose underneath this apparent formal diversity. This discourse strategy is mirrored variously throughout the novel and is ultimately a reflection of the epistemological unity of Laguna narrative esthetic and world view.

James Ruppert. Arizona Quarterly. 44:1,
Spring, 1988, pp. 78–79

In *Ceremony,* Leslie Silko brilliantly crosses racial styles of humor in order to cure the foolish delusions readers may have, if we think we are superior to Indians or inferior to whites, or perhaps superior to whites or inferior to Indians. Silko plays off affectionate Pueblo humor against the black humor so prominent in twentieth-century white culture. This comic strategy has the end-result of opening our eyes to our general foolishness, and also to the possibility of combining the merits of all races. Joseph Campbell wrote in *The Inner Reaches of Outer Space* of the change in mythologies away from the local and tribal toward a mythology that will arise from "this unified earth as of one harmonious being." *Ceremony* is a work that changes local mythologies in that more inclusive spirit.

Silko is the right person to have written this book. She herself is a mixed-blood, and her experience has evidently given her access not only to a variety of problems, but also to a variety of styles of clowning and joking. Although Elaine Jahner has mentioned the presence of jokes in the novel, I have known whites to read *Ceremony* as not comical at any point. Probably their power of recognition had been switched off by "the picture of the humorless Indian . . . so common in so much of the literature, in so many of the film and television depictions of Native Americans." . . .

Tayo's difficulty is grave, yet Silko jokes about it frequently. The belief among whites that Indians never laugh is contradicted continually by the sounds of Indians responding to subtle in-jokes or to a corrective kind of teasing crystallized in the work of ritual clowns. . . .

Whites with some appreciation for Indian culture sometimes express a surprising certitude that "this once great culture is being lost or replaced by an Anglo culture that does not have the same respect for nature . . . and is in some ways morally inferior to it." The celestial laughter Silko calls forth by her *Ceremony* shows that Indian civilization is living and has the potential to transform anglo culture.

Elizabeth N. Evasdaughter. *MELUS.* 15:1,
1988, pp. 83–84, 94

Not surprisingly, Silko's real subject involves her Pueblo heritage, but it is not limited to that. What really seems to interest and concern her is the survival of that heritage in the twentieth-century American world that surrounds and contains that heritage in usually destructive and often mindless— if not malicious—ways. . . .

Silko's novel, *Ceremony,* is in no sense a nostalgic celebration of the "old ways," though some of its characters are governed by such feelings. Like many first-rate novels, it questions not only the modern world but the old ways themselves in such a manner that her Pueblo heritage becomes a highly dramatic aspect of the book as a whole, partly because she doesn't really know (until she has finished writing this book) what the answers to the questions are: "Do the old ways have any meaning for today's Pueblo Indian? Are the traditions that have somehow managed to survive flexible and resilient enough not only to help us adapt to and live in the modern world but also to illuminate that same world in meaningful ways? In short, can the Lagunas survive as a community, as a people, in an alien and often hostile world?" . . .

Silko's *Ceremony* is not by any standard a modernist novel at first glance, nor is it the traditional storytelling that goes on in so much of her next book, *Storyteller.* She does make use of techniques developed in the twentieth-century novel—near stream-of-consciousness writing at times, for instance, where appropriate. And she does not use ordinary chapter breaks, largely because the narrative being developed is not straight-line conventionalized plotting. The significant action of *Ceremony* happens in the mind of the protagonist and consists of his affirming himself and establishing his identity. Breaks in the story line and transitions are effected by using mostly English versions of traditional Laguna poems, which themselves take on ever greater importance as the novel develops. In many ways, especially thematic, it resembles the near-contemporary novel, *One Flew over the Cuckoo's Nest,* the protagonist of which, like Tayo in *Ceremony,* is victimized by the machinery of a society he neither accepts nor understands—on one level, but only too well on a deeper experiential level.

C. W. Truesdale. *North Dakota Quarterly.*
59, 1991, p. 205–6

SILVA, CLARA (URUGUAY) 1908–76

When *La caballera oscura* (The dark horsewoman) appeared in 1945, there also appeared—especially for a first book of such maturity—a serious poetic voice, passionate and intense, that sang of great themes, bringing together a somber drama with a feverish lyricism. Poems based in substantive pain—life, love, death, time, eternity, nothingness—went together in solemn pace, like that of a statue, and were clad in verbal splendors with a personal tone all the poet's own.

This same serious voice now tells us its moving *Memoria de la nada* (Memory of nothingness), which is almost a continuation of the other book, connected by their essential themes and expressive forms.

This voice—in which every sensitive reader recognizes the great authenticity, the rare fidelity to herself of a woman as wrapped up in her work as a mother with her child—is raised here, as in *La caballera oscura,* singing the narrative of life's emptiness. The theme, the whole subject matter take priority in the slow rhythmic development; we hear a full, firm pulse, cut by partial breaks in the rhythm. . . .

Clara Silva, romantic, instinctive, intuitive, gives us the exaltation of her "I." But this I that she sings, she sings in the personal and the generic, she sings in its narrowness the narrowness of a species that is the victim of time and is disinherited, without faith or justifying certitude.

Born of a deep love for life and the world, of a bedazzlement that is not extinguished before terror, this *Memoria de la nada* unwinds like a border between light and shade and phosphorescence and sumptuous colors: white, black, golds, reds, green, blue. Ice, mirrors, ash return from nothingness to nothingness. (1949)

Isabel Gilbert de Pereda. *Escritura.* 7, 1969,
pp. 101–2, 104

The thirty sonnets in *Los delirios* (Deliriums) represent a double renovation within Clara Silva's poetic work. On the one hand, the passage from more or less free verse to the sonnet, on the other, thematic change that divides this book into two major subjects not hitherto gone into in depth in her lyrics: physical passion and the problem of God.

If the sonnet form was unexpected in this body of poetry, the same does not hold true for these themes, which were adumbrated in her earlier work, although only touched on or suggested. The figure that her books present evolves and follows its star without altering its essential lines: obstinate intensity, exasperated review of the self, tremendous egocentrism that, as well as being the center and the strength of communication, is one of its greatest obstacles.

In any case, God is the novelty, the novelty sometimes in accord with the rest of the work and in accord with that recurrent process in women's poetry that brings the most intense creatures—among us, Juana and Esther de Caceres—to religious poetry. Sometimes it is the same process that gets male poets in over their heads in metaphysical morasses.

Considered from a purely literary point of view, the change looks like a loss. The introduction of an interlocutor undoubtedly increases the poems' tension. But at the same time it limits, trivializes, reduces to human terms the conflict that gave both its depth and its title to her previous volume, *Memoria de la nada* (1948) (Memory of nothingness).

It is this God, however, that has to be attacked from all sides by arguments that are sometimes commonplace, sometimes highly original, with reproaches, name-calling, sometimes with submission, almost always as from one equal to another.

It could be called a mystical poetry.

Idea Vilariño. *Marcha.* 778, 1958, p. 22

[Silva is a w]ell-known author of poetry in Uruguay. Lesser known are her novels published later in life, which express the existential anguish of a Latin American woman caught in the dichotomy of the soul versus the body. Most of her novels explore the social and psychological traps that Latin American women suffer. Her techniques are stream-of-consciousness and interior monologues. There is no doubt that she is very original in her prose.

Lucía Fox-Lockert. In Diane E. Marting, ed. *Women Writers of Spanish America* (Westport, Connecticut: Greenwood Press, 1986), p. 348

Clara Silva presents sexual problems and the lack of communication between man and woman. Her protagonists are disgusted by the sex act and are full of anguish because they are searching for something more, something transcendent that does not come to them with or because of men.

The title of her book, *El alma y los perros,* shows the distance that exists between the soul *(alma),* representing woman, and the dogs *(perros),* representing man, dogs with the dominant animal instinct. . . .

La sobreviviente is a novel that presents the world as it is seen by the lone protagonist, Laura Medina, a young Latin American girl who passes through some of the great cities of the world: Florence, Paris, and a Latin American capital, possibly Montevideo, in the 1940s. At twenty, her purpose in life is to seek her vital relationships with the people and things that surround her. Without a normal plot, the novel presents chapters with titles such as "The Room as Witness," "Morning," "Purple," "The Body," "I Am Laura Medina," "A Boy of Solids," "Separation," and "City." The protagonist vacillates between God and nothing, sensuality and spirituality, poverty and wealth, love and indifference, masculinity and femininity. Existential problems fill the novel and cause the protagonist to abandon her position as spectator and become a participant in the anonymous, collective unit. This requires her to compromise herself, submerge, unite herself with the whole, the masses. The techniques used are subliminal and two constant literary devices are the stream of consciousness and the interior monologue.

Lucía Fox-Lockert. *Women Novelists of Spain and Spanish America* (Metuchen, New Jersey: Scarecrow, 1979), pp. 16–17, 198

SINCLAIR, MAY (GREAT BRITAIN) 1865–1946

A novel has recently been published—*The Helpmate,* by Miss May Sinclair—which appears to fall exactly into the category of those works in which the Edinburgh Reviewer traces most clearly the blight of the Convention. It is a novel, that is to say—written by an author whose performance, brilliant though it be, falls in some respects short of its promise—a novel which, though abounding in cleverness, must for various reasons be held to have missed a success very nearly attained, must on the whole be regarded as a brilliant failure. . . .

Now I will venture to say that this book, for all its cleverness, does not deserve the high praise it has received nor the kind of praise it has received. And I strongly suspect that most of the reviewers in the leading newspapers know that it does not. I seem to trace in all these reviews the restraining finger-prints of a Convention—not the British Convention. Here and there a bold spirit dares to find the story dull, improbable, irritating—but I observe in almost all these reviews a curious coincidence: the reviewers concentrate on the very dull and not a little improbable figure of the respectable wife, while her far more interesting and more lifelike husband is left severely alone, save for a few approving allusions that might have been dictated by the novelist: "dignified indulgence," "loving mildness," "unfailing tenderness," and the like.

Lady Eleanor Cecil. Living Age. September
21, 1907, pp. 579, 588

Miss May Sinclair has not failed to write an interesting book on Charlotte, Emily, and Anne Brontë [*The Brontë Sisters*]. How could she? After covering all the ground from Mrs. Gaskell to the Abbé Dimnet, she has remained herself; and this volume is the story of her experiences among the Brontës and their critics, written for those who are as well up in the matter as herself, but still eager to exchange opinions. It is part of the justification for books that they facilitate such exchange of opinions; yet to us it seems not wholly necessary that every stage in their formation should be perpetuated in print. Miss Sinclair's book is too long. She quotes a great number of Emily Brontë's verses in a manner more suited to a newspaper discussion. She should have quoted much more to arrest the ignoramus; far less would have been sufficient for the devotee. The book has only reached a half-way stage to finality.

Evidently Miss Sinclair set to work with some excitement, and that is well; but she must have continued when the excitement had abated, and not waited long enough for after-thoughts. She is too often unsettled without being strongly moved, tired without being calm. Not but what she has put good things into every part of the book, and more than good things. . . . But the whole is an exercise, not an achievement. It is rather the expression of a point of view than really individual. We feel that Miss Sinclair has sacrificed much to a desire to be impressive.

The Athenaeum. July 13, 1912, p. 33

Miss Sinclair's work is quite good enough to stand on its own merits without any apologia. She has undoubted power and sincerity. She is intensely sensitive, and is especially apt in dealing with the subtle emotions and fine-drawn distinctions, varying shades of light and color. It would be absurd to pretend that the eight stories which make up this volume [*The Judgment of Eve*] are

Miss Sinclair's best work. All are readable, but from the standpoint of the author's high achievement several are negligible.

Saturday Review (London). April 25, 1914,
pp. 542–43

It would be hard to find a better illustration of the gulf that divides Georgian from mid-Victorian fiction than that which is furnished by Miss Sinclair's choice of a hero *[Tasker Jevons]*. The heroes of fifty or sixty years ago were generally of the Admirable Crichton type: handsome, athletic, and distinguished. They took Double Firsts, played in the University Eleven, and rowed in the University Eight. James Tasker Jevons did none of these things. He had no social or educational advantages; he was undersized, and was only redeemed from physical vulgarity by the freakish irregularity of his features and his fine eyes. . . . But he was a genius, and he knew it; he had mapped out his career in advance and carried out his plans to the letter. . . . Miss Sinclair has given us a brilliantly written and extremely interesting book with a new type of hero, for whom, if we cannot love him, we come in the long run to entertain a feeling of intermittent affection.

Spectator. April 15, 1916, p. 504

In *The Divine Fire* . . . Miss Sinclair gave no indication of her dissatisfaction with the traditional method of novel-writing; she did no more in that book than give her readers a glimpse of under-currents. Her other novels, arresting pieces of work, were the well-told stories of the competent craftsman. *The Three Sisters, The Combined Maze, The Tree of Heaven,* were good in matter and in manner. . . . Miss Sinclair was one of a golden fellowship, but until she wrote *Mary Olivier* she did not stand out from among them as definitely critical of tradition.

Dissatisfaction, however, was in the air. A number of writers, weary of the iterated tale, of the melange of sentimentality, convention, faked incident and false psychology known as the popular novel, were making experiments of one sort and another; and when Miss Sinclair published *Mary Olivier,* she ranged herself definitely with the pioneers. Her position as a writer who has had the courage to look at life from an individual standpoint will be strengthened by her forthcoming book. In *The Romantic* she uses the direct method, presenting her story through the mind of one of the characters. This method is also employed by others of the group to which she belongs, for instance, Dorothy Richardson; but to say that Miss Sinclair derives from this writer would be doing her less than justice. For one thing, Miss Sinclair was experimenting with this method before Miss Richardson began to write, and for another their work has nothing else in common. Miss Richardson's is monumental. Having chosen a dumping-ground she is pouring on to it novel-load after novel-load of heterogeneous objects, and by so doing is raising an immense, an almost Cyclopean, mound. Miss Sinclair, on the contrary, is selective. She produces an effect of lightning, of concentrated seeing, of extraordinary and sudden brilliancy, and this effect is particularly apparent in her presentation of John Roden Conway in *The Romantic*. I do not know of any piece of writing more subtly forcible than the lifting of veil after veil from the man's personality until the creature stands revealed in pitiable nakedness. Miss Sinclair presents him to us, and the reader is left to find the pity of humanity for a soul so marred, to murmur in fear and trembling, "Can such things be?" and to acknowledge unwillingly, sorrowfully, that they are.

C. A. Dawson-Scott. *Bookman.* November, 1920, p. 248

Like *Mr. Waddington of Wyck,* Miss Sinclair's new book [*Life and Death of Harriet Frean*] is a study of the psychopathology of Peter Pan. Neither Mr. Waddington nor Miss Frean ever grew up. In the earlier book it takes the form of conceited selfishness. In the latter it takes the form of conceited unselfishness. And since we live in a post-Butler world, it is of course the unselfishness which causes the most unhappiness. . . .

The old army of psychological novelists, with Henry James at their head, left no act of their characters without a clear and conscious cause for it, and thereby justly deserved to be called academic. For life isn't like that. The new army, with Miss Sinclair not to be far from the van, are apt to leave no act without a clear cause for it in the subconsciousness. This novel in consequence resembles an X-ray photograph—the facts are there but not the likeness.

Miss Sinclair's skill is astounding, her brilliance never failing, but she writes a priori. She is an academic artist in the truest and least insulting sense.

Raymond Mortimer. *Dial.* May, 1922, pp. 531, 534

[May Sinclair] is too rebellious to see quite straight as an artist. *Anne Severn and the Fieldings* is, in any case, not one of Miss Sinclair's best books because, although it contains the essential truth about all its characters, it is not true enough to the appearances of the world. The myth she has designed to express her discovery hardly holds together. There is reality in the theme of Jerrold, the man who is everything that is noble and fine, but who is evasive and turns his back on unpleasantness. . . . But the circumstances of the book are so casually imagined that the mind is skeptical. . . . But more damaging to the effect of *Anne Severn and the Fieldings* than . . . mechanical defects is Miss Sinclair's reaction against the fluffy, feminine ideal. . . . Anne Severn is her author's declaration that a woman can be passionate and sexual and yet a cool and dignified human being. She is rather more that than she is a person. She has something of the almost priggish open-airiness and self-reliance that the early pioneers of the higher education of women strove to inculcate in their pupils. She interrupts the story to say "Yea" to a "Nay" that was uttered in controversy outside it. When she intervenes in the processes of the tractor . . . there is a surface on the description of her action, a glossy surface such as one sees on those big advertisements that hang in railway stations, which proceeds from Miss Sinclair's consciousness that many people have alleged from time to time that the things that women do with levers may be mysterious but are not efficient. It is this slight disingenuousness in the conception of the principal character that makes the book distinctly less impressive than Miss Sinclair's novels usually are. For it is primarily a novel about passion; and when one is shown Anne consumed by passion, the very power of her creator makes us shocked and incredulous. This is the real thing; but how startling it is that Anne should have felt it. One feels as a headmistress might if she discovered that the head prefect was engaged in an ardent love affair. This is not to say that Miss Sinclair is not a gifted and delightful artist. She has shown herself that in other volumes; she shows herself that here, in the description of the peace of Wyck on the Cotswolds, and in the characterization of the Fieldings. But perhaps just because here is a romantic theme, that might well involve its writer in adherence to the romantic conception of women, she has forfeited one tiny part of her artistry.

Rebecca West. *The New Statesman.*
December 2, 1922, pp. 270–72

The unifying factor in the work of May Sinclair is its humanity. The emotions are controlled by the intelligence, but ever and again we find them claiming their inalienable rights, and it is then that the author produces her finest work. This is not sentimental, but there is about it a naked truthfulness quite free from that conventional rhetoric which is the evil tradition of most writers in dealing with emotions.

Nowhere have I found more convincing truth than in *Mary Olivier.* This book is undoubtedly the toughest, the most compact of Miss Sinclair's works. It is built of even, well-laid bricks, bound together by a mortar which is consistently good in quality. The whole is a harmonious composition. *The Three Sisters* is Miss Sinclair's masterpiece, but *Mary Olivier,* equally among her works and among the best literary productions of the last few years, holds a special position. It is the model of modern romance, and is as far removed from the old convention as are the novels of Dorothy Richardson and James Joyce, except where it shows too great a respect for certain dead institutions or laughable professions of faith. But this defect is its sole weakness, and is weakness, moreover, only to the philosopher or anarchist. In avoiding cynicism, the author is sometimes betrayed into the use of ancient currencies. In any case, she is the least conventional of women writers.

The form of *Mary Olivier* is new; it is an experiment—a sudden intellectual gesture of the author. This experiment is a complete success. Besides being solid and compact, the book contains a quick succession of pictures. One gets the impression of an album of highly finished engravings, filled with useful details, well grouped, and not interfering one with another. Moreover—and this is most remarkable considering the complete revolution in Miss Sinclair's style—these pictures have her old perfection of finish.

Jean de Bosschère. *Yale Review.* October, 1924, pp. 82–83

Miss Sinclair's *The Dark Night* is the novel in verse (free of a kind) of an accomplished novelist who has already expressed herself again and again in her natural medium, and is now trying an experiment in a medium not naturally her own. The flavor of her poem is what might be known as *modern,* though the word has a shifting value, and perhaps a more fitting expression is *up to date. . . .*

Miss Sinclair . . . has, as her primary consideration, a story to tell. Her imagination moves in terms of personality, reaction, plot, the interplay of character upon character. *The Dark Night* is conceived primarily as a story, and could have been told, without any loss of interest, in the usual manner of the novel. Most readers will be instinctively disposed to judge it by the standards of criticism usually applied to the superior novel. Her motive, therefore, in substituting free verse for her excellent prose is open to conjecture.

Harold Monro. *Criterion.* April, 1925, p. 145

Poetry and metaphysics were her first lines of activity. She produced books of verse in 1887 and 1890, wrote reviews and articles for philosophical journals, and came only after some years to the art of fiction. Her first short story was published in 1895, and her first novel, *Audrey Craven,* the following year. It showed no very clear signs of genius; and neither did its two successors. The first novel which gave her the beginning of a reputation was *The Divine Fire.* She was a realist and at first tended to show the drabness and futility of life rather than the brighter aspects. *The Creators, The Life and Death of Harriet Frean, The Flaw in the Crystal,* and various short stories helped to consolidate a reputation that became so high that in 1916 William Lyon Phelps called her "the foremost living writer among English-speaking women." . . .

Her later novels were, perhaps, more finely contrived, surer in delineation, more subtle in character drawing, than anything she had done before. The short book, *A Cure of Souls,* is a delicious, mildly ironical portrait of a lethargic, comfort-loving rector, which perhaps shows Miss Sinclair at her best. It is complete, rounded, and humorous.

The Times (London). November 15, 1946, p. 7

A student of psychology and philosophy—it was she who, reviewing *Pilgrimage* in 1918, first borrowed the term "stream of consciousness" from William James—she must have been among the earliest English novelists to have been aware of the work of Freud. Neither *Mary Olivier: A Life* nor *The Life and Death of Harriet Frean* could have been written without a knowledge of psychoanalysis. Both describe the upbringing of young women during the second half of the Victorian age. The general attitude towards the age, at any rate as seen in the middle-class family, is akin to Samuel Butler's in *The Way of All Flesh,* though the modern reader may also see in them foreshadowings of the matter, though not the manner, of the fiction of Ivy Compton-Burnett.

Especially interesting now is May Sinclair's technique. Throughout the novel we are placed as it were in Mary's consciousness, but there is no stream-of-consciousness as such. Her thoughts are reported for the most part in *oratio obliqua,* usually in the second person. . . . At the same time, though not going anywhere as far as Joyce in *Portrait of the Artist,* May Sinclair very ably renders the increasing complexity of the mind from the simple terms of childhood.

> Walter Allen. *The Modern Novel in Britain
> and the United States* (New York: Dutton,
> 1964), pp. 15–16

Although at one time the name of May Sinclair . . . was linked with that of Dorothy Richardson as an innovator in the stream-of-consciousness mode, her name is now unfamiliar even to serious students of English literature. She was not one of the giants of modern literature, surely not a Joyce or a Woolf, nor was she a true inventor of fictional forms, like Dorothy Richardson. Instead, she wrote competent novels about many subjects during a long and successful career, and it is as a popularizer of themes and techniques which belonged to the avant-garde that she maintains her interest and usefulness for this study of the feminine consciousness.

Her novels are carefully constructed, clearly written, and contain only that amount of technical innovation which her readers could easily handle (and think of themselves as "modern" at the same time). She worked into her books concepts from psychology which were new and disturbing to those readers. She used Freudian concepts before any other English novelist, and notions such as repression, suppression, dream symbolism, and the like fill her novels. In addition, she was a serious scholar widely read in biology, psychology, and philosophy and concerned with such social questions as the war in Europe and feminism.

As a student of literature she produced criticism of considerable sensitivity and awareness, and she had the ability to put what she had learned in other fields immediately into a fictional form. The very term "stream of consciousness" belongs to May Sinclair. Actually William James used it first in discussing the workings of the mind, but she was the first to apply it to the content of a work of fiction—to give it a literary connotation.

> Sydney Janet Kaplan. *The Feminine
> Consciousness in Modern British Novels*
> (Urbana: University of Illinois Press, 1975),
> pp. 47–48

Sinclair's 1918 reference to Miriam Henderson's "stream of consciousness going on and on" in the early volumes of *Pilgrimage* . . . did not please Richardson . . . but the metaphor, borrowed from William James, has become commonplace in the vocabulary of literary criticism. Sinclair, a student of philosophy who published two books on the subject (*A Defense of Idealism,* 1917; *The New Idealism,* 1922), recognized the imprecision of the term. *Stream,* on one hand, connotes unity and continuity and suggests an active, creative self; on the other hand, it evokes multiplicity and change and a view of the self as a passive receiver of impressions. Richardson objected to the latter connotation, which she thought predominated. . . .

Probably because she too emphasized a unified, active self, Sinclair abandoned the term except as part of her characterization of a novelist in *Far End* (1926). His name, Christopher Vivart, suggests the vivid nature of his art, and he describes his experiment as "presentation, not representation." He presents only "a stream of consciousness, going on and on: it's life itself going on and on." . . .

Sinclair's own similar experiment, a female *Bildungsroman* entitled *Mary Olivier,* appeared in 1919. Often compared to *Pilgrimage, Mary Olivier* is the primary focus of the recent critics who discuss Sinclair's work (e.g., Kaplan). Like Richardson, Sinclair in *Mary Olivier* tries to present quotidian reality as directly as possible. In the face of many obstacles, including a mother with very traditional notions about woman's role, the main character struggles to develop her intellectual and artistic potential. Although Sinclair called this novel her "favorite" and "best book" . . . she did not consistently immerse herself in the consciousness of a single character in subsequent novels. Nor did she define her choices about point of view or her punctuation as "feminine," as Richardson did. Yet Sinclair had an abiding interest in the suffrage movement and its implications for women's roles in society . . . and in 1912 she wrote a pamphlet called *Feminism* for the Women Writer's Suffrage League. . . .

In her fiction . . . Sinclair recreates the thrust and parry of this period of rapid change in which editors and critics attack and defend artistic innovations with equal conviction. In "The Return" (1921), for example, reviewers disagree about a free-verse poet whose aims are very like those of the imagists, but the poet's own family dismisses him totally as incompetent and obscure. In *The Allinghams* (1927) one reviewer disparages Stephen Allingham's "Epithalamion" as inept, irritating, and eccentric and refuses to call poems such barbaric works that defy all poetic traditions. Another critic, however, insists that Allingham has substituted subtle for marked rhythms and simplicity for ornamentation.

In all these cases, actual and fictional, Sinclair closely associates aesthetic innovation with the metaphysical position she calls the "new idealism." Rejecting traditional linguistic and literary structures and themes is parallel, in philosophical discussion, to stripping away the abstract ideas about reality associated with traditional idealism. Directly presenting reality in such a way that manner cannot be separated from matter parallels apprehending ultimate reality, in a fresh and immediate way, through the temporal world.

> Diane Gillespie. In Bonnie Kime Scott, ed.
> *The Gender of Modernism* (Bloomington:
> Indiana University Press, 1990), pp. 436–40

SITWELL, EDITH (GREAT BRITAIN) 1887–1964

Whatever may ultimately be said of the permanent value of their work, few will deny that, while they [the Sitwells] were fighting for new values, they did pull down the Gates of Gaza, perfectly willing to break their own heads along with those of the Philistines. . . . in some sort they have won now, the gates are down, and the Philistines are at their oldest and most dangerous trick of attempting to persuade themselves (and the Sitwells) that they were on the side of the rebels all the time, and, indeed, that there was never any rebellion at all. . . . The Sitwells have not done more than prove that they have a vision, and they have not yet imposed it on their own minds. They are all young, and are all developing. . . . As a family and as individuals they have invented a new idiom, but if they do not now adapt it to express a new truth it will become a dead invention in their own hands.

> *Saturday Review* (London). March 26, 1927,
> p. 474

A summarized view, then, of the prolific fifteen or sixteen years of her activity suggest that she is no pioneer anarch building on tradition, but a romantic compelled by time-tyranny to be unromantic; that she is a verse-writer of talent (which may be called the feminine of genius); that she has had experiences varying from the valueless to the slightly valuable, but that on few occasions only has she succeeded in organizing them; that her limited class of experience has produced poems little more varied than the uprights of a circular railing and damaged by an unreasonable excess of irrationality.

> Geoffrey Grigson. *The Bookman* (London).
> August, 1931, p. 245

Her book [*The English Eccentrics*] is a friendly excursion rather than a guide, and fuller of acknowledgments than of references. The lesson to be drawn from it—if so heavy a draft as a lesson be required—is that eccentricity ranks as a national asset, and that so long as it is respected there is some hope that our country will not go mad as a whole. . . . Those of us who assume (perhaps wrongly) that we are sane, can learn from her pages the lesson most necessary

for a sane man; the need of a tolerance which is touched by pity but untouched by contempt.

E. M. Forster. *Spectator.* May 19, 1933,

p. 716

Miss Sitwell . . . has done her pioneering, and we are now able to regard her
work, not as controversy, but as poetry. The fact remains that she was one
of the writers who bridged the gap between the sterile years of the early war
and the post-war years of excited experiment; that she helped to keep the
interest in poetry alive when it was near extinction. . . .

Society has declared itself the modern Vanity Fair. The English countryside has proved bucolic beyond endurance. In the present there seems no
haven for this acute and irritable mind; there remains the past. And in the
past she finds the elegance, the grace, the soft civilized beauty which she
vainly seeks in the present. It is to her own childhood that she turns for
solace. . . . And in *The Sleeping Beauty* (1924) and *Troy Park* (1925) she
looks back to the dreaming summers of youth. . . . The "Troy Park" of the
collected edition is almost entirely autobiographical. . . . Within those walls
it is always summer. . . . She has never really left Troy Park; or, if from time
to time she has left it, the brutality and treachery without drove her hastily
back. So, living herself within the veil of a dream, the dream which was her
own childhood, she looks out at the external world and sees that, too, as a
dream. Her view of life remains in essence that of a child, a sensitive child
seeing everything in terms of its own private world. . . . Miss Sitwell has
retained a child's imagination while acquiring an adult's power of voluptuous
expression. . . . She has not merely recreated, she has created a world. . . .
In her verse the discords which torment her as a person suffer metamorphosis; they become poetry. And so for once we really are confronted with the
romantic poetry of escape.

Dilys Powell. *Descent from Parnassus* (New
York: Macmillan, 1934), pp. xiii, 111–12,
127–34

One cannot think of her in any other age or country. She has transformed
with her metrical virtuosity traditional meters reborn not to be read but
spoken, exaggerating metaphors into mythology, carrying them from poem
to poem, compelling us to go backward to some first usage for the birth of
the myth. . . . Nature appears before us in a hashish-eater's dream. This
dream is double; in its first half, through separate metaphor, through mythology, she creates, amid crowds and scenery that suggest the Russian Ballet
and Aubrey Beardsley's final phases a perpetual metamorphosis that seems
an elegant, artificial childhood; in the other half, driven by a necessity of
contrast, a nightmare vision like that of Webster, of the emblems of mortality.

William Butler Yeats. Preface to *Oxford
Book of Modern Verse* (Oxford: Oxford
University Press, 1936), pp. xviii-xix

With the appearance of *Street Songs* and *Green Song,* those who cared for poetry recognized a true poetic and prophetic cry which had not been heard in England since the death of Yeats. This was not merely exquisite poetry: it was great poetry; we felt once more the excitement of having amongst us a poet who could give us back our sight and our belief in the human heart, a poet on Shelley's definition.

Throughout Miss Sitwell's poetry a Swinburnian element persists. We are conscious of it in her elaborate technique, in her uncanny sensibility to the texture of language; and also, I dare say, in an occasional diffuseness, and in a feeling that the central core of her meaning is veiled in mist, and will dissolve if we approach it too closely. Miss Sitwell herself has accepted this kinship with Swinburne. . . . [Her] appreciation of Swinburne's verbal mastery is one of the most illuminating of all her critical studies, and one of the most personal. Many young people adored Swinburne in the early years of this century, but few mature poets would have admitted to an equal admiration in 1932.

After *Gold Coast Customs,* it is not surprising to find that Miss Sitwell wrote no poetry for many years. She was re-creating her spirit, seeking a belief or a vision which would enable her to transcend the evil and misery in the world; and during these years, evil was moving towards its catastrophe. We must suppose that much of her time was passed in reading, for these are the years of her anthologies of poetry with their critical introductions. And here I may say in parentheses that these introductions seem to me, with their self-imposed limits, to be among the most valuable pieces of modern criticism, and a merciful relief from that sheep in wolf's clothing, Taine's English Literature in a new disguise, the sociological criticism of Marxism. It is true that they endow the reader with a very subtle ear and demand from him very strict attention; and few readers, perhaps, can have followed Miss Sitwell in her discrimination of every nuance of sound. But anyone who has attempted to do so, must have had his capacity for enjoying poetry increased beyond measure; and what more can we ask of criticism?

In spite of Swinburnian and symbolist characteristics, it is clear from her latest poems that Miss Sitwell's place in English literature is with the religious poets of the seventeenth century. Again and again the audacity of her sensuous images reminds us of Crashaw; she has Traherne's rapture at created things, and Vaughan's sense of eternity. . . . Miss Sitwell is essentially a religious poet; that is to say, she has experienced imaginatively, not merely intellectually, the evil and misery of the world and has overcome that experience by the conviction—the full, imaginative conviction—that all creation is under the Divine Love.

Kenneth Clark. In J. G. Villa, ed.
Celebration for Edith Sitwell (New York:
New Directions, 1948), pp. 56–59, 66

With the publication of *Street Songs* in 1942 and *Green Song* in 1944 Miss Sitwell has not only won an almost unique place for herself among the poets of this war but abundantly fulfilled the highest hopes which her admirers have had of her. This great flowering of her genius is her reward for years of devoted and patient labor at her art. From her first beginnings she possessed an instinctive sense for the true essence of poetry and a sensibility so fine and delicate that it can detect all the subtle echoes and associations which float around the sounds of human speech. She set herself a hard task when she made up her mind to restore to English poetry the richness of texture which had been largely lost in the Edwardian and Georgian epochs. For this reason much of her early work was experimental. . . . Of this preparatory work, in many ways so brilliant and so fascinating, she is herself a stern critic. When she published her *Collected Poems* in 1930, she omitted many pieces that others would wish to be included. . . . Yet even in this remarkable volume she had not found the full range of her gifts. Though *The Sleeping Beauty* showed of what enchanting fancy and haunting melody she was capable and *Gold Coast Customs* showed what tragic power and prophetical fury were hers, it was not until the Second World War that she fused all her different gifts into a single kind of poetry and combined in noble harmony her delicate fancy, her uncommon visual sense, her tender sympathy, her heroic courage in the face of a shattered world and her deep religious trust in the ultimate goodness of life. . . .

The imagery of rain is developed with enormous power in "Still Falls the Rain," which has claims to be the most profound and most moving poem yet written in English about the war. It was inspired by the air–raids of 1940, but it has nothing transitory or merely contemporary about it. It is an intense, highly imaginative and tragic poem on the sufferings of man. . . . [T]he destruction wrought by the air–raids is transformed into an example of man's wickedness and punishment and redemption. He brings his own sufferings upon himself, but through them he may be redeemed. So Miss Sitwell passes beyond the horror of the present moment to a vision of its significance in the spiritual history of man and through her compassion for him finds a ray of hope for his future.

This assertion of positive values in the face of corruption and destruction is fundamental to Miss Sitwell's poetry and gives to it a special coherence and harmony. Against "Lullaby" and "Serenade" we must set such poems as "Harvest" and "Holiday." We shall then see how Miss Sitwell passes through the harrowing doubts and despairs of war to a constructive outlook. This outlook is religious. . . . Whatever wounds mankind may inflict upon itself, whatever it may suffer from decay and destitution, it can in the end be healed by finding itself in harmony with the powers of nature and with the light and the love that inform them.

Maurice Bowra. In J. G. Villa, ed.
Celebration for Edith Sitwell (New York:
New Directions, 1948), pp. 20–21,
26, 27, 38, 31

Edith Sitwell has . . . written many books of prose, notable among them a biographical study of Alexander Pope and a novel based on the tragic life-story of Jonathan Swift, *I Live Under a Black Sun.* She has also been an indefatigable and highly original anthologist, and has combined the chosen comments of others with her own *obiter dicta* in two unique anthology-journals, *A Poet's Notebook* and *A Notebook on William Shakespeare.* In all these works, or in the introductions to them, she has provided a great deal of valuable light on her views of what the lives of poets mean, what poetry is for and how it works; so that they are not only fascinating in themselves but also important for anyone who wishes fully to appreciate the oeuvre of this remarkable poet. . . .

I have remarked before on the fact that, though each phase of Edith Sitwell's poetry seems distinctly marked off from those that preceded it, the more carefully one studies them the more closely one sees that they are related. They are like a continuing argument between the two poles of her inspiration, between romance and satire, affirmation and irony; now one gains the ascendancy, now the other, in method as in content. In her poems from "Still Falls the Rain" to "The Canticle of the Rose" they seem to find a resolution within a larger synthesis: the depth of tenderness and compassion, the understanding of human desolation that so poignantly informed "The Little Ghost Who Died for Love" are there, and at the same time the savage mockery of *Gold Coast Customs;* the dream-like incantations of *The Sleeping Beauty* and the hard drumbeat of rhythms first evolved in *Nursery Rhymes.*

John Lehmann. Edith Sitwell (London: BC/
Longmans, 1952), pp. 7, 31

It has been firmly maintained by her critics that *Façade* derives its chief interest from the technical acrobatics of the work; that this collection of poems is noteworthy not so much for what it says as for the way in which it says it, not so much for its meaning as for its abstract quality, the sound patterns it makes from words. Yet this does not constitute the poetic totality of *Façade.* These poems are not merely impressionistic exercises in poetic technique. Had they been so, not even William Walton's scintillating musical accompaniment could have enhanced their literary value. . . . The dazzling virtuosity and concentrated brevity of the music provides a pungent, allusive commentary, and is a perfect embellishment of Dame Edith's incisive wit and parody.

Geoffrey Singleton. Edith Sitwell: The Hymn
to Life (n.p.: Fortune Press, 1960), p. 48

If ever a poet's personality affected the critical climate in which her work was considered, that poet was Edith Sitwell.

To anyone who had read her brother's autobiography, or who had heard Dame Edith talk about her upbringing, it was perfectly evident that the ornate flamboyance of her dress and appearance and the extraordinary manner of her public pronouncements were easily traceable to a very obvious inferiority complex. She was, in private, unsure of herself—and although we are all, I suppose, vulnerable to criticism where our work is concerned (and a poet *is* his work), she was more vulnerable than most, particularly to the personal criticism to which she was often subjected.

But critics very rarely consider poetry apart from personality where their contemporaries are concerned, and too many living critics have been blinded by "the enormous and gold-rayed rustling sun." It is true that Dame Edith's last years were made, all too often, sad by sometimes vicious attacks upon her. It was even suggested, in the month before her death, that she was incapable of being moved by the condition of others, which was to say that her poetry was insincere. She may indeed have been guilty of posturing in her public appearances and even in her writing on prosody; but poetry, as she said, was a kind of religion with her, and she was always and utterly true to her own conception of it. It is impossible to have too low an opinion of those ignorant critics whose lack of perception led them to think otherwise.

It is, however, true that it is difficult to disconnect the poet from her poetry: and for those who met her even occasionally, the difficulty is more subtle. When one's knowledge of her kindly patronage, her encouragement of numberless other writers, her practical support of the needy (often personally unknown to her), is joined to recollection of one of the most lovable and kindly human beings one has ever met, it is all too easy to overlook the faults in her work, and to take the will for the deed. . . .

One must I think dismiss her prose work as of far less value than the poems. She disliked writing prose, although some of her prose is good: there are passages in *Fanfare for Elizabeth,* particularly, which are (in a rather self-conscious manner) very finely wrought; *Pope,* although supplanted by later scholarship, contains some admirable complimentary passages; and there is some very witty occasional journalism. . . .

But her critical writing—both in *Aspects of Modern Poetry* and in the Forewords and Introductions and Notes on her own poetry—is frequently labored and tiresome. It is again perfectly obvious that it was her basic lack of confidence in herself as a poet that forced her into those public explanations of her technique, her constant reiteration of her own value as a prosodist. Her long Introductions to the Penguin selection and to her *Collected Poems* were irrelevant to the poetry in them: the pages of explanation contributed nothing to one's enjoyment of her work, and convinced no one of its value who was otherwise disposed. . . .

She was, however, a great anthologist—both of poetry and prose: her notes on Shakespeare, and on poetry in general, are, where they consist of a montage of apposite quotations, extremely valuable.

Derek Parker. Poetry Review. Spring, 1965,
pp. 18–19

Taken Care of, the autobiography of Edith Sitwell, would seem to be of clinical interest only (except to gossips) as a record of the largely paranoic ramblings of a poor old woman blighted by a most horrible childhood, if it did not contain a few pages that show the one peculiar good that managed to develop in this warped being.

Edith Sitwell appears to me to have been a monster, in a quite strict sense—"any plant or animal of abnormal shape or structure, as one greatly malformed or lacking some parts." But her ability to distinguish the affective properties of verbal sounds—the logic of melopoeia—was developed to a most extraordinary degree. This faculty is in itself a valuable phenomenon, and she was able to transmit its findings to her readers in some of her poems and in much of her critical writing, such as *A Poet's Notebook, A Notebook on William Shakespeare,* a book on Pope, some of her notes for *The Atlantic Book of British and American Poetry,* etc. But an autobiography asks the reader to look at the author as a human being; and it is hideous, shocking, painful, to witness the degree to which this one gift of hers was unaccompanied by any proportionate presence of other related properties. . . .

The human poverty self-revealed in all but a few pages of *Taken Care of* does, after all, throw light on an aspect of her work. Her later poems, with their tragic themes, obsessive symbols and seemingly compassionate point of view, have never moved me, as did the light, crisp early work—which she herself describes precisely as showing in some poems, "a violent exhilaration, [in others] a veiled melancholy, a sadness masked by gaiety." I see now—reading her words of cheap contempt for anyone who has criticized her, of vulgar self-praise, her passages of heavy sarcasm (in the style of Mrs. Wilfer in *Our Mutual Friend)*—that though she also had, in her fierce and loyal affection for a few persons and for many books, moments when she did envision "the warmth of love that makes all men brothers" (she is alluding to her wartime poems), it must have remained largely a theoretical experience, which was not only constantly at variance with the spite and pettiness in her but was also a projection that helped prevent her from acknowledgment of that spite. All the world's evil comes from "them"; "they" are the crucifiers; Edith Sitwell identifies consistently with the poor, the long-suffering, the crucified. It is this that, quite naturally, makes the later poems seem false, lacking in the very depth they seem to claim so fervently for themselves. They are overextended, and any such overextension inevitably shows up in the language and rhythm, the very substance, of a poem.

Denise Levertov. The Nation. June 7, 1965,
pp. 618–19

From the time [Edith Sitwell] wrote *Gold Coast Customs* there must have been a strong urge to take this step [conversion to Roman Catholicism]. In that poem she had for the first time fully and plainly realized a terrible range and depth of the truths she had been setting out in her earlier poems. She brought her intuitions sharply and fiercely down to earth; and thus for the first time a definitive statement of all that was implied by the alienating process of bourgeois society entered our poetry. A great deal of this realization came through the workings of her own mind in the creation of her poems, and through her swift response to Swift and Blake and to the tradition of Baudelaire and Rimbaud. I do not think that any directly political writings had affected her. The 1844 Manuscripts of Marx had not yet appeared in Moscow in their difficult German text. She had however read a good deal of Hegel and the German Nature-Philosophers. She told me that the originating image of the *Gold Coast Customs* was the spectacle of some Hunger Marchers led by a blackened man who was jestingly acting the part of a skeleton or death figure; she felt that she was looking at a modern Dance of Death, and the fused image of London and the Gold Coast, expressing the final deprivation and dehumanization of man, was born in her mind. . . .

Her thinking, as I have stressed, was emotional and intuitive rather than political and intellectual in the narrow sense. She was much taken up with the idea of revolutionary fires consuming a rotten society and clearing the earth for a better and cleaner growth; but always thought of the outbreak of fire as a sort of spontaneous combustion from below—something inevitable and finally necessary for the assertion of justice in the universe, but blindly violent and frightening.

Jack Lindsay. Meetings with Poets (New
York: Frederick Ungar, 1969), pp. 79–80

Edith Sitwell's criticism . . . is not all splenetic expression of a highly eccentric taste. To those who associate only the outrageous with her and her poetry it will be a surprise to discover in her criticism a continual concern for form and a unified texture of language. An examination of her critical work reveals a duality of temperament: there is indeed the one that might be called her "way" of passionate individualism, but it is found to be joined with an abiding interest in the organic discipline of art.

Especially significant in the exposition of the disciplined esthetic that can be found in Sitwell's criticism is her frequent and unique usage of "shadow" as a term to explicate certain purposive relationships within a poem. This term is prominent in her explication of what she calls the "texture" of a poem: embodying for her the essence of interconnection, the term "shadow" clearly reveals her commitment to an organic theory of poetry, a commitment further confirmed by her many appreciative references to Coleridge. . . .

In discussing the meaning of Edith Sitwell's poetry no one has disputed the symbolist function of her work. Yet, while many symbols—Ape, Lion, Dust, Sun, Bone are prominent ones—have been adduced as evidence of her role as a symbolist, no comment has appeared on "shadow." It is, however, not only a term of Sitwell's critical vocabulary but (with its cognate "shade") even more importantly also a persistently recurring image from her earliest to her last poetry. The image of "shadow" holds a central position in the symbolist significance of her work because it embodies in its implications of interconnection all the order that her critical and poetic visions discover.

James Brophy. Edith Sitwell: The Symbolist
Order (Carbondale: Southern Illinois
University Press, 1968), pp. xiv-xvi

In January 1922, *Façade,* the "entertainment" [Edith Sitwell wrote] in collaboration with William Walton, was presented to a privately invited audience at her brother Osbert's house in Carlyle Square. Eighteen months later, in June 1923, the first public performance was given at the Aeolian Hall.

To say that its reception was mixed would be an understatement. "Never, I think, was a larger and more imposing shower of brickbats hurled at any new work," she wrote, adding that "these missiles have now been exchanged for equally large and imposing bouquets." But at the time there was not a bouquet to be seen. Critics, she declared, asked the opinions of a passing postman and the fireman at the hall, and "These modern substitutes for the Delphic Oracle replied promptly, and in no uncertain terms. They opined that we were mad."

Façade resulted from "a kind of dare." "Willie gave me certain rhythms and said, 'There you are, Edith, see what you can do with that.' So I went away and did it. I wanted to prove that I could."

Her verse was written as a "work of gaiety" at which "the audience was meant to laugh." It was a surrealist experiment in which she was consciously placing assonances and dissonances in deliberate patterns for their effect on rhythm and speed. It reflected the attitude of the post-war poets to the language. The Georgians, they thought, had used a "tired language" and "sleepy family habits." With the peace had come a feeling of rebirth and, she wrote, "the physical world and its manifestations seemed to us to need reexamination as if we had suddenly burst into life or had gained sight after being blinded from birth."

New experiments in art are seldom appreciated at once. *Façade* became a connoisseur's piece, hailed only by a few as a masterwork and dismissed by many as incomprehensible.

Elizabeth Salter. *Edith Sitwell* (London:
Oresko, 1979), p. 12

What [John] Pearson's book [*The Sitwells: A Family Biography*] cannot give us—probably only a close reading of the notebooks and correspondence would do so—is a truly interior history of how [Edith,] this rare being, part show-off, part victim, part self-taught pedant, part holy-woman, suddenly came together [during the years with her brother, Osbert, at Renishaw]. There can be few progresses more unpredictable than the journey from *Façade* and *The Sleeping Beauty* to "Lullaby," "Tears," or "Once My Heart Was a Summer Rose." Yet the early poetry is there in the later one: the same love of color, something that she could lay on like a worker in enamels, the same love of strange words, the same personal rhythms as though a woman of 30 had just learned nursery rhymes. One small touch comes to mind: it is the use of the French nurse's sound "do-do"—the equivalent of "bye-bye"—as used in *The Sleeping Beauty* and in the wartime "Lullaby." In the early poem, a berceuse inserted into the flow of the story, the lullaby is sung to the fated princess who is compared to a tree that drips with gold. In "Lullaby" the same sound is used as materialism tries to comfort a dying world. . . .

[Her] two periods of most intense inspiration lasted a comparatively short time, and the critic or scholar who inquires into Edith Sitwell's poetry will have to try to create some pattern (if there is one) in the muse's visitations. Even the wartime apocalyptic vision soon dimmed, and the insights turned into mechanical tropes that do not even succeed as homiletic exercises. She adopted the mask of the sybil ("I an old woman in the light of the sun") and produced poems with long Blakean lines, but too often they read like self-parodies. In this last period of her life, clearly finding much of her early books alien, the work of another person, she tried to pillage her first poems for signs of the later significance. Thus *The Sleeping Beauty* was chopped up into songs and sections, a habit that Elizabeth Salter and Allanah Harper follow in their otherwise benign and sympathetic selection from Edith's work published some years back. Any reconsideration of the work as a whole demands complete poems, printed in the order they were written.

Richard Jones. *Virginia Quarterly Review.*
Summer, 1980, pp. 482–83

Edith's *The Mother,* published in 1915, was not a particularly striking first book and did not sell many copies. But it contained some remarkably individual lines that showed the genesis of an original poetic talent. In "The Drunkard," a poem in her first collection, the opening lines:

> This black tower drinks the blinding light,
> Strange windows livid white.

give an indication of what was to become a preoccupation with light and shade, whether in literal terms of color or to represent life and death. The couplet:

> Once more wild shriek on shriek would tear
> The dumb and shuddering air.

takes this vivid use of sensory impressions further by merging sound with feeling. The young girl's imaginative buttressing of the physical world had become a poetic strength in adulthood.

Unpromising and to a large extent unnoticed as *The Mother* was, it contains a theme that was to be developed and praised in Edith's later work: whether death of the body brings with it the spiritual death of the soul. Often in her early work Edith wrote of some act of treachery, where the problem of reconciling infamy and death is examined within the context of a firm belief in "good." In the title poem, "The Mother," the spirit or soul of a mother murdered by her son cannot rest, because of the thought, torturing to her, that she was murdered *despite* the love she had given him. The woman is not cast in the role of an accuser; neither does she blame her son for her own death. Instead he suffers in purgatory. . . .

Edith's determination to dedicate her life to poetry meant more than just writing her own. In 1912 Edward Marsh had published the first of an intended annual series of collections of Georgian verse called *Georgian Poetry*. It ran until 1922 and included the kind of work Edith disliked intensely. She felt that it dealt only with the ramblings of English village cricket matches and country-loving beer drinkers. This was a less than fair assessment, but in any case she wanted to oppose the bulk of pastoral sentimentality that the Georgians produced.

Geoffrey Elborn. *Edith Sitwell: A Biography*
(Garden City, New York: Doubleday, 1981),
pp. 23–24

Edith didn't just queen it in life, she also believed one should come the aristocrat in poetry. In her 1925 essay "Poetry and Criticism" she declared that it was "time we returned to an earlier [pre-Wordsworth] tradition in poetry, and left the peasant and words suitable to the peasant." Later she wrote that "poetry should never be middle class" (whatever that might mean) and used the word "suburban" as the most damning of epithets. . . .

[She] always saw [other women writers]—no matter whether they were dead or alive—as potential rivals. Contemporaries like Charlotte Mew, Vita Sackville-West, Nancy Cunard, Kathleen Raine and Anne Ridler were treated to her scorn, and even George Eliot was adjudged by her to be unreadable. A feminist case for Sitwell would be difficult to mount, given her attitudes to her own sex: "Women are Hell" was one of her sayings. . . .

Surely what's to be said on Sitwell's behalf as a poet—that in the odd line of "Colonel Fantock" she did manage to express something of herself, that "Still Falls the Rain" has a certain rhetorical power even if its ideas don't bear looking into, that children may perhaps enjoy some of her rhyming or assonance or mention of geese and goblins and foxes—can be managed in very few words indeed. Against that are the very considerable number of questions to be asked about her basic ability as a poet.

How, for instance, could she allow herself to be so appallingly repetitive even at a time when Yeats and Dylan Thomas had made acceptable the use of recurrent symbols? . . . .

Above all, perhaps, there is the question of Edith Sitwell's borrowings. As a critic she was well known to be a plagiarist, but rereading her poetry one is struck by how little of that, too, is truly hers: Remove Christina Rossetti, Walter de la Mare, Wallace Stevens, T. S. Eliot and Dylan Thomas and all that remains is airy Romantic nothings treated at length.

Blake Morrison. *Encounter.* 57, November
1981, pp. 89–90, 92–93

Edith's early experimental poetry, especially *Bucolic Comedies* and *The Sleeping Beauty,* stands up well. Her macabre masterpiece *Gold Coast Customs* deserves most of the praise it received. Her war verse, particularly *The Shadow of Cain, The Song of the Cold,* and *The Canticle of the Rose,* is still worthy of commendation. Chief among her prose works are *I Live under a Black Sun* and *The Queens and the Hive.*

What was especially important to Edith was that so many of her fellow poets, among them Yeats and Eliot, Dylan Thomas and Stephen Spender, spoke of her as one of the most creative artists of the century. Today admirers of her work rank the poems of her mature years higher than the verbal legerdemain of her experimental period. Louise Bogan, however, is one of the few who prefer Edith's earlier efforts to her later reflections on the world's evils. That Edith was a master technician, an adroit inventor of rhythms and of rhymes to mark them percussively, is obvious to anyone familiar with *Façade*—the work that first brought her notoriety and still draws an abundant number of readers to her other works.

Her *Collected Poems* still finds a substantial audience, though individual readers are not as enthusiastic as was the late Cyril Connolly, who once wrote: "When we come to compare the collected poems of Dame Edith Sitwell with those of Yeats, or Eliot or . . . Auden it will be found that hers have the purest poetical content of them all." Allen Tate tended to agree with Connolly, but he summed up Edith less extravagantly when, shortly after her death, he commented that she was "one of the great poets of the twentieth century . . . a remarkable and independent personality."

G. A. Cevasco. *The Sitwells* (Boston: Twayne, 1987), p. 140

The history of modern performance, especially the performance of poetry, is incomplete without a chapter devoted to the readings of Edith Sitwell, the first poet to be honored as a Dame of the British Empire. Dame Edith— poet, biographer, critic, novelist, anthologist, autobiographer, performer, and "practicing eccentric." . . .

Façade belongs to what is sometimes called the first stage of Edith Sitwell's poetry. The early poems include her experiments in marrying sound and meaning. While there is frequently a dark side to them, they are more often light and almost nonsensical, after the fashion of Edward Lear and Lewis Carroll. Alan Porter tells us that "Sitwell sometimes writes deliberate nonsense," while Jack Lindsay believes two fundamental things happen in her early poetry: "the Word comes alive; and . . . Rhythm comes alive." As a contrast to her early poetry, Sitwell's later poetry is often concerned with "expressing sympathy for unhappy humanity." John B. Ower sees her sharing "Eliot's concern with synthesizing a comprehensive poetic and spiritual system from the disorder of the modern world" and believes her "nightmare vision of evil, suffering, conflict and contradiction is for both theological and metaphysical reasons basic to her world picture." . . .

Sitwell's use of sound helps render her poems especially amenable to reading aloud and to being set to music. As exemplified by the poems in *Façade,* they are characterized by strong rhythms, internal and end rhymes, and various types of vowel and consonant patterns, including alliteration, consonance, and assonance. Denise Levertov credits the British poet with an extraordinary "ability to distinguish the affective properties of verbal sounds—the logic of melopoeia."

Robert M. Post. *Text and Performance Quarterly.* 11, 1991, pp. 128, 132–33

SLESINGER, TESS (UNITED STATES) 1905–45

Miss Slesinger's generation, which she calls "the unpossessed," is of a slightly later vintage than the well-known postwar company of Hemingway and Kay Boyle. She pictures them in the throes of a desperate effort to face the new discipline of collective action. Whoever read her brilliant and bitter indictment of the jittery era in "Missis Flinders"—which seemed to me the best short story of last year—will have been watching for this larger treatment of similar material.

And how does Miss Slesinger view this new, regenerative process? In the main, her colors are decidedly mordant. *The Unpossessed* pictures a group of younger New York intellectuals whose social protest remains pretty much in the realm of talk—Lenin toasted in gin, as it were, revolution served up with cocktails. Though a few of her youngest characters escape arraignment, the rest come in for large doses of ridicule. . . .

Since her ridicule cuts both ways [the] tendency [to facile smartness] is generally avoided. But as a novel *The Unpossessed* betrays a more fundamental weakness. Perhaps the fact that the short story "Missis Flinders" stands as the last chapter, with the book built back as it were from that entity, accounts for a certain brokenness both as to structure and theme. Its unity is threatened by the fact that Bruno now competes with Margaret (Missis Flinders) as the chief character, and their problems remain unrelated. Bruno's Hamlet-like straddle would be solved apparently by the courage to lose himself in collective action. Margaret's problem is quite different: it is sex, "womanhood," and her salvation supposedly lies in the most bourgeois of resources—have a baby. And incidentally, Margaret's story is not improved by its larger treatment; a certain sentimentality has crept in which was wholly absent from the short story. But the main weakness is that these two themes—on the one hand a sort of D. H. Lawrence critique of sexual integrity, and on the other redemption by social action—run separate courses through the book and are never really integrated. As a result, the book breaks down at important points where "talk" fails to bridge the gaps in underlying structure. A number of scenes, including the climactic "party," have the air of tours de force.

It is nevertheless a brilliant and cutting first novel. Miss Slesinger is harsh on her "fellow-travelers"; she does not pretend that their redemption has been accomplished, and it is even implied that for some of them, in the words of Bruno, the resolution is just another opiate. This seems to be salutary rather than not, and it is a credit to her honesty that the book does not end with a wishful red sunrise on the immediate horizon.

Ferner Nuhn. The Nation. May 23, 1934,
pp. 597–98

Finally, [among contemporary American short stories] there are the sentimental he-man and she-woman stories, wherein the heroes and heroines yearn for the recapture of the elemental pleasures because of their dissatisfaction with the bogus refinements and false innocence of contemporary sophistication. There is a mawkish toughness in them, as in the stories by Hemingway, and a touch of simple-minded or dishonestly flippant heartbreak, as in the fiction of Kay Boyle and Dorothy Parker. Such stories are generally little more than table talk mixed with picayune malice unredeemed by insight. Miss Slesinger's present collection of eleven stories belongs to [this] group. . . .

Miss Slesinger has a thin but real talent. Her sympathies are wider than Dorothy Parker's or Ernest Hemingway's, but she lacks their skill. She overwrites, and frequently she tries to hide lack of insight in verbiage. She is full of such meaningless phrases as "a lovely, hungry spring morning—perilously lovely." She is boisterously sensitive, and her discussions on sex are less enlightening than she seems to think. But she is a genuine short-story writer, because she has a good eye for the little tombstones of life. Her present book of stories [*Time: The Present*], for all its faults, is far better than her novel, *The Unpossessed.* In the latter she proved that the novel form was probably beyond her, because she has intellectual asthma. In *Time: The Present* she proves that the short-story form is well within her reach, but that she still has to learn that all inscriptions even on little tombstones, are best when brief and clear.

Charles Angoff. The Nation. June 19, 1935,
p. 717

The best story in Tess Slesinger's collection [*Time: The Present*] I think, is "The Mouse Trap," the tale of an abortive attempt to organize a strike among the employees in the outer office of an advertising agency, which is quelled by the adroitness and super-salesmanship of the head of the company. The story is told as seen through the eyes of his secretary, herself his more than devoted admirer; and this approach, permitting the use of that subjective style of writing which is Miss Slesinger's favorite method, also permits a full development of the ironical implications of the episode, while the handling of the long scene in which the employer cajoles, wheedles and browbeats the would-be strikers back into bewildered submission, reveals Miss Slesinger as being able to handle complicated situations with force and vigor as well as being in contact, however tentatively, with some of the larger realities of the day.

It is the success of this story, in fact, that contributes to one's disappointment with many of the others in the volume, for nowhere else does she go so directly to her subject nor seem to surround it with so thorough a comprehension. One of the faults of the "stream of consciousness" method is that in focusing all attention on thought processes it tends to disregard the active shell that encloses them, so that the impression remains, not of live human beings, but rather of a sort of ghostly parade of ideas. Miss Slesinger's method, moreover, adopts a convention of what might be called *vocalized* thoughts, or at least a stream of consciousness that is miraculously grammatical and ideologically compact. This, imposing another convention, that the thoughts be brisk and epigrammatic, dilutes the method still further, so that in some of the stories—such as "On Being Told That Her Second Husband Has Taken His First Lover," whose title practically tells all—one finds the narrative reduced to what amounts to a string of witticisms, sufficiently clever in themselves but hardly strong enough to carry the emotional tension desired.

The characters who figure in such stories as these are "intellectuals" indeed, but—after what she has shown she can do with pathos in "After the Party," with terror in "Mother to Dinner"—one wishes Miss Slesinger would turn her attention more consistently to less articulate personages.

Robert M. Coates. The New Republic.
July 24, 1935, p. 312

Tess Slesinger's remarkable novel [*The Unpossessed*] was published in early 1934, achieving immediate notoriety, especially in New York City. Nevertheless, her satirical *roman à clef* about the *Menorah Journal* group managed to lend itself to misrepresentation during the brief time before it was forgotten altogether. In retrospect, the book is limited; it captures, through imaginative literature, only certain specific tendencies of the group and its preoccupations. Yet, unlike the many products of the attempt to use "art as a weapon" (which was a fashionable Communist slogan in the early Depression), Slesinger's synthesis of art, ideas, and quasi-political themes is spontaneous and penetrating. . . .

When *The Unpossessed* appeared, the *New Masses* instantly reviewed it. Philip Rahv, the editor of *Partisan Review* who had yet to break with the Communists, gleefully seized upon the character "Comrade Fisher," who was supposed to be a member of a band of pro-Trotskyist agents attempting to "bore from within" as fellow-travelers of the Communist Party. Fisher, Rahv wrote, is "kneaded out of the same mud-pile as those insufferably clever young men, veterans of the Zionist Salvation Army, who are now writing articles for liberal weeklies on the strategy and tactics of the world revolution and the villainy of Stalin." Still, Slesinger's book was not without faults, Rahv concluded, for it did not present a "disciplined orientation" for radicalized intellectuals. . . .

The Unpossessed is an outstanding book—a prototype of the Jewish/ intellectual writings of Saul Bellow, and the social/satirical stories and novels of Mary McCarthy. Technically, *The Unpossessed* is grounded in the Modernist mode (using certain formal methods inspired by Joyce, Proust, the early Hemingway), and thematically it is informed by a strongly feminine perspective (suggestive of Dorothy Parker and Katherine Mansfield). Yet the novel also remains in the stream of earlier American books by and about radical intellectuals—particularly Max Eastman's *Venture* and Edmund Wilson's *I Thought of Daisy.* As in these two, personal and political themes run together in *The Unpossessed,* overlapping, intertwined, often infused with an intentional ambiguity. . . .

Furthermore, like its predecessors, Tess Slesinger's novel is rooted in the actuality of the historic moment: *Venture* is thematically locked in the "Golden Age" of pre-World War I radicalism; *I Thought of Daisy* expresses the discomfort of the twenties; and *The Unpossessed* transmits the disorientation of the early Depression. Slesinger's work communicates the pain and contradictions of the intellectuals trained and instructed by the special environment of the twenties, as they now struggle to relate to the new realities and demands of the thirties.

Alan Wald. Jewish Social Studies. 38, 1976,
pp. 311–13

Between 1935 and 1945 when she died of cancer at thirty-nine, Slesinger wrote the scripts for seven films which were produced and another eight which were, in Hollywood parlance, "shelved." Generally she worked in collaboration with her second husband, Frank Davis, who was originally a cutter and then a producer, and who became a writer after his marriage to Slesinger in March of 1936. In addition to *The Good Earth,* her credits include *Girls' School* (Columbia, 1938), which was based on her long short story, "The Answer on the Magnolia Tree": *Dance, Girl, Dance* (RKO, 1940), a protofeminist film directed by Dorothy Arzner. . . .

Hollywood gave Slesinger material for what would have been her next novel. *A Tree Grows in Brooklyn* (released after her death) was to be her last film, after which she would return to the novel for which she had been preparing not only by living and working in the Hollywood *milieu,* but also by systematically studying the various departments in the studios in a deliberate attempt to learn about the people in the industry, and the work that they did there.

Through Slesinger's novel remained incomplete at her death, the approximately 150-page manuscript, divided into sections labeled Notes, Characters and Beginning (of which there are several versions), is comprehensive enough to reveal her general intentions. Moreover, Slesinger discussed her plans for the book with her husband. Judging from both these sources, Slesinger's aim was to write about Hollywood not from the viewpoint of its elite, as Fitzgerald did in *The Last Tycoon*, nor from the viewpoint of its thrill-seeking aspirants and fans, as Nathanael West did in *Day of the Locust*. Instead, she meant to write something more comprehensive, a novel about Hollywood written from the perspective of the ordinary talented workers of the film industry in their personal, professional and political interactions.

Janet Sharistanian. *Michigan Quarterly
Review.* 18, 1979, pp. 430–31

Slesinger's current readers often find her fiction startlingly reflective of their own worries about sexuality, reproduction, heterosexual relationships, family conflicts, work, and social change. In particular, her filtering such issues through the voices, thoughts, and emotions of diverse, yet well-defined, female characters strikes a responsive chord. That her writing can be so contemporary despite its reliance upon stereotypes of male and female "nature" typical of the early decades of the century is undoubtedly due, in part, to her background. Unusually progressive in its childrearing practices and work patterns, Slesinger's family provided her with complex experience made generally familiar only recently as the movement of large numbers of middle-class mothers into wage labor, and contemporary feminism's insistence on generalizing about private experience, have exposed the complicated connections between domestic and public life.

Janet Sharistanian. Afterword to Tess
Slesinger. *The Unpossessed* (New York:
Feminist Press, 1984), p. 361

A 1930s contemporary: *The Unpossessed* (The Feminist Press) is a fifty-year-old novel that has improved with age. Tess Slesinger uncovers the downside of idealism among *The Big Chill's* grandparents, an ensemble of 1930s social reformers making a last, desperate reach for the grand illusions of their youth. But the book's eerily contemporary feel depends on Slesinger's witty look at changing sexual roles. The thoughtful working woman discovers that her marriage is too stifling to endure and too secure to abandon. The sexually liberated woman yearns for emotional involvement but keeps up a protective, jazzy façade.

Time has made Slesinger seem prescient, but it has given her style the quaintness of a period piece—a deft blend of social realism and high-energy stream-of-consciousness (echoes of Dreiser filtered through Katherine Mansfield).

When Slesinger dedicated the work "to my contemporaries," could she have guessed she'd be addressing us? Would she have been pleased at her foresight, or dismayed at how little progress we've made?

Caryn James. *Vogue.* November, 1984,
p. 274

SMEDLEY, AGNES (UNITED STATES) 1892–1950

Agnes Smedley's novel *Daughter of Earth* is an important and terrible book. As far as I know it is the first feminist-proletarian novel to be written in America. Do not shrink from those terms; the story of Marie Rogers forces you to face them. It bristles with labels and flat doctrinaire beliefs; it demands that you look at the society in which the dogmas of rebellion breed; and if you can ever forget the America that *Daughter of Earth* reveals—harsh, unjust, sordid, dishonest, sometimes tantalizingly beautiful and exciting— then you are nearly immune to the effect of words.

The author writes about life more intensely than most of us manage to live it. The story seems to have been propelled into being by an urgency too desperate to be denied. It is told as if sheer emotion had made the words and poured them on the paper; there is no evidence anywhere of deliberate, conscious artifice, no apparent pattern, no "style." "Here, my friends, is a chunk of life which has perhaps its own beauty and meaning. Certainly I should scorn to decorate, much less to disguise it. If you like life, you might try this one. If you fear life, run, friends, for your peace and security." So the author might have said.

Instead she gives us no warning but lets the chief character tell her own story. . . .

Her proletarian sentiment was as real and as harsh as her feminism and it began in the early days when she lived in a tent on the "other side" of the railroad tracks and faced the social distinctions that bred even in the class-room of a public school in a small Missouri town. But her class-consciousness matured when the State troopers brought terror into the mine camp in the foothills of the Rockies where her father hauled sand; there and in Trinidad she learned the meaning of the text "from him that hath not shall be taken away." There was never a moment when she and her brothers and sisters were not helpless victims of an impersonal system beyond their control; though their father did not know how impersonal it was when he clutched the throat of the little mine-owner who had cheated him out of a summer's pay. And it was many years before Marie focused her bitterness on the eco-nomic scheme of things which had made her life so fierce and angry a business. . . .

The story of her childhood is alive with feeling, its detail is rich and telling. The later pages are more diffuse and less moving. Yet they provide a fragment of social history that I have not seen written anywhere else: radical New York before and during the war; committees, parades, deputa-tions, more committees; government agents, War Department spies, the third degree; insane suspicions, plots and exposures, and, under them all, cold fear in the minds of the war-makers who saw in every radical an agent of destruc-tion. Marie's initiation into the movement for Indian freedom and her perse-cution by the authorities is told in appalling detail, the more appalling because there are many to vouch for its accuracy. Her personal tragedy emerges from these events with an air of absolute inevitability.

There are some who may object to this book for its tone of bitter, partisan violence. Let no one judge it without reading it through. Agnes Smedley knows that mountains can be beautiful and that love can be sweet. But when mountains are made the battleground of desperate men, their beauty becomes unimportant or at most a tragic note of contrast. And when love is killed by fear or shame or brutal indifference, it turns to bitterness. Bitterness is a valid part of this story.

Freda Kirchwey. The Nation. March 20,
1929, p. 347

Any book from the pen of Agnes Smedley, that redoubtable fighter for the rights of the underdog, is an exciting event, particularly at a moment when she is witnessing at first hand one of the great conflicts of history. For with the possible exception of Edgar Snow, no American is better qualified by temperament or experience to write of China's resistance to Japan from the viewpoint of the Chinese Communists, its most steadfast proponents. Since 1929 Miss Smedley has interpreted Chinese Communism to the world. She spent most of 1937 in the Communist districts and among the forces of the Red—now the Eighth Route—Army. Although suffering from a painful spinal injury, she traveled uncounted miles over rugged country, with a typewriter strapped to her back and an entourage of only a few guards. Pain, weariness, cold, hunger, and even, occasionally, the lack of candles prevented her from writing more than a rough draft for submission to her publishers. . . .

Scattered through the spare catalogue [in *China Fights Back*] of daily triumphs and tribulations of the Communists appear fascinating vignettes of Chinese life. The troops, politically disciplined and personally self-restrained to an extraordinary degree, think little of a seventy-mile march on foot in a single day. The first steps are taken to break down the medieval habits of Chinese who cannot be persuaded to believe in the existence of invisible germs, or who regard a needle as a precious treasure and gape in astonishment at locomotives, moving pictures, and other oddities of Western civilization. The diaries of Japanese captives and Japanese dead, expressing dissatisfaction with the war, are utilized with telling effect by a marvelous Communist propaganda machine. The old-line Chinese war lords fatalistically predict and suffer defeat, while those who survive it strive desperately to organize widespread popular resistance after the Communist model. Chinese intellectuals are challenged for their complacent indifference to the fate of the common soldier. Some foreign missionaries find it impossible to envisage successful Chinese armies; others, half instinctively, assist even the Communists in the struggle for an independent China.

Over and above the incidents and the explanations rises the blazing sincerity of Miss Smedley, a devoted partisan who confesses to "passionate likes and dislikes," yet strives always to tell the truth as she sees it. Today, in her mind, the social struggle in China must be subordinated to the overriding task of beating back the Japanese imperialist drive. But the final victory must and will be delayed until China is freed from the grip of entrenched wealth and privilege—until the reforms demanded by the Communists are consummated. To those who subscribe to it this is an inspiring, an intoxicating creed. Agnes Smedley's greatest contribution is to have transferred from life to the pages of her book something of the spirit in which it is being furthered.

David H. Popper. Saturday Review of
Literature. July 16, 1938, p. 35

Everything Miss Smedley has done in China, every belief she held, every sacrifice she made could be traced directly to her dreary childhood, her unhappy personal life, her physical ailments. Yet, this turmoil and unhappiness produced a passionate and fearless crusader, rather than a neurasthenic.

With brief gaps, Miss Smedley has lived in China for thirteen years. During these years, she has made herself an integral part of the Chinese revolutionary pattern, a leading champion of the poverty-stricken and the oppressed. She worked with the underground against the Blue Shirts and Tu Yueh-sen's sinister Green Circle Society. For thousands of painful miles, she marched with the Chinese guerrillas, ate their food, suffered with them, ministered to their spiritual and medical needs. She witnessed great events in Chinese history, and in some of them—such as the famous Sian kidnapping incident—she has played a role. As a spokesman for American democracy she regained friends lost by the American sale of oil and steel to Japan.

Battle Hymn of China, thus, is a record of Miss Smedley's work, adventures, and impressions. It is also an exciting gallery of incredible figures—heroes and villains and the layer of the common man in between.

Mark Gayn. Saturday Review of Literature.
September 18, 1943, p. 22

This book [The Great Road] is dangerous to the Free World precisely because it is so well done. The publishers say that it is a first draft that has been somewhat polished since Miss Smedley's death. It has been polished until it glistens.

R. A. Smith. The New York Times. October
14, 1956, p. 41

Hers were among the first works to be hunted out by the bookburners of the early 1950s, "cleansing" USIA libraries. Abroad initially, then at home, her books disappeared from library shelves. Publishers allowed her books to go out of print. . . . Bad enough a "Red sympathizer," but also one who described marriage as a "relic of human slavery" in a time when women were once again being pressed into home and consumerism, a feminist when abortion was only whispered about, a woman who extolled female strength and size and will in the blurry age of June Allyson. Never mind that her books had always been praised in the past; they were also called "fiercely honest," "urgent," "savage in tone"—no virtues in the land of Ike. Under the avalanche of McCarthyism, the indifference of America fattening through the 50s, her life and books (like so much else of left and feminist culture of the United States) were buried.

Paul Lauter. Afterword to Agnes Smedley.
Daughter of Earth (Old Westbury, New
York: Feminist Press, 1973), p. 423

The stories and portraits in this volume [*Portraits of Chinese Women in Revolution*] illustrate Smedley's insistence—made clear in *Daughter of Earth* as well—upon economic self-determination for all women as the key to their independence. Economic independence would, moreover, develop in the context of the liberation of *all* oppressed people. In these respects her views were similar to those being argued during the 1930s by the Communist Chinese Women's Association. The portraits further display Smedley's admiration for strong, aggressive women, not bound even by passing obeisance to traditional proprieties. To some extent, it may be that her own indifference to such proprieties generated tensions with her Chinese comrades. One can well imagine that she startled the austere Communists when, arriving in Yenan, she threw her arms around Mao, Chou, Chu Teh, and others and gave them "big kisses." It is possible, too, that her enthusiasms—teaching the Communist leaders to square dance, for example—were mistaken for an excess of sexual liberation. At one point she apparently did generate considerable hostility by announcing that all the wives who had survived the Long March with their husbands should be divorced because they were feudal-minded. These veteran women revolutionaries, who earlier had participated in experiments with the marriage law and family relationships in a rural context, were convinced that women would be victimized in a structureless situation at this stage in the revolution. Smedley and the Chinese women with whom she sided on this issue had just come from the city and had little experience in the countryside. Mao's wife at the time, Ho Tzu-chen, once even went so far as to threaten to kill Smedley. It is certainly true that both Smedley and the Chinese women envisaged relationships of sexual equality, especially among revolutionaries.

Jan MacKinnon and Steve MacKinnon.
Introduction to Agnes Smedley. *Portraits of
Chinese Women in Revolution* (Old
Westbury, New York: Feminist Press, 1976),
pp. xxv–xxvi

In styles used also by Lu Hsun, Smedley attempts, in two more ambitious stories, to write the histories of privileged women who crossed class lines in China to join the revolution. In "Shan-fei, Communist" and "The Dedicated"

Smedley is not simply telling her Western audience that women's lives are changing somewhat. She is frankly promoting the fact that women have taken a bold hand in changing their lives in order to effect revolutionary changes in all people's lives. She is, in short, attempting to write, within the framework of accurate history of two women's lives, the generic history of revolutionary Chinese feminists.

It is a difficult assignment, and Smedley adopts styles that are unfamiliar to her. They are also not what Western readers are accustomed to. They do not focus sufficiently on "scenes"; they contain virtually no dialogue; their view is generic not individualistic; their ideology is explicit—all of which we do not expect from fiction or reportage.

Not surprisingly, the results are mixed. If we are looking for individual idiosyncrasies in characterization and an emphasis on personal relations, we shall be disappointed. If we are interested in history and moved by social documentary, we will consider Smedley's efforts worthwhile, if flawed. These stories may also help to answer questions that Western feminists like myself have put to the Chinese, partly out of their own ignorance of Chinese history and ideology, partly out of their own confusion about the relationship between class and feminism.

> Florence Howe. Afterword to Agnes
> Smedley. *Portraits of Chinese Women in*
> *Revolution* (Old Westbury, New York:
> Feminist Press, 1976), pp. 180–81

For students of Smedley's later writings. "Cell Mates" [1920] presents an early expression of her lifelong principles and an example of the young journalist's experimentation with the techniques of her craft. Fascinating reading in itself, "Cell Mates" reveals three significant points about Agnes Smedley. We see her finding her voice, her confidence as a writer, and her will to write; finding a mode or form of expression in character sketches, developing a personal brand of journalism, and assuming a dual role as participant/observer; and finding a subject in women's welfare, the rights of oppressed people, and revolution.

Agnes Smedley wrote these sketches from her personal meetings with these women when she, too, was a prisoner in the Tombs, "a monument to the savagery within man.". . . .

"Cell Mates" shows Smedley finding her subject, as well as her voice, form, and vocation as a writer. The subject that captivates her interest and to which she dedicates her work and her entire life, is the welfare of all oppressed people. . . .

An essential point to note in considering the subject matter in "Cell Mates" is Smedley's feminism. It is clear, throughout her writings, that she is particularly concerned about improving the condition of women. In China, she worked with women revolutionaries, and often wrote of the traditional rules that restricted them, symbolized by the ancient custom of binding women's feet. Feminism, for Smedley, was a special interest, but she saw it as one aspect of the larger cause of all oppressed people. It is in this light that "Cell Mates" is best understood.

Judith A. Scheffler. In Alice Kessler-Harris
and William O. McBrien, eds. *Faith of a
(Woman) Writer* (1984; Westport,
Connecticut: Greenwood Press, 1988),
pp. 200, 203–4

Smedley's militant and creative use of personal rage evoke the same disturbing emotions as do the images of the poor we find in the etchings by her friend Käthe Kollwitz. Like Kollwitz and Emma Goldman, she did not romanticize the poor or the working class, and she never glorified their way of life. Indeed, most of her close friends were from the middle and upper classes. And it may have been precisely this, her success in sending a radical message across class boundaries, that most frightened such China lobbyists as Kohlberg and Judd. The events of the last years of her life led Smedley to believe that American capitalist interests were opposed to the interests of the poor—in China and India, but implicitly in America as well.

Throughout her life, in her writings and her public statements, Smedley's self-appointed task was to communicate the desperate, endless nightmare of poverty and ignorance. Her goal was the overthrow of these two dragons. Her life was a battle, without truce or compromise, to that end.

Janice R. MacKinnon and Stephen R.
MacKinnon. *Agnes Smedley: The Life and
Times of an American Radical* (Berkeley:
University of California Press, 1988),
p. 351–52

In many ways, Agnes Smedley's *Daughter of Earth* represents the Ur-text of women's proletarian fiction of the 1930s. Published in 1929, it signaled, according to many critics then and subsequently, the beginnings of proletarian realism as a literary movement in the United States. Its framing device provides the illusion of distance between narrator and subject—here, supposedly co-extensive: Marie Rodgers is a woman recovering from a breakdown reviewing her past. Smedley's frame sets up two spaces, American and Denmark, and two times, the past and the present, which illuminate the two sensibilities of the middle class and working class.

Moreover, within the main body of the narrative, two other discourses are established and set into combat—the dual narratives of desire (inscribed across the gendered body) and history (constituted within a class and anti-imperialist politics). These two opposed narratives are, of course, interrelated and, in fact, inseparable; it is the attempt to separate them that drives Marie crazy. The prescriptions of both narratives for the gendered body firmly connects one to the other, yet ironically renders the working-class woman un-scripted. Hence the crazy-quilt; hence Marie's craziness. . . .

Framing establishes beginnings and endings, sets up a distance between text and context, a distance which both confirms difference and erases its significance and so marks off the unruly complexities intervening. The fram-ing device suggests simultaneously that there are two stories and that there is only one story—the story of the innately creative artist cramped and suffer-ing within the confines of the socially imposed restrictions of class and gen-der. This, however, is the story of the working class subsumed and wrapped within the frames of bourgeois narrative. Because neither plot nor story can find a language to compose the "fragments" of class and gender as representa-tions of each other and themselves, the bodies of Marie and of the movement remain excluded from either the (gendered) frame or the (classed) narrative.

Paula Rabinowitz. *Genders.* 8, 1990,
pp. 68–70

Daughter of Earth is a novel about the profound destructiveness of not-knowing—of ignorance caused by poverty and isolation. It is also a novel of education. Its protagonist learns to live in the world of the literate, the self-possessed—those with choices. But like many who have made such a journey into knowing, she is haunted by her past, and it shapes her perceptions and actions. As a young child in the dirt-poor Missouri farming country of the 1890s, Marie Rogers is confronted brutally and violently with the stark truth about gender relations and social class in the culture of the frontier. Her only recourse is flight from each exploitative situation. Not until her late teens does she acquire the analytic power of mind to move from gut reaction to the beginnings of conscious understanding of working-class womanhood in the United States. Later her education broadens: She questions her U.S. identity not only on its own terms, but as it appears to non-Western people of color, a perspective the importance of which we are only beginning to realize fully now. But living on the borders between the unknowing silence of the working classes and the glib articulateness of leftist circles, Marie is nowhere at home.

More than any novel I have ever read, this novel demonstrates a painful irony: that the economic and social forces that cause deprivation irreparably maim the heart and the mind even as they strengthen the will to change the world for others.

Nancy Hoffman. In Florence Howe, ed.
Tradition and the Talents of Women
(Urbana: University of Illinois Press, 1991),
p. 171

SMITH, PAULINE (SOUTH AFRICA) 1883–1939

It is difficult to say whether Pauline Smith has sought [in *The Little Karoo*] to capture and preserve the feeling of this remote district and its patient humble people, or whether in writing of these folk she has all mankind at heart. Probably the first. Her childhood was passed in the Little Karoo, and her mind was packed, during the impressionable years, with the sound and smell and color and feel of it. One doubts that she has said to herself, Lo, I will be a Universalist. She is utterly unself-conscious, and she withdraws herself almost uncannily from the action of her stories. And she has succeeded overwhelmingly in breathing life in the Karoo, with its remote farms and hamlets, its laborious journeyings in a rumbling ox cart, its stern, sober, simple, shrewd men and women, its utter detachment from the world and civilization—especially this detachment, the Karoo's completeness in itself, economic and ethical; but she has succeeded also in picturing the man and woman in each of us, so that the people and the country of which she writes with strange brooding pity seem only incidental to her brooding upon mankind, and the Karoo is only her name for the world, conveniently isolated for sympathetic study.

Arnold Bennett speaks of her "strange, austere, tender, and ruthless talent.". . . . Austere in that Pauline Smith stands always aside, watching life as it goes by, interpreter and not participant. Tender, yes; infinitely tender and sympathetic [, able to compress] into a few small pages the material of a novel, and still convey a sense of time and space and growth and significance; and this is what Pauline Smith has done. Novelist or no, she is a great short story writer.

> Brooks Shepard. *Saturday Review of*
> *Literature.* April 25, 1925

Pauline Smith's simple but highly developed physical awareness gives these stories of the Little Karoo their remarkable faithfulness to external reality. She sees with such simplicity that her people, drawn entirely from the outside, seem to be inside out. She never intrudes, never even enters a room where a character lies sleeping, but stands apart too aloof to pause to enjoy personally the rose on a china cup or a little hand mirror rimmed with tiny shells. Her characters are the religious Dutch peasants of South Africa and she has given them such life that, to the reader, they have absolute permanence.

> *The Nation.* September 2, 1925

Although Pauline Smith's writing has become generally known only recently, she is not a modern writer. In many respects she is closer to the Victorian age than to this generation. She would have known a world which was socially and economically stable. The houses in which she spent her younger years were furnished with somber and heavy articles. Net and velvet curtains hung at the windows; family portraits were on the walls. Hers was a world of politeness and restraint.

Even when she was writing in the 1910s and 1920s, it is clear that she was thinking back to some earlier period, probably around the time of her own childhood. Her *South African Journal* of 1913–14 shows that she had many disappointments when she found that Little Karoo places and customs had changed—were no longer as in her girlish days. . . .

The motor-car was beginning to supplant the ox-wagon, and journeys from one part of the Little Karoo to the other were becoming swifter and easier. As a result, the remote settlements were being opened up. When Pauline Smith was moved so greatly by the sacrament service at Mill River— an event she was to use so powerfully in her creative work—she comments in her journal that even that was something which was passing away. . . .

Pauline Smith had no interest in reflecting this violent intrusion of the twentieth century in her work. It is possible that she was largely insensitive to it. While "the ceremony of innocence" was being drowned in Europe, she remained in the seclusion of her English cottage, dreaming of an earlier time. . . .

There are other ways in which Pauline Smith is closer to a past genera- tion, for instance in the unshakable moral framework of her writing. Although she is tolerant, sketching all her characters with an unbiased pen and a careful controlled passion, her conception of a just order remains. Her stories are set in a definite world; she is neither fluid nor uncertain.

Geoffrey Haresnape. *Pauline Smith* (New
York: Twayne, 1969), pp. 145–47

Pauline Smith, living in the 1920s in the isolation of the Karoo as Schreiner did before her, created a justificatory myth of the Afrikaner people that con- tinues to answer, in literature, to certain political pressures to this day. (I use the word "myth" not in its primary dictionary sense of a purely fictitious narrative, but in the sense the anthropologist Claude Lévi-Strauss does, as a psychologically defensive and protective device. A myth is an extra-logical explanation of events according to the way a people wishes to interpret them.)

Pauline Smith, a writer of Chekhovian delicacy, was not an Afrikaner and she wrote in English. She wrote of rural Afrikaners, in whom her stories see poverty as a kind of grace rather than a limiting circumstance. Why? I believe that she was faithfully reflecting not a fundamental Christian view, but the guilt of the victor (British) over the vanquished (Boer), and also the curious shame that sophistication feels confronted by naivety, thus interpre- ting it as "goodness." One of the main points represented by her characters is their total unfitness to deal with the industrial society that came upon them after their defeat by the British. Her story "The Pain" shows an old man and his dying wife terrified even by the workings of a hospital; the husband's humbleness is emphasized almost to the point of imbecility. This virtue in helplessness, in the situation of being overwhelmed by poverty, drought, economic depression, was to become a justificatory myth, in literature, of the Afrikaner in relation to the development of his part in the politics of domination. Based on it, at least in part, is the claim of Afrikaners to be a white African tribe.

Nadine Gordimer. In Christopher Heywood,
ed. *Aspects of South African Literature*
(London: Heinemann, 1976), pp. 105–6

For me, and arguably for other modern South African readers, there are a number of obstacles to entering and remaining comfortably within the world of *The Beadle*. One is Pauline Smith's rendering of a conceivable imagined Afrikaans into English; the second is the way her works contribute towards upholding certain myths about the Afrikaner—myths that have had and are still having important political implications; and the third is the temperamental narrowness of her characters, their tendency towards single, consuming obsessions.

Clearly Pauline Smith's choice to render Afrikaans into English was not made for the superficial purpose of displaying local manners and setting but, being closely linked to her writing intentions, was consistent with the essence of her vision of the Afrikaner. . . .

Certainly Pauline Smith has importance as a regional writer. She paints the topography of the Little Karoo, the farms, the houses and everything that is in them, with fine detail, and she even offers two full pages of historical background to the Afrikaner community of that region. It is because of this richness and the bold simplicity of her stories that both *The Beadle* and *The Little Karoo* are enjoying a current popularity and are generating a good deal of critical writing. But I cannot resist putting in my pennyworth of caution: I don't believe that her work is "informative about the social . . . character of the Little Karoo," nor do I accept that while she relaxed on Arnold Bennett's yacht in the Mediterranean writing, as the gossip goes, she intended to giver her readership a set of "universals." For me the Aangenaam community is a nostalgic, wish-fulling one and if its inhabitants are (because such a community never existed as Smith portrays it) allegorical of "human nature," then I would like to know *whose* "human nature"?

Sheila Roberts. *World Literature Written in
English*. 24, 1984, p. 232–33, 238

Pauline Smith questioned many beliefs and practices, and with respect to the injustice done to black Africans she was either unperceiving or silent. Esther Shokolowsky, the old "Jew woman" to whom terrible things had happened in her own country in eastern Europe "at the hands of Christians," is treated sympathetically. But the black Africans to whom terrible things were also happening in their own country escape her attention and therefore her sympathy. She does point briefly, by way of comment, to the Boers' reaction to the freeing of the slaves by the English—"an incomprehensible act of injustice." She makes a similar passing, ironic observation about the treatment and upbringing of indentured children: Spaasie prays, "Make me to be obedient" and Klaas prays, "Make me run quickly when my master calls."

Charles Ponnuthurai Sarvan. *World Literature Written in English*. 24, 1984, p. 249

I have noted some features of *The Beadle* which suggest that the Aangenaam valley is precapitalist in organization. Let me recapitulate them and add a few more.

1. The life of the (extended) family and the economy of the farm are closely integrated.
2. Production is, by and large, for household use or for barter; money is little used.
3. Social mechanisms exist to counteract rather than encourage extremes of wealth and poverty.
4. Bonds of attachment exist between people and the soil.
5. Authority is patriarchal.
6. Marriage is looked upon as a universal life-goal. Marriages tend to take place early, and within the district. They are often arranged.
7. The community is culturally homogeneous.

The features I have listed are common to what, following Alan Mac-farlane, I call classic peasant social organization. But the overlap is not complete. Certain features of classic peasant life are eschewed by Smith, while other aspects of life in the Aangenaam valley distinguish it from the classic pattern.

The feature added by Smith to which I would specifically point is hierarchy. . . .

The second departure is peculiarly Smith's. I take the reign of the Van der Merwes to be her vision of a patriarchalism purged of its tyrannical side, a benign Little Karoo patriarchalism to be set against a malign Great Karoo patriarchalism. . . .

More intriguing is the question of why there must be a *seignor*, why Smith did not envision, in her ideal valley, a society of more or less equal independent farmers with their various *bywoners* and tenants. For in creating her *seignor*, however benign, and despite her assurance that on feast days "rich and poor mingled together without distinction of class" Smith reintroduces the devil of class into her African Eden.

J. M. Coetzee. *White Writing: On the Culture of Letters in South Africa* (New Haven: Yale University Press, 1988), pp. 71–72

SMITH, STEVIE (GREAT BRITAIN) 1902–71

It has been interesting to find that a novelist, Stevie Smith, who made a success before the war with *Novel on Yellow Paper* (1936)—seriously gay, grimly comic, exquisitely inconsequent—has gone on since the war to achieve a greater (literary) success with *The Holiday* (1949). It is less effervescent in comicality but still has a lightheartedness which carries with it a terrifying burden of serious import, of apprehension, of awareness of the tragic problem of the individual and the corresponding problem of the human race in its present perplexities. A book amusing, serious and at moments profound.

> R. A. Scott-James. *Fifty Years of English*
> *Literature: 1900–1950* (London: Longmans,
> 1951), p. 187

It would be a manifest exaggeration to call her a neglected poet, yet as one of the most original women poets now writing she seems to have missed most of the public accolades bestowed by critics and anthologists. One reason may be that not only does she belong to no "school"—whether real or invented as they usually are—but her work is so completely different from anyone else's that it is all but impossible to discuss her poems in relation to those of her contemporaries. The dismissing adjective usually tacked to her verse is "fey," which is accurate enough for her less successful pieces—and she is a very uneven poet. Her poems either come off magnificently or collapse absolutely. Then she is that extremely rare bird, a great comic poet—though the word "comic" has in this connection an unfortunately pejorative connotation (one thinks of Thomas Hood, W. S. Gilbert, Ogden Nash). It will not do, either, though it is much nearer the mark, to classify her poems as "light" in the sense that Auden defined the word in the preface to his *Oxford Book of Light Verse*. Perhaps her nearest equivalent among contemporary poets is John Betjeman, who surfaces with deceptive gaiety an inherent gloom, except that in the case of Stevie Smith the gaiety is fundamental and does not deceive the gloom but defines it. A concise example is the comic-sinister title of her book: *Not Waving But Drowning,* taken from a poem about a drowned man (in this case no relation of that worn out upper-case archetype, The Drowned Man). . . .

The uninhibited wit and gaiety which she brings to her best poems plus the optimism they often express provides an appearance of frivolity which is in reality a mask worn to further the impact of truth which, were it declaimed from a lugubrious tripod, would be vitiated or diluted. The apparent geniality of many of her poems is in fact more frightening than the solemn keening and sentimental despair of other poets, for it is based on a clearsighted acceptance, by a mind neither obtuse nor unimaginative, but sharp and serious,

innocent but far from naïve, and because feminine having a bias toward life
and survival, of the facts as they are and the world as it is.

David Wright. *Poetry.* August, 1958,
pp. 311–12

It may be an indication of Stevie Smith's rapidly growing popularity as a poet
and her ability to reach all sections of the public, at one level or another, that
some of the younger poets, impressed by what she can achieve with her
apparent facetiousness of manner, and emboldened, perhaps, by her success,
are attempting to adopt her style—with somewhat disastrous results, let it
be said. For of all the poets writing today Stevie Smith is one of the most
original and certainly the most inimitable.

Her latest volume, *The Frog Prince,* consists of sixty-nine new poems
and a selection from her previous volumes, supported by her typically zany
drawings. Those who have acquired the taste for Stevie Smith will not be
disappointed; they will find fresh specimens to add to their collections of
extraordinary characters. . . .

Those who may not have had the complex experience of reading Stevie
Smith are advised to start with *The Frog Prince,* for here they will find poetry
of genuine merit quite unlike anything they can have seen or heard before.
A childlike vision combined with maturity of outlook, a sense of compassion
intermixed with a wry sense of humor, an acute feeling for humanity underlying the cold appraisal of the world in which we live, go to the making of
these poems.

Howard Sergeant. *Poetry Review* (London).
Spring, 1967, pp. 48–49

These adjectives, or some of them, could be applied to Stevie Smith's own
poetry: severe, austere, simple, bracing, impersonal. If "this is truly Greek,
and what the Greek is," then Stevie Smith is somewhat Greek. If to be
classical is not to be (in a number of senses of that peculiar adjective) romantic, then she is in some senses classical. Like these adjectives, she is equivo-
cal, not half so simple as she seems. . . .

If classicism is avoidance of the romantic, then one can adduce her best-
known because most obvious attributes: the perverse, off-rhyming (she goes
out of her way to rhyme impurely, but at other times thumps down on the
most obvious if pure rhyme), the inevitably comic and deflatory effect of
rhyming English words with French, and the bathos which W. McGonagall
achieved effortlessly but she had to work for. . . .

In its essence Stevie Smith's poetry is uncluttered, and hence must leave
out, for instance, the reservations and modifications and clarifications which
a denser and slower-moving writing admits. But it leaves out what it could not
accommodate and still be the kind of poetry it is: and that is all it leaves out.

D. J. Enright. *Encounter.* June, 1971,
pp. 53–54, 57

Florence Margaret Smith came by the more exotic name of Stevie as a side effect of her smallness. Her family is reported to have nicknamed her after the jockey Steve Donoghue, small even by the exacting standards of his profession. She was born in Hull in 1902, where her father was a shipping agent, who deserted the family for the sea. Her mother took Stevie and her sister to London three years later, and she was to live the rest of her life in the same house in Palmers Green. . . .

Stevie Smith's family context and private milieu are so important that it is necessary to get them straight from the beginning. Her poetry is continuously drawn from a setting of decaying gentility and a recognition of her own experience of Englishness. Personal loves and enmities expressed in her work issue starkly from her early experiences of domestic unhappiness; there is a feeling of unforgivingness. . . .

Stevie Smith is a problem poet to the critic. She encourages him to be too earnest, or too lax. Verse narratives no longer appeal to the critical or poetical imagination as they used to: the repeated poems of religious doubt, the to-die or not-to-die vacillations (not drowning but waving, it could be called), upper crust loneliness or malefaction, the despairs of the plain-faced, can be tedious at their worst. There is a great deal of moral captioning; many of her poems are as much "the higher doodling" as her drawing. But an interesting intelligence is engaged in her work—and it is a literary intelligence as much as the feeling that came from her despair: feminine, powerful, and far from inconsiderable. Too many people have read only the surface in which she disguised it. And if there are not true, plain love poems, no sonnets, no baroque cultural greetings sent out across the centuries, no masterful samples of orthodox iambic pentameter, it is because she was inscrutably loyal to her inner life and the styles she used to express it. Her career is a moving record of dedication, faithful to no fashion, astute and quirky perhaps, but unflinchingly honest.

(London) *Times Literary Supplement.*
July 14, 1972, p. 820

Stevie Smith had a wonderfully various mind and her work is a forest of themes and attitudes. In large part it was her intelligence and honesty that led to this—to the protean, compound substance we all are. She was rather fierce about the truth—a modern peculiarity. The encouragement the age gives to both acceptance and doubt, the way it leaves us with the museum of everything without much trust in any of it, made her at once diverse and sardonic. "We are born in an age of unrest," observes Celia, the narrator of her third novel, *The Holiday* (1949), "and unrestful we are, with a vengeance." Evidently Smith was prone to be sardonic anyway. Perhaps because her father had deserted to a life on the sea when she was young, she was quick to turn "cold and furious" about anything selfish or unjust. Calling the heroines of her novels after Casmilus, "shiftiest of namesakes, most treacherous lecherous and delinquent of Olympians," she seems also to have been nagged by

a sense of unworthiness that may have gained strength from the same experience. In any case, fatherless, she would be "nervy, bold and grim"; she would
fend for herself. And clever as the next person, in fact cleverer, she would
be nobody's fool, nor suffer foolishness. All this gives a wickedly unstable
and swift slashing quality to her work. She herself is not to be trusted—
except to be formidable, unpredictable, remorseless.

To a degree, however, Death stood in for Smith's father; she looked up
to it, ran to it when she was hurt, needed its love. In *Novel on Yellow Paper*
(1937), the heroine, Pompey, is sent to a convalescent home at age eight and
there appalled by a maid's "arbitrary" motherly feeling; "it was so insecure,
so without depth or significance. It was so similar in outward form, and so
asunder and apart, so deceitful and so barbarous in significance." Soon after,
she becomes afraid for her mother, who suffers from heart disease—and
terrified once again for herself, since there is nothing she can do: she is
reduced to "fury and impotence," "a very hateful combination." Thus startled
into distrust of life, she discovers the great trustworthiness of death. "Always
the buoyant, ethereal and noble thought is in my mind: Death is my servant."
Let life do its worst, the black knight can be summoned. . . .

Smith's combination of honesty and "wicked bounce" makes her work
a tonic. Considering the risks she ran, she wrote remarkably few poems that
are clever or zany for their own sake. If her novels are too clever by half,
the poems are as clever as they should be—clever beyond reasonable expectation. Much as she plays with her moods and insights, much as she remains
sprightly and astonishingly inventive in poem after poem from the first volumes of the late thirties to the posthumous *Scorpion, and Other Poems*
(1971), her work has almost always the dignity of disciplined seriousness.

Calvin Bedient. *Eight Contemporary Poets*
(New York: Oxford University Press, 1975),
pp. 139–40

Stevie Smith reminds you of two Lears: the old king come to knowledge and
gentleness through suffering, and the old comic poet Edward veering off into
nonsense. I suppose in the end the adjective has to be "eccentric." She looks
at the world with a mental squint, there is a disconcerting wobble in the
mirror she holds up to nature.

Death, waste, loneliness, cruelty, the maimed, the stupid, the innocent,
the trusting—her concerns were central ones, her compassion genuine and
her vision almost tragic. Yet finally the voice, the style, the literary resources
are not adequate to the somber recognitions, the wounded joie de vivre, the
marooned spirit we sense they were destined to express. There is a retreat
from resonance, as if the spirit of A. A. Milne successfully vied with the
spirit of Emily Dickinson.

The genetic relations which the forms of these poems often bear to the
clerihew and the caricature prevent them from attaining the kind of large
orchestration that they are always tempting us to listen for. And if they are

the real thing when measured by Auden's definition, ["memorable speech"]
they miss the absolute intensity required by Emily Dickinson's definition:
when you read them, you don't feel that the top of your head has been taken
off. Rather, you have been persuaded to keep your head at all costs.

Seamus Heaney. *Preoccupations: Selected
Prose 1968–1978* (London: Faber, 1980),
p. 201

Florence Margaret Smith, who retained her nickname *Stevie* throughout her
adulthood and published under its androgynous rubric, reveled in incongruities. Her poetic speakers shift from male to female, conformist to nonconformist, simple to complex, and adult to child; at times, indeed they are both alive
and dead. She frequently set her poems to well-known tunes and sang them
rather tonelessly to willing listeners, and she often appended sketches whose
relationship to the text is problematical. Her syntax is odd, her rhymes unexpected, her numbers idiosyncratic, and as a result her work is nearly always
lively and original. Her poems have an immediate appeal, and yet many of
them bear considerable re-reading. The frequent incongruities chiefly account
for this double effect.

Smith's odd juxtapositions and her love of paradox invite comparison—
not infrequently pursued by her critics—to Blake. She herself was aware of
the parallel, even calling one of her poems "Little Boy Lost." Like Blake she
writes parables, redefines Christianity, addresses animals, sees angels, uses
simple language, and illustrates her poetry, but in all essentials she and Blake
are significantly different. Blake's is a handy-dandy world where justice and
thief change places, and so is Stevie Smith's, but Blakes's humor is rarer and
more likely to serve an ultimate if not an ulterior purpose. Smith's humor is
embodied and pervasive, more like the sort of extra joy which Coleridge
called the "blossom of the nettle."

Death, both natural and induced, was Stevie Smith's primary subject, at
least partly because she knew that she could rivet an audience with it. . . .
Her interest in death was not a pose. Her central assumption, the core of her
nature, was the recognition that death is always available, the only friend
who is as close as the river, waiting in every bottle of aspirin: "'two hundred
and I am freed.' / He said, 'from anxiety.'" Death was "end and remedy": "I
cannot help but like Oblivion better / Than being a human heart and human
creature." Even in a 1970 anthology for children, Smith mentioned in her
introduction the freeing knowledge that death is available, and she chose to
include the "fiercer" romantic efforts, together with Blake's sick rose and
Nashe's falling brightness. Predictably, her American publishers insisted on
publishing the book as an adult anthology.

Janice Thaddeus. *Contemporary Poetry.*
Winter, 1978, pp. 36, 38

The kind of poet Stevie Smith is begins to emerge from a close look at the *Collected Poems*. She does not develop, in any helpful sense of the word: the first handful of poems announce her concerns as clearly as do the final, posthumous poems. The consistency of technique and craftsmanship is as sure in 1937 as it is in 1969. To say that, though, is to acknowledge the inconsistency too, in that quite often the reader is left wondering whether Stevie Smith knew or cared when she had written a poem not quite true to her Muse. The answer to that sort of nagging doubt is probably that she knew but didn't care all that much. There is a deliberate carelessness in much of her writing which reflects her own rather cavalier attitude both to the world and to poetry, and this carelessness is something the reader has to confront, because it becomes, oddly enough, one of her peculiar strengths. . . . Stevie Smith is sufficiently sure of herself to throw at her audience quite a lot of what, in another context, she calls "balsy nonsense," in the knowledge that, when she has to, she can redeem herself. This process of giving with one hand what she takes away with the other operates through all her work, and it is one which is itself disturbing for readers and critics. We do, after all, like our poets to develop, and to take themselves seriously. But the tendency to see all poets in terms of growth towards maturity, however natural and understandable, is not always illuminating: Keats has suffered because of it, so too has John Clare. Clare in fact provides a useful pointer in the argument, in that he has endured a fate similar to Stevie Smith's at the hands of critics prepared to acknowledge his presence but unwilling to absorb him into their patterns of critical discourse. You will not find Clare getting much of a mention in surveys of the Romantics and Victorians, and this is as much a hint as to his true stature as an indication of his supposedly minor significance. Furthermore, Clare evinces the same sort of inconsistency. Stevie Smith likewise stands outside any tradition of the day, and in so doing acts as a comment on what is happening elsewhere; she becomes a touchstone, just as to read Clare is to see him apart from his contemporaries and to see them in a new light.

Mark Storey. Critical Quarterly. Summer,
1979, p. 42

For some reason which the two editors don't reveal, nothing [in *Me Again: Uncollected Writings of Stevie Smith*], except for the letters, is arranged in chronological order. James MacGibbon, Stevie's literary editor, does not comment on this, but says in his rather cautious preface that their choice is "tantamount to an autobiographical profile." This is not quite so, but he is surely right in saying that the book will give most readers their first authentic idea of her religious convictions. These were self-convictions. She had almost made up her mind that God was one of man's most unfortunate inventions. What needed explanation was not man's failing but his continued demand to love and be loved, even when

> Beaten, corrupted, dying,
> In his own blood lying.

But that was not enough, and the frail poet hurled herself against Von Hügel, Father D'Arcy, Ronald Knox and all the propositions of the Catholic and Anglo-Catholic Churches. "Some Impediments to Christian Commitment," which is a talk she gave at St. Cuthbert's, Philbeach Gardens, just over two years before her death, is an account of her own spiritual history, a touching one, with her own particular sense of the sad and the ridiculous. It has never been printed before. "Torn about," as one might expect, by the loss of her childhood faith, she was driven year by year to conclude that "the Redemption seems a Bargain dishonorable to both proposer and accepter." Uncertainty, however, which she finally settled for, proved treacherous, and she had to admit finally that she was a backslider as a non-believer.

Among the ten stories retrieved for us is perhaps the most lyrical of all, "Beside the Seaside," a languorous *fin-de-saison* holiday impression, the pebbles of the beach still warm to the touch but deeply cold underneath, and her friends' tempers just beginning to fray. There is a variable delicate friction between the interests of wives, husbands and children, and between human beings and nature—one might say between the seaside and the sea. Helena (the Stevie of this story) detaches herself, unable to help doing so, and wanders away inland across the marshes, returning "full of agreeable fancies and spattered with smelly mud" to confront the edginess of the party with her artist's sense of deep interior peace. In "The Story of a Story" she again defends herself as an artist. This wiry situation comedy shows why Stevie sometimes longed, in her character as Lot's wife, to be turned into a pillar of asphalt, since she seemed to give offense so often. Her friends did not want to become her material, as they had in "Sunday at Home" (also reprinted here), and her publisher hesitated, afraid of libel. "The morning, which had been so smiling when her employer first spoke, now showed its teeth." Sitting alone in the rainswept park, the unhappy authoress regrets the loss of friends, but much more the death of her story. She had worked on it with love to make it shining and remote, but also with "cunning and furtiveness and care and ferocity." These were the qualities which went into Stevie's seemingly ingenuous fiction. . . .

In the end, one of Stevie's greatest achievements was to be not only a connoisseur of myths, but the creator of one. Out of an unpromisingly respectable suburb at the end of the apparently endless Green Lanes she created a strange Jerusalem.

Penelope Fitzgerald. *London Review of Books*. December 3, 1981, p. 13

"This is the talking voice that runs on," says the narrator of *Novel on Yellow Paper*. And all kinds of "speaking" are found in the poems: letters, confessions, prayers, songs, messenger speeches, dramatic monologues, addresses, advice-columns, conversations (some rather one-sided, like "The After-thought"), Socratic dialogues, debates and arguments. Invocations are frequent: "Away, melancholy," "Do take Muriel out," "Honor and magnify this man of men," "Girls!," "Reader before you condemn, pause," "Crop, spirit, crop thy stony pasture!," "Farewell, dear friends," and (most of all) "Come, Death."

This talking voice sounds simple and spontaneous, but is more cunning than it seems. Stevie Smith's manner can be baffling; at times, as D. J. Enright says, one simply asks: "So what?" The zany, scatty, somewhat Thurberesque illustrations, the eccentric reading manner—she would sing her poems off-key, or recite them in a rather childish voice—the cryptic off-hand oddity of some of the shorter poems, invite dismissive words like "batty" and "fey.". . . .

The novels and stories, though dominated by "the talking voice that runs on," are full of people very vividly characterized by their speech. . . .

Most of the fictional voices are based on Stevie Smith's friends and enemies (George Orwell, for instance, was split into two of the characters in *The Holiday,* Basil and Tengal). These impersonations were so sharply done as, on occasion, to get her into the kind of trouble that is described in "The Story of a Story."

The pleasure in satirical characterizations goes with a relish for parody, imitation and pastiche.

Hermione Lee. Introduction to Stevie
Smith. Stevie Smith: A Selection (London:
Faber, 1983), pp. 18, 23

How does Stevie Smith's strange doggerel poetry achieve its inimitable magic? This question is constantly asked both by her admirers and her critics, because she is an original voice in poetry with no back-up tradition and no imitators. "Eccentric" and "quirky" are words most frequently applied to her poems by baffled reviewers. . . .

But Smith's technical sophistication is only one of the many tools she used, and the unsettling effects she achieved through juxtaposition of inappropriate ideas expressed as much the person she was as the way she worked. Her funniest poems are always sad, poignant, and searingly honest. She was never without a feeling of deep sadness, but she "counted despair derisory" and saw it as her own weakness rather than the fault of the world. A small maker of mischief inhabited her head, a debunker of pomp and self-importance that sent her into a fit of giggling at serious moments.

Jeni Coupyn. The Bloodance Book of
Contemporary Women Poets (Newcastle-
upon-Tyne: Bloodance, 1985), pp. 37–38

Smith's poetry not only draws on children's culture for its form and content but knowingly exploits the interrogative play signal to challenge conventional literary and cultural frames and unsettle the reader's assumptions about the relationship with the text. Quite evidently her teasing segregates her readers into those who opt for the simple stability of the notion that "this is play" (and therefore need not be investigated) and those who pursue the ramifications of the challenge her teasing presents. That challenge is fundamental. In terms of conventional literary framing, Smith's flippancy, carelessness, and redundancies, her refusal to commit her authority to a single voice or point of view, her childishness, use of fairy tales, nursery rhymes, and oral literature all signal that her writing is nonserious, verse not poetry, fun not Literature. Read in this way, its obvious ironies, though recognizable, are contained and defused.

If, on the other hand, the reader pursues the destabilizing effects of the question "Is this play?" then he/she is forced to consider the nature of the complicity the poems invite and to recognize the ambivalent, carnivalesque quality of their laughter that is at once challenging, self-mocking, and subversive. From this perspective, it becomes evident that Smith juxtaposed the (private/secret) world of play and magical possibility with the (public) known world of the conventionally Real in order to contest cultural forms and assumptions.

Martin Pumphrey. Critical Quarterly. 28,
1986, p. 90

Her aim was to write poetry that comes to the lips as naturally as speech. In this she is an inheritor of a tradition that looks back to the *Lyrical Ballads* and beyond. But her liking for simplicity, her refusal to overdecorate her themes, is only one aspect of her poetics. Another is her constant use of quotations, half-quotations, travesties, echoes and allusions drawn from the work of other poets whose voices infiltrate her own. "The accents are those of a child," Christopher Ricks has written; "yet the poems are continually allusive, alive with literary echoes as no child's utterance is." Learning poetry by heart at school developed her auditory imagination which, in turn, fed her highly literary, referential poems. As John Bayley has argued, "these poems have in their own way as much disciplined digestion behind them as those of Yeats or Valéry." She wears this learning lightly and makes shrewd use of her sources. Some of her poems are translations, strictly or freely rendered; others rework famous tales, legends or plays, in which meaning turns upon a reversal of convention, disenchantment; her Persephone, also indicating a fear of life, prefers the underworld. . . .

Though much in her work is autobiographical she is not a confessional poet. Instead, she adopts a variety of personae, some of them animals, through which to voice her thoughts, fears and feelings. These do not cohere to construct a single, authoritative voice but remain multivocal and contradictory. Her writing upholds the importance of inconsistency and paradox. "In

Lear's mind run also the Fool's iconoclasms," she once wrote, this duality appearing also in her own work with its blend of the tragic and comical.

> Frances Spalding. *Stevie Smith:*
> *A Biography* (New York: Norton, 1988),
> pp. xvi–xvii

SÖDERGRAN, EDITH (FINLAND) 1892–1923

The small Swedish-speaking community in Finland saw the establishment of a strong Modernist movement relatively early—perhaps because of the unstable political climate in Finland generally and the anomalous position of the Swedish-speaking community in particular. The two pioneering poets of the movement were Edith Södergran and Elmer Diktonius. They were followed by Gunnar Björling and Rabbe Enckell, and the movement's domination of Finland-Swedish poetry was not seriously challenged until the 1960s.

Edith Södergran . . . was brought up partly in the cosmopolitan atmosphere of the Russian capital, St. Petersburg, and partly in the Finnish countryside of Southern Karelia. She contracted tuberculosis in 1908, and her short life was lived in the shadow of death, a shadow darkened further by the disasters of the Bolshevik takeover in Russia and the Civil War in Finland. Her first collection of poetry, *Dikter* (1916), was partly in the Symbolist style: it seemed daringly modern to the conservative literary world of Swedish-speaking Finland. Her following collections, such as *Septemberlyran* (1918), are wilder and more ecstatic, in the style of Expressionism. The poetess feels herself to be a stranger and prisoner in the world and can only realize her full potential in a cosmic setting. . . .

Her last poetry, however, published posthumously in *Landet som icke är* (1925), is in a quieter vein, as in the celebrated title poem where she dreams of [a] nonexistent country.

> Gavin Orton. In Irene Scobbie, ed. *Essays*
> *on Swedish Literature* (Aberdeen, Scotland:
> Aberdeen University Press, 1978), p. 127

"Every woman who writes is a survivor," says Tillie Olsen. Sixty years ago, Edith Södergran died in a remote village in eastern Finland. Her brief life was full of hardship. She experienced war at close hand. She knew what starvation meant. She lived in the shadow of a killer disease for most of her life. The four thin volumes of poetry that she published were met with scorn, laughter, or indifference by critics and public alike. And when she died, from tuberculosis and malnutrition, at the age of thirty-one, she could count on the fingers of one hand the number of her friends and supporters. Yet she could write

I lift my head. I have a secret. What could touch me?
I am unbroken, a hyacinth that cannot die.
I am a spring flower with pink bells
rising full of earth's carefree triumph:
to live unsurpassed, strong, without resistance in the world.

She exited life a survivor, her joy intact, her belief in the value of her poetry unshaken. And time has proven her right: unlike many poets of her generation, Edith Södergran has not faded. Her place in Scandinavian literature is secure: her poetry continues to influence and inspire, to be quoted, put to music, recited, anthologized, re-issued, analyzed—and translated. . . .

[At] her literary debut in 1916 with the collection entitled *Poems*. . . . one critic [asked] whether her publisher had wanted to give Swedish Finland a good laugh. The rest of the critical reception was in the same vein. . . .

Södergran's answer to all this [the negative criticism and the ravages of war] was another collection of poetry, *The September Lyre*, soon followed by two more: *The Rose Altar* and *Future's Shadow*. The critics continued to heap their scorn and to consider her, at most, "an interesting fool."

Edith Södergran arrived on the literary scene with the force of an explosion. Who did she think she was, this woman from nowhere, who dared to do away with rhyme and meter and call it poetry? There were, however, a few people who recognized her strength as a poet. One of them was another woman, the author and critic Hagar Olsson. She wrote a sympathetic review, to which Södergran responded, incredulous: "Could it really be that I am coming to someone? Could we take each other's hand?" . . .

Edith Södergran had many voices as a poet. She was expressing her feelings about separation and death. She was concerned with herself as a woman, and with the ambivalence of her feelings toward men. In some of her poetry, she conjures up a primeval force that aims to change the world. And in her last poems, she accepts death with a calm simplicity inspired by the Gospels and the Book of Psalms. But one theme runs through all she has written: her concern with freedom and her joy in life. To Hagar Olsson she writes:

Surrender yourself to my will, to the sun, to the force of life. . . .
Let life fight to the utmost. . . . I want to pour over you my
living reserves of strength. I am life, the joyous life.

Edith had a sister in American literature, and it is here that they touch each other most closely. Emily Dickinson wrote: "I find ecstasy in living; the mere sense of living is joy enough."

Stina Katchadourian. Introduction to Edith
Södergran. *Love and Solitude: Selected
Poems 1916–1923* (San Francisco: Fjord
Press, 1981), pp. 6–9

Long ago, the critic Bengt Holmqvist expressed a not unreasonable fear—that Edith Södergran would fall into the hands of cultists or, at any rate, uncritical enthusiasts. The pathetic and yet exotic circumstances of her life, the efforts of some of her contemporaries to surround her earthly existence, and her production, with sanctity's odor, the strong emotional appeal some of her poetry makes (to such disparate groups as unhappy adolescents, radical feminists, and fundamentalist Christians), the visionary quality of many poems in the middle collections—it is readily understandable how, and why, a canonization may occur. But we have seen what damage the cultic approach did to the study of Rainer Maria Rilke, obscuring his place in literary history, diverting his audience's attention from his remarkable poetic means to his several "philosophies," and, what was worst, driving away potential readers who were unprepared for full enlistment among his worshipers. It is to be hoped that, in the future, scholarship will grapple with Edith Södergran's language, in all of its aspects, with the expansion of our knowledge about the circumstances of her life . . . , and with the complex story of her reception in the North and abroad.

Certainly, she has been a major liberating force on Scandinavia's poetry, even as Rimbaud was on that of France. Holmqvist—who, by the way, does not hesitate to mention Edith Södergran in a single breath with Rimbaud and Rilke—speaks of "the great revolution" which her work caused; and poet after poet has willingly confessed an indebtedness to her. . . .

The extent of Edith Södergran's influence in Scandinavia . . . can be measured, however roughly. But what of that final and probably unanswerable question: how does Edith Södergran rank in the outside world, in the "museum of modern poetry" (to use the title of the Enzensberger anthology where the German poet helped bring her to the attention of an international audience)? For example, had she written in her "best language," German, would she have been accorded a rank as high as the one she holds in the North? Or had she been born in the English-speaking world, would her poems have a place, say, in every anthology of imagist poetry? (The Danish critic Poul Borum has observed a tone which is "astonishingly reminiscent" of Edith Södergran's in the verse of D. H. Lawrence; in the same volume, Borum has given Edith Södergran a chapter, called "Three Priestesses," in which she is coupled with two stars of German poetry, Elsa Lasker-Schüler [1876–1945], and Nelly Sachs [1891–1970] in a trio of "the century's great women lyricists.") The making of such comparisons, the uttering of such praise is as exciting, of course, as it may be misleading; Edith Södergran does possess a Lawrence-like sense of the magical moment (for example, Lawrence's "The Gods! The Gods!" could well be from her hand), she has the tormented erotic perceptivity of Lasker-Schüler, and, sometimes, Sachs's air of the tragic prophetess—but she is not just a Nordic version of any of these poets, rather the owner of a special genius. Still, how can that genius be defined to someone who does not know her work? Telling W. H. Auden about Edith Södergran, even Gunnar Ekelöf had to take recourse to comparisons: "She is a very great poet, as far as I can judge of Achmatova's class, or even beyond, a young Swedish woman in the *diaspora,* one of our Byzantines, brave and loving as your Emily Brontë. It is a pity that such a rare bird should be buried for the world in a grave over which the war has passed several times. She belongs to the world though her language might seem an Old Aeolian dialect."

George Schoolfield. *Edith Södergran:*
Modernist Poet in Finland (Westport,
Connecticut: Greenwood Press, 1984),
pp. 133–35

Formally, [Södergran's poem] "Vierge moderne" speaks with authority. The anaphoric "I am," implying a strong parading I, transforming itself into a promise of the future. At the same time a teasing, masquerading I, enunciation of mobility and heterogeneity.

A fashion statement, with as much playfulness as authority. A challenge, as bold as it is casual. Read as above it is a questioning of the basis of our culture: the categories of the sexes, the legitimacy of naming.

How does it come about that it can be read as a token of lack? As a deficiency in femininity? As a rejection of love? The main explanation is the loss of a context, the repression of the discourse of the new woman. The second part of the emancipation of [the] last century has been forgotten. The phase where emotional, creative, erotic emancipation was in focus. "Vierge moderne" is a performative. It has been read as a constative. Reading the poem like that is to deprive it of its authority, just as it is deprives its readers of its promise. A performative utterance, as was said above, can gain its authority from accepted conventions—like the "I do" of the wedding ceremony. If not, if the task is instead initiating new procedures, it will have to seize authority.

Edith Södergran, in her poetry, seized authority. Partly through sheer inner strength and creative power. Partly, though, through the historical moment. The moment can be seen as an interregnum in the rule of naming. *Before,* the concept of women as frail, passive, "opposite" reigned. *After,* a trivialization and commercialization of the new woman set in, the figure was turned into a joke or an advertisement. *Before,* a lack of desire characterized women. *After,* the Freudian or modern scientific definition of women's sexuality took over. The period where Edith Södergran belongs is the period in between, the period of Alexandra Kollontay, Lou Andreas-Salomé, Grete Meisel-Hess, Elisabeth Dauthendey, the period of female initiative and self-definition, of women's quest for their own desire, their own soul, their own eroticism.

Unfortunately the period was a short one, particularly as regards the erotic quest. By around the turn of the century, the new scientific discourse on sexuality was established. Women's passivity was defined as "normal" (Freud) or "natural" (Ellis). We are back in the dual oppositions: women's sexuality is passive and receptive, men's is conquering and active. We are back in "mastery," once so firmly rejected by women.

But, for a short while, the erotic field was open. Women stepped out, "Sorties," searching for new possibilities. Something seemed within reach. Then, with the words of Virginia Woolf (in another context): "the close withdrew; the hard softened. It was over—the moment."

The moment was over. It has almost been forgotten that it ever existed. "Vierge moderne" is a performative speech-act. If we ever want to see it in a felicitous light, the prerequisite is that we bring it back in its proper context: the new woman and her courageous and collective quest in the decades around the turn of the century.

Birgitta Holm. NORA: Nordic Journal of Women's Studies. 1, 1993, pp. 29–30

SOMERS, ARMONÍA (URUGUAY) 1920–

Armonía Somers . . . belongs by right of birth to what is called the Uruguayan generation of forty-five; however, she may be considered one of the exceptions that negate or justify the ultimate value of this category which is being so much questioned today. The problem is that in reviewing what it means to belong to this generation—themes, preferences, problems—we encounter something more than divergences; there is actually an almost complete disjunction between the preoccupations that typify the work of this writer and those toward which the rest of the group inclined.

Armonía Somers began to publish relatively late—1950—and her first work was a novel, <i>La mujer desnuda</i> (The naked woman). This narrative already shows the most characteristic and defining traits of her style, among them the most important, originality. . . .

In the context sketched out by the narrative, humor appears more like an act of revenge than of amusement; humor is no game, but rather denounces and cries out, and, for this reason, most often appears in the guise of black humor. Humor appears in different levels of signification, from the word, which may be a name, to the circumstances created by a broad and rich context. . . .

[A]ll of Armonía Somers's work reflects concerns of a moral nature, and lead us to reflect on human life and its circumstances. . . .

Her work translates automatically into a counterweight to an idealized image of the world, showing it to us in its nakedness and shame. . . . The writer commits herself to giving us the history of fraud and lies, demystifying this world so as to reveal the swamp of human misery. It is no accident that her themes are "the great inevitables, like destiny, death, and love."

José Manuel Garcia Rey. Cuadernos Hispanoamericanos. 415, 1985, pp. 101–4

Fear, repulsion, curiosity. . . [I]n a story by Armonía Somers entitled *El hombre de tunel* (The tunnel man), a woman dying after an accident remembers that all her life she has been obsessed by the smile of a man whom she saw for the first time at the age of six, while playing around a sewer. . . . In this story, Somers allegorizes the morbid character of an inevitably sadomasochistic image by using opposing terms that create discomfort and perplexity. Finally, it is a matter of a metaphorical interaction between love and death. Death that, for her protagonist, is at once loss and recovery. Death that recurs in Somers's fictional trajectory, as the *leitmotiv* of her shattered narrative universe. Death that will have a central function in an entirely different story, entitled *Un retrato para Dickens* (A portrait for Dickens). . . .

This is a linear narrative, in the first person, about the experiences of an orphan girl whom the asylum entrusts to an alcoholic longshoreman and his wife who is obsessed with stones. . . .

In this long story, almost a novel, sordidness is repeated and re-created as a topic, although the language overcomes its relationship to the referent, creating distance. The absurd, posited as a parable, appears to adapt itself to demystifying content which, however, acknowledges the protagonist's vulnerability.

Helena Araújo. *Plural.*
179, August, 1986, pp. 21–22

Somers has carefully separated her vocations as a school teacher and librarian from her career as a writer. In 1963, the noted Uruguayan critic, Angel Rama, described the unusual nature and importance of her fiction: "Everything is uncanny, strange, disconcerting, repulsive and, at once incredibly fascinating in the most unusual prose that the history of our literature has known: Armonía Somers's books." Her fiction fuses reality and imagination, this world and the beyond where living and dead share a common sense of emptiness and lack of communication. Her dense prose style and expressionistic imagery formed by the unconventional confluence of a visceral or repulsive or violent realism and a lyrical metaphysics is a unique accomplishment. . . .

Death and female/male relationships emerge as important constants in [*El derrumbamiento* (The fall), her] first collection of short stories: the sensations of sexuality, the unusually unencumbered naming of the body's humors—sweat, saliva, milk, blood, semen—the taste of mother's milk, of abortions, of intercourse. In most [descriptions of] sexual relations, indifference and pernicious eroticism prevail in Somers's explorations of misogynist aggression. Furthermore, Somers tests the taboos of her society in the unique desacralization of cultural stereotypes, both sexual and racial, in her characterization of the Virgin Mary and a Black man—"marianismo" and "machismo."

[The] short novel [*La mujer desnuda*] allegorical in nature, scandalized provincial Montevideo of the 1950s, whose critics condemned the author as a "gifted and pathological erotic," a "misguided pedagogue" and a "crypto-maniac recidivist." This work marked the start of a continuous and frank treatment of the problems of sexuality and eroticism in Somers's fiction, a narrative that challenges the hypocrisy of social and religious morality and portrays man as a solitary and cruel beast.

Evelyn Picón Garfield. In Diane E. Marting,
ed. *Women Writers of Spanish America*
(Westport, Connecticut: Greenwood Press,
1986), pp. 129–30

One of the least known (in the United States) yet most innovative and shock-ing authors in this anthology [*Women's Fiction from Latin America,* 1988] is the Uruguayan Armonía Somers, whose penchant for the sexually bizarre and the grotesque earned her the displeasure, distaste and disapproval of male critics during the 1950s. In "The Plunder," an uneducated, inarticulate man wanders the countryside, periodically raping women in an attempt to subdue his pathological fear of their bodies and reproductive organs. This plunderer is himself "plundered" in an unusual way when a peasant woman he meets on the road takes him to her breast, and, by suckling him, asserts her power over him. The real irony of the situation is revealed, however, when both he and the reader learn that the woman is able to produce milk just "from wishing it." It is his discovery that she in fact has never been "plundered" that makes her "rape" so disturbing to him.

Gabriela Ibrieta. *Hispanic Review.*
58, 1990, p. 425

SOMERVILLE AND ROSS (IRELAND) [E. O. SOMERVILLE 1858–1949; V. MARTIN (MARTIN ROSS) 1862–1915]

The literary partnership of Miss Edith Somerville and Miss Violet Martin—the most brilliantly successful example of creative collaboration in our times—began with *An Irish Cousin* in 1889. Published over the pseudonyms of "Geilles Herring" and "Martin Ross," this delightful story is remarkable not only for its promise, afterwards richly fulfilled, but for its achievement. The writers proved themselves the possessors of a strange faculty of detach-ment which enabled them to view the humors of Irish life through the unfamil-iar eye of a stranger without losing their own sympathy. They were at once of the life they described and outside it. They showed a laudable freedom from political partisanship; a minute familiarity with the manners and cus-toms of all strata of Irish society; an unerring instinct for the "sovran word," a perfect mastery of the Anglo-Irish dialect; and an acute yet well-controlled sense of the ludicrous. . . .

They reached the summit of their achievement in *The Real Charlotte,* which still remains their masterpiece, though easily eclipsed in popularity by the irresistible drollery of *Some Experiences of an Irish R.M.* To begin with, it does not rely on the appeal to hunting people which in their later work won the heart of the English sportsman. It is a ruthlessly candid study of Irish provincial and suburban life; of the squalors of middle-class households; of garrison hacks and "underbred, finespoken," florid squireens. But secondly and chiefly it repels the larger half of the novel-reading public by the fact that two women have here dissected the heart of one of their sex in a mood of unrelenting realism. While pointing out the pathos and humiliation of the thought that a soul can be stunted by the trivialities of personal appearance, they own to having set down Charlotte Mullen's many evil qualities "without pity." They approach their task in the spirit of Balzac. The book . . . is extraordinarily rich in both wit and humor, but Charlotte, who cannot control her ruling passion of avarice even in a death chamber, might have come straight out of the pages of the *Comédie Humaine.*

C. L. Graves. Quarterly Review. 219:436,
1913, pp. 30–33

It chanced that I was engaged, in another connection, with some criticisms, or, rather, with an appreciation, of The Two Ladies (as I always think of Martin Ross and E. O. Somerville) at the very moment that the sad news of Martin Ross's illness reached me. Two days later she died, and now part of the eulogium all suddenly and tragically becomes an elegy.

I had been reading aloud some of the sketches, and in particular "The House of Fahy," which I have always held was one of the best short stories ever written, with a last sentence that no one but a professional elocutionist with nerves of steel could possibly compass; and afterwards it had amused me to imagine a room filled with devotees of the *Irish R.M.,* such as might as easily exist as a Boz Club, capping quotations from that and its companion books and finding pleasure in expressing admiration in the warmest terms and in minute detail; and there are not many pleasures greater than that.

The discussion might, indeed, have begun by the old question, What are the best short stories in the world? and my own insistence on the claims of this very "House of Fahy" to a place high on the list; because, as I should have urged, it relates an episode proper only to the short-story medium; there is no word too many or too few; it has atmosphere and character; it is absorbing; it has a beginning, a middle, and such an end!

"But what about 'The Maroan Pony'?" some one might have inquired. "Isn't that a perfect short story too?"

And I should have replied that it is.

"And 'Harrington's'?" some one else might have urged. "Isn't that perfect? And it has an extra quality, for in addition to all the humor of it, and the wonderful picture of a country auction sale, it has that tragic touch. To my mind it is greater than "The House of Fahy.'"

And then I am sure that a most emphatic claim for "Trinket's Colt" as the best of all would have been formulated; and by this time we should have been right in the thick of it, all eager to speak and be heard.

To me The Two Ladies have long been the only contemporary authors whom it is absolutely necessary to read twice instantly: the first time for the story, which is always so intriguing—and the more so as you get more familiar with the ingenuity of their methods—as to exact a high speed; and the second time for the detail, the little touches of observation and experience, and the amazing, and to an envious writer despairful, adequacy of epithet. And having read them twice, I find that whenever I pick them up again there is something new, something not fully tasted before. . . .

And now the bond has snapped, and "Martin Ross," who was Miss Violet Martin, is dead. With her death, the series stops, for though neither was the dominant spirit, the prosperity of the work demanded both. As to The Two Ladies' method of collaboration I know nothing, and should like to know all; which held the pen I have no notion, or if one alone held it. But that it was complete and perfect is proved by this sentence from a private letter from one very near to them, which I may perhaps take the liberty of quoting, since it embodies a remark made by the survivor of the many, many years' partnership. "There isn't a page, there isn't a paragraph, there isn't a line which either of us could claim as her sole work." That is collaboration in the highest degree, two minds that not only work as one but are one.

E. V. Lucas. *Spectator.*
January 1, 1916, pp. 9–10

There is force in the criticism of Somerville and Ross that used to be made in the sour, wan yellow dawn of the Irish revival, when it was a crime for anyone to laugh in Ireland, unless they laughed for the right party: the criticism that these ladies were simply purveying the stage Irishman to English magazines and winding up the old parish hurdy-gurdy of Irish farce.

And, of course, they were. The tradition of Irish farce is permanent. The stage Irishman is permanent. He is as permanent as the Irish narrative gift and the use of words as an intoxicant. The puritanism of Maynooth and Merrion Square cannot put its gooseflesh on the warm native fancy. But there is more than one Somerville and Ross. An early novel, written before [*Some Experiences of an Irish R.M.*] made them popular, does attempt to say what the Anglo-Irish were like between one View Hallo or one petty sessions and the next. That book is *The Real Charlotte.* I don't want to be a spoil-sport, especially now the *R.M.* has been canonized by *Everyman,* and I write as a foreigner, but *The Real Charlotte* did something which had not, up to the 1890s, been done in Irish literature. It portrayed the Anglo-Irish with the awful, protracted mercy of the artist. It "placed" them as no novelist had thought of "placing" them before; as surely, for example, as Mrs. Gaskell knew how to place her world in *Wives and Daughters.* I do not mean that *The Real Charlotte* is as sound or as accomplished a novel as Mrs. Gaskell's.

It was a first novel, awkwardly built, and, like so many Anglo-Irish writers, the authors never got rid of an amateur, almost a juvenile streak; but *The Real Charlotte* was a beginning of great promise. One went to Ireland looking for the characters of the Irish R.M.; one found oneself, thirty years after it was written, surrounded by the disquieting people of this one serious novel. . . .

And though *The Real Charlotte* is a novel about jealousy and the never-ceasing intrigue and treachery of Irish life, its main stuff is this snobbery. Not a plain, excluding snobbery that tells us where we may go and where we may not, but a snobbery that is in the blood. Not a snobbery versed in distinguished ancestors only, but a snobbery bedeviling the character with the pretensions of second cousins and the mildewed memories of better times. It is a snobbery that has become the meaning of life. It permeates everything: good sense, idealism, hatred, tenderness, religion—even pity. We must allow something for the fact that this book is written in the 1890s; and when the Dysarts wince because Francie keeps her gloves on at tea, we are charmed by the comedy of the manners of a period. Anglo-Irish snobbery was pretty genial about such quaintness. But underneath this are the inturned passions of a small, defensive and decaying colonial society: Francie is a social casualty in the everlasting skirmish with the other Ireland. Only by exaggerating their exclusiveness and creating low comedy around them can the Ascendants keep their ascendancy. . . .

Fifty years of politics lie between us and these skirling *commères,* with their high-pitched domestic life and the loquacity of distressed Elizabethans. But the narrative writing has the Irish visual gift, so bold in its metaphors, so athletic in its speed, as if tongue and eye were racing against each other. . . . And then, though there is hardly a breath of Irish politics in the story, they are there by implication. For the characters are exclusively the Irish Protestants and their isolation gives a strength to the strokes in which they are drawn.

The faults of *The Real Charlotte* are obvious. The national malady of not "letting on" what you are up to enables the novelist to catch the changeableness of human character; but toward the end . . . the elusive becomes the frantic. It is unforgivable that Francie is killed out riding; especially as her death, one is pretty sure, is due to the profound snobbery of the authors. There is no way of making a lady of her, so she had to be killed. But after one has removed the old-fashioned trappings, the irony, the insight and portraiture of this novel show that Anglo-Irish society might have got its Mrs. Gaskell, if the amateur tastes of the discursive colonial had not breezily ridden the chance off the page.

V. S. Pritchett. *The Living Novel*
(New York: Reynal and Hitchcock, 1947),
pp. 150–52, 154

We should judge a book not by how we think it may affect a hypothetical foreigner, but solely by how it actually does affect ourselves. In short, if

Slipper's story and the *Irish R.M.* books in general do seem funny to us, they need no other justification. They will not, of course, seem funny if we feel, for instance, that their idiom is divorced from any living speech or that the scenes and traits of character that they describe have no roots in Irish life. But this is not the case with Somerville and Ross; they exaggerate, obviously, as every comic writer does, but their exaggeration is firmly based on Irish ground which they knew well and which in their own way they loved deeply. They lived in Ireland for almost all their writing lives and they had, as a writing team, a sensitive ear and a penetrating humorous eye. If their writing is not part of the literature of Ireland, then Ireland is a poorer place than many of us believe it to be. . . .

Three novels are more important than the rest—*The Real Charlotte, Mount Music,* and *The Big House of Inver.* Mr. Stephen Gwynn has said that *The Real Charlotte* is one of the most powerful novels of Irish life ever written. Its central figure, Miss Charlotte Mullen, is certainly a massive and formidable concentration of evil intent working in commonplace detail, without any thunderclaps or blue flame. Evil has often been more dramatically exhibited, but I do not think it has ever been more convincingly worked out in humdrum action, or brought home with such a terrible cumulative effect as an element in everyday life. . . . *The Real Charlotte* is generally considered the best of their novels, and I think it is so. It is also, unfortunately, the one most marred by evidence of lack of sympathy with outsiders. Professor [Daniel] Corkery, in a striking phrase, denounces the presence in our literature of "an alien ascendancy streaked with the vulgarity of insensibility." The verdict itself has a little streak of the same, and its harshness is unjust, as far as most of the work of Somerville and Ross is concerned. But in *The Real Charlotte* the streak is noticeable and it harms an otherwise splendid achievement. That does not mean, however, that I think *The Real Charlotte* is un-Irish. There is nothing un-Irish about aristocratic pride; a great part of our Gaelic literature throbs with a full and blue-blooded contempt for the low-born.

The two other main novels, *Mount Music* and *The Big House of Inver,* are much more loosely written, but with more generous feeling. The ice has melted—there are twenty-five years after all between *The Real Charlotte* and *Mount Music*—and the style has lost some of its edge, the edge that I think Martin Ross put on it, for good and ill. The central theme of *Mount Music* is one of which Irish writers have in general tended to fight rather shy, that of Religious Intolerance, on the part of both Protestants and Catholics. Miss Somerville calls it, cheerfully enough, the Spirit of the Nation and follows its devious workings and its double language with remarkable detachment. The whole subject is of course now utterly out of date, and such a spirit can scarcely be conceived by the modern Irish reader, who positively drips with tolerance. None the less the book may be read for its antiquarian interest.

Although both *Mount Music* and *The Big House of Inver* lack style as compared with *The Real Charlotte,* they have not lost the power of generating a demonic force in a credible character. Such is Dr. Francis Mangan in *Mount*

Music; such, in *The Big House of Inver,* is Shibby Pindy, the illegitimate great-hearted daughter of a gentle family, who has had a peasant upbringing, but whose passion is to restore, through her half-brother, the glories of the big house, which stands empty at the beginning of the novel and is in flames at the end. *The Big House of Inver,* were it not for something a little blurred and loose in the writing, would surpass *The Real Charlotte.* I am not indeed quite sure that it does not surpass it as it is, for if there is a blur in the writing there is no such smudge of meaningless character as is the Dysart family group in the earlier novel.

What we regret then, amid so much that we admire, is that, as imaginative sympathy deepened, style declined. The youthful arrogance which somewhat blunted the moral perception yet carried itself extremely well. The quality of unwavering intelligence is in the writing—an intelligence not worried by clichés, but never allowing a cliché to come between it and the reality of the given moment. This alertness flags in the later works which have a wider vision but a less precise one. Perhaps had it not been for the success of the R.M. stories, which diverted them for so many and such important years from their vein of tragedy, Somerville and Ross might have given us a work of their maturity which would have been as alert as it was humane.

Donat O'Donnell [Conor Cruise O'Brien].
Irish Writing. March, 1955, pp. 10–13

When Lady Gregory steps from her Big House, Lennox Robinson has written, "she never condescends, she knows her humble neighbors well, sits by their fire in the homelist fashion," but in Somerville and Ross there is "a touch—it is only a touch—of 'we' and 'they,' of the contrast between the Big House and the Cabin." This is much like saying that Faulkner writes of Negroes with just a touch of "we" and "they." Somerville and Ross were daughters of the Big House, and the Cabins belonged to the other Ireland. For that matter, Robinson's belief that Lady Gregory had blurred her pronouns was not shared by the country people of Kiltartan.

The contrast between Big House and Cabin looms large in Somerville and Ross because it loomed large in Irish life. Every Irishman knew that he belonged to one of these worlds, or believed that he did, or knew that he did but denied it. No Irish novel could fail to take this into account if it hoped to represent accurately the thoughts and emotions, the very look and feel of its society. . . . [T]he habits engendered by feudalism had not vanished: Ireland remains dominated and divided by fierce prejudices of class and caste.

The slow passing of that world is the subject of the novels of Somerville and Ross. Their career spanned the entire period during which their class fell from power, and their works respond to the stages of this defeat. *Mount Music* (1919) opens in the 1890s, when "the class known as landed gentry still ruled in Ireland." *An Enthusiast* (1921) "attempts to give a picture of the closing days of the old order of country life in Ireland." *The Big House of Inver* (1925) "is the history of one of those minor dynasties that, in Ireland, have risen, and ruled, and rioted, and have at last crashed in ruins." But this is also true, if in indirect and subtle ways, of their earlier novels, written when the old order enjoyed a deceptive sense of security.

The stories are seldom dispassionate, for they are written from a fierce though critical loyalty to the Big House and a harsh, often ungenerous opposition to its enemies. But they move steadily toward tragic knowledge, toward recognition of the fact that the Big House was not destroyed by the mutinous Cabins but by its own weakness and capacity for self-deception. The *Irish R.M.* stories are exceptions, but they are special precisely because they evade this subject. The world which Somerville and Ross loved is held suspended in these stories, its dissolution checked. "With Joyce's *Dubliners*," Frank O'Connor has written. "*The R.M.* is the most closely-observed of all Irish story-books, but, whereas Joyce observes with cruel detachment, the authors of *The Irish R.M.* observe with love and glee." This is true: they have been excelled only by O'Connor himself. But beyond the magic hedgerows of the *Irish R.M.* lay a darker world, existing and perishing in time.

Thomas Flanagan. *The Kansas Review.*
January, 1966, pp. 56–57

Summary of a literary career is never a simple matter. Even with the greatest there are things we would wish otherwise. The task is made yet more difficult when, as in the case with Somerville and Ross, we treat of a closely knit partnership, one member of which outlived the other by a whole generation. The knitting together of the two lives seems to increase in geometric rather than arithmetic progression the haps and accidents which control literary lives and the sundering of the partnership, instead of simplifying issues, creates new ones.

Cutting boldly through all the reservations which threaten to inhibit the formation of any conclusion, one would wish, first of all, to claim for these writers that they are great givers of pleasure, great entertainers. Edith reports of Violet that an old countrywoman said of her: "Sure ye're always laughing! That ye may laugh in the sight of the Glory of Heaven!" The old woman went to the heart of the matter. Preeminently, it is the "R.M." stories one thinks of in this connection, but many of the essays and articles, as well as the novels, contrive to amuse us with great good-humor. The writers' comic confidence is solidly based on their security within their social group, and, paradoxically, their interpretation of the tragedy of their class can be traced to the same source. Better than anyone else they knew the grave and the gay sides of their worlds. *The Real Charlotte* is, of course, their greatest achievement in any mode but it should not be forgotten that, after Martin's death, Edith carried on this branch of their activities very creditably in such novels as *Mount Music* and *The Big House of Inver*. Had Violet lived, as Edith did, to see the emergence of modern Ireland, perhaps they might together have provided in another great novel the sort of searching commentary on the new Ireland which they had already achieved about the old. This complex partnership, so tragically sundered in mid-stream, bristles with conjecture. If Martin had lived; if the need for money had not been so keen; if Martin's ill-health had not interfered, and so on and so on.

A truce to such pointless speculation! The achievement, after all, is solid enough. It includes what is, arguably, the finest Irish novel of the nineteenth century and a set of the funniest stories ever written. Somerville and Ross may not always function at their highest voltage, but when they do, their brilliance is undeniable.

Socially secure in a poor country, socially insecure in a declining class, they looked at their Irish world with clarity, geniality and much sympathetic insight. We should be grateful for what they did, not captious about what they did not do.

John Cronin. *Somerville and Ross*
(Lewisburg, Pennsylvania: Bucknell
University Press, 1972), pp. 100–101

The us-against-them dichotomy, Ireland of the Big House versus Ireland of the Cabins, is present in Somerville and Ross's work, but without the intensity of a cause. The "personal element" that reigns supreme in stories such as "Poisson D'Avril" also moderated their views of the public element, replacing the hasty passions and overly rigid categories of political rhetoric with a more generous sympathy for real people and actual experiences. When the Somerville estate at Drishane was forced to adopt "unusual defensive precautions" against Fenian activities in the mid-1860s, Edith, then a girl of ten, preferred to idealize the rebels and act the part of an Irish nationalist herself. Her dissenting role was expanded when the English dragoons offered her brother a ride on their horses; Edith, only a girl, was ignored; "I think that from that hour I became a Suffragist." Yet the various causes, whether women's rights, anti-Parnellism, nationalism, or unionism, never invade and restrict the literature. There the mildly rebellious and critical attitudes attach more significance to the internal weaknesses of the gentry than to the shifting economic and political forces outside its control.

Even as she continued to support the old economic system, therefore, Somerville also recognized the part that the gentry had played in its own ruin. Her 1925 novel, *The Big House of Inver,* uses the Prendeville estate to chronicle the entire history of the Protestant Ascendancy of the nineteenth century. From its earliest beginnings in nobility and splendor, the family line soon became corrupted by marriages into the lower class and, even more so, by its own brilliant but debilitating extravagance. . . .

Yet the deep-rooted sympathies and instinctive assumptions that had shaped *The Real Charlotte* in 1894 remained firm throughout both their lives. Prosperity for the large mass of people and bureaucratic thoroughness do not necessarily create moral ideals or provide acceptable substitutes for the cast-off traditional values. Somerville and Ross could understand the passage of the old order into history and appreciate the new social institutions; but their first and strongest loyalties remained always with the Big House.

They recognized, years before most members of their landed class, that the old system of land ownership and social privileges was nearing its end, paralyzed by its own feudal sensibilities and extravagances. Yet historical perception formed only one part of the authors' sense of their class. Literature also gave them a way of evoking the past and using it to measure and judge the new, rising interests. Their recreation of the old social order continues to mourn the loss of that way of life, even as it admits the loss. With all its strengths and limitations, the vantage point of the Protestant Ascendancy serves as the dominating center of their work. They accurately describe the fate of many once great estates, yet their work passes, perhaps too lightly, over the fate of the large mass of the peasantry.

Wayne E. Hall. *Shadowy Heroes: Irish Literature of the 1890s* (Syracuse, New York: Syracuse University Press, 1980), pp. 69–70

Somerville & Ross were traditional novelists: they were concerned with the way people behave in society. They wrote about what they knew intimately: the Anglo-Irish and, sometimes, the way their finely layered society was beset by political pressures. They focused on individual members of Anglo-Irish society with a subtlety of characterization which illuminates not only the social and religious conflicts of the time but the more general human condition. They threw into relief the troubles of an entire class and showed godlessness and greed in the most ordinary people. They were less concerned with the Gaelic and Catholic Irish, about whom they knew less; but when they did write about them it is often with a sense of pathos and their comedy never degenerates into the buffoonery of Lover and Lever. They have been misjudged. Their feminine laughter was sharper and more critical than anything which gave rise to the Stage Irishman, but it was usually reserved for those of their own religion. There was no malice in their attitude to the Irish people.

Their ability to capture the dialect of the people is remarkable. The Irish turn of phrase, the striking image, the singular inflection, never degenerate into stock stage brogue or Kiltartanese. They had no desire to change or improve the people, and they enjoyed them as fellow creatures. They were not blinded by the sentimentality which spoiled the work of many nineteenth-century writers, nor by the patriotism which colored the vision of many of their contemporaries. . . .

Their first collaborative effort, a dictionary of their families' speech, indicates their immense interest in words. They knew that because they were Anglo-Irish they spoke the English tongue differently from the English as well as from the Irish. . . . The speech of the Irish people around them was to them even more fascinating, because it was more colorful and poetic.

When they began to learn Irish in 1897 it was not in order to study ancient texts but to illuminate the things they heard said around them every day. They carefully preserved trial reports from local newspapers for the amazing dialogue recorded: "I did not say that I would keep her between the gate and the pillar until I would squeeze the decay out of her."

Their advantage over many of the writers of the Irish Literary Revival was that they did not live in Dublin but in daily contact with the people of the West of Ireland. The Ireland which their contemporaries visited to collect folk tales was their ordinary environment. They did not romanticize the peasantry nor exaggerate the unspoilt nature of their lives because they knew only too well the squalid conditions in which many of them were forced to live. And although there was always the tremendous barrier of the Big House and the differences in education and religion they still *knew* the country people. They went to their births, marriages and deaths, and attended them in sickness; they worked with them in stable and garden, and they met them at horse fairs, agriculture shows, races and hunting. Necessarily in a rural community there is more mutual dependence and helping each other than elsewhere. They knew the country people with an intimacy quite different from the observation—however sympathetic—of an outsider. And so they had the immense advantage of knowing another way of life and another way of speech.

> Hilary Robinson. *Somerville and Ross: A Critical Appreciation* (Dublin: Gill and Macmillan, 1980), pp. 3, 48–49

The claims made for Somerville and Ross as authors are high: according to Gifford Lewis, in her introduction to the *Selected Letters,* they wrote "the best Irish novel of the nineteenth century and the best set of comic tales of Irish life in the last days of the Ascendancy." I have to confess that I find one (*The Real Charlotte*) dull and the other wearisome, with its endless contretemps in the Irish countryside and singular turns of phrase—"'Many's the time Jamesy Geoghegan and meself used to be dhrivin' her to Macroom with gips an' all soorts,' says I."

The R M stories (the first volume published in 1899) stand as a monument to Irish incorrigibility and the knockabout approach to life; all very amiable and high-spirited, indeed, but savoring inescapably the stage-Irishness which, by the end of the century, had become a considerable source of affront to a good many people. While Major Yates, the Resident Magistrate, was being brought up smack against the antics of his social inferiors in colorful Skebawn, "Martin Ross's" relative, Lady Gregory, and her associates were in the thick of an opposing campaign to add dignity to Ireland, even if they had to bend over backwards to do it (in the wake of Lady Gregory, the amount of "peasant quality," or PQ, an Irish play contained, became the criterion by which to judge it).

Certain phrases and episodes from the letters do stick in the mind, it's true, like Edith Somerville's allusion to one "excellent supper," with "a huge pie like a Noah's ark with every sort of animal inside it," and Martin Ross's description of a dog that caught sight of her in the bath and promptly went into a fit. One literary prescription of Ross's seems sound—"to be brisk and candid and interested in common things"—as does the view of both authors that dialect is a matter of idiom rather than mispronunciation.

Unfortunately, the latter isn't borne out in their own work—"'If the tinker laves a sthroke of the pan on the misthress's dog, the Lord help him!' said Patsey"—and indeed their attitude to dialect (being funny about it, rather than by means of it) leaves one with a rather disagreeable impression. One of the merits of the letters is that Somerville and Ross aren't under any obligation to keep up a flow of comic Irishness and consequently project themselves, for the most part, as mettlesome and engaging.

Patricia Craig. *New Statesman and Society.*
August 4, 1989, pp. 29–30

SONO AYAKO (JAPAN) 1931–

Ayako Sono is not well known in the United States. Her literary career began in the fifties, but *Watcher from the Shore* is her first novel to be published in English. Like Sawako Ariyoshi, with whom she is sometimes linked, Sono is concerned with social issues, and her focus here is a particularly important and timely one: abortion. Although she is a Roman Catholic and a strong moral voice in the novel is a Catholic woman, the novel is no sectarian tract. Rather, it highlights a growing national unease in Japan about the widespread practice of abortion, conservatively estimated at one million a year. . . .

The effects of abortion on parents, especially the mother, is a common media focus, and *Watcher from the Shore* shows a range of responses from parental indifference to strong maternal guilt. Sono, however, concentrates not on family but on an obstetrician-gynecologist who runs a clinic in which abortions make up a major part of his practice. Sadaharu Nobeji, age forty-two, is aware of the irony of his being engaged simultaneously in supporting life and terminating it. Maintaining a common Japanese view that although abortion may not be good, it is necessary, he is outwardly comfortable with the duality; yet the novel's central concern is Sadaharu's growing inner discomfort about what he does.

The plot is simple, consisting of a series of case histories to which Sadaharu responds. Together the cases, which include aberrations such as malformed infants, mixed gender, and infanticide, raise questions that disturb him. . . .

Sono blends successfully the novel of character and the novel of ideas. Sadaharu Nobeji is a believable and appealing figure as one who insists that he does not take life seriously but does, who insists that he is at peace with himself but is attracted to a hymn with words that are an act of contrition, and who insists that he has no desire for faith but hears a divine voice in the blowing wind. The questions raised about abortion and its implications . . . are enduring ones for which, as represented in the painting of Christ with dirty hands, there are no simple or pure responses. *Watcher from the Shore* is a well-made, illuminating, and significant work.

Celeste M. Loughman. *World Literature Today.* 64, 1990, pp. 368–69

Bogged down by heavy-handed (perhaps poorly translated) dialogue, this slow-moving novel (*Watcher from the Shore*) about a Japanese obstetrician and his patients utilizes Dr. Sadaharu Nobeji's well–run clinic as a vantage from which to view multiple facets of Japanese society. Dr. Nobeji tries to be detached, yet he finds it impossible not to become emotionally entangled with his patients, whose problems are complicated, involving highly charged issues of infertility, adoption and abortion. Not only clinical ability but also great diplomacy are required to deal with the families of neglected infants, or babies damaged at birth. One particularly troubling case concerns the daughter-in-law of a prominent Japanese family of industrialists. When the young woman acknowledges that the child she is carrying is not their son's, the family, intensely aware of maintaining their image, demand a dangerous, six-month abortion. Dr. Nobeji discusses the moral ambiguities of many of his cases with a clear-thinking and non-judgmental Catholic priest. Sono's novels have been bestsellers in Japan; this, her first book to appear in English, is sentimental, sometimes maudlin, and fails to hold the reader's interest.

Sybil Steinberg. *Publishers Weekly.* January 19, 1990, pp. 98–99

Sono is very much published in her native Japan, but this is the first of her novels to be translated into English. Typically, there is minimal plot. Having located his clinic by choice in a rural shore area, a gynecologist describes and recounts his reactions to his practice: births, legal abortions, unwed mothers, and deformed babies all bring forth his comments and his discussions with his Christian cousin and her Catholic priest. The novel is more a vehicle for consideration of the doctor's intervention into human life than a fictional narrative. The original Japanese title, "The Soiled Hand of God," is more apt but probably less acceptable in English. Interesting but not likely to be widely popular.

Donald J. Pearce. *Library Journal.* March 15, 1990, pp. 115–16

SONTAG, SUSAN (UNITED STATES) 1933–

For me Susan Sontag's first novel, like her critical essays, beguilingly evokes an image of Lillian Gish playing Chopin on a piano to the Comanches in the shadows of her vast desert ranch in *The Unforgiven.* An alternate image might be Edna Best tending the stove on her family island in *Swiss Family Robinson.* In fact, any image suggesting a shrewd, serene, housewifely confidence in form which sustains and insulates, which reflects a sharp-edged and patient intelligence, would be applicable to Miss Sontag. In the *Benefactor,* a small, comic and charming work, she has given us a book whose protagonist, Hippolyte, tries to encompass life with just such a Sontaguesque sense of form, and whose hero *is* that sense of form. . . .

Although Hippolyte, a scholar and dilettante who runs through a great many adventures, fills pages with his personal speculations, these are nipped off by the precise, faintly inflected prose, like so many cubes snapped out of an ice tray. By the same token, the eclecticisms which embellish the story—tidbits from, among others, Gide, Rousseau, Voltaire—do not sour or oppress us nearly as much as they might: The bird–like purposefulness and persistent energy of Miss Sontag's writing infect us with her own bustling sobriety and cunning, and thus spare us the giddy sense of wayward burrowing.

Donald Phelps. New Leader. October 28, 1963, pp. 24–25

The Benefactor is an intricate, ambitious fantasia on themes suggested by European literary modernism roughly up to and including Simone Weil (her speculations on *grâce* and *pesanteur*) and Jean Genet (his deliberate choice of inauthenticity as a pretext for action in a hypocritical world) as seen through the eyes of someone deeply committed to the philosophical and psychological premises of the "cool" world of the 1960s, European *and* American. (I mean the word in no derogatory sense.) Not the mores or the latest jargon, but the idea and essence of the Cool is what she is after; her narrator's crisis straddles the wartime 40s, but she herself is closer in spirit to Robbe-Grillet and Uwe Johnson than to Weil or Genet. It is the prosy, circumstantial deliberateness of what might easily have been merely another flashy exercise in neo-surrealism that strikes one at first. Hence the peculiarly neutral "translator's English" of her by no means dull prose and her oddly spotty documentation, meticulous in many details, wholly vague in others. The novel, indeed, is very American in its combination of bookishness, philosophical literalness, and moral hypochondria.

R. W. Flint. Commentary. December, 1963, p. 490

The Benefactor was published with considerable fanfare and reviewed with some disappointment; it was charged with being too European, too obscure, and too fashionably involved with appearance and reality. It is all of these things, but it is more than involved with appearance and reality, it is an attempt to come to grips with this involvement—the involvement is the subject of *The Benefactor*. In the nameless city, very like Paris, Hippolyte has spent his life dreaming and arranging his life to correspond to his dreams. His dreams are more important to him than his life; the only object of interest in his life is a woman, Frau Anders, and she is more annoying than interesting. Hippolyte keeps trying to dispose of her, by selling her into slavery or burning down her house, and she keeps reappearing; she is a bedraggled, comical, and unexpectedly engaging representative of the external world that Hippolyte can almost, but not quite, extinguish. And it is Hippolyte and his dreams that finally triumph. With the kind of epistemological twist used by Gide in *The Counterfeiters*, we are left uncertain and apprehensive about what has been dream and what has not.

Geoffrey Bush. Yale Review. Winter, 1964,
p. 301

Style, dream, and banality: these notions cluster, however loosely, behind Miss Sontag's essays as they do behind her novel, *The Benefactor,* where the psychopathic narrator Hippolyte commits his life to his dreams, which are the style of his existence. Interpreting his dreams "did not relieve" Hippolyte, but only substituted irrelevant meanings for them. He detects, too, the falsity of lines "which people of taste insist on drawing between the banal and the extraordinary." Hippolyte trusts his dreams because they are at once extraordinary and banal. Today our most fantastic experiences are banalities. . . .

Obviously Miss Sontag takes positions, and she should. Above all she dreads the cliche in all its manifestations, as when she urges that religion must not be diluted to an acquiescence toward religion-in-general, or religious fellow-travelling, just as painting of a given period must not be diluted into admiration for Art, or cultural fellow-travelling. But in making these judgments she speaks for a new generation of critics who sense their distance from Culture, for they know it's foolish, or at least impoverishing, always to be requiring impressive meanings. Inevitably at a time when so much is banal, somebody had to tell us that "the discovery of the good taste of bad taste can be very liberating." Miss Sontag is a remarkably liberating writer because she has allowed herself to proceed by "immersion" in what she sees and reads. She calls it "immersion without guidelines."

Wylie Sypher. New York Herald Tribune.
January 30, 1966, p. 2

This is a hard book [*Against Interpretation*] to like and a harder one not to admire. In a free-wheeling collection of twenty-six essays—about half of which were originally published in the *New York Review of Books* or *The Partisan Review*—Susan Sontag indicates with impressive assuredness that she knows a lot about some things and at least as much as any other authority about everything else. What puts one off more than the extravagance of her judgments ("Most American novelists and playwrights are really either journalists or gentlemen sociologists and psychologists"), or the knowing, sometimes messianic shrillness of her tone, is Miss Sontag's concern with being, above and before all, fashionably *avant-garde*. One can't resist the suspicion that "the new sensibility" she heralds in these essays is her own, and that much of her esthetic doctrine is a complicated and unconscious self-promotion. . . .

Perhaps what makes *Against Interpretation* valuable and exciting is not so much its erudition, which is considerable, or its high level of intelligence, but its passionate irresponsibility, its determined outrageousness.

Jonathan Baumbach. *Saturday Review.*
February 12, 1966, p. 33

Strangely pedantic, confused, or timid about what she would hold to, and never more so than when she produces notes and aphorisms of a fine neatness and futility, Miss Sontag comes through as someone anxious to revise what she takes to be our mistaken view of art. But her cause appears to me less momentous than she seems aware, deriving from a view of art and of persons that belongs to what is by now a quite aged modernism. It is a cause unlikely to enlist readers unacquainted with the strawman philistine—stubbornly holding to the idea of "content" in the arts—who falls regularly before her sentences; and equally those who will find her not radical enough and who are getting by various means direct access to the "eschatology of immanence" that she finds laid out in Norman O. Brown's *Life Against Death*. But no matter; it is Miss Sontag herself who proves interesting and important as she utters the incorrigible Blakean demand on an "eschatology of immanence," a celebration of the body, the flesh, the sensuous appearances of things in the world; and as she records what corresponds to this, her deep disinclination to believe any longer in the self of psychoanalysis and the academic intellectuals—in the self as the New York literary culture conceives it.

Jack Behar. *Hudson Review*. Summer, 1966,
p. 347

Like everything Miss Sontag writes, *Death Kit* has strokes of wit in its pages. . . . There are quick thrusts of imaginative perception, for example about the inward experience of the blind. The graveyard spectacular produced as a finale—a pastiche of Thomas Browne, Rider Haggard and Kafka—has passages of force.

More important than any of this, there are moments when the reader can peer through the haze of abstract, overconfident cultural critique into a highly human torment and confusion—the suffering of a writer who seems bent on transforming self-hatred into an instrument of objective analysis, yet who nevertheless knows in her deepest self that this feeling cannot be thus elevated, since it is merely another style of pride. ("He who despises himself esteems himself as a self-despiser.")

Affecting as these moments are, they are too personal and infrequent to redeem the book as a whole. The plain case—no less visible here than in *The Benefactor*—is that the author's most powerful and most valuable impulse, the impulse to rage, is thwarted by novelistic form. Damnation-dealers and ravaged consciences are swallowed up, usually, in fiction. The conventions even of so-called philosophical novels—those forgiving fullnesses of view, obligations of understanding and compassion—tend to trivialize fury.

Benjamin DeMott. *The New York Times.*
August 27, 1967, p. 2

There was a delightful innocence about Camp and its followers that I found intriguing. It was determinedly and doggedly anti–intellectual, in a very, very intellectual way. Its devotees were trying so hard not to seem Profound, though there was really no danger at all of that, and yet they couldn't help but intellectualize everything, because they knew no other mode of perception. Miss Sontag's program was very simple: she was against thinking. But she was not really anti–intellectual. Indeed in a way she was the very epitome of intellectuality: she was all ideas, and her emotions were not so much felt as thought. She got her thrills out of abstractions, which she reified into attitudes. The kind of thinking she was against was the kind that attempted to make sense of ideas. She did not want to make sense out of anything: she preferred to revel in concepts, treating them as if they were form-fitting silken garments, to be enjoyed for the snugness and the sheen. What she affected to be for was emotion, feeling, texture; she wanted her art to reveal the Thingness of the world, she said. . . .

What she wants is something she calls "transparence," which means "experiencing the luminousness of the thing in itself, of things being what they are." Interpretation ignores the sensory experience of art and attempts to squeeze as much content out of it as possible. Our culture of excess and overproduction has brought about "a steady loss of sharpness in our sensory experience." We must recover our senses, learn to see more, hear more, feel more. "The function of criticism should be to show *how it is what it is,* even *that it is what it is,* rather than show *what it means.*" And finally, . . . "in place of a hermeneutics we need an erotics of art." . . .

For [Sontag], photography is an aggressive, appropriating act (one shoots/takes a picture) which "makes reality atomic, manageable, opaque . . . denies interconnectedness, continuity . . . confers on each moment the character of a mystery." Alienating us from direct experience, the photo provides a more intense second-hand experience, an illusion of knowledge; essentially discrete, disjunct, mute, ahistorical, the photo cannot tell the truth that comes only from words and narration. Photography levels hierarchies, fosters seeing for seeing's sake, "the didactic cultivation of perception, independent of notions of what is worth perceiving, which animates all modernist movements in the arts."

Along with modernizing and surrealizing our perspective on reality, however, the camera also consumerizes it. The world becomes "a department store or museum-without-walls in which every subject is depreciated into an article of consumption, promoted into an item for aesthetic appreciation." And governments exploit the photographic image as another medium for capitalist ideologies—stimulating artificial appetites to consume, replacing real political change by a change of images, and keeping populations under surveillance.

Sontag's six essays [in *On Photography*]—really linked meditations or even prose poems—all take up these themes again and again, placing them in progressively more complex contexts, squeezing (now and then with visible strain) every bit of significance out of each disquieting aspect of the photographic image and its ambiguous but potent force in the modern consciousness. There are no illustrations here, just lean prose studded with tight-mouthed, provocative aphorisms (the intellectual's equivalent of the stand-up comic's one-liners). . . .

A splendid performance—intellectual pinball on the French model where the goal is to keep a subject in play for as long as possible, racking up a brilliant score of cultural references and profound (if somewhat obscure) *mots*. Yet *On Photography* is less self-consciously self-advertising than that; more disenchanted with pure esthetics, less against interpretation than one might have expected. It is, finally, a moralistic (Marxist persuasion) indictment of our common lot as "image junkies." The last sentences of Sontag's book call for an ecology of images without specifying the meaning of that term. Rather than mindless delight and preservation (save the seals! save the snapshots!) or puritanical proscription (only the pure may survive!), *On Photography's* analytical exposé of the dynamics and extent of our addiction should serve as a definition by example of such an ecology.

Richard Kuczkowski. Commonweal.
February 3, 1978, pp. 88–89

Miss Sontag claims (no doubt correctly) that illness as metaphor is used at the expense of the literally ill: it compounds their physical illness with a cultural judgment, moralizes their position as other, abnormal, ill-omened. Metaphor has a tendency to naturalize a given condition, to make it, through the play of comparison, reconnect with accepted ways of looking at the world, with a moralized network of ideas and beliefs which must always imply, in the case of illness as metaphor, that the disease is somehow chosen; if not deserved, somehow justified. . . .

When Miss Sontag argues that it is not morally permissible to use cancer as metaphor, we may find her ethically noble but utopian, caught in a Platonic dream of a language which would give direct access to realities rather than the displaced symbols of realities. No doubt she is not so naive as to mean this literally: really she wants us to get rid of metaphors whose implications we can't control, which are loosely used and come to be taken as literal. What is needed is not elimination of the metaphor, but the constant showing up of metaphor for what it is, through countermetaphor, through the rhetoric of exposure, which Miss Sontag so effectively manages.

Illness as Metaphor is wholly successful as polemic and as provocation to the rethinking of cultural metaphors. . . . Otherwise, I cannot help but feel that Miss Sontag could tell us much more about the subject, that she is in a position to undertake, somewhat in the manner of Michel Foucault, a more sustained "archeology" of the idea of illness in our culture. In particular, one would like to hear her at greater length on the perception that madness has become the modern glamour disease: what was originally a brilliant metaphor for the decentering of perception (in Rimbaud, for instance) has degenerated into an irresponsible literalness, so that one can find serious writers proclaiming that the discourse of schizophrenia is the only authentic language of our time.

Peter Brooks. Partisan Review. 46:3, 1979,
pp. 438–39, 443–44

It was the great virtue of *Against Interpretation* (1966) and *Styles of Radical Will* (1969), Sontag's two early volumes of essays, to have responded so authoritatively to the question of identity, defining modernist performances in their abdication from the whole variety of traditional aesthetic values: sublimity, disinterestedness, harmoniousness, completion, etc. . . .

Yet her criticism relied then (as it continues to rely) on a partial estrangement from the vagaries of radical modernism. She has never relinquished her strong sense of the incommensurability of modernism, speaking of it always as a problem or a crisis, never simply as a cultural advent comparable to others. . . .

All of her stories are in some sense productions of the will. They do not (as she once said of the greatest works of art) seem the ripened analogues of nature's forms, but rather *constructs* of an artificer whose hand remains unfailingly in view. Yet at their finest her fictions construct the drama of moral antinomy: the human longing for freedom *and* for bondage; for the completion of knowledge *and* for absolution from knowledge; for the parent's invincible purview *and* the naked need of the child; for an autonomy of self *and* for the dissolution of self into collectivity; for a historical past that is "arrangement," pregnant with meaning, *and* for a past that is heaped, broken—wreckage upon wreckage, pleading no tale.

To say her fictions are willed is only to say that she pursues by means of words what she has already understood to be in excess of their aptitude. . . . In *I, etcetera* her talent extends to a new kind of narrative that is precisely *not* inventive, that in fact tenders nothing that cannot be summoned from the documentary basis of her own life. These pieces—which seem to me the best of the book—may as well be called essays as stories. Identifying them by means of that sizable word, we do well to recall its inventor. "Project for a Trip to China" and "Unguided Tour" . . . wield an authority that has its sources not in fiction but, like the essays of Montaigne, in the perplexity of being only an individual, a subject, apart and without recourse to any of the forms of "total imagination," whether Calvin or the French Catholic League, Hegel or Reverend Ike. These works comprise the I of *I, etcetera*: in them Sontag has invented nothing save herself. And it is, in fact, not the storyteller's workshop but instead the bare by-room of an exigent self that serves as the gathering place for her best impulses. Resolved to write what she has done, seen, willed, endured, she persuades us again and again to take counsel. Disciplining the tangle of private experience into words, Sontag declares a persistent, if diminished, possibility of wisdom.

Benjamin Taylor. The Georgia Review.
Winter, 1980, pp. 908–9, 911

In *Under the Sign of Saturn* Sontag is at work again reshaping the canon of modern European literature. Her particular polemic—a strong element in the general thrust of postwar New York literary criticism—is to celebrate the leopards in the temple of literature, not those cool and calm consciousnesses (like the Sophocles and Shakespeare of Matthew Arnold) who abided all questions and saw life whole, but those whose own derangement allowed them to explode the lies of order so that better forms might be discovered. In her criticism she labors to turn even the most self-isolating, uncompromising, and personally outrageous of such figures (I think here especially of Artaud) into humane teachers, whose flame, all the brighter for being trimmed, she will pass on to future generations. . . .

If *On Photography* is Sontag's belated neoplatonist turning away from that image of the critic in vogue, then *Under the Sign of Saturn* is her effort to reassess the public aspect of her pursuit of a career that has been defined historically by its distaste for public life and display. Searching for the shape of other careers, she implicitly meditates on her own: what am I to make of this pile of books that in some way is me? . . .

As always, her intelligence makes her essays refreshing, even though we may often learn less about her subjects than about what she thinks of them and how their ideas affected her. In pursuit of new connections she has fashioned a rhetoric of subordination that puts her forward as the humble lightning rod of culture. This is my tradition, she seems to say, these are my boys, and thus the Romantic project of finding the heart of a culture in its eccentrics winds up recommending instead the eccentricity of its own quest.

Leo Braudy. The New Republic. November
29, 1980, pp. 43, 45–46

Essays lie all over the land, stored up like the unused wheat of a decade ago in the silos of old magazines and modest collections. In the midst of this clumsy abundance, there are rare lovers of the form, the great lovers being some few who practice it as the romance this dedication can be. And romance for us, the readers, when certain names appear on the cover of periodicals. Susan Sontag: the name is a resonance of qualities, of quality itself. The drama of the idea, the composition, a recognition from the past that tells us what the present may bestow when we see her name. The term "essay" itself is somewhat flat as a definition of the liberality of her floating, restless expositions. . . .

Her writings are *hers,* intimately and obsessively one might say. They bear, each one, the mark of a large and coherent sensibility, the mark of her *interests,* her sense of the aesthetic and moral world around us. Almost none of her work comes out of the mere occasion, the book published, the film released, or the fad acknowledged. I suppose her theme is the wide, elusive, variegated sensibility of modernism—a reach of attitude and feeling that will include great works of art, the modern disturbance of the sense of self seen in "camp" and in pornography, and account for the social, historical disturbance represented by the contemporary glut of photographic images. Modernism is style and the large figures of culture she likes to reflect upon leave in their styles the signature of wishes, attractions, morals, and, always, ideas. . . .

In her novels and stories we discover what we have learned to expect from Susan Sontag; that is, that all is unexpected. Her fiction is angular, devious, and yet I would call it ruled by a special rationalism, and when we read we are trying to bring these aspects into harmony. Form, the narrative challenge, must be, will be, made to yield; it is a battle, but a lighthearted, good-natured battle. . . .

Thinking about Susan Sontag in the middle of her career is to feel the happiness of more, more, nothing ended. An exquisite responsiveness of this kind is unpredictable, although one of the intentions of her work is to find the central, to tell us what we are thinking, what is happening to our minds and to culture. There are politics, fashions, art itself, and of course the store-house of learning to be looked at again and again in her own way. I notice that in her late work she stresses the notion of pleasure in the arts, pleasure in thinking. Only the serious can offer us that rare, warm, bright-hearted felicity.

Elizabeth Hardwick. Introduction to Susan
Sontag. *A Susan Sontag Reader* (New York:
Farrar, Straus, 1982), pp. ix–x, xiii, xv

If . . . one believes with Bataille "how impossible it is at the present moment for anything human to arise except from the cesspool of the human heart," disburdenment is not the aim. Apocalypse cannot loom, though unimaginable destruction can. Allegories cannot be satisfying, because punishment is not sought. Instead one wishes to return, world to world.

But Sontag's practice, in its inner aim, is more severe. One returns to a stripped bare consciousness, as a descriptive process. She does not trust the politics of will and spiritual completeness, not if one reads her carefully: they "aestheticize." She does not trust photographs, because they too, with their ubiquity and prettifying, aestheticize. She does not trust the myths of modernist art nor the current metaphors of social constructions. She cannot yield to any theater of action that draws from or tries to imitate nature. She can defend only those works and that kind of consciousness that are perplexed by their subject, patronize themselves, and just as stubbornly, paradoxically, seek to simplify. . . .

Sontag's voice is never thin. She does share, however, with all her fictional characters, in all their appearances as "I," a manner of phrasing. To the pleasures of her writing—the beauty of distillation, the ghosts that come alive between juxtapositions, the spirited intrusions captured in epigrams—must be added its self-imposed restrictions. Her language is made up of principles, insistences, statements pulled from the flow of things against all temptation to reproduce the object she is thinking about. This is her philosopher's habit, her instinctual discounting of the tremulous behavior of writers after the abject, *écriture,* the sublime. But what her writing most often holds off is the amorphous tangle of the vivid. Whatever care she takes, overscrupulous and precise, to make sense of an argument, what is allowed to slip away is the unplanned, the mortal, the fecund.

Sohnya Sayres. *Susan Sontag: The Elegiac
Modernist* (New York: Routledge, 1990),
pp. 147–48

The Volcano Lover is a surprise. A historical novel by Susan Sontag? And a historical novel that declares itself (shamelessly, one almost wants to say) to be a *romance,* at that? Who would have thought it? Although she has written fiction in the past, Ms. Sontag is best known as a critic who for the last 30 years has been one of the leaders of the avant-garde in the United States, the American champion and interpreter of such quintessentially European figures as Roland Barthes and E. M. Cioran. Surely the author of that seminal essay "Against Interpretation" would look with nothing but scorn upon a modern-day attempt to produce something worthwhile in such a tired old genre as the historical novel? Well, not a bit of it. *The Volcano Lover,* despite a few nods of acknowledgment toward post-modernist self-awareness, is a big, old-fashioned broth of a book. Sir Walter Scott would surely have approved of it; in fact, he would probably have enjoyed it immensely. . . .

The novel opens with a prologue that invites us to accompany the author on a visit to the flea market of history: "Why enter? What do you expect to see? I'm seeing. I'm checking on what's in the world. What's left." Some readers may quail at this self-conscious and rather ponderous opening; Ms. Sontag, however, has set her aim on a broad audience, and very rapidly—indeed, at the turn of a page—we find ourselves set down squarely in a solid and recognizable world: "It is the end of a picture auction. London, autumn of 1772." . . .

In places, *The Volcano Lover* does become somewhat dropsical, swollen with the accumulation of historical evidence (no sources are cited, however), but for the most part it proceeds with an admirable lightness of step. There is an operatic quality to the tale (Baron Scarpia makes frequent, villainous appearances), and a grand, at times majestic, sweep to the telling. The style is confident, vigorous, witty. ("Ah, these English," reflects Goethe. "So refined and so coarse. If they did not exist, nobody would have ever invented them.") And, for the most part, the narrative is irresistible in its forward thrust. Some of the set pieces are worthy of a Marguerite Yourcenar or a Simon Schama, and there are wonderful touches of grotesque comedy. . . .

I find *The Volcano Lover* impressive, at times enchanting, always interesting, always entertaining; yet it also seems to me curiously hollow. I wish I could like it less and admire it more. What is missing is the obsessiveness of art, that leporine, glazed gaze that that confronts us from out of the pages of many a less densely textured but altogether more concentrated work. Will it seem cantankerous in the extreme if I say that Ms. Sontag *cares* too much? Art is amoral, whether we accept this or not; it does not take sides. The finest fictions are cold at the heart. For all the author's evenhandedness, we sense clearly behind her studied fiction a passionate moral intelligence hard at work; this is to Ms. Sontag's great personal credit, of course, but peculiarly damaging to her art. . . .

However, what will stay with me from *The Volcano Lover* are those moments when the author forgets about the broad facts of history and homes in on this or that detail of her grand pageant, letting her imagination have full and formidable play.

John Banville. *The New York Times.*
August 9, 1992, pp. 1, 26–27

[*Alice in Bed*] Sontag's . . . first stage play focuses on Alice James, the invalid sister of Henry and William and, since Jean Strouse's acclaimed 1980 biography and the publication of her diary, a feminist icon. It is in the latter role that Sontag casts the bedridden Alice, and playing off her name, she suggests, too, another, more famous Alice of fiction—to the extent that the center of the play's action is a tea party. The tea party becomes a gathering of independent women of imagination: Emily Dickinson, Margaret Fuller, Myrtha from the ballet *Giselle* and, as the somnolent dormouse, Kundry from Wagner's *Parsifal*. Alice's doting brother Henry makes a couple of appearances as well. Unfortunately, although Sontag acknowledges that her work is "a free fantasy based on a real person," none of the characters ever breathes with life; each lies flat on the page as a mouthpiece for Sontag's ideas about the imagination's dual role as liberator and jailer for a 19th-century woman of intelligence and about "women's anguish and women's consciousness of self." Moreover, her dialogue is arch and literary. Regrettably, Sontag can add her name to a list of talented novelist-critics whose stage work disappoints.

Penny Kaganoff. *Publishers Weekly.*
June 28, 1993, p. 70

SORIANO, ELENA (SPAIN) 1917–

Elena Soriano shows the frustrations of every woman, both the ordinary, normal women from the middle class as well as the rebellious, nonconformist and independent. Self-image, dignity and pride are cruelly subjugated in their day-to-day confrontation with men who decide what should occur in their marriage. The frank style of the author captures the horrible struggle of women trying to reconcile their feminism with the bitter realities of life. . . .

[The] three lives [in *(Espejismos)*] are condemned to repeat these hypocritical acts which are but mirages—*espejismos*—of what the true relationship between a man and a woman ought to be. There is no bridge between the three and no possibility of communication. Women are "disposable" when they grow old and it is as hopeless for them as it is for the protagonist of *La playa de los locos* to be loved for themselves. Pedro, like the doctor in the preceding novel, could have found an easy solution by going to war and replacing both women, but he is destined for trouble and is left with the two.

The two protagonists of *Medea 55,* Miguel Darguelos and Daniela Valle, met at the battle of the Ebro during the Spanish Civil War in 1938. She followed him and they were married during a truce. First they escaped to France and later they came to the Americas, where they traveled through various Central American countries. Both managed to live by their wits, he as a politician, she as an artist. In 1955 we find Miguel at the height of his political career, which he wants to solidify by marrying the young daughter of an important minister. To Daniela's surprise, he divorces her and she promises vengeance. Two weeks later he remarries and the young bride receives a gift: a complete history in letters and photographs of the previous marriage!

Daniela represents a modern Medea who abandons family and social considerations to follow her lover. When she is betrayed by him she decides on a last act of vengeance and carries it out against the young bride of her former husband, a girl of seventeen. We must make clear that her crime—different from that in the Greek tragedy—is much more subtle: she kills the faith and hope of an innocent girl by showing her, through letters, photographs, and newspaper clippings that her husband is capable of throwing the woman he "loves" into the waste heap when she no longer fits into his plans. Once again we have a man and a woman who disagree on what love is. For her it is something permanent, something that gives her reason to live. Miguel, on the other hand, sees her as a witness to his past and as a stumbling block to his future. He insists that he wants an "innocent" woman and he despises her for being a lusty female. As a practical man he cannot see why Daniela, at only thirty-five, is at a loss as to how to remake her life and perhaps he is right. Love, for Miguel, is associated with a sense of respectability, and he has never had it. His second marriage is a dream of security; his new wife must respect him as a father and obey him as a God with absolute faith—and

Daniela sets out to kill this image of perfection that he seeks, this last child of his male ambition.

Lucía Fox-Lockert. *Women Novelists in Spain and Spanish America* (Metuchen, New Jersey: Scarecrow, 1979), pp. 8–9, 101, 105–6

Soriano published four novels during the l950s, only the first with full censorial authorization. Her trilogy was not allowed to "circulate," i.e., she was permitted to print it at her own expense but not to have it distributed, since her treatment of female eroticism and passion and portrayal of marriage as something less than "happily ever after" was considered dangerous. Whether as the result of frustration or responsibilities to her children (born in these years), Soriano abandoned the novel after completing the trilogy. A writer of a very different sort, personal, subjective, and impassioned with little in common with objectivism, Soriano in purpose is closer to Ortega's theories on the novel (in fact, her novelistic practice is similar to Chacel's). She followed Ortega's principle that characters not be defined by the author but allowed to define themselves. Theoretically, Soriano is distant from the literature of *engagement* which came to the fore with the Mid-Century Generation in Spain.

Caza menor (1951; Small game hunting) with its baroque richness of vocabulary was adopted as a text in France and at some schools in the United States. Set in rural Castile, very similar to the area of Soriano's childhood and a spot well known to the author from many summers of residence, the novel spans the decade preceding the Civil War. Its atmosphere recalls Pardo Bazán's chronicle of the decadence of landed gentry in *Los pazos de Ulloa,* as well as that of Elena Quiroga's *Viento del norte,* published in the same year. Technique is essentially that of traditional Spanish realism, with touches of *costumbrismo* seen in the detailed descriptions of local customs. . . .

The trilogy, entitled *Mujer y hombre* (Man and woman), consists of three independent novels with no common characters or connections of plot. Thematic unity exists, since each examines a different love relationship, neither happy nor normal, as the novelist inquires into the complex, elusive, and sometimes surprising relationships between the sexes. There is also a certain unity of emotion, of anguish on the part of characters who have sought to make of love a substitute for faith, reality, and even decency, seeking in it a basis for their lives. In varying existential limit situations, they must confront the deceptiveness of this central "fact" of their existence. Of the trilogy's five most important characters, four experience crises as a result of the approach of middle age: physical aging, inescapable evidence of the finitude of existence, produces existential anguish. Other existential motifs include the problem of freedom, the issue of personal authenticity, and relationships between the self and the other. In each case the action of the novelistic present is precipitated by an individual emotional crisis and covers a relatively short time span. . . .

Medea 55 (a title from which the novelist dropped the 55 in subsequent editions) is a modernization of the Greek myth, set in Latin America—probably out of fear that to use a Spanish setting could bring serious political complications (one of the two protagonists is a totally unscrupulous politician). Restrictions imposed upon action and characterization by the mythic framework make this work the least realistic of Soriano's novels. . . .

The illusions on which love is based, the self-deception and deceits it occasions, the myriad forms love takes, its emotional and psychological perversions, are illustrated throughout the trilogy via a combination of the most diverse technical elements, from modified Aristotelian unities to the modern flashback and stream of consciousness for a highly personal result. Narrative intensity is achieved due to the singular unity of time, place, and action in the framework of personal crisis, while perspective is introduced by the use of introspection and retrospective recall. Soriano clearly draws upon observation, intuition, projection, and theoretical readings, and the influences of contemporary philosophy and psychology as well as specific literary theories are clear, as is a conscious experimentation with literary techniques. Soriano is a well-informed theorist who is embarked upon a simultaneous quest for artistic expression and answers to personal questions. It is unfortunate that she has not continued her novelistic output. For nearly three decades, her writing was limited to critical essays; a personal tragedy motivated her return to a more subjective form. The drug-related death of her son led to a long, anguished autobiographical exploration of the tragedy, *Confesión de una madre* (A mother's confession) in 1986.

Janet Pérez. *Contemporary Women Writers
of Spain* (Boston: Twayne) 1988, pp. 98–102

The protagonist of *La playa* (The beach) perceptively locates her ambivalence within a precise historical matrix, characterizing her youthful self as a true daughter of the times. Describing herself as "un complejo producto de transición, de crisis humana en todos los órdenes" (a complex product of transition, of human crisis in all its orders), she bitterly recognizes that she was "envenenada de errores y contradicciones" (poisoned with errors and contradictions). After recollecting her inability to surrender sexually to her lover, she works through a penetrating analysis of her ambivalent and confused imprisonment between alienating ideologies and possibly liberating alternatives. She recognizes her dogmatic, narrow, and puritanical moral and sexual information on the one hand and her free-thinking education on the other. Exposed to fascinating theories about primitive and pagan pleasures, she was forbidden to apply those theories to practice. Yet, though conditioned by the immanence of parental morality, she experienced the strain of her generation to touch a transcendent future painted with paradisiacal colors. Thus victimized by contradictions characteristic of women of her class and historical moment, she experienced the troublesome conflict. . . .

The consciousness that she was the product of historical crisis leads *La playa*'s protagonist to a growing awareness of how she was caught up in alienating texts that mediated between her and the resolution of her quest for fulfillment. . . .

This inclination of *La playa*'s protagonist to view character traits as sharply polarized into civilized-cerebral and natural-instinctual is instrumental in her attempt to mask and shrink and diminish her youthful self in order to fit the role of her culture's idea of the "natural" woman. . . .

Yet, in spite of her captivity within the polarity of masculine-feminine, active-passive, the narrator-protagonist of *La playa* intermittently offers acute observations of the restrictive cultural codes that underlie her choices. One recalled conversation between the young woman and her lover expresses her consciousness of the paternal law that underwrites female existence. . . .

Overcome by her ambivalence and entrapment within discourses of her alien Other, the protagonist of *La playa* is rendered diminished and hollow when her lover disappears, ostensibly to the war. Since her attempt to invest her libido in him failed, she is left with nothing in its stead, nothing but despair. The end of that unconsummated love affair signifies the end of her text; her life thereafter is summated in some twenty pages, a life of indifferent acts, mechanical and meaningless words, historical unconsciousness. Little wonder that her aging is frightening; it threatens to impose a second closure upon a constantly narrowing range of possibilities. Nevertheless, a text like *La playa,* about a bright and educated woman whose life figuratively ends when her fleeting first love evanesces before its consummation, stands as poignant testimony to the misspent power of unnamed female desire.

Elizabeth J. Ordoñez. *Voices of Their Own:*
Contemporary Spanish Narratives by
Women (Lewisburg, Pennsylvania: Bucknell
University Press, 1991), pp. 58–61, 64

SOW FALL, AMINATA (SENEGAL) 1941–

The growth of African creative literature in English since the publication of Thomas Mofolo of South Africa's: *The Traveller of the East, Pitseng* and *Chaka* at the turn of the century which were closely followed by those of two Ghanaians: E. Casely-Hayford's *Ethiopia Unbound* and R. E. Obeng's *Eighteenpence,* has been noted to be fairly impressive, especially after the monumental debut of *Things Fall Apart* by the venerable Chinua Achebe of Nigeria.

It has also been noted with a rather pretentious chagrin in some quarters that since the publication of *Eighteenpence* serious Anglophone writing has been preoccupied by the so-called stock themes of African Literature namely, culture clash, colonial domination and reaction against it, and corruption in politics on the one hand and anthroposociological documentation on the other. And as if to spite the critics vis-à-vis the latter theme, a Nigerian writer proudly titled his collection of short stories, *The Way We Lived!* This title seems to exemplify what the critics see as the preoccupation of Anglophone writing with the past and tends to undermine cogent arguments to the contrary.

When it comes to the theme of the interaction between the various strata of society however, Francophone African writing, made popular by Camara Laye and revolutionized by the one time docker, Sembene Ousmane, has blazed the trail.

It is, however, not only in the vein of the theme of conflicts of social stratifications that *The Beggars' Strike* should be examined, for the story is the study of the egoism of man in every society as typified in the character of Monsieur Ndiaye, the Director of the Department of Public Health and Hygiene and the prospective Vice-President of an anonymous Country with equally an anonymous capital City. The conflict is between Ndiaye, on behalf of the Establishment, and the *boroom battu,* the begging-bowl-bearers, who are considered to be inflicting themselves on the City.

The beggars pose such a threat to the Tourist Industry which the country is laboring to develop that it devolves on the protagonist's department to rid the city of them. After a great deal of strain at the task, the beggars are successfully harassed out of their usual haunts—the marketplaces, the pavements in front of the big shops, hospitals, banks and hotels as well as the mosques. This glorious achievement of the protagonist recommends him for the very high position of the Vice-Presidency of the Country.

It is here that the dramatic irony of the story is spawned, for the *marabout,* holy man, who divines the good fortune of the protagonist's imminent nomination as Vice-President prescribes an alms offering of a bull to the very beggars the protagonist has so successfully driven into hiding—without which the prophecy could not come true. What is more? The offering has to be made to the beggars in their haunts of public places from where they have been evicted. Ndiaye is determined to perform the sacrifice, as prescribed, but not even propitious bribes could convince the beggars to "go into town and take up your places in the streets" for the bounteous offering!

As the cover blurb of the novel aptly quotes. "The beggars have got the power in their hands . . ." They are on strike.

It is the commencement, the procedure and the underlying philosophy of the strike which offers the most exciting reading and the psychological insight into the study of the protagonist's character and that of human motives for that matter. . . .

Bravo to Sow Fall and all connected with the production of this, yet another of the trail-blazers in African writing, in which beggars, the dregs of society, defeat a war-lord of politics.

Kwakuvi Azasu. *West Africa*. May 17, 1982,
pp. 1329–31

Between *The Ghost* . . . (1976) and *The Beggars' Strike* . . . (1979), there is a decisive change. Aminata Sow Fall's desire to get away from the conventions of the traditional novel becomes apparent. From the linguistic point of view, her effort to locate the spoken aspect of writing appears in a blatant fashion; this is one possible response to the impasse in which Africans who write in European languages find themselves when the question "Writing for whom?" arises. If the survival and development of the vernacular languages remain an unquestionatile necessity for any colonized society, the zeal exercised by non-African criticism in preaching the return to traditional tongues often denotes an attachment to the imported standards of the "well written" and the "well spoken." The total intolerance with respect to any linguistic deviation [is] invariably deemed incorrect or "a bastardized language which is no longer either English or African," (L. Kesteloot on A. Tutuola). However, as Achebe declares, "The price that a universal language . . . must pay for being spread out over the whole world is to accept several types of different usages.". . . .

Aminata Sow Fall's characters speak a Senegalized French; whence the deliberate repetitions of clichéd expressions, the play of stereotypes in the dialogue, and the frequent intervention of Wolof to express realities foreign to the borrowed language. . . .

If the Wolof expressions in *The Ghost* are always matched by French equivalents or carefully translated in a note, the same thing does not happen in *The Beggars' Strike*. Only those words or phrases whose explanation seems to be indispensable to the comprehension of the narrative are put into the glossary. Everything happens as if the concern to make herself understood to a foreign audience was no longer essential. It is not, of course, a question of an elimination or a shutting off, but a shift in priorities. The choice, ambiguous in the first novel, has unequivocally settled, in the second, on a mass African audience. . . .

The significance of A. Sow Fall's works goes far beyond the boundaries of realism. The problems confronted are connected, as we have seen, with the language of the novel; they constitute not only a critique of the system in power, but also and above all a fundamental reexamination of the fundamental values of being human. Values that . . . I would bring together under the name of the gift. The multiple facets that the gift assumes and its close connection with oppression are woven together in a complex fabric that A. Sow Fall never ceases to unravel and recreate in the course of her narratives, starting with that of women. To say that *The Ghost* and *The Beggars' Strike* are speaking first and foremost about women is, either, depending on one's view of feminism, to limit them or to open them up. The protagonists of these two books . . . are men; however, their entrances on stage never occur without the presence or the observation of a female character. Every question raised also involves the subject of woman.

Trinh T. Minh-ha. *French Review.* 55, 1982,
pp. 780–85

Aminata Sow Fall's work exemplifies . . . contemporary satire. Her earliest and best-known novel, *Le Revenant* (The ghost), is social satire, attacking the evils of today's inhumane, materialist society without reference to whites. The African nature of the work is limited almost exclusively to the social custom which demands the distribution of large sums of money at ritual baptisms. In her second novel, *La Grève des bàttu* (The beggars' strike), three "patrons" are mentioned, only one of whom was white, and it is the vicious nature of a boss, not of a white, which is attacked. Selected for this study for its ironic satire, this work is typical of current trends in the absence of racial issues. Further, it illustrates classic western structure and treatment combined with a plot based on fundamentally non-western cultural traditions, intended to suit both African and western audiences. . . .

The plot, classically structured as tragic irony, presents a protagonist first making a decision he believes will further his ambition and eventually realizing that it is exactly that decision which has ruined him: he falls by his own fault. Like Oedipus, he can blame destiny, or the will of Allah, but it is each reader's belief in that destiny which determines to what extent that reader views the protagonist's own folly as responsible for his end. . . .

Among the diverse satirical techniques used by Sow Fall, it is irony that is particularly interesting, given the dual audience. Recognition of the irony of the plot depends on the knowledge the African audience shares with the author: the practice of Islam requires daily almsgiving, and almsgiving ordinarily requires beggars. . . .

The incongruity for the African audience is thus that the politician's plan to sweep the streets clean of beggars cannot work because of the religious law. [The] second step, to eliminate alternative interpretations, its readily accomplished by the African reader: the narrator is citing the newspaper, but in the absence of evidence, in Booth's words, that the journalist is "careless or stupid or crazy," there is no acceptable alternative. The third step, to decide on the position of the author (or implied author, but with irony we cannot avoid the question of authorial intent) is similarly easy for the African reader: no sane human being would have meant that one should ignore the precepts of Islam and run the beggars out of town. The fourth step is the reconstruction: the author intends us to understand that the newspaper proposes an impossible, improper, inhuman action; thus the African reader identifies a meaning contrary to what is written.

The western reader, however, might not so readily recognize the incongruity. Particularly westerners who know Dakar or other third world cities, might agree with the journalist: yes, the beggars are aggressive, tenacious and omnipresent. Unfamiliar with the precepts of Islam, the western reader might miss this first dash of irony. . . .

The irony of the whole work should be readily accessible to both audiences, and the satirical attack on the political situation is made chiefly through irony. Both audiences are led to stand with the author, agreeing that this society is turned upside down. The beggars have all the accepted virtues, cheerfulness, caring for others, courage, honesty, accurate assessments of themselves. . . .

For both audiences, the dramatic irony of the plot will be effective. Similarly, both audiences will appreciate social injustice as a common target for satire, and will find familiar the presentation of the evil rich and virtuous poor. Both audiences can appreciate the work as one whose covert irony derives from agreement with the author that the present system is bad. Moral satire of corrupt politicians is, certainly, as much a commonplace in the western world as in Africa. For the western audience, however, there may be an additional dimension to this moral satire. Mour plays out his scene with two wives, among lepers, believing *marabouts* may be part snake, and yet he is vicious and foolish in exactly the same ways as we are. Thus, for the western audience but probably not for the African, *La Grève des bàttu* exemplifies the universality of the vices and follies of mankind. Further, that significant cultural difference which provides for the success of the beggars' strike and the resolution of the action must lead the western audience, although perhaps not the African, to consider the implications of the difference: this resolution could not occur in the west, since charity, however warmly recommended, is not an essential part of our daily life. Determination of the author's intent in such an ironic message to the west, confident in our superiority, would take us outside the work into a different study.

Elinor S. Miller. *Irony and Satire in French
Literature.* French Literature Series,
(Columbia: University of South Carolina
Press), 1987, pp. 144–50

Aminata Sow Fall's fiction reveals an alert and pleasant style. The fluidity of her writings is never hampered by overly scholarly sophistication, and language is well adapted to the various contexts she chooses to illustrate. Although she writes in French, she knows how to embroider her work with Wolof words and expressions, thus providing the reader with the local flavor of Senegalese verbal authenticity and poetic lyricism. *L'Appel des arènes* (The call of the arenas) concerns a young boy's indomitable interest in traditional Senegalese wrestling in spite of the disapproval of his parents. *L'Ex-père de la nation* (The ex-father of the nation), her latest book to date, depicts the rise and fall of an African head of state. . . .

Sow Fall's stories take place in contemporary Senegal some fifteen years or more after the independence of this former French colony. Her incisive pen sketches a satirical portrait of Senegal's new elite in power and stresses as well the dramatic disproportionate dichotomy between the impoverished and the affluent. Beyond these social comments which are geared to readers on their primary reading level, the conjuration of Sow Fall's plots and style can hardly be missed. Her novels evolve within an African context, but their structure and characters contain elements that may be easily associated with fairy tales on a more universal level.

Although Aminata Sow Fall situates her stories geographically in Dakar, timewise no precise indication is given as to the period within which her characters evolve. A sagacious reader, however, recognizes immediately the traits of present-day Senegal. . . .

Although Fall's works are written, they bear the mark of Africa's oral literature. Since the novel is a genre imported to Africa, it is of necessity influenced by the original literary form of Africa: the oral tradition. Besides the many Wolof expressions which she uses, Sow Fall seems to take special interest in quoting . . . Wolof proverbs. . . .

Sow Fall's main characteristic as a writer is not her choice of themes, or even characters, but the fashion in which she treats them. Sow Fall's microcosm contains socially accurate elements, but her plot relies largely on the imaginary. She enlarges it with metaphorical perspectives. Her novels have the freshness and the flavor of tales deeply rooted in the African tradition. She has successfully merged two apparently contradictory elements: socio-realism, often perceived under the cloak of enchantment, and the symbolical appeal of African morality tales. In her case, those two components infer sociopolitical awareness.

A modern griot, Aminata Sow Fall is a genuine voice of Africa. Her style emanates humor, and the content of her novels expresses wisdom, popular beliefs, and social criticism. Her narratives, based on fictitious events, provide useful universal truths and at the same time entertain and arouse curiosity. In the true tradition, her artistry and "divertissement" are functional. Her stories contain the moral element present in all African tales. Sow Fall discloses that those events that "go wrong" in life are mainly due to the very nature of man. The reader has to discover those truths as they occur in most tales, as opposed to fables, where the message is emphasized. *Le Revenant* indicates that selfishness and corruption are finally punished. *La Grève des Bàttu* shows that one cannot solely rely on magic forces to achieve success and that it is the fairness of one's previous actions which leads to a successful future. Both Bakar and Mour have "sinned" and are punished.

Tales do not pretend to describe the world as it is, and the African storyteller—even as a contemporary novelist—possesses a key to a world of fairy-tale enchantment. In spite of some foreign influences, Aminata Sow Fall remains faithful to the legacy of her forebears. She espouses the traditional role of the woman in Senegal who, as a storyteller, preserves and transmits the culture of her people to the generations to come.

Françoise Pfaff. *CLA Journal.* 31, 1988,
pp. 340–42, 357–59

Mariama Bâ and Aminata Sow Fall, writing well after the advent of independence, are not interested in indulging in anti-West invective or in looking back into the past so that they can apportion blame. As spokeswomen for their society as it is now they describe the crisis of cultural identity in all its dimensions in a clear attempt to elucidate the divisions which exist not only in Senegal but in the whole of Black Africa.

The conflict which underlies all others and which is seen as the most fundamental difference between the traditional way of living in Africa and modem Western life is that between the community and the individual. It is presented in different forms in the novels. Sometimes we see a deliberate attempt on the part of an individual to break with the community, which is the case of Diattou in *L'appel des arènes;* at other times it is the community which rejects the individual, as with Bakar in *Le revenant;* and in some instances the individual finds it impossible to live between two worlds, as does Ousmane in [Bâ's] *Un chant écarlate.* To understand the significance of this break, whatever its causes, one must realize that in traditional African society, the community is of primary importance. To remain part of it, one must accept its norms without questioning them. In exchange, the community cares for and protects its members and gives them their spiritual and cultural identity. Nowadays, however, communal values are being challenged and what is referred to as Western individualism is becoming part of the African way of thinking.

This conflict between traditional communal life and modern individualism is represented spatially by the opposition between the country and the city. Even if collective values survive in the city, particularly in the poor districts, they do not have the same moral power that they have in the village. Interestingly, the main action of all the novels by Bâ and Sow Fall takes place in the big city, in Dakar, except for that of *L'appel des arènes* which is situated in a provincial town, but we do get some glimpses of village life. . . .

If in spatial terms, the conflict between communal norms and support and modern individualism or solitude is represented in part by the opposition between the village and the city, temporally it is revealed through rupture between the past and the present. . . .

The antagonism between traditions and modernity is sometimes presented as a direct conflict between the European and the African ways, not merely as an indirect link which may be asserted by some and rejected by others. In *Le revenant* there are no clear references to external influences but in *The Beggars' Strike* the relationship between the events described and the Western way of thinking is clear. The presence of beggars is said to threaten the national economy for damaging tourism, but, finally, it is shown that what is good for tourism is not good for the country as a whole, for the city can no longer function. Tourism thus becomes a symbol for foreign influence on the mentality and the political decisions of African leaders.

Susan Stringer. *SAGE: Scholarly Journal on Black Women.* Student Supplement 1988, pp. 36–40

For the last twelve years the Senegalese novelist Aminata Sow Fall has been relatively prolific. Between 1976 and 1987 she has produced four novels: *Le revenant* (1976), *La grève des bàttu*, (1979; Eng. *The Beggars' Strike*, 1981), *L'appel des arènes* (1982), and *L'ex-père de la nation* (1987). Following the publication of *La grève des bàttu*, she was shortlisted for the Prix Goncourt in 1979 and awarded the Grand Prix de l'Afrique Noire in 1980.

No doubt Fall's work has given a voice to millions of voiceless women in her society. Put together, her four novels also create a literary universe that goes beyond the already-classic theme of women's emancipation to explore the human predicament in a contemporary Senegalese society undergoing tremendous mutations. In each of her four novels the issue of social change is portrayed through the collective and individual dramas of her characters. More specifically, Fall narrates social, cultural, and political behavior to illustrate the negative impact of unbalanced social change. . . .

Fall's social vision goes beyond the issue of modernization to explore its implications for humans and their conduct. To reach such a depth of insight, she draws from an imagination fed by a strong knowledge of her countrymen and -women. . . .

Through a theme of mendicancy . . . Fall explores the dilemma and the duplicity of a society caught in a crossfire between the demands of an imposed model of development and the constraints of its own cultural heritage. More important, using the resources of her rich and creative imagination, she manages to display the devastating effects of such an imbalance on both the individual and the collective psyche.

From a portrayal of social and cultural behavior in her first three works, Fall's most recent novel, *L'ex-père de la nation*, deals with the hot topic of political life in an imaginary African country easily identifiable as Senegal. This reflection on political behavior is presented as the memoirs of Madiama Niang, former head of state, jailed after his dismissal from office. Through this flashback on his own past reign and personal tragedy, Madiama introduces the reader into the daily intrigues and vices of political life. . . .

L'ex-père de la nation goes beyond the personal drama of an imaginary head of state to explore the tragedy of African political life. The nation Madiama presided over is like a confiscated ship in which, like worms, public officials greedily thrive on the sweat of the people. In this atmosphere of tension and competitiveness, freedom, humanity, and justice are replaced by hypocrisy as a way of life.

As noted in my introductory remarks, Aminata Sow Fall's social vision goes well beyond the issue of feminine emancipation to embrace the general survival of a collectivity and a nation faced with the delicate task of finding a balance between the demands of what is improperly termed "modernization" and the preservation of its very foundation, its cultural genius. As a novelist, however, Fall draws from both social reality and her imagination to bring to life the destructive effects of this unresolved situation on human resources. Indeed, from *Le revenant* though *L'ex-père de la nation*, what she tackles is the human predicament in a changing society. Through Bakar's personal disillusionment, Mour Ndiaye's ambiguity, Nalla's search for threat-ened values, and Madiama's bitter prison memoirs, the reader discovers a vast *comédie humaine* of people searching for social, cultural, and political solutions to their unhappiness.

Nevertheless, Fall's approach to the issue of social change raises some serious ethical and ideological questions. . . . Her social realism betrays a failure to question the institutions that generated such conduct. In pointing at the consequences, not at the institutions that support and implement social change, Aminata Sow Fall's ideological stand goes beyond a choice of the status quo to advocate social reformism, but she does not prescribe thorough-going or revolutionary solutions.

Samba Gadjigo. *World Literature Today.* 63,
1989, 410–15

Traditionally, one of the key themes in African literature written in French has been the alienation of blacks when they come in contact with Western society, and their ensuing struggle to find a stable identity and to readjust to their native country. In the 1960s and 70s the topic of the French educational system inspired a number of *"romans de formation,"* (educational novels) where the protagonist, a black child or teenager, experienced the culture and education of whites either in Africa, at the high school level, or abroad, at the university level. . . . Such novels were centered around the conflict be-tween the young and the family (and the village at large) and a duality of attitudes concerning the validity of a Western education for their African children.

Since the early 1980s, education has remained a recurrent subject in many African novels written in French. Although the underlying theme has not been drastically altered, the approach reveals a new perspective towards the problem. . . . [This approach is reflected in] the novel *L'Appel des arènes* by the Senegalese woman writer, Aminata Sow Fall. . . .

With the aftermath of postcolonialism in the 1980s African literature . . . assumes a new discourse. To this extent, *l'Appel des arènes* acts as a pamph-let, and calls for a series of reassessments: on the part of the African intelli-gentsia as to their choice of an adequate lifestyle; on the part of writers as to their tasks and, more specifically, on women writers as to their commitment to Africa's future; finally on the part of the critics.

Sow Fall challenges readers, whether African or European, to question their attitudes, and to reassess the broad spectrum of Western education. For women, she stresses the dangers of blind emancipation that does not leave room for their African identity. From her own standpoint, she suggests that women writers be more creative and not so doctrinaire.

Finally she addresses African critics, who are so involved in their critical approaches that they tend to forget the text. The opening page, with the

African context devitalized, may then be interpreted as a parable for what Africanists have done when they analyze a piece of African literature.

Odile Cazenave. *Africa Today.* 38, 1991,
pp. 54, 62

SPARK, MURIEL (GREAT BRITAIN) 1918–

Memento Mori is an exceedingly adroit book but, in its rather conscientious heartlessness, not an entirely likable one. Miss Spark is clearly on the side of some characters as against others. But there is a certain glee about the precipitation with which they are all jumbled together in their common fate. Miss Spark manages to get a large number of sharply defined and entirely convincing characters, of a wide range of human and social varieties, into her picture. This life of an old people's ward in a hospital is described with gruesome convincingness, especially when one end of it is filled with "geriatric cases," who come in like some wild medieval carnival. But for all its smoothness and precision *Memento Mori* never quite loses the flavor of being a gratuitous curiosity.

Anthony Quinton. *The London Magazine.*
September, 1959, p. 85

Miss Spark has shown in previous books how workmanlike is her study of the society she describes: sometimes, indeed, she gives the impression that she is more sociologist than novelist. Certainly there has been no funnier or more revealing picture of spiritualist circles than this. [*The Bachelors*]

Many readers relish Miss Spark's novels chiefly for this: her characters may be improbably sinister, but they are larger than life and much funnier. Yet surely her talent is more original; it has something to do with a quick and in many ways unfeminine intelligence (her logic is ruthless) allied to a matter-of-fact acceptance of metaphysical thoughts which most of us ignore or fear. The tension thus created, between her sharp hilarious exposure of trivialities and the underlying mysteries of the soul, intrigues and baffles the reader, and is in itself a sort of satire.

The Bachelors is less baffling, less extraordinary, than *Memento Mori*, but the tension is still there, because even bachelors need to know what happens after the free meals and free love. Miss Spark may not encourage "the amendment of vices," but she makes it refreshingly clear that modern satire can be more than anger or tittle-tattle.

(London) *Times Literary Supplement.*
October 14, 1960, p. 657

The Prime of Miss Jean Brodie is a gloriously witty and polished vignette, and why, since the author has herself said she cannot help finding almost everything in life slightly ridiculous, should she not feel the same about the somber problems which beset society, and Roman Catholics in particular, in this troubled and insecure age of ours? . . . One may argue that Mrs. Spark is at her best in avoiding bulky themes, but if her admirers are right in thinking *Memento Mori* the most serious of her books, by far her best, it will not be long before she must tackle material tougher than the vaguely symbolic portrait of a memorable eccentric lady. . . .

(London) *Times Literary Supplement.*
November 3, 1961, p. 785

She enjoys certain evident advantages: wit, high-fantastic humor, a sense of style, a capacity to communicate human oddity and solitude. She is also fashionable in being a Roman Catholic, and a convert too. . . . Next, Mrs. Spark is a stylist, and this allows her to skim deliciously over the surface of things, using elegance as a device for holding anything incoherent, inchoate, or disagreeable at arm's length, even while acknowledging its presence. It also allows her, by the wit and precision of so many of her words, to conceal the fact that her novels tend to be static and even, by a paradox, circumlocutory. . . .

The remark "neurotics never go mad" occurs in two of her books, and is the prime consolation accorded Mrs. Spark's characters in their daily struggle not to appear too eccentric to others or too disturbing to themselves. It is because she can convey this and so persuade us to find it comic, that Mrs. Spark has, in twelve years of writing, become a minor monument.

Anne Duchene. *The Manchester Guardian
Weekly.* May 2, 1963, p. 11

If this book [*The Girls of Slender Means*], shrewd, economical and funny as it is, misses being absolutely top-notch Spark it is, I think, because she has caught the gaiety of the times but missed something equally important: their moral earnestness. . . . Muriel Spark's glittering surface poison always needs one deep incision to make it run in the veins. . . . Mrs. Spark has the wit, the Catholicism and the unkindness of Evelyn Waugh, but she has not yet mastered his skill at heartbreaking jungle deaths.

Katharine Whitehorn. *Encounter.* December
1963, pp. 80–81

A writer who interest me more [than Golding], and whose books are less allegories than moral or religious fables, is Muriel Spark. Her characters and backgrounds, and her use of dialogue, all have an authentic ring, but her purposes are those of the ordinary realistic novelist. She is a devout Roman Catholic (Golding's metaphysics are also Christian) and Mrs. Spark's gift for comedy is made portentous by her sense of the eternal significance of all human choices. . . .

Mrs. Spark's novels are at once very amusing and harrowingly penetrating; she is compassionately aware of how much of life is distraction in Pascal's sense, the search for trivialities and disguises that will divert our minds from the soul's sadness and loneliness, from life's uncertainty and transience, from the abyss.

G. S. Fraser. *The Modern Writer and His World* (London: Penguin, 1964), pp. 171–72

There are . . . as I see it, two high points to date in the output of [Spark,] this brilliant and unconventional writer. Each stands out from among works related to it but lesser in overall quality and effectiveness. *Memento Mori* is the more objective of the two, a Swiftian vision of the world which overshadows even such ingenious works as its predecessors *Robinson* and *The Comforters*. *The Prime of Miss Jean Brodie* restates the problems of these earlier books in somewhat more subjective terms. Here the Spark persona finds herself the absolute center of the novel.

There is no indication, however, that these two books, fine as they are, have succeeded in resolving what I believe to be the conflict that called them into being: the fundamental duality of Muriel Spark's worldview. There is in fact every reason to believe that Mrs. Spark's private war continues in unabated violence, and may shortly necessitate from her another gesture of dazzling virtuosity, perhaps this time a novel with an American setting. For unlike her great spiritual ancestor, she does not intend to stick pretty much to London, the British countryside, or to Bath. We are fortunate in this: if our time has brought forth new confusions, it has give us the writers to deal with them: new Jane Austens for new realities.

Charles Alva Hoyt. In Charles Shapiro, ed. *Contemporary British Novelists* (Carbondale: Southern Illinois University Press, 1965), p. 143

Perhaps because I first read Muriel Spark merely for the sake of reading, perhaps because I read her books in odd foreign parts where they had been untimely ripped from their dust-covers and hence bore no biographical data, I did not realize that she was a Catholic Novelist. The one thing that everybody knew about this author lay unknown to me. But this deficiency is now supplied, and I can see that the novels could be held to bear out the dustcover's directions: they have Catholics in them, and a good deal of reference to Catholic doctrine. Mrs. Spark's new novel, *The Mandelbaum Gate*, would itself suggest quite strongly, by its detailed and sometimes "loving" descriptions of the Holy Land, that its author could well be a practicing Christian, or else a practicing archaeologist, or (though less likely) a botanist with a particular interest in wild-flower seed-dispersion. And its characters might seem to indicate that their author is a Christian, or else a Moslem, an Israeli, or an Arab, a diplomat, or a spy—or even, come to that, possibly a novelist.

Not that I wish to take Mrs. Spark's faith—that "beautiful and dangerous gift"—away from her. On the contrary. But there is a difference between a Catholic who writes novels and a Catholic Novelist. This latter term evokes, even if it shouldn't, an unholy mixture of the Claudelic, the Mauriacesque and the Greenean, a browbeating either direct or indirect, a stifling odor of incense or of fallen sweat or of both. Mrs. Spark's writing seems to me altogether dissimilar: even a lapsed Wesleyan can approach her without too painful a sense of intimidation or exclusion. Yet most discussion in print of Mrs. Spark's work centers on her Catholicism—and rarely get far away from it. In an otherwise subtle article appearing in this journal on the publication of *The Girls of Slender Means,* Frank Kermode described her as "an unremittingly Catholic novelist"—unremitting? Mrs. Spark?—while Granville Hicks has faintly deplored her as "a gloomy Catholic, like Graham Greene and Flannery O'Connor, more concerned with the evil of man than with the goodness of God." Far from gloomy, I would even have thought her positively funny, and—though admittedly this new novel lends one more conviction on the point than might otherwise have been felt—concerned with the evil of man no more than is to be expected in a fair-minded though shrewd observer of humanity.

D. J. Enright. *The New Statesman.* October
15, 1965, p. 563

The Transfiguration of the commonplace. That is the title of pig-eyed Sister Helena's famous treatise in *The Prime of Miss Jean Brodie*; it is also an appropriate description of the fictive method of Muriel Spark.

Approaching the novel with all the suspicions of a poet accosting an alien, and perhaps inferior, medium, Miss Spark uses a dazzling assortment of techniques to accomplish in prose what she had first attempted in verse: to create by cutting through the barriers of overused language and situation a sense of reality true to experience, an imaginative extension of the world, a lie that shows us things as they are—a supreme fiction.

But although it admits of endless variation, her apparently complex method is simple. She uses a momentous, sometimes supernatural event violently to shift perspective and reveal the bizarre underpinnings of the superficially conventional. The agent of transfiguration differs from novel to novel; a character's involvement in the process of writing the novel of which she is part; an airplane crash on a lonely island; a series of phone calls reminding the elderly recipients that they soon must die; a diabolical intruder descending upon a working-class community; the trial of a medium for fraudulent conversion; the betrayal of a charismatic schoolteacher by her most trusted disciple; a catastrophic fire at a boardinghouse for single girls; a forbidden pilgrimage to the Holy Land. Each time, the cataclysmic event has the same effect. It forces the reexamination of circumstances long since taken for granted; it forces the protagonists to confront the terms of their existence.

Muriel Spark was born in Edinburgh in 1918. Her father Jewish, her mother Presbyterian, she was educated in the latter faith, an unlikely beginning for one of England's more important contemporary Catholic writers. Like Joyce's feelings for dear, dirty Dublin, Miss Spark's feelings for the city of her birth are ambivalent. . . .

The long title poem [in *The Fanfarlo, and Other Verse*] is a "symbolist ballad" based on some lines in Baudelaire's short story "La Fanfarlo." Narrative and allegorical, the poem anticipates the modes with which Miss Spark will ultimately be most comfortable. It also develops one of her novels' most persistent themes: the inadequacy of a self-indulgent approach to experience. The romantic, Samuel Cramer, in No-Man's Sanitarium, had in life projected his self upon the world; with Dantesque appropriateness, Death offers him neither Heaven nor Hell, either of which would be acceptable, but Limbo, the nonbeing he thoroughly fears. For Miss Spark, as for Hulme and Eliot, it is form, both in art and in life, that brings out what is decent in man. Without strict controls based outside the individual, art disintegrates, life becomes meaningless in the face of death.

Ultimately, the poems of this volume are of limited success, demonstrating that without concentrated, richly suggestive language, even sharp wit and a fine ear for rhythms may not be sufficient. For Miss Spark, the communication of experience is largely dependent on an intricate use of structure and pattern more appropriate to the novel.

Karl Malkoff. *Muriel Spark* (New York:
Columbia University Press, 1968), pp. 3–5

Muriel Spark has always been an interesting, and a very amusing, novelist; but observers of her recent work will have noticed that something fresh has been happening with her—she is turning into a very high stylist indeed. A new authority has come into her work, in the form of great tactical precision and a growingly high-handed manner both with her readers and her characters; and from *The Public Image* (1968) on she has given herself over to works in the novella form, very tight, very clear, works in which every compositional decision and every compositional device is traded at the same high economy as in Hemingway's better stories, though for very different reasons.

The result is in some ways a limiting of the pleasures—especially the comic ones—of the earlier books; but Mrs. Spark has not ceased, in the process of self-purification, to be a comic writer, a Catholic comic writer. She remains as macabre as ever; the tactics of indifference which make her aesthetic manner so poised are also part of an appalling *moral* manner, a splendid impudence; as with a number of our Catholic writers (who have contributed more than their proportionate share to aesthetic speculation in the English novel), an ingrained casuistry has always touched her dealings with the form, and these recent books have been open celebrations of it. As to the kind of Catholic aesthetics, it is not the tradition of humanism in the Catholic novel that lies behind her—Mauriac's "the heroes of our novels must be free in the sense that the theologian says man is free. The novelist must not intervene arbitrarily in their destinies" is hardly for her a conviction but a matter of witty speculation. She is much closer to the Catholic novelists of detachment, to Joyce's God-like writer, paring his fingernails, or to Waugh at the height of his comic powers—who, despairing of God's sensible presence in modern history, feels free to represent the contemporary world as chaos, and his characters as bereft of significant moral action.

This makes for an absurd and macabre universe, but at the same time for a sense of what is absent, a knowledge of true things and last things. Like Waugh, in fact, Muriel Spark is very much a *memento mori* writer, and indeed her novel of that title is a central testament—a farce which shows the comic unreality of human and historical concerns in its senile cast, and also evokes for the human lot a cool, instructive pathos. Unlike Waugh, though, she is decidedly an aesthetician, not only because she is a poet and one of our most intelligent novelists, but also because she senses a necessity for wholeness and coherence. Indeed that seems at present her main preoccupation; and it is the relation between the chaotic or contingent and the teleological that seems now to direct both her artistic and her moral interests and to make her recent books into very exact, very formal, and very duplicitous objects.

Malcolm Bradbury. Possibilities (Oxford
University Press, 1973), pp. 247–48

Since *The Public Image,* [Spark] has been putting her writing through a sieve, working towards a light, transparent, musical prose which is capable of supporting a heavy burden of meaning on the frailest of details. In *The Driver's Seat* and *Not to Disturb,* I felt that she was like a conjuror whose technique is so perfect that he loses the rabbit altogether and the point of his act disappears with the animal. Both novels were so scrupulous, so drained of the superfluous ordinary world, that they were hardly more than gossamer webs of theology and literary theory. In *The Hothouse by the East River,* the sleight of hand is brilliantly timed; the rabbit goes, then comes back again . . . and Miss Spark pitches her troubling parable exactly midway between pure metaphysical illusion and the solid landscape of bourgeois fact and society.

Her literary models now are professedly Robbe-Grillet and the nouveaux romanciers. She despises the novel as a form of mere social mimesis and writes a kind of polyphonic prose (the term is Amy Lowell's) which is closer to allegorical verse than to the loose fustian of conventional fiction. Every sentence *sounds*; each one poses what Miss Brodie would call Poise—its syntax is painfully simple, its stresses fall regularly, it has a contrived delicious clarity. One can almost scan a page of Miss Spark's writing, and its predominant rhythms are those of a nursery-rhyme of pure statement.

Johnathan Raban. Encounter. May, 1973,
p. 83

Despite her tape-recorder ear, her penetrating and retentive eye, Mrs. Spark is not attempting to give the illusion of life, for, in her terms, life itself can be illusion, dangerously obscuring basic truths by its swarming welter of diverse phenomena. She writes, she has pointed out, "always in the hope that everything will be said and done more clearly and more appropriately than in real life." And so, in her books, there is, behind the verisimilitude, a structure and a neatness that moves her art away from naturalism into the realm of the stylized and the self-contained. Though her material is taken with some shrewdness from the life, the use she makes of it, what she selects and how she organizes this, is openly artificial. Carefully disrupting normal chronology . . . making great play with time-shifts, flash-backs, glimpses forward, she attempts to bring to light fundamental patterns scribbled over by the gaudy scrawls of contingency, essential truths buried under human trivia, truths that man neglects at his own peril. Skillfully, using pattern and selection, reliant on strongly centripetal plots, Mrs. Spark endows the little world she is so exactly picturing with an additional dimension, changes it from something formless and contingent into an entity possessing the meaningful and necessary design of a work of art. Having scrutinized the society she is to concentrate upon for what she would call its "essence," she then so structures her plot, so chooses her characters and choreographs their actions, as to make this stand out vividly: the dictatorial behavior of an Edinburgh schoolteacher in the thirties thus becoming emblematic of Fascism; a scandal in the Roman film-world, with its subsequent circus of spurious publicity, standing as garish image of man's efforts to deceive and self-deceive. Mrs. Spark herself compares her art to parable. In fact, it also comes close to allegory, to that type of writing much favored in the Middle Ages, where the visible scene, concretely presented, is regarded as a kind of text, a fund of metaphor, which, properly interpreted, can yield important truths. In Mrs. Spark's fiction, the depicted society, precisely and humorously portrayed, becomes too a potent symbol of some fundamental tenet: a tenet, usually, indicative of human limitation, for these novels are ironic as well as allegorical.

Peter Kemp. Muriel Spark (Totowa, New Jersey: Barnes & Noble, 1975), pp. 12–13

The technique of a Muriel Spark novel is in fact exactly opposite to Jane Austen's: it works by continual *dislocation*, by setting up a fabric of faults and cleavages from one side of which the events of the novel can be construed in one way, while from the other they fall irrevocably (although we can recapture our first innocent vision by an effort of imagination) into another pattern. The pleasure of reading her lies in the unexpectedness and yet the justice of these discoveries. It is the pleasure of continually breaking out into a new-found world—a new level of sophistication—whereas the pleasure of Jane Austen is the pleasure of finding that each new vista, however surprising, is a vista of the same well-ordered park, and fits naturally and ineluctably with all the others. Muriel Spark's technique is inherently inimical to the setting-up of a single "authorial" or "ultimate" point of view from which alone every-thing in the novel can ultimately be seen as cohering with everything else (that point of view in a Jane Austen novel from which we stray only by dint of misreading or by ceasing to read the novel *as a novel*); although of course one can have a reading of a Muriel Spark novel which is *from a technical point of view* ultimate and "complete" in the sense that it catches all the force (although perhaps not all the reverberations) of all the dislocations.

The Prime of Miss Jean Brodie is in this sense organized round Sandy's betrayal. Read straightforwardly from the first page on, the book can for some time be taken as a piece of amusing but rather lightweight social satire about the startling effect of a flamboyant and strong-minded spinster upon the girls of a drably conformist Edinburgh school. Of course even on that level there is an undercurrent of resistance and discomfort stemming from the urbane, deadpan irony of the style (one can trace the acknowledged influence of Max Beerbohm here). . . .

However, even discounting style, the social-satire reading of the book runs steadily into choppier and choppier water. We pass from the idyll under the tree in the grounds of Marcia Blaine School for Girls, with Miss Brodie handing out to her enthralled little girls her colored, delightful, half-sinful scraps of knowledge of the exciting adult world (so much more real and alive than the school subjects), to the isolation of her set in the whispering, private world of their precocity, to the strange fruits of political and sexual craziness that grow so naturally in this microclimate, untouched by the frosts of Edinburgh winters. Throughout this there is a constant swell, as of wind and tide in opposite directions, of uncertainty about what we are to think of Miss Brodie.

Bernard Harrison. In Gabriel Josipovici, ed.
*The Modern English Novel: The Reader,
The Writer, The Work* (Totowa, New Jersey:
Barnes & Noble, 1976), pp. 238–39

[Muriel Spark] belongs [among] those novelists, Waugh, Firbank, Henry Green and Powell, who have attempted to understand the world by cultivating detachment; so that what they construct has a self-conscious artistry, which depends for its effect on the writer's oblique stance to his material. There is a clear preference for imposing form rather than interpreting what is immediately presented to the eye; it is the form which will give significance. In Muriel Spark's most completely successful works—which I would take to be *Memento Mori, The Bachelors, The Means, The Hothouse by the East River* and *The Abbess of Crewe,* she achieves the same sort of success that Waugh does in *A Handful of Dust,* Firbank in *Caprice* or *The Flower beneath the Foot,* Green in *Party-going* or *Loving,* and Powell in *Afternoon Men.* Drawing on the real world as in [Robert Louis] Stevenson's words "an inexhaustible magazine," she, like them, creates a stylized version, standing at an oblique angle, immeasurably different, being designed and significant; the design and significance being an illumination and criticism of the world the senses perceive. . . .

Fictional truth may be, as Muriel Spark has said, something less than absolute, but it is more intense than the truths revealed by sociology. The imagination perceives and realizes what reason is blind to. . . . It is this sort of truth that in her best work she achieves.

This being so, questions of her place in Scottish literature may appear irrelevant. And indeed there is something tiresome in the habit of thought which insists on establishing a nationality test. When, for instance, Maurice Lindsay, in his magisterial *History of Scottish Literature,* states that after *Jean Brodie* her work adorns English rather than Scottish Literature, one may somewhat wearily detect a note of parochialism. Nationality is not after all one of the most important of a writer's characteristics; the concept of it is in many ways a piece of rather jaded nineteenth-century provincialism. And it is only in a small country, conscious of a sense of inferiority, that the question can be asked. Not all small countries either; do the Irish feel a need to disown Beckett?

But since the question has been raised it may be worth asserting that she seems, throughout her work, to draw on her Scottish background and display qualities characteristic of it. She has . . . drawn attention to the importance of what she calls the "nevertheless" principle in her life and work; and it is clear enough that the dislocation, so marked a feature of her mode of seeing, derives from this principle that cannot allow things to be as they first seem.

Her awareness of the attractiveness of the forces of evil, of the bonny guise the Devil presents himself in, has deep roots in the Scottish psyche, the expression of which in Literature goes back beyond Hogg and may more recently be found in Stevenson and Buchan.

Her concern with style reflects Stevenson also and of all Scottish writers this still too neglected master is the clearest influence on her work; for influence at its most fruitful is to be discerned in manner rather than material.

Allan Massie. *Muriel Spark* (Edinburgh: Ramsay Head, 1979), pp. 94–96

Akin to what in the Renaissance was know as *sprezzatura*—an aristocratic "contempt" for one's own productions—this attitude has served [Muriel Spark] both well and badly in her recent work. In a brilliantly faceted novel like *The Takeover* (1976), the offhand treatment of characters and events is integral to her comic vision of the decline and fall of the international rich and enhances our sense of an ornate structure reduced to glittering chaos. In *Territorial Rights* (1979), however, where the bubbling of absurdity is less in evidence, we find something different: a refusal of fictional responsibility that verges on the contemptuous. Characters are simply thrown away at the end, and the annoyed reader wonders why he should care what happens when the novelist apparently doesn't.

Loitering with Intent is a much better book than its immediate predecessor. I had a very good time reading it. But the light hand to which Fleur refers creates certain problems having to do with fictional credibility and commitment within a comic scheme. . . .

These deficiencies, as I see them, would matter much more were it not for Muriel Spark's stylistic aplomb, the constant play of her wit, and above all the inspired creation of Fleur as her narrator-heroine. For Fleur, despite the ambiguities of her makeup, is a true heroine, one who engages the reader's sympathies; we cheer her on. Endowed with liveliness, self-confidence, and a touch of real madness, she is the perfected medium for voicing and enacting the paradoxes that have engaged Muriel Spark's fancy in this novel. She has the energy that the chief plot device lacks; she is the one character whose observations, actions, and imaginings supply the comic brio that sweeps the reader happily past all hesitations and dissatisfactions to the high-spirited finale. . . .

Though she has written three or four of the finest English novels to be published since the Second World War, my impression is that Muriel Spark is taken somewhat for granted these days and that she has received much less critical attention than, say, Iris Murdoch or Doris Lessing. Perhaps that light hand is partly to blame—that, and the exceptional lucidity of her style. She is, of course, a major resource of contemporary British fiction and likely to astound us again with a work as powerful as *Memento Mori, The Prime of Miss Jean Brodie,* or *The Girls of Slender Means.* If *Loitering with Intent* does not achieve that level, it is nonetheless intelligent comedy of a sort that will give more pleasure than nine-tenths of what is acclaimed as good fiction today.

Robert Towers. *New York Review of Books.*
June 25, 1981, pp. 45, 46

It has been Muriel Spark's singular achievement as a novelist to synthesize the linguistic cunning of poetry with the seeming credibility of prose. One of the most self-conscious of stylists, Spark has a fondness for scattering poetic quotations, like clues, throughout her fiction and it is no accident that several of the poets quoted are Metaphysical in technique or metaphysical in tone. Dr. Johnson's controversial essay on Cowley . . . suggested that in Metaphysical verse "heterogeneous ideas are yoked by violence together," a remark that acquires a novel application in Spark's treatment of murder, terrorism, blackmail, fraud and other crimes against the individual. Her subjects, frequently dislocated by large doses of black comedy, are her contemporaries, who coexist with the author (or her representatives) in a world whose sublime ideals tend in practice to become ridiculous. . . .

One of Spark's most effective conceits is the notion that characters, in actuality as well as art, can only face facts through fiction—a situation from which she extracts wisdom as well as wit. . . .

While Spark is intensely serious about her artistic calling, she uses her craft to portray life as a divine comedy that often collapses into farce when events overwhelm expectations. In her books, appearance is deceptive by nature. . . .

Dealing with a period ranging from the 1930s to the present, Spark is one of the most lucid and alert of contemporary writers. Even when her characters slip into solipsism her books do not ignore world events such as the rise of Fascism *(The Prime of Miss Jean Brodie)*, the Second World War and its aftermath *(The Girls of Slender Means)*, the Eichmann trial and the Middle East conflict *(The Mandelbaum Gate)*, the Watergate scandal *(The Abbess of Crewe*, 1974), the crisis of capitalism *(The Takeover*, 1976) and political terrorism *(Territorial Rights*, 1979). But Spark is never merely topical, for her novels are haunted by the spectre of a theological eternity.

Alan Bold. *Muriel Spark* (London: Methuen,
1986), pp. 11–13

Strange events and characters are . . . woven into the fine fiction of Muriel Spark, who has been described as an author with one foot off the ground. "It is all demonology," says one of her characters. Indeed, unusual personalities do flit about like wraiths—especially through the narrow halls of Spark's more recent fiction. *The Hothouse by the East River* is inhabited by a neurotic whose shadow falls in the wrong direction and sits by the window hour after hour "seeing things." In *The Driver's Seat,* a woman screams in disapproval when she learns that the gaudy [garment] she is about to buy will not show the blood stains she plans to [acquire] during an appointment with her murderer. And in *Not to Disturb* a group of ghoulish servants make elaborate plans with the media to tell the sensational "inside" story of their masters' imminent murder-suicide, which they have also helped arrange; meanwhile, thunder rolls, lightening cracks, and "him in the attic" lurches about in lusty madness. . . . Muriel Spark also has expressed an interest in moral philosophy. . . . Spark states that her career as a novelist began only after her conversion to Roman Catholicism. Although she does not want to belabor this sequence, she admits that her religion has provided her with a type of ground work from which to write . . . . Not unlike some of T. S. Eliot's poetic maneuvers, one of Spark's novelistic techniques is to create clear, sharp images of a moral wasteland, where the ethical statement is expressed more by what is missing than by what is present. Death-in-life situations, and characters who are often more spectral than human, underline the qualities of compassion and integrity by their conspicuous absence.

Richard C. Kane. *Iris Murdoch, Muriel
Spark, and John Fowles: Didactic Demons
in Modern Fiction* (Madison, New Jersey:
Fairleigh Dickinson University Press, 1988),
pp. 11–13

Magic is associated [in Spark's work] with fraudulence or misguidedness; mystery with either the finite and knowable or the infinite and unknowable. Magic is a snare, a temptation to what is delusory; and the basic trouble with magic is that it ironically employs matter to escape the claim, the reality, of matter. Mystery, by contrast, may be converted into the nonmysterious or known—if the mystery is the sort with which the police are finitely concerned. Or mystery may be that sort which is unknowable, the sort that induces awareness of infinite reality. This larger mystery must be believed, cannot be known. Understandably, Spark makes comic hay of the contrast between those characters who in good or bad faith will not acknowledge more than the finite kind of mystery and those characters who quite see the claims of the finite, but whose belief demands that these claims be accommodated with faith's firm reality. Spark's interest in the scope and manifestations of the real combines prominently with her concern for the creative act and has so combined from the beginning of her career. This in turn means that certain emphases upon balances between Being and beings, universal and particular, reality and realism, ubiquitous and here, eternal and now—that such emphases commonly tend to be shaped by the novelist's focus upon the mystery of making. My contention is that . . . structural, generic, and textural interests are subsumed within Spark's role as creator, and that this role is most richly seen in her special theistic-aesthetic terms. We see this creative focus most plainly in *The Comforters, The Public Image, Not to Disturb,* and *Loitering with Intent.*

Joseph Hynes. The Art of the Real: Muriel
Spark's Novels (Madison, New Jersey:
Fairleigh Dickinson University Press, 1988),
p. 136

The connection between Muriel Spark's conversion and her self-discovery as a writer has marked her work indelibly. Vocation in her own life has forged her authorial identity and supplied her with a theme to which she could resort in novel after novel. In this study I have attempted to trace its recurrence in widely differing books from different phases of her career. Even so, it would be a mistaken view of the writer that failed to detect shifts in, and adaptations of, the perennial concern. . . .

In [her] unyielding rigor is an aspect of the author's vision that some of her detractors find hard to accept. Such critics, viewing the novels in humanist terms, have been repelled by a discipline that subordinates individual desire to the immutable (and often exorbitant) demands of dogma and have regretted its entrenchment at the expense, say, of Caroline's and Barbara's sexual happiness. And here lies a rub that any admirer of Muriel Spark must address—the extent to which her beliefs impair the access of a non-Christian reader to her work. . . .

Whether or not one assents to the metaphysical framework that encloses the best of Muriel Spark's novels, there can be no doubting that it ensures against solipsism and vainglory, against being, as the Old Man of the Mountain says to Peer Gynt, "to thyself . . . enough." These, the negative bequests of a humanism that came to birth as an assertion of human dignity, have quite as often inflated the littleness of humankind as they have realized the excellence of its potential. With premises very different from Spark's, David Ehrenfeld has traced a number of global woes to the humanistic vision: "there are good and evil sides to humanism, and it is time to recognize the evil side for what it is and the damage it does." Novels that warn us of "that evil side," no matter how disconcertingly and uncompromisingly unfashionable the tenets of the warning, are novels to cherish. The . . . way to honor them is to read them in the terms that they offer: imaginatively, at least, to agree that it is in the severe limitation of the self, not its infinite aggrandizement, that moral health is to be found.

Rodney Stenny Edgecombe. *Vocation and Identity in the Fiction of Muriel Spark* (Columbia: University of Missouri Press, 1990), pp. 135–36, 156

Critics have been, understandably, fascinated by the original and confident way in which Spark writes; it has been tempting to define the terms in which she works, and to read from her work some intimation of absolute points of reference, be they spiritual or aesthetic. However, such terms are elusive. I have found it rewarding to consider the perspectives and motivation of some of her characters individually. By rebuilding their understanding of their lives, their problems, their needs and their ability to confront challenges, it is possible to see how Spark portrays an experience of life to which the individual will contributes. I have studied her women characters exclusively. This is because little attention has been paid to Spark's presentation of women, although her achievement in constructing female character is unrivaled in the twentieth-century Catholic novel. Spark is not a feminist in the sense that she asserts specific rights for women, nor is she interested in decrying a society which might seek to repress women. However, she has, in several of her novels, depicted women in a search for a dignity and possession of mind which, in its own way, vindicates a woman's spiritual integrity. Waugh's women are mostly mere social satellites; Greene appears unable to present the inner consciousness of a woman—the female characters in his books are shown through the eyes of men. Muriel Spark, however, conveys an insight into the minds of her women characters which enables the reader both to identify with and to appraise their behavior. She does not intend them to stand as exemplary figures; indeed, some are clearly flawed and willfully contrive their own malevolent relationships. Some, though, achieve their identity through their quest for self-respect, which involves an appreciation of all that they cannot understand.

Judy Sproxton. *The Women of Muriel Spark* (New York: St. Martin's Press, 1992), p. 18

STAFFORD, JEAN (UNITED STATES) 1915–79

From time to time there appears on the American literary scene an exceptional and original feminine talent. Several over the past few years have
exhibited brilliant facets, but Jean Stafford is the first in many years to spread
before our eyes a radiant stylistic network of dazzling virtuosity.

> Elizabeth Bullock. *Chicago Sun Book Week.*
> September 24, 1944, p. 1

There is no doubt that Jean Stafford, author of *Boston Adventure,* is a remarkable new talent. This is not to say that her first novel is a completely satisfying
experience but that Miss Stafford brings to the writing of a novel an unusual
native endowment; I would find it hard to name a book of recent years which,
page for page or even sentence for sentence, was so lively and so clever. By
the light of any one of the incandescent moments of *Boston Adventure,* it
may turn out that the book as a whole is strangely disappointing, reminding
us that in the final analysis no amount of skill as a writer substitutes for the
total novelistic power. But for its manner, for the way in which it stands up
to the literary job, Miss Stafford's novel unquestionably demands a place for
itself in the best literary tradition.

> Diana Trilling. *The Nation.* September 30,
> 1944, p. 383

Miss Stafford's remarkably fine novel [*Boston Adventure*] has been praised
for its range and perception, its style, and for a distinction, as I see it, that
springs from the meeting of genuine personal culture with deep independence
of sight. It has also, because of certain echoes, been analyzed for its Proustian
qualities. But not enough has been said of the real Proustian epic in it. . . .
Here, at last, is a novel in which sensibility is not sacrificed to representation;
in which the inwardness of man, at once the deposit of events and the shaper
of them, is functionally related to bold and objective visual power.

> Alfred Kazin. *The New Republic.*
> October 23, 1944, p. 538

[*The Mountain Lion*] is an even finer novel than *Boston Adventure,* though
less brilliant. It does not have the startling wealth of anecdote which Jean
Stafford offered in her first novel; but it has a deeper richness of child-myth
and child-lore—charms against the adult world, rhymes, ritualistic "dialogues" and shared "jokes," intimations of mortality—and the statement it
makes of good and evil, innocence and experience, is tantalizing in its possibilities of extension. In this narrower plot, the author has found, paradoxically, greater freedom of perception and utterance: her style here is cleaner
and more athletic.

> Henry Rago. *Commonweal.* April 4, 1947,
> p. 618

Miss Stafford writes with brilliance. Scene after scene is told with unforgettable care and tenuous entanglements are treated with wise subtlety. She creates a splendid sense of time, of the unending afternoons of youth, and of the actual color of noon and of night.

Refinement of evil, denial of drama only make the underlying truth more terrible.

> Catherine Meredith Brown. *Saturday Review*
> *of Literature.* March 1, 1947, p. 15

The Catherine Wheel—her third and perhaps most complex novel—is supported by few of those subsidiary virtues which gave vitality and idiosyncrasy to her earlier work; for all the elaborate rendition of locale and *décor,* it never really aims—as did *Boston Adventure*—at a systematic investigation of the social fact, nor does it attempt to frame a specialized personal crisis with the masterly precision of *The Mountain Lion.* Its scope is defined by intentions at once more limited and more ambitious than these: Miss Stafford has sought to convey, through two subtly interwoven though distinct narratives, a vision of emotional anarchy assaulting a world of "traditional sanctity and loveliness"—a vision in which the individual disaster is simultaneously symptom and result of the larger social decline. . . . Miss Stafford has written a novel to compel the imagination and nurture the mind; she has also written one in which pity and terror combine to reach us in the secret, irrational places of the heart.

> Richard Hayes. *Commonweal.* January 25,
> 1952, pp. 404–5

In her superbly controlled novel *(The Catherine Wheel)* Miss Stafford has shown a modern martyrdom; her story discloses the secret torture of two persons, a child and a woman, both caught in a tragic circumstance during a tranquil summer on the coast of Maine. . . . The village in this novel is named Hawthorne, but even without that reminder it is clear that Miss Stafford is concerned with the identical plight that Nathaniel Hawthorne pondered in his stories—the tragedy of human isolation, the devious, painful, perilous struggle for harmony and understanding. *The Catherine Wheel* is a novel of great restraint and of great beauty.

> Walter Havighurst. *Saturday Review of*
> *Literature.* January 26, 1952, p. 11

In each of her novels, she has begun with what her art and imagination can really create: a densely detailed, spatially narrated image of a place, some people, and their relationships, dramatizing the whole in a diffused, remembered time, rather than any too tyrannical chronological time. But then, toward the end, she seems to feel the need for a "memorable act," for some abruptly theatrical violence, which not only intrudes improbably upon the soft-grained texture she has been building up, but for which frankly she has no taste or instinct. . . . The result is false, mutilating, and unworthy of her.

Robert Phelps. *The New Republic.*
March 10, 1952, p. 21

Character is most important in these stories, but character does not play out a drama of isolated sensibility. Instead, Miss Stafford's people are seen, as it were, in a full round of experience, are set with their problems and conflicts in a milieu that is vital and charged both with intimate and external meaning. To an unusual degree, there is a significant rapport and reciprocal influence between these characters and their environments, and from this ability of Miss Stafford's to relate aspects of character with the details of scene and situation comes a major strength of these stories, their compelling believability.

Gene Baro. *New York Herald Tribune.*
May 10, 1953, p. 3

Maladies and misfortunes of one sort or other cause Miss Stafford's characters to retreat from the world of customary urges and responses into a never-never land of dreams and unfulfilled desires, a land where sickness is king and despair his consort. Within its boundaries, Miss Stafford writes with certainty, understanding, and beauty. Like her three novels, (her) stories within their impeccable frame-work, are meaningful and complex. They remind me of children's Japanese flower-shells which when submerged in water open silently to disgorge a phantasmagoria of paper flowers, richly colored, varied and vaguely grotesque in contrast to the bland, unrevealing walls of their temporary habitations.

William Peden. *The New York Times.*
May 10, 1953, p. 5

These three archetypal figures—the alien, the rebel, and the freak—serve, then, as a focus for exploring the cultural condition of the modern world. That condition is given an ethical dimension through a fusion of psychological, humanistic, and Christian terms. Moral judgment is couched in the language of Freud as well as of the Bible, and the fusion is effected through imagery. The serpent, referred to in crucial scenes of each of the novels, is equally at home in the worlds of theology and depth psychology, and possession by the devil may be construed literally or metaphorically. By seeing the eternal problem of innocence and guilt, good and knowledge, from this threefold perspective, Miss Stafford gives full scope to her other ironic vision while enriching and extending her material. The use of terms, concepts, and images drawn from a variety of ideologies is the language and technique of the ironist who seeks to show both the metaphoric, incomplete character of the insights they articulate and their inability to command single-minded belief.

Olga W. Vickery. *South Atlantic Quarterly.*
Autumn, 1962, p. 489

We might say that Miss Stafford knows the limits of her talent too well; neither in the Emily stories nor in any of the others does she burden her prose with a sense of personal urgency, of compulsion to speak. The stories mean just what they seem at first glance to mean; the plot itself *is* the meaning. Thus in one story we witness a beautiful lady's wasted career, and the only matter for reflection is that her career was indeed wasted. In another we see a retired professor disembarrass himself of a sycophantic disciple, and we experience relief: *that's* over with. Similarly, we share the sense of achieved freedom experienced by a young woman who deserts her provincial guardians in Colorado, and of two lovers who foil a pack of busybodies. If there is a recurrent idea in this book [*Bad Characters*] it is the idea of sheer escape, stripped of intellectual content.

Frederick C. Crews. *New York Review of Books*. November 5, 1964, p. 13

Jean Stafford loves the American landscape and the American past: the Colorado desert, the coast of Maine, the old streets of Boston, Miss Pride picking her way through an ancient graveyard, Katharine Congreve wandering about her father's old mansion. Yet she always sees the relevant modern comment and fits it in exactly. She is very conscious of the deodorant in the drugstore window, the giveaway formality of the *arriviste,* the blue or pink head of the dowager. Her great gift is to be able to place the vulgar detail in the center of the picture without making the picture vulgar, making it, on the contrary, something at once more vivid, faintly humorous, accurate, and at the same time fantastic. What she does to the American scene is to show it as a landscape with a billboard in the center, a billboard that represents the human encroachment on nature, at times funny, at times sordid, at times pathetic, but at all times the reader's and the author's principal concern.

Louis Auchincloss. *Pioneers and Caretakers*
(Minneapolis: University of Minnesota
Press, 1965), p. 159

Some months ago the major portion of Miss Stafford's interview with the mother of Lee Oswald [*A Mother in History*] appeared in *McCall's* Magazine. The compelling interest of this self-portrait—for the writer let Mrs. Oswald speak for herself—was equaled only by the nature of the reader reaction to the piece. Letter after letter poured in repeating words like "disgusted," "shocked," "outraged." . . .

None were more surprised at this storm of protest than Miss Stafford herself and the editors of the magazine. For what she had done was—and is—a most valuable analysis of a woman sick with a spiritual and emotional malignancy. Like a good analyst, Miss Stafford hardly speaks at all, letting the wild, interminable flow, alternately deluded and canny, outraged and cosy, spill from the woman's lips into a tape recorder as she exonerates herself and her son from all blame, points condemning fingers at a shifting host of

"Theys" and heaps scorn on the official establishment and the gullible public alike. . . .

Where Jean Stafford's great skill is manifest is in the brief interpolations, between Mrs. Oswald's copious stream, in which she describes the meticulously neat little house filled with small "decorative" objects the owner "just picked up" but empty of all roots; observes the owner's mannerisms and idioms, her bustling proffers of coffee and collaboration; tells of her own hideously hilarious struggles with the tape-recorder, of the harrowing visit with the mother to the son's grave; manages to convey the trauma of her own involvement with this woman without ever raising her voice.

Marya Mannes. New York Herald Tribune.
February 27, 1966, p. 4

Stafford wrote her best when she wrote about places and people she had experienced intensely. She said she shared the "sense of place" and "dislocation" of Henry James and Mark Twain. Certainly, in her own work she returned again and again to those places that had been most important in her life—Covina and Boulder, which she called "Adams," Heidelberg, Damariscotta Mills. When her characters have left their homes, they often express in one way or another their sense of dislocation, from the rather direct statements in such stories as "The Bleeding Heart" and "Children Are Bored on Sunday" to the less direct and meditative expressions in such stories as "A Reunion" and "The Lippia Lawn." As these remarks suggest, her fiction is often highly autobiographical. It is her own life as a girl and as a woman that has inspired much of her best work. Her first story, "And Lots of Solid Color" (1939), and the last story published before her death, "An Influx of Poets" (1978), are autobiographical bookends for the work that comes between.

The work that comes between is three novels—*Boston Adventure* (1944), *The Mountain Lion* (1947), and *The Catherine Wheel* (1952)—and nearly fifty stories, plus a substantial body of essays and articles. . . .

The central characters, the girls and women, are usually portrayed as powerless victims—of their poverty or of their wealth, of rejection by people they love, of the roles into which society forces them, of the devalued status of divorcées and even widows, of their own deep anger at their powerless state, of their inability to act, of all these things internalized as self-hatred. Often the relationship to the father is crucial; it is usually ambivalent and sometimes hostile. The orphan, often fatherless, sometimes motherless, is a dominant character type.

Mary Ellen Williams Walsh. Preface to Jean
Stafford (Boston: Twayne, 1985), n.p.

Stafford's ironic vision, though a particularly appropriate response to the modern condition, was reinforced by her inheritance of the American literary tradition. American literature has from its beginnings been characterized by antithetical impulses, the innocence and naive faith in a brave new world shadowed by the dark symbolism of the Puritan tradition. As Richard Chase illustrates, contradictions and dualities are endemic to American literature, so that as Alfred Kazin notes, by Stafford's era, "the greatest single fact about our modern American writing [was] our writers' absorption in every last detail of their American world together with their deep and subtle alienation from it." Stafford inherited and merged in her work the Gothic symbolic tradition of Nathaniel Hawthorne and Herman Melville; the social criticism and novel of manners of Henry James and Edith Wharton; and the comic frontier tradition of Mark Twain and the early local colorists. Her successful manipulation of the paradoxically varied yet similar strains in American literature lends to her work a diversity and vivacity that qualify her as an important minor American writer.

Ultimately, Stafford's modernist sensibility and her American heritage are mediated by a more fundamental birthright; Stafford the ironist and Stafford the American are tempered always by Stafford the woman. If, as Judith Fetterley maintains, in a patriarchal society, "bereft, disinherited, cast out, woman is the Other, the Outsider, a mourner among children," Stafford's affinity for the lost and lonely is the peculiar sympathy of one sufferer for another, a "painful communion," a "honeymoon of cripples," a "nuptial consummation of the abandoned." And, I would argue, her special sympathy for the sufferers in her culture derives from her sex.

> Maureen Ryan. *Innocence and*
> *Estrangement in the Fiction of Jean*
> *Stafford* (Baton Rouge: Louisiana State
> University Press, 1987), p. 7

Stafford would live for twenty-seven years after the publication of her third novel, *The Catherine Wheel,* in 1952, yet she failed even to come close to completing another. She won the Pulitzer Prize in 1970 for her *Collected Stories,* but by then her knack for short fiction had been effectively dormant for a decade. She survived by turning out book reviews, essays, and cranky polemics. Her nonfiction prose from the 1960s and 1970s includes pieces that are among the best journalism written during those decades; indeed Stafford seldom wrote even a personal note that is not in some way memorable. Nonetheless it is hard not to see the ephemeral articles of these years as a calculated avoidance of the greater demands of fiction.

The causes of Stafford's decline are several and elusive. For all the excuses she loved to make, at the deepest level she knew that she had no one to blame but herself; yet in some sense she was powerless before the tangled imperatives of her own nature. In any event, the novelist who had leapt so spectacularly onto the stage in the 1940s and who had seemed possessed of limitless promise was starting, by the 1970s, to be relegated to a defunct generation. Despite the Pulitzer, her fame faded drastically.

By the mid-1980s, however, Stafford was riding the crest of a revival. Legions of readers are now discovering her for the first time, marveling anew at her humor, her narrative power, her ironic verve, her disdain for all things shabby and chic—and at the perfect sentences she worked so hard to construct. What Robert Fitzgerald wrote about *The Mountain Lion* is true of all her best work: "Though you read it with amusement, you will feel it aching in you like a tooth for days."

David Roberts. *Jean Stafford: The Life of a Writer* (New York: St. Martin's Press, 1988), pp. 4–5

In 1944, critics hailed as a major literary event the publication of Jean Stafford's first novel, *Boston Adventure;* in the fifties, when her wonderful short stories were published in the *New Yorker,* her fiction reached a wider audience; and in 1970, after her *Collected Stories* was awarded the Pulitzer Prize, many people who had never read her work before discovered what a splendid writer she was. Yet until recently much of her fiction was out of print. Furthermore, over time the ardor of some of her early admirers cooled. Alfred Kazin, for example, who had praised *Boston Adventure* when it first appeared, devotes only one sentence to Stafford's work in his study of twentieth-century American writers, *Bright Book of Life.* Today it is largely due to the efforts of feminist scholars that Stafford's fiction is being rediscovered by a new generation of readers.

Charlotte Margolis Goodman. *Jean Stafford: The Savage Heart* (Austin: University of Texas Press, 1990), p. x

What comes across most strongly in Stafford's graceful fiction, as Ms. Goodman herself acknowledges, is not so much her female self-hatred but her almost overwhelming sense of isolation. She is a poet of loneliness: not a single one of her protagonists seems to feel at home in the world she occupies; most of them long to find refuge in someone else's life; each of them seems surrounded by hollow spaces full of echoes. This powerful sense of aloneness transcends gender: loneliness is not just a female complaint, nor is being a misfit a female prerogative. One senses always in Stafford's fiction the pain of someone who can neither find comfort in the world nor sever herself from it completely: hope is the eternal enemy, along with the wistful yearning for connection that afflicts the vilest-tongued child ("Bad Characters") or the most arrogant old New England spinster ("The Hope Chest").

Even without having read her biography, one could assume from the work that Stafford, like most of humanity, always longed for love and rarely felt that she got it. What she received instead was a gift that enabled her to transmute that longing into something at a safe distance from herself, and then the cold consolation of art.

Evelyn Toynton. *Salmagundi.* 92, Fall, 1992, p. 244

STARK, FREYA (GREAT BRITAIN) 1893–1993

Fourteen years ago Freya Stark wrote a book called *The Valleys of the Assassins,* which seemed to me then and still seems one of the rare and lovely travel books fortuitously thrown up from time to time by professional travelers, to take their place in the stream of English literature. . . .

Perseus in the Wind is the plump fruit now hanging on the boughs after the probationary blossom of her early experience. It should have been easy to foresee that if she could already write in those terms in 1934, by 1948 she would still be writing in the same strain. . . . Miss Stark is a serious person, and these essays must represent the philosophy she has worked out for herself after years of dangerous and adventurous living. Whether she has commanded happiness is only for herself to say; beauty she has recognized to the point, I should judge, of poignant pain; death she has valued at its proper estimate; enjoyment has always been richly hers; and as for the conquest of fear—well, that, like happiness, must remain for her to say. The reader has no business to pry into such private things; and Freya Stark is not only a serious person but is also a private person, whose last recesses of secrecy demand respect. . . .

These essays, then, must stand for the summing-up of a life's creed worked out in lonely and often perilous places. They reflect a fundamental optimism, if by optimism we mean a belief in all which is generous, beautiful, permanent and true, "such delicate goods as justice, love and honor, courtesy, and indeed all the things we care for."

V. Sackville-West. Spectator. November 26,
1948, p. 704

She has given much pleasure to many people. She has scholarship enough to give some plausible reason for venturing into places so remote that even the R.A.F. has been put to some trouble to extricate her; she has communicated her enthusiasm for such places with marked success—but one has always feared her awful promise to strangle a book with fine writing. On the whole her travel books escape with no worse injury than a wry neck. What happens when she tackles a more tractable *genre* is all too sadly evident in her new book.

Perseus in the Wind is a volume of twenty essays in which Miss Stark gives her reflections on such subjects as Service, Happiness, Education, Beauty, Death, Memory, Love, Sorrow, and Courage. It has to be confessed that her bearing in the presence of these abstractions is irreproachable; indeed, it is frequently admirable. But it is hardly original. . . . We could accept these reflections in the spirit with which they were offered (for Miss Stark modestly disclaims all intention of being original) were it not that she smothers most simple statements with figurative language.

P. H. Newby. New Statesman and Nation.
January 1, 1949, p. 17

Miss Freya Stark's writing seems to me wholly admirable; and so are her aims, her side-shows and her digressions. "Curiosity led me," she states, "pure, disinterested curiosity," and she adds that "if we are to criticize the British for anything, as we cannot get out of the habit of doing, even now that we are poor—it would be for lack of this virtue." Fortunately Miss Stark has always possessed the virtue in full measure, and one is glad to note her pronouncement that "curiosity ought to increase as one gets older."

Certainly in this new book [*Ionia: a Quest*] she has chosen a theme worthy of her own virtues and abilities. For the coast-line of Ionia is, as it were, the birthplace of curiosity. . . .

It shall be said that whether Miss Stark is looking for history or not, she is constantly looking at it, constantly plunging into it with the zest of a diver, and emerging with rare finds which she displays or strings together in an admirable pattern and in accordance with her "accuracy of a different mood." The severest professional historian may well be delighted at and even instructed by her manner of discovery and presentation, however much he may sometimes be shocked by her rapid generalizations. These are always forceful and fresh, like the rest of the writing, and may appear at any time. . . .

To have brought into clear light with love and knowledge, so much of what might have faded, to have so insisted on the concrete reality of what is immortal and with an accurate style to have transmitted to others, in detail and extent, the rarity of her own fine experience—these are great achievements, and many other readers besides myself will be grateful to Miss Stark for what she has accomplished.

Rex Warner. *Spectator.* November 12, 1954,
pp. 583–84

"This book" [*The Lycian Shore*], she says, "lays no claim to learning, but roams through space and time as books of travel should do." The reader may fairly complain that it devotes rather too much length to learning and does not roam through space or time half enough. In the case of so eminent and well-loved a writer of travel books, such a complaint would be based only on the excellence of her past achievement, and disappointment is no more than relative. It is what is missing that disappoints, not what is here; and perhaps what is most obviously missing is sympathy with her subject. Miss Stark does not hold the Turks in the same affection as she does the Arabs and Persians; and if, like other Britons, at heart she prefers the Greeks, like other Britons she is not going to say so.

C. M. Woodhouse. *Time and Tide.* May 12,
1956, p. 557

Born in Paris, raised in England and Italy by estranged parents, Stark escaped her Victorian upbringing through travel. From North Africa through Central Asia, she traveled, unmarried and poor, recording her impressions in countless photographs. Learning Persian, Turkish, Arabic and Kurdish, this independent woman mingled with sultans and ordinary people, was admitted into harems where no European men could enter and rode camel caravans. A minor celebrity and an agent for Britain's propaganda efforts during World War II, Stark campaigned against fascism and wrote travel books that now sound quaint and romantic. Her striking photographs, reproduced in this illustrated biography by her godson [*Traveler through Time*] capture a Bedouin wedding, barges on the Nile, Baghdad's squalor and beauty, Greek ruins in Western Turkey, Burmese pagodas, worshipers in Afghanistan.

Genevieve Stuttaford. *Publishers Weekly.*
September 5, 1986, p. 94

This sequel [*A Winter in Arabia*] to the author's *Southern Gates of Arabia* describes Dame Freya's second trip through southwestern Arabia for three months during the winter of 1937–38, when the area, recently pacified by Harold Ingrams, was little known to Westerners, much less to single women. An intrepid Englishwoman in the line of Hester Stanhope, Mary Kingsley and Gertrude Bell, Stark (now 94 years old) was strongly attracted to the hard life of the desert Arabs. In this attractively written travel account, originally published in 1940 and long out of print, she combines her knowledge of archeology, geography and history with an ability to recreate feelings, actions, dialogue and the idiosyncrasies and sensitivities of people at all levels of Arab society.

Genevieve Stuttaford. *Publishers Weekly.*
July 3, 1987, p. 52

After appearing in Eastern newspapers, these twenty-eight pieces were gathered into this volume [*Bagdad Sketches*] originally published in Bagdad in 1933. It was the first of many Stark would produce on the Middle East. Inside she unfolds her journeys from Damascus to Kuwait, detailing the people and places she encounters. With the changes that have occurred in the area since Stark's time, this now may be more valuable as a record of an era long gone than as merely a quaint travel journal.

Michael Rogers. *Library Journal.* September
15, 1992, p. 98

STEAD, CHRISTINA (AUSTRALIA) 1902–83

It was to be expected that Miss Christina Stead, after the rich and riotous fantasy of *The Salzburg Tales,* would try her hand at naturalism of one kind or another. Here, then, is *Seven Poor Men of Sydney,* a story about all sorts and conditions of men, but mostly the educated poor, in Australia today.

Naturalistic fiction it certainly is in one sense; the events are credible enough, there are no excursions into the supernatural, no comic or grotesque or fairy-tale extravagances. The characters, too, are apt to talk as people do in ordinary life—at any rate, for part of the time. Yet it is obvious at the start that Miss Stead's taste for realism has little of the liveliness and spontaneity of her sense of fantasy. Her breadth of curiosity, her detachment, her elusive wit and her delight in words are not less impressive than before, and are joined here to a fine practical intelligence in matters of political philosophy; but the total effect is nevertheless thin and insubstantial. Precisely because it abandons make-believe for an all too familiar reality, *Seven Poor Men of Sydney* is lacking in coherence on its own plane. There is no intelligible pattern in this assortment of strains and stresses, no urgency in the passions and dilemmas and mental intoxications of these odd men and women, all of them the victims of the depression, all searching for jobs or loves or happinesses which do not in fact exist for them. . . .

The clash of ideas and personalities among this little group lends itself to some brilliant passages of argument, in which Miss Stead's cool and ironical impartiality never falters. But it needs more than impartiality of this kind to quicken the scene of life.

(London) *Times Literary Supplement.*
January 30, 1934, p. 772

Christina Stead's books are rich and strange. These qualities of richness and strangeness run through her three books but their value is a highly variable quality. They play upon the surface of the theme and where there is harmony between the theme and the surface they have a cogency of their own, but where they are out of harmony with the theme, the glitter of the surface shows tawdry as tinsel in daylight. Her manner shows at its most brilliant and illuminating in *The Salzburg Tales,* its least in *The Beauties and Furies.*

The Salzburg Tales are fantastic tales told in the fantastic manner. They give full scope to the author's gifts and do not put too much weight on her failings. In this book her characterization is fantastic and the reader is not jarred because he has accepted the overtly fantastic world in which they move. It is Looking Glass Country in which anything might happen. But in proportion as her work depends on the creation of living characters, it becomes less convincing. In *Seven Poor Men of Sydney,* she applies a fantastic, half-grotesque technique to a rational theme, but the book is saved from the full consequences of this because its weight is thrown on the social rather than on the individual element in it, and it can stand a certain amount of patina. But in *The Beauties and Furies,* which is an intimate and individual study of a small group of people, the very life of the book depends on its characterization. No amount of meretricious glitter can animate these sawdust puppets, so that for all its undiminished surface brilliance the book fails, and fails helplessly. The failure of the book as a whole discredits even the rich ornament which was felt to be such a definite achievement in the early books.

M. Barnard Eldershaw. *Essays in Australian Fiction* (Melbourne: Melbourne University Press, 1938), pp. 158–59

For Love Alone is a title to scare most readers, but those who have met Christina Stead before will take the risk, confident of her wit, truth, and startling prose. By the time they have reached the end they will have understood that the author has chosen language which precisely describes her theme. . . .

It is not Christina Stead's way to sketch a character within select lines. She has the whole matter out and examines each thought under a microscope. Thus Teresa's burning need to leave Australia is not stated with a few raw arguments such as an ordinary novelist might think sufficient. A hundred pages are spent on proving the point, the evidence piling up before the reader as it piles upon the shoulders of Teresa. . . . The picture is painted and the analysis compiled in a torrent of language that is truthful, surprising, coarse and beautiful—an imaginative image like "the nights of pale sand" matched with the startling statement, "Of course she would never get a man, for she smelled and looked like an old pancake." Writing sometimes like an undisciplined Virginia Woolf or a disciplined James Joyce, she builds her story at length, determined to uncover every emotion, to examine each cause contributory to her argument.

It is a mighty undertaking, and the book, although remarkable, is not entirely satisfactory. The author has run her head against the old difficulty of how to describe the boring and the prosy without being boring and prosy.

Spectator. October 26, 1945, p. 392

The dust seems to have settled rather quickly upon the works of Christina Stead. Her name means nothing to most people. The title of one of her novels, *House of All Nations,* occasionally causes an eye to shine with cordiality and it may be noted that good things have been heard about this book even if it is not possible to remember precisely what they are. Is it perhaps a three-decker affair by a Northern European once mentioned for the Nobel Prize? The title of her great novel, *The Man Who Loved Children,* doesn't sound reassuring either; the title is in fact, one could remark, not good enough for the book, suggesting as it does a satisfaction with commonplace ironies. (But no title could give a preview of this unusual novel.)

At the present time none of Christina Stead's work is in print. Her name never appears on a critic's or journalist's list of novelists, she is not a "well-known woman writer"; she has written about finance, about Salzburg, Washington, Australia and yet neither place nor subject seems to call her image to the critical eye. Upon inquiring about her from her last American publisher, the information came forth with a *tomba oscura* note: all they had was a *poste restante,* Lausanne, Switzerland, 1947.

Elizabeth Hardwick. *The New Republic.*
August 1, 1955, p. 17

There is a bewitching rapidity and lack of self-consciousness about Christina Stead's writing; she has much knowledge, extraordinary abilities, but is too engrossed in what she is doing ever to seem conscious of them, so that they do not cut her off from the world but join her to it. How literary she makes most writers seem! [*The Man Who Loved Children*] is very human, and full of humor of an unusual kind; the spirit behind it doesn't try to be attractive and is attractive. As you read the book's climactic and conclusive pages you are conscious of their genius and of the rightness of that genius: it is as though at these moments Christina Stead's mind held in its grasp the whole action, the essential form, of *The Man Who Loved Children.* . . .

After you have read *The Man Who Loved Children* several times you feel that you know its author's main strengths and main weakness. The weakness is, I think, a kind of natural excess and lack of discrimination: she is most likely to go wrong by not seeing when to stop or what to leave out. About most things—always, about the most important things—she is not excessive and does discriminate; but a few things in *The Man Who Loved Children* ought not to be there, and a few other things ought not to be there in such quantities. . . .

I call it a good book, but it is a better book, I think, than most of the novels people call great; perhaps it would be fairer to call it great. It has one quality that, ordinarily, only a great book has: it does a single thing better than any other book has ever done it. *The Man Who Loved Children* makes you a part of one family's immediate existence as no other book quite does. When you have read it you have been, for a few hours, a Pollit; it will take you many years to get the sound of the Pollits out of your ears, the sight of the Pollits out of your eyes, the smell of the Pollits out of your nostrils.

Randall Jarrell. Introduction to Christina
Stead. *The Man Who Loved Children* (New
York: Holt, Rinehart and Winston, 1965),
pp. xxviii, xxxvi, xl–xli

[*The Puzzleheaded Girl*] consists of four long short stories, "The Puzzle-headed Girl," "The Dianas," "The Rightangled Creek," and "Girl from the Beach." They are not equally fine. "The Dianas" will be hard to recall a month or two from now. "The Puzzleheaded Girl" trades somewhat upon the reader's interest in the obliquities of character, but it is wonderfully delicate. The distinction of the stories is a quality of perception, the mind bodied against the rush of experience. . . .

Her best stories give the impression of having reached her imagination at one leap: she has only to transcribe them, as we fancy her transcribing

The Man Who Loved Children. . . . Miss Stead assumes that it is still possible to get things right, the line accurate, the graph precise. She has her own sense of the way things are, and she sees no good reason to give it up now in favor of anyone else's nonsense or the common nonsense. . . .

Miss Stead writes as if most of the work were already done by God or Satan or the seasons, and now she has only to deliver the material in reasonable order. In the light of eternity it may emerge that she was wrong, but in the meantime the assumption is good for her art.

Denis Donoghue. *New York Review of Books*. September 28, 1967, p. 5

Christina Stead's work began to appear in the early 1930's, but it was not until 1965 that a book of hers was published in Australia. (In passing it might be noted that many of the leading Australian novelists have been published mainly, or entirely, overseas.) Over a period of more than thirty years she has devoted much of her life to writing and has produced eleven books, all of them written outside her native land. She left Australia in 1928 and has never returned, and this is one reason why her work is less well known in her homeland than it should be. Furthermore, her early fiction, sophisticated, yet often passionate and strangely colored by fantasy, though praised by well-qualified judges, was not likely to appeal to those of her fellow countrymen reared largely on naturalistic novels dealing with such traditional Australian topics as the convict past and life in the outback. Like a number of important Australian artists Christina Stead has always had strong ties with Europe. . . .

Christina Stead has said "the object of the novel is characterization" and she is in this sense a thoroughly traditional novelist, even though her early work was not always naturalistic in its approach. She clearly believes the novelist's task is to present people as they really are—and in ways that will make them acceptable to her readers. Yet the most common criticism of her work (apart from its alleged lack of form) is that, for all her great talents, she does not possess the essential gift of the realistic novelist, the capacity for creating thoroughly credible characters or, as it is sometimes put, "the ability to create character in the round." This criticism, it is true, has been applied mainly to the early books but exception is sometimes taken to the characters in the novels after *House of All Nations* also. Such a judgment cannot be conclusively proved or disproved. The reader must finally decide for himself. It should be observed, however, that critics have always been prone to this particular way of condemning novels. Dickens and Dostoyvsky were taken to task on this account and their achievements were so great that one begins to suspect that the charge is often all too facile and misleading.

R. G. Geering. *Christina Stead* (New York:
Twayne, 1969), pp. 19–20, 158–59

One unfortunate consequence of the ready classification of Australian fiction into a city-country polarity is that the varieties of city life tend to be ignored. There have been some good chroniclers of suburban life, and of urban work, but there is more to the city than that. Australian stories have not traditionally been strong on the bohemian-artistic-intellectual areas. Perhaps in the past that would have seemed too self-conscious, too indulgent. Three recent collections redress the balance.

Christina Stead's four novellas in *The Puzzleheaded Girl,* set in Europe and America, brilliantly yet with an effortless obliqueness document the life styles of intellectual, radical, fringe bohemian groups during the late 1940s and the McCarthyite days, and the strange, motiveless, expatriate American girls in Europe, seemingly liberated yet blocked by all manner of neuroses. The novellas work not by conventional plot but by the great monologues of characters, and the compulsive, seemingly unwilled and unmotivated entanglements they live in. What is so powerful is the utter ease and unselfconsciousness with which Christina Stead handles her materials of sexuality, neurosis, obsession, art. She is writing from within the worlds she portrays, never presenting a sort of "most unforgettable character I ever met" but letting us get to know the figures as they talk and act.

Michael Wilding. Meanjin.
June, 1971, p. 263

Written by the great author of *The Man Who Loved Children*—among the most strange and powerful achievements of literary realism in our time—*The Little Hotel* deals in acidulous miniature with the very large subject of Europe's social transformations following World War II. The residents of Monsieur and Madame Bonnard's impecunious little Swiss residential hotel are baffled, touching, contemptible relics of European colonial administration and the homeless, compromised leisure class it once sustained. Filled with a quaintness based more on absurdity than on charm, they are not attractive people. Besotted with their political paranoia and genteel racism, they numbly live through their heartbreaking, insufferable rituals, clinging to dwindling bank accounts, which, instead of providing them with freedom, lock them all the more tightly into small and hopeless lives. The book describes these lives with a focus that is almost disorienting in its precision.

To say that Christina Stead writes well verges on the impertinent; what is basically the plain style of English expository fiction has rarely been rendered with such originality, given such a continuously absorbing texture. In the age of realism's exhaustion, Stead has sustained herself as a great realist by bringing to bear on the banal an intelligence so closely tuned and penetrating that it renders everything as compelling, eccentric, and bizarre. And though she is the least sentimental of writers, this focus provides her with an almost (she would hate the word) theological comprehension of human pathos and vanity. In passing, one might mention that the feminists' indifference to Stead is slightly baffling. She is, for example, a much more profound—and far more politically aware—writer than the justly rehabilitated, but now vastly overpraised, Jean Rhys. Quite apart from *The Man Who Loved Children,* one thinks of Stead's overwhelming novella, *The Puzzle-headed Girl,* standing in a class by itself as a treatment of a young woman in America. In *The Little Hotel,* as in all her work, Stead's eye is cold indeed, and the trivia she sees terrible indeed. But here, as elsewhere, her intelligence, toughness, and charm also give a strange voice to the even rarer quality that one must call wisdom.

Stephen Koch. *Saturday Review of Literature.* May 31, 1975, p. 28

[Stead's] small hotel in Switzerland holds, embraces, madmen and predators, snobs and sentimentalists. Her laconic brittle style, with transitions that look blind in their curtness but nevertheless allow us to glimpse some haunting insights, finds its dramatic correlative in the narrative voice of the woman who runs the limping hotel. "My English is not very good," the woman may say, but such words take their place within the way in which Miss Stead's English is very good. . . .

[In *The Little Hotel*] even English finds its imperial confidence shaken, finds itself sapped by having to be not only a mother tongue for those who are away from their motherland, but also the desperate Esperanto of these motley aliens. It is a tragicomic shabby-genteel world, in which the upper lip is stiff and the lower one is trembling, and Miss Stead has a great gift for sensing the words that escape from just such a divided mouth. . . .

The accents are no longer those of "the out-of-date English milords," but of English refugees from Attlee's England who are "beginning to worry about dying among foreigners." Their children are foreign to them, but then so are their parents. The desiccation of such a life, its fear of sexuality, its embittered clutch upon its ancestors and its descendants—all this makes *The Little Hotel* at once painfully impressive and yet painedly narrow, like a wince. The allied ironies which coursed through what is still Miss Stead's best book were more ample, for *The Man Who Loved Children* was open to larger failures of imagination in its terrifying family than those which fret and lacerate the denizens of the little hotel.

Christopher Ricks. *New York Review of Books.* June 26, 1975, p. 14

Miss Stead's venerable gifts are well known: ranging from her native Australia to the America and Europe in which she has lived, she is, after Graham Greene, the most intercontinental of modern novelists; she is a caustically keen observer of a wide spectrum of human scenes; she writes a direct prose that can rise to all but the largest occasions of poetry; she is politically thoughtful without being propagandistic, giving her characters a sufficient but not crushing burden of ideological significance; and she has traveled well in the human interior and can be devastatingly clear about some of its uglier turns. . . .

Among the gifts Miss Stead does not conspicuously possess is that of joy, which translates, in the narrative art, into the gift of lubrication. Her plots move chunkily, by jerks of hasty summary and epistolary excerpt; her dialogues are abrasive, full of dry, twittery self-exposition and clichés that may or may not be deliberate. . . .

If there is such a thing as a "woman's novel," it finds itself bound, at least in the honest hands of . . . Stead . . . to the figurative description not of an action but of a quality—the quality of femininity, static and wary, hugging to itself the bleak dignity of solitude.

John Updike. *The New Yorker.* August 9,
1976, pp. 75–77

Miss Stead's considerable powers of evocation were manifest from the start, in *Seven Poor Men of Sydney,* set in her native Australia. The grim world conjured up in that novel would seem derivative of the London depicted in *Keep the Aspidistra Flying* had it not prefigured Orwell's novel by a year: "the foetid rooms, eyes opening on littered streets, heavy wombs, market-gardeners' carts trailing a cabbage smell, mustaches washed in beer, working-men's tramcars rattling out to brown dusty suburbs, Alexandria, Redfern, Waterloo, pawnshop windows advertising their unredeemed pledges, grimy hands, sweat, unfolded papers relating the latest murder, wrinkles, hands with swollen veins, and eyes thick with the circular lucubrations of the dulled mind trying to escape." And in *The People with the Dogs* (1952), she brought to life the desolate tenants of a Harlem boardinghouse: Philip Christy, an alcoholic former radical; his proud sister Nell; Nan, a brazen, spirited boarder.

In her later novels, Miss Stead has tended to concentrate on middle-class women—many of them aspiring writers—who feel themselves oppressed; *The Beauties and Furies, For Love Alone* and *Miss Herbert* feature strong-willed, independent women made wretched by insensitive husbands or lovers, and determined to forge new lives. Yet however admirable or true, their resistance invariably seems willed. Unlike so many American novelists, she manages to imbue her working-class characters with a reality largely absent in her liberated heroines.

Miss Stead is sufficiently versatile to command several literary styles. She can strike off a Lawrentian image of a ravaged industrial landscape "full of coughing black smudges which had been born to be men and women"; produce a sustained burlesque—in *House of All Nations*—in which an obsequious dinner guest endures the importunate hospitality of a banker intent on stuffing him with one lavish course after another; infuse with pathos a vulnerable young man contemplating in the mirror "that single leaf of flesh which had been given to him to write his own history upon"; or re-create the haunted atmosphere of a Gothic novel, as she does in *The Rightangle Creek: A Sort of Ghost Story.*

Still, her proclivity for tendentious speeches can become tiresome, her plots laborious, her characters overwrought and wooden. And the intensity of her prose often lapses into melodrama. In *Miss Herbert,* when the middle-aged Eleanor Herbert falls in love with her daughter's suitor, Miss Stead observes: "This strange man whom she did not know yet to be Paul Waters came toward them and looked straight into Eleanor's eyes with the glance of a man who understands a woman wants him and who gives himself and means to take all, a dark look that existed long before language." This is the rhetoric of a drugstore novel.

The virtue of *A Christina Stead Reader* is that it displays the variety of her achievement in a single volume. However imposing the giant sprawl of Miss Stead's novels, one comes away from this collection wondering if she might not have been better served by that archaic literary form, the short story.

James Atlas. *The New York Times.*
February 4, 1979, p. 28

Seven Poor Men of Sydney is but the first of a number of Stead's novels with collective protagonists. While *The Man Who Loved Children* most brilliantly makes an entire family its center, this novel, *House of All Nations, The People with the Dogs,* and *The Little Hotel* all explicitly extend their primary focus to a group of characters rather than subordinating everyone else to a single individual hero. This structural choice itself indicates a faith in the equivalent interest of all individuals.

Stead's writing attends to the secrets that fascinate her in the concealed lives of individuals of every classification. Especially concerned with "these thousand and thousand grains of sand of individual lives" that have been only partly recorded, she makes literary record of many such lives. In spite of her persistent disclaimer of particular interest or origins in feminism, many of the unrecorded lives whose stories she tells are those of women; and the unrecorded story she tells best is her own. Stead's most coherently powerful fictions are her two autobiographical novels, *The Man Who Loved Children* (1940) and *For Love Alone* (1944). In them, Australian critic Dorothy Green finds "one of the most remarkable accounts . . . written of what it feels like to be a creative artist who is also a woman, a woman of intellect and passion, to whom both are equally necessary, growing from childhood through adolescence to the threshold of full adulthood."

Joan Lidoff. *Christina Stead* (New York:
Frederick Ungar, 1982), pp. 12–13

Perhaps the most pervasive features of Stead's novelistic world are the political vision which shapes it and the delight she takes in language. Stead is surely a political writer, with a leftish disposition, as numerous critics have remarked and Stead herself has suggested. Political in her case means a preoccupation with the ways that the familiar features of our world—love, say, or families, or finance, for that matter—are not given in nature but are rather products of struggle, arenas in which power is contested. Conversely, *politics* for Stead also involves the tracing of what one of her characters somewhat cryptically identifies as "the influence of Marx on character," which I take to mean that view of the world that regards persons more or less as products of their circumstances. Stead's preoccupation with language links her with other contemporary writers. Her novels investigate, among other things, the processes of signification and the conditions and determinants of meaning. But their main energy lies in a linguistic excess that takes a number of different forms across an unusually wide stylistic register: intense lyricism coupled with closely observed descriptions, aphoristic brilliance, heightened reproduction of the ordinary speech of quite distinct groups of people.

While politics and language structure Stead's imaginative world and define it in relation to the world that she and her novels inhabit, they do so quite differently at different times. Indeed, the meanings of both *politics* and *language* as well as the relationship between them change in significant ways over the course of her long and distinguished career. Stead's early novels are concerned with explicitly social and political themes; the novels written during the 1940s transpose her political vision from public life to the more "private" world of the family and shift their focus from questions of class, loosely, to questions of gender; her late novels describe the commodification of both public and private life and represent the fragmentation of a world composed entirely of words. These changes, and especially the narrowing of Stead's novelistic world, mark the trajectory of a left-wing female intellectual through a literary culture initially somewhat receptive, later indifferent, and finally hostile to the left.

Louise Yelin. In Alice Kessler-Harris and
William McBrien, eds. *Faith of a (Woman)
Writer* (1984; Westport, Connecticut:
Greenwood Press, 1988), pp. 191–92

Over the years I [have] brooded over aspects of her work that might have prevented its wider acceptance, notably that verbosity mentioned in a review of her first book, *The Salzburg Tales*—"Her verbosity is that of passion and genius" (Sir John Squire, *Daily Telegraph*). On the same jacket Rebecca West says, "Delightful miscellany . . . the work of a strong, idiosyncratic talent." That book, which I read long after the later books, had to me too many elaborate derivations, but is certainly as West says. I no longer have my copy of *The Beauty and the Furies,* listed in the American editions of her works as her third, but I recall that while every page had its brilliance, the total outpour did seem at times indigestible. *Dark Places of the Heart,* on the other hand, published abroad as *Cotter's England,* is transacted in household conversations, alternating with narrative in a tone so close to the down-to-earth characters and their concrete lives that it seems all but marred by them. Stead knew trade unionist life in all its fluid blend of working-class saltiness, socialist ethic, and rainbow ideals. Nor is Stead ever boring or instructive, in the way of some proletarian novelists of the era—and that world is only one of her worlds. In her work, people and their lives took precedence, and she had a gift for putting talk and life-story together. Her exploration of the nonsexual relationships between women, one that well precedes Doris Lessing's *The Golden Notebook,* may have gone unnoticed, perhaps because she performed without partisanship. She has the tolerant overview that all great writers have; everybody gets a fair shake.

Yet this can mitigate against "story" in a novel—even to those who do not demand too formal a path of progression, yet require a provided sense of its moving on. On the farther side there are those novels which we excuse as poems of action rather than accounts reasonably rendered. Stead's longer books fall somewhere in between. One follows the people and the talk. Simple as the single sentence may be, their tumbled abundance creates a style. Actions follow one another in a whirlpool of knowledge and allusion—she knows so much. Or one wallows in the locale. There Stead's sense of place—of any place—is as geographic as Balzac's and as descriptive, often with a comic sensuousness in which the very lay of the land contributes to the sardonic voice in which a novel sometimes unfolds.

Hortense Calisher. Yale Review. 76, 1987, pp. 174–75

Feminist criticism has alerted us to the ways in which women writers have subverted the conventions of romance plots, by frustrating the traditionally coded expectations of a death or a wedding as the ending of a heroine's quest or by "writing beyond the ending" to introduce a variety of alternative strategies. Although Stead uses few of the subversive strategies identified by Rachel Blau Du Plessis in her recent study, she writes "beyond the ending" in her own fashion. Even when her novels seem to have traditional endings— the failure of the bank in *House of All Nations,* the weddings in *Letty Fox* and *The People with the Dogs,* death in *A Little Tea, a Little Chat*—they have been prepared for in such a way as to suggest their inability to end the forces set in motion by the texts in which they appear. For example, by the time Letty Fox has made the marriage that ends her story, marriage has been totally devalued as a goal and canceled as an ending. Even Letty's alternative claim—that this wedding is her real beginning—fails to convince in the light of the context in which it has been presented. Here marriage is redefined as neither end nor beginning but merely another step—and possibly a self-defeating one—in Letty's struggle to get by.

In each of Stead's novels, the central character or more often, group of characters, give rise through their needs to the shape their stories will take. Sometimes she seems to go too far in her willingness to allow a character's context or a character's voice to override what we normally think of as plot, but the more fully one enters Stead's fictional worlds, the more such objections disappear as one begins to understand the complex patterns of alignment and the dialectical relations she is seeking to illuminate. Stead's fiction assumes unusual shapes and develops unexpected rhythms—but always to convey the specific shape of a particular experience. In her most memorable fiction, the dominant element is usually a character—yet on closer examination that character cannot be separated from the particular web of relations in which he or she is entangled.

Diana Bryden. Christina Stead (Totowa,
New Jersey: Barnes and Noble, 1987),
pp. 29–30

Stead's texts offer an especially vivid demonstration of the work of ideology in language, in discourses. There is little description and documentation, even less narratorial comment: the characters speak themselves and their world into textual existence, as it were. Dramatic monologues, spoken or "thought"—"great arias and recitatives of self-deceit, self-justification, attempted manipulation"—constitute the bulk of the novels, which are in general loosely structured in a series of scenes. The foregrounding of linguistic processes achieved by this structuring technique demonstrates the incessant inscription of ideologies in fantasy and dreams as well as rationally formulated ideas. The ideological structures and textures of mental life, with its fluid relations between the conscious and the unconscious, are the material of Stead's fiction.

Men as well as women are constructed in this way, as the writing presents the surfaces of their lives as the real, refusing the temptation to promise some essential truth behind the masks of gender. Stead's salutary refusal to idealize some essential woman beneath the melodrama and the clichés of contemporary femininity in these constructions is particularly notable, for it proposes, contrary to some feminist accounts of gendered subjectivity, that we *are* what we act, that femininity is lived as it is performed in society and culture. The narrative enacts splits between these partriarchal ideologies and women's desires, yet both are presented as equally part of their reality, and not, as in liberal humanism, as the shadow and the substance of experience. As we observed in Stead's comments on the powers traditionally attributed to women, the apparently "natural" sexual and aggressive desires which erupt to wreak havoc within the social order can be seen as themselves constructed by their very exclusion from that order's definition of femininity.

Susan Sheridan. Christina Stead
(Bloomington: Indiana University Press,
1988), pp. 12–13

Stead's characters manifest their identity in speech more than in action; they are walking mouths. Fragments of psychological drive often appear in Stead's imagery rather than through character, whereas the "objective" forces of history push her plots and receive exposition as chunks of authorial wisdom or as the wise words of a character modeled on her husband. Her best realized characters, on the other hand, cohere through their individual linguistic styles, like Henny and Sam in *The Man Who Loved Children* and Emily in *I'm Dying Laughing*. Although much of Stead's fiction seems "objective," focusing on public issues and on characters observed from the outside, recurrent psychological issues related to preoedipal parent-child dynamics, especially the dangers of narcissism and the necessity for autonomy, shape her work from the inside.

Female identity in Stead's work is constantly struggling for definition against overwhelming forces—in her earliest and some of her latest work, the disruptions of female sexuality and the engulfing power of parents. One of her best works, *House of All Nations,* escapes the problems of female identity through male identification, and it has therefore received little attention from feminist critics. The subsequent autobiographical novels *The Man Who Loved Children* and *For Love Alone* directly portray female identity in formation. Several of her late novels with female protagonists, especially *The Little Hotel, Dark Places of the Heart* and *I'm Dying Laughing,* dramatize the dangers to female autonomy from engulfment by the other and the destruction of both self and other through women's manipulative empathy.

Judith Kegan Gardiner. *Rhys, Stead,
Lessing, and the Politics of Empathy*
(Bloomington: Indiana University Press,
1989), pp. 54–55

The Man Who Loved Children goes beyond the narrative of family to wider issues—issues of gender and power in traditionally organized Western society. . . . Stead's interest in the gender/power theme may be traced through all her fiction. It forms part of her overall concern with varieties of exploitation: economic, social, familial, sexual, and personal. As in *The Man Who Loved Children,* Stead in other novels is largely concerned with the politics of interpersonal relationships, with the crossroads of the personal and the social. . . .

Boundaries . . . remain central to Stead's fiction—boundaries of gender, economics, politics. In her own life, she crossed national boundaries, leaving Australia early to live and write in Europe and the United States. So she is not a distinctively Australian writer. Although *Seven Poor Men of Sydney,* part of *For Love Alone,* and a few of the stories in *The Salzburg Tales* have Australian settings, most of her work is set elsewhere. She is too rich and varied a writer to be capsulated by typing or labeling of her fiction, by placing it within any national boundaries. Rather, she is best seen as a leading figure among international writers in English, one who enlarges the vision of the sexual politics that shape our culture and ourselves.

Phyllis Fahri Edelson. In Robert L. Ross,
ed. *International Literature in English:
Essays on the Major Writers* (New York:
Garland, 1991), pp. 242, 247–48

STEIN, GERTRUDE (UNITED STATES) 1874–1946

We find . . . that Miss Stein's method is one of subtraction. She has deliberately limited her equipment. . . . Obviously, any literary artist who sets out to begin his work in a primary search for music or rhythm, and attempts to get this at the expense of (the) "inherent property of words," obviously this artist is not going to exploit the full potentialities of his medium. He is getting an art by subtraction; he is violating his *genre*. . . . Miss Stein continually utilizes this violation of the *genre*. Theoretically at least, the result has its studio value. . . . By approaching art-work from these exorbitant angles one is suddenly able to rediscover organically those eternal principles of art which are, painful as it may be to admit it, preserved in all the standard textbooks.

> Kenneth Burke. *Dial.* April, 1923,
> pp. 409–10

In her detachment, her asceticism, and her eclecticism, Miss Stein can only remind us of another American author who lived in Europe and devoted himself more and more exclusively to the abstract. The principal difference between Henry James (whom Miss Stein reads more and more these days) and Gertrude Stein is that the former still kept within the human realm by treating moral problems. . . . Moreover, what Miss Stein has in common with James she has in common with Poe, Hawthorne, Melville, and several other important and characteristic American writers: an orientation from experience toward the abstract, an orientation that has been so continuous as to constitute a tradition, if not actually *the* American tradition. Of this tradition it is possible to see in Miss Stein's writing not only a development but the pure culmination.

> William Troy. *The Nation.* September 6,
> 1933, pp. 274–75

I was delighted to see that Miss Stein never mentioned her style, never said that she had a philosophy, and that her point of view was merely the natural way she had of walking and speaking English; even in her boldest creations she acted spontaneously and enjoyed the fun of amusing herself. I was surprised first because our French wits rather liked wondering at themselves and even being shocked at themselves but certainly explained to everybody how marvelous and queer they were. On the contrary this woman whose mind was so rich and so new seemed never to have time to stop, look and listen at herself. All her actions and all her attention she kept in herself. All her personality she carried inside herself, inside this space and this time which was herself.

> Bernard Fäy. Preface to Gertrude Stein. *The Making of Americans* (New York: Harcourt, 1934), pp. xii–xiii

I have never heard talk come more naturally and casually. It had none of the tautness or deadly care that is in the speech of most American intellectuals when they talk from the mind out. If sometime you will listen to workingmen talking when they are concentrating upon the physical job at hand, and one of them will go on without cease while he is sawing and measuring and nailing, not always audible, but keeping on in an easy rhythm and almost without awareness of words—then you will get some idea of her conversation.

John Hyde Preston. *The Atlantic Monthly.*
August, 1935, p. 192

It is little surprising that the ideas of William James have influenced his pupil. It is remarkable, however, to realize that Stein has, from her first work forward, created in an aesthetics which did not have its formal doctrination until as late as two decades after her first experiments with it. It is to be understood literally that the rudiments of a pragmatic aesthetic appeared in her work before contemporary philosophers, including William James, had expounded such an aesthetic. It was, then, with the voice of annunciation that she said, in 1926, "naturally no one thinks, that is no one formulates until what is to be formulated has been made."

Robert Bartlett Haas. Foreword to Gertrude
Stein. *What Are Masterpieces* (n. p.:
Conference, 1940), p. 21

Her writing is harder than traditional prose, as a foreign tongue is harder than a native tongue; at first glance we catch a word here and there, or a phrase or two, but the over-all meaning must be figured our arduously. Yet a tension is created, a question asked and in Miss Stein at her best, dramatic context mounts to a climax and then a conclusion. It's pure creative activity, an exudation of personality, a discharge, and it can't be defined more exactly. The mysterious surge of energy which impels a boy who is idling on a corner to race madly down the street is part and parcel of the same thing. When people call it elementary, they mean elemental.

W. G. Rogers. *When This You See
Remember Me* (New York: Rinehart, 1948),
pp. 69–70

"In writing a word must be for me really an existing thing." Her efforts to get at the roots of existing life, to create fresh life from them, give her words a dark liquid flowingness, like the murmur of blood. She does not strain words or invent them. Many words have retained their original meaning for her, she uses them simply. Good means good and bad means bad—next to the Jews the Americans are the most moralistic people, and Gertrude Stein is an American Jew, a combination which by no means lessens the like quality in both. Good and bad are attributes to her, strength and weakness are real things that live inside people, she looks for these things, notes them in their likenesses and differences. She loves the difficult virtues, she is tender toward good people, she has faith in them.

Katherine Anne Porter. *The Days Before*
(New York: Harcourt, 1952), p. 39

In almost all literature until Gerturde Stein, the act of composition has been used to recall, recreate, analyze, and celebrate an Object Time, the time in which the "thing seen" is happening. This is true whether this Object Time is in the historical past . . . or the historical present. . . . In Gertrude Stein, just the reverse is true. In almost everything she wrote, it is the Subject Time, the time in which she is happening as she sees and writes, which is realized. . . . When she says "The time of the composition is the time of the composition," she means exactly that. The time that goes on in her writing is *not* the time in which her "thing seen" is going on. Her complete works might very aptly be called, "A la recherche du temps présent."

Robert Phelps. *Yale Review.* Summer, 1956,
p. 601

She never relinquishes the strictest, most intimate relationship between her words and her thought. . . . The aphoristic style and the conciseness of the formulas express the energy of this writer's consciousness, which appears almost excessive. Her language is affirmed in slow tempo, with a marked degree of solemnity, as it seeks to acquire a certain weight of one-syllable words. It represents finally a summation of things felt, lived with, possessed. It is common language and yet it relates an experience of intimacy which is the least communicable of all experiences. A word used by Gertrude Stein does not designate a thing as much as it designates the way in which the thing is possessed, or the way whereby the poet has learned to live with it.

Wallace Fowlie. *Saturday Review of
Literature.* December 22, 1956, p. 21

If these works are highly complex and, for some, unreadable, it is not only because of the complicatedness of life, the subject, but also because they actually imitate its rhythm, its way of happening, in an attempt to draw our attention to another aspect of its true nature. Just as life is being constantly altered by each breath one draws, just as each second of life seems to alter the whole of what has gone before, so the endless process of elaboration which gives the work of these two writers (Stein and Henry James) a texture of bewildering luxuriance—that of a tropical rain-forest of ideas—seems to obey some rhythmic impulse at the heart of all happening.

In addition, the almost physical pain with which we strive to accompany the evolving thought of one of James's or Gertrude Stein's characters is perhaps a counterpart of the painful continual projection of the individual into life.

John Ashbery. *Poetry.* July, 1957, p. 252

Her "art" is one of subtraction and narrowing throughout. In her art she does not reflect, for reflection entails consciousness of identity and audience, an awareness fatal to the creative vision. She rules out the imagination because it is the hunting ground of secondary talent. She rules out logical, cause-effect relations: "Question and answer make you know time is existing." She rules out distinctions of right and wrong: "Write and right. Of course they have nothing to do with one another." She will have no distinctions of true and false: "The human mind is not concerned with being or not being true." She abjures beauty, emotion, association, analogy, illustration, metaphor. Art by subtraction finally subtracts art itself. What remains as the manner and matter of the specifically "creative" works of Gertrude Stein is the artist and an object vis-à-vis. This is not art; this is science. Miss Stein would turn the artist into a recording mechanism, a camera that somehow utters words rather than pictures.

B. L. Reid. *Art by Subtraction: A Dissenting Opinion of Gertrude Stein* (Norman: University of Oklahoma Press, 1958), pp. 171–72

As a scientific demonstration of Gertrude Stein's belief in the final absolutism of human character, *The Making of Americans* carries the weight of its conviction and the conviction of its enormous weight. As a work of literature, it is all but swept bare of the felicities of detail, color and anecdote that beguile the attention in great books as well as minor ones. But Gertrude Stein had had enough of the picaresque trappings and sentimental diffusions that recommend novels to the insatiable reader. She wanted to come to essentials— to ideas in action rather than ideas comfortably couched in formulation, and to character as an entity alive rather than character as an identity pinned to the wall like a butterfly. Her conception would test the power of the intellect to usurp the power of the emotions in communicating living experience, yet she was ready to face the challenge. . . . The pages of *The Making of Americans* are as full of rolling and repeated cadences as the Bible, but its more prevalent sound, like that of Oriental ritual, is the music of the continuous present, always going on and always, almost always, but not quite, the same. . . . Gertrude Stein had come early to a notion that was to dominate her creative life—the notion that the "continuous present and using everything and beginning again" was the final reality in fact and thus the final reality that words could communicate. Escaping from the conventions of beginning, middle, and ending, she simply laid out a space—a space of time as big in its proportions as a canvas of Jackson Pollock—and proceeded to make sure that it would be "always filled with moving."

John Malcolm Brinnin. *The Third Rose* (Boston: Little, Brown, 1959), pp. 94–95

She never had her tongue in her cheek; she genuinely believed in her own uniqueness and incomparable genius; she devoted to the prosecution of her "experiments" the single-mindedness and sense of dedication of the greatest of writers and thinkers. She was her own first victim. If her confidence was misplaced and her experiments ridiculous, she is at least to be commended for determination. . . . It also explains why she obtained a genuine *succès d'estime* denied to the glibbest of pure charlatans, and why the Forsters, Hemingways, and Eliots, though they could not possibly have brought themselves actually to read her work, still less to enjoy it, nevertheless felt constrained to praise it. . . . Nor indeed were her experimentations with language wholly without value, if only as a set of awful warnings; a wiser woman would have perceived that by their very nature they could only lead to abortions; a quicker woman would have perceived their uselessness after the first instead of the five hundredth page; a more modest, or a poorer, woman would not have published, or have been able to publish, them. The *Stanzas in Meditation* is perhaps the dreariest long poem in the world, offering the absolute minimum in reward or pleasure against somewhere near the maximum in obstruction. Let it stand as a perpetual witness against the myth of an inherent value in "experiment."

Hilary Corke. The Kenyon Review. Summer,
1961, pp. 387–88

In serious literary circles, as distinguished from the large public, Gertrude Stein's real accomplishments were always known. There, her influence was at one time considerable, though it worked in very different ways and degrees on different individuals. It was known that her writing had influenced, in certain respects, Sherwood Anderson and, later, Hemingway. It was supposed that Steinese had found echoes in Don Marquis's *archy and mehitabel* as well as in the difficult poetry of Wallace Stevens, who once wrote "Twenty men crossing a bridge, / Into a village, / Are twenty men crossing twenty bridges, / Into twenty villages." Her insistence on the primacy of phenomena over ideas, of the sheer magnificence of unmeditated reality, found a rapturous response in Stevens, a quiet one in Marianne Moore.

F. W. Dupee. Commentary. June, 1962,
p. 522

Her immediate perceptions, her thoughts about certain nagging problems, her questions about certain objects or themes that appear in her writing, the associations that a word or sound might set off in her conscious mind, all of these are for Gertrude Stein legitimate materials for her writing. Her method of composition seems to go something like this. She focuses directly on a particular subject for as long as it may stick in her mind. Then she may depart from the subject to follow an association or report something that has entered her consciousness. The subject at hand returns again and again, but the importance of this whole retrospective process is to express the continuous present on-going of her consciousness. This is, after all, the only pure knowledge according to her theory. If data other than that relating directly to the supposed subject intrude into her consciousness, then they must be recorded as a manifestation of Gertrude Stein's process of thought.

Michael J. Hoffman. *The Development of Abstractionism in the Writings of Gertrude Stein* (Philadelphia: University of Pennsylvania Press, 1965), p. 195

More extreme than Thoreau, Stein has an ideal of what we may call seeing without remembering, without associating, without thinking. She wants the eye to open to the reality of the material world as though it had never opened before: for then we catch reality at its 'realest,' unfiltered through the schemata of the sophisticated eye which is dimmed from too long domestication in the world. And even though she does not develop or push the comparison she clearly cites the child's way of looking as exemplary: naivety must be cultivated in order that we may see reality as it is and not as we remember it to be. This takes us back to the problem of how a child does in fact perceive reality. More basically, whether one can in fact see anything clearly at all without the aid of memory, the subtle reawakening of innumerable past visual experiences is open to doubt. Certainly, words are full of memories—are perhaps pure memory—and the impressions gained by the unremembering eye could never be transmitted by the unremembering voice. For without memory there is no metaphor; and without metaphor we would never have had language. Stein avoids live metaphors but to communicate at all she has to use those dead ones we all use continually in our daily speech. Her ideal properly carried out, if it did not lead to a visual confusion akin to blindness, would certainly lead to silence.

To draw these inferences is perhaps unfair. In fact what Stein wants is to purify the eye, to break old visual habits, to initiate a more vivid commerce between the sense and the real world.

Tony Tanner. *The Reign of Wonder* (New York: Cambridge University Press, 1965), p. 191

In "Melanctha" she simplified her diction in order to stress the developing patterns of repeated words. There too she began to stretch given moments in time to abnormal length. With *The Making of Americans,* she eliminated action, yet by using extended repetition broken by slight changes in phrasing that allowed slow conceptual accretion, she managed to conserve a dynamic subject matter. Finally in *Tender Buttons,* conventional subject matter disappeared except insofar as some single thing stimulated Gertrude Stein's mind into action. Words were arranged as objects sufficient in themselves upon the page; and both alone and in series they made their effects by the associations roused through their composition. The stylistic process was one of gradual loss of story (movement) and of subject (thing) until, at her most obscure, Gertrude Stein offered arrangements quite as abstract as those painted by her friends, Braque, Picasso, Gris, and Picabia. In so doing she emphasized the underlying structures of colloquial speech, even as the Cubists isolated and stylized the geometrical components of the human figure.

Richard Bridgman. *The Colloquial Style in America* (New York: Oxford University Press, 1966), pp. 193–94

Regarding the famous aria [in *Four Saints in Three Acts*] "Pigeons on the grass alas," in [Richard] Bridgman's view "anti-supernatural," he is quite wrong, for this is one of the few moments in the opera that Gertrude really explained to me. It is St. Ignatius's vision of the Holy Ghost and it represents a true vision. It begins with "ordinary pigeons" which are "on the grass alas," not doves against the sky as they maybe could be wished to be. But it goes on to a "magpie in the sky on the sky," exactly as one sees these birds in Spain, hanging there trembling, exactly as in many a primitive Spanish painting too, where the magpie, flat and seeming almost to vibrate, does represent the Holy Ghost. And the succeeding declaration, "Let Lucy Lily Lily Lucy Lucy," may indeed, as Bridgman suggests, be "an authorial statement stimulated by the religious context"; but when I treated it as proof of true vision, as a heavenly chorus heard chanting in some heavenly lingo, Gertrude was ever so pleased.

Virgil Thomson. *New York Review of Books*. April 8, 1971, p. 6

[Stein's] is a vision, paradoxically, of the "literally true." The phrase is used as the title for one of her works, and it might be the title of all of them. It compares with the vision of certain mystics who lived with the compelling sense of total illumination, with all the parts of everything seen plainly, in unbroken and simple and easily perceived harmonies, the highest and the lowest together. Stein's vision had that clarity, that intensity, and that ease. She saw the reality of relations—at first, relations of people, then of objects in space, and then of events in time—with as much force and clarity as though they were tangible. The substance of what she saw—or to put it more accurately, the summary of it—was more or less profound or trivial or remarkable as different occasions for observation can be for anyone. But the tangibility of relations, for her, did not blur. There was nothing for her to say *about* them but that they were there; they were so, literally and tangibly true.

Leon Katz. Introduction to Gertrude Stein. *Fernhurst, Q. E. D., and Other Early Writings* (New York: Liveright, 1971), pp. xxxii–xxxiii

What, finally, is our view of Gertrude Stein? A dominating figure, a *femme intrigante,* and a problematic writer. The importance of her language experiments to poets and writers is indisputable. . . .

This pioneering destruction of associative emotion bears its finest fruit in the enigmatic plays and droll librettos, which have the charm of a friendly sphinx. . . . But in the novels, and most notably in *The Making of Americans,* which she stubbornly insisted was her masterpiece, her zeal for classification and repetition asks language to bear too heavy a burden. Unlike Joyce and Proust, the only novelists she'd admit as her equal, her solipsism does not take us into "the secret grottos of the self" ([William Carlos] Williams's phrase). Compared to Joyce's Dublin and Proust's Paris, her universe is a defoliated landscape.

Herbert Leibowitz, *The New York Times.*
February 3, 1974, p. 2

What distinguishes Gertrude Stein . . . from nearly all of her chronological contemporaries in American literature (e.g., Dreiser, Stephen Crane, Vachel Lindsay, *et al.*) is that, even a century after her birth, most of her works remain misunderstood. The principal reason for such widespread incomprehension is that her experiments in writing were conducted apart from the major developments in modern literature. Neither a naturalist nor a surrealist, she had no interest in either the representation of social reality or the weaving of symbols, no interest at all in myth, metaphor, allegory, literary allusions, uncommon vocabulary, synoptic cultural critiques, shifts in point of view or much else that preoccupied writers such as James Joyce, Thomas Mann and Marcel Proust. Unlike them, she was an empiricist who preferred to write about observable realities and personally familiar subjects; the titles of her books were typically declarative and descriptive, rather than symbolic or allusive. Like other modern writers, she was influenced by developments in the non-literary arts; yet Stein feasted upon a fertile esthetic idea that the others neglected—to emphasize properties peculiar to one's chosen medium and it alone. As her art was writing, rather than painting, Stein's primary interest was language—more specifically, American English and how else its words might be used. Indicatively, the same esthetic idea that seems so acceptable in modernist painting and music was heretical, if not unthinkable, in literature.

From nearly the beginning of her creative career, Stein experimented with language in several ways. Starting from scratch, she neglects the arsenal of devices that authors had traditionally used to vary their prose. Though she was personally literate, her language is kept intentionally unliterary and unconnotative. Her diction is mundane, though her sentence structure is not, for it was her particular achievement to build a complex style out of purposely limited vocabulary.

Richard Kostelanetz. *The Hollins Critic.*
June, 1975, p. 2

There is probably no other writer who would be less comprehensible without reference to the time (the "composition") in which she wrote. While it may be a tautology to say that writers reflect their time and milieu, there are still certain periods of the past in which cultural upheaval seems, in retrospect, so apparent and inescapable that the works of art created during that time become functions of that revolution. During such epochs, certain writers emerge who can be best appreciated only within the context of that release of cultural energy, just as there are others who, in following these pioneers, become writers for all ages. . . .

It does not seem outlandish to suggest that Stein occupies a similar position in Modernist literature. Like "an event in chemistry," she seems in retrospect to have been an inevitable product of cultural energy. Heir to a century of Romanticism and its implications for authorial subjectivity and experimentation, and versed also in modern psychology, Stein had the good fortune to be drawn to an environment, Paris, where innovators in the other arts were attempting experiments similar to hers that ultimately changed the way all civilized peoples were to see and create the world. Her relationship with Picasso was crucial in this regard: for beginning with *Melanctha,* Stein's writings quite often went through the same stages of experimentation as the paintings of her Spanish friend. . . .

[Stein is the] first writer in English that I know of who came to see writing as *purely* a problem in composition; and her explorations of the limits of the English language made it possible for a number of important writers to go to school to her. . . .

To reject Stein any longer is to reject Modernism. While this rejection may be a luxury that some people will continue to permit themselves, it is one that no serious reader can afford to indulge. To deal properly with modern letters, we must face the work of Gertrude Stein head on, in both its intrinsic and its cultural significance. She is too large a fact to be ignored any longer.

Michael J. Hoffman. Gertrude Stein (New
York: Twayne, 1976), pp. 132–35

Gertrude Stein's erotic works are demonstrations of disguised autobiography. For many of the lyrical and revealing pieces in her early oeuvre, *Painted Lace* (1914); *Pink Melon Joy, Possessive Case,* and *No* (1915); *Lifting Belly* (1917); and *Not a Hole* and *A Sonatina Followed by Another* (1921), Stein invented a witty code that played upon the details of her sexual and domestic self. In such a private autobiographical style she can tell everything—and she does. The works also have inherent literary qualities which would make them worthy of notice, even if they did not show so much of the author's personality and habits. They speak in her private but authentic voice—warm, teasing, with exaggerated flights of fancy and whimsy that point to the more radical developments of her later years. The subject and style are, then, both testing grounds; in a sense, her lifestyle would become her art. Erotic, subconscious elements are allowed to interact with conscious craft to produce documents of the interior life. . . .

In her repetitions, mimicking, role playing as "author," Stein has always tried on attitudes like hats in front of the bedroom mirror. She creates a magic theater, in which she plays actor and audience at once. Her attitudes surface and change, coalesce and fragment. If at first she seems to affirm her passion, later she questions and mocks, even denies the worth and quality of her relationship. Autobiographical themes of identity, self-justification, narcissism, and pride occupy her as well as moral questions of guilt, innocence, sin, security, risk, and certainty, and all of these are juxtaposed against frank homosexual statements and naive, totally positive images of her relationship. She finally seasons her text lightly with a straight-faced romantic vocabulary that might in other contexts pass for heterosexual. . . .

Since Stein is never far from humor in any of her pieces, her frankest are no exception. The joyfulness and humor of her treatment of sexual themes breaks down social and linguistic barriers. The shock of juxtaposition of her unusual style forces Stein, as an observer and participant, into new and unexpected perspectives. Pushed by her own temperament to solve certain technical problems of rhyme and diction, to make up new words, to join others together, to treat her lines as a virtuoso singer might, Stein charms by the sweetness of her melodies, her sophisticated naturalness, her complex simplicity, her careful cheerfulness, her precarious self-acceptance. These private writings constitute her interior theater; she is the hero of an appreciative audience and the villain when the boos begin; and she is finally the audience itself, alternately caught up in the hisses and applause.

Elizabeth Fifer. Signs. Spring, 1979,
pp. 472–73, 483

In *Useful Knowledge* (1928), a collection of previously unpublished shorter pieces written between 1914 and 1926, Gertrude Stein makes the case for "redress" and "excess" in our sexual and imaginative lives. The composite text is a dramatic collage of changing styles, alternating between distinct voices and various roles. Its most inventive bursts of free rhythms invariably give way to tight rhyme schemes and exact meters. Surprising juxtaposition is its most basic resource, resonance and fluidity its basic procedures. . . . In *Useful Knowledge,* the language itself functions both as primary vehicle and disguise, simultaneously concealing and revealing her purposes. It is as if her extreme need to speak the unspeakable forced its way into a new channel—a way to both say and unsay at once.

In *Useful Knowledge,* Stein takes special delight in submerging her questions and lists, with their extensive sexual puns, into a distanced scientific and philosophic language. As in a philosophic inquiry, the questions asked are often "leading questions," which sharply narrow and carefully determine their response. Yet in another sense they also provide Stein with a release and a way to go forward—a technique that cuts through the themes of the book and allows her to step in and manage her own, and her audience's, perception. By using leading questions and other philosophic "proofs" to convince us her suppositions are correct, she balances between oppositions and creates extremes to dramatize all the sides of her argument. She addresses herself to a novice who needs instructions, hence the title, but she remains intensely conscious that her words will be overheard by a disapproving general audience, composed of guardians and witnesses, internal as well as external, bound to local values and traditional social behavior.

Elizabeth Fifer. *Journal of Narrative Technique.* 10, 1980, p. 115

Gertrude Stein's writing was undoubtedly influenced by the modes of modern painting she helped to discover and promulgate, particularly cubism. A good deal of Stein criticism has explored this influence, attempting to account for her perennially resistant radical work by discovering in it direct adaptations to literature of cubist technique. Though this notion of borrowed technique is problematic, comparisons of Stein's work to modern painting can be helpful in adjusting our vision to writing which continues to appear strange. Moreover, Stein's pre-World War I work *is* very similar to cubist painting of the same period. They share an orientation toward the linguistic or pictorial surface, a movement in and out of recognizable representations; both shatter or fragment perception and the sentence (canvas), and both render multiple perspectives. . . .

In her recent book on Stein's portraits, Wendy Steiner uses the fact that writing is not painting—that words are signs while paint need not be—to condemn Stein's fully experimental writing. She is able to do that because she begins with the assumption that Stein's radical work is literary cubism. Her argument runs as follows: 1) Stein's experimental writing is literary cubism, but 2) because writing is a second-level sign system it cannot really adopt a form indigenous to painting, a first-level sign system, therefore 3) the writing fails. More typically, analyses of Stein's work as literary cubism simply ignore the fact that words are signs, that their mode of signification need not be referential (representational), and thereby ignore the center of her writing: the creation of culturally alternative modes of literary meaning.

Marianne De Koven. *Contemporary Literature.* 22, 1981, pp. 81, 95

The somagrams of Gertrude Stein—hers and ours about her—illustrate this well-worn axiom. They reveal something else as well; attempts—hers and ours—to fix monstrous qualities of the female body. Like all monstrosities, we despise them, and thus, we seek to fix, to repair, them. However, like all monstrosities, we also need them, and thus, we seek to fix, to stabilize, them. We often toil in vain.

For those who would represent her, Stein's body presents an alarming, but irresistible, opportunity. For her body—the size of it, the eyes, nose, sweat, hair, laugh, cheekbones—was at once strange, an unusual presence, and special, an invigorating one. Increasingly indifferent to "feminine" norms of dress, style, and action, Stein herself appeared to behave as if that strangeness—like her writing itself—was more special than strange, at once original and right. . . .

Stein's texts warn us against going on to genderize grammar itself. Her literary language was neither "female," nor an unmediated return to signifiers freely wheeling in maternal space. It was instead an American English, with some French twists and a deep structure as genderless as an atom of platinum. It could bend to patriarchal pressures, or, lash against them. It could label and curse monsters, or, finally, respond to a monster's stubborn and transforming will.

> Catharine R. Stimpson. *Poetics Today.*
> 6:1–2, 1985, pp. 67, 80

Stein's most obscure texts, texts that have received attention only as important stylistic experiments, are in fact filled with ideas, and . . . the ideas are sophisticated and coherent. We might also fairly call them feminist ideas. Stein is more intelligible and more centrally interested in issues of gender than has been thought.

One implication of Stein's departure from Jamesian psychology is that the mental paradigm with which she replaced it enabled her to say things about women and their place in the symbolic order. In the short period between *Three Lives* and *Tender Buttons,* Stein moved from a Jamesian notion of selective attention to a psychoanalytic one. By 1912, the transition was complete. The interesting fact of mental life for her was no longer that we suppress or ignore certain facts in the interest of survival—James's point— but that we *repress* aspects of experience in the interest of instituting culture. What we repress is not trivial, as James has it, but important; the very fact that we are so intent on keeping it out of view says as much. And the repressed mental content—pre-Oedipal memories, for example, or discounted impressions—can be excavated at any moment. Her final point is that among the things cast into shadow by the culture are the mother and the female body; in the texts of 1912, she uncivilizes us by bringing these back into view.

> Lisa Ruddick. In Michael J. Hoffman, ed.
> *Critical Essays on Gertrude Stein* (Boston:
> G. K. Hall, 1986), p. 238

The point of Gertrude Stein's verbal experimenting is that, if words used without the rational object of saying something in particular, something definitively "thought," can produce an effect of amounting to something, it will have been established that coherent intellectual intent is not necessary for the successful employment of the resources of language. The writings of Gertrude Stein were seductive in the seeming elementalness of their verbal characteristics. Though they were canny contrivances of non-meaning, they invited reception as artifacts that might have been produced in an age of verbal innocence; and they were, indeed, so received, at first by the "advanced" literary public, and, gradually, by more and more of the general public, appreciation in the latter case showing in the form of good-humored tolerance rather than in that of critical satisfaction. There has survived from earlier approving attitudes to what Gertrude Stein did with and to words a settled view that exposure to this results in a healthy disburdening of the mind of the cliché procedures of sophisticated linguistic habit. The actuality is otherwise.

Gertrude Stein's work consists of studied deviations from rational continuity of thought; if allowed to affect the mind, they disrupt its natural rational proclivities. As a *spectacle,* the work looks massively, primitively, simple. But *read,* verbally followed, not just looked at, it could only take the mind on an ever-turning course in which reason is thwarted at every turn. The unhealthy effect of it was not perceived because readers thought of themselves as looking at it, not as reading it. But looked-at words must also be read. Where these words held the eye fascinated, they could make themselves be read, and induce belief that this was, linguistically, something. The procedure appeared to be, in the atmosphere of modernist sympathy with the new in word-ways, a reduction of the sayable to a verbal minimum, a salutary straining of mental simplicity to its extreme. But it went below this minimum, beyond this extreme. . . .

Through the years, now and then, a question has been insanely raised by someone as to whether I thought I was God. I recall commenting on that proposition very, very, long ago with an ascription to Gertrude Stein of being God rather than myself. This was in very serious play with the possibilities of extreme statement. I meant that I was my careful self, laboring with the difficulties of being exactly what I was as myself among others, and of speaking exactly what my mind thought through to the verge of words. Dismiss those difficulties of being, thinking, speaking, and you absent yourself to an ease of tireless deity-being. To whom? Gertrude Stein has actually won for herself the status of a figure of at least quasi-divinity in literary lore. Timidity of identifying themselves as non-comprehenders of her writing and her intent, or as irreverent disbelievers in the title of what she did to being taken seriously, has become the rule where quasi-worshipfulness is not the rule. Perhaps everyone up to the time of her self-deification was-is to blame, for the great emptiness that had accumulated in human self-knowledge—which Gertrude Stein tried to fill with herself for everyone's edification.

Laura Riding Jackson. In Michael J.
Hoffman, ed. *Critical Essays on Gertrude
Stein* (Boston: G. K. Hall, 1986),
pp. 241, 260

STERN, G. B. (GREAT BRITAIN) 1890–1973

Larry Munro is for other readers. Is this Miss G. B. Stern the author of *Children of No Man's Land?* In that novel she packed so many talents that it would not hold together; it flew apart and was all brilliant pieces, but in this! Larry Munro, we repeat, and once again Larry Munro. That is all there is to be said for it. Miss Stern herself strings a quality of more or less bright little beads in between, but they are scarcely visible for the gnashing, all-a-quivering Larry Munro of which her claim is composed. It is not stupid—it is silly; not clever—but bright; and it is so sentimental that it makes the reader hang his head.

K[atherine] M[ansfield]. *The Athenaeum.*
October 8, 1920, p. 472

Miss Stern has one of the queerest talents among contemporary novelists, for she lives by choice on a mental desert rich in natural beauties but unvisited by culture. One can imagine her sitting up among the palm branches, shamelessly clad only in the bright hibiscus flowers of her innate gifts, dropping coconuts on the heads of a party of missionaries from the *Times Literary Supplement* and the *London Mercury,* who had landed to try and get her to listen to the good news about Flaubert. She simply does not care for any of the literary conventions of to-day. Now, that is very unusual. . . . That is why she makes no attempt to stamp *The Room* with what are recognized to-day as the hallmarks of a good book. She writes jauntily; anybody who hastily turned over the leaves might jump to the conclusion that here was a respectable artisan of the Berta Ruck type. . . . But the literary snob would lose a great deal. For *The Room* is a very rich and jolly book. It shows Miss Stern's power of creating real people at its very best.

Rebecca West. *The New Statesman.*
April 1, 1922, p. 734

It is possible sometimes to wish that Miss Stern had a little less cleverness, a little less talent for light and amusing flippancy. She has other qualities which these sometimes obscure. She draws character originally and she really does see into the minds of her persons. But at the same time she has a light and facile pen and a distinct gift for making amusing phrases. It is a pity indeed that one side of her should seem to interfere with the other. But so it is. Her natural talent for psychology really ought to be developed even at the expense of her ability in inventing conversations and scenes which are as unsubstantial, though they are as pleasant, as meringues.

Edward Shanks. *London Mercury.*
May, 1922, p. 97

With her usual sureness of touch, her capacity for communicating experience, and her wide cosmopolitan outlook, this author presents not only the intriguing Toni Rakonitz in her relations with her English husband, Giles Stoddard, but the whole Rakonitz clan in their relations with each other. . . . The book [*A Deputy Was King*], indeed, may be said to represent Europe through the medium of this family, which, to a certain extent, at least, is chameleon-like in its adaptation to environment. . . . As for the odd entanglements of the central married couple curiously innocent as entanglements go, they are as nothing against the intricate tribal ramifications which Miss Stern has known how to weave into a pattern of living reality.

J. A. T. Lloyd. *Fortnightly Review.* May,
1927, p. 718

There have been many actresses among the lively characters with whom Miss Stern has beguiled her admirers. She catches their glamour and their fallibility, the hard work in the glare of the footlights and their gay fascination in private life as few contemporary novelists have done. In *The Donkey Shoe* she adds to her theatrical gallery the entrancing Jessica Marwood. . . .

G. B. Stern has never written and surely never intended to write profound novels; but she has never failed to entertain. If the peculiar enchantment of the actresses she writes about is convincing, her sympathetic portraits of the young are just as persuasive. It is the ability to present the beguiling and baffled Jessica with as much understanding as she does the unhappy Damaris [Jessica's daughter] which puts on this latest of her novels Miss Stern's own inimitable stamp.

Pamela Taylor. *Saturday Review of
Literature.* June 7, 1952, p. 23

Wooden is the last word for G. B. Stern, an elastic stylist if ever there was one. I remember at an early age being stunned into admiration of her nerve for daring to write something as solemn as a book in a style of tea-party gossip. On and on she goes—interjections, asides, explosions, slang, an overwhelming gush of reminiscence, anecdote, nonsense and chit-chit about nothing in particular, but all extremely well-done. She is, stylistically, what used to be called "a rattle," and rather refreshing it is, among so many prudent stylists, to meet someone as exuberantly verbose. But what is it all *about?* Well, *For All We Know* (a suitably airy title) is about one of those brilliant, fictional families with ramifications so complex that even with a family tree at the beginning you can hardly tell by the end exactly who is whose great-aunt or grandmother or second cousin. But it doesn't really matter; what does is the frightful, fascinating buoyancy of plot, characters, conversations, and, of course, plain narrative. It struck me as wildly untrue to life, but so have a lot of better books—and very agreeably so, if you are a fast reader and can speed up into the spirit of the thing.

Isabel Quigley. *Spectator.* January 13, 1956,
p. 58

As this semiautobiographical novel [*A Deputy Was King*] opens in 1921, Toni Rakonitz is weary of working at her exclusive London dressmaking shop; she dreams of a life of never-ending parties. Giles Goddard, nourished on a generous allowance and eager to have fun after fighting in World War I, seems Toni's ideal savior. They marry ten days after meeting, well aware that love is not the basis for their union. The most appealing part of the book follows the two through their early years of marriage, filled with the longed-for parties; the births of three children; profligate spending; the near-bankruptcy of Toni's business; and clashes of will. But Giles deserts Toni, running off with her magnetic, egomaniacal cousin, Loraine. This articulate novel, first published in Great Britain in 1926, is particularly intriguing for its incipient feminism. Stern *(The Matriarch)* delivers surprisingly current observations on women's roles in business and family: "Directly she succeeded in noosing a man's interest in the work she did," Toni learns, "she promptly loosened and lost it for the girl she was." But the later focus on Loraine is less satisfying, and the somewhat ambiguous happy ending wraps things up a bit too neatly.

Penny Kaganoff. *Publishers Weekly.*
July 5, 1991, p. 62

STOCKENSTRÖM, WILMA (SOUTH AFRICA) 1933–

Wilma Stockenström, a distinguished Afrikaans poet, has also written several critically acclaimed prose works, of which this short novel is the first—but surely not the last—to be translated into English. Within the context of recent Afrikaans literature, *The Expedition to the Baobab Tree* is a truly remarkable contribution, both for the lyrical quality of its prose and for its boldly imaginative theme.

Although set in an African past, this is no conventional historical novel. In form it is a sympathetic fictional autobiography, told with passion and resignation, of a slave woman who was primarily a sexual object. The nameless narrator's tale of her life's humiliations leads her ultimately to a giant baobab tree, which is her final refuge; hence the title. Both the period and the hybrid locale are never identified, a deliberate vagueness which both tantalizes and frustrates the reader. The vocabulary of the flora and fauna is drawn from the Cape of Good Hope, but there are clues (dhows, praus, slave processions from the interior) which lead the reader away from the Cape to a presumably East African setting. Likewise, the image of master-slave relations contains little that is specific to the Cape. This is in no sense a literal reconstruction of South African slave biography such as André Brink attempted in *Kennis van die aand*. Nevertheless, this theme is still a fresh and disturbing one for many South African readers, although others, like Brink, have begun to explore it. Stockenström is by no means a "dissident" Afrikaans writer (she escapes notice in Jack Cope's [1982] survey of these writers, *The Adversary Within* . . . , but she has provided a profoundly symbolic critique of South African history by focusing on master-slave sexual exploitation.

The English translation by J. M. Coetzee, the Booker Prize-winning author of *The Life and Times of Michael K* (1983), is a splendid rendering of the intense Afrikaans original. Indeed, it faithfully preserves some of the occasionally jarring phrases found there, such as "cat-speculation dissimulation," which could never conceivably have originated in the mind of the narrator, though they are attributed to her. These lapses, however, do not much detract from a moving and extraordinary book, one which for some readers may invite comparison with William Styron's *Confessions of Nat Turner* (1967).

> Jim Armstrong. *World Literature Today.* 59,
> 1985, p. 150

One picks up *Kaapse rekwisiete* (Cape Town theatrical props) with great expectations, coming as it does after the bold achievement of Stockenström's . . . *Expedition to the Baobab Tree.* . . . Between those two prose works she published a magnificent, albeit austere volume of poetry. . . . Poetry is her true métier; in this medium she uses her lyricism to express precise and abstract thought. In the novel discussed here, however, her lyric effusions are annoyingly intrusive. The reader is forced to notice the well-phrased, manicured sentences, which at times run to as much as ten lines.

The novel deals with a bunch of irrelevant superficial characters, members of a state theatrical company in Cape Town. It is only as one finishes the book that one realizes the author's aims: perhaps these drifting personages represent the feeling of helplessness and alienation of the white South African of the 1980s? They are the mere props of the title. The action, purposely theatrical, revolves around a female stage director, an erstwhile actress with the improbable name of Lefebvre. She and the rest of the company are effete bohemians who switch bed partners at the flick of a wrist. There are also the homosexual males with their easy alliances. The atmosphere is one of cynicism, and nobody is particularly inspired by what the troupe is doing or its relevance.

Still, the book is far from flippant. It possesses a tragically sad undertone, for the characters are such genuinely lost souls. The true protagonist of the book is probably the city of Cape Town itself, as what little action there is shifts from suburb (white) to suburb (white). Not that the iniquities of apartheid are brushed aside: the husband of one troupe member is a political activist and a prisoner on Robben Island, and Lefebvre ends up—joyfully for the first time—with a new lover across the color line. However, there is something too easy here: does she merely accept him because his name is Rufus, as she as a redhead had always felt an outcast in her adoptive family?

And why does the novel raise such flippant questions in the reader's mind? Did I misread it, then?

Barend J. Toerien. *World Literature Today.* 62, 1988, p. 501

Wilma Stockenström is a well-established poet, novelist, and dramatist as well as a professional actress. *Die heengaanrefrein* is her fifth book of verse. Of her four novels, it is *Die kremetartekspedisie* (1981; Eng. *Journey to the Baobab Tree*) which has brought her the most renown, having been translated into numerous languages and awarded Italy's Grinzane Cavour Prize in 1988.

The title of Stockenström's new work is difficult to render into English, for it has a certain ambiguity resulting from the word *heengaan,* which can mean both "going away, departing" and "dying." Both meanings are functional. The work was commissioned for the commemoration of the tricentennial of the Huguenots' landing at the Cape, and the title thus refers implicitly to their departure from France in the seventeenth century. Stockenström did not produce a boring epic poem, however; she used the historical material to write a satire about the Huguenots' progeny, the Afrikaners. Her perspective on the sociopolitical realities of South Africa in the 1980s makes *Die heengaanrefrein* into a harsh reflection of today's tensions. In the process of portraying the forefathers, she satirizes their descendants and shows without mercy how soft, lazy, and comfort-conscious this species has become. Thus *heengaan* also refers to the "perishing, dying" Afrikaner breed, whose corruption is juxtaposed with the Huguenots' dedication, hard work, steadfast belief, and loyalty.

Still, the poem is quite complex, with no simple historical or chronological line. Stockenström's intent is to portray Homo sapiens and his inherent weaknesses. The collective guilt of white South Africans is thus given shape within the description of the fragmented, tormented modern society: "The houses can scarcely groan under the repression. / The orchards are weighed down by the fruit of illusion. / . . . / And empty buses depart and arrive in the cities of misery / and there are sales and unrest and stray dogs, / and there are black flags and triumph in the streets." In contrast to the spiritual corruption which is leading to the downfall of the "whiter" sector of the community, the darker inhabitants of the country suffer despair. The poet's ideological stance can be deduced from her ironic question: "Who is it that copulates against despair / and rears children for the ash heap? . . . / Whose lips are a burnt scream?"

The poem ends with a lyric intermezzo in which the poet turns from the prevailing minor key to a hopeful view of the joys of the young language, Afrikaans, which remains in spite of the terrors of the fragmented society. However, this optimistic note on which the poem ends, this sudden turn toward a lyric hymn about the joys of Afrikaans, stands in strange contrast to the earlier sections. Perhaps it reflects something of the schizophrenia in the psyche of many South Africans of lighter hue. Are they really of Africa?

Through the consciousness of Afrikaans as an African language, the poet seems to point at local roots, at the shedding of the European "skin."

Die heengaanrefrein uses concentrated, dense images and possesses a philosophical veneer. The collection shows Stockenström as poet at her best: a sustained discourse on the paradoxes and ironies of life in South Africa.

Helize van Vuuren. *World Literature Today.*
63, 1989, pp. 355–56

The 1970s marked the emergence of a strong voice in Afrikaans, Wilma Stockenström. Her first published work was a volume of poetry entitled *Vir die bysiende leser* (1970; For the nearsighted reader), followed by *Spieël van water* (1973; Mirror of water), *Van vergetelheid en van glans* (1977; Of oblivion and of splendor), *Monsterverse* (1984; Monstrous verses), and *Die heengaanrefrein* (1988; Refrain of departure). Her work is in turn fiercely satirical of the monster, namely, humankind, and a nostalgic longing for a time when nature (and the African landscape in particular) still revealed its own significance. Stockenström has also published a number of novels, chief among which is *Die kremetartekspedisie* (1981; *The Expedition to the Baobab Tree,* 1983). Through the subject of a slave woman in 15th-century Africa, Stockenström explores the realm of dreams and death, in which polarities are fused and boundaries dissolved. The novel shares certain qualities with the novels of J. M. Coetzee, who translated it. Stockenström's latest work is the novel *Abjater wat so lag* (1991; Abjater, the laughing one), in which the subject is an old nurse, helping her wards enter into death.

Carli Coetzee. In Steven R. Serafin and
Walter D. Glanze, eds. *Encyclopedia of
World Literature in the 20th Century* (New
York: Continuum, 1993), p. 565

STORNI, ALFONSINA (ARGENTINA) 1892–1938

Alfonsina Storni tried her hand at all literary genres, but her major contribution is her poetry. . . . Her gaze, turned always on herself, led her constantly to look for new paths and for the key to what inspired her most nearly perfect poems. Critics have made various pronouncements about her work, but they seem unanimous in recognizing its great value. In an overview of the poetry of our country, Alfonsina Storni must be singled out as an illustrious figure, and as our finest woman poet. . . . Horacio Rega Molina well summed up her special gifts: "Her distinctive characteristics are irony, humor, calm contemplativeness, uncertainty, and a certain tough-minded interpretation of themes. One does not find these features in the work of Juana Ibarbourou or Gabriela Mistral. . . ."

María Teresa Orosco. *Alfonsina Storni*
(Buenos Aires: Universidad de Buenos
Aires, 1940), pp. 314–15

[Storni] who ofttimes speaks of love with cynicism and with irony as when, in a mood that recalls one of Edna St. Vincent Millay's, she says: "little man, I loved you half an hour, do not ask for more"; she who is forever intent on proclaiming the final "liberation" of woman, is also the one who says to the lover: "I shall lay myself at your feet, humble and meek"; "sweetly, I shall fall at your feet, 'neath the full moon"; "take my life; make it, if you will, your slave," in a tone which is not *feminist* surely, but feminine to the extreme. For many of her poems disclose a meekness and submission in the face of the "sweet torture" of love for which she ever clamors; and what she admires most in man is his virility, his physical strength. She speaks of iron muscles, of hands of steel, of a voice that makes a woman cringe, and dominates—a man's voice: warm and feared. And before this tower of strength she likes to feel small and humble.

This quasi-servile attitude of hers contrasts with the other she likes to assume in moments when she feels it incumbent upon her to express the muffled and stifled cry of other women who, like herself, wish to proclaim their equality with men, yet want nothing better, perhaps, than to be frail femininity in the steel grip of powerful and commanding masculine hands.

She never gives herself wholly to her passions, as do most women, for she is forever conscious of the mind—*the first nucleus,* as she calls it in *World of Seven Wells*—whose weight she cannot elude, and which she feels nailed fast within her by a cruel destiny. For she is aware that were it not for this propensity of hers to think, to philosophize, to rationalize, she might have found more happiness in life, more freedom. And so more than once she bemoans this cerebral chain that has the power to bind her to the stolid, cold and restricting fetters of thought, and to keep her from roaming freely in the uninhabited plains of instinct.

Perhaps because of this, many of her poems seem somewhat prosaic and *intellectual;* to reflect preconceived mental attitudes, rather than spiritual or emotional needs.

Sidonia Carmen Rosenbaum. *Modern
Women Poets of Spanish America*
(New York: Hispanic Institute in the United
States, 1945), pp. 224–25

In her important poems Storni is the contemporary cosmopolitan; she sees nature, the city, the sea, human relationship, not from the standpoint of any particular country or continent but as the land of reality seen through a poet's imagination and vision, anywhere on this planet. No special knowledge of any particular country with its tradition is necessary to understand her poetry. As a cosmopolitan she distinctly belongs to the twentieth century; consequently she is much, but not exclusively, concerned with the evolution in the position of women in human society. Great women of the past, as in "Great Women" and intellectual women, "the mental women" in "The Other Friend," are one medium through which she presents the conflict between the individual and the surrounding world. . . . The feminine resentment against the lack of understanding from merely comfort-seeking and pleasure-seeking man is present only in the background; the chief stress is on the discrepancy between imagination and reality which, in human relationships, is equally disappointing to either sex.

Living in the inner world of imagination and dreams is not sentimental romanticism in Storni. Instead, it is the frustrating experience of one who would like to think, fight, and live . . . with her surrounding world but who, disappointed by the shallowness and the lack of response of the outer world, returns to her own. . . . Earlier candidness of the poet in her effort to grasp and enjoy the universe, her compromise (when not finding the answers) in seeing, in the microcosmos around her, the beauty of the climbing rosebush on a modest house in the suburb, the glance in the eyes of a child whose fear of a snake she disperses with kindness, has become, in poems like "Pain," resignation, a deliberate restraining of her own nature into the will toward lethargy.

Gabrièle von Munk Benton. *Hispania*. 33,
May, 1950, pp. 151–52

Twenty-five years after her suicide, Alfonsina Storni's highly personal and accomplished work continues to attract devoted readers. The unevenness of her work—its strengths and imperfections—adds up to a totality that testifies to an intense life, as intense in the living as in the imagining. . . .

Juan Ramón Jiménez praised her complete naturalness and her genuine feeling for life and poetry; thus did her contemporaries view her, both in Argentina and abroad. Roberto F. Giusti reiterated these judgments in his study of her written shortly after her death. Nothing since then has been offered to modify this assessment in any significant way. . . .

She was not an exceptional poet because she was not able to master her instrument of expression, perhaps because she did not make the effort to seek perfection. But she was original both because she created a very personal poetic world and because she started a rebellion in poetry against the limitations and austerity of her environment.

Javier Fernández. *Cuadernos del Congresso*
por la Libertad de la Cultura. No. 84,
May 1964, p. 93

The first books of poems of Alfonsina Storni display a taste for cynicism, irony, bitterness, and rebellion, which corresponds to the circumstances of her life. . . . Alfonsina rebelled sincerely and authentically against the psychological, erotic, economic, and social limitations imposed on the women of her time. She explored . . . the feminine psyche, and was censured as an erotic poet. But, as María Rosa Oliver correctly pointed out in defining Alfonsina's personality, "She sang about physical and spiritual exaltation with purity." . . . Julio Noé, in his study of Alfonsina's poetry, states: "She was born to love freely with her body and her soul, with pagan happiness and with the tenderness of a gentle woman; but her alert intelligence prepared her to be on guard against man, the "master of the world," whose impure desires stain the deepest sentiments.". . . According to Ricardo Rojas, "She gave voice in female poetry to the mysteries of sex, using forms reflecting the innovations in poetic technique of her time." Sor Juana Inés de la Cruz, the beautiful "Tenth Muse of Mexico" (as her admirers called her), played a similar role in the seventeenth century regarding the emancipation of women.

Etelvina Astrada de Terzaga. *Cuadernos Hispanoamericanos.* No. 211, July, 1967, pp. 127, 129

Alfonsina Storni [was] one of the many illustrious contributors to Victoria Ocampo's review *Sur,* who began publishing her poems in 1916. Starting from the lyrical imagery of the "Ultraista" movement, she soon found a motif of inspiration in themes relating to the situation of women, the social and psychological stigmas which apply to them living in a *"patriarcado."* Her comedy *El amo del mundo* (1927) is based on the theme that man, in spite of the flattery and courtship with which he surrounds woman, is her enemy, *"el enemigo dulce,"* and looks upon her as morally inferior: "Being man he thinks himself master of the world. Woman in relation to him can be the object of his whims, a distraction or even a moment of madness. But never another being of equal moral integrity." Already defiant of the conventions which for thousands of years have hampered women's emotional expression and prevented them from revealing their sensuousness and the passion of their desire, had found expression in her poetry. . . .

In 1934 Storni published *Mundo de siete pozos,* in which her poetry assumes an allegoric thoughtful character, as she centers her vision on cosmic themes. The tone moves from lyrical or satirical to epic; the style acquires a baroque richness which comes from the author's preoccupation with language and her desire to explore its symbols and possibilities (probably the influence of James Joyce's *Ulysses,* also felt by other Latin American writers). The quality of Alfonsina Storni's writing and the reputation which she finally gained formed the first step towards including women at the same level as men in the history of Argentinean literature. Storni moved from "poetess to poet," as Rachel Phillips ironically says in the title of her study. Recalling one of the things which Victoria Ocampo had stated, that "a woman cannot really write like a woman . . . until she no longer feels obliged to respond to attacks and defend her intellectual freedom and equality," one realizes the inevitable presence of a transitional stage during which she cannot as yet write with the sole purpose of "translating her thoughts, feelings and vision." Only then, no longer concerned with defending her position, will she be able to turn her mind to the tasks which confront every writer within the literary and historical context in which she lives.

Psiche Hughes. In Mineke Schipper, ed.
*Unheard Words: Women and Literature in
Africa, the Arab World, Asia, the
Caribbean, and Latin America* (London:
Allyson and Busby, 1985), pp. 235–37

It is regrettable that anthologized selections of Alfonsina Storni's poetry usually do not include poems from *Mascarilla y trébol* (Death mask and cloverleaf, 1938), her eighth and last book of poetry, since this collection contains some of her best work and perhaps her most original approach to form. It is also understandable because the content of the poems is depressing and occasionally confusing. In these poems, written during a period of great personal stress, the author succeeded too well in making her readers confront the doubts and disillusions about the value of life itself, which she herself was facing. Early in 1935, Storni discovered she had cancer and a radical mastectomy left her with extensive physical and psychological scars as well as ever increasing pain from the metastasizing cancer; a very noticeable and rapid premature aging added to her unhappiness. She had always been emotionally unstable, suffering bouts of depression and paranoia, and nervousness at times to the point of breakdown, and she reacted to her personal tragedy by avoiding her old friends and withdrawing into herself. It was during this period that she wrote the poems of *Mascarilla y trébol,* and by the time the book was published, at the end of June 1938, she realized that she had terminal cancer. *Mascarilla y trébol* is evidence for the theory that in order to explain the nature of creative activity "we must account, first, for the relation between the finished product and both the experiences and intentions of the life and consciousness that feed it." Out of her most tragic and most inherently unshareable experience, Storni was able to produce some of her finest and most universally comprehensible poetry. She successfully shaped her suffering into art through a verse form that is both original and remarkably appropriate to her material. It is difficult for the reader, who is vulnerable to living or witnessing close at hand the same experience, to keep an emotional distance from poems that for the most part reveal bitter resentment over a real, imminent, early, and unwanted death. . . .

Mascarilla y trébol occupies the special position of being a conscious culmination of the poet's work as well as a reflection of a particularly tragic experience. The "anti-soneto" form, which is both a happy and original synthesis of the poet's contradictory impulses, and a fitting medium for her themes and vision, gives every impression of being an objective obtained. Even though the content of the poems is for the most part a projection of a very anguished state of mind, the control and skill exercised in the expression of that content suggests that Storni had achieved an artistic maturity that was not even a visible potential in her first books. It is unfair to the poet to ignore these poems.

Janice Giesler Titiev. *Hispania*. 68, 1985,
pp. 467, 473

Alfonsina Storni enjoys the well earned acclaim of being one of the first and foremost Latin-American feminist poets. Thus, Beatriz Sarlo places her at the head of a list of women "que abrieron camino" to whom she dedicates her book *El imperio de los sentimientos (Next in line is Victoria Ocampo)*. Similarly Irene Matthews, in a recently published article on Gabriela Mistral, notes that Alfonsina Storni is included in most reviews of literary feminism in Latin America as among a handful of "attractive standard bearers whose spite, charm, and intelligence—differential and iconoclastic—undermine the masculine norm." Needless to say, this undermining of the masculine norm was not always seen in terms of approval, particularly by contemporary male critics. What is more, in many cases it was simply ignored, sanitized out of existence; and Storni's feminism was presented in general terms of a woman writing about marginal women's preoccupations. . . .

There is today a general agreement that Storni's poetry matured as it grew from the somewhat neat sentimental, neo-romantic verses of her youth to the more complex poems of her last two collections, *Mundo de siete pozos* (1934) and *Mascarilla y trébol* (1938). . . . The overall validity of such criticism seems beyond dispute and I seek no quarrel with it; on the contrary, in looking at Storni's feminism, I too, can see a parallel maturing in her emancipation from the masculine norms of her society, and one which would seem to coincide with Elaine Showalter's perception of three main stages in the history of women's writing, namely, the feminine, the feminist and the female.

Evelyn Fishburn. In L. P. Condé and S. M.
Hart, eds. *Feminist Readings on Spanish
and Latin American Literature* (Lewiston,
New York: Edwin Mellen Press, 1991),
pp. 121–22

STRUCK, KARIN (GERMANY) 1947–

[In *Journal Einer Krise* (Journal of a crisis)] the acknowledgement of creative love, a love through which the woman proves her identity, goes hand in hand with her emancipation from a purely destructive love addiction. One such type of identification, however, is the strengthening of that style of "self-exposition" that has characterized the writings of Karin Struck from the beginning.

> Does another possibility exist, besides the "exposition of the self," considering the hypocrisy of that one? Believe me when I say that I do not want to have you at my disposal, by writing about you. Believe me when I say that writing is an act of love.

It is no coincidence that this speech, directed at the man she once loved, reads like a declaration of the axioms of women's literature in general. Appellation and self-justification balance one another out here. Karin Struck remains true to her literary form of expression; she "exposes" herself in her most recent work as well, in the name of love, and with courage as well as with confidence.

This writer, who like no other in the Federal Republic of Germany conceives of herself in all her womanhood as a representative of a class society, is able to explain herself now more than ever. . . . In harmony with Enlightenment ethics, she frees herself from her self-inflicted minority status, from her childhood of dependent love. Yet even as she comes of age, Karin Struck does not give up on trying to communicate with men. Dialectically, writing means both self-reliance, and symbiosis with writing. In her representation of herself as reference, we discern, time and again, a character trait that is generally applicable in women's literature. . . .

She has long recognized that there are many men who . . . are not interested in women's learning to read. The book closes with a calm and sober challenge: "I have a right to my own life." In her journal, Karin Struck does not yet share in the unique individuality for which she has declared her support. The journal deals much more with the theme of the crisis-ridden process of gradual self-discovery—and in this regard, it still represents a record of "representative existence" a personal sense of self-reliance. . . . Like hardly any other German-language female writer, Karin Struck refreshingly clarifies a basic conviction of feminism: The personal is political. The development of one's personality is a political deed, and a social act. . . .

Karin Struck's journal distinguishes itself through its documentary character, even in its fictionality. There are reasons for this. The work is made up of at least three books that were originally conceived of separately: a peace book, a book of dreams, and a diary chronicling the generation of a work. Women's literature between documentary and fiction: Karin Struck's *The End of Childhood* is constantly aware of its "intermediate form.". . .

As a dialectical means of identification, the quotation becomes "form, transformation, aesthetic" in the works of Karin Struck, integrating itself into the "invention" of its own self. That which is documentary turns into fiction, just as that which is fiction turns into documentary. The ability to change sociopolitically remains interrelated with the transformation of (women's) literature. To this extent as well, *The End of Childhood* represents a "Journal of Crisis." When a person's ability to change and his representational transformation do not determine one another, literature stagnates in noncommittal aesthetics and politics. Karin Struck's crisis of self-determination and self-reliance—the "end of her childhood"—presents her perception of an invention, her choice of a realization. Within this context, it is not surprising that dreams (again) play such a structurally significant role in this report of perceptions. They, too, represent individual documentary accounts, yet they are at the same time wish-projections, forming an expression of precisely that "intermediary form" which is distinctive not just in this work, but to a great degree in women's literature in general. She provides a documentary account of our imagination. Woman introduces herself as subject to change; she corrects the image that is forced upon her by an aesthetic principle based on patriarchy, both through her social politics and through her literature.

> Manfred Jürgensen. *Frauenliteratur:*
> *Autorinnen, Perspektiven, Konzepte* (Bern
> and Frankfurt: Lang, 1983), pp. 197–200

Struck is best known for her autobiographical works dealing with this question: "Can women reconcile erotic love with their intellectual consciousness while fulfilling themselves as lovers, mothers, and wives in a class society?". . . [*Klassenliebe* is a] heavily autobiographical account, written in the form of a brutally frank journal, with random passages, and quotes taken from various sources, [and] documents the author's childhood, her factory experience, her student days, her marriage, and her affair with the bourgeois intellectual "Z." All of this is narrated from the perspective of the author's awareness of her working-class background and the role class has played in setting up insurmountable barriers between her and "Z." Although much of the social analysis has been regarded as undigested student Marxism, and although the tone often borders on the pathetic, some critics have found this novel an interesting account of the student movement in West Germany. It is of interest to courses or studies on modern women's writing in the Federal Republic of Germany in that context. . . .

Lotte, the heroine of this novel, [*Lieben*; To love] is an older version of Karin, the heroine of *Klassenliebe* (Class-love), and Nora, the main character in *Die Mutter* (The mother). Again, the narrative is heavily autobiographical, despite the third-person narration and a conscious reference to Goethe's works. In *Lieben*, a woman of thirty, mother of two children and midwife, breaks out of her working-class marriage through an affair with a bourgeois intellectual, becomes pregnant, and chooses to have an abortion. After this, she experiments with loving women and younger men, but none of these graphically and stereotypically described encounters provide her with the "Wohnungen gegen den Tod" that she is searching for. At the end, she is disillusioned about ever realizing her ideals. Despite the themes, this cannot be considered a feminist book and is of limited interest as women's writing, unless one is searching for conservative texts. . . .

Nora, the heroine of this novel, [*Die Mutter*] has been named with Ibsen in mind. The text, alternating from the third to the first person and containing references to literary or sociological presentations of motherhood, relates the suffering of Nora, who argues that mothers have no place in capitalist society, that babies are mass-produced in "bearing factories," and that more attention is paid to abortion than to birthing. Her dream is of the primal, erotic mother; of developing a cohesive, maternal will and of regaining an "oral integrity." The "maternal" society she envisions for the seventies, which would produce the "new man," would arise when mothers found themselves, and when men became real lovers accepting their role as fathers. . . .

Anna, the heroine of this story [*Trennung*] represents a continuation of the experience of Lotte in *Lieben*. *Trennung* picks up where that novel left off, with the relationship of the heroine to a young drug addict. But here, the working-class heroine has become a writer, with the titular act of separation providing her motivation for writing. Guilt-ridden in a way that Struck's heroines rarely are—they prefer to accuse others of their misery—Anna recounts the events of her life, which we know from the other novels, and tries to discover who she is, where she should be in society, what her various work experiences and love affairs have meant for her. The terrain and the issues are familiar to Struck readers by now. The novel ends, however, with Anna's thirtieth birthday, and the intimation that she is ready to plunge from her balcony.

Susan L. Cocalis. In Elke Frederiksen, ed.
*Women Writers of Germany, Austria, and
Switzerland* (Westport, Connecticut:
Greenwood Press, 1981), pp. 231–33

Unlike the American poet Anne Sexton, Karin Struck will never place her psychoanalyst in the compromising position of posthumously revealing the details of her neuroses, since she herself has been recording her every thought and physical sensation in a series of thinly disguised autobiographical novels for years. Such is the stuff that dreams are made of, particularly ones that get related on an analyst's couch. Struck and her publishers apparently assume there is an audience that is interested in the minutiae of her biography, particularly her sex life, and in her renewed attacks on the sacred cows of the German women's movement (women's right to have an abortion) and feminism in general. The dustjacket copy promises the reader "literature as relentless attempt at self-definition" ("Literatur als schonungsloser Selbstversuch"), although the text that follows might be more aptly described as "relentless self-definition as an attempt at literature."

In her latest novel, *Blaubarts Schatten* (Bluebeard's shadow), Struck continues her autobiographical narrative in the thin guise of Lily Bitter (symbolic name!), a middle-aged writer living in Hamburg with her children. In the night of October 3, 1990, while contemplating the abortion statistics from the former GDR, Lily remembers the circumstances of her own abortion, which serves as the catalyst for an ensuing series of emotional diatribes on the topic of abortion, men as (fascist) "Bluebeards," feminist complicity with the Bluebeard-men (re: abortion) contra the glories of motherhood, father-daughter incest, the failure of socialism, and true women's emancipation. All the above are set in the context of bitter Lily's relationships with men (present, past, incestual, imagined, and mythical), her addiction to sex and alcohol, and her own abortion, all of which are represented at great length and in graphic detail. Interspersed in the narrative are intertextual allusions to the Bluebeard legend, Ingeborg Bachmann's works, socialism in the former GDR, and the contemporary literary scene. The mayor of Hamburg also makes a cameo appearance (telephone sex) after he has allegedly become sexually aroused by Struck's protagonist at a party. And so Lily's drunken, insatiable night-life goes on and on, with occasional forays into the daylight hours. To make a long story short, Lily eventually reclaims the "brains" her father had denied her and uses them to fashion her anger into a "dagger" with which she stabs ("penetrates") the latest Bluebeard in her life. In the end she renounces all the Bluebeards for another type of male lover, Bachmann's "men with name John" (Hans). Presumably Struck's next novel, the sequel in her autobiographical narrative, will be called "Undine's Revenge" or "Hans um Glück" (Lucky John).

This review began by comparing Struck to Anne Sexton, but perhaps a more fitting analogy for the Struck of *Blaubarts Schatten* would be Camille Paglia. Struck . . . girds herself in her leather and whips to do battle against the feminists. Although she is more self-doubting . . . than Paglia and less grounded in the academic arena, she is equally verbose and self-referential in her attacks on cultural irons. Where Paglia, however, uses sexuality verbally as a weapon in her attack on the intellectual establishment, one has the feeling that Struck is condemned to repeatedly reenact sexual transactions because she has been victimized by her father and the men in her life. Writing here is not metaphoric weapon as much as it appears to be a form of self-indulgence and therapy.

Susan L. Cocalis. *World Literature Today.*
67, 1993, pp. 177–78

SUCKOW, RUTH (UNITED STATES) 1892–1960

The method of Mme [Aino] Kallas is the dramatic one which befits the violence of incidents taken from the history of a people which lived precariously and upon which calamity, sudden and definitive, was likely to fall. Miss Suckow, dealing [in *Country People*] with a more tranquil life, chooses for her short novel of the German farmer of the Middle West the form of a simple chronicle. In it she can summarize the lives of three generations and depict a tragedy (if tragedy it is) not of decisive violence but of attrition. In her story no passions rise high, her characters measure their achievement by solid, material things, and the pity is chiefly that men and women who have worked so hard for a living should live so little. She traces the history of a family from the grandfather who came as a settler to the grandchildren who go their separate ways in a changing civilization, and their story is typical. Change comes but it comes slowly. The purchase of a Ford marks an epoch in the life of the second generation, but a Victrola comes only with the third, and meanwhile the elders, worn by labor, drop aside. Their lives are without the terrible sufferings which Mme Kallas describes, but they are also without the passionate defiant joys. Happier but less intense they live their lives in labor and pass on to each succeeding generation a little more comfort and a slightly changed civilization.

Miss Suckow's method is no more showy than her story but it has the advantage of wide observation, absolute honesty and the knack of selecting just those incidents calculated to picture to the imagination the life which she is describing. Moreover, she has no ax to grind and she neither satirizes nor idealizes. No more unprejudiced record has been written of this particular epoch and this particular region. It gives an impression of completeness without being either ponderous or dull.

J. W. Krutch. *The Nation.* August 20, 1924,
p. 194

Born to a poverty to which she cannot reconcile herself, Cora Schwietert [in *Cora*] struggles for independence through work. She achieves a certain amount of success: overcomes the business world's prejudices against women, makes money. Instead of bringing happiness, this success only begets new problems. Fundamentally romantic, Cora would like to marry, but the men she meets are her inferiors. Their jobs are not so good as hers. Nevertheless she succumbs to an attractive suitor whom she encounters while on a vacation outing in Yellowstone Park. She gives up her work and for the first time in her life, mistress of her own home, knows real happiness. Unfortunately her house is built upon sand. Her husband, whom she still loves, turns out to be ne'er-do-well, loses his job, and, frightened by his wife's pregnancy, deserts her. After the birth of her child Cora returns to her family and renews the old round of work. Having known, however briefly, better things, she is no longer satisfied with money-making as the end of life; and the book closes with her accepting the attentions of a wealthy married man.

As a study of the deadening effect of poverty, conflict between security and conventional success as opposed to happiness, evolution from romanticism to cynicism in an individual, *Cora* has all the elements of an important novel. The motivation, the events in the heroine's life and their effect, are convincing. But the characterization is thin. Cora herself lacks warmth; one would like to sympathize with her but one cannot. Intellectually the author has made her point: she has outlined an authentic, pitiable life; emotionally she has not convinced us. It is as if she were engrossed with the scene and the action to the comparative exclusion of the characters. Only old Mr. Schwietert stands out as a truly human being. Had Miss Suckow done as well for his daughter, her book would be worth reading for its character portrayal as well as its admirable theme.

The Bookman. November, 1929, pp. 312–13

In Miss Suckow's latest novel [*The Kramer Girls*], along with her usual excellence in pure representation, there is, perhaps, a stronger emotional current than in any of her previous books. She has yielded a little of her aloofness, and she has gained in power and depth. The story is of three sisters in the familiar Iowa environment. Miss Suckow's characters are never to be summed up in a sentence. It is only at first glance that they seem to be types. For she has developed to perfection her own technique of word portraiture—that of approaching a character from many angles, disregarding inconsistencies, until the figure emerges, three dimensional, astonishingly like life. If Miss Suckow has not achieved as yet in sustained power all that her admirers have hoped from her, the fact remains that she is one of the few of our important novelists whose powers are still on the increase.

The Nation. April 30, 1930, p. 523

The children and older people who make up the present short stories [in the collection entitled *Children and Older People*] are not sketched to prove this social philosophy, any more than Katharine Mansfield's or Selma Lagerlöf's characters have an ulterior motive for being. Miss Suckow is too individualistic to be a violent propagandist. She has seen with extraordinary clarity into the conscious or unconscious motives of her Iowa country and small-town people. She is too close to the soil to be cynical, and, while no frailty is too small to escape her notice, the sum of weaknesses and strength is in such honest and untheatrical proportions that generally if not admirable the characters are at least memorable as human beings. . . .

Here is an unsentimental picture of ordinary people who are living natural and hence rather sentimental lives. There are no violent passions, ambitions, crimes; none of the elements of small-town life that "nice people" would not know about. Yet here is what at least most women would find to build upon if they went back to their home towns and belonged to the women's club. To this New York emigrée it brings back a picture too well remembered to be a serious challenge. But Miss Suckow revives memories that are pleasant, and for moments of nostalgia these and others of her stories are commended to the attention of not too earnest and not too civilized readers.

Catherine Royer. *The Bookman*. October,
1931, pp. 191–92

This volume, [*Carry-Over*] which contains *Country People, The Bonney Family,* and sixteen short stories, gives a very fair view of Miss Suckow's scope. The two novels deal respectively with farm and small-town life in Iowa and both converge toward the World War. In her revealing introduction Miss Suckow repudiates the overemphasis on locality placed on her work, and I agree with her that the deeper implications are most certainly not bounded by state lines. But in the long run her work appears to rest considerably on the delight readers feel in recognizing known things. The warm folksy flavor and conscientious detail almost lead one to complete acceptance, and it is only on second thought that one wonders if sympathy, no matter how patient or intelligent, is enough to bring to the scene and the time.

Country People is an unpretentious, moving story of a farm family written about an era when farmers' sons and hired hands alike hoped to buy and did buy farms of their own. The patient struggle toward ownership is typical. Nothing was to be bought "until all this got paid for," wife and sons were so many hands, "August wasn't going to pay for help when he had boys of his own," a better barn always came before a better house. The simple daily occupations of self-respecting folk whose sensitive qualities had little time for blossom—"the cows had to be milked," marriage following scanty courtship brought intensive cooking and childbearing—are detailed with a fine degree of accuracy and insight. Within its limits this appears to be actual farm life as the more steady, well fixed farmers lived it.

What is wrong with this picture? Miss Suckow herself evidently feels some uneasiness. In the light of the present she analyzes the period of *Country People* as the "breathless moment" before the storm of today. She says in her introduction that she thinks she stuck too closely "to the facts"; she does not seem to recognize that a point of view determines one's choice of facts. Her attitude quite evidently is a Christian one and her selection of materials, rich as they are, was nevertheless motivated by a conscientious sense of wanting to be just to characters and scene without fully realizing the deep integration between the two. As a result there is a calmness and even tone that does not adequately hint at the incipient violence within farm life. The storm of today was at least a cloud at the time of *Country People.* I miss in these pages the constant fretting worry of farm people, their anxiety about the weather, the crops, "if the heat don't let up the corn will burn," the undertow, in short, that finally washed up in the years following the War, culminating in disaster much deeper than any predicated merely on drought or the present economic crisis.

Miss Suckow feels the need to bridge the gap between the past and the present, and this need, it seems to me, would not be felt if the groundwork had been more amply provided for. No one expects mortgage sales to be stopped by united action in the time of *Country People,* but something of the germ that made such events possible might be implied. Miss Suckow in her synopsis of the future careers of her different characters allows Frank to keep his farm by virtue of the united action of farm neighbors, but she hastens to add that it was done through mutual agreement of those present and "there were no guns or tear gas." This repudiation of the idea of violence is extremely important as a clue to her basic attitude.

It permeates *The Bonney Family*. Miss Suckow claims for this novel that it "has something of the pastoral quality of a small town on an inland river," and she is correct. One is justified in questioning how realistic such a conception may be. My own researches would lead me to repudiate the notion that any small town anywhere at any time, realistically conceived, had quite that complete sunny quality—any more than a "breathless moment" actually occurred in the pattern of the farm struggle, properly understood. The conflict was there, working underground like a mole, and Miss Suckow by ignoring it softens all the material in the novels and short stories. She earns great credit by her choice of simple, ordinary people and her refusal to exploit them by melodrama. An important aspect of American life is portrayed in these pages, but the author's point of view is limited by an organic weakness, revealed in Miss Suckow's notion that the recognition of individual characteristics is somehow separate from recognition of the background and its social implications. This divided vision weakens the force of her novels and at the same time endows her characters with a too complacent tenderness. One may compare "The Bonney Family" with a much earlier novel, also about a minister's family in Iowa, *The Damnation of Theron Ware*, by Harold Frederic, to see the difference between the searching mind and a searching mind too saturated with the milk of human kindness.

Josephine Herbst. *The New Republic*.
October 21, 1936, pp. 318–19

Two years in the life of an Iowa town around 1900 [are chronicled in *New Hope*.] The new minister comes with his family as the book opens; at the end he is leaving for another parish. In between, Miss Suckow creates a snug, neighborly little world, in which fried chicken and hot biscuits go nicely with the milk of human kindness. A happy epitaph to a safe and simple period of our history.

The New Yorker. February 28, 1942, p. 81

Seven plaintive, formless pieces [*Some Others and Myself*] written in a sentimental, neighborly fashion, about small-town people and country people. There is also a long memoir of Miss Suckow's religious development.

The New Yorker. January 12, 1952,
pp. 83–84

To anyone born after World War I, Ruth Suckow's new novel may seem no more contemporary than an old-fashioned Sunday sermon, no closer to modern literature than Horatio Alger. It may be hard to believe that she was once praised as a realist, and that so joyous a literary . . . [cynic] as Henry Louis Mencken cheered her on and gave her houseroom in his *American Mercury*.

The fact is, Author Suckow has not changed at all, but life has. The Iowa that was her childhood home is still the source of her fictional plots. In *The John Wood Case,* her first novel in seven years, the period is Teddy Roosevelt's time, and the theme is the . . . [morality] of that era.

In modern fiction's psychological jungle, the homespun plot seems both soothing and revolutionary. John Wood, trusted employee of a land-company, is regarded as a paragon of virtue in his town. . . .

The fact is that that best of fathers and husbands, John Wood, has been stealing the firm's money to speculate on the Chicago stock exchange. What interests Author Suckow is how the old Iowans she knew so well square the dreadful event with conscience, with character based on Biblical supports, with the responses of common humanity. Some, including old friends, are uncompromisingly unforgiving. Others, knowing that John Wood broke the code in the hope of easing life for his sick wife, want to be charitable. But for young Philip, life seems smashed, and his agony is the greater because he had worshiped his father. In working out an ending to this story, Author Suckow is still the realist who stirred Mencken's enthusiasm.

Time. May 11, 1959, p. 103

The name Ruth Suckow was well known in the 1920s, when Realistic treatments of the Middle West were the vogue in American fiction. During the first fifteen years of her writing career, she published some forty short stories and critical essays, three novelettes, and six novels. All her fiction had Iowa settings; all bore the hallmark of convincing authenticity. The young author possessed a truth-telling temperament and a total disdain for pretentiousness. Her literary style, acquired through unremitting self-discipline, reflected these qualities. Quiet and restrained, it was characterized by detachment and almost stark simplicity. Yet her critical comments struck home. The rebels of the Realistic movement claimed her as their own.

In the 1930s, when regional writing was under scrutiny, Miss Suckow's works were often noted as exemplars. As Sinclair Lewis put it, they were "genuinely native." Gifted with a poetic sense of place, the young writer valued the local quality as "that which gives form, color, and flavor"; but she hastened to add that "It does not give ultimate significance." She discovered beauty in commonplace surroundings, worth in ordinary lives, and pathos in undistinguished human struggle. In the Midwestern character, she perceived "a certain downright quality, a plainness, a simple freshness." Her assessment of the "folks" culture, dominated by the common desire to "get ahead," was central in all her early works and culminated in her important novel *The Folks.*

Though Ruth Suckow was justly classified as a Realist and as a regionalist, she was something more. That "something more" has never been adequately assessed. Most of her early critics were satisfied to exclaim over her scrupulous fidelity to her chosen locale and its people; later, as her books and stories appeared less frequently, commentators failed to analyze them in depth. Scholarly appraisals of her works are rare, and are confined for the most part to brief (though laudatory) mentions in general studies of fiction of the period. Aside from one unpublished doctoral dissertation, no full-length study of her work in its entirety has appeared. It is a regrettable fact that at the time of her death in 1960, Ruth Suckow and her works were not as well known as they had been thirty years earlier at the height of her career. Yet her books are not period pieces or local-color oddities. Though they reflect their region and their era, they have universality. They deserve a place in the chronicle of American literary achievement.

Leedice McAnelly Kissane. *Ruth Suckow*
(New York: Twayne, 1969), n.p.

Only a few American women novelists and short story writers have achieved and preserved a position among the foremost of American authors. Ruth Suckow in the 1920s appeared to be destined for such distinction. But in the decades that followed this role seemed to become less secure as writers and readers responded to changing moods and forces in America. . . .

Cherishing the common and universal in her fiction, she shunned the critics' term of regionalist as a misinterpretation of her intent. An examination of her entire work leads us to accept Ruth Suckow's sense of the enduring in the rural life styles of her narratives and the folkways of her people. For the 1970s her "folks" thesis as the basis of American civilization has particular interest. . . .

Her originality stems from her choice of the Iowa scene as subject matter, to which she brings knowledge, talent, and compassion. Genuine affection and intimate acquaintance are combined to create an authentic delineation of scene. Her eye for visual detail imparts to the scene a convincing reality, created by a faithfulness to minutiae. In her interiors, every object has the preciousness of the familiar and cherished, and the power of her landscape descriptions is the result of her aesthetic response to the scenic beauty of Iowa.

Her narrative technique is most successful when she concentrates upon the small incident which has deeper implications for thought. The incidents themselves are commonplace; they become significant through her capacity to suggest these overtones.

Her portraiture also reveals sympathy and perceptiveness. Comprehension of the child's emotions of pleasure and pain enables her to portray him with convincing sensitivity. The old people, experiencing a variety of ills, are treated compassionately to evoke pathos. And in all age groups, she makes poignant the sufferings of the inarticulate.

Margaret Stewart Omrcanin. *Ruth Suckow:*
A Critical Study of Her Fiction
(Philadelphia: Dorrance, 1972), pp. 1, 181

Iowa Interiors tells of the generations, the difficult hours and days working the land, the parents and children caught up in family, small town and village anxieties. Every situation and theme is recorded in a quiet but singularly skillful and serious manner. Ruth Suckow is especially interesting with old couples who have lived together in a compromise that always denies part of their feelings; they live, these enduring couples, usually in a social structure or with the mere bad luck of nature that does not justly accommodate their efforts and needs.

In one story, a "golden wedding" party is accomplished with brilliant accuracy and without sentimentality. There is a sense in the old people, particularly the women, that life is to be endured as a destiny and dignity finally accompanies a certain rough good sense and hard work.

Questioning is nearly always an inchoate anxiety driven away by the bustle and the drudgery of duty and routine. The stories are brilliantly alive, truthful, and alert to the rhythms of speech and feeling.

Elizabeth Hardwick. Introduction to Ruth
Suckow. Iowa Interiors (1926; New York:
Arno, 1977), pp. 2–3

Probably no one has given us as true a picture of Midwestern life as Ruth Suckow has. With the accuracy of a photograph, her fiction describes little towns and farms and rural crossroads. The people living there have the faces of Iowa and speak with the accents of Iowa. A person who has actually lived in this region is likely to recognize it instantly in the pages of a Suckow novel.

Willa Cather's quiet, almost poetic narratives, Sherwood Anderson's accounts of frustrated people, Sinclair Lewis's satire—all these stories of the Midwest are valuable in their way, and our literature would be the poorer without them. But without the music of Willa Cather, without the pathos of Anderson, and without the sting of Lewis, Ruth Suckow makes us conscious of the very texture of Midwestern life. She takes one into her world, doing so in a quiet way that seems to have nothing to do with art. One is rarely conscious that he is reading about events in a certain place. He knows only that he is there and that he cares about what is happening.

Everything she wrote fits into the over-all pattern of her art. It is an art that has to do not only with surface matters of sunny fields and tree-lined streets, of small-town banks and schools and churches, of middle-class rituals such as High School commencement exercises and Memorial Day services. It is an art that does what all true art must do: it anatomizes the crises of the human spirit.

Abigail Ann Hamblen. Ruth Suckow (Boise:
Boise State University Western Writers
Series, 1978), pp. 5–6

Despite the praise of so distinguished a critic as H. L. Mencken, who compared her favorably to Sherwood Anderson, Ruth Suckow has not received a great deal of critical attention. When her fiction has been discussed, most of the interpretation and praise have been given to her novels of generational change and family conflict, *Country People* (1924) and *The Folks* (1934), and to her first book of short stories, *Iowa Interiors* (1926). One volume that has received almost no attention is her last book of short stories, *Some Others and Myself* (1952). The neglect of these stories is no doubt due to what one critic has called "their relaxed and somewhat discursive" manner. Clearly the stories in *Some Others and Myself* do lack the tight plotting and disciplined concentration of effect that one expects from the short story. In their sprawling, meditative style, they seem at times more properly reminiscences or personal essays. But I would argue that this style is precisely suited to the purposes of these stories and that the significant aesthetic effects of *Some Others and Myself* must be sought in the volume as a whole rather than in its individual parts. Looked at in this way, *Some Others and Myself* reveals both its great beauty, which is a beauty of resolution rather than of conflict, and Suckow's best quality as a writer, a certain Jamesian fineness of mind that refuses ever to simplify the human. . . .

If *Some Others and Myself* is a book of women it also is a book of persons, for Suckow repeatedly emphasizes the concrete person's transcendence of all categories. In this purpose lies the reason for her stories' relative looseness and meditative quality. Suckow is not so much interested here in the hard edge of character, which the tightly unified short story can brilliantly reveal, as she is in depth of character, which develops and discloses itself only through long experience. The depth of her characters' lives emerges not from a single dramatic action or gesture but from long-sustained, repetitive actions. Because the drama of her "half hidden" women plays itself out only over a long course of time, Suckow turns to a relatively free form that combines a focus on the present with recollection and meditative interpretation of character. This is not to say that she abandons the devices of the short story altogether. Several of the stories lead to moments of climactic perception or epiphany, and her command of the significant surface of detail to reveal character is everywhere apparent.

Two purposes of *Some Others and Myself*, then, are to make visible the lives of otherwise invisible women and to insist on the irreducibility of concrete persons. A third purpose is suggested by the book's title, which points not only to the fact that it contains stories and a memoir but also and more significantly to the self's necessary relationship to others. Whatever the self is, Ruth Suckow insists, it becomes so only among other selves. The narrator of several of the stories realizes this as she returns to the others who have been such a part of her own past. Again and again she discovers the close, sometimes suffocating, interdependence of others and at the same time the role of those others in making her what she is.

Fritz Oelschlager. *Western American Literature.* 21, 1986, pp. 112–13

Always respected as a regional fiction of depth and integrity, Ruth Suckow's spare, sometimes almost plotless character studies and examinations of thwarted or narrow Iowa lives were often, during her lifetime, criticized for being too unpleasant and for piling up excessive detail. This criticism now seems overdrawn, accurate perhaps only for *Country People,* her first novel, and for some of her short stories. The novels of her middle period, studying Iowa women and families, are more even-handed, although their emphasis on relatively shallow characters living unconsidered lives and dreaming only limited dreams lends them also an air of pathos. However, her two last novels, *New Hope* (1942), and *The John Wood Case* (1959), more symbolic as well as more overtly concerned with moral issues, balance bolder dreams and goals against deeper disappointments. In both novels, a central theme is a loss of innocence, and the passing of the optimism of the frontier, or at least of early settlement, is mourned, even as the strength and endurance of those worthy of the dream is revealed. *New Hope* dramatizes this tension through the growth into awareness of a child, and *The John Wood Case* reveals it through the device of the discovery of a long-concealed crime.

Ironically, perhaps, Suckow's last novel, the only one directly centered around a clearly identified evil, is also her most optimistic. Beginning with an almost idyllic view of a family and its environment, it moves through the revelation that the idyll has always been merely an appearance to a final, hard-won sense that one at least of the participants is worthy and will be strengthened by his suffering.

Mary Jean De Marr. *Midamerica.* 16,
1989, p. 65

Ruth Suckow's sensitive and realistic fiction is filled with portraits of women and of their families. Among the novels of the productive middle period which produced her finest work, *The Bonney Family* (1928), *The Kramer Girls* (1930), and *The Folks* (1934) concentrate on families, including portraits of fathers and sons as well as of mothers and daughters. In these novels, however, the female characters tend to be the more fully rounded and completely characterized; their choices and their fates, no matter how mundane, are in general far more compelling than the stories of their male counterparts. As its title indicates, *The Kramer Girls* studies a family consisting in fact almost entirely of women. In that same period, *The Odyssey of a Nice Girl* (1925) and *Cora* (1929) focus primarily on their protagonists, while studying also the women—and to a much lesser degree, the men—who influence them. *Odyssey* and *Cora* are unique among Suckow's novels in that each follows a single female protagonist on her life quest from childhood to maturity, exploring her professional goals and attainments (or lack of attainments) as well as her personal, emotional questing. They differ importantly in that *Odyssey,* like most of Suckow's fiction, is set among the middle-class, while *Cora,* the subject here, centers on a character from a working-class family.

Cora is Suckow's most focused treatment of a theme which underlay much of her fiction about women in her middle period: the conflict for an intelligent woman between love and work or, to put it another way, the difficulties for a woman in a patriarchal society who attempts to find both personal and professional success and fulfillment. In this novel, Suckow approaches the theme in two primary ways: through following the search of Cora Schwietert for a complete and fulfilling life, and through contrasting Cora's experiences with those of several other women who struggle through different circumstances or make different choices. Suckow's habitual effective use of the Midwestern scene and her characteristic flat or repressed tone combine well with her realistically grim assessment of an Iowa woman's scant likelihood of success in balancing personal and professional goals in the 1920s.

Mary Jean De Marr. Midamerica. 18,
1991, pp. 80–81

In her novel *The Folks,* Ruth Suckow describes the lives and times of the Ferguson family of Belmond, Iowa, in the first three decades of this century. Recently reprinted by the University of Iowa Press, this book describes the conflicting desires of American middle-class families to sink roots and establish communities, while at the same time restlessly seeking out alternative communities and details.

Ruth Suckow . . . an Iowa author . . ., wrote of the rural and small town "folk" of the midwest. The word "folks" stands for the people who collectively make up the community, who share beliefs and goals—for "folklife" as Suckow believed—but it is also a midwestern euphemism for "parents" or older generation.

The "folks" in Suckow's book are Fred and Annie Ferguson; Suckow devotes the first and last of the six sections of the book to them. The other four sections describe their four children: Carl, Margaret, Dorothy, and Bunny. In graphic and poignant detail, Suckow penetrates the repressed psyches of these people, the said and the unsaid, their hidden shame and frustrated desires.

Suckow also beautifully illustrates the constant gravitation between geographic poles these people feel in an increasingly mobile society, and what these poles represent psychologically. . . .

While historical events of the period—the roaring twenties, prohibition, and the Depression—are secondary to detailed psychological portraits of the characters, *The Folks* should interest cultural historians and literary critics alike. Suckow's book testifies to the complexity of the inner lives of white middle-class families as they worked out their relationships with each other and their culture in a conflicted era.

Lynn Cothern. American Studies
International. 30:2, 1992, p. 112

SWENSON, MAY (UNITED STATES) 1919–89

May Swenson, in her second book, *A Cage of Spines* . . . is lively, ingenious, and fanciful. She enters the world of things, animate and inanimate, without self-consciousness and with a rare sense of play. She tells riddles, observes the weather, and turns her mind toward pebbles, birds, and small animals as readily as toward people. Her faults, by no means extensive, are perhaps too continuous a sparkle and an occasional lapse in the sense of scale, for some things *are* larger than others. She is an accurate naturalist, however, and an imaginative one.

Louise Bogan. *The New Yorker.*
April 27, 1958, pp. 237–38

May Swenson . . . is a poet who sees singly, and she is, to my personal taste, one of the most ingenious and delightful younger poets writing today *(To Mix with Time: New and Selected Poems)*. She has, at any rate, probably the best eye for nature. . . .

Her attention to nature gives May Swenson's poems a directness of gaze that is sometimes lacking when she turns to other, apparently broader subjects. She needs, perhaps, the concreteness of things close at hand in order to see deeply; it is as though language, in her hands, responded naturally only to the actual and palpable. She has a staggering poetic equipment: visual acuity, a sense of form, a fine ear for rhythm and the colloquial. Among her recent poems there are too many with high pretensions, in the shapes of arrows or zigzags or earthquakes, dealing with the Scheme of Things. A series of travel poems—with the exception of one about a bullfight—strikes me as terribly self-conscious, as though someone had been Taking Notes. But even if, in her straining for fresh ways of saying things, this poet's sureness sometimes deserts her, she just cannot go wrong with nature poems. They are *seen;* the husks and kernels of nature are *there.* And sometimes, at moments of great simplicity, her poems go almost as far in eloquence as poems can—as in a favorite of mine called "Question". . . . A poem like this, in its simple lyricism, makes us forget all questions about the direction of poetry, about schools and generations. It is, after all, a song; and songs hold their own secrets. This one may hold the secret of long life.

Peter Davison. *The Atlantic Monthly.*
December, 1963, pp. 84–85

No one today is more deft and lucky in discovering a poem than May Swenson. Her work often appears to be proceeding calmly, just descriptive and accurate; but then suddenly it opens into something that looms beyond the material, something that impends and implies. You get to feeling that if the world were different she would have to lie in order to make her point, but that fortunately the world is so various and fortuitous that she can be truthful and also marvelously effective.

So graceful is the progression in her poems that they launch confidently into any form, carrying through it to easy, apt variations. Often her way is to define things, but the definitions have a stealthy trend: what she chooses and the way she progresses heap upon the reader a consistent, incremental effect.

An example poem is "The Little Rapids." The words nimbly leap, at their best; they know what they are about. And the reader finds that they are about the heart, "its zest constant / even in sleep, / its padded roar / bounding in the grotto of the breast." The words, vivid and apt as they are, are not enough to account for their success; the reader finds himself encountering adventures that converge into the one steady vision of the whole poem.

In the continuing work of Miss Swenson the question becomes: will her luck provide worthy encounters? Will she become distracted by this poking so interestedly in a dilettantish way into stray things? Sometimes, as in "The Secret in the Cat," you think that she is just clever, apt with diction, able to maintain a chosen topic and to rev it up. But that same cleverness often leads into wilder and more interesting regions, as in "A Bird's Life." Some of the cleverest poems, just through their intense unity, succeed in becoming greater things, as in the heart poem mentioned earlier, or in "Sleeping Overnight on the Shore," or in a wonderful poem about "The Watch." Partly, the most successful poems succeed through the ambition, the scope of the curiosity, of the writer; she pursues remote things, how the universe started, what will happen when . . . if. . . .

William Stafford. *Poetry.* December, 1967,
pp. 184–85

May Swenson is the poet of the perceptible. No writer employs with greater care the organs of sense to apprehend and record the surfaces of the world. She is the exemplar of that first canon of the poet—*Behold!*

From the time her poetry began appearing in the early 1950s in such places as *New Directions in Prose and Poetry, Discovery,* the *New Yorker,* and *Poetry,* Miss Swenson's work in its concentration on the sensible has been very much her own. The preoccupation with perception dominates the poetry of her successive volumes—*Another Animal* (1954), *A Cage of Spines* (1958), *To Mix with Time: New and Selected Poems* (1963), *Poems to Solve* (1966), and *Half Sun Half Sleep* (1967). One can name, however, if not influences, at any rate some poets whose work runs parallel to hers. Her development of visual detail has some relationship to the accurate reporting of Marianne Moore. It is sometimes close to that other remarkable declarer of what is there, Elizabeth Bishop. Her interest in nature, its small creatures and their large implications, is reminiscent of Emily Dickinson. In form, her work may have had some relationship to the experiments of E. E. Cummings, though it has always been a distant one, her experiments having gone farther into the visual and less into the verbal than his. . . .

It is as an observer that May Swenson has become best known. Such a comment as Robert Lowell's "Miss Swenson's quick-eyed poems should be hung with permanent fresh paint signs" represents a common reaction. Miss Swenson achieves this freshness by a good eye enlivened by imagination. But however imaginative, her poetry is continually tied to accuracy of sight, to truth, to the literal, and concrete. This is so even when the truth is conveyed by metaphor or in a spirit of aesthetic play. From the beginning, Miss Swenson has demonstrated an unusual ability to set down accurate and detailed observations. . . .

Miss Swenson's involvement with the perceptibly solid is further seen in her placement of the poem on the page. Lines and spaces are carefully arranged in patterns appropriate to the subject. Some words are given typographical emphasis by being set off and repeated. Even punctuation and capitalization—or the lack of them—are arranged for visual effect. . . .

This linking of the parts of the poem, the care in its visual physical arrangement, is not related to form alone. It reflects the careful observation, the respect for the whole range of the senses, that goes into the language and concepts that Miss Swenson presents. Her poems are not limited to linear time; they are patterns in space as well. The shaped poem represents the poet's response to the aesthetic need for structure, a need met in other poets by the formal stanza or the syllabic or metric line. The enclosing of the poem within spatial boundaries rather than auditory-rhythmic limits is especially appropriate to the perceptual qualities of Miss Swenson's art.

Ann Stanford. *Southern Review.*
Winter, 1969, pp. 58–59, 68–69, 71

She is known as a nature poet, "one of the few good poets who write good poems about nature . . . not just comparing it to states of mind or society," as Elizabeth Bishop has remarked. You can easily cull a bestiary from her work, which would include geese, turtles, an owl and its prey, a bee and a rose, frogs, fireflies, cats and caterpillars, landscapes and cityscapes, and always with a wondering, curious eye, an intense concern about the structure and texture of her subject, an extraordinary tactility. "The pines, aggressive erect tails of cats," begins a poem on "The Forest." A poem called "Spring Uncovered" begins, "Gone the scab of ice that kept it snug, / the lake is naked," and ends where "a grackle, fat as burgundy, / gurgles on a limb" with "bottle-glossy feathers." She watches things over long periods, and tracks her metaphors through itineraries of implications, with pleasure.

But beyond the naturalist's patient observation lies something else. What critics have called Swenson's "calculated naïveté" or her ability to become "a child, but a highly sophisticated child," is actually that childlike ability to envision something freshly, to ask incessant questions and always be prepared for unexpected answers—required of the creative scientist. "What things really are we would like to know," she murmurs, and what else is the motive of the speculative intellect? Swenson's poetry asks as many questions as a four-year-old, and she wants to know not only how things are made and what they resemble, but where they are going and how we fit in. . . .

While Swenson does not write on feminist themes most of the time, she does so occasionally, with electrifying results. . . . Most often, she blends, she balances. Science, technology, the mental life of observation, speculation: she has invaded these traditionally "masculine" territories. Yet her consistent intimacy with her world, which contains no trace of the archetypal "masculine" will to conquer or control it, seems archetypally "feminine." So does the way she lets herself be precise yet tentative and vulnerable about her observations where a comparable male poet, perhaps driven by the need to overcome alienation, might be pretentious (Snyder?), pedantic (Olson?), nervous (Ammons? James Wright?) or agonized (Kinnell?); and her affinity for the small-scale object, like Emily Dickinson's, also reads like a feminine characteristic. . . .

Swenson has always had an individual style, though bearing traces here and there of Cummings, Marianne Moore, and especially Emily Dickinson. She has always been committed to formal experimentation, and she has often played with the shapes of poems. . . .

Swenson does not theorize on the subject, but her work shows some ways to express our relation to the natural world as we comprehend it. The shapes in *Iconographs* are shapes of speculation, balanced between the patterned and the random—for so we presently guess Nature to be—and attempting to capture both the ways we fit into the world and the ways we cannot fit. They are playful, quirky, eccentric, and imply that these are qualities intrinsic to the world as well as ourselves. But Swenson is modest as well as mentally fearless, and will not let us pretend that our model-building is more than that.

Alicia Ostriker. *The American Poetry Review.* March–April, 1978, pp. 35–36, 38

These poems [in *New and Selected Things Taking Place*] mutter in the passive voice: "it is observed"; "it happens." The event, the text, stands out even as our guide to it steps back so as not to block the view. May Swenson indeed camouflages herself marvelously, and her protective coloration conveys respect. So we see "The World" clarified but glean only hints of "her world." For the poetry has no heroine and no heroics. In this she differs a great deal from so many modern women poets who attempt to find themselves—or at least such fragments of self as are retrievable—in their work. May Swenson, on the contrary, effaces herself, blends into the landscape. . . .

Swenson searches heaven and earth for a vantage point. The problem is, none exists. The meanings of God's spangled heavens have long since split out into the Einsteinian universe. Matter is motion. Fixed viewpoints swirl away and Swenson so much needs a firm footing and a clear view at first hand of things taking place. The sun, moon, and earth spinning in space are for her, and nearly everybody else, news—acceptable hearsay—third-hand reports. Remote. . . .

May Swenson can fairly be described as gun-shy. *Homo sapiens* makes her nervous. If she cannot declass man a notch or two, fur and feather him as it were, objectify him, she nerves herself and resorts to anthropomorphiz-ing, as she does in the brilliant pot-calling-the-kettle-black, male-female dia-logue of "Bleeding," with its text slashed diagonally by a white ribbon of alienation. Generally May Swenson fumbles whenever she has human preoc-cupations—sporting, social, whatever—on her mind. The voiced-interaction poems drum along, their cross-cutting repetition of words monotonous and mind-numbing, like a mantra. . . .

May Swenson lives on the Eastern seaboard, writes with a Western accent, and sees with a certain amused, clear-sighted naiveté. One has the impression most poetry written by women still is an interior matter and is set within four walls. Although she is not oblivious to the problems of being female, May Swenson is not indoors enough, let alone enough in her own skin, to accommodate herself to the woman poet's present persona. She does not want to "make waves" in the sense of stirring up trouble. She leaves the problem of gender pretty much alone, if only because it could be messy (cf. "Bleeding"). She edges away from the subjective, yet she holds with Romanticism, by which I mean an interest in the particular over the general, the single over the recurring. In selecting events, animals, men, scenery, topics, she is drawn to the non-nondescript, the unique occasion: a moon-landing, the strange animal (bison not cow), the odd man out (a blind man), the picturesque canyons, lakes, or into the gothic and the magical.

But when she is put on her mettle and forced to catch the meaning of the antithetically banal or the flux and flurry of water and snow, wind and weather, then she gives up poems such as "Working on Wall Street" and "Looking Uptown" and her *Iconographs*. Then she shines.

Rosemary Johnson. *Parnassus.*
Fall–Winter, 1978, pp. 47–50, 52, 59

May Swenson's *New and Selected Things Taking Place* collects nearly thirty years of her remarkable poetry. At sixty, she may well be the fiercest, most inquisitive poet of her generation; certainly few are more brilliant or more independent of mien. Her poems . . . are characterized by an extreme reti-cence of personality, an abundant energy, and an extraordinary intercourse between the natural and intellectual worlds. She has always been as formal as poets come, demonstrating early and late a skilled employment of tradi-tional verse as well as a passion for invented patterns. There are two central obsessions in her work: the search for a proper perspective and the celebra-tion of life's embattled rage to continue. Her poems ask teleological questions and answer them, insofar as answers are ever possible, in every conceivable poetic strategy: she writes narrative, catalog, image, concrete, interrogatory, and sequence poems (often mixing these in a single work). Her language is generally sonorous, remarkable for its Anglo-Saxon stress, alliteration, extensive word fusions, and a devotion (now declining, it appears) to rhyme. She has made language an instrument for pursuit of ideas, but always ideas discoverable only in things of the experiential world. She believes, apparently, that the world functions according to some hidden final purpose, and further-more, that a right apprehension ultimately reveals a Coleridgean intercon-nectedness of all parts. . . .

Nothing so excites Swenson's imagination or reveals her poetic investi-gation as that image of flight. In poems about airplanes, birds, insects, and especially space exploration, she celebrates the joy of flight. Motion is both her subject and her image, being life itself. Flight, however, rarely means escape; it is her means for exploration, penetration, for travel to and through the world; it is what humans cannot naturally do, but . . . what becomes the passage toward and into vision. . . .

Vision, seeing, looking, recording are so pervasive in her poems that one almost forgets how active she makes all the senses in the service of penetrat-ing surfaces. Flight is not only the revelation of human bondage, it is also the vehicle of imaginative and intellectual possibilities. . . .

Never a poet of ennui or cynicism, though often a poet of elegiac grief, she believes that all is beautiful if seen properly. . . .

Dedicated as they are to angles of vision, avoiding autobiography and personality, Swenson's poems necessarily emphasize structure—sometimes to the point of mannerism. Often enough they possess a wonderful lyricism that celebrates; but primarily they nominate, and this occasionally leads to an annoyingly indiscriminate series of similes; a thing that looks like this. Or this, or this. This mannerism reveals a kind of "scientific" attitude in her work, an attitude also marked by often esoteric and technical terminology— not in itself a problem though it helps create the impression of a dispassionate stance when there is passion present and the need to show it. Swenson's reticence may sometimes mean the difference between a powerful experience and no experience, as in riddles or dry humor. Indeed, one of Swenson's characteristics is a wry wit which sometimes trails off into whimsy, into the glib and clever. . . .

If Swenson sometimes generates consternation and dismay, the fault is born of a poetry urgently trying to tell us that everything matters, a poetry so affirmative that we cannot escape knowing we matter. Even random read-ing here produces surprise, delight, love, wisdom, joy, and grief. May Swen-son transforms the ordinary little-scrutinized world to a teeming, flying first creation.

Dave Smith. Poetry. February, 1980,
pp. 291–95

Nobody writes poetry quite like May Swenson anymore. She is a genuine anomaly: mischievous, inquisitive in the extreme, and totally given over to the task of witnessing the physical world. . . . Her most obvious precursor is Marianne Moore. Unlike Moore, she rarely makes literary allusions (she does have a fine poem here [*In Other Words*] addressed to Elizabeth Bishop upon hearing of her death), yet she shares Moore's enthusiasm for detail, especially as it pertains to nature.

Never solemn or self-indulgent, eschewing the big finale, Swenson is intent on noticing everything around her while preferring herself to remain in the wings. Sometimes she subjugates the self to such an extent that it may seem on the verge of disappearing altogether from the poem. But her language is so sensuous and her eye so exacting, one instead comes away from her writing feeling one has been in the presence of a mind as comprehensive as Darwin's, as chimerical as Herbert's or Dickinson's, as felicitous as Donne's. . . .

A person from another planet reading her poetry might believe there were no wars on Earth and that death and the postmortem realm do not receive here the kind of attention we in fact spend on them. Only infrequently do we get to see the darker side of Swenson.

Dennis Sampson. Hudson Review. 41,
1988, p. 387–88

May Swenson's new book [*In Other Words*]—her first since *New and Selected Things Taking Place* some nine years ago—is a welcome addition to a paradoxical oeuvre. Few writers who on occasion strongly remind us of others have created so fully recognizable and inimitable a world. A playful spirit for whom writing is a (very exacting) game—as even the titles of *Poems to Solve* and *More Poems to Solve* suggest—she has in her typographical and syntactical ingenuity recalled, and often surpassed, e. e. cummings. Her penchant for scientific subjects, and her scientist's patience for documentation, evoke Marianne Moore and W. H. Auden. More surprisingly, this very modern poet who exuberantly breaks lines, and rules, in unexpected places takes one back to the 17th century—to the far sterner-minded George Herbert— to find another poet so dedicated to fashioning the right form for the fresh occasion each poem presents. . . .

We have too few comic poets. Swenson provides comedy in two senses: marrying her words off in one happy ending after another, she makes us laugh as she does so. But whether she writes in jest or in earnest, she belongs to that rare company of poets who convert the arbitrary correspondences among the sounds of words into what seems a pre-existing order. *In Other Words* confirms that there are no words other than her own, exactly, for what the language discovers in May Swenson, or for what she gives back to it.

Mary Jo Salter. The New Republic.
March 7, 1988, pp. 40–41

The posthumous publication of May Swenson's poems celebrating Eros adds luster to the reputation of a major American poet. Swenson (1913–89) came from Logan, Utah, to enter the world of honors, awards, and fellowships as her poetry became known. She writes a language rich in sensual texture, rich in rhyme, and strong in rhythm. Still, however enchanting her word-play or music, what strikes the reader more deeply in these poems is the intelligence of her understanding. Love, as she tells us about it, has little of the narrative or dramatic interest we might expect. Instead, she exposes the nature of attraction with the precision of a physics text revealing nature's laws. Love for her is akin to Martin Buber's definition of God: a power to be found, from time to time, "between me and thee." Dialectical relationships of all kinds arrest her eyes: tree to tree, bee to flower, human male-female lovers, but also human to self, mind to heart, even a human to his shadow. She feels, and makes us feel, the dialectical form of our most vital moments. . . .

Erotic appeal addressed to the ear, eye, and mind together makes Swenson's most powerful poems memorable. This is a sophisticated poetry in its use of line length, refrains, typography, and tone. The short, one- or two-word line of "A Couple" brings us like a zoom lens into the mating of a bee and a flower. A delicious feeling of a rondo is created in the irregular repeat of the title line in "All That Time," enacting the meaning of the poem in the form. The intricate beauty of love matches between the sentence and the line, as in the virtuoso "Four-Word Lines," indicates a familiarity with the traditions of Western love poetry. The talking tone of a very erotic poem such as "In Love Made Visible" reminds one of the way Anna Akhmatova speaks coolly of intimate things. This tone unites the physical and spiritual dimensions of love. For Swenson, the very truth of our identity remains with the lover, as she says in "You Are": "no one / can be sure / by himself / of his own being."

Appropriately, pairs of poems have been arranged on facing pages to speak to one another. A mating scene of water birds in "The Willets" is similar to the nonchalant, impersonal bonding of two people in "Holding the Towel." Love and death are juxtaposed in both "Satanic Form" and "Night Before the Journey." In the first, artifacts of civilization (clocks, metal boxes, glass bricks) are overcome by "the intricate body of man without rivet or nail" and other natural forms "not cursed with symmetry." In the second, love asserts its power to enchant and bless as the world ends. Single lines, of course, come to dwell in the reader's imagination. Swenson's words about fear impress me: "Empty of fear and therefore without weight," "our very skin— / a sheath to keep us pure of fear," and the lilting "O love the juice in the green stem growing."

Doris Earnshaw. *World Literature Today.*
67, 1993, p. 185

The familiar voice in May Swenson's *In Other Words: New Poems* speaks with a naturalist's love for the variety and particularly of the world. In poems that take great delight in discovering the shapes and associations hidden in the natural world, Swenson pays homage to Marianne Moore and Elizabeth

Bishop, yet her poems are quirkier, more playful and more celebratory than [those of] her two precursors. . . .

Although May Swenson often writes about nature and geographies she is not a poet of place. Instead she is a steadfast and faithful visitor who masks her restlessness with a clear-eyed optimism and curiosity. As a result she searches with patience for "the scene beyond the apron of the eye / about to shift," as she writes in "From a Daybook." Sometimes we may feel that a poem has missed this subtle "shift." When this happens, Swenson's poems can be too purely descriptive. But even when this occurs, as it does in "Teddy Bears" and "Shuttles," the writing is always full of exuberance as the poet looks for ways to praise and enjoy the world. . . .

In Other Words is a spacious book. It is May Swenson's seventh volume of poetry and unfortunately her last. (She died in 1989.) Appearing more than two years ago, it has received scant attention yet it is a book that deserves to be read widely, for it contains a vision of incredible integrity, a vision that "lives in bodies of words."

Michael Collier. *Partisan Review*.
58, 1991, pp. 586–87

Maybe I had too high expectations for this collection [*The Love Poems of May Swenson*] when it was first announced. A new book by May Swenson is always welcome, and this time normal anticipation was heightened by the possibility that her estate had decided to publish work that shyness or prudence had prevented her from making available during her lifetime. Hopes slipped a notch when the credits page stated that only thirteen of the poems were previously unpublished; five have before now appeared in magazines, but the remaining thirty-seven can be found in earlier volumes of her poetry.

The title isn't quite accurate. For "love" we should substitute "erotic." In a quite good poem called "Café Tableau," the eroticism involved is not even the author's but high-voltage description of the visible attraction between a white woman and a black waiter. Only in the poem "Year of the Double Spring" (one of the poems already collected) is the poet's beloved portrayed in non-erotic contexts so as to emerge as specific and individual— one result being that painful currents of feeling are allowed to appear as they inevitably must when love beyond pure eroticism is dealt with realistically.

Alfred Corn. *Poetry*. 161, February, 1993,
pp. 295–96

SZYMBORSKA, WISLAWA (POLAND) 1923–

Wisława Szymborska is a contemporary of such important Polish poets as Tadeusz Różewicz, Zbigniew Herbert, and Miron Białoszewski. She was born in 1923 in Kórnik (the Poznań region), but moved to Cracow at the age of eight and has lived there to this day. Her first published poem dates from 1945. As with most Polish writers who made their debuts after World War II, much of her early work was infused with the ideology of socialist realism as then forcefully propagated by the Communist Party. These poems were collected in the volumes *Dlatego żyjemy* (That's what we live for, 1952), and *Pytania zadawane sobie* (Questions put to myself, 1954). In retrospect, the best that can be said about them is that they are not so strident in tone as similar exercises produced at the time, and that they do contain a few personal lyrics. It was in 1957, with the volume *Wołanie do Yeti* (Calling out to Yeti), that Szymborska abandoned overtly political themes, found her true voice, and began to build the enormous reputation she enjoys in Poland today.

A painstaking craftsman, she has published a volume of twenty-five to thirty-five poems every five years or so since 1957. They are: *Sól* (Salt, 1962); *Sto pociech* (A million laughs, 1967); *Wszelki wypadek* (There but for the grace, 1972); *Wielka liczba* (A great number, 1976). Though slim, each volume has been hailed as a major event in Polish literature. The most recent of them, *Wielka liczba,* appeared in a printing of 10,000 copies and was sold out within a week. Szymborska is that rare phenomenon which has not been seen in Poland since the days of "Skamander": a serious poet who enjoys a large audience. Perhaps even rarer, she scarcely ever gets a bad review. All the important critics of poetry in Poland—Artur Sandauer, Ryszard Matuszew-ski, Jerzy Kwiatkowski—are consistently enthusiastic about her work. Her readers are attracted by the unusually wide range of themes; by her skill at blending the traditional and the avant-garde; by the innovative uses of lexicon and syntax; by the balance struck between skepticism and love in her view of the human condition; by the combination of high seriousness, gentle humor, and indulgent irony. Better than any other contemporary Polish poet, her work exemplifies the ideal of poetry put forth by Pushkin in *Eugene Onegin:* "ishchu soiuza / Volshebnykhzvukov, chuvstv i dum" (I seek the union / Of magic sounds, feelings, and thoughts).

Magnus J. Kryński and Robert A. McGuire.
Polish Review. 24:3, 1979, pp. 3–4

Wisława Szymborska's poetry is—above all—marked by a striking universality which allows for widely variant readings. In his review of Szymborska's 1976 collection, *A Great Number (Wielka liczba),* Stanisław Barańczak primarily stressed the sociological aspect of her poetry as it is revealed in her use of language. Her language and images, he argues, are nearly always concrete and situational. In his introduction to her 1977 *Poetry (Poezje),* a retrospective collection, Jerzy Kwiatkowski, relying heavily on a vocabulary sprinkled with philosophical terminology, presents her primarily as an existentialist poet, though he does admit, "that doesn't mean at all that Szymborska's poetry is some kind of theoretical treatise on the various possibilities of the means of being laid out in verse." Czesław Miłosz, who once wondered

whether she might be a poet of limited range, now also ranks her as a philosophical poet whose "conciseness is matched only by Zbigniew Herbert."
Szymborska maintains a much more modest appraisal of her own works.
When asked in a 1975 interview to comment on the critics' naming of her as
an existential poet, she replied, "The label is flattering, but also disconcerting.
I do not engage in great philosophy, only modest poetry." In fact, poetry
itself—or to be more exact, the paradox of poetry's possibilities and limitations—is frequently the focus of Szymborska's work. . . .

"A Great Number," representative of much of Szymborska's work,
touches upon several of her common themes: 1) The element of chance or
fate, that is, the random quality of the universe, and, more importantly, the
random quality of the poet's perception of it; 2) The potential endlessness of
the universe, its vastness which cannot be comprehended in its entirety, but
can only be comprehended by perceiving selected minor elements of it; 3)
As a corollary, the importance that microscopic elements of the universe
play in making up reality: Thus, at least on perceptual grounds, meaning is
possible only because of smallness, individuality and solitude; 4) Poetry as
a means to achieving what understanding is possible. Poetry is a repository
for and preserver of life's individual elements. Consequently, poetry is the
surest element for giving meaning to the things and experiences of life, at
least insofar as meaning can be found to exist at all, and insofar as it can be
grasped by the poet. . . .

Like [contemporary Polish poet Tadeusz] Różewicz, she both affirms
and negates at the same time: negates by what she says, and affirms by the
fact that she says it. But in such lines she goes beyond Różewicz's minimalism
and achieves something akin to Bialoszewski's latent spiritualism, wherein
the bare-bones images of stoves reduced to "gray naked holes" seem to grow
out of Różewicz's bankrupt world of ruin, somehow renewed and imbued
with a new significance. Szymborska's is a poetry of healing which, while
understanding the unpleasant nature of the disease, nevertheless finds reason
to rejoice.

John Freedman. *Polish Review.*
3:2–3, 1986, pp. 137, 146–47

Polish publishers have a tradition of publishing original works written in
foreign languages. The present volume . . . [*Poezje—Poems*] a reprint of a
1981 bilingual selection of Wisława Szymborska's verse (*Sounds, Feelings,
Thoughts: Seventy Poems*) . . . belongs to that category. Given the present
shortage of paper in Poland and the resultant price tag of 2,500 złotys—a
student's entire monthly stipend in the 1970s—such an undertaking can only
be justified by Szymborska's status as one of the finest postwar Polish poets
and by the desire to acknowledge her popularity abroad.

Surprisingly missing from the Polish edition, however, are the comments
and the bibliographic note contained in the American edition; the Polish
volume remains silent as well about the translators, on whom a note would

have been appropriate, especially in light of the recent death of Magnus J. Kryński, a prominent Polish émigré. The American edition's introduction by the translators has now become the afterword. Its opening lines about Polish critics' unabating praise for Szymborska have been deleted. Later, one paragraph referring to the poems written under Stalinist rule and two paragraphs mentioning political themes, the poet's recent protest against Stalinist politics, and her involvement in the Flying University have been deleted. As a result, the footnotes have been considerably abridged. Szymbroska's poetry stands bare here, a grim reminder of taboos that are still bridling Polish society.

Alice-Catherine Carls. World Literature Today. 65, 1991, p. 519

Szymborska is a distinguished Polish poet, admired for her witty, often wry, coolly intellectual poems—poems that at the same time radiate warmth and, through their attention to the particular, often subvert the intellectual categories through which we view the world. Adam Czerniawski has translated 36 of Szymborska's poems published over the last two decades. The present volume [*People on a Bridge: Poems*] is not the first collection of Szymborska's poems in English translation. *Sounds, Feelings, Thoughts*, a selection of 70 poems (the earliest of them from the mid-1950s) in translations by Magnus J. Kryński and Robert A. Maguire, was published ten years ago (1981). That volume offered a much richer introduction to Szymborska's poetry, having a more varied and therefore more representative selection and an essay by the translators that is both longer and more informative than Czerniawski's crisp five-page evocation of Szymborska's "particular imagination." *Sounds, Feelings, Thoughts* had the additional virtue of being a facing-page, bilingual edition. Of the 36 poems in *People on a Bridge*, 20 also appear in *Sounds, Feelings, Thoughts*. But Czerniawski's translations are more felicitous, and his selection includes 16 new poems written in the 1980s.

M. G. Levine. Choice. January, 1992, p. 752

Long recognized in Poland as a leading voice in contemporary Polish poetry, Wisława Szymborska has not achieved the same popularity in the English-speaking world as other poets of her generation such as Zbigniew Herbert and Tadeusz Różewicz. Still, *People on a Bridge* is not the first introduction of Szymborska's verse to English readers. Czesław Miłosz included poems by her in his seminal anthology *Postwar Polish Poetry* (1965), and in 1981 Princeton University Press published a selection of her poems translated by Magnus Kryński and Robert Maguire. . . . Let us hope that the present volume, a welcome addition to those earlier translations, will help bring Szymborska the recognition that she deserves.

The poems selected by Adam Czerniawski came from four different collections and span a period of twenty years. Rather than adhere to chronology, Czerniawski has grouped the poems according to recurring themes, most prominently the problem of art's relationship to time, death, and reality. Thematic unity is further emphasized by a ring composition. The poems opening and closing the book (the only two given both in English translation and in the Polish original) deal with the precariousness of human life, symbolized both times by the image of a bridge, and the inability of art—despite its futile attempt to resist the flow of time—to penetrate the mystery of death and existence.

At the center of Szymborska's attention is the disparity between the limitations of the poetic imagination and the unlimited vastness of reality: "Four billion people on this earth, / but my imagination is as it was" ("Big Numbers"). The mathematical value of π comes closer to expressing the infinite richness of the universe than does the poetic imagination: "It cannot be grasped *six five three five* at a glance, / *eight nine* in a calculus / *seven nine* in imagination, / or even *three two three eight* in a conceit, that is, a comparison." Art catches only individual facts and existences, a fraction of reality. Poetry, marked by insufficiency and imperfection, is a selection, a renunciation, a passing over in silence, and a "sigh" rather than a "full breath." The poet, like anyone else, is unable to transgress his or her own "I," his own particular existence. Being himself, he cannot be what he is not.

In the opposition between reality and art, life and intellect, Szymborska declares herself on the side of reality and life. Ideas are most often pretexts to kill, a deadly weapon, whether under the guise of an artistic experiment ("Experiment"), a political Utopia ("Utopia"), or ideological fanaticism ("The Terrorist, He Watches"). Szymborska sides with reality against art and ideology, and this choice situates her in the mainstream of postwar Polish poetry alongside Miłosz, Herbert, and Białoszewski.

Like Białoszewski, although in a different idiom, Szymborska extols the everyday and the ordinary. Her "miracle mart" is made of barking dogs, trees reflected in a pond, gentle breezes and gusty storms, the world "ever-present." Even in dreams she appreciates most of all their ability to create the illusion of reality. In the theater she is moved by a glimpse of actors caught beneath the curtain more than by tragic tirades. Her poetry reverses the accepted view of what is important and what is unimportant; it puts forward common and humble reality at the expense of history and politics: "Pebbles by-passed on the beach can be as rounded / as the anniversaries of insurrections" ("May Be Left Untitled").

Pervaded by the spirit of contestation, Wisława Szymborska's poetry thrives on paradox. A mixture of "loftiness and common speech" ("Unwritten Poem Review"), it is subtle, witty, and ironic.

Bogdana Carpenter. *World Literature Today.*
65, 1992, pp. 163–64

TAFDRUP, PIA (DENMARK) 1952–

Assent to life takes the place of a blocked assent to the self: an open ending is inevitable. An aspect of this relentless subjectivity is—for some of these [contemporary Danish women writers]—a new awareness of their own bodies. This . . . produces a security which facilitates an opening to a "you."

"I am the one who/ porous for your insights/ opens up in desire." With these words Pia Tafdrup rejects isolation ("Do not lock the world out/ or me in") and opens up her erotic universe of poetry. In her poems, and also in the work of Juliane Preisler, Dea Trier Mørch and Inger Christensen, the representation of sexuality connotes a feeling of community—reaching a climax in Inger Christensen's "I am you."

Annegret A. Heitmann. Introduction to *No Man's Land: An Anthology of Modern Danish Women's Literature* (Norwich, England: Norvik Press, 1987), p. 11

Is poetry splitting or healing? In his 1985 book on poetics *Mit lys brænder* (My light is burning) Søren Ulrik Thomsen . . . answered that consciousness of a splitting between the One and the Other was a radical condition for his poetry. In *Nye digte* (New Poems; 1987) Thomsen tried to write lyric poetry on this theme of splitting. Pia Tafdrup . . . can in part declare herself in agreement with Thomsen in *Over vandet går jeg: Skitse til en poetik* (Above water I walk: outline of a poetics): "I exist alone, as I, separated from the absolute other."

As far as it goes, these two prominent representatives of Danish poetry of the 1980s are on the same wave length as classic modernism, Baudelaire, and Rimbaud. In their poetry Thomsen and Tafdrup seek clarity and intensity; the aim of both is to permit a condensed experience of existing *now*. To this Tafdrup adds that the poetical "point of illumination" (with its beauty and pain) lies in the dialectic between splitting and absence on the one hand and unity and presence on the other; this dialectic, she explains, is "a prior condition" of the birth of her poems. Tafdrup does not have the uncompromising split consciousness of Thomsen.

[Tafdrup's] *Over vandet går jeg* consists of hundreds of small aphoristic prose bits divided into fifteen chapters without headings. All the themes are related to Tafdrup's ideas of the poetic work and of the poet: inspiration, esthetics, time, language, and poetry related to the reader, to nature, to mimesis, and to criticism. All the very brief texts are separated by a light-blue "poetic" asterisk, which accentuates the coordination of all statements.

Tafdrup often refers to other poets, as when she pins down the main points of her poetic inspiration, the state of prearticulation: after having described the making of her own poetry "between hunger for life and mortal dread, passion and thought, language and silence," she cites Paul la Cour (who wrote the most famous work of Danish poetics, *Fragmenter af en Dagbog,* in 1948), Inger Christensen (whose poetry of the 1960s is a central incentive to her), Rimbaud, Mallarmé, and T. S. Eliot. In all she describes the modernism which broke open the classical ideal of beauty: "Not our feelings, but the pattern we create of our feelings, is the essential."

As a poet, Tafdrup combines a strong self-consciousness with an ability to submit to the unknown, the reader included. She creates a "room" for the reader's senses and thoughts concerning the inexpressible contents of poetic creation with her identity as "poet, woman, Jew, Dane." Thus, in her 1986 collection of poems *Hvid feber* she involves the reader and draws his attention to her own presence (in "The Dream of the Reader") by rolling him out of his "own shadow" and making him take off like "a bird / that can fly out of my dream / and into yours" ("Avian Yearning"). In fact, Tafdrup finally describes *Over vandet går jeg* as "a poetics of gliding, because all meaning comes from within. Reality is only reality." So, writing is, to her, "an uplifting and opening process, which gives me a feeling of walking above water. And the poem may, with its grips, make the reader glide for a moment." These lines explaining the title of the book contain the essence of Tafdrup's emotionally strong staging of her poetics.

Both as a universal poetics and as an entry to the work of Pia Tafdrup, *Over vandet går jeg* is valuable. It is "an outline" and no *Theory of Literature* à la Wellek and Warren (1958); but it holds a personal radiating power, and its transcendence of poetry is intense.

Svend Birke Espegård. World Literature Today. 67, 1993, p. 192

During the 1980s, Tafdrup clearly emerged as one of Denmark's most outstanding poets, and in 1988, at a remarkably young age, she became a member of the prestigious Danish Academy. She graduated in 1977 from the University of Copenhagen; she has traveled widely, including the U.S., and her experiences as a traveler have echoed in her poetry.

Tafdrup's debut, *Når det går hut på en engel* (1981; When an angel has been grazed), reflects a young person's double experience of knowing that the world is fragmenting—wars, relationships, sudden death—and of being able to probe that world with and through words: to write poetry. This dual attitude, simultaneous desperation and joy, marks Tafdrup's body of poetry and gives it an undeniable tension. Tafdrup is, however, not an ideological or philosophical writer, for her emphasis is always on experience—often in its minutest nuances. In particular, she devotes much detail and attention to sexual desire and that awareness of the body, or bodies, to which such sensuality leads. Perceptively, she has characterized her own poetry in that vein as not merely trying to write about desire but to demonstrate it through language—what she calls "the syntax of desire."

Tafdrup's collections of poetry—*Intetfang* (1982; No-hold), *Den inderste zone* (1983; The innermost zone), *Springflod* (1985; *Springtide,* 1989), *Hvid feber* (1986; White fever), and *Sekundernes bro* (1988; The bridge of the seconds)—may not startle the reader with any abrupt changes in form or outlook, but the language gradually seems more vibrant and rhythmical. Tafdrup is a skilled performer of her own texts, and the oral quality of them suggests very strongly that they be read aloud and not merely read. As is the case in all oral poetry of quality, the full impact of the nuance of detail, the suggested pauses, the implied intonation are realized only when the text is given voice.

Tafdrup, whose background in literature is impressive, once in an article—which might be seen as the draft for a poetics—noted that aesthetics should not be perceived as a straitjacket from which the poem dreams of being liberated; aesthetics is, rather, the reason why the poem is not destroyed by chaos. Tafdrup's texts may be seen as acts of resistance against chaos, and in her exploration of desire and the language of desire, the moments of lust, ecstasy, intimacy, and joy grant her a sense of a fullness and fulfillment that, at least momentarily, keeps the existential darkness at bay. In some ambitious poems she attempts, as did the poets of yore, to reach for the unfathomable. Such sensual moments offer, in addition, a sense of self and self-assurance, which permit an openness and sensitivity to a partner; thus, Tafdrup's poetry, even if it records much loneliness, cherishes a sense of togetherness.

Such moments, however, never make Tafdrup's experience of the world simplistic or idyllic, for she is astutely aware that her world, as well as the world in general, is fragile and that death may be imminent. In fact, her rhythmic, sensuous language—laden with rich, innovative images—refutes any clear-cut, mundane perception of existence but conjures up, rather, the complexity of richness of the experience of the one whose senses are open to the world.

Lately, Tafdrup has tried her hand at drama, *Døden i bjergene* (1988; Death in the mountains), and in *Sekundernes bro* there are rhythmic prose sketches that suggest that she may attempt the form of the short story.

It is, however, as a poet the Tafdrup has earned her prominent position in Danish letters. Her quest for fulfillment is rendered with a burning, pleading, proud, painful, and joyful intensity; thus, she has found for desire a language that is her own.

Niels Ingwerson. In Steven R. Serafin and
Walter D. Glanze, eds. *Encyclopedia of
World Literature in the 20th Century* (New
York: Continuum, 1993), p. 586

TAGGARD, GENEVIEVE (UNITED STATES) 1894–1948

The new selection, made by herself, of Genevieve Taggard's poems—*Traveling Standing Still*—brings her literary personality before us as none of her previous volumes did. She has here chosen from these three earlier volumes twenty-eight poems; and she has exercised, in dealing with her own work, the same excellent critical judgment which has distinguished her literary reviews. One had always been aware before of this distinction of Genevieve Taggard's and of the integrity of her art; but one had never seen her outline so clearly as that of certain of her sister-poets. One had been aware of her originality but would have found it a little difficult to say precisely in what that originality consisted. . . .

The impression of Miss Taggard that one gets from this is a little unexpected. If one had tended vaguely to confuse her with a familiar school of women poets—a school which one of their number has recently herself described as the "Oh-God-the-Pain Girls"—Miss Taggard has excluded from this book anything that might encourage it. What we find is a kind of poetry which, however else it may move us, is not in the least "poignant," and we see that Miss Taggard's point of view, her temperament, and her intention must somehow differ from those of the poets with whom, as I say, we tend to class her. She seems, in fact, to differ from her sisters in certain fundamental respects, and I believe that they are in some ways more like one another than Genevieve Taggard is like any of them. . . .

In the poetry of Genevieve Taggard, we become aware of . . . [The] Pacific sun. If most of the lyric poetry we know owes its vividness, its pathos, its fierceness, to the coldness, the stoniness, the bleakness, the meagerness, the illness, the death, with which the poets see themselves surrounded—so Genevieve Taggard's is the wisdom of the Western spaces and suns; and it is something quite other than the wisdom of our keen Eastern winds and constricted streets. The most striking feature of Miss Taggard's temperament, in contrast to the writers of the East, is the fact that her poetry is so rarely the result of a sharp reaction from one extreme to the other: a girl from the Pacific islands does not react against nature, as so many of our New England writers have done. . . .

What we finally get is a poet of our common human experience who, despite her fastidious and busy mind, which embroiders it sometimes like lace, stitching it in and out, is singularly close to the ground. Whatever she may say in her bitterer moments—expressing herself in the admirable verses of *The Quiet Woman* and *Dissonance Then Silence*—she accepts what life brings her as natural and right. (1928)

> Edmund Wilson. *The Shores of Light: A Literary Chronicle of the Twenties and Thirties* (New York: Farrar, Straus, 1952), pp. 345–47, 349–50

Genevieve Taggard of Waitsburg, Washington, has been writing poetry for the past ten years, and recently issued a small selective volume, *Traveling Standing Still:* a tribute to her integrity toward her own work. A member of the University of California group fathered by the genial [Witter] Bynner, Miss Taggard came East about eight years ago and, with some other young poetics established *The Measure,* a magazine faithful to conservative forms. But the Washington poet is anything but a conservative. In her effort to find an exact likeness for her emotion and thought—a metaphysical ideal—she has invented a number of metrical turns and cadences. The faults she falls into are the result of the difficult medium she works in: at their worst, obscurities and eccentricities. Since she goes in for power in preference to delicacy, and for universal rather than intimate things, she often reaches too far or not far enough, and does not achieve complete communion with the reader. In short, she is an erratic poet who errs on the side of spaciousness, rather than littleness. I feel that Miss Taggard's best work lies ahead of her, and will always lie ahead—an admirable trait in perspective. She does not devote herself to the much simpler task of perfecting minutiæ. The less than thirty poems she has saved from the past are decidedly varied. There are some in which woman borrows natural symbols for self-interpretation; others which interpret Hawaiian myths, people and scenes; and others, as in Louise Bogan, wherein woman is shown in love's aftermath.

Alfred Kreymbourg. *Our Singing Strength:*
History of American Poetry (n.p.: Tudor,
1934), pp. 552–53

Genevieve Taggard has always been a conscious and conscientious poet. She seldom accepts the trite or obvious expression, and seldom expresses a tedious opinion. A follower of her work from her first public appearance in *For Eager Lovers* must be aware of what she is trying to achieve and of how far she has progressed. The same motives that first impelled her to use rhythms like recurrent hammer-blows, rhythms within rhythms, and that prose syncopation which is peculiar to her poetry, are still the motives with which her latest book [*Not Mine to Finish*] were written. . . .

Often I recoil from the image too thoroughly carried to completion, the point too forcefully driven home. My mind puts up a defensive shield. But Miss Taggard's poems are not accomplished by understatement, and if one accepts them, one must accept their vigor as being their most salient characteristic. She never shrinks from a difficult theme, but carries it through triumphantly. . . .

Three of the poems in this latest volume are about the most time-honored and fundamental of themes—unsuccessful marriage, motherhood, middle-age. They are moving, as such poems deserve to be, and they are not mawkish.

J.N.N. [Jessica Nelson North]. *Poetry.*
December, 1934, pp. 168–70

Miss Genevieve Taggard is a little too prone to think of verse as a kind of poetic comment on the news. In much of her verse, she seems the sort of writer who would write poetry, war or no war, because all she has to do is comment on what is happening, and if what is happening is horrible and shattering, she simple writes *about* it. . . .

The clues to Miss Taggard's incidental weaknesses are in the banality of "True Fable," with its refrain, "It was poetry, poetry and the human heart," in the coquettish triviality of "Dialogue on Cider," in the spurious solemnity of "Exchange of Awe" ("Marvelous now is man"). The subjects cover the limited but cluttered assortment of a suburbanite's ruminations—there is a proper "Salute to The Russian Dead," a poem tackling the whole problem of American culture, and one about the paper geraniums in a Greenwhich Villagey café. I do not mean that Miss Taggard has not the right to make one subject do as well as another; but I cannot find in her that quality of simultaneous vision and technique which Marianne Moore once call "unanimity," and which Miss Moore happens to exemplify: a basic seriousness (in the French sense) with which the poet can address all things and with which he can bring our concentration to his *way* of seeing things rather than to the things themselves. I simply get weary following Miss Taggard around.

Henry Rago. *Poetry.* February, 1947,
pp. 289–90

Genevieve Taggard has a distinctly critical perspective on [the] rhetoric of aestheticization, a stance which may be seen as integral to her own necessarily complicated relation to contemporary love discourse. The particular shape of her poetics is largely determined by her need, as a bohemian woman poet, to reconcile contradictory imperatives; that is, by a desire to deconstruct certain cultural myths—such as the "aesthetic" character of sexual love—while preserving certain others, most importantly, the notion of the heterosexual dyad of artist-lovers as inviolable.

Taggard's love poetry of the 1920s testifies to her affiliation with Greenwich Village ideals. Most central is her use of the Romantic artist as paradigm for the human subject: a sensibility elevated above and alienated from the social world. Consistent with Village culture, this has a determining effect on her depiction of heterosexual love, which constitutes her major thematic preoccupation in this period. She is, moreover, openly critical of bourgeois materialism and implicitly treats love as a force of resistance against it. Finally, art and love, artist and lover are so closely identified in her work as to be almost interchangeable. . . .

Taggard holds the assumption of the inviolability of heterosexual monogamy in common with both her immediate bohemian milieu and the broader mainstream culture, yet the investment which motivates this assumption is different for each of them. As the voice of mainstream values, sexology was concerned to preserve the heterosexual couple as a productive social unit and hence worked to channel the contemporaneous preoccupation with sex and gender to traditional bourgeois interests. Taggard was in fundamental disagreement with this model of sublimation, as "Doomsday Morning" clearly illustrates. Her position may be more closely identified with that of her immediate community of Village bohemia. She represented love as an enclave apart from society and further identified love with art, thus producing the same metaphoric concretization which served to structure and focus bohemian oppositionality to the mainstream. . . .

The intricate structures of compromise and denial attending a woman writer's participation in a masculinist subcultural milieu need not close off the possibility of real protest. The example of Taggard suggests, however, that the political valences of a given poetic discourse—the costs or courage entailed therein—may only be visible in the context of fairly local historical parameters. When, in the 1930s, Taggard produced a volume of social protest poems, conventionally recognizable as "political," she was widely criticized on artistic grounds for what amounted to her directness. Edna Millay herself made a single foray into political poetry with *Make Bright the Arrows* (1940), with similar results. (To the end of her life, she was apologizing for this "lapse" in her artistry.) Any feminist investigation of women's relation to the public sphere of cultural value needs to take seriously the penalties to womanly—and writerly—identity that direct participation may entail. Local historical focus allows for the possibility of broadening what at any given cultural moment may constitute public discursive space for a woman speaker. In particular, Taggard's work opens up the possibility of bringing women's love lyrics into history from the ahistorical imaginary to which they have been relegated.

Nina Miller. Genders. 11, 1991,
pp. 41–42, 52, 54

With the publication of her collection of verse *Calling Western Union* in 1936, Taggard turned her attention openly to social reform and lost her early critical acclaim. This publication marked a departure from her first poetry which may be classed with what Edmund Wilson called "O, God-the-Pain-Girls" poems, lyrics in conventional form on the subjects of love, death, and loss. The poems in *Calling Western Union* not only confront the political issues of the time but also demand active political engagement. Taggard's vision becomes collective rather than private as she creates a brand of modern poetry different in that it values audience accessibility rather than "aloof indecipherability" and social relevance rather than universality.

In *Calling Western Union,* Taggard uses images of women to call for social reform. Taggard draws portraits of individual women to reveal the nature and scope of social problems. . . .

Most of the poems in *Calling Western Union* go beyond simple identification of social ills to call for direct collective action. In these, Taggard represents groups of women as moving forces in working class reform. . . .

The most powerful vision of change comes in the opening poem in *Calling Western Union,* "Night Letter to Walt Whitman," a highly stylized piece which not only replicates Whitman's style but also recreates the night-time static of a radio transmission. The poem predicts a future reuniting of City and Land which will bring "order plenty equal work with ease" to displace the contemporary city with "wealth spliced with want streets / Strewn with Refuse" and the earth "to bad land returning . . . farms and mills dead-locked." This renewal is appropriately embodied in the image of the land, not as Mother Earth, but as "A swarthy sister with strawberry mouth" who joins with her brother, urban industrial culture, to bring a new moral order. Taggard pictures an earth with "fences gone / trespass antique" and "goods and peace" for all in her prophetic vision of the future. Here, as elsewhere, Taggard represents women as essential agents in the collective action necessary for socialism's ultimate triumph.

Martha A. Wilson and Gwendolyn Sell.
Arkansas Quarterly. 2, 1993, pp. 129–31

TAN, AMY (UNITED STATES) 1952–

Snappy as a fortune cookie and much more nutritious, *The Joy Luck Club* is a jolly treatment of familiar conflicts (between mothers and daughters, immigrants and natives) in a new guise. The club's four mah-jongg-playing ladies are Chinese, but their daughters (three of whom have Chinese fathers) are American. Or so *they* say. Even after forty years in San Francisco, certain behavior patterns do not unravel. When a girlfriend advises Waverly Place Jong to tell her mother "to stop ruining your life. Tell her to shut up," she replies, "Well, I don't know if it's explicitly stated in the law, but you can't *ever* tell a Chinese mother to shut up. You could be charged as an accessory to your own murder."

The Joy Luck Club is lively and bright but not terribly deep. The stories resolve themselves too neatly and cozily, and are often burdened with symbols (a spindly-legged table or a weed-choked garden for an unhappy marriage) that flatten them out. One cannot help being charmed, however, by the sharpness of observation, the mixture of familiarity and strangeness, and, finally, the universality of Tan's themes: I was amused by how Jewish the Chinese mothers sound, with their honey-voiced, dragon-hearted competitiveness over children and food, their insistence that they are not criticizing, merely remarking. . . . *The Joy Luck Club* becomes a happy illustration of its own subject, a combination of Chinese subtlety and American ingenuity.

Rhoda Koenig. *New York.* March 20, 1989,
p. 82

The Joy Luck Club is a segmented novel eloquently blending the voices of four Chinese immigrants and their daughters. The mothers become friends, meeting regularly in what they call "the Joy Luck Club" to play mah-jongg, buy stocks and gossip. The novel is narrated horizontally as well as vertically; friendships and rivalries develop among the daughters as well as among the mothers. . . .

Tan's book is organized into four chapters—the first relating the separate lives of the mothers; the next two focusing on the daughters' stories; the last returning to the mothers. Tan is a deft, vivacious conductor, evoking spirited individuality as well as harmony. . . .

Throughout *The Joy Luck Club,* Tan tests the distance between expectation and reality. Jing-mei Woo explains, "America was where all my mother's hopes lay. She had come here in 1949 after losing everything in China: her mother and father, her family home, her first husband, and two daughters, twin baby girls. But she never looked back with regret. There were so many ways for things to get better." But she goes on:

> In the years that followed, I failed her so many times, each time asserting my own will, my right to fall short of expectations. I didn't get straight A's. I didn't become class president. I didn't get into Stanford. I dropped out of college. . . . For unlike my mother, I did not believe I could be anything I wanted to be. I could only be me.

Each of these first-generation daughters is a guardian angel, helping her mother negotiate the baffling San Francisco culture. And the mothers remain loyal to their often-disappointing daughters. The women in each family are held together by pride, embarrassment and longing. They are, indeed, the loves of one another's lives.

Tan has a remarkable ear for dialogue and dialect, representing the choppy English of the mothers and the sloppy California vernacular of the daughters with sensitive authenticity. These stories are intricately seamed with the provocative questions about language that emerge from bilingual and trilingual homes. In families where verbal exchanges can prove problematic, one sometimes turns to other kinds of oral communication: Tan's cooking scenes are drawn with subtle intensity. "My father hadn't eaten well since my mother died. So I am here, in the kitchen, to cook him dinner. I'm slicing tofu. I've decided to make him a spicy bean-curd dish. My mother used to tell me how hot things restore the spirit and health. But I'm making this mostly because I know my father loves the dish and I know how to cook it. I like the smell of it: ginger, scallions and a red chili sauce that tickles my nose the minute I open the jar."

The segmented structure of *The Joy Luck Club* encourages readers to think simultaneously in different directions. There are some flaws. Several characters, particularly Rose Hsu Jordan and Ying-ying St. Clair, could be more fully developed. Occasionally a device used for narrative effect—such as when Jing-mei Woo asks in the last chapter, at age thirty-six, what her Chinese name means—defies credibility. Generally, however, *The Joy Luck Club* is a stunningly auspicious debut. Tan is a gifted storyteller who reaches across cultures and generations:

Valerie Miner. The Nation. April 24, 1989,
pp. 566–67

The Joy Luck Club is a huge hit in America: number two on the *New York Times* bestseller list (after *The Satanic Verses*); U. S. paperback rights sold for one and a quarter million dollars. It's good, but not *that* good: what it is is ethnic, and about mothers and daughters. I can just see the jubilation when this perfect combination of flavors-of-the-American-month arrived on the publishers' desk. By contrast the English reaction to ideological correctness has always been deep suspicion. If *The Joy Luck Club* is successful here I hope it will be for its intrinsic qualities, and in proportion to them.

It has many. The oriental artist starts with an advantage: a culture of indirection and artifice; the knowledge that successful stories (all successful communication) must be cunningly crafted. *The Joy Luck Club* is *very* cunningly crafted—thus disproving one of its own themes, that American children lose Chinese values. It has four mother-daughter pairs, four parts of four chapters each, four corners of the mah-jong table at which the women of the Joy Luck Club tell their stories. In part one the Chinese mothers begin their stories; in parts two and three the daughters tell theirs; finally in part four the mothers' stories are resolved.

This is very clever. The Chinese stories can't help but be fascinating, and so we are caught and held to the end. They're also cleverly planned to cover every sort of Chinese woman's character and experience: strong and weak, rich and poor, wife and concubine. . . .

In parts two and three we see what happens to these women in America, through the eyes and fates of their daughters. Some of this is realistic and amusing: the daughters' embarrassment over the mothers' unAmerican ways, the mothers' fierce competition. . . .

But some of it, I feel, Amy Tan's teacher, writers' group and editors should have cautioned her against. *The Joy Luck Club* is *over*-schematic. We move too often from one corner of the table to another to remember or care enough about each. And at the same time it is over-significant. In the end it gives you indigestion, as if you've eaten too many Chinese fortune cookies, or read too many American Mother's Day cards. Each part begins with a Chinese parable; each chapter title is deeply meaningful; each story, event and name is packed with messages about life, love, dependence, memory.

Finally, in all this craft and care there is a central imbalance. Most of the stories come out of Amy Tan's own family; out of her life, her mother's and grandmother's. Suyuan Woo's Joy Luck Club is real; so are her twin daughters left by the roadside in 1949. Even if I hadn't learned this from the publicity handout I would have felt it from Jing-Mei Woo's role as our central story-teller, and from the special drive and passion of Suyuan's story. But Amy Tan gives half her mother's story to An-Mei, so that we learn less of Suyuan's story than of the other mothers'; and she tells us less of Jing-Mei's grown-up life than of the other daughters'.

That is (I think after reading this novel) very Chinese. But it left a gap in a book otherwise as strictly balanced as an equation. Who said that all writers should burn their first, autobiographical novels? That's nonsense. Of course, all autobiographical first novels aren't good but all good first novels are autobiographical. Amy Tan's first novel would have been better if it had been about her mother and grandmother; then she could have left the others for her second and third. And they would have been better still. As it is, I hope her too early and too easy—her too American—success won't have spoilt her altogether. I bet her mother has a Chinese proverb about *that*.

Carole Angier. New Statesman and Society.
June 30, 1989, p. 35

Her first [novel,] *The Joy Luck Club,* took the U. S. by storm two years ago with a central mother-daughter relationship so powerful that it pulled the book away from any literary or ethnic ghetto. Tan has done it again with a big, bold story [*The Kitchen God's Wife*] set in pre-revolutionary Shanghai and framed by a contemporary family drama whose near-misses of communication, secret trade-offs, and emotional culs-de-sac brilliantly describe its own culture while refusing its limitations.

Chinese-American Pearl cannot tell her mother that she has multiple sclerosis. Winnie, in turn, has never told Pearl the truth about her life before she arrived in the States in 1949. Thanks to the dislocation of emigration and the chaos of revolution, it has been easy to reinvent the past, to change, names, places and people. Only the threat of Winnie's friend Helen (real name Hulan) to tell Pearl what really happened galvanizes Winnie (real name Veili) into setting the record straight.

Winnie's story of her life in Shanghai in the 1930s and 1940s is stuffed with documentary detail. We learn about tea, hairdressing, dowries and going to the lavatory in pre-revolutionary China. We catch the decadence, the sweet-sour smell of an over-ripe culture on the turn. Teenage girls from genteel business families gossip about Ginger Rogers, kept in line by a phalanx of formidable aunts and mothers-in-law who nonetheless are powerless to protect them against the weakest and cruellest of men.

Reluctant to comment on the importance of its own project, *The Kitchen God's Wife* tells its story without a scrap of literary self-importance. Yet its very lack of pretension, its refusal to puff its own processes, draws attention to our own lack of stories by women from immigrant cultures: in Britain we have, as yet, no female equivalent of Mo or Rushdie.

Kathryn Hughes. New Statesman and Society. July 12, 1991, p. 38

In her new book, *The Kitchen God's Wife* . . . Tan juxtaposes the China-born mother's inner turmoil with the U.S.-born daughter's trepidation. The cultural distance between mother and daughter contributes to the fears they have for (and the secrets they keep from) each other. As daughter Pearl tells it, "To this day it drives me crazy, listening to her various hypotheses, the way religion, medicine, and superstition all merge with her own beliefs. She's like a Chinese version of Freud, or worse."

But the mother, Winnie, bears the weight of a tragic past that she cannot share with her daughter. Abandoned by *her* mother—one of five wives—at age six, she is raised by uncaring relatives. To escape, she marries a charming actor who turns out to be an unscrupulous brute; he tortures her through beatings, public humiliation, and rape. She endures the hardships of war-torn China with him, bearing three children, eventually burying each. Her planned escape to the U. S. to join her new love is nearly botched when her estranged ex-husband tracks her down, beats and rapes her. Nine months later, Pearl is born. "I have tried to think how I would tell my daughter," Winnie muses. "But every time I begin, I can hear her voice, so much hurt."

When a family friend tricks mother and daughter into disclosing their secrets, Winnie's tale of her life in China is a gift to Pearl—a large but missing piece of her own identity.

Helen Zia. *Ms.* November–December, 1991,

p. 76

Here's cause for celebration: a handsome new storybook by Amy Tan. . . .

Ms. Tan makes details from her Chinese-American background totally accessible. Indeed, many of the finest moments in her adult novels are when she evokes the particular and peculiar texture of a childhood world most of her readers will never experience.

The Moon Lady is an invitation to young children to attend a long-ago moon festival in China. The reader travels along with seven-year-old Ying-ying, spending a wide-eyed day of pleasure, waiting to encounter Lady Chang-o, who lives on the moon and who once a year fulfills the secret, unspoken wishes of the heart. This is a story with deep, satisfying meanings, a tale of a lost child who for a prolonged and terrifying moment risks losing even her sense of self. . . .

I may seem greedy to want more, but there are structural flaws in the first and last pages, which are also marred by stilted dialogue and spurious morals. These bookends aren't needed. *The Moon Lady* can stand alone without the extra baggage of flashback and update. There is no need to place Ying-ying's adventures within the long and honorable tradition of the "grandmother's tale." Perhaps Ms. Tan overestimates the need of her audience for reassurance that Ying-ying lived to tell her tale or underestimates children's capacity to grasp character through action rather than announcement. There is no need for *this* grandmother to insist she once fidgeted; any reader who spends five minutes with Ying-ying easily discovers this first-hand.

Ellen Schecter. *The New York Times.*
November 8, 1992, p. 31

The multivalent structure of *The Joy Luck Club* resists reduction to simple geometric designs; nevertheless, two figures—the rectangle and the circle— help to chart Tan's play on the theme of maternality. As the novel begins, June takes her place with three Joy Luck aunties around the mah-jong table. Her position at one of the table's cardinal points determines the direction of her journey east which ends in China. At the end point of June's story, the trope of the rectangle merges with that of the circle: June's arrival in China brings her full circle to the place where her mother's story began, and her meeting with her half-sisters sets into motion a circulation of mirrored relationships blurring identities, generations, and languages. Because it repudiates linearity and symmetry, the circle is a privileged motif in feminist writings, one that suggests the possibility of reconfiguring traditional familial dynamics and dismantling the hierarchical arrangements of the Oedipal triangle and the patriarchal family. For instance, in her book on the reclamation of the pre-Oedipal in women's novels, Jean Wyatt envisions "the possibility . . . of imagining alternative family relations based on preoedipal patterns— family circles whose fluidity of interchange challenges the rigid gender and generational hierarchies of the patriarchal family." In Wyatt's analysis, there persists, in women's writings, the fantasy of a nurturant family where "family members come forward to share the work of fostering others' development [so that] the responsibility for nurturing [is extended] to a whole circle of 'mothering' people."

In *The Joy Luck Club,* the discrete identities of familial members are woven into a collectivized interchangeability through the novel's parataxis— its use of contiguous juxtapositions of voices, narratives, and motifs. Through the novel's interweaving of time frames and voices, three generations of women are included within a relational network linking grandmothers, mothers, daughters, aunts, and sisters. For these women, however, mutual nurturance does not arise from biological or generational connections alone; rather, it is an act affirming consciously chosen allegiances. As Wyatt suggests, mothering as a "reciprocal activity" generally presupposes "a strong mother figure who has a central position in the family," but even "when the mother is not there, the circle remains, its diffuse bonds extend a circle of equals who take turns nurturing each other." In *The Joy Luck Club,* the death of June's mother, Suyuan, invites the Joy Luck aunties to step into the circle of "mothering reciprocity"; indeed, it is Suyuan's absence that inaugurates the meeting between June and her half-sisters, when they confirm their mutual identification as each other's sisters *and* mothers.

As we have seen, the maternal voices in *The Joy Luck Club* begin to shift from "I" to "you" to engage the discrete subjectivities of mother and daughter in a tentative exchange of recognitions and identifications. In the same way, the novel's resonant structure and its use of parataxis effectively write the reader into the text as a crucial participant in the making of meaning. The reader of *The Joy Luck Club* is a weaver of intricate interconnections who must, like Suyuan's unraveling of an old sweater, randomly "pull out a kinky thread of yarn, anchoring it to a piece of cardboard, [roll] with a sweeping rhythm, [and] start [a] story." This way of engaging the reader as an active constructor of meaning allows the feminist novel to project a community of sisterly readers. In tracing a family history that blurs the demarcations between the roles of mothers, daughters, and sisters, *The Joy Luck Club* breaks down the boundary between text and reader in order to proffer the notions of sisterhood as a literary construction and as a community constituted through the act of reading. At once disintegrative and constructive in its operations, the novel holds its dual impulses in unresolved suspension and fulfills its fundamentally transformative project—a mutation from daughter-text to mother-text to sister-text.

Marina Heung. *Feminist Studies.* 19, 1993,
pp. 612–13

TAYLOR, ELIZABETH (GREAT BRITAIN) 1912–75

At Mrs. Lippincote's, by Elizabeth Taylor . . . [is a] witty, sharp, extremely casual story about a middle-class Englishwoman who, without possessing any of the qualities that are now standard equipment for contemporary heroines, is one of the most engaging young females in the current crop of novels. Here is one more proof that the English can do a certain kind of novel—intelligent, ironic, and just this side of penetrating—better than anybody else. Even if it does not seem to some people as worthwhile as chronicling the growing pains of American youth or life among the homicidal inhabitants of the Georgia gullies, it is at least vastly more entertaining.

The New Yorker. April 13, 1946, p. 101

In her two brief and totally dissimilar previous novels, Mrs. Taylor studied, with engaging wit, the feelings of extremely small groups of people; in this book, she takes on a whole English seaside village of characters—a likable woman novelist whose husband is having an affair with her best friend, a paralyzed, bawdy old woman, a lonely young widow, a predatory retired naval officer, and a funny, intolerable brat, among others—and produces not only a subtly observant study but a highly original narrative. If you needed any further proof of Mrs. Taylor's genuinely fresh and enchanting talent, this book should furnish it.

The New Yorker. October 25, 1947,
pp. 132–33

A Wreath of Roses is her fourth, and it has the same lightness and speed; the same clairvoyance at catching ripples of feminine feeling, as her first, *At Mrs. Lippincote's.* Since there is nothing very busty or blustery about all this, Mrs. Taylor will probably have to be content with a lot fewer readers than she deserves.

Like Jane Austen, one of her models for the art of fiction, Elizabeth Taylor has lived a quiet life in rural England. . . .

A Wreath of Roses is not the "perfect novel" that she has confessed she would like to write, but it contains three extremely well-drawn characters: two young women and a baby. Confidantes and friends from girlhood, Camilla Hill and Liz Nicholson are spending their summer holiday together again in an old village, full of gardens which ooze sunny peace as a honeycomb oozes honey. Liz's new baby creates all kinds of subtle estrangements, hilarities and tensions. A more serious tension arises when a handsome young stranger arrives at the local inn; though Camilla knows that he is dangerous, she is attracted to him.

Novelist Taylor comes a cropper in dealing with the handsome stranger—a psychotic who is a good deal more dangerous than Camilla at first suspects. Mrs. Taylor suggests facets of his character, all neatly and plausibly, but no individual emerges. At the climax of the story Camilla is filled with understandable terror at learning that her new friend is a murderer. The motives and behavior of the young man at this point are, however, by no means made credible to the reader. The novel ends rather helplessly with his suicide.

Elizabeth Taylor's best novel is still her third, *A View of the Harbour,* in which she managed a greater range of characters and moods with more solidity of style.

Time. March 21, 1949, pp. 112, 114

A Game of Hide-and-Seek, the new novel by Elizabeth Taylor . . . is that rare and difficult thing, a love story. It is about "nice" people, who pay the nice people of real life the extreme compliment not merely of thinking and speaking in sentences that parse but of having something interesting to think and say. It is ambitious as well as exquisite, revealing on every page that the author has intended to produce a work of art and maybe, with luck, a masterpiece. If *A Game of Hide-and-Seek* is not a masterpiece, and as a work of art has crucial flaws, it is nevertheless often beautiful and touching, and will give pleasure to many people. Indeed, the degree to which it gives pleasure is the degree to which, in the end, it proves disappointing, for though Mrs. Taylor has provided a great deal, she has not provided enough. She has skimped, a grave fault in a hostess, graver still in a writer. Readers of novels are always ravenous and importunate, and their howls cannot be silenced with almonds and canapés. They must be fed until gorged. In reading *A Game of Hide-and-Seek,* we are like guests who, over cocktails, have glimpsed a dinner table gleaming candlelit in the next room, with its promise of a substantial feast to come. On being called to the table, we are offered a delicious clear soup, salad, ices, a plate of fruit. At last it dawns on us that, for all the elegance and enchantment of the scene, something has gone wrong. The main dish has been omitted; there is to be no roast beef and Yorkshire pudding. In Mrs. Taylor's novel, beautiful as it is, she has unaccountably left out the climax, with the result that her marvelous preparations have been in vain, and our interest, after mounting from page to page, turns to exasperation. All the sensibility in the world, we protest, cannot take the place of having things happen. If the action of the story is not complete, it is not a story; the end of a story must be more than "The End," it must be the particular end for which the story was begun.

Brendan Gill. *The New Yorker.*
March 24, 1951, p. 104

One way of praising Mrs. Elizabeth Taylor is to say that if Chekhov had known the sad, ugly twentieth-century English reality of ribbon development and roadhouses and railway buffets, he might have written just such stories as appear in *Hester Lilly.* The analogy should not be taken too literally. Mrs. Taylor has little of the bitter-sweet nostalgic quality conveyed by the Russian word *toska,* her view of the world is in many ways sharper and more incisive. What she does share with Chekhov is a keen and wonderfully compassionate insight into the workings of private defeat, a sympathy that never falters into sentimentality. She is aware that, in one sense, we are all defeated in the long run, and is not unnerved by her knowledge. For that reason, although her characters are often pitiable the final effect is far from depressing, but conveys rather that little upsurge of exhilaration we feel at each fresh glimpse of the difficult truth.

The quality of her sympathy is perhaps best shown in "Spry Old Character," the story of an aging Cockney called Harry who goes blind and is sent to a home filled with twittering gentlewomen, where the incomprehension on both sides soon becomes complete and invincible. She does not try to soften the fact that Harry is a self-centered and disagreeable old windbag—so much so that, when he is befriended by a number of busmen who can at least speak his own language, we are almost persuaded that he does not deserve his luck. The result of this devotion to truth that is not one but many-sided is to release a deep spring of compassion and recognition. The same might be said of any of these characters—of the heroine of the long title-story, who is not particularly attractive or intelligent or endearing, but whose inarticulate misery is immediately convincing; of the embittered Sybil in "A Sad Garden," a story remarkable for its glimpse of the absolute of childish terror. In short, Mrs.

Taylor confirms, in *Hester Lilly*, her calm and confident possession of one of the brightest talents to have emerged in English fiction since the war.

(London) *Times Literary Supplement.*
November 12, 1954, p. 725

Elizabeth Taylor's heroine [in *Angel*], while given to us as an Edwardian novelist, is, in fact, all the ladies who ever have written trash in the name of literature rolled into one revolting entity. . . .

Like *Gone with the Wind*, her [first] novel is a critical flop but a popular success and so, with the press against her and the public for her, Angel goes on from triumph to triumph, until she is rich enough to buy everything she wants, including a husband of sorts. . . .

Mrs. Taylor gives us a heroine who is self-centered, unrealistic, capricious . . . unteachable . . . and she contrasts this with Angel's image of herself. . . . But she does allow Angel such virtues as integrity. . . .

Mrs. Taylor's book has been out for . . . weeks now; for a work of such perceptiveness, charm and elegance, it has received too little critical attention, and seems likely to be forgotten fairly soon.

The explanation of this general neglect is probably that the Angels of the world have written so many bad novels about novelists that readers shy away. . . . Another explanation is that the publishers of the book—Viking Press—have gone to considerable lengths to misrepresent their product. . . . There is a double irony here. One is that a distinguished publishing house would choose to send out one of its best novels disguised as a cheap romance. The other is that the jacket would be appropriate to a book *by* Angel rather than to one *about* her. No doubt a witty practical joke has been played, though on whom it remains to be seen.

Robert Evett. *The New Republic.*
October 21, 1957, p. 19

Miss Taylor . . . is a passionate defender of the shy and has little sympathy for the people who are not. To be a sympathetic character in her book, you must always say and do the wrong thing. You must never enter a drawing-room without blushing, tripping, knocking over a vase and then saying, in a much too loud voice, something so stupid that you feel obliged to spend the rest of the evening brooding about just *how* stupid it was. Display any presence of mind, and you are out—you become one [of] the pushy, vulgar, brutish, insensitive unshy.

I exaggerate somewhat. But I did often wish, as I read the collection [*The Blush*] that Miss Taylor would stop insisting so on her equation of social maladroitness with moral and intellectual superiority. Some of the nicest people are not shy, and some of the shyest people are dreadful. (I recently read in the newspaper, in an interview with his sister, that Adolph Hitler was a very shy boy.) More specifically this schema makes it too easy to predict how a character will behave.

But this is only to say that Miss Taylor's stories do not "collect" as well as one might have expected when one read them in *The New Yorker,* where (with two exceptions) they first appeared. Individually they are delightful.

Janet Winn. *The New Republic.*
June 1, 1959, p. 21

Kate Heron, the central figure of this novel [*In a Summer Season*], is a woman in her early forties who, after the death of her first husband, has married a man who is ten years younger and has all the qualities that make a man attractive to women and is in love with her. Only one shadow lies across their happiness; he has no work, and it is difficult to imagine a job that he would be happy in, let alone one that he could be trusted with. Kate has enough money for both of them, but his days are long and empty, and he is restless and touchy in ways that men who have an office to go to are not. He is, in fact, a beautiful child. With this as the first subject and, as the second subject, the love affair between Kate's grown son and the sexually uninhibited, quite heartless daughter of Kate's dearest and now dead friend, Mrs. Taylor has constructed her story along patterns as formal as the patterns of music. It is terribly funny, and at the same time as melancholy as looking at oneself in the mirror.

The New Yorker. February 11, 1961, p. 124

Miss Taylor, that past mistress of narrative, again [in *The Soul of Kindness,*] writes a story that holds one's interest from first to last. Yet I found it disappointing, as if I'd just finished reading brilliant notes for a novel instead of the finished product. My mind was full of questions. It is the story of a (we are told) devastatingly beautiful and charming girl. She has been spoiled by her doting and widowed mother, and after her marriage she sets about putting everyone's life to rights with a thoughtful, gentle touch. Instead she causes near-disaster in every case, yet at the end everyone is coming back for more— except, oddly enough, her mother, who suddenly shows a strength for which the reader is not prepared. . . . The real weakness of the book, it seems to me, lies in the fact that though the heroine is described again and again as exquisite and charming, the reader is not convinced. One can't see why even weak people would fall under the spell of what seems a transparently selfish character.

However, Miss Taylor couldn't write an inelegant sentence if she tried and her prose is a delight as always; there is a wonderful supporting cast and secondary plot, and the London backgrounds are all vivid enough to touch and smell.

Harper's. August, 1964, p. 104

There is a peculiar and soothing Englishness about everything Mrs. Taylor writes, which is, no doubt, part of her appeal for readers of *The New Yorker,* in which these twelve stories [*A Dedicated Man*] were first published.

Whether her subject is maiden ladies holidaying in Greece, the teenage off-spring of the Jewish commuter belt, or what goes on below stairs in Thames-side hotels, it is impossible to imagine not only more quintessentially English characters and settings, but also any other writer who so quietly and skilfully evokes the particular loneliness, or embarrassment, or hypocrisy, or discontent, which Mrs. Taylor's compatriots know to be a national disease, even while disliking those who point an accusing finger. Perhaps it has something to do with the enervating climate of the Thames Valley, but more with the whole fabric of class and respectability, those two social albatrosses which have inspired so much of the English literary tradition. Mrs. Taylor is the Pont of fiction, only she has outlived that remarkable artist long enough to observe a backwash of coarse hysteria into the scene he so delicately imposed. . . .

The best, because the quietest and most poignant, of these sketches of middle-class emotions, are the stories about women on their own, women who, because they have somehow missed out on the busy satisfactions of their sex, have time to observe and regret and discover some kind of private solace. . . .

Maybe these stories, so accurately set in a world which to a younger generation will seem both petty and ridiculous, so lulled in the mood and tempo of a society where appearances mattered and words said less than they implied, do not add up to a very exciting or urgent contribution to current fiction. But the smoothness of Mrs. Taylor's style and her patience in recreating tiny, valuable moments of truth show once again that she is among the most craftsmanlike of any English novelists now writing.

(London) *Times Literary Supplement.*
July 1, 1965, p. 553

Miss Taylor has always been able to show up ordinary-seeming people as capable of unusual depths of good and evil. In this novel, however, she starts with an unusual group—a Catholic family sect which lives by itself on a little self-sustaining hillside estate within commuting distance of London, doing its own farming, baking, etc., and mingling with other townsfolk not at all. One of the eighteen-year-old daughters finally rebels, goes to the village to find a job, and eventually marries a young reporter who lives there with his charming mother. In the strange relationship that exists among the three—the mother, son, and daughter-in-law—and later with their son, Miss Taylor is at her best. It all seems so matter-of-fact and everyone so delightful right up to the last few pages when suddenly one gets a frightening glimpse of the kind of undercover selfishness which if allowed to run its course can destroy individuals and even families. Setting this ordinary suburban triangle against the religious community where another kind of selfishness exists, masked in holy guise, makes an effective counterpoint, a delicious ironic comment, and a thoroughly engrossing tale.

Katherine Gauss Parker. *Harper's.*
April, 1968, p. 106

Elizabeth Taylor must surely now be among the four or five most distinguished living practitioners of the art of the short story in the English speaking world. Some have reservations—this reviewer among them—about her
range as a novelist; there is an assumption of English middle-class habits,
preoccupations, and woes which, however accurately and indeed sometimes
waspishly documented, excludes perhaps too much of modern experience to
give her broader canvases the significance she herself might intend. And
harking back to Jane Austen is not, in the media-influenced society we now
have, a relevant rejoinder.

But when it comes to the isolation—in the symbolic as well as technical
sense—of a particular relationship, a particular incident in which the apparently ordinary, stock individual is momentarily exposed, then there is no
writer so skilled at imprinting forever on the reader's mind *how* significant
that moment can be. Like the best snapshots—and holidays, with all their
high anticipations, remembered delights and revisited disappointments, figure
in six of these eleven stories—Mrs. Taylor's evocations are painfully apt to
jerk the memory, not into sympathetic nostalgia but into the irony of those
strenuous escapes into pleasure we embody in the word "holiday." The dingy,
mosquito-plagued hotel, for instance, at which one arrived too late to see the
cathedral, dined disgustingly, and lay awake to the reverberation of snores
through cardboard walls; here, on honeymoon, Melanie begins to smell the
murky adjustments of marriage as the next-door couple's quarrel mounts and
yet, next morning, appears grotesquely and recognizably glossed over by the
pursuit of pleasure. Here, in a snatched escape from the giggles and prurient
condescension of youth, a lonely dull widower is cruelly thwarted (by gout)
from his idyllic chance with lovely fat gallant Phyl, the publican's wife getting
over her hysterectomy with blistering sunburn; this tender and tragi-comic
non-affaire is a perfect example of the way Mrs. Taylor, in a few deft words,
transforms   the   banal   stereotype   into   an   endearingly   vulnerable
individual. . . .

The Devastating Boys has, indeed, so many varied moments where appearances and "standards" are turned topsy-turvy that a less generous writer
might have allowed this collection to seem satirical and even malicious. But
the gentle reminder, implied even in Mrs. Taylor's most sardonic descriptive
details, that we are all as ludicrously self-seeking, as blind and petty as these
faded snapshot figures, is enough to shake any such glib critical comment.
Perhaps it is the humble wisdom of experience that all story-tellers need to
focus the moment against the insignificant wastes of time that lie around.

(London) *Times Literary Supplement.*
June 9, 1972, p. 525

Elizabeth Taylor . . . is not generally thought of as a writer concerned with
philosophical issues. Her twelve books about life in suburban England are
usually called "genteel" novels of manners and praised for "meticulous craftsmanship." And yet Taylor judges her characters less by their social interac-

tions than by their ability to perceive "ultimate truths" about the nature of "reality." Even though this reality includes the drawing room, its ultimate truths are ugliness, violence, loneliness, and death, a reality stark by anyone's standards and difficult to accept. Hence, much of Taylor's work concerns how people deceive themselves and others as they fall into and promote illusion.

Taylor's novels are peopled with writers and painters, her pages, peppered with allusions to works of art and artists. And yet the artistic imagination is only one manifestation of what Taylor sees as the human propensity for illusion. I optimistically label this propensity the "creative imagination"; in Taylor's work it is not the sole property of the artist, but, rather, a common human trait that frequently finds its paradigm in the more specific creativity of the artist.

Taylor's work is not unrelated to the novel of manners; the main difference between Taylor's "good" and "bad" characters—whether artists or not—is that her less sympathetic characters only use their imaginations to aggrandize and protect their egos, while her more sympathetic characters, although equally isolated, express through their illusions a solidarity with other lonely people. . . . Taylor's attitude toward the creative imagination changes from dark suspicion to hopeful celebration when she realizes its strange social dimensions; characters in earlier works only come to grief through their addiction to illusion; characters in later works tend to achieve a certain admirable success through their ability to create and promote illusions. Thus Taylor weaves together philosophy and drawing-room observation to create novels that are more than merely "genteel."

Taylor's work may be divided into three stages. In the early period, she is unfailingly critical of the distorting blandishments of the imagination: *At Mrs. Lippincote's* (1945), *Palladian* (1946), *A View of the Harbour* (1947), and *A Wreath of Roses* (1949). In her middle period, Taylor moderates her criticism: *A Game of Hide and Seek* (1951), *The Sleeping Beauty* (1953), and *Angel* (1957). Finally, the novels of her later years celebrate the creative imagination: *In a Summer Season* (1961), *The Soul of Kindness* (1964), *The Wedding Group* (1968), *Mrs. Palfrey at the Claremont* (1971), and *Blaming* (published posthumously in 1976). . . .

This schematic presentation of Taylor's shifting attitude is perhaps more useful for assessing her work than strictly accurate as a description, because in all her novels—early, middle, and late—she struggles with two major paradoxes: the novelist's use of "fiction" to unmask "illusion" and depict the "real," and the solitary novelist's condemnation of egotistic isolation. Much of Taylor's justly praised craftsmanship may be seen as an exploration of this first paradox; her abundant allusions, spare prose style, and preference for inconclusive closure are formal ways of confronting the problem of telling the truth with lies. Her subject matter, meanwhile, explores the common isolation of humanity. . . .

If Taylor has not joined the ranks of such contemporaries as Barbara Pym, in whose work Christian faith is more likely than art to lead from the depicted world of clumsy human foolishness to an implied realm of divine grace, neither has she joined the ranks of such true believers in art as [Henry] James himself. For Taylor, man's salvation lies in the realm of human imagination, yet unlike James, whose artists manqué suffer because they have the souls but not the skills of artists, Taylor extends the salvation of the imagination to the nonartist (Nora, Cressy), the bad artist (Angel), and even the false artist (Ludo)—who nevertheless has the wit to recognize the "true" artist in Mrs. Palfrey, who works in "life." In Taylor's hands, the creative imagination undergoes a democratization that is a fitting accomplishment for a writer who, despite her reputation as a genteel novelist of manners, was a professed Socialist living in a Socialist state.

Jane Brown Gillette. *Twentieth Century Literature.* 35, 1989, pp. 94–95, 111

Another 70-year-old widow who befriends a young man is Laura Palfrey in Elizabeth Taylor's *Mrs. Palfrey at the Claremont*. Laura, somewhat estranged from her only daughter, moves to a London hotel, where she resides with three other widows and one widower. She lives comfortably but frugally, supported by the interest from her husband's estate. By accident she encounters Ludo, a poor young writer. Ludo, seeing Laura as a subject for his novel, poses as her grandson for the benefit of the Claremont's guests, who have been waiting in vain for the appearance of the much-talked-about but absent family member. In return for the entertainment at the Claremont, Ludo creates a splendid evening for Laura at his basement apartment, where he prepares a meal. In turn Laura obliges Ludo with a loan of fifty pounds, even though she is worried (needlessly) about her financial situation; during her husband's life she had never bothered to learn how to handle money. This perceived self-sacrifice on behalf of the young man stands in sharp contrast to her rejection of a marriage proposal from her older co-resident at the hotel, who is seeking a nurse-wife in his declining years.

E. M. Nett. *Women's Studies.* 18, 1990, p. 180

Elizabeth Taylor's *At Mrs. Lippincote's* is another testament to the way definitions of home and homeland are feminized in wartime domestic novels. . . .

In *At Mrs. Lippincote's* the contiguous communities of home and army are seen to reflect an uneasy alliance, a cold war which questions the purpose of a nation. Through the expression of power and patriotism represented by army life, women are shown to be manipulated into believing that they must repress their needs for individuation and submit to the higher purpose of protecting the nation.

At Mrs. Lippincote's is structured as a process of Julia awakening to her individuality by testing herself against women's traditional roles. . . .

One way Taylor dramatizes Julia's development is by having her read earlier women's novels. In order to assess the governing conventions of her life, Julia must become a critical reader, reinterpreting the conventions of romance and realist fiction. . . .

As Nancy Armstrong has observed, Taylor's novel suggests that domestic fiction is a successful form of those chapbooks that prescribe the formation of female character according to traditional codes of conduct.

Phyllis Lassner. *Mosaic.* 23:3,
1990, pp. 95–96

There are twelve stories in this collection, [reprint of *A Dedicated Man*] and all of them charged with a peculiarly English lucidity, whether the setting is the Home Counties, Greece or Marrakesh. One of Elizabeth Taylor's aims, indeed, is to cast light on various facets of English social life—quintessentially, during the 1950s, when decorum was on its last legs but niceties still had a place. Wryness and fastidiousness are the author's traits, while a kind of muted willfulness or discontent shapes the characters. This author is often funny—as in the story, "Vron and Willie" about a kleptomaniac brother and sister and their drunken aunt—but a more characteristic tone is an ironic sedateness. She is good on a whole range of adolescent behavior from the wistful to the awful—and in this collection in particular, she turns her attention to the strategies that prevail when people of opposing temperaments are thrown together.

It's not that there is anything very dramatic about these convergences, which typically take place between couples on holiday (the title of one story, "In a Different Light," suggests the theme of all of them) but, in some mysterious way—and always in the lowest possible key—she gets to grips with the jarring note. Makeshift alliances form one strand running through the collection, while another has to do with the make-believe element in people's images of themselves. In the title story, "A Dedicated Man," this crosses and recrosses with reality, until the two get hopelessly entwined. The author herself has no moral stance: she is far too practiced and subtle an observer for that. But she directs our attention to those dubious areas in which romance, self-delusion or bad judgment cause a crucial unsatisfactoriness.

Patricia Craig. (London) *Times Literary
Supplement.* January 15, 1993, p. 22

TEASDALE, SARA (UNITED STATES) 1884–1933

Sara Teasdale stands high among the living poets of America. In an age of outpour, her constitution and her method combine to reaffirm the beneficence of limitation. Nature, rich in her gifts to Miss Teasdale, has been wisely severe in her refusals, and the poet's forbearing and chary art has enforced the continence of nature. She writes brief poems on few subjects; her diction is culled rather than copious; her imagery is unmarked by range or change. Even the verse-forms are few and obvious, though certain unrhymed poems offer to the caprice of the hour the distant courtesy of a passing salutation. I find in her no proof of that more than Gallic unreserve which a press notice sent me by her publishers is sharp enough to discover in her work; if it be there, I applaud the cunning with which Miss Teasdale has hidden her openness.

Still further, I am not sure that Miss Teasdale's second-best, which naturally exceeds her first-best in volume, is notably superior to the second-best of many other expert artists among her living compatriots. It is in her brief, passionate, unfalteringly modeled lyrics, at once flame-like and sculpturesque like fire in a Greek urn, that her true distinction becomes manifest.

The passion which these lyrics embody is a strong, but also an unhurried, unimpetuous, clear-sighted, and self-guiding passion. Most poets in our day utilize their transitory fervors hastily, anxiously, as they might consume their hot tea and waffles in alarm lest the life-giving heat should vanish. The stay of the feeling in their minds seems only long enough to insure its rebound to the page. With Sara Teasdale the case is different; her passions endure, and she can wait. Hence the rare combination of fervor with a high, serene discretion, a poised and steadfast art, which makes the expression of feeling in these compact poems, "half-ardent, half-austere." . . .

Miss Teasdale scars her pages with the spelling "thru." I shall retaliate for the sufferings I have undergone from the practice only be calling my persecutor "up-to-date"—a revenge which is indistinguishable from homage in the ears of all lovers of that fashion of orthography. In other points, I should sum up Miss Teasdale as the inheritor rather than the copyist of the great English tradition, the tradition of refined vigor, vigor enclosed and ensheathed in comeliness, of feelings intensely personal yet delicately human, of a life whose springs are central and intimate, however great the variety of its individual outflowings.

O. W. Firkins. *The Nation.* January 6, 1916, p. 12

No one of these word-musicians has more completely and melodiously mastered her craft than Sara Teasdale, possibly the most gifted singer of them all. With the utmost simplicity of phrase and style, she achieves effects that are little short of magical; her stanzas, usually without a single figure of speech, are more eloquent than a poem crammed with gorgeous tropes and highly colored similes. This utterance which, as Miss Teasdale's schooling has proceeded, has grown less and less studied, is already recognizable among many echoes in the early *Sonnets to Dusé and Other Poems.* . . . But in *Helen of Troy and Other Poems* . . . it is far stronger. And yet, excellent as are many of the short poems, Miss Teasdale has not attained her full singing power in this volume; her songs are surpassed by the six monologs that open the book. Helen of Troy, Beatrice, Sappho, Marianna Alcoforando (the Portuguese nun), Guenevere, Erinna ("pale Erinna of the perfect lyre,"

Sappho's favorite pupil)—these are all made to live in a blank verse so musical that it has an almost lyric intensity. Classical in subject, the treatment is as modern and searching as any of Oppenheim's analytic probings; the figures are vitalized by a new interpretation that is as penetrating as it is passionate. . . .

Direct, eager, without ostentation or ornament, her lines move with a potency of their own. Sparing of metaphors, almost sparse in their clear expressiveness, these poems, usually limiting themselves to two or three simple quatrains, contain more sheer singing than those of any other living American poet. Miss Teasdale has a genius for the song, for the pure lyric in which words seem to have fallen into place without art or effort. . . .

Her most recent volume, *Love Songs* . . . is a gathering of her old amatory verses, a few new ones and a lovely interlude, "Songs out of Sorrow." This collection emphasizes again how bare of verbal subtleties and startling images her verses are, and yet how full of a deeper magic they seem. . . . For the greater part Miss Teasdale fulfils her promise; she gives us the lyric in its most concise and chiseled form; she responds to the passion of beauty that is, for all its disguises and evasions, as energetic as the passion for life.

Louis Untermeyer. *The New Era in
American Poetry* (New York: Holt, 1919),
pp. 264–65, 267, 269–71

A new volume by Sara Teasdale must be opened with anxiety—anxiety lest its author's old intensity of metaphor and meter be felt to have lessened, lest the glowing shapes of her love be seen to have paled and grown vague. The Sappho of this century and continent must be free, if anyone can be free, of poetical cant. Thus considered, at least a fourth or a third of *Flame and Shadow* meets the eagerest expectations. There is much in the book that is not fine, but there is enough that is. Sara Teasdale seems constantly assailed with two temptations, and it is only at intervals that she entirely surmounts them. One is the temptation to make effective endings, to save up points and appeals for a last line. This may come from having been set so often to music; she keeps her eye and ear too much, perhaps, on a possible singer whose audience will reward a neat conclusion with ripples of pleasure and applause. At any rate, it faintly tends to cheapen her product as poetry. The other temptation is to deal exclusively in stock love-lyric materials—in herself as "singer," in abstract Beauty, in the "call" of her love to this or that creature or thing, and in personified Pain. To handle these things complacently and forever is to be a minor poet, in whatever age you live. By now, for instance, the "Pain" of the twentieth century poetess is as conventional and irritating as the "pains" of Augustan Damons and Strephons had become by 1720. Sara Teasdale only reaches her perfection when, defeating her temptations, she interpenetrates pain with metaphor and metaphor with pain, when she finds the proper balance between fire and form, between the complexity of a condition and the simplicity of a cry.

Mark Van Doren. *The Nation.*
January 5, 1921, p. 20

Miss Teasdale's . . . work has been second only to Miss Millay's in the extent of the public response. . . . Miss Teasdale's love poems are more restrained and quite as skillful as Edna Millay's. Melancholy, wistful, sentimental. They have been compared with Heinrich Heine's, because of epigrammatic similarities. But they lack the intensity, the power and irony of the German's masterly lyrics. The Teasdale songs are closer to folk songs, handled with sophistication. Often their spontaneity is obvious, or depends on formulas the poet has employed many times before. Such poetry seems, on the whole, an excellent accomplishment, rarely a profound achievement. There are entirely too many Aprils, too many muted strings, too much wistfulness and weeping.

Alfred Kreymbourg. *A History of American
Poetry: Our Singing* Strength (n.p.: Tudor,
1934), pp. 446–47

The fascination of this volume [*The Collected Poems of Sara Teasdale*] lies in the fact that it exhibits so clearly the poet's development. As the years went by, the themes did not alter much, but the cadences became more varied; the mood more reflective, the expression more sensitive. Gradually, the irony that pointed the best of the early lyrics deepened and strengthened the poetry of Miss Teasdale's maturity. She was moved by the same things, rejoiced by the same natural beauties, overcome by the same loneliness, haunted by the same recurrent terror. But the personal relation is realized with a keener sense of the nuances of human intercourse, the terror is measured by a fuller awareness of man's fate, even the landscapes are viewed with a more perceptive eye. With these sharpened responses to the world about and the world within, came also a better control of her instrument. The later poems do not require, as so many of the early ones seem to do, the accompaniment of voice and strings in order to give them a suggestiveness that they fail to achieve. The riper pieces are, as their author came to be, self-sufficient. It is no strange and bitter brew that Miss Teasdale offers—it is the wine that one expects with dinner in a civilized place. But with the years, one finds that the bouquet is finer and the flavor delightfully dry.

Aware, as every sensitive person must be, of the cruelties that beset mankind, Miss Teasdale scarcely ever touches upon the problems that are the subject of current poetry. . . .

Here, plainly, is no revolutionary, in any sense of the word. The technique is traditional. The prevailing temper is one of acceptance—joyous, mournful, or resigned. But though Sara Teasdale's scope was limited, it enlarged with the years, so that her mature work delights one with its deeper music and frosty beauty. Even the long-for achievement of the good society will not appreciably lessen private griefs. While these remain, one can find some assuagement in the melody of such lyrics as these, and take courage from their quiet irony.

Babette Deutsch. *Poetry.* December, 1937,
pp. 150–51, 153

The work of Sara Teasdale . . . had begun to free itself, in the 1920s, from very nearly all traces of a romantic vocabulary and a romantic tone. The poems in *Flame and Shadow* (1920) are so naturally put together that they seem to be spoken, rather than written—spoken at the direct urging of passionate impulse. Miss Teasdale's lyrics, moreover, accompanied her experience of life step by step; they became increasingly lucid and tragic with the passage of time. She expressed not only the simplicities of traditional feminine feeling, but new subtleties of emotional nuance, and her last book, *Strange Victory,* published posthumously in 1933, shows classic depth and balance.

Louise Bogan. *Achievement in American
Poetry* (Chicago: Regnery, 1951), pp. 75–76

Her haunting and poignant poems, written in a pure, lyrical music, illuminated the moods of love in all their rainbow splendor as few singers before had illuminated them. She laid bare the soul of one woman when rapture, anguish, solitude, longing, or loveliness had burdened the heart to overflowing. And because her lyric testimony communicates emotion that is the same for all men, all hearts everywhere, her poetry possesses a timeless quality.

Her work is almost totally without figurative or ornamental imagery, without a large and pretentious vocabulary; it is not scholarly or cerebral. It is completely free of the influences that sifted through the poetic world during her lifetime: the awakening of a social conscience, the experimentation with new verse forms, new idioms of expression, poetry devoid of capitalization and clarity, and poetry depicting the emptiness and shallowness of the twentieth century. Essentially an individual in her life as in her art, she was affected by none of these.

For she did not see the world either through a social conscience or as an empty Waste Land; she wrote from the world within, a many-colored land whose shifting lights fell over the horizons of solitude, love, and beauty. The objective world was never as real or important to her as the castle of her own heart and mind.

It is true that her poetic latitude was limited: she was not closely concerned with the everyday struggle of the common man and his problems, or with the great philosophical probings of the world, or with the contemporary scene. But her range was wide enough to include the infinite spaces in the human heart—the eternal emotions of joy, sorrow, longing, and love that are of grave importance to every human being. . . .

If one word could be used to describe the poetic artistry of Sara Teasdale, it would be the word *pure*. From a purity of spirit, she gave the world poems of pure music, pure emotion, and pure beauty. Even the suffering and resignation of later years could not mar this quality of purity; for as the darkness grew deeper the true essence of the spirit shone even more luminously.

Margaret Haley Carpenter. *Sara Teasdale: A
Biography* (New York: Schulte, 1960),
p. 330–31, 348

In an age when love has almost been reduced to charts and diagrams and surveys, that Sara Teasdale continues to draw a loyal audience might, at first glance, seem surprising. That she does is evidenced by the fact that her *Collected Poems* has gone through twenty-three printings since its first publication in 1937, and a new edition, with an introduction by the distinguished American poet Marya Zaturenska, was published in 1966. Despite the fact that she was surrounded by the ferment of the "new poetry" during her lifetime, she made no effort to incorporate any of its tenets or techniques into her own work. She went serenely on her own path, marching to the music of a different drum, and even the formidable Amy Lowell had to agree that she was right to do so. . . .

For while Sara Teasdale did not consciously try to surprise her readers, her knowledge of language, and her skill in using it for the utmost connotative effect, could evoke the fullest overtones of emotion all the more effectively because it was not deliberately set down in so many words.

Rosemary Sprague. *Imaginary Gardens: A
Study of Five American Poets* (Philadephia:
Chilton, 1969), pp. 99–100

Sara Teasdale's place in American poetry has no parallel. Temperamentally, through the sheltered childhood that held her an unwilling prisoner of the past, she belonged to the tradition of women's poetry that flourished through the middle and late nineteenth century. But, thrown as she was into the conditions of a new age that arrived with shocking suddenness, she responded with courage, turning her girlish lyrics from conventional sentiment to a mature and unflinching exploration of the realities of her emotional life. Nowhere else in our literature has such a transition been recorded so clearly and articulately. She spoke for all women emerging from the humility of subservience into the pride of achievement, recognizing that her art sprang from the conflict of forces that pulled her in opposing directions. . . .

Sara Teasdale's heritage was the divided self—a personality ready for self-fulfillment, rich in outgoing emotion, sensuous, and keenly sensitive, attuned to esthetic rather than moral imperatives, but stricken with a paralyzing obedience to the rigorous proprieties imposed on her in childhood, mainly by her mother. Sara withheld and privately worried her natural impulse of emotion before releasing it, so that she appeared reticent and austere, except to the few with whom she felt free. The shrinking from life just at the point of ebullience was the paradox out of which she produced her poems, balancing passion against restraint, easy flow against containment, apparent simplicity against suggested complexity, desire against despair. Tension was the keynote of her life, although she hid it beneath her gentleness and let it show least when it was most intolerable.

William Drake. *Sara Teasdale: Woman and Poet* (New York: Harper and Row, 1979), pp. 1–2, 5–6

One of the difficulties in assessing Teasdale's poetry is understanding her use of images. Her range was narrow and her application deceptively simple. In her earliest poetry she relied heavily on classical and medieval material culled from her wide reading and revealing, apparently, little or no understanding of real life. A closer inspection, however, reveals that she was using this material for a unique personal statement. Her Helen of Troy was not the usual pawn of men's desires, but a strong determined woman bent on revenge. Neither of her "fallen women"—Guenevere and Marion Alforcando—regrets her actions; they only wonder at the behavior of other humans. . . .

It is the world of nature . . . to which she most frequently referred in her poetry. And here, too, her use of images has created misunderstanding. She focused on three major features—givers of light, sources of life forces, and carriers of messages. . . .

It may have been to maintain [the] sense of herself as a translator of the messages of nature that led Teasdale to prefer the musicality and the simplicity of her style to the more modern approaches that were being developed during her career.

The great themes of love and death dominated Teasdale's poetry, but in her treatment of them she sought to capture the intensity of her emotional response. It was probably this intensity that she meant when she spoke of "beauty." Beauty for her was a matter of perception. In her earliest poetry, the physical attractiveness of the actress Eleonora Duse provided the intensity of her portrayal of these themes. Later she would believe that the elements should be reversed, that it was love that provided the impulse necessary to perceive beauty, that is, to experience an intense emotional effect. When love failed to provide her with her sense of completion in life, she sought another way to express the sense of intensity in her art. The mode that she used was the moment of poise between two extremes, such as the moment in "Beautiful Proud Sea" when the watchers "Burn, like stretched silver of a wave, / Not breaking but about to break." The best of her poetry and of her thought was achieved in poems where this moment is captured, but even in her less successful works, it is present in the ironic twist with which many of her poems end. The apparent simplicity of Teasdale's poetry masked an intensity just as the disarming naturalness of her technique masked extraordinary artfulness.

Carol B. Schoen. *Sara Teasdale* (Boston:
Twayne, 1986), pp. 172–74

Teasdale's formal variations compose a melody suggestive of Verlaine's dictate in "Art Poetique": "Car nous voulons la Nuance encoreé / Pas la Couleur, rien que la nuance!" Unfortunately, even though Teasdale experimented with English verse forms in the same way that Verlaine stretched French verse, he is recognized as an innovator and she is not. In part Teasdale's label of traditionalist can be explained by the difference in the nature of English and French poetry. Because French verse had stayed metrically the same from the mid-sixteenth century until the dawn of the nineteenth, slight metrical changes, like those Verlaine made, appeared as revolutionary. On the other hand, Teasdale's innovations when placed against Pound's and Eliot's sweeping changes in English metrics seem insignificant. However, appearance is not necessarily reality. Although melody, metrics, and rhyme have fallen on hard times, in twentieth-century English verse, and Teasdale has been caught writing in a style that is currently out of fashion, her skill at inventing new melodies within formal limits demands a reevaluation of her poetry.

Mary Ann Mannino. *Turn-of-the-Century
Women.* 5, 1990, p. 41

TELIHA, OLENA (UKRAINE) 1907–42

The importance of the work of Olena Teliha, the greatest Ukrainian woman poet after Lesya Ukrayinka . . . cannot be confined to her well-known and often reprinted poems "Vechirnya pisnya" [The Evening Song] and "Povorot" (The return). To be sure, the first of these two poems is unsurpassed in lyric artistry in modern Ukrainian poetry, and the second poem contains the source of her theories and ideas. . . . One should add that the profound and sincerely pious regard of our entire nation for Teliha's social activities and for her heroic death, should not . . . cause us to forget the fact . . . that the most important and the highest measure of any great artist is his art.

Teliha achieved a classical form by gradually removing declamatory-rhetorical and stereotyped elements from her work. . . . The declamatory-rhetorical elements most strikingly jarred in her love poetry, for this particular genre is least suited to a programmatic approach; it requires an original touch, even if only an apparent one. Teliha's love poetry often conveys the impression of being too rationally planned and (despite its wealth of stylistic devices), too "prosaically" expressed.

Volodymyr Derzhavyn. *Mur.* 1, 1946,
pp. 183–85

The extraordinary sobriety of [Teliha's] poetic thought . . . is revealed in the general structure of her themes and the poetic detail of her works. Let us take, for example, the theme of the future return of emigrants to their native land. Other poets usually exploit this in scenes depicting triumphant marches and general rejoicing. Teliha, on the other hand, sees in it harsh reality: the encounter of strangers with strangers; cold and inimical souls meeting in an unfamiliar land. She foresees that the emotions of the moment will be despondency and resentment. The same can be said about the details: at the same time that our "poets" still swing their classical *swords,* Olena Teliha writes about "*planes* and . . . *machine guns.*"

As a poet of life's passions, she sought to discipline her soul by pride and by fidelity. She needed a frame for herself and for her poetry, and she found it in the most stagnant of poetic genres—album poetry [poetry addressed to someone.] She tightened this frame by subjecting her poetic expression to rigorous structural rules and metrical regularity. But this black frame only accentuates the red element: the color of blood and wine. Self-pride and fidelity only emphasize the depth of her intoxication with the fullness of life, just as the formal aesthetic rules accentuate the colorful profusion of her poetic imagery. Teliha remains in Ukrainian literature a unique example of romantic self-control.

Hryhoryy Shevchuk. *Arka.* July, 1947,
pp. 11–12

Despite all the things she had in common with Lesya Ukrayinka, Teliha's poetic vision was completely her own, sincere and unadulterated. Her poetry was perhaps the first in Ukrainian literature to express forcefully and in a manner heretofore unknown to us what we call the feminine mystique. In Lesya Ukrayinka this was an attitude of immaturity; in Khvylovyy one of superiority; in Olena Teliha, however, it was a completely harmonious component of pure poetry, or, to use Khvylovyy's words, the result of certain Freudian biological conditions. . . .

Teliha had a grandiose feeling for the greatness of woman, a feeling of emancipation that openly formulated its own spiritual world. The feminine mystique in her poetry became an element of dramatic tension, a conflict that captures one's attention and emotions. All this resulted in a singular personality in Ukrainian poetry who was "subject to her own and not foreign laws." Even those rare masculine moments in her poetry, which might have appeared artificial in the works of other women poets, appear quite natural and sincere in her verse.

Svyatoslav Hordyns'kyy. *Svoboda.*
March 2, 1952, p. 2

[Teliha's] first, and later, verses conformed to the rigid nationalistic standards of the literary-political journal *Vistnyk* ("The Herald, edited in Lvov by the uncompromising theoretician of Ukrainian nationalism, Dmitro Dontsov), in which they were extensively published. In 1929 she and her husband settled in Warsaw and lived there till the German invasion of Poland, when she moved to Cracow to lead the nationalistic movement in that region. During the German occupation of Ukraine, she returned to Kiev and there edited a literary journal, *Litavry* (Kettle-Drums). In 1942 the Gestapo arrested her and her collaborators and executed the entire group for its activity in the Ukrainian national cause.

In her voluntaristic patriotism, as in the determination of her convictions, Teliha was akin to Lesia Ukrainka. Her verses are of a tense, nervous temperament, and in them she makes plain that the Ukrainian woman, to play her role in her country's struggle, must adopt a severe Spartan attitude devoid of any idyllic preconceptions, and must arm herself with spiritual strength equal to the physical power to endure heroically not only the buffets of war but also the despair of solitude resulting from it. Teliha is often referred to as the Joan of Arc of Ukraine. The powerful, steel-couched, clashing idiom of her verses make her stand out rather as a Ukrainian Amazon.

Constantine H. Andrusyshen and Watson
Kirkconnell. *The Ukrainian Poets, 1189–1962*
(Toronto: University of Toronto Press, 1963), p. 463

TELLES, LYGIA FAGUNDES (BRAZIL) 1924–

The Brazilian writer Lygia Fagundes Telles's eighth short-story collection *(Tigrela and Other Stories)* has an extraordinary variety of characters, plots and narrative strategies yet never seems academic or willfully experimental. She has certainly read her Kafka and Borges, but while sharing some of their thematic concerns—time, memory, infinity, identity confusion—she writes with a pixielike touch that gives her work a strange buoyancy. She is by no means incapable of moral outrage, yet even when she writes about political corruption or the mistreatment of women she never becomes didactic or self-indulgent. Instead she relies on her imagination to create radical transformations of the quotidian, like the magical invasion of the rats (an image of the oppressed, rebellious masses) in the Secretary of Welfare's mansion, in the brilliant political satire "Rat Seminar." At times she is too relentlessly surrealistic; a number of stories end in perfunctorily strange ways, like routine episodes of "The Twilight Zone." Though she's known as a fabulist, her strongest stories are the most realistic ones. In "The Sauna" a middle-aged self-absorbed artist holds a kind of trial inside his mind as he guiltily recalls the women he manipulated to help his career. In "Dear Editor" she uses a similar technique to describe a sixty-year-old virgin schoolteacher's attempt to write a letter of protest against the rampant sexuality in Brazilian society, even as the teacher regrets her exclusion from it. Like so many of these stories, translated elegantly by Margaret A. Neves, it is funny, poignant, contradictory, and intriguing.

Richard Burgin. *The New York Times.*
May 4, 1986, p. 40

Certain of this Brazilian author's fourteen stories gathered here *(Tigrela and Other Stories)* are chilling and subtle. Told with a sensitivity to detail and character development, they portray universal fears and desires. For example, in "The Ants," two terrified students watch as a dwarf's skeleton is reconstructed. In "The Consultation," a servile psychiatric patient assumes his doctor's identity and determines another patient's fate. However, Telles has executed other stores less skillfully. "Yellow Nocturne," in which a woman conjures up events from her youth, suffers from an inadequately explained plot that gets lost in a surfeit of imagery. Telles also tends to overdramatize scenes that are incidental to the story. This is an uneven collection; the better passages effectively illustrate our terror of impending death and our yearning for love and immortality, but overall Telles disappoints.

John Mutter. *Publishers Weekly.*
April 18, 1986, p. 64

Unlike her contemporaries, João Guimarães Rosa and Clarice Lispector, who became famous as experimenters and stylistic innovators, Lygia Fagundes Telles chose a less spectacular, more traditional approach to narration. This has made her one of her country's most popular serious writers. Her stylistic profile is defined by her concern for craftsmanship and by a gradual refinement of her narrative voice toward utmost economy of expression. Located well within the modern tradition of psychological realism, Lygia's style achieves remarkable plasticity and expressive range, in keeping with the breadth of her thematic concerns. . . .

Lygia Fagundes Telles' preferred fictional milieu is the great São Paulo bourgeoisie. Within that milieu, her range of themes is large. In her novels, she has concentrated on portraying the moral decay of the middle class by focusing on young women protagonists trapped between their own aspirations for self-fulfillment and the stifling code of their social class. This element figures strongly in her short stories as well, but in her short fiction, the author favors the darker side of the human psyche. She has written many macabre tales and prefers morbid or pathological characters. In this sense, *Seminário dos Ratos* is a typical collection of her stories.

Jon M. Tolman. *Review.* 30, Fall, 1991, p. 65

Lygia Fagundes Telles exerts a notable equalizing force in her literary portrayal of the sexes. She elevates women from the traditional position of subservience and passivity to a position of stability, rationality, and, to a certain degree, social autonomy. She diminishes the traditional concept of men as pillars of strength with unchallenged authority to entities who are insecure, frequently demented, and otherwise morally and socially weak. Women, however, in the short stories of Fagundes Telles, are not anointed with sainthood, and men are neither ridiculed nor portrayed as imbeciles. The reading public can easily sympathize with most of her characters regardless of their sex or their dilemma. Over the years Fagundes Telles has consistently presented men and women as psychological and social equals in a maze of realistic and imaginary situations. . . .

Fagundes Telles is primarily interested in the psychology of her characters and intentionally neglects their physical attributes, except to emphasize or contrast a psychological trait. All the stories in *Antes do Baile Verde* (Before the green ball) serve as a framework for psychological confrontations. These confrontations may be between men and women, women and women, men and men, or they may simply be self-confrontations. A confrontation, of course, implies some sort of conflict, and Fagundes Telles is a master at presenting conflicts, although she chooses not to resolve them.

In the twenty short stories of *Antes do Baile Verde,* women are more apt to be cast as principal characters than men. The most consistent characteristic of these female characters is their sense of psychological and social independence. While such women seem to control their own lives and destinies, they are not superwomen. Men, on the other hand, are frequently portrayed in some sort of personal crisis which causes them to lose control of their own lives and destinies. They seem to be searching for peace of mind, because of a lost sense of essence.

Whether by intent or coincidence, Fagundes Telles is a literary iconoclast. In the Brazilian context, she has to a great degree departed from the stereotyped portrayals of women and men. By doing so, she has contributed to the cultural liberation of her country and to the intellectual liberation of both sexes worldwide. The equalizing of the sexes in *Antes do Baile Verde* is subtle, so it is not clear that Fagundes Telles is an intentional iconoclast. It is very likely that her ability to destroy images is a by-product of her ability to invent extraordinary plots which tend to invert or modify the traditional roles of men and women.

Lygia Fagundes Telles has earned a well-deserved reputation as an innovator of contemporary Brazilian letters. She has won the hearts and captured the imagination of the Brazilian reading public. Now she is well along the way to international renown due to her keen sense of human nature and her polished manner of presenting it in literature. Lygia Fagundes Telles seems to have attained that nebulous, but coveted sense of universality.

Richard L. Brown. *Romance Notes.* 32:2,
Winter, 1991, pp. 157, 159, 161

Telles's first published novel, *Ciranda da pedra* (1954; The marble dance, 1986), introduced the dialectic of imprisonment and liberation that moves through her entire oeuvre. Like in Clarice Lispector's fiction, family ties are prison chains that impede the protagonists from achieving growth. This theme is encapsulated in the metaphor of the aquarium in *Verão no aquário* (1963; Summer in the aquarium), which in the novel signifies the childhood that dooms the protagonist to dependency. The claustrophobic social ambience of most of Telles's narratives is that of an upper middle class bankrupt of both money and morals. Telles documents the inner turmoil of women who need to escape but are ill equipped to function in a rapidly changing world.

Telles is best known for her novel *As meninas* (1973; The girl in the photograph, 1982), which opens new directions in her prose style and introduces the element of specific political protest against the military dictatorship, then in one of its most repressive phases. The three women in this story are inmates not of the family home but of a pension in São Paulo. The fluid, alternating narrative perspectives of the novel offer intimate portraits of lives complicated by the contradictory dynamics of megacity life in a regressive moment of Brazilian history.

Telles's most recent work is *As horas nuas* (1989; The naked hour), which continues the revolutionary path of *As meninas* and has been compared to Clarice Lispector's *A hora da estrela* (1977; The hour of the star, 1986). This book, which won the Pedro Nava Prize for best novel of 1989, is the story of an aging alcoholic actress, a character as "polluted" and devastated as the country Brazil, for which she is clearly a symbol. The vision of São Paulo is one of prevailing misery; the city is "occupied" by street people, economic refugees of ecological and economic decline. One of the several narrators is Rahul, the cat, who gazes on the chaos with a calm, experienced eye.

Telles distinguishes herself from peers such as Lispector and Nélida Piñon with a direct testimonial prose that contrasts with the famous abstract approaches of Lispector and Piñon to the themes shared by these three writers. Telles offers keen observations on contemporary Brazilian society and politics, addressing the precarious situation of women in this aggressive environment. While they are very different stylists, Telles and her colleagues find common ground in their commitment to social change.

Elizabeth Lowe. In Steven R. Serafin and Walter D. Glanze, eds. *Encyclopedia of World Literature in the 20th Century* (New York: Continuum, 1993), p. 592

TERRY, MEGAN (UNITED STATES) 1932–

American King's English for Queens is the most clearly articulated of Megan Terry's language plays of the 1970s, explicitly concerned with the ways in which the text and context of language mold thinking, seeing, and believing. In four full-length plays, *Tommy Allen Show, Babes in the Bighouse, Brazil Fado* and *American King's English for Queens*—all "musicals" performed at the Omaha Magic Theatre—although ostensibly savaging television, Middle American family life, marriage, sex, or prison, Terry challenges the perceptions molded by language itself and the clichés about language as a vehicle for communication. Whereas words seldom say what they mean, the reverse (that they mean what they say) is often true. What is conveyed between characters onstage, or between them and the audience, is seldom confined by either the connotative or denotative meanings of the words used; and yet these deliberately chosen words and phrases are capable of creating meaning for both speaker and auditor.

Using the notorious American snipe hunt as a metaphor in *American King's English for Queens,* Terry identifies the parameters of language-meaning discourse. But action and reaction also create a context for meaning which either validates or rejects language's implications. Two features are vital to Terry's context for language: the transformations which illuminate the shifting realities purported to have acknowledged meanings; and the songs which redefine the circumstances of the characters and storyline seriously or mockingly. Unlike the absurdists, Terry does not investigate language to devalue it, nor meaning to abandon it, nor action to replace them both. Instead, all of her challenges testify her reluctance to allow the idea of meaninglessness to mask the uses made of language, action, and meaning. . . .

In the four full-length musicals named above, Terry admits that a speaker does not always say what she or he means, but does mean what she or he says; something is communicated by language. And in a structured world, socialized auditors recognize general language use as well as irony, clichés, and stereotypes to which they react. These responses may have been conditioned by the social climate, and the word choice of the speaker or the verbal response of the listener may not actually correspond with what they believe themselves to be saying, but these factors do not lessen communication. Normal utterances, lacking the precision of poetry's language choice, expand rather than contract the range of communication, especially when joined with action rather than separated from it.

Kathleen Gregory Klein. Modern Drama.
27, 1984, pp. 574–75

Megan Terry's early transformation plays—*Eat at Joe's, Calm Down Mother, Keep Tightly Closed in a Cool Dry Place, Comings and Goings,* and *Viet Rock*—represent a further response of the Open [Theatre] to the "setup." Abjuring the rigidity of appointed and anointed roles, the Open made transformational drama a staple of its early repertory, creating theatrical exercises and plays in which actors shifted freely and suddenly from one character, situation, time, or objective to another. As Terry's colleague Peter Feldman put it, "Whatever realities are established at the beginning are destroyed after a few minutes and replaced by others. Then these are in turn destroyed and replaced." From the perspective of two decades of subsequent theater, it should now be clear that Terry's work with transformation challenged more than the individual actor seeking versatility and range. In freeing the actor from the prescriptiveness of the assigned role, transformational drama challenged the prevailing character of realistic theater, which reinforced social and theatrical expectations. Terry's work in neutralizing fixed assumptions, dismantling the stereotype, and reevaluating the institutional hierarchy proved seminal in forming the emerging principles and modes of New York's alternative theater.

Chief among these emerging principles was off Broadway's conception of character. . . .

Any of Terry's transformation plays might serve to illustrate the Open's contribution to redefining dramatic character, although her technique is not always the same. . . .

Keep Tightly Closed in a Cool Dry Place, like all transformation plays, does not ask its actors to find some coincidence between themselves and the characters they are portraying, nor does it ask its actors to create subtexts. In place of this psychological work, it offers a sequence of opportunities for verbal and nonverbal behavior, each involving an abrupt shift in roles. Transformational drama is clearly both a challenge and an opportunity for the actor wanting to see himself or herself not as a trade magazine type but as an actor capable of moving with facility among diverse roles. Yet transformational drama is not simply "for the actors," as Gerald Weales suggests in his unappreciative assessment of Terry's work. Transformational drama, like all drama, is for the audience, whose response to the abrupt changes the form demands helps create this alternative model of presenting dramatic character, one that says more about the epistemology of character, onstage and off, than realistic drama can. . . .

If Terry's work with redefining character has found legitimacy in the American theater, so also has it been instrumental in establishing feminist theater. In *Feminist Theatre*, Helene Keyssar calls Terry the mother of the phenomenon. Yet in the 1960s, when Terry was active in New York, feminist theater did not even have a name. Today's Terry calls herself a feminist—and a humorist, and a humanist, and, most importantly, a theater person—yet her motherhood rightly began at the Open, not because she was writing plays for and about women (which she was) nor because she was shaping a feminist party line (which she wasn't), but because she was writing transformational drama. That form's theatrical efforts at dismantling the stereotype, freeing the actor from the prescriptiveness of an assigned role, and reevaluating the institutional hierarchy speak with force to the comparable goals of feminism. Whether or not Terry was writing plays at the Open that we would now call feminist, her work in neutralizing fixed assumptions was seminal in preparing off Broadway for the gender deconstructions of the burgeoning phenomenon we now call feminist theater.

June Schlueter. Studies in American Drama,
1945 to the Present. 2, 1987, pp. 59–62,
67–68

In over thirty years of writing more than sixty plays for the American theater, Megan Terry remains one of our most politically sensitive dramatists. Her *Viet Rock*, (1966), the first rock musical, protested early the aggressions of the war; *Babes in the Bighouse* (1974) focused on the problems and roles women were forced to accept in prison; and *Kegger* (1985) bewailed teenage alcoholism. Praised for her transformational dramas performed at the Open Theatre, which she founded with Joseph Chaikin, Terry assaults the traditional definition and depiction of self by having characters blend into each other. Too often, Terry holds, an individual's sense of self is stereotyped by external, oppressive forces, such as big government, pop culture, or a victimizing supermachismo.

Amtrak, which premiered on February 26, 1988, at Omaha's Magic Theatre where Terry is the resident playwright, is her most recent attack on forced role playing in America. . . .

Amtrak seems like a compact, naturalistic play, a Strindbergian battle of the sexes 1987-style, but Terry's naturalism is only surface deep. *Amtrak* reminds me of a politicized *Sexual Perversity in Chicago*. And like the hustlers in another Mamet play, *Glengarry Glen Ross*, Terry's Bruce and Rick are programmable males who acquire their identity from their jobs. They are never far away from their "business" (as Rick affirms, "My whole being is classified"). The duo speak a "winning bid English" on cellular phones to work on Contra deals in high places. Discussing "Colonel X," Bruce admits "That guy would steal from his grandma's pocketbook," and continues "Those guys were dirty before they ever discovered the Contras." . . .

Terry's comedy turns grim at the end. Throughout *Amtrak* the characters have been aware that something is wrong with their train. . . . The fate of these characters riding on Amtrak, America's public railroad, is charged with political symbolism. America, like the railroad and the Contras it subsidizes (secretly), is off its proper course. Both the fatal train and the embarrassed government suffer from power failures. Appropriately, the characters who have adopted various roles informed by Contragate tactics are foiled. Bruce and Rick thought they had the inside track, but a bumbling train crew ends their plotting. These men, like the women, thought they were going to fly high on this mission.

Philip C. Kolin. Notes on Contemporary
Literature. 20:2, March, 1990, pp. 3–5

One out of every eight people in the United States cannot read a sign or a medicine bottle. This statistic, and others equally alarming, are quoted early in *Headlights*, the Omaha Magic Theatre's contribution to raising awareness and dealing with the problem of illiteracy in this country. As part of their continuing commitment to exploring issues of immediate social relevance and to collaborative artistic development, Jo Ann Schmidman, Megan Terry, and their colleagues at the Magic Theatre have produced an exciting theatrical collage that celebrates the joy of reading and learning while it reveals the fear, insecurity, and disenfranchisement of nonreaders in an increasingly complex world. . . .

Terry developed *Headlights* from personal interviews and research on literacy, and the piece was subsequently structured by Schmidman in workshop. Schmidman, as Artistic Director, and Terry, as Playwright-in-Residence of Omaha Magic Theatre, have continued to expand on the legacy of nontraditional style and artistic development from their days with the Open Theatre. They lead a company whose social commitment serves as a model for both collaborative working methods and community involvement.

Kathy Fletcher. *Theatre Journal.* 42, 1990,
pp. 170–72

Buttressed by the company's energized, often transformational, acting and experimental designs, the OMT [Omaha Magic Theater] texts of the 1970s and early 1980s, usually by Megan Terry (with Jo Ann Schmidman as ubiquitous performer, as well as designer or director or both), typically mock and demystify a variety of political and cultural sins. I'm thinking of *Babes in the Bighouse* (1974), *Brazil Fado* (1977) and *American King's English for Queens* (1978), the latter featuring the human prairie dog Silver Morgan who queries the audience: "Do you bark, therefore you are?" sending up not only Cartesian logic but also, in a sound-babble lullaby sung by humans and non-humans, the idealizations of the pre-Oedipal in 1970s feminist scholarship. In their unabashed humanism, their feminist irreverence, these spectacular texts build on Terry's justly famous *Calm Down Mother* (1965), *Comings and Goings* (1968), *Approaching Simone* (1970), and reach ahead to the OMT's *Goona Goona* (1979) and *Kegger* (1982).

Body Leaks, created jointly by Terry, Schmidman, and visual artist Sora Kimberlain investigates subjectivity differently. In this multimedia performance piece, with an original jazz "sound structure" by Luigi Waites, coherent humanist frames are less apparent, while the psyche's desires and wounds emerge through a blurring [of] body art and plastic art. *Body Leaks* confronts censorship, what cannot be said, what we prevent ourselves from saying as "protection," but in this work, feminist resistance is rarely presented as a positivity, as a set of irreducible truths, but rather as a series of stunning effects that pun on truth-making. As though in playful duet with Luce Irigaray, Terry, Schmidman, and Kimberlain give us a mimetic mirror that does more than trap female thought and body into a pale reflection of the masculine. In *Body Leaks* reflection itself is mimicked. . . .

Fluids on surfaces might have generated some of the most powerful lines of the piece: "The glass is no longer transparent, / beaded and sweating, / it cries from the inside / longing to get through to you." Pushing the limits of Irigarayan mimicry, the mirror of *Body Leaks* no longer reflects the body but becomes the body, "beaded and sweating." No longer a medium of alienation, it cries to "get through to you." As set in motion by Terry, Schmidman, and Kimberlain this leaking, excessive body/mirror becomes an inspired kinetic image, one that not only extends the field of feminist performance but also creates dangerous new metaphors for feminine writing in the 1990s.

Elin Diamond. *Theatre Journal.*
44, 1992, pp. 518–19

THIRKELL, ANGELA (GREAT BRITAIN) 1890–1961

If there is any criticism to be made of *Ankle Deep* it is that the author has fallen a victim to the modern vice of facetiousness and refused to take her sentiment seriously. Constantly the lovers are being called "this pair of imbeciles" or the like, which prevents one from feeling the pity as well as the ludicrousness of their situation. But I hesitate to say anything that would suggest that Angela Thirkell has not the nicest taste in satire—or it may be irony—and gives the greatest promise of being a first-class writer of light humor. But she must keep in the background of her stories. Her opinions we should be glad to see in essay form. In a novel—I regret to appear ungracious—it is her characters we want, not herself.

Sean O'Faolain. *New Statesman and*
Nation. January 21, 1933, p. 76

Mrs. Thirkell's volume [*The Demon in the House*] about that plague of a little boy, Tony Morland, has a most distressing verisimilitude. No man can read it, if he be honest, without recalling his own capabilities of being tiresome to his elders, no woman without wondering at her sex's miraculous patience with the blunt-headed pertinacity of the human male. . . . He is the best boy in fiction since Mr. [Hugh] Walpole's Jeremy, and Mrs. Thirkell has none of Mr. Walpole's desperately avuncular conviction that grown-ups know better than the boy what is good for the boy: her Mrs. Morland is content—and oh! how justly—to know what is more convenient for mothers.

Life and Letters. December, 1934, p. 361

The peace which breaks over Mrs. Thirkell's lovingly chronicled Barsetshire families is . . . dilapidated. Just as war was for them, in the previous novels, more a question of annoyance and patient contriving than horror and privation, so peace is almost frustration—the commission nearly won, the skimping and make-do prolonged. Peace has failed to come as a great, dramatic climax; even its announcement is confused, its celebrations aggravating as all the bakers are closed.

If Mrs. Thirkell's legions of admirers have worried lest a Brave New World alter or disturb her county families they may relax and enjoy this new story [*Peace Breaks Out*] as usual. Life goes on much as before in village and close . . . bazaars are held, tennis matches arranged, house parties achieved. . . .

When problems and grim realities confront us on every side, it is perhaps ungrateful to complain of such undemanding entertainment. Yet at the risk of seeming captious, a plea is entered for a new field for Mrs. Thirkell's delicious and penetrating talents. She has now evolved such a well-recorded circle that there are no surprises left. The non-sequitur (of which she is undoubtedly the most ingenious creator); the old lady who never gets to her feet but in a landslide of impedimenta; the innocent and beautiful young women, or the hearty and wholesome ones, still, figuratively at least, brandishing their hockey sticks; the gallant young men, the equally gallant older ones, bungling a bit but adroitly managed by their wives; the snobberies of the servants' hall; the lower classes who may be kind, courageous, or difficult but who may never, never escape from their vulgarity—Mrs. Thirkell has drawn them all so neatly that one almost feels she is playing with stock figures from a kind of Pollock's Penny Plain and Tuppence Colored Children's Theatre. They may be manipulated into different positions but they never vary. And, too, she has developed a style which, while (deceptively) easy and confidential, has now become so involved that it verges on tea-table conversation with an elderly, delightful, but just faintly tedious aunt.

Pamela Taylor. *Saturday Review of Literature.* May 24, 1947, p. 14

Never too Late, if my calculations are accurate, is the twenty-fifth volume of Angela Thirkell's Barsetshire chronicle. Its characters are nearly all old friends. Its settings are wholly familiar to Thirkell readers. . . .

Mrs. Thirkell, like her own Mrs. Morland, whose experiences, sentiments and "snipe-flights" of observation one often feels she shares, has never professed to take her novels seriously. They are her bread-and-butter work, her annual habit, the means by which she earns or supplements her living. She rates them, as writing, far lower than her first book *Three Houses,* a collection of childhood memories associated with her grandfather, the painter Burne-Jones, and his circle. In this she shows clear judgment, for the now rare and little-known *Three Houses* is a small jewel, beside which the interlocking units of the Barsetshire chronicle seem like a bright string of Poppit beads.

And yet it does not do to dismiss the Barsetshire stories lightly. Not only have they given pleasure to thousands of readers on both sides of the Atlantic, but they have set out a pattern of a certain sort of English life in the first half of the twentieth century, which social historians of the future would be foolish not to follow.

C.-A. Lejeune. *Time and Tide.* June 9, 1956, p. 685

Even Angela Thirkell and Barsetshire have finally conceded that times have changed. This is a memorable admission, but not to be rated as a defeat. It simply means that Mrs. Thirkell has become the most relaxed social historian in England, and Barsetshire natives, freed from years of martyrdom to the stiff upper lip, are more like their best selves than at any time since peace was declared.

The army of occupation has come to stay in Thirkell Land. New ideas, strange words, unfamiliar attitudes and bizarre combinations of possessed and dispossessed gentry are accepted as fixtures in a world where change once spelled treason. Released from her Emily Post-duties, the author is at her best as a shrewd rocking-chair critic. True, the scene [*Close Quarters*] is set in one of those peculiarly depressing English summers. . . . Yet the general effect is of deep contentment and simplicity. Barsetshire has gone back to first causes and likes it. So, needless to add, will every reader who prefers the Barsetshire variety of the past to the present. . . .

Perhaps Mrs. Thirkell herself has been suffering from the exigencies of a stiff upper lip in recent years. Certainly this candid-camera shot of Barsetshire unmasked has put it right back into its niche of immortality.

Isabelle Mallet. The New York Times.
September 21, 1958, p. 40

Mrs. Morland, not the least agreeable of Mrs. Thirkell's permanent *dramatis personae,* admits to writing the same book year after year because her public likes it. If Mrs. Thirkell's own admirers were to voice a criticism it would not be that her books are all identical, for they do vary considerably according to which part of Barsetshire she happens to be visiting, but that she constantly repeats herself in little things. The same quotations appear in book after book, and even in the mouths of totally different people in the same book. And she will not let sleeping dogs lie. It is quite a while now since Noel Merton flirted with Peggy Arbuthnot, but we are reminded of it with unfailing regularity every time the Mertons appear on the scene.

Many old friends appear, some briefly, in *Love at All Ages,* but as Lady Graham's youngest daughter is now married to a clergyman who is also a Duke's son we are introduced to a new household, that of the Duke of Towers, with his American wife. Mrs. Thirkell is perhaps a little perfunctory with them; they are not as interesting as the Pomfrets or even the Omniums.

(London) Times Literary Supplement.
July 7, 1959, p. 421

Angela Thirkell wrote middle-class novels for middle-brow tastes. They were novels about well-mannered families who were living in a society increasingly threatened with extinction. As novels, they were neither vulgar nor lewd, nor profound, but they were read all over the world; readers outside England found them a valuable guide to the nuances of English social life. . . .

There are a few contemporary women authors who are called "lady-novelists," as Angela Thirkell was in her day. The term now has a pejorative ring. Egalitarianism and mass-marketing have crushed the middle-class middle-brow English novel almost out of existence. The people Angela Thirkell wrote about went out of fashion, as Angela Thirkell herself did, and the society revolving round an English cathedral city and its attendant villages lost a valuable chronicler. She and they have, in a sense, gone to earth. Yet the same sort of people are still there—clergymen and their families, the district nurse, the gentleman farmer, the doctor's wife, the gardener, the squire, and the charitable wives, widows and spinsters who make up country society. Has the literary genre become extinct? Whether it has or not, the Thirkell novels continue to be read.

> Margot Strickland. *Angela Thirkell: Portrait of a Lady Novelist* (London: Duckworth, 1977), p. ix

If the word "charm" makes you reach for your revolver, then Angela Thirkell's novels are not for you. They will, however, delight anyone who enjoys the novels of E. F. Benson *(Make Way for Lucia)*, Ben Travers *(Mischief)*, and Margery Sharp *(Cluny Brown)*. All show the influence of Jane Austen and P. G. Wodehouse: Clear-eyed, sensible people confront and rout the dippy, self-dramatizing ones; food, match-making, and gossip are on everyone's minds; and an air of intense coziness quietly covers all. Ironically, though these novels all stand square on the side of rationality, they are written in a spirit of wholesale denial. These authors—and Wodehouse himself, of course—wrote as if the First World War and the Great Depression hadn't changed anyone's perceptions or standard of living. No one is disillusioned. . . .

These three Angela Thirkell novels [*Before Lunch, The Brandons,* and *Pomfret Towers*] of the late 1930s are set in Trollope's imaginary county of Barsetshire, which besides the cathedral town of Barchester, contains the villages of Worsted, Fleece, and Little Misfit. Life for the well-off there sounds like a reward that awaits the blameless in heaven. . . .

Sometimes Mrs. Thirkell indulges in too much wishful thinking—sons who call their mothers "darling," children who are terrified of losing their tempers with parents they don't like. And, since she works for small, telling effects, her plots are often restful to the point of sedation (the country-house weekend in *Pomfret Towers* goes on for 145 pages). But the Barsetshire novels have the flaws of their virtues: delicately sly characterizations, affectionate satire, and the evocation of a vanished, stable world that served as a perfect backdrop for elegant comedy.

> Rhoda Koenig. *New York.* February 4, 1980, p. 55

THOMAS, AUDREY (CANADA) 1935–

Blown Figures is the fifth book by this already accomplished writer of fictions, and to date her most ambitious. In it Audrey Thomas approaches the height of her powers as a spinner of prose, a teller of surprising and engaging tales. With each of her books, the reader feels that the next will be not only better but different in some unimaginable way, and *Blown Figures* is unlike any of its predecessors, in technique at any rate.

The book returns to territory familiar to readers of *Mrs. Blood* and *Songs My Mother Taught Me,* and like these it is a self-contained unit. The heroine again is Isobel, who lost her unborn child in Africa in *Mrs. Blood* and whose hideous childhood is described in *Songs My Mother Taught Me.* In *Blown Figures,* Isobel returns to Africa alone, leaving her husband Jason and her two children behind, searching for the child she has lost—she's obsessed with her failure to find out what was done with the body—but searching also for expiation. She feels the death of the child was her fault, an absurd guilt left over from an earlier affair which ended in a traumatic abortion. . . .

On one level, *Blown Figures* is about Isobel's attempts at exorcism. On another it is about the exorcism of Isobel herself. Isobel must be taken to the end of her journey, her nightmare, so that the narrator can finally some-how get rid of her, return to the present, stop creating her. Isobel is haunted but she is also a pathetic and irritating ghost, fixed in time and repeating herself endlessly. "'Isobel doesn't live' said Jason to a friend, 'she exits.' He had meant to say 'exists.'" "How to rescue Isobel . . . without becoming oneself an Isobel," muses the narrator. Perhaps *Blown Figures* is her answer.

Margaret Atwood. *The New York Times.*
February 1, 1976

This year marks the tenth anniversary of Audrey Thomas's debut as a writer. *Ten Green Bottles* was first published in the States in 1967. It was out of print for many years, but Oberon has now re-published it, and offers a new book, *Ladies & Escorts,* as a "companion piece." In a way, everything Thomas writes is a companion piece to everything else. More than most writers, she is constantly weaving and re-weaving, cross-referencing, overlapping, even repeating her materials. Both these books are collections of short stories; but, though Thomas's novels threaten to fragment, to splinter into their com-ponent images, the experience of reading these books together is much like reading a novel. The stories reinforce and echo each other, even across that ten-year space. . . .

The distance between men and women is only one of the "terrible gaps" Thomas writes about. Her characters often exist in a state of prolonged culture shock. Men against women, reality against arcadia, Europe against America, and, even more starkly, the white West against some country further south, Africa or Mexico—these are the collisions whose psychic contusions she traces. . . .

Thomas is a writers' writer, which shouldn't prevent her from being a readers' writer as well. She has enormous verbal skills: a passion for words—words as games, words as magic or refrain, words as puzzle or multi-leveled pun—a wonderful ear for dialogue and dialect, a flexible style. . . . She is at her best when her stylistic gifts and her obsession with language are reflected by her material. Her finest stories not only demonstrate language, they are about language: the impossibility, and the necessity, of using it for true communication.

Her best stories, too, are about the difficulty of doing whatever it is that she does as a writer. She is not at heart a "story-teller," that is, a constructor of plots which will carry in themselves the weight of her meaning. In fact, she is at her least convincing with her most "finished" plots. Instead she is a fictionalizer.

Margaret Atwood. *Toronto Globe and Mail.*
April 16, 1977, p. 25

Audrey Thomas has acknowledged that writing about her own suffering is a form of therapy and that this very fact contributes to the strength of her work: "Going back over my own words, I reread my first 'real' story, real because it *had* to be written, it seemed to be the only way I could organize the horror and utter futility of a six-months long, drawn-out miscarriage in a hospital in Africa." This episode forms the basis not only of the early story "If One Green Bottle" but of Thomas's first novel, *Mrs. Blood* (1970) and the later work *Blown Figures* (1974). While it is understandable that so disturbing an experience might have to be relived and interpreted more than once, it is less clear as to why, in novel after novel, apparently identical episodes, characters and settings of not so traumatic a nature reappear. Being jilted, trying to lose one's virginity, working in a mental hospital are among the experiences we encounter in similar form more than once, reworkings which, however therapeutic for the author, must have some more artistic justification, if they are not to seem merely repetitive and self-indulgent. When one looks closely at all of Thomas's novels, it becomes apparent that the episodes are not in fact repeated; each telling is in a different form and for a different artistic purpose, as a painter might give the same model in different poses. Whatever the origins in real life might have been, the experiences are altered by their fictional contexts and it is the artistic shaping that gives them universal significance. Rachel, the writer who narrates the novel *Latakia* (1979), comments on the need for such formal control in art. Looking at a friend's painting she thinks, "Yes, the pain is there and very real, but where is the organization? She is at the beginning of a long, long road." That is a road Audrey Thomas has traveled in her six novels, where the pain may be very real, with its origins in actual experience, but where it is controlled and given meaning by fictional organization.

Audrey Thomas's novels . . . do in some sense form a continuous semi-autobiographical narrative, a kind of *roman fleuve,* and it is clear that the narrative voice belongs to the same person at different phases of experience. The split in the narrator/persona is similar in many respects to the split between Mrs. Thing and Mrs. Blood: Isobel is the girl and woman who struggles to be defined in terms other than someone's granddaughter, daughter, mistress, wife, or mother; Miranda/Rachel is the self-conscious artist and craftswoman who is able to insist on her own identity and purpose even at the cost of losing the men she loves. As the author herself sums it up: "I think that's what I was trying to deal with in my writing, the two different sides of me." Each novel is completely self-contained and very little is repeated in exactly the same form. The reader can respond to each novel as a shape in itself but may find totally new levels of response in remembering the others while reading any one. The demands on the reader's memory are considerable but the results are rewarding.

Joan Coldwell. Canadian Literature. 92,
1982, pp. 46–47, 55

After reading Audrey Thomas's *Blown Figures* some years ago, I approached *Latakia* with caution and excitement because of the intense complexity of the former. But *Latakia* does not disperse into a cloud of highly-charged loose ends that somehow fit together at dissolution. Even the book's layout is more compact, simpler, and easier to follow. *Latakia* is written in fragments, but the particles are separated by lines across the page, not by empty space. Negating an original suspicion that design was a function of cost, I realized that the two novels are based on entirely different concepts and, thus, also have different visual and literary structures. The fragments in *Blown Figures* explode in a contemporary version of tragic dissolution. *Latakia,* although it chronicles the story of a failed relationship between Michael and Rachel, is, ultimately, an elaboration on the traditional unity of romance. . . .

The novel actually takes place in Rachel's world after her tragic romance with Michael and at the end of her voyage around the Eastern Mediterranean. She is writing in the present, observing herself, her past, Michael, the people who were on the boat with her and Michael, the violence of people and systems in Latakia: her present, Heleni, the people in the square, in the stores, and on the beach. So if the novel is to be considered a romance, the present structure should also be in the form of a romance. Rachel's past romance with Michael can only be a fragment. The formal paradox of a dissolved romantic relationship and a romance form can be partly solved by considering that Rachel's ultimate romance is with her *self,* her female-defined identity, and not with Michael nor with the patriarchal world that he represents. Throughout the novel, Thomas is concerned with definition. How does one define and what creates unity or dissolution? Thomas recreates and redefines unity in character, linguistics, literary structures, and mythology in terms of the female self. Naturally, this involves the dissolution of traditional unities. . . .

Thomas and [her character] Rachel are both, ultimately, enabled to move beyond the traditional definitions of unity and dissolution, for the act of dissolution, the deviations from tradition, create the unity of a self-defined woman and a self-defined literary structure. The traditions of romance, the distribution of sexual power between men and women, the insistence on linear and logical rhetoric, and patriarchal linguistics, mythology, and culture are all challenged by Rachel's search for a self-defined life and Thomas's insistence on a self-defined structure. Dissolution creates unity, while the traditional concepts of unity create dissolution. But this is not a simple and absolute reversal of terms. There are points where elements that we traditionally perceive as unified or dissolute—the breakdown of communication, the tight control of structure by placing all disparate elements within the unity of one letter and the romance structure—do not transmute into their opposites. Consequently, there is also a dissolution of any absolute definition of unity and dissolution.

Ellen Quigley. *Essays on Canadian Writing.*
20, 1980–81, pp. 201–2, 218–19

Audrey Thomas does two things in her stories which allow her to transform the images of women in her fiction. First, she doesn't fictionalize in the usual sense of the word; she doesn't "invent" character and situation. The shift in content to an autobiographical base, in turn, frees her to make significant changes in the story form. Structurally, the stories are quite loose. Images of braiding or weaving best picture her method. She works in the story like an archaeologist gathering together the shards from the rag-bag of her experience, and piecing them together, as she finds the coherence and shape inherent in that material. Only the slenderest of threads—the path of the writer writing—serves as a "track" through. Thus the story form is not predetermined by the author's inventions nor by fictional paradigms. And this more open form in turn frees the image to take its shape from the material at hand, rather than from given models.

A metamorphosis of both the particular woman in this story and of the general image of women that we all carry around with us takes place. Thomas achieves this by first drawing on the details of her own life for her stories, rather than inventing her material. She then views those details with an archaeologist's "detachment," as "shards," which is what life becomes when separated from the paradigms of myth and story. Having de-constructed the traditional images of women in this and preceding stories, by giving us "real" mothers in actual situations, she then reconstructs, out of the material at hand, new models—both "real" and imaginary. Like a good anthropologist though she recognizes the subjective and tentative nature of the reconstruction: "And she doesn't look back. In *my story,* that is. She doesn't look back." The change in both the form and process of the story brings a transformation of the image.

Pauline Butling. *Canadian Literature*. 102, 1984, pp. 195–97

Most of the fictions of Thomas's first two collections are visibly constructed of variant scripts. In some a second script is implicit in the first, as in "One is One and All Alone" in which the young wife of a British official in Africa enacts a self-assured self to mask pervasive feelings of fear and ineptitude. When she loses a filling from a tooth, this fabricated self, like the tooth, crumbles, exposing the "raw nerves" of her irrational fears. In "A Monday Dream at Alameda Park" a married couple have created the story that they are "very liberated, very liberal"—a story which partly collapses when the husband finds himself drawn into group sex with another couple. In other fictions the alternative scripts are embedded in the first. In "Omo" the embedded diary of one character disqualifies the perceptions of the story's narrator. . . .

Like the narrator of "A Winter's Tale," most of Thomas's characters find it easier to "conjure up" a false story than to accept "the pulse of truth." As here, the false story is usually fabricated of familiar materials.

Frank Davey. *Canadian Literature*. 109, 1986, p. 6

Audrey Thomas's typical form emerges in this collection of thirteen recent stories [*The Wild Blue Yonder*] as the sketch *engagé/dégagé*. She finds an impetus, a core story, in recent history, usually violent—the Hungerford massacre, Tianamen Square, a generic newspaper story of a young murderer who preys on older women. In reshaping this story, Thomas expresses her strong social commitment, but more so her interest in how these public events affect the individual psyche and distort, however subtly, the narrative of the soul. Interrupting, disfiguring, and generally providing an alternative is the story that language tells itself. The metalinguistic element is not invariable, as in Daphne Marlatt, and seldom affects syntax, as in Gertrude Stein, but slides into parentheses (either actual or virtual) where homophones, morphemes, and etymologies press their case. In such byways, character and author become detached: each contemplates the universe as a labyrinth of words, and an impossible patchwork of paradox. The word play has a narrative function: it often diverts the story into the fantastic and then the grotesque. A reader is never sure when the placidly quotidian narrative will turn sharply into the bizarre, or when the weird will drop abruptly into a bathetic joke. . . .

Often in my reading notes for this book I find question marks following verbs. My uncertainties indicate that the binary of *engagé/dégagé* is triangulated in almost every Thomas story by the absence where a reader expects resolution or conclusion. Usually this strategy sends me to reading and re-reading. A wife may have drowned her own child rather than live the life of a missionary to Africa. *Why?* "Blue Spanish Eyes" ends with an idyllic flirtation, but it begins with a brief piece of journalese that points to an incomprehensible rape and murder. *Who?*

The narrative gaps are a way of extending the *engagé/dégagé* irony. The stories are left in suspension—for reader or character—are frustrated, hypnotized curiosity. Such a pattern compels attention in almost all the stories, and nowhere more intriguingly than in "Ascension," for me the strongest story in the collection. "Ascension" searches for the psychologies of a friendship between an island tourist and a resident Greek mother, and discovers the shared perceptions of very different women coming together in their necessarily shared lives. The story ends with a bizarre turn and a narrative gap *and* with a skillfully old-fashioned tying up, by Thomas's repeating with alterations the story's beginning. Mrs. Papoutsia will "try make bread in space." Christine will also rise up lighter than air. This blue yonder is truly an ascension to celebrate.

Laurie Ricou. Canadian Literature. 135,
1992, pp. 139–40

Audrey Thomas's *Graven Images* is primarily a novel about writing, about the ambivalence of anchoring the flux of life in words. Thomas plays with the idea that the images that carve themselves irrevocably into memory are both fluid and fixed, both inspiration and impediment to the writer of fiction. Images graven on memory (grave images, images of the grave) expand and glow in the mind of writer-narrator Charlotte Corbett, but they illuminate only obliquely the lives of her mother, [her] friend Lydia, and herself. . . .

After a first reading, one is tempted to feel cheated by the book, as if it were merely notes towards a novel yet to be written (as indeed it might be— Charlotte's novel). It becomes clear, however, that plot does not concern Thomas (it rarely does, in her novels), and that the European trip is merely a device to facilitate some intensive introspection on Charlotte's part. What is important, what resonates throughout the novel, is the image that first impels Charlotte to fix her mother's life in fiction: the image of a baby floating dead in a bucket of water. This is the shocking childhood memory that, unsolicited, Frances Corbett suddenly divulges one day, shattering forever the ossified testiness of her nursing home existence. Charlotte becomes obsessed with the "water-baby" image; each of the italicized entries that signal her attempts at novel writing deals evocatively with circumstances surrounding the dead baby in the bucket.

"Still-life" is Frances's malapropism for "stillborn," and the term is oddly relevant to the differences between *Graven Images* and two other Thomas novels in which a miscarried child is a recurring preoccupation. In 1970, Thomas wrote *Mrs. Blood,* the first-person narrative of a white woman in Africa undergoing the horror of miscarriage. Her next novel, *Blown Figures* (1974), follows this same woman in her solitary return to Africa several years later, her pain still raw, her sanity questionable. That the reader cares more about the woman in *Mrs. Blood* and *Blown Figures* than about Charlotte in *Graven Images* seems somehow to be related to the difference between engaging an image and simply using it as a means to an end. . . .

Graven Images is not an easy novel to read. Thomas asks much of her readers, demanding that they accomplish what her writer-narrator Charlotte spends the novel trying to do, namely make connections. ("There are times," Charlotte says, "when I seem to be doing several jigsaw puzzles at once.") Despite its trademark wit and its tender moments, *Graven Images* is an unsettling novel. Perhaps it's too accurate a measure of our fear of engaging the elderly, the past, family, relationships in general. Detailing a struggle that pushes towards illumination but remains a struggle, Thomas presents the ambivalent point of view of a would-be synthesizer, an author.

In *Graven Images*, Audrey Thomas allows all of us to experience the irony, the contortions, the wry in wry-ter.

Gwendolyn Guth. *Canadian Forum*.
July–August, 1993, pp. 39–40

THORUP, KIRSTEN (DENMARK) 1942–

Originally published in 1973, *Baby*, a first novel by Kirsten Thorup, was selected as the best Danish novel written in the 1970s. It was awarded the distinguished Pegasus Prize for 1980 and thus translated into English.

The novel describes life in the working-class and slum district of Copenhagen, where men, women and children are all victims of money or the lack of it, a condition which leads to divorce, prostitution and crime. Thorup stresses the hopelessness and monotony of their situation: they have no future, no way out in a society built on money and violence, drugs and sexual abuse. They have given up all hope for change—a big difference from the attitude of the 1960s, when there was still some hope for a better world. The situation of women and children is especially depressing: they are much more vulnerable than the men because they are more dependent on men. The different people described in the novel are socially and culturally without roots. They feel completely alienated in the society in which they are living; they only "exist on the surface." The novel's vigorous depiction of society's exploitation of the poor, particularly of women, is especially pertinent to the problems of society today, from both a sociological and a feminist viewpoint.

The novel is also interesting from a purely stylistic point of view. Thorup's style—which must have been a formidable challenge for the translator—manages to permeate the atmosphere of the world in which these people are living. By heaping sentences on sentences, by interweaving the characters' thoughts and emotional responses in a stream-of-consciousness style, Thorup successfully conveys the utter monotony and repetition of their thoughts and conversations. As an example of a modern Danish novel for English readers, the choice of *Baby* must be considered excellent, in great part thanks to the extremely good translation by Nadia Christensen.

Although several of Thorup's poems have the title "Trieste," this geographical location is not of significant importance. It is furthermore questionable whether they really are poems and not lyrical prose pieces. Published in Denmark in 1969, *Love from Trieste* gives snapshots of the thoughts and actions of a few individuals whose lives are intermingled as friends and sexual partners. In almost surrealistic scene paintings we follow their aimless wanderings in the city, their eating and drinking in restaurants and outdoor cafés and on picnics in the countryside. Somewhat schizophrenic, they all long for human contact, unable to cope alone with their lives: "I always have had to have somebody around me, I could neither eat nor sleep alone. And I never travelled to a strange place unless I had friends there who could take care of me," one of them confesses.

Together with her novel *Baby,* the collection *Love from Trieste,* now available in an outstanding, faithful English translation, is a good introduction to Thorup, one of the foremost Danish writers of today.

Ingrid Claréus. *World Literature Today.*
55, 1981, p. 495

In *The Long Summer* five years have passed since the twelve-year-old "Little Jonna" entered the *realskole,* five years since her family split up and two of her three brothers left home. The novel is a continuation of *Lille Jonna* (1977), the story of a young woman's development as she grows up in a country milieu on Funen.

The action in this sequel takes place in the summer between Jonna's passing of the *realskole* exam and her entrance into the gymnasium. The summer is filled with new experiences for Jonna, all of which take on a special significance in her continual development from adolescence into womanhood. She works first at an asparagus factory, later at a state institution for the mentally ill, where she has her first erotic experience. She watches as her two brothers who had left home return to the milieu from which they came; she notes with curiosity her third brother's arguments in favor of his own conscientious-objector status. Finally, as the relationship to her parents becomes more conflict-ridden and her need to know herself becomes more acute, Jonna moves to Copenhagen. The reader is led to believe that her decision reflects not only her desire to find herself, but also her attempt to escape the class into which she was born.

Though we come to know all the characters in this novel through the eyes of the young Jonna, the author has carefully managed to preserve their identities. The characters who surround Jonna are not merely caricatures of her own imagination, but are well-developed and realistic forces in her life.

These two books taken together serve essentially as an *Entwicklungsroman*—a young woman's personal development from adolescence into womanhood. It is unfair, however, to say that the strengths of *The Long Summer* stop there. Jonna's history is also the history of a larger group, one which follows the daily lives of her working-class and provincial milieus. Furthermore, the reader gains valuable insights from these two perspectives into the postwar period in Denmark up to and including the relative affluence of the 1960s. Thus the novel works on several complex levels, as Thorup demonstrates an uncanny ability in integrating a specific personal history, the setting in which that history takes place and the appropriate historical context.

Kirsten Thorup is no stranger to good novel writing. She has recently received the International Pegasus Prize for Literature (for *Baby*), and her novels to date are landmarks in modern Danish letters. *The Long Summer*, an extremely thought-provoking novel, continues that tradition.

Scott de Francesco. *World Literature Today.*
55, 1981, p. 117

In his summation of the [Pegasus Prize] jury's choice of *Baby*, Mr. Barfoed said of it: "Permeating the everyday lives of these characters is an experience which perhaps a woman best can formulate: the experience of being a thing, an object rather than a subject, a receiver—of bribery, of blows and bruises, or caresses, of persuasive words. And perhaps a woman's sensitivity is also particularly suited to describing this state with the unsentimental tenderness that Kirsten Thorup manifests in *Baby*."

Unlike the introspective characters present in most contemporary Danish literature, the characters in *Baby* live fragmented, unreflective lives. Inhabitants of Copenhagen's working-class Vesterbro section, they are presented en masse in the novel's first chapter, then scatter into separate, but uniformly unfulfilled relationships. They are preoccupied with money, and its paucity reflects the elusiveness of their personal satisfactions.

Kirsten Thorup is the author of two additional novels—*Little Jonna* and *The Long Summer*. She also has written poetry, short stories, and plays for television. Since receiving the Pegasus Prize, she has been awarded the Hans Christian Anderson Prize from the Writers' Union. *Baby*, which has just been reissued in paperback by its publisher, Gyldendal, has been described by one critic as "the most important novel of the '70s.". . .

In translating *Baby*, . . . [Nadia Christensen's] greatest challenge was to preserve the tone and rhythm of a book containing long sentences which suggest that everything has the same emotional weight.

Introduction to Kirsten Thorup. *Baby*
(Baton Rouge: Louisiana State University
Press, 1980), p. vi

There are only very few first-person passages in her Jonna-novels. We seldom encounter the relentless kind of investigation into identity which dominates [Thorup's] poetry. Whenever it does occur, it signals distance, modernistic emptiness and alienation: "At times I was in doubt whether I existed at all.

I was sort of outside everything, as if I were in a bell jar." But she generally uses an omniscient mode of narration which, by the rules of convention and logic, cannot be sustained by the I-narrator Jonna. When she looks into other people's letters, diaries, bedrooms and minds, the reader is meant to be puzzled and to be reminded of the fictionality of the narration. Having been nudged out of a naive, realistic reading habit, the reader can recognize that there is an unresolved tension between Jonna's fear of saying "I" and her closeness to her milieu. Her act of writing is in the first instance an escape route, but becomes increasingly a confrontation with repressed experience. Before we discover whether Jonna has found herself, however, she starts on a new escape route and enacts different kinds of possible female identities in the novel *Heaven and Hell* (1982). The final reunion of the narrator and the character Jonna in one self is yet to come.

Annegret Heitmann. No Man's Land: An Anthology of Modern Danish Women's Literature (Norwich, England: Norvik Press, 1987), p. 10

She was the only member of her family to go to gymnasium [high school] but felt an outsider in her new academic surroundings, at the same time becoming estranged from her old, nonliterary background. Her own early poetry naturally focused on the theme of alienation, lack of identity, and difficulty of communication.

Thorup's poetic debut in 1967 was already technically sophisticated with her aesthetic approach, her particular cutting technique—also used in some of her many television plays—and cool distance from the subject. Thorup's modernist interest also led her to French absurdism as well as to modern psychology (R. D. Laing) as reflected in *Love from Trieste* (1969; *Love from Trieste*, 1980).

Although widely read herself, Thorup's fiction almost exclusively embraces the nonliterary world as in her novel *Baby* (1973; *Baby*, 1980), which describes the lower-class urban milieu. The characters in *Baby* are without many resources in all senses of the word, and their "stripped" existence manifests itself through the dominating physical aspect of life as well as in an "attitudinal relativism" underscored technically by the frequent use of the coordinating "and."

After the portrayal of the jungle life in the city, Thorup returned to the simple provincial milieu of her own childhood Funen with the Jonna books. Her novel, *Himmel og helvede* (1982; Heaven and Hell), is a broad social and psychological epic involving many characters and fates. Again the focus is on the outsiders of the social mainstream who seem to differ from the more staid bourgeoisie in their greater mobility. The implicit dream of a better society lies with these more open, less conforming people. The descriptions are realistic and full of vivid details, but the plot is also constructed to allow the unlikely incident: it is an epic of possibilities.

Although Thorup is already a renowned author with a distinct physiognomy on the Danish literary scene, she—like her fictional outsiders—is open for new impulses; her literary image is still in its promising development.

Charlotte Schiander Gray. In Virpi Zuck,
ed. *Dictionary of Scandinavian Literature*
(Westport, Connecticut: Greenwood Press,
1990), p. 617

When Kirsten Thorup made the transition from modernistic poetry and prose pieces to the expansive, comprehensive narrative, the transformation of style and genre seemed great indeed. Her broad, mimetic reproduction of contemporary society seemed quite remote from her early quest for identity through verbal experimentation. However, a closer look at the character portrayals in her later novels will reveal significant similarities in the description of identity, and this particular perception of identity has left its distinct imprint on her narrative form as well as her style. Thorup's novels after *Baby,* 1967 (*Baby,* 1980) have been compared to a Bildungsroman, and the comparison is justifiable insofar as they share the quest for identity through an expansive narrative which focuses on the interaction between the protagonist and his or her surroundings. Comparing Thorup's series of novels to the Bildungsroman, however, reveals how her atomistic perception of identity is reflected by a similarly disconnecting tendency in the structure of the narrative: causative and chronological narrative has been cut up into separate, open-ended sections, each of which is added to but not continuing the preceding section.

If we agree that the Bildungsroman—or, novel of formation—deals with the growth of an individual within his or her social relationships, and that the protagonist develops through stages in a fairly linear manner, then Thorup's novels differ mainly in three ways: 1. there is more than one protagonist; 2. although some of the major characters gain some insight, there is no gradual development or real growth of personality; 3. the chronological process has been slowed and severed into open-ended, separate entities.

Even though Jonna is present as narrator throughout the novels, this does not necessarily mean she is the main character. Her function as narrator can be seen apart from her role as a character and seems rather a technical device to hold the long and fairly loosely connected sections together. Seen in the context of all the novels, Jonna becomes an important character on the same level as two other female characters, Maria and Miss Andersen. The novels thereby, like the earlier *Baby,* deal with a whole group of people—with emphasis on the women—whose fates create mirror images, parallels and contrasts in a manner that produces a pattern of female (and male) destinies. Like *Baby,* the novels are collectively oriented underscoring social interaction and interdependence and deemphasizing the notion of an autonomous development and sense of self. . . .

Thorup's atomistic view on identity of necessity must make her depart from the Bildungsroman model. Her adherence to a structure of coordination, with its implicit refusal of causal sequences, is contrary to the causal and dynamic progression inherent in the ideology of the Bildungsroman. Thorup's view of identity thus influences the structure of the novels: where there is no gradual human development the linear progression must be broken. The narrative is therefore divided into sections—like very long chapters—focusing on separate periods which unfold the lives of the many characters in stages. The narrative units thus also fit into the lace pattern metaphor where each narrative stage is represented by a section in the pattern which is then held together by a larger interconnecting pattern of mirrored fates. The metaphor thus functions on two levels: that of the description of individuality and that of the narrative structure.

From the point of view of the crucial identity search, the metaphor illustrates how everything seems to dissolve into amorphous particles when close to the characters while a more distant view may reveal the contour of some pattern. But the pattern is not visible by nature; it first has to be woven like identities must be expressed through social interaction as well as verbally in order to come into existence. The disconnecting tendency, which can be traced to Thorup's own experience of modern life, seems the most pervasive feature. The uniting tendency, as reflected by the old Marie's imaginary weaving, seems more tentative and wishful than real. The intimation of a pattern—with its implication of fatalism—has been perceived of as part of a family tradition. But this kind of "fatalism" may as well reflect a knowledge of and agreement with Jung's concept of the collective unconscious. Thorup's novels present a successful amalgam of modernism and traditional realism expressing simultaneously modernist aestheticism and social interest. But whether the pattern is believed in or not, once it has been formulated, it has come into existence as a work of art. That is why it is not just any pattern but a lace pattern.

Charlotte S. Gray. *Scandinavian Studies*. 63,
1991, pp. 214–15, 219–20

TIKKANEN, MARTA (FINLAND) 1935–

What happens in Märta Tikkanen's eighth book, *Storfångaren*, is this: recently widowed (as every devotee of Finland's literature must have learned by this time), she falls head over heels in love with "this man I think I know inside and out, an old companion, a good friend, a comrade, yes . . . a comrade from the barricades of long ago." (By "long ago" we assume she means the social and political engagements of the 1960s.) Then she goes to Greenland on a reading tour and, we are assured, experiences with special vividness nature and people because of her erotically stimulated condition: "How would the Land of the Human Beings [after "Inuit," "human beings," the native Greenlanders' name for themselves] have looked with [*sic*] my eyes but without the membrane of your skin?"

The sections of the book in which Tikkanen presents her ejaculatory impressions of Greenland itself are interesting enough: she meets artists (whole clans of them) and poets, mostly women; she gives snippets of history (with the obligatory reference to the Norse settlement and its disappearance in the fifteenth century); flitting across the land- and seascape in a helicopter, she sees the ruins of the church on Hvalsø, where a "great Nordic wedding" was celebrated in 1408, just before the curtain descended; she lambastes Brigitte Bardot and the Greenpeace do-gooders for their alleged failure to grasp the necessities of Greenland life; she hearkens to the song of the "great hunter" (and its catchy refrain, "ajaa-ajajaa"), which gives her book its title. Further, she interviews "Greenland's only woman mayor," is herself subjected to a disastrous radio interview with an overinformed and loquacious announcer (male but unappealing, and a chain-smoker to boot), takes notes, admires children, signs books, and generally behaves like the Nordic celebrity she is. Every once in a while she tries to resist the lure of the absent lover's "intellect" and "potency," but of course in vain; not even the distasteful circumstance that he is also a smoker (in bed) can cool her ardor. Again and again, memories make her drop her punctuation ("your voice your smell your breathing your taste"), move her to orgasmic outcries ("quickly and slowly, violently hard and gently and quietly, for a long time"), and inspire self-plumbing reveries ("Do I love you as men love, is that why this love is unlike all others?").

Could not Tikkanen's public have been treated to her hodoeporicon yet spared the trying chronicle of intimacy? But then her fans would have been disappointed by the absence of the Tikkanen cachet they so adore. Besides, her erethism is quite compatible with an ancient arctic tradition: when Hans Egede undertook the conversion of the Inuit, he discovered that Greenland's icy mountains were a veritable hotbed of lustful activity, easily more aphrodisiacal than India's coral strand.

George C. Schoolfield. World Literature Today. 64, 1990, pp. 655–56

Her first two novels, *Nu imorron* (1970; Now tomorrow) and *Ingenmansland* (1972; No-man's-land), deal with a couple, easily recognized—with the aid of her own later works and her husband's autobiographical books—as a somewhat fictionalized portrayal of their marriage. The wife's situation is made ever more difficult by the husband's alcoholism, erotic adventures, and jealousy, and by her constant exhaustion (as a working woman, a mostly loving wife, and a conscientious mother), her growing awareness of male domination, and her sense that she is wasting her own gifts. Tikkanen's next two books, sometimes characterized as "pamphlet novels," turn away from immediate personal concerns to other problems of oppressed or neglected women. In

Vem bryr sej om Dori Mihailov? (1974; Who cares about Doris Mihailov?) the central if invisible figure is a lonely and emotionally damaged single parent; the story of her life is pieced together by a female television reporter and a self-centered male psychiatrist. Tikkanen's *Män kan inte väldtas* (1975; Manrape, 1977) marked her entrance into international fame, not least because of its sensational nature: Raped by a man whom she has accompanied to his apartment, a divorcee plots and triumphantly (if somewhat unbelievably) inflicts a counter-rape on her assailant. Widely translated, the book was made into a film (1978) by Jörn Donner. From this *succès de scandale* Tikkanen went on to *Århundradets Kärlekssaga* (1978; Love story of the century, 1984), in which, using what might be called a narrative series of prose poems, she took revenge on her husband for his complaints about her emotional coldness and aggressiveness. Concentrating not only on the husband's drunkenness but his egocentricity, the book (and a subsequent dramatization) reached a huge audience of women who found it a reflection, in some measure, of their own marital lot; Tikkanen's remarkable reputation in Germany in particular was built upon her bitter story of an unbearable but evidently inescapable relationship.

As the health of her husband declined, Tikkanen's attention went to other domestic miseries. In *Mörkret som ger glädjen djup* (1981; The darkness that gives happiness depth) she interlarded—in still more narrative-lyrical poems—the account of a contemporary adolescent's emotional illness with the tale of the devotion, and self-accusation, of the mother of Josef Julius Wecksell (1838–1907), a Finland-Swedish poet who had gone incurably insane while still in his early twenties. A companion work, in topic if not in tone, *Sofias egen bok* (1982; Sofia's own book), was the factual chronicle of the illness and treatment of her youngest child, afflicted with minimal brain dysfunction. With *Rödluvan* (1986; Little Red Ridinghood) Tikkanen took up her own case for analysis: the little girl with a gently domineering father and a compliant mother who moved into the lair of a demanding husband, a shaggy wolf more vulnerable in life than in the fairy tale. Nonetheless, aware though she was of the childhood situation that, she believed, created her acquiescence to male tyranny, and proud of her revolt, she told, in *Storfångaren* (1989; The great huntsmen), of her longing for her new love, a distinguished Danish author, during a visit to women's centers in Greenland.

Tikkanen is one of Finland's best-known authors, because of her ability to combine feminist messages with personal revelations in a variously passionate, wry, or sentimental way. Her ejaculatory style is a particularly apt instrument for attracting and holding her readership: Extremely conversational at the start of her career, her verbal mode has grown more and more exalted with the years, so that it is almost impossible (save in the case history of her daughter) to draw a line between prose and poetry. Similarly, the genre description "novel" on the dust jacket of what is probably her best book,

Rödluvan, seems to be a misnomer for what is part of her own ongoing autobiography.

George C. Schoolfield. In Steven R. Serafin
and Walter D. Glanze, eds. *Encyclopedia of
World Literature in the 20th Century*
(New York: Continuum, 1993), pp. 595–96

TLALI, MIRIAM (SOUTH AFRICA) 1933–

The second well-known South African writer is Miriam Tlali. While on a visit to the Netherlands her colleague Mothobi Mutloatse (1978) described the situation in South Africa, which made it impossible for black writers like himself to write anything but short stories. The tension and political unrest do not allow writers the extended periods of repose which are needed to set up and work out a novel. For this reason he was amazed to discover that "an important novel" had been written, and "by an ordinary housewife at that!" Miriam Tlali's work is rooted in "the situation." She is outspoken in her criticism of the authorities and "the system" and her books are banned in South Africa.

Mineke Schipper. *Unheard Words: Women
and Literature in Africa, The Arab World,
Asia, the Caribbean, and Latin America*
(London: Allyson & Busby, 1985), p. 59

In the mid-1970s the South African publishers Ravan Press began to produce novels by black South Africans. The aim was similar to that of their journal, *Staffrider:* to produce literature by South Africans for South Africans. Ravan Press aims at as wide a readership as possible and tries to keep prices low. They, and other publishers of works by black writers, face the financial loss brought by bannings with courage, and will make no concessions by exercising censorship themselves. One scene in the novel *Muriel at Metropolitan* by M. (Miriam Masoli) Tlali, for instance, was bound to draw official disapproval. It speaks of a cleaner who hires out his rooms to lovers at night and charges a special fee to a police sergeant from Marshall Square and a black cover girl. *Muriel* was duly banned. Published by Ravan in 1975, it was subsequently included in Longman's Drumbeat series, and translations have begun to appear.

Muriel at Metropolitan is largely autobiographical, based on Tlali's experiences in a hire purchase firm in Johannesburg. Like [Ezekiel] Mphahlele's *Wanderers,* however, it has a theme which goes beyond the beginning and end of the contents.

Metropolitan, the H.P. firm, is a microcosm of South African life, with its variety of people and their relationship to each other. Muriel is unhappy there, not so much because of the way she is treated by the white staff but because she has to become part of the system of charging unduly high interest rates to black purchasers who can ill afford it. . . .

Irony is the moving force in the story. It sets the tone in which the absurd situations forming the action are told, and it underlies the description of the characters. It provides the humor with a sharp and serious undertone. . . .

The tolerance with which Tlali views the outrageous set-up is a new note in black fiction; it contrasts with the bitterness of La Guma and Mphahlele, as well as with the devil-may-care attitude of Boetie and some of the short story writers. It coincides, however, with the note of new confidence we have found in black poetry during this period. It does not necessarily mean that the author is willing to forgive. . . .

Tlali's tolerance for the situation at Metropolitan and for the white characters is derived from strength. The black characters are not afraid to answer back! . . .

The dialogue is faultless. Tlali has an ear for the intonation of the black characters, both the educated and those who know little English, for the Afrikaans-speaking women and for the Jewish boss. Her keen powers of observation are in evidence everywhere. Her skill in articulating people's thoughts led to her being asked to contribute a column to *Staffrider* magazine, "Soweto Speaking," in which she tells the stories of various people on their behalf. She brings this genre, introduced in America by Studs Terkel, to South Africa, where it has been followed by such popular books as Carol Hermer's *Diary of Maria Thele* and Elsa Joubert's *Die Swerfjare van Poppie Nongena*. . . .

Miriam Tlali's second novel, *Amandla*, meaning "Power," was published by Ravan Press in 1980. The censors probably did not go further than the title and the picture of the clenched fist on the cover, both symbols of the struggle for freedom, before banning it. *Amandla* is a very different novel from *Muriel at Metropolitan* in every respect. Gone is most of the easy humor, the ironic approach, the tolerance. As in Sepamla's *The Root is One* the bitterness of the earlier writers and the hope which was emerging from it has given way to rage, frustration and confrontation. The characters in *Amandla* and their creator have experienced the Soweto uprisings and it has altered their outlook. . . .

Tlali's method of telling the story is also very different from that of [the] other writers [whom we have discussed]. As narrator she is a "witness to history." Her authority "rests on the fact that (she) was present at the critical moment when history took a new turn." Yet she is not a historian or a reporter. "Where the historian and the reporter are supposedly objective and concern themselves with bare facts and where the historian seeks to deal with events and their causes and effects" the work is "creatively subjective.

(It) deals with idea-forms, and subjective moulds in which events are first cast." The novel is a "vehicle for developing the collective wisdom or strength of the family, the clan or the nation." . . .

In the course of the narrative we learn about every aspect of life in black townships in a period of crisis: how the students organize demonstrations and strikes, meeting literally underground (in a bunker under a church) and swearing oaths of secrecy based on traditional initiation formulas. We see the mourners at the graveside of children killed in confrontation with the police. There is fear, but the dominant mood is one of defiance. The liberation of women, in the black South African context, means that women must play their part and this they do courageously.

Ursula A. Barnett. *A Vision of Order: A Study of Black South African Literature in English (1914–1980)* (Amherst: University of Massachusetts Press, 1983), pp. 157–59, 161–63

Setting down a liberation struggle in the making presents writers immediately with problems of perspective. The struggle, clandestine perforce and inevitably confused, not a phenomenon easily analyzed and ordered, yields up a mine of bewildering material for writers who, themselves immersed in the center of the whirlwind, are unable to make the neat artistic detachment of plot or theme and objective viewpoint customarily demanded by the western bourgeois novel form, even if they were to consider such a form suitable to their purpose.

One possible consequence of all this, and certainly a consequence evident in Miriam Tlali's novel, is a very confused literary product. *Amandla* certainly captures the immediacy of events and draws the reader into the confused apprehensions which must be the lot of many of the participants in such a period of social turmoil. She allows the reader to stumble on events, on connections between characters and on sequences of cause and effect in much the same state of bewildered ignorance as must have been the lot of many of the citizens of Soweto. This could have welded itself into a brilliant artistic play to draw the reader into significant experience of the action of the novel. But somehow it never does: it remains accident rather than design. The writer's rejection of western structural devices may have been as deliberate as it was necessary, nevertheless the confusion of the action merely seems to reflect a confusion in the mind of the writer which is never resolved. It may be that the Black South African reader, familiar with township relationships and interconnections, is less at a disadvantage here than the western reader. And, after all, the novel is aimed at the black South African reader. However, there seems a low level of organizational awareness even on the part of the central characters, though their prototypes in the real event obviously constructed some loose organizational framework to control their activities and their destiny as much as they could in the teeth of accelerating events. Thus even for the black South African reader there is a failure to transmit an important element of revolutionary consciousness. . . .

Tlali's problem arises from this attempt to incorporate, erratically, too much historical and political material in her framework. Instead of selecting a small number of events and limiting her historical and political explanation of these to what the situations themselves make necessary, she allows herself to be seduced into making comprehensive surveys and using situations as an excuse for serving them up to the reader. . . .

The work's ultimate flimsiness rests on this tendency to clothe ideas and information in situations, instead of the other way around, and in the absolute absence of any sense that the characters are a people in charge of their own destiny.

> Jane Watts. *Black Writers from South Africa: Towards a Discourse of Liberation* (New York: St. Martin's, 1989), pp. 222–24

South African black women have tended to make distinctions between their own aspirations and those of European and white American feminist movements, which have influenced the thinking of many white South African women. Miriam Tlali, for example, has said that she would call herself a feminist, "but not in the narrow, Western kind of way of speaking about a feminist." They have perceived western feminism either as in pursuit of trivial gains or as separatist in a way that black South African women, as members of a community striving for the extension of human rights to all its members, cannot afford to be. When Tlali was asked if she would focus in her writing on the lives of black women, she replied that she would not make an explicit decision to concentrate on women: "Our liberation is bound absolutely with the liberation of the whole nation, so I'll always combine the two." . . .

Tlali's [*Footprints in the Quag*] is the more clearly documentary [as contrasted with Sheila Roberts's *This Time of Year*] partly because the law has created a condition and a mode of life that almost all Sowetan blacks are forced to share, and it is therefore easier to read the stories as a record of the Sowetan black community on the Rand in the 1980s. . . .

Tlali's indignation . . . is directed not only, or mainly, against the male oppressor, but against the life-impoverishing physical settings and inhuman laws that whites created and that encourage Musi to oppress. Roberts too sees the white male oppressor as produced by and dependent on unjust privilege, handed down by his own male ancestors and accepted by him as his right. . . .

In her frequent depictions of the oppression of women by men, Roberts's women (and, it seems, Roberts herself) enjoy as Tlali's never could the humiliation of an exploitative man. "This Time of Year," "My Turn to Go," and, most grotesquely, "Knobs and Nikes" all center their narration in the consciousness of women who enjoy the sight or the thought of a would-be exploiter's humiliation.

Tlali's stories cannot contain such humiliations for a second reason, which she shares with other black women: that matters directly related to the marital relationship, especially sexual ones, are private, private at least to the extent that they may not be discussed in writing. Lack of marital privacy, for example, is not mentioned in "Mm'a-Lithoto" as a strain on the couple because such a lack would imply a strain on their sexual relationship, which is not open to discussion in fiction. . . .

Tlali's assumption that women can make each other's lives bearable by supporting each other in everyday trials comes much closer to [Alice] Walker's understanding of womanism than does Roberts's treatment of women's relationships. A key element in six of the ten stories that make up *Footprints in the Quag* is the womanist support that women of the urban black community feel they owe each other. This is the main subject of the story "Fud-u-u-a," which deals with the miseries, as experienced by women, of traveling on overcrowded commuter trains. "We're all alike; we're women. We need each other when things are difficult" is Tlali's summary of the roadside fruitsellers' attitude. Prevented from escape by the crowding of the trains, all three of the women who meet in the station have experienced the humiliation of being groped by a man, concealed in the crowd.

Margaret Lenta. Tulsa Studies in Women's Literature. 11, 1992, pp. 103–4, 106–7

TOLSTAYA, TATIANA (RUSSIA) 1951–

The young writer Tatiana Tolstaya, whose first short story appeared in 1983, includes both positive and negative portraits of women in her rostrum of characters. Many of Tolstaya's women characters pursue the kinds of lives so often associated with the heroines of "women's writing." Tolstaya's command of narrative, however, her handling of her writer's tools, allows her to create these negative prototypes yet avoid any identification with them. Her story *Okhota na mamonta* (The hunt for the woolly mammoth, 1985) provides an excellent example of this technique at work. The plot of the story concerns a beautiful woman's attempt to capture a husband for herself. Tolstaya creates a heroine, Zoya, who is both a parody of the nineteenth century sentimental heroine and a representative of vacuous middle class morality which Tolstaya sees as prevalent in Soviet society today. . . .

The devices which Tolstaya uses to distance herself from . . . clichéd morality show obvious borrowings from at least two of her male literary predecessors. Her debt to Nabokov and his use of the untrustworthy narrator can be seen in her manipulation of the narrative voice which at one moment merges with that of the heroine and then completely rejects any identification with her. Her debt to Gogol is also evident, and it is appropriate that she chose this most misogynist of nineteenth-century writers to borrow from in dehumanizing her heroine. Gogol's own fear of, and consequent dislike of, women caused him to reduce his female characters to inanimate objects. One remembers his hero Chichikov in *Dead Souls* "falling in love" with a woman whose face Gogol compared to a freshly laid white egg or the "Lady Delightful in Every Respect" from the same novel who becomes a bird of prey as she spreads rumors about Chichikov throughout the town. Tolstaya not only distances herself from her heroine but does so using the devices of her male literary predecessors. . . .

The critical response to this new and gifted writer, whose emergence has been one of the literary events of the 1980s, has brought much of the traditional antipathy to women's writing to the surface. It has also revealed that the issue of women's writing has become a foil for an even more serious debate among Soviet writers today, namely the issue of talent versus hackwork. In an interview published in *The Moscow News* in 1987, Tolstaya made the point that women's writing ("feminine prose" as she put it) is still alive and well in the Soviet Union today. She characterized it as "the confusion of daily routine with life, a saccharine quality, beauty smacking of a fancy goods store, and the author's mercantile psychology." Moreover, she added, "feminine prose today is mostly written by men." Tolstaya's point was that virtually any work which is superficial and which reflects the author's own Philistine values can be classified as "feminine prose." In saying this she was clearly directing her criticisms at the literature of dubious literary merit which is still being produced by members of the Writer's Union today.

Tolstaya has since been attacked in the press for her remarks by members of the conservative literary establishment such as the critic and writer Pyotr Proskurin who responded angrily to her redefinition of "feminine prose" and to her disparaging remarks about the novel *Vsyo uperedi* (Everything is ahead) by the conservative writer Vasilyi Belov who makes no secret of his misogynist views. The controversy between Tolstaya and the deeply entrenched, male-dominated literary establishment relates only superficially to her criticisms of Belov or even to her remarks about what constitutes "feminine prose." Subsumed within the gender issue is the larger one of talent. As writers such as Tolstaya gradually redefine the term "women's writing," it is becoming increasingly more difficult to pass the work of a woman writer off as mere "women's writing." To paraphrase Tolstaya, men write it too! Tolstaya, however, seems to have become the focal point of a debate which transcends her own specific work, namely that between those of undeniable literary talent and those whose acceptance into the literary establishment years ago was due more to their Party stance than any inherent literary proclivity.

Adele Barker. *Studies in Comparative Communism*. 21, 1988, pp. 360, 362, 364

The author of the thirteen short stories collected in *"Na zolotom kryl'tse sideli"* (They sat on the golden porch) is well known in the Soviet Union but still virtually unknown abroad. Drawings by G. Eshkov appear on the front cover and in the text. The back cover features a small photograph of Tolstaya, which reveals that she is still a young woman, and a few lines about her higher education in the Department of Classical Philology at Leningrad University. We also learn that her stories have been published in leading Soviet literary journals such as *Novyĭ Mir, Oktiabr'*, and *Neva*. At the end of the book there is a three-page critical afterword by A. Mikhailov on Tolstaya's art as a writer of short stories. Mikhailov praises her successful blending of sensitivity with realism, her laconic style free of superfluities, and her skill in handling the passage of time as a tangible compositional reality.

The book's title story is typical and contains elements that appear in all the other stories in the collection. It depicts simple, ordinary folk: husbands and wives, old men and women, and, above all, children. In all the selections the real heroes are most often children and old people. For the most part, the tales are narrated from a child's perspective. The way in which these children see the world and everything around them appears to be filled with magic, mystery, miracles, and sometimes with horrors. Everything is perceived as swaying, either in the water or on the branches of trees. However, the child's experience of exploring new worlds is not always a happy and joyful one. For example, in "Svidanie s ptitsei" (An encounter with the bird) Petya, the boy hero, experiences the death of his grandfather. He learns of the existence of a bird of death called "Sirin," who strangled his grandfather. No one can escape fate; everyone will eventually die. Still, Petya dreams of marrying a mysterious beauty named Tamila and going off with her on the *Flying Dutchman* to search for the vanished Atlantis. Such childish dreams are typical of almost all of Tolstaya's short fiction.

As Mikhailov has pointed out, in Tolstaya's tales the divine simplicity of childhood often comes into conflict with the harsh realities of adult life, which invariably include losses and disappointments. However, for all of Tolstaya's sober, realistic outlook on life and her clear, unadorned prose style, her stories are also saturated with charm and romanticism. These aspects of her art provide a certain balance to the harsh, inimical, often sad realities of life which she portrays. One also feels that Tolstaya's "insignificant, simple people"—children or lonely and forgotten "old folks"—have hearts full of dignity and human treasures. Indeed, the precious element of human dignity stands out in all the stories here, a refreshing breeze from the land of socialist realism.

Victoria A. Woodbury. *World Literature Today*. 62, 1988, p. 471

On the Golden Porch, containing thirteen [of her remarkable short stories] in all, appeared in Moscow two years ago. It sold out immediately, as good and necessary books do in the USSR; but on this handful of short stories, mostly running to a mere fifteen or so pages in large print, her reputation was firmly established. They show an exceptional virtuosity in language which, unlike Nabokov's, makes for itself no ostentatious claims. Their originality can be appreciated best after a glance at the work of other women writers in *Balancing Acts*.

Sergei Zalygin claims that the short story is an indispensable genre in Soviet literature. The main literary journals need to publish at least one in every issue, which would otherwise look "incomplete and unusual" to their readers. Yet he has included only three women in his anthology—the well-known veteran I. Grekova; Lyudmila Petrushevskaya, anecdotist and also playwright, and Tatiana Tolstaya. In her anthology of Soviet women writers, Helena Goscilo has, of course, also chosen one story by Tolstaya—"Peters," about a sad boy who is kept away from other children, her first to be published in *Novy Mir* and the one that alerted the public to her significance.

Henry Gifford. The New York Review of
Books. June 1, 1989, p. 3

Old women in outlandish hats, children who mind what happens to the people painted on their dinner plates, men who wish to have their hearts removed: these and many others come and go throughout these Russian stories [in *On the Golden Porch*] like the ordinary beings they truly are. They chafe at the present, yearning towards the future or the past. The Crimean sun dazzles, a lost astrakhan coat is still mourned, unknown parents are invented, lip-gloss is suddenly on sale at a street stall. Hope and disillusion keep up some sort of balance.

At first, it is hard to guess what era we are in. With nannies, summer dachas, white tablecloths, fur coats and crocodile shoes the atmosphere is hardly the dreary one associated with contemporary Russia. But the phrase "after the war" keeps recurring. Though memories stretch back further, this is Moscow and Leningrad in the late twentieth century, with tiny apartments, quests for pâté and Rubik cubes, hats traded for books, and the life of the imagination burning bright.

Tatiana Tolstaya's people spend a great deal of their time imagining. Some of them, like Sweet Shura or kind, silly Sonya, manage to protect themselves. They write letters to their lovers rather than meet them, and die with their dreams unshattered. But for most of the characters disappointment is woven in, integral to the poetic way they see their lives. Little Petya is given a magical egg by his beloved. The egg will ensure that, all his life, he will feel longing. But the beloved is not what she seems, and Petya's tremulous career of joys and disappointments has been launched.

Simeonov is in love with Vera Vasilevna, whom he believes to be dead. He only knows her through her voice on old 78 records, but its divine storminess moves him far more than all-too-available Tamara, with her offers of fresh laundry and flowery curtains. He pictures Vera buried in Paris or Shanghai, selects the tinge of the light as the rain drizzles over her grave, insists that it was for him only that she sang. Small wonder, therefore, that when reality breaks in, Simeonov can only half welcome it.

Time runs through these stories. People are constantly searching for gaps, for doors that might lead them through the solid walls of reality, for the reappearance of missed opportunities. Rivers flow, the light changes, some lose heart. But others, often unlikely ones, just can't be kept down. The approach of a new season is all they need to buoy up their spirits, to encourage them to pitch in again.

Though the characters are full of dreams and objects have a life of their own, fantasy does not get out of hand. These people live through their senses. They enjoy delicious jam and hot baths, listen to the sounds of the winter city, appreciate the feel of good clothes. But above all, they look. Tolstaya is an intensely visual writer. The world she conjures up is almost cinematic, larger than life. Antonina Bouis, her translator, must surely have enjoyed herself there. Now, thanks to her lively and sparkling English, we can too.

Ruth Pavey. *New Statesman and Society.*
June 9, 1989, p. 41

Time, language, and imagination are the reigning divinities of Tolstaya's fictional universe. With the aid of myth, folklore, and numerous intertexts, her inordinately condensed narratives offer meditations on eternal universal concerns: the elusive significance of a given life in "Sonia" (1984; "Sonia," 1989), "Peters," "Samaia liubimaia" (1986; Most beloved, 1991), "Somnambula v tumane" (1988; Sleepwalker in a fog, 1991); the isolation of the individual personality in "Peters," "Spi spokoino, synok" (1986; Sweet dreams, son, 1989), "Krug" (1987; The circle, 1989); the conflicting claims of spirit and matter in "Okhota na mamonta" (1985; Hunting the woolly mammoth, 1989), "Ogon' i pyl'" (1986; Fire and dust, 1989), "Poet i muza" (1986; The Poet and the Muse, 1990); the complex nature of, and interplay between, perception and language in "'Na zolotom kryltse sideli . . .'" "Fakir" (1986; The fakir, 1989), "Noch" (1987; Night, 1990), and "Liubish'—ne liubish" (1987; Loves me, loves me not, 1989); and the transforming power of imagination and memory in "'Na zolotom kryltse sideli . . . ,'" "Svidanie s ptitsei" (1983; Date with a bird, 1989), "Reka Okkervil" (1985; Okkervil River, 1989), and "Milaia Shura" (1985; Sweet Shura, 1989). Yet throughout her oeuvre, as Tolstaya herself has acknowledged, style has primacy over thematic novelty and psychological insight.

Tolstaya's narratives move at an irregular pace, combining minimal plots and sparse dialogue with extravagant poetic description as they slip unobtrusively in and out of temporal frames and characters' thoughts through quasi-direct discourse. Those characters, often situated at the two extremes of the age spectrum, are rendered memorable through Tolstaya's vividly grotesque depiction of their simultaneously risible and pitiable features. A comparably synthetic technique for portraying "losers" in amorous endeavors allows Tolstaya to demythologize romance, as in "Peters" and "Vyshel mesiats iz tumana" (1987; The moon came out, 1992), just as multiple perspectives on a given individual destabilize a single, unilinear interpretation of character.

Tolstaya's fiction teems with dreamers, self-abnegators, failures, pragmatists, egotists, and misanthropes shuttled between largely unrealizable desires and brute reality. That gap may be bridged by the transfiguring capacities of the imagination, which flourishes virtually unchecked in childhood, but diminishes with time's passage. Hence the melancholy sense of loss and helplessness that permeates Tolstaya's texts.

Tolstaya compensates for her protagonists' deprivations by conjuring up for the reader an Aladdin's cave of stylistic riches. To enter Tolstayaland is to step simultaneously into one magical realm of the fairy tale and the oppressive dinginess of a grimy kitchen. The endless array of startling contrasts yields not only sensual pleasure, but also fresh perspectives on phenomena that acquire multiple dazzling hues. Scrambling temporal and spatial categories, alternating poetic lyricism with satirical irony, shifting from one narrative perspective to another, leaping from colloquialisms and popular slogans to elevated diction and citations from "sacrosanct" sources, Tolstaya packs her kaleidoscopic narratives to the brim. Critics have responded above all to the bold originality of her metaphors, which sometimes swell to Homeric proportions; to her breathtakingly unconventional, subversive juxtapositions; to her idiosyncratic, garrulous Sternian narrator; and to her skill at creating a densely palpable atmosphere through eloquent detail and accumulation of rhetorical devices. Her iridescent, luxurious prose—laden with vivid tropes, apostrophes, exclamations, rhetorical questions, and allusions—isolates her stylistically from the majority of contemporary Soviet authors. It allies her with such creative innovators of the 1920s as Yury Olesha and Isaak Babel, as well as Nikolay Gogol (1809–1852), Ivan Bunin, Andrey Bely, and Vladimir Nabokov. Moreover, it corroborates Tolstaya's claim that the desire to display the spectacular range of the Russian language, to explore its boundless expressive powers, was the chief stimulus for her metamorphosis into a writer.

Early in her career Tolstaya focused on the lost paradise of childhood, relying on the Edenic myth as algorithm. Whatever the diversity of her subsequent narratives, including experiments in moral allegory, notably "Serafim" (1986; Serafim, 1992) and "Chistyi list" (1984; A clean sheet, 1989), they never addressed nakedly political issues or engaged in topical debates. In that regard, her latest publication, "Limpopo" (1991; Limpopo, 1992), signals a dramatic reorientation. Longer, more digressive, and less tightly constructed than any of her previous stories, it verges on a novella and offers transparently ironic commentary on Russia's current situation of impotent chaos and spiritual indigence: Crushed by a compromised past, Russians foresee no tenable future and dwell in anomie. Its verbal pyrotechnics and hilariously comic passages notwithstanding, "Limpopo" has affinities with the apocalyptic strain of literature that has proliferated during Gorbachev's policy of glasnost.

Since her debut in 1983, Tolstaya's texts have grown progressively longer. One could reasonably classify her last two publications, "Somnambula v tumane" and "Limpopo," as *povesti* (novellas) rather than short stories. If her recently professed intention of authoring a novel in the near future signals a search for new directions, then the first phase of her creative development unequivocally guarantees her status as the stylistically most venturesome and complex modernist practitioner of the short story in Russia during the 1980s. Although modest in quantity, her oeuvre amply justifies Joseph Brodsky's assertion that Tolstaya is "the most original, tactile, luminous voice in Russian prose today."

> Helena Goscilo. In Steven R. Serafin and
> Walter D. Glanze, eds. *Encyclopedia of
> World Literature in the 20th Century* (New
> York: Continuum, 1993), pp. 596–98

TRABA, MARTA (ARGENTINA) 1930–83

In 1966, Marta Traba, known to all as an art critic and to some as the author of a beautiful book of poems, *Historia natural de la alegría* (The natural history of joy), revealed herself as a novelist. In Havana, a jury made up of Alejo Carpentier, Manuel Rojas, Juan Garcia Ponce and Mario Benedetti conferred the Casa de las Américas Prize on *Las ceremonias del verano* (Summer ceremonies). . . . Encouraged by the prize, she published with a Colombia press a stupendous *Homérica Latina* (Latin Homeric), complex, rich, seductive, sustained not by anecdote but rather by the general atmosphere, its own narrative replacing dramatic tensions. The characters are those who are content with little and don't have the means to feed or clothe themselves. At the same time she achieved the feat of publishing seven books [of art history and criticism] in three months in different countries: Puerto Rico—a country that she knows very well—Mexico, Colombia, and Venezuela. . . .

I don't know at what point Marta Traba began to feel that living life was a terrible feat. Perhaps it was on account of the situation in Argentina. Perhaps something changed inside her or was no change, but rather that there suddenly rose to the surface a Marta of flesh and blood that had never broken out before. Because her two latest novels, *Conversación al Sur* (Conversation in the South) and *En cualquier lugar* (Anywhere at all) have brought out what was already present in *Homérica Latina*, but what now opened up like the red flowers of passion. . . . Marta started to tear herself apart and that is when she wrote *Conversación al Sur*, published in 1981: two women talk to each other about despair and torture, exile and mourning; they tell the story of their losses, knowing that, at the end, the police will come for them, too. . . .

I turned her book *Conversación al Sur* into a shroud, I carried it in my bag for many months, I loved it intensely. I had never read anything better, tougher, more moving than what Marta wrote about the mothers called "The Madwomen of the Plaza de Mayo." It is at one and the same time literature and accusation. It is also Marta uniting in herself a great woman writer and a splendid human being.

Elena Poniatowska. *Revista Iberoamericana.*
51, 1985, pp. 888–89

Briefly . . . Traba's tale features two women. Irene is middle-aged, middle-class, and basically apolitical: Dolores is young, working-class, and politically engaged. *Mothers and Shadows* [*Conversación al Sur*] is constructed from their dialogue, some of which is exteriorized or voiced and some of which takes place as interior conversation. The scene is Argentina under military rule; the women's topics include popular resistance, "the disappeared," and the disciplinary powers of the Argentinian and Uruguayan states. Each speaker stirs up memories in the other by her presence and conversation. "[H]and in hand" they piece together what has happened into an indictment of the juntas and a commemoration of the disappeared, "lest we forget." In *Mothers and Shadows,* forgetting is a feature of isolation—of ignoring the bonds between peoples and suppressing/repressing the link up of events. Missing links make for a disjointed sort of history, whose incompleteness is reflected in the fragmentary character of Traba's book. On the whole, it's rather like a jigsaw puzzle—made of pieces which require (re)arranging for the picture to take shape. We might think of the novel's readers as players, then, who are at work on discovering a pattern or filling in an historical sequence.

The novel's dominant history is largely a matter of suppression and re-pression. On one hand, suppression "disappears" bodies and information; it is properly an operation of the state. On the other, repression is exercised by subjugated subjects, who may be thought of as acting out an obsessional defense. They keep their distance from what is happening, these subjects— the torturer's mutilation of the human body finding its counterpart in their refusal to recognize, touch, or be touched. An oppositional history is simulta-neously kept alive by Dolores and Irene; its distinguishing characteristic is its emphasis on touch. Not only do the two women draw close to each other in conversation, but as active readers of events in Argentina and Uruguay they keep us in contact with events that the two regimes would suppress. As the first in a series of interpreters, they are in a position to (re)define reading, which they posit as a constitutive activity, a labor through which the world is reconstructed and "the disappeared" in a sense returned. "In a sense" represents a significant qualification in the women's history, however. It's significant because the bodies of "the disappeared" remain missing, their names and histories alone coming back to haunt. With missing bodies, we have reached the limits of idealism, then, for the body's materiality is pre-cisely what stories cannot restore. Nor does Traba finally believe they can. Rather, her readers' idealism is sharply qualified by the final event of the novel: torturers break in upon the two women and military rule continues as before. With her ending, Traba suggests that if a different history is to happen in Argentina, words will not be enough; bodies will also be called upon to act.

Kate Cummings. *College English.*
52, 1990, p. 555

Traba's novels are implicated with the death and birth of language, and would seem to engage with a central set of problems evolving around the opposition between language as communication on the one hand and silence as erasure or cancellation on the other. However, these texts also *dissolve* the opposition between language and silence: if silence, gaps, and erasure can be construed as possible forms of expression, then the texts may concentrate on making those silences *speak* by "reading between the lines," reading for a repressed subtext or uncontainable surplus of meaning beneath the surface oppositions of monological discourse. On a more sinister note, however, inscription, signification, and identity are very often experienced as forms of cancellation of the human—seen as a Kafkaesque, tortured writing *onto* and writing *over* the human body.

A dual yet complementary approach emerges. On the one hand there is the possibility, for Traba, of "locating" a kind of silence which is not the withdrawal from expressivity but rather, following Ernst Cassirer, a "mythical space" of self-protection, a search for expression through the presence of symbol rather than the absence or dis-placement of sign. Parallel (yet in apparent contrast) to this is the overtly political context of *silent* "disappearances," *hushed-up* torture, and exile in which Traba sets her later novels. In such a context, silence can no longer be symbolic gesture: it is outright scandal. . . . The struggle to save the expressive possibilities of language is by no means an abstract philosophical problem in the context of a military régime whose field of battle extends from the gratuitous destruction of the human body to the annihilation of the signs by which the body identifies itself and conserves a sense of its own dignity. The very concept of dictatorship suggests an implicit relation between power and the control of words, and much of Traba's work is involved in exposing this functioning of oppression at the level of the sign, felt as a distortion or mutilation scored across the body of the text. . . .

The repression of multiple meanings in the novel is associated disturbingly with the torture, "disappearance," and silencing of anyone who dares to express an alternative to the official story, so that the "death" of language cannot be dissociated from physical mutilation and biological death. Nevertheless, even the briefest study of Traba's narrative and the textual theory she explicitly puts forward elsewhere will reveal that text and body are not unequivocally conflated in her work, but are mediated through a materialist analysis. . . .

Throughout her work Traba constantly attempts to project this whole process onto a socio-historical plane whereby a material method might open up the necessary space for people (in particular the people of that colonized space termed "Latin" America) to gain possession of the text of history, largely written and controlled by others. In order to achieve forms of historical awareness and thereby undo chains of dependency, Traba suggests that it is necessary to bind oneself to the material body, that which cannot be expropriated, and proceed "against the grain," positing the negative for the positive and the positive for the negative. Only through the unleashing of dialectical tension might it be possible for body and thought to unite and appropriate the text of history, to create that point of rupture which she termed the "silent zone," through which the other may emerge once more into history, take possession of it, and cover herself at last with its images, as Traba bade us to do with the paintings of Martínez, Gerzso, and García Guerrero.

Ella Geoffrey Kantaris. *Modern Language Review.* 87, 1992, pp. 83, 90–91, 101

TREADWELL, SOPHIE (UNITED STATES) 1885–1970

There is no effort to make melodrama sympathetic in Sophie Treadwall's new play of American life in Mexico [*Gringo*]. Plot and counterplot abound, with fiercely contending passions of love and hate and considerable sums in gold dust at stake. Now and again there is the swirl of a machete or the flash of gunplay. But the quarry that is chiefly hunted in "Gringo" is the sheer character and the starkly real emotions of white men of the North and of their Indian and halfbreed environment.

There is a socialist draft-dodger living in exile who hails the peon as "brother" and is eventually all but murdered by him in a spasm of craven fear. There is an upstanding mine expert who loves and is loved by the draft-dodger's wife, yet runs true to his gods of honor, as she does.

There is an American squaw-man sodden with drink and with love of his woman. Especially there is his daughter, who is taught to call herself an American, but whose young blood is alive with Indian passion and treachery. Then there is the "revolutionist" bandit, played to the life by José Ruben, and his gang of Indian and half-breed followers. The whole problem of the two races and their mongrelization is shown in miniature, and is shown with a vitality and a color of reality that make this play for the most part of absorbing novelty and interest.

It is a study in warring racial inheritances. Weak as her father is and overmastered by his vices of love and drink, he has yet the pride of the white man and a full measure of love and ambition for his child. But the boredom of his home oppresses her and the wild blood of her race comes uppermost.

Infatuated with love at first sight for the American engineer, she betrays the secret of the gold-dust hoard for an Indian love philter, and when she is captured with the others by Tito, and is forced to become his mistress, her passion as quickly shifts to him, and she follows him to bear his burdens and cook his tortillas. The portrait is as vivid and convincing as it is true to biology.

With all its wealth of character and atmosphere, there is little in this play that commands the sort of sympathy essential to melodrama. A perfectly good plot is deployed with the necessary skill, but one remains strangely indifferent to the fate of the dramatis personae, even when absorbed in the development of their characters. A play that through two acts promises to be a sensational success perceptibly flags as popular entertainment in the concluding scenes. It remains, however, an achievement of great distinction and of greater promise on the higher levels of drama.

John Corbin. *The New York Times*.
December 15, 1922, p. 26:3

Atlantic City was the scene of the première—barring a single night in the sticks—of *Loney Lee,* which has Helen Hayes for its star. The play is the work of Sophie Treadwell, who will be remembered as the author of *Gringo.* The *Atlantic City Gazette-Review* gives this account of the piece:

"*Loney Lee* depicts cleverly the adventures of Appolonia Lee, known more familiarly as 'Loney,' and her attempt to 'make the stage' after she has had exceptional success in the high school auditorium back in a little town in Kansas. How her illusions are shattered and she finally attains happiness and love, not as she had pictured, but in a decidedly opposite direction, develops a comedy and a role which appear to be adapted perfectly to her personality.

"The opening scene, which is laid in a studio of the big town, affords an opportunity for Miss Hayes to present herself as the young girl overflowing with ambition and enthusiasm, and paves the way for a series of interesting developments, which feature a French marquis, who lives on his wife's bounty, and his episode with the aspiring and disillusioned young girl, 'strong and wiry.'

"Complications begin and the unsophisticated Miss Lee is offered her 'big chance,' inasmuch as a great producer and a famous star are present, through the request of the Marquis, at a dinner in the studio.

"The scene serves as a means of dispersing her fond hopes and presenting a star and a producer as they are, minus the glare of footlights and the fascination of the theater.

"Hamilton Revelle, as the Marquis de Severac, portrays with exceptional ease a polished character, and the work of Harry Minturn, who is seen as Lawrence Gormont, the noted producer, although featured only in the critical dinner episode, is of convincing quality.

"Miss Hayes offers a role worthy of her past successes and makes, through her appearance and efforts, a production to afford an evening of excellent entertainment."

John Corbin. *The New York Times.*
November 11, 1923

Sophie Treadwell has come close to writing an excellent comedy in *O Nightingale.* As it is, she has turned out a well-written play that is almost consistently entertaining, and which provides several unusual and interesting characters. It is basically a story of a young girl who comes to New York with stage ambitions, but it is worked out with less theatrical background than you might imagine. Only near the final curtain, does one rub up against the stage in the person of a leathery manager and his popular star.

This comedy of Miss Treadwell's has fought its way slowly to the Broadway stage—a position to which it is considerably more entitled than approximately half of the current play list. Some two seasons ago, when the play was known as *Loney Lee,* it got as far as an out-of-town tryout with Helen Hayes in its leading role. Now, presumably re-made a little, it reaches the Forty-ninth Street Theatre with Miss Treadwell programmed as its sponsor, although Mary Kirkpatrick stands with her as co-producer. Moreover, the play comes to town with the author in the cast, although, presumably in the hope of fooling at least two or three people, she is programmed as Constance Eliot. For it seems that Miss Treadwell, in years and years of writing, has never quite got over the ambition to be an actress. . . .

The play falls a bit short as drama primarily because Miss Treadwell has elected to keep her story rather thin, and sometimes because scenes are permitted to run a little down hill at the finish instead of building to their climaxes. It remains, however, an amusing and generally well-written comedy.

Stark Young. *The New York Times.*
April 16, 1925, p. 25:2

From the sordid mess of a brutal murder the author, actors and producer of *Machinal,* which was staged at the Plymouth last evening have with great skill managed to retrieve a frail and sombre beauty of character. In superficial details the story resembles the Snyder and Gray murder case. But Sophie Treadwell who is Mrs. W. O. McGeehan in private life, has in no sense capitalized a sensational murder trial in her strangely-moving, shadowy drama. Rather has she written a tragedy of submission; she has held an individual character against the hard surface of a mechanical age. And Zita Johann acts the leading part with a bewildered droop and a wistfulness that quite redeem the chief character from the commonness of the environment. Subdued, monotonous, episodic, occasionally eccentric in its style, *Machinal* is fraught with a beauty unfamiliar to the stage.

Throughout the rather commonplace story Miss Treadwell has kept the young woman pathetically individual. The first scene, treated expressionistically, discloses her in a business office, fumbling about her work, unhappy and afraid. She marries her giggling, complacent employer as the easiest way out of her private muddle. Successive episodes chronicle her career through marriage and motherhood. Once, vaguely pursuing some ideal, she falls in with an engaging adventurer; and now happy for the first time she takes him for her lover. In the last half of the play she is on trial for the murder of her husband. In conclusion, one scene shows her in prison on the eve of electrocution, and the last, played in darkness, reports bits of descriptive conversation and her frightened scream from the electric chair.

It is difficult by description to communicate the precise quality that distinguishes *Machinal* and that casts a subtly moving spell on the audience.

J. Brooks Atkinson. *The New York Times.*
September 9, 1928, p. 26:3

In case Arthur Hopkins should be interested, be it known that in *Machinal* he has produced a play impossible to tuck away comfortably in the familiar circumlocutions of the reviewing craft. Usually we regard plays in terms of resemblances; and in point of fact *Machinal* resembles more than one bespattered murder tale. The woman who marries helplessly for protection, takes a lover and kills her husband is no fresh conception on the stage or in life. In *An American Tragedy* we have already peeped in at the gruesome horror of the prison death quarters. Furthermore, the episodic treatment of the story, the skeletonized settings, the descriptions of the dull routine of office life through the medium of adding machines, filing cabinets and typewriters and dogmatic tatters of office conversation, recall *The Adding Machine, From Morn to Midnight* and the whole mad tumble of expressionistic drama. Yet, from all these factual resemblances, *Machinal* emerges as a triumph of individual distinction, gleaming with intangible beauty. . . .

Long experience has taught us to prepare ourselves for flaming passion and crowded excitement in murder plays. The emotional ordeal of the nameless Young Woman in *Machinal* would be well suited to such torrid treatment. Hating her office duties she marries her employer, whom she cannot endure, goes slumming timidly in the speakeasies in quest of enjoyment, succumbs to the gentle advances of an adventurer, kills her husband, stands trial in a court room scene, listens to the sonorous consolations of a priest in the death cell and stumbles, frightened and ghastly, to the electric chair. The news columns have chronicled that tawdry yarn before.

They have never disclosed it, as *Machinal* does, in terms of an impersonal exposition of character in conflict with environment. In the ten scenes of this play all the emotions well up, but crisp and austere—like intellectual images of what we are usually asked to feel. Flinging overboard the usual sentimentalities, neither excusing nor forgiving, Miss Treadwell dogs the Young Woman's disasters through their successive steps to the chamber of death, linking the end with the beginning, keeping her play restrained and tidy.

J. Brooks Atkinson. *The New York Times.*
September 16, 1928, p. ix:1:1

The Sophie Treadwell whose *Machinal,* an arresting tragedy of a submissive girl caught in the toils of our mechanized age, was brought out a year ago by Arthur Hopkins, last night turned to a different Hopkins and to a different sort of playwriting. *Ladies Leave,* which was presented by the Charles Hopkins who rules the destinies of a tiny theater in West Forty-ninth Street, may be catalogued as a drawing room comedy. . . .

To sustain the artificiality of high comedy is no small task. It demands a definite point of view, a skill in character drawing and a steady flow of wit. Miss Treadwell's play possesses these necessities to some extent, but they do not manage to keep the ball of gayety floating in mid-air all evening. On occasions the play hits ground with a hollow plop, to rise again a few minutes later through an amusingly written scene or a fresh twist in the dialogue.

Brooks Atkinson. *The New York Times.*
October 2, 1929, p. 28:3

Sophie Treadwell, who once wrote an original play entitled *Machinal,* has renovated the legend of the scarlet sisterhood in *Lone Valley.* . . . [You are well into] Miss Treadwell's play before you realize that Mary's past has been lively. Although she is now leading a clean and healthy life as a lone farmer-ette in some Western valley, her feathery wrapper and her mastery of the vernacular betray the sporting-house training. She is discovered in the second act by one of her old patrons, and very quickly the town knows her for the sordid critter she used to be. Be assured that she does not drag down the innocent adolescent next door. He wants to marry her in spite of it all. But he is the first man she has ever loved and she knows that he ought to go to college. Being loath to interfere with the bookish part of his education, Mary goes out into the night to take the rattler, bound back to a life of shame.

When Miss Treadwell takes an old legend she believes in taking it thoroughly. She has missed none of the characters, the turns of event or the feats of symbolism. The performance is colorless and hackneyed. Excepting Raymond Sovey's beautifully lighted set of a farmhouse interior, *Lone Valley* is out of the theater's old clothes closet. In view of the mental agility that *Machinal* disclosed, it is surprising that Miss Treadwell did not recognize the frailties of *Lone Valley* before she placed it in production.

Brooks Atkinson. *The New York Times.*
March 11, 1933, p. 18:6

Both Sophie Treadwell and Henry Hull have a respect for Edgar Allan Poe that verges on awe in *Plumes in the Dust,* which was acted at the Forty-sixth Street Theatre last evening. She is the author of this three-act sketch of the life of America's most singular genius, and he acts the raven-headed poet whom disaster followed like one of the Furies. It is an earnest pageant of desolation and melancholy, bedecked with bits of verse and bedeviled with orotund literary writing, and Arthur Hopkins has seen it nicely staged. But with all sincere respect for the talents that have been generously bestowed upon a dirge to a great poet's memory, this column suspects that the life of Poe is a chilly subject for stage discussion. Poe would blush for many of the vainglorious speeches he has to make in his own defense across the footlights.

Miss Treadwell, best known as the author of *Machinal,* has dogged close on the heels of Poe from the day he leaves his foster-father's house in Richmond in 1826 to the day he dies obscurely in a hospital bed in Baltimore in 1849, a-babbling of life's anguish. All his principal associates are here—his devoted foster-mother, his aunt, his child-wife, Virginia, and many of the literary celebrities of New York who whirled around in their smug circle while Poe starved and froze in his wretched cottage. It is the story, by now familiar, of an isolated poet who was outside all time and all trends and who was cursed with some psychopathic illness that drove him periodically to drink. Poe was a writer of pure literature; he was untouched by the times through which he lived, and his life was not only wretched but lonely.

In the circumstances it is difficult to relate it on the stage without turning it into a minor *Hamlet.* Miss Treadwell and Mr. Hull have rather conspired toward that end. She has done it by putting on his lips opulent literary phrases that sound a little egregious when Mr. Hull speaks them with an actor's exuberant swagger.

Brooks Atkinson. *The New York Times.*
November 7, 1936, p. 14:2

Among serious plays, a distinguished example of the fusion of expressionism and Freudianism in the American drama was Sophie Treadwell's *Machinal* (1928). In the style of *Roger Bloomer* and *The Subway,* but without the dream, Miss Treadwell explores the unconscious processes that might motivate a young girl such as figured in the famous Ruth Snyder murder case. The heroine, simply named The Young Woman, is a gentle, tender, sexually baffled creature in a hard, mechanized civilization teeming with sexual threats which arouse her anxiety. Craving emotional satisfaction yet having been brought up to view sex as loathsome, the Young Girl is in constant panic at her libidinous urges which threaten to break through wherever she turns, in her mechanized office or the closely packed subway train. Her boss has fat, flabby hands which she fears, and her mother has a drab mind that can discuss only garbage and potatoes while the Young Girl probes her about love and marriage. The Young Girl marries the boss only because it represents escape from her mother and the tenement. Her honeymoon with an earthy, lusty man is a magnificent depiction of embarrassment, sexual panic and hysteria; she undresses in the bathroom and cries for her mother as her husband approaches her.

In the hospital after she has had a baby, she can't endure her husband's visits and projects death-wishes toward her baby. Associating God with her fat-handed husband, she identifies herself with the Virgin Mary and mumbles that "I'll not submit" to any further relations with him.

In a barroom scene that veritably crawls with sex in a variety of forms— a woman needing an abortion, men waiting for pick-ups, and a homosexual trying to seduce a young boy—the Young Girl accepts a man's offer of an affair. Alone with him, she relaxes and finds new freedom. In a tender and warm love scene that is not expressionistic, repressed memories of her childhood return to her—nursery rhymes and childhood images which purify her. Her lover, who has killed two men in Mexico, gives her the hint that leads her to kill her own husband with a bottle filled with pebbles. But her lover signs a deposition betraying her and she confesses in court that she killed her fat-handed husband to be sexually free of him. Just before the execution she again fights "submitting" to the barber who would shave her head, and she goes to her death as an escape from a life that had been a sexual hell. Miss Treadwell's portrait of an emotionally starved woman driven to murder by her fixated loathing of sex is a full-blown psychological study, although the others in the play have less dimension. *Machinal* shows the origins of frigidity in the mother's own disgust with her marriage which she conveys to the daughter. In form the play is notable for the free-association soliloquies which attempt to project the kind of unconscious turmoil from which crimes of violence erupt.

Miss Treadwell wrote a number of other plays including a study of Edgar Allan Poe, *Plumes in the Dust* (1936), and a somewhat inept drawing room satire on psychoanalytic faddists, *Ladies Leave* (1929), in which she depicts a bored wife having an affair with her psychoanalyst and following him back to Vienna in what one critic called "a doorslam louder than Nora's." There was another unhappy lady in the play who couldn't eat or sleep until after she was psychoanalyzed, and then "my dear, she went right out and divorced her husband and opened a tea room." Unlike *Machinal,* the other works of Miss Treadwell were not departures from realism.

W. David Sievers. *Freud on Broadway: A History of Psychoanalysis and American Drama* (New York: Cooper Square, 1955), pp. 90–92

The [Theater] Guild's last social play before Pearl Harbor, Sophie Treadwell's *Hope for a Harvest,* opened on November 26, 1941, and closed after thirty-eight performances. This drama tells the story of a woman who has inherited a ruined ranch, which she decides to restore to its original fertility and beauty by means of hard labor. The playwright points the moral that more work could solve the problems of decaying farms and decadent farmers, but a rise in prices caused by the war helps solve the farm problem at the end of the play, thus diminishing the strength of the pro-work thesis.

The *Daily Worker*'s critic, Ralph Warner, denounced this analysis of the farm situation. The decay of American farms, he asserted, was not caused by sloth and other vices, but rather by "monopoly control of markets, prices, and crop production" and by government refusal to supply mortgage relief and farm machinery. The reviewer for *New Masses,* Alvah Bessie, was displeased to note that the Okies, whom the playwright depicted as lazy tramps, were introduced just for laughs. Neither Miss Treadwell nor the producers had treated the exploited proletariat with sufficient solemnity. The Guild's decade of social plays ended on this note.

Morgan Y. Himelstein. *Drama Was a Weapon: The Left-Wing Theatre in New York 1929–41* (New Brunswick, New Jersey: Rutgers University Press, 1963), pp. 151–52

Machinal, written by Sophie Treadwell, was first produced and directed by Arthur Hopkins at the Plymouth Theatre, New York City, on September 7, 1928 and ran for ninety-one performances. A "failure" commercially, it was generally acclaimed by the critics as one of the finest productions of the season and was considered one of Arthur Hopkins's ten best stagings in his forty-year career as a stage director/producer, as well as being Sophie Treadwell's best play. Condensations of the script appeared in *Theatre Magazine* in 1928 and in *The Best Plays of 1928–1929* edited by Burns Mantle; the complete script was included in John Gassner's collection *25 Best Plays of the Modern American Theatre (1916–1929).*

The most remarkable aspect of the piece was its use of expressionist techniques to tell an otherwise common story. . . .

Expressionism, while considered exotic, was not new to Broadway. O'Neill, Rice, Kaufman, and Connelly had all previously experimented with this style. Nor was it new to call attention to mechanization's crushing effect on individual sensitivity and expression. But this was a particularly well-received use of expressionistic means that, according to *New York Herald Tribune* reviewer Percy Hammond, successfully "blended the terms of art and box office."

Jennifer Parent. *The Drama Review.* 26:1, 1982, p. 88

Machinal, at the Public [Theater], is a revival of a 1928 expressionist play, by Sophie Treadwell, about a young stenographer who feels stifled and oppressed by all the circumstances of her life. She yields to the urging of her mother—a coarse creature who gobbles her bread, and may even wipe her plate with it—and agrees to marry her fat boss, repulsive though she finds him. Eventually, she takes a lover, and then she kills her husband by smashing his head with a bottle filled with stones. Under the obtrusive direction of Michael Greif, the production is expressionist to its eyeballs; scene follows scene amid flashing lights and crashing sound effects, so it's a wonder that the story seeps through at all. Not that it would matter much if it didn't, for the story is where the trouble lies: the script is earnest and humorless and deeply condescending toward working people and toward its heroine as victim. (In this instance, audience as victim, too; Sophie Treadwell may have felt downtrodden, but *we* didn't step on her.) The point of view expressed in the title was a standard left-wing cliché until, seven years later, Clifford Odets' *Awake and Sing!* broke the mold of "social protest" and cleared the air.

Machinal, according to a note in the program, is based on the actual case of Ruth Snyder, who, with her lover, Judd Gray, killed her husband and ended up in the electric chair. The original production opened to almost universal critical approval. One holdout, or partial holdout, was Charles Brackett, who reviewed plays for this magazine in the early, pre-Benchley days, and it was on this matter of "victim" that he also balked. "In comparison with Ruth Snyder . . . the young woman in *Machinal* becomes a nebulous and incredible figure," he wrote. "Whatever her faults Ruth Snyder had fire, and vigor, and a great lust of life. This heroine is a whining, neurotic girl full of self-pity and repressions. . . . I should say that she was the kind of girl whose miseries might lead her to develop asthma or hay fever. That she could ever rise to murder I will not admit." He approved of the acting of Zita Johann and Clark Gable as the young woman and her lover, and of Arthur Hopkins's production. What left him cold was the play.

Edith Oliver. The New Yorker. October 29,
1990, p. 114

[In *Machinal,* The Young Woman's] story could have been told through conventional sentimental realism, but Treadwell prefers to use expressionistic devices that emphasize the context over the woman herself. Whether the playwright is using the heightened realism of the kitchen scene and the intimate scene with the lover or the antirealistic cacophony of the office scene, she depends on cliché and repetition, reiterated platitudes that signal the attitudes toward work, marriage, motherhood, possessions, and money that provide the protagonist's only choices. The characters in the cast list are designated by role—Young Woman, Mother, Husband, Lover (more properly "Man" in the printed play)—and the names that appear in the text—Jones, Smith, Roe—are almost as generic as the labels. The expressionistic devices can be funny—as they are here when Marge Redmond (Mother), a master of the querulous cliché, and John Seitz (Husband), a master of the pompous cliché, are on stage—but within the laughter there is the hard edge of anger and sadness. Treadwell's highly efficient antimachine machine keeps the attention as much on society as on its victim. . . .

It has been—and still is—customary to suggest that Sophie Treadwell's play found its origin in the Ruth Snyder-Judd Gray murder case, but except that the young woman in *Machinal* dies in the electric chair as Ruth Snyder did (the first woman to be so honored by the American justice system), there is little similarity between the play and its presumed source. *Machinal* has much more to do with Broadway's essays in expressionism in the 1920s than with a current event, however lurid. The play's devices, and its indictment of a society in which routine devours the individual, place it in the generic line that includes Elmer Rice's *The Adding Machine* (1923), *Beggar on Horseback* (1924) by George S. Kaufman and Marc Connelly, and more gentle doses of the decade's fascination with cliché, like J. P. McEvoy's *The Potters* (1923), which I wish someone would revive, and the Gershwins' "The Babbitt and the Bromide" from *Funny Face* (1927). Where *Machinal* differs from its brothers under the scrim is that it is a play by a woman with a woman protagonist. That, feminist critics have suggested, is why it fell into obscurity after its initial success, but it was never as lost as later criticism has suggested.

Gerald Weales. *Commonweal.* November 23,
1990, pp. 698–99

I was not overly fond of this play [*Machinal*] when reviewing its previous off-Broadway revival (could it have been thirty years ago?). Then, as now, I thought it had value largely as a parade ground for the precision marches of an imaginative director (Gene Frankel in the 1960 version). *Machinal* has all the mechanical simplicity of early American Expressionism—the style that came to us via Germany, through the plays of Georg Kaiser and Ernst Toller. Unlike the Expressionistic work of Strindberg, who invented the form as a means of exploring his dream life, German Expressionism was propelled primarily by socio-political considerations. And it was these implicit Marxist critiques of the system that informed later American manifestations, most notably Eugene O'Neill's *The Hairy Ape* and Elmer Rice's *The Adding Machine.*

Like Rice's Mr. Zero, Treadwell's Miss A (otherwise known as Young Woman) is identified by a generic name, and, like Mr. Zero, she works at dehumanizing tasks. After the stage lights go on, industrial lamps are raised, and a stertorous voice announces, "Episode One: To Business" over a large radio mike. The various automatons constituting the office work force begin their mechanical functions: typing, adding, telephoning, mimeographing. Miss A is late ("all those bodies pressing—had to get out in the air"), and when she arrives—a pert little thing in black bobbed hair—her tender ears are assailed by a cacophony of homilies ("The early bird catches the worm," "Haste makes waste").

Machinal is based on an actual story, the Ruth Snyder murder case. Snyder was the first woman to die in the electric chair; the playbill displays a photograph of the execution taken off the front page of the *Daily News* (the headline screamed "DEAD!" in monstrous capitals). This celebrated case inspired a number of fictional works, including James M. Cain's *The Postman Always Rings Twice* and an unproduced play by William Styron and John Phillips called *Dead: A Love Story*. Male authors tend to treat Snyder as a ruthless lech who persuaded a hapless lover to murder her wealthy husband. Treadwell, ignoring the complicity of the lover, treats her as a neurotic victim of sexual and social oppression, driven to murder as the only alternative to madness and despair. . . .

When Miss A is asked in the courtroom why she didn't choose divorce rather than murder, she answers, "I couldn't do that. I couldn't hurt him like that." It is the only startling thought in the play. Otherwise, this tale of a sensitive plant wilting in the age of the machine is declarative, predictable, simplistic. What remains vital and lively, however, are the theatrical possibilities.

Robert Brustein. *The New Republic.*
December 17, 1990, pp. 27–28

Sophie Treatwell's *Machinal* transmits a terse, telegraphic message: the institution of marriage is a breeding ground for anger, desperation, and violence. This 1928 expressionist drama imparts the story of an ordinary young woman's marriage to her employer and the societal and psychological pressures that lead her ultimately to murder him. Trivialized by theater critic Robert Brustein in 1960 as "one of those banal tabloid stories . . . about how a sensitive dish of cream is curdled in the age of the machine," Treadwell's slighted work often has been characterized as a derivative drama of social criticism targeted at the effects of mechanization on the individual. Treadwell's social protest, however, reaches beyond the machine age of the twentieth century. Augmenting a female tradition of literature that dissects the restrictive institution of marriage and its effects on women, *Machinal* stands as an early twentieth-century piece of subversive drama, conveying the message that female insurrection can lead to "one moment of freedom" before the patriarchal "machinery" crushes the revolt. . . .

Although an analysis of Treadwell's dramatic canon reveals a broad spectrum of dramatic forms ranging from light comedy to melodrama to social criticism, it is her longstanding "partisanship of feminism" that marks the majority of her works. Plays such as *Oh Nightingale* (1925), a conventional comedy about an aspiring actress in New York City; *Lone Valley* (1933), a melodrama of a reformed prostitute; and *Hope for a Harvest,* a realistic drama of a woman's attempt to restore her family's farm, all feature female protagonists who struggle for autonomy (albeit not always successfully) in a male-dominated society. Perhaps the strongest declaration of Treadwell's commitment to feminist concerns is her play *Rights,* an unpublished biographical drama of Mary Wollstonecraft, the eighteenth-century author of the seminal feminist work *A Vindication of the Rights of Woman.* Copyrighted in 1921 but never produced, *Rights* frames Wollstonecraft's bid for personal freedom against the broader struggle of the French Revolution. Criticized as didactic and unfocused, *Rights* nevertheless capsulizes some feminist issues that receive powerful, searing dramatization in *Machinal* seven years later, particularly the role of women in the institution of marriage. The bold, vibrant character of Wollstonecraft in *Rights,* who lashes out, "I am opposed to marriage. . . . I will not submit to an institution I wish to see abolished," stands behind the docile wife portrayed in *Machinal.*

Like *Rights, Machinal* (French for "mechanical") voices Treadwell's feminism with a particular vehemency and radicalism that is softened in many of her other plays. Combining expressionistic techniques, such as repetitive dialogue, audio effects, numerous short scenes, and the distortion of inner and outer reality, Treadwell creates, with the evocative disorientation of an Edvard Munch, the picture of an ordinary young woman driven by desperation to murder. . . .

Sophie Treadwell belongs to the coterie of early modern women playwrights who portrayed with relentless honesty women's struggle for autonomy against a patriarchal system. Concentrating on women's issues and employing the male-dominated mode of drama, feminist playwrights such as Treadwell have threatened to subvert the traditional theater by seeking their own powerful public voice. Their efforts until now have condemned them to a literary anonymity of unpublished works and hasty critiques such as that suffered by Treadwell. The contributions of Sophie Treadwell and women dramatists like her merit reassessment. The story in *Machinal* of one ordinary woman's attempt to strike back at a repressive institution needs to be communicated. Perhaps instead of being misread or misinterpreted by male critics, *Machinal* has been comprehended all too well. Silenced for decades by the literary "machine," Sophie Treadwell still has a message to telegraph to her "daughters."

Barbara L. Bywaters. In June Schlueter, ed.
*Modern American Drama: The Female
Canon* (Madison, New Jersey: Fairleigh
Dickinson University Press, 1990),
pp. 97–99, 108

Treadwell, who graduated from Berkeley in 1906, came of age with the century's industrial boom. An actress, journalist, and feminist, and the author of four novels and more than thirty plays, six of which were mounted on Broadway, she seems to have reflected, as well as chronicled, the era's restless obsession with productivity. In *Machinal,* the heroine is not a corporate highflier but a young, poorly educated stenographer who is swept up in the slipstream of the century's velocity, where she cannot find "any place, any peace." (Neither, really, could men, although, as the Adams quotation indicates, men built this world, which then trapped them in a different kind of alienation.) In *Machinal* . . . the city is the antagonist, and its inhabitants are merely cogs in the inexorable drama of production.

John Lahr. *The New Yorker.*
November 22, 1993, p. 83

TRIOLET, ELSA (RUSSIA–FRANCE) 1896–1970

Elsa Triolet is the wife of Poet Louis Aragon, one of whose recent volumes was named *The Eyes of Elsa*. In 1944, she won France's *Prix Goncourt* with her short stories; but readers are not likely to find her new book a prizewinner.

The White Charger is a novel about Michel, an illegitimate son. Father spends most of his time at sea, mother spends most of hers smoking opium, so Michel soon learns to look after himself. He grows into a talented pianist and crooner—but so indifferent to the life of post-World War I that he scarcely bothers to sing for his supper. Women—princesses, chambermaids, doxies, chorines—are all bowled over by Michel's fascinating indifference. At twenty-five, Michel is the western world's most bored Casanova, married to an aging American moneybag and hopelessly in love with a frigid Swede.

Mme. Aragon tries earnestly to explain that Michel's gigolory results from his being at heart a frustrated knight-errant in today's ignoble world. She redeems his calloused soul by making him die nobly in World War II. But three-fourths of *The White Charger* is simply a listing of Michel's tedious romantic conquests. Only the most dogged reader will remember, by the end, just what made Elisabeth different from Mary, or from Marjorie, and Riri, and Gisèle, and Irène, and Francine, and Nicole, and Mariana, and Lucette, and Lily—to mention only a few.

Time. January 6, 1947, p. 68

I think I can understand why the French wartime public liked *The White Charger* so well. It is a picture of freer, wickeder days, and it has the quality of having been written in prison, as if by a woman dreaming of Paris and a phantom lover, which makes it an intensely feminine book. It has no plot; it is simply the story of a charmingly indifferent Parisian hero, whose adventures take him from city to city and into beds that are rarely his own. "And why," Louis Hector Berlioz asked in the foreword to his *Damnation of Faust,* "did the author dispatch his hero into Hungary? Because he wished to include a piece of music with a Hungarian theme." Elsa Triolet dispatches her hero to Berlin and New York, not because the story requires those particular journeys but, chiefly, because she has comments to make on German and American women. Michel, the hero, has affairs with ladies of both these nationalities. In fact, he conquers or yields to almost every woman under sixty who appears in the novel; he is the *homme fatal,* the male counterpart of the girl in the green hat. He is also a psychological type portrayed with more acuteness and more suggestions of tangled motives than one expects in this picaresque sort of story. Adored by his mother, a famous singer who has lost her voice, he is indifferent to other women even while embracing them; emotionally, he is honest only with men. He is unable to fall in love until he meets a Swedish girl even colder and more abandoned than himself, but she soon leaves him for his closest friend, whom he has come to regard as a second father. Other women desire him even though they despise him. One of them takes him to lunch and tries to reform him; then, at parting, she whispers, "You are a whore, Monsieur, a whore. See you later." They all see him later. And they all shower gifts on him, but he dreams only of riding into a beleaguered city on a white charger to rescue a spotless maiden.

I have not been able to find a copy of the French edition, but those who have read it tell me that the dialogue is a lively echo of Paris before the war. In the translation, the dialogue doesn't echo Paris or Manhattan or any other place on earth inhabited by human beings. When the translator speaks of a man without a vest, you nod your head and say to yourself, "Good! She writes American; she wouldn't let them bully her into saying 'waistcoat,'" but then you read the sentence again and decide that in the original the man was probably without a coat—*sans veston*. When the translator speaks of one-story houses in Greenwich Village, you can be certain that they began as *maisons d'un seul étage,* or what we other Americans call two-story houses. Throughout the book there is a feeling of haste, as if the translator hadn't stopped often enough to revise a sentence or look into the dictionary. The result is something like a Paris confection reproduced for the mail-order market.

Malcolm Cowley. The New Yorker.
January 11, 1947, pp. 81–82

Three very feminine narratives [*A Fine of 200 Francs*] of the French underground, which are certainly not novels, as the publishers call them, though it is hard to find a better label for them. They are more like poignantly written case histories of how three very different people reacted to the necessity for resistance to the Germans, and as such they form an artistically presented footnote to history. Mlle. Triolet, whose sympathies are obviously with the Communists, writes extremely well, but she seems almost intentionally to avoid making the perils she recounts particularly moving or vivid. She has skillfully crystallized the concerns of certain Frenchmen during the Occupation (she assumes that everyone knows all about the Resistance movement by now), but it is doubtful that readers will be either enlightened by, or even greatly interested in, her narrative as the recent tragedy of France grows more remote.

The New Yorker. September 20, 1947, p. 98

Elsa Triolet . . . [along with] Louis Aragon, edited an underground newspaper during the Occupation. Her most recent book, *A Fine of 200 Francs . . .* subtitled "Three Short Novels of the Resistance," won the Goncourt Prize.

These stories are the best I've read among what has come to be called "Resistance Literature," and first of all for the negative reason that they are not concerned with the more flamboyant heroisms which, however authentic or admirable in themselves, seem sensationally exploited when recounted in fiction. Although several of her characters are actively involved, they are presented rather as people with their individual human problems altered and constricted under the *conditions* of occupation during the *time* of the Resistance. "The hope of peace hangs over us like a sword . . . everyone eats cold food, drinks any old concoction. . . . The danger lies not in doing this or that, but in happening to be there."

To describe the atmosphere of this time—the suspense, the daring, the exasperation—her prose style is admirably suited: quick, sharp and edgy.

John Farrelly. *The New Republic.*
October 6, 1947, p. 30

Elsa Triolet (née Elza Iur'ievna Kagan) is known to readers of French literature as a prolific, frequently impressive novelist and as a kind of *monstre sacré*. A decisive woman, with clear pro-Soviet principles and loyalties, she was a major power in French literary politics for forty years. She is also one of the major *characters* in modern French poetry, the object of the public, published adoration of the poet Louis Aragon. He enshrined her in such works as "Elsa," "Cantique à Elsa" (Canticle for Elsa), "Le fou d'Elsa" (A fool for Elsa), and "Les yeux d'Elsa" (Elsa's eyes) at least as solidly as Vladimir Maiakovskii did her older sister, Liliia Iur'ievna Brik, in his "Pro eto" (About this) and "Fleita-pozvonochnik" (The backbone flute). Elsa Triolet is also a heroine of Russian literature. Long before being so fulsomely adored by Aragon, she had appeared as the cosmopolitan, comfort-loving, and elusive Alia of Viktor Shklovskii's *Zoo, ili pis'ma ne o liubvi* (Zoo, or, Letters not about love). Although she later wrote seventeen novels and a number of other books in French, Triolet's own first novels, written in Russian in the late 1920s and published in the Soviet Union, can stand comparison with any Russian prose of the period. Throughout her career, she continued to translate in both directions and to promote Russian literature in France and French literature in Russia.

Elizabeth Klosty Beaujour. *Alien Tongues:*
Bilingual Russian Writers of the "First"
Emigration (Ithaca, New York: Cornell
University Press, 1989), pp. 58–59

Late in 1944, she started what was meant to be a long short story but eventually became the novel, *Personne ne m'aime* (Nobody loves me). . . . In the course of the novel, Elsa developed a second heroine, whose full career needed a new work, *Les Fantômes armés* (Armed ghosts), published in 1947. To this great desolate pair of novels she gave the collective title *Anne-Marie.* . . .

Armed Ghosts shows how the past corrupts the present and how, more insidiously, the present corrupts the past. It answers the final question of *Nobody Loves Me*, whether there is anything for whose sake people can love each other, and postulates the necessity of permanent struggle. Peace is the continuation of war by other means. The choice is between an uncaring boredom and commitment. Jenny turned herself, as Aragon said, into a work of art, and the end of that is suicide. Does Anne-Marie, "La Demoiselle" in the Resistance, take on what Juliette in "The Lovers of Avignon" might have become? If so, her experience is the "banal" one which is also universal. . . .

Le Cheval roux (The russet horse) appeared in 1953 after Stalin's death, but it had been written before the news came. The Russet Horse is a long novel of apocalyptic terror. It begins after an atomic war in which Elsa, named as such, has been terribly disfigured. She and an American pilot, Henry, join up to make what they can of their predicament. The novel ends with a flight into the distance and a cry of "Adieu, Louis!" Elsa was proud that the physicist Frédéric Joliot-Curie had advised her on the scientific data it contains, but despite this and its semi-allegorical content Elsa's "anticipated autobiography" is too locally topical to read well. . . .

Elsa published a new novel Le Monument (The monument) in 1957. Here, she takes up the quarrel between socialist realism and the avant-garde. Lewka, an avant-garde sculptor, is asked to make a monument to Stalin. Elsa had in mind Picasso's drawing of him and a story she had heard of a Czech sculptor who had killed himself when his monument to Stalin was unveiled, artistically crippled and hideous. Like Lewka, he wanted to leave all his money to the blind who could not see how Stalin and their city had been disgraced. This decisive break with the Party's insistence on realism, a celebration of the freedom of the imagination was, as Pierre Daix observes, particularly significant because Elsa was renouncing all that she had led Aragon towards. . . .

Elsa completed The Age of Nylon trilogy with L'Âme (The soul), published in 1963. This is a metaphysical fairy tale about a child prodigy with, as Elsa averred, a long literary pedigree. All together, The Age of Nylon, with the forest simplicities of Roses à Credit, the erotic energies of Luna-Park and the studied eccentricity of The Soul show that her spirit was achieving a new freedom in the wake of The Monument. Her work lost here a sense of dutifulness which had marred much since Anne-Marie.

Lachlan Mackinnon. The Lives of Elsa
Triolet (London: Chatto and Windus, 1992),
pp. 164, 167, 182, 187, 190–91

In addition to her work with the Resistance, she found time to write two novels and a dozen short stories. In 1945, she became the first woman to win the Prix Goncourt, for a collection of three stories published as Le Premier accroc coûte deux cents francs (A Fine of Two Hundred Francs). . . .

In spite of her many achievements as a journalist, a biographer, a translator of Russian prose and poetry, and as a novelist whose fiction is an intriguing blend of fantasy and political engagement, Triolet has remained an undeservedly neglected writer. . . .

Bitterly disillusioned with the failure of wartime ideals to survive the Cold War, she wrote movingly of the révolution manquée (aborted revolution). In her two-volume novel, *Anne-Marie,* Célestin of *The Lovers of Aragon* reappears. But now he is a general involved in a sinister plot against the Republic. We also learn that Juliette, his one true love, did not survive the war. The novel *L'Inspecteur des ruines* also reflects the pessimistic postwar mentality of the Left. The hero, Blond, returns from a German prison camp having lost his family. Utterly adrift, he meets a black marketeer who hires him to sift through the rubble of bombed out cities in search of valuables. . . .

Her most controversial novel, *Le Monument* (1957), marked the end of her involvement with *PCF* organizations, such as the *Conseil national des écrivains,* of which she was vice president. She was also attacked by Party chief, Maurice Thorez, because her book questioned the validity of socialist realism.

In her last major work, *Le grand jamais* (Absolutely Never; 1965), a witty novel of ideas that explores the nature of historical truth, Triolet continued to assert her independence. Madeleine, young widow and former student of Régis, a famous historian, wishes to uncover the truth about her dead husband, who had made his reputation with a brilliant new interpretation of Catherine the Great. But the book was a hoax. Régis, whose favorite character is Mad King Louis of Bavaria, sees history as a joke and denies the possibility of historical truth. Needless to say, such a pessimistic perspective on history scarcely conformed to the Party line, but was further proof of Triolet's independence.

Her last book, *Le Rossignol se tait à l'aube* (The nightingale stops singing at dawn), a moving meditation on old age and loneliness, was published just before her death in 1970.

Helena Lewis. *Belles Lettres.* 9, Winter,
1993–94, pp. 33–36

TROTZIG, BIRGITTA (SWEDEN) 1929–

A collection of short stories by Birgitta Trotzig entitled *I kejsarens tid* was published in 1975 and carried the subtitle "legends." The seven tales that comprise the slim and remarkable volume presented a new departure for this most original of Sweden's contemporary writers. *I kejsarens tid* baffled the critics who had hardly begun to grasp the rich metaphorical meanings of the previous works, all of which had been cast in more conventional literary modes. As soon as the effects of the shock of novelty dissipated, however, it became clear that Birgitta Trotzig's central themes and concerns were unchanged. Only here they found expression in a more abstract and metaphorical language. Love and power have been Birgitta Trotzig's focal themes since her first novel and they are the very themes that unify the seven tales of *I kejsarens tid.* The legend that gives its title to the volume, is a most vividly drawn image of a patriarchal order of an unspecified time and place which is marked by stifling repression and conformity and which comes to a sudden apocalyptic end. This kingdom of Caesar evokes previous images of "the time of the law" *(De Utsatta)* and of "the time of the emperor" *(Sjukdomen)* that are familiar to the Trotzig reader. It recalls the moving pictures of the only film based on a Trotzig novel entitled *Kejsaren.* The kingdom of Caesar depicted in this very short tale can well stand for all the fictional worlds that Trotzig has created and recreated throughout a writing career that spans three score years and more.

The women characters that inhabit these fictional worlds must be viewed within their social context—a context of hierarchical, oppressive and invariably patriarchal conventions. It is impossible to isolate the individual characters in Trotzig's fiction from either their natural or their social environments. The natural landscape in which the characters exist, Trotzig herself has repeatedly said, is her starting point. . . . And the social conditions—the accommodations that aim at subjugation and ownership are only the other side of the indifference, narcissism and violence that lie within the individual human psyche. Impotence and rage are common responses to the process of victimization which is built into the power structures described in Trotzig's works. These structures have not changed essentially. They have only become more ruthless and efficient in her most recent novel which is set in a modern period.

It is important to note that Birgitta Trotzig's fiction, which places women in the subservient position where they realistically belong in the patriarchy, does not designate them as the sole victims. . . .

Only a love that is capable of affirming another human being, or in St. Augustine's words, a love that allows the other *to be* is capable of bringing about change in the houses of power and of leading the way out of captivity— out of the increasingly tightening social systems of control and dehumanization. Trotzig's novels and short stories point to those moments of promise in the lives of men and women and record in most vivid and concrete terms their limited success and their tragic and pervasive failure. . . .

Careful reading of Trotzig's fiction leaves no doubt that the philosophical issue transcends sexual politics. A grave injustice is done to her texts if the reader overlooks the power of Eros that touches so many of the male characters at the very core of their being. Although many are defeated, it is important to note that for a number of the male characters, the journey is, at least, begun. . . .

Birgitta Trotzig does not write from a conscious and explicitly feminine point of view. It is impossible, therefore, to extract from her fiction an oversimplified statement about the role of women. Rich and varied are the images she projects of women as mothers, as wives or lovers and as daughters. In attempting to trace the fate of some of them, it becomes clear that they are drawn within a social environment that limits their full development as persons as it limits the development of men. Within the restricting context of the patriarchy, however, hope lives that human life may be redeemable. A light shines through Eros in the realm of darkness and "peaceful death."

Adma d'Heurle. *Scandinavian Studies.* 55, 1983, pp. 371–73, 381

Her first novel, *Ur de älskandes liv* (1951; From the life of the loving ones), was well received in Sweden, but it was *De utsatta* (1957; The exposed) that established her reputation as a gifted and profound writer. This major novel, as well as *En berättelse från kusten* (1961; A tale from the coast), is set in a remote historical period in rural Scania, whereas the later works, *Sveket* (1966; The betrayal), *Sjukdomen* (1972; The illness), and *Dykungens dotter* (1984; The Marsh King's daughter), are set in more recent times.

The Scanian landscape, with its icy desolation and its warm softness, is the background against which her characters are usually drawn. The plains of Scania provide a suitable background that keeps in view the metaphysical dimensions of the novels. A direct sense of self and rootedness in the world of nature distinguishes the major characters in Trotzig's fiction. The realism in all her novels is that of the visionary artist. The patterns of vivid images of landscape, characters, and events carry a particular moral force because they cannot be separated from a broader view of human life. The novels transcend the time and space that they depict so vividly.

The events of *Sjukdomen* are significantly framed by the two world wars. It is the tragic story of the retarded and mentally ill Elje Ström, who is cared for by his father, a lonely, poor, and religiously fanatic laborer. Elje's illness and the psychological drama of father and son are intertwined with the social conditions of rural Sweden and the political events in wartime Poland.

Dykungens dotter can be read as a sequel to *Sjukdomen*. It transposes the theme so that a young man's search for his mother becomes a young woman's search for her father and her lost child. The novel retells the Hans Christian Andersen fairy tale whose title it bears, but it is also a new tale whose mythological dimensions are immediately evident. The prevailing imagery in *Dykungens dotter* is that of the pulsating, teeming, creative life of the marsh. Opposed to it is the "cage"—any of the man-made structures that confine the ever-creative force of the organic world. Humankind is one with the interwoven and interconnected parts of the universe of nature. The novel brings together the Christian and pagan worlds of body and spirit that are set apart in Andersen's "Marsh King's Daughter."

Trotzig's shorter prose narratives include novellas, short stories, and a collection of allegorical tales. Her versatility, her religious sensibility, and her breadth of vision have been widely recognized. It is, however, the intensity of her language and the purity and lyricism of her prose works as well as her poetry that make her one of the most important and original of Sweden's contemporary writers.

Adma d'Heurle. In Virpi Zuck, ed.
Dictionary of Scandinavian Literature
(Westport, Connecticut: Greenwood Press,
1990), pp. 627–28

From her debut in 1951, Trotzig—unaffected by the vagaries of literary fashion—has remained faithful to an original vision of existence and presented a profile uniquely her own. She is the recipient of a number of prestigious literary prizes, among them the Selma Lagerlöf Prize (1984) and the Pilot Prize (1985), and has enjoyed critical acclaim, not least in France.

Trotzig's vision of existence is basically religious, but her novels and short stories (she often refers to the latter as fairy tales or legends) are not vehicles for abstract theological discourse; they are palpably and painfully concrete; the concept of God-made-flesh is fundamental in her works. Her early novel *De utsatta* (1957; The exposed) is set in Skåne against a background of war in the seventeenth century. The novel *En berättelse från kusten* (1961; A tale from the coast) is set in Skåne in the Middle Ages. Her later novels, *Sveket* (1966; The betrayal), *Sjukdomen* (1972; The illness), and *Dykungens dotter* (1984; The marsh king's daughter), are set in more recent times. In most of Trotzig's stories the protagonists are from the lowest strata of society, people who are poor, downtrodden, and betrayed by life and fellow beings. They are suffering pain, hardships, and indignities, sometimes to the limits of the endurable; the pessimistic vision of existence that emerges through Trotzig's descriptions is relentless and seemingly unrelieved by grace and only redeemed by the dark intensity of her language. Critics have suggested that Trotzig has made her uncompromising vision an end in itself, effective and compelling, but ultimately aesthetic. It may also be tempting to suggest a deliberate "pious manipulation" behind the creation of such a bleak, implacable, and hopeless universe in order to offer redemption through Christ as the only possible salvation. Trotzig had an early traumatic experience of unmitigated evil when confronted with the exposed horrors of Nazi concentration camps; she also repeatedly points to the predominance of hunger, poverty, oppression, and torture in the world at large as ample justification for her vision. The suffering of children in particular makes Trotzig approach the timeless theodicy problem: how to reconcile the concept of a loving God with the existence of so much evil. Although Trotzig's political orientation toward a socialist-Marxist worldview may at times conflict with her religious convictions, the search for justice, divine or social, remains a constant. The descriptions in Trotzig's stories are often unstated indictments of intolerable social conditions; *Dykungens dotter,* for example, is on the mythical and allegorical level patterned on the Hans Christian Andersen fairy tale of the same title; on the realistic level it offers a highly critical account of the social development in Sweden, seen from the perspective of three generations of disenfranchised people. *De utsatta* is more than a historical novel; the descriptions of war in seventeenth-century Skåne reverberate with the author's strong emotional involvement with contemporary events in Algeria. The malady implied in the title of the novel *Sjukdomen* is not only that of the mentally retarded protagonist: his birth in 1914 and his first internment in 1939 are significant dates in his life, but also in world history. Trotzig admits that she intended the novel to be both an individual story and a myth of our century.

Trotzig's primary concern, however, is to depict the individual at the intersection of life and death, order and disorder, hope and despair. The ritual movement is downward, to the lowest and the most degraded state, in an imitation of or rather identification with the passion of Christ toward metamorphosis and resurrection.

In her essays Trotzig offers comments on her own activity as an author. Repeatedly she asserts her belief in the potentials of art and in the power of the artist as outsider and rebel: Unfettered art is one of the most effective weapons against what she terms "the insufferable order."

Lars G. Warme. In Steven R. Serafin and
Walter D. Glanze, eds. *Encyclopedia of
World Literature in the 20th Century* (New
York: Continuum, 1993), pp. 602–3

TSUSHIMA YUKO (JAPAN) 1947–

The stories in Yuko Tsushima's *The Shooting Gallery* are somewhat misleadingly described on the back cover as being about "a changing Japan, where spirited women, no longer bound by traditional values, find themselves free to lead lives of sexual freedom, economic independence—and, sometimes, loneliness." The women in these stories do possess a sort of painful, unwanted freedom, but they remain heavily shackled by convention if not tradition. They are by no means the aggressive women who have made themselves over into the equals of men and whom we are taught to admire in the West. They are rather more subtle and appealing in their basic helplessness in the face of ineluctable social circumstances. . . .

These stories offer as revealing a glimpse as any I have read of contemporary Tokyo to those who have not been there, and to those who have, they effectively recall that eclectic hive of a city beneath whose Westernized surface old folkways of feeling persist, if only vestigially, and behind whose brave affluent facade most people continue to live cramped, frugal, and matter-of-factly self-denying lives.

Lane Dunlop. *Literary Review.*
32, 1989, pp. 288, 293

Tsushima's fiction is nearly always deployed around the persona of an indomitable though solitary woman. She can be a young mother (as in *Child of Fortune* [*Choji*], 1978; *The Territory of Light* [*Hikari no ryobun*], untranslated, 1979; and *Woman Running in the Mountains* [*Yama o hashiru onna*], 1980), an adolescent (as in *Burning Wind* [*Moeru kaze*], untranslated, 1980), or a grown woman paired with an adolescent (as in *By the River of Fire* [*Hi no kawa no hotori de*], untranslated, 1983). She can be from the middle class or the working class, but either way she is utterly uncompromising in guarding her idiosyncrasy. The fierceness with which she keeps herself free and independent is what runs through each of Tsushima's works, be it a short or a long *shosetsu*.

It is almost as if to keep this fierceness untamed that the author keeps her prose relentlessly short and trimmed. There are no convoluted qualifications, nor are there many *gitaigo*—words that function to loosen up a tight syntax and to colloquialize prose. Tsushima modulates the tautness of her prose with dexterity, although her phrases never run lax and loose.

> Masao Miyoshi. *Off-Center: Power and*
> *Cultural Relations Between Japan and the*
> *United States* (Cambridge, Massachusetts:
> Harvard University Press, 1991), pp. 212–13

The daughter of the famous novelist Dazai Osamu, Tsushima Yūko, has firmly established her own place in the literary world. Her works often deal with themes that seem to derive from her own life: the absence of father, divorce, single mother, death of her son. However, her work cannot be confined within the convention of the *shishōsetsu* or "I-novel," for it often incorporates surreal situations and appropriates classical literature as its framework. Her ability to produce the unforgettable image of a female physicality that is solitary yet inseparably tied to the flow of all-inclusive life on earth, marks her as one of the major writers of contemporary Japan.

> Hosea Hirata. In Steven R. Serafin and
> Walter D. Glanze, eds. *Encyclopedia of*
> *World Literature in the 20th Century* (New
> York: Continuum, 1993), p. 335

Tsushima's first published short story, "Rekuiemu—inu to otona no tame ni" (1969; Requiem for a dog and an adult), was written in her senior year of college. Her early stories present a closed world of family relationships, often from a child's viewpoint; many contain macabre and surreal elements. Inevitably first identified as Dazai's daughter, Tsushima soon began to establish an independent reputation. "Kitsune o haramu" (1972; Conceiving a fox) was nominated for the Akutagawa Prize; the collections *Mugura no haha* (1975; The mother in the house of grass) and *Kusa no fushido* (1977; A bed of grass) were awarded the Tamura Toshiko Prize (1976) and the Izumi Kyōka Prize (1977), respectively; and the novel *Chōji* (1978; *Child of Fortune,* 1983) received the Women's Literary Award (1978).

The protagonist of *Chōji* is a thirty-six-year-old divorced mother who believes herself to be pregnant again. Through her experience of the pregnancy and the conventional attitudes of the people around her, the novel explores two of Tsushima's major themes: the tensions between motherhood and other dimensions of identity and sexuality, and the social marginality of a woman raising a family alone. (Tsushima married in 1970 and divorced in 1976, when her daughter was four; her son was born the same year.) Tsushima's characteristic use of light and water images as symbols of vitality and sexuality is at its most effective in this work. Tsushima has carried on the efforts of earlier women writers such as Okamoto Kanoko . . . and Enchi Fumiko . . . to portray sexual love as experienced by a woman. Often employing narrative techniques close to those of the confessional *shishōsetsu,* or "I-novel," she has reexamined the language available to express a woman's sexuality—a concern she shares with many contemporaries writing in other languages.

The newspaper serialization of her novel *Yama o hashiru onna* (1980; *Woman Running in the Mountains,* 1991) brought Tsushima a wider audience, while the story "Danmari ichi" (1982; "The Silent Traders," 1984) earned her the Kawabata Yasunari Prize (1983). Both works employ vivid images of nature in the interstices of the city, and draw on folkloric sources. The novel's heroine, a young single mother, dreams of living like the indigenous hunter-gatherers of the far north. The deadening urban routine and the control of bureaucracy over her life (through records of her child's illegitimacy) can barely contain her intuitive, wild energy. Associations with the *yamanba,* or mountain witch, and Japan's preagricultural peoples give mythic force to a novel of minutely detailed realism.

After the sudden loss of her son in 1985, Tsushima turned to an intensely personal contemplation of grief in which she strips away modern technological society's insulation from the inevitability of death. The novel *Yoru no hikari ni owarete* (1986; Driven by the light of night) retells the eleventh-century romance *Yowa no nezame* (*The Tale of Nezame,* 1979). In three chapters in letter form, the contemporary narrator addresses the woman author of the tale, Sugawara no Takasue no Musume (1008–?). In her lifetime, death must have been an ever-present reality, yet her words have survived for nearly a thousand years—facts that sustain the narrator, herself a writer, as she resolves to continue her own work.

Tsushima's prolific output and the autobiographical basis of her writing have resulted in some repetitive reworking of materials in her short stories. Over her twenty-year career, however, her fiction has evolved a distinctive fusion of realistic social content, critically observed from the margins, and transcending elements of myth, dream, and natural imagery employed with considerable imaginative power.

Geraldine Harcourt. In Steven R. Serafin and Walter D. Glanze, eds. *Encyclopedia of World Literature in the 20th Century* (New York: Continuum, 1993), p. 605

TSVETAEVA, MARINA (RUSSIA) 1892–1941

Marina Tsvetayeva (in the book *Vecherni albom* [*Evening Album*)] is innately talented and innately original. Although her book is dedicated to "the brilliant memory of Maria Bashkirtseva"—and epigraph taken from Rostand—the word "mama" is on almost every page. This leads to thoughts about the poetess's youth, thoughts that are confirmed by her own words of admission. There is a good deal new in this work: a new, brave (almost excessive) intimacy; new themes—a child's love, for example; a new spontaneous, mad predilection for the trifles of life. And, as is to be expected, here the main laws of poetry are instinctively guessed, so that this book is not only a book of a young girl's confessions but also a book of excellent poetry.

Nikolai Gumilyov. *Apollon.* 5, 1911, p. 78

Tsvetayeva's poems are very well conceived and polished. She is a great master of the word, with a predilection for poetic effects. First of all, she endeavors to give her verse a conciseness approaching aphorism. She wraps thought and infinity in a form polished and concise to the limits. She speaks almost in formulas, in sharp sentences. What is called "darkness" in Tsvetayeva's poetry is in fact concentration, lightning speed, which sometimes requires decoding. In Tsvetayeva, every word carries meaning and does not fail to evoke an image or thought. Perhaps that is why it is not easy to read her, even her best works, such as "Poema gory" ("The Mountain Poem") or "Poema kontsa" ("The Poem About the End"); it is necessary to follow her every word with the greatest attention. . . . Tsvetayeva's images are only hinted at: she never elaborates them, so that even here her sharpened precision is like the piercing of a knife.

Tsvetayeva's interrupted, nervous verse is verse in flight, in motion. Hence its dynamism, its pathos, its avoidance of the superfluous. As in Akhmatova, in Tsvetayeva's poems the expression and the poetic punctuation are more important than the melody of sound. But while Akhmatova is inclined toward the common speech, to what is known as "vulgarization of the poetic diction," Tsvetayeva's words are rich in sound and playful. Her poems reflect literary richness and the brilliant and capricious manner of people's speech, unexpectedly accompanied by witticisms, of which every average man is capable.

Marc Slonim. *Ruski arhiv.* 4, 1929, p. 108

She belonged neither to the Pushkin nor to the Lermontov school of Russian poetry, although in view of her romanticism, Pushkin had to be (and was) closer to her than Lermontov, whom . . . many of the Parisian émigré poets were attracted to. . . . Pushkin's poetic style is not reflected in Tsvetayeva's: in the realm of poetry they had nothing in common. Nevertheless, Tsvetayeva's poetic tastes were in some sense eclectic. Perhaps it should be said that she could be unselfishly and enthusiastically carried away by any authentic poetry she found: in Blok, Bely, Balmont, Bryusov, Akhmatova (Tsvetayeva's verses to Akhmatova are full of unexpected tenderness, revealing their closeness in some mystic Russian depths). Voloshin, Mandelshtam, Pasternak, Mayakovski. She speaks of them all both in prose and in verse with truly poetic generosity (I don't recollect her speaking of Gumilyov). Tsvetayeva has little in common with other women poets in Russian literature, such as Akhmatova, Zinaida Hippius, Carolina, or Pavlova. Contrary to Adamovich's judgment of her "decadent female egocentrism," in her verse there is little specific femininity, and insofar as there is femininity, it is of different gender from theirs, not decadent but hearkening back to folk laments. Here, perhaps, can be found a secret, deep kinship with Akhmatova.

Gleb Struve. *Russkaya literatura v izgnanii*
(New York: Izdatelstvo imeni Chekhova,
1956), p. 151

Marina Tsvetaeva learned her *métier* (we have seen that she took a Russian synonym of this term as the title of one of her books) from two very different sources. One was the "grand style" of the eighteenth century, as exemplified by Derzhavin, with his lofty rhetorics and weighty archaisms. The other was the popular tradition of the heroic or lyric folk song. Yet she learned also from her contemporaries, for instance Khlebnikov, whose example perhaps she followed when she freely reinterpreted in *King-Maiden* ancient Russian myths and old folk motifs. But the poet of her time who taught her most was the early Pasternak, whom Tsvetaeva resembles in her romantic temper, as well as in her expressionistic technique. As in Pasternak's case, the marks of her style are a tight syntaxis and an elliptic imagery, a discordant sound pattern and a rigid metrical design.

Tsvetaeva's poetry is deeply feminine, but of a femininity which is neither soft nor weak. Unlike Akhmatova, who cannot express her experience except personally and directly, by means of poems which read like fragments from a private diary, Tsvetaeva is often able to convey her vision of life through historical or legendary "masks." It is from the Biblical and the Christian tradition, as well as from mythological and literary lore, that she takes all the exalted figures of saints and knights, lovers and poets, heroes and heroines whom she turns into objects of praise: David and Saint George, Phaedra and Hippolytus, Don Juan and *Manon Lescaut's* Chevalier des Grieux, Pushkin and Byron, Napoleon and Marina Mniszek, the Polish princess who married the Pseudo-Dmitrij to seize with him the Russian crown. Tsvetaeva does not hesitate, however, to seek her idols or *personae* even among the women and men of her circle, paying her homage in verse to Anna Akhmatova or Aleksandr Blok. To the latter she consecrated a lyrical cycle full of loving admiration and of lucid psychological insight.

Renato Poggioli. *The Poets of Russia*
(Cambridge, Massachusetts: Harvard
University Press, 1960), p. 314

I do not believe that in my life I have met a more tragic figure than Marina. Everything in her life history is vacillating and illusory: political ideas, critical opinions, personal dramas—everything except poetry. There are few people still alive who knew Marina, but her poetry is only now beginning to become familiar to many people.

From her childhood until death she was lonely, and this alienation was connected with her constant rejection of her environment. . . . She liked many things just because they were "out of place": she applauded when those around her did not, stared alone at the lowered curtain, walked out of the auditorium during a performance, and wept in a dark, empty corridor.

In her youth Marina had admired *L'Aiglon* and the conventional romanticism of Rostand. Later, her enthusiasms went deeper: Goethe, Hamlet, *Phèdre*. Sometimes she wrote poems in French and German. Yet she felt a foreigner everywhere but in Russia. Her whole being was closely connected with her native landscape, from the "hot rowan" of her youth to the final elder tree stained with blood. Love, death, and art were the basic themes of her poetry, and she resolved them in a Russian manner.

Ilya Ehrenburg. *Novy mir.*
January, 1961, pp. 100–101

I place Tsvetayeva highest; she was a formed poet from her very beginning. In an age of affectations she had her own voice—human, classical. She was a woman with a man's soul. Her struggle with everyday life was what gave her strength. She strived for and reached perfect clarity. She is a greater poet than Akhmatova, whose simplicity and lyricism I have always admired. Tsvetayeva's death was one of the great sadnesses of my life.

Boris Pasternak. In Olga Andreyev Carlisle,
ed. *Voices in the Snow* (New York: Random
House, 1962), p. 199

Tsvetaeva is in essence a religious poet, an appellation which should be taken as a necessary but by no means a limiting or sufficient description. The religious current in her poetry is particularly evident in her cycle (and sixth book) of poems, *Poems to Blok* [*Stikhi k Bloku*], one of Tsvetaeva's major achievements and an outstanding monument of modern Russia poetry.

First, a brief description of the structure of the work. The natural analogy and the probable model for the cycle was, of course, Aleksandr Blok's own famous early volume of Symbolist poetry, *Poems on the Beautiful Lady* (1901–1902). The cycle consists of three parts, the first of which is almost as long as the other two combined. It is also divided in time—the first part was written in 1916 (except for its conclusion, written in 1920), while the two shorter sections were written in 1921, presumably on the occasion of Blok's death. As then might be expected, there is a marked difference in tone between the parts. In the first portion the "high and lofty" language which has been frequently noted in Tsvetaeva—it is worth noting that one of her favorite

Russian poets was the eighteenth-century poet Derzhavin—sounds most clearly. The second part is a threnody to Blok in the folk manner: the theme "in which cradle do you lie?" recurs continually, and such motifs as "a prince without a country" and "a friend without friends" bear a distinct folk imprint. The third part is an apostrophe to Russia symbolized as the grieving Virgin; it combines the disparate styles of the first two sections in an intense and stirring counterpoint of imagery and language. There is a valid question, it should be said, as to whether or not *Poems to Blok* ought to be read as a unified work rather than merely a book of poems, but the thematic order and progression of the poems lend great weight to the former reading—it might be best to say that Tsvetaeva, like Eliot, took individual poems on a single theme and "at some point" decided to use them as the basis for a larger whole work. . . .

Marina Tsvetaeva may best be characterized as a Mayakovsky of the Middle Ages, a heretic in an age of non-believers. Her *Poems to Blok* are a living liturgy of Russia and the Russian language.

Peter Viereck. *TriQuarterly.* Spring, 1965,
pp. 58, 61

The deliberate stylistic mixture in *Fedra* [*Phaedra*] was received by the émigré critics with a veritable howl of outrage. Xodasevič wrote of an "inexcusable and tasteless confusion of styles." Adamovič wrote that *Fedra* is "howled and screamed rather than written," and Vladimir Vejdle complained of a "total absence of feeling for words as responsible and meaningful *logos*." The critics compared *Fedra* to Racine's tragedy and to *Penthesilea* by Kleist and found Cvetaeva verbose, inelegant, and incoherent by comparison. The reception of *Fedra* by the émigré criticism is the most obvious example of a condemnation on the basis of irrelevant comparisons and inapplicable criteria. Even as astute a critic as Xodasevič failed to see that the essential intention of Cvetaeva was considerably different from either classical or romantic poets and that the unfamiliar "mixed" style was adequate for conveying her conception of the myth. The reception of *Fedra* demonstrates how the tyranny of what is considered the current good taste can seriously impede a comprehension of valid forms of artistic expression which happen to be outside such current definition.

We know of no attempt to produce any of Cvetaeva's dramatic works on the stage. With the possible exception of *Konec Kazanovy* [*The End of Casanova*], they would offer considerable difficulties both in terms of staging and interpretation. In her preface to *Konec Kazanovy*, Cvetaeva pointed out that anything she might write for the theater should be considered a poem in dramatic form rather than a play. Read as poems, many of her plays make exciting and rewarding reading. "Fortuna," the best of the early plays, is an elegant piece of ripe romanticism, while "Tezej" is not only a magnificent poetic accomplishment but an impressive philosophical conception as well. On the whole, Cvetaeva's plays, while not being the striking and unique contributions to Russian literature that her lyric poetry and *poèmy* are, remain a significant and respectable part of her total literary accomplishment.

Simon Karlinsky. *Marina Cvetaeva*
(Berkeley: University of California Press,
1966), pp. 264–65

Now and then, in reading the early verse of Tsvetayeva, one is struck with the feeling that here a character has jumped out of the *dramatis personae* of Blok and that his elemental traits have been developed with particularly sharp expression. In this case, I do not mean at all to deny the distinctive originality inherent in the poetry of Tsvetayeva. It is important, however, even in so sharp, sometimes whimsically expressed a manner as her own to see the general peculiarities of the times, a general line of development in Russian poetry of which the most significant innovations are Blok's. Tsvetayeva, with the expressive directness so peculiar to her, sometimes even demonstrably underscores her own longing to express the national feminine character. . . .

Everything in the poetry of Tsvetayeva is as if woven from contrasts and contradictions. Here is the contrast between naturalness and bookishness. Naturalness should stress the dismissal of broad social relationships and the historical perspective. The characters in Tsvetayeva are really possessed of enormous emotional power. Of all the poets of the "Blok school," Tsvetayeva is the most organically given to elementality, to an explosive strength of the poetic temperament. It often happens that a great poet's perspective of historical movement, instead of disappearing, strives to enter into a character, as if to feel at home in it. In this instance, bookish conventionality becomes not so much a reminder of the finished model as the particular method for great poetic generalization. If, let us say, Tsvetayeva stylized her character according to the prose of Leskov or Dostoyevski, then as a result there would appear not only stylization but the disclosing of certain traits in the national feminine character. Bookishness becomes the means of broadening the possibilities of the poetic image. The vitality of Tsvetayeva contrasts to the conventionality of social relationships. But Tsvetayeva expresses this contrast between vitality and conventionality only through generality carried to the extreme and only through characters almost theatrically contrived.

Pavel Gromov. *Aleksandr Blok: Ego*
predshestvenniki i sovremenniki (Moscow:
Sovetski pisatel, 1966), pp. 453–55

She gave the impression of a woman, full of creative inventions, who had put off her problems, but a woman who did not look into herself, who did not know her vital (and feminine) possibilities, who had not matured towards a consciousness of her present and future reactions. The part of a misfit, which she adopted and about which she wrote beautifully in the poem "Roland's Horn" ["Rolandov rog"], after many years betrayed her immaturity:

being a fish out of water is not, as was once thought, a sign of originality in a human being who stands *above* others, but is the misfortune—both psychological and ontological—of a man who has not matured to the point of uniting with the world, of fusing with it and his time, that is with history and other people. Her involvement with the White Army was foolish; it was to a certain degree the outcome of her attachment to her husband, Sergey Efron, to whom she "promised a son." Thus she said to me: "I will have a son, I have sworn to Serezha that I will give him a son." She had a certain faith in dreams, she trusted in certain fantasies. In Marina this maladjustment was the more tragic in that with the years she began to seek fusion, that her built-up peculiarity gradually began to oppress her; she outlived it and nothing arose in its place. She matured slowly, like the majority of Russian poets of our century (in contrast with the preceding one). But having understood, perhaps in the last years of her life, that man cannot all his life remain an outcast, and that if he does the blame rests with him and not with his surroundings, she did not achieve maturity; her conflict was aggravated in that, as a poet in emigration, she had no readers, there was no reaction to what she wrote, and perhaps she had no friends of her stature. The poet carrying his gift like a hunchback his hump, the poet on an uninhabited island or descending into catacombs, the poet in his tower (of ivory, brick, or whatever), the poet on an iceberg in the ocean—all these are tempting images, but they hide a romantic essence that is sterile and dangerous in its deadliness. You might insert these images in immortal or simply good verse, and someone undoubtedly will react to them inwardly, but they will bear with them one of the most insidious elements of art—escapism, which, if it embellishes the poem, destroys the poet. The Prague isolation of Marina, her role of outcast in Paris, could only lead her to silence in Moscow and tragedy in Elabuga. In her own personality, in the character of her relation to people and the world, this end was already masked: it was foretold in all those lines where she cried to us that she was not like everyone else, that she was proud that she was not like us, that she never wanted to be like us.

She yielded to the old decadent temptation of inventing a new self: the poet as a monster deformity, unrecognized and misunderstood; the mother of her children and the wife of her husband; the lover of a young ephebus; a heroine of a glorious past; a bard, singing the doom of an army; a young disciple; a partner in a passionate friendship. From these (and other) "personality images" she made verse—great verse of our time. But she had no power over herself, did not create herself, did not even know herself (and cultivated this ignorance). She was defenseless, reckless, and unhappy, enclosed by a "nest" and lonely: she found and lost and erred without letup.

Nina Berberova. *The Italics Are Mine*
(New York: Harcourt, Brace & World, 1969),
pp. 204–6

The best way to define Marina Tsvetayeva's place in modern Russian poetry is to say that she had none—this was her personal tragedy and her lonely distinction as an artist. . . .

Marina Tsvetayeva's unflinching integrity in the employment of her genius puts her among the small band of Russian poet-witnesses who felt themselves to be, and recognized in each other the voices of the country and the keepers of its values during what Blok called the "terrible years." There were only four of them—besides Tsvetayeva: Pasternak, Akhmatova and Mandelstam. The last of them to die was Akhmatova who, towards the end of her life, in 1961, wrote about them all in a remarkable poem entitled quite simply: "There are four of us." By numbering Marina Tsvetayeva—the only one mentioned by name—among this chosen few, Akhmatova at last gave her the place she was never able to find in her life.

Max Hayward. Foreword to *Marina
Tsvetayeva: Selected Poems* (New York:
Oxford University Press, 1971), pp. vii, xi

Although, talking about Rilke, Tsvetayeva speaks of poems as *prayer,* she did not make the mistake of blurring the distinction between poetry and religion, any more that she would ever allow for poetry the utilitarian hope that Art can do civic good. Both were as much *limitations* she recognized in poetry, as magniloquent claims made for it. In the closing passage from "Art in the Light of Conscience" she makes that clear: "To be a human being is more important, because it is more needed. . . . The doctor and the priest are humanly more important, all the others are socially more important."

It is always a false polarity to set life in opposition to art except in this way; to see the limitations of the claim that can be made for it. Certainly it is in what Tsvetayeva's poetry *includes* that we sense its greatness; there is no censor between her and her experience, nothing that checks what is given to her from finding its shape upon the page. And yet she understood very well the ambiguous relation she took up to the external world. "I don't love life as such; for me it begins to signify, that is to acquire weight and meaning only when it is transformed, that is—in art. If I were to be taken beyond the ocean, into Paradise, and forbidden to write, I would refuse the ocean and Paradise."

There is nothing willful in this; it is simply the other side of the truth she records sadly and honestly, in another letter. "Externally, things always go badly with me, because I don't love it (the external), I take no account of it, I don't give it the required importance and demand *nothing* from it. Everything that I love changes from an external thing into an inward one, from the moment of my love of it it stops being external." She takes no pride in this, though as she makes clear at the conclusion of "Art in the Light of Conscience" she "would not exchange her work for any other. Aware of greater things, I do lesser ones, this is why there is no forgiveness for me. Only such as I will be held responsible at the Judgement of Conscience. But if there is a Judgment Day of the word, at that I am guiltless."

Elaine Feinstein. Translator's Introduction
to *Marina Tsvetayeva: Selected Poems* (New
York: Oxford University Press, 1971),
pp. xvii–xviii

One of the two or three greatest Russian poets, she took to writing prose especially in the last decade before her suicide, because it would sell and she needed to feed herself and her family. All of her prose is, in a sense, autobiographical; but in prose Tsvetaeva writes not of the pain of the instantaneous, present self as she does in poetry. She writes primarily of the past: her past family, her past friendships, and of past reactions to people—all stylistically transformed into the passionate subjectivity of the present. Our sense of the author's self comes to us directly through the style; there is no coherent exposition of a life-view as it developed, something we have found in other, nonmodernist autobiographies. Rather, the past is judged by a self already formed and in a uniquely acute tone of voice. The text itself becomes the only truth.

By choosing a style of highly-mannered subjectivism when *not* talking ostensibly about herself, Tsvetaeva is declaring her freedom from conventions of objective narration while still retaining the right to historicity (the family chronicle) and to critical judgment of her fellow poets. She establishes her own identity through her evaluations of other poets, as well as through her juxtaposition of self with family. She is alternately epigrammatic—as in her judgment of two symbolist poets: "All that is not Bal'mont is Briusov, and all that is not Briusov is Bal'mont"—and digressive, as we will see. Simulating anti-logic, she makes judgments whose logic then becomes inescapable. . . .

Tsvetaeva's most important self-definition through prose, in memoir-criticism, comes (logically for the poet Tsvetaeva) in her various discussions of Aleksandr Pushkin. As a remembered child, she recalls her earliest memories of the poet. As a woman, she deals directly with the three women of the Pushkin myth: his unfaithful wife, his devoted nurse, and his most famous female creation. As a Russian poet, she must identify with her greatest predecessor; but, as a Russian woman poet, she must also separate Pushkin's maleness from his meaning as a poet. . . .

Marina Tsvetaeva, because she was never anything but confident of her role as poet ("I am a craftsman and I know my craft"), felt free to choose a wide range of poetic voices from the neutral or masculine to those of deliberate, vigorous femininity. Her lack of heed that her public might find the vigorous female voice too strident, abrasive, hysterical, or immodest constitutes a great part of her appeal to the feminist reader. Her lack of self-regard, the skill with which she inverts strength into vulnerability, marks a good deal of Tsvetaeva's poetic intonation. Her poetry, not yet absorbed into either Russian or non-Russian culture, is beginning to be studied in all its metrical and semantic complexity. . . .

As with other women poets, only some of Tsvetaeva's poems contain a speaker with an explicitly female identity. Whenever the world of her poetry divides into a masculine/feminine opposition, Tsvetaeva allies herself with femininity: Ophelia against Hamlet (one, in defense of Gertrude), Phaedra against Hippolytus, Lilith against Adam, and Helen of Troy against a whole tradition that blames her for the Trojan war. Her heroines of myth and tradition are rescued from their portraits as either destructive or victimized beings—the familiar dual interpretations of masculine tradition—to be reclaimed as new female self-definitions.

Abandonment and power are both regarded by Tsvetaeva as necessary givens, prerequisites to creativity. They no longer exist sequentially (as in Akhmatova) or in opposition. If customary male-female relationships are reversed in Tsvetaeva, with the female calling upon the male to love, care, understand, and obey, there is in her poetry the knowledge that this reversal is as futile as the masculine assertion of power. Only the power of the speaker to reintegrate the two through poetic speech emerges as something saved from the wreckage of emotion or nonemotion. . . .

Tsvetaeva has carried the female imagery [of] the split self to its ultimate position as the enemy of all creation. Her poetry, women's poetry at its most female and universal, is the model for future Russian poetry by women. It is a model evoked rather than technically exploited. Tsvetaeva has had no real successors among women poets so far. She, of all women writers, travels farthest into her own female myth reversals, anger, romanticisms, into the female voices buried within her, and into a terrible perfection of craft in *After Russia* and in many poems preceding and following it. Her elliptical style, like that of Emily Dickinson, should elicit endless serious involvement on the part of the reader when we learn to leave aside our fascination with these poets' lives.

> Barbara Heidt. *Terrible Perfection: Women
> and Russian Literature* (Bloomington:
> Indiana University Press, 1987),
> pp. 96–97, 133–34, 143

Tsvetayeva's poems plunge the reader into an atmosphere of emotional intensity, limitless feelings ("this limitlessness in the world of limits!"), constant dramatic conflicts with the norms of the surrounding world. Never calm and contemplative, Tsvetayeva's poetry is work of dynamism, strength, and a rapturous, "heathen" love of life. "To love the sea means to become a fisherman, a sailor, and still better—a Byron (a sailor and a singer, in one!). To lie by the sea . . . does not mean to love it."

In her life this immensity of feeling had disastrous results: people were "horrified by the dimensions of emotions they aroused in me." Yet the nature of Tsvetayeva's feelings was not what it often seemed to the men who were targets of her obsessions. . . .

The "love" that Tsvetayeva spoke of existed in the world of the spirit, in the world where the unattainable, the impossible was real. For Tsvetayeva it was a given that the touching of words was as real as the touching of hands.

The "elements," i.e., a spiritualized Nature, for Tsvetayeva were synonymous with soul. "Nothing touches me but Nature, i.e., the soul; and the soul, i.e., Nature," she wrote to her friend Teskova on December 12, 1927. In her work the intensity of thought, speeding upon the wings of emotion, proves the fearlessness of her confrontation with (and the expression of) the elements, her irrevocable refusal to don the "armor," i.e., to appear before a reader (and the elements) arrayed in the psychological defenses of feminine lyrics—melodiousness and languor, both variations of the poetic posturing that uses feeling (i.e., what poetry is said to reveal) as a psychological defense (i.e., conceals the self, in life or art). This paradox of self-revelation/self-concealment is most conspicuous in the assortment of "poses" that lyric poetry as a genre has at its disposal: e.g., a pouring forth of feeling can assume the mincing posture of more traditional feminine love lyrics. It is clear that the force of Tsvetayeva's emotions cannot be confined by conventional strictures. Yet even her dramatic and hyperbolic speech cannot fully express the power of her feelings: "The limitlessness of my words is but a weak shadow of the limitlessness of my feelings." . . .

She saw mere estheticism as an unpardonable sin against true life and true art. True life means a complete surrender to the elements. True art comes as a result of this psychological openness to experience; it is the voice of the elements speaking through the poet.

Nina J. Kossman. Introduction to In the
Inmost Hour of the Soul: Selected Poems of
Marina Tsvetaeva (Clifton, New Jersey:
Humana, 1981), pp. viii–xi

Her early poetry was her most obviously autobiographical. In her first two books she portrays herself, with some archness, as the child of an elegant, and happy, bourgeois family. She writes about her relationships with her mama and sister, about events of family importance, and about friends, among them young men. Some poems are fantasies in which those close to her are cast in fairy-tale roles and in the conventions of literary romanticism. Her air of false innocence is somewhat sentimental, and she is at pains to show that she was a clever child. She mentions German authors and uses German words. She admits to self-indulgent regrets on leaving her sheltered childhood. She clings to the past, but she also looks forward to love. In the course of her second book, *The Magic Lantern* (1912), she shows a growing awareness of life's impending dangers and of real separations.

If she had written nothing beyond the two volumes called *Milestones*, published abroad in 1921 and 1922, her place in European poetry would have been secure. In these books, however, her love of country comes to the fore. The books create a mirror of the Russian mind, sometimes at the peasant level.

Tsvetaeva's poetry is, in general, stimulating and often written with passion. At the same time, she had a tendency to function as an observer, or even as a Greek chorus. The result was a certain diffuseness. Her artistic aims—the examination of her own childhood, of the Russian psyche, and finally of the nebulous spheres of morality and desire—are not, in any visible way, inevitably linked. Perhaps her greatest drama was a search for a stable identity. Tsvetaeva's prose is more directly autobiographical than is her poetry, and perhaps contains more clues to her character. In "The Rain of Light" (1922) she praised Pasternak's *My Sister Life* for its lyricism. In *Mother and Music* (1935) she tells in whimsical tones of her youthful decision to make poetry, not music, her métier. *My Pushkin* (1937) is also about her youthful years. In it she describes how her view of the world was steadily enlarged through her expanding knowledge of Pushkin, who wrote about country and history as well as about love and friendship.

Evelyn Bristol. *A History of Russian Poetry.*
(New York: Oxford University Press, 1991),
pp. 241, 244

TŪQĀN, FADWĀ (PALESTINE) 1917–

This new collection has no introduction; the poet is content merely to preface it with an extract from the title poem, "I Found It." It is this poem that gives the collection its spiritual core. The poet proclaims that she has discovered the way to her inner self, and she announces this discovery with all the joy of Archimedes on the day he discovered the solution to his problem. She cries out, "I found it!" with all the enthusiasm of a child who has discovered a treasure he has dreamed about for a long time and about which he has heard many tales, with the ardor of a long-lost wanderer who suddenly finds the road again. . . .

Tūqān has discovered herself through her poetry; her personality is crystallized in it. Through poetry she has broken out of prison, namely, tradition. Through her poetry she lifts the voice of womanhood and breaks out of that prison as she embraces life with a new élan. Through poetry she can experience the achievement of some meaning in her existence; neither the dust of neglect nor the gloom of incarceration can blot it out. . . .

In *I Found It* we see a new Fadwā Tūqān. The one who was forever *Alone with Days* has found companionship. She has set sail and ventured forth on a long journey in search of love. After a long period of wandering and alienation, she has now discovered the way to selfhood under the guidance of poetry and love. Whereas before, her voice groaned, now we hear it powerful and free. In so doing, she leaves her place among the poets of pain and takes up a middle position between them and the love poets. In this new collection the predominant psychological experience is that of love; sometimes it is forbidden, other times it makes her fearful of the future, at still other times it fills her with happiness. . . .

As with other poets, she has rid herself of the constraints of traditional meter and rhyme and writes in a contemporary fashion; her verse is simple, devoid of complexities and ornamentation, and sweetly cadenced. . . . From the point of view of content, she is still in the caravan of romanticism, addressing herself to the distant beloved, dreaming of a meeting with him and recalling her memories, as she simply and sincerely complains of her loneliness, her grief, and the departure of her beloved.

Khuzāmā Sabrī (Khālida Saʿīd). Shiʿr.
Autumn, 1957, pp. 103, 105–6

It is impossible to talk about Fadwā Tūqān's latest collection, <i>Give Us Love,</i> without making some reference to the two previous volumes, <i>Alone with Days</i> and <i>I Found It.</i> Her latest collection is simply a further chapter in the continuing love epic this sensitive poet has been writing throughout her career.

Love, then, is the principal topic of these three collections. Her first collection contains some poems in which you will find some mystical reflections, intimate conversations with nature, and some discussion of the poet's soul, yet her heart seems hardly to open to the first thrill of love. Eventually, however, she finds her place and a means of expressing the way she feels personally about love. It is, of course, inconceivable that the Palestine tragedy could touch a sensitive Palestinian poet without shaking her and arousing her innermost feelings. Thus, toward the end of this collection there are five poems on that subject. <i>I Found It</i> has two such poems: one, "Call of the Earth," is almost a narrative, while the other, "Dream of Remembrance," mingles memories of her brother, who died fighting for the Palestinian cause, and an exploration of the problem itself, which led him to fight. There is also another poem, "Torch of Freedom," dedicated to Egypt for its struggle against the tripartite invasion of 1956.

This latest collection, <i>Give Us Love</i>—with the exception of the remarks made above with reference to the first two collections—is also monopolized by the subject of love; there are pictures of various situations, and of their emotional impulses and the human attitudes involved. . . . This collection also shows the poet's continuing interest in nature as she produces images pulsating with its rhythms and steeped in its perfume. . . . Her feeling for nature is a perfectly authentic one even though she chooses to make use of it in the service of love, to the point that this feeling almost assumes the status of a mystical experience.

Malik ʿAbd al-ʿAziz. Al-Ādāb.
January, 1961, pp. 33, 36

It is to be noted that [Fadwā Tūqān] stays away from the kind of poetry that offers advice and spiritual guidance; she does not adopt the role of preacher or moral guide who relies on the vocabulary of valor to instigate revolution and anger. She has abandoned the editorializing style; we do not find words like "kill," "revolt," "destroy," words that die as soon as the event itself does. She speaks quietly and with a clear logic that allows her words to reach both heart and mind. This is because she tells a heartbreaking story in which she describes the sufferings of the displaced refugees. In much of her poetry she paints eloquent and humane portraits of such people, portraits that arouse deep sympathy. One such story occurs in the first poem of *I Found It*. Even though the style is quite close to that of prose and is not as purely poetic or well polished as that of some of the leading modern Arabic poets, the poem treats its subject through vivid imagery and reveals its ideas with great eloquence. Her poetry can stand with the best in world literature in that her imagery forces people to share and participate, and that is better than poetry of valor that glorifies war, fighting, and destruction. While poetry of valor may serve a purpose sooner or later, Tūqān's poetry penetrates people's hearts and prepares people to deal with the issues logically. . . .

Our poet has tasted the bitterness of loneliness, spiritual deprivation, and social angst. She has given a beautiful portrayal of the tragedy, and in [*I Found It, In Front of the Closed Door*, and *Give Us Love*] the diligent reader can find evidence of this pain and the political, social, and intellectual tragedies involved. Her personal poems have been more numerous than poems about her homeland, but once her homeland was occupied by the Israelis, she began to write more about it. Three of her poems are both the most beautiful and the most accurate portrayals of the occupation ever written by a poet.

Yūsuf ʿIzz al-din. *Fi al-adab al-ʿArabī al-hadīth* (Baghdad: Dār al-Basrī, 1967), pp. 312–13, 317

Were we to use the topics of the poems in *In Front of the Closed Door* as our only gauge . . . we would consider it to be almost a personal collection whose focal point consists of the memories and sorrows of the poet and her family. The first poem is about a Palestinian from Jordan living in England; there is one dedicated to William Faulkner, followed by a large number of poems about her dead brother. Then we find a poem by another woman poet, Salma al-Jayyūsī, along with a poem by Fadwā Tūqān dedicated to her; a poem to Tūqān's friend, "Y," in which she talks about her experience in love; and so on. . . .

In some of the poems in this collection Tūqān succeeds in escaping from the confines of the self so that she can come to grips with reality, but on several occasions she tends to resort to traditional visions or to indulge in excessive introspection. . . . Her vision of love is a traditional one, as is her view of death. When a poet turns inward and his sense of his own self assumes large proportions, he is unable to be sensitive or sympathetic to others and resorts to condemning them; the problems he deals with cannot be seen in their full dimensions. For this reason, Fadwā Tūqān prefers friendship to love, since she feels she is the only one who knows the real meaning of profound love and hence cannot establish any love relationship with anyone else in this world. . . .

Judging from the titles and subject matter of her poems written after June, 1967, a radical revolution seems to have taken place in her poetry, or at least a complete change, from one opposite to another. The titles assume a new tone, one in which Tuqan abandons all introspection and faces the issues head on. . . . A general perusal of these poems shows that each of them has a distinctive tone. It is as if some entity wanted to assume some form so that it could take on a new guise, yet is as yet unable to settle on the particular guise to use. The poet is trying to rid herself of the old world, and these poems show us clearly the difficulty she is having in tearing herself away from it. All this shows that changes in literary tone do not happen suddenly, but need a prolonged and painful gestation. Thus, we cannot give a general picture of the poems she has written since June 1967, because what we are hearing is a number of melodies rather than a single one. Some of them remind us of the old Fadwa, while others come close to having an entirely new sound, which we all hope will be used by her to its fullest extent.

ʿAbd al-Muhsin Ṭāhā Badr. Al-Ādāb.
March, 1969, pp. 20, 136–37

Fadwā Tūqān . . . comes, like Nāzik al-Mala ʿika, from a family with a tradition of poets. Her early poems concentrate on her emotions, but even when they speak of lost love and the end of youth they radiate a warmth derived from a fundamental vitality and an optimistic attitude to life. In her later poems she has mastered the techniques of the "free verse" movement, but she is known chiefly because in these poems she has introduced what for her are new themes. The situation on the West Bank since the Israeli occupation in 1967 has extended her experience and her poetic range; her poems dealing with the tragedies of separated families, the suffering and humiliation which are part of life under the occupation and the unbreakable will of the Palestinians to liberate themselves often attain an epic tone. Her language is rich in allusions to themes and images of classical Arabic poetry and full of references to the well-loved land, its olive and orange trees and its rich fertility so typical of Palestinian poetry.

Hilary Kirkpatrick. In Mineke Schipper, ed.
Unheard Words: Women and Literature in
Africa, the Arab World, Asia, the
Caribbean, and Latin America (London:
Allyson and Busby, 1985),
pp. 77–78

For Fadwā Tūqān . . . isolation from her society made her "lose her commitment to life" and at times she found it impossible to write. While her father was demanding that she write political poetry for the Palestinian cause, the frustration of seclusion was driving her almost to suicide.

Her autobiography [*A Mountainous Journey*], is a patchy book, the sententious style reflecting the difficulty of translating from Arabic, the occasional naïvety (in her descriptions of visits to Oxford and Stratford, for example) perhaps a result of such a secluded life. But it is worth reading for the personal story—the sense of non-entity she had from childhood, the oppressiveness of life at home in Nablus with two families hardly on speaking terms, and her struggle for education. Though she makes comparisons throughout between the oppression of women and the oppression of occupation, in fact we get little idea of the sources of her poetry or her life as a well-known political poet, probably a reflection of the split between public and private imposed by being a woman.

Kitty Warnock. *New Statesman and Nation.*
August 10, 1990, pp. 34–35

Unlike her two contemporary female scriptors, [Nawal] al-Sa'dâwî and ['Abla] al-Ruwaynî, Fadwâ Tûqân has a unique relationship to the Arabo-Islamic tradition. The centuries-long Arabic literary tradition, albeit male, did permit the female poetic voice to exist under carefully circumscribed conditions. As a poet, Fadwâ Tûqân has a long line of Arabic poetic women's voices with which to identify and against which to react. As a prose autobiographical writer, however, she carves out her own territory, creates her own literary voice. These two poles lead to literary tensions important to Tûqân's odyssey. The act of writing that generates the literary voice in this autobiography is problematic, indeed, tied as it is to both the corporal and poetic identity of the heroine. Fadwâ's life in the text creates relationships (both literary and biological) that will at once recast and redefine familiar, and very old, ones. . . .

Fadwâ Tûqân's earliest work was predominantly intimate and, in Fadwâ's words, concerned the self and not the collectivity. After the 1967 War, however, her poetry showed a greater concern with the Palestinian cause and became more openly political. Her poetic collections include *Wajadtuhâ* (I found it); *A'tinâ Hubban* (Give us love); *Wahdî ma'a al-Ayyâm* (Alone with the days); *al-Layl wal-Fursân* (Night and the horsemen), dedicated to "The Palestinian Freedom Fighter"; *Tammûz wal-Shay' al-Akhar* (July and the other thing); *Amâm al-Bâb al-Mughlaq* (In front of the locked door); and *'Alâ Qimmat al-Dunyâ Wahîdan* (On top of the world alone). The title of this last collection is explained with reference to the novella *Mâ Tabaqqâ lakum,* by the Palestinian writer Ghassân Kanafânî. Her autobiography was first published serially in 1978–1979 in *al-Jadîd. Mountain Journey, Difficult Journey* is clearly defined as an autobiography (and not as a memoir) on the cover of the book. Tûqân, thus, joins the long line of Arabic literary personalities who felt the egotistical and narcissistic urge to bare their lives before readers. It is, however, the male voice that dominates the classical or medieval genre. . . .

Fadwâ Tûqân is perhaps the ideal female vehicle for an effective criticism and recasting of Arabo-Islamic discourse. Unlike the medieval voice, the twentieth-century scriptor is responsible for the form and means of her discourse. But more than that: Fadwâ Tûqân is first and foremost a poet. It is not accidental that it should be a poet, since poets are highly favored in the Arabic tradition, who should question the tradition in a prose text, the medium of her contemporaries. . . .

The subversion of *Mountain Journey* is fundamental. Writing in Arabic, the language of the rich Arabo-Islamic textual tradition, she dissembles this very language. Speaking of "the family atmosphere which man controls," Fadwâ declares; "Woman should forget the existence of the word *no* [*lâ*] in language, except at the time of the creed ('There is no deity but God') in her ablutions and in her prayers. As for *yes* [*na'am*], it is the parroting word that she whispers from her suckling infancy, to become thereafter a gumlike word that sticks on her lips during her entire life." The body and the word have been brought together in a devastating attack on gender and the Arabic language. Woman is turned into an eternal child. The Arabic term for "word" here is *lafza,* an utterance—not the word as semiotic unit but the embodied corporeal word of speech. The Arab woman may, in Fadwâ's autobiographical vision, be restricted to *na'am,* yes. But Fadwâ Tûqân herself has very effectively said *lâ,* no.

Fedwa Malti-Douglas. *Woman's Body, Woman's Word. Gender and Discourse in Arabo-Islamic Writing* (Princeton: Princeton University Press, 1991), pp. 161–62, 177–78

When this autobiography was published in Amman in 1985, it looked quite different from the version that the Project of Translation from Arabic Literature (PROTA) has now presented to the English-speaking world. Published by a mainstream Jordanian press, it comprised Fadwa Tuqan's prose reconstruction of her life until 1967, together with an introduction by Samih al-Qasim. In addition to the inclusion of poems that frame the text, the English-language version has been "feminized." It is published by the Women's Press; it is translated by a woman, Olive Kenny; the poet and intellectual Salma Khadra Jayyūsī has edited the work and written a foreword and afterword; and the introduction to the original Arabic text has been replaced by one written by the scholar Fedwa Malti-Douglas. The female dimension of this book is thus highlighted.

As in all PROTA translations, the scholarly introduction and end materials are insightful and impressive. Jayyūsī's foreword offers personal accounts by Palestinians that are powerful assertions of cultural and political identity. Malti-Douglas's introduction places *A Mountainous Journey* in the tradition of Arab autobiography that was historically male-dominated and only recently has begun to include female exemplars. Malti-Douglas asserts that this work marks a break with autobiographical convention that "[sanctifies] family structure." . . .

By placing [Tūqān's] poem ["Unshudat al-Sairura"/(Song of Becoming)] at the beginning of this translation, Jayyusi stresses the significance of the national struggle to the writing of this autobiography. As in other parts of the world, a national crisis allowed a woman to question her identity and attempt to construct a new self, less bound by others' expectations and needs. Although *A Mountainous Journey* tells the story of the tragedy of the Palestinians and their incessant wars, it is also the narrative of a woman poet's retrospective awareness of hardships endured merely because she was a woman.

Tūqān has written this autobiography for herself but also for others. It is to be a guide to those who, like her, have longed to escape the "prison of the home," that "bottled-up harem." She describes the few individuals who have helped her, especially her brother Ibrahim, a famous poet, and the many who have blocked her, including women inside and outside the family. When she began to compose poetry, those who had tolerated her began to mount an active opposition. They quite rightly feared the urge to create. It is not surprising that her relationship with her mother should be marked by ambivalence. How could the daughter break out of the vicious circle if she did not first break from her mother?

Tūqān was born in 1917, the fateful year of the Balfour Declaration. Her story parallels that of Palestine as it passed through Ottoman, British, Jordanian, and finally Israeli hands. Her family was involved in the resistance; her father was twice imprisoned and her brother Ibrahim earned the title of "the voice of the Palestinian people." She does not shy away from a subject considered taboo during a time of national trouble, however, as she writes of a woman's unenviable situation in a conservative community like Nablus, her hometown. She identifies her own liberation, and that of the women of Nablus, with "the Arabs' struggle against new western imperialism" and with the death of her father. As it was for her people, so 1948 was a turning point in her personal as well as in her poetic career—with her father's death she was finally able to do his bidding and write political poetry. Her earlier hesitation, owing to her anxiety at her literary inexperience, lessened when she was no longer coerced by him. It is only after 1967, however, the subject of the sequel to this book on which she is currently working, that she became totally engaged in writing political poetry.

The last fifteen pages fragment the flowing prose into a staccato recording of both personal and political events of 1966–67. The final half page includes four separate entries that chronicle her own silencing as the cataclysm of war approaches.

The publication of this first piece of prose writing by "Palestine's Outstanding Woman Poet" allows the English-speaking reader to gain a glimpse into the life of a Palestinian woman who had the courage to challenge patriarchy and the love to defend and sing of her homeland. *A Mountainous Journey* is eloquent testimony to the power of the soul to endure the unendurable.

Miriam Cooke. *Middle East Journal.* 45,
1991, pp. 320–21

TUSQUETS, ESTHER (SPAIN) 1936–

"The first sexually explicit novel from Spain," Tusquets's *Love is a Solitary Game,* is profoundly dull. This is a tale of a sticky-licky triangle: Ricardo, "grubby longings," young, spotty and devious; Elia, a rich married woman in her thirties "discontent and enormously bored" (and enormously boring); and Clara, young, pure and in love with Elia. The whole is peculiarly unerotic and not even funny when the three of them end up in bed together after what seems a very long time.

Grace Ingoldsby. *The New Statesman.*
August 9, 1985, p. 26

Read mimetically, Esther Tusquets's *El amor es un juego solitario* creates an illusion of narrative normalcy. The actional code of the story lacks visible complexity. An omniscient narrator recounts the events of a triangular love relationship which unfolds sequentially in a closely defined interlude of time. The three principals are Elia, an indolent, wealthy matron; Ricardo, a university student and aspiring poet who successfully appeals to her to initiate him sexually; and Clara, Ricardo's classmate, who is also attracted to Elia. Although there are no chapters, the syntagmatic unfolding of the story is marked by discernible spatial units which correspond to the differing perspectives of the three characters. Structurally, grammatically and lexically, the work evinces seeming compliance with orthodox practice and propriety.

A hermeneutic reading of *El amor* nonetheless suggests a contrasting interpretation. When integrated paradigmatically, the novel's signs enter into a different network of relationships that creates a deviation from the norm. Characterized by perverse pairings, this deviation is heralded by the dialectic interaction of the linguistic and visual signs inscribed on the book's cover (i.e., the novel's title and the images of two windows). Both sign systems adopt a code of irony and self-reflexivity which, through defamiliarization, undermines the initial mimetic reading.

The novel's visual signs appear to be contradictory and alien. The bottom of a window, mysteriously severed from its rest, occupies the uppermost space of the page. An image of the full window is placed at some distance below the first, offering a graphic statement of disjunction and difference. Yet the spatial aloofness created by these discordant signs is mitigated by the viewer's gradual awareness of their interaction, for the meaning of one is yoked to the other. The disquiet created by the first image of truncation rests largely with its discrepancy from the conventionality of the second. While acknowledging them as different entities, the viewer is impelled to join them visually and conceptually thereby creating an unorthodox gestalt.

The linguistic signs of the novel's title, placed equidistantly between the two visual images, enter into an engagement with them that amplifies this discordance. Unlike the other two novels of the Tusquets's trilogy, *El amor es un juego solitario* offers the reader a title with a fully articulated sentence. Yet despite its grammatical orthodoxy, the title is riven by contradictions that defy the experiential and poetic conventions associated with love. The sign love, sacramentalized and mythified by cultural convention, celebrates the union of two subjects rather than the rivalry and calculated contrivance of games aimed at producing "winners" and "losers." The disruption of meaning is exacerbated by the use of "solitario" as a predicate adjective which further undermines the semantic correlation of subject and predicate and subverts a basic principle of game theory, namely that the different categories of play presuppose company rather than solitude. The copulative verb ("ser") thus joins the clashing codes of the subject and predicate in an "unnatural act" which, like the conflictive union of the visual signs, requires the reader's interpretation. Read referentially, the title is perplexing. Read figurally, however, it provides a rhetorical codification of deviance by employing language to mean something other than what it says. . . .

Taken together, the complex relationship of incompatible codes found on the cover of *El amor* suggests a system of signification that is both copulative and differential.

Mirella d'Ambrosio Servodidio. ALEC. 11,
1986, pp. 237–38

The story outline of Esther Tusquets's *El mismo mar de todos los veranos* evinces the characteristic markings of the traditional novel of rebirth and transformation. The mature heroine, a professor of literature, detaches herself from her familiar surroundings and withdraws to the two focal sites of her childhood: the vacant, city apartment of her parents, where she ponders her husband's newest infidelity and the callous indifference of her estranged mother and daughter; her grandmother's seaside house to which she retires for an extended period (some twenty-seven days) in the company of Clara, her student-lover. Here, with Clara acting as herald and initiatory guide, and in apparent response to the "Call to Adventure," the heroine passes through the first portal of transformation calling for severance from the outside world. As she recounts her life story to her lover, she initiates an inward journey to the causal zones of the psyche where childhood attitudes and attachments are reviewed and made available for transfiguration. The framing myths and fairy tales that guide the heroine's narration and which give symbolic expression to consecrated *rites de passage* heighten the reader's expectation of the forward movement associated with novels of regeneration. The heroine's ultimate return and reintegration with society seal the work's apparent conformity to the monomythic archetypes as described by Joseph Campbell.

However, this prima facie evidence is sabotaged early in the novel by violations of the archetypal paradigms encoded in the rituals of male rebirth novels. . . . The promise of progression and fluidity held out by the traditional Bildungsroman aborts and is displaced by the static patterns and frozen frames of spatial form which, instead, presents the reader with a *Bild* or portrait of a heroine who is incapable of change.

A useful optic for viewing the psychological and narrative stasis of *El mismo mar* is provided by current feminist psychoanalytic theory which highlights the mother-daughter relationship as the dominant formative influence on female development. . . .

Syntactic complications, verbal complexity and density of style, characterized by the abundant use of figures of speech, heighten the effect of retardation, slowing the reader's progress. There appears to be a desire to infinitize the writing process with endless, run-on sentences, some taking several pages. Clauses are elongated or held in suspension by digressions, disjunctions, parenthetical insertions and interpolations, and by the persistent use of locutions like "acaso" "tal vez" "quizá" which introduce exhaustive explorations of all the permutations of the narrator's tortured thought-processes, creating a syntactic embodiment of a "pozo dentro de un pozo que está dentro de otro pozo." This type of sentencing and the refusal to paragraph serve an important architectural function of rhythm and sequence which reduces the reader's speed of reception and fortifies the work's thematic concerns.

Thus, the compulsive ruminations that rotate eternally in the narrator's mind come to rest in the immutable patterns set by narrative structure, language and style. *El mismo mar de todos los veranos* is a saga of desperate fixation in which mothering, mirroring and textual production are inextricably entwined.

Mirella Servodidio. *ALEC*. 12, 1987,
pp. 157–58, 172

Esther Tusquets's recent trilogy of novels—*El mismo mar de todos los veranos, El amor es un juego solitario* and *Varada tras el último naufragio*—provides the reader with a fascinating study of the dynamics of women reading, rereading, misreading and rewriting the male literary canon. It constitutes an endless play of mirrors in which character and reader alike are compelled to reevaluate a myriad of textual patterns which have shaped their lives and transformed them into receivers or resisters of a work's implicit code. From the perspective of a feminist literary analysis, the novels present a still unexplored terrain for a careful examination of how a feminist critic reads Esther Tusquets obliging her characters to read themselves in or out of the patriarchal tradition.

In each text of the trilogy, the scenario is somewhat different, but certain patterns emerge. First, each one deals with the upper-class Catalan society of the 1970s, a social setting which enables Tusquets to focus on her characters' emotional insufficiencies rather than on their economic dependencies. Secondly, in each novel, many of the names of the characters are the same and certain structures of "three" emerge. There are three main characters: Elia, Clara and Jorge, subsequently joined by three other players: Ricardo, Pablo and Eva, cast into three different sexual patterns: heterosexual, lesbian and bisexual, and defined against the backdrop of three literary models: traditional myths, fairy tales and revisions of the two.

It is perhaps this last aspect which seems most significant in the intense intertextual dialogue each novel sustains with the others. For literature itself is the true protagonist of these tales and the formidable enemy that the characters must confront to achieve a level of personal freedom. As I began to examine this topic, a chorus of critical voices shouted in my ear countless words of theory and praxis which coalesced in harmony when applied to Tusquets's novels. Harold Bloom has hypothesized that "you are or become what you read." Recent feminist literary criticism has added that reading is a "learned" experience and that we are not condemned to become what we read but are also empowered to "resist," subvert and revise the literary canon. Reading for women thus becomes rewriting, an act of "literary warfare" designed at changing not just one text, but "the whole system of texts" it is immersed in, a powerful exorcism of "the male mind implanted in us." . . .

Tusquets's trilogy creates a new mirror for her readers and the author herself becomes a possible precursor and muse for women authors seeking freedom from the male canon. As my analysis of each novel has revealed, the results of this arduous process of revision are not always positive. Women do succumb to silence at times; they do fall prey to entrapment; they do occasionally lose and misuse their creative voice; they sometimes misread themselves and others. But they are also capable of rereading and rewriting the male çanon and of bringing together in an intense bond their own creative discourse and intimate sense of female sexuality. Maybe they all do not live happily ever after, but then again, we're only now writing our own ending for their tale.

Linda Gould Levine. *ALEC*. 12,
1987, pp. 203–4, 215

[*The Same Sea as Every Summer*] is an absolutely remarkable novel that should illustrate—formally and thematically—what's possible for a feminist writer to do, although I suspect that it will go unnoticed by most reviewers (will the *New York Times Book Review* give space to a novel that uses almost no periods and might confuse the readers of Bobbie Ann Mason?) and most feminists because, above all, Tusquets is, by American standards, the most contemptible of all things, an artist. The story revolves around a middle-aged woman's attempt to make sense of her failed life—an unfaithful husband, a mother and child who have little sympathy for her, the death by suicide many years ago of the only man she ever loved, and a current lesbian affair with a young woman whom she will wind up taking advantage of in a way that she has always been taken advantage of by others. The novel exists as a kind of howl of remorse, anger, and desperation as its first-person protagonist relives her past and attempts to figure out how, nearly fifty years old, she will get on with her future. Near the end, she thinks to herself: "I have finished the repertoire of my stories—although it is only a feeling, since stories are almost infinite—I have the feeling, then, of having finished the repertoire of my stories, stories that are almost always similar, and that I renew, revive, and repeat in the face of each possibility of love, as if loving were only finding the best of pretexts to recall, or perhaps to invent, to take dusty old memories out of the closet, to open the costume trunk and to put on the costume of ancient sorrows—at bottom the same, single sadness—the costume of innumerable, renewed periods of loneliness that constitute a life." By the end, she seems not to have succeeded in finding a new life; she, instead, seems about to return to her unfaithful husband and the world of her mother. Given the politics of America, no one will want to hear that a woman's attempt at change might lead only to understanding and paralytic fear.

Martha Kolintz. *Review of Contemporary Fiction.* 10, 1990, p. 192

Para no volver, Esther Tusquets's fourth novel, follows the protagonist Elena through a series of psychoanalysis sessions as she tries to deal with her mid-life crisis. . . .

Throughout her fiction Tusquets has focused on the psychological turmoil of middle-aged women who find themselves bored or trapped by married life. In most of her novels her protagonists embark on a quest, an inward journey across their troubled psyche and into the hidden corners of their past. In *El mismo mar de todos los veranos,* for example, working within a mythical mode, Tusquets, as Elizabeth J. Ordóñez points out, uses a lesbian relationship as a kind of quest myth through which the narrator is reborn. In *Para no volver* Tusquets continues the psychological penetration that has characterized her other novels, but changes her tone and substitutes the lesbian adventure with a psychoanalytic experience and mythological referents with cinematographic ones. She continues to explore the persistent effects of past patterns ingrained on the human psyche and to use the potentials of language to transform reality. . . .

Besides words and epithets, the narrator wages her attack on psychoanalysis through absence. Elena culminates her debunking of the psychoanalytic method by insisting upon her analyst's failure to find evidence in her of the oedipal and the castration complexes so central to Freudian doctrine. Elena openly criticizes her analyst for not considering her present problems instead of probing into her childhood and adolescence, which were, as she explains, unhappy and full of conflict like everyone else's. When Elena does find an example of "ese dichoso complejo de castración" in her inability to "mear un ocho contra la pared," its insignificance and ludicrousness confirm the mockery made in the book of essential psychoanalytic beliefs.

If it is true, as Bakhtin says, "Everything has its parody, i.e., its comical aspects," then modern psychology can be no exception. The originality of Tusquets's treatment of psychoanalysis lies in her juxtaposition of its serious and comical aspects revealed, on one hand, by a careful assimilation of its tenets into the characterization and plot of her novel and, on the other, by a studied confrontation with its pretensions. In this way, Tusquets's latest novel emerges as both a novel of adult rite of passage and an irreverent postmodern satire. Parody creates a tension between its model and the imitation it produces. This tension, in turn, generates hostility while it discloses dependence on the parody's underlying referent. It is precisely the imitation, ambivalence, and conflict at the heart of parody that account for the interplay in *Para no volver* between acceptance and resistance, submission and subversion, and assimilation and confrontation.

Catherine G. Bellver. *Romanic Reviews.* 81,
1990, pp. 368–69, 375

[Tusquets] has published a trilogy of novels, *El mismo mar de todos los veranos* (1978), *El amor es un juego solitario* (1979), *Varada tras el último naufragio* (1980); a series of short stories, *Siete miradas en un mismo paisaje* (1981); and a fourth novel, *Para no volver* (1985). Her texts evince an unrelenting obsession with the past and its effects upon the present. The central characters, all women, repeatedly fasten on their own psychic development; and her fiction clearly avoids the articulation of an explicit program for socio-political change, although much of the general malaise running through her work stems from an indictment of what Elizabeth J. Ordóñez terms "the roots of collective neurosis . . . in the Catalán bourgeoisie" . . . the psychological implicates, but does not directly elaborate upon, the social.

If it eschews prescription, Tusquets's fiction also makes clear the limitations of marginalizing novelists, relegating them to a literary "ghetto," on the basis of their dissimilarity from the recognized and accepted "masters"— the male novelists in Spain who continue to dominate, and hence define, the canon. The prevalence of certain so-called "women's themes" invites critics such as Jones to place Tusquets squarely within the second "generation" of women novelists. Female characters and female experience determine the locus of meaning; the narrative emphasizes women's existential dilemmas and their pursuit of authenticity in a duplicitous and hostile society; and the texts acknowledge the value of recovering women's voices.

By the same token, Tusquets's preoccupation with the textual boundaries and effects of literature and language likens her to several male novelists who are synonymous with the contemporary Spanish novel. Writers such as Juan and Luis Goytisolo, Gonzalo Torrente Ballester, and Juan Benet bring to the genre stylistic innovations and new theoretical concerns, among them the issue of self-referentiality. Self-referential novels interrogate notions of authority and authorization in order to question and ultimately undermine social constraints and conventions. Because they consistently investigate the dynamics of self-referential narrative, the aforementioned group is usually classified as the standardbearer of the contemporary self-referential novel in Spain.

If Tusquets has much in common with the recent group of women novel-ists who concentrate on novelizing feminine voices, she has equally as much in common with the self-referential novelists: she experiments with literary and linguistic forms, explores the inventive and constrictive potential of liter-ary language and of literature in general, and takes as her subject narrative itself. She interweaves explicitly female experiences and perspectives with a consciousness of the strategies, discursive limitations, and cultivated art of narrative. And if Tusquets shares a presumably male predilection for self-referential narrative, what consequences does her choice hold for the estima-tion of her own fiction and for women writers in Spain?

Nina L. Molinari. *Foucault, Feminism, and Power: Reading Esther Tusquets* (Lewisburg, Pennsylvania: Bucknell University Press, 1991), pp. 15–16

TY-CASPER, LINDA (PHILIPPINES) 1931–

The Peninsulars is a "book of the magistrates" which, at the same time, concedes the difficulty of keeping purity of human motive and means intact. The very longing of its figures for heroic proportions often exposes their imperfections and leaves them vulnerable to unforeseen contingencies. San-tistevan tries to obscure his having betrayed Agbayani with Araceli, by blam-ing the unfortunate governor for the rebel's death and by deserting the governor's cause. His new father-image, perversely, becomes the privateer Segovia who resembles the self-seeking royal fiscal. During the fearful attack on Negros by Moro pirates, Santistevan's sense of guilt returns, overwhelm-ingly disproportionate and destructive of all his confidence. Later, on his return, when the rescue of Manila is placed in his custody, undirected, uncom-forted, utterly anguished, he sees the city of the Virgin disintegrating before his eyes—as irrecoverable as Araceli's chastity; and his romantic dream of personal glory deteriorates (as it had earlier for Agbayani, the patriot-*manqué*) into a death-wish.

The novel gives no sentimental allegiance to one nationality or class against another. Something of magnitude miraculously is recovered in a Pe-ninsular and is discovered in an *indio*. Having been transported safely out of the confusion which he has helped create, the governor general plans to make one final attempt at immortalizing himself by delivering the city from Falkener. Luckily, his fever of pride is purged—the governor becomes a proper tragically ennobled figure when, recognizing his *hubris,* he delegates deliverance to Santistevan, Carre, and Licaros. The first two have been like sons to him. Licaros, the *indio* priest who, refused a parish, has mortified and prepared himself equally through meditation and through battle with the infidels, recapitulates some of the governor's complex self-division. Far from having perfected himself, he is constantly worried that he may be a better *indio* than a priest. In the battle on Negros, Licaros contemplates the possibility that Moro raids in part may be justified as self-defense; and he cannot help admiring their refusal to submit to Spain. Later, he is slow to absolve Santistevan who, he fears, may be confessing his sins of deed and intent out of weakness and not out of true contrition. He himself can concede that Santistevan may have desired "not to defile Araceli but to be incarnated in her, to be protected forever from all change by her virginity—perhaps to be immaculately reconceived"—a folly perhaps, but only questionably a sin.

Licaros's broad-mindedness represents the breadth of the novel's vision, just as the governor general's ultimate purgation represents its inevitable thrust toward affirmation, through the slough of scruple and despond. Both men see that pursuit of personal honor, at another's expense, can be self-corrupting. The major relationships and countless devices in *The Peninsulars* imply acceptance of man's need to discover himself through others. The images of Araceli as saintly virgin and of the governor general as god-father help to define Santistevan to himself; but he reduces them to less than person, he permits the ideal no aspect of reality and therefore is mortally bewildered by each new casualty of circumstance. Similarly, the governor general, pretending to sacrifice himself for the defense of his people, uses them for his personal ends. Each inclines to make the other his "colony" in miniature, his store of ready resource.

> Leonard Casper. *New Writing from the Philippines* (Syracuse: Syracuse University Press, 1966), pp. 135–36

The wealthy family of Don Severino Gil has gathered in his Manila home for his wake and funeral. After Don Severino's sudden, mysterious death, his casket has been ordered closed. Was Don Severino murdered? They are a self-important lot, overly concerned with appearances, so the Pope's impending visit has them in a tizzy. There is much talk about how best to make a show for the occasion, and three elderly sisters compete for control, though Maria Esperanza, the oldest and most calculating, feels confident she will win. Enter Telly, a glamorous, rootless niece who, never having recovered from her former husband's betrayal, finds it an effort to keep living. At the wake Telly meets her cousin Sevi, a priest who questions whether he turned to God because his father, Don Severino, ignored him as a child. Through Sevi, Telly rediscovers desire. The complex drama of a gathered family shares equal time with the political and religious mood of the Philippines in 1981. Linda Ty-Casper pulls no punches in this unusual novel, which she describes as "a pasión—traditionally, a lengthy, chanted chronicle of agonies"—yet she wears silk gloves. With jabs so deft they avoid the didactic but sting mightily, she indicts everything, from the values of the well-to-do to martial law to the Roman Catholic Church. It is not surprising that she felt *Awaiting Trespass* could not be published in the Philippines. As Telly says, "What we need are memories, not arms. Arms can misfire, be used against the self. But words, writers, memories. Someone should be writing about our times. Silence, self-imposed, serves the censors."

Chéri Fein. *The New York Times.*
October 27, 1985, pp. 40–41

Small print from last week's paper disclosed the discovery of twelve headless bodies, business as usual in the Philippines, and in this context it is hardly surprising that Linda Ty-Casper's novel has not been published there. *Awaiting Trespass* is purposely slow moving; subtitled *a pasión,* a chanted chronicle of agonies, it circles round the wake for the wealthy playboy Don Severino and is prefaced by its author as "a book of revelations about what tyranny forces people to become; and what, by resisting, they can insist on being." The intense Roman Catholicism of the Severinos, well heeled and well connected—"they can't understand how anyone can be content with enough," is considerably upset during the wake by speculation concerning the casket which, in a severe break with tradition, is discovered to be securely sealed. The mores of the three elderly sisters are questioned by other members of the family as they face the political and personal, possibly financial, repercussions of opening the dreadful box. Spattered with poetry it doesn't really need, the novel does however move with grace to its conclusion, making a political and moral point that stretches right back to Antigone: how best to honor our dead?

John Spurling. *The New Statesman.*
October 18, 1985, p. 29

Awaiting Trespass: A Passion is a short novel set in the Philippines in 1981. While its form, a canticle of sorrows, draws the story of one death, one family together in a sober eulogy, Linda Ty-Casper's style is mostly brilliantly satiric. Ty-Casper has written several novels, but, so far as I can see, she's never been taken note of in America. It can't be that difficult for a publisher to discover one of our own talented "colonial" writers (her work also comes to us by way of Readers International). What's more, they might have cashed in, for *Awaiting Trespass* is, in part, a close look at privileged life in Manila during the Marcos regime.

Ty-Casper is not concerned with scandal-sheet items and Swiss bank accounts but with the real and terrible despair of those who understand the sticky moral climate they live in. Now that the secrets of Imelda's closets have been exposed to all the world and Cory is, with some difficulty, holding her own, *Awaiting Trespass* might be published in the Philippines.

The dead man in the novel, Don Severino Gil, was rich, powerful, corrupt—a caricature of the swaggering playboy. His sisters, three haughty and pious old ladies who aim to keep the past untarnished, still worship their brother (white linen, flower in his buttonhole) as a godlike male whose worst sins are mere peccadillos. A comic chorus in their black finery, they're as competitive as the aunts in *The Mill on the Floss,* checking out their linens and the stores in their pantries. What they represent is lusty, dead, and laughable, but still a weight that pulls down upon the younger members of the family. Don Severino's son is, not surprisingly, a priest, though even that protest has been co-opted by the great man. Big Daddy, yes, but Ty-Casper is not simplistic: the priest has doubts about his vocation; and Don Severino's favorite niece is a sophisticated divorcée drawn to self-destruction, a poet who puts as little faith in her psychiatrist as she does in a fortune-teller.

I was at once reminded of *Leaf Storm,* Gabriel García Márquez's first story—violent death, coffin center stage, the life of the patriarch assembled from each mourner's reverie—but in its fine arguments between poet and priest, its inclusion of a revolutionary nephew who may be "right on" in his heroics but is only one corner of the puzzle, this novel is more like the mature Márquez of *The Autumn of the Patriarch* in scope and moral complexity. But Manila is not Macondo: *Awaiting Trespass* resists nostalgia, and the novel's lyric swirl is not ahistorical; indeed, there is a clear investment here in the immediate risk of rebellion. The cut of society in this requiem is exactly the world that President Aquino comes from, and her allegiance to it may finally be one of her great problems. It is surprising that we have not heard of Ty-Casper: I can only suppose that *Awaiting Trespass* is too subtle a fiction.

Maureen Howard. *Yale Review.* 77,
1988, pp. 247–48

The nameless narrator of Linda Ty-Casper's latest novel [*A Small Party in a Garden*] is an Americanized Filipina of uncertain years, emotionally speaking at the end of her tether. She is discovered amid a gathering of former Cornell students, where the women vie with one another in cattiness as they jostle "to eclipse each other in flinty gowns and trendy Dior-cut *barongs,*" and the men's talk, equally competitive, is all cynical advice as to how best to exploit "the crazy economic situation." Washed by waves of disingenuous camaraderie, they are eager to believe that external suffering is an illusion ("poverty is only psychological") or else that it is susceptible of facile solution—which is perhaps only to be expected of the arrivistes and nouveaux riches of Manila under martial law, during what feels for all the world like the period just before Ninoy's murder.

"B" can be forgiven for being of two minds about the circumambient vulgarity, frivolity, and cruelty. The daughter of a prominent liberal lawyer, she is in conscience keenly exercised by all she witnesses. As Imelda's Girl Friday, on the other hand, "responsible for the first lady's trips abroad, checking out her itinerary to spare her unpleasant surprises, and going over her speeches to make sure there is the seriousness of a statesperson against the coquetry of a woman," she feels herself to be deeply compromised, with a stake in perpetuating institutionalized wickedness abetted by extravagant personal fancy. A heartsearchingly long conversation with her father follows, revolving around the question of moral and political allegiance. This peters out inconclusively and forms the prelude to disaster, as they stumble upon a scene of carnage—whether the result of NPA depredations or ministrations of an army special unit in mufti, who can tell? "B" is arrested, beaten, and, in a sickening episode accompanied by portentous introspection, gang-raped, the narrative fading out as consciousness, presumably, dies.

The theme of *A Small Party in a Garden*—personal and political depravity in a nexus of cause and effect—echoes that of Ty-Casper's earlier novels *Wings of Stone* and *Awaiting Trespass* (both 1986) and its heroine is recognizably akin to the vulnerable and deluded characters adrift in the former work. The new novel, however, does not return us to the world so unflinchingly dissected there, does not—superficial resemblances aside—resurrect any earlier characters. It is far more lightweight and far less serious than its predecessors, seeming more fable than fiction. Its interest lies most of all perhaps in determining why, judged by the standards the author has set, it must be seen as a relative failure, lacking both conviction and compulsion.

Ty-Casper's strength has always been the creation of a stressfully introverted political environment, a fraught ideological atmosphere: Manila under the Spaniards in the eighteenth century and under Ferdinand and Imelda in the 1970s and 1980s. Anyone wishing to feel what it was like to live through those decades in the Philippines (more precisely, in the metropolises and among the various dissenting and complicit elements of the bourgeoisie) could do worse than read Ty-Casper's novels. They are prompted not so much by a sense of the future foreseen as by an imaginative sense of the future-in-the-present. This quality, accounting as it does for vivid description and absorbing narration (absorbing inasmuch as it draws us ineluctably into the center of a tormented state of affairs), is conspicuously absent from her new novel. In its place there is an authorial tendency to balloon self-indulgently: "I call myself names. Co-conspirator of martial law. Henchman. No, henchwoman, I correct myself. I work on things that do not count for anything; with superficialities. I help distract the people from the real issues. I call myself other names, burying the hurt in my flesh like a plow left in the field." The loss of credibility signaled by such verbose and banal musings opens a hole into which the rest of the narrative crumbles. Disbelief cannot be suspended for long, as the style, by turns unbearably mannered and coarse-grained in a journalistic way, reinforces the artificiality of dialogue, situation, and character. As a pessimistic parable, the book perhaps works, but not as a novel which engages complex issues and vivifies an actuality with depth and tact. *A Small Party in a Garden* is a notably bad book, by a reasonably good writer. It shows, in every way.

D. M. Roskies. *World Literature Today.* 64,
1990, pp. 198–99

[In her writing] she [has] persisted in dramatizing the difficulty of Filipinos, during centuries of Spanish and American colonialism, to find satisfactory terms for self-definition and -determination.

The Peninsulars (1964) set a precedent for reconstructing confrontations in Manila, during the nineteenth century, between Spanish liberals and conservatives, which so weakened the colonial administration that incursions by the Dutch and later by the British were possible. In 1979, Ty-Casper published *The Three-Cornered Sun,* a novel of the ill-fated revolution of 1896–1898. Not only were the Spaniards far better equipped militarily than the Filipino insurgents, but the latter were divided into factions. The novel shows how aristocratic dilettantes, at first in combat as if at play, learned in their defeat the rightness of the national cause and the need for solidarity. The same pattern of naïveté gradually and painfully enlightened appears in *Ten Thousand Seeds* (1987). This time, however, it is the Americans who, coming as liberators, found themselves substitute rulers instead, and understood such realities better only at the outbreak of the Philippine-American War in 1899.

Ty-Casper's later novels have concentrated on oppression of Filipinos by their own countrymen who have put greed, nepotism, and factionalism before the national interest, especially during the martial-law years of President Ferdinand Marcos (1972–1981). *Dread Empire* (1980) reveals how a provincial strongman managed to imitate Marcos's tactics locally; *Hazards of Distance* (1981) pictures how ordinary citizens became caught between government violence and the Communist New People's Army; and *Fortress in the Plaza* (1985) dramatizes the impact on decent families of the political opposition's actual massacre, in a Manila public square, in 1972. As censorship tightened, Ty-Casper found her audience in London, with *Awaiting Trespass* (1985), a novel of the martyrdom of a presumed wastrel secretly helping imprisoned detainees; and *Wings of Stone* (1986), a tale of an expatriate's return from America during the election of 1984 which, along with the 1983 assassination of a more illustrious returnee. Ninoy Aquino, ignited the final stages of revolt against Marcos. *A Small Party in a Garden* (1988) personalizes the régime's brutality through the gang rape of a politically neutral woman, one of Imelda Marcos's lesser staff, by men in uniform.

Despite marriage to an American, Ty-Casper has retained her Philippine citizenship. Yet she has tried not to be chauvinistic in her judgments, but to distinguish persons of good will among the Spaniards and Americans, as well as—when necessary—to indict Filipinos who have betrayed the ideals of self-sacrifice and service.

Leonard Casper. In Steven R. Serafin and Walter D. Glanze, eds. *Encyclopedia of World Literature in the 20th Century* (New York: Continuum, 1993), p. 609

TYLER, ANNE (UNITED STATES) 1941–

One of the better things about *If Morning Ever Comes* is its title. It accurately suggests the unpretentious, mildly questioning quality, and the tentative little moral of Anne Tyler's first novel. . . .

The trouble with this competently put-together book is that the hero is hardly better defined at the end than he is at the beginning. Writing about a dull and totally humorless character, Miss Tyler has inevitably produced a totally humorless and mainly dull novel. That it isn't entirely dull is a tribute to Miss Tyler's restrained, unshowy style, a very pleasing niceness of observation (although an absolutely feminine one; what mind Ben Joe has is only vestigially masculine), and an excellent but unobtrusive use of symbols. Anne Tyler is only twenty-two and in the light of this her knowledge of what she is doing, her avoidance of obvious pitfalls and her refusal to take risks are a bit puzzling. I'd like to see what she could do if she stopped narrowing her own eyes and let herself go. It might be very good.

Julian Gloag. *Saturday Review of Literature.*
December 26, 1964, pp. 37–38

The fact that twenty-four-year-old Anne Tyler, who was born in Minneapolis and now lives in Toronto, grew up in Raleigh, N.C., must seem to her significant enough to make her publishers note on the jacket of this book that she "considers herself a Southerner." And this novel, in so far as it goes in for regional subject matter, does report upon life in still another rural Southern pocket. Her characters [in *The Tin Can Tree*] are the eight inhabitants of a three-family house on the edge of backwater tobacco fields—two bachelor brothers, two spinster sisters and the Pike family, whose small daughter has just been killed in a tractor accident when the book opens.

There are, indeed, some fine scenes and sounds of a regional sort, especially in one chapter in which a group of women talk over the Pike tragedy while tying tobacco. Here, as elsewhere in the book, she makes use of a nice specificity of local detail and neatly captures the casual and yet complex movement of Southern rural speech with its indirections and interruptions, its reticences and awkwardnesses which manage to express emotion.

Yet, rurality and Southernism are not really Miss Tyler's chief interest. Despite some obvious debts to the tradition of the Southern novel, she has none of the Faulknerian anguish over a present rooted in past wrongs. Nor does she share the late Flannery O'Connor's sense of a religious soil out of which characters are thrust forth into the withering present, taking grotesque and tragic shape—though Miss O'Connor's style, with its austere notation of scene and dialogue, may have taught her to make an eloquence of spareness. If she reminds me of anyone, it may be the Carson McCullers of twenty-five years ago—who, then as young as Miss Tyler, also wrote of human disconnection and the need for love in a stagnant community. . . .

Like [Sherwood Anderson's] Winesburg stories, *The Tin Can Tree* shows us human beings frozen into fixed postures. . . . Life, this young writer seems to be saying, achieves its once-and-for-all shape and then the camera clicks. This view, which brings her characters back on the last page to where they started, does not make for that sense of development which is the true novel's motive force. Because of it, I think, her book remains a sketch, a description, a snapshot. But as such, it still has a certain dry clarity. And the hand that has clicked its shutter has selected a moment of truth.

Millicent Bell. *The New York Times.*
November 21, 1965, p. 77

It's hard to classify Anne Tyler's novels. They are Southern in their sure sense of family and place but lack the taste for violence and the Gothic that often characterizes self-consciously Southern literature. They are modern in their fictional techniques, yet utterly unconcerned with the contemporary moment as a subject, so that with only minor dislocations, her stories could just as well have taken place in the 1920s or 1930s. The current school of feminist-influenced novels seems to have passed her by completely; her women are strong, often stronger than the men in their lives, but solidly grounded in traditional roles. Among our better contemporary novelists, Tyler occupies a somewhat lonely place, polishing brighter and brighter a craft many novelists no longer deem essential to their purpose: the unfolding of character through brilliantly imagined and absolutely accurate detail. . . .

Less perfectly realized than *Celestial Navigation,* her extraordinarily moving and beautiful last novel, *Searching for Caleb* is Tyler's sunniest, most expansive book. While etching with a fine, sharp wit the narrow-mindedness and pettishness of the Pecks, she lavishes on them a tenderness that lifts them above satire. Consider Daniel Peck. A cold and unoriginal man, aging gracefully but without wisdom, he is yet allowed moments in which we glimpse his bewilderment at a life that has been in the end disappointing. . . .

Reading *Searching for Caleb* one is constantly being startled by such moments: gestures, words, wrinkles of thought and feeling that are at once revelatory and exactly right. But at the center of Tyler's characters is a private, mysterious core which is left, wisely, inviolate. Ultimately this wisdom is what makes Tyler more than a fine craftsman of realistic novels. Her complex, crotchety inventions surprise us, but one senses they surprise her too.

Katha Pollitt. *The New York Times.*
January 18, 1976, p. 22

Anne Tyler's standards are high; she works both hard and fast. Of her earlier novels, this seems most similar to *A Slipping-Down Life*—the antagonists and circumstance and action are equivalent—but *Earthly Possessions* is far better done. If not precisely a sequel to her previous works, it's nonetheless a companion-text; the narrative is supple and the world a pleasant place.

Violence and lust are rare, or offstage; the characteristic emotions are abstracted ones—anger comes to us as vexation, bliss as a kind of contended release.

Yet I do not feel this novel represents advance. The wheels are a touch too audibly clicking, and inspiration seems second-hand. It's as if her sense of continuity overruled the chance of change; the book is programmatic and the program feels over-rehearsed. Still, anyone who wrote the splendid *Celestial Navigation* and *Searching for Caleb* should be allowed to take a breather—and Anne Tyler's average work is more than good enough. *Earthly Possessions* is deft, good-humored and never less than engaging; one hopes its author, next time through, will once more be fully engaged.

Nicholas Delbanco. The New Republic.
May 28, 1977, p. 36

A marvel of a book deserving full critical recognition, *Morgan's Passing* covers twelve years in the life of its middle-aged hero, Morgan Gower, tracing the history and disintegration of his first marriage as well as his acquisition of a new wife and a new identity. As in Anne Tyler's other novels, the center of human interaction is family life with all of its perils, limitations, and rewards. . . . A man with and for whom life is difficult yet never boring, Morgan is a genuine eccentric in an urban setting, a comic anti-hero "acting out some elaborate inner vision" of himself.

In *Morgan's Passing* as in several of her previous novels, Anne Tyler shows her genius at creating such a figure. Morgan at once reminds us of other mild, at times tragicomic, eccentrics in *Celestial Navigation* (1974), *Searching for Caleb* (1976) and *Earthly Possessions* (1977); of Jeremy Pauling and Charlotte Emory and of Duncan, Justine, and the elusive Caleb Peck. Yet, like these other Tyler characters, Morgan is also unique, a highly individualized figure in a contemporary American landscape. . . .

On the surface, *Morgan's Passing* is primarily the story of one man's handling of change and aging, although clearly the growth and change of Emily Meredith, the young puppeteer Morgan eventually marries, is also central to the plot. It is an elusive novel, however, at times zany, at times sad, a book preeminently concerned with marital mistakes and marked by Miss Tyler's characteristic sense of distance. . . .

It may be that . . . Tyler is holding back something of her narrative skill, but if there is a key to this distance in Tyler's work, it lies in the central metaphor of *Morgan's Passing:* puppetry. In many ways, Morgan Gower is a deliberate, conscious mask for the novelist. Like her, he is a small-scale impostor who laments having one identity, one life. . . .

It is precisely this sense of distance and respect for character and the privacy and inviolability of even fictional lives which Tyler invites her readers to share. She is, I think, remarkably successful. *Morgan's Passing* is a testament to that success.

Stella Nesanovich. Southern Review.
Summer, 1981, pp. 619–21

New work by a young writer who's both greatly gifted and prolific often points readers' minds toward the future. You finish the book and immediately begin speculating about works to come—achievements down the road that will cross the borders defined by the work at hand. Anne Tyler's books have been having this effect on me for nearly a decade. Repeatedly they've been brilliant—"wickedly good," as John Updike recently described one of them. *Dinner at the Homesick Restaurant* is Anne Tyler's ninth novel; her career began in 1964 with a fully realized first novel (the title was *If Morning Ever Comes,* and there are piquant links between it and her latest book); everything I've read of hers since then—stories, novels and criticism (Anne Tyler is a first-rate critic, shrewd and self-effacing)—has been, at a minimum, interesting and well made. But in recent years her narratives have grown bolder and her characters more striking, and that's increased the temptation to brood about her direction and destination, her probable ultimate achievement.

The time for such brooding is over now, though—at least for a while. *Dinner at the Homesick Restaurant* is a book to be settled into fully, tomorrow be damned. Funny, heart-hammering, wise, it edges deep into truth that's simultaneously (and interdependently) psychological, moral and formal—deeper than many living novelists of serious reputation have penetrated, deeper than Miss Tyler herself has gone before. It is a border crossing. . . .

Dinner at the Homesick Restaurant is, from start to finish, superb entertainment. . . . Much as I've admired Miss Tyler's earlier books, I've found flaws in a few—something excessively static in the situation developed in *Morgan's Passing,* for instance, something arbitrary in the plotting of *Earthly Possessions.* But in the work at hand Miss Tyler is a genius plotter, effortlessly redefining her story questions from page to page, never slackening the lines of suspense. There are, furthermore, numberless explosions of hilarity, not one of which (I discover) can be sliced out of its context for quotation—so tightly fashioned is this tale—without giving away, as they say, a narrative climax. There are scenes that strike me as likely to prove unforgettable. . . .

Seriousness does insist, in the end, that explicit note be taken of the facts of this career. Anne Tyler turned forty just last year. She's worked with a variety of materials, established her mastery of grave as well as comic tones. Her command of her art is sure, and her right to trust her feeling for the complications both of our nature and of our nurturing arrangements stands beyond question. Speculating about this artist's future is, in short, a perfectly natural movement of mind. But, as I said before, I'm reluctant to speculate and I expect other readers, in quantity, will share my reluctance. What one wants to do on finishing such a work as *Dinner at the Homesick Restaurant* is maintain balance, keep things intact for a stretch, stay under the spell as long as feasible. The before and after are immaterial; nothing counts except the knowledge, solid and serene, that's all at once breathing in the room. We're speaking, obviously, about an extremely beautiful book.

Benjamin DeMott. *The New York Times.*
March 14, 1982, pp. 1, 14

The world as Tyler perceives it is a decidedly messy affair. In addition to the burden of personal and familial pasts, her characters suffer from peer pressure *(A Slipping-Down Life)*, child abuse *(Dinner at the Homesick Restaurant)*, genetically-based predispositions *(Searching for Caleb)*, and poor self-image *(Morgan's Passing)*. Most live in terror of the outside world, like Macon Leary compiling guidebooks to minimize contact with it *(The Accidental Tourist)* or Jeremy Pauling holing up in his studio in agoraphobic panic. Others try to escape but cannot, like Charlotte Emory, whose only successful departure is as the hostage of a befuddled bank robber *(Earthly Possessions)*. Much of the apparent chaos in Tyler's fictional worlds is due to the fact that everything seems to happen as an incongruous blend of utter chance and utter doom: Jake Simms just happens to take Charlotte hostage, while Ethan Leary just happens to be in a fast-food restaurant when a teen-aged thug decides to murder all the customers; the Pecks seem destined from birth to buy only Fords and to despise plaids *(Searching for Caleb)*, while Emily Meredith is destined to embark on a career in puppetry that seems genetically encoded *(Morgan's Passing)*. The Tyler characters who do try to remain functional in this chaotic world rely on various strategies. One such strategy is the cultivation of ritualistic behavior, like the purchase of a new red toothbrush every winter *(If Morning Ever Comes)*. Others try to create the illusion of control by assuming identities (Morgan Gower in *Morgan's Passing*) or acting more integrated than they really are (Elizabeth Abbott of *The Clock Winder*). Others immerse themselves in the world of games (especially Monopoly and solitaire), where the rules are clear and winning a real possibility. Others frantically demand to know "the point," be it the point of pursuing an unsuccessful music career (Drumstrings Casey in *A Slipping-Down Life*), of getting to class on time (Justine Mayhew Peck in *Searching for Caleb*), or of holding a funeral for a cremated husband (Serena Gill in *Breathing Lessons*). Others just as frantically try to blame someone, anyone, anything for all that happens, since blame implies an understood order and a feeling of control. Still others use a medium that is quite appealing to Tyler: the fine arts. Most notably in Janie Rose's "tin can tree" and Jeremy Pauling's "pieces" *(Celestial Navigation)*, Tyler's characters try to integrate the seemingly antithetical fragments of the world, rendering incongruous images, ideas, and events into meaningful wholes over which they, as artists, exert control. Photography likewise is a frequent pursuit in Tyler's novels, as characters attempt to "freeze" particular moments, to save them from the exigencies of change, of passing time, and of seeming chaos.

In the course of writing her eleven novels, however, Tyler seems to have evolved a means of dealing with these exigencies that has little in common with rituals, role playing, or games. In their stead, her characters have come to rely on a strategy that exerts a measure of genuine, rather than illusory, control over their lives and the world. It is seen as early as *Searching for Caleb,* in which the fortune teller Madame Olita explains to Justine Peck that one of the most painful elements of man's existence, the weight of the past, need not be overwhelming: "you can always choose to *some* extent. You can change your future a great deal. Also your past. . . . Not what's happened, no . . . but what hold it has on you." In a similar vein, Macon Leary of *The Accidental Tourist*, buffeted by the shocking death of his son and the dissolution of his twenty-year marriage, eventually comes to the realization that one may "choose what to lose."

It is an upbeat stance, and one quite unusual for the contemporary American literary scene. No wonder she defies classification. Humanists like Anne Tyler are, after all, very rare indeed.

Alice Hall Petry. *Understanding Anne Tyler*
(Columbia: University of South Carolina
Press, 1990), pp. 14–17

Tyler's particular territory is Baltimore, where she has lived since 1967 and where she places her characters, almost all of whom find their primary identity as members of a family. Tyler emphasizes the family situation throughout her work, exploring the quirks and foibles of characters who long for happiness that often remains elusive. Family members suffer disappointments, misunderstandings, and tragedies, yet these families endure. Humor pervades Tyler's fiction as a natural device to help balance life's disappointments. Family members face broken marriages, unhappy children, lost dreams, illness, and loneliness. Through it all these families survive. Tyler is primarily interested in day-to-day endurance; her characters generally succeed through effort.

Tyler's novels are popular and readable, not the characteristics critics generally praise. Some critics chide Tyler for avoiding sexual, political, and social issues in her work and for taking few technical risks; Tyler's novels and stories, however, deal with the problems most people must face every day. Although Tyler cannot be labeled an outspoken feminist, her novels present strong women characters. If these women fail to live independently, they at least attempt to gain a better sense of their lives.

Tyler has established a network of appealing characters who reside in Baltimore, and when a minor character has a cameo appearance in a later novel, we begin to wonder if all these fictional people might really know one another. Tyler looks on her characters as if they were next-door neighbors she cherished. However bizarre or eccentric readers sometimes find her characters, Tyler knows that ordinary people often have within them unique characteristics that set them apart from other "ordinary" people.

Most of all, Tyler *likes* her characters. "I like to think," she has written, "that I might meet up with one of my past characters at the very next street corner. The odd thing is, sometimes I have. And if I were remotely religious, I'd believe that a little gathering of my characters would be waiting for me in heaven when I died. '*Then* what happened?' I'd ask them. '*How* have things worked out, since the last time I saw you?'"

Elizabeth Evans. *Anne Tyler* (Boston:
Twayne, 1993), pp. ix–x

TYNAN, KATHARINE (IRELAND) 1861–1931

It was in the pages of *The Irish Monthly* that Katharine Tynan first won recognition as a poet. She was one of that brilliant company that gathered about Father Matthew Russell, and that was first introduced to the world through the pages of this magazine.

It is a far cry to 1885, when Katharine Tynan published her first volume of verse. Now there comes to us for review her *Collected Poems.*

In an age in which literature—and even that branch of literature that is poetry—is wrested from its high purpose and forced to serve as the vehicle of decadent thought and pagan concepts of life, it is a joy to come upon something worthy of so rare a gift as that of the poet. . . .

Katharine Tynan, in her songs, has maintained the Victorian tradition for pure, clear and direct singing—the tradition of Wordsworth and Tennyson. One agrees with Æ in his introduction to this volume when he dwells on the natural ease with which she writes poetry. The meter in which the majority of her poems are written is peculiar to herself. It was this meter of hers, if I mistake not, that no less a poet than Francis Thompson praised. The form in which her poems are cast is individual. She created a form to suit her thoughts and moods, just as Tennyson created a form; as Hardy did.

Her subjects are many and varied. She is the poet of human love and longing and loneliness, just as she is the poet of hope and happiness in a spiritual world beyond the stars. Her *Collected Poems* are divided thus: "The Old Country," "Mother and Child," "Songs of Love, Life and Death," "Saints and Angels," "Prayers and Desires," "Heaven and Earth," "In War-time," "Birds and Flowers and Beauty of Earth," "Legends and Fantasies," "The Tree-lover," and "Personalia." . . .

I shall conclude by quoting from Æ's Foreword: "Katharine Tynan says of herself that she was born under a kind star. It is true. She is happy in religion, friendship, children, instantly kindling at any beauty in gardens, flowers, in sky and clouds. She has, too, that spiritual bravery which makes beauty out of death or sorrow. A friend passes, and he is sped on his journey, not with despair, but with hope, almost with imaginative gaiety. It is a great gift this, which on a sudden changes our gloom to a glory."

Michael Walsh. *Irish Monthly.*
December, 1930, pp. 627–31

Although Mrs. Tynan is a modern novelist, we seem to step a long way back in her novels. We are away from the novel, so popular in our own day, which is scarcely a story. We are aeons away from any sordidness, any beastly eroticism, the backwash of so much of our modern fiction. Mrs. Tynan is not in any sense a great novelist. She has no place in the same rank as Sheila Kaye-Smith, she has not a masterly touch of creation, but she can give us a very good story. I do not want to be misunderstood if I say that Mrs. Tynan is more than anything else the type of novelist who gets a rather obvious but good plot. Sometimes we are in danger of forgetting exactly what a plot is. In so much modern fiction, excluding detective fiction, there is no plot at all. We are simply gazing at the map of a mind. But in the stories of Mrs. Tynan we are introduced not only to a good plot but to an exciting tale and a tale which is always perfectly clean. A great deal of the fiction of our era can be best described as perfectly dirty. Mrs. Tynan is clever without being in the least subtle. She is smart without letting her fiction become merely shallow smartness.

> Patrick Braybrooke. *Some Catholic*
> *Novelists* (London: Burns, Oates and
> Washbourne, 1931), p. 209

W. B. Yeats was twenty and Katharine Tynan twenty-four when they first met. She was the daughter of Andrew Tynan, a strong farmer of Whitehall, Clondalkin, County Dublin; had published her first poem in a Dublin paper when she was seventeen and in that year of 1885 had won considerable notice as a poet with her first book of poems *Louise de la Valliere*. The means of their introduction was Professor Oldham of Trinity College, Dublin who was then editing the *Dublin University Review*. He said to her abruptly one day, much as one might announce the capture of a rare moth, "I've got a queer youth named Yeats," and brought the poet to see her soon afterwards. . . .

It would be a mistake to judge her solely by the mountain of mediocre fiction which she produced. Yeats probably overvalued her poetry, as he overvalued Todhunter's plays, because of friendship and the dominance of a literary tradition which both of them disliked; but his criticism of her work . . . is generally clear about her limitations and he may not have been far out in considering her an Irish Christina Rossetti, with all that this reckoning implies. The selection of twenty-one of her poems which he made for the Dun Emer Press in 1907 shows that she was a considerable minor poet and her anthologies of Irish poetry deserve to be remembered more than they are. George William Russell's [AE] tribute to her the year before she died [Introduction to *Collected Poems of Katharine Tynan*] will be found to coincide in many points with Yeats's view of her. Yet when all this has been said, the respective literary careers of Yeats and of Katharine Tynan, who were both subject to many of the same influences and both often employed upon the same themes, show most clearly the difference between the quality and the singleness of purpose of a major poet and the occasional felicity of a minor one.

> Roger McHugh. Introduction to *W. B.*
> *Yeats's Letters to Katharine Tynan* (Dublin:
> Clonmore and Reynolds, 1953), pp. 11–14

Her first book of poetry, *Louise de la Vallière and Other Poems* [appeared in 1885]. In a biography of Tynan, Marilyn Gaddis Rose says, "As a girl launched on her career, sponsored by Father Mathew Russell, editor of the *Irish Monthly,* as an intimate of the Meynells, a visitor of Christina Rossetti and Lady Wilde, it was inevitable that she meet W. B. Yeats." By way of introduction, Oldham showed Tynan Yeats's *The Island of Statues,* and she always retained a fondness for this work, judging it his "first considerable poem." . . . During March of this year, Oldham, in his *Dublin University Review,* had been responsible for the first publication of Yeats's work, an excerpt from *The Island;* then from April to July of 1885, he printed the play in its entirety in the *Review.* . . .

Tynan's *Louise de la Vallière,* originally published at her father's expense, ran into a second edition in the following year, for it pleased the Catholic members of the reading public. Of the volume's success, she said, "The priests had sent my first little volume of poems into edition after edition, to the bewilderment of my publisher, Mr. Kegan Paul, who used to say that mine was the only poetry that sold with him." By modern standards it is not a very good book of poetry: the language is anachronistic, replete with "thou," "thee," "methinks," and "eth" inflections; it employs consciously poetic diction, such as "even" for "evening" and "i' the" for "in the"; throughout, the poems have obvious morals, often restated in philosophic tags at the end; the meter is a pronounced iambic, sometimes accomplished by stressing "ed" inflections; grammatical inversion strains into rhyme; and characterization proceeds along the line of the late Dickens, that is, through a select description of physical features, such as eyes, hair, and hands for women. Nevertheless, the book "was reviewed quite respectfully by the London literary papers, by the London dailies, and the big provincial papers." One might suppose, then, that in the beginning of their friendship, Yeats paid Tynan homage and she lent him prestige. . . .

Tynan published her second book of poetry, *Shamrocks* (1887), which Yeats reviewed. One of Yeats's reviews of *Shamrocks* is the lost *Gael* review. . . . After this review in May, Yeats published a second review, "Miss Tynan's New Book," *Irish Fireside,* 9 July 1887, in which he praised *Shamrocks* over *Louise de la Vallière* because in her second volume Tynan seemed to have found "her nationality." He organized this review around the comparison of "the metaphors of things" (as in *Louise*) to "the things themselves" (as in *Shamrocks*). Always careful of her feelings, he wrote to her about the review, "I hope you did not mind my fault-finding." Two poems that Yeats especially liked from *Shamrocks* were "The Heart of a Mother" and "St. Francis to the Birds," the latter of which he included in the 1907 Dun Emer volume of Tynan's selected poetry. That he should so highly praise this poem is ironic, for, as Sister Francis Inés Moloney observes, the poem is "reminiscent of Longfellow who also wrote on the subject of St. Francis's sermon to the birds" in his poem "The Sermon of St. Francis," and Yeats had previously expressed amazement at Tynan's poor taste in admiring Longfellow. . . .

Shamrocks is, as Yeats pointed out in his *Fireside* review, a better book of verse than *Louise de la Vallière,* even though it repeats the same themes of nature, motherhood, and religion, and is didactically optimistic. (The epigraph to the volume is from Richard Henry Horne's *Orion:* "'Tis always Morning somewhere in the world.") Its superiority depends, at least in part, upon the Irish subject-matter of its longer narrative poems, a change that Richard Ellmann attributes to O'Leary's influence.

> Carolyn Holdsworth. In Richard J. Finneran,
> ed. *Yeats Annual, No. 2* (London:
> Macmillan, 1983), pp. 60–63

[Tynan] had risen to sudden fame with the 1885 publication of her first volume, *Louise de la Vallière and Other Poems.* Influenced mainly by Longfellow and the Rossettis, *La Vallière* was well received in Ireland, England, and America, particularly by the Catholic press. . . .

In 1887 Tynan became the first to review Yeats's work, and she reviewed his early books several times each. In 1893 Tynan published the first known interview with Yeats. Her speeches on Irish poetry featured Yeats prominently, and she published many essays introducing him to Irish, English, and American readers. Altogether, Tynan published eighteen volumes of poetry; more than thirty-five romance novels; uncounted biographical studies, anthologies, essays, and reviews, and five volumes of memoirs. In 1907 Yeats edited a selection of Tynan's poetry for his sisters' Dun Emer Press, although he later declined Tynan's request to edit her 1930 *Collected Poems.* Long before then he had come to think of Tynan, the poet Lionel Johnson, and himself as the founders of the Irish literary renaissance.

> James J. McFadden and Daniel Kiefer.
> *Modern Philology.* 88, 1991, pp. 261–62

UKRAINKA, LESYA (UKRAINE) 1871–1913

[Ukrayinka] in the beautiful cycle *Sl'ozy—perly* [Tears—Pearls] raises a great lament not over her own fate, not over the fate of some hero or some whimsical artist, but over all of her native land, over people in chains. There have been many similar laments in our poetry, especially after Shevchenko. Lesya Ukrayinka, however, is the first and the only one able to control this wide scale of emotions, ranging from a quiet sorrow to a savage despair and a proud, powerful scorn. . . .

Her body is sick, but her soul is healthy and her thought is lucid. Her own suffering does not conceal from her the beauty of nature and those exquisite dreams that beauty inspires . . . or the beauty of peace and happiness of other people. It does not weaken her desire for the good of all people; on the contrary, it strengthens the desire, although it simultaneously overshadows it with a gentle mist of sadness and resignation. [1898]

Ivan Franko. *Tvory v dvadtsyaty tomakh*
(Kiev: Derzhavne vydavnytstvo, 1955),
vol. XVII, pp. 247–48

Many of [Ukrayinka's] lyric poems from the cycle *Vidhuky* [Echoes] and *Nevil'nychi pisni* [Songs of slaves] sound like dramatic monologues. We find dialogues in almost every longer poem. . . . These are, to some extent, prototypes for her future dramas. The dramatic poem is a transitory stage between the lyric and the drama: and it is this genre, rather than the drama, that marks the work of Lesya Ukrayinka in the second period of her literary activity. In the dramatic poem we find everything: the lyrical element, a well-developed plot, and a dramatic collison. Here Lesya not only creates a mood and suggests certain ideas in their dialectic development; she also provides us with an epic view of things and she achieves the highest degree of flexibility and perfection. The refined, architectonic structure of her work leads her at times away from realism. She omits insignificant facts; she does not harken to the noise of everyday life and does not drown in it.

Lesya's works of the second period contain lofty ideas. But they are not tendentious, although some critics maintain that "among Ukrainian poets there is no woman more tendentious than Lesya Ukrayinka." . . . According to Cherkassenko: "The tendentiousness of Lesya Ukrayinka's work lies in her desire to awaken her people to life. This is the object of her creativity; her device is the beautiful, fiery, prophetic Ukrainian word, cast into wondrous forms." If one equates such a desire with tendentiousness, then almost all Ukrainian literature must be labeled as tendentious, most of all the works of Taras Shevchenko. . . . Admittedly, she often champions the national idea in her works in the first and second periods, but this theme is dressed in such artistic form and contains so much authentic feeling and life-creating force that any tendentiousness is out of the question. . . . She [also] deals with problems of art, religion, moral obligation, and she is interested in social problems. To reduce this wide span of her creativity to the "desire to awaken her people to life" is to misunderstand Lesya Ukrayinka or to understand her very one-sidedly.

Mykhaylo Dray-Khmara. *Lesya Ukrayinka:*
Zhytta i tvorchist' (Kiev: Derzhavne
vydavnytstvo, 1924), pp. 106–7

The lyric poetry of Lesya Ukrayinka is not generally considered to be the crowning achievement of her work, although she displays true strength and courage in her social poems as well as a moving feminine quality in poems describing her intimate moods and feelings. The crowning achievements of her work, however, are her dramatic poems. The lyrics of her middle period, those written from 1895 to 1900, for the most part lack artistic perfection. Even after overcoming the influence of the "old school" in *Dumky i mriyi* [Thoughts and Dreams], it took her a long time to find the artistic balance that makes a work classical, the certitude that fears nothing. She did find it in the . . . collection of lyric poetry *Vidhuk y* and in a number of monologues and dialogues of her verse dramas. . . .

Her later works are, according to these apt words of M. Yevshan, "no mere fragmented reactions of the poetic spirit, or fragmentary pictures thrown together in a moment of inspiration, but rather always conscious acts of the creative will. . . ."

Intellect, poetic intuition, the profound tenderness of the female mind, strong creative will, the lofty eaglelike soaring of her thoughts, which enables her to tie every insignificant occurrence of our daily life . . . to the eternal problems of the human spirit . . . all this has been intertwined in Lesya Ukrayinka's works into an harmonious whole. Here we find . . . all of human life reflected, just as the universe is reflected in a drop of dew.

Mykola Zerov. *Do dzherel* (Cracow and
Lvov: Ukrayins'ke vydavnytstvo, 1943), p. 169

Apart from the intrinsic value of her work, the chief merit of Lesya Ukrainka was that she exercised the function of a beneficent innovator in the field of Ukrainian poetry, an introducer of fresh new forms as well as ideas. Emerging from the imitative influences of the post-Shevchenko tradition, she labored consciously to lead Ukrainian literature out of its provincialism and the preoccupation of its writers with purely domestic themes and subjects. With the clear conviction that every national literature must have its own peculiar native coloring, she also was convinced that it must necessarily profit by conforming to universal standards and develop itself within the framework of the ideas common to all humanity. This point of view can be seen even in her adolescent lyrics. . . . Such themes were a novelty in Ukrainian poetry then. At the same time she successfully experimented with European forms hitherto unused by Ukrainian poets. . . .

Lesya Ukrainka's attitude . . . was one of faith in the innate strength of an indestructible nation, and consequently, the compelling necessity of battling on with a firm conviction of ultimate victory. Of course, there is at times a melancholy overtone in the bold assertions of her verse, but it is not always possible [even] for those who enjoy rugged health continuously to maintain a mood of calm and untroubled assurance in the future, and Lesya Ukrainka had no such advantage. In any case, not to look backwards, never to lose heart, incessantly to keep on fighting, and never to doubt of eventual victory—this is the main ideological content of her poetry.

The appreciation of Lesya Ukrainka's contribution to Ukrainian literature began to be widely expressed only after her death. . . . The heroic tone and the neo-Romanticism of her dramatic poems based on hitherto unfamiliar themes did not meet with a wide response at first . . . except among the discerning, but admiration and appreciation is steadily growing as the years go by. It is now realized that she possessed a remarkably strong poetic imagination, a universalism in her choice of themes, a profound penetration of the variations of human psychology, together with a style both highly lyrical and charged with dramatic power.

> Percival Cundy. Introduction to Lesya
> Ukrainka. *Spirit of Flame: A Collection of
> the Works of Lesya Ukrainka* (New York:
> Bookman Associates, 1950), pp. 36–37

[Ukrayinka's] poem "Romans" ("Romance"), written in 1897, is a classical example of the love lyric. Though it consists of only two anapest stanzas of fourteen lines, it creates a deep impression through its intensity of emotion, laconic expression, effective acoustics, fortified by alternating feminine and masculine rhymes, and inter-stanza anaphora. Her portrayal of the various facets of her emotions, and the delicate utterance of her soul do not obscure the lucidity of thought and image. Absence of any affectation makes her verses sincere and deeply persuasive. . . .

"Robert Bruce, King of Scotland" ("Robert Bryus, Korol' Shotlands'kyy") is an excellent indication of her new concern for serious social themes. Robert Bruce, the only Scottish lord who remained faithful to his people in their struggle against the invading English army, scores a great victory over the King of England and saves the independence of Scotland. Although still hampered by some stylistic difficulties (she applies, in places, the stylistic devices of Ukrainian *duma*), Lesya begins to demonstrate the ideological pathos which was to saturate both her lyric and dramatic works.

Her interest in Robert Bruce's struggle for Scottish independence no doubt
was inspired by the struggle of her compatriots for their own national cause.

                              Constantine Bida. *Lesya Ukrainka* (Toronto:
                              University of Toronto Press, 1968), p. 33

Unlike most playwrights, Lesya Ukrainka as a student of dramaturgy moved
in an opposite direction from what could be expected, that is to say, from
the modern idiom to the ancient, from Ibsen, Hauptmann, Maeterlinck to
Aechylus, Sophocles, Euripides. Her "theater" became classic not merely in
formal ways, including techniques and [the] three unities; it involves moreover, elevated themes, high style, overall structure.

She began her career of a playwright with a prose drama *The Blue Rose*
(Blakytna troyanda), written in 1896, which is based on a present-day topic
and to a high degree influenced by Ibsen. As Alfred de Musset and Heine in
her early poetry, so Ibsen proved to be her mentor in the initial stage of her
dramatic endeavors. This was followed by a period of fervent searching and
conscious intensive study during which Lesya Ukrainka familiarized herself
with and explored new achievements in the Western dramaturgy and, consequently, succeeded in developing her own immanent idiom and style. Her
play becomes, like the Greek prototype, poetic drama in form, charged with
insurmountable conflict that leads to a crisis, and marked with spiritual overtones. Although not necessarily scenic, her plays should not be called, however, "closet dramas" even though a pure "show element" is lacking. This
external shortcoming is sufficiently compensated by the inner dramatism that
imbues them with vibrant life. Besides, Lesya Ukrainka's work excels in
values identifiable with supreme quality literature which implies both form
and the content. As a rule, they are permeated with lofty ideas, universal in
scope, as they are dressed in the beautiful and fragrant linguistic garment.
Beyond this impressive façade their functions in fulfillment of the stage re-
quirement assume of necessity secondary position, in which they differ from
the Greek pattern.

                              Roman V. Kuchar. *The Ukranian Review.*
                              Summer, 1970, p. 18

The dramatic poem, *U pushchi* (In the virgin forest), was completed in 1907,
at the time Lesya was informed of the critical state of her health. She proceeded to concentrate on her unfinished works. This poem is concerned with
freedom of the creative spirit and conscience, as well as with freedom of
artistic expression, values that were a constant part of the poetess' *Weltan-*
schauung. The story deals with an Italian sculptor, Ayron, who comes to
Puritan Rhode Island in quest of freedom of expression. The Puritan leader,
Godvinson, strives to persuade him to create utilitarian articles (e.g., a
dummy for the tailor). Caught between noble dreams and cold reality, inspiration deserts Ayron, and he resigns himself to death: "When will the angel of
death call me? I have a premonition that he will come soon." The prototype

of Richard Ayron is Roger Williams, sentenced to exile in 1635 by a Massachusetts court for his opposition to the State's interference in religious affairs.
The ideals of Roger Williams—freedom of conscience and the right of an
individual to determine his destiny—echo in Lesya's drama.

The dramatic poem, "Cassandra" ["Kassandra"], written in San Remo
on the Italian Riviera, in 1902 and 1903, stands in a long line of ancient and
West European oeuvres on the Trojan War and the prophetic role of Priam's
fair daughter Cassandra. Lesya makes Cassandra her central personage, and
places the main accent on the antithesis of ideas, revealed in dialogues, in
which is disclosed the deepening of Cassandra's tragedy (although she possesses prophetic powers, Cassandra is powerless to change the course of
events). She considers herself a true descendant of Prometheus, like Iphi-
genia; consequently, she refuses to submit to the will of the gods, who are
not free, being slaves of Fate (Moira). Cassandra is an embodiment of absolute truth, her only Master. In time even Cassandra comes to blame herself
for her tongue, which must speak of the unavoidable. Because the credo of
Lesya's life and work in every respect was the truth of her beliefs, she chose
this eternal plot to express it pathetically and with full mastery and skill.

Natalia I. Pazuniak. *The Ukranian
Quarterly.* Autumn, 1971, pp. 14–15

UNDER, MARIE (ESTONIA) 1883–1980

She is, like [Yeats] not an inter-national but very much an extra-
individualistic artist. (By extra-individualistic I mean such an intensification
and deepening of personal experience that it ceases to be individualistic and
assumes universal validity.) Her work is regarded as being the most richly
rewarding and interesting in Estonian literature. But she is undoubtedly also
one of the most outstanding poets of the twentieth century. . . .

A poet of remarkable linguistic ability, Marie Under delves deep into the
essence of things, and with the various means of expression at her command
she adumbrates their innermost secret. She penetrates into the core of their
existence, seeks to grasp it spiritually from within and, working outwards
from the very center, to render their outer appearance comprehensible. Her
power of abstract thought grows in her years of maturity; fully conversant
with the metaphysical and religious problems which life presents, she has
gained a thorough mastery of life.

Side by side with her purely contemplative poems we find others which
carry immediate conviction by their weight and breadth. These are her ballads and legends. In this medium, too, she shows herself the most outstanding
exponent of Estonian poetry, particularly in her works in which, with illuminating symbolism and discerning portrayal, she evokes her own native land-

scape and the moods and the emotions peculiar to a Nordic people—as other great Scandinavian and Baltic artists have similarly done. . . .

Gifted with exceptional powers of contemplative thought and with the liveliest of emotional responses, Marie Under has attained real greatness and uniqueness in her work. The ultimate value of her poetry does not lie in its sensuous appeal, the appeal of form and color, but in its spiritual content, in the moral intensity and insight which distinguish all her poems. From earliest youth deeply moved by an inner faith, she has found for herself the ultimate meaning of life, and her spiritual explorations have led to moments of blinding truth.

"Suffering without singing is a sad venture. Singing without suffering— that is what the throat is for," says Sainte-Beuve. To Marie Under, suffering is also singing. And the wonderful resilience with which she savors and renders sorrow lifts and transmutes the weight of her tragic experiences into sound and light.

Aleksis Rannit. Books Abroad. 37, 1963,
pp. 125, 128–30

In 1963, Marie Under, the great Estonian poet who had lived in exile since 1944, overwhelmed her readers once more with a collection of new verse entitled *In Borderlands*. The poet, who in her earlier verse had rushed, whirled, and burned with the times, now listens to "time to untime all times": "My watch ticks slower, clearer. / All distances grown nearer, / Green hour when yearnings come . . . / Sea, fount of founts, reliever / Of burdens, solve all fever / In foaming waves. . . ." The vital mystery of the sea, which acts as a central leitmotif through the whole work of Marie Under, retains even now the white glow of foam and seagulls, and an intimation of search for and promise of a fulfillment. . . . Under sets her whole work in the perspective of her quest for transcendence, identified with the very gift of poetry. This hope lends unity to an exceptionally rich, feverish, and passionate creation, which extends through the first sixty years of our century. . . .

Under's early verse vibrates with the joy of telling the light, colors, motion, sounds, smell, and touch of things felt, and of her own feeling body. Her poetic words start from concrete sensations and things; they are full-bodied and shimmering things themselves and part of a huge awe-inspiring community of nature. They are given as a gift and they come straight from the heart. The world Under depicts in her first three collections is that of man's happy unison with natural fullness, a world of erotic candor, and immanence of Being. Occasional hints of a fear, an absence, the passing of time, a dichotomy between soul and body, reveal an underlying anxiety, but they are overruled by new gusts of full-blooded vitality.

A radical change occurs in her poetry around 1920. Her world of sensual union with nature is torn in shreds: death, not growth, is the law of life. Separation and isolation are the lot of the soul. War dead march through the poet's dreams and claim their share of life. The poet voices their request, cries for help, justice, pity. She denounces social evil and physical distress of men in sharply-drawn realistic depictions of city scenes. But her inner anguish breaks out in still more desperate visions of refusal, forsakenness, void, and contradiction, leading to hallucinatory evocations of cosmic gloom ("Moon of Death"), where man and beast feel the breath of the same all-pervading doom. Yet out of this existential despair a new sense of participation spreads in Under's poetry: the communion of the silent victims of existence whose truth is want and whose symbol is shadow.

Henceforth, a new light coming from the very depths of despair, as it were, permeates the poetry of Under. It envelops the poems of *Delight in a Lovely Day,* 1928, with the glow of a quasi-Franciscan solicitude for all creation. In the ballads of *Eclipse of Happiness,* 1929, tragic destinies of a legendary past are told with the same inner vibration, making them equal to many masterpieces of world literature.

At the same time, the theme of unquenchable thirst for life, which runs through all Under's verse, takes a definitely metaphysical turn. . . .

Yet the poet so genuinely gifted to embrace the world, to convey man's agreement with creation, has suffered to the hilt the agony, fear, and hostility of our times. Some of her most impressive verse dates from World War II ("With Mournful Lips," 1949) and its aftermath ("Sparks in Ashes," 1954) reflecting the impact of events that have cut . . . wounds in the soul and body of her nation. From shame to indictment and maternal care for the victims, her verse rings with the same resonance to universal existence as it does in her happiest poems. The soiled and terrible world is never closed in her poetry. And the increasing silence of her latest poems still vibrates with the expectation of an ultimate miracle.

The vitality of hope, the unusual range of human experience imbedded in her poetry, and the depth of her responsiveness to and responsibility before the universe make of Under's poetry one of the truly significant creations of our time.

Alexander Aspel. Books Abroad. 43, 1969,
pp. 363–64

The chief representative and president of this [Young Estonia] movement was the poet Marie Under. In her first book, *Sonnets* (1917), Marie Under surprised her audience with her genuine and esthetically well-executed portrayal of nature, which heralded the birth of a great talent; however, conservative readers were shocked by her frank display of eroticism. The same motifs dominate her collections *The Early Spring* (1918) and *The Blue Sail* (1918). Influenced by German expressionists, she wrote *The Bleeding Wound* (1920), *The Heritage* (1923), and *Voice from the Shadows* (1927). Amid glimpses of delight, one senses the ominous presence of dismal moods. . . .

The ballads in *Eclipse of Happiness* (1929) conjure up legendary episodes; atheism and depression are present. Already at this stage, Marie Under had attained a distinctive and vigorous style. Her trips to Paris (1926), Rome

(1929), and Vienna (1929), as well as the influence of her religious mother, transformed her outlook into a stronger, more optimistic perspective, and her next volume, *A Stone Off the Heart* (1935), contains such poems as "The Harp of David," "Adam," "Jacob and Leah," and "Mary Magdalene." The poetess announced that man has his roots in God. Her despair had subsided considerably, as if she had been relieved of a burden. Of all Marie Under's books, *With Sorrowful Mouth* (1942) held most appeal for Estonians, for it expressed their feelings about the tragic annexation of their country by the Nazis and the Soviets. During the Soviet invasion in 1944, Marie Under entrusted her fate to the Baltic Sea and escaped to Sweden in a tiny boat. She had dedicated some of her best poems to the Baltic Sea, and it responded. In spite of another stone on her heart, the gentle and frail poet took courage and became a speaker for her nation. . . .

Widely diverse phenomena of life are encompassed within the scope of Marie Under's contemplative and transcendental cognition. In "Ecstasy" (1917) the poet eagerly accepts the blossoms of life and admits that her "every nerve vibrates to rapt delight." However, she also acknowledges death, for it "grants her something that life had not given her: the ability to sustain a total, ultimate experience."

Aleksis Rubulis. *Baltic Literature: Survey of
Finnish, Estonian, Latvian and Lithuanian
Literature* (Notre Dame: University of
Notre Dame Press, 1970), pp. 83–84, 86–87

Attempts to translate Marie Under have been made repeatedly in a number of languages. A French selection from her verse sponsored by UNESCO is about to appear. Yet nothing has been done so far that could convey more than a vague notion of the vitality of her art. Apart from her compatriots, only a few scholars who have mastered the difficult Finno-Ugrian language in which she writes are as yet in a position to appreciate it fully: for these, however, she counts as one of the really major poets of our time. . . .

Now, in exile, uprooted, "unselfed," as she feels herself to be, she has still, more impressively than anyone else, been voicing the collective feelings of her nation, but in her unique personal manner, both soothing and strengthening. In her last two volumes, *Sädemed tuhas* (Sparks in ashes, 1954) and *Ääremail* (On the brink, 1963), her language retains its capacity for flowering forth suddenly in exciting metaphor and transcendental vision. Hers is still the clearest and most probing eye in Estonian literature, and her voice the most audible even when most subdued. No one has expressed indignation more strongly than she, but never blind indignation. Now, "on the brink," her plea is still for steadfastness and resistance, but not for hatred. Through all the racking discords of her life she has reached concord. Yet not "calm of mind, all passion spent": her feelings remain stirringly alive—as much so as anyone's in the literature of our time.

Ants Oras. *Sewanee Review.* 78,
1970, pp. 247–48, 267

Marie Under has left us an important statement which she calls her legacy. It was written in response to Aleksis Rannit's request and bears the title "My Testament" *(Minu testament)*. In this statement, Under makes reference to her personal views and her poetic production since the subjugation of Estonia to the Soviet Union. She also singles out ten poems in particular, written between 1941 and 1953, which express her firm stand for justice and deep compassion for human suffering. In these poems, theme, subtle imagery and various poetic devices combine to form beautiful art—a conscious and gracious bequest which appoints all its readers as beneficiaries.

Although "My Testament" is dated June 24, 1968, it was not published until immediately after Marie Under's death in September 1980. The ten poems are from two separate collections: *With Sorrowful Lips (Mureliku suuga)*, published in Estonia in 1942, and *Sparks in the Ashes (Sädemed tuhas)* published in Sweden in 1954.

The poems are: "Christmas Greeting" *1941 (Jõulutervitus 1941)*, "Soldier's Mother" *(Sõduri ema,* January 1942), "Homeward Journey" *(Kojuminek,* 1942), "Remembrance and Pledge" *(Mälestus ja tõotus,* 1943), "The Rest Stop" *(Peatus,* Autumn 1944), "Nocturnal Journey" *(Öine teekond,* Autumn 1944), "Kassary Cemetery" *(Kassari kabeliaed,* Autumn 1945), "One Wind Chases Another" *(Tuul ajab taga teist,* Autumn 1945), "The Most Beautiful Evening of the Year" *(Aasta kauneimal õhtul,* December 15, 1945) and the tri-partite cycle "Accusation" *(Päälekaebamine,* Autumn 1953). . . .

[Through Under's metaphorical language,] her consummate artistry forms a poetic legacy which rivals the majesty of her passion and the dignity of her compassion. The vigor of her thought is matched by the intense beauty of her spiritual sensitivity. Hopefully, these examples of her poetry illustrate how successfully she has combined profound social comment with artistic integrity as the poetess of a nation. Also, hopefully, we her beneficiaries will know how to treasure her bequest.

Laurence P. Kitching and J. Kõvamees
Kitching. *East Meets West: Homage to
Edgar C. Knowlton, Jr.* (Honolulu:
University of Hawaii Press, 1988),
pp. 168, 175

Under started as a poet of flaming youth in the decorative fin-de-siècle style and a writer of experimental sonnets. Within that style she expressed the rebelliousness, erratic temperament, and emancipation of the 1910s: the fervent heart she gave voice to was even more dramatic than Anna Akhmatova's or Edna St. Vincent Millay's with a much more demonstrative eroticism. Her first published book (the second she wrote), *Sonetid* (1917; Sonnets), contained lines like "Oh, those [my] stockings that do not want to end," which shocked and delighted Estonian readers and critics. Her subjective approach to love themes continued in *Eelõitseng* (1918; First flowering) and in her most sensual book, *Sinine puri* (1920; Blue sail); her use of broken yet musically convincing metrical schemes made her the fountainhead of twentieth-century Estonian neoromantic poetry. The initial swiftness of her thought and feeling was matched by a sometimes unfortunate haste of execution, but in general, even in her early, less significant poetry, the freedom and certainty of her pen made for vitality and freshness. As a young lyric poet she seldom had composure or repose, but her poetry is not purely emotional; it is abundant, even overabundant, with thought.

Although critics have characterized her early work as impressionistic, Under lacked the impressionist trait of antimonumentality. She seldom used the technique of blurring the outlines of tonal progression of wording, and even as an impressionist she did not avoid hard, melodic edges and sudden, sharp contrasts of images. Thus, because she was a born poet of energy, it was easy for her to modulate her style and become an expressionist of strong rhythm (specifically, of innovative techniques in accentual verse) and of driving power of thought. Under's collections *Verivalla* (1920; Gaping wounds), *Pärisosa* (1923; Heritage), and *Hääl varjust* (1927; Voice from the shadow) express the full profundity of her anxiety and show her as a person feeling all emotions with authentic intensity. Prepared by her reading of Rimbaud, Whitman, and Émile Verhaeren, Under accepted the aesthetic and spirit of the expressionists, especially of Georg Heym and Georg Trakl, and, applying their ideals to verse translation, she published the anthology *Valik saksa uuemast lüürikast* (1920; Selection of new German poetry). Her dynamic lyricism found a new affirmation in *Õnnevarjutus* (1929; Eclipse of happiness), a collection of ballads in a style to some extent reminiscent of those of the German poet Agnes Miegel.

It is with *Rõõm ühest ilusast päevast* (1928; Joy at the beautiful day), and especially with *Kivi südamelt* (1935; The stone off the heart), that Under's mental vigor found a more classical structure, although to the very end of her life she remained an emotionally and intellectually restless master of open form. In the choice and treatment of subject, *Kivi südamelt* also reflects the Christian fervor and philosophical, symbol-laden character of her late work. Under started producing political poetry under the Soviet and Nazi occupations (1940–41 and 1941–44) and, escaping from the second Soviet occupation to Sweden in the autumn of 1944, she continued to write it there. She showed remarkable mastery as a committed writer, working with precision and tension, but without calling the Nazis or Soviets by name; and although strongly tied in her dramatic nature lyrics to her native soil, she never even mentioned the name of her beloved Estonia in any of her poems. Under's Christian attitudes kept her from becoming overly nationalistic, but her late verse has especially captured Estonian hearts and minds because it is the essence of her own humane patriotism, sense of right, and inward serenity.

One of Under's finest collections is her last book, *Ääremail* (1963; In the borderlands), in which her metaphysical insight and symbolism found its final, somber, philosophical tonality. She fulfilled her task in her hours of gloom, showing again the true power of introspection and passion. She was a master of both inductive and deductive thinking, but throughout her life her verse was persuasive essentially because all of it is permeated with lyrical flow.

Under was active as a critic primarily in the 1920s; her especial interest at the time was modernist theater. Later, and until her death, her sympathies in the arts lay more with Beethoven's music and El Greco's paintings. She was exceedingly active as a verse and prose translator, rendering twenty-six major works into Estonian, starting with Goethe and Schiller and ending with Pär Lagerkvist and Boris Pasternak. She never imposed her own diction on any of her renderings, but tried to follow precisely the outer structure and integral style of the original.

Under's popularity and reputation are constantly growing, and she is regarded as the foremost Estonian lyric and lyrophilosophical poet of the twentieth century. As such, her achievements complement those of her follower Betti Alver, Estonia's leading intellectual poet.

> Aleksis Rannit. In Steven R. Serafin and
> Walter D. Glanze, eds. *Encyclopedia of
> World Literature in the 20th Century* (New
> York: Continuum, 1993), pp. 505–6

UNDSET, SIGRID (NORWAY) 1882–1949

Jenny has been labeled immoral by some reviewers, probably because an illegitimate child appears in it, and Jenny Winge, the heroine, is loved by her fiancé's father. But the sad fact about Jenny Winge is that, in spite of undeniable appearances, she is stiffly and terrifyingly moral, if morality means having high ideals and going as far as death because they can't be lived up to. . . .

Jenny is not one of Sigrid Undset's best books. It is too rigid, too full of fine-spun agonies. If humor is defined as a lack of the sense of proportion, then it fails by being humorless. It seems to justify ever so little those who speak about Norwegian gloom. And yet there is in it so much ability to ensnare visual beauty and so many wise and delicate perceptions that one must hope for translations of Sigrid Undset's maturer works.

> Signe Toksvig. *The New Republic.*
> October 5, 1921, pp. 165–66

Sigrid Undset is a capable writer. She knows how to tell a tale engagingly, and her present narrative of Viking life in old Norway is entertaining enough. Yet *The Bridal Wreath* is not unusual in substance or in form and its technique is time honored. It is the type of book which, once read, is put on the shelves for good or taken off only to make room for another novel. That the ripples created by it in the vast ocean of novels should reach the shores of America is amazing.

The Nation. August 22, 1923, p. 200

With *The Cross,* Sigrid Undset completes her remarkable trilogy of medieval Norway, the first two volumes of which, *The Bridal Wreath* and *The Mistress of Husaby,* had brought the heroine to the threshold of middle age. Kristin Lavransdatter is in no sense an epic character, a symbolic figure such as we have come to expect from modern Scandinavian authors. Her development from waywardness and caprice to steadfastness in the face of misfortune, from intolerance to mellowness, is a not unusual human phenomenon, and it is described without recourse to the glamour which the period of the novel might well have afforded to a more romantic novelist. The work glows with a finer light than those flashes thrown off by romanticized history. The theme of the book is the illusion of earthly happiness; the illusion of happiness chased through a thousand sins and desires, disappointments and rallyings, to be relinquished at last, almost with a sigh of relief, in the serenity of at least one conviction: that no dream worth anything to the spirit of man can ever be realized.

It is this theme, tragic in the noblest sense, which Sigrid Undset plays upon Kristin Lavransdatter as upon an instrument. To carry the metaphor further, we might liken the trilogy to a concerto, Kristin being the solo instrument against a background of the full orchestra. And from that point of view, the work is well orchestrated; the writer handles the world of personalities which she calls into being to accompany Kristin with clarity and verisimilitude. . . .

Sigrid Undset's method is devoid of shrillness and dramatization. She writes patiently, and she must be read patiently. She never once rattles the stage thunder of history; though the transition period between paganism and Christianity in Scandinavia was thunderous enough. . . .

In view of this positive, or objective, quality, I find it regrettable that the translator feels called upon to "poeticize" the style of the book. In any prose such fancy contractions as *'twas* and *o'er* are out of place. In a work as straightforward and sinewy as *The Cross,* they are more than a little annoying.

Robert Hillyer. *The New Republic.*
June 8, 1927, p. 79

Sigrid Undset here [*The Axe*] gives us the first volume of her second trilogy, a sufficient proof that she does not take the novelist's calling lightly. Like her previous *magnum opus, Kristin Lavransdatter, The Axe* presents Norway in the Middle Ages with an intimacy of psychological and physical detail that reminds one of Balzac. It may at least be said that no one to whom Balzac's method is repugnant will enjoy a book in which the salient events are few, and the minutiæ abundant and predominantly disagreeable.

It is on the courage of truth, not on the seduction of beauty, that Sigrid Undset bases her appeal. She has realized her people, major and minor, with an energy that leaves us unable to doubt them and, furthermore, she has realized them as individuals. In this respect we are reminded less of Balzac than of George Eliot and Sheila Kaye-Smith. The result in connection with her antique background is both disturbing and stimulating. . . .

It may have been gathered that, despite its sordidness, there is a bracing quality in the novel as a whole. Such is decidedly the case. The landscape backgrounds are done with fine sympathy and reserve. The picture of medieval Norwegian life and customs is most interesting, particularly in the complicated legal questions that arise as to blood-money, marriage tithes, etc. These are skillfully woven into the main story. In fact, so complete is the representation that on laying down the book one has to rub one's eyes in order to be sure than one is in modern America, not on the estate of an ancient Norwegian baron.

Charles Wharton Stork. Saturday Review of
Literature. June 2, 1928, p. 930

I think no one can fail to recognize Sigrid Undset as one of the greatest of living writers. One might question just why so great a talent should choose to express itself through the pageant of medieval Norway, for there have been few great historical romances. But a reading of the book stills the question. Man at odds with fate is an eternal figure. The most variable element is the name and form of fate. Moreover, a historical romance is a term loosely used. Often it seems to be applied rather because a story is inadequately realized than because it is set in an earlier day than the writer's. *War and Peace* and *Don Quixote* both antedated their authors some but they are too intolerably real to seem to us "historical." Their authors were more interested in their characters than in a stained-glass past. And so is Sigrid Undset. Although she reproduces medieval Norway in all the rich pageantry of color and form, although she spares us neither sounds nor smells, her story also is intolerably real. She can transport us eight centuries and several thousand miles more effectively than most writers can take us into the house next door.

The Snake Pit is the second in a tetrology of novels called "The Master of Hestviken." *The Axe* preceded it and it will apparently be followed by *In the Wilderness* and *The Son Avenger.* I am not quite able to say why this second book interests me less than *The Axe.* Perhaps one can feel only once the first fine enthusiasm over the discovery of a new writer of the first rank, and afterward one settles down to a more humdrum enjoyment. . . .

And yet under the irritation we see that two superb portraits are slowly emerging from the painful pages. Sigrid Undset succeeds marvelously in projecting character in the round, with every fleeting shade added to make the elusive whole.

Alice Beal Parsons. The Nation.
March 13, 1929, pp. 316–17

In her latest novel Sigrid Undset completes her monumental tetralogy "The Master of Hestviken." The volumes in the order of their appearance are: *The Axe, The Snake Pit, In the Wilderness,* and *The Son Avenger.*

No proper estimate of this work should overlook Mrs. Undset's stride from a *succès d'estime* to a very high order of general popularity in America. She has, within five or six years, risen from a writer whom nobody read and somebody appreciated to one whom many will read whether they appreciate her accomplishment or not. The award of the Nobel Prize for Literature in 1928 had something to do with this, but less, perhaps, than appears on the surface.

For, possessing a style which is so effortless as to appear no style at all, narrowing her delineation of character down to a chiaroscuro of simple action and superficial description—employing, in other words, the most primitive and time-honored of all the devices of the story-teller—she is able to create an atmosphere and a sensation of power. This old method, in a period satiated with the new, the super-analytical, and the exotic, appears marvelously fresh and original. And to say that it *is* fresh is only to remark that the grace of simplicity is perennial.

She writes of the North countries in their heroic age, and it is difficult to see how any other place but the North could have produced her. The lapse from drama into lethargy, the slow accumulation of passions, the towering melancholies producing their own sense of predestination—all these are reflections of a brooding winter land. *The Son Avenger* brings out her method and temperament very clearly. It is a less graceful story than *The Axe,* and also far less gracious. In it, the storm of the whole tetralogy rises to a final height of blood and thunder. But is also contains some of the author's finest descriptive writing. And it is a fitting climax to a dramatic whole.

Eugene Löhrke. The Nation.
September 10, 1930, pp. 273–74

The difficulty with reporting on Sigrid Undset's *The Wild Orchid* is that it is so obviously the first half of a two-part novel that any decision on it will have to be tentative. It is full of excellences, but all the lives and situations in it are held suspended at the end. . . .

If this novel is somewhat disappointing to those who admired Sigrid Undset's great books of mediæval Norway, it may be because she has conceded too much to our age. *Kristin Lavransdatter* and *The Master of Hestviken* are epic dramas of conscience. But sin, repentance and redemption are hard words for the twentieth-century tongue; we use them awkwardly or without conviction when speaking about our contemporaries. Fru Undset knows this, and has either hesitated to confront us with them or has herself felt that they were out of key. As a consequence *The Wild Orchid* has not the intensity of her mediæval sagas; but it is possible that its sequel, *The*

Burning Bush, which must inevitably treat of Paul's conversion to Roman Catholicism, may bring the completed novel back into the true Undset line.

Dorothea Brande. *The Bookman.*
December 31, 1931, pp. 466–67

Considered with *The Wild Orchid,* to which it is the sequel, *The Burning Bush* must take an honored place among the world's most tedious works of fiction. Specifically, these two volumes are made up of approximately three hundred and fifty thousand words conveying information about the life of Paul Selmer, a Catholic, the son of well-to-do, liberal, divorced parents. The episodes the author selects from Paul's career for particular emphasis are his unhappy love affair with a girl of the lower classes, his religious conversion, his unhappy marriage, and the complicated troubles resulting from innocent meetings with his former mistress.

The two books are also conscious propaganda for the Catholic faith. In comparison with their other departments, the propaganda is the best part of them; that is, the propaganda *for* Catholicism is much more interesting and much more intelligently conveyed than the propaganda *against* so many other things—against liberalism, the Protestants, against communism, divorce, spiritualism. Sigrid Undset has one major objection, apparently, to everything in life which is not Catholic; her reason for objecting, by a beautiful logic, is that these things are not Catholic, and consequently they are works of the devil. She is militant; she is direct; she is willing to make her position on these matters clear if she has to repeat it on every page for eight hundred and seventy-eight pages. And so she does.

There is another little twist to the propaganda which enlivens the last two hundred thousand words—enlivens it provided you are interested in studying the ways in which propaganda is or is not effective. It is all, evidently, propaganda for the lesser evil. . . .

There is very little more in this long book. There were a few good character sketches in *The Wild Orchid*—that of Paul's mother was very good—but even so slight a reward for the industrious reader is omitted from the second volume. There would be no point in reviewing the book at all if it were not that it is the work of Sigrid Undset, who once won the Nobel Prize and is a distinguished writer whose name commands a certain respect from those who have never read her works. . . .

The weakness of the author's point of view is evident in the excessive length of these two books. They are long, not because the material demands such exhaustive treatment, but because the author repeats herself so frequently: it is as though she were conscious of the weakness of her case, and so repeats herself because she fears she will not be understood or believed.

Robert Cantwell. *The Nation.*
September 21, 1932, pp. 263–64

Ida Elisabeth [in Undset's novel of that title,] marries a man of the infantile type and gives herself over to his family, a weak lot who depend more and more upon her to face realities for them. Frithjof, the husband, cannot hold a job, and Ida must keep a little dressmaking shop. Of four children, two are lost. The excuse for divorcing Frithjof is so sufficient that even the family cannot deny it. In another village Ida provides her sons with a secure home. But even when her own most legitimate desire as a woman is to be satisfied, by marriage with Tryggve the lawyer, she can rationalize herself into repeating the sacrifice, this time that her children may not suffer. The book has body, and Sigrid Undset's descriptive force is quiet and sound as ever. She has the power to give any human life of which she writes a rich detail, which in its turn makes her moral qualities all the more persuasive. Nevertheless, at certain turns in the present story, her moralizing gives rise to writing best described as stuffy.

The New Republic. December 6, 1933, p. 112

An agnostic in her school days, unable to affirm even disbelief, she came into the Catholic Church through perceiving that a stable moral system is impossible with[out] the premise of revealed religion. Fidelity between man and woman simply cannot be, she says bluntly, apart from an ideal which demands fidelity. "But true to a man—no, I don't believe any woman can be that." Therefore, she concludes: "We have no right to assume that any part of European tradition, cultural values, moral ideas, emotional wealth, which has its origin in the dogmatically defined Christianity of the Catholic Church, will continue to live a 'natural' life if the people of Europe reject Christianity and refuse to accept God's supernatural grace."

Many of the legends of the saints she admits arose for much the same reason that today people make up legends about film stars. And on heresy her pithy epigram is: "It is not doubt which makes a man a heretic, but belief." From such pungencies *Stages on the Road* derives its refreshingly tart flavor, as its charm flows from Sigrid Undset's gallant spirit and poetic feeling.

Theodore Maynard. *Saturday Review of
Literature.* October 20, 1934, p. 12

Just why the publishers term this book [*The Longest Years*] a novel is difficult to understand, for despite its paraphernalia of fictional names it is straight autobiography. Miss Undset, of course, exercises the novelist's art of selection, choosing her incident with effectiveness and shaping it so as to achieve dramatic emphasis, but her background, her personalities, her happenings are all from her own experience, the emotional crises of her chronicle take on poignance from remembered delight or bitterness, and the narrative gains intensity from the sincerity of its feeling for the figures which live in its pages.

Miss Undset has sketched in it such a childhood as knows no radical differences wherever it is lived,—a childhood passed in pleasant places, wisely guarded and abundantly warmed by parental love, rich in simple plea-

sures, given purpose by simple duties, and invested with the delight of untrammeled companionship with the young and the gay. And always in the
background the elders appear, good people who faced life with earnestness
and integrity, with enough of intellectual distinction to lend vivacity to the
interests of their children and enough of the Scandinavian love for nature to
give them frequent opportunity for mountain or seaside holiday. Among them
the child Sigrid, or Ingvald, moves with the passionate interest in life and
people which later found reflection in her tales.

> Amy Loveman. *Saturday Review of*
> *Literature.* October 26, 1935, p. 15

Gunnar's Daughter . . . takes its place among her minor works but shines
there with a firm and natural light. As she tells the story of how the lovers,
Vigdis and Viga-Ljot, destroyed each other in their pride she seems to be
entirely ignorant that there are such things in writing as tricks. This happened, then that; and such and such things were said quite in the order
imposed by impartial time. By the end, however, a definite and distinguished
tragedy has taken shape and half a dozen persons have lived lives which
were both individual and intelligible. How one tells such a story is probably
not to be known except by those who can do it; and they do not talk to their
readers. Sigrid Undset probably could not enumerate the measures she took
to keep her feud from being squalid or her lovers from being pettish. Everything manages to be large in her story, no single word of which escapes from
her hysterically or self-consciously. The reason must be that she is a novelist;
that she is content to write in the tradition of novelists; and that what she
has to say she knows how to say in terms of events which appear to have
nothing whatever to do with herself.

> Mark van Doren. *The Nation.*
> August 1, 1936, p. 135

This is a novel [*The Faithful Wife*] with a rich Scandinavian background,
human, penetrating, and neither didactic nor argumentative. It is a family
story in which not only are very interesting people made interesting, but also
their life, summer and winter, country and city. Beyond and behind the intense drama of marriage and divorce, is this realized Scandinavian existence,
which in itself, as with Undset's historical novels, is worth the price of admission. But the wife's emotional problems, which might be any wife's anywhere,
keep this book from being, like too many American regional novels, a study
in description and behaviorism.

> Henry Seidel Canby. *Saturday Review of*
> *Literature.* October 9, 1937, p. 14

Even in her minor efforts, among which this [*Images in a Mirror*] should
doubtless be classed, Mrs. Undset is both penetrating and wise. Her heroine
is a woman who neglects the current business of her husband and children

for vain regrets over an abandoned career. Mrs. Undset manages to bring her back home in time with an appealing but not oppressive little sermon for all such ladies.

The New Yorker. August 27, 1938, p. 58

This novel of eighteenth-century Norway is primarily a character portrait of a deeply human and courageous woman, [the title character,] Madame Dorthea, who finds her life beginning to fall to pieces when her husband disappears. Nothing Sigrid Undset writes lacks distinction, but this must be placed among her lesser books. It has some fine passages, particularly in the second half, but is somewhat dull, with a confusing narrative line and an array of characters who seem too numerous and complexly related.

The New Yorker. August 3, 1940, p. 52

Sigrid Undset provides that thing rare in Europe and anti-Nazi literature—the background of a good world that is not of the future. In her book, the Nazis have to stand up to Norway and one of the products of that admirable and successful democracy, Miss Undset herself. They suffer by the comparison. Sigrid Undset is thoroughly at ease in the liberalism and natural internationalism that are the reflections of her whole country's attitude. She simply cannot help being sane and sensible. "To ordinary healthy and normal Norwegians," she complains, rather exasperated, "the whole National Socialist ideology is so alien." . . .

At the back, there is always Norway. Without saying very much, Sigrid Undset drives home the senselessness and indecency of invading a country whose very values were useless to the invaders. A few bases and some salt fish were the Nazi estimate of a country that had quietly achieved a pattern of life which is still in the pre-blueprint stage in most of the democracies. "We," says Miss Undset, "had learned by experience that it is possible to live quite well in a poor country if industry, forethought, reciprocal helpfulness enter into the effort to make the most possible out of all sources of livelihood. Our state economy was, accordingly, a thoughtfully developed, fine, sensitive mechanism; after a year of German power it has practically gone to . . . ruin."

The strength of Sigrid Undset and the effectiveness of her book lie in the fact that hers is not the voice of an isolated high-minded individual, but that of her country. The Norwegians doubted that they would ever have to fight. When they were confronted by howling divisions munching cocaine-filled chocolate bars, the Norwegians may not have known what they were fighting against. But they knew what they were fighting for—a *status quo* that had a present as well as a future.

Sybille Bedford. *The New Republic.*
March 2, 1942, p. 40

This, [*Sigurd and his Brave Companions*] like everything Madame Undset writes, has a certain distinction, but it is one of her less successful tries. The adventures of three little boys in thirteenth-century Norway are too diffuse to be very satisfactory to American children. The stained-glass medieval background, on the other hand, is beautifully done.

The New Yorker. December 4, 1943, p. 130

Sigrid Undset's writing takes its place as one of the truly remarkable phenomena in the literature of the twentieth century. She is, wrote a Swedish critic in 1927, the year before she received the Nobel prize, one of the very few contemporary authors of whom one may well use the adjective "great." That is no exaggeration. In scarcely any of her contemporaries do we find human life treated with comparable breadth of vision and depth of insight. In her thought and imagination, subjects from the present and from distant times are touched by the same convincing assurance and creative power. On her stage she presents characters from the Middle Ages who are as much alive as any of her creations from the present. "I am one who has lived two thousand years in this land" was her remark on a recent ceremonial occasion, with a playful reference to the famous reply of the Government minister, Skogstad, in Gunnar Heiberg's play *I Shall Defend My Country* (*Jeg vil verge mit land*). Sigrid Undset has no relish for the pathetic style, least of all when speaking of herself, but here there was no reserve. Two thousand years—why, it was self-evident! She is in fact not only contemporary with her own time but also with the past, with history. In 1909, two years after her first book *Mrs. Marta Oulie* (*Fru Marta Oulie*), a story of married life in an Oslo setting of the most palpable everyday reality, she published *The Story of Viga-Ljot and Vigdis* (*Fortællingen om Viga-Ljot og Vigdis*), a historical novel set in the period at the end of the tenth century. Both books were magnificently alive. An interviewer asked her how it was that she had come to write about characters from such remote times. "One can only write novels about one's own contemporary world" was her answer. . . .

Sigrid Undset is the Christian realist *par excellence*. More than any other writer she gathers together the threads of the European realist tradition. Her writing has grown organically out of the powerful presentation of everyday reality which we meet in the nineteenth-century novel and which is the essence of literary realism.

A. H. Winsnes. *Sigrid Undset: A Study in Christian Realism* (1954; rpt. Westport, Connecticut: Greenwood Press, 1990), pp. 7, 8

At first sight Catherine of Siena would seem a strange choice for the pen of Sigrid Undset. Whether one thinks of her in the unearthly loveliness of Andrea Vanni's great portrait, or in the heaven-storming aspirations of her own *Dialogue,* or in the brilliant legend still haunting the magic settings: Papal

Avignon and her own Siena, this most exquisite of ecstatics would hardly seem the appropriate subject for one of the most robust and realistic talents ever to pierce the medieval. . . [frame] of the modern romancer. Sigrid Undset's Catherine is certainly a more startling and even at times disconcerting personality than the usual vision of hagiography, but it is easier to believe that this woman did do the things that Catherine historically did. The great medievalist's effort to present her heroine in her daily habit as she lived in her particular world of time and place, and all too human humanity, has resulted in a portrait at once more full-blooded and, surprisingly, more edifying than the traditional image. . . .

It is this extraordinary sense of Catherine "hovering on two wings . . . over the abyss between time and eternity," which gives Sigrid Undset's passionate realism such persuasiveness in the very remarkable book, finished not long before her own death.

Helen C. White. *Commonweal.*
August 6, 1954, pp. 444–46

What is a little masterpiece? Little in subject, or in quality, or in size? Too often and quite wrongly we drift into the latter assumption. So let us avoid all equivocation and state that these four stories by Sigrid Undset are masterpieces—big ones. Certainly they are big in subject, for they deal with the deepest of human passions, with diurnal and endured tragedy; certainly they are fine in quality, for they are written with a compassionate heart and a deceptively simple-seeming hand; certainly they are not very long—I would say gracefully long, around the fifty-page mark, a very satisfactory length.

Sigrid Undset has that rare ability of bringing you materially into touch with her characters in a few lines with few words, into touch and almost touching. One is reminded of the essence of Joyce of *The Dubliners,* or of Katherine Mansfield at her least whimsical. . . .

At times the reader may suspect that this writer is something of a blue stocking who has never come to terms with the black silk stocking—yet she constantly retrieves herself, and one is left with the feeling that she knows all about everything. At only one point does the note of compassion fail: when she gets her teeth into a big, open-air, hearty bully of a woman booming with terrible cheerfulness. Suddenly no sympathy here at all. It is only terribly funny, and malignant and pitiless. Yet from the pen of a woman whose honesty, tenderness, compassion, and artistry are otherwise deeply moving and of the finest order.

William Sanson. *The Saturday Review of*
Literature. April 18, 1959, p. 42

The themes of Sigrid Undset's novels and essays are remarkably limited. As a woman as well as an author she has a deeply committed social awareness. She believes in the old virtues of wisdom, justice, truth, mercy, moderation, and above all loyalty and a sense of responsibility. Loyalty is reflected first of all in man's relationship to the family unit, the pivot of society, for Sigrid Undset believes in the sanctity of marriage and the inviolability of the home. As she sees it, most men and women look upon loyalty as the most precious possession they have; others with their restless hearts are incapable of loyalty and are forced to suffer the tragic fate of isolation and loneliness in a godless world. A. H. Winsnes writes: "It is the capacity for loyalty in men and women which is put to the test. The conflict of conscience which results from disloyalty—the conscience tormented with the conscience saved—is the theme which constantly recurs. For this reason, her writing revolves around the central relationships in life in which loyalty is demanded, whether a pact must be kept or service rendered—between husband and wife, parents and children, the individual and his home, family and country.

As a deep religious faith was added to her moral idealism and ethical convictions Sigrid Undset raised this concept of loyalty into a higher sphere. With Christianity a new significance was given to man's position in a supernatural world of the spirit. . . . A violation of his code of honor is a wrong against society, but beyond that it is also a sin in the face of God. Often a conflict arises in man's mind between the longing to do God's will and the desire to follow his self-will. In *Olav Audunssön* Sigrid Undset tells of the battle that has been waged in the universe since the beginning of time between God and His enemies. Every human being must take part in this struggle on one side or the other, for man has been given the free will to choose between loyalty and disloyalty and must therefore serve God or break the pact made with Him.

Such is the nature of the dramatic struggle waged by Olav Audunssön and Kristin Lavransdatter. Both are proud protagonists who may not always have lived in the light, but who nevertheless have never repudiated life. It takes them both a lifetime of struggle and suffering before they learn how to find satisfaction in accepting the full burden of their responsibilities and it is only at the very threshold of death itself that they finally submit in self-surrender to a spiritual authority. Every aspect of their lives is brought into harmony with their religious development, for to the medieval mind everything in the world was ultimately dependent on God.

Sigrid Undset as a devout Christian knows that religion can never become outmoded. The plight of modern man is no different from that of medieval man six hundred years ago, and the message of the Church has as much relevance today as it did then. The heroes and heroines of her contemporary novels are forced to wage the same battle as Kristin and Olav, even though not in such a dramatic or psychologically penetrating way.

Carl Bayerschmidt. Sigrid Undset (New
York: Twayne, 1970), pp. 158–59

After she received the Nobel Prize for Literature in 1928, Sigrid Undset was world-famous. Her books were translated into the major European languages and were best-sellers in Europe and the United States. But since here death in 1949, interest in Sigrid Undset has declined and very little critical attention has been given to her books.

Unlike many of her famous contemporaries—Proust, Mann, Joyce, Virginia Woolf—she used the conventional narrative form and experimented with no new literary techniques. This helps to account for her neglect in academic circles. Then there is her moral vision. In a recent anthology of women's fiction, a modern critic says, "Her religious worldview is an embarrassment to critics who have established that nihilism is the only accurate description of the way things are in the post-Christian era. Above all, her belief in the old virtues of loyalty, moderation and a sense of responsibility seems decidedly out of step in a narcissistic age." . . .

It would be gratifying to think that the recent publication of *Kristin Lavransdatter* in paperback (by Bantam) for the first time may signal a renewal of interest in Sigrid Undset. The neglect she has suffered, despite the reasons for it I suggested earlier, is surprising in an age of militant feminism, when obscure women artists—literary and otherwise—are being resurrected, and when women of high achievement are the focus of so much attention.

Surely Sigrid Undset ranks as a woman of high achievement. Her range as writer was vast, her knowledge of history and literature encyclopedic. In addition to *Kristin Lavransdatter* and *The Master of Hestviken,* the medieval epics which are her acknowledged masterpieces, she wrote seven novels set in contemporary Norway, another, *Madame Dorthea,* set in the eighteenth century, several volumes of short stories, translations of Icelandic sagas, as well as numerous articles, essays and book reviews. . . .

Sigrid Undset was a true novelist, not a religious propagandist, as is sometimes charged. But in her greatest works she concentrates on the individual's relationship to God and our eternal destinies. It is the material of tragedy—and divine comedy. To read one of them is to step into a world of truth and light.

Maura Boland. Commonweal.
November 7, 1980, pp. 620–21, 623

For Undset, who had lived her early adult life as an educated, emancipated and free-thinking young woman, sexuality alone, in isolation, is perhaps the only language which certain women, painfully inarticulate, know how to use with men. It is not that it is the best, or necessarily the most natural or obvious one, but simply that because such women are immature and insecure, they can find no other. They are not more, but rather less, womanly as a result of this incapacity, even if they are apparently more feminine. In her commonsense way, she see sexuality as a fact of life, and not as its "meaning and object" or as any more a liberating and enhancing experience than its concomitants of marriage, domestic commitments and family life. What she would see as the childish attributes of sexuality—a movement towards irresponsibility, the cult of the momentary sensation, the short-term relationship—are for her incomplete, unserious, unsatisfying. Stability is more important and, significantly, more desired and desirable. In her novels it is adult sexuality which is important and satisfying, because it is humanizing as it grows and matures. Sexual distractions are precisely that: irrelevant, escapist, pathetic. In her fictional world, sexuality must be consciously and willingly accepted, but it must be adult and related to the whole life. . . .

Undset's chief concern is to write about the daily lives of a number of intelligent, attractive and often thoughtful, but by no means extraordinary, men and women whose chief concern is to live their lives properly and in a way which will in all respects be as deeply satisfying as one can reasonably expect, with proper regard for their own nature and that of their fellow human beings, at peace with themselves and their neighbors.

J. C. Whitehouse. *Journal of European Studies.* 16, 1986, p. 17

Marta Oulie, Charlotte Hedels, Edele Hammer, Jenny Winge, Rose Wegener, Uni Hirsch, and Harriet Waage all gaze repeatedly at their own reflection, find the image too exquisite for such common surroundings, and wonder where the perfect "other" might be whose eyes will return the same idolatrous reflection they see. But the endings of their stories suggest several different levels of growth in self-knowledge, leading to different resolutions of the problem. Marta and Harriet, like Narcissus, experience erotic awakening, but are unable to fasten their desire on a suitable object. They love the image of themselves in love, but when that reflection takes on the ugly features of an adulteress they resign themselves to loss and despair. Edele and Jenny, who are bound by an inner vow of chastity until the "right" man should appear, in their loneliness and impatience succumb to men they do not love and then resort to suicide because they cannot live with the contaminated reflection they see. Rose and Edele, after surviving despair, discover that love is not their right, but their responsibility—something they must work for. They must stop waiting passively for validation from a heroic lover and work actively to love the vulnerable human being they have elected to their care. . . .

Undset was once asked whether she thought religion was just a substitute for sex. Her reply was, "No, I would say the opposite is true." This opinion, like many of her others, sounds notably less cranky and puzzling if we view it in a medieval mirror, rather than through the Freudian lens that has so massively altered our view of eroticism in this century.

Sherrill Harbison. *Scandinavian Studies.* 63, 1991, pp. 464–65, 472

Neo-Thomism seemed to confirm for Sigrid Undset all the conclusions about human nature she had already experienced in her life and so unflinchingly depicted in her fiction—the destructiveness of selfishness and the delusions of mortal love that blinds its victims to the inevitable disaster it will cause. The doctrine also called for the application of those principles not only to

the individual's life but to society at large, at a time when European civilization was worshiping Mammon, and totalitarianism had begun its tragic rise.
No European writer of the 1930s answered the neo-Thomist call to battle
more vehemently than did Sigrid Undset, insisting in novels, speeches and
essays that dogmatic Catholic authoritarianism must replace postwar materialism if society was to survive. . . .

In one area, however, Sigrid Undset "managed to shake off . . . the
narrower aspects of a purely Catholic dogma in the interests of a more inclusive, universal Christian view," the peak of her spiritual growth. *Stages on
the Road* (1934), her retellings of the self-sacrificing loves of Catholic married
saints, humanely demonstrates that speedy martyrdom may be far less demanding than the day-to-day struggle to live in obedience to God's laws. In
Men, Women and Places (1938), she went surprisingly further, declaring her
unanimity of spirit with none other than D. H. Lawrence, whom she called
"a visionary and a poet of genius." Perhaps alone of her generation, Undset
fully understood the difference between Lawrence's preaching and prophetic aspects.

Mitzi M. Brunsdale. *Religion and Literature.*
23:3, 1991, pp. 93–94

UNO CHIYO (JAPAN) 1897–

Although Chiyo produced quite a few short stories and essays in the first ten
years of her career, it was not until 1933 that she published her first significant
work, a novel entitled *Confession of Love* (*Iro Zange*). Chiyo had in the
meantime dissolved her five-year marriage with Ozaki Shirō, her second husband, and started quite a different life with Tōgō Seiji, a well-known painter
who had lived in France for many years and who had once been involved in
a sensational double suicide attempt. The couple met when Chiyo visited
Tōgō to interview him about the suicide attempt—she was writing a novel
with a double suicide scene and needed information. The next day, they
decided to live together. The novel *Confession of Love,* which established
Chiyo as a serious writer, is largely based on the suicide story Tōgō told
Chiyo. Although Chiyo characteristically made a self-effacing statement that
if the work was any good it was because of Seiji's skillful narration, it stands
out as one of the finest novels treating the theme of love written in the pre-
World War II period. . . .

Chiyo has written repeatedly about herself, hinting at secrets of her long,
successful life and career. In a short but revealing story called "Happiness"
(*Kōfuku,* 1971; tr. 1982), the narrator, a thinly disguised Chiyo, says that she
can find pleasure in things that might appear odd to other people; standing
in front of the mirror, naked after her bath, she sees, with the help of her

failing eyes, a body resembling Botticelli's Venus. In such a way she collects "fragments of happiness one after another." Like this narrator, Chiyo knows that satisfaction comes from pursuing the objects of her affection; she feels she has achieved independence from the world of disquieting affairs.

Uno Chiyo's inner strength and integration of life and art sustained her over many decades of writing. The painstaking care with which she approached her craft distinguished her from other writers—though she modestly shrugged off such recognition. In 1977, when Chiyo turned eighty, the first of the twelve-volume collection of her works was published. She stated on this occasion that after nearly four decades, she still looked forward to more years of writing. She did indeed publish two more books in 1984, a testimony to her enduring dedication as an artist.

Yukiko Tanaka. *To Live and to Write:*
Selections by Japanese Women Writers
1913–1938 (Seattle: Seal Press, 1987),
pp. 185–88

Confessons of Love offers to readers both "a good read" and a fascinating study of the psychological interplay in the relationships of a "modern" Japanese woman with a "modern" Japanese man as well as a tantalizing glimpse at the nature of the modern love suicide. The quality of the translation is exceptional, and the work well deserves the Friendship Commission's Translation Prize for the Translation of Japanese Literature, which it was awarded. *Iro zange* (as the original was titled) was well received, and though the novelist has won several literary honors such as the Jōryū Bungaku Shō or Women's Literature Prize (twice), the Noma Hiroshi Prize, and the Art Academy Prize for her later books, it is still considered one of her most representative works.

Uno Chiyo, along with other women writers who were her contemporaries—Nogami Yaeko, Hayashi Fumiko, Miyamoto Yuriko, and Enchi Fumiko. . . to name just a few—participated in a renaissance of female authorship. These writers, whose works were and remain quite popular, have been undervalued by many critics as "female school literature" but have contributed extensively nonetheless to the development of modern Japanese literature. Uno Chiyo is, so to speak, like many of the writers in the mainstream of Japanese literature in that she unflinchingly examines the experiences of modern life and, with a penetrating sincerity and a profound intellectual capacity to understand that life and its implications, has created literature that contextualizes her vision both historically and socially while making an intensely personal and dynamic statement. Still, her books are a joy to read, no matter how perplexing, provocative, or frightening they may be at times.

Confessions of Love features a male narrator and protagonist. The author based the character and the plot on a highly publicized love-suicide attempt by the artist Tōgō Seiji, with whom Uno subsequently had a liaison of nearly five years. Part of the fascination of Uno's writing is founded on just such an interplay of autobiographical/biographical fact with the contrary demands of fiction and art. Rather than a realism which is after all the creation of an illusion of reality, writers like Uno are expected to create in the reader a sense of the authenticity of the human experience presented and the sincerity of the authorial voice that presents the story. Despite the basic unreliability of the narrator and main male character Yuasa Jōji, the reader harbors no doubt that the author has examined and knows from personal experience the allure and the dangers of this weak man, whose talent, neediness, and irresponsibility both enthrall and threaten to destroy the women who love him. Knowing the folly does not prevent the loving, as Chiyo herself was well aware.

Marilyn Jeanne Miller. *World Literature Today.* 63, 1989, pp. 742–43

Confessions of Love is Uno Chiyo's longest work and also one of her best known. It was an instant success when published serially in *Chūō kōron* in 1934–35 and as a book in 1935, partly because it was based on a sensational incident in 1929, the failed double suicide of the painter Tōgō Seiji. . . .

Although Uno says she wrote down exactly what Tōgō said, being a meticulous writer she must have carefully rearranged and re-created the story. Uno's format, in which both the male protagonist and the women are described through the words of the protagonist himself, is quite effective. She depicts Yuasa as a vain, frivolous, irresponsible man through his interactions with the women. This depiction could be a small measure of revenge against Tōgō, whom she divorced a short while later. The emotional and mental reactions of the women who fall for him, too, are skillfully described through the eyes of Yuasa. Individual differences aside, all three women are alike in defying social conventions. They are eager to break away from the old virtue of submission to authority. In this sense, this is a genre novel, depicting the historical age of Taishō democracy, when progressive women tried to assert their rights by fighting for the improvement of their role in society. These women were called "modern girls," or *moga* for short.

Uno herself was known to be one of the *moga* and that is probably why she treats these unconventional women with empathy. They resemble the author herself in their impulsiveness and reckless passion. It is interesting to note that Uno has little sympathy for Yuasa's wife, who should be allowed at least a little pity for having such a thoughtless husband. . . .

[Uno] had more lovers and husbands than any other woman writer, and she came to be know as a master writer of love, or even "lust," stories. Many of her stories were drawn from the emotional experiences of her own love life. With each love lost, writing became her salvation from experience. . . .

At age ninety-one Uno not only still writes but also carries on a tradition of successful iconoclasm. Her works are windows onto a rich and beguiling world.

Yoko McClain. *Journal of Asian Studies.* 48, 1989, pp. 881–82

Uno's other occupations allowed perspective, and, more important, permitted her the freedom to pursue her art unencumbered by financial considerations. And so, aside from all her other accomplishments—kimono designer, magazine editor, and village head—her writing will be her legacy. "What I write today I want to be better than what I wrote yesterday. I'll do what I can to go on living, and while I'm alive I'll work with all my might. Death'll be the final stop."

That final stop will invite a new assessment of Uno's art and contributions. She will most likely not be counted among the major writers in the literary pantheon; she lacks the breadth of a Natsume Sōseki, or the poetry of a Kawabata Yasunari. But then, Uno never really intended to be a literary heavyweight. Dreams of such magnitude were beyond the realm of imagination for women of her generation. Even those who did approach writing with more apparent seriousness will have a difficult time finding a place alongside the likes of Sōseki and Kawabata. Women's writing at the time was simply not accorded the same value as men's. Women who did "attempt the pen" were regarded more as anomalies than as serious writers, and more often than not they were thought to be slightly scandalous.

But Uno very cleverly manipulated the prejudice and suspicion that surrounded intelligent, outspoken women during the early twentieth century. She subverted the status quo and used her femaleness to her advantage by turning what the world saw as scandal into personal profit. "No one is as fortunate as a woman writer!" she could exclaim with little hesitancy. And of her propitious debut in the literary world she acknowledged: "I now feel lucky, being born a woman." In part Uno's disclaimers are traditional modesty. She worked hard and often under less than encouraging conditions to achieve recognition. Moreover, she surprised her peers, and perhaps herself as well, by becoming in later years a significant writer and one extremely proud of her craft. Once she lost the aura of femme fatale and gained an appreciation of herself as "a woman whose sense of purpose comes from within," the works she produced were beyond compare. "The Puppet Maker," *Ohan*, "Happiness," *Story of a Certain Woman Alone*, and many others will remain as lasting testaments to her talent. These stories are artfully told and beautifully crafted and will remind all who read them of the resiliency and subtlety of Japanese literature. And Uno Chiyo will long be remembered for her zestful optimism and for her unfailing passion for life and love and art.

Rebecca L. Copeland. *The Sound of the Wind: The Life and Works of Uno Chiyo* (Honolulu: University of Hawaii Press, 1992), pp. 84–85

Born in 1897, the Japanese writer Uno Chiyo (sometimes called Chiyo Uno in the West) grew up at a time when "respect men, despise women" was a common dictum in Japan. Ms. Uno, however, flouted such conservative teachings and lived with verve. She took lovers and left them, married three times and supported herself with a variety of pursuits, including publishing a fashion magazine, designing kimonos and, above all, writing about her life and loves. After reading the engaging biography *The Sound of the Wind,* by Rebecca L. Copeland, who teaches Asian literature at Washington University in St. Louis, one is eager to read her translations of three stories in the second half of the book. Yet, unfortunately, many readers will find Ms. Copeland's account of the writer's life far more interesting than Ms. Uno's work, even though the translations are excellent. "The Puppet Maker," based on Ms. Uno's friendship with an octogenarian craftsman, is repetitious and plotless. "The Sound of the Wind," a complex tale of a husband's infidelity, becomes unintentionally hilarious to the modern-day Western reader as the submissive young wife forgives and endures increasingly flagrant indiscretions. The final story, "This Powder Box," is a first-person account of Ms. Uno's life with a lover. His first wife comes to visit, and the author writes, "It is strange, but if he had told me that she and I would have to live together, I believe I could have managed it." These stories reveal the ambivalence she must have felt about herself, driven to take risks yet wanting also to conform to the accepted standards of behavior for Japanese women.

Elizabeth Hanson. *The New York Times.*
September 20, 1992, p. 47

Uno Chiyo, born in 1897, attributes her long life to having lived "just the way I wanted to"; that is to say, recklessly. *The Story of a Single Woman,* which its translator refers to as an "'I-novel', a distinctly Japanese form, not fiction but not strictly autobiography either," takes Uno Chiyo, alias Kazue, from infancy to 1930. We leave her at a moment of characteristic impulsiveness, moving in with a painter whose failed suicide pact with another lover has caused a recent scandal.

Alone in his house, the blood that Kazue finds still caking the quilt and the distant sound of the wind transport her back to 1913. Her dying father, crawling forward over windswept snow, frightening off helpers, is coughing blood. This image, springing to mind at a pivotal moment, makes her question, at least in retrospect, whether falling in love with the painter is just a way of following in her father's self-destructive footsteps.

Kazue's hard and headstrong father is certainly a presence to be reckoned with. In the novella entitled *The Sound of the Wind,* his compliant wife views his passion for horses and for his mistress in a romantic, forgiving light. Kazue's insistence that she never resented her father's autocratic treatment is in similar admiring-doormat vein.

Among her father's child-rearing ploys was to call Uno Chiyo "Blackie," assuring her that men dislike dark-complexioned women. His death, and her teenage discovery of the dramatic changes to be wrought with white face powder, enabled her to burst forth as "a tree peony in full bloom."

Emboldened by her mask and the elegant clothes she was good at contriving, she embarked on her dual, entwined career as *femme fatale* and writer. She relinquished the former, with some regret and relief, in her sixties, but maintains the latter into her nineties. As a sideline she ran a fashion magazine and still has a kimono shop.

Quite how she has been able to flout so many of the restrictions imposed on Japanese women and still be honored with the Third Order of the Sacred Treasure and be named a Person of Cultural Merit is something of a wonder. Writing, she claims, was simply a way of making more money than she had as a teacher, seamstress or waitress. But it also became a form of endless reshaping and re-evaluation of her own eventful life, with its volatile mixture of passion, waywardness and submission.

However breezily she may have started as a writer, the fine, fleeting lightness of her mature style, with its appearance of guileless candor, is as much suggestive of painstaking craft, skillfully disguised, as of naïvety. A European writer with whom she is in some way comparable, although less steely, is Marguerite Duras.

Several recurring threads—the mask-like face, the man worthy of respect, the crafted expression of feeling—are drawn together in the novella *The Puppet Maker*. In 1942, Uno Chiyo happened upon a puppet carved for an old, tragic *bunraku* play. Of this encounter, she writes: "As I gazed at the puppet I felt implicit in her face the very depths of a woman's sorrow, and I grew curious about the person who had carved her."

Accordingly, she set off to interview the eighty-five-year-old Yoshioka Kyukichi. Finding him still busy in the workshop he had occupied for sixty years, she settled to listen over a period of ten days. His unaffected account of himself, quickened by comments about the subtle interventions of art within a strictly traditional craft, make magical reading.

Ruth Pavey. *New Statesman and Society.*
November 27, 1992, p. 43

VALENZUELA, LUISA (ARGENTINA) 1938–

El gato eficaz (The efficacious cat) a novel by the Argentinean Luisa Valenzuela, opens up a transgressive fissure in the ethical-aesthetic tradition, one that goes beyond destructive boundaries by achieving a constructive mutability, a renovative virtuality, the sign of the literature of modernity. By joyfully and actively confronting death, the narrator and protagonist devotes herself to cultivating a vital nihilism against the paralyzing Christian morality of the West, and a parodic critique of its defensive bulwarks. The text and its narrator are dissociated from cultural norms and are committed to change, a characteristic of an essentially modern attitude. . . . Metamorphosis—relativity and alterity—proposes to rescue man from the sclerosis and slavery of tradition.

The incarnation of this principle of rupture, the protagonist is female, a violator of all taboos, who spreads fear and horror in men so that they can save themselves from an empty "dogslife." An accomplice of the symbolic cats of death, she sows the turbulent and changing clairvoyance of mortality. . : .

Valenzuela's novel implies a "violent rupture of the old order" and maintains the necessity of the "establishment of a more just and rational social order." . . . But, etymologically, revolution means the "turning of worlds and stars," circular time, the eternal return of the past, of the mythic. Valenzuela breaks with the most immediate tradition—the historic—and searches in anthropological roots; she returns to the old question of continuity and discontinuity, of life and death. In this search, she has encountered the imperceptible music of eroticism.

Evelyn Picon Garfield. Insula. 400–401,
March–April 1980, pp. 17, 23

Unquestionably, one of the most characteristic qualities of Valenzuela's prose is the plurality to which Cortázar referred, for her work inevitably offers or demands a multiplicity of readings and interpretations. At times deceptively simple, always subtly political or feminist but never sententious, her prose rarely offers solutions to the problems it posits, for that is not her intent. Instead, her work examines life, reality, and our sociopolitical structures from different vantage points and in a variety of contexts in order to suggest new definitions or even a plurality of interpretations for situations not necessarily recognized as problematic. Much of the wealth and beauty of her writing rests in the fact that she often touches those areas and topics that are ostensibly irrefragable, already settled, or even taboo.

Her work continually undermines our social and political myths, but unlike so many writers with a political bent, Valenzuela steadfastly refuses to replace the old mythic structures with new but equally arbitrary and potentially equally authoritative substitutions. As she herself has noted, her works are not designed to imply that she alone knows the truth or the answers to the problems. Instead, she attempts to present situations in ways that subject them to different interpretations and possibly unique, more productive solutions, but again, the final diagnosis or cure for these social ills, if any exists, rests with the reader who must be actively involved in the text and also in life outside of the text. She hopes that the reader can discover some value in her words and do something about the predicaments which tyrannize contemporary life.

In this sense her work is characterized by an eternal search, always pursuing those uncharted truths which will necessarily challenge and redefine that absolute orthodox Truth (which, as Valenzuela insinuates, may well be a misnomer), which is so facilely accepted as it surreptitiously dominates and engulfs us all. And, of course, this search is necessarily predicated on and conducted through the medium of language, and Valenzuela is a virtuosa of language. Her unique style is unfailingly vibrant, crisp, and clever, paradoxically, at times almost classical, at others patently baroque. For example, *Como en la guerra* (As in war) is neatly structured on the classic heroic myth with its preordained discovery, subsequent loss, journey, and final encounter. *El gato eficaz*, at the other extreme, is filled with the conceptism and linguistic play typical of the baroque. Continually self-conscious, with narrators frequently critical of their stance as well as their task, her prose has been correctly labeled a verbal adventure, as we are caught up in and by the language and the linguistic twists and turns.

Nevertheless, to speak of language as if it were a separate entity does not mean to suggest that language in Valenzuela's work is somehow alien to her thematic concerns. Quite the contrary. Her discourse is not only the means of expression but also the subject of that expression, for Valenzuela's work centers on three intricately related preoccupations: language, women, and politics.

Sharon Magnarelli. *Reflections/Refractions:*
Reading Luisa Valenzuela (New York:
Peter Lang, 1988), pp. 2–4

The popularity and importance of her work reside both in the themes she dramatizes and in the means she employs to effect this drama, and if Valenzuela reminds one of times of García Márquez or Lydia Cabrera, Donald Barthelme or Paul Bowles, her fiction nonetheless achieves a distinctive voice that allows her to address issues she has clearly made her own.

As Valenzuela's first story collection since *Up among the Eagles* (*Donde viven las áquilas*) appeared in Spanish in 1983, *Open Door* provides both something new for American readers and a selection of the author's best earlier short fiction. The book opens with the fourteen stories comprising the 1983 collection, gathered together for the first time in translation, and follows with eleven selections from *Strange Things Happen Here* and seven stories from *Clara* (or *Los Heréticos*). As Valenzuela remarks in her Preface, "For the time being, here are my favorite stories from the three collections. But I must hurry, now, and write others: it is the only way I know of jamming a foot in the door so it won't slam in our faces."

Readers familiar with Valenzuela's work will recognize in *Open Door* the author's characteristic heterogeneity of subject matter, artistic method, and thematic concerns. Shamanistic figures, folkloristic superstitions and ritual magic, cultic beliefs and indigenous legends jostle urban settings, café life, state-of-the-art state terrorism, and the amorous doings of vacationing bourgeoisie to yield modern political parables and twice-told (albeit revamped) myths, small comedies of manners and mocking parodies of middle-class conventionality, ironic illuminations of religious realities and secular tales of physical and/or psychological terror. Similarly, traditional narrative techniques combine with a postmodern experimentation (fragmented narration, magical realism, randomness, and linguistic pranksterism) in the service of themes that are as timeless as the search for truth, community, or control over nature's mysteries, and as topical as sexual and political persecution in present-day Argentina or the nature of power relations within and among contemporary social classes. Here, in short, are stories that explore the boundaries of what is currently thought possible in fiction while reminding us of what must be demanded from fiction in our time.

As one moves through this collection, changes in focus are evident. The newest selections are the most artistically adventuresome and, according to their author, speak to "my love for Latin America and my passion for reinventing its myths." Stories gathered from *Strange Things* look most unswervingly at a Buenos Aires given over to violence and government-sanctioned illegalities, whereas those of her first volume "walk in writing the tightrope between religious fanaticism and heresy." Yet different as these stories may be one from another, they all reveal Valenzuela's dislike of "dogmas and certainties" and share her sense of urgency, of knowing something that desperately needs saying. All witness to her efforts to jam that foot in the door, the door of her title, which is also the name, so we are told, "of the most traditional, least threatening lunatic asylum in Argentina."

Brooke K. Horvath. *Review of Contemporary Fiction.* 9:1, 1989, pp. 243–44

Language is certainly one of the spaces where feminist struggles are staged, but it is difficult for feminist demands in Latin America to dissociate themselves from other social, ideological struggles. One can therefore find a noticeable difference in the kind of questions that Valenzuela prioritizes in her fiction. It is "milk-cow" words capable of disturbing the conventional mind/body polarity that interest her; that is, words as they materialize and can be rehabilitated for use by specific bodies at a specific place and time. "Who told whom all these facts? Who spoke all these words? At what moment? Where?" the narrator asks in the opening story "Fourth Version." "Who sees and who is seen? Who sees being seen?" These are questions that emphasize agency, readership, and historical circumstance, questions which, along with the contestation of the truth claims behind documentary evidence, the refusal of closure, and the disclaiming of authority from any single narrative voice, give us a sense of the multiple mediations—including those of women reading other women's narratives—through which the voice of the silenced other reaches us.

Valenzuela urges us to undertake a historical cultural analysis as a way of confronting what she calls "the ambivalences of protection" which can turn custodians and protectors into "watch dogs."

If I speak of Valenzuela's stories as revolutionary, I would like to specify that this is so primarily in relation to the supposedly "revolutionary" changes that took place at the level of Argentina's political economy during what William Smith refers to as "the second experiment in authoritarianism" in which her stories take place (though it was really the first authoritarian rule in 1966 that pompously called itself a capitalist revolution). I am referring to the repressive period of the Process of National Reorganization to which President Videla referred as "a final chapter of one historical cycle and the beginning of another." It is this ideological concept of revolution and of history as what Hannah Arendt called "a totally self-fulfilling logic by which the movement of history is explained as one consistent process"—a logic that leaves no gaps in the understanding of a historical process and justifies the dirty war against civilians—which Valenzuela will first need to disrupt. . . .

What is clear, however, is that the weakening of the authoritarian state and a strengthened female consciousness are closely related issues. What is also clear is that any attempt to change history or phrase it in a different language and from a different perspective, will have to work with the awareness that any other weapons, any other words about to be refashioned cannot assume purity, not only because "to clean, to purify the word is the best form of repression" but because, as the play on the words "lapidador" and "lapidario" [lapidator and lapidary] in "Fourth Version" suggests, women have not only been stoned and commerced with as precious stones; they have been inscribed in stone.

Like many feminist thinkers, Valenzuela is aware of the power of language to subordinate and exclude women. She is convinced of the need for women to reshape language as part of a broader social and political project. Yet, in OW [Other Weapons] she has refused to understand women as free of determination from participation in domination, and is reluctant to assume the oppressed have a privileged relation and ability to understand reality.

Laura García-Moreno. *Latin American Literary Review*. 9:38, 1991, pp. 8–9, 18

From what she terms the "Argentine darkness," from the metaphorical alphabet city of New York's Lower East Side, and from the wild zones of "authority," gender, and language itself, Luisa Valenzuela has won a brilliant, difficult, involving text. In a 1986 interview Valenzuela said she was "stalking" rather than writing this novel, and signs of the five-year struggle for its production are evident in the narrative(s) of its protagonists, who are also authors: "To write about the immediate, almost an impossible task. One's arm must extend way beyond its reach in order to touch what is virtually clinging to one's body." In fact, the story-within-the-story is the recording of what seem to be meditations by the writer-characters, Agustín Palant and Roberta (whose patronymic is not given), on various aspects of its composition. . . .

Like its characters, the text is preoccupied with traces. Agustín is concerned about inscriptions of blood on his jacket, the identifiable details in vomit, the traces "which are impossible to erase," which are hidden, appropriated, sublimated. Roberta worries about the evidence in his manuscript, which she hides in an S&M parlor, the suitable submergitory for repressible objects and oblivious encounters. Some traces read like circumstantial evidence, graffiti "left with graphomaniac zeal" in the narrative, and it is difficult to assess their importance to the engine of the novel. In this category I place the references to, and the stylistic or structural autographs of [Alain] Robbe-Grillet, [Jorge Luis] Borges, and [Djuna] Barnes; the gender almost arbitrarily marked in names like Edwina, "Vic" (for victim), and Roberta; and the traces of horror and worship implicit in the Tompkins Square setting, "vortex of the forlorn": Ave. A, Ave. B, and so on. Yet, these tricks with letters retain the occasionally mystifying suggestiveness they held for the characters themselves, as if they were metaphors of great meaning.

There is no question that the novelist, herself an Argentine currently living in New York, deals profoundly with the exiles' burdens of traces of an "other" life. Memories of the past and in particular of the "desaparecidos" in Argentina threaten, particularly in Agustín's dark, incoherent case, to overwhelm attempts at their erasure. Valenzuela's interests in censorship, self-censorship, and objectification of the "other" lead her into an exploration of sado-masochism, where the complicity between agents and customers of pain forms a perverse mirror of the political relationship between dominators and dominated. Thus, she restores the regressive and political subtext to pornography, which is carefully depicted as such in passages rife with casual violence and sinister metonymies ("There are the torturers and the tortured, thought the ear"), and implicitly confirms the obscenity of the wanton exercise of power, as well.

There is a certain postmodern claustrophobia to this enterprise. I have to admit that I wanted to put the book down, as its motives led its characters to visit various urban temples of the desolate—the homeless shelters, surreal soirées, the necrophiliac death chambers of artistic renown, the lengthy confinements in apartments so well described that you can see the cartons of takeout foods rotting in ethnic splendor in the refrigerator. Valenzuela's trademark "way" with secretions and contaminants is evident here, too; but the text is so well constructed that it provides a tight alibi for her sense of language as a secretion, "the most terrifying of all perhaps because of everything it conceals while revealing, or vice versa." One reviewer wrote that you have to wear rubber gloves to read this novel; he or she is striking, possibly unwittingly, at the heart of the author's notion of catharsis. Readerly sweat notwithstanding, I'd say that the source of the novel's grandest question, and Roberta's means of answering it, are unforgettable.

Marisa Januzzi. *Review of Contemporary Fiction.* 12:3, 1992, pp. 175–76

Luisa Valenzuela would rather, you suspect, be writing about love than politics: women's desire is a powerful current in her fiction, leading to brave acts of self-knowledge. But as an Argentine writer, she has said in an interview in *Ms.* that she feels "politics has been imposed on" her, and she's always seemed to be searching for a way to do both. Although she writes forcefully about the turbulence of the space between two people—the way violence enters into, or perhaps originates in, relationships between men and women— she's come at this nexus of romance and power from a different angle every time. In her 1985 short story collection *Other Weapons* (Ediciones del Norte) she wrote about women in love with revolutionaries, or explored the tension between violence in necessary fantasy and in forbidden action. In *The Lizard's Tail* she began to sketch out a revolutionary consciousness of her own. And in her most recent work, *Black Novel (With Argentines)*, set in New York City (where she lived for much of the 1980s), she's come closer than ever to a female understanding of the public and erotic operations of power, and of the origins of the torturer's sadomasochistic impulse.

The *Lizard's Tail,* which was first published in English in 1983 and has been reissued here by Serpent's Tail, applies a fragmented narrative to a very Argentine political geography. Dedicated to Kathy Acker among others, and owing as much to postmodernism as to magic realism, it takes place in an unnamed country ruled by military might and witchcraft, power and its symbolic representation. . . .

If *The Lizard's Tail* probes the unconscious of politics, *Black Novel (With Argentines)* searches out the politics of the unconscious. Where the one takes place in an imagined Argentina, the other is set in a very real New York, at a time of sexual excess and urban decay—the New York where Valenzuela lived in the early 1980s. A very different kind of story, *Black Novel (novela negra* suggests *novela rosa,* a "pink" or racy novel) is much more linguistically subdued than *The Lizard's Tail.* In a return to the style of *Other Weapons,* the language here is colloquial, plain; in Toby Talbot's clear but toneless translation, it seems almost flat, and its images distanced by their setting in the world of exile. Magic seems to operate less easily in this unfamiliar city— but that might be because, in its decadence, it has brought the realm of the unconscious deliberately to the surface. Pretending to be hard-boiled and objective, *Black Novel* employs familiar events from the above-ground world of "relationships"—and then mirrors them in the subterranean world of sex clubs and rituals of domination.

Julie Phillips. *Women's Review of Books.* 9, July, 1992, pp. 20–21

VEGA, ANA LYDIA (UNITED STATES) 1946–

Ana Lydia Vega . . . dares to run greater formal risks than [Carmen] Lugo [Filippi], and for this reason succeeds in producing more innovative short stories, although there are several failures among hers, as well, for instance "Ahi viene mama Yono," with its undeniable roots in "Los funerales de la Mama Grande." With long lists that border on litanies, this is the most obvious example of a failure among Vega's narrations in her collaborative collection with Lugo. However, I must emphasize that the stories that dominate are those whose salvation lies in the word and that leave the reader convinced that he or she is encountering a worthwhile writer. Vega takes the achievements of Luis Rafael Sanchez in his most recent narrative a step further, although along other paths. Sanchez . . . marked the appearance of a new way of dealing with popular speech in our narrative. . . . In a personal and original fashion, Vega continues Sanchez's advances along a different road, and both authors make their respective routes join up with the Antillean neobaroque that is so fashionable in our day. "Letra para salsa y tres soneos por encargo" is Vega's best example of this salvation by means of popular language.

Efraín Barradas. *Revista/Review Interamericana.* 11, 1981, p. 466

In contrast to [Rosario] Ferré's controlled literary narrative, Vega lets loose a language of the streets, "the lumpenized ideolect" of Puerto Rican popular culture, to parody and serve as a counterpoint to the voice of official public rhetoric. Vega examines, with a delight and a vengeance, the distortions and contradictions of traditional values and the absurdities of colonialism and Puerto Rico's consumer-oriented lifestyle.

Her characters are members of the working class and of the lumpen proletariat which today make up the majority of the island's urban dwellers. The female characters are in the "pink collar" professions, still dependent on male bosses but earning money, and sexually at least, liberated from traditional mores. Her language moves with the popular rhythm of the "salsa," combining satire, irreverent humor, and biting criticism. . . .

Although Vega's stories do not deal solely with the condition of women and are a general cultural critique, certainly the female characters in "Pollito chicken" and another story, "Letra para salsa y tres soneos por encargo" (Salsa rhymes and three short-order tunes) reveal much about the man-woman relationship as it applies to a large sector of the population. They recall the views of José Luis González in his recent essay "El país de cuatro pisos" (The four-storied country), in which he discusses popular culture versus that of the elite and the changing status of women as a result of North American political and economic domination. According to González, North American colonialism caused an internal upset in Puerto Rican cultural values: "The vacuum created by the dismantling of the culture of Puerto Ricans from 'above' has not been filled, in any way, by the intrusion of North American culture, but rather by the ever obvious rise of the culture of Puerto Ricans from below. . . .

Vega incorporates the popular tradition in her work and represents what González refers to as an "ideological rupture," that is, a break with the ideology of a colonized society which produces fixed, stereotypical images of each of its members. She shares with Rosario Ferré and other women writers a sense of purpose which combines their feminist concerns with the social and cultural problems of Puerto Rico. These women are producing a very *human* work that proposes an inclusive reality no longer limited by gender or class, and offers a new perspective, an authentic vision, and a genuine contribution to contemporary Latin American narrative.

> Margarite Fernández Olmos. In Doris
> Meyers and Margarite Fernández Olmos.
> *Contemporary Women Writers of Latin*
> *America* (Brooklyn: Brooklyn College
> Press, 1983), pp. 86–89

Ana Lydia Vega, [is] co-author with Carmen Lugo Filippi of *Virgenes y martires* (Virgins and martyrs, 1981), and the collection *Encancaranublado y otros cuentos de naufragio* (Threatening Skies and other stories of shipwrecks, 1982), which received the "Casa de las Americas Prize" in 1982. Her work also explores the problem of identity within a Caribbean context and the question of cultural unity, and *mestizaje* (admixture of races) that is characteristic of the Caribbean experience. Although her stories are marked by feminist consciousness, the world she depicts also contain a great deal of violence, assassinations, assaults; the reader is hit as well with stylistic world play and humor, that can be noted in the tongue-twister title "encancaranublado," a world typical of the Caribbean, to describe the skies that predict storms (hence my attempt to translate it as "threatening skies"). Like Ferré and co-author Carmen Lugo Filippi, Vega records the rapid and uncertain social and economic changes in Puerto Rico, where both national and personal concepts of identity are under attack. The stories grouped under the first section "Nubosidad variable" (Variable clouds), refer to the different Caribbean nationalities, adrift in the sea of uncertain political status and unsettling social and economic changes. In the title story, "Encancaranublado," Vega brings together protagonists from several Caribbean countries—Haiti, the Dominican Republic, and Cuba—and explores their interactions as they attempt an escape by boat to the United States. Their brush with shipwreck, their subsequent retrieval by the United States Navy, and the ultimate lessons they learn about "Caribbean" solidarity and their place in North American society, can be read as a political allegory in the best tradition of universal political literature.

"Puerto Rican Syndrome" is another exploration of pan-Caribbean identity, using violent actions and images which culminate in the apocalyptic tidal wave that overcomes the Island. Vega parodies the language of the media, of politicians, of those who would convert the Caribbean into a costumbristic island paradise of food, fun, sun and sand. She discounts the paradise in favor of a realistic picture of the problems which confront the people of the Caribbean today, and she offers no easy solutions. Although her themes question traditional social values and the absurdities of colonialism in the tradition of Maria Bibiana Benitez, Lola Rodriguez de Tio, Julia de Burgos, "her language moves with the popular rhythm of the 'salsa,' combining satire, irreverent humor, and biting criticism."

Sandra Messinger Cypess. In Carole Boyce
Davies and Elaine Savory Fido, eds. *Out of
the Kumbla: Caribbean Women and
Literature* (Trenton, New Jersey: Africa
World Press, 1990), pp. 84–85

The eight "false chronicles of the south" in Ana Lydia Vega's collection bearing that title are inspired by certain historical events and characters as well as by the oral traditions of Ponce and the southeastern Puerto Rican cities of Guayama, Arroyo, Patillas, and Maunabo. Each story is preceded by a page of comments by the author, and epigraph, and a print. Like many of Latin America's New Historical Novels of 1979–92, the predominant tone is carnivalesque.

One-half of the volume is taken up by "El baúl de Miss Florence: Fragmentos para un novelón romántico," a short novel featuring a Jane Eyre-type American tutor who gradually falls in love with her adolescent pupil, whose father, an autocratic womanizer, lusts for her. Miss Florence's only genuine suitor is the French doctor Fouchard, but in spite of their sincere attraction for each other, she is frightened off by his abolitionist ideas. The setting is the Lind sugar plantation near Arroyo between 1856 and 1859—Mrs. Lind is the daughter of the inventor and artist Samuel F. B. Morse. In addition to being a well-executed pastiche, "El baúl de Miss Florence" captures the social conditions of both owners and slaves.

Of the other seven authentic short stories, four are set between the 1890s and 1913; one portrays the Easter Sunday 1937 Ponce Massacre of the Nationalists; the final two are contemporary pastiches, respectively, of a crime of passion and a Chaucer-like public limousine ride. Except for "Cosas de poetas," which ridicules the local unpublished poet of Guayama and his unsuccessful attempt to secure the backing of visiting poet José Santos Chocano, the historical stories subtly fuse a Puerto Rican patriotic sentiment, directed against both Spain and the U.S., with a variety of narrative forms. "Cupido y Clío en el Bazar Otero" is a political mystery story set in the late nineteenth century in which an *independentista* disguises himself as a priest and, with the help of his sister, who pretends to be pregnant, and the owner of a music store, succeeds in escaping from the island.

"Un domingo de Lilianne" alternates three different plot threads in order to portray most originally the 1937 massacre of the Nationalists. The principal narrator is a woman who recalls in the first person her wealthy family's Sunday excursions to her grandfather's *finca* on the outskirts of Ponce. As she and her family, although aware of the impending Nationalist parade, leave the city in their Packard, the two other focal figures look for vantage points from which to view the parade. San Juan photographer Carlos succeeds in snapping a picture of the massacre from a rooftop, whereas Angel, who had returned on his bicycle from the beach after collecting shells, is struck in the head by a bullet and probably dies. The political message is purposely downplayed until the final page, when the "official story" of the "plot" is contrasted with the red letters painted on the white walls of the convent: VIVA LA REPÚBLICA, ABAJO LOS ASESINOS, directed against the Americans.

Vega's delightfully humorous feminist criticism of Puerto Rico's *machos,* rich in dialect, is applied to the patriotic theme in "El regreso del héroe." The triumphant return to Arroyo in 1895 of an ex-political prisoner is focalized by the womanizer and voyeur "Chebo Farol, príncipe de las letrinas, rey de los frescos." The same picaresque spirit with modern-day popular slang and a discreet dose of metafiction informs the final two stories, "Premio de consolación" and "Cuento en camino."

With this fourth volume of first-rate stories, Ana Lydia Vega secures her reputations as one of the best Latin American short-story writers of her generation. Utilizing a carnivalesque tone, linguistic ingenuity, and a *pasión de historia* (title of the short story which earned her the 1984 Juan Rulfo International Prize in Paris), she also joins forces with the New Historical Novel that has been predominant in Latin American fiction since 1979.

Seymour Menton. World Literature
Today. 67, 1993, p. 159

VILALTA, MARUXA (MEXICO) 1932–

The recurrence of certain thematic concerns and the search for a suitable form in which to cast these ideas may indeed be considered a trademark of Vilalta's theater. But the shift that has occurred properly begins with *Esta*

noche juntos, amándonos tanto (Tonight, together, we'll love each other so).
Vilalta made her first mature contribution to the theater with *El 9*, a play
that, although it has a socio-economic theme, incorporates all the allegorico-
expressionistic devices that characterize the Theatre of the Absurd. In *Esta
noche juntos, amándonos tanto,* however, she moves away from strictly absurdist form to a theater that combines absurdist techniques with Brechtian
Verfremdungseffekte to accommodate an overt social message. In *Nada
como el piso 16* (Nothing like the sixteenth floor), on the other hand, she
uses representational techniques. But despite the patina of realism here, it is
clearly something other than the conventional realism we associate with social protest writing. . . .

The advent of the absurdist revolution in the 1950s and the almost simultaneous rediscovery of Brecht's politically-oriented theater constitute the
two most significant trends of influence on the avant-garde theater in Latin
America. While during the 1960s the avant-garde tended to favor the absurdist
mode which rejected overt social commitment, the latter part of the 1970s
has seen the return of a theater concerned with social issues. Vilalta's shifting
away from absurdist form coincides with this change in the climate of the
contemporary theater, which one critic has identified as the "demise of the
age of the absurd in drama." It would be wrong, however, to view this return
to a more overt social commitment as a regression to a dated social realism.
In the interval, under the influence of Brecht and absurdism, it has taken on
a new strangeness. It is in this sense that Vilalta's achievements in the theater
can best be understood.

Tamara Holzapfel. *Latin American Theatre
Review.* 14:2, 1981, pp. 11, 17–18

The Mexican Playwright Maruxa Vilalta said in a conversation with the late
Grace Bearse and myself that she belongs to no particular school of drama.
However, when pressed by us to name a literary affinity, she offered the idea
that her dramas may bear a likeness to those of Ionesco. Indeed, she follows
Ionesco in the concentration on single, illogical situations, the lack of real
communication among characters and the dramatists' obvious pursuit of
irony. But while Ionesco probes the limits of language, Vilalta pursues social
critique and protest, a mode which is so characteristic of Latin American
theater. . . .

Her concern with politics did not surface directly in her first play, *Los
Desorientadoes* (Drifters), of 1959, which deals with the frustrations of the
younger generation and attacks their passivity. The youths are bound by
convention, by the traditional standards of their parents and by their own
impractical ambitions. The conclusion is not well drawn and the play may be
seen as a stepping stone to a later, more sophisticated theater.

In her more recent plays she vividly presents the most serious global
problems facing present day society, problems to which she does not believe
in offering obvious solutions. Rather she exposes schematic situations, which,

because of their starkness, demand the intellectual participation of the audience. In the theatrical aspect, Vilalta is constantly experimenting with lights, rhythms and multiple roles for her actors in order to heighten the impact of her message. She uses explicit stage directions, music, dance, pantomime, and motion picture screens to avoid a static effect. Yet her concept of theater is not avant-garde.

In Vilalta's dramatic evolution, the political roots of social problems and the social roots of political problems are expressed in a universal and contemporary language. Her plays are schemes created to illustrate a point about mass society of our century rather than to demonstrate any shadings of character, to quicken the consciousness of her audience rather than to create an imaginative world of their own. It is paradoxical that Mexico and its dilemmas are virtually absent from her plays, as if she were a spiritual expatriate. But it is clear that Vilalta, determined to adhere to a nationalistic "temática" is struggling to express a vision that is both Latin American and also consonant with the humanistic views that she imbibed early in life. The plays that stand out in this sense are *El 9* which exposes the tyranny of the rush toward North American-style modernization and *Esta noche juntos, amándonos tanto,* which caricatures the fascist mentality that Vilalta sees as a universal threat. The twentieth century and its political and social horrors are Maruxa Vilalta's negative obsessions and as an idealist, daughter of fighting idealists, she has staked her dramatic career on combating these formidable giants.

Grace Bearse and Lorraine Elena Roses.
Revista de Estudios Hispanicos. 18, 1984,
pp. 399–400, 405

Since her beginnings in 1960, Maruxa Vilalta has experienced an uninterrupted activity as dramatic author and stage director. Her works have been conceived strictly for the theater, without useless literary concerns. Whence comes her effectiveness and the salience that occur when her texts confront the vital space of the stage.

The first works followed the paths traced by didactic expressionism; they led to very well-coached conclusions concerning the social imbalance of bourgeois structures, the boundless power of material goods over spiritual values, and the negation of the most legitimate aspirations of the human being.

The author's most recent works exhibit a greater complexity and are connected with other Latin American authors who are attempting to harmonize two dramatic modalities that appeared irreconcilable until only a few years ago: on the one hand, the concern with historicity, conceived as a central theme of any theatrical creation; on the other, the inscription of the problem of the being in its most intimate essence and its responses to the conflicts that life, by the very fact of being dynamic, provides.

The epic theater and the descendants of Bertolt Brecht's drama analyze man as a mere historical circumstance: the characters of this theater have been depersonalized, determined solely by the events of History. Archetypal or generic characters, each of them represents a sector of society and the dramatic conflict has its origins in the diversity of positions that these characters encounter within the social group. This tendency dominated in the early works of Maruxa Vilalta, which was understandable if we accept that the immediate problems of our society originate in poverty, ignorance, and inequality. For this reason, these early works are emphatically affirmative; they denounce, signify, and seek means for rectifying the vicious practices of bourgeois society.

On the other side, the mark that the theater of the absurd has left on contemporary dramatic literature is so much deeper, and its signature is always a system of questionings that shows the individual in eternal struggle with the group. . . . Ionesco and Becket interrogate the very reasons for existence, the uselessness of all struggle, the absurdity of any redeeming value, especially in the face of the imperative of death and silence.

Carlos Solórzano. Latin American Theatre Review. 18:2, 1985, pp. 83–84

What we do find unquestionably in Vilalta is a complex theater in which she employs the technique and form most appropriate to the specific message. For that reason, her approach is sometimes essentially naturalistic, at others mostly absurd. Her theater is also frequently marked by violence, if not physical, at least psychological. It is consistently sociopolitical, protesting the contemporary condition of mankind, but there is an underlying recognition that the sociopolitical problems are products of the individuals as much as vice versa. Her works are often circular, ending where they began with no apparent progress or resolution for the problems presented, and thus reinforce the notion that we cannot improve society without changing the individual, and conversely we cannot alter the individual without revamping society, in a never ending vicious circle of inertia.

One of the main currents we also find running through Vilalta's works, although a characteristic not generally emphasized by critics, is the question of discourse, the emptiness of language and the ever growing distance between the signifier and the signified. Discourse is repeatedly employed by her characters, consciously or not, to divert and misdirect attention, to disguise reality or truth. . . .

Her dramatic works certainly suggest that the problem is not limited to politicians but rather permeates all of society. Surely her message is that we all need to change our lexicon and bring it into line with our experience. At the same time we cannot lose sight of the fact that language is inherently a political gesture.

This preoccupation with discourse may be less overt in some of Vilalta's other works, but it is surely even more important as she subtly employs a language which is multifarious and polysemic. . . .

Vilalta's later work, *Esta noche juntos, amándonos tanto,* makes a parallel use of multifarious discourse and the theme of time. I have already noted the distance between the signifier and the signified epitomized in the characters' incessant reiteration of their love for each other. In her analysis of the semiotic systems of the play, Kirsten Nigro has noted, "el decorado y los personajes son dos conjuntos de signos visuales que, al combinarse, producen una contradicción." Once again the one to one relationship between signs and their referents breaks down, and nothing is quite as it seems. . . .

Vilalta's three most recent works, *Historia de él, Una mujer, dos hombres y un balazo,* and *Pequeña historia de horror* evince a growing awareness of the theatrical event itself and of theater as discourse. In each play there is conscious application of the Brechtian V effect; we are forbidden a willing suspension of disbelief as the actors talk about their characters, assume their roles or costumes on stage, and set their own scenes. In addition to providing the sociopolitical awareness and criticism which was sought by Brecht, the technique in the Vilalta works also encourages us to recognize the theatricality of our everyday life and language.

Sharon Magnarelli. *Hispanic Journal.* 9:2,
1988, pp. 99-100, 103, 105, 109

VILLANUEVA, ALMA (UNITED STATES) 1944–

The archetype of Terra Mater, Earth Mother . . . function[s] in the mythicization of "la abuelita" in the anthology entitled *Poems* by Alma Villanueva. The collection may be divided into three parts. In the first section Villanueva presents a seven-poem biography of the poet-speaker consisting of recollections of the process of maturation from childhood to womanhood. The second section is introduced in the last poem of the first part and an appropriate title might be "Cantarlas Claras: Canto de Mujer: Song of Woman." This section reveals woman's situation in the general scheme of contemporary life. Part three consists of three poems and might be entitled "Revelation and Recognition"—of certain truths and the task that woman has before her to become "a woman of clarity," a woman of understanding. . . . This woman is the exemplary system of values and standards, the image on which humanity will base its heroes of contemporary myth. . . .

Mamacita, the emerging mythical heroine of the story, is formed after the images of Coatlicue, La Virgen de Guadalupe, La Soldadera, and La Abuela, all of whom have in common one or more characteristics of the Earth Mother archetype. We have seen that through memory the poet has restored to Mamacita the role of imitator of the archetype and reproducer of archetypal gestures. Mamacita's story and what she has generated through her grandchild is the unifying narrative of the collection.

The myth structure described at the beginning of this essay is central because in that structure Mamacita's story finds its function and meaning. Her story constitutes the history of the acts of a historical figure who is gradually transformed into a mythical Supernatural Being who then provides positive values and an exemplary model to live by in the modern world. The story is considered to be absolutely true because it concerns itself with everyday life and with mythical and historical realities of humanity. The story has survived because it offers alternative values and ways of life. Mamacita's story is related to creation. First, the creation of Mamacita herself based on past Supernaturals who are in turn based on the Earth Mother archetype. Second, the creation of a woman based on Mamacita's guidance and teachings. Third, the creation of a Woman Warrior Poet of Resistance based on Mamacita's gestures of resistance. Fourth, the creation of a "woman of clarity," a Supernatural Being based on the revelation and understanding of archetypal characteristics and actions learned from Mamacita. This Supernatural Being will guarantee the continuation of the cycles of creation.

These four transformations are recorded in the three sections of the anthology. The four have occurred in one woman, the poet, who throughout the story acquires understanding of the qualities of the Earth Mother archetype, gradually becomes an imitator of the archetype and accepts the role of reproducer of archetypal gestures.

The myth structure describes the creation of a myth. And in this case it constitutes the mythicization of Mamacita. By knowing and recognizing the myth, the paradigms for all of Mamacita's significant acts are revealed. In Mamacita's case, one is aware of why the Earth Mother acts the way she does and thus one can control and manipulate at will the explanation of the actions of this archetype within the context of the myth.

It is appropriate here to interject the idea that the archetypal Earth Mother, Mamacita, and the poet are the results of individual histories that are both mythical and historical and tied to a culture that is dynamic, creative and responsive to experience. Archetypes and myths cannot be studied in a vacuum; they must be related to a historical process of change.

Mamacita's story is a knowledge that one feels, experiences ritually, either by recounting the myth or by reading a story that is based on the myth. The myth of Mamacita, like that of the Pachuco, is a true living force because Mamacita will always be here to offer the proof.

Alejandro Morales. *Bilingual Review/Revista Bilingue.* 7, 1980, pp. 124, 140–41

Villanueva's work is pervaded by a constant quest to affirm the woman, the natural or "relatedness" principle, as she throws down her peaceable gauntlet of female power before an overly technological, rational, and masculinized culture.

Some recurrent themes in Villanueva's work, which affirm the poet's challenge to a lopsided culture and her passionate desire to transcend its limitations, are the interconnectedness of all living things with each other and with nature both animate and inanimate; the wholeness of the self (particularly the female self; metamorphosis and transformation; rebirthing and renaming. Many of her works engage in a process of myth-making, rediscovery and redefinition of the female—and often, matrilinear—principles through poetry, poetic drama, and short fiction. As does one of her literary models, Adrienne Rich, Villanueva considers the creation of literature and life to be one: an organic unity. Villanueva's poetry is dynamic, vital, and personal, but her "I" is almost always a "we" as she speaks of woman's common experience, and contributes significantly to the enrichment of a common female literary culture, as well as to the creation of a renewed and transformed society. . . .

Bloodroot has been remarkably well received. As the editor, James Cody, wrote: "What I saw astounded me because I saw a clarity of line, a forthrightness, a subconscious and assumed rhythm perfectly suiting all the possible circumstances that can confront a poem." Juan Rodríguez in his inimitable style in *Carta Abierta* has give hearty praise to Villanueva: "la ruca echa chingazos poéticos left and right. Reading this book was like holding a stick of dynamite—con el mechón encendidio" (the gal flings poetic outbursts left and right. Reading this book was like holding a stick of dynamite—with a lighted fuse.)

In his essay "Terra Mater and the Emergence of Myth in *Poems* by Alma Villanueva," Alejandro Morales correctly identifies the archetype of Earth Mother and the mythification of *la abuelita* (the grandmother), but his interpretation stops short of identifying the feminist dimension essential to the "emergent" or transformative power of myth in the author's poems. The poet's portrayal of *mamacita's* (dear mother figure) resistance to Anglo-American society is significant, as is her poetic admiration of *mamacita's* defiance of the much greater threat of death to the spirit. Also important is the poet's discovery of the way in which *la abuelita's* mythical power is transmitted from generation to generation: "grandmother to mother to/daughter to my daughter." The matrilinear chain of wisdom emerges as a mythical pattern and a source of power: "men come/and go/your friends/stay./women stay." Morales's interpretation of "The White Goddess," in the poem "Of Utterances" overlooks the ribald elements of stanzas such as: "The cunt all acceptance/opening wide/of the mind of man and/giving birth to their children/The Poem. The Painting. The Sculpture." The goddess is not seen as a degraded muse or symbolic of the state of art today, but as a foil to appraise the entire tradition of Western patriarchal art. Villanueva, better yet, refuses the phallus as a definer of womanhood and as the source of her poetic inspiration. The Muse, or its male counterpart, is simply not woman's to accept or reject, for "we women just don't have any." So it is at this juncture that woman must turn to herself for inspiration, thus shaping a female literary culture and inventing herself. For example, Villanueva explores the recreation of the witch within the female tradition—as Phoenix. She consequently manages to redefine the witch from a feminist perspective as a symbol for the female poet filled with the immortal potency of her love, her blood, and her words: "I burn, self/imposed/in a fire of my/own making/my witches' secret: the poem as/my witness./ this cannot be destroyed./they burn in the heart, long after/the witch is dead."

Alma Villanueva is driven by her private demons to create a direct and energetic poetry. While her output is uneven, her poetry represents an inner force that is never trite or hackneyed.

Elizabeth J. Ordóñez. In Julio A. Martínez
and Francisco A. Lamilé, eds. *Chicano
Literature: A Reference Guide* (Westport,
Connecticut: Greenwood Press, 1985),
pp. 415–19

As a poet Alma Villanueva is consciously preoccupied with a search for a universal female community. The influence of the women's movement in the United States seems to have reached her without significant interference from the Chicano social movement of the 1960s and 1970s. . . . Villanueva is the product of a process of socialization; yet, unlike the rest, she has an overriding objective: to transform her concrete experience into a vision of a personalized myth. She achieves this objective in *Mother, May I?* her most interesting and dynamic work.

In 1977, a year before *Mother, May I?* appeared, Villanueva published two poetic autobiographies, *Bloodroot* and *Poems*. The latter won first prize in poetry at the University of California, Irvine, in the year of its publication. Collectively these three works demonstrate that Villanueva is a poet who senses her personal development in terms of time. In fact, among the poets discussed in this volume, she is not only the most sequential in presentation but also the only one to write a poetic autobiography, an achievement that makes her unique also among Chicano poets. . . .

Villanueva seems to have had the most urgent need to compose an auto-biographical poem. Because this literary genre necessitates a retrospective look at the author's life, including an explanation of his or her arrival at a certain point in that life, an autobiography gave Villanueva an opportunity to confront compelling questions about her personal development which stood in the way of her desired poetic vision. . . .

In light of the absence of both a mother and a father, it is understandable that Villanueva's protagonist in *Mother, May I?* must achieve the birthing of a personal self, or her "I." Her search for continuous participation in a mythi-cal, female community may stem from a deeper wish to transcend the inter-ruptions she perceives as having marred her own relations with her real mother. The fact that Villanueva was raised by her Mexican grandmother until she was eleven years old may account for her emotional identification with Mexican culture. Since her closeness to her grandmother is part of her childhood, her Chicana, or Mexican-American, identity plays a minor role in her adult poetic persona, which lies more within a community bounded by gender than within one bounded by race or ethnicity.

When compared with the poetry of [Lorna Dee] Cervantes and [Bernice] Zamora, Villanueva's shows the least awareness of a Chicana consciousness. Her solution of the dilemma of being both a woman and a Chicana is to respond primarily as a woman to the dominant masculine society. . . .

By juxtaposing the two identities of "woman" and "Chicana," Villanueva is at once expressing a hope for their reconciliation and asserting her inability to achieve a synthesis between them. She chooses a mythical community of women because she is thereby permitted to speak to alienated women everywhere, regardless of race. The consequence of her choice is the silence of her poetry on the subject of Chicana experience. In a curiously paradoxical way, Villanueva shows that the search for a female identity is especially complex when considered in relation to a Chicana self-definition. She challenges her readers to discover how to include a Chicana identity in a female identity.

Marta Ester Sanchez. *Contemporary Chicana Poetry: A Critical Approach to an Emerging Literature* (Berkeley: University of California Press, 1985), pp. 24–25, 84

She published two poetry collections in 1977, *Bloodroot* and *Poems;* the latter volume won the first prize for poetry in the third Chicano literary prize competition at the University of California, Irvine. Her third volume, *Mother, May I?* was published in 1978. Villanueva's work is autobiographical and focuses on her emergence as woman and poet.

Bloodroot expresses Villanueva's "nostalgic desire for a return to an original, maternal womb from which, presumably, both women and men emerged." This vision of the cosmic womb is conveyed through such images as blood, milk, and breasts, as well as earthy images of trees and birds. The woman seeks to give birth without the aid of man through union with the earth, suggesting a common origin for everyone. In "ZINZ" the poet similarly affirms the oneness of human beings, male and female, in images referring to a common origin. The poet eventually speaks in a more personal vein in a poem reminiscent of Walt Whitman. "I Sing to Myself" describes the emerging self which cannot be held back: the woman gives birth to herself.

In *Poems* the personal voice is heard more strongly as it challenges male sexual and literary dominance. The speaker boldly asserts female sexual superiority and claims a magical witch nature in images and metaphors that continue to underscore the theme of the self emerging. This self, which is female *and* poet, also attacks the tradition of the woman as muse who inspires art. She goes on to assert that she will be her own muse and grow her own wings.

Mother, May I? is an autobiographical narrative poem that traces the poet's development from childhood to her thirties in three sections. The theme of birthing treated in previous works continues to be developed here, but it is enhanced by the autobiographical shape of the volume and its narrative sequencing. . . .

Alma Villanueva's chief poetic concern is with exploring her feminine self rather than her Chicana self, a dominant theme in Bernice Zamora and others. Villanueva plumbs the themes of birth, renewal, and survival in her own idiom. As Marta Ester Sánchez says, "The poetic enterprise of *Mother, May I?* is to create from concrete experience a personal myth of a universal womanhood." Villanueva accomplishes this in part by challenging the restrictive psychic environment imposed by men and society, and sometimes even by other women. Her poetry stands up to this threat to authentic—that is, free—existence.

Carl R. Shirley and Paula W. Shirley.
Understanding Chicano Literature
(Columbia: University of South Carolina
Press, 1988), p. 43–45

In a similar manner as [Carmen] Tafolla, Alma Villanueva revises the myth of Eve and Adam in her poem "Of/To Man." . . . In both poems, the poets respectively reinterpret, recover, redefine, and re-appropriate woman's role, rejecting the passive "chingada" as a model. Most importantly, both poets turn what has been regarded as a negative into a positive image in the process of demythification. This is indeed what Alicia Ostriker calls "revisionist mythmaking," a necessary strategy for "It is thanks to myth we believe that woman must be either angel or monster." It is precisely this mode of constructing reality that is being challenged by these Chicana poets. They are aware that over the centuries of patriarchal domination, whether as object of derision or idealization, woman has been the object of androcentric fictions which make sure her place and role uphold the patriarchal order of things at the expense of her own oppression which sometimes is insidiously disguised as the most "sublime" of idealizations. . . .

In her poems of *The Irvine Collection* (1977), Alma Villanueva deals with another infamous role associated with women: witchcraft. Villanueva turns all the negative associations of witchcraft into a celebration of woman's archetypal power, playing with man's fear of it. Two of the poems, "Witches' Blood" and "The Last Words" constitute disturbing and defiant examples of "revisionist myth-making" in its most effective, subversive demythifying. . . .

In "The Last Words" Villanueva dedicates the poem to Anne Sexton and Sylvia Plath, "and all those that burned before them in Salem and other places." The poem is also a celebration of woman power as well as a defiance to men by reappropriating the role of the witch which basically is one of the most concrete symbols or constructs of male fear of women's power. . . .

The inversions and disruptions of the "order of things" in the poems of Villanueva come from her keen awareness of the suffering and exploitation women have endured through the centuries in the name of everything, including themselves.

Carmen M. Del Río. *Revista Canadiense de Estudios Hispanicos.* 14, 1990, pp. 437–41

Even though the spirit and the mood that inform the writing of Ron Arias's *The Road to Tamazunchale* and Alma Luz Villanueva's *The Ultraviolet Sky* seem very different, these two books exhibit many similarities. While *The Road* has a male hero and belongs to the tradition of the picaresque novel and the chivalric romance and *The Ultraviolet Sky* relates more to a tradition of feminism and feminist literature which evolved out of the 1980s, both novels (or should we call them "tales"?) portray a journey and a quest through time and space. Their protagonists go to the "edge" of the world, where life and death meet, where rebirth temporarily challenges destruction, where knowledge and clarity can momentarily replace confusion, and where some degree of wholeness and truth seem to be attainable in spite of all the flaws, the errors, the inadequacies. In their struggle to survive, Fausto and Rosa pursue with unwavering commitment several quests which may be seen as so many rites of passage. Both abruptly leave their familiar environment with impatience, anticipation and dread; both, visited by dreams and fantasies, set out to explore—beyond the horizon of their everyday life—expanses where their private memory interacts with the collective memory, history encounters myth, and their personal truth merges with some global truth.

From their dreamy and wakeful experiences, both retrieve fragments of realities and eagerly put them together, in a play or in a painting, to create some meaningful design. In the process of retrieving they reinvent not only their own lives but life itself. Their wanderings in the collective memory and imagination help them reach some understanding about their identity as members of a community whose experience is grounded in the same myths and history. In their re-creation of life they also give evidence of that poetic activity which informs the Chicano sensibility and can act as regenerative spirit and a saving grace. Leave-taking is the first step toward rebirth, a resurrection in life. . . .

Rosa sets out on her journey with impatience and determination and, like Fausto, as though she were summoned by inner forces. She places herself under the spiritual protection and guidance of two women figures whose "truth" she seeks to retrieve: her grandmother, Luz, whose memory must live on and Quetzalpetlatl, the forgotten Goddess "ever-present, infinite, ever-loving, holding her myth inside herself" whom it would be "sin" not to remember.

Rosa's regeneration has to take place away from the setting of her ordinary life, away from the city, in Lupine Meadows, within the proximity of bears, rattlesnakes, coyotes, and wolves (they will all belong to her own bestiary), of earth, sky, ocean, and mountain. In that remote, lonely place, "ruled by the sun and the moon," she feels less exposed than in the city. There, she can move between light and darkness, dawn and dusk, and between two paintings in which she tries to capture the mystery of the lilac sky—"the color that could be seen at sunrise or at sunset . . . the color of beginnings and endings"—and of the black shawl with the empty fold ("and the shawl was the night that belonged to Quetzalpetlatl."

Stunned by the beauty and the intelligence of the earth, she is haunted by the "ancient warning of extinction" and by the question "How will we survive?"—a question she does not ask but feels daily "like a wild animal's mute desperation when it feels itself being hunted to its death, and the wild wisdom of the body, of the instinct, the cellular knowledge."

Like her grandmother, Luz, who would always say "Estoy juntando," "I am gathering," Rosa tries to gather everything around her: the darkness for the difficult time ahead; the silence, disturbing and soothing; the rainbow sky; the sharp edge of the coming winter; the warmth of promising mornings, "true lilac mornings" and "sunsets promising change"; the delight and the pain: the loving and the horrifying memories. The island and the great white spray constantly moving against it in the daytime become reassuring images. She identifies both with the waves in their endless movements and with the rock which can command the dark and hold its own against the sea. She is herself both on the edge and firmly rooted, always wavering between a sense of precariousness and separateness and one of complete belonging. . . .

In her paintings she tries to assert feminine themes, the prevailing presence of mothers, sisters, grandmothers; of goddesses; of witchgoddesses (the Feathered Serpent Woman set on fire because of her power and who survived the fire); of *brujas;* and she praises the force and intensity present in the woman's body: "I've just completed a view of Earth from space, with the continents in the shape of a woman's body nursing her child, laying on her side, the oceans surrounding them like blue light." Her paintings, even if they are doomed to remain incomplete, must capture the essence of the feminine body, its autonomy and strength, its dependence and relatedness, its immersion into earth, sky, and ocean.

This exploration of femininity through her paintings during her self-imposed exile—"her pictorial images are inspired by her own emotional experiences and sensory perceptions"—parallels her friend's, Sierra's, exploration through poetry ("words are like flesh"). Rosa establishes herself as a modern woman firmly rooted in the late twentieth century, in the history of the 1980s, and participating in a gathering of all women, now firmly holding their own ground. She is anticipating the coming of a new century and of a new generation, that of her new-born daughter, Luzia. She also tries to reach a more universal meaning by capturing the mythical dimension of womanhood.

The experience of a Chicano living in the United States in the late 1980s cannot be grasped fully if it is not seen in its various settings. Rosa is an American, a Chicano woman who is also German, and whose life span stretches between two wars—World War II and the Vietnam War; the imperialistic pursuits of the United States in Latin and Central America have affected countries whose scars have also wounded her. She is also a woman whose ancestry reaches farther to her Mesoamerican and Indian heritage, a daughter of the Earth whose existence has universal cosmic significance.

All these women in her must resist all threat of domination and destruction, and challenge death in all its forms.

Genviève Fabre. Bilingual Review/Revista Bilingue. 16, 1991, pp. 171, 176, 178

VILLEMAIRE, YOLANDE (CANADA) 1949–

"To canonize" a young woman writer, whom it has been collectively decided to include in the company of the great classics, always poses a certain number of special problems. The absence of prior critical readings—except for reviews in the specialized or general press—makes one even more uneasy about a choice whose precise relevance is not always clear at the time of going to press. The writer's very youth forces a reading of a body of work whose few great moments are barely sketched out and whose overall project so far appears only in fragments. . . .

Yolande Villemaire comes to us nonetheless like a ripe fruit. A dozen books published in as many years trace the itinerary of her writing from experimentation as practiced in magazines like *Cul-Q* or *Hobo/Québec*, to the working out of a neo-realism whose high quality was hailed by critics as soon as *La Vie en prose* (Life in prose) and *La Constellation du Cygne* (The sign of the swan) appeared, making Villemaire one of the leading figures of the new Québécois literature. . . .

Lucie Robert. Introduction to special issue on Villemaire. Voix et Images. 33, 1986, p. 388

How can one speak of this rotatory and encyclopedic novel without stopping it in its gyrating course? How to describe *Life in Prose* leaving both the life and the prose intact, as they move with the mad rhythm of modernity? To place the vibrating thing under the lens of the microscope to study its contours and its colors means, in a sense, reducing the field of investigation. Let us be aware of it. Let us give up from the beginning the idea of seeing and grasping everything. Without thereby implying that we can't say anything about this book. . . .

Fiction. The rallying point of modernity. But *La Vie en prose* with its kit of accessories and disguises mixes together the lines of the real and the paths of the dream, the features of life and narrative, the thread of words, the grain of things, at will. How far to trace the real when realism is possible in literature but when literature is not possible in reality? . . . A novel that contains the principle of its own proliferation, that manipulates a series of amusements, digressions, substitutions, that programs and disguises the return of the same to such a point that one never succeeds in touching "the origin," "the first term," "the authentic subject," which keeps itself apart from the written but which gives itself up to it at the same time, thus testifying to the equal love of life and of prose, playing at moving the boundary between reality and fiction, producing therein that "quake of the real" that is perhaps what modernity is about.

Lise Potvin. Voix et Images. 33, 1986,
pp. 406, 425

For a dozen years, now, Villemaire's literary production has not cease recreating—not to say repeating—itself, within the same narrative schema (and whatever the genre employed: poetry, novel, essay, short story, mixed media), which is the source of this supposedly original vacillation. [In Villemaire, we observe a] systematic use of the same narrative schema, in prose as well as in poetry; repetition; recurrence of certain motifs, certain themes. . . .

In Villemaire, prose and poetry are linked in their content and in their constructions. The "laboratory" of which she speaks is that of a writer proud of her discoveries.

Claude Sabourin. Voix et Images. 33, 1986,
pp. 428, 439

La Constellation em-bodies the cruci-fiction of a *jouissance* whose astral resurrection constitutes the placing "into the light" of a subject of enunciation. Thus, in Villemaire, "Jacob's struggle with the angel," that of a hand-to-hand with the unnameable lays bare the inscription of a void that breaks the surface of a discourse that this act essentially consists in renaming.

Anne Élaine Cliche. Voix et Images. 33,
1986, p. 452

Now, this book, *La Constellation du Cygne,* it came to me like a mesh of interrogations, about the novel itself and about the reading that had been done of it. More than that, this text published by Editions de la Pleine Lune [Full Moon Press, a women's publishing house] makes it necessary to reconsider the writer herself. . . .

La Constellation du Cygne seemed to me an excellent example for approaching the question of the persona and the political, since the plot concerns the love relationship between a Jewish prostitute and a Nazi officer, a relationship that begins on August 15, Assumption Day, 1940, in Paris, and ends in August, 1944, thus covering the four crucial years of the last war.

A knot of interrogations, this novel. For me. For others, as well. For Jews in particular. And also for those concerned with politics. The discomfort that this novel can produce is evident in the editorial signed by Bernard Andres [in the special issue of] *Voix et Images* who entitles his contribution, "From the Literary to the Spiritual." . . .

History with a capital H has, in this novel, been assimilated to the love story, whereas it's the opposite one expects from a novelist, that the small history be integrated into the larger one, because *she's the one playing the tune, and not the other way around.* The Jews did not have the choice to die in their beds or in Auschwitz. And this Yolande Villemaire has not taken into account.

If, as a reader, I take a heavy responsibility—with respect to the sacred position Yolande Villemaire enjoys in Quebec—it is because I can thereby call upon *her* responsibility as a writer. I do not challenge her belief in previous lives. I say only that the subject does not interest me, since I already have enough to deal with in this life down here. But I cannot allow this belief of hers to serve as a panacea or an escape route. . . .

Just who is Yolande Villemaire to forgive Hitler and Nazism this way?

Suzanne Lamy. *Voix et Images.* 37, 1987,
pp. 19, 27

The pleasure of the body and experimentation with drugs are also central themes in Yolande Villemaire's novel entitled *Vava.* But the readers who, because of the title, expect to meet again the exuberant Vava who's a character in *La Vie en prose* and also encounter once more the jubilant avant-garde writing of that novel will be disappointed. Written for the mass audience— according to the author's own admission—*Vava* . . . utilizing a traditional narration, recounts the life of Vava Lafleur from 1968 to 1986. What happens in the life described at such length (707 pages)? Not much, unfortunately. In search of her identity, Vava recounts chiefly her numerous voyages and her sexual experiences. Does this mean that an erotic discourse enriches the text and gives it a certain destiny? No. We are dealing, rather, with a discourse of carnal adventures where the absolutely dizzying succession of male lovers (with mention as well of a female lover and a threesome) completely banalizes the representation of sexual relations. It is notable, moreover, that the narrative is set in a certain period by the numerous allusions to drugs, to travels, to mysticism, and to important political events like the War Powers Act, the Referendum, and the conflict in Afghanistan. But since everything is filtered through Vava's consciousness, this dimension is only slightly developed and, in the end, the personal articulates very little with the social. What do we get from this novel? Hard to say. One sure thing, this narrative reveals a strong tendency to narcissism, a tendency that, as in *L'Ange de la solitude* (The angel of aloneness), expresses the pain of woman's life.

Janet M. Paterson. *University of Toronto Quarterly.* 60, 1990, pp. 19–20

The heroine [of *Vava*] is brimming with urgent self-awareness and an energy too powerful to be contained in a single identity: each therefore has to invent a multiplicity of personae to accommodate this force. . . . Vava evokes various incarnations of herself from previous existences, mainly the Parisian Jewess Liliane Katz who died at Auschwitz. . . . (She) lives in the *milieu des arts* in Montreal and moves among literati and film-makers and theater people and photographers and artists. It is a world remote from conventional social forms, and [Vava] perceives such forms from a great distance. Vava pays occasional visits to her grandmother who has lived a modest, steadfast life surrounded by her garden; it is not simply the years and the miles that separate these two women, however, but rather the grandmother's conviction that men are superior to women. . . .

The endless affairs conducted by Vava are diversionary tactics in the quest for union with the shadowy Michel Saint-Jacques, who is her holy grail; between his brief and inconclusive appearances sexual union is achieved in apartments in Montreal, Vancouver, New York, in hotels in Paris and Egypt, on a beach in Mexico, in a canoe in Quebec with men whose presence in Vava's life may be fleeting or of long duration. The randomness of the encounters is emphasized by the fact that the one time she becomes pregnant it is by someone whose name she does not even know.

All this provides the filling between the interstices of the creative life of the narrator whose literary output resembles closely that of Yolande Villemaire: the Liliane Katz topos has an independent form in *La Constellation du Cygne,* which also has in common with *Vava* a preoccupation with heavenly bodies and even references to an Egyptian blue porcelain hippopotamus; *Ange amazone* (Amazon angel) foregrounds Hawaii, shamanic powers, reincarnation.

This novel deals with the circumstances around the creative act rather than the product; Vava recounts in detail the parties after the plays, the socializing around the presentations made at conferences, but is less fulsome about the plays and the presentations themselves. And in spite of celebrity and world travelling she remains naive and childlike. Her story is told in the present tense and in short sentences; she is surprised to find herself in certain situations, and feels that this is not her true self. In order to find this true self she enrolls in course after course of self-realization techniques and is constantly driven to tears by any set-back or rejection—as, for example, when she is expelled from one workship for being "too weird." In the turbulent late 1960s she seeks self in alcohol recognizing this has gone too far— she turns up to teach a class one day in a drink-sodden stupor, and has no recollection of what she has been saying to the students—she swears off and turns to other drugs in the 1970s and 1980s. Like a child she needs the reassurance of contact with certain family members and older, wiser mentors.

Whether her chaotic search ends with the finding of the grail and inner tranquility is something I will not reveal; but I must say that I cannot forgive Vava for what she did (and as the homonym with her previous incarnation exists only in English, I really don't think there's a pun intended) to her cats.

Vivien Bosley. *Canadian Literature*. 131,
1991, pp. 219–20

VORSE, MARY HEATON (UNITED STATES) 1874–1966

If you have an abiding love for the water: if the smell of tarred rope, the salt tingle of brine, the quiver and plunge of any and every sort of craft beneath your feet, from a punt to a racing yacht, are things that fill you with joy; then Mrs. Vorse's whimsical little volume, *The Breaking in of a Yachtsman's Wife* will lay strong hold upon you, and you will take it off quietly by yourself, safe from interruption, and laugh softly over it and be grateful for its humor and its insight. And if, on the other hand, you are one of those who have tried valiantly to qualify either as a yachtsman or a yachtsman's wife, and have owned yourself vanquished, you will still find in the book abundant entertainment, and an ironical appreciation of your point of view, even though the laugh is often against you. Furthermore, one may justly pay it a compliment rarely due to fiction of the episodic sort, of feeling that instead of there being a superfluity of episodes, there is on the contrary no page that we would willingly have sacrificed.

Bookman. July 8, 1908, p. 502

This [*The Very Little Person*] is a very little book about a "very little person," but the adjective, in both cases, has reference to quantity not to quality. The "very little person" is the first baby in the Greatrax family and the author describes with delicious humor the great changes wrought by such a tiny traveler. The exaggerated importance of the young parents, the naive manner in which Mr. Greatrax tells his friends, the hopes and fears of the first few months in baby's development, all are told with a delicate satire and loving sympathy, and even the baby's point of view is recognized in its first acquaintance with its own hands and feet. The difference between the methods of our parents and the modern theories in regard to the proper bringing up of children is laughably illustrated and every smallest event in a baby's life delightfully related—first smiles, first discipline. It can not be described, but it is delightful reading, and Miss O'Neill's pictures are fitting attendants for such a charming little book.

Literary Digest. June 17, 1911, p. 212

The promise of a love story, implicit in the title [*The Hearth Country*] is thoroughly borne out. It is less, however, the romance of two souls than a consistent analysis of a girl's mind and emotions under the stress of three successive courtships—the last a successful one. The book has the atmosphere of New England fifty years ago. The closest friend of Ellen Payne tells how the latter, a lovely and ardent girl of eighteen, meets and falls in love with a serious young teacher; how she outgrows this passage to carry on a whirlwind affair with a young man of her own fiery temperament whom she is at last compelled to give up through fear of a nameless undercurrent in his character; and how at last an accident, endangering the life of an old chum, reveals to her that he is the long-sought object of her real affection. . . . The study of a sensitive and attractive girl's heart is done with sympathy and with insight. To those who do not mind introspection, and who are not wedded to complexity of action, it should make a wholesome appeal; though the book is wholly feminine in outline and tone.

The Nation. May 7, 1914, p. 528

Mrs. Vorse's analysis [in *The Prestons*] is wonderfully true, though through all the extremely funny situations there runs a current of sadness reminiscent of *The Autobiography of an Elderly Woman.* The family she describes is typical of Our Town in Illinois—a far more frequent and American type than that of Our Hill on the Hudson. Being Mother on the Hilltop was a delicious interlude in a career. Being Mother in Our Town is an all-the-year-round "familiar task of meeting Jimmie's difficulty and smoothing out Henry." Henry Preston is like a thousand American family men, leaving everything to the mother, and interfering *hardly* ever but always at the wrong moment. Partnership in parenthood is so rare among us and vision so limited that parents still persist in believing that their children are being brought up instead of seeing that they are persons growing up. Careers are no longer issued under sealed orders; in abandoning this ancient right of parenthood the elders too often sit back to let youth run its swifter pace unaided. There is, of course, the occasional mother who begins a university course on psychology while her baby is in the nursery, only to find him in the grades before she is ready to practice her child-study on him; and the less frequent mother who "takes up her Thomas à Kempis for guidance in trying where all others have failed." On the other hand there is the wartime mother who has received from the young people of her family a written vote of thanks for allowing them to be born and to grow up at this particularly interesting time—a mother worth having, and one doubtless inspired to "carry on." But most of us make no effort to keep up beyond jogging along comfortably with the children in easy sight, till they suddenly strike their stride and are gone.

The Nation. February 1, 1919, p. 173

Greenwich Village receives for once a not unworthy treatment in *I've Come to Stay*, by Mary Heaton Vorse. . . . Mrs. Vorse writes well; the characters maintain a high level of conversational cleverness, and Sonya, the super-child who turns cart-wheels in the street to express her individuality, is an entertaining creature. The reader becomes at once a joyful partner in this gay romance.

The Dial. May 17, 1919, p. 526

With *Men and Steel* the trilogy of the steel strike is complete. [William Z.] Foster's book told what may be called, in no slighting sense, the professional labor leader's story. The Interchurch Report set down with authority the facts and figures about the labor policy of the employers and its result. Mrs. Vorse speaks as a poet. An incalculable, a terrific thing happened in the soul of the nation when three hundred thousand steel workers and their families arose to demand justice and were crushed back into the maw of the furnaces, into their own helplessness and discouragement. Foster gave us the blue-print, and the Interchurch Commission the statistical survey; Mrs. Vorse has written the tragedy. . . .

Mrs. Vorse has built up this picture by vivid spots of color which seem for a while chosen at random, just as they would flash upon a sensitive observer as he looked about him at this strange country. Gradually the things of steel take form before the eyes, then the people of steel, then the revolt of the people against the things. We receive the same sense from the book which those of us who were there received from the reality, and which none of us but Mrs. Vorse has adequately expressed: that this was not merely a quarrel for domination, that it was a heroic thrust of humanity upon "chaos and the dark," that it was symbolic of the high drama of the earth. How hopeless was the struggle of these simple people against the impersonal power of the corporations, against the cold and hypocritical hostility of officials and institutions, against the ignorance and prejudice of the public, against the silence which robbed them of the knowledge of their own achievements and insulated them from the courage of their fellows! Each man in his own house, waiting, waiting, drawing every day nearer the time when there would be no more bread for his wife and children, had to nourish himself against doubt by a superb faith. And at the end, the breaking of that faith was far more cruel than blows from State constabulary or the return to a life of nothing but toil and sleep. . . .

It is a beautiful and a terrible book, because like a true work of art it embodies the elemental beauty and terror of life. If we think of the sacrifice of individual persons and individual causes, and of the vengeance that some day is likely to be exacted for those sacrifices, it will depress and frighten us. But if we think of the mighty faith of the humble that some day must triumph, it will strengthen our courage. Mrs. Vorse might have ended with the prophecy of Zephaniah: "Woe to her that is rebellious and polluted! to the oppressing city! . . . Her princes in the midst of her are roaring lions; her judges are evening wolves; they leave nothing till the morrow. Her prophets are light and treacherous persons; her priests have profaned the sanctuary, they have done violence to the law. . . . Therefore wait ye for me, saith Jehovah, until the day that I rise up to the prey; for my determination is to gather the nations, that I may assemble the kingdoms, to pour upon them mine indignation, even all my fierce anger; for all the earth shall be devoured by the fire of my jealousy. . . . Behold, at that time I will deal with all them that afflict thee; and I will save that which is lame, and gather that which was driven away; and I will make them a praise and a name, whose shame hath been in all the earth."

George Soule. *The Nation.* January 19, 1921, p. 87

Fraycar's Fist, by Mary Heaton Vorse, is a collection of short stories dominated by two *leit-motifs:* the sea, and divinely ordained love at first sight. The action of the stories is varied, and in almost every case speeds along like a swift horse directed by a practiced rider. The ocean and the rough Atlantic shore are delineated with devotion and an occasional touch of magnificence. But the characters are phantoms far too similar to one another in their dark beauty and imperiousness. They loom up for a moment through seacoast storms, only to be driven into unreality by mystical tempests. The book is fairly well managed melodrama that satiates before it is done and then falls away like froth.

The Dial. 77, November 24, 1924, p. 437

Mrs. Vorse has been the war correspondent of the labor movement in the United States. In the midst of her preoccupation with three generations of family life, and her career as a writer on which this family depended for bread, and in spite of the dislocation of war, which took her to Europe for long periods, she succeeded in being on nearly all the active fronts of the labor struggle for the decade 1912 to 1922—the Lawrence strike of 1912, the Mesaba strike of 1916, the attempt to wipe out the I.W.W. by frame-up in court and killing in the street, the Palmer raids, the steel strike of 1920, the Amalgamated lockout, the judicial murder of Sacco and Vanzetti, the children's crusade in behalf of the wartime prisoners. In addition Mrs. Vorse gives an account of the Women's Peace Movement of 1915, of the warring countries in that year, of Europe after the Armistice, from England to the Balkans, and of Russia in the year of the great famine. Especially enlightening are her impressions of the revolutions in Italy and Hungary before those movements were suppressed in blood and terror by Mussolini and Horthy.

Mrs. Vorse was fortunate through her ability as a writer in gaining access to important magazines, while working in the labor movement, sometimes acting as organizer, and writing for the labor press. She was thus able to compel interest and sympathy for the worker from an indifferent and even hostile audience. And writing for this audience made her a responsible journalist, developed her power of persuasion, and taught her the value of moderation, of understatement. Her record of the atrocities of modern life, of all the evil done under the sun in that terrible decade, is factual and restrained. Now and then a comment has a note of bitter but salutary truth, as when, in speaking of wartime hysteria, she says: "One group of people tortured another. The suppressed hatred and sadism of the frustrated was unloosed in the name of patriotism. War unloosed the idealism and heroism of a generous people, but it unloosed them for destruction."

Upon the reader, however, the effect is of a deep and purging indignation. Those who followed events in those years will recall, and it will be good for them to recall, the cold cruelty of the Lawrence mill owners, refusing to let the children of the strikers be sent to other cities to be fed, the crafty cynicism of Judge Landis in procuring the indiscriminate conviction and sentence of over a hundred victims of patriotic rabies on the charge, not always proved, of being members of the I.W.W., the fanatical ferocity of A. Mitchell Palmer introducing illegal methods into the Department of Justice, the sickening duplicity of Hoover using the power given him in the name of humanity to betray the cause of a better world in Europe—the very cause for which we fought.

Another grateful aid to recollection is Mrs. Vorse's Who's Who of the labor leaders of those years—Frank Tannenbaum, Bill Haywood, Ettor, Giovanitti, Elizabeth Gurley Flynn, Carlo Tresca, Sidney Hillman. Her portrait of little Ann Craton in the organizing campaign for the Amalgamated Clothing Workers is charming, and memorable is that of William Z. Foster in his direction of the great steel strike, of whom she says: "He was probably the ablest labor organizer this country has ever known."

In finishing her book Mrs. Vorse tells us that she realized that while she thought she was writing about the labor movement, imperialism, war, she was all the time writing about children. "For when you come down to it, the labor movement is about children and about homes. In the last analysis, civilization itself is measured by the way in which children will live and what chance they will have in the world." This is the theme of the book. Always in a strike, a war, a famine, Mrs. Vorse touches the essential human interest through the child. There are a score of pictures of children, en masse, as at the New Year's party on the East Side of New York during the Amalgamated lockout or starving together at Samara; and as individuals, such as the homeless Milorad Bachinin, "a symbol of all the children of Serbia—a silent accusation of the children against war"; or six-year-old Gene Benefield on his way to Washington to ask for his father's release from prison. When asked, "What do you play when you are at home?" he replied, "I pick cotton and I chop cotton." It is this theme of childhood that gives its pathetic beauty to this book and determines its mood—that of abounding compassion.

Robert Morris Lovett. *The New Republic.*
January 1, 1930, p. 234

It is unfortunate that Michael Gold should have proclaimed that Mrs. Vorse's new novel, *Strike!* is a "burning and imperishable epic"—that is, a book to be classed with Homer and Milton. It is more unfortunate and less to be condoned that the publisher should have repeated Mr. Gold's generous but misguided words on one of those natty detachable bands that publishers like to place, like sashes, about book jackets. For so frantic a blurb would prejudice any reviewer or book buyer who did not happen to know Mrs. Vorse and her own modesty and craftsmanship.

By the device of combining Marion and Gastonia in one fictitious town, she has given a clear, honest, and often dramatic account of the horrors of the Southern textile mills. Most important in the book is her sympathetic picture of the mountain women who have been enticed to the mills, and who join the union only when they discover that the bossmen—devils mysterious as their native savage God—are condemning them to sick starvation. They are union members who do not know that there is an international labor movement. They are Communists who have never heard of Russia. They are Fine Old Americans who live more meagerly than Tibetan villagers. They are passionately pious Baptists who are not without earthly humor.

It is a beautiful irony that this book should have been issued at almost the same moment with the utterance by the Immaculate Herbert of the words: "In the American system, through free and universal education, we train the runners, we strive to give to them an equal start . . . The winner is he who shows the most conscientious training, the greatest ability, the strongest character. Socialism, or its violent brother, bolshevism, would compel all the runners to end the race equally; it would hold the swiftest to the speed of the most backward."

I do not suppose that Herbert the Immaculate meant in his slyly humorous way, his devotion to good clean fun, to give an opportunity for publicity for *Strike!* Yet whether or not he meant it, his platitudes gave to the book an especial pertinence. For he uttered them in those very Carolinas whose abominations are described by Mrs. Vorse!

She makes it uncomfortably clear, in this book, which is more a statement of facts than a novel, that our lovely American system does not, particularly in the region where the Immaculate droned his inspiring, his almost Bruce-Bartoning words, give anything like a universal education; that it does not train the runners—that, in fact, it is very likely to jail the real runners; and that, in innumerable cases, the winner is not he who shows the most conscientious training, the greatest ability, or the strongest character, but rather he who commands the services of the largest number of policemen with clubs and of militiamen with machine-guns.

But are the Southern mill towns really as horrible as Mrs. Vorse asserts, and the strikers really as gallant and as innocent? I maintain on my word of honor as a man who is not a Quaker or a Great Engineer, and who will certainly become neither immaculate nor President, that she has exactly and understandingly described what is happening in the Piedmont today. I have been there, through some of the very scenes which she chronicles. I know several of the characters in the book. She tells the truth—and dramatically.

I wonder if a lonely and confused man in Washington by the name of Herbert Hoover will read this book? Or if (to make the fantasy utterly mad), reading it, he might conceivably do anything, or say anything pertinent, about it?

There was a time, no doubt, as an Iowa farm boy, when he respected the Mothers in Zion: the honest, earnest, kindly, quiet women who bore children, who worked sixteen hours a day, who had always a bowl of milk for the wayfarer, who went for days or weeks to help neighbors in their need.

Such women still exist. Perhaps Mr. Hoover can no longer find them in Washington, or near his mansion in California. But if he will read *Strike!* and have such genius as to believe that it may be true, he will learn—and even a President of the United States might, perhaps, be able to learn something!— that the intolerable state of labor in the region where he oozed his goose-fat words has less to do with Socialists and Bolsheviks than with the slavery of just such women as once mothered a little boy named Herbie and gave him cookies.

If I were a publisher named Horace Liveright I would not talk about anything so vague as "burning and imperishable epics." I would, day after day, by the crudest modern ways of advertising, by newspaper page and radio and billboard, demand: "Your Excellency, Mr. Hoover, have you read *Strike!* by Mary Heaton Vorse? And if you have, what do you think of evicting families in which there is a child with smallpox, of policemen blackjacking unarmed old women, of whole American communities receiving an average wage of twelve dollars a week?"

And if the Immaculate most immaculately refused to answer, I would ask the same questions of Owen Young and Henry Ford and Dwight Morrow and Governor Roosevelt and William McAdoo and Al Smith.

I wonder if Al and Dwight Morrow might not answer?

Sinclair Lewis. *The Nation.*
October 29, 1930, p. 474

Above all it is her love of human beings, whatever their rank or kind, that illumines Mrs. Vorse's understanding of labor's struggles and labor's victories. One cannot know her, however briefly, without becoming aware of this. It is in her insatiable curiosity, her humor, her courtesy, her tact, and in a kind of gallantry that is so much a part of her. . . .

Mrs. Vorse's study of the C.I.O. has taken her from Florida to Seattle and almost all points in between. It has not been through mere accident that she has been on hand for the most critical happenings of the past five years. An uncanny prescience for what is about to be exciting and important took her to Flint for the sit-down strike in Chevy 4 and she witnessed there the victory of the auto workers with all its drama.

To other reporters on the job there is something a little startling about the way in which Mrs. Vorse manages to find herself in the thick of things. Calm, unhurried, she succeeds nevertheless in arriving at the right place at the right time. Perhaps it is because of the friendships that she has made through the years. While she is a first-rate reporter, she is more than that, more than an observer. Her sympathies are deeply engaged in the struggle that she has witnessed. . . .

Mrs. Vorse's interests are as varied as the titles of her books, which range from *The Breaking in of a Yachtman's Wife* to her autobiography, *Footnote to Folly*. The folly, incidentally, is not the author's personal folly but that of a war-torn world to which she has written what is indeed a brilliant footnote. But always she has come back to labor's struggle for the right to organize. Calling the roll of the strikes she has been through is to list the battles of a veteran warrior: Lawrence, Paterson, the strike on the Mesaba iron range, the great steel strike of 1919, the Kansas miners, Passaic, Gastonia, and Marion, in 1931 the Kentucky miners. And finally she has followed the rise of the C.I.O.

For those who have had a part in the struggle as well as for those who have stood outside it this book will mean a great deal. The participants have been too preoccupied with immediate tasks to record for the future this significant phenomenon. And what is more they have seen only one part of the nationwide growth of a new kind of unionism. Here is an observer who does not pretend to detachment. She is ardently concerned with the future of the organization that she describes. She has seen it all and she writes of it out of a lifetime of experience, a lifetime that has taken her from a prim Victorian drawing room to the picket lines of America.

> Marquis W. Childs. Foreword to Mary
> Heaton Vorse. *Labor's New Millions* (n.p.:
> Modern Age, 1938), pp. 1, 3–4

Mrs. Vorse has a contribution to make which is peculiarly hers. Never content to be just a conventional hall and union headquarters reporter, she has always somehow got to know individual workers and their families as labor reporters rarely get to know them. Through an intense sympathy she succeeds in becoming part of the very group she writes about. And as a result, she is able to break down our customary abstractions and figures into their component human elements. If the term did not carry unpleasant associations, she might be called labor's human-interest reporter. . . .

Because of this immediacy, because you cannot take refuge in the aloofness of objectivity or caution or indifference or whatever you wish to call it, *Labor's New Millions* is often uncomfortable reading. It is a record of unspeakable brutality by police, strikebreakers and vigilantes, of the deliberate fomenting of community hysteria by spies and citizens' committees, of the cynical defiance of the National Labor Relations Act by employers. On the other hand, though, much comfort can be got from seeing how an unorganized and oppressed mass of workers found within itself the strength to overcome the seemingly unyielding obstacles of its organization and liberation. Let us hope that *Labor's New Millions*, thanks to its low price will win a large popular circulation. There is a desperate need now for such books to counteract the abundant and skillful propaganda of the hardbitten anti-union camp.

Samuel Yellen. *The Nation.*
September 7, 1938, p. 138

The story of Provincetown between 1907 and 1942 would be a prime haul for any regional chronicler, and [in *Time and the Town*] Mrs. Vorse makes the most of the Yankee and Portuguese fishermen and the painters, rumrunners, Provincetown Players, and summer people who gave the town its legend. She does a little better than that, too: she shows us how the outside world made social changes in Provincetown and how her own affection for an old Cape Cod house survived three decades of change. Salty and easygoing.

The New Yorker. July 18, 1942, p. 60

The IWW leaders, and other beleaguered union organizers, were quick to recognize the supreme importance of publicity efforts by sympathetic and established reporters. Four years after the Lawrence strike, Bill Haywood would call on Vorse to serve in a similar fashion on the Mesabi Range. From that point on, Vorse was continually sought out by proponents of industrial unionism, from the IWW to the CIO, to provide the news coverage which could bridge the communication gap between union leadership and the general reading public. Her writing could compel interest and sympathy for the worker from an indifferent and even hostile audience. Vorse's measured, knowledgeable reports found easy entry into such middle-class journals as *Harper's, Scribner's, The Outlook,* and *The Independent,* outlets which were normally closed to writers too closely identified with left activists, and thus labeled as "propagandists" by the mainstream press. But Vorse also wrote for liberal intellectuals and reformers in such publications as *The Masses, The Nation,* and *The New Republic,* and for the workers themselves in her hundreds of dispatches for union newspapers, newsletters, and broadsides distributed by the labor press.

A consistent theme in her work is the need for industrial unionism. Year after year she exposed the failures and limitations of the AFL's goals and leadership. Her writing helped to convince many middle-class and working-class Americans of the wisdom of industrial labor organization.

Unlike many labor journalists, Vorse was often a participant in strike revolts. Her inside knowledge of union strategy and leadership, combined with her fervent commitment to accurate reporting, brought uncommon depth and passion to her work. Her middle-class readers, as well as her union friends, knew her version of events could be trusted. Always her writing was designed to make one feel, as well as think. For Vorse, a news story must include a re-creation of the human drama, as well as a recital of factual detail. . . .

But Vorse's most unique contribution to the labor journalism of her time is her consistent attention to the role played by women. Throughout her career, women and children interested her most. The worker's wife, the Serbian orphan, the starved children, the mean tenement home, the courage of girl pickets—these were the core of her material. Even today, the stirring epics of labor history are chiefly a tale of male leaders and activity. Through Vorse's eyes, we see a wider span, and are awarded tantalizing glimpses of the crucial contribution of women to labor advance.

> Dee Garrison. Introduction to Mary Heaton
> Vorse. *Rebel Pen: The Writings of Mary*
> *Heaton Vorse* (New York: Monthly Review
> Press, 1985), pp. 23–24

The writing career of Mary Heaton Vorse spanned the first half of the twentieth century. Her early articles and short stories were published during the years of Theodore Roosevelt's Presidency. Her last published effort appeared in 1953 during the first month of the Eisenhower Administration, when she was in her late seventies. She was an extremely well-received, commercially successful writer of popular fiction and reportage. Later in her long career, Vorse—who devoted herself to radical and feminist causes—became a politically committed journalist who hewed closely to the Communist Party line in much of her writing. . . .

Even so, however, it does not seem to me that this anthology [*Rebel Pen*] does Vorse justice. The selections have a sameness about them. In her day Vorse was an able, compassionate, dedicated speaker for the downtrodden, the exploited, the oppressed—whether male or female, adult or child, black or white. Yet all too often the anthologized material, especially the labor journalism, is special pleading that now reads like hack work for the ideologically committed reader. No matter what year she is writing or what situation she is discussing, the pieces in this collection deal with stalwart workers, brave spouses, militant women, oppressive management, pompous bosses.

> Daniel J. Leab. *The New York Times*.
> January 12, 1986, p. 28

Why reprint a historical novel [*Strike!*] that does not have much value as literature, especially when the real historical story has been reported by such good writers as Irving Bernstein, Ray Marshall, and Jacquelyn Hall and her fellow authors in the acclaimed book *Like a Family* (1987)? Rutgers University historian Dee Garrison, the author of a first-rate 1989 biography of Vorse, makes the case in an excellent introduction to the novel. She sees *Strike!* as the best of a forgotten genre, the strike novel of the 1930s, written at a time when the Left momentarily flourished. Briefly, she argues that Vorse was an early feminist writer who celebrated the courage and strength of working women, and that the novel reveals "the lost world of the mill family and the southern poor white women" without Communist party cant.

Unfortunately, Garrison's essay summarizes the strike better than the novel does. Read her essay and skip the novel. Vorse romanticizes the workers. And although she recognizes the problems of low income and owner oppression of unionism, she otherwise shows little understanding of the complexities of southern workers' lives. To acquire a better understanding of the historical issues that surround textile worker culture, read Robert Zieger's essay "Textile Workers and Historians."

James A. Hodges. *Industrial and Labor Relations Review.* 46, 1993, p. 604

VOZNESENSKAYA, IULIA (JULIA) (RUSSIA) 1940–

Have you heard the one about the mother and daughter who sawed off their lover's legs when he wouldn't hand over his thirteenth-month pay packet? He kept saying he wouldn't succumb to their torture, he'd been a partisan. And what about the little ice skater whose male trainers decided to "free the ligaments" in her legs? Her mother drowned herself when she found out. These and many others among the one hundred anecdotes which make up Julia Voznesenskaya's *Damskii Dekameron* are painful, bloody and horrific, and more evidence of the bizarre quality of Soviet Russian life. It has a particular failing for women. From the meat queue to the pleasures of the flesh Russian women are happy, but they crave a little civilization on the side. Voznesenskaya's title, which might have been better translated as *The Ladies' Decameron,* is an ironic pointer to the bourgeois graces and comforts Soviet culture excludes. Significantly none of the sex in this book is erotic.

Voznesenskaya, most prominent among the Soviet women activists at the end of the 1970s, founder of the group "Maria" before she left in 1980, has chosen fiction to explain the Soviet female lot. Ten women each tell one story a night to pass the ten days they spend quarantined in maternity hospital. Their physical preoccupations may have something to do with their having just given birth, but the cameo social documentaries have a fearful life of their own. The best of them transcend the casual manner in which they are told—like the story about Albina, the skater, who grows up to be a promiscuous, sentimental Aeroflot hostess. The melodramatic, operatic conclusion to her childhood undoing is in the best Russian tradition, while the allusion to Nabokov points up the eternally childish mind of the narrator.

Yet the social and political implications of the stories are never far away. Albina's tale is satisfyingly destructive of the official ideals of youth, sport and chastity. The Western reader is given to understand that unlike our own discontented Freudian relic this is not a society which values sublimation. Daily life is brutal, needy and pervasively policed, and thank Lenin for that, because the arrival of the militia can sometimes save a life. The whole is glued together by chance and tenderness, which is not quite enough when the cultural habit is for people to go at each other hammer and tongs. The anecdotal form corresponds nicely to the reality of Soviet communal living, where the day proceeds by unexpected leaps and bounds, jabbed by conflict and appetite.

Voznesenskaya, a balanced and unprogrammatic writer, doesn't set out to make her women consistent or good. They contradict each other and relish their triumphs. You might think they had had enough of male brutes as they make their way through dispiriting accounts of first love, seduction, desertion, farcical sex, infidelity, jealousy, rape, money and revenge. But they go on being delighted. They talk about being bitches to each other but who cares? Bitchiness is one of the subtler ways of surviving in the pursuit of happiness, better certainly than resort to the axe. Marriage, even if it is temporary, matters for that bit extra material comfort and security it can bring. The women narrators have their sensual whims and tricks and not all the men are beasts.

The women's political prejudices are neatly exposed. The so-called "Party bigwig" Valentina, who initially inspires fear and distrust, turns out to be rather subtle and human. The quarantine allows the dissident Galina to get to know Valentina, and in turn these two orderly women learn what it is to be Albina. As the women tell of furtive sex in overcrowded apartments, romantic weekends on the Black Sea and public couplings in labor camps, if any one of them is an outsider it is Galina with her high-minded lack of passion.

Voznesenskaya's language is appropriately pithy and colloquial. The English translation of this book, which has appeared in Russian only in the West, drops some words and uses dated slang, but otherwise it races along.

All is richly well in the end: the tenth night is given over to distilled happiness. The women compare themselves with Western women and consider our lives dull and inferior.

Lesley Chamberlain. (London) *Times Literary Supplement*. March 14, 1986, p. 276

Ms. Voznesenskaya's novel is not so much, as the jacket copy would have it, about "a society torn apart by suicide, divorce, and alcoholism"—rather, it is a poet's vision of how men and women struggle to live with each other. It is a bleak and distressing vision, but vision it is.

A wardful of mothers (willing and unwilling) lie in quarantine in a Leningrad maternity hospital and to pass the time tell one another tales, just as did the ten young men and women of Boccaccio's *Decameron* in their enforced isolation from the medieval plague. (Interesting that of these Soviet women half should have read the *Decameron,* or claim to have!)

Motherhood has taken by surprise or otherwise an amazing assortment of women—we have the "tramp," the music teacher, the prostitute, the biologist, the dissident, the party functionary—but the gentle and enduring passions of motherhood seem to be the last thing on their minds. Their tales are of love, lust and loose living, of horrible revenge and agonizing pain, of drunken women cutting off the legs of even drunker men, of rapes and castrations and, like a gleam of light, of the "daisy game," in which young women arrange themselves on the floor like the flower, heads together, legs apart, and young men pleasure each by turn; and one is grateful that at least there is pleasure.

Ms. Voznesenskaya, an activist and poet in the Soviet Union before she went into exile in West Germany in 1980, presents a harsh society—but human nature is even more so. A survivor returns with her child from Auschwitz only to find her husband with another woman; she is turned away from her own front door, grateful to be given the fare to another city. A child athlete who survives years of sexual torture from her two coaches one day rashly tells her ambitious mother what's going on, whereupon the mother promptly drowns herself. No help there!

Don't let me put you off reading *The Women's Decameron*. You should. It is profoundly interesting. I suspect it is nearer the truth of female experience than we gentle, self-censoring, educated, elitist Western women writers ever allow ourselves to get.

I do not, by the way, find the tales that make the Leningrad women laugh in the least funny, but humor is the most difficult thing in the world to translate, and you may have better luck than I: if, to start with, you find things like castration and the humiliation of men by women funny, you should laugh your head off with no trouble at all. W. B. Linton's translation is uneasy—I suspect it of being too faithful to the original. Phrases unheard of in practical English, such as "crazy types" and "gilded youth," coexist selfconsciously with "wimps" and men "getting their leg over." Never mind. Julia Voznesenskaya's vision shines through the opaqueness of cruelty, indecency, pornography, and out the other side into the sheer delight and wonder of just being alive, and female, and fighting back, albeit in a bullying, bewildering world.

Fay Weldon. *The New York Times.*
October 26, 1986, p. 9

Julia Voznesenskaya's . . . drastic solution in *The Women's Decameron* is to steal the liberating formality of mediaeval story-telling. As in Boccaccio, ten characters tell a tale on each of ten successive days.

Here, the narrators are mothers quarantined in a Leningrad maternity ward. Speaking of first love or rape, of jealousy or revenge, they tell of the casual brutalities of Soviet men and of the system that rewards them. This is history from below, its terrors softened by the laughter of a shared predicament. Stupidity and inertia open up fissures in the fabric of male and state power. A woman with her wits about her can crawl through these rents to find pleasure and security.

Boyd Tonkin. *The New Statesman.*
February 13, 1987, p. 30

In the closing pages of this book, [*Soviet Psychiatry*] which provides a constant reminder of the vulnerability of psychiatry to abuse, David Cohen pays tribute to the changes brought by *perestroika*. He concludes with a hope that the remaining dissidents will be set free and those whose lives have been ruined by misused psychiatry will be rehabilitated and compensated, a wish that also lies at the heart of a remarkable and touching collection: *Letters of Love: Women Political Prisoners in Exile and the Camps.*

There are said to be no more women left today in Soviet camps. Julia Voznesenskaya, who has collected and edited these letters, was herself a prisoner and an exile before she emigrated to West Germany in 1980. Her purpose in publishing them now is to provide a testimonial to the courage and resilience of these exceptional women, who, during the 1970s and early 1980s travelled vast distances on prison trains into exile, leaving behind them, often for many years, children, husbands and friends.

There are no names. *Letters of Love* is divided into three sections: those to friends, to relations, and to lovers. If the letters written to children are the most obviously moving, with affectionate references to a domestic existence painfully unlike conditions in labor camp, those written to friends, and particularly women friends, strike the clearest note, a wry, uncomplaining, even apologetic tone that comes across as immensely strong.

The tales the women have to tell are terrible: brutality, fear, theft, loneliness, despair and boredom. Yet these letters exude determination, even exultation. "I am saying farewell to you until 1981," writes one women as she leaves for exile in the mid 1970s. 'A five-year sentence isn't life,' our father used to say . . . especially five years exile. Don't worry about me. I continue to survive. . . . And whenever we meet, it will be as friends."

Caroline Moorehead. New Statesman and
Society. November 24, 1989, p. 46

WACIUMA, CHARITY (KENYA) n.d.

The social organization within the Kikuyu tribe is so central to the individual's sense of self that Waciuma explains both the general network and her family affiliation in the first chapter of *Daughter of Mumbi*. The title of her autobiography itself suggests the importance of these ties to her identity, as Mumbi is the legendary mother of all the Kikuyu, and Waciuma's description of the traditional system of division within the tribe links her with many generations of ancestral forbears:

> We all belong to a Clan (muhiriga), which includes all the descendents through the male line of one of the daughters of Gikuyu and Mumbi, and this is further divided into Sub-Clans (mbari), and then into lineage groups of four to six generations (nyumba) . . . We are the clan of Achera, which is also called Giceri, and we are the descendents of Njeri, the daughter of Gikuyu.

Waciuma learns of her lineage and related Kikuyu folklore from her paternal grandfather: as members of the Giceri clan the boys would become "self-sufficient and independent," and the girls "hard-working and devoted to their men." Inherited family traits, as well as clan affiliations, become important guidelines as the young mature from childhood to adulthood and accept the full responsibilities of all Kikuyu.

Carol E. Neubauer. *Journal of Modern African Studies.* 21, 1983, p. 118

Daughter of Mumbi is an autobiography which presents national history in a favorable light. Into the narration of childhood experiences are integrated the hopes and fears of a nation in the grip of the worst manifestations of imperialism and colonialism. . . .

A special feature of this work is the convincing picture it gives of the original beauty and solidity of Kikuyu culture. The reader is given enough information about the people for him to feel truly acquainted with them and their way of life. The author realistically presents many aspects of village life—belief in witchcraft and the existence of ghosts, ancestor worship, adherence to polygamous practices, the use of cattle as the currency for various transactions, the role of the council of elders, and the place of oral traditions in the life of the people. In each case the novelist gives sufficient detail for the background against which she writes to be fully realized. She achieves great success in the way she links the past with the present. . . .

The author undoubtedly has a fascination for this culture. But she is not sentimental in her presentation of facts. Just as there are merits, there are weaknesses. For instance, people with supernatural powers use them mostly to destroy their enemies. There are frequent inter-tribal wars, especially between the Masai and the Kikuyu, and these bring untold hardship to the people. The novelist looks at the situation from very varied points of view and at times puts these simultaneously before the reader. The aim certainly has been to present a culture that has a root in reality.

Since the work is autobiographical, it is appropriate that the author devotes a lot of space to Wanjiku, her heroine. We see her move from humble beginnings in the village to achieving the status of a college student in the town, exposed to all the temptations of city life. She acquits herself creditably both academically and morally. She personifies Kenya of the future, free from superstitious ideas and ritual worship, liberated from the shackles of imperialism, restored in honor and dignity to its ancestral land, and accepted as a respectable member of the international community. . . .

In *Daughter of Mumbi* Wanjiku dominates the scene because the whole work is about her personal development. Every other character plays a subordinate role. In this matter every [African] female novelist tries to make a contribution to the feminist ideals and helps to lay the foundation for a female literary tradition which is yet to be fully established in Africa.

Oladele Taiwo. *Female Novelists of Modern Africa* (New York: St. Martin's, 1984), pp. 33, 35, 37, 45

Charity Waciuma's autobiography, *Daughter of Mumbi* (1969), is certainly less well known than either [Josiah Mrangi Kariaki's] *Mau Mau Detainee* or [R. Mugo Gatheru's] *Child of Two Worlds* but is no less representative. *Daughter of Mumbi* belongs to the group of self-portraits written by Kenyans who remained in their country throughout the period of Emergency and experienced the conflict between the Mau Mau followers and the British colonials and Home Guard firsthand. Charity Waciuma, however, does not stand out among other Kenyan nationals as a prominent political figure, as do J. M. Kariuki, Mugo Gatheru and Tom Mboya among many others, and for this reason her autobiography has long been overlooked in the field of African literature. She neither developed strong party ties nor assumed a public role in the conflict beyond the scope of her own village. Nor is Charity Waciuma known as a professional literary writer in the sense that Ngugi wa Thiong'o and Grace Ogot are, for example. *Daughter of Mumbi* is not an autobiographical statement among a larger corpus of fiction or poetry by the author; rather it is Waciuma's single major literary effort and as such presents her story of a young Kenyan woman coming of age during the Mau Mau conflict. Her individual story, moreover, tells the story of many Kikuyu who arduously struggled to protect the stability offered by family and communal life and [were] threatened from both sides by the Mau Mau and the British colonials.

She has chosen to write her life story to document the gradual deterioration of traditional religious and social values within the scope of her own family.

Daughter of Mumbi narrates the period of Waciuma's childhood and adolescence in Fort Hall in the Central Province of Kenya. Her story begins with an account of the naming ceremony after her birth and ends just before she reaches full adulthood and her country gains national independence. Until her early college years, which coincide with the beginnings of the Mau Mau movement, order and security largely characterize her life both on an individual and on a communal level. Two different yet complementary influences create and sustain the order of childhood: her family life and the tenuous balance between traditional social and religious beliefs and the spread of Christianity. As long as these two interdependent structures, her family and her religious beliefs, remain mutually supportive, Waciuma benefits from the sense of fulfilling a significant role in her family and just as crucially, of belonging to the community and sharing its social values and traditional folklore. Unlike many Kikuyu families who had not converted to some branch of Christianity, the Waciuma family as members of the Church of Scotland must actively maintain a mutually beneficial synthesis between Christian doctrine and traditional values. Yet as long as a viable compromise which is ultimately not detrimental to either interest is sustained, the family benefits from a broader basis of support and order in their lives. . . .

From her father, Waciuma learns to interrelate social and religious values of the clan and her education through the Church of Scotland. The balance between traditional and Christian beliefs provides the single strongest source of order in her childhood. Waciuma underscores the importance of certain age-old clan customs, such as the ritual of naming children. Not by accident does she choose to begin her autobiographical narrative with an account of the ancestral association linked to her own name. The first chapter of *Daughter of Mumbi* is entitled "Names" and the first words explain her parents' reasoning in the choice of her Kikuyu name. An autobiographer Waciuma recognizes the historical ramifications of her name, Wanjiku, and links her names and the traditional process of naming children to her Kikuyu heritage and the order it lends to her life. . . .

Her name alone symbolically ties her not only to generations of her own family but to all Kikuyu people as well. Her Kikuyu name links her to the spirits of the dead and to the unnumbered children of the future. Most importantly, the title of her autobiography, *Daughter of Mumbi,* identifies her as merely one individual—one more daughter of Mumbi, the legendary mother of all Kikuyu people—who emulates the heroic models of her clan ancestors and brings order and meaning to her life through traditional beliefs. . . .

By concluding with a reference to her deceased father and the connection between his house and his father's house, Waciuma extends her personal story beyond her own family. The familial ties between Nyumba ya Gacii and Nyumba ya Waciuma in some sense touch all sons and daughters of Gikuyu and Mumbi and expand the story of one woman and her family into a folk history pertaining to many generations of Kikuyu people. In writing her life story, Waciuma makes the pledge as many Kenyans have to carry on ancient traditions into the post-Independence era despite strong pressures from Western influence and Christianity. For the African writer, autobiography is a means to restore the balance between tradition and change that has been threatened and in some cases destroyed over the years. Through autobiography a writer can give her life a sense of meaning and an order that is perhaps more far-reaching and more lasting in the text than in life itself. For Charity Waciuma, writing her life story in some ways answers the pervading sense of separation and ambiguity precipitated by her father's death and the widescale conflict. Her story documents her traditional heritage and ties her to all members of her clan who suffered a similar sense of dislocation and disorientation in relation to the Kikuyu land and cultural values in general.

C. E. Neubauer. *World Literature Written in English.* 25, 1985, pp. 213–15, 219

The Christian religion, as it was introduced into Kenya in colonial times, condemned the practice [of female circumcision]. Charity Waciuma in *Daughter of Mumbi* explains it this way:

> [T]he Church of Scotland missions decided they had to stamp out the circumcision of women. Instead of doing this in a subtle way, they went about it so badly that they actually increased the people's attachment to their old customs. Both the girls themselves and their parents were turned away from the Church if the girls had the operation performed.

According to Waciuma, young females are placed in a tug-of-war position where they are refused membership of the Christian Church if they have committed the "sin" of circumcision, and are also refused a position within their community if they are not circumcised. An uncircumcised female was considered to be "unclean" and often not allowed to marry because "it was believed that a girl who was uncircumcised would cause the death of a circumcised husband. Moreover, an uncircumcised woman would be barren." In *Daughter of Mumbi* the Christian school girls who had not "been to the river" to be circumcised were segregated at school from those who had been circumcised. In the village it was the uncircumcised girls who "became a laughing-stock, the butt of their jokes"; at school the tables were turned and it was the circumcised girls who were ridiculed and isolated and even prevented from advancing in their education at the Christian mission schools. The Christians were attempting to eradicate this "barbaric" tradition but instead exacerbated the culture clash. Both circumcised and uncircumcised females were made to feel ashamed of their bodies and their sexuality.

Jean F. O'Barr. In Eldred Durosimi Jones, et al., eds. *Women in African Literature Today* (Trenton, New Jersey: Africa World Press, 1987), p. 60

WADDINGTON, MIRIAM (CANADA) 1917–

A review of this small volume [*Green World*] is long overdue, especially since most of the poems within it are worth close consideration rather than neglect. Mrs. Waddington is a social worker by profession, and it is perhaps not surprising that the best of her poetry reflects the daily experiences of her professional life. Poems such as "The Bond" and "Investigator" are not only skillful demonstrations of the author's ability to handle the poetic form, but they also show a true awareness of social problems, as well as a rich humanitarianism in her approach to them. But for those readers who are skeptical about the poetry of social work, it is perhaps well to note that Mrs. Waddington by no means restricts her poetic reactions to her own professional field. She can write a good love lyric; and her power of description is not slender.

Technically her poems show a rich variety, and she is always willing to experiment. Her vocabulary is rich; her metaphors and similes are often daring, but usually successful. Though she is seldom trite, she usually marshals her ideas in an orderly manner, and, generally, it is not difficult to arrive at the core of the matter. At times she can be annoying by her disregard of what might have been helpful punctuation, but this in itself is a small matter. What does matter is the delicacy of her perceptions, as well as her awareness of social problems, both large and small. She is a good poet, and she is still developing.

S. E. R. *Canadian Poetry Magazine.*
December, 1947, p. 44

In [Miriam Waddington's] two books, *Green World* and in particular *The Second Silence,* social responsibility and human response rest on a faltering, recovering human will. If her later poetry is to be called religious, it is a very daily religion, whose shrine is everywhere. Living and Loving are work and choice, a series of imperfect acts and revisions of acts. But we carry with us the memory of a green world of free acts, symbolized in children, accessible in dreams, and prophetic of some last act: "the magical release of final definite decision." . . . Her tone alone, with its combination of sharpness and tenderness, of wit and incantation, would link her with the Evangelical tradition in English literature—as, say, a kind of cross between Cowper and Blake. I should add that she is a very uneven, often unsatisfying poet, whose work as a whole is more impressive than any poem or selection of poems can make it seem. She is at her best when the daily imperfections of the will are in the foreground and the second silence is evoked but not emphasized in a peroration. Judging from the poems I have seen since 1955, her third volume promises to be her finest.

Milton Wilson. In A. J. M. Smith, ed. *Masks of Poetry* (Toronto: McClelland and Stewart, 1962), pp. 129–30

The Season's Lovers is Miss Waddington's third volume of poems. In it she makes metaphysical lyrics that are governed by venerable images like the city as a macrocosmic being, the paradox of intermingled selves that remain ultimately strangers, the word as creator, and the dream that outreals reality. These images are exciting ones that have long been the matter of good poetry, and precisely because of this they are very difficult to manipulate well. Their very richness is embarrassing, in using them it is difficult to avoid using, for instance, the seventeenth-century manner. While there is no particular virtue or merit in "being original" (tables of degrees in originality are a device of lazy reviewers), there is great virtue in putting things meaningfully for one's contemporaries. In *The Season's Lovers* it seems to me that the meaningful poetic statement, or the modern manipulation of old images, has been on the whole successfully brought off. . . .

Miss Waddington is a passive lyricist. The movement of her poetic self is almost invariably responsive. The situations she projects are of the sensitive and intelligent self in the various attitudes of response from ecstatic to revulsive. The ultimate theme of *The Season's Lovers* is in fact the horrific glory of responsive self. Hence there is in Miss Waddington's work a peculiarly direct relation between the lyric form and its content; her content is almost lyricism itself. This proposition is neither meliorative nor pejorative: her way, though striking, is just one way of doing things.

Ian Sowton. *Dalhousie Review.*
Summer, 1959, pp. 237, 239

The fifty-five poems in *The Glass Trumpet* deal with "man woman child" and the reader must ask what is the "what" of them? They are headed "Things of the World," "Carnival," and "The Field of Night." They are printed in a small type down the center of the page. Gaps are often used instead of punctuation and may be a guide to the reader-aloud who has not been taught punctuation in an advanced school. The more orthodoxly written and set poems are more attractive to eye and mind. The content consists of personal experience—the apparently autobiographic content of, say, "saints and others"—of random reflections, as in "Summer Letters," of family, as in the Judith Wright-like poem, "The Gardeners." There are more consciously literary poems in the "Carnival" section (reflections of Yeats, Eliot): while in "The Field of Night" there are Biblical echoes, and a sense of an inarticulate poetic cry moving into the deliberation of words.

What is the achievement? The reflection, certainly, of an intense, imaginative, intellectual woman's responses to the world of natural phenomena, ideas, and human beings. This is poetry which is based on wide reading and on a sensitive capacity to match emotions with words, disciplined in most cases, into a cohesive form. From these poems some Canadian flavor emanates: but not obtrusively. It is there as background to poetry—which might have been written by this poet anywhere in the world where her thoughts and feeling were engaged. It is written out of experiences many of which will be accepted as part and parcel of modern life, with its movement, strain, self-awareness, intensity and complexity.

A. Norman Jeffares. *The Journal of
Commonwealth Literature.*
June, 1971, pp. 135–36

Mrs. Waddington's poems in her fifth book of verse [*Say Yes*] give us pictures of love, small joys, and the grand disillusions of our urban landscape. Some of the poems build neither to climax nor to complaint but to a finale that seems halfway between a bad imitation of Gertrude Stein and a bad imitation of A. A. Milne. . . .

Others head for the heart of what she feels she feels. They chase after those images for whose sake she writes, whom we might say she propitiates in verse. Neither classically pure nor modernistically precise, the images which she has "begun to worship" have a biographical immediacy and vitality, and they are, for her, firm enough to be treated like old photographs. She can "prop them up on bureau tops in hotel rooms." . . .

Mrs. Waddington sees and is fond of the "little fringes" of the frayed, everyday world. She responds to drabness with sprightly charm and a little girl's imaginativeness. The more personal she is, the more engaging is her work.

F. D. Reeve. *Poetry.* July, 1971, pp. 236–37

I think most of Miriam Waddington's poems in her recent collection of new and selected poems, *Driving Home,* are boring. But as this collection spans thirty years of work, boredom here is perhaps not entirely her fault: the worst poems reflect the fashions of times they were written in. It is difficult not to be bored with intricate little home-made myths and texts designed to fill up with sentiment the empty prairies or an empty life. And it is difficult now not to be bored with the careful encapsulating into *rhyme* of the passions and anguish of a social worker in the 1940s and 1950s, and of the lives of those she was in contact with.

But I wonder if Waddington doesn't share these views. The best of the poems in *Driving Home* are mostly in the section of new poems (since 1969). Here she is able sometimes to get inside her present life and show it to the reader in a convincing way. In "Eavesdropping" she imagines all the wonderful things she hopes for at the sound of the telephone: literary fame, academic recognition, and long-distance love. . . .

Some hint of the powerful poems Waddington might have written out of her social work in clinics, jails and as a welfare official can be seen in "Investigator" (1942) where she captures for a moment something of the inside of the homes and lives of the poor. . . .

In "The Women's Jail" (1956), an unrhymed poem, Waddington tells of how she secretly admires the beautiful young girls in jail for check-forging. . . . It is the tag of "evil" applied to these girls or their crime, plus the self-doubt expressed as the easy comparison of the social worker to the inmates, that bothers me. As someone raised with the left-wing background that Waddington mentions, plus having experienced her work among the poor, could she really believe that check-forging is "evil"? I can't help feeling that there is something awfully genteel about this poem and its neat final comparison—as though the poem is a careful, conventional mask for a more jagged and powerful response to this situation. And so with a number of her other social poems.

My lack of complete belief in what Waddington is saying appears even in the new poems of this collection. Something is missing, for me, in a poem like "Transformations" when she says she wants to spend her life in Gimli listening to the silence. . . . Granted, this poem is doubtless meant to be a bit of *joie de vivre,* but even so I'm not convinced there is much *joie* in concentrating all winter on Henry Hudson adrift in a boat. Henry Hudson strains the credibility even in the midst of a willing suspension of disbelief.

Tom Wayman. *Canadian Literature.* Winter,
1973, pp. 85–87

Miriam Waddington has always maintained a rigorous, even stern intellectual approach in her poetry, though the surface of idiomatic flow sometimes may paradoxically obscure the hard thought behind the poems. The development of her poetry has centered around the development of a completely personal voice, and this search for a unique voice has become one of the critical cruxes in any discussion of her work. The tone of the voice, certainly in the writing from *The Glass Trumpet* on, has been achieved through the emergence of a specific speaking persona within the poems. One critic has called it an "uneasy voice" which expresses "hesitant, sometimes almost shy revelations." The voice she has certainly developed for herself, but its tone may be akin to what she feels are essentially Canadian moods in the work of a painter she much admires, Phillip Surrey. In a review of his paintings, she stated that Surrey is Canadian in tone because of a kind of tentativeness that creates tension because he is "investing his pictures with more emotion than he is willing to confess to."

Although this voice is Canadian in these terms and although she has adopted it as part of her distinctive style, in some ways the timbre and tension may come from the influence of American poet Alan Dugan, a poet she very much admires. Dugan has also fashioned a unique, colloquial voice in his poetry: tough, slightly jaded, and self-deprecatory, it is a voice that assesses the speaker's chances in the world with some humor, that is occasionally cynical and sometimes downright bleak, and that reveals only so much, with the persona remaining outside life even as Dugan suggests his own commitments to it. This voice is similar to Waddington's though perhaps it is more direct, less tentative in its American-ness.

Peter Stevens. In Robert Lecker, et al., eds.
Canadian Writers and Their Work, vol. 5
(Toronto: ECW Press, 1985), pp. 282–83

WAKOSKI, DIANE (UNITED STATES) 1937–

Still in her twenties, Diane Wakoski has already gained recognition as a poet of genuine talent. A Southern Californian with a Berkeley B.A., she now lives in New York, where she teaches in a junior-high school. . . . [Her work] is youthful, spacious, sunny, exuberant, excited, and though filled with teaching, it is free from pedantry. Among the many virtues of her poetry, the rarest and most wonderful is its ease, its grace, its naturalness. This is not to say that her poetry is "easy." Indeed, her surrealistic symbols are often extremely demanding, but her poems never demand exertions from the reader whom they do not repay with immediate and abiding joy.

> Robert Regan. *Library Journal.*
> March 1, 1966, p. 1231

In her *George Washington Poems* [Diane Wakoski] has revived the figure of the Father of Our Country as a genuine living fictional personage, but in totally unexpected ways—at least to me. He becomes neither the historical figure, nor a mythological one; but instead a changeable person, variably George, the General, Mr. President, a father figure, an enlightened aristocrat, and ultimately a projection of the poet herself, slipping back and forth in time, with whom she converses, or to whom she declaims, in the cheerfullest terms imaginable, about her own life, her actual father and husband, her sense of relationship to her country, and many other themes. The ramifications are endless. Her body becomes a map, for instance; her personal being, the history of that nation. If Miss Wakoski's scheme has a flaw, it is the playfulness that pervades it, but perhaps this is essential, perhaps the scheme would collapse without it.

Readers who insist that poetry cannot be poetry which does not rise from and return to a sense of conviction, will be dissatisfied with *The George Washington Poems,* as will those who prefer a stronger, more complex language than the post-Beat idiom used by Miss Wakoski (as I generally do myself). But poetry or not, this book delights me. It is exactly the sort of book I should like to find, but never do, at my bedside when I go visiting in somebody else's house.

> Hayden Carruth. *Hudson Review.* Summer,
> 1968, p. 408

I have been following Miss Wakoski's career for several years, listening to her read in public and brooding over her poems in books and periodicals. I have been consistently impressed by her ability to convey the emotions of terror and desire, the experience of a vulnerable spirit in an environment of overwhelming verticals and horizontals. Bright, arresting images and perceptions leap from the pages of her poems, some of them whimsical and naïve, others profound and breathtakingly original. Yet, though her flights are imagi-

native, she permits a great deal of reality to enter her poems, often transmo-
grified, to be sure—as it inevitably would be under pressure of strong feelings
of anger, alienation, or frustrated love.

It is the feeling of love that is particularly interesting. The speaker of
her poems is forever reaching out for love and withdrawing in pain, as though
she has touched atomic waste. In fact, many of the poems are addressed,
rather reproachfully, to an unnamed male figure who is both lover and be-
trayer. This figure is sometimes a father and sometimes a husband and, occasionally, George Washington, who serves as a sort of paragon of virtue, a
great generative and controlling force, in Miss Wakoski's private mythology.

Stephen Stepanchev. *The New Leader*.
December 2, 1968, p. 18

Diane Wakoski's new book, *Inside the Blood Factory*, presents at first reading
a bewildering array of talent. She can work in many different forms: prose
paragraphs, the short, tight lines of Williams or H.D., the free surrealistic
movement, the loping Whitmanesque line. In one poem, "Sestina for the
Home Gardener," she creates a witty variation on that ancient form, maintaining the precision of the mode, while lengthening the lines and pouring
out the images in a profusion that threatens to break the pattern, but never
quite does so. At the same time the volume shows a similar range of themes
and materials: an elegy to the dead, a memorial of a father in the Navy,
images of ancient Egypt, George Washington, Beethoven, a sequence to a
man who drives a "silver Ferrari," a sequence based upon the Tarot deck,
or a poem about a scene where a mother slices oranges for her invalid son.

This list of subjects may suggest a little of the range of Miss Wakoski's
vision, which touches with a generous affection the things of life and finds a
home for them within the self. . . . All this variety of movement, whether in
rhythm or in image, builds up to the total impact of a powerful poetic mind,
continuously absorbing and recreating the current of experience, pooling it in
sections that hold together by her deliberate technique of repetition. . . . Out
of it all comes some of the most striking poetry produced in New York City
during the past decade.

Louis L. Martz. *Yale Review*. Summer, 1969,
pp. 603–5

The dominant theme in this latest volume of poems [*The Motorcycle Betrayal
Poems*], in case you haven't guessed, is *betrayal*. It's in the title, in the dedication, and in most of the poems. "The only man who's never/betrayed me/is
my accountant," she says, which tempts us to conclude, syllogistically, that
he is, therefore, no man. The assumption throughout her work is that men
are by nature as prone to betrayal as mortality. Just as she can not resist
mentioning it in a poem, we find it hard to resist mentioning that her father
left when she was two. But psychiatry and poetry are antipathetic; it's unnecessary to violate her psyche. In spite of the fact that she insists that her life

is laid bare in her poems, we should force ourselves to act as though there is a gap between life and art, between Diane Wakoski the private person and Diane Wakoski the public artist. Let her deny it; it's still true. It is always true—of every writer. So any comments we make here must really be about the voice in the poems, not the author's personal voice. Everybody acts a little funny in front of a camera. . . .

That Diane Wakoski has talent few people can deny. Sometimes that talent produces a startling image, a great passage, or even a near-great poem. But at other times that talent is ruined by speed, ambition, and self-pity.

Robert DeMaria. *Mediterranean Review.*
Spring, 1972, p. 55

[Wakoski] cultivates the longer poem; although there are short poems in [*Greed*], she often requires considerable length to say what she wants to say . . . yet she says it, and that is what counts. The reader has the feeling of a strong, centrifugal force, rarely centripetal. . . .

Her facility is particularly apt for describing *desires,* pleasure, and wishful thinking. When she writes about pain she is less convincing; there is much violence in her book—blood, bruises, scars. . . .

Her desires are open, liberal, attractive, and spendthrift; she has a marvelous desire to encompass everything.

John R. Carpenter. *Poetry.* June, 1972,
pp. 165–66

Diane Wakoski knows how to make words into poems. Her precise and straightforward style organizes not-quite-reality, and pushes it into the right contact. At all times in these two books [*The Motorcycle Betrayal Poems* and *Smudging*] Wakoski is in control, she is the craftsman. Although her poems are not traditional structures, she builds them solidly with words which feel chosen, with repetition of images throughout a poem . . . and with exact observation. . . .

These two books are remarkable because Diane Wakoski has successfully balanced the life of emotion against the life of intelligent reflection, through the medium of poetry. The poems sound true in your heart, true in your mind, and true in your ear.

Debra Hulbert. *Prairie Schooner.* Spring,
1973, pp. 81–83

Diane Wakoski has been unreadable for five years. Our good writers are liable to terrible slumps, though none has beaten Wordsworth's record. Personalists are always by definition in danger of substituting liking for principle. In *Greed, Parts 8, 9, 11* she's pulling out of it. As it was you had to tell students what books of hers not to read (everything after *Inside the Blood Factory*). The words are still too conceptual, moving at speech's rate without its weight, but that rate and the lumber-pile of line *become* weight (again) in this. You have to read her with love, though, to see it. She's *over* writing to audience expectations (or to a mythic self-image, as in the hideous Breadloaf lecture), by the brave device of parts 8 and 9, and begins to be clear what metaphor, for instance, won't do. She's never (or only once) *merely* cute. *Greed* 11 really begins to be a way to write lines that are sense-units but not for that reason stupid. The book is anchored on her but no longer exploits her. She may write bad things again, but after this won't print them. Bet.

Gerald Burns. *Southwest Review.* Summer,
1973, p. 280

Diane Wakoski published her first book of poems in 1962. *Smudging* (1972) and *Greed, Parts 8, 9, 11* (1973) are her thirteenth and fourteenth books respectively—an average of more than a book a year. Such feverish production—many would say overproduction—can be explained by examinig Wakoski's aesthetic. "Poetry," she believes, "is the completely personal expression of someone about his feelings and reactions to the world. I think it is *only interesting* in proportion to how interesting the person who writes it is." This super Wordsworthian formula places a heavy burden on the poet, for poetry is the "completely personal expression" of one's every feeling and reaction to the world, how does one maintain consistent interest? Wakoski strives for a voice that is wholly natural, spontaneous, and direct. Accordingly, she avoids all fixed forms, definite rhythms, or organized image patterns in the drive to tell us the Whole Truth about herself, to be *sincere.* . . .

There is something appealing about . . . the poet's admission that although she longs to "dream past all my lower class barbed wire" and "walk down the street in a silk glove," she must always come back to the "faded colors, lumpy shape" that is her peasant heritage. But despite the stress on ordinary particulars—teeth that are "strong but yellowish" and "lumpy mashed potatoes"—Wakoski's is not a poetry of *attention,* a celebration of the phenomenal world.

Marjorie Perloff. *Contemporary Literature.*
16, 1975, pp. 90–91

Diane Wakoski leaves no doubt about her feelings toward Marjorie Perloff's review of her work and toward criticism in general:

> That's what I think enraged me so much about Perloff's criticism that my poetry was superficial or easy, that whatever she did not like about the emotional facade or plain language, that plain language did not indicate a lack of struggle. If she as a new critic likes to see the struggle in the language (which is why she loves Ashbery. There's the language—I mean, the words are practically fighting with each other from word to word. And because she's a formalist she prefers to have that struggle go on within the language, whereas I'm not a formalist, and to me

that's not the struggle that is most interesting), it seems unfair not to look for the author's intention.

Certainly Wakoski has a reason for anger at Perloff's review. Yet her own argument is curiously naive, as if there were conflicts carried out in language that interest some poets ("formalists"), and conflicts carried out in more substantial ways ("form is an extension of content" is a familiar formula of Wakoski's) that interest other poets. All the critic has to do, like a piece of litmus paper, is register the author's intention in a particular case. Her more elaborate descriptions of poetic process as the creation of a "personal mythology" betray a similar naïveté, ignoring the work of any number of critics, philosophers, psychologists, and others who have questioned the very idea of "personality," of "subject." If the result of that ideological "battle-ground" for critics has been the escape from any immediate contact with poems, it would seem as though for poets the conflict engenders an acute distrust of critical intelligence in any form. . . .

If one turns to Wakoski's poems, her comments about Perloff's review begin to make a certain sense. For these poems in fact offer one of the most compelling challenges to someone like myself, and most of us, tuned to detect the slightest distortion, the barest hint of squall line approaching to disturb "plain," straightforward language in a poem: "I tear up my mother's letters / because she is a sad woman who has given me / the gift of her sadness." Faced with lines like these from a poem called "Tearing Up My Mother's Letters," there is somthing painfully silly about resorting to all one's heavy French artillery to reduce them to an effect of discourse, erecting a kind of Maginot line to protect criticism's hard-won territory. Even if Wakoski's argument seems naive, at least it provides sufficient warning that the poems will not leave one's critical assumptions neatly in place.

Evan Watkins. Contemporary Literature. 22,
1981, pp. 562–63

The "new poetry" toward which Wakoski [Toward a New Poetry] would have us move is based on the longer narrative poem, the "personal narrative" of the poet. This "new art" is not the traditional lyric with its forms of meter and strophe, but "a kind of cross between religion, philosophy, and story telling. It is a meditative art, and it's very personal, as opposed to the story teller who feels much more involved in telling the stories of other people." Epic has moved into fiction, she tells us, and poetry is the contemporary speech of our most sensitive people. Her gripe against critics is that they are historically minded and judge a modern poet with the sound of seventeenth-century diction in their heads. She teaches for a community of poets, those who understand. Defending herself against elitism, she claims that a self-selected group of poetry lovers is not anti-democratic.

Wakoski's essays, "poem-lectures" and interviews are arranged in five sections. Columns from the American Poetry Review published between 1972

and 1974 are followed by published and unpublished pieces. The five interviews take up one-third of the book. She comments on many areas of life
and poetry: dreams, oral readings (she is a very popular reader on the college
circuit), academic critics (Helen Vendler comes in for heavy opprobrium)
and specific opinions (she disputes Adrienne Rich's objections to Stevens's
"The Dolphins"). Her critical judgment is professional; the "Letter to the
Finalists of the Walt Whitman First-Book Poetry Contest" illustrates the
application of her principles to a specific situation and is full of interest.

   In spite of the sound doctines put forth here, many readers will be exasperated by the aggressive narcissism; "I," "me," "mine" and "my poems"
stud each paragraph with monotonous repetition.

D. Earnshaw. *World Literature Today.* 55,
1981, p. 327

Diane Wakoski's poetry, which strays about as far as possible from the detached irony of a well-made modernist poem, undertakes, nevertheless, precisely the task which Eliot outlined. Her work suggests that while the
"prejudice in favor of reason" which Nietzsche distrusted might lead to a
misguided and futile search for modernist order, there is in post-modern
poetry both an order and a method. In her attempt to confront the "futility
and anarchy which is contemporary history," Wakoski not only accepts but
embraces the experience of loss which underlies so much of her poetry. She
begins with traditional or inherited myths and develops out of them her own
malleable, often contradictory mythology, one which responds to irreversible
absence by elaborating and thereby continuing desire. George Washington
becomes the father of our (her) country; The Man With the Mustache reappears as frequently and as much on cue as Yeats's Maude Gonne; and The
Man Who Shook Hands exists solely as an enigma. As the moon goddess,
"Diane" either enchants men or wonders why she doesn't. George Washington's deflated image hardly replaces a stable father figure, and the elusive
King of Spain dissolves into his crippled brother. In spite of this, Wakoski's
quest for a personal mythology succeeds just because she controls and or-
chestrates every experience. Personal but very deliberately not confessional,
Wakoski's poetry acknowledges loss—of children, of love, of sustaining
myths—and develops out of that a coherent body of work in which desire
functions as an enabling drive.

Taffy Wynne Martin. *Boundary 2.* 10:3,
1982, p. 157

Diane Wakoski's *The George Washington Poems* [are] twenty-three deadpan
surrealist farces woven like Maypole ribbons around the stiff figure of the
father of our country. As Wakoski explains in a preface, the poems "address
some man in my life as well as his alter ego, George Washington"; both figures
represent "'the man's world,' with its militaristic origins and its glorification
of fact over feeling.". . .

The systematic derangement of chronology reinforces Wakoski's tacit undermining of objective history. The seriousness of history and the dignity of male leadership and power within it are deflated not by direct and solemn critique, but by the poet's spirit of play, and by her aggressive foregrounding of her own fascinations and obsessions. Interpolating Washington into dramas of disconnection and failure suggesting the flip side of the American Dream, she manipulates him much as political leaders manipulate populations. The hero of national fame is at the personal level false and stiff, a wooden puppet containing so little emotional sap that Wakoski, with her sweeping loves and hates, her moments of arrogant haughtiness and abject humility, her terror and pain on the one hand, and her penchant for wicked nonsense on the other, easily upstages him. Upstaging is the poet's form of victory, of course, not simply over this particular man, but over the mental and institutional structures mandated by masculinty. As political commentary, *The George Washington Poems* is both a fool's holiday and a declaration of independence, reminding us that authority resides where we the people bestow it, disappears where we withdraw it.

At the same time, to understand *The George Washington Poems* as predominantly satiric is to ignore their forceful emotionality. The long central poem "The Father of My Country" reconstructs the child Wakoski's desperate love and need of the absent, indifferent father who has both created her identity and betrayed her.

Alicia Ostriker. Feminist Studies. 10, 1984,
pp. 490, 493

After almost twenty full-lenth collections, Wakoski continues [in *Medea the Sorceress*] to break new ground. Using the collage technique, she intersperses the long pseudo-autobiographical poems that are her trademark with quotes from Nick Herbert's *Quantum Reality: Beyond the New Physics* and Mario Puzo's *Inside Las Vegas,* letters to two friends, and an exploration of her poetic heritage. These might seem unlikely juxtapositions, but Wakoski makes them work. Intended as the first installment in a projected series, "The Archeology of Movies and Books," this collection is inspired in part by coming-of-age movies: "I know that I have avoided movies most of my life, when what I should have been avoiding was sex." More than anything else, she presents an explanation of woman's middle age, offering stunning insights. Highly recommended.

Rochelle Ratner. Library Journal.
February 1, 1991, p. 81

WALKER, ALICE (UNITED STATES) 1944–

Miss Walker's poems [in *Once*] lack little in poetic quality, in the traditional, *i.e.*, white sense. I was frequently reminded of Emily Dickinson while I read her. Miss Walker has the tight tongue, the precise wordings, the subtle, unexpected twists, the reversal of the anticipated order of words and understatements for plus emphasis, or the shifting of emotions. . . .

Her poetry is dignified, unobtrusive, almost, at times, matter-of-fact. There is a lack of celebration or affirmation that one finds so exhilarating and so often in today's black literature. Her poetry is timid thunder. Black people are explosions of love, hate, fear, joy, sorrow, *Life*. Their literature should be that way.

The reader will hear a soft hum; a lovely delicate melody will brush him and he will think, "I want to hear more." He will re-read, lean closer and strain to touch, or be pulled by the magnetic *is*ness of a lovely sound. He will wait and search and wait for the melody to break forth into some wildly glorious song which will roll and roll and roll like a chorus of thunder, under him, through him, swelling him, so that he too might burst forth, join in and sing. Though the song might be terrible, the notes are our Black life's blood. But our singer does not here sing. In *Once,* she hums a haunting, poignant, yet certain, distinctive song.

Carolyn M. Rodgers. *Negro Digest*.
September–October, 1968, pp. 52, 12–13

[*The Third Life of Grange Copeland*] is an ambitious novel, for [Alice Walker's] attention is focused on a man wavering between the traditional poverty in Georgia and the glimpse of freedom that can never be his. Uprooted, he goes north, only to be disappointed by the confusing life of New York and the bitter cold. He returns to Georgia to find that his son has grown up, but little else has changed: The son, Brownfield, is satanic, methodically brutalizing his wife and children in a way which appalls even Grange, who is no angel. . . .

The violent scenes are numerous, but the arguments between husband and wife, father and son, are if anything more harrowing than the shotgun murders. It is hardly an idealized portrait of three generations of a black family, but the passions are enacted against a landscape which is carefully drawn: Baker County, the cotton fields, the ramshackle houses pitched in misery. Mrs. Walker has no lack of compassion, but has an essential detachment and so avoids being racially tendentious: She records skillfully the fakery and guilt of the cracker and the cotton picker, the awakening of Grange to his corrosive self-pity.

If the novel fails in parts it is because it attempts too much—too many years, too many characters. The movement is occasionally ponderous; elsewhere the years skip glibly by leaving the reader breathless. At times Mrs.

Walker clumsily stitches episode to episode. Her strength is in her control of character rather than all the "business" that goes on in a family chronicle.

Paul Theroux. Book World. September 13, 1970, p. 2

Alice Walker's graphic first novel [*The Third Life of Grange Copeland*] delivers a powerful statement by letting the narrative, characters and episodes speak for themselves. In describing the lives of black sharecroppers from 1920 through the 1960s, the twenty-six-year-old black novelist—author of a book of poems, *Once,* as well as a quartet of stories on insanity—could have taken the easy, tiresome way out by haranguing for militancy, revenge and separatism. Instead, she allows the reader to make his own assessment of Southern conditions and the desperate need for change. . . .

Miss Walker's novel—infused with poetic images that unfold visually as though performed on stage—is remarkably similar to Athol Fugard's excellent play, *Boesman and Lena.* In both works the black wives, constantly forced to move their few tattered possessions from one makeshift home to another, are tormented mainly by their husbands rather than the world. In both, the characters are castoffs lurking on the fringes of an oppressive white society, who see life as a perpetual cycle of hope and despair. . . .

Miss Walker deftly sculpts her people and delineates their relationships. Indeed, since they generally transcend the plot, the one episode involving civil rights workers seems an intrusion that neither advances the story nor enhances our understanding of the characters. Fortunately, it does not detract significantly from an otherwise compelling novel that emphasizes the humanity we share rather than the horrors of dehumanizing experiences.

Paula Meinetz Shapiro. The New Leader.
January 25, 1971, pp. 19–20

In 1966, Langston Hughes commented on one of Alice Walker's short stories: "Neither you nor I have ever read a story like 'To Hell with Dying' before. At least, I do not think you have." Hughes's early recognition of the uniqueness of Walker's artistic voice is equally applicable to the twelve other stories in Walker's new book, *In Love & Trouble: Stories of Black Women.* This collection would be an extraordinary literary work, if its only virtue were the fact that the author sets out consciously to explore with honesty the textures and terrors of black women's lives. Attempts to penetrate the myths surrounding black women's experiences are so pitifully rare in black, feminist, or American writing that each shred of truth about these experiences constitutes a breakthrough. The fact that Walker's perceptions, style, and artistry are also consistently high makes her work a treasure, particularly for those of us whom her writing describes.

Blood and violence seem the everyday backdrop to her characters' lives—a violence all the more chilling because it is so understated. It affects the ten-year-old girl who discovers a lynched man's headless body just as surely and ruinously as it destroys the middle-aged wife trapped in a loveless marriage or the ancient black woman ousted from a white house of worship. . . .

I believe that the worst results of racism in this country have been to subvert the most basic human relationships among black men, women, and children and to destroy their individual psyches. It is on this level of interpersonal experience that Walker succeeds in illuminating black women's lives. Some of her characters are damaged by material poverty, but what they suffer from most often is emotional destitution. These portraits are not pretty. When the reality is prettier, as a result of the implementation of black *and* feminist goals and values, the stories will be prettier too.

Barbara Smith. *Ms.* February, 1974,
pp. 42–43, 78

Revolutionary Petunias, Alice Walker's second book of poetry, is a major achievement by a poet who deserves more critical attention than she has received. The promising seeds she planted in *Once* have blossomed into poems of extraordinary grace, wisdom, and strength.

What especially recommends this volume to readers, makers, and scholars of poetry is Miss Walker's sensitive and intelligent use of black Southern roots, the primal sources of much that gives definition and tone to Afro-American writing. Unlike poets who, in the words of Eugene Redmond, "dismiss the legacy and anger of their ancestors by practicing various forms of heresy and sacrilege," she celebrates the legacy, probes it to find practical methods for handling contemporary problems. Her preface tells us the "poems are about Revolutionaries and Lovers; and about the loss of compassion, trust, and the ability to expand in love that marks the end of hopeful strategy." Yet the poems are hopeful strategies for recapturing one's humanity. And from the gifts and lore of ethnic heritage the poet draws strength to love and to be fully human amidst the crises of twentieth-century American life. It is a sure understanding of how to apply ancestral wisdom that informs these precise, lucid and skillfully crafted poems.

Jerry W. Ward. *CLA Journal.* September,
1973, pp. 127–28

My initial reaction to the first several stories of *In Love & Trouble* was negative. Miss Walker's search for ways to be new and different struck me as too willful and strained. I felt the same way about her earlier novel, *The Third Life of Grange Copeland,* whose style seemed too fine for the rough subject— the way two black men, a son and a father, try to degrade and destroy each other. But as I read on through these thirteen stories, I was soon absorbed by the density of reality they convey. They contain the familiar themes and situations of conventional black political and sociological fiction. There are black revolutionaries who read books and meet in small study groups, radical lady poets who read before black student audiences shouting "Right on!," and sharecroppers victimized by white landlords. But we see all these from genuinely new angles, from the point of view of the black woman or man totally absorbed in the pains of their inner life rather than the point of view of the protester or the newspaper headline.

The subtitle of the collection, *Stories of Black Women,* is probably an attempt by the publisher to exploit not only black subjects but feminine ones. There is nothing feminist about these stories, however. Neurosis and insanity, hatred and love, emptiness and indifference, violence and deceit—that is what they are about.

Jerry H. Bryant. *The Nation.*
November 12, 1973, pp. 501–2

Meridian, Alice Walker's second novel, is the story of Meridian Hill, a young Southern black woman, from her early childhood on through her thirties. Set in the South, Meridian's story also invokes the impact of the Civil Rights movement, its major psychological and social stresses, as borne out in the lives of the three main characters, Meridian, Truman Held, a black artist and activist, and Lynne, his white wife, also a civil rights organizer.

Written in a clear, almost incandescent prose that sings and sears, there is great breadth and depth to Ms. Walker's imagination that ranges, in *Meridian,* from treatment of earlier vestiges of African and Indian life, back woods poverty, a college for black girls named Saxon (formerly a slave plantation) on to the grim confrontations of the Civil Rights era. It is an extraordinarily fine novel. . . .

In this novel as in her other works, one is aware of the very considerable size of Alice Walker's talent, the ease with which she handles language, her ability to see the essence of life in all things and take joy in it in an almost pantheistic fashion reminiscent of Tolstoy or Shakespeare.

One senses here, too, a dialectical tension between the values and practices of the black Christian tradition on the one hand and the black secular tradition of militant struggle on the other. While *Meridian* embodies one resolution of this tension, one anticipates future development of this theme, by this very talented writer, who is emerging as one of the major humanistic voices of our time.

Robert Chrisman. *The Black Scholar.*
April, 1976, p. 3

A close look at the fiction, especially the shorter pieces, of Alice Walker reveals that she employs folklore for purposes of defining characters and illustrating relationships between them as well as for plot development. By so doing, she comments on the racial situation in the United States and, in some instances, chastises her black characters for their attitudes toward themselves. The folklore materials Walker uses and the ways in which she uses them are especially evocative of Charles Waddell Chesnutt and Zora Neale Hurston. Therefore, interpretations of Walker's uses of folklore and folk culture place her in a tradition that goes back at least as far as the late nineteenth century. . . .

Alice Walker is assuredly in the literary and historical traditions of the recording and creative use of black folk materials. Like Chesnutt, she uses such material for social commentary. But her environment allows more freedom of usage than did Chesnutt's; where he had to embed his statements about slavery in an elaborate framing device and filtered them through the eyes of a white Northerner, Walker can be obvious, blatant, and direct about social injustices. Like Hurston, Walker reflects a keen insight into the folk mind. As Hurston reflected the nuances of relationships between men and women in *Their Eyes Were Watching God* (1937) through the use of the folk culture, so too does Walker use this culture to reflect relationships between the characters in *The Third Life of Grange Copeland*. Like [Jean] Toomer, she feels that the folk culture is an inseparable part of the black folk at any level of existence—the college bred and the illiterate black are equal in their heritage. Although class and status may be allowed to distort how one views the culture, it can never be erased. Alice Walker does not attempt to erase it from her works.

Trudier Harris. *Black American Literature Forum*. Spring, 1977, pp. 3, 8

As a craftsman, Walker sorts out the throwaways, the seemingly insignificant and hidden pieces of the lives of Southerners, particularly black families, and stitches them into a tapestry of society. Who is to blame for the waste in our lives, she asks? Ourselves? The society that seems at every turn opposed to blossoming? The wrath of God? The question of responsibility for personal action and societal change is one recurrent motif in the complex quilts that Walker makes out of thrifty sentences, knotted questions, tight metaphors, terse sections. Her novels continually stitch a fabric of the everyday violence that is committed against her characters and that they commit upon one another in their search for regeneration, and regeneration is what they as black people desire.

The exploration, then, of the process of personal and social growth out of horror and waste is a motif that characterizes Walker's works. For her, the creativity of the black woman is essential to this process. . . . In searching for the means to her own artistic and political freedom, Walker investigates the legacy of the past. To deepen our understanding of the plight of her maternal ancestors, she not only calls upon her own personal history but upon Jean Toomer, who perhaps more than any other writer of the past had focused on the repressed creativity of black women. . . .

For this author, the black woman, as a result of her history and her experience, must be in struggle against these two distortions of life. Until she is free, her people cannot be free, and until her people are free, she cannot be free. Walker stresses the interrelatedness of these two obstacles to wholeness, for the struggle against them is not merely a question of replacing whoever is in power; rather it is a struggle to release the spirit that inhabits all life. Walker's quilts reiterate the basic concept that "the greatest value a person can attain is full humanity which is a state of oneness with all things," and that until this is possible for all living beings, those of us who seek wholeness must be willing to struggle toward that end.

Barbara Christian. *Black Women Novelists*
(Westport, Connecticut: Greenwood Press,
1980), pp. 180–81, 237–38

Alice Walker's unsparing vision of black women's victimization in sexual love—their isolation, degradation, or grotesque defeat by despairing or aspiring black men—has been a major element in her growing body of work. . . . Somewhat less prominent in defining her concerns has been Walker's active commitment to civil rights issues involving all black people. The commitment suggests a hope that societal change may help solve the type of private dilemma her fiction particularizes. The appearance of her second novel, *Meridian* (1976), did not so much negate this implied optimism as express a need to consider moral and philosophical issues raised by a political awakening.

At the same time, *Meridian* represents a shift from a preoccupation with commemorating black women's suffering to a concern with probing an individual black woman's situation for its roots and possibilities. Again Walker's optimism is less evident, however, than her need to explore questions of responsibility even, or particularly, among those with valid historic claims to having been victimized.

Martha J. McGowan. *Critique.* 23:1, 1981, p. 25

It's true and important that a disproportionate number of people who seek out Alice Walker's sparsely distributed books are black women. She comes at universality through the path of an American black woman's experience and is even brave enough to write about such delicate fictional themes as interracial sex and the oppression of women by many cultures in Africa. . . . But white women, and women of diverse ethnic backgrounds, also feel tied to Alice Walker. The struggle to have work and minds of our own, vulnerability, our debt to our mothers, the price of childbirth, friendships among women, the problem of loving men who regard us as less than themselves, sensuality, violence: all these are major themes of her fiction and poetry. . . .

The storytelling style of *The Color Purple* makes it irresistible to read. The words belong to Celie, the downest and outest of women. Because she must survive against impossible odds, because she has no one to talk to, she writes about her life in the guise of letters to God. When she discovers her much-loved lost sister is not dead after all but is living in Africa, she writes letters to Nettie instead. The point is, she must tell someone the truth and confirm her existence. . . .

The result is an inviting, dead-honest, surprising novel that is the successful culmination of Alice Walker's longer and longer trips outside the safety of Standard English narration, and into the words of her characters. Here, she takes the leap completely. There is no third person to distance the reader from events. We are inside Celie's head.

In the tradition of Gorky, Steinbeck, Dickens, Ernest Gaines, Hurston, Baldwin, Ousmane Sembene, Bessie Head, and many others, Alice Walker has written an empathetic novel about the poorest of the poor. (In fact, her first two novels meet that high standard, too.) But, unlike most novels that expose race or class, it doesn't treat male/female injustice as natural or secondary. (And unlike some supposedly feminist novels, it doesn't ignore any women because of race or class.) Just as unusual among books about the poor and powerless, it is not written *about* one group, *for* another. The people in this book could and would enjoy it, too.

Gloria Steinem. Ms. June, 1982,
pp. 37, 89–90

The Color Purple is an American novel of permanent importance, that rare sort of book which (in Norman Mailer's felicitous phrase) amounts to "a diversion in the fields of dread." Alice Walker excels at making difficulties for herself and then transcending them. . . .

Love redeems, meanness kills—that is *The Color Purple*'s principal theme, the theme of most of the world's great fiction. Nevertheless—and this is why this black woman's novel will survive a white man's embrace—the redemptive love that is celebrated here is selective, even prickly. White folk figure rarely in its pages and never to their advantage, and black men are recovered only to the extent that they buckle down to housework and let women attend to business. For Walker, redemptive love requires female bonding. The bond liberates women from men, who are predators at worst, idle at best.

Peter S. Prescott. Newsweek. June 21, 1982,
pp. 67–68

Perhaps Alice Walker alone of her generation of black women Southern writers persistently identifies herself and her concerns with her native region— the deep South of Georgia and Mississippi. "No one," she has concluded, "could wish for a more advantageous heritage than that bequeathed to the black writer in the South: a compassion for the earth, a trust in humanity beyond our knowledge of evil, an abiding love of justice. We inherit a great responsibility . . . for we must give voice to centuries not only of silent bitterness and hate but also of neighborly kindness and sustaining love." Her heritage is complex; nevertheless, like Louisiana native Ernest Gaines, Walker grounds her fiction and poetry primarily in the experiences of the South and Southern blacks. Her three volumes of poetry, three novels, and two collections of stories, all depend upon what black life is, has been, and can be in a specified landscape that becomes emblematic of American life.

While Walker's paradigm communities are nearly always black, rural, and Southern, they become viable emblems by means of her creation of familial and social generations that underscore her concerns with familial identity, continuity and rupture, and with social roles, order and change. In shaping her fiction and much of her poetry according to patterns of generations, she has established a concrete means of portraying who her people are and what their lives mean.

Thadious M. Davis. *Southern Quarterly.*
21:4, 1983, p. 39

The focus on the struggle of black people, especially black women, to claim their own lives, and the contention that this struggle emanates from a deepening of self-knowledge and love—are characteristics of Walker's work. Yet is seems they are not really the essential quality that distinguishes her work, for these characteristics might be said to apply to any number of contemporary black women writers—e.g., Toni Morrison, Paule Marshall, June Jordan. Walker's peculiar sound, the specific mode through which her deepening of self-knowledge and self-love comes, seems to have much to do with her contrariness, her willingness at all turns to challenge the fashionable belief of the day, to reexamine it in the light of her own experiences and of dearly won principles which she has previously challenged and absorbed. There is a sense in which the "forbidden" in the society is consistently approached by Walker as a possible route to truth.

Barbara Christian. In Mari Evans, ed. *Black
Women Writers (1950–1980)* (New York:
Doubleday-Anchor, 1984), pp. 257–58

The Color Purple subverts the traditional Eurocentric male code which dominates the literary conventions of the espistolary novel. As a genre, the English epistolary novel, a form invented by men writing about women, embodies male control of the literary images of women. By appropriating a form invented and traditionally controlled by men, but thematicizing the lives and experiences of women, Alice Walker asserts her authority, or right to authorship. Signing herself as "A.W., author and medium," Walker suggests that her purpose has been not only to create and control literary images of women, and black women in particular, but to give voice and representation to these same women who have been silenced and confined in life and literature. *The Color Purple* is a novel which deals with what it means to be poor, black, and female in the rural South during the first half of the twentieth century. In an interview in *Newsweek* in June 1982, Walker explains that Celie, the protagonist of *The Color Purple,* is modeled after the author's own grandmother, who was raped at the age of twelve by her slave owner (and Walker's grandfather). Celie's fate, however, is brighter. "I liberated her from her own history," remarks Walker, "I wanted her to be happy." Walker hopes that "people can hear Celie's voice. There are so many people like Celie who make it, who came out of nothing. People who triumphed." Thus, for Walker, art is liberational and life-saving; it is an act for reconstruction and reclamation of self, of past, of women, and of community.

Mae G. Henderson. Sage: A Scholarly
Journal on Black Women. 2:1, 1985

The 1970s feminist discourse informs *The Third Life (of Grange Copeland)* discursive formation. The text takes certain heterogeneous facts—the domineering patriarch, the violent and oppressive male, the battered abused mother and child—which are essential to feminist ideology. Then, it establishes a group of relations between these facts which enable it to make a particular enunciation, to formulate a particular feminist ideologeme.

The Third Life—along with other feminist texts like Ntozake Shange's *For Colored Girls,* . . . . Gayl Jones's *Corregidora* and *Eva's Man,* Toni Morrison's *The Bluest Eye* and *Sula,* which reconstruct and emphasize the same American and Afro-American facts and categories as *The Third Life,* and other feminist series in political science, sociology, history, psychology, etc.—gives meaning, coherence, validity, and a history to the strivings and yearnings of a contemporary feminist set of assumptions about women's reality and existence. But, more importantly, we see how *The Third Life* and other feminist texts are "socially symbolic acts" which invent imaginary or formal solutions to the unresolvable social contradictions. These texts function as indices and cultural messages for Americans and Afro-Americans who embrace feminist ideologies because they explain certain lived experiences. With *The Third Life,* Alice Walker produces new myths about the American and Afro-American historical past—and especially about black women—to counter past and existing myths which have not portrayed women, and particularly black women, as complex human beings who have existed in oppressive and sexist historical constellations.

W. Lawrence Hogue. MELUS. 12, 1985,
pp. 61–62

In *Meridian* Walker pursues the African-American subconscious through the inner voice of a young black woman. She confronts the desperation of the late 1960s and early 1970s when, despite the successes of the Civil Rights movement, Black Elk's words seemed a fitting epigraph for the chaos of America. "The nation's hoop is broken and scattered," he said, grieving over the violent end of his people's dream. On a preliminary page of *Meridian* Walker uses Black Elk's words to announce the political and spiritual desolation that must be overcome in the lives of individuals and society. Symptomatically, for her generation, the hoop of language—that continuum of voice going back to slavery and embodied in fiction by *The Autobiography of Miss Jane Pittman*—was broken and scattered. During the 1960s, as James Alan McPherson notes in *Elbow Room,* words "seemed to have become detached from emotion and no longer flowed to the rhythm of passion." That is the condition Walker and her character seek to overcome in *Meridian* as, together, they work to restore language, self, and nation.

For Walker and Meridian, silence and solitude become an essential prologue to speech and social action. Like Invisible Man, though for different reasons and in a different context, Meridian suspends the pursuit of eloquence. Like Zora Neale Hurston, Walker is a friend to her character. But she does not tell the story in a frame directly associated with the oral tradition. For one thing, she knows that Meridian, though brave and eloquent, is too preoccupied with her survival and the struggle of the people she works among, to focus on telling her story. For another thing, Meridian goes in search of a loving political voice after she finds that revolutionary rhetoric is often a mask for hate and emptiness and that the debased political language of the late 1960s upholds the condition of violence, egotism, and injustice she and her radical contemporaries seek to overthrow. To heal her soul and restore the spirit of words, Meridian listens and responds to the voices of the dead, particularly those black and Native American ancestors who haunt Walker's Georgia as they did Jean Toomer's. Consequently, the story unfolds gradually through visions and in remembered snatches of song and speech stitched together by Meridian's simultaneously meditative and political voice. And for her part, Alice Walker's pursuit of intimacy with her readers begins in her relationship with Meridian.

John F. Callahan. *In the African-American Grain* (Urbana: University of Illinois Press, 1988), pp. 217–18

The Color Purple broadens the scope of literary discourse, asserting its primacy in the realm of academic thought while simultaneously stirring the reflective consciousness of a mass audience. Unlike most novels by any writer, it is read across race, class, gender, and cultural boundaries. It is truly a popular work—a book of the people—a work that has many different meanings for many different readers. Often the meanings are not interesting, contained as they are within a critical discourse that does not resist the urge to simplify, to overshadow, to make this work by a contemporary African-American writer a mere sociological treatise on black life or radical feminist tract. To say even as some critics do that it is a modern day "slave narrative" or to simply place the work within the literary tradition of epistolary sentimental novels is also a way to contain, restrict, control. Categorizing in this way implies that the text neither demands nor challenges, rather, that it can be adequately and fully discussed within an accepted critical discourse, one that remains firmly within the boundaries of conservative academic aesthetic intentionality. While such discourse may illuminate aspects of the novel, it also obscures, suppresses, silences. . . .

To critically approach *The Color Purple* from an oppositional perspective, it is useful to identify gaps—spaces between the text and conventional critical points of departure. That the novel's form is epistolary is most obvious, so apparent even that it is possible to overlook the fact that it begins not with a letter but an opening statement, a threatening command—speaker unidentified. "You better not never tell nobody but God. It'd kill your mammy." Straightaway Celie's letter writing to God is placed in a context of domination; she is obeying orders. . . .

Throughout *The Color Purple*, sexuality is graphically and explicitly discussed. Though a key narrative pattern in the novel, it is usually ignored. As readers approaching this novel in the context of a white supremacist patriarchal society wherein black women have been and continue to be stereotyped as sexually loose, a black woman writer imagining a black female character who writes about sexuality in letters to God, using graphic and explicit language, may not seem unusual or even interesting, particularly since graphic descriptions of sexual encounters conform to a current trend in women's writing. But this is most unlikely, as it is the culture's fascination with sexual autobiography that has led to a burgeoning of fiction and true-life stories focusing on sexual encounters.

> bell hooks. In Harold Bloom, ed. *Alice*
> *Walker: Modern Critical Views* (New York:
> Chelsea House, 1989), pp. 215–16

Temple of My Familiar (1989) is likely to remain a novel often begun and seldom finished. Any novel that attempts to provide a spiritual history of the universe hardly makes for light reading. One that also demands a belief in transmigration of souls is doubly difficult. Place all that within the context of what Walker herself has called "a romance of the last 500,000 years," and the extent of the challenge the novel presents to its readers begins to emerge.

In *Temple*, Walker brings back from *The Color Purple* some characters whom she simply could not bear to abandon, most notably Miss Celie and Miss Shug. Yet, in spite of the familiar faces that may bring pleasant glints of recognition to *The Color Purple* admirers, the coincidences of fate that bring them into contact with Walker's new characters call for a willing suspension of disbelief that may be too much to ask.

Still, close readers of Walker's works should not have been surprised by the turn that her work took with *Temple of My Familiar*. In fact, *Temple* provides not so much a turn as a logical extension of what had gone before. Once Walker had shown her female characters capable of breaking the bonds of oppression and defining themselves as whole persons, and once she had, at the same time, discovered divinity in all human and nonhuman elements of the universe, it was actually a small step to making women into goddesses. With one possible exception, the novel's goddesses constitute part of womankind's distant past, yet the ancient matriarchal religions discovered by Walker's contemporary characters in the novel allow them to redefine relationships between the sexes. They are thus able to cure themselves of some of the same varieties of dis-ease based on societal expectations that plagued characters in Walker's earlier works. The lessons they learn about the need for balance between the flesh and the spirit help them redefine themselves.

Donna Haisty Winchell. Alice Walker
(Boston: Twayne, 1992), p. 115

In *Possessing the Secret of Joy,* Walker focuses on female circumcision, telling the story of one African woman whose life is practically destroyed after she submits to the mutilating operation. . . .

Possessing the Secret of Joy is an unabashedly polemical novel. It is Walker's activist attempt to expose readers of her fiction to the horrors of female circumcision and thereby invigorate the movement to ban it worldwide. . . .

The novel takes place in an unnamed part of Africa (probably Kenya) and the US and focuses on the experience of Tashi, who in *The Color Purple* was an African friend of Celie's children Adam and Olivia. In *Possessing the Secret of Joy,* she has become a bitter and dysfunctional old woman. Her story unfolds in fragments of memory in a first-person serial narrative that also incorporates the voices of her family and the *tsunga* M'Lissa, who in the name of tradition circumcized Tashi and the other girls of her Olinka village. In the course of the novel, we see Tashi's descent into madness and her eventual revitalization. . . .

The most moving sections of *Possessing the Secret of Joy* are made up of the dialogue, broken up and dispersed in their narratives, that takes place between the elderly Tashi and the very old M'Lissa when Tashi has come to kill her. . . .

Walker feels she has a right, as an African American, to confront African traditions she sees as antithetical to women's health. She commented in . . . [an] *Essence* interview that she speaks for her "great-great-great-great-grandmother who came here with all that pain in her body." But in her zeal she, like other Western critics, lumps African countries and cultures together into a single entity. In *The Color Purple,* Tashi's Olinka village appears to be situated somewhere in West Africa. In *Possessing the Secret of Joy,* it is located in East Africa.

Gay Wilentz. Women's Review of Books. 10,
February, 1993, pp. 21–22

WALKER, KATH (NOONUCCAL, OODGEROO) (AUSTRALIA) 1920–

Having for the moment forgotten about Evonne Goolagong, Kath Walker admits that she is probably the most famous of all Aboriginals. She is perhaps the best-selling poet in Australia, and her leadership in the 1960s civil rights movement helped win basic rights for Australia's indigenous people. An Australian magazine shows pictures of her chatting with the prime minister. She has been awarded the MBE by Queen Elizabeth. She has even been on a hijacked plane during her world travels. She says unabashedly that in Australia—and throughout the Pacific—she is "loved." "The whole of the Aboriginal people are proud of me. Whenever anybody goes overseas it's me. I travel in their behalf."

Her work—her name, her cause—is unfamiliar to Americans, few of whom could name the prime minister of Australia. The history of the Aboriginals comes as a surprise as well. She recites this history in cold, matter-of-fact tones, shocking American students unaware of the grim facts behind the European settlement of Australia. . . .

Her poems sparkle with ironic humor and the painfulness of the clash between primitive tribal life and technological society. When she published *We Are Going,* in 1964, she became the first Aboriginal to publish a book of poems. She wrote a book of children's stories, *Stradbroke Dreamtime,* and two more books of poetry, *The Dawn Is at Hand* and *My People.*

Her poetry is not good as poetry, but it is compelling as a repository of Aboriginal legend and custom. Much of her poetry is simply bad verse. . . . But much of it is poignant and infused with a lyrical honesty. She speaks of her people as outcasts in their own native land; their ancient customs are holding on pathetically or dying out ("No more boomerang / No more spear; Now all civilized— / Colour bar and beer.")

The theme of time recurs with irony and sadness. . . . Poems such as "Assimilation—No!" and "Integration—Yes!" are explicit political statements, and "Aboriginal Charter of Rights" is a poem accepted by her people as an official declaration.

"*We Are Going,* my first book, was pure propaganda—to make people sit up and take notice," she said. "I make no excuses. I'm proud of it. It sold seven editions in seven months. I'm the highest-selling poet in Australia." She added with a smile, "Not the best, but the best-selling."

Walker's poetry is a valuable lament for the loss of a culture, but it is not as a poet that she will be best remembered, for Aboriginal literature is at a very early stage. Without a tradition or even models (Aboriginals have only recently gained the right to education), it is unsophisticated, awkward, and didactic. There have been only three Aboriginal novels so far, and few poets. . . .

Walker is able to speak as an Aboriginal and as a modern Westerner. She claims feminism has no application whatsoever to Aboriginal culture, even as it is forced up against the modern world. "In the Aboriginal world, man and woman stand together."

Bobbie Ann Mason. *Denver Quarterly.* 15,
1980, pp. 65, 67–68, 70

Black American influence is also evident in the works of Kath Walker, Australia's most popular Aboriginal poet. Like the other Aboriginal writers she perceives an obvious parallel between black Australian and black American experiences. . . .

She too has interesting American connections. She has the distinction of being the first Australian writer to be inducted into the Mark Twain Literary Society of America. Her first collection of poems, *We Are Going,* sold sixteen editions in the United States within six months of its initial publication there. This American interest in her work is matched by Walker's own interest in the American, expecially black American, literature. She states that her interest in Afro-American writers, which she says is part of her interest in ethnic literatures in general, stems from the fact that she shares with them the "same passion for rejecting oppression." She recognizes the "example and encouragement" of the militant black American writers of the 1960s.

Walker points to Richard Wright, Ralph Ellison and James Baldwin as writers [who inspired her, and signals] Amiri Baraka for special admiration. . . .

Baraka, a founder of the Black Arts Movement and the chief exponent of the Black Aesthetic, is one of America's most militant poets. Like Walker, he is a public poet who views his art as an instrument for liberation. She can, without any difficulty, identify with his rhetoric of racial outrage; and she probably has relatively easy access to his poetry because much of it is forcefully clear.

Against this background it is possible to grasp the pronounced shift in the tone of her recent poetry. Much of her early poetry, though occasionally angry, is largely conciliatory. Sometimes she naively trusts white liberals and expects them to be redeemers of the Aborigines. . . .

In her most recent work, however, Walker sounds much more assertive. Her new cultural confidence may be due to numerous factors: her widespread popularity, her personal maturity, her fuller involvement with Aboriginal issues and the substantial civil rights gains made by the Aborigines during the last decade or so. But her acquaintance with Afro-American writing, especially the aggressive and angry poetry of the Black Arts Movement, and her personal contacts with black intellectuals (Afro-American, Afro-Caribbean and African) during her visits abroad have also certainly contributed to her new racial assertiveness. Representative of her new tone is one of her most recent poems, "Black Commandments," which unapologetically celebrates the legitimacy of the Aboriginal cultural consciousness.

Emmanuel S. Nelson. Westerly. 4, 1985,
pp. 50–52

Kath Walker recently adopted the name Oodgeroo, after the old woman from one of her own legends. In that story, Oodgeroo, so named because of the paperbark tree on which she writes her stories, travels the land recovering the history of her people. It is a fitting title for a woman who has spent close to thirty years recording the voice of Aboriginals. Kath was one of the leaders of the Civil Rights Movement which led to the 1967 referendum which finally allowed Aboriginals to vote. Through poetry, prose, essays, and recently, artwork, Kath Walker has articulated the concerns of Aboriginals, and has protested against the many injustices which still beset her people in modern day Australia. . . .

In 1964 her first volume of poems, *We Are Going,* was released by Jacaranda Press. It sold out before it could be launched and soon went into seven editions in as many months. Her second book, *The Dawn is at Hand,* published in 1966, was equally popular. This was followed in 1970 by *My People* which collects her previous work and includes additional poetry and prose pieces. *Stradbroke Dreamtime,* her first complete work of prose, features both autobiographical material as well as modern Aboriginal legends of her own creation. This was published in 1972. It was followed, almost a decade later, by a personally illustrated children's book, *Father Sky and Mother Earth,* which tells the story of creation from an Aboriginal perspective. In 1985, Ulli Beier released a book entitled *Quandamooka: The Art of Kath Walker* . . . which features a series of Kath Walker's illustrations, accompanied by her brief commentary on each work.

Gerry Turcotte. *Kunapipi.* 10, 1988,
pp. 17–18

WALKER, MARGARET (UNITED STATES) 1915–

Straightforwardness, directness, reality are good things to find in a young poet. It is rarer to find them combined with a controlled intensity of emotion and a language that, at times, even when it is most modern, has something of the surge of biblical poetry. And it is obvious that Miss Walker uses that language because it comes naturally to her and is part of her inheritance. A contemporary writer, living in a contemporary world, when she speaks of and for her people older voices are mixed with hers—the voices of Methodist forebears and preachers who preached the Word, the anonymous voices of many who lived and were forgotten and yet out of bondage and hope made a lasting music. Miss Walker is not merely a sounding-board for these voices—I do not mean that. Nor do I mean that [*For My People*] is interesting and moving poetry because it was written by a Negro. It is too late in the day for that sort of meaningless patronage—and poetry must exist in its own right. These poems keep on talking to you after the book is shut because, out of deep feeling, Miss Walker has made living and passionate speech.

Stephen Vincent Benét. Foreword to
Margaret Walker. *For My People* (New
Haven: Yale University Press, 1942), pp. 5–6

Miss Walker's poems [in *For My People*], though they are songs and portraits of American Negroes of today, are suffused with the prayers and hopes of the submerged and semi-submerged of all times. . . .

Miss Walker's poems for her people everywhere show that she has thought long and felt deeply about the sorrow laden past and present of the American Negro. Out of a rich experience in the lower Mississippi Valley and in Black Chicago at the head of that valley she has seen the substance of poetry in the blind struggle of her people. The Yale Series of Younger Poets, whose choice she is this year, has here launched a career indeed. Miss Walker's poems are not new to *Opportunity* readers, for several of them have appeared in these pages, but the intensity of her sustained effort may come as a surprise to those who know only her shorter pieces. Her symbols, the South, the "L," the delta, the white gods, cotton, 1619, are familiar, but her use of them is with new strength.

A full pride in the past and a healthy view of the present give her poems distinction. She is no mournful weeper wearing her pen out over the twin literary tragedies of lynching and color. Her sorrow and her pride find themselves in more tangible and commonplace symbols: the grandmothers who were strong and full of memories, the money-gods who take life away, the strange contradiction of beauty in the bitter low cotton country. Her hearty portraits of Molly Means, Stagolee, Kissie Lee . . . and of Gus the Lineman are not, fortunately, of the how-I-have-loved-thee school of feminine poets. Perhaps Miss Walker's volume marks the end of a school of Negro women poets; she is more struck by the fact that "We with / our blood have watered these fields / and they belong to us" than she is in the crenellated visions of archaic sorrow so freely indulged in by the "lady poets" in their small black and gold veined volumes. *For My People* contains some of our strongest recent verse. "Sorrow Home" is a dirge of real power.

Ulysses Lee. *Opportunity*. December, 1942,
pp. 379–80

To appreciate the extent of innovation *Jubilee* brings to a thoroughly quarried, frequently hackneyed genre of writing, it is only necessary to recall that the Civil War novel has been the source of some of the crudest stereotypes of Negro characters in American fiction. As Robert A. Lively pointed out in *Fiction Fights the Civil War:* "the Negro is rarely a central figure in Civil War novels—he only hovers near the white heroes and heroines, to whom space and interest is given." Margaret Walker has reversed the picture completely. With a fidelity to fact and detail, she presents the little-known everyday life of the slaves, their modes of behavior, patterns and rhythms of speech, emotions, frustrations, and aspirations. Never done on such a scale before, this is the strength of her novel. As it unfolds one sees plantation life as it was seen by Negro slaves, feels the texture of American history as it was felt by Negro slaves: the Civil War with the hopes it aroused, its sordid and grim realities; the participation of the Negroes in the fight against slavery;

the ugly and frustrating rise of the Ku Klux Klan; the postwar waves of terror in the South to keep the Negro down and prevent emancipation from becoming a reality.

The author is so intent on presenting her historical data as accurately as possible, on correcting the distortions which have crept into so many Civil War novels, that at times she fails to transform her raw material into accomplished literary form. There are passages of very pedestrian prose. Fortunately, the colorful and musical speech of the Negro characters in the novel transcends the stilted prose of the narrator. . . .

And there is Vyry, the heroine of the novel, who distills out of her life as a slave, and the trials of the Civil War, and the frustrated hopes of the Reconstruction years, a hard realism, a fierce spiritual force and hope. . . .

Abraham Chapman. *Saturday Review of Literature*. September 24, 1966, pp. 43–44

[*Jubilee*] serves especially well as a response to white "nostalgia" fiction about the antebellum and Reconstruction South—especially Margaret Mitchell's poor but popular *Gone with the Wind*. One cannot read one of these novels without repeatedly contrasting it with the other. On dialect: Miss Walker's is thoroughly researched and linguistically accurate; Miss Mitchell's ranges from rather accurate to absurd. On the role of blacks: Miss Walker reveals the various levels of black mentality, as well as the devotion of some slaves to, and the intense hatred of others for, their masters; Miss Mitchell presents blacks before the Civil War as happy darkies completely devoted to "missy" and "massa." On "social controls": Miss Walker portrays vividly the savagery of white vigilante repression; Miss Mitchell portrays the Ku Klux Klan as an organization of noble and dedicated men with the highest moral objectives. In short, the novels make for an interesting and enlightening companion study—a study of painful historical reality and romanticized self-deception.

Roger Whitlow. *Black American Literature* (Chicago: Nelson-Hall, 1973), pp. 138–39

After a lapse of twenty-eight years Margaret Walker has brought out a new volume of verse. Entitled *Prophets for a New Day*, it was printed by the Broadside Press. Though a very thin volume (it contains only thirty-two pages), the work is impressive. It is the best poetical comment to come from the civil rights movement—the movement which came to a climax with the march on Washington and which began thereafter to change into a more militant type of liberation effort.

In *Prophets for a New Day* Miss Walker, with poems like "Street Demonstration," "Girl Held without Bail," and "Sit-Ins," catches the spirit of the civil rights age, when young blacks gladly went to jail for the cause of freedom. "The Ballad of the Free," another liberation poem, treats as kindred souls Nat Turner, Gabriel Prosser, Denmark Vesey, Toussaint L'Ouverture, and John Brown. The inclusion of the last name shows that Miss Walker, though much "blacker" now in her thinking than she was in her early works, has not lost her respect for men of good will, whether black or white. Unlike most present-day Negro writers, she is willing to honor not only abolition heroes like John Brown but white martyrs of the civil rights movement as well.

Arthur P. Davis. *From the Dark Tower*
(Washington, D.C.: Howard University
Press, 1974), pp. 184–85

After this glorious and busy period [the Harlem Renaissance], the country and black literary activity went into a slump. What poetry exists is tinged with depression, socialism, and sometimes protest. Between 1930 and 1945 the major poet was Margaret Walker and the most important poetic event the appearance of her 1942 volume *For My People*, which was published as no. 41 of the Yale Series of Younger Poets, making her the first black to appear in that prestigious group. At the time Walker was a twenty-seven-year-old professor of English. . . .

The form of "For My People" is the most immediately striking thing about it. Drawing on free-verse techniques, on the Bible, and on the black sermon (her father was a preacher), Walker fairly overwhelms the reader with her rhetorical brilliance. She continues this same method and approach in the poems that follow—reciting her heritage of "Dark Blood," tracing black people's blind belief in gods from Africa to America, singing of her "roots deep in southern life," and in the simple poem "Lineage" decrying the fact that she is not as strong as her grandmothers were. . . .

Part II of *For My People* is made up of ballads about black folk heroes known and unknown, famous and infamous. Two of the best have heroines as their central figures—Molly Means, who was "a hag and a witch; chile of the devil, the dark, and sitch," and Kissie Lee, a tough, bad gal. . . . In these tall-tale and ballad narratives, Walker adheres pretty closely to the traditional ballad stanza, varying it with four-beat couplets and spicing it up with dialect speech, which she is successful at orthographically representing.

The final section, composed of only six poems, is much shorter than the first two. These are freely handled sonnets in which Walker gazes back on her childhood, writes about experiences she has had since leaving the South (such as talking to an Iowa farmer), and expresses needs and struggles common to all human beings.

For My People was and remains significant for many reasons. First, its mood coincided with the depression and hard times of the 1930s, and also with the social consciousness and militant integrationism of that decade and the following. In style, it was different in a worthwhile way from what had been written during the Renaissance. Walker's attention to black heroes and heroines was also timely and helped to communicate the "negritude" of the volume and delving for roots which is one of its major themes.

Gloria Hull. In Sandra M. Gilbert and Susan
Gubar, eds. *Shakespeare's Sisters: Feminist
Essays on Women Poets* (Bloomington:
Indiana University Press, 1979), pp. 174–76

Margaret Walker as a poet and as a writer was not dependent on the academy for her subject matter, for her style, for her authorial posture. Indeed, the rhetorical power of the poem, "For My People"—the verbal arpeggios, the cascading adjectives, the rhythmic repetitions—has its roots in the "preacherman" rhetoric of the Black South. Similarly, Vyry's eloquent prayer in *Jubilee* came from the Blacks' past and from the deep folk memories of a trouble-driven people. . . .

Not only does *For My People* have word power, but it is a poem filled with subtle juxtapositions of thought and idea. When the scene shifts from the rural South to the urban North—to "thronging 47th Street in Chicago and Lenox Avenue in New York"—the poet describes her people as "lost disinherited dispossessed and happy people." At another point, they are depicted as "walking blindly spreading joy." This Donnesque yoking of opposites linking happiness with dispossession and blind purposelessness with joy reveals the depth of Margaret Walker's understanding of the complexities of the Black experience. In fact, the poet here is writing about the source of the Black peoples' blues, for out of their troubled past and turbulent present came the Black peoples' song—a music and a song that guarantee that happiness and joy will somehow always be found lurking behind the squalor of the ghetto or behind the misery of the quarters or in some sharecropper's windowless cabin in the flood-drenched lowlands. For whenever there is trouble, a Bessie Smith or a Ma Rainey or a Bill Broonzy or a B.B. King or someone with the gift of song will step forward to sing it away. In fact, the song gets better when one is real lowdown and disinherited and even suicidal.

Richard K. Barksdale. In R. Baxter Miller,
ed. *Black American Poets between Two
Worlds, 1940–1960* (Knoxville: University of
Tennessee Press, 1986), pp. 105–7

The reader [of *For My People*] experiences initially the tension and potential of the Black South; then the folk tale of both tragic possibility and comic relief involving the curiosity, trickery, and deceit of men and women alike; finally, the significance of physical and spiritual love in reclaiming the Southern land. Walker writes careful antinomies into the visionary poem, the folk secular, and the Shakespearian and Petrarchan sonnets. She opposes quest to denial, historical circumstances to imaginative will, and earthly suffering to heavenly bliss. Her poetry purges the Southern ground of animosity and injustice that separate Black misery from Southern song. Her themes are time, infinite human potential, racial equality, vision, blindness, love, and escape, as well as worldly death, drunkenness, gambling, rottenness, and freedom. She pictures the motifs within the frames of toughness and abuse, of fright and gothic terror. Wild arrogance for her speakers often underlies heroism, which is often more imagined than real.

The myth of human immortality expressed in oral tale and in literary artifact transcends death. The imagination evokes atemporal memory, asserts the humanistic self against the fatalistic past, and illustrates, through physical love, the promise of both personal and racial reunification. The achievement is syntactic. Parallelism, elevated rhetoric, simile, and figure of speech abound, but more deeply the serenity of nature creates solemnity. Walker depicts sun, splashing brook, pond, duck, frog, and stream, as well as flock, seed, wood, bark, cotton field, and cane. Still, the knife and gun threaten the pastoral world as, by African conjure, the moral "we" attempts to reconcile the two. As both the participant and observer, Walker creates an ironic distance between history and eternity. The Southern experience in the first section and the reclamation in the second part frame the humanity of folk personae Stagolee, John Henry, Kissee Lee, Yallah Hammer, and Gus. The book becomes a literary artifact, a "clean house" that imaginatively restructures the Southland.

But if Dudley Randall has written "The Ballad of Birmingham" and Gwendolyn Brooks "The Children of the Poor," Walker succeeds with the visionary poem. She does not portray the gray-haired old women who nod and sing out of despair and hope on Sunday morning, but she captures the depths of their suffering. . . .

Patient nobility becomes the poet who [in *Prophets For a New Day*] has re-created Martin Luther King, Jr., as Amos. She has kept the neatly turned phrase of Countee Cullen but replaced Tantalus and Sisyphus with Black students and sit-ins. For her literary fathers, she reaches back to the nineteenth-century prophets Blake, Byron, Shelley, and Tennyson. Her debt extends no less to Walt Whitman and to Langston Hughes, for her predecessor is any poet who forsees a new paradise and who portrays the coming. As with Hughes, Walker is a romantic. But Hughes had either to subordinate his perspective to history, or to ignore history almost completely, and to speak less about events than about personal and racial symbols. Walker, on the contrary, equally combines events and legends but reaffirms the faith of the spirituals. Although her plots sometimes concern murder, her narrators reveal an image of racial freedom and human peace. The best of her imagined South prefigures the future.

R. Baxter Miller. In *Black American Poets between Two Worlds, 1940–1960* (Knoxville: University of Tennessee Press, 1986), pp. 119–20, 133–34

From this [early sample of her] published poems (*The Crisis*, May 1934) to the benediction of "A Poem for Farish Street Green" (February 27, 1986),

the penultimate poem of *This Is My Century: Black Synthesis of Time,* Margaret Walker Alexander mines the depth of heritage: music *(melos),* memory
(ethos), and community *(epos).* And it should not surprise us that one of
America's most distinguished and senior Afro-American poets, twelve years
before the millennium, has delivered for posterity the poem of the century.
For each of Margaret Walker's published volumes, beginning with the famous
and award-winning *For My People* (1942), has signaled a major poetic event.
It is true that twenty-eight years intervened before the poet published another
volume after *For My People* sounded the second phase of modern poetry
written in the United States. For while it interrupted the sound created in
the earlier, modernist phase by poets, on one hand, like Ezra Pound, T. S.
Eliot, Amy Lowell, and Wallace Stevens, and, on another, like Countee Cullen, Claude McKay, Georgia Douglas Johnson, and the earlier Langston
Hughes, the *For My People* collection stood as the sole book-length publication of Margaret Walker's poetic voice. But in 1970 when *Prophets for a
New Day* entered publication through Dudley Randall's Broadside Press, we
received our singular poetic memorial to the Civil Rights Movement of the
mid-1950s through the 1960s. In 1973, *October Journey. . . ,* a collection of
autobiographical and occasional poems written over Margaret Walker's lifetime, provided the link between the earlier two volumes and those poems
written since and included in the present volume, *This Is My Century: Black
Synthesis of Time.* Thus, what may appear to be a discontinuous record is,
actually, the record of a poetic vocation consistently practiced for over fifty
years. But those fifty years become immortal here, not only as the journey
of a Self as it creates the features of its wonderful plentitude, but as the
journey of a people and the voice of an age. *This Is My Century: Black
Synthesis of Time* is a poetic biography of the twentieth century.

Eleanor W. Traylor. Callaloo. 10, 1987, p. 571

In radical opposition to notions of discontinuity, confronting us as a fictional
world of consecrated time and space, *Jubilee* worries one of the traditional
notions of realism—the stirring to life of the common people—to a modified
definition. Walker completed her big novel in the mid-1960s at the University
of Iowa Creative Writers' Workshop. She tells the story of the novel, twenty
years in the making, in *How I Wrote Jubilee.* This novel of historical content
has no immediate precedent in Afro-American literary tradition. To that extent, it bears little structural resemblance to Hurston's work before it,
although both Hurston and Walker implement a search for roots, or to Morrison's work after it. *Jubilee,* therefore, assumes a special place in the canon.
    From Walker's own point of view, the novel is historical, taking its
models from the Russian writers of historical fiction, particularly Tolstoy. In
its panoramic display, its massive configurations of characters and implied
presences, its movement from a dense point of American history—the era
of the Civil War—toward an inevitable, irreversible outcome—the emancipation of ten million African-Americans—*Jubilee* is certainly historical. Even
though it is a tale whose end is written on the brain, in the heart, so that

there is not even a chance that we will be mistaken about closure, the novel unfolds as if the issues were new. We are sufficiently excited to keep turning the page of a twice-told tale accurately reiterating what we have come to believe is the truth about the "Peculiar Institution." But the high credibility of the text in this case leads us to wonder, eventually, what else is embedded in it that compels us to read our fate by its lights. My own interpretation of the novel is that it is not only historical, but also, and primarily, Historical. In other words, "Historical," in this sense, is a metaphor for the unfolding of the Divine Will. This angle on reality is defined by Paul Tillich as a theonomy. Human history is shot through with Divine Presence so that its being and time are consistent with a plan that elaborates and completes the will of God. In this view of things, human doings are only illusions of a counterfeit autonomy; in Walker's novel agents (or characters) are moving and are moved under the aegis of a Higher and Hidden Authority.

For Vyry Ware, the heroine of *Jubilee,* and her family, honor, courage, endurance—in short, the heroic as transparent prophetic utterance—become the privileged center of human response. If Walker's characters are ultimately seen as one-dimensional, either good or bad, speaking in a public rhetoric that assumes the heroic or its opposite, then such portrayal is apt to a fiction whose value is subsumed in a theonomous frame of moral reference. From this angle of advocacy and preservation the writer does not penetrate the core of experience, but encircles it. The heroic intention has no interest in fluctuations or transformations or palpitations of conscience—these will pass away—but monumentality, or fixedness, becomes its striving. Destiny is disclosed to the hero or the heroine as an already-fixed and named event, and this steady reference point is the secret of permanence.

The blending of a material culture located in the nineteenth century with a theme which appears timeless and is decisively embedded in a Christian metaphysic reveals the biographical inspiration behind Walker's work. *Jubilee* is, in effect, the tale translated of the author's female ancestors. This is a story of the foremothers, a celebration of their stunning faith and intractable powers of endurance. In that sense, it is not so much a study of characters as it is an interrogation into the African-American character in its poignant national destiny and through its female line of spiritual descent. A long and protracted praise piece, a transformed and elaborated prayer, *Jubilee* is Walker's invocation to the guiding spirit and genius of her people. Such a novel is not "experimental." In short, it does not introduce ambiguity or irony or uncertainty or perhaps even "individualism" as potentially thematic material because it is a detailed sketch of a *collective* survival. The waywardness of a Sula Peace, or even a Janie Stark's movement toward an individualistic liberation—a separate peace—is a trait of character development engendered by a radically different Weltanschauung.

Hortense J. Spillers. In Shari Benstock, ed.
Feminist Issues in Literary Scholarship
(Bloomington: Indiana University Press,
1987), pp. 186–87, 191

In these essays we are ever mindful of Walker's need to defend the often unspoken values that belie a common Afro-American consciousness and define the chaos and disruption that constantly threaten America. We are ever mindful of the poet in these essays who is constantly searching for ways of giving meaning to her culture through its own formal and structural devices. The essays create a literary landscape that encompasses the past, present, and future. The writing is noticeably passionate, yet thoroughly discriminating. For the reader who has become accustomed to Walker's poetry, the voice in these essays recalls a familiar style and orientation. Like the poetry, these essays are inextricably bound to Walker's own history. Like the poetry too, the essays show a single driving force: a dramatic tension between social activism and artistic imagination. Moreover, Walker, in "The Humanistic Tradition of Afro-American Literature" makes no pretense about assigning a profoundly revolutionary role to art. . . .

As for most of our best writers, for Walker socio-political criteria have always been as important as literary criteria. This is not, however, a pedestrian concern. Walker's preoccupation has led her to explore the internal and external dynamics of the Black experience: to see its manifold cultural products, its philosophical humanism, its militant activism. It is this broader perspective, which always challenges the literary imagination, that has given her critics such difficulty, perhaps, in finding for Walker a "place" in the literary canon.

One thing we might look to these essays to do for us is to help establish what it is that gives Black American literature its distinctive life and voice, why there is a persistence in its mode of expression. For Walker it is that "feeling tone," the abstracted content of the Black experience ever seeking to express itself through the culture's reservoir of verbal landscapes, some spoken, some sung, some preached, some known only through their silence. For Margaret Walker, life and work, as these essays reveal, represent the kind of literary engagement with ideas that should mark its own place in the literary canon and in history.

Maryemma Graham. Introduction to
Margaret Walker. "*How I Wrote* Jubilee"
and Other Essays on Life and Literature
(New York: Feminist Press, 1990),
pp. xix, xxi

WANG ANYI (CHINA) 1954–

In China to make the world "better and better" through fiction has always required that one write in a realistic narrative style with clearly understandable, didactic, or even tendentious thematic messages and that one not let the unavoidable ambiguity of excessive artistry interfere with the seriousness of one's purpose. In the seven stories included in *Lapse of Time,* written between 1981 and 1984 (at age twenty-seven to thirty), Wang Anyi has not deviated from this time-honored norm. Stylistically, linguistically, and esthetically (i.e., in everything pertaining to artistic form) there is nothing particularly striking about the stories, either in the original Chinese or in translation. The English versions, especially those by Howard Goldblatt, Daniel Bryant, and Michael Day, are faithful reproductions of Wang Anyi's style of writing.

The themes are uppermost in the stories, and any reviewer would be remiss if he did not summarize them. The theme of "The Destination" (1983) is that "life in Shanghai is not easy"; this line occurs no less than three times in the course of the story. "And the Rain Patters On" (1980) is an uplifting tale which teaches us that a young girl should never give up what Zhang Kangkang had one year earlier called her "right to love." "Life in a Small Courtyard" (1983) demonstrates that love can overcome poverty and make a life devoid of material comforts bearable. "The Stage, a Miniature World" (1983), though suffering from the same repetitiveness that plagues all of Wang's works I have read, is the only selection containing a touch of nonromanticized irony; in it we learn that the new, in the form of Western-influenced songs and dances, is more popular than the old traditional (meaning 1949–78 traditional) entertainments. The highly autobiographical story "The Base of the Wall" (1981) is the most interesting and successful in the book because of its depiction of the lives of those without culture who lived on the wrong side of the wall until the Cultural Revolution put them temporarily on the top of the heap. The irony is that were they still on the top of the heap, Wang Anyi would not be a writer writing about them and a little rich girl longing to be one of them. No matter. Her theme is that Disraeli's "two nations" living in China separated yet by the base of an old wall that still "sticks up from the ground in stubborn silence" share a common humanity is well taken and mercifully unobtrusive. "Between Themselves" (1984), the story of a hyperactive young student and an ineffectual teacher who is pushed too far and actually slaps the boy, is the only one of the selections that left me wondering, "What does it all mean?" It was a refreshing feeling.

"Lapse of Time" (1982) is a hundred-page novelette designed, it seems, to assuage the "guilt about her past comforts" mentioned in Jeffrey Kinkley's preface and containing all the major faults of Wang's writing: excessive wordiness, repetitiveness, unrealistic or stereotypical characterizations, overly abrupt changes in moral character, didacticism, and shallow moralizing. The theme of the work is what Bertrand Russell once called the "moral superiority of the oppressed" and (its obverse) the moral inferiority of the oppressor as well as the uselessness of the rich and the worthiness of the poor. When the main character is a poor laborer, she is strong, decisive, useful to society, and spiritually fulfilled; but when she becomes rich again, she goes right back to being useless, idle, and overcome by a sense of the meaninglessness of existence. Not to worry. In the end she discovers "the meaning of life": "The true meaning of life is simplicity itself: supporting yourself through your own labor." Or: "Use your own strength to row this little boat called life to the other shore." "Simplicity itself"—a fitting characterization of Wang Anyi's moral imagination.

Michael S. Duke. World Literature Today.
63, 1989, pp. 535–36

In "The Destination," one of the stories in *Lapse of Time,* a . . . character returns to Shanghai after years of life on the frontier, where he had volunteered to go in place of his brother. He has forgotten that Shanghai people stand in crowded buses in a certain stoic way. He realizes slowly that the city is not as glamorous as he remembered it. His family tries to marry him off to an unappealing woman—"a dead crab"—just because she has a room. All this is sparely told and poignant. But Wang Anyi must have an upbeat ending—is this Mao's influence at a great distance, or simply prudence on her part? "He believed," she writes, "that once he arrived at his true destination, he would have no doubts, troubles, or sense of rootlessness." Nothing in the story makes us believe this for a moment.

The title story, "Lapse of Time," is a novella, wonderfully translated by Howard Goldblatt, about Ouyang Duanli, a spoiled young married woman from a rich Shanghai family who is reduced to a pariah during the Cultural Revolution. Her husband and in-laws turn out to be either weak, bickering, or greedy. Like her children she learns to manage, lining up to buy food in the early morning and fighting not to get jostled out of her place. She comes to like making a bit of money by doing dreary manual work. Her working-class comrades are more interesting than most others in recent Chinese fiction: they are helpful to her, yet make her feel the anger of class envy. The bad time ends and the family becomes rich again. Duanli slowly realizes that while she now has plenty of money again she misses working, but she can't quite find the strength to go back. Her story is delicately and deftly outlined, like good caligraphy. Wang Anyi's inevitable final sentence about how time "never made its passage in vain" seems simply irrelevant.

Wang Anyi's *Baotown* is a short novel about life in a small town remote from the great shifts in Chinese politics. At first its people seem poor but kindly. They share their food and houses with orphans and stray travelers and boast about their willingness to help each other. But when a single lonely woman goes to bed with a boy she adopted as a child, their Baotown neighbors beat them up. With a few exceptions, such as Ding Ling in her early work, Chinese writers are not good at describing sexual feeling, which is often compared to flowing warm water. Wang Anyi also uses this image, but she also can describe, in language coy to us, but almost pornographic to Chinese readers, the mute, Oedipal longing of her odd couple, who sleep head to foot:

> His feet were resting in Aunt's bosom, warm, soft, warm and
> soft. Very gently he moved his toes and found an even softer

> spot, even warmer—and now the skin on his head began to
> tingle. He did not dare move as he felt his heart begin to pound.
> A breeze came through the brick-hole, the grass outside was
> wrestling.

Wang Anyi tells the story of a little boy in Baotown who is drowned in
a flash flood. The Party, needing a model hero for the county, decides to turn
him into one. A professional writer is commissioned to concoct an inspiring
story of his heroic death for the public, the family is given a better house,
and a memorial hall is planned. None of the little hero's belongings, however,
can be found to be placed on exhibit in the hall. Only his signature survives
on the mud wall of an outhouse. But is it really his handwriting? "Absolutely,"
says a young friend. "The two of us were taking a shit together and we just
wrote our names for fun." The committee tries to lift off the signature for
display, but the walls of the privy crumble, "so in the end they had to leave
the Youth Hero's signature where it was." Wang Anyi's quiet sense that there
is a continuing Communist comedy to be observed in China sets her apart
from her contemporaries.

Jonathan Mirsky. *New York Review of
Books.* October 26, 1989, p. 28

Baotown is a droll metacommentary on the roles of the writer in society. Bao
Renwen, nicknamed "Word Crazy," is an eager, naïve villager whom others
consider educated beyond his usefulness. Ultimately he becomes a kind of
wise fool facilitating village change.

> He wrote without regard for day or night, wrote on the unused
> parts of exercise pads from school, wrote until he had seven
> several thick books' worth of writing. His parents wanted him
> to think about finding a wife. He refused. "Writing first, family
> second": this too was his secret motto.

Word Crazy's deepest impact is on the family of Bao Yanshan. Bao
Yanshan has three sons: Construction, the eldest and slowest, whom everyone is eager to marry off; Culture, an intelligent youth who falls in love with
a transient named Little Jade; and Dregs, so named because he is the last of
the family. Dregs, a gentle, sensitive child, befriends a bitter old man named
Fifth Grandfather and invites him home to eat from the meager family pot.
(Like the rest of the village, Bao Yanshan's family is struggling against
starvation.)

Floods have shaped and reshaped Baotown over the centuries, and once
again disastrous rains inundate the remote town, killing some villagers.
Among the drowned are the wife of Bao Yanshan's neighbor Bao Bingde (she
falls or jumps off his back), and Dregs, who loses his life in a failed attempt
to rescue Fifth Grandfather. People search desperately for the child, but it is

the reviled newcomer Picked-Up who dives into the deadly waters and retrieves Dregs's corpse.

After the flood, villagers reconstruct their world. Dregs's family deeply mourn him, but press on. Bao Bingde remarries and soon becomes a father. Picked-Up achieves new status for his courageous recovery of Dregs's body. And Word Crazy creates a romantic tale about the small lad who had put his life on the line for Fifth Grandfather.

The heroic story draws outsiders to Dregs's home, and the government erects a monument to the Youth Hero. Dregs's parents are given materials to build a bigger house. This enables their son Construction to find a wife, which frees the second son, Culture, to marry Little Jade. Meanwhile, Word Crazy is rather startled by what the pen has wrought.

Wang balances with eloquent irony a number of tricky themes—turgid party bureaucracy, community responsibility versus individual enterprise and intergenerational romance. Her portrayal of sexuality (heterosexuality) is strikingly candid for contemporary China. Wang writes with sympathy about Communist ideals and the villagers' daily crises, but her work is never rhetorical or sentimental.

Disappointingly, most of *Baotown's* major characters are male. Most of the women we do meet are named in relationship to men—Aunt and Second Aunt, Bao Bingde's wife, Bao Yanshan's wife. I'm not looking for Ms. Youth Hero, but I do want to know the girls and women more fully.

Otherwise, *Baotown* is a very satisfying novel—deft, original, tragic, funny. This is one of the most felicitous translations of Chinese I have read in a long time. Martha Avery elegantly uses idiomatic English and allows the novelist's wit to shine through.

Valerie Miner. *The Nation.* March 19, 1990,
pp. 389–90

Wang Anyi is one of the many young writers who have appeared in China since the political changes following the death of Mao Zedong. "Socalist" China is the society which produced her. She was born in 1954.

Love in a Small Town is a novelette telling the story of a sexual relationship between two dancers who are members of a rural ballet troupe. We follow them for twelve years, beginning when the boy is sixteen and the girl twelve. Wang herself was assigned at the age of sixteen to a rural performing-arts troupe during the Cultural Revolution, and the novelette is said to be based on a "true story," events which happened in the company to which the author belonged.

After years of often dreary "socialist realism" and "revolutionary romanticism" in Chinese literature, it is refreshing to read a piece of fiction in which the author's only interest is in a universal human impulse. Though the story is set in the period of the Cultural Revolution, not a word of politics or "ideological consciousness" intrudes. The narrator only notes without comment the death of Mao and some other "leaders" in 1976.

The mode is ironic. The lovers are physically repulsive and of low intelligence. The intellectual narrator mostly looks on with lofty dispassion on the progress of their affair, but sometimes there is a break: "They live in a time of bleak ignorance; there is no forerunner to help them see the light. . . . We can only grope, search, crawl and scramble in the dark, trying to find a way out of the filth and mire. Adam and Eve are our examples."

Love in a Small Town is a step in the development of the modern Chinese literary consciousness. It is an allegory which ends with the birth of illegitimate twins, a boy and a girl, whom the mother claims were fathered by no one but are hers alone. Here is a place to start, a way out perhaps, from the ugly, brutish society and spiritual world in which the characters live. Contemporary China's intellectuals are the most severely oppressed in the modern world, but the human spirit of a writer like Wang Anyi is ultimately not cautious.

Russell McLeod. World Literature Today.
64, 1990, pp. 192–93

Of all the interesting young writers who emerged in China in the 1980s, Wang Anyi must be one of the most prolific. She has written at least half a dozen collections of short stories and several novels, but perhaps her most famous (or infamous) works are the three "novelettes" (as translator Eva Hung calls them) known collectively as the "Three Loves," which first appeared in literary magazines in China in 1986 and 1987. *Love on a Barren Mountain* is the second story in the trilogy to be translated, the English version of the first (*Love in a Small Town,* also translated by Eva Hung) having appeared in 1988.

The book is apparently based on a true story which Wang watched unfolding when she was sent down to the countryside during the Cultural Revolution. The two main characters, referred to throughout only as "he" and "she," are a cellist in a small performing arts troupe and the girl who becomes his mistress, and with whom he eventually commits suicide; but it is far from being a clear-cut moral story where right is immediately discernible from wrong—Wang is too good a writer for that, and although her choice of subject-matter may have caused considerable unease among more "ideologically sound" members of the literary establishment in China, she handles this exploration of human sexuality sensitively and convincingly. Her belief that women are by nature stronger than men comes across very clearly in her depiction of both the mistress and the cellist's wife: she actually writes "Women are in fact superior to men in strength as well as wisdom, but since they do not have their battlefields, they put everything into love." The cellist appears to be a weak and rather cowardly character, but because, in the first chapter, Wang has shown us scenes from his youth, we can at least begin to understand why this might be. These scenes, including a strangely beautiful one where the family home goes up in flames, are interspersed in a kind of counterpoint with scenes from the childhood and youth of his mistress, whose background is morally dubious in Chinese terms but who is drawn sympathetically, almost as an innocent victim of her own sexuality.

Wang's rather cinematic technique of cutting from one scene to another can sometimes be confusing, but I found the parallel development of the histories of the two protagonists mostly quite effective, and I was impressed by the author's eye for detail and her descriptions of profound human emotions and their mutability. I think she has interesting and important things to say about relationships between men and women, and anyone familiar with the Chinese literary scene over the past few years will quickly realize how courageous she is to have tackled this subject so honestly and openly. Eva Hung's translation reads smoothly, on the whole, in spite of some minor inconsistencies, and she has coped successfully with what I suspect was a somewhat problematic style in the original.

Caroline Mason. *China Quarterly.* 129, 1992,
pp. 249–50

WARNER, SYLVIA TOWNSEND (GREAT BRITAIN) 1893–1978

She has no Platonic consolations for her green Dorsetshire world [*The Espalier*], brooded over by the sardonic melancholy of Hardy and Powys, except a wry, good-tempered humor. The fact that she imitates Hardy at times with a closeness within the forbidden degrees, cannot disguise her originality. Less skillful technically than *The Unknown Goddess* [by Humbert Wolfe], her work lends itself less to quotation.

Yet there is the firm impress of a personality one likes and respects in the allegory of "The Virgin and the Scales," or the brief, bold strokes of the narrative in "Nelly Trim," with its swift, Homeric opening. . . . Some will complain that Miss Warner, like most happy possessors of both youth and cleverness, overdoes the second; but time will cure. Some, again, will find her view of life too ironic; but so is life. Miss Warner should be heard of again.

F. L. Lucas. *Authors Dead & Living*
(London: Macmillan, 1926), pp. 253–54

In comparison with Mr. Yeats or Mr. Monro, Miss Sylvia Townsend Warner is occupied with a smaller problem. Her work is infused with that rare quality, a genuine rural sentiment. This is not the faked-up rural sentiment of most of the Georgians, but that more homely and genuine thing, the actual country outlook of Burns, Herrick, Barnes, Herbert, or Hardy. That Miss Warner has to admit a certain indebtedness to these predecessors, goes without saying. Yet her book is a perfectly honest performance, and her craftsmanship is both sure and subtle within its limits. Her general outlook has grown a little more fanciful and less poignantly tragic than when she wrote her earlier book *The Espalier* which was an exceptionally fine performance. Now that Miss Charlotte Mew is dead, I think Miss Warner should be proclaimed the best woman poet in England, outside of Chelsea—which, as we know, has its own ideas.

John Gould Fletcher. *Criterion.* June, 1929, p. 133

Miss Townsend Warner has been criticized and is likely to be criticized again for the fact that in her new novel, *The Corner That Held Them,* she views her fourteenth-century nuns through twentieth-century eyes. I can only feel thankful that she does. How bitter this mediaeval concoction would be without the jam of modern wit and irony!

In literature reality is relative only to our willingness to believe, and, because I can believe in them, Miss Warner's nuns are for me much more like fourteenth-century nuns than could be any tedious puppets talking pseudo-Chaucerian. As far as period details are concerned I do not know whether the novel is accurate or not, but it is something more—it is entertaining. Miss Warner's survey of thirty-three years of life in the convent of Oby is from start to finish a mild, sustained delight, never during its three hundred and ten pages jarring one by any obvious error in the drawing of her long pageant of characters. She treats them all with equal insight and interest so that, as far as importance is concerned, they are all much of a size and rouse the same sympathy. The resulting effect is slightly flat but one of complete realism.

Olivia Manning. *Spectator.* December 3, 1948, p. 744

Miss Sylvia Townsend Warner . . . is a true professional: she has a style of her own, a distinctive outlook on life, a sly, pungent, poetical way of expressing what she sees. She does not always see anything very new; her imagination turns more readily backwards, preferring to evoke and interpret the atmospheres of the past rather than the tricky materials of our own time. She is one of those writers who have an unmistakable *flavor,* recalled with pleasure long after the story and its persons are forgotten. It is a flavor deceptively smooth, and even prim, for she writes with a grace and polish; but there are undercurrents of earthiness and poetry, and the two things together, the smoothly raked surface and the surprising subsoil, are what give her work its distinctive and pregnant quality.

James Michie. *The London Magazine.* January, 1955, p. 90

Ordinarily, our sensible parent, *The New Yorker,* doles out Sylvia Townsend Warner's stories one at a time. But her collected stories, like her favorite sweets, *marrons glacés,* make way for immoderate consumption and some indigestion.

The unfaltering texture and taste of the latest in *Swans on an Autumn River* are admirable, but disconcerting too. Small talents seem properly more restless in the United States than in England. Truman Capote feels new literary forms thrust upon him; both he and we envisage the writing career as an infinite beanstalk to climb, an ascent which Miss Warner would snub as otiose, also ungainly. She herself minds her neat, confined talent like a shop for gourmets; her products aim at the choice modesty of kumquats and button mushrooms. . . .

A collection of such stories is like an annual surprise party: within the total predictability of the gathering, each story calls out, in its well-bred accent, "Surprise! Surprise!" And we experience, against our will, the same small ridiculous sensation of pleasure we felt the year before. In the past, Miss Warner's interest in the preternatural was more distinct, but it is sensed still in the titivations of her new stories. Across the placid surfaces of her characters run inexplicable tremors. Minute unseen forces play minute tricks, equivalents of curdling milk and dropping stitches and hiding best umbrellas. Each story is allotted its moment of witchery: a sudden, often mischievous, seldom malign, and never prolonged interruption of the habitual state.

And how it is told fits like hook and eye what is told. Each sentence too executes its tweak of the mind. A shock, slightly more emphatic than others to come, sets the story in motion. Miss Warner likes to make the start startling and seemingly disconnected, a shopping list, a notice posted in a French dining car. (Eventually, of course, these things will be unremittingly connected.) A short, level plain ensues, time to cross our legs and wind our watches. Then come the dips and turns of observation ("Dissatisfaction is a mildew, and creeps"), the near crises ("An instant later, deftly and deliberately, she knocked over her coffee-cup"), a dark tunnel with small shrieks, moments of birdlike suspension above beechwoods and bungalow roofs. The pace quickens, to outdistance ennui, and then we absorb the sharp, conclusive jolt, the laconic solution of a telegram: MOTHER DIED CLIMBING BOX HILL.

Mary Ellmann. *The Nation.* April 11, 1966, p. 431

With the publication of her first, and still most well-known novel, *Lolly Willowes* (1926), [Sylvia Townsend Warner's] reputation was made—and to some extent fixed. Early successes must be paid for. In her case, however, the success was earned. This story of a maiden aunt, who, wearying of dependence, withdraws to the country and becomes a witch, is exactly the kind of offbeat theme that makes a fashionable talking point. But the charm and oddity mask a serious purpose, and in the 1920s, when there was such a tragic residue of unmarried women, the novel could be read as a disguised feminist manifesto. The Devil, the "loving huntsman" of the subtitle, is the resort and protector of all wild and single beings. . . . *Lolly Willowes* is no mere piece of delicate urban whimsy: it is a novel with bite, and improves with each rereading.

Mr. Fortune's Maggot ("Theo's" book) [for Theodore Francis Powys] came out the following year, and likewise lends itself to a whimsical interpretation. Mr. Fortune, a middle-aged missionary, feels called to evangelize the remote South Sea island of Fanua: but once established there he only makes one convert, a charming native boy with whom he most Christianly falls in love. But time, the climate and an earthquake do their work: his own faith is lost, and he returns disconsolate to his superiors. It is the subtlest of tragedies. . . . The author's tone is compassionate. "My poor Timothy," she writes in the Envoi, "I do not know what will become of you."

She did, however, try to find out—if my reading of her novella "The Salutation" is correct. It is surely Mr. Fortune who turns up as the anonymous stranger befriended by an elderly widowed Englishwoman on a South American farm. But here too the personal outlook for the lone outsider is a bleak one. A persistent theme is beginning to emerge, the tragic pull in human fate between romantic adventurousness that has nowhere to go, and acceptance of one's lot which ends up in stagnation. It is a distinctively post-Christian dilemma, and the author has no ameliorating belief to offer save that in "some integral pity that nourishes the universe."

That pity is the informing spirit of her third and most mellow novel, *The True Heart* (1929), which re-tells the Cupid and Psyche story in a nineteenth-century Essex setting. The tale of the orphan girl Sukey who makes her way into Queen Victoria's presence on behalf of her true love, the idiot son of a snobbish vicar's wife, sounds bizarre or folksy: but it is neither. The Victorian world is so graphically described, the landscape so true and real, that the fable becomes an affirmation of love as a power that overcomes all odds. *Imaginative* love: there is no pandering to easy sentiment. Her most optimistic presentation of what she wanted to say, this is the last of her books to tempt one to use the epithet "delightful."

Glen Cavaliero. Powys Review. Summer,
1979, pp. 7–8

Under such disarming headings as "My Father, My Mother, the Butler, the Builder, the Poodle and I" and "Stanley Sherwood, or the Fireman's Revenge," Townsend Warner [in *Scenes of Childhood, and Other Stories*] airs the glamorous and charming eccentricities of her upper middle-class background with a telling irony. Her material is presented in a way that seems effortlessly natural, with none of the coyness and snobbishness that might have infected a lesser writer (and, one is tempted to add, lesser person). A ghastly butler can be mocked with moral impunity, since at the same time he is presented as an individual, a person with his own peculiar integrity; and because, too, the word of which butlers are a part is treated with equal stringency. . . .

It is easy to place too much emphasis on the Wodehouseian quality of her social world and not enough on her more private perceptions. The book is in fact shot through with a dark sense of morality and the passing of time.

One of the most disturbing, though far from humorless, anecdotes hovers with fearful delicacy round the approaching death of a cheerful and stylish young coachman, Ted Hooper, laid low by tuberculosis. . . . [The] alternation of an intensely felt emotion and a sharp, ironical criticism of the limitations of a particular society is the crux of Townsend Warner's art.

But the prevailing mood of the collection is undoubtedly sunny. Its author's wit can be devastating: "Major Beldam was, as my mother's fashion magazine would have put it, a simple confection in red and gray." Animals have a minor but significant role, and their quirkiness is often more than a match for that of the humans; Lord Kitchener ("the only cat I ever knew who chewed his own moustachios") gives Sylvia's mother "a biting, monosyllabic glance." Sometimes the narrative is interrupted to let us look into another world, rich and strange as a stained glass window or a magic box. One hilarious anecdote concerning Lord Kitchener and the mouse he fails to catch ends with a sudden marvelous evocation of life in an Indian nursery, experienced as if at first hand by the young Sylvia via her mother's recollections. . . . That supreme gift, displayed to the full in the novels, of capturing the very light and smell of places as dissimilar as a South Sea island and the Essex marshes, is tantalizingly glimpsed in such passages. They remind us that Sylvia Townsend Warner was a poet too, and that it is a poet's awareness of verbal nuance that helps give her prose its unusual distinction.

Carol Rumens. (London) *Times Literary Supplement.* November 6, 1981, p. 1302

Reading this book, I gradually realized that almost everything that mattered to the author was either left out or skipped past or splashed over with a rather urgently whipped-up froth of spoofing. *Almost,* I have to emphasize: There are passages of sudden, seemingly involuntary spellweaving that match the best pages of her other works. That is saying a lot, both qualitatively and quantitatively. She published seven novels, thirteen collections of short stories, six volumes of verse, and two biographies, besides her early political articles and literary studies, including a translation from Proust. She wrote a libretto for an opera based on the last days of Shelley, and when very young, having trained as a musicologist, was one of the editors of a ten-volume history of Tudor church music.

I had hoped to find in *Scenes of Childhood* the answers to some of the puzzles left by my acquaintance with the author. But I should have remembered the fashions that helped form the patterns of the *New Yorker,* where the pieces gathered here originally appeared. . . .

In the frailest anecdote, though, characteristic notes ring out: "The cat went up the stairs like an arpeggio passage in a cadenza"; the brass bed had "a starched white valance usually stenciled with dogpaws." Parts of some stories rise tantalizingly above the whole. In a tale of the mother's demented battle against mice, genuine emotion suddenly takes over, revealing "the astonishing storehouse" of the mother's memories of her Indian childhood, memories of scent and sound and color that become the author's own.

Is it unreasonable to wish that Warner had invariably written from the heart? Not, I think, when the difference in quality is so striking. . . .

It adds to one's desire to know what really concerned Warner when the first of these sketches was published in 1936. Titled blithely "My Mother Won the War," it looks back on her mother in a fierce and lengthy feud with the head of the local Red Cross committee over whether a soldier's pajama trousers should have a button, suggesting that the mood of 1914–18 in England was hilarious. Yet Warner felt a bitter revision against the "mass madness," the "brutal bungle" of war. At the time she wrote the story she was a committed Communist, contributing to the *Left Review* and trying desperately to place articles about Spain wherever they might help the Republican forces fighting Franco.

In 1938, *After the Death of Don Juan* appeared; although set in eighteenth-century Spain, it expressed her passionate antifascist convictions. In 1939 (the same year as the trifling "Madame Houdin" and "How I Left the Navy" in this volume), she published one of her most remarkable novels, *Summer Will Show,* the story of a woman's escape from her marriage into a strong erotic and political involvement with her husband's mistress. The background is Paris during the 1848 revolution, and the book ends with the heroine, after seeing her lover Minna stabbed to death on the barricades, staggering home a few days later and sitting down absently to glance at one of the leaflets she had been distributing. Then, "obdurately attentive and with growing absorption," she reads on in the Communist Manifesto.

Hope Hale Davis. *The New Leader.* March
8, 1982, p. 16

Sylvia Townsend Warner's prose is always sharp and fast-moving; time and again she pulls the carpet from under the reader's feet. But in the poems, in general, she is content to leave the carpet be, to settle down on it before that potent Warner symbol, the hearth. With its many Georgian flourishes, and yet little of the vitiating sentiment and deliberated significance which characterize that school, Sylvia Townsend Warner's early poetry did not appeal to many of her contemporaries. Behind all that is derivative and superficial in the style of *The Espalier* and her second collection of poems, *Time Importuned,* one can begin to hear the tone which became distinctively her own as she sloughed off the poetical and moved towards the plain style of the late poems. . . .

Louis Untermeyer added to his advocacy the phrase, "like a feminine Thomas Hardy." Sylvia Townsend Warner's poetry resembles Hardy's understating tone and themes sufficiently to suggest the comparison whenever it has attracted anything by way of commentary. Circumstance itself seems to encourage it; since the summer of 1981, Sylvia Townsend Warner has shared a place with Hardy and the Dorset Worthies in Dorset County Museum, and the implications are more than geographical. . . .

In a more general way, Powys must be held responsible for the proliferation of graveyards and dark, empty houses in Sylvia Townsend Warner's early poems, and for the element of horror which mars some of them. His work strengthened her growing suspicion that "the English Pastoral is a grim and melancholy thing" which she expressed in her own version of the Powysian perverse. In her writing, no convention is sacred, no presupposition assured. The world has been turned upside-down, and we must stand on our heads to view it clearly.

[We] might say of Sylvia Townsend Warner what she said of John Taverner in *Tudor Church Music:* "The honest admirer . . . must be ready to admit that such and such specimens . . . are not great works. The admission need cost him little, since he can say with conviction that the most insignificant of them betrays, somewhere and somehow, the master hand."

Claire Harman. Introduction to Sylvia
Townsend Warner. Collected Poems
(Manchester: Carcanet/New York: Viking,
1982), pp. xv–xvii, xxiii

She has no critical cachet whatever, this writer. Her fifteen volumes of fiction are not examined in studies of the modern English novel—even *Mr. Fortune's Maggot* (1927) fails to appear in bibliographies of gay writing, though it is, with Stein's *Things as They Are,* the most passionate homosexual novel I know. She is not "taught," and I have never heard her mentioned on those occasions when poets are "ranked." Women's studies have neglected her, too, though her status among the serenely Sapphic householders is irreproachable. . . .

I suspect the point of the poetry would be considerably sharpened if we did not know the prose to be so masterful and so attractive: it is difficult to believe that even this great quantity of verse is more than a second string to her bow. But this is not the case; Warner is a poet of great and consistent achievement. Our difficulty is with the *mode* of her verse rather than with its amount. She is not a modernist, and her fashion is not our fashion; ease, profusion, recurrent pattern and confidence in natural presences are *démodé* among us, and what we admire in Crabbe and Edward Thomas, in Hardy and de la Mare, we find suspect in a writer still active (till 1980!) among us, a writer who would rather be interesting than excruciating, who prefers centers to edges, meetings to sunderings, who chooses not so much to anatomize a state as to fix a vision.

Richard Howard. The Nation. March 19,
1983, p. 343

In male discourse the city is a female body. In women's fantasy novels the city is a hostile male body, and the heroines of Rebecca West's *Harriet Hume* and Sylvia Townsend Warner's *Lolly Willowes* retreat to nature, the garden or the forest to find nature and the body of the mother. . . .

In *Lolly Willowes* Laura restrains her grief at her mother's death and only breaks down when she finds a gardening glove of her mother's which still holds the shape of her hand. The rest of her life is spent getting back in touch with Mother Earth. The city's hostility to her spinsterhood and nature itself isolate her from the natural female world. When her nephew violates her space in the wilderness, he is driven away by a swarm of bees, the creatures Erich Neumann describes as sacred to the mother goddess, not only because of the nourishing quality of their honey, but because of the minimal role the male plays in their community life.

The anti-Apollonian discourse of the feminist fantasy narrative reproduces the magical lost woman's wilderness. Feminist fantasy fiction recovers the song of Daphne and speaks with the rustling tongues of laurel leaves. Like Joyce's "leafy speafing," it releases the maiden imprisoned in the lettering leaves. The discourse of Artemis is pure, savage, and antiurban, signifying both selfhood and sisterhood and a powerful sexuality in virginity. Artemisian discourse is directed against male desire. . . .

The prophecy in *Harriet Hume* that "the trees will get us yet" was fulfilled in Sylvia Townsend Warner's *Lolly Willowes* (1926). There is no need to ask who is Sylvia, for she has created a world of trees and given her heroine to the forest as heartily as other authors give them in marriage. There is no more exquisitely powerful evocation of the joys of spinsterhood in print. The rapture of St. Teresa as the bride of Christ matches Lolly's rapture at her dance with the devil. The prose is as sharp and delicate as Lolly Willowes's nose and chin. The single woman's passion for adventure and her flight into freedom are portrayed without guns and policemen in the plot. The humor is not that bitterly intellectual Scotch brew of Rebecca West, but a lighter and more domestic concoction like the dandelion wine Laura sips with her landlady, Mrs. Leak.

> Jane Marcus. In Susan Merrill Squier, ed.
> *Women Writers and the City* (Knoxville:
> University of Tennessee Press, 1984),
> pp. 138–39, 148

Sylvia Townsend Warner's *Summer Will Show* is a fictional account of collisions among classes, genders, and sexualities, a *Well of Loneliness* with antiracist, antiimperialist politics, a lesbian *Sammy and Rosie Get Laid* set in the revolutionary crisis of 1848. Dedicated to Townsend Warner's lover, Valentine Ackland, the novel was originally published in 1936 and is now being reissued. . . . Sammy and Rosie are in this case Sophia Willougby, an upperclass Englishwoman of country background, and Minna Lemuel, an East European Jewish artiste—a pair whose affinity transcends class and cultural barriers although, this being 1846/1848, they never do get laid.

The 1930s are also present in the novel's portrait of political turmoil and imminent violence (reflecting the revolutionary possibilities of Popular Front alliance as well as Fascist repression in Germany and Italy); in Minna's history of pogroms and current endurance of anti-Semitic insult; in the status of . . . Sophia's illegitimate half-caste nephew, sent from some colonial outpost to train for a life of dutiful clerkship. At the same time Townsend Warner sets her nineteenth-century stage: she phrases the issues of women's relation to class and money in terms of married women's right to own property and flourishes *The Communist Manifesto* as the latest word in political analysis. Townsend Warner tells us her story even in the way she tells the story: This novel is a virtual catalogue of devices for preliberation lesbian narratives. . . .

The particular achievement of *Summer Will Show* lies in the interweaving of sexual and historical stories, politics and form. . . .

Although Townsend Warner retains her realistic predisposition throughout the novel, the Victorian propriety of the first part's English family life gives way, when Minna's Paris is introduced, not to the wildly experimental, but to one striking absence. She suddenly discards the business of narrative connections, so that the scenes begin to cut one into another without any transitions from drawing room to bedroom or bedroom to street; they enact on the page the characters' relinquishing of control over their personal destinies and the author's abandoning of narrative responsibility to the historical event. *Summer Will Show*'s nineteenth century becomes modern at the advent of sexual disruption. Then the political season will show.

Finally, there remains the particular pleasure of twentieth-century suggestions (if not fulfillments) in nineteenth-century dress(es), for those of us who always wanted *The Bostonians'* Verena Tarrant to choose Olive Chancellor, and Olive to have her historical stage.

Julie Abraham. The Nation. March 19, 1988,
pp. 389–90

Lolly's age and her spinsterhood make her an unusual heroine, especially for a bildungsroman. Yet *Lolly Willowes* is revolutionary and subversive in more than its portrayal of an old maiden aunt who casts off the role society has created for her and rejects other middle-class values that define what is good and proper. Warner also mocks both social and literary conventions when she transmutes her seemingly innocent and comically realistic bildungsroman into a satiric fantasy, flouting literary conventions by combining the two types of fiction. In Part 1 of the novel, the narrator realistically details Lolly's life at Apsley Terrace, the London home of Lolly's brother, and relates in a flashback the details of the Willowes family history and the first twenty-eight years of Lolly's extended youth in Somerset. In the next two parts of the novel, she combines realism and fantasy; Lolly achieves womanhood by making a pact with the devil and becoming a witch.

Warner realizes that a radical re-visioning of Western culture and the literary tradition that expresses and imparts Western values is necessary if women are to come to know themselves and create their own stories. Anticipating Virginia Woolf's call in *A Room of One's Own* (1929), *Lolly Willowes* retells social and literary history from the perspective of a woman who refuses to cast herself as Eve. For a woman to achieve adulthood, in Warner's view, she must use her independent income to claim more than a room of her own. She must, like Lolly, challenge what Adrienne Rich has called the male prerogative of naming.

Barbara Brothers. In Laura Doan, ed. *Old
Maids to Radical Spinsters: Unmarried
Women in the Twentieth-Century Novel*
(Urbana: University of Illinois Press, 1991),
pp. 195–96

What then *is* a lesbian fiction? Taking Sylvia Townsend Warner's *Summer Will Show* as our paradigm, we can . . . begin to answer the question. . . . Such a fiction will be, both in the ordinary and in a more elaborate sense, non-canonical. Like Townsend Warner's novel itself, the typical lesbian fiction is likely to be an under-read, even unknown, text—and certainly an under-appreciated one. It is likely to stand in a satirical, inverted or parodic relationship to more famous novels of the past—which is to say that it will exhibit an ambition to displace the so-called canonical works which have preceded it. In the case of *Summer Will Show,* Townsend Warner's numerous literary parodies—of Flaubert, Eliot, Brontë, Dickens and the rest—suggest a wish to displace, in particular, the supreme texts of nineteenth-century realism, as if to infiltrate her own fiction among them as a kind of subversive, inflammatory, pseudo-canonical substitute.

But most importantly, by plotting against what Eve Sedgwick has called the "plot of male homosociality," the archetypal lesbian fiction decanonizes, so to speak, the canonical structure of desire itself. In so far as it documents a world in which men are "between women" rather than vice versa, it is an insult to the conventional geometries of fictional eros. It dismantles the real, as it were, in a search for the not-yet-real, something unpredicted and unpredictable. It is an assault on the banal: a retriangulating of triangles. As a consequence it often looks odd, fantastical, implausible, "not there"—utopian in aspiration if not design. It is, in a word, imaginative. This is why, perhaps, like lesbian desire itself, it is still difficult for us to acknowledge—even when (Queen Victoria notwithstanding) it is so palpably, so plainly, there.

Terry Castle. *Textual Practice.* 4, 1990,
pp. 200–201

WARNER-VIEYRA, MYRIAM (GUADELOUPE) n.d.

By "accepting" the label of madwoman, Juletane [in the novel of that title] is, in effect, "domesticating" madness, as it were. It is no longer just madness "in the sense that a life of total isolation is a form of madness" but also madness as the only way for her to behave in the situation she finds herself in. . . . And to the extent that no one really pays much attention to what a madwoman has to say, it affords her some protection . . . and this in turn becomes a vehicle for self-revelation, enabling her to write about and ponder her own experiences.

It is here that one sees Africa emerging as nothing less than a prisonhouse for this Afro-Caribbean woman. The myth of Africa as the Mother-continent or the Guinea of voodoo worship to which one returns upon being "set free" by death is replaced by the harsh reality of a social system that daily reminds Juletane of the fact that she is and remains an outsider and, therefore, a "prisoner" of others' perception and their way of categorizing her.

Jonathan Ngate. Callaloo. 9, 1986,
pp. 556–57

Suzette and Juletane, the anti-heroines of Miriam Warner-Vieyra's two companion novels *(Le Quimboiseur l'avait dit* [The sorcerer said so] and *Juletane)* are figures of dislocation, isolation and alienation, victims of misguided efforts to escape from their initial restricted situations. Both are associated with closed spaces, severely circumscribed worlds. Suzette, a young West Indian girl, confined to her room in an insane asylum in Paris, looks back nostalgically to her island and what had once seemed to be a restricted environment comes to be in retrospect an idyllic paradise. Suzette's selective memory evokes an image of simple, communal life in a tiny village on an island "as big as two coconuts." In terms of the fate of woman's ambitions Vieyra's novels are pessimistic. Suzette affirms that she ought never to have left her village. The journeys to Europe *(Le Quimboiseur . . .),* and to Africa *(Juletane),* attempts at self-actualization and escape, end in catastrophe. The woman who is not content to limit herself or to "be satisfied with the known domestic world," Suzette seems to suggest, is doomed to failure, to a last state worse than the first, partly because of her society's taboos, but also because of false, misplaced ambition. Juletane in Africa goes mad because she has been betrayed by her husband but also because she is unable to accept and be content with the sort of life typified by her husband's first wife, for whom "the entire universe was limited to a mat under a tree and three children around her" ["Pour elle, tout l'univers s'arrête à une natte sous un arbre et trois enfants autour"].

Similarly, Suzette in Paris is driven to madness because her dreams too are betrayed. She is exploited and degraded by her ambitious and egotistical *créole* mother (a symbolic representation of Guadeloupe or that part of Guadeloupean society which espouses and pursues white values) and her French lover (her false vision of France). . . . Having strayed too far from home, now, with no way out, she longs to recover the safe haven of her father's boat, the comfort of the island womb.

The closed space can function generally as both a positive and a negative image. In later West Indian novels it is a trap which forces a confrontation with self, a confrontation often too painful to endure. It is a prison which is accepted and transformed by an effort of the woman's imagination into a refuge from a reality perceived as intolerable.

Elizabeth Wilson. In Carole Boyce Davies
and Elaine Savory Fido, eds. *Out of the
Kumbla: Caribbean Women and Literature*
(Trenton, New Jersey: Africa World Press,
1990), pp. 48–49

Femmes échouées (Fallen women) is a collection of nine stories by the Guadeloupean-born writer Myriam Warner-Vieyra, who has made Senegal her home for the last twenty years. The book is her third following the two novels *Le quimboiseur l'avait dit . . .* and *Juletane. . . .* The stories are set in Guadeloupe, the beautiful French-speaking Caribbean island, and the rich mixture of its cultures permeates the stories with an exotic flavor, either through the local variety of the "fruit of passion" or through the life-styles of its inhabitants.

The protagonist in each selection is a woman. A black servant girl dreams of winning the first prize at a Paris music academy when her gift for music is discovered by her (female) employers ("Premier prix"); a married woman finds herself slowly dying from marriage to a cool, indifferent, uninterested husband, whom she calls "Wall" ("Le mur, ou les charmes d'une vie conjugale"): a wheelchair-bound wife castrates her husband when she learns that their young maid is expecting his child ("Sidonie"). All the stories are written in a wholly realistic style except "Heure unique" (Unique hour), in which the burial of a loved one triggers impressions of a revival of the love affair.

Nadežda Obradović. *World Literature
Today.* 64, 1990, pp. 185–86

With undeniable forcefulness, Warner-Vieyra's short stories hold the reader's attention while capturing the essence and ambience of the contexts within which she has elected to set her vivid plots and well-defined characters. *Femmes échouées* has a sensitive simplicity of form and is enriched with lively dialogues reflecting comic, serious, lyrical, and surrealistic moods. Moreover, her frequent use of certain cinematic techniques lends unique and concise style to her accounts, which have an implicit or overt morale.

In *Femmes échouées,* Warner-Vieyra offers striking profiles of women. Except for a young doctor, male protagonists are generally seen in a dimmer light. As the title indicates, the female characters suffer many failures in the stormy waters of life. In these short stories, the writer paints with brisk impressionistic strokes the whole range of Guadeloupean life-styles. Furthermore, as she depicts love and betrayal, hope and despair, Warner-Vieyra intersperses social and political comments in her narrative to stress facets of Guadeloupe's history and to denounce the inequities of its class structure, political status, and economic conditions.

Like her compatriots Maryse Condé and Simone Schwarz-Bart, Warner-Vieyra knows how to embroider her works with magic realism, and her highly imaginative and sometimes provocative short stories enthrall the reader by switching from the world of the living to the ancestors' realm.

Myriam Warner-Vieyra is indeed one of the most original talents to appear on the Francophone literary scene in recent years. As has happened with her prior writings, it is hoped that *Femmes échouées* will one day be translated into English. When this happens, let us hope that the translation will maintain the verve and compelling qualities of the initial text.

Françoise Pfaff. *CLA Journal.* 33, 1990, pp. 457–58

Warner-Vieyra attacks polygamy and the selfishness of the African man, rather as does Mariama Bā in *Une si longue lettre* (1980). Warner-Vieyra's protagonist, however, has no female models within her own or another society, unlike Bā's Ramatoulaye, who can find strength in memories of her mother, who knows she belongs to Africa. Just as Bā's novel is a letter addressed to another woman, Juletane's diary is read by Hélène, an educated West Indian woman working in Paris, who has suppressed her emotions in order to get ahead with her career, but who finds herself moved by the diary. Thus the story of the woman who dies from having chosen the wrong "African chief" (but could there be a right one for a romantic like Juletane?) is poised against the story of the woman who wants complete independence.

The structure of interwoven plots, with events in the past affecting the life of the woman who reads of them in the present, is similar to that Ruth Prawer Jhabvala uses in *Heat and Dust* (1975). Women learn by reading what other women have written, especially their autobiographical writing, as many feminist critics have observed. Like Jhabvala, Warner-Vieyra is (of course) not writing autobiography. Rather she uses women's need to relate to one another through written language as a way of constructing her story, while keeping herself at a distance from both her characters. Juletane and Hélène, neither of whom has clearly made a better choice of life, tend "to dissolve and merge into each other," a model that Judith Kegan Gardiner has found to be frequent in modern women's writing. When she starts to read, Hélène finds that "fragments of her own life came back to her and forced her to make comparisons." Halfway through the diary, Hélène dreams of vengeance and seems to share Juletane's growing madness: "She wanted to make every man on earth suffer, to humiliate all men, to emasculate them." . . . At the end she thinks: "Was she right to be getting married? Ousmane [her fiancé], of course, was nothing like Mamadou [Juletane's husband] and she was the exact opposite of Juletane, but still. . . ."

Adele King. *College Literature.* 18, 1991,
pp. 100–101

For Warner-Vieyra, who has lived in Senegal for the last thirty years, the body is the privileged symbolic site which serves to represent the conflicts issuing forth from the fatal clash of cultures: African and Caribbean, Islamic and Catholic. And so, in *Juletane,* the subject's distress translates into a steady diminution of her physical and mental capacities, a decline leading to a sort of "gentle death," since the character fades away into a tranquil forgetfulness.

Juletane considers suicide because she cannot let herself be "tamed" either to the idea or the reality of the polygamous marriage which her husband Mamadou imposes upon her. She gives in to a self-destructive violence which leads her to the brink of madness.

She imposes upon herself a series of physical mortifications which reveal a desperate and futile effort to master "un destin [qu'elle] ne maîtrisai[t] pas" [a destiny (which she) did not control] . . . an effort which, according to philosopher Susan Bordo, is an integral part of the psychology of women labelled "anorexic": that is, women who engage in self-destructive behavior in order to compensate for their lack of social power.

Françoise Lionnet. *Callaloo.* 15, 1992,
pp. 35–36

WATSON, SHEILA (CANADA) 1919–

The style of *The Double Hook* is "a more complex and symbolical way of writing" than most readers are used to. The novel *appears* to be written in the clichés of the regional idyll, the Western, the ethnic-group novel, just as Hemingway's *The Old Man and the Sea* appears to be a simple story of a disappointed fisherman. Yet they are both symbolic novels; their use of cliché is ironic. What lifts them above the ordinary is that their symbols do not belong to a private world but to the great heritage of symbols in the "collective unconscious" of the race. All significant fiction unfolds with a hero, a romantic interest, a battle, and a resolution. Those readers, and there will be many, who find the symbolic groundwork laid out at the beginning of *The Double Hook* difficult to follow, might well keep in mind the outline of the story.

The Double Hook opens with a murder. James Potter, the main character in the novel, has just killed his mother: "James was at the top of the stairs.

His hand half-raised. . . . The old lady falling. . . . Into the shadow of death. Pushed by James's will. By James's hand."

Following this dramatic opening, each member of the straggling hill community imagines that he sees Mrs. Potter fishing, as was her custom, somewhere along the river that winds through the settlement. . . .

Mrs. Watson wished to make her story universal in scope. James Potter is not simply James Potter. Mrs. Potter is not simply his mother. They and the other characters stand for larger and deeper concepts. To accomplish this, as we have seen, she has built up the novel around a basic symbolic pattern. But it is not a symbolic pattern that is "invented" or one that is superimposed upon the story. The symbols are well known: the fish as Christ the God, Son, and Savior; the coyote, in Amerindian legend, as the nameless fear of the unknown. This is made clear, too, in the novel itself: "I don't know about God, William said. Your god sounds only a step from the Indian's coyote." But Mrs. Watson goes deeper than Christian truth and Amerindian myth. Her pattern is based on those elements, fire, earth, air, and water, that are basic to the "collective unconscious" of the human race, to the racial memory of man.

This symbolic pattern in its turn determines certain other aspects of the novel. The town James visits has no name. Its bank, hotel, bar, and brothel could be made of cardboard, put up for a day for the filming of a Western. This is deliberate. It is as though the author had said: "Take any town. Call it X." The setting must be somehow familiar yet universal. In addition, Mrs. Watson wishes to demonstrate that the film Western, although it contains all the materials for a great work of art, has so far failed to produce one. Popular culture has its limits. These she "explodes," creating what she has called an "anti-Western."

If her story is to become universal, she must overcome also the limitations of the "ethnic-group novel." This form has become very popular and is seriously studied in university circles—perhaps the most famous example is Willa Cather's *My Ántonia,* which describes the life of poor Swedish immigrants in the Middle West in the early years of this century. One notes that *The Double Hook* is saturated with the "folk wisdom" found in this type of novel, even to the point of caricature. There is a purpose. The "ethnic-group novel" is essentially condescending to the people it describes, and invites the reader to say: "How quaint!" In doing so, it prevents the characters from becoming universal or even fully human, since the basic hypothesis is that they are particular and singular in some way. To a certain extent, then, *The Double Hook* is somewhat of a literary manifesto.

A third literary ghost must be laid before the novel can attain the true structure that is inherent in the material, and that is the regional novel. Many authors have restricted themselves, not to some ethnic group, but to some region, usually one that has aspirations to cultural identity, such as the southern part of the United States. When Mrs. Watson refers to *The Double Hook* as an "antiregional novel," she implies that this approach limits and in so doing falsifies a novel's picture of human nature. Her method this time is not caricature so much as parody, and she has had the courage to tackle the great master of this *genre,* William Faulkner, in his own lair.

John Grube. Introduction to Sheila Watson.
The Double Hook (Toronto: McClelland and
Stewart, 1969), pp. 5, 12–13

The stark, closely circumscribed lives of these settlers in a small community in British Columbia unfold under the eye of Coyote, the North American Indian culture hero and trickster par excellence. The Faulkneresque characters speak through a third-person narrative voice that seems to issue from the land itself. . . . Watson achieves this voice largely through her use of folk motifs. But this old lady of the north is psychology's Terrible Mother, the constricting death-force that prevents her children from living full lives. As the novel opens James has murdered the old woman by pushing her down the stairs, but her spirit continues to haunt the community. Character after character sees her fishing at different points along the stream. But as Ara, the old woman's daughter-in-law, realizes, "it's not for fish she fishes." The novel traces James's desperate attempt to break free from this fisher of souls, Greta's inability to break free in any way short of suicide, and the struggle of Ara, William, Kip, Felix, and Angel to live meaningful lives.

Sheila Watson does not take her plot of characters from Coyote tales, she does not build her novel on folk motifs concerning the Coyote, nor does she adopt the straightforward, playful tone of the tales. Because she uses folklore in a more complex manner, a folkloric approach to her novel not only illuminates this specific text but also suggests approaches and questions that we can bring to other literary texts. For example, to understand *The Double Hook* we must identify the Coyote as an Indian folk figure, locate probable sources, determine how Sheila Watson's Coyote is like and unlike her sources, and we must see the way the author interweaves the tradition with her own plot, themes, and characters. The result should be a fuller understanding of all aspects of the novel. . . .

Watson has created [in Coyote] a voice which resonates with the Indians' past, the settlers' present, and with prophecies of their future. The critical debate over the function of Coyote in *The Double Hook* will probably continue. But for those who are outsiders to the Indian traditions and to the settlers' way of life, a folkloric approach provides the information needed to understand the all-important dualities of the novel. Coyote brings death and life; he is a fool, but he is a wise fool. A knowledge of the Indian tales shows us how Watson has altered the tradition to create a voice who speaks a universal, archetypal language. Post-Nietzschian, post-Einsteinian, and post-modernist we may be, but we still tend to look at the world and at literature from our own culturally biased perspective and we still tend to think of dualities as mutually exclusive opposites. Indian Coyote tales tell us that the hook is one, and double.

Steven Putzel. *Canadian Literature*. 102,
1984, pp. 8–9, 15–16

The language of [the] zero zone is, strictly speaking, silence. Not until this silence is perceived for what it is—a kind of naming—can a language appropriate for speaking of it become possible. We have—a double hook.

A silence of this kind underlies the literature of Canada, and Sheila Watson addresses it directly in *The Double Hook*. *The Double Hook* is an activity of language reflexively moving in on its own energies, moving out from them along channels of liturgy and ritual, floating inside a medium, a surround, of silence. The silence is physical, emotional, theological, eventually metaphysical. It invades character and event; it saturates words and dampens reference and resonance.

Why is *The Double Hook* so unusual in this way? And why is it, in spite of this unusualness, so authentic—as the contributors to George Bowering's collection of critical essays seem to agree? Because *The Double Hook* is *an* archetypal North American fiction and *the* archetypal Canadian fiction of this strange estranged space where allegory, symbol, and language float with such self-consciousness. This is why it is a very important book—one that awakens echoes, teases out memories, builds uncommon images, and uninvents the world. . . .

Watson avoids the distinct historical and social framework to which the Canadian imagination is so often leased and the public language so frequently used. She refuses to posit Canada as a secure social structure with eternity in place. It is impossible for anyone outside *The Double Hook* to walk the valley as if it is the universe, but peculiarly that is exactly what Watson's figures do. The world-in-itself phenomenon is not the condition of Canada, but some things in *The Double Hook* very nearly are. Watson strips the work of all surface level conventions, lets the world float, and makes the setting nowhere, demanding recognition of the silence and invisibility that surround the experience of Canada. She realizes that it is necessary to maintain the authentic meaning of words or risk everything, that the limits of language are indeed the limits of the world. Ultimately, inauthentic meanings destroy a culture more finally than silence ever could. Watson's language is not referential, but with it she creates a world that was not previously visible and that cannot usually be seen in Canada or in Canadian literature.

Margaret E. Turner. *Ariel*. 18, 1987,
pp. 66–67, 77

After having written one very short but just about perfect novel, Sheila Watson can certainly be forgiven for retiring from the profession. *The Double Hook* was our great modernist fiction, the hope, in the post-war period, that

Canada would not be consigned to hewing and drawing formula novels about dashed dreams under prairie snows.

Yet haven't we all regretted the irony that such a superior writer should write so little? It is probably normal then, that *Deep Hollow Creek* will be read in the light cast by *The Double Hook*. Is this the ur-novel? Did it deserve to be withheld all these years? Is it gratifyingly autobiographical?

Deep Hollow Creek was written twenty years before the last version of *The Double Hook*. While there are similarities, notably in Watson's inventive observations, there are interesting differences. Chief among the latter is in the spirit of structure—*The Double Hook,* with its quests and fire and rebirth, resembles myth; *Deep Hollow Creek,* with its indeterminacy and modesty, resembles life. Or rather living.

If the book had been published shortly after it was written, which would have been highly unlikely, would-be readers would have said that it had no story. Curiously, story is what it is all about. . . .

In *The Double Hook* there is no central character but a strained community in agon under Coyote's eye. Here there is a central character, but in relationship to story she is the reader in the text. Young Watson was very smartly uncovering a version of modernism in which the conventions of the well-made late-Victorian novel were flouted in the interest of a particular real. We are perhaps less disconcerted by the absences we apprehend than 1939 readers might have been. We have the advantage of our reading experience, and Sheila Watson has been responsible for showing our way to that advantage. . . .

In this (presumably) first book Watson is already skilled at the sharp edges her readers have always enjoyed. There is a porcupine "crossing the rock pile, with a rattle of quills." Readers of the later novel will not mind seeing again that someone "rode stiffly, slipped over the horse's back like a clothes-peg." Riders of the frozen sage will recognize Stella's sentiment: "I can't stand the feel of the stirrup iron at twenty below."

The "carelessly" gathered fragments have the effect of enjoining the reader outside the text to engage in assemblage and reconfiguration, just as the reader inside the text must do with these people's spoken and gestural narrations. These people are adept at recombining their own stories. To that end the valley telephone system serves well, there being no private lines.

It should be said that the young Watson had not yet learned to get her flame to white heat, a process that is well documented by F. T. Flahiff in his "Afterword" to the most recent edition of *The Double Hook,* wherein he demonstrates Watson's unerring revisions.

George Bowering. *Canadian Literature.* 136,
1993, pp. 132–33

WEBB, MARY (GREAT BRITAIN) 1881–1927

Mrs. Webb has not written a *Wuthering Heights,* but she is of contemporary novelists the one least unlikely to do so. If the passions which she describes tear less painfully the poor flesh harboring them, they are, like Heathcliffe's, rather the spirit of a waste than the comfortable affections of humankind. And Mrs. Webb, like the great Emily, is often at a loss how to reduce to a common formula her appreciation of the homely, solid life of the countryside and her sense of the dark mysteries latent in nature, both organic and inorganic. Unlike the great Emily, she has, too, a considerable talent for comedy. This is sometimes, and I think, unfortunately, expressed in satire.

H. C. Harwood. *The Outlook.* November 11,
1922, p. 406

The pity was that, though her books are full of wise and witty sayings, she did not sufficiently exploit her humor. Yet, withal, in her first four books at least, one recognizes that she was one of the few real humorists of the twentieth century. We have had, we still have, plenty of funny men; but hers is the humor that springs from creation of character. Her humor has kinship with the humor of Dickens, which trusts not in clowning and buffoonery— excellent qualities in their way and time and place—but relies wholly for its effects on the observation and study of average human types. It is impossible to convey that humor, or to do it faint justice, as it is impossible to convey Dickens's humor. . . .

Her wit is so elusive and at the same time so profound that even now . . . I can never dip into her pages without lighting upon fresh examples. . . . And to her wit she brought a power of imagery unexcelled by any modern work. Only an author endowed with an equally acute sense of beauty and proportion, born of humor, could have put such gems of fancy into words without seeming a bit high-flown.

Edwin Pugh. *The Bookman* (London). July,
1928, p. 194

The strength of the book is not in its insight into human character, though that is not lacking. Nor does it lie in the inevitability with which the drama is unfolded and the sin of an all-absorbing and selfish ambition punished. It lies in the fusion of the elements of nature and man, as observed in this remote countryside by a woman even more alive to the changing moods of nature than of man. Almost any page at random will furnish an illustration of the blending of human passion with the fields and skies. . . .

One reviewer compared *Precious Bane* to a sampler stitched through long summer evenings in the bay window of a remote farmhouse. And sometimes writers of Welsh and Border origin, like William Morris, have had their work compared to old tapestries. But while these comparisons suggest something of the harmonies of color they fail to convey the emotional force which glows in these pages. Nature to Mary Webb was not a pattern on a screen. Her sensibility is so acute and her power over words so sure and swift that one who reads some passages in Whitehall has almost the physical sense of being in Shropshire cornfields.

Precious Bane is a revelation not of unearthly but of earthly beauty in one bit of the England of Waterloo, the Western edge, haunted with the shadows of superstition, the legendary lore and fantasy of neighbors on the Border, differing in blood and tongue. This mingling of peoples and traditions and turns of speech and proverbial wisdom is what Mary Webb saw with the eye of the mind as she stood at her stall in Shrewsbury market, fastened in her memory, and fashioned for us in the little parcel of novels which is her legacy to literature.

Stanley Baldwin. Introduction to Mary
Webb. *Precious Bane* (London: Jonathan
Cape, 1929), pp. 10–11

With this heart to love and mind to labor, Mary Webb had in her service rarely delicate senses. All poets are for their own purposes good "observers"; though most of their "notes," maybe, take themselves. But by no means all poets are very exact and comprehensive observers. Mary Webb, whose world was "a place of almost unbearable wonder," had senses almost microscopic in their delicacy. She could—most rewardful of feats—seize the momentary. "It may be all illumined, like a somber pine at the advent of wood pigeons." That for sight. And for sound: "The peewits wheel and call continually, and from amid the ripple of their wings their cry sounds lost and lovely as some Naiad's voice beneath running water." And this of the wind—with how far a journey: "It is like a whisper in the night, when you cannot tell whether a child or a man is speaking. . . . We never see the gates of its dark house swing open, nor watch it fall beyond the waters into its tomb beneath the yellow sunset." And for scent she tells of the resinous sweetness of agrimony on a dusty highway in July; the curious redolence of a rock in hot weather.

In these moods she had no need of "fine" writing—the writing that is pitched above the voice. Her imagination went abreast with her feeling, and her words embodied both. *The Spring of Joy* wells over with a grave and sweet happiness, the happiness "of the minds of the simple-hearted, who are the Magi of the world." Trees, leaves, buds, flowers, fruits; country scenes and ways and work and pleasures; wind and waters, cloud, meadow and woodland; these are its never-failing joy.

Walter de la Mare. Introduction to Mary
Webb. *Poems and The Spring of Joy*
(London: Jonathan Cape, 1933), pp. 15–16

Mary Webb's poems have been extolled for their music—but as that word is capable of many interpretations, we should like to ask, before we accept the verdict, in what way her poems conform to that mysterious law which is the essence of music? Mr. Robert Lynd truly refers to the "imaginative energy" of her writings, but this energy is a result as well as a cause. Mr. Walter de la Mare in describing her appearance has called her "bird-like," and she also possessed the poet's "wood-bird soul," but he does not reveal the secret of her flight and song. Mr. Baldwin has praised her "acute sensibility," but this very quality of acuteness has its hidden springs which we would try to discover. . . .

Poetic art has its own "countless variations," and may give us the highly trained technique of a Robert Bridges or a de la Mare (which one may call scholastic or rational poetry), or the naïve song of a singer who has an un-trained but instinctive ear for his music—such as we find in the work of Mary Webb (which one may call natural or intuitional poetry). Such a singer may truly be termed "bird-like," for his song is as dependent as that of a bird upon the inspiration of the moment. All forms of poetry, however, whether trained, or spontaneous, include three chief factors—beauty of imagination, energy of expression, and rhythm of form, and all three are evidenced in the poems of Mary Webb. Surely it is rhythm in its widest sense which at the same time distinguishes and unites her verse and prose?

Lorna Collard. *Contemporary Review.*
April, 1933, pp. 456, 458

Mary Webb died just over twenty years ago at the comparatively early age of forty-six. Her contribution to English literature consists of but six novels, a volume of essays and poems, and more recently a further selection of hitherto unpublished poems have been printed. During her lifetime Mary Webb's writings received little recognition, and were known only to a small circle of appreciative readers. In 1926 The Right Hon. Stanley Baldwin was given a copy of *Precious Bane* for a Christmas gift, by one of his secretaries, and he read the book with keen delight, and a week or two later sent the author a letter expressing his admiration. Mary Webb was deeply touched by this recognition, especially in view of scanty acknowledgement which the wider public had given to the book. The following year the Prime Minister when presiding at the Royal Literary Fund Dinner referred to her as a "liter-ary genius who had recently died without public mention," and at last public interest was awakened, and a special edition of her works became imper-ative. Ironically Mary Webb had passed beyond "the world's blames and praises." . . .

When one turns to criticism of Mary Webb it can be said that her range was limited, for she frequently introduces the same characters in differing guise. There is a use of symbolism which leads her into inconsistencies, and a tendency to become vague and verbose. Sometimes she plays the part of the rustic philosopher, and story and dialogue are but the vehicle of her meditations. Her strength lay not in invention, but in imagination. While we readily grant that she may lack originality as a story-teller, in perception, in feeling she excels. She has a noble conception of human nature, a love for the homely, and is wholly sensitive to the mystery of life, and its fortitude born of beauty, love, and laughter. She is a true creative artist in that she portrays the oceanic storms which rage in the lives of the lowly, the way in which the suffering spirit transforms the homespun and the commonplace.

Wilfred Shepherd. *The London Quarterly and Holborn Review.* October, 1949, p. 305

The appeal of her earliest published story, "A Cedar-Rose," which first appeared in *Country Life* (1909), is in the gentle lyricism of its telling. Here already we find that lucidity of style and use of symbolism so characteristic of her novels. The other stories I have selected were written in the final years when, migrant between London and Shropshire, she was declining physically, yet trying desperately hard to place the shorter writings she was producing when not working at her novels. "Mr. Tallent's Ghost is an intriguing parable told with wit and verve. It has a fine opening manner and is compelling from start to finish. "The Cuckoo Clock"—for children of all ages—is an amusing fable imbued with rather sinister overtones. This story is invested with her typically sharp descriptive power, humorous observation and imaginative energy. . . .

For Mary Webb the physical world was "almost intolerably lovely" and her spiritual response to it was that of a mystic. But there was nothing indefinite or hazy in her attitude, and as a naturalist endowed with the keenest of senses, she looked for precision in the nature books she was reviewing. Nothing less than accuracy will do when nature is the subject. Not hesitating to point out mistakes (particularly critical of illustrations to bird books), she is generous in her praise of exactitude, admiring a writer who "says exactly what he saw, and the plainer the writing, the more rapture his memories bring to the reader. Only the true naturalist dares to be terse and simple." She herself, as the reviews show, had "the sure touch of the lover of earth who not only loves but knows." Neither was there anything sentimental in her attitude: she stresses nature's indifference to man, and tells us in a typically aphoristic comment, "It is as unwise to be sentimental towards Nature as it would be to sonnetize in her presence the rosy lips of a cannibal queen." . . .

Described by a contemporary critic, Geraint Goodwin, as "one of the most sensitive and best equipped of women writers," Mary Webb, though not an innovator extending the frontiers of her art in the technical sense, does, in page after page, extend our awareness, sharpen our perceptions.

Gladys Mary Coles. Introduction to *Mary Webb, Collected Prose and Poems: A Selection of Mary Webb's Hitherto Uncollected and Unpublished Work* (Shrewsbury, England: Wildings, 1977), pp. x–xii, xiv

Unfortunately, though Mary Webb's novels are more than just rural romances or regional works, the wave of popularity swept over them superficially and while numerous articles were written about her, none made a penetrating evaluation, none succeeded in clarifying the essential nature of her achievement—and so this was neither understood nor established critically. The change in literary tastes during and after the Second World War also went against her, the novel becoming predominantly urban and readers requiring increased sophistication, a drier tone. So the pendulum swung—Mary Webb went "out of fashion," her public reputation waning rapidly in the post-war decades, her critical reputation still awaiting illuminating interpretations (such as continental writers had made in the early 1930s). . . .

There has always been, and probably always will be, an ambivalence of attitudes towards her—no doubt her work will continue to have its vehement admirers and equally vehement detractors. At times her writing can be luminous, but she has obvious weaknesses and excesses, faults especially prevalent in her earlier novels (such as insufficient dramatization, a tendency to didacticism and overuse of suggestive atmosphere). Yet it should be remembered that she was still developing as a novelist when her career was cut short. And without the flaws we would not have had the writing. . . .

As a novelist of country life, Mary Webb holds a special place, uniquely combining mystical and regional elements. In her work outer and inner landscapes occur as one; and her writing, shot through with poetry and insight, has, at its finest, an irreducible quality. Yet she is an authentic novelist—imaginative rather than inventive, warmly human and concrete, rich in humor, irony, passion and compassion. Scholars are now recognizing that she is a peculiarly modern writer. Though not an innovator (she uses traditional narrative procedures and does not extend the boundaries of her art in the technical sense), she writes out of a twentieth-century consciousness, her work informed by deep intuitions of the modern spirit. . . .

In evaluating her we need to set aside the conventional frames of reference, the usual tenets of criticism. She fits into no definite category. But critical attention directed to her imaginative organization, her assimilation of universal myth and folklore, her treatment of nature and landscape, her symbols, her binding themes, will reveal the unity and coherence of her work, the strength and significance of her intensely individual vision. Her work functions at several levels of meaning; by her visionary quality she conveys truths for her time and those to come; and she beckons us not back to nature but forward to it. In reading her receptively (and allowing for flaws) we gain sharpened perception, extended awareness.

Gladys Mary Coles. The Flower of Light: A
Biography of Mary Webb (London:
Duckworth, 1978), pp. 327–30

It is easy to be critical of Mary Webb's novels, their faults are so apparent—contrived plots, didactic tone, romantically idealized heroes and overly emotional prose. It is understandable that she has been reduced to a historical footnote, her five novels, hundreds of poems, essays and reviews all but forgotten. And yet, her best work is surprisingly powerful. The word "primitive," so often and justly applied to her lack of sophistication, applies as well to her major strength: the use of nature and myth, which gives her best novels the force of legend or fairy tale.

Webb's ability to integrate nature and myth into her fiction derives from her attachment to Shropshire, where she was born and grew up, and which she never emotionally left. . . .

Of Webb's five novels, only *Gone to Earth* has neither an idealized hero nor a happy ending, and it is that tragic ending, its inevitability and the author's ability to confront it, that gives the book its power. Published in 1917, *Gone to Earth* was Webb's second novel. It was well received upon publication—Rebecca West, who reviewed it, called Webb "a strange genius"—and it is on this work, along with *Precious Bane,* that her reputation may at length be built. . . .

In Webb's philosophy, which sustains the best of her work, the individual's relationship with nature parallels his or her relationship with fellow human beings: if kindness, cruelty or sensitivity characterizes one set of relationships, it will characterize the other set as well. In her weaker novels, philosophy overwhelms fiction—with excessive romanticism in *The Golden Arrow* and *Seven for a Secret,* with didacticism in *The House in Dormer Forest.* But in *Gone to Earth* and *Precious Bane,* ideas give dimension to the narrative.

Although Webb may never be viewed as a major writer, she is certainly worth reading, and Virago Press deserves thanks for bringing *Gone to Earth* back to print. Erika Duncan's introduction is unfortunate, though, in its gushy and clichéd language ("And through Hazel, at a time when women could not really fly or sing, Mary Webb gave all of us this stirring woman's song") and in its several inaccuracies including, inexcusably, a misreading of the book's conclusion, for Hazel is not torn limb from limb. But the edition makes a timely appearance and may awaken readers to Webb's work. Perhaps in time, critics will acknowledge Webb's novels without the obligatory reference to their many flaws, and readers will enjoy them without apology.

Gail Pool. *The Nation.* September 25, 1982,
pp. 279, 281

Webb presents a number of difficulties for the feminist critic. During the last decade, when feminist criticism developed and burgeoned, the works most often given attention were those which had the surface appearance of "feminism" or which could be read as "code"—as telling feminist tales in secret, as filled with covert rebellion. Yet Mary Webb's life gives only small indication of "feminist sympathies," and her work is filled with deflected insights into the nature of women's conflicts, woman's oppression. She would be the last to suggest that the complexities of her history and psyche were the result of her gender or of patriarchy. While *The House in Dormer Forest* and *Gone to Earth* contain explicit criticism of the terrible lives endured by those women and men who accept their social roles and shape their lives to fit the patterns created by others, and while she clearly abhors the false convention of sexual modesty decreed for both men and women, Webb nonetheless chose not to examine closely the structure which created such roles, values, and conventions. . . .

What evaluation, then, is the feminist critic to render when considering Mary Webb? Or, to put this question into different terms, what does the study of Mary Webb add to our understanding of the nature of women's writing? Because authorship is an act of power whereby the individual creates the world she desires, an examination of Webb's novels expands our understanding of the world women would create. Since writing is an act of power, those women who write, whether covertly or overtly rebellious, perform an action clearly in opposition to their society's expectations. And in so doing, the woman writer—even one who denies independence to the creatures of her own imagination—asserts her ability to create what she would have. As an individual Webb starved herself, but as an author she found the means for her satisfaction. . . .

Despite the ambivalencies and griefs of Mary Webb's life, and despite the frequency with which they mar her writing, as a woman writer she deserves critical appraisal rather than elegiac sentiment. . . .

She denied what she would have and sought it nonetheless. She refused what she wanted even as she gave that wanting creative life and literary breath. Arguing for romantic love's supremacy, she still desired fame and immortality; she is, most simply and most complexly, a woman who wrote.

Michèle Aina Barale. *Daughters and Lovers:
The Life and Writing of Mary Webb*
(Middletown, Connecticut: Wesleyan
University Press, 1986), pp. 166–68

Just when the predicament of Hazel Woodus, the heroine of *Gone to Earth,* seems to allow for no resolution, Webb ends the novel by dropping her into a hole. By what might be considered a sort of poetic justice, Webb, as author, has been in danger of suffering the same treatment from readers for some time now. Despite the seductively beautiful paperback editions of her books published in the late 1970s and early 80s, Webb remains unfamiliar even to most professional readers. The current lack of interest in her work is understandable because Webb's elegiac vision of a pastoral England and often expressed admiration for Thomas Hardy inspire comparison of their novels. And those judging by anything akin to formalist standards will rank Hardy much higher; despite all the criticisms that have been made about their form, his novels are decidedly better composed, if better means more smoothly plotted and linguistically sophisticated.

However, all readers do not judge by such standards and ordinarily, we might expect to find numerous appreciations of Webb among the works of the Anglo-American feminist critics who are engaged in the construction of a women's literary canon. But, unfortunately, Webb repeatedly dramatizes masochistic female behavior, while her narrators assert its naturalness. Faced with a "minor" novelist whose work might be regarded as supporting the old critical assessment of women writers as conservative and imitative, and, even more troublingly, might seem to substantiate psychology's past claim that women are naturally masochistic, even scholars of women's literary traditions may be inclined to let her drop back into obscurity. Yet it is a pity for Hardy's novels to eclipse Webb's, because hers have their own virtues, among which is the light their revisionary responses to his shed on the ways modernist texts in defense of women connect *male* masochism and the colonialist impulse.

Carol Siegel. *Novel*. 24, 1991, pp. 131–32

WEBB, PHYLLIS (CANADA) 1927–

Phyllis Webb has compelled the attention of readers with a remarkably small production of poems. The *Selected Poems* of 1971, though it contained the pieces she wished to retain from twenty years of work, amounted, if one leaves out John Hulcoop's long introduction, to only one hundred and sixteen sparsely printed pages. *The Vision Tree,* appearing eleven years later, contained one hundred and thirty-four pages of verse; *Wilson's Bowl,* the result of fifteen years of work after the appearance of *Naked Poems,* contained seventy-three pages of poems.

Even if one could envisage Phyllis Webb sanctioning a Collected Poems, including the pieces that have been dropped successively in compiling the *Selected Poems* and *The Vision Tree,* it would still be a relatively slight volume, for though Webb began publishing in Alan Crawley's *Contemporary Verse* in the early 1950s, her publication—if not her production—has always been sparse. There seems to have been a reluctance involved in all her decisions to release a poem into print or oral reading. In fact, the extent of her publication has become steadily less copious over the years.

Phyllis Webb collaborated with Eli Mandel and Gael Turnbull in a joint volume, *Trio,* in 1954. Two years later, in 1956, she was able to publish a volume of her own, *Even Your Right Eye.* It was six years before her next volume, *The Sea is also a Garden,* appeared in 1962; this was followed three years later by *Naked Poems,* a collection of poems honed to a hard gem-like transparency and abstraction. Then followed a long period of apparent silence. The *Selected Poems* of 1971 contained nothing written after 1965, and during this period Webb contributed few poems to periodicals. Yet she continued to write in reclusion, to polish, and, very often, to discard. The

"Kropotkin Poems," on which she worked for years until they became—as she herself wryly admitted—a "legend," never reached completion as the self-contained suite she had planned. Yet finally a new book, *Wilson's Bowl,* appeared, which showed she had moved into more expansive views and more complex forms than those so sparsely delineated in *Naked Poems.* In 1982 a tiny volume of short poems, *Sunday Water: Thirteen Anti-Ghazals,* appeared, and when *The Vision Tree,* the second selected poems of her career, was published in 1982 it contained a scanty half-handful—three poems of moderate length—written after the publication of *Wilson's Bowl.* . . .

Always in her poetry, but increasingly as time goes on, Phyllis Webb shows herself hostile to conventional systems of morality, to political organization of any kind, and to consolatory religions that offer fragile hope or anything less rigorous than the question she poses in a slightly later poem than "Marvell's Garden": "What are we whole or beautiful or good for/but to be absolutely broken?" ("Breaking," *The Sea is also a Garden*). But there is the other morality of the craft that too demands its denials and its deprivations, its willing self-disciplines. The link between the sentiments and the forms of moralist—as distinct from moralistic—writing has always been close; the compact, undecorated and largely unmetaphorical forms of the *récits* of André Gide and Albert Camus, of the 1930s parable-novels of Morley Callaghan, are directly related to the fact that these writers are using their fiction to project moral problems, and that in the process of creating an austerity of word as well as of thought they bring together a morality of art and a morality of action that are parallel, that resonate together, but are neither identical with each other nor necessarily interdependent.

Thus it is no accident that Phyllis Webb, as she has proceeded according to the morality of art towards the impoverishment of form for the sake of greater ultimate richness, has also practiced austerities and simplifications in her life, and has sought the reclusion that all good artists, like all saints, find necessary at some time in their careers. . . .

Since *Wilson's Bowl* appeared, Webb has been writing, as is her wont, slowly and with much discarding, and has published few poems. But whatever comes now, her deliberate small *oeuvre* has already entitled her, for the clarity of her vision and the dedicated impeccability of her craft, to a first place not merely among recent Canadian poets, but in the whole poetic tradition of our land.

George Woodcock. *Queen's Quarterly.* 93,
1986, pp. 529, 538, 545

Phyllis Webb's *Water and Light* (1984) was at least five years in the making, a fact entirely characteristic of this master of musical phrase and meticulous image: "I play by ear. And the eye." The verse-form Webb works with in *Water and Light,* subtitled "Ghazals and Anti Ghazals," owes something (not much, technically speaking) to the lyric usually associated with Persian literature (its appearance is also common in Urdu, Arabic, Turkish, and Pashto literatures). The first public manifestation of the Middle Eastern drift in

Webb's poetic and political attentions can be dated by referring to a villanelle written five years ago (January 16, 1979) entitled "The King of Kings has left the Peacock Throne." However, as I've suggested elsewhere, Webb's adaptation of the old Persian lyric to suit her new poetic needs represents a solution (almost certainly temporary) to a complex problem which first made itself felt much longer than five years ago. . . .

The reason this project was never completed is, in my opinion, closely related to Webb's eventual discovery and subsequent adaptation of the ghazal. In the late 1960s, while she struggled to endow "sweet old Prince / Kropotkin" with long-lined life, the feminist revolution entered a new phase of consciousness-raising. Gradually, Webb came to identify the long line in English poetry with men and aggression: "It comes from assurance (or hysteria), high tide, full moon, open mouth, big-mouthed Whitman, yawp, yawp, & Ginsberg—howling. Male."

Uneasy with the tacit assumptions that underpin an essentially male poetics, Webb sought not exactly to reject but to transform the long line, bringing it from the soap-box and pulpit (on or in which Whitman, Ginsberg, and Dylan Thomas often seem to be standing) down to the kitchen tables at which women write.

The struggle to effect this transformation is most obvious in *Wilson's Bowl:* in the transformation of "The Kropotkin Poems" into "Poems of Failure," and in other poems, prose-poems and paragraphs which "proceed before the amorous invisible, governed by need and the form of its persuasions." The "amorous invisible" might be thought to look ahead to the "amatory" ghazal, with its "clandestone" order; certainly, the easy mixing of line-lengths in her ghazals—"The pull, this way and that, ultimately into the pull / of the pen across the page"—proves the success of Webb's struggle to transform: she can now extend her lines "across the page" without resorting to oratorical yawp and without falling under the spell of a voice that imposes itself aggressively, forcing the reader to read on and on. . . .

What's important here is to understand and appreciate how the family subject and the panoply of feminist issues (social, moral, economic, artistic, political) get transformed by the poet into the text and textures of the ghazals and antighazals she has been working on since the Fall of 1981. Idealized and universalized love between the poet and his female beloved, subject of the traditional ghazal, is particularized *and* politicized, becomes the poet's love for her own sex ("the good neighbor policy," which disrupts the poetic process), the poet's relationship with mother and brother, the poet's love of visual images and the sound of words. The lyric form—

> A lozenge of dream
> sticks on my tongue
>
> Soulange, Stonehenge
> sugar-mite, maple—
>
> a candy poem

—is compelled to accommodate dialectical material (particularized *and* politicized), to dramatize vision (the "I Daniel" section is a dramatic monologue or, more accurately, a dramatic lyric in the tradition of Browning's "James Lee's Wife"), to carry crypto-narratives (the writing of the first "thirteen Anti Ghazals," for example), to allow the poet vox when she wants to play frivolously in the shallows of sound poetry, to rewrite history and so generate a new secrecy, and to indict/lament "the whole culture leaning. . . ." Introduced to the ghazal by a man (the sender of the "card / with a white peacock spreading its tail") who presumably directed her attention to John Thompson's *Stilt Jack,* Webb performs a feminist act of liberation, freeing the form from a male history and a male monopoly in practice.

John Hulcoop. *Canadian Literature.* 109,
1986, pp. 151–52, 155

In review, most of the poems in Webb's first three volumes, and certainly the best of them, can be seen (though this is *only one* kind of seeing) as dramas of the insurrectionary struggle to escape, to break out of that which confines, to break into that which is rightfully hers—where she can be herself and speak in her own voice. Confinement can take a thousand forms: our bones, our bodies, our bourgeois desires and fears; our birth-place, geographically and psychologically speaking; our living-space, historically and socially speaking; our face, which may be (or be hostile to) our fortune, professionally and sexually speaking. Hope and despair, faith and disbelief, love and hate can all assume the shape of gray walls and towers in which the Lady of Shalott (who prefigures the modern woman writer's struggle for freedom) finds herself a close-kept prisoner, weaving her web by night and day until, finally, she declares she is "sick of shadows." . . .

Naked Poems, like *Water and Light,* is a landmark volume in Webb's career. These poems exemplify, with almost comic text-book accuracy, the "technical development of the modern lyrical poet" which, as Frye said in 1953, "is normally from obscurity to simplicity." Initially, the lyric poet must pass through "a social, allegorical, or metaphysical phase, an awkward and painful phase for all concerned," Frye observes. "Finally, a mysterious but unmistakable ring of authority begins to come into [the poet's] writing, and simultaneously the texture simplifies, meaning and imagery become transparent." . . .

These poems do so successfully what Webb says they must do, they speak with such clarity/transparency from their "absolute location," that, six years after publishing them, the poet confessed, "I admire them as if someone else had written them. Somehow they are apart from me. . . . If they are intensely personal love poems (and obviously they are), who am 'I,' then, and what are 'they'? Did the eagle descend for a moment in the form of a hummingbird? In any case, the air was very clear; sound came through as very plain song."

John F. Hulcoop. In Robert Lesker, et al., eds.
Canadian Writers and Their Work, vol. 7
(Toronto: ECW Press, 1990), pp. 278, 288

Although Phyllis Webb has not previously been associated with the language poets, her earlier poetry—some ten volumes in all—has been highly experimental in form. And thus it is no surprise to find that her newest book, *Hanging Fire*, takes up language itself as its subject. Webb makes the link to surrealism abundantly evident in her opening note, in which she explains that the "titles of poems in quotation marks are 'given' words, phrases, or sentences that arrive unbidden in my head." She then adds, in words that Breton might have written, "I've been tracking them for some time to see if there are hidden themes, connections, a sub-rational rationale. It seems there are. . . ." Webb allows the hidden meanings to leap from the language so that the verse can find its own direction. The opening poem decries the idea of "A Model of the Universe," the poems replacing such stultifying order with creative confusion, the poet finding "meaning meandering" in the river of "biologic soup"—a river "on which we move undulant, / forsaking all else for this infectious cruise."

Throughout *Hanging Fire* Webb seeks to subvert the notion of an autonomous ego. She begins by *voicing* Descartes's famous adage—"I speak, therefore I am, / or so I say"—instead of *thinking* it or *writing* it. Drawing on a famous scene in *Hamlet,* she observes how the idea of an autonomous ego divides against itself as it continually sees "the egoless Transcendent / poised on the parapet, / armed & dangerous." Such a transcendent "I" sees itself armored in self-righteousness come to tell the perceiving "I" what it must do. For all the delightful word play in Webb's poems, one cannot help detecting a dark undertone of personal unhappiness, and one suspects that the volume's strength derives from the interaction between the flashes of word play and the more sombre meditative tones. Indeed, as the volume proceeds, the "I" becomes progressively more prominent, as though by the end of the volume Webb had already begun to abandon the impersonal language style for something closer to the heart.

University of Toronto Quarterly. 61, 1991,
pp. 60–61

It is not surprising to find Phyllis Webb going outside the mainstream of English poetry for inspiration since her whole career has been one of rigorous self-scrutiny and ceaseless experimentation. In many ways the ghazals, as oriental lyrics, are a natural progression from *The Naked Poems,* her 1965 volume of sapphic haiku. In that book Webb created a larger narrative structure out of intense lyric moments by writing in suites, and then organizing these suites (five, like the five ghazal sequences of *Water and Light*) into a "story." In this way the static form of each brief poem was transcended, and a different kind of unity was discovered than that of the single lyric. A minimalist vocabulary of images—not metaphors, but colors and objects—was replayed again and again, so as to accrue value merely by the fact of repetition. . . .

From her earliest publications Webb has shown herself skeptical of the poetics which she practices so elegantly. Although a loving maker of brief lyrics, Webb has never fully trusted the lyric's illusion of unity and control, of "energy recollected in tranquillity." There has always been a nervous energy in her work, questioning the very artifice which gives that work shape. . . . The ghazal represented one solution for Webb's on-going struggle with form. . . .

It was not *the* solution for Webb whose career has been one of continuous experiment; once she solves a problem, the solution itself becomes a problem if it threatens to become habitual and restrictive. This is the way any good poet works, but for Webb it is also one of the great topics of her poetry. Given the rich results of her attempts to solve her dilemma as she is forced, again and again, to confront it, one trusts that "the amorous invisible, governed by need" will find a new form for its persuasions.

Susan Glickman. *Canadian Literature.* 115,
1987, pp. 51–52, 59

Although Phyllis Webb's public profile has never been as high as Leonard Cohen's, her very reclusiveness has itself become a part of her image. In many ways, this has had a more seriously distorting effect on the reading of her work than Cohen's notoriety has had on his. For, though Webb's poetry is often private and solitary, it has always had also a dimension of public care and political concern. The great weakness of Webb criticism has been to preset her as inward-turning and solipsistic, to the exclusion of that political world on which Jacobo Timerman turns his astonished eye in "Prison Report." As recently as 1987, George Woodcock could still write that "for Phyllis Webb, growing maturity as a poet has meant growing withdrawal— a narrowing of contacts with the world paralleling a narrowing of the circle of the creative self," and that she "has also practiced austerities and simplifications in her life and has sought the reclusion that all good artists, like all saints, find necessary at some time in their careers." This not only demonstrates a limited appreciation of Webb's work for CBC radio (collected in *Talking*) and her active engagement in the work of Amnesty International; it also represents a drastically reductive reading of her poetry. . . .

Phyllis Webb . . . has been highly influential on all these [main] currents [of contemporary poetry]. One way of assessing the variety of this influence, and also of appreciating at a glance the tension between modernism and postmodernism in her work, is to look at the back-cover blurbs for her 1980 volume, *Wilson's Bowl.* The writers who here pay tribute to Webb range from Northrop Frye, whose role as the mentor of the 1950s "mythopoetic" poets places him at the center of Canadian modernism, to bpNichol, the very epitome of postmodern experimentation and open form. . . .

Both Cohen and Webb reach to the end(s) of modernism. Cohen, one might argue, is stuck there: like F. in *Beautiful Losers,* he could say of himself "I was the Moses of our little exodus. I would never cross. My mountain might be very high but it rises from the desert." For Webb, the ends are definitely plural. Her work shows that there is no single end or purpose to modernism; by the very intensity of the questioning which her long silence subjected it to, modernism in her poetry breaks through to its complementary pair, its waiting Other.

In the works of both writers, modernism and postmodernism play against and with each other in ways which present, in exemplary form, the issues Canadian poetry has faced in the last three decades. This movement is not yet finished; the compression of contemporary literary history is such that our canonical figures are still alive, still changing, still writing. The emerging canon has been slow to recognize the full challenges of postmodernism: Leonard Cohen, for all his outrageousness, has been easier to assimilate than Phyllis Webb. But the canon *is* an emerging one, and any account of it now has to be provisional. It would certainly be my hope that the breaking down of the modernist/postmodernist distinction, so evident in recent criticism, will also be reflected in the evolution of canon-formation: and in this process, the examples of such writers as Leonard Cohen and Phyllis Webb may well be more useful than those of more easily categorized figures.

Stephen Scobie. In Robert Lecker, ed.
Canadian Canons: Essays in Literary Value
(Toronto: University of Toronto Press, 1991),
pp. 63–64, 67, 70

WEIL, SIMONE (FRANCE) 1909–43

Since her death, Simone Weil has come to seem more and more a special exemplar of sanctity for our time—the Outsider as Saint in an age of alienation, our kind of saint. In eight scant years, this young French-woman, whom scarcely anyone had heard of before her sacrificial death in exile at the age of thirty-four, has come to possess the imagination of many in the Western world. Catholic and Protestant, Christian and Jew, agnostic and devout, we have all turned to her with the profound conviction that the meaning of her experience is our meaning, that she is really *ours*. Few of us, to be sure, would find nothing to dissent from in her religious thought; fewer still would be capable of emulating the terrible purity of her life; none could measure himself, without shame, against the absolute ethos toward which she aspired. And yet she does not seem strange to us, as other mystics and witnesses of God have seemed strange; for though on one side her life touches the remote mysteries of the Divine Encounter, on the other it is rooted in a world with which we are familiar. . . .

Before her death, scarcely any of Simone Weil's religious writings had been published. To those in France who thought of her still, in terms of her early political essays, as a somewhat unorthodox Marxist moving toward anarchism, the posthumous Christian books must have come as a shock. Surely, no "friend of God" in all history, had moved more unwillingly toward the mystic encounter. There is in her earlier work no sense of a groping toward the divine, no promise of holiness, no pursuit of a purity beyond this world—only a conventionally left-wing concern with the problems of industrialization, rendered in a tone at once extraordinarily inflexible and wonderfully sensitive.

The particular note of conviction in Simone Weil's testimony arises from the feeling that her role as a mystic was so *unintended,* one for which she had not in any sense prepared. An undertone of incredulity persists beneath her astonishing honesty: quite suddenly God had taken her, radical, agnostic, contemptuous of religious life and practice as she had observed it! . . . She refused to become, in the typical compensatory excess of the convert, more of the Church than those born into it; she would not even be baptized, and it is her unique position, at once in and out of institutionalized Catholicism, that determines her special role and meaning. . . .

To what then does she bear witness? To the uses of exile and suffering, to the glory of annihilation and absurdity, to the unforeseen miracle of love.

Leslie Fiedler. Introduction to Simone Weil.
Waiting for God (New York: G. P. Putnam's
Sons, 1951), pp. 3–5, 9–10

What makes us in the end unwilling to accept her claims? What is it that more often than not distorts her genuine love of truth? . . . She claims too much (St. Joan heard rightly when she was told to tell no one of her visions), and sometimes too stridently. She talks of suffering "atrocious pain" for others, "those who are indifferent or unknown to me. . .," and it is almost as if a comic character from Dickens were speaking. We want to say, "Don't go so far so quickly. Suffer first for someone you know and love," but love in these pages is only a universal love.

Graham Greene. *New Statesman and
Nation.* October 6, 1951, p. 374

When she reviews and interprets the modern political history of France, or when she lists the needs of the soul of man, needs which must be taken into account in any social planning, what she has to say is of immense importance and should be studied with care, for it is beautifully penetrating and balanced. Her specific recommendations are not by any means always so, however.

Nor is the overall impression to be gained of her mind, for all her brilliance, one of balance. Her thinking is sometimes idiosyncratic in the extreme, displaying a lack of objectivity that seems almost willful, and some of her outbursts are so emotional as to be almost altogether untrustworthy.

S. M. Fitzgerald. *The New Republic.*
August 18, 1952, p. 186

I cannot conceive of anybody's agreeing with all her views, or of not disagreeing violently with some of them. But agreement and rejection are secondary: what matters is to make contact with a great soul. Simone Weil is one who might have become a saint. Like some who have achieved this state, she had greater obstacles to overcome as well as greater strength for overcoming them, than the rest of us. A potential saint can be a very difficult person: I suspect that Simone Weil could be at times insupportable. One is struck, here and there, by a contrast between an almost superhuman humility and what appears to be an almost outrageous arrogance. . . .

Certainly [Simone Weil] could be unfair and intemperate; certainly she committed some astonishing aberrations and exaggerations. But those immoderate affirmations which tax the patience of the reader spring not from any flaw in her intellect but from excess of temperament. . . . The intellect, especially when bent upon such problems as those which harassed Simone Weil, can come to maturity only slowly; and we must not forget that Simone Weil died at the age of thirty-three. I think that in *The Need for Roots* especially, the maturity of her social and political thought is very remarkable. . . .

Many readers, coming for the first time upon some assertion likely to arouse intellectual incredulity or emotional antagonism, might be deterred from improving their acquaintance with a great soul and a brilliant mind. Simone Weil needs patience from her readers, as she doubtless needed patience from the friends who most admired and appreciated her. But in spite of the violence of her affections and antipathies, in spite of . . . generalizations . . . I find in the present book especially a balanced judgment, a wisdom in avoiding extremes, astonishing in anyone so young.

T. S. Eliot. Preface to Simone Weil. *The Need for Roots* (London: Routledge and Kegan Paul, 1952), pp. iv, vi, xi

In spite of her remarkable mental endowments, [Simone Weil] was deficient in one important quality. She lacked the historical sense. It is difficult to define this sense with accuracy, because it involves a combination of rare qualities; its absence is therefore all the more noticeable. True, Simone had a strong sense of the past. Her knowledge of ancient civilization is extensive. But she has a habit of referring her historical explanations to a point in time at which they become either unverifiable or merely fanciful. Her preoccupation with pre-history encouraged, if not dictated, this tendency. . . .

While too much attention has perhaps been paid to Simone's reasons for refusing baptism, her attitude to Catholicism is admittedly colored by serious prejudices and perversities. It is a wonder that her Catholic friends preserved their equanimity as well as they did. . . . However genuine her reservations and criticisms, her attitude to Catholicism is fundamentally unhistorical. She attacks the Church not merely because it has been marred by corruption and worldliness, but simply because it is in the world. . . . If Simone had been able to demonstrate how a church, any church, can exist on earth without taking institutional form, then her criticism of the Church in its human manifestation would have carried more weight.

E. W. F. Tomlin. *Simone Weil* (New Haven,
Connecticut: Yale University Press, 1954),
pp. 37–39

The progressive aberration in [Simone Weil's] thought illustrates the terrible harm that an excessively developed but isolated intelligence can do to the life of the spirit. Simone Weil's system constitutes a proof, one of the most terrifying negative proofs I have encountered, of the necessity for the Church to assert its authority. Left to herself, removing herself from her condition as a woman, Simone Weil was devoured by her own intelligence. Her spiritual drama was an obsession with mathematical certainty in matters for which only faith in the Word of God can bring ultimate clarity. . . .

I am not saying that Simone Weil was a consciously perverse heretic. She was the victim of her intellectual solitude; she was tragic proof of the futility of the wish to deny one's condition. If Simone Weil had had children, she never would have written as she did, because she would have understood that the physical act of maternity is participation in creative Love.

I daresay that almost everything she wrote—which often resembles a novel, but a tragically inhuman novel—is dead wood, because her fundamental intuitions are false.

Charles Moeller. *Littérature du XXᵉ siècle et
christianisme* (Tournai, Belgium: Casterman,
1954), Vol. I, pp. 254–55

[Simone Weil's] love for God—and for Christ, whom she equates with God—does not seem to lose anything from her religious isolation. Her spiritual autobiography *(Waiting for God)* reveals a soul extremely attentive to its sacred vocation. The crux of her thinking can be formulated as follows: absolute detachment from and annihilation of the self so that God may work in the soul; the human being offers his humanity to God so that through this process he can come into contact with others. Her masters are principally Eckhart and Saint John of the Cross. Simone Weil has a perfect understanding of the beauty of the religion of Christ, and because she is fully aware of it, she suffers when she sees its disfigurement in the course of its history. Had she lived, Simone Weil would have undoubtedly written a Christian manifesto comparable to her earlier social manifestos. . . .

Simone Weil seems to have had a mysterious knowledge of the briefness of her existence. She was in a hurry and strode with giant steps. At no time could diversion or simple distraction gain her attention.

Marie-Magdeleine Davy. *Simone Weil* (Paris:
Éditions Universitaires, 1956), pp. 26–27

[*The Notebooks of Simone Weil*] is not always attractive, but it compels respect. She is sometimes unbalanced and scarcely accurate. She whitewashes Plato, suggesting that he really disapproved of slavery and disliked only decadent art. She refuses to say any good word for the Jews: the only city over which she does not lament is Jerusalem. "Practically the only thing the Hebrews did was to exterminate, at any rate prior to the destruction of Jerusalem." She seems at times almost too ready to embrace evil and to love God as its author; many readers may find a repellent and self-destructive quality in her austerity. (A figure which obsesses her is T. E. Lawrence.) She endorsed the Greek view that "to philosophize is to learn how to die"—and it is hard not to believe that she in some way willed her own early death. Yet the other side of this is the sense of a profoundly disciplined life behind her writings: the union of a passionate search for truth with a simplicity and austerity of personal living, which gives to what she writes an authority which cannot be imitated. She is one who, like Kiekegård's "subjective thinker," does not simply convey information, but is most properly to be understood as an example.

Iris Murdoch. *The Spectator*. November 2,
1956, p. 614

The hair's breadth which separates Simone Weil's philosophy from vulgar determinism is the mysterious factor, among all the others which acted upon her, which compelled her to face . . . ultimate tests and to challenge the stony-hearted egoism which she perceived everywhere, and in herself, so much more clearly than most of us dare to do. This is the mysterious factor which compels the fool to persist in his folly until he becomes wise and makes it true that he who endures to the end shall be saved. It is strange, but it is a fact, that Simone Weil, for all her unrelenting realism, was martyrized by compassion not only for the suffering in the world around her but even for the sufferings of slaves in the distant past. It is surely no exaggeration to say that her place is with the heroes and geniuses who incarnate the conscience of the human race.

Richard Rees. *Brave Men* (London:
Gollancz, 1958), pp. 209–10

She was a fantastically dedicated participant in the most crucial experiences of our time, who tried to live them directly in contact with the supernatural. Her real interest for us lies less in what she said than in the direction of her work, in the particular vision she tried to reach by the whole manner of her life. What she sought more than anything else was a loving attentiveness to all the living world that would lift man above the natural loneliness of existence. . . . When a French apprentice who is new on a job complains that the work hurts him, the older men usually say that "the trade is entering his body." This saying, which Simone Weil picked up in the Renault factory, had a special pathos for her. It expressed her belief that there is a particular closeness we can reach with the world, that the truth is always something to be lived.

Alfred Kazin. *The Inmost Leaf* (New York:
Noonday, 1959), pp. 211–13

In her last years Simone Weil seems to have sought enlightenment by a systematic cultivation of maximum hypertension. Her thought proceeded by no other way than paradox. This is not new. . . . But there is a tension of life and a tension of death. Simone Weil was a dying girl. Hers was a spastic, moribund, intellectual, and spiritual agony. We can sympathize with it, be moved to tears by it, much as we are by the last awful lunacies of Antonin Artaud, but we imitate it, allow it to infect us, at our peril. This is a Kierke-gaard who refuses to leap. *Angst* for *angst*'s sake. Anguish is not enough. When it is made an end in itself it takes on a holy, or unholy folly.

Kenneth Rexroth. *Assays* (New York: New
Directions, 1961), p. 199

[Simone Weil's] passionate and uncompromising love for Christ and His poor (for her His true Church) was that force which drove her to share both the depersonalizing life of the factory workers and the exhausting but rewarding life of the peasant farmer. It drove her to the cause of anarchy and human dignity in the Spanish Civil War. It drove her into the streets of war-time London, into the slums of Harlem. To sacrifice her own personality in the face of injustice, for the cause of justice, was the end which directed her action from the time that she slept on the floor as a student so that a student poorer than she could have her bed, until the hounding ended in tuberculosis, malnutrition (she would not eat as long as her countrymen in occupied France were starving) and death at the age of thirty-four. . . .

The genius of Simone Weil's mind is peculiarly her own, even though it is in the tradition of Charles Péguy and Léon Bloy in its mysticism and its concern for the poor. It is also a powerful expression and extension of the European intellect of the twentieth century, an intellect which has absorbed the classical and Christian heritage in philosophy, history and social thought with a thoroughness that leaves it free to range back and forth through time from fifth century Athens to contemporary France. In its ranging, her mind draws parallels, suggests analogies and makes connections (both safe and wild) in a tireless effort to increase man's understanding of his own nature and of his society in order to create new possibilities for action.

John Ratté. *Commonweal.* March 22, 1963,
pp. 669–70

What else can we do, however uneasy or inferior we feel, but admire her passionate, sometimes maladroit devotion to the working class, her intense and unsectarian religious zeal, her capacity for self-denial, her attempt to convert pain into something wholly fruitful, her brilliant disruptive mind and painstakingly trenchant prose, her audacity in teaching the young, her almost peasant simplicity in aphorism, her refusal to defer to evil wherever she found it, her will, her guts, her crabbed truthfulness? We admire, but with a hunch that much of it amounts to a frenetic displacement of womanhood. Something crackpot emerges alongside what is her evident genius and her almost pernicious goodness.

Paul West. *The Nation.* April 19, 1965, p. 422

Propelled by the heroic voluntarism characteristic of the great mystics, Simone has flashes of inspiration, springing from an urgency to look more deeply into the ideas and feelings of men, so as to discover where the evil, hidden by compromises and by hypocrisies, really lies: in Weil's writing, therefore, there are no reassuring commonplaces.

To contemporary man, encouraged by sociology and psychoanalysis to avoid making distinctions between good and evil; to contemporary man, who would like to find unity in the assimilation of neutral values, in the substitution of politics for religion; to contemporary man, who has been enticed by a humanitarianism requiring no sacrifices (merely an alibi for an absence of morality)—Weil brings back choice, that area in which personal commitment can really be measured.

Antonio Sfamurri. *L'umanesimo cristiano di Simone Weil* (Florence: L. U. Japadre, 1970), p. 116

Simone Weil certainly occupies a special place in the history of French thought, in which religious reflection has always shied away from speculation. The mystics, protected by the solid walls of scholastic theology and philosophy, dedicated their writings to the "practical" problems of prayer, of contemplation, and of moral conduct; while the philosophers who concerned themselves with religious questions armed themselves with the conceptual instruments of metaphysics or epistemology, or else were content to meditate on God and on man without attempting to construct any sort of system. Simone Weil's manner of thinking, in which metaphysics and mysticism are joined and become inseparable; her penetrating ability to transpose moral actions and religious acts onto ontological planes—these approaches are not part of the French tradition. . . .

She is in the tradition of Plato and Kant. She shares with these two great philosophers a prudence that consists of not pushing to a conclusion the speculative perspective that a fine idea offers, and of being humbly contented with the unfinished and the incomplete. The entire range of possibilities will not be exhausted by choosing only one—this caution is perhaps the secret of the strength and fruitfulness of all thought, and Simone Weil shares with Kant and Plato the calm humility that governs this kind of modesty.

Miklos Vetö. *La métaphysique religieuse de Simone Weil* (Paris: Libraire Philosophique J. Vrin, 1971), p. 143

In writing about Simone Weil it seems inevitable to begin with a discussion of her personality; but it is also ironic, because she regarded personality as an obstacle to all the highest human achievements, and her essay on the human personality, which is in fact about the destruction of personality, is one of the most important and least understood, and sometimes when understood one of the most disliked, of all her essays. . . .

Unique and unclassifiable as a thinker, she was neither a reactionary nor a progressive. She was something altogether exceptional—a great soul and a brilliant mind, as Eliot expresses it, "with a kind of genius akin to that of the saints."

But these are dangerous words. An attribution of saintliness is almost a kiss of death in an enlightened age like our own, in which barbarous words like good and evil are falling into disuse. In place of evil we now have maladjustment and antisocial or reactionary complexes, and in place of good we have maturity and successful social adaptation. I shall try . . . to avoid quarrelling about words . . . and as regards saintliness . . . follow George Orwell's advice that saints should always be held guilty until their innocence has been proved—or, in modern language, that eccentric behavior should always be attributed to immaturity or maladjustment, unless it can be shown to result from a more perfect maturity and a finer adjustment than the normal.

Richard Rees. Simone Weil: A Sketch for a
Portrait (Carbondale: Southern Illinois
University Press, 1966), pp. 11, 8–9

Original sin is not something apart from the Creation and which came afterward; it is inseparable from it. It is the very existence of the distinct, thinking human being that is guilty. That is why, in speaking of the self's need to renounce itself, Simone Weil refers to this by the forceful term of "decreation." By withdrawing, God has allowed us to exist; he has done so for the sake of love and so that we ourselves, for the sake of love, can renounce the being he has given us.

But what is this being he has given us? Is it veritable being? More than once Simone says that the ego is in reality nothing, that man's being is nonbeing. And indeed, what is left that could properly be considered man? From the start the personality seems dissolved, split on one hand between the power to reject good, a power that is the self itself but is only a false power— because in one way or another we do in the end obey God, if not for the love of good, then by being subjugated by necessity—and, on the other, the power to accept good that, basically, is identical with good itself, identical with God. For only God can love God.

Simone Petrémont. Simone Weil: A Life
(New York: Pantheon, 1976), p. 497

There are not two facts; there is only one. Simone Weil is a *genius-woman*. She is a moral genius in the orbit of ethics, a genius of immense revolutionary range. By reviving the inward quest of man in history, she has discovered the key to a wisdom which can be applied to the daily life of every man on both the individual and the social plane.

She is a woman inasmuch as she has all the feminine characteristics of spiritual fruitfulness: the importance of nurturing, of tending, of protecting in accord with the physiological exigencies of beings, vicissitudes and things; attention to preservation, healing and use; the prevalence of weakness over force; the importance of words, of language that communicates; the significance of participation and warmth in relation to sensibility, in the way one lives, works, studies and teaches; the emphasis placed upon the practical application of wisdom for the greatest possible happiness of man on earth.

These two basic characteristics of her personality find expressive unity in her work. Her contradictions are there reconciled in an equilibrium above the biographical plane of her existence.

> Gabriella Fiori. *Simone Weil: An Intellectual Biography* (Athens: University of Georgia Press, 1989), p. 309

It is good for us to read Simone Weil today, if for no other reason than to encounter a powerful countercurrent to the slow seeping mediocrity of our times. When as today professional theologians are preoccupied with fantasy, play, hope, the future, and the psychology of life-adjustment, it is chastening to hear the voice of one who regarded the gift of life and the gift of death as one, and who could assert without qualification, "It is in affliction that the splendor of God's mercy shines, from its very depths, in the heart of its inconsolable bitterness."

The genius of Simone Weil lay in the depth and clarity with which she analyzed the perennial questions about evil, suffering, justice, war, labor, love, and God. But she did more than merely probe intellectually; throughout her life she disciplined her body and mind to make of them a single instrument of precise, relentless reflection on the deepest matters of the soul. She reminds us of Kierkegaard by caring more for ideas than for food. She mortified her flesh as Kierkegaard did, and like him went early to the grave. Like Kierkegaard, too, she concerned herself more with experience than with doctrine, more with questions than with answers, more with the troubled spirit of unbelievers than with the confident faith of believers. And she had as Kierkegaard did that marvelous spirit of inquiry which makes it impossible to rest easy with any truth or teaching until one has reached down into the earth and found its roots in experience. She earned the respect of André Gide, T. S. Eliot, Jacques Maritain and Nicholas Berdyaev. Simone de Beauvoir and Raymond Aron, [her] fellow students in Paris . . . stood in awe of her personality which combined ruthless intellect with a compassion that could reach around the world to sense the suffering of human beings she had never seen.

Charles de Gaulle thought her political ideas mad. But Albert Camus spoke of her as "the only great spirit of our time."

Thomas A. Idinopulos. In Thomas A.
Idinopulos and Josephine Zavosky Knopp,
eds. *Mysticism, Nihilism, Feminism: New
Critical Essays on the Theology of Simone
Weil* (Johnson City, Tennessee: Institute for
Social Science and Arts, 1984), pp. 17–18

Eating, looking and waiting are bridges between [Weil's] life and thought. By looking closely at them we see *that* she transforms embodied experiences into images of spiritual stances, even if we cannot explain how she does so. There are so few virtuosos of the spiritual life about whom we have enough biographical information even to see this transformation that it would be overly fastidious not to learn what we may about it from Simone Weil.

If these three images are bridges for us between her life and thought, for her waiting was the bridge between looking and eating, which were in irreconcilable contradiction "here below" and were an indissoluble identity in the "realm of God." For her, the mechanics by which the soul moves from a natural to a supernatural orientation are controlled by attentive waiting; it is the way the contradictory acts—eating and looking—become one.

Judith von Herik. In Thomas A. Idinopulos
and Josephine Zakovsky Knopp, eds.
*Mysticism, Nihilism, Feminism: New
Critical Essays on the Theology of Simone
Weil* (Johnson City, Tennessee: Institute for
Social Science and Arts, 1984), pp. 59–60

Simone Weil, surely an outstanding woman religious figure of our culture's twentieth century, is separated by a deep and enormous chasm from contemporary feminist theology and religious thought.

. . . [F]or Weil, who was always in solidarity with all oppressed people, "women" did not exist as a group. She could write an entire scenario for the spiritual revitalization of France *(The Need for Roots)* without mentioning them as a collectivity.

Behind this lies a much deeper and, to feminists, more distressing problem. Weil's life and work can be appreciated for many reasons, but its stark loneliness, suffering, and self-destructiveness cannot be wished away. Weil's very spirituality made her a "priestess of pain;" this is hardly what women today want or need. Appellations such as "masochism," or the suggestion that Weil suffered from *anorexia nervosa*, raise this question in a different way. Surely what women should hope for are models of health, strength, and liberation, rather than a pattern of self-immolation, fanatical purity, and extreme denial of the body. If Weil is of any use to feminists, it would seem to be only as a negative example.

Lucy Bregman. In Thomas A. Idinopulos
and Josephine Zavosky Knopp, eds.
*Mysticism, Nihilism, Feminism: New
Critical Essays on the Theology of Simone
Weil* (Johnson City, Tennessee: Institute for
Social Science and Arts, 1984), pp. 91–92

Weil's acceptance of death "falls into line with the Christian mystical tradition" especially because it is accompanied by affliction and feelings of abandonment. Thus the soul must continue to love God even if it thinks itself abandoned by God. "The soul has to go on loving in the emptiness, . . ." Weil says. "Then, one day, God will come to show Himself to the soul." And for Weil this is possible only for those who, through expiatory suffering, have been rooted in death.

In the final analysis Simone Weil could never accept her own humanity, and ultimately her desire to flee toward purity and death was also her failure to accept the reality of her own existence. "The misery of man," she once wrote, "consists in the fact that he is not God. He is continually forgetting this." Simone understood all too well the misery of not being God. Her affliction was not being able to accept it.

Josephine Zakovsky Knopp. In Thomas A.
Idinopulos and Josephine Zavosky Knopp,
eds. *Mysticism, Nihilism, Feminism: New
Critical Essays on the Theology of Simone
Weil* (Johnson City, Tennessee: Institute for
Social Science and Arts, 1984), pp. 134–35

Weil . . . is often thought to have forsaken her earlier political concerns as a result of her religious experiences.

This picture of Simone Weil's life and thought is seriously misleading. Her life cannot be neatly divided up into "political" and "religious" periods. She never abandoned a concern for political and social questions; they remained at the heart of her thinking through her turn to Christianity. She never wavered from her central preoccupations: the problem of the dignity and spiritual condition of the most vulnerable and powerless in society, particularly the manual worker; the question of work and its place in society; and the role of science and technology in shaping the moral character of a civilization. In fact, Simone Weil's turn toward Christianity must be understood at least partly in terms of her search for answers to precisely these concerns. Although she came to feel that these answers could not be found in the secular realm alone, she never ceased considering their political dimension.

We do not mean to deny the traditional picture's emphasis on the substantial changes that Weil's views underwent in the course of her life. But there were also some important continuities. In particular, her assessment of Karl Marx and orthodox Marxism remained strikingly constant throughout her life and writings, at least from 1934 on. Both earlier and later in her life, she saw Marxism as making some contributions of permanent value: Marx's affirmation of the dignity of labor; his analysis of how capitalism can degrade the worker; and his taking of society as the basic unit of inquiry and studying it in terms of relationships of power. At the same time, at every period in her life Weil was deeply critical of Marx's theory of history and of the primacy given, especially within orthodox Marxist social analysis, to purely economic forces in society. Finally, Weil was also critical of Marxism as a guide to political activity in the service of the oppressed, charging it with fostering both passivity and an illusory sense of power in the proletariat as well as undermining the necessary moral foundations of political activity.

Lawrence A. Blum and Victor J. Seidler. *A Truer Liberty: Simone Weil and Marxism* (London: Routledge, 1989), pp. xvi–xvii

One lesson she gives us, and perhaps it is the most important, is that of doubt. She was Alain's faithful pupil and invites us to be. Everything she wrote, even though so often in the limpid style of French analytical tradition, deserves to be held at an intellectual arm's length. Throughout her brief maturity she wrote skeptically, that is, experimentally. She set down ideas as they came to her, in bold intuitive strokes that resist systematic development. Significantly, many of her writings are entitled "reflections," and the aphoristic brilliance that frequently flashes out in them (and even more in her *cahiers*) might be likened to the commanding lines of a sketch. There is consequently an attractive incompleteness in her work. . . .

She is taking one along the uncharted course of her thoughts. The steadfastness with which she looks at a problem or an issue becomes the guide. Doubt is a kind of mainspring to this steadfastness, a vigilant reckoning (or intellectual fussiness) that kept Weil from being taken in by easy resolution of very real difficulties. She always preferred the harder way, that of keeping the difficulties in focus. This dubitative power of her intellect kept her finally free of the mighty fanaticisms that beguiled so many of her fellow intellectuals. By reading her skeptically, we are not only responding to her in kind; we assume the necessary distance of doubt from which to assess the value of her ideas.

Her style is in a sense a snare. The clarity of her presentation and its intellectual forcefulness may be too easily taken (impetuous readers as we are) as evidence of final conviction, as though she had assumed some definitive vantage, just as her longing for purity, intellectual, spiritual, and otherwise, may be too easily construed (and has been by some) as evidence that she was a pure being. . . .

Her writing at its best has a meditative quality, and meditation forbids the snatching which, in Blake's terrible words, "doth the winged life destroy."

That is why, again following her example, we do well not to grasp her and her thinking in an appropriative way, putting her under a house arrest convenient to our own sensibility. This point must be underscored if only because she has so often been seized upon or pulled at, particularly by Christians with canonical urges.

Thomas R. Nevin. *Simone Weil: Portrait of a Self-Exiled Jew* (Chapel Hill: University of North Carolina Press, 1991), pp. 384–85

Simone Weil's philosophy is one that interrogates and contemplates our culture; it makes us aware of our lack of attention to words and empty ideologies, to human suffering, to the indignity of work, to our excessive use of power, to religious dogmatisms. Rather than set out a *system* of ideas (like a theory of justice or a theory of the good), Simone Weil uses her philosophical reflections to show us how to *think* about work and oppression, freedom and the good, necessity and power, love and justice—even to think, or not think, about God. In this way we are asked to examine the human condition and learn to discern a way through it.

Richard H. Bell. Introduction to *Simone Weil's Philosophy of Culture: Readings toward a Divine Humanity* (Cambridge, England: Cambridge University Press, 1993), p. 3

The claim placed upon us by Simone Weil's call for a new civilization is not remarkable. Other prophetic figures throughout history have made such demands for a revitalized order, and some, including Gandhi and Marx, have understood the centrality of work in this transformative process. Weil is asking, however, that revitalization be tied to an understanding of work which is spiritual. Unique in her call and relentless in her belief that civilization could be bettered, in spite of her ambivalence about the extent, and efficacy, of social change, Weil provides an important message to those struggling with work's meaning. . . .

Nine years before her death in 1943, Weil wrote the long essay on oppression and liberty which she referred to as her "testament." In her systematic effort to grasp the obstacles to free and fulfilling labor, Weil dismissed the expectations of ideologues and the polemical arguments for revolutionary change. Liberated work had much to do with the status of the manual laborer, in this classic essay, and the possibilities of integrating thought and action which would fortify the working class in their struggle for authentic participation. Her essay advances an image of the primacy of this form of labor over supervisory or intellectual work, and signifies an early indication of Weil's partiality to manual labor. It is only in her later writing that this partiality

assumes spiritual significance and becomes the basis for her appeal to a restored social order of spiritual laborers.

Clare B. Fischer. In Richard H. Bell, ed.
*Simone Weil's Philosophy of Culture:
Readings toward a Divine Humanity*
(Cambridge, England: Cambridge University
Press, 1993), pp. 189, 194

Though the spirit of Simone Weil is basically the spirit of the gospels, she
belongs with the "outside Christians" (as do Tolstoy and Wittgenstein, who
also had "no official religion") though in love with the New Testament. For
her the gospels are seen through the eyes of Homer and Euclid, and broadened by Eastern thought, all of which share the same impersonal sense of
the divine in individual terms as Jesus Christ did.

The "communality of humanity" will not be found in the old sense of an
"enlightenment" metaphysics of empty liberalism, but rather in the new sense
of "survival metaphors" which we need as a dying man needs a drink of
water. The center of a future civilization—a "new" Renaissance—must be
freedom of the thinking spirit in poetic and discerning genius, the intimate
work relation between the human body and its environment, and the common
human bond arising from every human's root expectation that good will be
done to him or her.

It is very necessary (above all for the sake of the next few generations,
Simone Weil says) to change our conception of human greatness so that we
no longer think of mass-fixated, mean-spirited men of power, like Hitler and
Stalin, as "great" men, nor of "empires" (economic or militaristic) as "great"
societies, but reserve the term of "greatness" for those humans and those
smaller communities who truly deserve it. We must each become more like
educators and spokespersons of *a divine humanity*—receptive to God coming
into our midst so that we may be truly lifted up. Because we are not open
and attentive to this, Simone Weil's prediction is not an optimistic one.

H. L. Finch. In Richard H. Bell, ed. *Simone
Weil's Philosophy of Culture: Readings
toward a Divine Humanity* (Cambridge,
England: Cambridge University Press, 1993),
p. 308

WELDON, FAY (GREAT BRITAIN) 1933–

Fay Weldon . . . has written *Down Among the Women,* which speaks for
itself. Indeed, the novel speaks very persuasively, despite the short, sharp
sentences which, snapping out at first, take on the tone of a tolling bell as

the half-dozen girls we meet begin to contract the habits that will come to rule them. Fay Weldon has a remarkable eye for these, succeeding in matching the habit to the girl even in the context of 1950. The men, meanwhile, are seldom predictably selfish, but range from the pathetic and insistent to the artistic and heedless, lend many scenes involving both the sexes an atmosphere oddly reminiscent of *The Horse's Mouth.* Miss Weldon's dialogue is sharp and her sense of timing excellent, as they need to be when complemented by a risky, stripped-down narrative style [which] sometimes reads like a drama synopsis: but her point remains unproved. The elegiac defiant conclusion "We are the last of the women" comes after she has smitten . . . [the] cleverly individual-ized group with such undifferentiated doom that they cannot help appearing gray and lifeless.

R. R. Davis. The New Statesman.
September 3, 1971, p. 308

The troubled and confused characters in Fay Weldon's new novel [*Remember Me*] are Londoners of a fairly ordinary sort, and by the time they are through leaping over the obstacles and dealing with the bizarre problems Miss Weldon invents for them, they are a bedraggled lot indeed. Rather like people in a breathless, ongoing comic opera, they speak to the reader directly, introduc-ing themselves in the most imaginative of ways, defining themselves almost exclusively in terms of two or three other people. . . .

A doomed young woman in Miss Weldon's second novel, *Down among the Women* (1972), complains of being no more than a puppet manipulated by men; she commits suicide at the age of thirty-six, convinced that her own life and life in general are pointless, a matter merely of suffering. Madeleine of *Remember Me,* similarly bitter about having been rejected by her husband, does not exactly commit suicide, but she drives a car in poor condition at such high speeds that an accidental death is inevitable. Dead, she wills herself to return in order to make life miserable for those who have survived her. If she does not quite cause the breakup of her former husband's marriage, or the death of his new young son, she comes close to it in a series of fast-paced, comic episodes that remind one of a film deliberately speeded up— or of a puppet show in which the puppets have twitched and jerked almost out of control. . . .

Down among the Women, a dizzyingly crowded short novel, took six main characters, all women, through various sexual adventures that are really contests of a sort with an elusive enemy—maleness itself. Several of the women in it are victims; one or two appear to have turned out well, though, like Margot and Lily, they tend to define themselves only in terms of men. *Down among the Women* is characterized by a certain bold, high-powered energy. . . .

Remember Me is a better-constructed novel, and its time-span is neatly truncated. Yet, apart from the teen-age Hilary, who is the only sympathetic person in the narrative, the characters are again one-dimensional. It is difficult to be patient with Madeleine, who is reputedly intelligent but who behaves with monotonous stupidity, centering her life exclusively on her former husband. Similarly, it is difficult to take Margot very seriously, since she spends so much of her time catering to her husband and her two teen-age children; she seems, moreover, not to have glanced through any women's magazines in years—surely, had she taken the time, she would have discovered that her role in life, her very character itself, has become one of the great Women's Liberation clichés of the decade.

While writers with the patience and sensitivity of Margaret Drabble or Penelope Mortimer can still make us respond to the plight of the oppressed housewife, the theme itself has become a very familiar one. The startling revelations of one decade become, all too frequently the shopworn clichés of the next.

Miss Weldon's scorn for her characters is expressed in frequent authorial intrusions; she cannot resist patting her characters on the head and saying patronizingly, "Good Lily!" "Kind Lily!" "Oh Jarvis!" "Disloyal, disconnected Margot!" The effect is that the reader soon loses sympathy with them, for if an author is contemptuous of his or her characters, how can the reader feel otherwise?

Remember Me has the breathlessness of an Iris Murdoch novel, and some of its inventiveness. But it lacks depth and resonance, and it resolves itself as glibly as any situation comedy, despite the seriousness of the issues involved. Is it possible that feminist concerns with the exploitation of women by men, while still painfully relevant to our lives are no longer viable as subjects for serious fiction?

Joyce Carol Oates. *The New York Times.*
November 21, 1976, pp. 7, 54

Praxis, the British writer Fay Weldon tells us, is Greek for action, turning point, and orgasm, and Praxis Duveen's long life [in the novel entitled *Praxis*] includes a generous supply of all those things. At present old, poor, barely able to hobble about her basement apartment and to scribble these memoirs, Praxis has been at various times Willie the student's common-law drudge, a prostitute, Ivor the businessman's suburban doll-wife, Philip the film maker's glamorous working wife, mother of two, stepmother of three, a highly paid copywriter of ads glorifying the stay-at-home wife and a famous feminist leader. She has committed adultery, incest and infanticide, for which last she spent two full years in jail. She has been raped. As a child she was the horrified witness of her father's violence, her mother's madness. In fact, into these 251 pages Fay Weldon has managed to cram at least one instance of just about every kind of manipulation and aggression that men use to get women where they want them, and just about every nuance of guilt and passivity that keeps women there.

Praxis is by no means as well shaped as it could be. I had carefully noted, for example, that Praxis is about five when her memories begin, in the mid-1920s, and since she claims to be very old in the novel's present, I kept wondering if she was speaking to us from some unspecified moment in the future; it is only at the very end that we learn that she has mistaken sickness and malnutrition for old age, a confusion which seems unlikely on the level of reality and a trick on the level of art. Miss Weldon's purposes, moreover, seem divided with regard to her heroine. As the survivor of a traumatic and genuinely bizarre girlhood, Praxis is presented as a particular, even unique individual; yet having carefully established our sense of Praxis's strangeness, Miss Weldon goes on to use her as a sort of incarnation of all that is typical and shared in women. I was never certain when Praxis was acting as an individual and when she was just being "a woman."

For all that, I read *Praxis* with great excitement. As a narrative it is perhaps too ambitious, but as a collection of vignettes, polemics, epigrams, it is often dazzling, pointing up the mad underside of our sexual politics with a venemous accuracy for which wit is far too mild a word. "'Women are so fundamentally immoral,' Philip would complain, admiringly enough, at dinner parties. 'They go after what they want, red in tooth and claw. Whether it's babies, or a man, or sex, or promotion, they let nothing stand in their way. They're barbarians,' That was in the days when men were prepared to generalize about women, and women would not argue, but would simper and be flattered by the attention paid." The male, fatuous with power; the female, toadying in the hope that some of it will rub of on her: It would be hard to say which disgusts Miss Weldon more. The relentlessness with which she savages both may discomfort you—it did me—but the energy with which she urges us to blunder our way into a fuller humanity could not be more exhilarating.

Katha Pollitt. *The New York Times.*
December 17, 1978, p. 7

I suspect Fay Weldon types with her teeth. Her prose is always biting, but she *will* keep chewing on the same old themes: the complicated, often sinister interplay among spouses, ex-spouses, lovers, and children; fleeting youth and cheating lovers; and wifely hostility, usually repressed. In *Watching Me, Watching You,* a collection of eleven short stories and one recycled novel, Weldon channels the wifely hostility into tales of things that go bump in the night: ghosts, of course, and husbands, delivering their customary biffs, kicks, and condescending pronouncements. "Women," announces one, about to eat bloody beef off Rosenthal china, "are what their husbands expect them to be; no more and no less. The more you flatter them the more they thrive." (It sounds like talk-to-your-plants time.) The ghosts are less clammy, and they don't sleep with their secretaries.

In Weldon's stories, most of the spirits are projections of female misery marching—or wafting—through the ages. . . .

Oddly, most of the women in these stories are capable professionals, able to hold down jobs, tend their broods, and make great omelets. For some reason, though, they allow their husbands to dictate their self-worth. They buy the whole patriarchal package, in which the perfect woman is a doll that, properly wound, does everything well, but that cannot, God forbid, wind itself. When you're tired of it, you toss it out, probably with a little alimony, and get a new one—"someone young some man hasn't had the chance to wear out yet."

The Fat Woman's Joke, first published in 1968 as . . . *And the Wife Ran Away,* is not as sharply observed or as scathing as Weldon's best accounts of suburban angst. A turner-outer of plays and television scripts as well as of stories and novels, Weldon has done a lot of writing between this book and the stories, and the practice shows. The stories are so economical, the novel so blatant. *The Fat Woman's Joke* is composed almost entirely of conversations—which would be fine if the characters didn't speak in snippy, polished paragraphs, like Fay Weldon. Still, this is an interesting Weldon blueprint: All the basic ideas are here, except for a notion of "sisterhood" she seems to have acquired over the past decade or so. . . .

The novel, Weldon's first, is awfully schematic, and after a while it gets to seem like *The Prophet,* with assorted pilgrims.

Carolyn Clay. *New York.* January 25, 1982,
p. 53

Fay Weldon's heroine, Ruth [*in The Life and Loves of a She-Devil*] is a woman so thrillingly ugly she inspires dread even in herself. Energized by a well-orchestrated hatred, she determines to change her life and transforms herself into a she-devil. Weldon has never been better than in this outrageous satire of self-improvement. Her vision is as mordant here as it is accessible and funny.

Good wife Ruth, tall, dark and heavy, has a jutting jaw and a nature delicate enough to be offended by her husband Bobbo's passion for Mary Fisher, a petite blond romance novelist who lives, with her classic features, in the High Tower of her fiction. Ruth, Bobbo and their two children live what Bobbo calls the good life in the suburb of Eden Grove.

When Bobbo leaves her to live with Mary Fisher in the High Tower, Ruth's lifelong weeping turns to a hatred that liberates the she-devil within her; she is not afflicted by doubt like the good. She knows what she wants—revenge, power, money, "to be loved and not love in return." Ruth burns down her house, dumps her now homeless children on Mary and Bobbo in their love bower and manages to prod Mary's aging, incontinent mother out of her rest home and back into Mary's unwilling care—the better for trysting lovers to discover the messy details of love. Thus begins Ruth's raving quest through the dungeon of life for the grail of earthly beauty, acceptance and love.

Here, as in her other books, *Female Friends, Down among the Women, Praxis* and *Puffball,* Weldon is dazzlingly inventive, a symphonic she-devil. Absurdity works for her as it does for few writers. Her exaggerated parable of love and power boasts rounded characters, a marvelously intricate plot and a style so polished and sure that it bites and snarls, then leaps to a lyrical kiss or to deadpan philosophy.

If the horror of transforming revenge is too much for you, you can decide it's fantasy. But it's real enough.

Alice Denham. *The Nation.* March 16, 1985,
pp. 315–16

Home truths never have much zing. Abuse may be "hurled" but home truths, blunt and thudding, are "delivered"—and, in Fay Weldon's latest novel, the reader is on the receiving end. Set around Glastonbury, her tale "of the wickedness of men and the wretchedness of women" is a game of consequences: what happens when Harry leaves Natalie, a silly woman whose only "cred" is with the delicatessen. With Thatcherism in full swing there's little need for the "primitive malevolence" that so undid Liffey in *Puffball.* This is the age of "two legs bad": of computer consultants, Hinkley Point, illegally imported agricultural chemicals, intensive pig-breeding units, unemployment, divorce, professional malpractice. For *Heart of the Country* read state of the nation; all the gang are here.

Abandoned with two children, a Volvo and a dog, Natalie, as is obvious from her shoes, is never going to cope. Peep-toed heels are for enjoying life, not "for the getting through." Natalie is as silly as a Victorian doll: "All wide eyes, smooth cold skin and silent blinking." So silly that Sonia, who points her in the direction of the DHSS, could kill her and very nearly does. It is Sonia, single parent, lentil-eater, who tells this story. "You can't get blood out of a stone," she suggests as the DHSS motto, but squeezing the stone properly helps. Natalie must cease to be a supplicant and become a claimant: "You mustn't talk about wanting this or that, about your feelings or pride or whatever. You must talk about your rights as a citizen half the time and cry the other half. That gratifies them both ways. . . .

Weldon's an astute and witty chronicler who doesn't miss a trick—it's sadly fitting that Sonia's sanity should land her in a madhouse and that Natalie's story should become therapeutic for her in turn—but her style remains professional and chatty; her tone, as in her *Letters to Alice,* at once intimate and from the plinth. Her prescriptions for coping, for instance, read like Shirley Conran's *Superwoman,* except that instead of "Don't polish floors, seal them," we read: "If you're thinking of going on social security why not cook and eat the dog?" And bracketed statistics punctuate the prose— Unemployment among the rural under-twenty-fives . . . sixty percent of men . . . forty-three percent of women . . .—making this less a novel than a message from someone who knows and cares about what's happening at the front.

Sonia rejects a happy ending—"No. She must get on with changing the world, rescuing the country. There is no time left for frivolity." But it's neither frivolity, nor Weldon's habitual lack of sentimentality, that are missing here.

It's that her characters inform us but don't make us care, while readers looking for the rough magic of a novel get short shrift.

Grace Ingoldsby. *The New Statesman.*
February 6, 1987, pp. 27–28

This British novel [*The Shrapnel Academy*] is a grim, funny parable of our
time. It is about a house party that gets out of hand. Neither truth nor fact,
it is about incendiary possibility.

Some unlovely people converge one blizzardy evening at the fictional
academy, which is dedicated to that, alas, utterly historic military shithead,
Henry Shrapnel, he who invented the exploding cannonball. The randy, sep-
tuagenarian general Leo Makeshift—who is, on the morrow, to deliver the
Wellington Lecture—arrives with his blond-haired young hussy, Bella. Then
come various members of the military-industrial complex and the women
who love them—no flower children, these, either. With so many well-
accented, respectable, racist rotters about, rotten things seem likely to happen. And that's only Upstairs.

Downstairs the teeming hordes of Africa and Asia live in some squalor
and illegality, but safe from deportation. Their self-appointed leader is the
imperfectly politicized black butler, Acorn, who is quite insane. Weldon
plunks in an honorable, bisexual, feminist journalist with a penchant for high
heels. There is also a golden-haired chauffeur of low intelligence and moderate decency. Do they get together? What an old-fashioned question. . . .

Weldon is not above cannibalizing her old works: whole paragraphs have
sometimes reappeared. Here, instead, she reuses a tried-and-true structural
gimmick that works, though not so well as in *Puffball.* There, amid the psychological bric-a-brac of one woman's pregnancy, is inserted a chronicle of
everywoman's pregnancy; the *The Shrapnel Academy,* capsule summaries of
the great battles and battlers of history are proffered like vitamins during the
mounting hostilities of dinner and afterward. Soon you long for another mor-
sel of the academy's caribou patty or a sip of dry dialogue.

Weldon realizes it too. Unwilling to give up on her structure (and why
should she?), she cajoles: "Reader, you now fear you are going to hear all
about Gustavus Adolphus. How right you are." . . .

Not only did Weldon voice, with exhilarating candor, the feminist consciousness that arose in Britain in the 1970s, but she latched onto the comic
tradition in women's writing. Women have always had a sense of humor;
particularly feminists, who would need it, wouldn't they?

Fay Weldon is a major writer. In *The Shrapnel Academy,* she is, as ever,
witty, honest, vicious.

Adrianne Blue. *Ms.* April 1987, pp. 34–35

Providing a paradigm neither of New Critical unity nor of poststructuralist
dissemination, *The Life and Loves of a She-Devil* evades both modernist and
postmodernist categories but, in its persuasive freedom from theory and la-

bels, offers what may well be a truer picture of our current intellectual climate than either. Indeed, one can go further: precisely because the *She-Devil* does not intend free play or *jouissance* but nevertheless provides us with a concrete image of the unresolved and unresolvable; precisely because it presumably intends unity but, thanks to the clash of its extremist intention and its moderating intentionality, fails to achieve it, it speaks with a special urgency and power to the confusions of the present. Straddling the distance between an older literature and a new, and between two kinds of criticism, it proclaims, willingly or not, the residual strength of those habits of thought and those forms of desire that have, until now at least, defined Western thought. The *She-Devil* may not tell us where we are going, but it says something—a good deal in fact—about where we are now. That is, after all, no small accomplishment.

Alan Wilde. *Contemporary Literature.* 29,
1988, p. 419

Once a writer has a respectable oeuvre it becomes possible to pick out thematic obsessions, recurring characterization, even repeated phrases: in short, we can make generalizations with impunity. It's an art to which Fay Weldon is no stranger.

To practice it on her: Weldon writes about Women's Lot; her heroines are downtrodden housewives and mothers in their thirties and forties, the repressed who return as harpies and heretics to wreak revenge on faithless husbands and the banalities of housewifery. Her world divides between men and women. Men are vain, insensitive creatures, drunk with ambition, careless of wives and children, weak, yet commanding obedience to domestic rules. Women are either beautiful, hard-headed and sexy (the mistresses) or resentful, neglected and plain (the wives). Hubby leaves wife for mistress; wife, the blemish on his power and virility, issues a curse on his new life.

Weldon delights in coincidence and chance encounters to score political points; her harpies are never individualized, isolated characters, but symbols of generations of women's oppression—a sisterhood of witches, in fact. The new lover is haunted by the ghost of the woman she has displaced, literally possessed by the dispossessed. It's all very clever, very sharp, the spoilt bourgeois mistress (or second wife) buys her happiness second-hand; she turns heel on her sister's demands at her peril.

Both *The Hearts and Lives of Men* and her novella *The Rules of Life* extend these themes—one with a light touch, the other with higher claims to seriousness. *The Hearts and Lives of Men* was first serialized in *Woman* magazine, which perhaps explains its gentler tone. . . .

The Rules of Life is altogether bleaker. . . . This is Weldon in grim garb, embellishing her historical fable of joyous infidelities with a little social awareness. . . .

I think, that irony rarely disrupts. And, in Weldon's case, it's usually a veiled moralism. Its sardonic detachment and high-handed tone have always made me feel that she really doesn't like women much at all, much less have a grip on contemporary differences. Women interest her because she relishes the fictional possibilities of what she perceives to be their condition. In *Hearts* the ironic "dear Reader" asides effectively march hand-hand with the idea of goodness and enduring pragmatic love. We can all laugh at the jokes, buy the book, watch the series, wear the T shirt—and continue to make the mistakes. Giggles of recognition do nothing to change the arrangements Weldon believes to be so unjust.

Helen Birch. *The New Statesman.*
December 4, 1987, p. 28

With her recent novels Fay Weldon doesn't so much use a plot as a ploy, a device to get things moving. There's a strong idea, or motif, at the center of the narrative, and a lot of smart social comment and contemporary vicissitudes surrounding it. *Darcy's Utopia* is in this mold. The blueprint for a pleasanter society, one without money or overpopulation, is ascribed to a Professor Julian Darcy, currently in prison; but really it's his second wife Eleanor who is at the bottom of the notion. Eleanor is issuing her life story, bit by bit, to the features editor of a woman's weekly by the name of *Aura,* and at the same time submitting to a more intensive grilling on the subject of Darcian monetarism (and other things) by a journalist from the *Independent.*

The two interviewers of Eleanor Darcy, Valerie Jones of *Aura* and Hugo Vansitart, find themselves seated side by side at the Media Awards dinner, and the next minute they're holed up together in a Holiday Inn, while the world—or at least the part of it affected by their behavior—goes hang. They only emerge to continue the two-pronged examination of Eleanor Darcy, who seems to have spent her life sloughing off various skins: born Apricot Smith, to an incipient alcoholic and an off-hand banjo-player, she has passed through the stage of being Ellen Parkin, before coming to fruition as Eleanor Darcy.

Eleanor has trouble with dates. Married at seventeen to a Bernard Parkin, a Catholic on the verge of converting to Marxism, she stayed married for fifteen years before taking up with Professor Darcy, yet gives her age as thirty. (The author's confusion over dates is even more striking, unless we're meant to believe that Eleanor's grandmother Rhoda gave birth to a daughter at nine or ten.) Still, what with the devil hovering outside the window of a polytechnic, household ghosts playing havoc with the ornaments and episodes of ill-wishing taking place at college, Eleanor's concern with chronology is perhaps understandably perfunctory. Her aim is to tamper to the fullest extent with social usages, though whether in the interests of regeneration or mischief-making, it is hard to say.

The author's aim is a bit clearer, but not much. She is, as ever, out to point the finger at social abuses, and the "Utopia" motif enables her to proffer some extreme solutions to certain miseries in her usual playful manner. She keeps our attention through all the throwaway enormities, colorful side-issues and teasing didactics of her newest work of fiction, but fails to indicate exactly what it is that these add up to. Too much randomness, and not enough firm control, mar *Darcy's Utopia*.

Patricia Craig. *New Statesman and Society.*
September 21, 1990, p. 42

Leader of the Band and *The Cloning of Joanna May* have a family resemblance to the earlier books. (There are fourteen previous novels and short-story collections.) They have the regular jumble of characters leading lives that we recognize as modern by their snarled netting of impulse, incoherence, and battering by uncontrollable forces. They are lightly spiced with Weldon's beloved metaphor, magic, without which her readers would feel they had not gotten the genuine article. Her wrath is everywhere in evidence, her ideas skitter and glitter in every direction.

But in these recent books, something has happened to her writing. It's as though Weldon, who like the rest of us must feel the despair-a-day that comes with the morning paper, has finally been overwhelmed. The crush of all that anger, all that desperation, appears to have squeezed out of these novels what Weldon, as a novelist, does best. Both books sound as though they were written from the top down. So many topics tackled—heavy topics, too: feminism (especially as it applies to women inching into middle age), heredity, power, ambition, love and marriage, sexual mores, free will, the hollowness of the middle class, the absurd social order, the wickedness of unbridled science, the sins and futility of war, and more. In *The Cloning of Joanna May* there is a lot of wheel-spinning over what constitutes the self, many paragraphs on the "eye" that sees and the "I" that is. . . .

When Weldon stops carrying us along in the rush of events, when her characters have no vitality, then we are forced to confront her less as a novelist who is engaged and more as a pure idea-monger. And then we are in trouble. Of course we recognize that she still stands on the side of the angels. But now the ideas have the ring of boilerplate bombast, the writing sounds choked-up and deadened, or pumped up into "cute" or simply soap-box shrill. . . .

When Weldon can bring herself to resist the temptation to write tracts, she is once again the Weldon we remember. Otherwise, there is a sense that she is too obviously miming her own pain, not her characters', that the gestures have grown too frantic, or, finally, too exhausted.

Judith Dunford. *The New Republic.*
August 20–27, 1990, p. 42

Novels derived from TV drama usually have cheap allure. *Growing Rich* is based on Fay Weldon's Anglia TV serial and, ironically, she uses this form to create a complex, ambitious and heretical book.

The basic story is a soap opera about unexceptional lives. Set in Fenedge in East Anglia, a bit of land at the end of nowhere, where opportunities are nil, it evolves into a saga of psychic and surreal phenomena, loss of innocence, infidelity, destruction of the planet and the arrival of the Devil. "Dramas happen everywhere if only you hang around for long enough.". . .

Fay Weldon writes in elliptical chunks, not continuous narrative. This gives her freedom to interrupt these life stories with all manner of encyclopedic information: on women's rights, the destruction of the environment, governmental hypocrisy, frozen chickens, the fecundity of nature, the virtues of the spotted orchid, dog-rose and crossbill, and how extruded egg is produced.

A narrator underpins the chaos with a voice of commonsense and love. Husbandless, childless and paralyzed, Hettie Upton is spirit and thought. She knows about calmness in adversity, and from her wheelchair watches, with a benign accepting eye, all that is happening in the external world.

When young she was operated on for a bodged pregnancy termination. A wasp stung the surgeon. The scalpel slipped and Hettie was paralyzed. "So you understand why I am preoccupied with concepts of 'lucky' and 'unlucky' to be paralyzed: 'deserving it' . . . but deserving what? The luck or unluck? Forget it."

Despite such moral conundrums, the machinations of the Devil and the clairvoyance of Annie's mother, the final impression is that chance, not luck or fate, creates destiny and chaos in Fenedge. Like life, *Growing Rich* is fecund, capricious, surprising and odd—and like life, elusive of meaning in the end.

Diana Souhami. *New Statesman and Society*. March 6, 1992, p. 46

"Long Dong Silver," an actor in a pornographic film, played an important role in the recent public confirmation hearings of Justice Clarence Thomas. It was shocking—even in America of the 1990s—to hear in public a discussion about the generosity of a man's genitalia. Yet Fay Weldon, born in New Zealand and now living in London and Somerset, has based her sixteenth novel [*Life Force*] upon (to quote the dust jacket), "a very vital ten inches belonging to one Leslie Beck, aka Leslie the Magnificent." The novel concerns sexual pleasure, especially how Long Dong Leslie bestowed it upon four female friends: Nora, Marion, Rosalie, and Susan—and the havoc he provokes when he returns to rekindle old rivalries and infidelities. The "life force" of the title is of course Leslie's cock, or dong, or dick, or willy (it gets called all of these, and more, during the novel's course [or coarse]). The object of desire, alas, has somewhat shrunken when Beck reappears, a sixtyish widower in search of new relationships. . . .

For all its inadequacies of characterization, this new novel does end well. Plot elements begin to be resolved neatly—too neatly: A husband presumed dead returns, a cat presumed strayed is found in a closet, an awkward daughter makes the college hockey team. . . . Then Nora admits she has abandoned writing autobiography for writing fiction—the latter was found to be easier and much more fun. Then she tells us what *really* happened in the real world—the husband actually is never heard from again, the cat is lost forever, etc. It is a trick on the reader but a good trick. . . . Weldon's ending almost, but not quite, redeems her shallow, old-fashioned novel.

Robert Phillips. *Hudson Review.* 45, 1992, pp. 493–94

"Once you have felt love . . . you do not feel competitive any more: you do not believe you will be loved, or not loved, because your make-up is right or wrong. You do not worry because your breasts are small, or your hair greasy. . . . You know that all these things are trivial, that love strikes in spite of them." This is the exceptional book that brazenly asserts the primacy of private affairs, like love, over public; politics are dismissed as "men's games." But politics might kill Isabel, who loved a senator, secretly bore his son, and is in danger because the bachelor father's sleazy handlers regard potential news of the romance as threatening to his Presidential hopes. Isabel is a famous talk-show host, married to a man inclined toward housework. She shares a world of comforts with a cozy group of female neighbors, which, however, always holds sinister undercurrents from the world of external affairs—both kinds. The British Weldon gets some minor Americanisms wrong here, but she gets absolutely everything in the moral and emotional universe brilliantly, emphatically, and entertainingly right.

The New Yorker. November 9, 1992, p. 147

WELTY, EUDORA (UNITED STATES) 1909–

She proceeds with the utmost simplicity and observes with the most delicate terseness. She does not try mystically to transform or anonymously to interpret. The parallel forced upon us, particularly by those of Miss Welty's stories which are based on an oblique humor, is her likeness to Gogol. . . . Like Gogol, Miss Welty opens the doors and describes the setting, almost inch by inch. . . . Miss Welty's method can get everything in; nothing need be scamped, because of romantic exigencies, or passed over, because of rules of taste. Temperamentally and by training she has become mistress of her material by her choice of one exactly suitable kind of treatment, and—a final test of a writer's power—as we read her, we are made to believe that she has hit upon the only possible kind.

Louise Bogan. *The Nation.* December 6, 1941, p. 572

Now I happen to think that to make a ballet of words is a perversion of their best function and I dislike—because it breeds exhibitionism and insincerity— the attitude toward narrative which allows an author to sacrifice the meaning of language to its rhythms and patterns. . . . Miss Welty constantly calls

attention to herself and away from her object. . . . This is the sin of pride—
this self-conscious contriving—endemic to a whole generation of writers
since Katherine Mansfield and most especially to the women of that generation. . . . I have spoken of the ballet quality of Miss Welty's stories: in this
connection I am reminded of the painter Dali and—via Dali—of the relationship between the chic modern department store and much of modern fiction.

Diana Trilling. *The Nation.* October 2, 1943,
pp. 386–87

It is her profound search of human consciousness and her illumination of the
underlying causes of the compulsions and fears of modern man that would
seem to comprise the principal value of Miss Welty's work. She, like other
best writers of this century, implies that the confusion of our age tends to
force individuals back upon conscience, as they have not been since the
seventeenth century; for in the intervening centuries, values were more
closely defined, behavior was more outwardly controlled. Miss Welty's prose
fiction, like much of the poetry and fiction of this era that seeks to explore
the possibilities of the imagination, is comparable to the rich prose of Sir
Thomas Browne; and reminiscent of the poetry of the seventeenth century.

Eunice Glenn. In Allen Tate, ed. *A Southern
Vanguard* (New York: Prentice-Hall, 1947),
pp. 89–90

Let us admit a deep personal preference for this particular kind of story,
where external act and the internal voiceless life of the human imagination
almost meet and mingle on the mysterious threshold between dream and
waking, one reality refusing to admit or confirm the existence of the other,
yet both conspiring toward the same end. This is not easy to accomplish, but
it is always worth trying, and Miss Welty is so successful at it, it would seem
her most familiar territory. There is no blurring at the edges, but evidence
of an active and disciplined imagination working firmly in a strong line of
continuity, the waking faculty of daylight reason recollecting and recording
the crazy logic of the dream.

Katherine Anne Porter. *The Days Before*
(New York: Harcourt, 1952), pp. 107–8

There is one young woman who is accepted as "different" and "authentic"
even by the best celebrants of the black mass in Taos and Carmel and Greenwich Village and Norfolk: the Eudora Welty who, with her two recent volumes of short stories, *A Curtain of Green* and *The Wide Net,* has become
possibly the most distinguished of the new story-tellers. Oh yes, she has
heard of Symbolism, but her writing is as clear—and free of obscenity—as
the Gettysburg Address.

Sinclair Lewis. *A Sinclair Lewis Reader*
(New York: Random House, 1953), p. 212

Miss Eudora Welty . . . deals in overtones and moments of implication; she . . . compels our acceptance by the spell of words and symbols. The significance of her characters and scenes lies as much in the past behind them and in the future before them as in the moment snatched from the moving reel and set before us in a vivid "still." . . . The unsaid and the implied are essentially human, and human sophisticated at that, for although the characters of her creation are usually simple folk the reader is never for a moment unconscious of Miss Welty's sophisticated eye. Here is a wonderfully clear vision, humorous, tender, and always shaping the raw experience before her to our satisfaction. Nevertheless, as I read each successive book of Miss Welty's, I am less and less satisfied. She is so entirely successful on her own home ground, but she hardly ever wins an away match.

Angus Wilson. *New Statesman and Nation.*
Novenber 19, 1955, p. 680

From her earliest published work to her latest collection of stories Miss Welty has drawn heavily upon the worlds of myth and folklore and, while handling many of the same motifs again and again, has consistently absorbed them more and more fully into her own meaning, so that in her most successful work it is impossible to say that here is Cassiopeia and here Andromeda. The reader can only be aware that these legendary figures, along with similar ones from Germanic, Celtic, Sanskrit, and numerous other folk sources, are suggested by the characters that Miss Welty is drawing. . . . Quite consciously Miss Welty has taken the characters common to several mythological systems and translated them into present-day Mississippians. Although a faintly fantastic element remains in her stories, her characters and her atmosphere are too thoroughly Southern to be mistaken for those of Siegfried's Germany or Perseus's Greece. So typically Southern are they, in fact, that many critics damn her for her provincial approach to life.

By patterning her characters closely after folk heroes Miss Welty has avoided exactly such a strictly regional approach as that for which she has been blamed. Since her first published story she has been working toward a fusion of the universal mythic elements embodied in various culture-heroes with the regional world that she knows first-hand. The effect of this attempt on her work and her degree of success with it may be followed throughout her work.

William M. Jones. *Southern Folklore
Quarterly.* December, 1958, pp. 173–74

Eudora Welty is an imaginative writer. With her, nothing comes out of stock, and it has been impossible for her to stand still. Her art is a matter of contemplation, susceptibility, and discovery: it has been necessary for her to evolve for herself a language, and to arrive, each time she writes, at a new form. . . .

[*The Golden Apples*] is great, tender, austere stuff, shot through from beginning to end with beauty. . . . In *The Golden Apples,* Miss Welty would seem to have found, for her art, the ideal form. But, for a writer of her stature, nothing is conclusive—what comes next? American, deliberately regional in her settings, she "belongs," in the narrow sense, to no particular nation or continent, having found a communication which spans oceans.

> Elizabeth Bowen. *Seven Winters &*
> *Afterthoughts* (New York: Knopf, 1962),
> pp. 216–18

When Miss Welty says that she is "touched off by place," she suggests a journey beyond the region of the touching off. And indeed her imagination molds her material into beautifully symmetrical essences and shapes. She participates in the life around her with such perception and fidelity that she catches it exact, and then she colors it and carves it into an entity beyond the realism of daily life, which is just what the people of her region have done with the often shallow and monotonous basic material of their lives. The result is an ironical tension between form and content, in which prosaic experience is enveloped in a mist of rhetoric, and irrational action is reported in the most attractive of verbal forms.   .

> Robert B. Holland. *American Literature.*
> November 1963, p. 35

With her wide range in style, point of view, subject matter, and fictional modes, Miss Welty has thoroughly investigated the possibilities inherent in the short story form, enriching and extending the potential of this demanding genre. Through her constant experimentation she has literally defied the genre's limitations and boundaries, and in exploring the mysteries of the inner life she has used dream and fantasy in a manner that has enabled her to produce a heightened realism. Her vision of relationship as a "changing and pervading" mystery is consistent throughout her fiction, and her characters are continually probing into these mysteries trying to surmount the separateness existing between themselves and others, and undergoing experiences in which they are "initiated" or "reborn" into the world.

> Alfred Appel. *A Season of Dreams: The*
> *Fiction of Eudora Welty* (Baton Rouge:
> Louisiana State University Press, 1965), p. 256

In *Losing Battles* the traditional drama of Agrarian *versus* Industrial—appearing obliquely and yet in a completely significant way—takes on a complexity demanding an explication hardly even to be begun in a summary comment. In this story—which may well be Miss Welty's greatest achievement and one that assures her, if any further assurance is needed, of her place among the great American story tellers of this century—we are again in the domain of a fictional country. It is Boone County in the northeast hill country of Mississippi. . . .

[The conflict] sounds a little like Thomas Hardy, and it is to some extent. What finally comes from the clash between Miss Julia and the family tribe of the Banner community, however, is the result of Miss Welty's genius for seeing life not so much in the manner of Hardy as in that of her favorite novelist, Jane Austen. She transforms the drama of the disposession of the country people in America into a highly ironic comedy of universal human motives.

Lewis P. Simpson. *Southern Review.*
Summer, 1970, pp. xxii–xxiii

It is not craftsmanship which has been the most important factor in determining [Eudora Welty's] new place in American letters. One suspects that critics have finally begun to realize that, far from being narrow in scope, her work is prodigious in its diversity and reveals a mind and sensibility capable of almost anything. There is no typical Eudora Welty story in the sense that there is a typical Ernest Hemingway story. She may have stolen from herself on occasion, but she has never precisely re-created an earlier work, and most of her stories are unique in the way that true literature always is. There is nothing like "The Wide Net" anywhere else in fiction, and at least a dozen of her stories stand alone in the same way.

On the other hand, quite apart from these earlier works, *Losing Battles* is itself a novel on which to build a literary reputation. Like *Delta Wedding,* to which it bears some superficial resemblance, it is essentially a story about the family and its larger manifestation, the community. But *Losing Battles* has social, historical, and philosophical dimensions which are not to be found in the earlier work, and it is these dimensions which have undoubtedly convinced some of the more sociologically-minded critics that Miss Welty deserves a place in the first rank of contemporary novelists.

Thomas H. Landess. *Sewanee Review.*
Autumn, 1971, pp. 626–27

Eudora Welty's novel, *The Optimist's Daughter,* which first appeared in *The New Yorker* of March 15, 1969, is a miracle of compression, the kind of book, small in scope but profound in its implications, that rewards a lifetime of work. Its style is at the service of a story that follows its nose with the instincts of a good hunting dog never losing the scent of its quarry. And its story has all those qualities peculiar to the finest short novels: a theme that vibrates with overtones, suspense and classical inevitability.

Known as a "Southern regionalist," Miss Welty is too good for pigeon-holding labels. Though she has stayed close to home, two interlocking notions have been demonstrated in her fiction: how easily the ordinary turns into legend, and how firmly the exotic is grounded in the banal. They are subjects only partly dependent on locale. In *The Optimist's Daughter,* we are in the South once more, but a South where real distinctions are made between Texas and Mississippi, and Mississippi and West Virginia. And if place has been Miss Welty's touchstone, the pun implicit in the word "place" comes alive in her new novel; its colloquial meaning—caste, class, position—is as important as its geographical one.

Howard Moss. The New York Times.
May 21, 1972, p. 1

Innocence enmeshed by schemers, gullibility abused, a harmless, hopeless simplicity too grand for deceitful living has been a theme in Eudora Welty's fiction since *The Robber Bridegroom,* 1942. . . . But in Miss Welty's new novel [*The Optimist's Daughter*] this very innocence ceases to be comic or charming and becomes lethal, a crucial failure to do business with the world, a special vulnerability, not a peculiar state of grace; not innocence at all, finally, but a form of guilt, the weakness both of individual men and a whole Southern style. . . . The book is so powerful . . . stern, and funny in a way that has nothing to do with Miss Welty's earlier comic writing. Or rather, that has all too much to do with it, since it is concerned with taking it back. The engaging and irresponsible Uncle Daniel, say, of *The Ponder Heart,* has become . . . the helpless judge of *The Optimist's Daughter,* dignified but too delicate, not half as fit for life as he thought.

Michael Wood. New York Review of Books.
June 29, 1972, p. 9

The Optimist's Daughter is an unlikely triumph, combining Chekhovian understatement with Faulknerian verve, displaying the author's powers at their best. She has lost nothing over the years: her unerring ear, the comic vitality of her characters, the authenticity of furniture and flowers and small-town mores remain compelling. And the profundity of her moral imagination has deepened. Little of obvious significance happens in this book. An old man dies, his daughter grieves, his young second wife feels an injustice has been done her (on her birthday!). There is a southern funeral, unexpectedly invaded by the wife's implausible relatives. The daughter, Laurel, returns to Chicago, where she works. She thinks about her own long-dead husband, and about what her marriage meant. What makes such events important is the penetration with which the characters are judged and the intensity with which they are loved.

Patricia Meyer Spacks. Hudson Review.
Autumn, 1972, p. 509

Eudora Welty's fiction is the richest in human understanding and in power to shape and convey that understanding of any living writer known to me. In all of American fiction, she stands for me with her only peers—Melville, James, Hemingway, and Faulkner—and among them, she is in some crucial respects the deepest, the most spacious, the most lifegiving. . . .

Eudora Welty—in the wide centrality of her vision, in her fixed yet nimble scrutiny of what might tritely be called "the normal world" (the normal daily world of the vast country called the American South) and in the nearly infinite resourcefulness with which she has found means to convey the discoveries of that scrutiny—has opened to a whole generation of writers the simple but nearly unattainable possibility of *work*. We read her fiction, we recognized our world, we knew that our world was therefore the possible source of more good fiction. It had been done once; it could now be done again, and differently.

> Reynolds Price. In Louis Dollarhide and
> Ann J. Abadie, eds. *Eudora Welty: A Form
> of Thanks* (Jackson: University Press of
> Mississippi, 1979), pp. 124–25

For Welty, as for most serious writers in English since James, the vision of the existence of man is not a simple relationship between stimulus and response. Behavior has its roots in history—not simply the history of the immediate past from which habits derive, but in an ancient, archetypal past. This dimension of history exerts a more basic, defining force on men, which over the course of human evolution has shaped the ways by which men have come to understand their relationships to nature, each other, and the universe. These shaping forces reside in the psyche but are more often than not unconscious. They are most clearly observed in out-croppings of myth and fantasy that to the artist's eye occur all around us. But the interest in myth and fantasy rests solidly in the present, real world. In "Place in Fiction" Welty writes that "the novel from the start has been bound up in the local, the 'real,' the present, the ordinary day-to-day of human experience." . . . It is significant, however, that the statements in which she seems to espouse allegiance to the photographic depiction of surfaces or appearances are quickly qualified. Place for Eudora Welty has a dimension of "mystery" because "it has a more lasting identity than we have." The "realism" that she finds essential to the novel applies equally to any kind of successful fiction. . . .

The Golden Apples can be seen perhaps as a merger of Welty's realistic method with the allegorical, but the notion hardly seems to do justice to so fine a book. It is more helpful to think of Welty's use of myth and fantasy in terms of three methods defined from a structural perspective. The demands she makes on her readers' imaginations are great no matter which sort of structure may be found. Her narrators may use myth and fantasy to define character; or with fantasy she may imaginatively create the interior of a mind or an allegorical landscape to investigate "the truth of the human heart"; or, finally, she may create characters who, like Virgie, are as aware of the dimension of myth and fantasy as the reader is asked to be.

> Robert L. Phillips, Jr. In Peggy Whitman
> Prenshaw, ed. *Eudora Welty: Critical Essays*
> (Jackson: University Press of Mississippi,
> 1979), pp. 56–57, 67

Welty's constant theme is communication itself, the state of human existence in which individuals, because of some connection with each other in the natural world, become more than the simple integers they might seem. Every hero and heroine. . . . leaving the private, silent world of memory, grief, or dream, crosses a threshold into a real world that is enriched by that very entry, by that self so long withheld.

Also part of this passage is the reader of Welty's fiction. He must be attentive to the totally and artistically synthesized vision of the world that sustains her work. The moment of vision is built upon the particular world each fiction summons into existence. The climactic experience of each of Welty's fictions is not only the resolution of a plot but a denouement of the form, in which the world appears in its integrity before the reader, allowing him to realize how and when the parts become whole. . . .

Welty has given, and will continue to give (for these works are soundly made and will stand), a literature that reaches great stature in its theme of love. Few writers understand that the most complex human emotion, love, is also the most simple, and that a true statement of the theme is both discussable and not.

> Michael Kreyling. *Eudora Welty's Achievement of Order* (Baton Rouge: Louisiana State University Press, 1980), pp. 174–75

Placing Welty within the "Republic of Letters" is important in itself, but it has the greater advantage of focusing her final control of southern materials. Because of its vivid frontier settlement, its complicated plantation ethic entailing slavery, civil war, and the gradual decline of hereditary values, the South in general and Mississippi in particular present the modern literary imagination with unusually clamorous circumstances. As her fiction, essays, and interviews reveal, Welty's sense of a regional identity was deepened appreciably by the civil rights movement of the 1950s and 1960s and by the merging of distinctive American cultures which was accomplished in the following decade. Living continuously in Jackson, Welty observed closely this process of modernization, the small provincial capital of her birth transformed in the next seven decades into a metropolitan center with a diverse, highly mobile population approaching 300,000. But Welty's historicism has behaved admirably throughout. This ability to reconcile process and stasis, time and eternity, self and community, is, it seems clear, a reflection of Welty's citizenship in the modern "Republic of Letters." Relieved of the extremes of belief and rationalism, Welty discovered in this realm a suppleness of mind which is essential to the reconciler's art. More specifically, she discovered the means of forming an *image* of the South, one stripped of its historic defensiveness, romance, and ready applicability. There is finally a coolness at the core of Welty's work, a reserve or restraint that Walter Sullivan quite accurately notes, but it does not preclude her fulfilling the role of the modern vocation of letters. "The man of letters is primary in keeping open the possibility of man's apprehension of the truth of his destiny beyond time." Although etched in irony and pictured in displacement. Welty's preserved "Southern character" testifies to the strength of this moral "possibility." Her Mississippi chronicle is finally the outward shape of a passionate interior drama that has preoccupied all serious writers of the modern South and, before that, all chroniclers of Western culture.

Albert J. Devlin. Eudora Welty's Chronicle:
A Story of Mississippi Life (Jackson:
University Press of Mississippi, 1983), p. 212

Despite readers' agreement that her settings and the dialogue of her characters are unmistakably Southern, despite reviewers' responses to hers as a Southern world, despite Welty's own repeated testimony to the importance of place to fiction, only in the last few years has her portrayal of the South become a major theme of Welty scholarship. The orthodox view has held that Welty is a versatile writer who renders Southern dialogue with precision and humor but whose concerns are not regional but universal, her varied fiction speaking not of history and social conditions but of the lives of individuals. Even reviewers' occasional criticisms of her vision of the South have seldom stimulated study of her South. On the contrary, to the charge, for example, that her vision is nostalgic and uncritical, her defenders have often answered by turning the argument aside: her subject, some insist, is not the South and her kinships are not Southern in particular. . . .

Comedy reigns as Southern talkers come alive. Allen Tale . . . [has said] that Southern conversation isn't about anything except the "people who are talking." At the heart of much of Welty's comedy is the truth of this statement. Tate also says that the purpose of Southern conversation "is to make everybody happy." Welty might agree. As a comic-realist, however, she knows that not everybody is made happy by Southern conversation. In her fiction, the listeners are affected in many different ways, depending on their individual dispositions and their positions within, or outside of, the group, while the person made happiest by Southern talk is usually the person doing the talking. But Welty would probably suggest that this characteristic is true of oral traditions in general, not just of Southern ones. . . .

In reading Welty's fiction, Cleanth Brooks is reminded that "Homer, the father of the poetry of Western civilization, was himself a poet of the oral tradition, even though he was to become the very cornerstone of the written tradition." Welty, Brooks observes, is another who achieves "a true wedding" of the oral and written traditions, successfully incorporating the oral into the written and thus "giv[ing] it an enduring life." I would add that not only has Welty preserved the oral tradition; she has built much of her fiction on a recognition of connections between the oral and the written—and between Southern storytelling and other story or storytelling traditions. She reminds us that the oral and written traditions have been intertwined since the time of Homer and perhaps nowhere more so, in the twentieth century, than in the American South.

Carol S. Manning. *With Ears Open Like Morning Glories: Eudora Welty and the Love of Storytelling* (Westport, Connecticut: Greenwood Press, 1985), pp. ix, 198–99

Few critical studies of Eudora Welty have observed that she writes fiction that reflects a specifically female appropriation of traditional narrative structures. Although her style has been described as "entirely feminine" by Louis D. Rubin, most critics do not try to find out how this feminine style works. Rubin uses the term "feminine" as a characteristic of "elusive," "fastening on little things," "rich in allusions and connotation." He characterizes Welty's style as being both "feminine" *and* "muscular," implying that feminine style can include control and preciseness in narration. But Rubin does not relate his observations to the author's sex, nor does he take into account that it is exactly the duality generating from "feminine" and "muscular" that has its own dynamics. Peggy Prenshaw is one of the first critics who insisted on Welty's status as a woman writer using gender-determined language. In her essay "Woman's World, Man's Place: The Fiction of Eudora Welty," she sets out to prove that in Welty's fiction the presence of the matriarchal world dominates. She distinguishes furthermore between a "matriarchal and feminine presence" and the masculine. Her title "Woman's World, Man's Place" is chosen to illustrate that the presence of the matriarchal (biological life; relation to the mother) and the feminine (the feminine archetype of the unconscious; according to Neumann also the archetype of psychic development) have more influence on Welty's characters than the masculine principle (realm of the heroic-egoistic).

Franziska Gygax. *Serious Daring from Within: Female Narrative Strategies in Eudora Welty's Novels* (Westport, Connecticut: Greenwood Press, 1990), p. 5

WEST, JESSAMYN (UNITED STATES) 1892–1984

Fourteen unpretentious and agreeably old-fashioned stories [*The Friendly Persuasion*] about a likable Quaker family—a thoughtful, industrious father, an affectionate and capable mother, their flock of clearly individual children—and their mild but not uneventful life on a nursery farm in Indiana about the time of the Civil War. Miss West, whose first book this is, has produced neither a standard piece of period nostalgia nor the equally standard album of lovable eccentrics, and it is even more to her credit that she has had the sense and taste not to patronize or exploit the gentle piety that directs the lives of her characters.

The New Yorker. November 10, 1945, p. 102

[In *Cress Delahanty*] Miss West recounts the growing up of a nice, bright girl in a nice, bright family on a ranch in southern California. Her adventures are about what we would expect: she writes poems, she falls in love with a shy classmate, she cultivates "personality," she takes piano lessons, she goes away to college. We have read of such adventures in novels before; what induces us to read of them again? Nothing but Miss West's uncanny reckoning of how much weight of telling each of these adventures will support. They are like so many delicate but strong bridges reaching back and back into our common childhood; the deeps they span are by no means fearful, they are only wide. In the lost country to which they lead, it is ten in the morning and the sun is just above the trees. The one ogre is death, and at the ages of twelve and thirteen we have it in mind that if worst comes to worst, we can sit down and somehow talk him out of claiming us. We don't, in any event, *have* to go, as grownups do. Miss West never tries to be very funny or very sad; she gives us a dear child, lets time take her away from us, and the book is finished.

Brendan Gill. *The New Yorker.* March 13, 1954, pp. 129–30

This is a novel [*South of the Angels*] of Chaucerian dimensions and certainly the most ambitious which Miss West has attempted. Her method is to move from household to household: from the spinsters Opal and Eunice, each in her way so hungry for love, to Asa Brice, the bachelor with his ingenious plans for developing the arroyo; from the Reverend Raunce, the revivalist who has found God, to Tom Mount, carpenter and philanderer who has found sex, from Shel Lewis and his lovable wife and children to Base and Elizabeth Cudlip, the embittered Southerners. These are a precious few of the many whom she has brought to life and who respond in their varying ways to the two magnetic poles of love and hate.

Miss West is the master of the swift descriptive phrase and of the intimate revelatory action. Her story has many gleaming moments; I think she is at her best in writing of young love and of adolescence; I think she gauges her women more acutely than her men; and I am not myself too much put off by the constant change of perspective which her method necessitates. Yet sometimes it is a wrench to pull oneself out of a scene which is just beginning to reach its depth and to reopen one's mind to a different and less compelling situation. This is not a book to be read at a canter; it must be taken up and put down and started afresh; and it would have been kinder for the reader had a cast of characters been supplied.

Edward Weeks. *The Atlantic Monthly.* July 1960, p. 96

The historian Frederick Jackson Turner once said that the American frontier was not a place but rather a spirit—"of determination, of endurance, of independence, of individualism, of optimism." Jessamyn West's works embody this spirit. In *The State of Stony Lonesome,* as in her other books, readers find characters they would be proud to call friends: Ginerva Chalmers, a vibrant—yet proper—teen-ager; her uncle Zen, whom she secretly loves; her delicate, obstinate mother, Birdeen; even Sarah Loomis, the "blowsy" mistress of the local post office—and of uncle Zen. They inhabit a lush, moral Valencia, California, and their meetings, partings, sentiments and conflicts are as revealing of place and time as fiction has a right to be. The structure is plain. On the eve of Ginerva's marriage to a young, suitable man, Zen invites her to "walk the memory" of their relationship. They do so in a series of simple, evocative flashbacks. The themes of an unspoken attraction, a girl's coming of age, California life in the early 1920s, will be familiar to Miss West's fans, as will the economy of voice, rectitude of detail and stylistic grace with which they are, for the most part, handled. Although Zen and Ginerva recall characters from *Cress Delahanty,* both seem as fresh and juicy as the local Yorba Linda oranges. Yet the framing story is curiously out of focus. When the "Come, walk memory" tone appears at the beginning and end, the narrative stutters, the beautifully rendered landscape withers and the reader longs for the straightforward action of Zane Grey. With this one prominent exception, *The State of Stony Lonesome* is quietly effective, even though, compared with Miss West's nineteen earlier frontier books, it is a relatively minor outpost.

Jacqueline Austin. *The New York Times.*
January 6, 1985, p. 20

From *Friendly Persuasion* onward West seemed intent on proving the critics wrong, proving that she could go beyond the bounds of Quaker experience, be more than a one-book writer, and be *un*ladylike whenever she pleased. As her husband wrote to me in his notes circa April 4, 1991, "J. often [after completing such a book] said something along this line: '*That* will stop them thinking of me as *just* a Quaker writer!' This seemed to bother her more than most critics' comments." A reader who has read nothing further of West's than the Jess Birdwell and Cress Delahanty stories might make the mistake of believing that she never dealt with the dark aspects of life. But all one has to do is read *Witch Diggers, South of the Angels, The Life I Really Lived,* and *Massacre at Fall Creek* to see the other side of the coin. Comparatively speaking, nevertheless, hers was usually a quiet voice heard amid the hubbub of the multitude. Probably owing to her Quaker background, West had a disconcerting habit of avoiding violent confrontations, for the most part ignoring popular trends, writing to please herself rather than the passing whims of the reading public, while all the time following the precedent of her beloved Thoreau in marching to a different drummer.

Alfred S. Shivers. *Jessamyn West* (Boston:
Twayne, rev. 1992), pp. 139–40

WEST, REBECCA (CICILY ISABEL FAIRFIELD) (GREAT BRITAIN) 1892–1983

The conjunction of Miss West and Henry James is a curious one; for Miss West has precisely the kind of acute, modern, probing, flippant, traditionless, open mind that seems so alien to the mind of Mr. James. Miss West, I imagine, abhors reticence, while Mr. James, I also imagine, detested revelation. The oddity of this conjunction of very dissimilar minds is extraordinarily apparent in Miss West's book [*Henry James*]; for she has remarkable difficulty in concealing her dislike of most of her author's writing, and is only able to allay the reader's suspicion of her attitude towards him by periodically be-praising him with a generosity that is entirely beyond his merits. . . . All these sentences lifted casually here and there from Miss West's book do denote that on the whole Miss West thinks that Mr. James was a tedious old gentleman even when he was a youth; and it was probably her sense of this irritation with him that induced her to such generosity as her final sentence: "He died, leaving the white light of his genius to shine out for the eternal comfort of the mind of man." It is as if she wished the reader to forget that she had been praising Mr. James with faint damns, and had tried to accomplish this purpose by damning him with loud praise.

St. John Ervine. The Bookman (London).
September, 1916, p. 169

Miss West's long-expected novel [*The Judge*] impresses one first as being beautifully written. That of itself would not take one far, but the rich and humorous imagery, the signal vitality of her style, are used to construct a most sympathetic portrait of a young Scotch girl. . . . All the elements of a great novel are here, if they are not quite satisfactorily combined. To applaud the sympathy and intelligence of the author I can find no sufficient words. But when she is content to try to do either test at once, or is able to compose more cleverly, she will, I think, so deeply impress the delighted reader that *The Judge* will be dismissed as immature.

H. C. Harwood. The Outlook.
July 1, 1922, p. 14

Her literary reputation has till now been resting upon a high-spirited little book on Henry James, the best psychoanalytical novel yet published, and the best regular reviews now appearing of current fiction. Admirers of her *Return of the Soldier,* and her critical articles in the English *New Statesman* are at last given the work which they have so long been promised, a long and important novel entitled *The Judge*.

Before the reader has finished three pages of it, he will settle himself more comfortably in his chair, and surrender himself to the powerful and lamentably rare pleasure of reading a writer who can write. Miss West does not use the *staccato* style *As Now Worn by Leading Literary Ladies;* her writing is rich, closely packed, highly colored, and individual. It seems impossible for her to be careless, to take the easy, faded word, or to fall short of precision. Her imagination is primarily visual, and her landscapes stand out with mineral hardness and brilliance. Her style reflects her subjects like a metal mirror varying with their colors, but burnishing them all to an ardent, almost truculent, loveliness.

Raymond Mortimer. *The Dial.* October,
1922, p. 441

It must be obvious to anyone who reads the work of Miss West that in her is to be found what I may call a germ of grim brilliancy. She is brilliantly conversant with the more serious side of life. Miss West writes as if she was rather angry with humanity, as if she viewed the mass of people amongst whom she moves and has her being with a slightly malicious smile. Perhaps at present, and I say this advisedly (for Miss West is comparatively young), she cannot see the sun because the clouds obscure it, yet she would do well to remember that though not seen the sun is still there. Miss West has of course had a remarkable success in a comparatively short literary career and in every way she deserves it, for if Miss West is as yet somewhat uncertain of her own feet and much more certain of the feet of other people, she has every chance of a most distinguished career in the world of letters. But Miss West would do very well to beware of the newspapers. Lately she has written many superficial articles, in which she attacks men, in an extremely cheap kind of way. Miss West is too good an artist, she has too brilliant gifts, she has too great powers of really fine writing, to develop into a kind of woman, to whom the Editors of the cheaper press write, when they wish to secure an article that is merely written to cause correspondence.

Patrick Braybrooke. *Novelists: We Are
Seven* (n.p.: C. W. Daniel, 1926), p. 141

Miss Rebecca West's rather vaporish little expedition into the realms of fantasy, *Harriet Hume,* has made me regret the ponderous but respectable feminism of her earlier novels.

Life and Letters. November, 1929, p. 482

Miss Rebecca West's *The Thinking Reed* is a big book, both in bulk and in subject; there is a good deal more matter than the afflictions of wealth here. Her writing covers a really immense field with an air of athletic ease: intellectual writing, in the exact sense, but at the same time flexible, vivid and never cold. *The Thinking Reed* seems to me to be a classic novel, such as is not often written today: imagination (or vision) and sheer top-form professional ability now seldom go together; it is hard to find a mean between satire and good faith. The settings have depth, they are not only painted; they are not abstract, or there to illustrate moods. . . . The book as a book appears to

me to have almost no imperfections; it rounds itself off, it is impossible to
think beyond it.

Elizabeth Bowen. *New Statesman and*
Nation. April 11, 1936, p. 571

Miss West's book [*The Meaning of Treason*] is rich in argument and impression and one elaborates the other. She is satirical but on the side of authority,
scornful, at times even snobbish about her victims, sizing them up with the
drastic wit of an undeceived hostess and yet unexpectedly, surprisingly fair,
and even compassionate. No doubt there is a touch of strain and rhetoric in
her moralizings. We are not always sure when we hear the words of common
sense that the voice is free of the tremor of the extremist. Like many brilliant
writers, she has a mind that is too incessantly being made up; it is like
listening to doors slamming one after the other through a house. If I could
have been an American rebel or a Sinn Feiner, I would have been puzzled
to know what her advice to me would have been. But there is no doubt of
the people she portrays with such alarming moral verve—the mad, the simple, the frightened, the liars, the shameless, the eccentrics, the conceited,
caught in a world that was shabbier and more exacting than they suspected.

V. S. Pritchett. *New Statesman and Nation.*
September 24, 1949, p. 332

The Meaning of Treason is the title: but I am not sure what is the meaning
of the title. I can only suppose that Miss West thinks that she has provided
a psychological explanation of treason in her occasional analyses of the characters and minds of various traitors of the last war. For myself, I cannot
derive any coherent "reason for treason" from her pages, for all the various
Freudian diagnoses of compensation, mother-complex and what not.

Sir John Squire. *The Illustrated London*
News. October 1, 1949, p. 490

This is the fundamental dilemma which is hidden in all Rebecca West's writings, the problem of God dying in the cookery class. Her most complete
statement is in the terrifying and marvelous essay called *Letters to a Grandfather.* Few people seem to know of this work. It has probably alienated the
religious by its extraordinary symbolism, a transcendent God appearing as a
tired Negro in a worn scarlet dress suit, and the Holy Ghost as the light
reflected from the whites of his eyes. The irreligious probably realized that
this was a deeply religious work and rejected it. It is however exceedingly
important. . . . The final vision of the *Letter to a Grandfather* is in fact stated
to be essentially the same thing as the Crucifixion, and the crucified Christ
acquires splendor by being an explorer, stretched out in space trying from
one point to embrace and understand all, and therefore the supremely worthy

object of the devotion of the lady hung on the opposite wall.

G. E. Hutchinson. *The Itinerant Ivory Tower*
(Oxford: Oxford University Press, 1953), p. 253

Actually, rather more fatiguing than Miss West's occasional overabundance in *A Train of Powder* is the endemic ascendancy of her intellection over her feeling. Although there is evidence that Miss West would herself be the first to announce that no cause is searched out and no justice allotted by the mind alone, operating without the support of natural emotion, throughout her essays emotion shows itself as the selfconsciousness of education rather than as the free impulse of the heart.

Miss West's pictures of Mrs. Hume, of the parents of Marshall, of the families of the Greenville lynchers are all portraits which, although shrewd, lack the kind of truth which is finally supplied only by simple warmth and compassion—the wall of her superior powers would seem to rise between Miss West and these suffering human beings. Of course, if tenderness were also within her gift, it might incapacitate Miss West as a reporter. It is quite possible she must do without this one more talent in order to make such full use of her superb intellectual gifts.

Diana Trilling. *The New York Times.*
March 20, 1955, p. 3

Miss Rebecca West dwells, and has dwelt for many years on the summits. Intellectually and morally, in temperament and outlook as much as in practical achievement, she towers above contemporary practitioners in popular journalism. She is one of the few really great reporters of our time. Her latest book [*A Train of Powder*] is a collection of a few of her essays in reporting over the past troubled decade—studies in crime, ranging from the greatest of the Nuremberg trials, through a lynching in South Carolina, the case of the hapless Mr. Setty (the Warren Street motor trader, bits of whom were cast up on an Essex marsh), and the even more hapless youth, William Martin Marshall, the Foreign Office radio operator who gave information to an official in the Soviet Embassy. The unity of the book—and it is a remarkable unity in spite of the wide diversity of experience recorded—is supplied by Miss West's maintenance and exposition of the feminine principle.

John Connell. *Time and Tide.* June 4, 1955,
p. 740

If Jonathan Edwards were living in our time, and if he were a gifted literary critic, he might well have written this volume of Rebecca West's. . . . [T]he chapters of *The Court and the Castle* indicate to us what a very "high" Calvinist Miss West has become—a supralapsarian even, one suspects, of a more rigorous sort than John Calvin himself. She is studying here a series of writers, mostly but not entirely English—beginning with Shakespeare and including Proust, Henry James, Kipling, Trollope, Kafka—from the point of view of their acceptance or rejection of two Calvinist dogmas, that of total depravity and that of predestination or absolute decrees. . . .

This is a great theme, and since the issues of corruption versus innocence and of predestination (or determinism) versus free will are as profound as any with which great writers deal, Miss West's concentration on the theme makes it possible for her to get well under the surface of most of the works she deals with. In general, she is guiltless of the vice of distorting a writer's picture of things for the sake of demonstrating a thesis triumphantly, and in general, too, she is quite free from the small vice of undervaluing a writer because he is guilty of some theological or social heresy. Of some of her terribly mistaken Pelagians, such as Fielding and Emily Brontë, she writes with the liveliest appreciation.

Newton Arvin. *The New York Times.*
November 3, 1957, p. 28

Wondering, as we all wonder, "whether the universe is good or bad," Miss West has attentively read the great writers of Western Europe—not going to them for easy formulations, for "answers," but accepting them as companions in the search. As a result, her criticism of their work [in *The Court and the Castle*], though it is subordinated to a purpose, is not unbalanced; there is no trace of the squashing, distorting and lopping common among critics who write to a thesis. . . .

In reviewing this book, the temptation is to quote and quote again. It is so full of passages which are too striking to be hurried over, too beautifully expressed for paraphrase to be possible. What I have written is not a review in any critical sense, for the book is too profound and densely packed for me to be able to assess it until I have had time to live with it, to keep it beside me as a companion to my reading, as one keeps *The Sacred Wood* or *Countries of the Mind* or *The Wound and the Bow.* Meanwhile, I hope I have at least conveyed my sense of the book's importance and my feeling of obligation to its author.

John Wain. *The London Magazine.*
December, 1958, pp. 62–63, 65

[*The Birds Fall Down* is] a fascinating story, so contracted in time and focus as to resemble a thriller rather than a conventional novel, but a thriller infinitely superior in style and imaginative power to most of the breed. Miss West suggests in a foreword that the incidents recounted are more than symbolically true. Her allusions are appropriately sibylline, but they hint at real persons and real events. In any case, she proposes that the collapse of the liberal-idealist-terrorist groups, discredited by instances of police spying like that depicted in the story, opened the door to the professional revolutionaries like Lenin—presumably less romantic and less ambiguously "Russian" in their goals and methods.

As historiography, the hypothesis seems at least incomplete; the shape assumed by the Russian Revolution of 1917 cannot be explained on grounds of individual psychology alone. But Miss West's historical thesis is explicitly presented only in her brief foreword. In the novel itself, her psychological notations are perfectly convincing, the divided mind of the traitor—presented by indirection, but no less forcefully for that—provokes an answering anguish in the reader. It will be remembered that Miss West has examined the question of treachery on another occasion. I found *The New Meaning of Treason* objectionable for its cavalierly offered insights into the minds of convicted traitors. It seemed to me faintly indecent to clap a gloss upon the work of criminal tribunals, psychologizing the man in the dock with as much familiarity as if we had made him, when in fact we could only unmake him. But *The Birds Fall Down* is Miss West's own excellent invention, its characters are her creatures, and she may analyze and exhibit them as she pleases. That she has done and most happily.

Emile Capouya. *Book Week.*
October 2, 1966, p. 2

Rebecca West's literary career is outstanding both in scope and durability. She began writing reviews at age nineteen for *Freewoman;* the following year (1912) she joined *Clarion* as a political writer and has continued to write for British and American periodicals. Setting aside her hundred-odd early magazine pieces, the interval between her first and most recent book spans fifty years. Her output during this busy career is richly varied: political journalism, literary criticism, biography, history, travel sketches and fiction.

If this vast and varied output holds together, the unifying core must be the Augustinian doctrine of original sin. An effect, argued Augustine, cannot be greater than its cause. If we are nothing ourselves—not good or bad, but nothing—none of our strivings can have any reality. Although she has written an interpretive biography of St. Augustine (1933), she has never exorcised him. Her books continue to insist that there is more evil than good in our world and that the evil is more vivid. Man's depravity energizes the two myths symbolically designated in the title, *Black Lamb and Grey Falcon* (1941). It undergirds Rebecca West's distrust of the worldliness usually equated with the male principle. It saturates her reading of Shakespeare: the palace intrigues in the histories and tragedies show what happens when the will acts in a milieu where the will counts as nothing; *The Court and the Castle* (1953) claims that Calvin, who insures the salvation of a few, sparkles and glints sunshine next to Shakespeare, who damns all. Rebecca West's own characters seem determined by what they *are,* not by what they do. Their choices do not create new opportunities. Alice Pemberton, of "The Salt of the Earth" (1934), does evil things in order to punish herself for a nonspecifiable crime. This self-destructiveness, all the stronger for its involuntary nature, recurs in Rebecca West's criticism.

Peter Wolfe. *Rebecca West: Artist and
Thinker* (Carbondale: Southern Illinois
University Press, 1971), pp. 1–2

Rebecca West might be called a literary Paganini. She has written and published many words, most of them words of wisdom and wit, in almost every prose medium—journalism, history, literary criticism, short stories, novels. She is probably most famous as an interpreter of contemporary history, and *A Train of Powder* and *The New Meaning of Treason* justify this fame. Yet many consider her genius to lie essentially in literary criticism, and *The Strange Necessity, The Court and the Castle* bear this out. But what engages us here are the six serious novels, published over a period of almost fifty years from *The Return of the Soldier* in 1918 to *The Birds Fall Down* in 1966, novels which display an incredible eclecticism in style, structure, content, subject matter and technique.

What unifies her work is its brilliance of style and the wholeness and coherence of her world view. Whatever Miss West writes is distinguished by the tough elegance of her prose, by sentences as soundly conceived and executed as those of any living stylist. . . . The business of the artist, Miss West says in both *The Strange Necessity* and *The Court and the Castle,* is to analyze his experience and construct from his examination a synthesis for his readers which will clarify and focus, often correcting, their view of the universe. Miss West observes experience with an innocent and unclouded eye, accurate and farseeing. She constructs her syntheses out of a full understanding of what the eye has seen, coupled with a deep understanding of the culture and the literary tradition within which she works. And she contrives to perfect the form of the synthesis with grace and concentration.

These qualities account for much, but they do not explain her virtuosity. Nor is her rich eclecticism to be confused with experimentation. The six novels, in their startling and wide-ranging differences, give no evidence that the author has tried first one medium and then another, searching for the one which best suits her. On the contrary, she has been able to choose, out of limitless resources, whatever style and type of novel her analysis demands for its synthesis. To speculate *why* she has never needed to repeat herself is both impossible and absurd with so articulate an artist, who would share her motivations if she wished to.

Turner S. Kobler. *Critique.* 13:2, 1971,
pp. 30–31

Rebecca West's greatest period of creativity began with *Black Lamb and Grey Falcon,* and one can see now how the books that follow depend on it and derive from it. The two books of trials, *The Meaning of Treason* (1949) and *A Train of Powder* (1955), relate to *Black Lamb* in two ways: they extend Dame Rebecca's "world" into the realm of law, and they complete her meditation on the meaning of modern history. Law must obviously be a crucial concept to one who sees the world divided between civilization and barbarism, for law is the wall that men build against disorder. Treason is a willful breaching of that wall, and fascism is a denial that a wall can exist, and so of course Dame Rebecca would be fascinated by the case of Lord Haw-

Haw, and the judgment at Nuremberg, and would see those trials as political tragedies. Her accounts of the trials are, in a sense, journalism, but they are journalism raised to a high level of art and thought, with the richness of understanding that makes *Black Lamb* a great book. Character and setting are created with extraordinary vividness, action and dialogue are as convincing as in a novel. Yet they are scrupulously factual, and because they are factual (as *Black Lamb* also is), they perform an important moral function.

Dame Rebecca writes: it is the presentation of the facts that matters. . . . The face of the age in these cases is the face of a traitor, a Nazi, a murderer, a lynch-mob. But one must confront that face for the sake of reality, and once more it is art that comes to our aid. Dame Rebecca's art takes us beyond the facts, to the questions they raise: what in men leads them to betray their fellows? What are the foundations of stability and chaos in human societies? What defenses can men build against the strain of evil in themselves? These are moral questions, and those three "factual" books—*Black Lamb* and the two books of trials—are moral books; but they are also artful and imaginative. Here Dame Rebecca has found her true form, in which art and fact meet, and keep faith with reality.

Samuel Hynes. Introduction to *Rebecca West: A Celebration* (New York: Viking Press, 1977), pp. xv–xvi

The celebration in *Rebecca West: A Celebration* belongs as much to the reader as to the author. Here are her writings that you set aside to read; her major works that deserve to be reread; and the surprises of watching criticism and reportage mellow before your eyes into philosophy and permanence. The sum is a literary and political history of a large part of this century.

To say that Rebecca West is "an extremely clever young woman who can handle a pen as brilliantly as ever I could and much more savagely," as George Bernard Shaw wrote in 1916, is almost to take something away from her staying powers, in 1977. The cleverness is still there, to be sure; it often breaks out in letters to the literary sections of the London weeklies—put-downs of women she regards as too clever by half in their novels or criticism. Always with, if not far ahead of her times, she and her work have shunned trendiness—the blight of modern writing, in newspapers, magazines and even books. . . .

A good hallmark of the thoroughness of *Rebecca West: A Celebration*, which her publisher has selected from her writings with her help, is that it includes the opening section of her unpublished *This Real Night.* Her ability to establish a time and do so in a universal idea has not diminished. . . . The unfinished novel is a sequel to *The Fountain Overflows,* published twenty years ago, which is not included in this collection. But there is a fair amount of fiction here: *The Return of the Soldier,* a World War I novel written from a woman's perspective; *The Salt of the Earth,* a short American murder novel; and self-contained sections of *The Thinking Reed* and her last novel,

The Birds Fall Down, published in 1966. The fiction leaves the reader resolved to turn to the fuller works. A useful bibliography shows that West has written fiction steadily across her career: *This Real Night* will be her twelfth novel. . . .

The collection also includes the keenest explanation of the Italian travel books of D. H. Lawrence. West observed him in Florence, tapping out an article a moment after his arrival. "I was naive," she writes, believing that he had not done his homework. "I know now that he was writing about the state of his own soul." She describes how he rendered the city and people in symbolic terms, rifling the visible for his own vocabulary. Only a fellow-artist could recognize the longer reach of such inner travel. . . .

Rebecca West took her name early in the century from the rebellious Ibsen heroine in *Rosmersholm* who had modern ideas, replacing her real name, Cicily Fairfield, which sounded too genteel. Her own identity by any name shines through the pages of this celebration.

Herbert Mitgang. *The New Republic.* June
18, 1977, pp. 28–30

Rebecca West has accomplished the difficult, and I should have thought the impossible: She has sent me back to the *Confessions* of St. Augustine, back, as it were, to that wretched pear tree, looking for the partridge I never found in my youth. Dame Rebecca is now eighty-five years old; her short book, *St. Augustine,* was published in 1933, long before it occurred to anybody to hoke up a new category of letters called "psychobiography." As usual, she was ahead of her times. *St. Augustine* is psychobiography with style. It suggests that when Augustine abandoned his mistress for the monastery, the West lost a great imaginative writer and gained a lot of unnecessary guilt about sexual and other matters.

Dame Rebecca can also be said—in her accounts of the Nuremberg and Lord Haw Haw trials, in her stunning crime reportage and in her shrewd literary criticism—to have anticipated Mary McCarthy and Hannah Arendt and Truman Capote and (sigh) the New Journalism. Her masterpiece of history and travel, *Black Lamb and Grey Falcon* (1941), surpassed anything done in the same vein by her beloved D. H. Lawrence. She ought, leaving aside the lapse of those years as the chattel of H. G. Wells, to be considered a heroine of the modern feminist movement: After all, she created herself, taking her name from Ibsen, and refused to be marooned inside a fine, domestic sensibility. Art, politics, history and religion are her realms. She has also written seven novels. . . .

Of [her] work in progress, *This Real Night,* the most that can be said is that Dame Rebecca still writes English prose better than almost anybody else. This prose, whether lyrical with a spine, or savage with a wink, or so wise in its cadence that the emotions prance, is in the service of an affirming humanism, a tough desire. Art, she insists, does not tell us what we know, but much more than we could ever imagine. "This strange necessity," in its triumphant moments—King Lear, Beethoven's Quartet in C sharp minor, Michelangelo's waking woman on the Medici tomb, Molly Bloom's soliloquy, Ingres—"is part of a system; it refers to one of the rhythms of which we are the syntheses." Art denies death, and thus makes possible "a distinguished humanity."

And so she is fascinated by the anti-artists, by killers, traitors, Fascists. . . . And by nations that "go soft like so many sleepy pears." These rhythms, also and alas, are part of the synthesis.

John Leonard. *The New York Times.*
September 26, 1977, p. 33

1900 is a skillful blend of documentary history, illustrations, and personal reminiscence. It contains a month-by-month calendar of events, and a good deal of further factual information listed under subject headings such as "Literature and Thought," "Music," "Architecture and Design," "Science, Technology and Medicine." Emphasis is placed on Europe rather than simply Britain with France receiving as much attention as England, and America shuffling restlessly on the sidelines.

Facts come first, as a kind of sustained preface or list of contents. They provide a frame and a constant point of reference for the text that follows. Presented in this way, they also free Rebecca West to write as both historian and participant. She is able to evoke the turn of the century as it appeared to the eight-year-old girl, and, at the same time, draw on the many and varied experiences of a committed lifetime that spans the century then about to be born. The result is an attractive, personal interpretation that offers a reliable view of the past without becoming trapped in the cold distancing of objective history.

The strong personal element comes only partly from the reminiscences: it owes just as much to Dame Rebecca's historical approach, which is almost entirely through personalities. The Conference on Labour Representation held on February 27 can be described as "the most important event in 1900," but the issues underlying this moment when the British Labour Party was formed are treated with nothing like the relish that appears later in the portrait of Beatrice Webb: "She had ability, though it was a pity that she had devoted it to the cause of lifting the poor out of poverty, for, as her diaries show, she disliked the poor, largely because they were so often stupid."

It is not that ideas, issues, and events are ignored. They are here all right, but presented always as inseparable from the people who formulated or enacted them. Even when she is writing of the Boer War, with tactics outlined and national characteristics compared, it is the personalities involved who leap most forcefully into life—Kruger, Chamberlain, Rhodes, and most notably Milner who is treated so unsympathetically that he could well be seen as the villain of *1900;* if, that is, someone apparently so incapable, unimaginative and boring could possibly summon up enough energy to be villainous.

Dame Rebecca's selection of French men and women to represent the turn of the century is particularly interesting because her affection is fully engaged with what she describes as "the wholeness of French experience," an ability to assimilate diverse experiences without feeling them as threatening or destructive. Proust is seen as typifying this quality at its finest, while Colette is invoked as a more ambiguous case. . . .

There are, inevitably, gaps in *1900*. There is little about sport, not enough on the music hall, not much about working conditions. We are asked to take some sweeping generalizations as self-evident truths ("Men and women do not really like each other very much"), and a few judgments that demand contradiction. It does not seem sensible to describe Thomas Hardy as "the most chaste of writers," and whatever the quality of Zola's fiction in 1900, he hardly deserves to be dismissed as "not a very good novelist." But such errors of judgment are only to be expected if one put one's faith in people, and that is what Rebecca West has unashamedly done in this very good book.

Peter Keating. (London) *Times Literary Supplement*. March 5, 1982, p. 247

All her life Rebecca West has written in praise of virtue and condemning wickedness. She finds moral relativism ridiculous, and says so in essays and her fiction. She was a propagandist of genius. Of the thousands of articles produced for and against the feminist movement in the first two decades of the century, Rebecca West's are among the finest. . . .

Covering a wide variety of subjects from suffrage, national politics and trade unionism to domesticity, sex-antagonism and crime, and including many reviews of books and plays, she wrote then as a convinced socialist (notwithstanding her critical feelings about the emergent Labour Party) and a dedicated feminist, and consequently provoked a storm of correspondence. . . .

Rebecca West's articles in *The Freewoman* and *The New Freewoman* were serious and unsettling, no less for radicals than the rest of the population. She was a first-rate critic, whether reviewing books, criticizing anti-suffragist philosophy, assaulting confused socialist thinking (albeit from the position of a socialist), or defending the cause of women. . . .

Her articles were daring, and often joyously so—a counter to all those who felt then, as too often now, that feminism represents something gloomy and sour. They are good examples of a level of anarchist feminism in literary criticism. They demonstrated again and again her wide reading, her original and extraordinarily good judgment, her wit, and her astonishing grasp of the complexities of political and emotional life. When she was provocative, it was always to a purpose. She had a remarkable capacity to reach the core of the issue.

Jane Marcus. Introduction to Rebecca West. *The Young Rebecca: Writings of Rebecca West 1911–17* (London: Virago/Bloomington: Indiana University Press, 1982), pp. ix, 8, 10

According to Jane Marcus, who has edited this imposing collection of reviews and essays [*The Young Rebecca: Writings of Rebecca West 1911–1917*], "the young Rebecca West stood for revolution, free love, equal pay, the working class, votes for women and the most advanced ideas in literature." A formidable list, you might say, denoting unusual vigor and progressivenesss; to uphold such ideologies in 1912 or thereabouts was tantamount to proclaiming oneself an advocate of upheaval—not the easiest course to follow, socially or otherwise. But Rebecca West was nothing if not wholehearted in her views.

The *New Freewoman* and the *Clarion,* which published her earliest writings, are well named to indicate the line Rebecca West was taking at the time. She is often on the offensive, lashing out at cant and injustice, repudiating facile habits of thought, castigating the faint-hearted and the misinformed, pouncing on instances of silliness wherever she finds them. At twenty or so, she is struck forcibly by the flaws in society's arrangements. Piety bores her, anti-feminism appalls her, drudgery gets her down. As a literary critic she is sharp and sardonic. From the start, she adopted an entertaining manner to deal with inferior novels. "The immense significance of this work lies in its binding," is as pertinent a comment as any on Hall Caine's *The Woman Thou Gavest Me.* Mrs. Humphry Ward too comes in for an appropriate measure of detraction: "For an example of her complete lack of sense, let us turn to *Daphne.*" In this piece Rebecca West makes sure that no thinking reader will ever turn to *Daphne* in anything other than a spirit of mockery. . . .

For those who confuse feminism with motherliness, or soulfulness, or womanliness . . . Rebecca West has . . . no time at all. This collection often surprises us with its perceptiveness on subjects that still cause agitation today; and it shows the author at her most agreeably contentious—resolute, energetic, and frivolous even while she is being doctrinaire.

Patricia Craig. The New Statesman.
May 28, 1982, p. 26

What Rebecca West was, and to my mind this excuses all personal error and all bad behavior, was an extraordinary, marvelous—albeit rather ill-disciplined—writer of fiction; a woman born to her literary vocation, in love with the human race as she could not be with individuals, unerring in her fictional vision; a novelist of wonderful animation, courage and compassion, and with an ability to see the world through the eyes of even those whom she most disliked. (The person may dislike many, but the person as writer can afford to dislike none.) But most of all because, flickering in and out of the black and white printed pages, as if richly colored gems were hidden there, offered casually as gifts to her reader, there for the treasuring, are a wealth of somehow thrown-away observations, brilliant little glimmers of insight, exquisite, which make the hairs at the back of the literate neck rise. . . .

I am prepared to forgive anyone anything if they can write like this, and she can, and quite often, not always, does. May I recommend three books of hers to you, if you are not already acquainted with her writing? *The Return of the Soldier* (1918), *The Judge* (1922) and, to my mind, the greatest and the best, *The Fountain Overflows* (1956).

They do not, unlike most novels written today, make easy reading. The last two are, to modern tastes, wandering, idiosyncratic, willful and unlikely, and the first is stuffed with sentiments not acceptable to modern liberal thinking. Rebecca West's distaste for poverty shines through *The Return of the Soldier* and her dislike and fear of the servant classes through *The Judge;* only in *The Fountain Overflows,* written in her maturity, does she appear truly rich and kind, and to have finally forgiven herself (and everyone else), for which the reader can only be grateful.

Fay Weldon. *Rebecca West* (New York:
Viking Press, 1985), pp. 14–15

Rebecca West wrote her way into the major cultural dilemmas of the twentieth century: suffrage, socialism, women's employment, sexual liberation, war, treason, and communism. She grappled constantly with the laws of patriarchy, and was obsessed with dualism. Deconstructionist and feminist critics have come to regard the binary principle as fundamental to Western thought, lending importance to West's engagement with this structure.

West has been appreciated and anthologized by materialist feminists for her early, outspoken, even pugnacious liberal feminism, but she has not been considered sufficiently within the context of modernism. . . .

Compared to other modernist women writers like Gertrude Stein, H. D., and Virginia Woolf, who are also being rewritten into modernism, West was more deeply drawn into heterosexual relations. She also exhibits what might be considered a masculine tone in writing. West had all the independence, motivation, and intelligence of the fin de siècle new woman, combined with a sexuality that challenged and attracted Edwardian men. West exhausted much of her energy and creativity over attachments to men, repeatedly reentering the binary of the heterosexual couple. . . .

West "re-figured" binary reasoning in two modernist works, *The Judge* and *Harriet Hume*. As with St. Augustine, she consistently saw gender as a factor. Her refiguring embraces several activities: a "figuring out" or philosophical reconsideration, the use of "figures" of speech, particularly metaphors of nature and culture, and the cultivation of strong and beautiful female figures, whose powers of observation and wisdom are a blend of practical, individual female experience and collective myth. An overarching figure is the generative cycle, which offers a complex binary involving time and gender. The constructive cycle is gendered feminine; the disruptive/violent incident is typically masculine, and it necessitates reconstructive female effort to initiate the cycle anew and to reach for an alternate form. . . .

Amid the seemingly inexorable cycles of life, West's central females experience moments of passionate connection to nature and the past, and visions of survival. They become celebrants and conservators of love, art, and natural beauty. With careful moves, they attempt to defuse evil and deny it figuration in the politics of men.

Bonnie Kime Scott. *Twentieth Century*
Literature. 37, 1991, pp. 169–70, 172–73, 186

West's interests in the Woman Question could not be contained within these parameters, and an examination of the genealogy of her fervent early rhetoric shows that her prime commitment was to a Romantic vitalist philosophy. The broader scope of her early sense of the Woman Question is best indicated by her support for the *Freewoman* and the *New Freewoman,* largely anarchist journals which "mentioned sex loudly and clearly and repeatedly and in the worst possible taste." West remained committed to a "scientific humanism," but she moved beyond Fabian political and economic theory to engage with sexology and psychoanalysis in an effort to understand sexuality and gendered difference. . . .

In West's elaboration in *The Judge* of the manner in which many layers of fantasy collapsed the vitalist ideal of romance, she tried to formulate the relationship between patriarchal fantasies and social and economic ideologies and realities. During the late 1910s and the 1920s West came to the view that an economic interpretation of women's oppression was inadequate; she began to articulate fictional and discursive arguments that masculine psychosexual neuroticism was manifested in patriarchal repression of women and that the primal scenes of fantasies, men's and women's, were culturally informed. She daringly neuroticized capitalist class relations.

West's account of female nature and vital passivity was to be elaborated in more essentialist ways during the 1920s. She argued in 1925 that women are more psychologically stable because their historically continuous primary nurturing roles as wives and mothers ensure that their present selves are not at war with their primitive selves and that "in the modern world most men have for their destiny mechanical and machine-like work which does not call for courage or initiative; therefore man's present-day self is always at war with his primitive self and is apt to be unstable and hysterical." This argument was to be one of the themes of the unfinished novel *Sunflower.* The gist of her argument seemed to be that neurotic modern men, overwrought by anxieties about their masculinity, should abdicate political power to more psychologically stable nurturing women whose greater closeness to nature mitigated against damaging sexual anxieties. West was certainly challenging the traditional relegation of women to a private sphere, but in terms which only reinforced antifeminist essentialist categories of gender difference. She even suggested, albeit in a superficially feminist joke, that the man who lacks the confidence of his primitive maleness—"courage and initiative"—has lost his charm. In *Harriet Hume* (1929) West married her Romantic vitalism to Jungian ideas of anima and animus; in 1931 she collapsed female vitality back into a stabilizing maternal instinct and the capacity to give "birth" to art which celebrates harmony, both being vigilant celebrations of the will to live. Men, she stated, are psychologically predisposed on biological grounds to violence and confirmation of the will to die.

Sue Thomas. Genders. 13, 1992, pp. 91, 103

WHARTON, EDITH (UNITED STATES) 1862–1937

I take to her (Mrs. Wharton) very kindly as regards her diabolical little clevernesses, the quality of intention and intelligence in her style, and her sharp eye for an interesting *kind* of subject. . . . She *must* be tethered in native pastures, even if it reduces her to a back-yard in New York.

Henry James. In Percy Lubbock, ed.
Letters, vol. 1 (New York: Scribners,
1920), p. 396

One of Mrs. Wharton's greatest distinctions is that she is not sentimental; when she succeeds in awakening an emotion in the reader, it is a legitimate one; and she accomplishes it by her art, not through parade of her own feelings. . . . She is detached from her plot. She can stand over and away from her structure and let the story tell itself, absorbing all our attention with a few light touches, and giving finality to all of them. The tenseness of her style and the manner in which she combines eagerness with discipline, poise, and perfection of phrase with lack of mannerism, are the tangible bases of her talent. She plots her stories, sees in her mind's eye the persons who participate in them, how they look, dress, and act, what their background is. She seeks to tell the truth about them, impartially and unemotionally.

Joseph Collins. Taking the Literary Pulse
(New York: Doran, 1924), pp. 54–55

Mrs. Wharton . . . has been far too much the professional novelist to sustain the qualities which first and very justly brought her fame. These were . . . an unflagging distinction of manner and a very high and very penetrating wit. Nor was this all. Her people were very much alive and several of her earlier books at least have that virtue so immensely rare in our letters: architectonic beauty, beauty of inner structure. Yet her work is fading and crumbling and will probably be almost forgotten until a time so detached from the present arises that people can go back to a little of it as to something quaint and sweet and lavendered, wondering that at so late an age a woman as intelligent as Edith Wharton could have taken seriously the conventions of a small and unimportant social group, could have in ultimate judgment identified herself with these futile and fugitive notions and confronted the moral world with the standards of a silly and cruel game.

Ludwig Lewisohn. Expression in America
(New York: Harper, 1932), p. 466

Nothing was ever more unmistakable in Edith than the quality of the foundations of her culture. She was never delayed in trifling with the easy, the showy, the quickly and cheaply rewarding; she went straight for the best, and no time lost; and she set up her standards once for all, to serve her lifetime. She seemed to be excused the long labor of trying the wrong turnings, following the wrong leads, discarding misfits, such as most of us have to worry through with patience; and this was fortunate, for she had no patience at all or any time for second thoughts and anxious renewals, only an eagerness, never exhausted, for further exploration and acquisition. . . . She was all that was right and regular in her smooth clan-plumage, but the young hawk looked out of her eyes. . . . She actually grasped what she was about, this one, as she settled down to her work and stuck to it; and on fire as she was with her ambition, her head was cool, she knew her place, and her pride in it was as sound as her modesty. The sagest and sternest of the craftsmen must admit that she meets them on their ground.

> Percy Lubbock. *Portrait of Edith Wharton*
> (New York: Appleton-Century, 1947),
> pp. 13, 244

It is interesting to see how Henry James's insistence on "form" in the novel was simplified by his friend and follower, Mrs. Wharton, into mere adherence to plot. The plot must proceed, through all its ramifications, even though characters be wrenched out of shape to serve it. Minor figures, put in purely to prop up the plan, soon are shuffled away, and are featureless from the beginning. The long arm of coincidence snaps up the roving actors and places them down neatly in surroundings cleverly arranged to suit their situation. . . . Mrs. Wharton's work formed a bridge from the nineteenth-century novel to the magazine fiction of the present where, in a superficially arranged scene, manners, clothes, food, and interior decoration are described carefully and at length; how she contained in herself, as it were, the whole transitional period of American fiction, beginning in the bibelot and imported-European-culture era of the late 1890s, and ending in the woman's-magazine dream of suburban smartness.

> Louise Bogan. *Selected Criticism*
> (New York: Noonday, 1955), p. 84

To be haunted by George Eliot is a fine, but awesome experience. That great moralist (who was also a great artist) is a convenient ghost at anyone's writing desk, but a formidable presence at the dinner table. Moving as she did in both the literary and the social world, Mrs. Wharton may have felt (other writers have done so) that putting pen to paper was in itself a moral act. This may be one explanation for the unevenness of her writing. She could be sharp and she could be dull; this was true of her not just in her later years but throughout her career.

> Wayne Andrews. Introduction to *The Best
> Short Stories of Edith Wharton* (New York:
> Scribners, 1958), p. xiii

The technique for her major characterizations moves, as it were, in two directions, both inward and outward. The theory of morality helps her to get at the inner truth of personality, the unique quality which individualizes and sets apart. Convention supplements morality in two ways: first, by providing a basis for contrast, a standard or norm by which the divergences from the usual and typical may be underlined; second, by serving as a control or guide rope for keeping morality within the bounds of the familiar and away from mere eccentricity. Thus Mrs. Wharton's basic technique for creating her central figures is to endow them with certain qualities which fail to fit into the established social pattern but are yet related to it, in this way giving them a greater value and interest than the generality of persons possess. Often the most trivial details are sufficient indication of individuality.

Marilyn J. Lyde. *Edith Wharton: Convention
and Morality in the Work of a Novelist*
(Norman: University of Oklahoma Press,
1959), p. 150

Ethan Frome, when he plunges towards what he considers certain death, is a failure but not a mystery. His behavior is not unmotivated; the tragedy is not contrived. The very heart of the novel is Frome's weakness of character, his negation of life. Behind that is his true, unfulfilled, relationship with Zeena. Wharton's economy of language in the novel is superb. There is hardly a word unnecessary to the total effect. Her final economy is the very brevity of the book. It fits the scene and character. There were depths to plumb; her people were not simple. To overcome the deficiencies of their natural reticence (and perhaps her own), to retain the strength of the severe and rugged setting, particularly the "outcropping granite," she resorted to a brilliant pattern of interlocking imagery and symbolism.

Kenneth Bernard. *College English.*
December, 1961, p. 184

Within these traditional limits, and despite her coolness to modernist innovations, Mrs. Wharton was a restless writer, forever seeking new variations of tone and theme, and in her several important novels after *The House of Mirth* rarely troubling to repeat a success. In *The Reef* (1912) she composed a subtle though tenuous drama of personal relations, Jamesian in manner and diction, which deals largely with the price and advantage of moral scruple. In *The Custom of the Country* (1913) she turned to—I think it fair to say, she was largely the innovator of—a tough-spirited, fierce and abrasive satire of the barbaric philistinism she felt to be settling upon American society and the source of which she was inclined to locate, not with complete accuracy, in the new raw towns of the mid-West. Endless numbers of American novels would later be written on this theme, and Sinclair Lewis would commonly be mentioned as a writer particularly indebted to *The Custom of the Country;* but the truth is that no American novelist of our time, with the single exception of Nathanael West, has been so ruthless, so bitingly cold as Mrs. Wharton assaulting the vulgarities and failures of our society.

Irving Howe. Encounter. July, 1962, p. 46

Ethan Frome, I have no doubt, will always be read, but it is out of the main stream of her work. I believe that she will be remembered primarily for her two great novels of manners: The House of Mirth and The Age of Innocence. In these she succeeded in re-creating an unadventurous and ceremonious society, appropriately sheltered behind New York brownstone, looking always to the east rather than to the west, and the impact upon it of the winds that blew from both directions. There were plenty of minor writers who attempted to delineate this society, but among those of the first rank Mrs. Wharton, at least in the first decade of our century, had it to herself. . . . The reason Mrs. Wharton succeeded where so many others have failed is that in addition to her gifts as an artist she had a firm grasp of what "society," in the smaller sense of the word, was actually made up of. She understood that it was arbitrary, capricious, and inconsistent; she was aware that it did not hesitate to abolish its standards while most loudly proclaiming them. She knew when money could open doors and when it couldn't, when lineage would serve and when it would be merely sneered at. She knew that compromises could be counted on, but that they were rarely made while still considered compromises. She knew her men and women of property, recently or anciently acquired, how they decorated their houses and where they spent their summers. She realized that the social game was without rules, and this realization made her one of the few novelists before Proust who could describe it with any profundity.

Louis Auchincloss. Pioneers and Caretakers
(Minneapolis: University of Minnesota
Press, 1965), pp. 53–54

Mrs. Wharton seems to be saying that, from a spiritual perspective, society, considered as the supreme lawgiver, is an illusion or a downright fiction. It is an arena of distraction, a kind of Vanity Fair. What The House of Mirth asserts is that no life possesses spiritual vitality until it is motivated by belief in its own significance. Obviously, the enigmatic and revelatory word that Lily does not achieve until the end of her life is "faith." Only with it can a successful quest be pursued against all the equivocating counter-claims and inducements of society, against the ostensible absurdity of life itself. . . .

Faith, as Edith Wharton defines it, is no generalized and temperamental optimism; it is, instead, an almost mystical assurance that only moral action can save the ever-threatened continuity of human existence. Beset by dangers inherent in social arrangements, man clings to survival by the thread of his moral instincts; he is, at his best, motivated by what Mrs. Wharton calls, in Sanctuary, "this passion of charity for the race." In other words, goodness is useful, and men and women must, under pain of extinction, bequeath it to their children.

James W. Gargano. *American Literature.*
March, 1972, pp. 140–41

In her best, most representative works, Mrs. Wharton continually returned to the idea of tradition and the need of viable modes of cultural transmission as important factors affecting the character of man's social history. She continually argued the necessity of the individual's commitment to the cultural tradition; the danger of alienation from it; the catastrophe which ensues when social upheavals like revolution, anarchy, and war destroy the slowly and delicately spun web of that tradition; and the necessity of imaginatively preserving—if necessary even reconstructing—the precious values of the past. Her artistic treatment of the theme of tradition usually involved two methods. The first was to dramatize the importance for men of the web of culture, manners, and mores that encloses them and to warn of the disaster in store for those who become culturally deracinated or alienated and for those who destroy the delicate web in a radical obsession to reform it. And the other method, evident in the final years of her life, was an impulse to reconstruct— archeologically, as it were—the social world of her youth: the traditions which vitalized the culture of Old New York in the period from about 1840 to 1880. She hoped to revive the memory of a set of slowly evolved cultural values suddenly wiped out by a succession of destructive changes in American life beginning in the 1880s—including the rise of the industrial plutocracy ("the lords of Pittsburgh," as she called them); massive immigration which totally altered the ethnic character of New York City; the first World War, the depression, and the New Deal; and the nationalistic hatreds, at the close of her life in 1937, building toward the Second World War.

James W. Tuttleton. *The Yale Review.*
Summer, 1972, pp. 564–65

The value of [Wharton's] work may have little to do with its hidden origins; but creative work, as a writer, gardener, and interior decorator, was clearly what rescued her. Without that she would have succumbed to the panics of her childhood, the breakdowns of her early married years, and the neurotic depressions and exhaustions of maturity. A woman of incredible energy and vitality, she kept her balance with the help of a relentless social round, but it was literary accomplishment that supplied the gyroscope of her selfhood.

From the abundance of her bleak frustrations Wharton wrung a view of human possibility that must touch any perceptive reader. She may seem to deal with the evolution of manners and the woes of marriage. But she really employs these materials to illustrate deep and persuasive moral insights. A story like "Bunner Sisters," a novella like *Ethan Frome* or *Summer,* achieves its immense power by the victory of her imagination over the apparent straitness of her background. In these amazing works she deals with the most impoverished of American lives, always implying that in the lowest as in the highest strata of society the chance of sinking yet farther or of aspiring yet higher remains present. No class is exempt from the dangers of pride or the chastening rod of humiliation.

Irwin Ehrenpreis. New York Review of
Books. November 13, 1975, p. 6

In her major works Edith Wharton was able to evoke the metaphysical and symbolical implications of the situations which she was presenting. She knew how to maintain the single point of view while juxtaposing the narrator's varying depths of consciousness in order to achieve intense dramatic effects. She was also able to give moments of significant experience permanent form as viable works of art. She was adept at suggesting dimensions of experience that would ordinarily escape a literal transcription of it. As a result, she furnished the sensitive reader with fragmentary clues enabling him to divine implicitly her interpretation of her subject. . . .

Edith Wharton, seen in perspective, is a novelist who provides a link between the morally and psychologically oriented works of Hawthorne and James, who preceded her, and the later Realists like Sinclair Lewis or F. Scott Fitzgerald with their tendency toward the sardonic and iconoclastic. Edith Wharton may not have been capable of Hawthorne's moral inclusiveness, infinite perceptiveness, and imaginative reach which, as James said, made him "a habitué of a region of mysteries and subtleties" where he took as his province "the whole deep mystery of man's soul and conscience . . . the deeper psychology." She may also have been incapable of James's firm but infinitely subtle probing of the human mind and of his dissecting of the various nuances of behavior, conscious or unconscious, in any given scene.

But, like both Hawthorne and James, Edith Wharton was sensitive to the ambiguities in inner experience, in human behavior, and in many generally accepted ethical and metaphysical formulations. More than they, she, of course, understood the intricacies involved in living as a woman in a world set up for the social, economic, and sexual advantage of men. Sensitive as she was to the complications inherent in human motives and values, she tended in her work, as James did in his, to illuminate rather than resolve the complex issues and situations that she subjected to her scrutiny. She drew few simple conclusions about class, society, or individuals. More than James, she had the ability to assimilate natural landscape and urban milieu into her art and to make consummate use of such settings as active factors in the unfolding psychic drama in her work. In this respect she seems closer to Hawthorne than to James. . . .

She is a moralist as well as a mannerist. She transcends the realistic aspects of her world by striking intuitions into the psychic motivations of her characters. Thought she did not herself use some of the later techniques of dream, association, distortion, and imagery that enable a writer to penetrate the innermost recesses of a character's psyche, she was, essentially and at her best, a psychologist in fiction. She continued the Jamesian propensity for disengaging "crucial moments from the welter of existence" to ascertain their true worth and significance and to determine how they affect the psyches and moral life of her characters.

Margaret B. McDowell. *Edith Wharton*
(Boston: Twayne, 1976), pp. 142–44

The emotional problems that had dominated Wharton's earlier fictions—the sense of desolation, the need to place sexuality—had been problems that she knew at first hand. Now that is no longer the case. She may have felt driven to write repeatedly about the feelings of parents toward their children; however, she could only infer the nature of such feelings. She may have longed for family (the tone in fiction after fiction suggests as much), but she had none. In fact, although she made wholehearted efforts to get to know "les jeunes," she was more and more alone, and she felt increasingly alienated from the manners and practices of the younger generation. The inability to marshal her energy efficiently in these works bespeaks her uncertainty, and the tone in many of them is mixed. When she is at her best, Wharton captures the poignancy of aging. At other times, her management of the fiction grows less felicitous: increasingly, her satire lapses into an uncharacteristic querulousness, and everything about the postwar world is dismissed as vulgar and cheap. . . .

In her last novels, for the first time, if we do not read carefully, we might be misled into accepting the stereotype of "Edith Wharton: The Author" that has prevailed since her death: a haughty woman, cold, faintly supercilious, with the imperious remove that only breeding and great wealth can confer. That persona is there sometimes, on the surface; yet below, there is someone quite different. Defensive and wary, with desperate (and hopeless) longings, loneliness, and apprehension. Wharton's own epoch had passed, and she had never truly lived in it; now, too late for reconciliations, it was gone forever.

Cynthia Griffin Wolff. *A Feast of Words:*
The Triumph of Edith Wharton (New York:
Oxford University Press, 1977), pp. 343–44

She moves beyond the subject of literal motherhood to meditation on the maternal principle itself and, combining literary, anthropological, and religious ideas, evokes the gods of which she believes the modern world stands in need. Those gods are female. They are the Mothers to whom Goethe had his Faust descend; they are the primordial maternal center of life whose loss to the Western world is recorded in Aeschylus's *Oresteia,* from which Edith Wharton at an early age took the image of the Furies that was to stay with her throughout her imaginative life but only in old age acquire the power of gender. They are—the Mothers of Wharton's last finished work, which she needed two volumes to contain—her mystical solution to a lifetime of tough-minded analysis, argument and debate on the subject of woman. . . .

In her last two novels Wharton, it could be said, absorbed rather than feared the Furies. With them, so to speak, she tried to call America back to the ancient Mothers, the awesome matriarchs of Bachofen and then before him Goethe and then before either, so she seems to have believed, all human thought itself.

If this final, highly romantic vision of Wharton's is saddening—and in many ways it is: it conceives of women in totally maternal terms, it writes men off once and for all, it reverses rather than equalizes or eradicates the hierarchy of gender—it is also intriguing. . . .

It is tempting to imagine that she might have returned to the issues of power, creativity, and healing raised in her last two novels about modern Americans and found a way to harmonize her newly articulated mysticism about femaleness with her old concern for women's lives in the here-and-now. But that perhaps, given the vitality of her argument with America on the subject of women from *The House of Mirth* through *The Age of Innocence,* may be a little like wanting to modernize an old house. Maybe we don't need less than what we have.

Elizabeth Ammons. *Edith Wharton's*
Argument with America (Athens: University
of Georgia Press, 1980), pp. 189–91, 194–96

Wharton's greatest talent was the ability to recognize the secret gods of American society and to approach them with an air of irreverence, an attitude nearly sacrilegious, to expose them as the empty idols they are. She understood that what America worshipped more than anything else was wealth. She knew that her mother's dictum, "Never talk about money, and think about it as little as possible," reflected not a disdain for wealth but an attempt to hide an obsession. She watched (and chronicled) the rise of the Beauforts, the Rosedales, and the Abner Spraggs of the world to the position of national heroes, and she showed the results of this overwhelming materialism. Novel after novel depicts the consequences of regarding the world as a marketplace, describes the dehumanization of those frozen in materialism, especially of the women who become commodities. In old New York the most salable woman, Wharton perceived, was the virginal child bride, May Welland; later a taste developed for the more sophisticated but equally ornamental type of Lily Bart; in the 1920s a more corrupted but equally decorative type, the flapper, Lita Wyant, prevailed. But each was the commodity demanded by a materialistic world—a woman without soul, without self, distorted and twisted from her true nature into a marketable product, one whose nightmare form was Undine Spragg.

Wharton knew it was not only women who suffered from this worship of wealth. If women lost their souls to become pretty things, men sold their souls—Ralph Marvell to attain his fantasy of egotistic escape, Selden and John Amherst to maintain secure positions in worlds they pretended to disdain. And the business of acquiring, protecting and increasing one's wealth, Wharton saw, kept one from the business of living. . . .

Money, that supreme American god, was Wharton's first target. This obsessive materialism degraded and destroyed many, and its power ruled in every period of American life that Wharton observed. But Wharton saw another American deity as almost equally dangerous, for she understood the consequences of the country's veneration of another false god—the idol of pleasure.

Pleasure is perhaps too strong a word to describe the secret god of old New York, for there the hidden idol was the milder goal of peace of mind, freedom from unpleasantness. Wharton knew that everyone seeks this peace, but she also perceived that what made old New York evil was its desire to achieve this peace at any cost. . . .

Conflict, tragedy, and pain were terrifying to Americans, and Wharton saw that their way of dealing with them was through belief in another god— the easy answer. Wharton knew that what America expected of life was "a tragedy with a happy ending.". . . America did not want to; believe that "things are not always and everywhere well with the world," and preferred to retreat to the formula, to the answer that avoided conflict and required no thought.

Carol Wershoven. *The Female Intruder in the Novels of Edith Wharton* (Madison, New Jersey: Fairleigh Dickinson University Press, 1982), pp. 164–67

She believed that all human ties were subject to the society in which they were formed, and any new tie realigned an old one. Yet her work shows a persistent effort to make all relationships between men and women and women and women more honest and more inclusive. . . .

The strength of Wharton's fiction comes from what Herbert Marcuse defines as "the hidden categorical imperative of art," the impetus to make the fictitious or the ideal real. This impetus can be traced in Wharton's efforts to present a model of female cooperation, which runs like an underground railroad throughout her work [and is reflected in her] exposure or the false simplicity of female stereotypes and her portrayal of the complexity and individuality of her heroines.

Susan Goodman. *Edith Wharton's Women: Friends and Rivals* (Hanover, New Hampshire: University Press of New England, 1990), p. 155

Wharton's best stories succeed in achieving the goal she sets in "Telling a Short Story" of being jewels that simultaneously give out many fires. Certainly the form of the ghost tale helped Wharton achieve the organic wholes she sought. The form legitimates the death-in-life atmosphere and unexplained mysteries that often jar in the realistic tales. No wonder she became so partial to the genre that in "Telling a Short Story" she hurries to discuss it before introducing the basic elements of the story. But the often made point that the ghost tale gave Wharton a "literature apart" can also be overworked. We have seen that she actually speaks the unspeakable in stories of many different types, and if the ghost tales are sometimes better, there are clear exceptions. I have to agree with Lewis's assessment of "Bewitched," for instance, as "an artificial yarn which strives for effect by converting the figurative into the literal." Moreover, the two best stories of Wharton's late period, "After Holbein" and "Roman Fever," are not ghost stories.

Or are they? "Roman Fever" concerns a past ghost, and "After Holbein" has been called a ghost story.

Barbara Anne White. *Edith Wharton: A Study of the Short Fiction* (Boston: Twayne, 1991), p. 106

Identity for Wharton is inextricably bound to culture, to one's material and social environment. "Traditional society," she argues . . . "with its old established distinctions of class, its pass-words, exclusions, delicate shades of language and behavior, is one of man's oldest works of art, the least conscious and the most instinctive." She might have said "one of woman's oldest works of art," in that women have traditionally been seen as the creators and guardians of the social world, especially in American culture.

The bond between the individual and the social group, "the web of customs, manners, culture," lies at the heart of Edith Wharton's fiction. Her novels and short stories depict individuals enmeshed in what she metaphorically called the social "web" or "net," an elaborate weave of manners, mores, rituals, expectations, gestures as well as physical environment, houses, streets, rooms, decor, costume that define the parameters of human experience, even human nature. As she knew from her own experience as a woman in Old New York, society is a "hieroglyphic world," a coded world of signs that individuals must learn to read and interpret in order to make the personal adjustments, however difficult, between individual desire and social necessity. Human nature, for her, was clothed in the social fabric; she saw no possibility for life denuded of that garment, no essential "human nature" outside the elaborately woven social context. The story she had to tell in her fiction delineated the dialectic features of the social bond: the bonds or restrictions society places on the individual and the resulting bond or covenant between the two. . . .

Her novels—especially *The House of Mirth, The Fruit of the Tree, Ethan Frome, Summer* and *The Age of Innocence*—stress the bonds put upon the individual by the social group. Protagonists from Lily Bart to Newland Archer must learn the coded meanings and values of their culture in order to exert any control over their destinies and, in spite of their attempts, they are more often blind-sided by messages they are unable or unwilling to read and interpret clearly. Yet in each case the protagonist measures individual bondage against social bonding and, in the end, adheres to the social covenant.

Katherine Joslin. *Edith Wharton* (New York:
St. Martin's, 1991), pp. 29–30, 36

An understanding of shame in the context of affect theory allows us an entirely new entrance into Edith Wharton's fictional universe, highlighting what has been overlooked and clarifying what has often been misinterpreted or simply ignored. A novel like *The Glimpses of the Moon,* which has been classed as a thin and melodramatic failure, seems less flawed when one examined the ways in which Wharton portrays shame disrupting a marriage. *Sanctuary,* which is often mocked by critics for Kate Orme's decision to save a child she hasn't had, is more substantial when that decision can be seen in the context of an emotional reality hitherto unexplored. When looked at from the perspective of affect theory, *A Son at the Front* emerges in part as a fascinating exploration of shame in the wake of divorce and as it works out in new relationships created by remarriage. Wharton's stories about artists and writers have been considered romantic products of an amateur, but they reveal themselves to be insightful recreations of situations in which shame impacts a creative artist's life. A number of Wharton's portraits of men seem richer and more subtle than has previously been acknowledged or understood.

Lev Raphael. *Edith Wharton's Prisoners of
Shame: A New Perspective on her
Neglected Fiction* (New York: St. Martin's,
1991), p. 318

Novels such as *The Age of Innocence* are seldom discussed as naturalistic fiction because of the critic's assumption that if a novel is naturalistic in its central impulse it cannot be a successful novel and because *The Age of Innocence* is clearly successful. But another tack would be to recognize that most literary movements produce in their opening stages ungainly and awkward expressions of the movement—much pre-Shakespearean Elizabethan tragedy, for example—and that American naturalism is no exception to this general rule. The major naturalistic novels of the 1890s are indeed often crude and melodramatic both in theme and form. But in *An American Tragedy* and *The Age of Innocence* the movement comes to maturity, both in the discovery of a fuller range of experience available for the representation of naturalistic themes and in the skill of the dramatization of these themes.

Donald Pizer. In Alfred Bendixen and
Annette Silversmit, eds. *Edith Wharton:
New Critical Essays* (New York: Garland,
1992), p. 140

Edith Wharton never forgave old New York for its way of "taking life 'without effusion of blood.'" . . . Though World War I gave Wharton an intense appreciation for the past—she grieved over the war's "uprootings and rendings" which swept away "all the thousand and one bits of the past that give meaning to the present". . . it did not reconcile her to memories of old New York's determination to ignore the unpleasant. Her criticism of the society that had shaped her was the creative impulse behind much of her earlier work. In describing the genesis of *The House of Mirth* (1905), Wharton noted that "a frivolous society can acquire dramatic significance only through what its frivolity destroys. Its tragic implication lies in its power of debasing people and ideals." . . . And after the war, though making the claim that "after all, there was good in the old ways." . . . Wharton explores through Newland Archer the stultification of the individual by society's constraints.

Though American manners of the 1920s repelled her—her later fiction becomes increasingly strident in its criticism of the contemporary social scene—Wharton never permitted her yearning for the "old ways" to obscure her sense of the past's shortcomings. In *Old New York,* a collection of four novellas published in 1924, her criticism of the past reaches a sharpness unparalleled even in *The House of Mirth.* While *House* depicts the broad spectrum of a society where the dollar determines social standing, *Old New York* focuses on New York's "aristocracy" of the decades prior to Wharton's birth, the families who trace their ancestry to English and Dutch colonists. Though not overtly materialistic, *Old New York* is provincial, and in all four novellas Wharton's concern is the manner in which the narrow rigidity of New York's prejudices makes no allowance for individual growth. And in one of the novellas, *The Old Maid,* Wharton concentrates directly on the problem of finding fulfillment, sexually and emotionally, in a society that ignores those needs, especially in its women. . . .

In *The Old Maid* Wharton uses the mother-daughter relationship to examine a woman's need to go beyond motherhood to find selfhood. While *The Old Maid* attempts in part to define what it means to be a mother, the novella's imagery suggests that the need to define a sense of self encompassing past dreams and present realities is of paramount importance. In the end, Delia is vouchsafed a glimpse of a shepherd stealing a kiss and a "vision of requited love." That a woman must turn to clocks and mirrors to realize her dream and her destiny is Wharton's most damning commentary on old New York.

Judith E. Funston. In Alfred Bendixen and
Annette Silversmit, eds. *Edith Wharton:
New Critical Essays* (New York: Garland,
1992), pp. 143–44, 157

The Children . . . is Edith Wharton's revision, from a woman's view, of one of mainstream Modernism's central and most compelling tropes: its romanticization of the erotic immaturity of the perennial bachelor and its insistence that this figure was the age's new Representative Man, whose acutely self-conscious sensibility, won by the sacrifice of adult sexuality, was "the very type of the great creative artist." Through Martin Boyne's complex love affairs with Rose Sellars and Judith Wheater, Wharton rereads what Eve Kosofsky Sedgwick calls the "tradition of fictional meditations on . . . male homosexual panic."

Judith L. Sensibar. In Alfred Bendixen and
Annette Silversmit, eds. *Edith Wharton:
New Critical Essays* (New York: Garland,
1992), p. 159

I do not mean to suggest that [in *The House of Mirth*] Wharton was capable of imagining an alternative for Lily in the world of unskilled woman workers: Lily Bart, Sweatshop Operative; Lily Bart, Shirtwaist Striker; or even Miss Bart of the Women's Trade Union League. Rather, I believe that the novel's references to the masses of women who worked because they had no other possibility in life gives resonance to Lily's fate. Hers is a tragedy that could occur only to a woman from the class into which she was born, a woman whose poverty, as judged by the standards of that class, turned her only asset into a fatal liability. In their last interview, a shaken Simon Rosedale offers Lily a loan, saying that theirs would be "a plain business arrangement, such as one man would make with another." *The House of Mirth,* the novel that contains this offer, and Lily Bart's life, which the novel documents, are testimony that no such arrangement can exist, that in "good" society, the workings of capital invariably have a gender—and a sex.

Lillian S. Robinson. In Shari Benstock, ed.
The House of Mirth, by Edith Wharton.
Case Studies in Contemporary Criticism
(Boston: Bedford Books/St. Martin's Press),
1994, p. 358

WHITE, ANTONIA (GREAT BRITAIN) 1899–1980

This story [*Frost in May*] of a heavy burden laid upon a young child, unfitted for the discipline of a convent school, is only saved from being too painful by the simplicity and sincerity of the telling. Nanda Grey, daughter of a recent convert to Roman Catholicism, is sent at nine years old to the Convent of the Five Wounds. She has already been received into the Church, has had instruction and learnt the catechism, and is full of ardor for the religion-shadowed life she is to lead. Her progress is not easy. The discipline of the school is not unduly harsh, but it makes demands which Nanda cannot meet. The discouraging of individual friendships, the embargo on the giving of presents, even birthday presents, the censorship of books sent from home ("*Dream Days* . . . apart from its being by a non-Catholic writer, is morbid, rather unwholesome, and just a *little* vulgar"), all fill Nanda, who is too gentle to think her elders can be wrong, with a sense of limitless inferiority. The culminating moment of young religious experience, the First Communion, leaves her unmoved, to her own horror; and she suffers secret terrors, fearing that she may become the owner of a "vocation." During an illness Nanda writes a novel, in the finest Ouida style, about a beautiful violet-eyed heroine and an ugly masterful hero, who is to reject the beautiful heroine and retire into a Trappist monastery. This effort, which appears innocent and amusing enough, is discovered, and Nanda is expelled. Unfair as this may seem, the author makes out a fair case for the attitude of the Reverend Mother, but Mr. Grey's attitude to his little daughter is brutal and incredible. The book is in no way controversial, and, as a study of emotional, innocent adolescence in rather unnatural surroundings, it can be read with much interest.

(London) *Times Literary Supplement.*
July 20, 1933, p. 497

There has been a long pause since Mrs. Antonia White wrote that neat, accomplished account of life at a convent school called *Frost in May*. Her new novel, elaborating a somewhat similar theme, is longer, more serious in tone, and perhaps a shade less spontaneous; but at the same time *The Lost Traveller* achieves a depth lacking in the earlier book, and presents with great vividness the somewhat unusual circumstances of the story it tells.

Clara, the heroine, is the attractive and intelligent daughter of Claude Batchelor, an unusually gifted classical master at St. Mark's School, in West Kensington. By becoming a Catholic convert at the age of thirty-five, her father has compromised his chances of preferment in his profession so far as a headmastership is concerned; while his marriage with a rather foolish woman of somewhat higher social standing than himself has not been entirely happy. The author is particularly successful in depicting the hive of trying relations and friends that makes the Batchelor household an uneasy one for a sensitive child; and Claude's eccentricities, bad temper and bursts of generosity are all completely convincing.

Clara has to leave her convent school, one of the more eminent of such institutions, because her parents can no longer afford to keep her there. She eventually becomes governess to a little boy at a large house in the country. There, through no particular fault of her own, a tragedy takes place; and Clara has a nervous breakdown. Finally, the implication of the last pages seems to be that she decides she has a "vocation," and all points to her becoming a nun.

Like not a few other recent novels, *The Lost Traveller* is inclined to emphasize the advantages of belonging to the Roman Catholic Church rather as if the intention were to advertize a salable commodity; and much that is expressed explicitly the reader might have found more acceptable as implicit in the background. However, this does not prevent Mrs. White's novel from being an admirable piece of work, and perhaps it would not be going too far to say that the book carries on the tradition of Charlotte Brontë, in its unfolding of a young girl's experiences in coming to grips with the world.

(London) *Times Literary Supplement.*
March 31, 1950, p. 197

Fifteen years ago Antonia White published *Frost in May,* which won a good deal of praise both in England and America. Her second novel is concerned with the theme of her first: the pains and blights of a young girl growing up, first at convent-school (her parents are converts to Catholicism) and later in the England of the years between 1915 and 1917. But *The Lost Traveller,* on a theme almost fatal—that of the sensitive adolescent—is not the novel of sensibility you would expect, with its usually too protective attitude toward the favorite. Rather, it is a chronicle of unfolding and developing relationships between the girl and her parents, and in various ways it is equally divided among girl, mother (oversensitive and dissatisfied) and father (a self-made intellectual not quite born to the middle class). And as a chronicle during which all the characters happily change and develop, the girl, above all, gently deflected from the fate of a dyed-in-the-wool blue-stocking, you are reminded of methods and styles just possibly close relatives to Miss White's—Arnold Bennett's and Dorothy Richardson's.

There are brilliant scenes—the family party after the funeral, the night the father takes his daughter to the opera—but it is not by brilliance that Miss White achieves her effects: rather it is by the very solidity of her structure through which life is allowed to flow. For her grasp, down to every grain of detail, of what she is writing about is firm and clear. Incident seems to flow effortlessly out of incident, there is no necessity for overemphasis, scenes never seem arranged or forced. The voice that speaks is often astringent in tone, usually grave, but never need it exaggerate by shout or declamation. Such ease and poise, though not exciting, are admirable, and produce a delicate truthfulness.

Jean Garrigue. *The New Republic.* May 29,
1950, p. 20

To the lay reader Roman Catholic novels present a difficult problem. Hovering over the scene of action is a conception of life which somehow explains or excuses the characters in a way not deducible from their temperaments or actions. A great deal has to be taken on trust. Thus the reader is aware in Miss White's Clara series of a kind of moral superiority in the Catholic characters which, turning their sins into misdemeanors, gives them an unfair advantage over the rest of the world. Clara herself is an egotistic, cold young woman who suffers a neurotic anxiety about her friends, lovers and family which is unrelated to real love or sympathy. Her father, a very well-drawn character, is a bigoted, conscientious convert who works up every domestic situation into a moral crisis of the first magnitude. It is clearly he who is responsible for Clara's inability to feel or act naturally. Yet there is always a suggestion that these devastating personalities are in possession of a secret code which, once deciphered, will transform their lives. In the meantime they must be accorded a special sympathy.

A continuous series of novels of this kind should probably, therefore, not be judged until its close, when the characters have worked out their destiny. For the present it can be said that Miss White is brilliantly successful in her account of Clara's collapse into madness. Miss White's exact, realistic and uncharged prose, which often produces a flatness in her ordinary scenes, is absolutely right for her terrible description of the asylum and of the hallucinations, a distorted reflection of real problems, which chase each other through Clara's disordered mind. This is not simply a clinical dissection of madness but a most moving evocation of a spirit still suffering though loosed from its controls. What horrifies is the assumption by the spectators outside the bars of unconsciousness in the victim. With the events leading up to this madness Miss White is far less successful. It is impossible to believe for a moment in the idyllic love-affair whose violent contrast to the unhappy marriage which has preceded it precipitates the crisis. A reader feels that Clara's brief period of intense happiness should have proven completely unreal, whereas the experience of the lovers is presented as something lasting and true. Miss White, in fact, has a curiously divided literary personality which expresses itself in one aspect in a gravely exact realism and in the other in a sentimentality of the most naive kind.

(London) *Times Literary Supplement.*
November 12, 1954, p. 717

Frost in May was written by a non-Catholic, the trilogy by a Catholic: one would expect the first novel to be anti-religious, the latter ones pro. But in fact religion plays a larger role in *Frost in May,* and is treated with tense ambivalence (like Stephen Dedalus, Miss White's mind was saturated with the religion in which she said she disbelieved). It is scarcely evident in the later books, except for one stage property in the final scene: Clara clutches a rosary as she whispers her last lines, and one is slightly embarrassed. But in general, Miss White's religion is in keeping with her style: bare and unobtrusive, neither warm nor comfortable. She has said that even during her years outside the Church she never doubted that a spiritual life existed, but she has also said, with characteristic bleakness: "The hardest article of faith for me to swallow is that God loves human beings." Hers is a religion that offers, not consolations, but Moments of Truth, a religion for a comfortless world. That world—the world of Antonia White—is a world worth knowing, though one would not want to live there.

Samuel Hynes. (London) *Times Literary*
Supplement. March 7, 1969, p. 733

The Dial Press is now publishing the Virago Modern Classics Series, which originated in London at the Virago Press, a small but growing feminist publishing house. The Virago Series concentrates on "rediscovered works" by and about nineteenth- and twentieth-century women; this year's titles include novels by Rebecca West, Radclyffe Hall, and Emily Eden, all of whom may already be known to American readers, and by Antonia White, whom this reader found a wonderful surprise. . . .

[White] wrote *Frost in May* (1933) under pressure from her husband. She produced no other novels for almost twenty years: her publisher comments on the "virulent writer's block" and the attacks of mental illness that disabled her. She did, however, translate many novels from the French. (An introduction by Elizabeth Bowen pairs *Frost in May* with Colette's *Claudine à l'École*.) *The Lost Traveller* (1950), *The Sugar House* (1952), and *Beyond the Glass* (1954) continue the autobiographical fiction begun in Antonia White's first novel. All are well made and interesting as social history; the last is an especially believable portrait of mental illness. None of the 1950s trilogy, however, has the purity of *Frost in May*. . . .

White's unpretentious prose renders honestly and quite without condescension the adult complexity of early adolescence; *Frost in May* portrays with vivid simplicity both the Paradise and the Fall. Antonia White thoroughly deserves her rediscovery.

Frances Taliaferro. *Harper's*.
April 1981, p. 102

Antonia White's first novel, *Frost in May,* is a girls' school story that was recognized as a classic soon after it was published in 1933. It became the first in a quartet of novels about an introspective young British woman, the last of which was published in 1954. All of them are well worth reappraisal.

The central figure in *Frost in May* is a nine-year-old girl, Nanda Grey, who struggles to keep her lively nature within the confines of a stringent convent, and the novel ends unhappily with her expulsion. Nanda's character reemerged in 1950 with a new name, Clara Batchelor, in White's *The Lost Traveller,* in which Clara becomes a governess and suffers her first major tragedy when her beloved pupil dies suddenly in an accident while he is under her care. In *The Sugar House* (1952), Clara grapples with a catastrophic marriage that is mercifully annulled. Clara's story concludes with *Beyond the Glass* (1954), a haunting novel of her retreat into madness in the midst of an overwhelming love affair.

All the works are largely autobiographical. . . .

The introduction to *The Lost Traveller* mentions that White changed Nanda's name because she wanted this "to be a real novel—[not] so much my own life." Her concern is not really justified, because these books, however autobiographical, succeed as novels. For all of Clara's—or White's—somber concerns, the books are infused with plenty of well-placed levity and spicy humor. White transformed her experience into a fluent prose quartet that displays a range of intensity, depth, wit, and acute understanding of human nature—qualities that always age gracefully.

J. B. *Harper's*. December, 1982, p. 72

The book for which Antonia White is best known, *Frost in May* (1933), is not merely an unusually vivid "school story" set in a convent. It pits an emergent individual will against a highly formalized discipline of behavior and thought. There is a clash between Nanda's developing aesthetic sense and the restrictive intellectual authority of the Church ("I don't want poetry and pictures and things to be messages from God, I want them to be complete in themselves"), between her strong emotional needs and the nuns' disapproval of intimate friendships, and between her self-conscious, anxious assimilation of a new faith and the habitual belief of the girls who are born Catholics. . . .

The pull between the controlling writer, digging up her past as though she were her own analyst, and the unredeemed, "untreated" self in the fiction, unable to make coherent shape of, or distance herself from her state of mind, is characteristic It's a strain which is both risky (the story may fail to get itself written at all) and fruitful, in that it informs the best of Antonia White's work: *Frost in May,* "The Moment of Truth," "The House of Clouds" and its matching section in *Beyond the Glass*. . . .

All Antonia White's stories have a susceptibility to material details which emerges in the lighter pieces simply as sharp decoration: the scum on the tea-cup and the "white ring round the iris" of Miss Hislop's eyes in "The Exile"; the smell of the nurse and the vulgar statuette on the Cottage Hospital mantelpiece in "Strangers"; Aunt Rose's mildewed clothes and the dusty furnishings of her tiny flat in Vienna. In the more disturbing stories details become alarming, unreliable.

Hermione Lee. Introduction to Antonia
White. *Strangers* (London: Virago/New
York: Dial, 1983), pp, i, v–vi

The content of her existing work and the fact that White lived for twenty-six years after publishing her last novel show that out of a long and varied life, the only experience available to her as a novelist occurred as she went through adolescence and into young womanhood and concerned her relationship with her father. In *Frost in May,* White presents Nanda enduring a traumatic humiliation when her father reads something she has written and interprets it as the revelation of a loathsome self hidden within his daughter. Seventeen years later, *The Lost Traveller* repeats the scene of the father's rejection of the daughter after his reading of a similar revelation of her guilt, this time in a letter. In this novel, which was the one White had the greatest difficulty in writing, the complex meaning of the father's rejection of the daughter is established. . . . White noted that she was surprised at how easily and quickly she wrote the next two books. In *The Sugar House* and *Beyond the Glass,*

White takes the daughter through her devastating attempts to become accept-able to her father. In the last book, having brought the heroine to the brink of extinction in the effort to achieve this impossibility, she shows the daughter writing yet one more letter revealing herself to her father. This one he receives with joy. In the fourth book, then, the father-daughter conflict is resolved, the daughter's humiliation is undone, her injury is healed.

White's novels are as much about her difficulties with writing as they are about her personal history. Because of her identification with the heroine, the novels tell us that White saw the act of writing as the assertion of a self who will be hated. . . .

White's novels show why she did not produce fiction without autobio-graphical content. For her the act of writing is an insistence on the integrity of the self. To invent characters beyond herself and her experience of others in intense relation to herself would threaten that hard won integrity. She wrote in 1940 that her "job in life" was to "give a form in writing to certain experiences." Her job in life seems to have been considerably more complex than that, but in her four novels she gave form to what was the central reality of her life and self.

Jeanne A. Flood. *Critique*. 24, 1983,
pp. 132, 149

The British novelist Antonia White . . . , whose work is enjoying renewed attention with the reprinting of all of her major books and the televised adap-tation of her first novel, is an example of creativity overcoming cruel personal circumstances. Her four autobiographical novels describe, in an achingly vivid way, the difficult early years of a life that had a full share of misery. They were written, with the exception of the first, in her more tranquil middle age, and it is part of her achievement that, from the perspective of her fifties, after failed marriages, successful motherhood, distinguished success as a translator from the French, and the loss and recovery of her Catholic faith, she wrote perceptively of her childhood and young womanhood without fore-shadowing her later career. Restricting their narrative to her early years, all of these books nevertheless present Christian belief in the sacrificial terms in which that faith commended itself to her throughout her life. . . .

The principal theme of her autobiographical fiction is the obscurity of Providence and the consequent necessity of faith. Other important themes of the novels include the first World War, and the problems of growing up with a cultivated intelligence, high ideals, and no money. The subject of insanity, presented with rare objectivity, takes over the final chapters of the fourth volume. Almost as rare even today is the unembarrassed seriousness with which White takes a young woman's desire and need to make her way in the world. The novels are unified, despite this diversity of content, not only by the central role of Nanda/Clara and the regular return to the family as the basic context and setting of events, but by the continued preoccupation with the demands of the life of faith. Patience in incomprehensible suffering always bears fruit in her fiction, but not always so as to provide direct consolation to the sufferer.

Philip F. O'Mara. *Cithara.* 28:1, 1988,
pp. 33–34

Antonia White's four autobiographical novels, *Frost in May* (1933), *The Lost Traveller* (1950), *The Sugar House* (1952), and *Beyond the Glass* (1954), constitute a whole discourse on the writing woman's life in the twentieth century. The revival of White's reputation with the reprinting of her work was one of the first projects undertaken by Carmen Callil at Virago Press in London. White wrote her life as she lived it in a series of fictions and an enormous series of diaries drawn upon by her two daughters for their heartbreakingly hostile memoirs. . . .

The Hound and the Falcon (1965) is the story of her reconversion to Catholicism. From 1949 to 1967 she translated thirty-four novels from the French; her version of Maupassant's *Une Vie* won the Clairoun Prize, and she translated many of the works of Colette. Like Colette, she loved cats and wrote about them in *Minka and Curdy* and *Living with Minka and Curdy.* In 1983, after her death, her daughter Susan Chitty published *As Once in May,* which contains a four-part sequel to the *Frost in May* quartet, five sections of another novel, sixteen chapters of her autobiography up to age six, stories, essays, and poems. . . .

White's gender anxiety appears to be enacted in narrative structure. Unlike other women modernists, she does not open her text for co-making by the reader. *Frost in May* is cold and distant in narrative stance, and the third-person authoritative narrator effaces the teller in the telling. The events of Nanda's education, her invitation as a convert into the Edenic garden of the convent and her expulsion after she has been trained to submit her will to the rules of a strict authoritarian regime, are told without emotion, as if still participating in the idealized order of the Order. It is the reader in the world who judges Mr. Grey and the Mother Superior as evil. A Catholic reader could read the breaking of Nanda's spirit as a triumph of ideology. Elizabeth Bowen identifies in White's style a cool exactness and a lack of "kindness," and Samuel Hynes expands this definition by calling the writing "icily objective" and "heartless." She seems to know that one slip into narrative sympathy for this oppressed child will send her subject sailing into sentimentality, one plea for pity will exile the autobiographical fictions to the shelves of the unread. Even now, all of Antonia White is out of print in the United States.

Frost in May and its sequels, *The Sugar House* and *Beyond the Glass,* are constructed autobiographically as participants in and subverters of the two overlapping discourses of "confession," the Catholic church discourse, and the discourse of popular women's magazine and fictional "confessions," dismissed from the canon because they are "personal." The novels and *The*

Hound and the Falcon also participate in the conventional discourse of spiritual autobiography as confession, from Augustine to Rousseau. . . .

After the initial recuperation begun by Virago, White's extraordinary work threatens to be inundated by the swamp of her daughters' biographical script, which figures her, not as a writer, but as a bad mother—much as Rebecca West's reputation, revived by 1970s feminism, was reinscribed by biography into the bad mother posture created by her son and his defenders or the wronged mistress posture in which she is defined by her relation to H. G. Wells. White's career was a lifelong attempt to write her life as a woman, and her contribution to modernism is a major redefinition of female autobiographical forms. Her particular contribution is the suppression of the "I-narrative" common to women diarists and the appropriation of the authoritative third person for the female voice. . . .

One way to read *Frost in May* in the context of the revision of modernism is to set it next to Joyce's *Portrait of the Artist as a Young Man*, since it was consciously written as a gendered reply to that work. . . .

The resistance to dialogue with the listener is, in this case of Catholic discourse, a conscious feminist literary strategy, not a retreat to traditional form, but the recovery of a lost public subject position for writers marginalized and privatized by Catholicism and patriarchy. The critical balance achieved by recent feminist Joycean readings of the personal and autobiographical is strengthened by analyzing Catholic female modernism in White as an elimination of the authority of the listener-reader position in autobiographical narrative as a form of confession. . . .

Frost in May creates its own tradition for a Catholic female narrative, pleasure and conversion (the story of the continental aristocratic girls) or transgression and expulsion from the fold (Nanda's story). As firmly as the daughter's tale is embedded in the Father's and the church's, a subtext of female solidarity and mythology ironically undercuts the master plot. . . .

White's fiction reinforces the urge to study women writers in relation to their own history, a narrative in which what are called the prewar years are in fact the high point of fifty years of struggle for equality. The war crushed this powerful movement, and their writing often articulates ambivalence about the reproductive or nurturing roles demanded of women. It is ironic that Antonia White's daughters fix her reputation as a bad mother, reproducing the cultural prescriptions that were ideological torture for women modernists.

> Jane Marcus. In Bonnie Kime Scott, ed. *The
> Gender of Modernism* (Bloomington:
> Indiana University Press, 1990), pp. 597–602

There is something a little strange—not to say ironic—about a woman who could write so fluently and so prolifically (over a million words of diary) about herself, and then be unable to convert this material into novels that are confessedly autobiographical. She noted the strangeness herself, but could not change it: year after year, entry after entry, thousands of words upon thousands of words, about the need to write, the impossibility of writing, fearing insanity when she did not write, fearing insanity when she did write, psychoanalysis to help her write, abandoning psychoanalysis, lest it threaten the writing. The portrait is of a genuinely sensitive and hard-working woman who wants to do her job and cannot.

Then, on the other hand, the same diaries present a completely different portrait: of a thoroughly tiresome woman constantly and greedily engaging in obviously inappropriate love affairs; a woman with insane expectations of others, and unreasonable fury when they failed to deliver. This woman is an unspeakably appalling mother with a massive egotism and capacity for self-deception, an obsessive fascination with her own health, with money, and with her bizarre religious fantasies, projected onto a Catholic church that seems unrecognizable now.

But what comes over most clearly is that Antonia White was, without question, a remarkable woman. Nothing seems to have daunted her courage for living: one reads the diaries wanting to pity her, but compassion is not the true response. Although the diaries do not mention it, one can easily glean from them the bold wit for which she was notorious among her friends. She won a boasting competition at a party once by declaring that *her* virginity had been certified by the Pope.

Perhaps it would have been easier for her if she could simply have "invented" things; her own life was too much. For autobiographical fiction requires a kind of confidence that cannot be comfortable to maintain.

In *Frost in May*, the plot revolves around the fifteen-year-old heroine's expulsion from her convent school for writing an "immoral" novel. Antonia White believed this to be true. Fiction writing, and letting other people see her fiction, held a dangerous potency for her. After the publication of *Frost in May*, she learned that she had never been expelled; that her father had himself withdrawn her from the convent.

All her experiences of self, even those of her own desire, turned out so frequently to be deluded. However would one write autobiographical fiction, and how could one avoid paranoia, in the face of such an obdurate and unobliging real world?

Sara Maitland. *New Statesman and Society.*
August 30, 1991, pp. 43–44

WICKHAM, ANNA (GREAT BRITAIN) 1884–1947

Searchers like May Sinclair, Virginia Woolf, Dorothy Richardson, are working in a prose that illuminates their experiments. In poetry, a regiment of young women are recording an even more rigorous self-examination. The most typical and, in many ways, the best of these seekers and singers is Anna Wickham.

Anna Wickham has published two books: *The Contemplative Quarry*, a first venture of forty small pages, and *The Man with a Hammer*, a longer but scarcely richer volume. Two other vivid collections, *The Noiseless Propeller* and *The Little Old House* are to appear shortly. The most casual reading—if such a thing were possible—of Mrs. Wickham's work reveals the strength of her candor, the intense singleness of her purpose. . . .

Her very mercurial temperament is representative of the nervous spirit of her age; mood follows mood with abrupt intensity. She is, in quick succession, burning hot and icy cold; she is driven from fiery antagonisms to smouldering apathy; she is acutely sensitive, restless, harassed. . . .

There are more than a few hints in these lines of the eventual freedom of women. Yet this promise of liberty, instead of causing fresh jubilations, brings only fresh questions. Woman is being freed—for what? Is she to be liberated only to be caught up in new entanglements? Free for larger discontents? For a more relentless fury in the sex-duel? She hesitates. She realizes that it is not possible to live long on a fight. She has dreams of peace even in the midst of battle.

Thus the fluctuating thoughts of Anna Wickham. And so, for the greater part, her poems present the drama of woman still struggling between what is difficult to repudiate and what is still more difficult to accept. Here we see her torn between dreams and domesticity, between being the instrument of love and love itself; making some sort of adjustment to the conflicting claims of modernity and maternity.

Louis Untermeyer. *The New Republic*.
April 27, 1921, pp. 269–70

For better or for worse these women [Marianne Moore, Edna St. Vincent Millay, and Wickham] have contracted marriages with wit, have committed themselves to careers of brains. Seventeenth-century England, where all of the three would have been at home, would have prized them well. Twentieth-century England and America will not do badly to accept their poetry now for better or for worse, since by many a sign it is here to stay a while; almost certainly more of its sort remains to be written and read. It is independent, critical, and keen, a product oftener of the faculties than of the nerves and heart; it is feminine; it is fearless; it is fresh. . . .

Anna Wickham's book [*The Little Old House*] is a highly valuable document both on poetry and on woman. It is the work of an inspired metaphysician, one of England's most honest and inviting minds today, a very contemporary John Donne absorbed to the soul in what she rebelliously, painfully believes and sees. She invents her own curiously uneven, potent rhythms; she rejects no pungent metaphor because it stinks or stings; when she likes she rhymes very cunningly, or misrhymes, or rhymes not at all:

> Rhymed verse is a wide net
> Through which many subtleties escape.
> Nor would I take it to capture a strong thing,
> Such as a whale.

Her demon is unrest; her muses instead of singing to her whip her to intellectual appetite and artistic execution. She is the growing, aching mind of woman asking for hunger that she may think and peace that she may create. She gives herself in love, she is willing to kiss until she is blind; but

> There is the sexless part of me that is my mind.

She would be lonely occasionally, and fast

> In still, kind, perfect night.

Man in the long run she would have more frank—not "sane and solemn," "merciless as a beast," chaste, decorous, possessive, but openly and freely enjoying her as she openly and freely enjoys him. The furtive knight, the slothful husband in the dark, she would make over sometimes into the noonday lover with the kindness and courtesy that human beings are so proud to command:

> Kiss me sometimes in the light.
> Women have body's pain of body's love.
> Let me have flowers sometimes, and always joy.
> And sometimes let me take your hand and kiss it honestly.

The appeal of such a book is great because it is both passionate and ascetic, and because its protests are intense without being shrill. Its author's voice is low, an excellent thing in prophetesses. Thinking will soonest save her, and she perpetually thinks.

> My love is male and proper-man
> And what he'd have he'd get by chase,
> So I must cheat as women can
> And keep my love from off my face.
> 'Tis folly to my dawning, thrifty thought
> That I must run, who in the end am caught.

Who else would have thought of "thrifty"? Only a few books of recent poetry are so continuously interesting as Anna Wickham's, and scarcely any is so civilizing.

Mark Van Doren. The Nation.
October 26, 1921, pp. 481–82

Despite setbacks—or maybe because of them—she was by the 1930s a poet of international repute, appearing in numerous anthologies, *International Who's Who* and the Fourteenth Edition of the *Encyclopedia Britannica*. In 1938 she drew up a manifesto whose slogan was "World's Management by Entertainment."

However, despite these ambitions—or, again, *because* of them—her work has during the last half century been ignored by all but a passionate few. A selection of her poems was published by Chatto in 1971; and in 1984, to celebrate the centenary of her birth, Virago published a four hundred-page paperback edition of her writings compiled and edited by R.D. Smith.

Anna Wickham loved to sing. The sound of song enters many of her poems despite the fact that they are often "prose poems" "free verse" or "formless." She used rhyme a great deal too, especially where it suited her purpose. . . .

Her verse is not only free but also full of ideas, inspiration and guidance for fellow poets. . . .

Her verse is various too. It may in one instance lament, in another rejoice, but is essentially exploratory. All the time the poet invites her reader to look again at life, to probe and to prod it. In particular the unnecessarily *ordered* life. She cries out against such anti-life and declares herself on the side of things that stir and have spirit. . . .

The strengths of Anna Wickham's poetry [include]: its accessibility without sentimentality, its strong and simple language, its power to speak plainly *and* to suggest, to point to the *un*spoken; and its capacity to rejoice and be thankful. Whether it protests or celebrates, Anna Wickham's writing is truly "a critical rejoicing in life." Read it and see.

Matt Holland. *Poetry Review.* 78:2,
Summer, 1988, pp. 44–45

Wickham was prolific (nearly 1,400 poems in twenty years) where [Charlotte] Mew was spare, yet both wrote overtly feminist poetry that has escaped notice for its failure to adhere to the experimentalist demands of a masculinist modernism. Thomas Hardy called Mew "far and away the best living woman poet—who will be read when others are forgotten," and Anna Wickham had by 1932 an international reputation. Anthologies of the day printed more of her poems than those of de la Mare, Graves, and, in some volumes, even Yeats. . . .

Like Charlotte Mews's, Wickham's formal conventionality is often the very vehicle of her politics: her forced rhymes are meant to be funny and irreverent and to set off the political conflicts of which her poetry is made; they should not be read as merely unsophisticated concessions to the popular conventions of the day. "Meditation at Kew," outlining a poignant but humorous utopian program for marital reform, is the poetic version of her 1938 feminist manifesto, *The League for the Protection of the Imagination of Women. Slogan: World's Management by Entertainment.* . . .

When Wickham writes at the head of her extraordinary autobiography, "I am a woman artist and the story of my failure should be known," she compels the kind of rereading the inclusion within this anthology guarantees, one which accounts not only for her disappearance from modernism's archives but also for the politics of feminist collusion in that exile. Wickham's poems of class consciousness are a salutary addition to a modernist canon insufficiently concerned with the differentials of class and ethnicity. Her poems range from feminist pieces on marital relations and on the conflict between mothering and writing to analyses of the domination of one class by another. . . .

I do not mean to suggest that the enormously uneven Wickham corpus remains undiscovered as a pre-text of literary Modernism. Mew must be admitted to the canon as an undiscovered treasure, while Wickham remains important for reasons other than either experimentalism or formalism in verse. Still, the personal and material specificity of "The Mill" should have its history among our modernisms, reflecting—alongside [T. S.] Eliot's phlegmatic portrayals of deceptive lovers, Joyce's spoofs on the magazine romanticism of the day, [Mina] Loy's send-ups of the masculine sexual principle, and [Djuna] Barnes's decadent New Woman poems—its own particular vision, neither ironized nor sentimental, of the way we loved then.

Celeste Schenck. In Bonnie Kime Scott, ed.
The Gender of Modernism (Bloomington:
Indiana University Press, 1991), pp. 613–16

WILDER, LAURA INGALLS (UNITED STATES) 1867–1957

In a dugout on the bank of Plum Creek in Minnesota, the Ingalls family found a home after the long journey from Indian Territory. Here at night Laura "listened to the water talking and the willows whispering." In the daytime when there were no chores to do she and Mary played in the shallow water or on the long gray rock out on the prairie. The first winter and spring were happy seasons and then just before harvest there came a cloud of grasshoppers which ate every growing thing. With the courage which sustained all pioneers who survived the hardships of frontier life, the Ingalls family met their problems and solved them. Mrs. Wilder tells the third story of her own childhood so simply and vividly that the period of the opening up of the great west lives again for the children today.

Elizabeth D. Briggs. *Library Journal.*
December 1, 1937, p. 915

One cannot be too grateful for Mrs. Wilder's series of books, which started with *The Little House in the Big Woods* and of which this, [*The Long Winter*] is the sixth volume. In them the author is writing of her frontier childhood in fictionized form. The new book tells of the Ingalls family's blizzard-bound winter of 1880–81 in a prairie town of the Dakota Territory. It is a dramatic story which children from eight to high-school age will read and reread.

The New Yorker. December 7, 1940, p. 109

In *The Long Winter,* the plucky Ingalls move from their claim on the Dakota prairie into their store in town to escape the severe winter weather, but when blizzard follows blizzard, the train stops, the school closes and the family struggles to keep warm, to keep up their spirits and. . . [to] keep from starvation. . . .When the train finally manages to reach the suffering settlement, they celebrate Christmas in May, with Laura always the main character. A beautiful picture of family life and of the indomitable spirit of our pioneers. May not be as popular as her other books.

Sonja Wennerblad. *Library Journal*.
December 15, 1940, p. 1093

In the seven books of Ingalls Wilder's autobiographical series a submerged metaphorical drama takes place in which recurring types of scenes or descriptive set pieces express conflicting concepts of self. The "emigrant" self, a combination of child and androgyne, emerges when Laura is alone in nature in its aspects of open expanse (prairie), energy and rapid motion (wind, flooding river, runaway horse), or immersing bounty (water, wild grass, hay). In such various scenes the self is pleasure-seeking, solipsistic, amoral, and oceanic. The contrary scene or description expresses a bounded, socialized self, feminized, physically and morally constrained. Included here are episodes of guilt or punishment for indulging the self, or awakening to the realities of necessity and work, or learning to wear (indeed to like) restrictive fashionable clothing and hair styles. The subject's linear progress toward acceptance of social structures is marked with ambivalence. Laura as pioneer and emigrant is enfranchised from communal norms and rules but is by definition a carrier of them, is indeed a sort of missionary for the ideologies of civilization. The emigrant self comprises both a state and a direction; the state is that of enfranchised pre-social self; but the direction is always towards the re-establishment of social structure. The account of Laura's transformation into respectable married woman coincides with the epic of American "manifest destiny" in which wilderness and autochthons are conquered and displaced. Laura participates in that drama. In the forward necessitarian thrust of narrative, personal history is determined by historical destiny, and individual consciousness accommodates to that destiny. But countering that thrust are the subject's elegiac moods, which serve as unacknowledged mourning for the emigrant self whose passing is felt, though not admitted, to be tragic. . . .

Ingalls Wilder's play on the concept "house" marks it as the autobiography's most subtle and complex transactional symbol. House and wilderness are logically antithetical to each other; pioneering can almost be defined as houselessness, the covered wagon replacing the house and enabling the ideal, mobile, liberated emigrant life and self. But of course the end, the goal of emigration is the construction of a house, and the re-establishment of social structure. Emigration only temporarily resembles nomadism. The books record a series of temporary habitations in houses, always followed by abandonment. Gradually, Laura's sense of delight and freedom at moving on (her father's feelings) are replaced by her adoption of her mother's wish for security and permanency. The series moves from *Little House in the Big Woods* to "Little Gray Home in the West" (the last chapter of *These Happy Golden Years*). But this conservative movement contains its own opposite momentum; it enables and indeed legitimizes the evocation of the lost emigrant self. In chapter 7 of *Little House on the Prairie,* wolves surround the Ingalls's house. Pa (as so often offering Laura a delicious glimpse of the dangerous and forbidden) calls Laura to the window to look at them. Thus Laura is able to see and even sympathize with and admire the wolves because of the very barrier which protects and separates her from them. Here, it is the frame—window as synecdoche for the house, and both window and house as synecdochal for the autobiography itself—that reveals and makes accessible the realm of the unframed and unbounded. The series similarly frames, with its overall house-to-house ("settlement of the West") narrative structure and with the predominant thematics of religion-based morality and patriotism, expressions of desire for the forbidden, the excessive, the dangerous. The *Little House* books record a series of endings and losses: childhood's end, the taming of the West, the expulsion of the Indians from their lands, the disappearance of the buffalo and other wild animals, Pa's relinquishing his desire to keep pioneering forever. The series concludes with Laura's marriage, whereupon she finally and irrevocably becomes "Laura Ingalls Wilder." But that is both the name of the conventionally closed (socialized and feminized) self and of the author of the series which so powerfully resurrects the emigrant/child-self. To bring what is lost into the frames of literary art is, if not to save it from extinction, to resist in some small measure consenting to its loss.

Sarah Gilead. *Criticism.* 30, 1988,
pp. 45–46, 49

In many ways, *The Long Winter* is the central volume in Laura Ingalls Wilder's extraordinary sequence of seven Little House books. It is the most intense and dangerous of the novels, and it covers the shortest span of time, a single legendary seven-month winter. The Ingalls family has made its fullest commitment yet to one spot on the Dakota prairie. Although Pa yearns to start again in Oregon, Ma insists that they settle so the daughters can "get some schooling." Laura, the autobiographical protagonist, is approaching adulthood. This book, darkest of the series, does indeed provide her with powerful "schooling"—it is a sober and disquieting crash course in what it can mean to live out a female life on the Western prairie.

All the Little House books chronicle the education and maturation of Laura and her sisters, and with the onset of Laura's adolescence the powerful role of gender in establishing parameters of possibility becomes more apparent. Ma looms larger as influence and model, and Laura's relationship with her becomes more problematic. Ma urges her daughters to perpetuate traditional women's culture wherever they find themselves. Yet the exigencies of Western life push the girls into positions and tasks that are traditionally male; for example, Laura shares Pa's work and finds it more to her taste than housework or teaching. . . . Under the stresses of the frontier, women typically clung to gendered culture for security, as does Ma. Thus a gynocritics . . . . which studies women's culture as a sustaining and ambivalent phenomenon, is particularly appropriate to Wilder's series, allowing us to read the Little House books as something more complex than a euphoric romance of prairie childhood.

The Long Winter especially lends itself to such a reading; its brief span presents the crux of Laura's adolescence. She is forced by violent weather to live a life of confinement and housework as circumscribed as her mother's and to contemplate the very different possibilities open to a young man through the exploits of Almanzo Wilder, whom she will someday marry. Almanzo and Ma are the heroes of this book because they successfully enact traditional plots of gendered culture. Almanzo triumphs with a daring journey across the frozen prairie and Ma triumphs by staying home and contriving to feed her family. Laura's growing awareness of her own limits and duties as a woman brings new weight and sobriety to the Little House series in *The Long Winter*, which can be made apparent by a feminist reading grounded in an understanding of women's culture. . . . As readers of whatever age, we respond profoundly to the archetypal power of Laura's situation as a female adolescent in Dakota territory. Because of the exigencies of Western life, she has an especially urgent stake in preserving the domestic world, keeping the bread rising and the fire burning. For the Ingallses, these are matters of life and death. But Laura's very consciousness, the spark of her selfhood, is threatened by this necessary routine. As a girl, faced by the twin pressures of gender and weather, where can she go? What can she do?

The book's ending provides no answers to these pressing questions. . . . The suffering has stopped, at least briefly, because spring has come. But the weather is still in control. *The Long Winter* explores what that inexorable fact can mean to a spirited girl, eager to invent herself a life in the nineteenth-century West. As the central volume of Wilder's enduring series, this novel is a powerful introduction to the myths, the art, and the realities of women's culture on the American frontier.

Ann Romines. Great Plains Quarterly. 10,
Winter, 1990, pp. 36–37, 46

Despite Wilder's praise of stoicism, the *Little House* books do not paint a picture of cold people. Wilder evokes, through cumulative portraits of Ingalls family life, a sense of well-being that gives vicarious pleasure to the reader. The family often has to depend on their own resources for companionship, but the time spent together is almost always peaceful or fun, rather than tension-filled. Ma and Pa love Laura even though she is naughty sometimes. The Ingalls children are both eager and able to please their parents. Whatever the situation, Ma and Pa can find ways to provide for their four girls. In volume after volume, Wilder firmly associates these gratifying characteristics of Ingalls family life with other aspects of their experience: hardship and deprivation, gratitude for little rewards, family self-containment and isolation, individual self-sufficiency, parental ingenuity and skill. Conversely, whenever government appears in the books, it is associated with bungling and stress, as in the homesteading allocations and regulations. Also, whenever heightened emotion is introduced, it is connected with undesirable behavior.

These links are present throughout the *Little House* books, along with many other illustrations of the ethical and political principles to which Wilder and [Rose Wilder] Lane [her daughter and collaborator] had become increasingly devoted. They imbued all the meticulous details in the books, how to build a chimney or make sour-dough biscuits, with an ideology of self-sufficiency. Ma and Pa refuse to be beholden to anyone, even for a few nails, a slate for school, an invitation to a party, or a pail of wheat to ward off starvation. A comparison of the less adorned, more strictly autobiographical "Pioneer Girl" manuscript with the more developed *Little House* series reveals that over time Wilder and Lane further accentuated the family's ingenuity and its geographic and economic separateness from its community, while minimizing the degree to which Pa had been dependent upon wage work. . . .

Wilder's and Lane's reinterpretations of their personal and familial history in light of the political changes initiated by the New Deal caused the two women to reshape their goals as writers. Wilder came to believe that she had a larger purpose in her writing. She had written the "Pioneer Girl" memoir hoping to preserve her father's stories and to make money. Later, with the publication of the first books in what became the *Little House* series, she desired prestige and wished to please her appreciative audience. Nonetheless, by the late 1930s, she viewed the *Little House* books as an important seven-volume novel for children, capturing the essential aspects of the American frontier and agricultural experiences. Later, Lane claimed that her mother specifically intended the series to be a criticism of the New Deal.

Anita Clair Fellman. *Signs: Journal of*
Women in Culture and Society. 15, 1990,
pp. 536-38

Whatever its apparent shortcomings may be, *Farmer Boy* has been unnecessarily neglected, and deserves recognition in its own right. Its setting does, to be sure, as Janet Spaeth points out, provide a "backdrop of 'the East'" against which Wilder can contrast the rigors and requirements of frontier existence, and it introduces Almanzo Wilder, who figures prominently in later volumes of the series and ultimately marries Laura. . . . Nevertheless, the book makes an even greater contribution to the larger series. In its portrayal of Almanzo's boyhood on a large, successful farm in the settled environs of New York State, *Farmer Boy* establishes the social, economic, and national backgrounds against which the opening of the West takes place. It supplies, therefore, at the beginning of the series, distinctive cultural elements that are thematically essential to the completion of Laura Ingalls Wilder's accounts of the American westerning experience. . . .

The greatest part of Laura Ingalls Wilder's story is carried, not surprisingly, by the Ingallses, her family and the family of the western frontier, energetic, resourceful, self-sufficient, and westward-looking. Complementing and completing the story, however, are the Wilders, the family of the farmer, equally resourceful and equally independent-minded, but socially assimilated, economically aware, and conscious of their part in the driving spirit of the greater nation. Brought into the series in the pages of *Farmer Boy* and developed by the later interweaving of Almanzo's life with Laura's, they constitute the other component of the dialectic from which emerges the American synthesis. That synthesis requires many things. It requires, to be sure, forthright and sturdy individuals—persons like Pa, Ma, and Laura Ingalls, like Almanzo and his parents, who can deal with the exigencies of life yet retain their sense of themselves as persons and as citizens. It requires settlement, as well, those waves of civilization that follow the frontier, domesticating nature and establishing the communities that bring law, education, religion, and commerce to the wilderness. Most of all, though, the American synthesis requires the coalescing of the people's separate endeavors into a cohesive national enterprise, in which individual, society, economy, and nation collaborate to create the vital, democratic realization of the westering dream. . . .

In the best Turnerian fashion, Laura and Almanzo, frontier settler and American farmer, blend their qualities to shape, even as they are shaped by, the westering experience. The powerful elements of the western myth come together at last, and in the fullness of their message is the affirmation of *Farmer Boy*'s integral place among the "Little House" books.

Fred Erisman. *Western American*
Literature. 28, 1993, pp. 123, 129–30

WILLIAMS, SHERLEY ANNE (UNITED STATES) 1944–

Some One Sweet Angel Chile, by Sherley Anne Williams. . . speaks in tongues and sings in many voices. It begins with an elegant and revelatory series of epistolary poems, "Letters From a New England Negro," written in the persona of an educated young black woman gone south, in 1867, to teach her newly-freed people. She learns as much as she teaches; the contradictions and rewards of the life she has left, as well as the situation she has come to, are unfolded with a clarity and complexity that were as satisfying to this reader as a five hundred-page novel. In a completely different vocabulary and rhythm, the middle sequence of poems celebrates Bessie Smith, and illuminates another facet of the history and heroism of black women. Here, in cadences echoing the blues, the author animates a chorus of men and women around the legendary Bessie to give a rounded and reverberating oratorio. The book's last section, in contemporary voices, often has for landscape the poet's native Southern California. The primacy of music continues as a theme, along with the complexity of relationships between black women and men. With a different perspective, the poet re-examines family, history, and the interstices between.

Marilyn Hacker. *Commonweal.* 109,
1982, p. 668

"The Darky," "The Wench," "The Negress": three chapter headings, which reflect three casual assortments of racism and sexism as much as they describe Dessa Rose, one of the two heroines of this demanding three-chapter novel [*Dessa Rose*] set in the summer of 1847. Dessa Rose is a pregnant black slave condemned to die (once she bears her child, a valuable commodity) for her part in a slave uprising in Kentucky; the other heroine is a white woman harboring runaway slaves on a North Carolina farm, where she has been abandoned by her husband. An author's note explains that the two heroines are derived from historical records; a 1971 essay by Angela Davis prompted Sherley Anne Williams to speculate about what might have happened if the slave and the harborer had met. Her narrative, much of it rendered in dialect, takes several unexpected turns—west, for instance, not north—as the women change their minds about who has been a victim and who is a friend. Sherley Anne Williams, a published poet whose first novel this is, is a native of California.

The New Yorker. September 8, 1986, p. 136

A Californian poet and academic, Sherley Anne Williams moves into fiction in *Dessa Rose* with a neat stroke of historical sleight-of-hand. In 1829 a slave uprising in Kentucky led to a death sentence for its pregnant ringleader, here called Dessa. A year later in North Carolina, rumors circulated of an eccentric white woman who harbored runaways on her ramshackle estate. Shifting the action to 1847, the novel makes Dessa and Miss Ruth meet, first as enemies; then rivals; then sisters: "Maybe it is only a metaphor, but I now own a summer in the nineteenth century."

Williams's writing about the ante-bellum South treads a knife-edge between tenderness and rage. Slavery grants her women the occasions of power and love, for instance as the adored "mammies" of their owners' children, at the same time as it leaves scars without and within. She traces the moves of black and white, male and female, over this chessboard of authority and deference with a poet's eloquence and an anthropologist's eye for pattern. Yet, since a piece of wishful thinking lies at its core, *Dessa Rose* finally shirks history in favor of romance.

Boyd Tonkin. The New Statesman.
April 24, 1987, p. 29

"Meditations on History," Sherley Anne Williams's novella about discourse and struggle, achieves much of its meaning through its own struggle with previous modes of discourse. Engaging works by William Styron and Thomas Gray, Williams explores the discourses of history and fiction. Although Williams references neither Styron nor his work in "Meditations," her title signals not only that Styron's *Confessions of Nat Turner* is the primary anterior text for her work, but that her purpose is to produce a text which engages Styron as a kind of literary interlocutor. . . . Williams's work suggests, however, that Styron's interventions result in the misreading of his historical subject, while her own work represents not only an attempt to reconcile the literary treatment to the historical subject but, in the process, to deconstruct her predecessor's methods. "Meditations," then, becomes a gesture of what Henry Louis Gates calls "critical parody," in that Williams revises and thus problematizes the structuration of Styron's *Confessions*. . . .

Williams's "Meditations" suggests that we must revise our expectations of white and male-authored literary and non-literary texts about blacks and women; that we must learn, in the words of Adrienne Rich, to enter "an old text from a new critical direction"; and, furthermore, that the act of "seeing" an old text "with fresh eyes" is "an act of survival." As Rich puts it, "We need to know the writing of the past, and know it differently than we have ever known it; not to pass on a tradition but to break its hold over us." In the sense that Rich uses the term, "re-vision" allows us to reclaim authentic historical and literary models and, in doing so, to liberate ourselves from old stereotypes.

The major significance of Williams's text is that it draws the reader's attention to the representational and interpretative strategies of those who dominate formal discourse. It becomes a decoding device for reading texts by those who control social and literary structures. In this regard, Williams not only reveals the presumptions and pitfalls of racial- and gender-inflected cultural misreadings but, perhaps more importantly, provides the reader with a model of how to read formal texts in which black and women's voices have been muted, suppressed, or misunderstood.

Mae G. Henderson. Black American
Literature Forum. 23, 1989,
pp. 632–33, 656–57

In Sherley Anne Williams's *Dessa Rose* (1986) . . . the protagonist, Dessa Rose—herself unnamed in a patriarchal sense since she lacks a patronymic—

recites a concise genealogy of her family, naming them for posterity lest they be forgotten.

This torrent of family names appears in a novel intensely concerned with onomastics, names, nicknames, pet names, misnomers, and name-calling, for example. In fact, Williams's entire novel is a "signifying" text on many levels. Three personal names, a pet name, and an epithet are used ironically and symbolically: Adam Nehemiah, Kaine, Mammy, Rose, and "devil woman," an epithet conferred upon Dessa Rose. Moreover, Dessa literally reclaims her given name and figuratively reclaims her personal history. Consistently misnamed "Odessa"; referred to successively as "The Darky," "The Wench," and "The Negress" in the titles of three major sections of the novel; and called out of her name with expressions like "devil woman," "treacherous nigger bitch," and "uppity, insolent slut". . . this ex-slave narrator, formerly illiterate, transforms herself into the Dessa Rose Anti-Defamation League. By the time of the action in the novel's Epilogue, she has begun to inscribe her own history in her own hand for her descendants and others who might peruse her tale. Henceforth, to paraphrase James Baldwin, everybody will know her name. . . .

Through her complex "signifying upon" several names. . . Williams critiques the flawed language and the flawed world-view of the slavocracy, and she substitutes counter-text in which the slave's voice can be heard. In so doing, her novel admonishes novelists, historians, and all guilty parties to stop their insidious misnaming of the slave. She demands that everyone call the slaves by their true names.

Mary Kemp Davis. Callaloo. 12,
1989, pp. 544–45, 556–57

In *Dessa Rose* Sherley Anne Williams creates a break in the grammar of racism. The intercalation of the discourses of slavery makes the textual work of *Dessa Rose* where the author opens a space, creates a day in the calendar of discursive history, for the African-American woman's text. Williams (un)-writes the plantation novel, separating the white woman from white racism (the socioeconomics of the planter class) and the white academic and literary discourses of slavery; she (dis)places white stories of black men's and women's lives (the "authoritative" written texts by which African-American experiences have been "known"), and, in a project sharing certain features with [Leslie Marmon] Silko's in *Ceremony,* (re)writes the slave narrative, freeing the black woman so that she can figure her story. She converts the monolithic character of group and generic identity (black woman/white woman)—moves instructive to me as I try to unsettle the oppositional terms feminist and theorist—to individual identities (Dessa/Ruth) in order to destroy the mechanics of stereotypes, the very machinery by means of which they work. Through structural intervention, Williams creates a break, a potential for relationship beyond the historical monolithic (white) master/(black) slave dialectic of oppression. She writes (in) the gap: a romance of race, a *u-topic* fiction of hope and a "happy ending."

Elizabeth A. Meese. *(Ex-)Tensions: Refiguring Feminist Criticism* (Urbana: University of Illinois Press, 1990), p. 135

Generally, Williams's novel is a much more optimistic if less complex book than Morrison's [*Beloved*]. Throughout, it teaches sophisticated lessons in pluralism and cooperation, accentuating the necessity of breaking down racial barriers, of establishing friendships across color, culture, and gender lines. Its final pages bring *Dessa Rose* to a tidy, romantic close; Dessa sits safely among her descendants, engaged in activity to ensure *"the childrens . . . never have to pay what it cost us to own ourselfs."* Still, one cannot close the book free of a sense of obligation. For in the last section, Williams describes in rich, sensual language the lovemaking between Dessa and Harker, and in bestial terms Dessa's shame at the literal marks of slavery she bears. Scars have transformed the center of Dessa's womanness to "a mutilated cat face. Scar tissue plow[ing] through her pubic region." In addition, through Dessa's recollection of her jail experience, Williams bluntly reminds her readers of the horrors of slavery. . . .

Through her title character, Williams speaks to the pathos and heroism slavery occasioned.

Jocelyn C. Moody. *Black American Literature Forum.* 25, 1990, p. 645

That Dessa resists [the] impulse toward self-destruction and survives to describe it to her children suggests that passive resistance must be exchanged in favor of articulated rebellion. Nevertheless, the impulse to silence the self has an invidious logic within the system which makes of the woman's body a text to be marked upon. The defiant heroine of *Dessa Rose* is herself one of those so marked. Walking in on her friend Nathan making love with Rufel, Dessa envisions the patterning of black and white bodies in bed as a text, with the black reduced to print to be read and discarded like a used newspaper: "He wasn't nothing but a mark on them. That's what we was in white folks' eyes, nothing but marks to be used, wiped out." That she is pregnant, and almost to term, does not prevent the men who find her from engraving their authority on her body. It is, in fact, the "R" branded on her thigh and the whip scars about her hips which almost lead to her repossession by the scholar Nehemiah, from whose jurisdiction she has escaped. Significantly, however, the schoolteacher's authority is itself dependent on the word of the slave, for in recording Dessa's history from her own lips, Nehemiah intends to produce the text he hopes will become canonical, *The Roots of Rebellion in the Slave Population and Some Means of Eradicating Them.* As the master

anticipates using the child to be born from Dessa's womb, so the scholar expects to appropriate the words issuing from her mouth for his own profit.
Anne E. Goldman. *Feminist Studies.* 16,
1990, pp. 322–23

Dessa Rose ends with *her* writing/righting her own story for her grandchildren, as she braids their hair—another nonscribal way of storytelling and maintaining history. She also ensures that the children know the story and that it is written down and then re-oralized. Hers is definitely mother write/right, not mother-as-written. She foregrounds the need for some memory of a past of struggle and not of defeat. Nehemiah's text is erased: "Miz Lady was turning over the papers in her hand. 'And these is blank, sheriff,' she say."

Dessa finally writes/rights her own story. Hers is a much more empowering gesture, with more human agency, than is Sethe's. The move from being the-mother-as-she-is-written to being the-mother-as-she-writes . . . is one of the text's most radical strategies. She becomes speaking subject, while the authorial or narrating "I" is submerged. The move is also one of re-oralizing, which decenters the text's narrative control.

> This why I have it wrote down, why I has the child say it back.
> I never will forget Nemi trying to read me, knowing I had put
> myself in his hands. Well this the childrens have heard from
> our own lips.

In the continuing discourse on motherhood and mothering which is being articulated in black women's fiction, there is a contest of interpretations. Any notion of an exclusivist, nativist, nationalistic articulation of an exoticized, reified, or romanticized black motherhood becomes limiting. Motherhood is both annihilation and empowerment; marking and renaming; the locus of change and growth but as well of pain and loss. Painful rememberings and liberating narratives seem necessarily to interrupt each other's dominance. All of these intersect at different points, as the narrative of the mother becomes more prominently articulated.
Carole Boyce Davies. In Brenda O. Daly
and Maureen Reddy, eds. *Narrating
Mothers: Theorizing Maternal Subjectivity*
(Knoxville: University of Tennessee Press,
1991), p. 56

In *Dessa Rose,* Sherley Anne Williams offers us a complex and nuanced exemplum of a slave narrative written by a woman. This is an especially noteworthy achievement in light of the fact that extant and published slave narratives in the historical record were written by black men. Black women wrote less than twelve percent of published slave narratives. By daring to call forth from the historical past the "voice" of "[d]e nigger woman . . . de mule uh de world," as Zora Neale Hurston so aptly put it almost half a century ago, Williams complicates a historical record that has almost entirely excluded or misrepresented the female slave voice. She invites us to imagine how such a woman might have assessed her world and notably asserted her subjectivity in writing. Like Toni Morrison's *Beloved* and Margaret Walker's *Jubilee, Dessa Rose* fits firmly into the tradition of contemporary fictional rewritings of slave narratives by African-American women.

In a contemporary setting, Williams also dares to inject ethnicity as well as gender into current literary debates on authorship, "voice," and "truth," thus complicating an already complicated postmodern agenda. Readers hold in their hands not only a "liberation narrative" by a black woman slave (Dessa Rose) but also a novel by an African-American woman. Williams's achievement is that she doubly subverts the anomaly of the black woman writer. The doubling of "voices," as a narrative strategy of protagonist and author both, engages readers in an interrogation of the very underpinnings of "authority" and "truth," vexed notions that plague contemporary discourse today. Both women in different times and places claim authorship and speak with authority.

Marta E. Sanchez. Genders. 15, 1992, p. 21

In the end, there is only one African American slave in *Dessa Rose*—and that is Dorcas. The rest are all fugitive slaves—Dessa, Harker, Nathan, Ada, Annabelle—all of them. It is worth noting, then, that Williams places only one voice beyond the realm of freedom and, coincidentally, represents only that voice as always a reconstruction of someone else's imagining. Perhaps Williams's most astonishing accomplishment is her implicit representation of the proper respect due the enigma and the ambiguity of the slave's voice. The fact that Williams ensures we never directly hear Dorcas's voice or immediately encounter her words except through others' representations suggests something about the limitations on our ability to hear the slave voice. Beyond "written history and outside of printed law," wrote Du Bois in another context, "there has been going on for a generation as deep a storm and stress of human souls, as intense a ferment of feeling, as intricate a writhing of spirit, as ever a people experience." This experience, he continued, comes to us in "the voice of exile" which is full of "eloquent omissions and silences" and conveyed in the "naturally veiled and half articulate" manner employed whenever "the slave spoke to the world."

Williams employs two interrelated strategies to represent that "voice of exile" in *Dessa Rose*. First, she defers the representation so that Dorcas's voice appears as always the recreative supplement of Rufel's narrative imagination. Second, she insists that the only humane way to recreate that voice is to supplement it by placing it amidst a chorus of voices of people who have lived the same life and experienced the same condition as Dorcas.

Ashraf H. A. Rushdy. African American
Review. 27, 1993, pp. 385–86

WILSON, ETHEL (CANADA) 1888–1980

This little novel [*Hetty Dorval*] introduces a new Canadian writer. It has in it just enough solid merit to make its ultimate failure a matter of regret. Mrs. Wilson's story deals with a young girl's infatuation for an older woman and her final rejection of this woman with the sure knowledge that "Good is as visible as green." There is nothing homosexual in their relationship—this is a very old-fashioned story. . . .

Now, Mrs. Wilson's book is in the way of being a moral primer. Hetty Dorval is Attractive Evil in every way—and Attractive Evil must be put down for everyone's sake. So far, so good. It is in the literalness of her one-to-one equation—Hetty equals Bad—that the author runs a little thin. You can't sustain a work of imagination on the color black, just as you can't write a good morality play without first writing a good play. And Mrs. Wilson hasn't done the first job.

> Seymour Krim. *The New York Times.*
> September 14, 1947, p. 16

Miss Wilson lovingly presents [in *The Innocent Traveller*] the portrait of a lady living long and with ceaseless vigor. One hundred years is the time allotted Topaz Edgeworth for sojourn on this planet. She takes joy in it, enriching her spinster state with sisters, brothers, nieces, nephews, and generation after generation of collaterals. From an English Victorian childhood to an excessive venerability in Western Canada her scope increases while her personality grows proportionately more colorful. A splendid old party results. Invulnerable, mannered, inordinately loquacious, rich in importance, ever ready to do battle, eager for callers or a new idea, this grande dame makes marvelous material. Gladstone, Matthew Arnold, Kipling, and Queen Mary strew her path with prestige. Once she meets Otis Skinner, who, in his shining person, forever cleanses the theater of evil.

Based partly on fact, padded with inventive fiction. *The Innocent Traveller* is gentle, engaging, quietly wise, and nostalgic without being dated.

> Catherine Meredith Brown. *Saturday*
> *Review.* December 10, 1949, p. 17

I have not come across either of the two books previously published by Miss Ethel Wilson, who is a Canadian writer, but *The Equations of Love* suggests an interesting talent in the making. Acute and tough-minded, following cheerfully in whatever direction a robust sense of comedy leads her, Miss Wilson is as yet deficient, I would say, in the kind of self-criticism which is a sixth sense for the writer of fiction and which is perhaps no good to anybody else. The book consists of two long short-stories, each of which seems to have borrowed something of style or idiosyncrasy from a different model: in the one case—most incongruously—from Henry James and in the other from Mr.

Maugham. "Tuesday and Wednesday," set among slovenly types in slatternly lodgings in Vancouver, is about a ridiculous, self-dramatizing drab of a woman with an equally absurd and feckless fish of a husband, and is, I fear, altogether a mistake. Miss Wilson's Jamesian or quasi-Jamesian deliberation here, though festooned with all sorts of feminine trimmings, sits grotesquely upon a theme that is really trivial and humorless; her Myrtle and Mort are, in the end, only boring.

The other tale, however, "Lilly's Story," is uncommonly shrewd and amusing, and is told with the most assured irony. An abandoned child, sluttish and knowing, is a small monster of duplicity even before she is introduced as a waitress in a Chinese joint in Vancouver. Lilly's life, after her own child is born, is a brilliantly sustained campaign to achieve respectability. I am not sure that, like several of Mr. Maugham's spectacular moral heroines, she is not a little too flagrantly "made-up," but the story is an excellent one for all that, though nearly ruined by the farcical touch at the close. A writer who may be worth watching.

R. D. Charques. The Spectator. March 21, 1952, p. 378

The opening pages of Swamp Angel, perfectly controlled, effective, firmly snaring the reader's interest, give immediate promise of enjoyment to come. These first pages present Maggie Lloyd's final evening with her husband as, one by one, she takes the meticulously planned steps which carry her out of the house to freedom.

The reading enjoyments which follow are real, but they are not those of a compactly plotted story which the opening promises. Rather, the author presents a detail from "the miraculous interweaving of creation," with sharp insights into a half dozen characters and a perceptive and often finely poetic examination of man's fellow creatures on the earth. . . .

The novel contains many passages of great beauty. A little fence-enclosed burying ground with three white crosses on a wild hillside, a fawn and a kitten in the first light of dawn, a loon over the lonely lake, the rainbow trout flashing on the surface of the water are a few of the scenes which are described with a moving simplicity that makes the reader catch his breath.

The author is able to delineate an emotion with the same skill, and the volume is full of small and bright surprises. The essay on the mystique of fly-fishing is one which would hardly be expected from a feminine pen. But the story, as a whole, is inconclusive.

Coleman Rosenberger. New York Herald Tribune. September 5, 1954, p. 4

Here [Mrs. Golightly, and Other Stories] are the macabre, the fanciful, the sensitive stories about women and very much for women—yet most of them do not live up to what they seem to be aiming at: there are good ideas but perhaps not always good story ideas. There are impressionistic studies—of

a fishmonger contending with his customers, of a City church, of a business
convention—but too often the twist is either missing altogether or disappointingly semi-detached from the heart of the story, a "good idea" in itself but
not a natural outcome of the plot. Perhaps these comments tend towards the
carping: to write one short story, let alone a whole book full, requires a
particular skill in selection and organization which many authors of full-
length books do not possess. I do not wish to carp, but I do think that
nowadays anyone trying to write short stories should recognize what a difficult form it is: should make up his or her mind, in short, as to whether what
they are trying to achieve is the perfect moralizing of a Tolstoy or the technical perfection of a V. S. Pritchett.

Gillian Tindall. Time and Tide. February 1,
1962, p. 37

It is . . . [the] ability to weave all elements of the art of fiction into a single
fabric that is Ethel Wilson's highest distinction. She has a shrewd insight into
social behavior and individual character, a strong sense of place and abundant
gifts for description, a wise and balanced view of man and his relationship
to the universe, an eye for the revealing symbol or image, and a clear, simple
and yet almost unerringly deft style; but each of these capacities is employed
to reinforce the others. . . .

Ethel Wilson lays no claim to being a major novelist, but she is a minor
novelist of genuine distinction whose work will almost certainly be read when
that of many more pretentious and prolific writers is forgotten. In the narrower context of the still emerging literature of Canada, she is a figure of
great importance. She is one of the very few Canadian writers for whom one
need make no apology in offering her work to the world. She belongs in the
main tradition of the English novel, has her affiliations as we have seen with
Defoe, Fielding, Trollope, Bennett and Forster, and yet she is unmistakably
an artist of twentieth century Canada. She neither pleads for nor repudiates
her own country, but writes of it with balance and dignity. She seeks to be
neither fashionable nor defiantly unfashionable, but expresses her own vision
honestly and in the form which suits it best. Self-consciousness, both in the
personal and national sense, has perhaps been the chief bane of writing in
Canada, situated as we are between the mellow traditions of the Old World
and the aggressive experimentation of the New, and it is Mrs. Wilson's special
legacy that her work is not self-conscious at all. Like the writers she most
admires, she has a limpid style, lacks pretentiousness, has something to say,
and says it with skill and with good heart. Like theirs, her work gives "inexpressible pleasure."

Desmond Pacey. Ethel Wilson (New York:
Twayne, 1967), pp. 174, 179–80

Not all of Mrs. Wilson's figures show the perception of Frances Burnaby [in
Hetty Dorval]: not all are conscious of what motivates them. But all are

observed in relation to an environment that becomes their "genius," and the author's balance of character with place becomes part of her exploration of man's relationship with himself, with others, and with the philosophical traps and supports which he invents to trouble and to comfort him. Such concerns do not make the author's works distinctively "Canadian" but such a demand is irrelevant in any estimate of literary worth. Ethel Wilson's sensitivity and her stylistic restraint have made her one of Canada's most accomplished novelists, and that is enough. . . .

There is a fluidity in both time and place, and because a person creates his identity in terms of these two, his identity is fluid as well. It is this fluidity that Mrs. Wilson is conscious of and that, through her imagery and her successive explorations of travelers-through-life, she has detailed in her work. In recognizing their "genius of place," her perceptive characters become conscious of the fact that lives can be molded, and hence also sensitive to their own potential in a specific place and time. What they must do is locate this world—"create their own system or be enslaved by another's"—if they are to know in their lives not only passion but also some peace. Frankie Burnaby can do this; so can Rose, the autobiographical grandniece in *The Innocent Traveller:* so can Maggie Lloyd, for whom the others are prototypes, in the most successful *Swamp Angel.* This, then, is Ethel Wilson's statement. It offers a strange combination of a romantic vision and an acute perception of reality—which is not distinctively Canadian, but is quite characteristic of Canadian irony. Mrs. Wilson's technical facility in presenting her statement—through character and symbol rather than through simple exposition—raises her work to the level of ordered, vital, and artistically satisfying fiction.

William H. New. *Journal of Canadian Studies.* November, 1968, pp. 39, 46–48

"Do we always live on a brink, then, said Nora to herself, lying there in the dark. Yes, I believe we do." This quotation, from Ethel Wilson's novel, *Love and Salt Water,* reflects the thoughts of the heroine's sister, soon after the heroine, Ellen Cuppy, meets an accident that leaves her face permanently scarred. Why should this disaster occur so unexpectedly during an ordinary outing in which Ellen takes her nephew to the seaside? Are all ordinary, everyday actions marked by unpredictability and filled with the same potentiality of disaster? These are some of the main questions that Mrs. Wilson's novels and stories try to answer; and altogether, they brilliantly project the luminous truth of Nora's observation—that we all live continuously on a brink, and that our commonest actions have the capacity constantly to frustrate, delight or, at any rate, surprise us. Since we live on a brink without knowing the exact outcome of our actions, we are innocent. It is the underlying purpose of Mrs. Wilson's fiction to record the facts of our innocence by illustrating the critical significance of seemingly trivial events in our lives; and her underlying theme, throughout, is an unpredictable future which, by means of coincidence or unimportant incidents, asserts an unfailing ability to inflict apparently undeserved grief and unmerited injury on unsuspecting individuals. . . .

All Mrs. Wilson's books illustrate the sudden shocks and abrupt shifts of fortune, like Ellen's accident, which can be produced by unforeseen events. Mrs. Wilson's universe is one of complete chaos, where anything can happen to anyone at any time; but she shows no willingness to question this disorder. She takes her strange and haphazard universe for granted, and nowhere reveals the slightest interest in investigating its philosophical foundations. Thus her books do not probe or analyze the action which they describe. Instead, they impose on this action a view of life that is slightly whimsical and which effectively neutralizes the actual risks and inherent dangers of an unpredictable future. The two essential features of Mrs. Wilson's fiction, therefore, are her illustration of the inimical capacity of the future and a predilection for a whimsicality that evokes the supernatural realities behind everyday appearances. . . .

The desire to protect her characters from the harsher elements of her theme opens Mrs. Wilson to the charge of "escapism." But if "escapism" means that she alters or distorts real dangers and threats posed by the future, then the charge cannot stick. The cruel adversities endured by all her chief characters prove beyond doubt that Mrs. Wilson does not evade or escape the real issues of an unpredictable future. She advocates neither escapism nor aggression. She compromises rather than opposes, acknowledges rather than investigates.

Frank Birbalsingh. *Canadian Literature.*
Summer, 1971, pp. 35–36, 46

Wilson writes about what she knows. That knowledge is based on a traditional women's culture where the roles of wife and mother are a woman's natural fate. Within these roles, a woman may be completely fulfilled but she lacks power and identity outside the private sphere. When these roles are thwarted or put aside, Wilson's women do surprising things. None of them achieve power in the traditional male sense but some manifest a spiritual power which touches and influences the lives of others. These powerful women extend the traditional role of nurturing; they give to each other and to the world not at the expense of self, as in the conventional housewife/mother role, but in the fulfillment of self as in the essential Christian mystery. The distinction is clearly seen [in *Swamp Angel*] between Maggie who is triumphant and Vera who is merely martyred and so becomes a burden to everyone else.

Wilson sees certain women as preservers and maintainers of the fragile balance of life, as synthesizers who draw together that which has been severed. The women of the Edgeworth family hold together their extended kinship network like the four points of a mandala. Maggie holds together the Gunnarsen family and so enables the genesis of a new community beyond the nuclear unit. In these novels, Wilson demonstrates how, within the web, we are all responsible for each other. No women is an island and we are all part of woman kind.

Donna E. Smyth. In Lorraine McMullen,
ed. *The Ethel Wilson Symposium* (Ottawa:
University of Ottawa Press, 1982), p. 95

"I had handled dynamite," Frankie Burnaby thinks at the end of Ethel Wilson's novel *Hetty Dorval:* "I had handled dynamite, and in so doing had exploded the hidden mine of Mrs. Broom to my own great astonishment."

I start with this image of a hidden mine in Ethel Wilson's fiction because I am an American reader, accustomed by my literature to explosions of violence in the novel and also to abundance, to the presence within a vast and varied landscape of rich deposits—the inexhaustible resources of art. Canadian critics, as they describe the abundance contained in Wilson's fiction, its richness of natural and social detail, have praised the surface serenity of her art: the detached tone; the compassionate and comic insights into the foibles of the great human family; the faith that remains unshaken even when these foibles, our seemingly innocent but obsessive meddling with each other, turn into destructive or coercive acts, violations of each other's freedom. I wish to excavate to a depth hidden beneath the surface sustained so beautifully by Wilson's style and tone and the seemingly casual meandering of her form; I wish to dig for the dynamite I suspect she has concealed. By her own image she has alerted us to the possibility of hidden mines and so validated the process of excavation, which I take to be the critic's essential act. First of all, I want to extract from Wilson's fiction the violence that lurks beneath its serenity. In these dangerous depths, I expect to find also abundance—a rich subterranean treasure of motives and meanings that constitute the source of Ethel Wilson's art.

Blanche Gelfant. In Lorraine McMullen, ed.
The Ethel Wilson Symposium (Ottawa:
University of Ottawa Press, 1982),
pp. 119–20

Ethel Wilson was the Edwardian child of a Victorian world. Her values were very much of her time. And in writing of her time, she managed deftly to establish on the page both the early years of this century in England and provincial Canada, and the social climate of Vancouver in the 1940s, the feel of the place. The place was isolated; the society was stratified; and one mustn't forget either of these observations. Part of her intent was to chart the dimensions of the life that was open to Canadians at the time—particularly to women—in urban and rural communities, in city and suburb, in occupational group and religious denomination, with or without economic or social access to summer cottage, train travel, Member of Parliament, Europe, or a taxi ride to New Westminster. It was a world deeply affected by *British* notions of culture and social propriety. "Americanisms" are not widely applauded in

Ethel Wilson's world, and traditional uppermiddleclass rituals are: they constitute for the author (and perhaps for the person behind the author) a public enactment of the cumulative values of civilization, part of a social contract that she regards as a necessity to carry on. . . .

The tensions of such a depicted world invite serious psychocritical responses—which we have yet to write. They may be no more reliable guides to Truth-with-a-capital-T than the legends and the known facts we already have, but they may illuminate the *text:* illuminate the tensions that women faced at least in a particular generation, and document the not necessarily fulfilling resolutions which women consequently chose or saw their society choose for them.

What I am saying is that there is more politics in Ethel Wilson's work than we have commonly recognized—governmental politics, as in "We Have to Sit Opposite" and other pieces—and sexual politics both directly and indirectly expressed.

W. H. New. In Lorraine McMullen, ed. *The Ethel Wilson Symposium* (Ottawa: University of Ottawa Press, 1982), pp. 142–43

In the conventional narrative of *Swamp Angel,* Wilson gives form to the drama of this struggle in her portrayal of Maggie's escape from a restrictive perspective on her environment to a fuller view—her search for her "place." *Swamp Angel* is literature about literature, but more than that, it explores those complex operations of the mind—an author's mind or anyone's—which are attempts to possess somehow the world around it. Wilson makes a connection between Maggie's search for her place, and a reader's search for belief; the richness of *Swamp Angel* lies in the interplay between these two quests. The reader's new role in relation to *Swamp Angel* produces a greater sensitivity to the exhilaration and danger of Maggie's quest. Likewise, Maggie's story is a cautioning guide to the reader who is hoping to possess a world.

The world around Maggie is clearly different from the environment in which many other creatures of Canadian literature, contemporary with the appearance of *Swamp Angel* or earlier, find themselves; whereas Maggie's world ultimately balances the hope of possession and the consequences of the absence of hope, theirs is often either a cheerful place unfamiliar to us or a terrifying wilderness empty except for a force of efficient and anonymous destruction.

Brent Thompson. *Canadian Literature.* 102, 1984, p. 20

Ethel Wilson's novel *Swamp Angel* (1954) has been praised for its vivid presentation of character, its accurate depiction of the British Columbian scene, its special handling of time, for the richness of its symbols as well as the depth and subtlety of its theme. It has nowhere been pointed out, however, that all these achievements are closely related to Ethel Wilson's counterpoint technique. For the characterization of the two main characters, Maggie Lloyd and Nell Severance, is made more suggestive by a variety of parallels and contrasts between them. The vividness and significance of the setting is enhanced by the contrast between the city, Vancouver, and the countryside, near Kamloops. The differing significance of time for the Severances and for Maggie is part of the thematic essence of the novel. The pervasive symbol, the Swamp Angel, appears not only in the narrative past and present in connection with the Severances, but also grows into a powerful symbol for the development Maggie has taken. Finally, the thematic content is enriched by, and partly hinges on, the parallels and contrasts between essentially two different strands of narration. Thus the staple elements of any counterpoint technique, parallelism and contrast, are effective in *Swamp Angel.* They weave characterization, setting, time, symbolism and thematic context into a complex system of interrelationships.

Reingard M. Nischik. *World Literature*
Written in English. 23, 1984, p. 375

The attempt to create and capture Canadian myth in the 1950s was animated by the spirits of the muse and the museum. Poetic exploration of inherited, classical and Christian myth and research and publication of indigenous tales were both part of a larger impulse—to summon the powerful spirits of this country.

Ethel Wilson's *Swamp Angel,* published in 1954, is centered in this complex of motives. It is a myth story, a journey to the wilderness and to greater conceptual and linguistic freedom, in a narrative which is frequently poetic, at times mystical, and which offers a plurality of signification. It calls upon the avatars, gods, God and silences of nature. This formal variety, of realist novel, poetry and philosophical speculation, is furthered in a range of styles and points of view, an enrichment of possible meaning at the expense of clear view and reliable interpretation. How the figurative, semantic, syntactic and formal levels of *Swamp Angel* all variously but harmoniously develop the idea of the inter-dependency of language and land is the subject of this article. Wilson's "message," I suggest, lies as much in a highly unusual use of metonymy and simile as in the characters' stories or the narrator's commentary. . . .

Swamp Angel is . . . based on a complex of metaphor and metonymy. It is metaphor, as is all literature, although within that category as prose it moves more to the metonymic than the metaphoric, and this is reinforced by the overarching story structure. Yet, while a novel and metonymic, it violates realist convention in refusing to provide that narratorial assurance which tells us that there are lessons to be learned, and that this book is a true synecdoche for our world. Opposing patterns—logos and mythos, human nature and Nature, the line of Christian progress and the wheel of birth and death—are all antinomies whose elements are grounded in the metonymic and metaphoric respectively.

On the level of organization and diction, this non-realist novel is distinguished by the language of realism. Juxtaposition may suggest both difference and likeness through proximity. Metaphor, when used, is subservient to the context, and the tenor of metaphor is drawn from it.

The rule of metonymy in *Swamp Angel* suggests, as Maggie's experiences do, that the individual must resist all assimilation, whether social or natural; and that even the cycles of birth, death and wilderness will fall before the gradual progression to Grace.

Heather Murray. World Literature Written in
English. 25, 1985, pp. 241, 250–51

[T]he history [in *The Innocent Traveller*] of the irrepressible Topaz, unmarried, without profession, sheltered and cared for by her large family for a hundred years, enjoyable as it all is to read about, may leave us with an overwhelming sense of its insignificance. Indeed, Wilson deliberately creates and reinforces our sense of triviality of Topaz's life: she is compared to a water-glider, an insect that skims along the surface of the water, "unaware of the dreadful deeps below"; she is "like a warbling unimportant bird" with a "funny little flute voice"; "She inscribes no significant design. Just small bright dots of color, sparkling dots of life"; when she is dead, "there is no mark of her . . . no more than the dimpling of the water caused by the wind." The significance of Topaz's life is not even that it is typical, for she is a "character," an *enfant terrible* whose outrageous behavior is described with mingled affection, admiration, and exasperation, and it would be difficult to find a universal pattern in a life so fortunately sheltered as hers. Nevertheless, the novel does achieve a significance that transcends Topaz's life. By various strategies, both structural and thematic, Wilson continually makes us aware of a broader context of meaning for human affairs.

This context consists only in part of the dichotomy between the secure, loving shelter that Topaz finds in her family—the comfortable rituals of the well-to-do Victorian middle class—and the terrible pitfalls that life and time have organized, willy nilly, for the Edgeworths and their descendents. These "nebulous agents of causality" do indeed provide a powerful ironic subtext for the book. . . .

Through the novel's structure and imagery Wilson both celebrates and deplores the conformity necessary for free spirits like Topaz if they are to survive economically and emotionally. Harmonious, close family living seems to demand the sacrifice of an imaginative, adventurous approach to life for fear of the fall into deep waters which might result from real risk-taking. To view the novel in this way is not to deny that actions of worth take place in it, but it is to become painfully aware of the other areas of human experience that must be excluded. Heterosexual relationships—except for those between relatives—are scarcely present. The pepper-pot house consists entirely of women, with the exception of the cook, Yow. Such relationships as exist are either comfortably familial, as with Father and the Stepmother (referred to only by their family roles); or, if truly sexual, disastrous, as with the case of Mr. and Mrs. Porter (she finds his sexual advances repellent), or Mary and Edward, or Topaz and Mr. Sandbach; or else they are simply omitted, as with Rose and her husband Charles, whose courtship and relationship, though presumably romantic and occurring well within the timespan of the novel, are never described. No serious disagreements or lasting animosities are allowed to exist among the major characters. . . . What people want, and receive, from each other in the book is comfort, shelter, and support, not excitement or stimulation. The rich variety of scene, incident, and character in the novel gives the illusion of a rich and full world until we consider the large areas of human experience that are excluded from it, and the conformity of all action to a predictable and circumscribed pattern. Ethel Wilson's considerable achievement, in this complex and stylistically accomplished book, is the use of structure and imagery to promote a constant awareness of the limitations of Topaz's world, as well as its delights.

Mary Ann Stouck. *Canadian Literature.*
109, 1986, pp. 18, 29–30

WISEMAN, ADELE (CANADA) 1928–92

Wiseman's technique clearly shows the debt she owes to the Yiddish tradition. The folk figures on which she bases some of her characters may be universally familiar, but they are characteristically Jewish manifestations of those more general types. Similarly, her point of view, at once close to her characters and ironically distanced from them, is not exclusively Yiddish, but certain features of it, like the use of "inner dialogue," make it quite distinctive. Above all, Wiseman's emphasis on the Yiddish language, on its particular forms and idioms, places her fiction unmistakeably in the Yiddish literary tradition.

Allan Weiss. *World Literature Written in*
English. 24, 1984, p. 406

Adele Wiseman is one of our most supple yet eloquent stylists. Winner of the Governor General's Award for the epic *The Sacrifice,* her collection of essays is an exquisite blend of meditations on her development as a woman and Jewish writer; she was among the first generation of women, along with Margaret Laurence, to break into the special ranks of distinguished post-war writing. Here we have Wiseman's powerful feminist reading of Henry James, reflections on ethnic marketplaces, travel notes on China, and contemplations of Canadian landscape in an age of ecological crisis. A producer of some of our most energized prose, earthy, robust, crackling with humor both bawdy and delicately ironic, her enthusiasm for language and experience is seductive and inspiring. The essays and reflections presented here add up to a mixed autobiographical album, taking the reader in jagged chronological order from the rites of childhood and initiation into the pleasures of literature to later poignant explorations of human suffering. To prevent this collection from lapsing into too dark a pitch, Wiseman concludes with her angry, comic, and defiant complaint against the incompetencies and injustices of civic life and property inspectors in Toronto.

Wiseman's prose signals the distance that women writers have come since Emily Carr's generation, a generation that could not speak with Wiseman's ebullient and colorful confidence about sexuality, political life, and the morality of literature. Wiseman has the ability, rare in any writer, both to tell us what it feels like to be gripped by the pleasures of the book and to engage us in her passionately moral vision of literature's purpose.

Glenn Deer. *Canadian Literature*. 120,
1989, p. 152

Intended for young children . . . Adele Wiseman's *Kenji and the Cricket*, which recounts the quest of a Japanese war orphan for a family, addresses every child's desire for love and security. Kenji, a starving street boy, adopts a pet cricket that leads him to a childless couple who in turn adopt him. The warmth of the narrative is enhanced by Shizuye Takashima's watercolor illustrations, whose blurred edges relieve the harshness of the details of Kenji's daily life and give the story the cast of memoir or fable. The style and length of the narrative indicate that this is a story to be read to children rather than by them; as the parent who read it aloud, I felt that some pruning of the language could sharpen the focus.

Carole Gerson. *Canadian Literature*. 129,
1991, p. 175

An examination of the female subject in Adele Wiseman's novels charts the radical shift from complicity with the patriarchy of orthodox Judaism in *The Sacrifice* (1956) to subversion of that culture in *Crackpot* (1974). Both works describe insular communities whose ideologies rather than their practices reflect a traditional and orthodox Judaism and which participate minimally in the large society. Each novel configures one female character as whore who exists on the periphery of the community. *The Sacrifice* finally refuses to accommodate the prostitute. An example of "a female character who cannot properly negotiate an entrance into teleological love relations, ones with appropriate ends, a character whose marginalization grows concentrically as the novel moves to the end" . . . Laiah is murdered for challenging Judaism's patriarchy. In the figure of Hoda, *Crackpot* seeks retribution for Laiah's death and provides a revisionist reading of the earlier text which attempts to recover a place for women within Judaism and fiction. *Crackpot* is written against *The Sacrifice* as a critique where "community and social connected-ness are the end of the female quest, not death.". . .

The Sacrifice and *Crackpot* construct a female subject as prostitute in order to free her from the limitations imposed on all women, married or single. While *The Sacrifice* does not embrace the prostitute, who already exists on the margins of society, and castigates her for desiring freedom, *Crackpot* celebrates her life and rewards her with integration. Whereas Laiah weakens over time, Hoda literally and figuratively proves larger than the constraints of the patriarchy. *Crackpot's* revisionist reading of the earlier novel is an atonement for the unholy, parodic "sacrifice" of Laiah and an attempt to locate a place for women within Judaism and fiction which will foster their independence and accommodate rather than repress their individuality.

Ruth Panofsky. *Canadian Literature.* 137,
1993, pp. 41, 47

WITTIG, MONIQUE (FRANCE) 1935–

In a critique of *féminité* as praise of women's difference from men, the name of Monique Wittig must be mentioned. Active in the early 1970s in the Fémi-nistes révolutionnaires and a contributor from the beginning to *Questions féministes,* Wittig has written four quite different books, which are nonethe-less related through her focus on women among themselves: the schoolgirls of *L'Opoponax* (The Opoponax), the tribal sisterhood of *Les Guérrillères* (The female guerrillas), the passionate couple of *Le Corps lesbien* (The les-bian body), the users of the postphallocentric vocabulary laid out in *Brouillon pour un dictionnaire des amantes* (Outline for a dictionary of women lovers; Lesbian people's materials for a dictionary). Wittig writes her novels, her monologues, and histories to explore what social relationships among women-identified women are or might be. She rewrites traditional culture in mocking takeovers: one entry in *Brouillon pour un dictionnaire* is "Ainsi parlait Frederika, conte pour enfants" ("Thus Spake Frederika, children's story"), surely one of the least reverent allusions to Friedrich Nietzsche to come out of French critiques of culture. She also invents new settings, such as the ceremonies and festivals of *Les Guérrillères* and *Le Corps lesbien,* and new modes, such as the feminized epic of *Les Guérrillères* and the lyric dialogue of *Le Corps lesbien,* to represent what a female/female life—separat-ist but not isolationist—might be.

As Wittig's talks at recent conferences in the United States show, she is suspicious both of the oppositional thinking that defines woman in terms of man and of the mythical/idealist strain in certain formulations of *féminité.* In her argument for a more politically centered understanding of women at the Second Sex Conference in New York (September 1979), she used a Marxist vocabulary which may be more familiar to U.S. feminists than the philosophical and psychoanalytic frameworks in which Irigaray and Cixous work:

> It remains . . . for us to define our oppression in materialist terms, to say that women are a class, which is to say that the category "woman," as well as "man," is a political and economic category, not an eternal one. . . . Our first task . . . is thoroughly to dissociate "women" (the class within which we fight) and "woman," the myth. For "woman" does not exist for us; it is only an imaginary formation, while "women" is the product of a social relationship.
>
> Ann Rosalind Jones. *Feminist Studies.* 7, 1981, pp. 256–57

Wittig's literary career spans more than these last ten years. In 1964, she made her debut with the appearance of *L'Opoponax,* published by Editions de Minuit, well known and respected for their promotion of the *nouveau roman* of Camus, Sarraute, and Butor. The book, which is in fact germinal to Wittig's feminist ideology, was myopically received and reviewed as a *nouveau roman* about "everybody's childhood," awarded the prestigious French Prix Médicis, and rapidly translated into several different languages, earning Wittig a literary reputation as a promising young talent. The publication of *Les Guérillères* in 1969 and *Le corps lesbien* in 1973 elicited far more mixed critical reception, as did *Brouillon pour un dictionnaire des amantes,* which Wittig coauthored with Sande Zeig, and published with Editions Grasset in 1976. Each of the books, by virtue of style alone, issues a profound challenge to canonized literary tradition, to the very process of reading as an exercise in community understanding. At the same time, each sets forth a vision of woman, derived from a particular feminist ideology, which poses an equally profound challenge to socially accepted, and very deep-rooted "norms": the vision defies these norms, threatens them, exposes their limitations and their destructiveness, and offers serious alternatives to them.

The American translations were not received very differently by the institution of literary criticism in this country. But a broader readership in the feminist community both on and off college campuses reacted immediately to these radical texts; and American feminist scholars and critics, albeit in limited numbers, have helped to illuminate the value of Wittig's works as literature. *The Opoponax,* first translated in England in 1966, before the advent of a vocal women's movement, has remained the least well known of Wittig's books. This early publication date, as well as the subtlety of the book, may be responsible in part for its relative obscurity. This is regrettable because the serious reader of Wittig would quickly discover that already germinal in *The Opoponax* are all the elements of the feminist ideology which are developed further in the later works. *The Lesbian Body,* an esoteric and erotic Sapphic "Song of Songs," is the most notorious of Wittig's works, and probably the most difficult to read. Thus, it has elicited a most curious response: feminists who were thrilled by the figurative and literal violence of the *guérillères* against the patriarchy, were appalled by its prevalence in *The Lesbian Body*. Dissatisfied with the translations of her previous books, Wittig and Zeig decided to translate *Brouillon pour un dictionnaire des amantes* themselves as *Lesbian Peoples Material for a Dictionary* in 1979; its critical reception is yet largely unknown. Read as a dictionary from A through Z, this book can serve as a companion piece to the previous books, providing the definitions and contexts for understanding their ideology.

Wittig is probably best known in the United States for *Les Guérillères* written in the political climate of the May 1968 student-worker revolution in France. This book urges women to battle and describes the fictional overthrow of the old order through guerilla-type attacks and the accompanying systematic destruction of patriarchal institutions and language. The goal of these *guérillères* is a new order, and a new language to reflect and promote the new values, as the old language perpetuated the old order. Appearing in translation in 1973, it was hailed as a feminist manifesto and is probably the most widely read and frequently cited non-American feminist work of our times. . . .

Read in sequence then, Monique Wittig's books chronicle a progression, an ongoing constitution of the female person as a speaking, acting subject of her own discourse, and her own battle to create a new order. For Wittig, language can and must be taken back from the patriarchy, forced into feminist political constructions which in turn can alter old ways of thinking. As opposed to the playful word games in *écriture féminine,* Wittig's alteration of language is conscious, controlled, and directed at radically redefining women as political beings. Woman begins to rethink and recreate herself in relationship to self, to others, to language, and to culture. Wittig's female protagonists emerge as more than the sums of their biological parts, their sexual differences.

In this journey through language, Wittig is not content to retreat to the dark recesses of traditional women's genres—the novel, the memoir, the autobiography still evident in much of *écriture féminine.* Instead, she appropriates and inverts those traditional male genres that have held the power to shape and reflect their language and their reality. Thus, each of her works rewrites a major literary genre, redefines and reinvents it. *The Opoponax* creates the female Bildungsroman, opening up female children's potential to defy and transcend feminine socialization. *Les Guérillères* mocks the traditional epic poem in which armies of men fight for God, king, and country, leaving women at home, outside the game and the text; here, armies of women annihilate the very patriarchy that sired the epic genre in its image. In *The Lesbian Body,* the lovers reclaim the "Song of Songs" from the Bible, as well as all of Western mythology; but here, lovers and "heroes" are lesbians. And finally the *Lesbian Peoples Material for a Dictionary* creates a tentative lexicon that redefines, but does not confine words and women to narrow meanings.

Under the subversive pen of Wittig, *bildungsroman,* epic poem, Bible, and dictionary—all powerful tools of patriarchal discourse—contribute to the genesis of another language, from which another culture is already clearly emerging.

Hélène Vivienne Wenzel. *Feminist Studies.* 7, 1981, pp. 264–65, 284–85

Though Monique Wittig's first two books, *L'Opoponax* (The Opoponax) and *Les guérillères* have been the focus of considerable attention, her last two, which have the word "lesbian" in the title, have been relatively ignored. . . . *Le corps lesbien* [is] an important contribution to the epistemological revolution now being carried out by feminist thought, especially the aspect of the revolution that attacks the semiological problem of "phallogocentrism." Wittig's reorganization of metaphor around the lesbian body represents an epistemological shift from what seemed until recently the absolute, central metaphor—the phallus. . . .

By comparing Wittig's recrafting of the phallic figure, Osiris, and Hesiod's recrafting of Pandora, we may see the significance of her transformation of myth for the history of consciousness. As she reidentifies the phallic figure as lesbian, Wittig operates a reversal in the signifying system and a displacement of subjectivity. By producing Olympian metaphor (specifically in metamorphosizing unalienated feminine figures into alienated ones), Hesiod also operates a reversal and displacement. Hesiod historically displaces a prepatriarchal order by emplacing the brow of Zeus (metaphorically the male-identified subject) at the absolute center of his signifying system. In *Le corps lesbien* Wittig displaces this phallic body and subject with the lesbian body and the lesbian subject. (See, for example, her ironic recrafting of Zeus as Zeyna in poem 43.) The reversal operated by both of these crafters of words signifies a shift of the biological body of reference for human consciousness.

Namascar Shaktini. *Signs: Journal of Women in Culture and Society.* 8, 1982, pp. 29, 37

The rapport between women and language within an androcentric culture is especially problematic in the works of Monique Wittig. While she feels it is imperative to write female experience in order to bring it to consciousness and so insert it into symbolic discourse, she aims ultimately to eliminate the very notion of "woman." To create a "woman's writing" or "woman's language" would perpetuate the very duality "man/woman" which maintains women as an oppressed class. Writing as a function of a female subject's relation to language must confront the structures of masculine culture, including the very structure that defines humans in terms of two castes—"men" and "women." In so doing, "political writing" must create the means to express a new culture not founded upon sexual difference.

Wittig insists that biological differences have no meaning outside the historically determined discourse of our patriarchal culture. . . . While feminists generally affirm this politically, Wittig notes that there is an underlying division within the movement. . . .

While insisting that "woman" is a political class rather than a biological entity, Wittig is conscious of the importance of the female body in the development of feminist awareness. Unlike proponents of "woman's writing," she never uses the body as a metaphor for the act of writing. I know of no author for whom the body is so insistently concrete. Indeed, one of the primary tasks of "lesbian writing" is to strip the female body of its heavy burden of metaphor and imagery imposed by male culture and to trace the steps necessary to restore the body intact to women. . . .

Wittig is under no illusion that writing alone will transform masculinist society. The Amazon for her is not a romantic figure evoked in nostalgia for a prepatriarchal past. She is the activist lesbian feminist of the present fighting to transform the future. Wittig is aware of the danger that writing can substitute for confrontation, as women turn inward, lost in utopian dreams or the exploration of the unconscious.

Diane Griffin Crowder. *Contemporary Literature*. 24, 1983, pp. 118–19, 131

On first sight, Monique Wittig's second book *Les Guérillères* (1969) could not be more different from that which preceded it, *L'Opoponax* (1964). The epic quality of *Les Guérillères,* its appeal to esoteric myth and symbolic promotion of the geometric figure, and its composition in terms of a number of short pieces of prose with no obvious thread of continuity distinguish it sharply from the day-to-day evocation of the childish world of *L'Opoponax.* However, the two novels share a fundamental interest in the emergence of awareness through the achievement of a certain linguistic virtuosity. While the children of *L'Opoponax* acquire standard linguistic skills before they challenge authority and assert their individuality, in *Les Guérillères,* the women start off by challenging male-dominated language and literature. Furthermore, the *je* which displaces the impersonal *on* at the end of *L'Opoponax* finds a correlative in the emergence of the first-person-plural pronoun at the end of *Les Guérillères.* The first novel stopped at adolescence and the realization of individuality. The second novel is trying to arouse a sense of solidarity and sex-consciousness in half of the adult human population. . . .

On the level of the fabrication of a new, alternative language, Wittig's enterprise is, perhaps inevitably, dogged by self-contradiction simply because she must have recourse to a common code in order to communicate her ideas. Considered in this light, the neologisms and individual semantic changes remain witty but quirky, superficial challenges. The real strength of the book lies in the combination of a subversive exposure of the way in which language is used to control and restrict and a positive revelation of the variety of the world and of more general semantic polyvalence. The emergence of the first-person-plural pronoun at the end of the book is the result of rigorous ideological de-programming. The change in shifter from "elles" [they/them] to "nous" [we/us] is a suitably subtle mark of the maturation of female self-awareness in a work so concerned with the liberating power of language and constitutes a convincing expression of an educated solidarity which accommodates both individual and ethnic variation.

Jean Duffy. *Stanford French Review.* 7, 1983, pp. 399, 412

The lesbian relationship as it unfolds in the prose poems of *Le Corps lesbien* is not analogous to the male-female experience. The dominant culture's obsession with penetration and intercourse has been replaced with a multiplicity of amorous encounters in which the lesbian lovers now heal and give birth to each other, now pursue, kidnap, devour, peel and dissect one another. In the absence of a vocabulary that would express the infinite depth of feeling between women, Wittig uses anatomical descriptions as a way of achieving this intensity. In her work, the contact between lesbians is not simply a matter of sexuality, but a cultural issue, one which involves the return to the strength, the statehood and the majesty of the ancient Amazons. As Elaine Marks has observed in her recent analysis of French lesbian writers: "[Wittig's] texts go beyond idiosyncratic sexual preferences toward the creation of a new mythology in which the female body is undomesticated." It is not surprising, therefore, that the struggle for identity between the *I* and the *you* also symbolizes the lesbian writer's marital tensions, her battle with a language that does not recognize her as subject. And just as violence must be done to the sexist grammar, so too must the female body, fragmented, fetishized and traded under the patriarchy, be created anew. But in this Amazon space, the scattered body is reassembled and made whole, lovingly, with reverence and infinite care.

Marthe Rosenfeld. *Mosaic.* 17, 1984, p. 240

Monique Wittig is a unique and often lone voice in French feminist theory. Despite all the scholarly attention that has been lavished upon Continental poststructuralist thinkers, her works, which elaborate an ungendered, universal theory of the subject, have been largely neglected in contemporary debates about feminism, antifoundationalism, and the political public sphere. This neglect . . . is more than an academic oversight: it is symptomatic of the presumed ontological categories of heterosexuality which organize, legitimate, and give meaning to the political relations of society and which are all too often inadequately interrogated by their postmodern critics; it is indicative of the blind spot in many French feminist theories of postmodernism— theories which purport to critique but in subtle ways reproduce gender as the central category of albeit fractured identities and of the subject in process; and it is expressive of the general silence that surrounds any serious discussion about universalism in contemporary feminist theory. . . . Heterosexuality [Wittig] contends, be it naturally, socially, or discursively theorized, gives the lie to universalism; but so too does universalism give the lie to gender as sexual difference. Whereas French theorists of difference use the feminine to deconstruct the universal, Wittig will employ the universal to deconstruct the "feminine." Working within a poststructuralist context and with a materialist theory of language, however, Wittig's writings negotiate critically the related problems raised by those who would critique androcentrism by reconstituting the "female" subject as a whole, positive, and unified identity as well as those raised by the liberal feminist search for an androgynous citizen self. Moreover, as we shall see, it is her radical and unflinching critique of a heterosexual episteme that allows Wittig to deploy the universal in ways that suggest challenging directions for feminist political theory. . . .

When deployed as a war machine . . . Wittig's subversive pronouns appropriate first by inhabiting and then by displacing the fictional category of the universal subject constructed in and through heterosexuality. These pronouns work like the Trojan Horse, that is, as simulacrums of that Absolute Subject which would deny those individuals called women the status of the subject while claiming to speak in their name. Wittig's "I," in short, forces the universal to live up to its promise by turning it upon itself, thus revealing its pretensions. In Wittig's hands, what Butler calls "doing gender" as performance becomes what might be called "doing universal." It is a strategy, literary and political, that ought not be reduced to naive humanist pipe dreams. If the "doer," as Nietzsche wrote, "is merely a fiction added to the deed—the deed is everything," so too is Wittig's lesbian "subject" one which demonstrates how the so-called ontological status of the "doer" is sustained through the ontology of heterosexuality. Thus, I would conclude, Wittig's deployment of the universal as a critique of heterosexuality invites feminists to reconsider the subversive acts that might yet be invented in the name of universality and its Absolute Subject.

Linda Zerilli. Social Text. 25/26,
1990, pp. 146, 149, 168

In all of her writing, Wittig deploys what we may call, borrowing from the situationists, a strategy of "detournement," an appropriation and redeployment as "lesbian" literature of the old war horses of Western culture. These range from accounts of the ancient Egyptians and Greeks, Christological accounts, the works of Ovid, Petrarch, Dante, Cervantes, and Scève, to those of Baudelaire, Genet, Proust, Barthes, Benveniste, Bakhtin, Deleuze, Levi-Strauss, Beauvoir, and others. In "One is Not Born a Woman," Wittig (1981) appropriates and redeploys Beauvoir's assertion that women "are not born, but rather become." In Wittig's hands, Beauvoir's utterance becomes a weapon against compulsory heterosexuality—certainly a possible usage, but not an immediately obvious one within the context of Beauvoir's work. What Wittig makes explicit is that if one is not born a woman but becomes one in and through socio-cultural practices, then every movement and moment of the shaping or manufacture of any "woman" (or "man," for that matter) is accomplished by some kind of ruse and *can only be countered by another, different ruse.* While the first (patriarchal) ruse operates in a deceptive fashion, the second (feminist) counter-ruse plays upon an older etymological sense—from the French *ruser,* to force out of place, to drive back or down, itself derived from the Latin *recusare,* to refuse. Wittig's second ruse is thus more primary, and operates as a resistance to being overtaken by another, derivative and more deceptive ruse. This combative ruse which Wittig reintroduces by way of strict attention to language I will call "lesbianization," a practice of the *detournement* of the presumptions and language of heterosexuality used as a strategic weapon in the battle for the liberation of "women" from the oppressions and omissions of dyadic logic. Just as the first "Trojan horse" was a bomb of sorts, an implosion of Greeks within the city of Troy, so Wittig's practice of lesbianization . . . aims to decimate what we may call patriarchal reasoning internally, to turn over and make "lesbian" the universalizing capacities of thought and language. If . . . "appropriation" has been the "specific nature of the oppression of women,". . . then reappropriation and deflection, *detournement* of the designative and appropriative powers of thought and language are what Wittig calls the materialist means of bringing to light and combating the (mis)appropriativeness that is "male" privilege.

Karin Cope. Hypatia. 6:3, 1991, pp. 75–76

Looking back at the corpus of Wittig's fictions from the past twenty-five years reveals that hers has been a constant journey, indeed a *voyage sans fin.* A continual quest for renewal, it has led her to abandon known territories, established traditions, past discoveries, and even domains successfully conquered, in order to push on to other explorations, and to further new ventures. In this pulling up of stakes, or forsaking of outworn modes of perception and creation, renversement proved to be a most useful travel accessory, the fitting accoutrement for a voyage of upheaval, overthrow, and transgression, as well as the ammunition for the functioning of her "war machine," the weapon concealed in the body of her "Trojan Horse."

But what of the present—and the future? Over five years have elapsed since the publication of her latest work, *Virgile, non.* It is natural to wonder what further renversement her next work will contain or how "it will sap and blow out the ground where it was planted." At the present moment, the only answer to these questions is silence.

However, knowing that lacunae, intervals, and instances of nonenunciation do not denote sterility or defeat—either in her individual fictions or in the course of her literary career—but instead, indicate a turning point that leads to renewal, it can be expected that this period of silence is simply a time that must elapse before words can pour forth afresh. This is in keeping with numerous occurrences of a similar kind found in Wittig's fictions: the cyclical patterns of destruction, pause, and regeneration in *Les Guérillères* in regard to the "féminaires," objects linked to women's "histoire," literature, and even language itself; the fragmentation and reconstitution of the pronoun *I (J/e)* and the dismemberment and reassemblage of the beloved's body that is symbolic of the actions of the lover (the writer) upon the body of the beloved (literature), in *Le Corps lesbien;* the frontal attack on the repository of language in order to arrive at a positive transformation, or the destruction of words that have lost their power and must die in order to be reborn—either in the form of neologisms (or even a neolanguage)—in *Brouillon pour un dictionnaire des amantes;* and finally, the decade of silence (which most closely resembles the present one) that occurred before the publication of *Virgile, non.* In addition, the use of phrases in English, which appears for the first time in Wittig's fictions in *Virgile, non,* is a clue to the renversement par excellence that Wittig is now contemplating, for her newest "war machine" is the intention to write fictions in English instead of in her native French.

This would indeed be a major upheaval, a schism so radical as to resemble a cataclysm. It would certainly "sap and blow out the ground where it [her work] was planted," for it would indicate a break with an entire literary tradition (an Old World in terms of language), the abandonment or destruction of tools she had perfected as a writer, and the refutation or even annihilation of her first language, her "mother tongue." So drastic is such a move, that it would be compared to the end of a civilization, indeed a world. For any writer, but especially for Wittig, who has been so preoccupied with "word work," this change would be astounding and certainly more audacious than any renversement she has undertaken to date.

Erika Ostrovsky. *A Constant Journey: The Fiction of Monique Wittig* (Carbondale: Southern Illinois University Press, 1991), pp. 167–68

The method of *Les Guérillères* enacts on one level what *Combat [pour la liberation de la femme* (Combat for women's liberation)] proposes on another: the emancipation of women from the ideologies that isolate and silence them. *Les Guérillères* achieves just those goals that all political manifestoes pursue: it centralizes, in its own terms, a previously marginalized history; it reconstructs the crimes of the oppressor; it appeals successfully to a violated code of justice; it defines its own potential audience by providing a model for a provisional coalition. What happened when Wittig moved from this transformed utopian manifesto to a contradictory and circumscript Marxist manifesto for women's liberation?

The answer must lie at least partially in the semiotic and structural differences between utopian and political methods. . . . *Combat* is not a lapse into programmatism so much as a self-conscious feminist attempt at political and discursive intervention, an intervention in a form that is especially resistant to discursive transformations by women. If it is neither so aesthetically or so politically untroubled as *Les Guérillères,* then it at least takes more risks and provides a more calculated agenda for a wider (albeit more fractured) audience than the latter work.

Janet Lyon. *Yale Journal of Criticism.* 5,
1991, pp. 115–16

WOHMANN, GABRIELE (GERMANY) 1932–

The inability to communicate with one another, to understand one another or merely establish contact is one of Gabriele Wohmann's major themes. . . . People are imprisoned within themselves. They live in more or less burdensome and ugly bodies.

We shall leave aside the question as to whether the body is actually a jail or simply a symbol of inescapable loneliness. One fact is certain: Gabriele Wohmann's people hope for liberation, for salvation. By what means? Ideology or religion are not mentioned as instrumentalities. Sex is just a distraction. Love would be a possibility but is never realized in tangible form. Death? The main protagonist of *Jetzt und nie* (Now and never) yearns for it but can never decide to commit suicide.

. . . What the author offers the reader is good but already familiar: passionate, infatuated girls, women with their decisions for or against a man. The reader has the impression Gabriele Wohmann is not moving forward. She has not accomplished much when measured by her talent. With all due respect, the reader wishes for her what she denies her own creations: development.

Rainer Hagen. In Klaus Nonnenmann, ed.
Schriftsteller der Gegenwart (Olten and
Freiburg: Walter, 1963), pp. 327–28, 330

Erzählungen (Stories). In these fifteen chronologically arranged *Erzählungen* we meet everyday characters in everyday situations with everyday problems; the unmarried seek companionship; the married seek freedom; friends misunderstand and betray one another; most see theoretical solutions for their unhappiness but are unable to act. But since these are the themes of much modern writing, what sets this collection apart?

First, the author captures both individual personalities and general types in relatively few words and the degree and circumstances of the emotion and weakness shown fits each character. The imagination with which she develops the stories keeps them from becoming trivial. . . .

Of interest too are the various narrative techniques. The author experiments in the first person. . . . Some of the third-person usage is traditional while variations include a stream-of-consciousness or framed dialogue.

Elizabeth Greaves. *Books Abroad.*
1967, p. 319

Gabriele Wohmann belongs to the best storytellers of the generation born in the 1930s. There are very few writers in the entire German-speaking world who surpass this author or even equal her. The fragility of relationships, the problematic nature of people, the misunderstandings that divide them—these are some of the elements that constitute Gabriele Wohmann's theme. . . .

This exact and spare prose never violates its own logic, is never too fastidious in its choice of adjectives . . . and comparisons. . . . It is too natural and musical ever to come close to those sterile and deliberately inventorylike texts by which we have been bored so often in the last few years. Most of the short stories in the volume sum up a life, as is appropriate to the form. However, they are exclusively concerned with female characters. It is probably an indication of the limit to Gabriele Wohmann's possibilities that she succeeds in presenting the intimate, private, and individual in exemplary form only when women are the protagonists. But this does not diminish the value of her stories.

Marcel Reich-Ranicki. *Literatur der kleinen Schritte* (Munich: Piper, 1967), pp. 284–85

In the second decade of Wohmann's activity as a writer, her novels became more frequent and appeared in increasingly rapid succession. Between 1970 and 1980, the author published six novels, as well as five omnibus volumes made up primarily of new stories. Also available since autumn 1979 are two volumes containing collections of stories that have appeared over the last twenty years. In addition, there are two volumes of "prose and such" from the years 1971 and 1972, the titles of which complement one another: *Self-Defense* and *Counter-Attack.* The texts so entitled represent an apex as well as a turning point in Wohmann's experimentation with language. This high point was to remain unique . . . because such a linguistic expression of concrete confrontations could scarcely lead beyond itself without "the plot-based reality" gradually getting lost behind a "reality based in language."

A volume of poetry appeared for the first time in 1974, under the title *Here's the Situation,* followed just four years later by a second, very different sort of lyrical collection entitled *Reason for Getting Worked Up.* In answer to the question posed in an interview with Southern German Radio as to whether "there is a genre that you prefer above the rest," the author replies: "Yes, it is prose, to put it generally, but not just the short story any more. Perhaps because I've written too many of them. So let's say: prose, because my poems are practically prose as well, that is, not lyrical poetry in the true sense of the word." . . .

When one attempts to delve a little more into the content and themes of Wohmann's prose, the . . . danger of over-generalization emerges. Furthermore, one learns little about a Wohmann text by conveying its content or plot, because her stories and novels deal almost exclusively with the concealed relationships between individual people, the relationships to one another, and, above all, with themselves, the silhouette of which appears within the intimate circle of a friendship, a marriage, or the family; this often also embraces one's career, frequently as a teacher or an artist. As critics repeatedly emphasize, her works deal with everyday situations from middle-class life, though it is an everyday life that also happens to include holidays and vacations. This notwithstanding, Wohmann's characters are seldom confronted with terrifically unusual events; the author is much more inclined to derive conflicts and tensions from the unarticulated aura of personal confrontations, from constellations comprising social insiders and outsiders, from reactions evolving among and between the sexes, quite often from age and generational differences, only seldom from class differences, and frequently from frustrated personal wishes that find only temporary ecstatic fulfillment. Though her attention to detail and her facility for precise reproduction have earned her frequent praise, her depictions only rarely approach detailed epic quality; even in her best stories, things remain only sketchily hinted at, and it is left to the reader to put things together, and to do the major portion of the thinking.

The earlier stories privilege the perspectives of young people, or of children, who occasionally lend these texts an Impressionistic tone. . . .

The question posed initially as to why this author remains so productive, and why she is driven like one possessed to continue writing, may well find its answer in her relationship to the times. She herself has frequently used the term graphomania to describe this drive toward writing . . . without caring to provide a more lucid explanation. Surprising perhaps, and revealing as well, is the author's admission that she in no way feels relieved or redeemed upon finishing a larger work, but rather finds herself already setting her eyes on her next project and yearning for its realization. On the other hand, she has spoken of the "fear of no longer being able to write" on the occasion of her novel *Late Autumn in Badenweiler,* a feeling that is reflected perhaps in the closing verses of the poem quoted above: "Right away, just to be sure / I gulped down the entire portion." Nonetheless, the language-works by this author ultimately tend much more to depict a sort of giving, of sharing and of sharing oneself, a phenomenon that must be regarded as a welcome rarity within our emotionally encoded private world and the world that surrounds us.

Sigrid Mayer. *Selecta.* 2, 1981,
pp. 449–50, 453

Gabriele Wohmann in her novel *Ausflug mit der Mutter* (Running away with mother) presents an adult daughter, the narrator, whose life is already self-defined. Her conflict lies in her difficulties with playing the role of the traditional daughter to her recently widowed mother. By analyzing her neglected mother, she reveals that these obligations cause great anxieties within her. She attempts to combine a family life with that of a writer. . . .

A certain ambivalence marks the daughter's relationship to her mother. She feels drawn to her through childhood memories, but at the same time has outgrown the needs on which this attachment was based. She therefore experiences an alienation toward her mother which in part arouses her guilt feelings. . . .

Wohmann seems to pose the question sincerely: isn't it enough to live a happy, complete life in dependency within a family? If it is, it must be remembered that children soon lose their need for mothering, and that years of emptiness often loom as an inevitable fate. Anyone who has made life so dependent on others may experience this predicament. Such a possible outcome heightens the problem, as well as the potential horror of the widow's existence in this novel. . . .

Wohmann does not offer a clear feminist message. . . . Yet, she presents a naked picture of the lamentable fate many traditional women experience. And through the portrayal of the daughter's horror at the mother's helplessness, the need for autonomy is at least indicated.

Much pessimism filters through Wohmann's writings, more than we are able to find, for instance, in Brecht's short story *Die unwürdige Greisin*. He envisioned a different type of old widow who succeeds in changing and living a full, alternative life, despite the condemnations of her children and the "proper" society. Brecht recognized that women must create their own, autonomous life aside from their involvement with the family. However, women authors, who often illuminate brutal realities, are as yet unable to produce such ideal images. They focus on the absence of power and lack of autonomy which mark their lives as a gender.

Helga W. Kraft and Barbara Kosta.
Germanic Quarterly. 56, 1983, pp. 81–85

Over a period of nearly thirty years Gabriele Wohmann has fought her way into the forefront of contemporary German writers. Recognition as an author of short stories and novels came fairly early in her career, with literary prizes and membership in the select circle of writers published by Luchterhand. Her detractors, however, have suggested that she has been too prolific and hence inconsistent in the quality of her work. Even her admirers will agree that her tight-lipped approach to psychological problems does not necessarily make her work accessible to a wide readership. Her accurate observations and detailed descriptions of people in mundane settings of ordinary life require a fair amount of patience on the part of the reader. It is perhaps for this reason that no English translations of Wohmann's novels or short stories are available (although some have been announced as forthcoming).

The long novel *Der Flötenton* (The sound of a flute) essentially tells the story of a man and woman who, on a trip to the "white city" of Lisbon, try to leave behind the well-established and often burdensome bonds of a comfortable middle-class existence. Anton is an architect with a filmmaker girlfriend, a handicapped son, a widowed mother, and a crotchety schoolteacher sister. Sandra, somewhat plump and apparently happy-go-lucky, teaches music (in particular the recorder) and has an unemployed husband, two children, and a father-in-law who is in love with her. Constantly moving between the protagonists' German home and their temporary abode in Lisbon, the novel presents a multitude of characters struggling to cope with life against the background of the Chernobyl nuclear accident. As Wohmann has one of her characters state: "I've always been interested in observing eccentrics." Reading *Der Flötenton* is like eavesdropping. Indeed rewarding.

Rita Terras. *World Literature Today.* 63,
1989, p. 94

In *Ein gehorsamer Diener* (An obedient servant) the prolific writer of fiction Gabriele Wohmann presents three of her sixteen radio plays: *Das hochgestreckte Ziel* (1983), the title play (1987), and *Es geht mir gut, ihr Kinder* (1988). All three were broadcast in stereo by Westdeutscher Rundfunk. Considering the traditional high standards of speakers, directors, and sound technicians on such broadcasts, it is safe to assume that the plays made a certain intellectual and emotional impact on the listeners. However, the experience of a detached reader is bound to be different. The characters of all three works are drawn from the upper middle classes, are well off, and do not have any credible problems. In short, they are not very interesting.

The author's chief concern, almost a topos, in all three plays is a phrase uttered by the protagonist of *Ein gehorsamer Diener* (an obedient servant), "occasions for dealing kindly with one another." He carries on an interior monologue, musing about his failure as a professor of philosophy, about his illness, about his "mania for isolation," about his association with the vagrants in the railway station. Again and again he interrupts his musings with direct apostrophes to his *Lebenslebewesen* (living being of his life) or *Lebensliebling* (darling of his life): i.e., his wife of some thirty years. He is in a hotel in another city, where he is to give a lecture. On the one hand he regards the separation from his spouse as a sort of rehearsal for his widowerhood, but on the other hand he says that he has vowed not to survive his wife by even a single day. Suddenly, at the very end of the play, the voice of his wife is heard. She is seated next to him in the hotel lobby, and she urges him to get up and go sightseeing with her. His entire long interior monologue has been a reverie.

The stylistic and linguistic tour de force of *Ein gehorsamer Diener* is sustained over twenty pages or about fifty minutes of air time. The same cannot be said for the other two plays. Both are considerably longer and feature two couples. In each work the four essentially shallow personalities and their trivial "problems" quickly grow tiresome. There is never any genuine dramatic agon. The characters' foibles and idiosyncrasies are presented, are dealt with "kindly," then fizzle out. If one were driving along the Autobahn late at night, these two plays would make for nice listening on one's car radio. Great literature they are not.

Franz P. Haberl. *World Literature Today.* 65, 1991, p. 295

WOLF, CHRISTA (GERMANY) 1929–

After an excursion to West Berlin, Rita from East Berlin says, "It is worse than being abroad, because one hears one's own language. One feels oneself in a strange land, and it is terrible." Rita cannot stop her friend, Manfred, from leaving what she would call the German Democratic Republic, though he might prefer to call it the Soviet Zone. But she refuses to stay with him. She goes back to her comrades in the East.

The story of this young couple is the nucleus of a novel *The Divided Sky (Der Geteilte Himmel),* by Christa Wolf, a very talented East German author. I don't think there is a female novelist of her generation (she is thirty-six) of equal literary standing in Western Germany. Ingeborg Bachmann and Ilse Aichinger come to mind; but Frau Bachmann has written no novel, though she has some stories to her credit. Frau Aichinger's novel *The Larger Hope (Die Grössere Hoffnung)* was published in 1948 and has not stood the test of time so well as her short stories, especially "The Fettered One" ("Der Gefesselte").

Christa Wolf's novel is among the few works by younger East German authors that have also been published in West Germany. Still, in a *Handbook of Modern German Literature,* just published in West Germany (*Handbuch der Deutschen Gegenwartsliteratur,* edited by Hermann Kunisch), you will find small fry like Karl Heinroch Waggeri and Leo Weismantel, Ernst Weichert and Martina Wied, but you will look in vain for Christa Wolf.

Rudolf Walter Leonhardt. *The New York Times.* September 12, 1965, p. 18

Both [Uwe Johnson's] *Two Views* and [Wolf's] *Divided Heaven,* one a novel from the West and the other from the East, make large efforts to wrestle with the tragic ambiguities of a divided Germany. Neither, I feel, wholly succeeds. There are superficial thematic resemblances. In *Two Views,* a West German photographer helps an East Berlin nurse to escape; in *Divided Heaven,* an East German technician defects to the West and then tries to persuade his girl to follow him. In both cases it is the impatient, individualistic male who most naturally identifies himself with the West, while the female is pictured as more passively integrated and more conditioned by her roots and by inculcated values. Uwe Johnson's Beate, a young woman increasingly alienated by the conformities, scarcities and restrictive rules of the hospital and city in which she works, nevertheless disperses only with difficulty her vision of the West as sinful and doomed. The bonds that link Christa Wolf's Rita to her native East are those that bind the fetus to the womb.

Although *Divided Heaven* is only mildly didactic, it never travels far from a familiar formula. The heroine must make her choice against and in spite of the transitionally negative features of a Socialist society in its first, formative years: acquisitive instincts, inertia, the complacency and dogmatism of party functionaries in whom harsh slogans have displaced the human dimension.

The individual who, like Rita's lover Manfred, allows his private resentments and his skepticism to accumulate to the point of physical defection is depicted as a lost soul, the victim of a tragic heritage, of an original and perpetually re-emergent sin. He is seduced by the false gods which lie both within himself and to the West.

Christa Wolf is not a writer who penetrates deeply. Although she writes sensibly and her story moves along, one is again struck by the fatigued traditionalism of style and structure which stands between so much Socialist literature and real artistic achievement. Frequently *Divided Heaven* echoes the banal and trivial tone of the romantic novel: "My little brown girl, Manfred called her"; "his look made her tremble"; "she had never before seen a man's face reflected in the water beside her own." Yet there is a difference. Rita's loyal and difficult commitment to the proud and frustrated technician, Manfred, holds the attention mainly because it is rooted in a real social milieu containing its own, intelligently observed contradictions. In the Western magazine serial, the heroine's perception of the masculine universe rarely transcends a keen bourgeois preoccupation with the size of her fiancé's income and the style of expenditure which it offers her. But Rita works in a predominantly male factory brigade, turning out railroad wagons. Through her eyes and those of her co-workers we are shown, quite plausibly, the technical problems and human tensions peculiar to a central state economy on the German model. Novelists have always found it easy to ignore work, particularly proletarian work, which is the source of all our lives and pleasures. It is therefore hardly surprising that in the modern Socialist novel the intrusion of this theme sometimes appears gratuitous and false. Even so, the effort is rewarding.

David Caute. *The Nation.*
February 13, 1967, p. 215

Christa Wolf's novel *The Quest for Christa T.* . . . pieces together the life of a sensitive young woman growing up against this background, and employs a keen eye for place and a [Uwe] Johnson-like technique of narration to wrap up a surprisingly hard ethical core. The publication (on both sides of the Atlantic) of a good English translation of this small masterpiece is something of an event. More than any other work of art to date, it seems to open up the Wall.

Unlike its very successful predecessor *Divided Heaven,* Frau Wolf's third novel scarcely has a plot; instead it is an inquiry, or more precisely a reflective, reminiscent inquiry in which the narrator is herself deeply involved—the *Nachdenken,* thinking back, thinking after, of its German title. The loan of the author's own Christian name suggests some autobiographical, introspective element, but the blend of love and detachment with which she writes seems anything but self-indulgent, and in any case this hardly matters. What she does, then, is to reconstruct the evolving character of a girl of her own generation whose education was interrupted by the debacle of 1945, using three crisscrossing and intermittently converging beams to light up different moments and aspects as they happen, in a staggered chronological order. The "beams" are objective narration, the narrator's subjective memories of her friend, and a random selection of the latter's posthumous writings and letters.

The events are not in themselves undramatic. There are the hardships of the war years and the defeat; there are an unpredictable marriage, an irrational love affair which breaks into it, finally a slow, then suddenly accelerating leukemia which leaves the husband with three young motherless girls to bring up in their isolated house. The tone however is subdued. The concern is not with tragedy so much as with thinking around tragedy, with unrealized options, with transitoriness itself, with what might have been.

This is matched by the author's open-ended technique, which allows her, for example, to conjure up a revealing conversation with one of her former colleagues, then suddenly to decide: "No."

> I shan't go to her, shan't visit Gertrud Dölling. The conversation
> won't take place, we'll save ourselves the emotions.

—as well as by Christa T.'s own elusive personality: "At home everywhere and a stranger everywhere," as it seemed to her school friends.

If the search, then, is a search for identity it is identity in a specifically East German setting; even the epigraph ("This coming-to-oneself—what is it?") is taken from the country's most approved poet, Johannes R. Becher. The awareness sought comes to Christa through writing, and although this might seem a discouragingly familiar literary remedy she is so ultra-sensitive to all that writing involves that the impression left is surprisingly fresh. "Writing means making things large." "The difficulty of saying 'I.'" "She thought life can be wounded by what one says" (though this isn't quite the same as the German *"Sie hielt das Leben für verletzbar durch Worte")*—these and other phrases suggest an unusual consciousness of the implications of putting pen to paper And this in turn comes from a larger moral sensitivity which rises to the surface each time the East German writer's traditional commitment clashes with the more discouraging facts of East German life:

> What she wished for more intensely than anything . . . was the
> coming of our world, and she had precisely the kind of imagina-

tion one needs for a real understanding of it. Whatever they may say, the new world of people without imagination gives me the shudders. Factual people. Up-and-doing people, as she called them.

So Christa T. doesn't like "the vehement overplayed words, the waving banners, the deafening songs," still less "the frightful beaming heroes of newspapers, films and books." Then in 1956, when she and her contemporaries find that "the iron believer" is finished, they come to realize that "we'd have to get used now to seeing by the sober light of real days and nights." "A word came up, as if newly invented: truth." Playing a pencil and paper game with her husband and friends a year before her death, she is asked to write down what humanity most needs if it is to survive.

I know her handwriting and afterwards I looked to see what her answer was. Conscience—there it was in her handwriting. Imagination.

We piece together an individual from such oblique touches as these, and she ultimately proves to be concerned with humanity itself.

John Willett. *New York Review of Books.*
September 2, 1971, pp. 21–22

I intend to take the narrative situation in *Christa T.* at its word, to "believe in" two separate and juxtaposed characters. The structure is dialogical rather than monological. The author's cautionary note at the text's outset is also to be understood literally: "Christa T. is a fictional character. Several of the quotations from diaries, sketches, and letters come from real-life sources. I did not consider myself bound by fidelity to external details." There was, then, a real person who is transformed in the book into the character, Christa T. But the book does not present itself as the result of this transformation; it demonstrates the creative process. This process has a demanding goal. It aims to retrieve the "actual" from the coincidences of history; to distill the "truth" from reality, and to present this all in the literary figure of Christa T. The real friend is meant to be "preserved" *(aufgehoben)* in the literary figure. Once present, the figure is expected to have an effect. We can suggest a new explanation for the paleness of the narrator-figure, who appears only to probe and to question—as the creative intelligence. The subject and object of the narrative are not identical; the novel's narrator and author, however, are the same. The narrator is not transformed into a literary figure—or, perhaps, only on occasion; for this reason she must remain faceless and nameless. The anonymity of the narrator is the price Christa Wolf pays for her own presence in the novel, suggesting a direct commitment of the author.

This results in a new perspective. Christa Wolf is undertaking a serious project of moral and political relevance: she wants to establish truth by means of fiction. The task is circumscribed in a prefatory chapter of the book; indeed, it is given already in the book's first sentence: "The quest for her: in the thought of her." Thinking and remembering are the two poles of the "work" the narrator does in regard to her dead friend; the goal is that she might "stand and be recognized." "So that people may see her": this is repeated like a leitmotif, often and with pathos. It functions as a kind of watchword that spurs one on and, at the book's end, recapitulates the narrative situation of the beginning, appeals to the present time: "So that the doubts may be silenced, so that she may be seen. When, if not now?"

The goal determines the structure of the book. To label *Christa T.* as a "novel of remembrance," as some have done, says little and is partially misleading. We remember something we have had and that we want to keep. The remembering person has a defensive relationship to time. But that is only one aspect of *Christa T.* The narrator is not satisfied with a literary recapitulation and preservation of the reality of the dead woman's life; she wants to find and establish her "truth, to elicit her essence and make it present; thus, she may have an effect. In the process of "re-collection" *(Nachdenken),* remembering becomes productive and points toward the future.

Heinrich Mohr. In Reinhold Grimm and Joel
Herward, eds. *Basis 2* (Frankfurt:
Athenaeum, 1971), pp. 192–93

The theme of alienation in contemporary East German novels is most pronounced in Christa Wolf's *The Quest for Christa T.* Here, a young woman, as narrator, tries to piece together the life of her friend Christa T., who died of leukemia at the age of thirty-five. We learn that Christa T. experienced the chaos of the Nazi years, fled from her hometown, resettled in East Germany, completed her high school education, studied German literature at the University of Leipzig, became a teacher, left her job because of a clash with bureaucratic regulations, married a veterinarian, and moved to the countryside in Mecklenburg where she had three children and did some writing. Though devoted to her husband, her marriage was not a happy one, and she fell in love with a hunter. Nothing ever developed out of that affair, and nothing ever developed out of Christa T.'s life, which was cut short by cancer.

In outline form, the story seems trivial. There is nothing outstanding or remarkable about Christa T. But, that is exactly the point. Christa Wolf writes about an average woman in East Germany, and she wants to understand why this woman is "drained" of her exuberance for life. In this respect, a disease, leukemia, is used metaphorically, as Solzhenitsyn uses it in *Cancer Ward:* Christa T. is suffering from a social sickness, which emanates from pathological conditions in her society. The narrator of the story feels compelled to analyze this sickness because she too, may become "infected," and hence, seeks a cure.

As in [Hermann] Kant's *Die Aula,* there is a dialectical relationship established between the narrator and her material. The past life and development of Christa T. are critically examined in the present so that the future may be changed. Using notes and diaries bequeathed her by Christa T., the narrator reconstructs the picture of a woman who had great hopes about contributing as a teacher to socialist development in the German Democratic Republic. However, these hopes were dampened by the hypocrisy and rigidity of petty bureaucrats. As a woman, she felt manipulated, and the result is that Christa T. withdrew into herself, reluctantly, in order to escape being reified by the social system. However, Christa T. never gives up hope for the socialist revolution, as one of her last dreams reveals. She is only overcome by the "disease," and the cure for this disease is partially suggested in the telling of Christa's story:

> One day people will want to know who she was and who it is that's been forgotten. They'll want to see her, and that's only natural. They'll wonder if that other figure was really there, the one we obstinately insist on when we mourn. Then people will have to produce her, create her, for once. So that the doubts may be silenced, so that she may be seen.
> When, if not now?

This refrain, "when, if not now?" occurs throughout the novel, and it becomes clear that the narrator has written about Christa's growing alienation in order to question the conditions which led to her withdrawal and death. This life of an average young woman in East Germany must be made known *now,* because the narrator, as a woman and citizen of the German Democratic Republic, shares the alienation of Christa T. and conveys it continually in her narrative. In this respect the narrative is more of a struggle than a quest, a struggle against the insidious disease which cuts man off from both himself and the rest of mankind.

Jack D. Zipes. *Mosaic.* 5, 1972, pp. 13–14

Christa Wolf's concept of subjectivity is also grounded in the tradition to which the stories in *Unter den Linden* generally refer. Neither for E. T. A. Hoffmann, Friedrich Schlegel, Arnim, Brentano nor for Ingeborg Bachmann was work a means to productive integration into society. On the contrary, in their opinion work trapped the human being in a social cycle that not only reproduced but even increased the alienation of the human being. If, with Christa Wolf, one understands self-realization in the socialist sense, then this task involves everyone and thus also requires single individuals to cooperate in improving general conditions for their universal realization. The activity of the subject assumed necessary for the achievement of self-realization must thus be internal *and* external. The hoped-for productivity of creative writing would logically have to include the impulse for renewed, revised, increased practical activity.

But—this needs to be emphasized once again—the strategic effect of the stories treated here would be misunderstood if one were to take their object to be the "inner life" of a few single individuals. The presentation of the stories and the expressed intentions of Christa Wolf leave no doubt that the author is reaching out to all society via the single reader and hopes to achieve an objective universal effect by refraction through several singular subjects. In this regard, she is once again different from Ingeborg Bachmann, for whom the social isolation of the human subject was hopeless, and also from the Romantics, for whom the achievement of the human ideal seemed possible only in the realm of poetry, art, God, or in "simple" forms of life that were more or less outside society. Christa Wolf's conception of the effect of her prose, in contrast, demonstrates a certain kinship with the Classical idea of an "aesthetic education toward humanity." As a program for social change, this idea was utopian. As long as individual humanity opposed the social interests of the exploiting classes, the influence on social development by "aesthetic education" was of little note. Under the conditions of socialism, such a concept may perhaps again achieve socially useful significance. Just how it might be related to other notions of aesthetic effect, what specific possibilities it contains, and where it fails—these questions remain to be considered.

> Hans-Georg Werner. In Gunter Hartung, et
> al, eds. *Erwurbene Tradition: Studien zu*
> *Werken der sozialistischen deutschen*
> *Literatur* (Berlin and Weimar: Aufbau,
> 1977), pp. 296–97

The project of Wolf's writing does not demonstrate the concepts of literary production and progress, but rather, regressing into history, it seems to retard progressive development and brush history against the grain. At the same time, this project seeks the promise of subjective agency and historical self-realization: "The difficulty of saying 'I.'" Wolf's literary creation of self (and history), however, rests in neither the teleological development of the bourgeois individual nor the decentering or deconstruction of this very same individual. In each of her works, the authorial identity and the narrative voice seem entirely redefined, different, and "other": There are many selves and many histories at work here. Rather than demonstrating the unified and progressive developmental career of the writer, Christa Wolf's work exhibits both a retrogressive and expansive unfolding of many *different* authorial lives.

> Helen Fehervary. *New German Critique*. 27,
> 1982, p. 163

Christa Wolf, one of the most eminent contemporary writers of the GDR, began her literary career as a loyal Party member and strict adherent to the concepts of socialist realism. Her first novel *Moskauer Novelle* can be labeled a model of socialist realism in that it abides by all five criteria of that literary movement. Consequently, this work may be classified as refined literary propaganda in that its primary purpose is the promotion of stronger ties of friendship between the inhabitants of the GDR and USSR. Fourteen years after the publication of this work, Christa Wolf acknowledges the lack of literary merit of the *Moskauer Novelle* and attributes it to youthful naivité.

The second decade in the existence of the German Democratic Republic was accompanied by a greater sense of maturity and confidence in the viability of the fledgling socialist nation. This new state of mind was reflected in the "Ankunftsliteratur" that focused on the achievements of the GDR under socialism. The new-found sense of security, however, also fostered a yearning for greater freedom of expression among the artists and writers. *Der geteilte Himmel,* the second work by Christa Wolf, marks a breakthrough in the quality of GDR literature as a result of its deviation from the strict guidelines of socialist realism. Instead of presenting another "expected" portrait of a utopian socialist order, *Der geteilte Himmel* represents an unprecedented realistic account of life in the GDR that is characterized by a "verschleierten Himmel," "Unrast," and "Schatten." While this work still abides by the characteristics of objective reflection of reality, partiality, and national orientation, these concepts are no longer characterized by political subservience but rather by honesty and truth. Of greatest significance is the abandonment of the socialist realism elements of the typical and the positive hero and their replacement with genuine flesh and blood characters. This gradual abandonment of socialist realism concepts and their replacement with universally recognized literary criteria earned Christa Wolf international acclaim.

Christa Wolf's third novel, *Nachdenken über Christa T.,* continues the trend away from socialist realism by abandoning the public sphere for an examination of the private domain, the self, in the search for self-actualization. Thus, such Kafkaesque phenomena as personal isolation and alienation are depicted in such uncharacteristic socialist realism forms as stream-of-consciousness, extensive use of interior monolog, and a complicated collage of flashbacks and foreshadowings.

Form and content of this work, therefore, represent not only an abandonment of, but even a direct challenge to, the principles of socialist realism. *Nachdenken über Christa T.* may be characterized as a direct repudiation of the concepts of objective reflection of reality and partiality in that Christa T. openly rebels against the socialist realism mentality of the "Hopp-Hopp-Menschen" and seeks fulfillment in discovering the essence of her being. The concept of national orientation also has been transformed in this novel in that the GDR no longer serves as the center piece for the evolving socialist society. Instead, the socialist state only serves as the canvas upon which Christa Wolf reveals the eternal struggle confronting all human beings— whether to lead a life as a "Mitläufer" and "Anpasser" or whether to chart a course for greater independence and self fulfillment. Finally, this work marks a complete rejection of the elements of the typical and the positive hero in that Christa T. represents the inauguration of the socialist anti-hero in the novels of Christa Wolf through her rejection of the herd syndrome and its replacement with the quest for individuality and self fulfillment.

Kein Ort. Nirgends marks the complete break with all five socialist realism criteria. This work has been cleansed from all the traditional socialist realism characteristics which advocate a transition from capitalism to communism. Political consideration no longer play a role in this novel.

George Buehler. *The Death of Socialist Realism in the Novels of Christa Wolf* (Frankfurt: Lang, 1984), pp. 174–76

Beginning with *Christa T.,* the work that established her own unique style, Wolf has accompanied her literary writings with essayistic and verbal commentary. She has introduced the concept of "subjective authenticity" to describe her personal moral engagement as an author in her literary production. Subjective authenticity can manifest itself, as in *Christa T.* and *Patterns of Childhood,* through the introjection of authorial consciousness in the literary text or, as in *No Place on Earth* and *Cassandra,* as essayistic commentary that illuminates the text and clarifies the relevance of the material for its maker. As the concept of "subjective authenticity" makes clear, all of Christa Wolf's writing is ultimately autobiographical. In her early and middle works, the correlation between authorial biography and fictional narrative is more readily apparent than in her later narratives where authorial subjectivity tends to be displaced into essays that elucidate the fictional texts. By creating an interdependence between personal, subjective essayistic commentary and the literary text, she undermines traditional generic categories and breaks down what she considers to be an artificial distinction between life and art.

The unique position Christa Wolf enjoys today, both in her own country and in the West, is largely due to the moral integrity she has displayed in her personal life and in her writing. Pursuing questions of personal conscience, she has criticized not only the policies of the West but increasingly those of the East as well. She has relentlessly scrutinized her own behavior and that of her compatriots and has refused to compromise her ethical standards, even when they have brought her into conflict with Party policy. As a consequence, she has come to be regarded as a voice of public conscience. Clearly Wolf's national and international reputation affords her special status within the GDR. Thus while the Party has the ultimate authority, Christa Wolf has become a force to be reckoned with. And that she *is* forcing a reckoning can be seen in her recent bout with the censors. Wolf insisted that the excised passages in the East German edition of *Cassandra* be marked by ellipses to signal censorship to her readers—and she prevailed, an unprecedented victory for a GDR writer.

Ironically, Wolf's position in the GDR today is the outgrowth of another function that often falls to literature in socialist countries: in the absence of an open public sphere, political and social issues are often debated in the literary arena. The symbolic, multivalent nature of literary language, as opposed to more restrictive and ideologically charged political discourse, allows for greater freedom of discussion of volatile issues. Thus literature, which officially has a proselytizing function, can simultaneously serve as an impetus for implementing internal reform. The socialist writer's dual function as proselytizer/supporter and critic means that she walks a fine line between the accepted, the acceptable, and the taboo. A morally responsible writer such as Christa Wolf, who is acutely aware how precarious her situation is, has helped extend the boundaries of the accepted and the acceptable as she has ventured even further into the realm of the taboo.

Anna K. Kuhn. *Christa Wolf's Utopian Vision: From Marxism to Feminism* (New York: Cambridge University Press, 1988), pp. 18–19

The East German writer Christa Wolf has produced a haunting novel about . . . the Chernobyl accident, and its complex effect on one woman. The nameless narrator is a writer, a mother and a grandmother, a concerned human being. The novel takes place in a single day in April 1986, and recounts the thoughts, feelings and phone conversations of the narrator as she goes about her daily routine alone in her home in a small village. She is trying to navigate the unknown territory of life after nuclear disaster and, at the same time, await news of her brother, undergoing surgery to remove a brain tumor.

Accident's focus is the destructiveness of modern technology and the mysteries of the soul that impel it to invent such self-annihilating marvels. "No surgeon could penetrate through to that hectic group of neural connections in the brains of those men who thought up the procedures for the so-called peaceful utilization of nuclear energy," the narrator thinks bitterly. And yet she is helplessly awaiting news that the cold-blooded expertise of medical science has been skillful enough to heal her brother, to return him to the state of thinking, feeling "selfhood" that scientific knowledge threatens to obliterate on a global scale.

Wolf's prose is as dense and spare as poetry and similar in its method. There is no narrative imperative to the book's structure, no "events" to propel the action. There is only the narrator thinking and waiting. Thought follows thought and all connect metaphorically to the novel's theme. At one point a friend calls to "hear my voice" and ask "whether I actually knew that she liked me." This leads the narrator to ponder what people really want and to conclude it is "to experience strong emotions and they want to be loved." From there she meditates on the possibility that the world of scientific research is really a "substitute gratification . . . a substitute life" for those who have lost their sense of what life can and should be. Next, wandering into her garden she notices that the zucchini plants have sprouted, recalls happy family feasts which may now never recur and worries about how her daughter will safely feed the grandchildren. Nature itself has become alien, fearsome, toxic. Finally, she muses on "the problem of what to do with the libraries full of nature poems." "Calling [the nuclear eruption] a 'cloud'"—one of the classic images of Romantic nature poetry—she thinks "is merely an indication of our inability to keep pace linguistically with the progress of science." . . .

While there is no resolution to the book's dilemma—how could there be?—it is, in a strange way, ultimately comforting. In its necessarily futile efforts to understand and come to terms with a terrifying situation, it becomes what it mourns, an experience of wholeness and integration. The narrator's very effort to face the meaning of nuclear power, to accept its unfathomability and yet to take responsibility for whatever can be understood or done, is cathartic and healing.

Wolf's sense of personal isolation may seem politically irresponsible to some. After all, we can protest, we can organize, we can act. But that is such a narrow reading of this profound and courageous work. Wolf is recording an experience of loss, impotence and terror. To read this novel is to plunge into that abyss in the best possible company.

Elayne Rapping. The Nation.
July 3, 1989, pp. 28–29

Wolf cannot . . . be simply aligned with the authors of postwar West German literature, modernism, or feminism. Her position in the German literary tradition is better understood, initially, at least, in respect to a particular literary heritage and aesthetic theory as they are fostered in a specific political atmosphere. Wolf's acceptance of socialism endows her early works with positive vision and remains the foundation for her narrative structure, now much refined; her training in German literature and socialist literary theory prescribes conventions and critical judgments from which she frees herself only gradually, while her familiarity with the canon of the eighteenth and the nineteenth century is always referentially present in her work. Later she is less convinced that systematic politics can offer solutions to the individual, but she never reveals the cynicism or resignation that often mark the works of her Western colleagues, for she retains the conviction that the dialectics of history affect society and the individual primarily by sustaining movement and change. She pushes aside the traditional masters of German literature— the accepted great men of the "cultural heritage"—and dominant socialist theories (particularly those of Lukács) in the process of discovering and delineating her own literary lineage and personal aesthetic. . . . Seeking new direction, she turns to other women writers (her predecessors Annette von Droste-Hülshoff, Marie Luise Kaschnitz, and Marieluise Fleisser; her contemporaries in the GDR, especially Maxie Wander, Irmtraud Morgner, and Sarah Kirsch; her English precursor Virginia Woolf), and feminist theoreticians. She locates herself, finally, in respect to those works whose value is revealed by her understanding of them as she comes increasingly to identify self understanding as a process of reading. Wolf internalizes the dialectic to conform to this personal experience, in which it denotes the confrontation of the "reader" with the "text," both terms understood in their broadest sense. Her readjustment of this oppositional stance involves a move away from its implicit polarity in the suggestion that reader and writer operate synchronously and that the text is re-formed in the reader/writing process. But the dialectical underpinning keeps her narrative perspective, as sophisticated as it might become, always in the realm of social interaction; her "subjectivity" and her internalization do not signify a withdrawal from society.

The notion of self-understanding as an act of reading is present already in *Divided Heaven,* where the protagonist "reads" her past during her physical and psychological recuperation in the hospital, and in *Christa T.,* in which the narrator bases her story partly on the posthumous writings of Christa T. and partly on her own recollection of her. The idea is further substantiated in Wolf's later works: in *Patterns of Childhood* we might overlook the narrator's references to the many hours spent in libraries verifying her recollection of past events, and we may not know, unless we read the accompanying theoretical essays, that *No Place on Earth* emerges from and is constructed around Wolf's reading of the works of her protagonists; the essays that accompany *Cassandra,* finally, are clear evidence both of the function of the reading process in the development of the narrative *and* of the manner in which the subject/author is merged with the object/textual material. To trace Wolf's references to her reading—of actual written texts or the less concrete record and recollection of personal experience—is to recognize that reading (which is to say: interpreting, seeing, evaluating, recognizing patterns) provides for her the network for the self's identity.

Her repeated epistemological question—articulated most succinctly in the motto to *The Quest for Christa T.*: "This coming-to-oneself—what is it?"—gives thematic unity to her oeuvre as it progresses through its several phrases. Wolf's unrelenting penetration into her own truth (her "reality") leads toward profound self-recognition; the resistant aesthetics of her oeuvre are anything but arbitrary. Rather, they manifest the rigorous adherence to the logic of her personal quest, taking her from ideologically motivated confession to humanistic revelation, from manifesto to epic prose.

Marilyn Sibley Fries. *Responses to Christa
Wolf* (Detroit: Wayne State University
Press, 1989), pp. 32–33

Christa Wolf clearly is not a feminist in some Western sense of the word. She neither wants contemporary women and women writers to establish their separate and often hostile spheres, nor does she wish to join the male world as it is and accept its standards, its traditions. She speaks to men *and* women but leaves no doubt that at this point in history woman must make herself an important, if not for a while the most important, voice in her culture because she is not yet totally trained to the "structures of thought and observation he [man] established." Woman must make use of her past outside the "citadel" of male reasoning, "instrumental thinking," to save both men and women.

If Christa Wolf speaks of "the memory of the future" (for this essay I prefer to render it "remembrance of things future") as the task of writing, of prose, then this task assumes a special significance in the context of her concern with women as writers and participants in history. For women there is the need to reflect back and to realize as well as express the radical utopian nature of a traditionally female existence of "mutual recognition and nurturant activity which may guide us in our struggle against instrumental rationality." Such activity, Christa Wolf suggests again in *Cassandra,* is not necessarily only women's domain (in that story men like Aeneas and Anchises share in it). But it has been assigned to them by the split that has divided the world into male and female, aggression, high achievement, instrumental rationality on the one hand, and subjugation, ordinary everyday living, and sensitive thinking ("fühlendes Denken") on the other. And unless women in general and women writers in particular can heal that split by recalling, reexamining, and applying what values the female experience has given them, their fate at best will parallel that of Cassandra, the woman and seer who could foretell the fate of Troy but could not prevent it.

Christiane Zahl Romero. In Marilyn S.
Fries, ed. *Responses to Christa Wolf*
(Detroit: Wayne State University Press,
1989), pp. 122–23

By the beginning of the 1970s at the latest, Christa Wolf was discussing her methods and intentions as a prose writer in public with critics and reviewers. The most important document in this discussion is her 1973 "Conversation" with Hans Kaufmann, "Subjective Authenticity," which first appeared in 1974. In addition to this relatively polemical document, it is useful to examine the more personal interview with Joachim Walther of 1972, which was printed in 1973, and also the self-critical essay, "Über Sinn and Unsinn von Naivität" (On the sense and senselessness of naiveté), written on commission in 1973. The common factor in these three documents is that Christa Wolf openly acknowledges the individuality of her prose based on her particular concept of experience. At the same time she clearly distinguishes between the cultural-political norms of a dogmatic socialist-realist conception of literature and her own work.

Proceeding from the demands made on the writer by modern prose, as she outlines them in the essay "The Reader and the Writer" of 1968, Christa Wolf develops her concepts of "inner" or "subjective authenticity" and makes it her concern to discuss the large questions of humanity and reality, of thinking and acting. She uses the concept of "subjective authenticity" only "provisionally." Since then the term has been applied widely to literary tendencies in the GDR in the 1970s, without its origins always being appropriately acknowledged. For Wolf it is the result of an unconditional demand for truth in dealing with one's own experiences. That requires a new relationship to reality: instead of trying to create an objective reproduction of facts in which the subjective element is submerged and which, at its most negative, becomes a mere reflection of reality, Wolf includes the subjective element, which involves the thinking, judgment, and experience of the individual in the writing process. From this position she rejects the idea that she, as the author, is sheltering behind her "material," her "theme," her "subject," or her "work" to make out of it "something they can play around with at will (and of thus treating readers as objects too)." Against this stance she sets the interaction of work and author in a process that "accompanies" life itself.

Karin McPherson. In Marilyn S. Fries, ed.
Responses to Christa Wolf (Detroit: Wayne
State University Press, 1989), pp. 149–50

In her own interpretation of Cassandra, . . . Wolf mainly intended to portray Cassandra and other figures as exactly and with as little prejudice as possible: "I wanted to reveal the psychological and social tendencies in this figure as precisely and as carefully as possible. I wanted to refrain from judgment, that is, *not* to say: this is right, or: there she should have behaved in an entirely different manner."

But [Wilhelm] Girnus disputes this; from his traditional Marxist perspective he argues that Wolf overemphasizes the repression of women throughout history and the cultural differences between the sexes:

> From the fact that Christa Wolf further implicitly connects the problem of oppressed women—in a manner incomprehensible to me—with the "murderous who-whom," the impression is suggested to the reader—possibly unintentionally—that history is at bottom not the struggle between exploiters and exploited, but rather between men and women—indeed, even more grotesquely: between "male" and "female" thinking, between causal and acausal, between rational and emotional behavior, so to speak. It simply cannot be true that such obvious nonsense gets published in a socialist country.

Girnus's polemical statement is an important document: in addition to refuting any emotional, cultural and historical differences between women and men, it confirms Wolf's accomplished break with the officially proclaimed Marxist ideology of the GDR. Wolf now goes her own way. Instead of continuing to see the modern world crisis in the orthodox light of class antagonisms, as Wilhelm Girnus does, Wolf introduces her own feminist thinking to the issue.

Wolf's new, independent thinking, however, is not anti-Marxist. In refuting the validity of present-day GDR ideology, she rather confirms basic historical assumptions. By reinterpreting history from a female perspective, she returns to the fundamental problem of the origin of all exploitation. This was explored by Friedrich Engels in *The Origin of the Family, Private Property, and the State:* "The first class law to appear in history coincides with the development of the antagonism between man and woman in monogamous marriage, and the first class oppression with that of the female sex by the male.

From this fundamental tenet of Engels's theory, Wolf has developed her own process of exploration, her own way of seeing which clearly acknowledges the differences between women and men. *Cassandra* illustrates this process. In its thematic and formal structure, Wolf's work acknowledges an autonomous female experience and demonstrates the search for new forms in which to express and interpret it authentically.

Heidi Gilpin. In Marilyn S. Fries, ed.
Responses to Christa Wolf (Detroit: Wayne
State University Press, 1989), pp. 362–63

The thematization of prophecy, clairvoyance, and psychic healing in Wolf's writings is difficult to place in context. My first impulse was to historicize the subject: to treat it as yet another indicator of Wolf's affinity or indebtedness to Romanticisim, or to analyze it as an extension of her critique of the mechanical materialism into which the Marxism of the GDR has degenerated. Then I considered writing about it as an aspect of Wolf's critique, most strongly stated in *Cassandra* and the *Cassandra*-lectures, *Conditions of a Narrative,* of the mind-body split, which is itself a part of her larger critique of the blind spots of western civilization, including the exclusion of women and of what has come to be termed "the feminine" from western civilization's definition of what is rational, valid, and real. The concept of the "feminine" has, at least since the beginning of modernity, been the repository for all that has to do with intuition and the soul, which are neither scientifically verifiable nor amenable to "rational" elucidation. Perhaps it is this equation of the feminine and the irrational that has mitigated against scholarly discussion of the psychic, intuitive, and even spiritual elements that recur in Christa Wolf's writing from *The Quest for Christa T.* through *Sommerstück.* . . . Words, so we are informed by the text of *Cassandra,* have a physical effect; "no" causes contraction and "yes" relaxation. And relaxation is nothing other than the release of tension through expansion on the physical level. I believe that expansion is the key word for what Wolf, perhaps unintentionally at first, has accomplished in the course of her development as a writer and as a human being. Her writing has evolved from the restricted materialism of Socialist Realism to the brink of an art form that integrates social and spiritual concerns without degenerating into occultism or irrationalism.

Wolf has repeatedly described her writing as the expansion of the limits of what can be said and as a struggle to transcend the boundaries, conscious or not, of what she allows herself to know. Perhaps even more important, however, than her broadening of what can be known and said is her deepening of our awareness of how knowing can transcend the boundaries of the "citadel of reason" by undermining the separation of the knower from the known. For many of us feminist academics, somewhat uncomfortably entrenched within the "citadel of reason," the possibility of such knowledge can be both profoundly threatening and profoundly liberating. It challenges us to rethink our relationship to even the most avant-garde modes of academic theorizing. It gives rise to irritation and to hope.

Myra Lowe. Women in German Yearbook. 7,
1991, pp. 1–2, 19

Christa Wolf might have subtitled *Was bleibt* (What remains) "Ein Tag in dem Leben einer DDR-Schriftstellerin," (A day in the life of an East German woman writer) for in the brief narrative she tells of the close observation by the East German secret police to which she was subjected in 1979 as a result of her stand on the expatriation of her colleague Wolf Biermann. The work is remarkable for the almost unmediated account it gives of wiretapping, break-ins, and the attempt to undermine a public reading that Wolf gave in East Berlin on the evening in question. Wolf conveys the anxiety, the helpless frustration, and—above all—the nausea that she experienced at the hands of the Stasi.

More important than the book itself is the critical dispute that has grown up around it throughout Germany. Wolf has been called by some a "state poet" of the GDR who, because she never broke with the regime, supported it through the mere fact that she remained in the country. However, no less a colleague than Günter Grass has come to Wolf's defense in a *Spiegel* interview, in which he praises her for her desire to live in peace with all parties while serving the high humanitarian goals that were at the center of her concern.

Was bleibt is a deeply personal document of inhumane persecution by unjust authorities that, precisely because it was written by a (the?) major author of the GDR, will undoubtedly achieve classic stature a decade from now. For the moment, however, the book raises the old and always painful questions about the role of the intellectual in society. Should Wolf—like Biermann, Jurek Becker, Sarah Kirsch, and Monica Maron, to mention only a few—have turned her back upon her native land long ago? (Those who feel this way overlook the fact that Biermann did not leave the GDR willingly.) Has Wolf not, precisely through her efforts to work for reform from within the country, contributed to its long-term survival? This is a question, of course, of special relevance to Germans who look back upon a half-century of their history.

Although the title *Reden im Herbst* (Speaking in autumn) is intended only as a literal location in time for Wolf's public contributions to the *Wende* or "turn" that began the revolution within the GDR in the autumn of 1989, it further cloaks the volume's seventeen brief essays, speeches, and letters—quite appropriately—with an aura of autumnal melancholy, for, as the author admits in her brief foreword, they had become the artifacts of a now-lost hope even before their publication. The title involves a certain inaccuracy, for the longest item in the book is a 1988 interview in which Wolf tellingly defines her position within—and on—the GDR. Her open letter to the East German PEN Club asking support of the organization for the then-imprisoned Václav Havel is dated February 1989. Beyond that, however, the emphasis of the collection is upon Wolf's public role in the tormented events surrounding the fortieth anniversary of the GDR and the fall of the Berlin wall. Even if Wolf's richly critical thought is now, alas, nothing more than a documentation of a major moment in history, *Reden im Herbst* will remain essential to a full understanding of the author and her literary work.

Wes Blomster. *World Literature Today.* 65,
1991, p. 111

The title of Christa Wolf's latest work, *Was bleibt,* is conspicuously without a question mark—that form of punctuation, or as she has deployed it in her writing, anti-punctuation, which has become a significant feature of her literary signature. *Was bleibt* could mean "what remains" in the sense of "what remains to be done," or more pitifully, "what else could we have done" *("was blieb uns übrig").* Or perhaps more exactly, "what is/will be left" (in the sense of "when this whole mess is cleaned up"); or it could mean something more positive, an abbreviation of *"etwas bleibt" ("etwas muss bleiben"),* to suggest that out of the chaos—that was and in a way still is the GDR—surely some good must be salvaged. Finally the title also carries a more personal message, about growing old, and scanning the significance of one's life. *Was bleibt* is both the culmination of this author's work and her casting around for new beginnings. Set in the "last days" of East Berlin (the story is actually set in 1979: thus the decline of East Berlin was being recorded on Christa Wolf's calendar for at least a decade), a day in the life of the author, its continuous present documents the self-destruction of a place and a time but not of the central character, who is threatened but holds firm, just as we have seen it before in Wolf's earlier works, *Moskauer Novelle* (Moscow novella), *Der geteilte Himmel* (Divided heaven), *Nachdenken über Christa T.* (The quest for Christa T.), *Kein Ort. Nirgends* (No place on earth), and *Kassandra* (Cassandra: A novel and four essays). "Holding firm" suggests a special sense of gravity. . . .

Placing aesthetics in the service of ethics and becoming subjectively authentic has not been easy for her. Firstly, it was unfashionable and secondly, it was uncomfortable. For in its most immediate expression, "subjective authenticity" is wholly dependent on the most consistently intense physical and emotional reactions. I would not like to postulate that there is no complexity in this process and I would not like to suggest that there is no pleasure. But it seems that in the work of Christa Wolf the purest form of subjective authenticity is in the experience of pain. *Angst* (fear), *Schreck* (shock), *Zorn* (anger), *Enttäuschung* (disappointment), *Kummer* (grief), *Unruhe* (anxiety),

Schlaflosigkeit (insomnia), *Trostlosigkeit* (despair), *Beklemmung* (oppression), *Verletzungen* (injury), *blankes Grauen* (sheer dread): such is the catalogue of pain from her latest and shortest novel. . . . What kind of pain? The pain of alienation. "Ich war in der Fremde" (I was in a foreign land). . . .

Her writing is always in the service of memory, as a recognition of one's responsibility for the past. And ultimately it is memory, as a repeated moral act, which is her work, writing being merely the form it takes. Thus, for Christa Wolf, memory is a craft to which even narrative and poetics, and certainly the comfort of the reader, must at times be sacrificed. When accused of complexity, her response has been that some things cannot be expressed otherwise.

Evelyn Juers. Cambridge Quarterly. 21,
1992, pp. 210–11, 220–21

The Quest for Christa T., which was published in 1968 [is] about a young woman who cannot, will not, live the rhythm of her society (and dies young). It's an exploration for Christa Wolf, through Christa T., of what it means to say, to be "I," "the difficulty of saying 'I.'" In "Interview with Myself," she asks: Will others be interested? She's not sure, but trusts that her whole life and experience, which grow out of an intense concern for the development of her society, will evoke problems and questions in *her* that are important to others. "My questions are what structure the book—not events." The book did provoke discussion, criticism and censorship. For many years it was more available in West Germany than in the East. . . .

Patterns of Childhood was published in 1976. It is another fictional autobiographical journey, this time to the near, unspoken, hardly-to-be-borne German past, in which the child who saw, who knew, is hidden. The adult who pushed her aside, forgot and suppressed her, now must find and know her. Wolf called this kind of labor "subjective authenticity," in which "authenticity" makes the word "truthfulness" look like a barely scratched surface. How hard that must have been to write, how much harder life itself became.

In that year, Wolf Biermann, a popular singer and composer, was allowed to travel to an engagement in West Berlin. He was not allowed to return. Wolf wrote: "1976 was a caesura in cultural policy development in our country, outwardly indicated by Wolf Biermann's expatriation. . . . A group of authors became aware that their direct collaboration, the kind they themselves could answer for and thought was right, was no longer needed. We are socialists, after all. We lived as socialists in the GDR because that's where we wanted to be involved. *To be utterly cast back on literature* brought about a crisis for the individual, an existential crisis." It must have been a political crisis, too. As one of the signers of a protest letter to the government, Wolf was dismissed from the executive board of the Berlin section of the Writers' Union. A rumor was spread by the Stasi that she had secretly withdrawn her signature. Her denial resulted in more intense harassment from the secret police. . . .

These conflicts, this falling back on literature, became *No Place on Earth,* which I think of as a play of mourning for the Romantic writers of the early nineteenth century—Günderrode, Kleist, Büchner—who were sentenced to suicide and madness. "They wrote hymns to their country," Anna Seghers said, "against the walls of whose society they beat their heads." . . .

I have not talked about *Accident: A Day's News,* a book I admire. It's about Chernobyl, a brother's brain operation, a woman's ordinary anxious day, "the significance of daily structure." . . .

And then *What Remains:* a collection of older stories, including the title novella describing Wolf's surveillance by the East German secret police a number of years ago. This story infuriated West German critics, who thought she should have published it much earlier. It was a jumping-off point for a scapegoating attack on Christa Wolf that held her responsible for all GDR corruption, bureaucratic crime and political repression. This campaign chose to disregard Wolf's work, which, in fiction and talk and interview, dealt with the life of the individual in a stultifying society, the pathetic condition of education, which she pointed out prepared young people for a life of dependent thinking, the untold stories of German literary history, as well as German difficulties in facing the Nazi past and the complicity of those still alive—her own generation.

Grace Paley. *The Nation.* April 5, 1993,
pp. 454–57

WOOLF, VIRGINIA (GREAT BRITAIN) 1882–1941

To the Lighthouse is a story about Mrs. Ramsay, but in a sense her death is a minor incident brought in to show how her influence lived after her; things center round her in the third part just as continuously, with just as little natural climax, as they did in the first. You might indeed say that it is hopeless to look for an orderly plot about such a heroine, because the things that are interesting about her make a plot irrelevant. And yet it is a mistake to suppose that you can say even those things in a novel without a plot.

Mrs. Woolf's later style is very beautifully adapted to the requirements of this subject; so much so as to attack very directly the problem of motivation. Indeed I think it is for this that she will chiefly be remembered; in this administrative but domestic setting, by the very structure of the sentences, we are made to know what it felt like for the heroine to make up her mind. Of course in itself this is not new; it is the main business of a novelist to show his reader, by slow accumulations, all the elements and proportions of a decision, so that the reader knows how the character felt about it; but Mrs. Woolf, so as to be much more immediately illuminating, can show how they are at the back of a decision at the moment it is taken.

We arrive, for instance, with some phrase like "and indeed" into a new sentence and a new specious present. Long, irrelevant, delicious clauses recollect the ramifications of the situation (this part corresponds to the blurring of consciousness while the heroine waits a moment to know her own mind; and it is here, by the way, that one is told most of the story); then by a twist of thought some vivid but distant detail, which she is actually conscious of, and might have been expected to finish the sentence, turns her mind towards the surface. From then on the clauses become shorter; we move towards action by a series of leaps, each, perhaps, showing what she would have done about something quite different, and just at the end, without effort, washed up by the last wave of this disturbance, like an obvious bit of grammar put in to round off the sentence, with a partly self-conscious, wholly charming humility in the heroine (how odd that the result of all this should be something so flat and domestic), we get the small useful thing she actually did do. . . . All one can say against the willful and jumping brilliance of Mrs. Woolf's descriptive passages is that, as part of a design, they come to seem unsatisfying; however delicate and brightly colored they seem cut in low relief upon the great block she has taken for her material, and even when you are sure that some patch is really part of the book you often cannot (as you can in my two examples) see why it should be. Of course her methods catch intensely a sense of period, of setting, of the immediate person described; are very life-like, in short; and I do not know how far it may be due to just this quality; to the fact that so many of her images, glittering and searching as they are, spreading out their wealth of feeling, as if split, in the mind, give one just that sense of waste that is given by life itself. "The great revelation perhaps never did come. Instead, there were little daily miracles, illuminations, matches struck unexpectedly in the dark."

"How far that little candle sheds its beams"; but still it is the business of art to provide candelabra, to aggregate its matches into a lighthouse of many candlepower. If only (one finds oneself feeling in re-reading these novels), if only these dissolved units of understanding had been co-ordinated into a system; if only, perhaps there was an index, showing what had been compared with what; if only these materials for the metaphysical conceit, poured out so lavishly, had been concentrated into crystals of poetry that could be remembered, how much safer one would feel.

William Empson. In Edgell Rickword, ed.
Scrutinies, II (London: Wishart, 1931),
pp. 210–11, 215–16

But what of the subject that she regards as of the highest importance: human beings as a whole and as wholes? She tells us (in her essays) that human beings are the permanent material of fiction, that it is only the method of presenting them which changes and ought to change, that to capture their inner life presents a different problem to each generation of novelists; the great Victorians solved it in their way; the Edwardians shelved it by looking outward at relatives and houses; the Georgians must solve it anew, and if they succeed a new age of fiction will begin. Has she herself succeeded? Do her own characters live?

I feel that they do live, but not continuously, whereas the characters of Tolstoy (let us say) live continuously. With her, the reader is in a state of constant approval. "Yes that is right," he says, each time she implies something more about Jacob or Peter: "yes that would be so: yes." Whereas in the case of Tolstoy approval is absent. We sink into André, into Nicolay Rostoff during the moments they come forth, and no more endorse the correctness of their functioning than we endorse our own. And the problem before her—the problem that she has set herself, and that certainly would inaugurate a new literature if solved—is to retain her own wonderful new method and form, and yet allow her readers to inhabit each character with Victorian thoroughness. Think how difficult this is. If you work in a storm of atoms and seconds, if your highest joy is "life; London; this moment in June" and your deepest mystery "here is one room; there another," how can you construct your human beings so that each shall be not a movable monument but an abiding home, how can you build between them any permanent roads of love and hate? There was continuous life in the little hotel people of *The Voyage Out* because there was no innovation in the method. But Jacob in *Jacob's Room* is discontinuous, demanding—and obtaining—separate approval for everything he feels or does. And *Mrs. Dalloway?* There seems a slight change here, an approach towards character-construction in the Tolstoyan sense; Sir William Bradshaw, for instance, is uninterruptedly and embracingly evil. Any approach is significant, for it suggests that in future books she may solve the problem as a whole. She herself believes it can be done, and, with the exception of Joyce, she is the only writer of genius who is trying. All the other so-called innovators are (if not pretentious bunglers) merely innovators in subject matter and the praise we give them is of the kind we should accord to scientists. . . . But they do not advance the novelist's art. Virginia Woolf has already done that a little, and if she succeeds in her problem of rendering character, she will advance it enormously.

E. M. Forster. *Abinger Harvest* (London: Edward Arnold, 1936), pp. 110–11

In its structural severity *Between the Acts* resembles a musical composition, or a poetic drama. Like these it rewards vigilant attention and increasing familiarity and yet gives immediate pleasure at a first reception. Few novels have this kind of form. In some ways *Between the Acts* is an advance upon *Mrs. Dalloway, To the Lighthouse* or *The Waves* because, without loss of depth, it has greater width of interest and greater variety of effect than they have. It owes more to the comic spirit. All her novels include the humor that depends upon fantasy and a perception of the grotesque, but the later and more characteristic work does not elsewhere include as much of the comedy of manners. At the surface the book is predominantly about contrasted manners and values. The characters, shrewdly observed and amusingly presented, are juxtaposed so as to offset one another, the scenes are comic, at times even farcical, as often as they are moving. It is a picture of present-day English life and manners in a setting which evokes the past history of England and forbodings of the future. But the full significance of the book depends, as in all her characteristic work, upon the sequence of scenes, the juxtaposition of experiences which throw light on one another, the recurrent images or symbols and (even more here than elsewhere) the variations of rhythm.

At the heart of the book lie the ageless paradoxes: man's insatiable thirst for the ideal and his constant preoccupation with the trivial; the "dateless limit" of human history and the "brief candle" of an individual life.

Joan Bennett. *Virginia Woolf* (New York: Harcourt Brace, 1945), p. 150

Virginia Woolf seemed to have the worst defect of the Mandarin style, the ability to spin cocoons of language out of nothing. The history of her literary style has been that of a form at first simple, growing more and more elaborate, the content lagging far behind, then catching up, till, after the falseness of *Orlando,* she produced a masterpiece in *The Waves.*

Her early novels were not written in an elaborate style. Her most significant early book is *Monday or Tuesday* (1921) and demonstrates the rule that Mandarin prose is the product of those who in their youth were poets. In short it is romantic prose. Not all poets were romantic prose writers (e.g., Dryden) but most romantic prose writers have attempted poetry.

The development of Virginia Woolf is the development of this lyrical feeling away from E. M. Forster, with his artlessness and simple, poetical, colloquial style, into patterns of her own. The reveries of a central character came more and more to dominate her books. In *The Waves* she abandoned the convention of the central figure and described a group of friends, as children, as young people and finally in late middle age. In a series of tableaux are contrasted the mystery of childhood, the promise of youth, the brilliance of maturity and the complex, unmarketable richness of age. If *The Years* seems an impressionist gallery with many canvases, landscapes, portraits, and conversation pieces, then *The Waves* is a group of five or six huge panels which celebrate the dignity of human life and the passage of time. It is one of the books which comes nearest to stating the mystery of life and so, in a sense, nearest to solving it.

Cyril Connolly. *Enemies of Promise* (New York: Macmillan, 1948), p. 49

Perhaps of all writers on literature, Virginia Woolf is the least "critical" in the day-of-judgment meaning of the word. She writes plastically, molding little busts and cameos of people, times and places; her every word is a revelation of her individual sensibility, and one might suspect that she has no regard for general principles at all, so little does she parade them and so modestly does she qualify the range and validity of her wider judgments. When speaking of Russian or American literature, for instance, she is careful to stress the fact that she is a foreigner, an Englishwoman, a lover of gardens, quiet, and Jane Austen. But this does not prevent her from seeing that Miss Austen may be likened to the Greek tragedians, "though with a thousand differences of degree; she, too, in her modest, everyday prose, chose the dangerous art where one slip means death." She is one of the few imaginative writers who can apply their own artistic methods to criticism without ever violating its first canon: to bring the reader closer to the book, the particular, than he could have come unaided—to "make it new," as Pound tried to do, and so often ended by making it Pound. She can instill a deeper awareness of the nature of writing by analyzing a page of Flaubert, as she does in "Re-reading Novels" in this new volume, than you could get from an entire treatise, even a good one, on truth and value in art, or contemporary significance in fiction. No writer about books surpasses her in immediacy, in the ability to convey "knowledge of" as distinguished from "knowledge about."

Frank Jones. *Partisan Review.*
May, 1948, p. 592

Now come the extracts from the diary [*A Writer's Diary*] she kept, irregularly, from 1915 to within four days of her death in 1941, a deliberate revelation and pitiless self-examination of that strange make-up which was her mind. She regarded it as good practice, rather as an athlete regards his exercises for limbering up. . . .

No one could seem dull to her, with her capacity for making people up; the portrait might bear no relation to reality, or perhaps she had a reality of her own. Yet people were a worry, for she was much sought after, and the interruption got between her and what she most wanted to do: she has again been held up by her accursed love of talk. "Incessant company," she writes in a moment of excerbation, "is as bad as solitary confinement." For there was only one thing she wanted to do, and that was to live her own arduous inner life as a writer. It is here that we begin to reach the depths and to uncover both the anguish and the ecstasy. To lead this life was perhaps harder for her than for most writers, not only for reasons of health but because the balance of what she wanted to say and the way in which she wanted to say it was so exceedingly precarious; how to keep the flight of the mind, as she puts it, and yet to be exact. A false step, and she will be off the stretched wire. It is the problem of seeing with the intensity natural to her, and at the same time of exercising the craftsman's control; the eternal problem of the artist, in her case rendered the more acute by her peculiar temperament and the ever-experimental character of her work. What she was reaching after we shall never quite know, and perhaps she did not quite know it herself. There is a groping, and from time to time a hint, a moon of light at the end of a tunnel; but of the intensity there can be no question. . . .

We may smile at her uncertainties, but here is no smiling at the profound sense of tragedy which underlay her high spirits and her fun. Outright she says that no one knows how she suffers, walking up a London street, nor how deep is her great lake of melancholy. . . .

As the years go by the diary makes it clearer and clearer that she had no desire to follow obediently in the accepted tradition of narrative and characterization. She is in pursuit of something far more elusive, which could be attained only by oblique methods of her own. She was trying to do something very difficult, trying to express the inexpressible, like someone gifted with seeing a color not visible to human eyes, or hearing a sound not audible to human ears. She was perfectly well aware that her interests as a writer—she calls it her *only* interest—lay in "some queer individuality of my own, not in strength, or passion, or anything startling, but then I say to myself, is not 'some individuality' precisely the quality I respect?" And then, her acumen as a critic suddenly shooting out its chameleon tongue, she captures Donne and Peacock into the same company as herself.

V. Sackville West. *Encounter.*
January, 1954, pp. 71–72, 74

Because it is in almost continuous state of moral and intellectual relaxation that Mrs. Woolf's characters draw out their existence, they can be projected only through a more or less direct transcription of their consciousness. Such a qualification is necessary, however, for the method here is rarely if ever as direct as that of Joyce or his followers. Between the consciousness and the rendition of it there is nearly always interposed a highly artificial literary style. This style remains practically uniform for all the characters; it is at once individual and traditional. The effect of its elegant diction and elaborately turned periods is to make one feel at times as if these sad and lonely people were partly compensated for the vacuity of their lives by the gift of casting even their most random thoughts in the best literary tradition. . . .

Here also Mrs. Woolf is pre-eminently the poet; for as an unwillingness to use motives and actions led to her substitution of poetic symbols in their stead so is she also compelled to use a metaphorical rather than a narrative style. In this practice of course she is not without precedent; other novelists have relied on metaphor to secure their finest effects of communication. But while such effects are ordinarily used to heighten the narrative, they are never extended to the point where they assume an independent interest. In Mrs. Woolf's books metaphorical writing is not occasional but predominate; from the beginning it has subordinated every other kind; and it was inevitable that it should one day be segmented into the purely descriptive prose-poems of *The Waves.*

William Troy. In Morton Dauwen Zabel, ed.
Literary Opinion in America, vol. 1 (New
York: Harper, 1962), pp. 333–34

Beneath the apparent variety of her writings, Virginia Woolf's work possesses remarkable unity. The fact that her novels represent less than half her production should not mislead us. Her reviews, her portrait sketches of literary figures, her general criticism, even her biographies, even *A Room of One's Own* betray a single preoccupation: the novel.

These writings are only a prolonged commentary in the margin of the various manifestations of that form of art to which she devoted her genius; thus she devoted her talent to it too, seeking, by setting her own experience against that of her predecessors, a definition, a formula for that literary genre which cannot be defined and knows no law. She acquired, in this field, a fame which none will dispute.

Her analyses are consulted by every critic. But we must not forget that such research was never for Virginia Woolf an end in itself; it was at once a preparation for her work as novelist and a residue of that work. However interesting, however highly esteemed these critical writings may be—and some attribute to them a surer and more enduring value than to her novels—they should be relegated to the secondary place and the accessory role that Virginia Woolf ascribed to them. By considering them from this point of view, moreover, we shall avoid the common error of believing that she took an interest in technique for its own sake, and that her perpetual experimenting with new forms was merely an aesthete's game, intended to compensate for or to disguise certain deficiencies in her creative genius. . . .

It is not because of her attack on the Holmeses and Bradshaws of the world, the Lord Mayors, the Church or the Army, commercialism, patriotism, or fascism, that Virginia Woolf will survive the test of time. I have stressed these examples of "commitment" to contemporary issues, not because they add any virtue to her work—I should be inclined to assert the contrary—but because they betoken a vitality, an awareness of the world, an infinitely richer kind of interest and contact than has commonly been ascribed to her. The figure of Antigone, which she evokes more than once with a sense of kinship, Antigone with her passion for truth, independence and integrity, holds undoubted fascination and wins our sympathy.

Jean Guiguet. Virginia Woolf and Her Works
(New York: Harcourt, Brace, 1965),
pp. 459–60, 464

The generation to which Virginia Woolf belonged was in revolt against Victorianism. Mrs. Woolf was extremely sensitive to the present, that is to say, to the spirit of modernism. She was also linked to the past by unusually strong bonds. Her father had believed in a certain kind of moral strenuousness, and although Virginia and her friends were serious young people, it was almost a point of honor with them to adopt an attitude as far removed as possible from that of their elders. . . .

Almost every writer on Virginia Woolf has commented on the fundamental dualism in her work. Unlike some of her contemporaries, she wished not only to criticize the tradition which she had inherited, but in a sense to renew it. Her goal was to write in such a way as to satisfy the utilitarian philosophy of her father, while remaining true to the artistic mood of her own generation. The former demanded that her books contribute something to the welfare of mankind, the latter taught her that every work of art is autonomous, a purely aesthetic skirmish in the struggle to achieve "significant form." The moralist in Virginia Woolf is most in evidence in her feminist writings, and the aesthete in her novels; neither is entirely lacking in anything she wrote.

Herbert Marder. *Feminism and Art: A Study of Virginia Woolf* (Chicago: University of Chicago Press, 1968), pp. 16–17

An understanding of Mrs. Woolf's concept of the creative reader brings to light more sharply the contemporary nature of her work. She died in 1941. Nearly thirty years later, ideas and trends whose shape could be glimpsed in her novels have become visible, not only in fiction—as in the *nouveau roman* of Nathalie Sarraute or Alain Robbe-Grillet, which carries subjectivity to its outermost limits—but also in music and especially in the theater of the absurd. The participating audience, the random act; the emphasis on the global rather than the linear, on the kinetic instead of the static; experiments with mass, rhythm, and space—all suggest a creative and innovating intellect whose ideas fit intuitively into emerging patterns of artistic thought.

Her approach to certain philosophical and psychological problems was also far ahead of her time. One may be reminded of Bergson, William James, and Freud in reading her novels. But contemporaries like Edmund Husserl's disciple Merleau-Ponty, the Swiss psychologist Jean Piaget (whose studies of the child mind bear out many of Mrs. Woolf's own observations), the school of Cassirer, Whitehead, and Susanne K. Langer, seem just as pertinent. Indeed—and every generation approaches a great writer from its own perspective—Virginia Woolf belongs to the moment of now. On her work, as in her concept of the moment, the future already lay "like a piece of glass, making it tremble and quiver"—by which she meant that the immanence of the future in the present brings it vitally alive.

This is not to imply, however, that Mrs. Woolf conforms to this or that current mode of thought. One does not draw a particular philosophy or discipline from her work. One can only conclude that her examination of her own encounter with lived experience was transmuted into the novel's form: modes of life became modes of fiction. And since a writer's apprehension of his methods, as Virginia Woolf was only too ready to admit, is apt to be mainly unconscious, so is the reader's participation in them.

Harvena Richter. *Virginia Woolf: The Inward Voyage* (Princeton: Princeton University Press, 1970), pp. 244–46

Virginia Woolf's researches into the comparative poverty of women were prompted, she says, by her visit to Oxbridge. It is the marked contrast between the spacious richness of the men's foundations and the beef-and-prunes atmosphere of Fernham, the women's college, that made her ask why women are poor. The university stands for a whole world of leisure, elegance, and luxury that *A Room of One's Own* treats as essential to the creation and perpetuation of art. The university is the bastion of that "intellectual freedom of which great writings are born," and the important fact about it in *A Room of One's Own* is that in recent times almost all the great writers of England had "procured the means to get the best education England can give."

But whereas *A Room of One's Own* is a book about money, sex, and culture, *Three Guineas* is a book about money, sex, and power. In the later work, the important facts about the university are that "the great majority of men who have ruled England for the past five hundred years, who are now ruling England in Parliament and the Civil Service, has received a university education," and that "an immense sum of money . . . has been spent upon education in the past five-hundred years." These facts lead her to recognition of what the university is really about, whom it really serves, and thence to rejection of the entire ruling class culture *A Room of One's Own* is so ready to embrace. She envisions, instead, a new kind of institution, one that will foster neither the old culture nor the system whose vehicle she now perceives education to be.

Lillian S. Robinson. In Louis Kanpf and
Paul Lauter, eds. *The Politics of Literature:
Dissenting Essays on the Teaching of English*
(New York: Pantheon, 1972), pp. 401–2

Throughout Mrs. Woolf's work, the chief problem for her and her characters is to overcome the space between things, to attain an absolute unity with the world, as if everything in the environment were turned into water. This desire for absolute union can be expressed in both physical and spiritual terms, and in Mrs. Woolf it nearly always has sexual connotations. . . .

The generally erotic nature of her art has never received proper emphasis from critics, though many have pointed to lighthouses, pocketknives, bodies of water, and windows as evidence of sexual symbolism. She has been portrayed as a prudish lady, a "peeper," as Wyndham Lewis once called her. It is true that her novels are often reticent about sex (Lytton Strachey's chief criticism of *To the Lighthouse* was that it avoided reference to copulation— a remark that tells as much about Strachey as it does about Mrs. Woolf), and sometimes she is manifestly prudish, as in *The Voyage Out*.

This does not mean, however, that her work is sexless. On the contrary, her prose is full of erotic impulses, and sexual themes are major elements in all her books. Again and again she either hints at or explicitly portrays homoeroticism: consider, for example, St. John Hurst, Clarissa Dalloway, Lily Briscoe, Neville, Orlando, and William Dodge. Mrs. Woolf's indirection in some of these cases may reflect her concern for decorum, or Bloomsbury's proclivity to a love that even in the 1920s was careful not to speak its name. On the other hand, when she does portray sexual emotions, she often injects an element of fear. Her nervous, barely concealed eroticism is . . . related to the wish to find some permanent, all-embracing union: in effect, to the death wish.

> James Naremore. *The World without a Self:*
> *Virginia Woolf and the Novel* (New Haven:
> Yale University Press, 1973), pp. 242–43

Virginia Woolf would have agreed with D. H. Lawrence that human beings have two ways of knowing, "knowing in terms of apartness, which is mental, rational, scientific, and knowing in terms of togetherness, which is religious and poetic." . . . Virginia Woolf associated these two ways with the two sexes. In *A Room of One's Own* she suggests that every mind is potentially bisexual. But she finds that among writers, and particularly among her contemporaries, most men tend to develop only the analytic, "masculine" approach, what Lawrence calls "knowing in terms of apartness," and most women only the synthetic, "feminine," that is, "knowing in terms of togetherness." In her opinion, however, to be truly creative one must use the "whole" mind.

In keeping with this, the greatest writers are "androgynous": they use and harmonize the masculine and feminine approaches to truth. They do not suffer from what T. S. Eliot calls the "dissociation of sensibility" or what Carl Jung calls the "split consciousness" of modern man; for in Jungian terms, they have discovered the "self," "a point midway between the conscious and the unconscious," in which there is a reconciliation of opposites. Like Jung, Virginia Woolf felt that neither an individual nor an age can find its point of equilibrium without frankly confronting and understanding the exact nature of the opposing forces. Thus, her interest in what it means to be a male or female was related to her quest for the self or the point of balance that would stabilize her personality and give her the sense of wholeness and unconsciousness which characterizes the androgynous writer.

> Nancy Topping Bazin. *Virginia Woolf and*
> *the Androgynous Vision* (New Brunswick,
> New Jersey: Rutgers University Press,
> 1973), pp. 3–4

To establish at once that *Mrs. Dalloway* is a novel with a plot of mental search, [Virginia Woolf] dramatized consciousness, embedding the thoughts and feelings of many characters in the movement of a single subsuming mind. In addition, by patterning its seemingly miscellaneous experience, she indicated that its movement would lead to insight. The interplay between the confusion of the consciousness and the logic of the structure produced that balance toward which she had been working during the writing of three earlier novels. She herself sensed this new power when she finished *Jacob's Room*.

Although she had clearly described the principles and the effects of the technique of *Mrs. Dalloway* years before, she had not easily arrived at this compression and control. In *The Voyage Out, Night and Day,* and *Jacob's Room* she had experimented with techniques of order and disorder that she now brought successfully into relationship. On the one hand, there is freedom in the lifelike rendering of Clarissa's thought. Her mind stands in a double relation to her outer experience, being both distanced from and penetrating the visible world: "she sliced like a knife through everything; at the same time she was outside looking on." Her dual response to the outer world is intermingled with her memories, but, on the other hand, there is clear control of the mixed impressions. Her thought takes flight through time and space, but its discontinuity is balanced by the logic of the associational and symbolic cluster that holds together both present and past; morning—flowers—youth—freshness—children on the beach. And wherever the complexity of her view might produce confusion, there is the tactful presence of the narrator to provide direction.

The effect is a blending of lifelike intensity and artful rhythm. The method is controlled economy—so perfect a dovetailing of inner and outer, past and present, that it becomes not balance but unity. [Virginia Woolf's] taste as she wrote *Mrs. Dalloway* was for poetry: "It is poetry that I want now—long poems. . . . I want the concentration and the romance: and the words all glued together, fused, glowing: have no time to waste any more on prose."

Jane Novak. The Razor Edge of Balance: A
Study of Virginia Woolf (Coral Gables:
University of Miami Press, 1975), pp. 68–69

The creative illusions that Virginia Woolf saw human beings weaving around them were after all only attempts to escape the constant threat of the unknown and unknowable forces and the painful knowledge that everything, including man himself, that is generated must be prepared for its dissolution. They were only different types of stances taken in an attempt to counterbalance these alien forces and to defy death. Although Virginia Woolf found these illusions, which took different forms on the imaginative, intellectual, social or mystical levels, as having more positive value than the sheer acceptance of the naked truth, yet she did not think they possessed the absolute power to resolve the threat of the void. These creative illusions, however fascinating, could at best conceal the fact of death, like Mrs. Ramsay's shawl hiding momentarily the ugliness of the skull before it is torn and shorn. Even the haven of bliss that she had created with her own imaginative and creative powers was engulfed by the devouring tide of Time. Her children died, the house decayed. The desolation and destruction prevailed where once she had created harmony and unity. How infantile and dwarfish these creative efforts of the individuals looked in the face of the vaster forces operating in the universe. It was at such moments that Virginia Woolf turned toward aesthetic order as having more permanent value than human efforts. At times she seemed to agree with Lily Briscoe that everything changed but "not words: not paints." As in Henry James and James Joyce, there is a suggestion in Virginia Woolf that the demands of the "architecturally competent" novel can alter the free flow of life. James's structurally integrated novels are symbolic of the formal beauty and grace, the ideal geometry of relationships that he sought but did not find in life. Joyce's choice of a style that has classical severity and precision was a counter attack on his vision of paralysis and dissolution of life in his Dublin stories. Proust embraced aesthetics as another "way of life," and art as eliminating the fear of death and the despair caused by nothingness. On the other hand, Virginia Woolf . . . did not wholeheartedly share this aesthetic view. She treated art only as one of the creative illusions employed to find a way of arresting or reversing the irreversible flow of time toward death. Virginia Woolf's artistic alter egos in her novels, although engaged in an untiring pursuit of art, do not conceal their general dissatisfaction with the power of art to retrieve life from death and mutability. Lily Briscoe knows that her painting will be forgotten in a remote corner of an attic. Bernard looks with remorse at his notebook of phrases lying on the floor of the dining hall from where it would be swept away next morning by the sweeper. Miss La Trobe is worried whether she has made her audience see her vision or not. Would all this effort, strain and strife be set at naught? Would her pageant be "a failure, another damned failure"? In the face of all this distrust and confusion it is impossible to believe that Virginia Woolf would accept and take solace in an aesthetic order as a possible escape from the temporal human existence.

Vijay Laxmi Kapur. *Virginia Woolf's Vision
of Life and Her Search for Significant Form*
(Atlantic Highlands, New Jersey:
Humanities Press, 1979), pp. 158–59

Virginia Woolf's renaissance is one of those unexpected events that have puzzled cultural historians. In one sense, of course, it need not be surprising at all. Woolf is too fine an artist, too secure in her imaginative range with a mind too subtly responsive to life outside and within to have been ignored forever. Still, in another sense it is surprising, for in her recent incarnation she has communicated aspects of herself which had seldom been noted in earlier years. Although she had shared the social and political ambience of Bloomsbury, and although her feminism was widely known, her essential reputation had been that of a highly accomplished writer of poetic prose. But now many readers take this latter role for granted and focus instead upon her sociopolitical stance, which they find equally innovative. They are raising important question about Woolf's pivotal place between the fact and the vision of art. . . .

Virginia Woolf is not just a survivor of the great age of Modernism who has been given artificial respiration. She owes part of her renaissance to a reading of her texts beyond fictionality. This is by no means a negative criticism: a revaluation of that self-conscious artist as a radical and feminist model is partly a revaluation of fiction itself, an expansion of the language of narrative into the language of life. Betty Flanders, Clarissa Dalloway, Mrs. Ramsay, as well as many of Woolf's male figures, can be seen not as characters of fiction but as aspects and illustrations of a single consciousness envisioning and clarifying its themes. The revaluation of Woolf is based on a revolution in the conception of language, of reading, of literary art. It is one of Woolf's paradoxes . . . that the dissolution of artistic language and fictional characters into a sum of persons caught in the discourse of life has taken place in the work of a writer who produced the most artful lyrical prose of our time.

> Ralph Freedman. *Virginia Woolf:*
> *Revaluation and Continuity* (Berkeley:
> University of California Press, 1980),
> pp. 3, 7–8

[Virginia Woolf's] preoccupations were much the same in her first novel as in her later ones; it is only the techniques that were subtilized, beginning with *Jacob's Room* (1922) and with some of the short stories and sketches immediately preceding that work. In *The Voyage Out,* she utilized a nineteenth-century longhand by which she conveyed inclusively the social environment of her heroine, Rachel Vinrace, and the people who surround—and crowd about—her, together with an extended analysis of the motives of her main characters. Virginia Woolf's twentieth-century "shorthand," used to re-create instead of to describe emotional, mental, and spiritual states, is present mostly in embryo. But the fact that she is on her way to achieving the shorthand "notation" present in the later fiction is one of the novel's chief fascinations. With this interesting and aesthetically substantial novel, she heralds, moreover, many of the insistent themes, situations, character types, and methods of presenting the subjective life that are prevalent in her books of the 1920s and 1930s. In the most perceptive account of the book to date, Avrom Fleishman maintains that it is "one of the finest first works by any author," and I must agree. In *The Voyage Out,* perhaps her most traditional novel, Woolf's vision is closer, I believe, to that expressed in *The Waves* (1931), her masterpiece and her most consciously experimental work, than it is to that found in any other of her novels.

> Fredrick P. W. McDowell. In Ralph
> Freedman, ed. *Virginia Woolf: Revaluation*
> *and Continuity* (Berkeley: University of
> California Press, 1980), p. 74

It has been suggested by Victoria Middleton that *The Years* is "anti-visionary," aimed at the very heart of "literary creation itself." This is true only if we are prepared to call *The Waste Land* anti-literary and anti-visionary. What *The Years* is, I think, is counter to the visions which have already made Woolf justly famous. When the same critic observes, like Leonard Woolf, that in *The Years,* Woolf "chose to work in a mode contrary to her deepest creative instinct," we recognize how extraordinary it is, in one's fifties, to search out a new creative vein, to allow one's anger to drive one to the discovery of new forms. This measures the terrible daring of Woolf's, and all the best, feminist writing: by its nature it opposes what we have learned from the great art of the patriarchy, that anger is inimical to creation.

> Carolyn G. Heilbrun. *Twentieth-Century*
> *Literature.* 27, 1981, p. 25

However much she herself valued it, Woolf could not in *The Waves* fully confront female authoring, female creativity. The choice of a male center to repress her own voice, the static, conventionalized portraits of widely separated males and females in which the perception of the female is subtly devalued, then the friendly mocking of male attempts to be androgynous and write—all these both suggest her greater comfort as a writer with the male persona and at the same time reveal her profound unease with any such persona. For writing was an ambitious act, one she could not finally separate from the egoism she so detested in males. Her only hope of accommodating these conflicting impulses toward creativity and anonymity was her idea that the sexes could enter that cab and drive off together—that writers at least could be truly androgynous. From underneath the serene surface that the would-be utopia of androgyny *The Waves* attempts to portray emerge traces of this conflict—traces which show the concept of androgyny as a strategy of evasion and suppression.

> Eileen B. Sypher. In Elaine K. Ginsberg and
> Laura Moss Gottlieb, eds. *Virginia Woolf:*
> *Centennial Essays* (Troy, New York:
> Whitson, 1983), p. 210

If *The Years* is one of Woolf's most political novels . . . what were her politics? They were, of course, feminist. But they went far beyond the dictionary definition of feminism as "the theory that women should have political, economic, and social rights equal to those of men," with its suggestion that feminists want nothing more than, as she put it in *Three Guineas,* to join "the procession of the sons of educated men . . . preaching, teaching, administering justice, practicing medicine, transacting business, making money." In fact, Woolf rejected entirely the sort of society created by men which she delineates with such care in *The Years.* Instead, she valued the qualities enforced on her as an "Outsider" (a person who has not only been excluded from positions of power in society, but subordinated to those who are in power), and longed for the world which her characters outline in the "1917" chapter of *The Years,* a world in which people might "live differently," a world in which people might establish a sense of community through candor in speech. In this paper I argue that Woolf's feminist vision in *The Years* is dual: that she both attacks patriarchal society directly and hints at a vision of society based on what she thought of as "women's values."

Woolf's attack on patriarchal society takes three major forms in *The Years*. First, she vividly illustrates the social repression inflicted by that social system on all her characters, male and female. Second, she subverts the family chronicle form in order to indict the patriarchal family and the literary forms which celebrate it. And, third, in an early example of feminist "revision," Woolf reverses the significance usually attributed to events and persons in a novel, trivializing historical persons and events in *The Years,* while elevating to political significance people, events, and conventions generally considered trivial or ordinary.

Laura Moss Gottlieb. In Elaine K. Ginsberg
and Laura Moss Gottlieb, eds. *Virginia Woolf: Centennial Essays* (Troy, New York: Whitson, 1983), pp. 215–16

In *To the Lighthouse,* Woolf looks homeward, like Milton's Angel. Perhaps filling in the gap in the lyric poem between this passage and the ensuing consolation with a narrative, Woolf sees her "homeward" glance at her memories of Cornwall as not only reviving her own hope but giving her mother new life. As her sister Vanessa testified, *To the Lighthouse* was no less than an act of resurrection, in its portrait of Julia Stephen in Mrs. Ramsay accomplishing the "rising of the dead." Enacting one of Milton's worst nightmares in "Lycidas" by placing her mother in the fictional setting of the "stormy Hebrides," Woolf as mariner "visits the bottom of the monstrous world" to transform her own status as castaway into that of someone who has completed the work of mourning. In the process she enables her mother to live again recapturing her in literary portraiture.

Especially in her use of [Cowper's] "The Castaway" in *To the Lighthouse,* by incorporating poetry Woolf transformed the novel. It was a triumphant experiment which would lead Woolf to further "elegiac novels" in which the sound of the waves associated with the response of nature to human desires would become ever more pronounced as the mutual infiltration of poetry and prose continued in her work. In Woolf's work, elegy becomes not just a ritual enacted through the explicit invocation and then transcendence of mourning, but one embodied in the very form of narrative. Woolf's lyricization of narrative results in the diversion of narrative from mimesis. Instead, narrative alludes to a deeper reality which it occasionally embodies, as at moments the entire structure becomes symbolic. This power of narrative to evoke a visionary reality, however, remains at best a work of invocation. Elegies seek, by immortalizing the dead one, to bring him back and so affirm a realm beyond death, but for Woolf, reaching that realm remains a power outside the grasp of the novel and of language.

Elissa Greenwald. *Genre.* 19, 1986,
pp. 54–55

Virginia Woolf's first novel [*The Voyage Out,*] depicting the initiation of a female artist-figure, captures the paradoxical relation of female initiation to female authority in the late-Victorian culture of Woolf's girlhood. On the one hand, Woolf's story of the semi-autobiographical Rachel Vinrace shows how the paradigms of female initiation encourage the young woman to identify with nature rather than culture and to imagine marriage and maternity as the destiny that will fulfill her life. On the other hand, Woolf endows Rachel with a powerful desire to evade or transcend this culturally determined destiny; in other words, to break out of the female initiation plot that her culture imposes upon women, constituting them not as fully legitimated participants in history and culture but as culture's material support. Neither the strength nor the resources of Rachel's desire are equal to the powerful cultural currents that oppose it, however, and the history of Woolf's heroine ends not in triumph but in death. Rachel's death represents not only the power of female initiation structures to overwhelm female desire when it ventures to imagine a different future, but also the difficulties that Woolf confronted in her first attempt to imagine an alternative to the female initiation plot. If Rachel's death records the failure of Woolf's imaginative project in *The Voyage Out,* it is also a symbolic, initiatory death that precedes the rebirth of Woolf's authority in the more powerful representations of female creativity in her later female *Kunstlerromane.* In *The Voyage Out,* Woolf augments the genre of the *failed* female artist-novel. Although her career might have ended here, it did not, and the existence of Woolf's later female artist novels enables us to interpret her representation of female initiation and female authority in *The Voyage Out* not as an ultimate failure but as a challenging and transforming critique, and further, as an allegorical measure of the very great odds that Woolf herself conquered in forging her own powerful artistic authority.

Christine Froula. *Tulsa Studies in Women's
Literature.* 5, 1986, p. 63

[The] conspiracy of woman reader and woman writer is literally a "breathing together" as we rock or are rocked to the rhythm of her words. In *A Room of One's Own,* the con-spirators are also the in-spiration for her talks to women students. In this chapter, which, like Woolf's, is a written version of a talk, I want to explore with you the ways in which she makes sexual difference an asset for women, makes the male the other, defines his language as different from the natural, normal speech of women together, and asserts the superiority of women's speech as a demotic and democratic instrument of communication, as opposed to the egotistical male "I" that lies like a "shadow" across the page, "a straight dark bar *(A Room of One's Own)* on the prison-house of language. For our texts we will take "taking the bull by the udders" a seemingly casual spoken phrase recorded in a letter; "A Woman's College from the Outside," an essay written at the same time as the lectures that compose *A Room of One's Own* and also concerned specifically with women's education; and a section of "The Pargiters," originally intended to be part of *The Years.* My concern is with Woolf's role as a feminist literary critic, her experiments with a female grammar and with a rhetorical strategy that I have called "sapphistry," which masters the principles of classical rhetoric and subverts them at the same time.

Sexual difference for Woolf is not a simple matter of male and female, power and desire. Lesbianism and homosexuality are equal others, and androgyny is a privileged fifth sexual and literary stance. In her life as in her work, celibacy is also singularly important in her own sense of sexual difference.

One may argue, moreover, that class difference extends her five-finger exercise to the other hand. For the salient subtext in every Woolf novel is the voice of the working-class women, the heroic charwomen mythologized into a collective Nausicaa washing the dirty linen of the patriarchal family, her perpetual subject. The caretaker's children, who sing for their supper at the end of *The Years* speak in tongues with the hard "k's" of a Greek chorus, a prophecy of the British mother tongue's responsibility for the exploitation of her colonial children. If women speak to each other in "a little language unknown to men" because of the male control of language, Britain's future workers, the Indians, Africans and West Indians of her former empire, speak to each other in pidgins and creoles, languages less "little," but equally "unknown" to the powerful. Their music, their art, may be a mystery to the elite, but it is a culture of its own. *A Room of One's Own* may appear to be merely a primer for valorization of female difference, but its eloquent peroration to the absent women washing up the dishes, assuring us that Shakespeare's sister will be born of the uneducated classes, declares that it will also serve as manual for the subversion of class difference and racial difference. . . .

The brilliance of *A Room of One's Own* lies in its invention of a female language to subvert the languages of the patriarchy. Like her novels, it is about reading and it trains us to read as women. Its tropes figure new reading and writing strategies, enlisting punctuation in the service of feminism with the use of ellipses for encoding female desire, the use of initials and dashes to make absent figures more present and transforming interruption, the condition of the woman writer's oppression, as in the citations to Jane Austen's experience, into a deliberate strategy as a sign of woman's writing. The narrator of *A Room* continually interrupts herself. In following the interrupted text the reader reproduces the female experience of being interrupted and joins Woolf in making interrupted discourse a positive female form. The tyranny of the interrupter is forgotten as the woman writer interrupts herself. I began by insisting on the contextualization of *A Room of One's Own* as historically the last in a series of women's suffrage pamphlets. I will end by suggesting that the literary strategy of interruption in the text is derived from the political strategy of the interruption of male politician's speeches, developed by the suffragettes after Christabel Pankhurst and Annie Kenney interrupted Sir Edward Grey and were thrown in jail. The tactic enraged the men and it was continued successfully throughout the campaign for the vote. Virginia Woolf's lasting contribution to "the Cause" was to transform a feminist political strategy which truly voiced women's rebellion at enforced silence into a literary trope which captures the radicalism of the movement in a classic tribute.

> Jane Marcus. *Virginia Woolf and the Languages of Patriarchy* (Bloomington: Indiana University Press, 1987), pp. 138–39

Jacob's Room is a thorough examination of class and sex in English society, in which the upper class feeds on the lower and, as it feeds, the upper-class male grows stronger; while the upper-class male sucks his power from the lower class, particularly the lower-class woman, his female counterpart grows even more fragile and sickly. This view of women in a hierarchical English society is best delineated through particular characters and relationships in *Jacob's Room*—through the complex pattern of interrelationships of the Barfoots, Dickenses, and Betty Flanders, of the Pascoes and the Durrants.

> Kathleen Dubie. In Jane Marcus, ed. *Virginia Woolf and Bloomsbury: A Centenary Celebration* (Bloomington: Indiana University Press, 1987), p. 196

That Woolf's sixth novel represents an act of comic tribute to her loving friend Vita Sackville-West has been well documented. However, a return to the diary record of *Orlando*'s conception suggests that the work was more than the playful tribute to Sackville-West or the escape from works of a more "serious poetic experimental" nature which some critics, following Woolf's lead, have judged it to be. Instead, *Orlando* completes the labor of self-creation which Woolf began in her autobiographical novel, *To the Lighthouse* (1927). In that earlier novel, she laid to rest the ghosts of her parents, establishing herself as an adult woman independent of their potentially eclipsing examples. In *Orlando* (1928), which bears "the clear stamp of her mind in its maturity," and "might in a sense have been called an autobiography," Woolf went further. Claiming her *literary* majority, she confronted the influence of both literal and literary fathers to reshape the novel, and so to create a place for herself in the English novelistic tradition which was their legacy to her.

> Susan M. Squier. *Women's Studies*. 12, 1986, p. 167

Virginia Woolf's career as a novelist makes two great lines crossing on one major problem—the formation of narrative strategies that make a critique of both gendering and hegemonic processes by rupturing the sentences and sequences of romance and related materials in quest plots. Both of her very first novels draw on the traditional concerns of love plots—the production of newly joined heterosexual couples, and of quest plots—the *Bildung* of the protagonist. That is, in *The Voyage Out* (1915) and *Night and Day* (1919) Woolf considers the endings in engagement to marry and death. After these novels, heterosexual romance is displaced from a controlling and privileged position in her work. It will never again appear as the unique center of narrative concern; it will never again appear assumed or unquestioned. *Mrs. Dalloway* (1925) offers thematic and structural debates about romantic love, the structural debate centering on the cunning device of a nonsexual yet secretly bonded couple—Mrs. Dalloway herself and Septimus Smith—as the bifocal center of the work. *To the Lighthouse* (1927) has a critical relation to the marriage plot and proposes a special passage through "reparenting" for Lily. *Orlando* (1928) and *Flush* (1933) close the issue of heterosexual love by drastic changes in its definition—the latter by describing the burning and yearning passions of a jealous pooch. . . .

The novels along the second major line of Woolf's career—*The Years* (1937) and *Between the Acts* (1941) as well as *The Waves* (1931)—ask a fundamental ideological and structural question: what "social" desires will empower stories and characters if a writer does not depend on the emphases and motivations of romance? Here Woolf displaces the emotional aura and structural weight of individual quest and of hero and heroine onto a communal protagonist. This protagonist—a large family, a group of friends, an audience, containing many close bonds and, importantly, including equalized members of all ages and sexual persuasions—creates a structure in which couples, individuals, walls between public and private, polarized sexes, and closures in (and of) family houses are subject to strong oppositional formations. In general, Woolf separates *eros* from any forced or conventional bonds, especially such institutions as heterosexuality and marriage.

Rachel Blau DuPlessis. Novel. 21, 1988,
pp. 326–28

It is grandpa's grammar and grandpa's myth that *Finnegans Wake* elaborates and celebrates. The oedipal drama is assumed to be *the text* of the human race. A violent, abusive oedipal scenario is portrayed as the human condition, while the *felix culpa* leitmotif stammers its ambivalent blessing over cycle after cycle of the *status quo*. It may be that the central myth of the Wake is not the oedipus myth itself, but *the importance of* the oedipus myth. *Finnegans Wake,* like *Ulysses,* affirms the myth that there *is* a myth of the race.

The radically contraband comedy of *Orlando,* by contrast, challenges the assumption that such a myth or symbol-system exists. The supposedly central and ultimate codes have changed as the spirits of different ages have spoken them. They may change again, Orlando well knows, as she realizes that she progresses not from rhetorical illusion to transcendent truth, but from one rhetorical illusion to another. And the things that she identifies as illusions are not simply the manners and dress of an age, but those large cultural codes which a less radical comedy would identify as truth and norm. Orlando perceives the rhetorically constructed "nature" of love, and the verbal politics that (en)gender the "nature" of the sexes.

Judy Little. *Women's Studies.* 15, 1988,
pp. 190–91

What was at stake for Virginia Woolf was the difficulty and challenge of writing with a difference. Woolf herself articulated her differences with her Edwardian predecessors, in "Modern Fiction" and "Mr. Bennett and Mrs. Brown"; her differences with the Victorian patriarchy surface in *The Pargiters* and then *The Years* as well as in *A Room of One's Own;* and the differences between canonical readings of Woolf and new feminist readings have begun to highlight the extent to which her writing seems to have represented an opportunity for her to grapple with her differences with herself, as well as to "use writing as an art." . . . Virginia Woolf set herself the impossibly complex task of re-telling in fiction a story she had never really been able to tell herself: she lacked the framework as well as the vocabulary she would have needed to represent fully the conjunction of impeded sexuality with chronic and debilitating loss. These are aspects of a common dilemma, of course, but the particular designs they compose in the history and writing of Virginia Woolf are her own: unique, as well as crucially important, to her. This particular vision—of a story now composed of gleams and glimmers of light, now obscured by partial or total darkness—was all she had to go on. It was her own: the particular, fractured design which represented her own subjectivity, her own creativity. She did not want to—could not—make it whole, or conclusive without losing her fundamental sense of its *shape:* its contrasts of light and shade, its ever-fluctuating rhythms. She wrote it exactly as she perceived it, though she experimented, from time to time, with different methods and forms. The attempt to offer a theory of the writing which ensued, to cast light on the dark places, to fill the empty spaces with new, enlightened narratives, cannot really serve to penetrate the exact nature of the mind of Virginia Woolf. We can only experience for ourselves, through the activity of reading her writing, both the light and the dark places of a peculiarly innovative, sensitive and fundamentally honest mind at work, and make whatever deductions we can.

Sue Roe. *Writing and Gender: Virginia
Woolf's Writing Practice* (Brighton:
Harvester/New York: St. Martin's, 1990),
pp. 171, 174–75

The first and the single indispensable work of feminist literary criticism is a slim volume by Virginia Woolf called *A Room of One's Own.*

In the 1978 preface to my first book, *Sex, Class, and Culture,* I tell the story of how I became a feminist critic, sitting up all night mesmerized by news of the Tet offensive and reading *A Room of One's Own.* Dissertation-blocked and Vietnam-obsessed though I was, I wanted to bring Woolf's arguments up to date. Some months later, in the fall of 1968 and as a private commemoration of the fortieth anniversary of the lectures that were to become *A Room of One's Own,* I wrote a long essay, the first piece of what has turned out to be my life's work. Provocatively, I called it, "Who's Afraid of A Room of One's Own?"

Although I believed that *A Room of One's Own* was one of the most beautiful books ever written, I felt it had flaws, particularly in its understanding of sex and class and the relation between them. I thought Woolf didn't know enough about politics—my kind of late-1960s style street-fighting anti-imperialist politics. But I thought I could help her out. Having been born on April 18, 1941, the day Virginia Woolf's body was found, I was all of twenty-seven years old.

Since then I have read and reread *A Room of One's Own* a number of times. I do not believe in sacred texts. Much of my career has been spent, after all, thumbing my nose at canons. So I will not say that *A Room of One's Own* is my Bible. But if Melville could say that a whaling ship was his Harvard and his Yale, *A Room of One's Own* has certainly been my whaling ship—my pirate ship, my tugboat, and my spaceship as well.

At each stage of my evolution as a feminist critic, as I brought different social and literary problematics to bear on the project and explored the intersections of class, race, gender, and sexuality, as I contemplated the revolution of the word and the revolutions beyond that, I have found that Virginia Woolf has been there ahead of me. Not that she provided comprehensive answers that made my own efforts redundant. Rather, the much thumbed-through text showed that she had posed most of the hard questions and recorded the consequent search for answers with elegance. With elegance.

Whether the issue was class or color, war or empire, she offered neither blueprint nor road map but, rather, served simultaneously as forerunner, companion, and comrade in the struggle. In 1968 I set out, with all due respect and a whole lot of chutzpah, to teach Virginia Woolf a thing or two. Well, my recursive reading of *A Room of One's Own* over the past twenty-two years reveals that the old girl has certainly learned a lot.

Lillian S. Robinson. *Women's Studies Quarterly.* 19:3–4, 1991, p. 11–12

When *Three Guineas* appeared in June 1938, the "Virginia Woolf" evoked by readers and reviewers enjoyed the status of one of the most eminent literary figures of the period, a position that ensured the book a public hearing and influenced the public reception of the work. Yet if Woolf's name assured the book's coverage in the press, the constructions of the author that emerge from the reviews illustrate both competing perceptions of what counts as effective, or authoritative, public discourse and a number of strategies for denying Woolf's text access to it. Within these competing discourses, the representation of Woolf's tone, in particular the care taken by both sympathetic and unsympathetic critics to distance the tone from anger, serves to locate the text not in the realm of the public debate about culture and war but in the realm of the aesthetic, with its implications of the private, the interior, the feminine. From its beginnings, then, the reception of *Three Guineas* raises one of the central questions confronting women who write cultural criticism or speak in the public realm: how to find a tone of voice, a rhetoric, a strategy for intervening or participating in a discourse that inscribes the institutionalized authority of men and that associates women's speech with the private and aesthetic. The result of the emphasis given to Woolf's style and voice was to undercut the authority of her arguments, in particular those about dominance and the origins of war that belong most clearly in the masculine realm. Instead, the arguments were all too often subsumed in praise of the art.

Brenda Silver. Signs: Journal of Women in
Culture and Society. 16, 1991, p. 348

On or about December 31, 1991, the fortunes of Virginia Woolf's reputation changed. Released from the distinguished Hogarth Press, the publishing house she and her husband founded when they bought a hand printing press in 1917, Virginia Woolf's books came out of copyright in Britain in January, 1992, fifty years after her death. Now the English reading public is being faced with her worldwide fame in their own bookshops. With the escape from the copyright straitjacket of the Hogarth Press into a myriad editions, cheap and scholarly, the image of upper-class madwoman may now be dispelled in Britain by the simple availability of Woolf's books on a common publishing circuit. Attitudes, once frozen in class fear and loathing, are altering. Familiarity breeds . . . well, familiarity. The English are at last discovering Virginia Woolf. And high time, too.

To what can we attribute the change? The answer is simple. Much as I would like to claim the credit for American feminist critics, I have to admit that our missionary tactics failed to convert the natives from their wicked and misogynist ways. It was the publishers who did it. Like a lusty Victorian maiden escaped from her corset and stays, Woolf has been rejuvenated by her release. Brightly dressed for the mass market of European railway bookshops and London tube station kiosks, the novels are being bought and read by the curious in ordinary editions.

That she also comes wrapped in the stars and stripes, trumpeted by the praise of American feminists, seems to be all to the good. Let's face it. The author was never a heroine to her nephew and biographer. Stepping briskly out of copyright, the debutante writer returns to her native soil—this time, one hopes, not as a suicide or a Bloomsbury bubblehead with no social conscience, but as a writer. . . .

There's something distinctly postmodern in the fact that such a great intellectual coup as the repackaging of Virginia Woolf is the work of publishers, not academics or biographers. But I am tempted to think that it was not only time and the economic tide which changed the climate for Virginia Woolf in Britain. It was also what we might call feminist criticism with a human face. . . .

Part of the confidence of tone comes from the sheer body of feminist critical work on Woolf, mainly American, on which these writers may draw for support or argument. Am I saying that the Penguin paperbacks are so much sheep's clothing in which the naked Woolf can enter the fold of the English canon? Yes.

Jane Marcus. Women's Review of Books. 11,
March, 1994, p. 17

WRIGHT, JUDITH (AUSTRALIA) 1915–

"The Moving Image" is not grounded upon a fine invention—is not, essentially, lyrical or narrative or dramatic poetry but is one of those mystical and philosophical explanations of the universe that every poet since Eliot has felt obliged to attempt: and all of which do a little smack of the Inkehorne. A fashion of darkly philosophizing may be just as dangerous to poetry in the long run as a fashion of Euphuism [was in the sixteenth century]. Considering *The Moving Image* as the first book of a young—but not so very young—writer, one must note the comparative smallness of output; a certain lack of joy, spontaneity and simplicity; and, in consequence, an impression of seriousness and, sometimes, strain. "Our unfortunate century," it has been said, "was born middle-aged." One can hardly hope that, as it grows older, it will grow younger.

Judith Wright's serious and analytical verses hardly deserve in themselves this criticism. . . . The title poem is not really obscure, not even difficult when given the [close reading] it deserves; moreover it is written with a power and passion altogether rare in philosophical poetry. The imagery is rich and beautiful and one is aware all the time of the masterly handling of rhythm; strong, like a heart beating. It is the *tendency* that is dimly alarming, for it is toward abstraction. . . .

But the tendency of the other poems—expressing Australia in terms of heat and surf and cattlebells, humanity in the figures of drovers, bushrangers, the half-caste girl, the "mad old girl in the hill" and the gently terrified "Brothers and Sisters"; and expressing the writer's own richly feminine genius in the imagery of blossoming trees—these promise anything everything the world.

Douglas Stewart. The Flesh and the Spirit
(Sydney: Angus & Robertson, 1948),
pp. 272–73

The impression which any individual poem [by Judith Wright] makes is deepened and intensified if one has a knowledge of the rest of her poetry: certain themes appear again and again in her poems, and there are certain human problems with which she seems to be constantly preoccupied. These themes and problems are, moreover, related to one another—the comprehension of one helps to illuminate all the rest. It becomes obvious, once one is familiar with the main body of her work, that Judith Wright is a poetic thinker, someone with a coherent view of life, a view of life which is not only stated but also initially conceived in poetic terms. The problems with which she is concerned are seen through the eyes of a poet; even more significantly, poetry itself is seen to be an important part of their solution.

There is nothing unique about the problems with which she is most deeply concerned—they are those which have engaged the minds of most serious writers for the past fifty years or so: the problems of discovering, in an age of cultural disintegration and confusion, some significant pattern or purpose in life; the problems of merely existing which are presented by an age in which for so many people, as William Faulkner has remarked, "There are no longer problems of the spirit. There is only one question: when will I be blown up?" . . .

Although there are some fine poems in *The Gateway,* and, as always, the standard of poetic craftsmanship is remarkably high, one misses the depth and passion which makes the best poems of *Woman to Man* so outstanding. This slackening of tension, and the emphasis on speculation rather than symbolic statement, are due perhaps to the fact that she has lost some of the philosophical certainty on which her earlier work was based. Judith Wright is after all a remarkably honest poet, and one cannot blame her for trying to work out her difficulties in her poetry. The results however do not seem to me to be always satisfactory. In particular the attempt to create some sort of private mythology, as in poems like "Legend," "Nursery Rhyme for a Seventh Son," "Fairytale"—and some earlier poems—are flat, disappointing, and obviously artificial.

R. F. Brissenden. Meanjin. Spring, 1953,
pp. 255–56, 267

Judith Wright seems to me essentially an Australian poet. She uses with ease, without either diffidence or aggressiveness, the scenery, the idiom, and the myth of her own country, and she uses it for poetry that is no sense limited or provincial. And this ease has not come without effort. There is, of course, a large basis of truth in David Wright's criticism in *Encounter;* it is difficult to write good poetry when there is no tradition established in which to write. But the solution is not, surely, to follow the latest London fashion and be "second-hand Europeans." . . .

Judith Wright was born a year later than Dylan Thomas. Like him she is a regional poet, who uses the language and the scene of her native place and the recollections of her childhood easily in her writing. The recurrent imagery of drought . . . is as natural to her as it would be strange to Dylan Thomas in his wet Welsh hills. She escapes from "the local but provincial into the regional but universal" because she is deeply concerned with problems that affect us all and uses the things she knows as a means to explore these problems, not for their own sake alone. It seems to me that by the end of her fourth book, Judith Wright has carried this exploration beyond the point at which Thomas wrecked himself by his insistence on remaining the boy genius. The comparison is one of development; I do not suggest that she has surpassed his achievement or even equaled it. But she is still alive, and I can think of few poets who have come to prominence since the war, whether "on the fringes of the sometime Empire" or at its hub, whose work, by its consistent quality and serious concern, shows such promise for the future.

F. H. Mares. *Durham University Journal.*
March, 1958, pp. 77, 84

Some verse is made to be sung, some intoned, some declaimed, some spoken—and some mumbled. Judith Wright's belongs to the last category. . . . It is necessary to be thus unhandsome at the outset because it has become universal practice for Australian critics to write of Judith Wright's verse no more responsibly than does the writer of the dust-jacket blurb of her latest book *(The Two Fires)*. . . .

Quite probably it is this quality of *fervor* that accounts for the high prestige in Australia of Judith Wright's work. As Yeats remarked, "They don't like poetry; they like something else, but they like to think they like poetry." Other detracting characteristics of Judith Wright's work, of which critics to date have been equally oblivious, would be abstractionism (notice how characters like Old Gustav, Mr. Ferritt, the Prospector, are generalized *before* being realized), a didacticism that generally blows up in bathos.

William Fleming. *Shenandoah.* Summer,
1958, pp. 33–35

Equipped as we are nowadays, we get a shock when we read of the primitive and naked struggle against nature in the new countries in the nineteenth century. It is a grinding, monotonous war, accumulating its casualties, impoverishing some lives, hardening others, operating with all the brutality of a fate. This is the subject of a scrupulous and sensitive Australian family history [*The Generations of Men*], written by an Australian poetess [Judith Wright]. From family diaries she has constructed a year-by-year account of the lives of her forbears who were opening up New South Wales and Queensland from 1820 onwards. The book may not enlighten us about the growth of Australian society, but in the intimacy of its account of the daily struggle, it gradually becomes an absorbing document. We are made to see what is done to a man who by temperament and gift was unsuited to the solitude, the natural disasters, the sheer physical claims that were made on him. . . .

The story of Albert Wright must have occurred in varying forms in all the new countries. It is the story of the making of a new man at the expense of his spiritual life, a process of hardening and martyrdom. At the point where he is racked no longer and has triumphed over his own character, he dies. It is a fable of the breaking or numbing of a civilized man. . .

It is odd and a great relief to read a book of pioneer life which scarcely mentions religion, and which does not push down our throats the conventional colonial optimism or the thick porridge of moral self-commendation. Miss Judith Wright is a skeptical writer, or at any rate, one who is austerely aware that a price has to be paid for new worlds. She is also free of that family complacency which affects so many writers when they are describing their family forbears. She has avoided the patriotic clichés, she has genuinely uncovered the daily life of a century and offers us no moral. A good style and a graceful, independent mind have given a dramatic interest to a subject which is usually overburdened with moral sobriety.

V. S. Pritchett. The New Statesman.
September 5, 1959, pp. 280–81

As often as not the iambic (particularly iambic pentameter) is the Cressida whom the English-speaking poet panders into the wrong bed. Such is sometimes the case with Judith Wright. One is a little surprised that a poet with her passionate concern for the mating of halves should let all her themes surrender, apparently, to the same succubus. At a first reading, [*The Other Half*] seems monotonous—a pity, as there is a great variety of subject matter. Words become enslaved by the meter. . . .

The collection could, I think, have gained from some excising and tightening up. But I don't want to exaggerate that. Growing acquaintance leads one to turn her pages admiringly and (not common these days) affectionately. Her Australian landscape—snakeskin, red rock, creek and jungle-bird—is the setting for her attempt to connect self and not-self, microcosm and macrocosm. Language is the point at which they touch. . . .

Whenever she is most passionately engaged with these major themes—and passion there is, in these love-poems between man and the cosmos, behind the deceptively slight-looking feminine body of her work—the basic iambic line moves with an athletic grace to her voice's sincere, gentle resonance; becomes, as the above stanza shows, skillfully varied with caesuras and alexandrines. There are at least a dozen poems here where the other half has brilliantly come. She is a very fine poet, still outrageously neglected in this country.

D. M. Thomas. London Magazine. May,
1967, pp. 70–71

Preoccupations in Australian Poetry merits attention, chiefly because its author is Australia's foremost poetess. Critics of her poetry will find here a systematic statement of her attitude to the Australian poetic tradition, espe-

cially in relation to the writers whose poetry has at its best the same imaginative grasp of reality as her own. . . .

It is probably true to say that, with the exception of her comments on
writers close to her own position, she is best on detail of criticism, rather
than conclusions. . . . To cavil at what we have is perhaps churlish, yet Miss
Wright is proving a peculiarly limpid critic of Australian writing (the novel
too is illuminated at various points), and the best of her observation is found
when she is less concerned to establish the continuity of certain concepts
than to allow the poetry to speak through her sympathetic interpretations.

J. S. Ryan. *Modern Language Review.*
January, 1968, pp. 237–38

Caught between her Australian identity and the identity deriving from the
use of English, [Judith Wright] attempts to revive "the song that is gone";
"the dance / [that is] secret with the dancers in the earth" manifests itself in
terms of the most traditional of themes, love. The search for "the hunter
[who] is gone" fructifies in "ordinary love" which offers to Judith Wright
"the solitudes of poetry," and also a sense of personal identity. . . .

Although Judith Wright has written poems about war, and although her
vision encompasses life and death, love and pain, her faith in existence, in
the certitudes of beauty, is unflinching. Her relationship with the external
world has a strong sense of family. So has her relationship with her lover
and child. . . .

Judith Wright never gets breathless even when she is at her most intense
in *Woman to Man*. In "To Hafiz of Shiraz," she suggests that with the repetition of experience, there is corresponding simplification of words but that
repetition and simplification need not mean the loss of intensity, for "every
word leads back to the blinding original Word"; there are no two ways for
her, "the way up and the way down," but one way only.

It is an unconscious irony in Judith Wright, one ventures to say, that she
is concerned with words in the sense of a theme in poems which seem, on
the whole, inferior to those in *Woman to Man*. The tone of most of these
poems is discursive, and although one notices the simplicity of the words one
also misses in fact, the blinding light of the original Word. In *Woman to Man*,
she does not *seek* to assert explicitly the power of words as she does, for
example, in *The Other Half*, because, in the former, language is a mode of
feeling and thus the power of words is felt in the power of the experience of
love that she undergoes.

Devindra Kohli. *The Journal of
Commonwealth Literature.* June, 1971,
pp. 43, 49, 51

Judith Wright, like other poets, is defined by what she is not and does not
attempt, as well as by what she makes peculiarly her own. She is primarily
lyric in her approach; on the whole she eschews the dramatic stance in which

the author lets some other character speak for himself. Her themes, too, are primarily Australian and contemporary. She has shown little interest in the themes of the European tradition, the myths and legends of Rome and Greece, or those of the Bible and the Christian religion, though she will occasionally use the latter in a half-humorous way as in "Eve to Her Daughters" *(The Other Half).* So that it comes as a surprise to find in "Shadow" two poems side by side which are genuine dramatic monologues, "Eurydice in Hades" and "Heloise Wakening," and both assured and successful poems in their genre.

Another essay into the dramatic monologue is the "New Guinea Legend: The Finding of the Moon" *(The Other Half),* a series of poems on this legend where the speakers are all members of the supposed New Guinea village where the events take place. It is a bold venture into that dangerous country where the white, civilized European poet attempts to make a primitive native race speak in their own persons through the medium of the alien English language and the equally alien European poetic conventions. It is never very convincing and Judith Wright has wisely refrained from trying to "go native": she has stuck firmly to the literary methods and the language of her own people and, as it were, translated the legend into terms of European mentality, just as a recent Chimbu story I heard successfully translated the story of Hansel and Gretel from the brothers Grimm, into a story purely Chimbu in ideas and setting and unaffectedly told with great charm in the local pidgin. Another unusual experiment occurs in *Alive:* five short poems about the words "unless," "therefore," "enough," "never," and "forever," not important or impressive poems but interesting as excursions into a new sort of poem and in a new verse technique.

A. D. Hope. *Judith Wright* (Melbourne:
Oxford University Press, 1975), p. 25

Judith Wright's collection of talks [*Because I Was Invited*] has as its main concern poetry in general. It also presents a further group of poets treated in the manner of her previous book *Preoccupations in Australian Poetry.* The great merit of that book lay in her rejection of the usual critical approach, with its emphasis on style and technique at the expense of theme and philosophy. . . . For all the seriousness and the prophetic content of her message these talks are never sermons. She is too good a poet to generalize. Her detail is always concrete, sharp, significant. . . .

It is currently fashionable in reviewing musical performances to ask whether there is a visible "face" behind the performance. Because of the mixture of humor, compassion and understanding, I find here more of a face of the real Judith Wright than even the collected poems afford.

Val Vallis. (London) *Times Literary
Supplement.* April 9, 1976, p. 432

In a recent comment upon her own poetry in *Poetry and Gender* (edited by D. Brooks and B. Walker), Judith Wright has stated that "my failure to write 'Bullocky' more than once has weighed heavily against me." It is certainly true that, to most Australians, Wright is the poet of "Bullocky" and "South of my Days," poems which reinforce populist notions of nationalist origins and identity; or "Women to Man," "Woman's Song" and "Woman to Child," poems which are powerful expressions of feminine sensuality. Yet Wright's poetry is much more important than these few poems, and their specific concerns, indicate. In the long term she will almost certainly be viewed as a significant lyrical poet whose images reflect yet transcend the Australian context and whose lyrics express a philosophy of vitalism, of language and the imagination. To appreciate these aspects the poetry needs to be seen as a whole, and the current imbalance in its critical reception is possibly due to the recurrence, on school and undergraduate syllabuses, of a limited number of poems which are certainly impressive, but which are usually studied in isolation. There has also been a marked preference, in scholarly articles, for the earlier poetry, up to and including the poems of *Five Senses*. There has been a strange neglect, apart from a number of brief and complimentary reviews, of the three latest volumes, *Alive, Fourth Quarter* and *Phantom Dwelling*. The publication of *A Human Pattern: Selected Poems* (1990), containing a strong representation from these last three volumes, may well reawaken interest in Wright as a poet whose best work is not necessarily her earliest, whose opus spans the period from the 1940s to the 1980s, and whose latest poems are energetic, innovative and powerful.

It is obvious . . . that Judith Wright is a poet of consistent and passionately held ideas. The poems, even when apparently spontaneous responses to nature, are permeated by these ideas. The *Collected Poems,* for instance, commences with a long and often labored poetic disquisition on the state of the time-ridden modern world, and "Patterns," the concluding poem of the last volume *Phantom Dwelling,* ponders the relationship between atomic power and Heraclitean philosophy (with a passing reference to Indian mythology). Wright's obsession with ideas and her consistent expression of them in the poetry has provided difficulties both for herself as a poet and for her critics. The difficulty for the critic who wishes to discuss the poetry as a whole is that of maintaining a balance; of preserving the immediacy and individual qualities of any one poem whilst, at the same time, relating it to a central core of ideas. . . .

The difficulties for a philosophical poet who is also a lyricist are considerable. Many of the poems carry a heavy philosophical loading for which the lyric is sometimes inadequate. There has been for the poet, too, the difficulty of finding objective correlatives for complex and powerful emotional states— love, exhilaration, nostalgia, despair, fear—which are simultaneously subject to self-conscious intellectual analysis. The poet is often, as it were, watching herself looking at nature and simultaneously registering both her immediate response and her philosophical analysis of that response.

Shirley Walker. *Flame and Shadow: A Study of Judith Wright's Poetry* (Saint Lucia, Australia: University of Queensland Press, 1991), pp. ix, 14–15

While believing strongly in poetry as an art, Wright is also a moralist. . . . In her case, this connotes no fixed or inflexible program of belief and behavior but the achievement of a delicate balance among individuals, communities, and the environment, which will vary according to time and circumstance around the earth's surface. Throughout her work, from the earliest poems written and published in the 1940s to her book on the conservation of Australia's Great Barrier Reef, *The Coral Battleground,* and beyond, Wright has espoused the notion of ecology in its broadest sense, as it derives from the Greek word *oikos,* meaning "household, home, or place to live." In dealing with the organism in relation to its environment, ecology has been said to concern itself with "the economy of nature." From an anthropocentric perspective, the "ecosystem" described by ecologists can be considered as a life-support system composed of the air, earth, water, minerals, animals, and micro-organisms, which all function together—with humans, who are part of the system—and maintain the whole. Wright's various problems and questions in understanding herself and the universe, as they are posed in the *roman fleuve* of her literary and critical writings, lead her toward the totalizing concept of ecology and away from the narrow specialist categories she has perceived as a feature of contemporary industrial societies. Having chosen our *oikos,* or home territory, according to Wright, we should become active participants in achieving and maintaining an "economy of nature," although this may involve a radical break with prevailing notions of economic management. Furthermore, Wright is critical of the many contemporary artists who opt out of the ecosystem to become exiles; perhaps unfairly, she is inclined to consider the choice of exile, and its accompanying mentality, as a "sickness" and a general weakening of the system as a whole.

Bruce Bennett. In Robert L. Ross, ed. *International Literature in English: Essays on the Major Writers* (New York: Garland, 1991), p. 206

WYLIE, ELINOR (UNITED STATES) 1885–1928

A lyric voice slight, but clear and fine, may be heard in this book [*Nets to Catch the Wind*], the voice of a free and lightly ranging spirit. The sound of it is now gay, now grave, but always it holds a little aloof—one detects that something "austere, immaculate" for which the poet herself holds her Puritan ancestry responsible. . . . But always the emotion is shy and delicate, as of a cool small wild-flower growing, by some whim of Nature, not in the woods, but in the protected area of a garden. The flower is very simple and of quiet color, but it has an individual vitality nevertheless.

Harriet Monroe. *Poetry.* January, 1922,
pp. 220–21

The apparent coldness in Elinor Wylie's work has been misunderstood by readers who were looking for the ruddy stupefactions of sentimentalism. Here is neither a case of cold nor warmth, but rather one of rhythms, and by rhythms I mean the curious capacity of thought for circumscribing static points of passion with melodic and luminous nuances. This is partially an *amor intellectualis,* but because it burns with a steady lambency and a concentrated fierceness, instead of flaring into ragged flames, there is no reason to doubt its intensity. Mrs. Wylie's best poems are jeweled instances in the fluctuating toils of Time. They are abstractions given a body and a shape and accoutred in armor. . . . I should say that she is cerebral in the sense that Dr. John Donne was cerebral. More than any woman of this generation she may claim to be a spiritual daughter of Donne. Through an intellectual chemical process, she crystallizes her emotions and yet retains their vitality.

Herbert S. Gorman. *North American
Review.* May, 1924, pp. 680–81

The despair and disillusionment setting in after the World War found its most tragic voice abroad in T. S. Eliot. On this side the Atlantic, it found a feminine counterpart in the marvelous brain of Elinor Wylie. Her work was not a direct reaction to the aftermath, but was raised on the private life of an aristocratic nature in no wise akin with the mob or democracy. Among the new aristocracy of intellects rearing ivory towers out of independent domiciles, Eliot was the prince, Elinor Wylie the princess. Each has had a long line of retainers and imitators. The despair of the woman was a positive thing; it was composed, not of self-pity, but of heroic acceptance.

Alfred Kreymburg. *Our Singing Strength*
(New York: Coward-McCann, 1929), p. 459

We may grant, nevertheless, that this kind of romance writing is a poetry—a "making"—to which the unhappy contribute. They contribute so widely and so very variously that where a wastrel like Marlowe from out of his pothouse squalor may augment this branch of literature with a *Hero and Leander,* a restrained schoolmaster like Charles L. Dodgson, from out of the forlorn stuffiness of that atmosphere which is thought most suitably to develop the minds of the young, will bring forth an *Alice in Wonderland.* We may grant also that this is a branch of literature to which, through plain enough reasons, do belong *Jennifer Lorn* and *The Venetian Glass Nephew*.

I must here of necessity approach to matters which as yet stay delicate. It suffices to remark that the corporal life of Elinor Wylie was but too often at odds with her circumstances. The nature of this very beautiful and tragic woman was not ever in all adapted to that makeshift world in which perforce moved her superb body. She had found, after marrying several of them, that this world was over full of disappointments. She, who possessed the needed ability and an urgent need to use it, created therefore quite another sort of world, building amid desolation a baroque pagoda to be the sanctuary of wounded dreams and unfed desires. She created, in brief, a retreat wherein the rebuffed might encounter no more inglorious fiascos of the spirit and of the affections.

James Branch Cabell. *Virginia Quarterly Review*. July, 1930, p. 340

An agile wit was the factor which propelled her from charm to charm in her choice of materials: from historic themes of the most ingenious fragility and inaccessibility, to familiar encounters rendered desirable by the humor and elegance of imagination she brought to them. Thus seventeenth-century Venice had no riches to strike envy in the heart of a pioneer farmer on the Chesapeake: for each of them she conjured an experience of equal splendor. There was a prodigality in her verbal invention which certainly stemmed from something deeper than museum catalogues or encyclopedias; if we are to praise phonetic dexterity in Byron and Browning, we must praise it in her. The pictorial and impressionistic efforts of the 1890s wilt feebly in comparison with the brittle imagery of her designs. In the tradition of *Émaux et Camées* she is, on first acquaintance at least, an austere and distinguished disciple.

Morton Dauwen Zabel. *Poetry*. August, 1932, pp. 276–77

. . . she was born to welcome the most intensely arduous mental labor in passionate exploration of the utmost resources of the English language in order to express every finest shade of thought and feeling that she experienced. She was abnormally sensitive to the powers latent in language. She had an altogether unusual intuition for the exact word, and had assimilated a large vocabulary. She was unusually erudite, and had her life led her in another direction, might have been a great scholar. . . .

Elinor Wylie wrote with extraordinary precision; but it was a precision that never for a moment sacrificed the incalculable turn of phrase, the spontaneously felicitous expression, that intuitive visitation of words that seems to us who have it not as a gift from the gods. Her subconsciousness was constantly preoccupied with the shape, look, color, and sound of words; just as

the rhythms of poetry were matters to her of second nature, and her sometimes intricate interior rhyming, art concealed by art, in the same kind.

William Rose Benét. *The Prose and Poetry
of Elinor Wylie* (Wheaton, Massachusetts:
Wheaton College, 1934), pp. 12–13

She could not bear being less than first in any company. Nothing on earth
would do but that a few of her close friends should join her in another room
and hear her read some poems—say some poems, as she always put it. Her
friends humored her in such tantrums of vanity and went to all lengths in
flattering her. She liked flattery as a lizard likes the sun. . . .

. . . I remember her best for these perfect sonnets [*One Person*] and her
broken commentary. What she and the sonnets together said was that this
final love had come to her like first love, and had dissolved her to her youngest
elements, but that she was no less a poet than before, and she could instinctively find ripe, skillful words for emotions which ordinarily go no farther than
sighs and tears, timid raptures and pitiful despairs. For once in the world,
youth knew and age could. The heart of sixteen spoke with the tongue of forty.

Carl Van Doren. *Harper's.* September, 1936,
pp. 365–66

The sonnets to "One Person" are generally accepted as the consummation
of Elinor Wylie's poetry. There certainly is no other group among her poems
that leaves so much satisfaction on so many counts. There is a warmth of
feeling and directness of thought that is not usual in her work and the circle
of experience that is touched upon has a much more general appeal than
formerly. Technically the sonnets show a complete mastery of the form. Her
experience in handling words in fanciful moods and in light, quick cadences
stands her in good stead and she moves perfectly at her ease within the
narrow limits of the sonnet structure. But she does not allow it to dissolve
in the easy flow of the lines.

H. Lüdeke. *English Studies.* December,
1938, p. 248

Elinor Wylie's closest literary kinship, which began in early childhood and
lasted throughout her lifetime, developing as an obsession in her life and
work, was Percy Bysshe Shelley. The best and the greater part of her prose
and poetry reflect his subtle influence. Seven of her eleven essays and
sketches in *Fugitive Prose* are a key to her sources and methods in regard
to Shelley. In her four novels there is a progression of interest in the same
poet: *Jennifer Lorn* contains a background resembling that of the Shelley
family; *The Venetian Glass Nephew* stems from some of Shelley's thought
and the philosophy of his age; *The Orphan Angel* brings Shelley to life again;
and *Mr. Hodge and Mr. Hazard* is a composite picture of Shelley and Elinor
Wylie. Of her four volumes of verse, the last two books *Trivial Breath* and

Angels and Earthly Creatures, which contain her finest poetry, also show an increasing preoccupation with Shelley himself and with his thought.

Julia Cluck. *PMLA*. September, 1941, p. 841

Once devoted to the rococo, the artist can break its spell only by shattering himself: what is required is a clean break, a fresh start, a new confronting, however painful and terrified, yet humble and thankful, of reality. The risk of this necessity Miss Wylie's integrity could not have long postponed. She might have shirked it for a while, because, like everybody else, she had her peculiar foolishness; and rather more than most, she might have been spoiled by adulation. Against these risks her besetting sin was her saving virtue, that fierce fine pride. . . .

It is good to hear this voice again, not only because it is familiar, but because even when it is being fantastical or fancy, it is always firm and fine. Apprehensive, yes, but gloomy never; amused, amusing, ironical, exquisite, precise, and proud.

Rolfe Humphries. *The Nation.*
April 3, 1943, p. 494

If Elinor Wylie's self-absorption may be defined in terms of what the eighteenth century called a "ruling passion," like all overwhelming and consuming emotions it carried with it the conviction of having an importance beyond the mere reflection in a glass; and she conveyed . . . "passion" with all the art her skill could master. To this day we [find] . . . unconsciously amusing parodies of her style, poems that speak of pretty boys running in the wind, poems of equally proud, fastidious, well-dressed good-looking women who yearn to possess the "hard heart of a child," to own things that contain the qualities of quicksilver and of crystal—but it is the attitude and not the essence that her imitators have caught—and she, like many a good artist before her, cannot be held responsible for the inept vanities and empty gestures of the school which followed her.

Horace Gregory and Marya Zaturenska. *A History of American Poetry* (New York: Harcourt, 1946), pp. 284–85

The gifts of Elinor Wylie . . . brought to the feminine lyric a mature emotional richness, as well as an added brilliance of craftsmanship. Mrs. Wylie early caught the note of Eliot's shorter poems. *Nets to Catch the Wind* (1921) revealed, as well, a first-hand apprenticeship to Donne, Herbert and Marvell. For a time she seemed overwhelmed by her own virtuosity but she became more tellingly controlled as time went on, and in her last volume achieved a power that was directly structural. Although an undertone of rather inflated romanticism was constantly in evidence, her work as a whole was far more complex than that of any feminine predecessor.

Louise Bogan. *Achievement in American Poetry 1900–1950* (Chicago: Henry Regnery, 1951), p. 80

It is in *Angels* . . . that Mrs. Wylie comes into full richness of statement which ranges from the opening sequence of unusual sonnets entitled "One Person" to the touchingly simple and lovely conclusion of "Little Elegy." This sequence, in which she protests most humbly her love and her sense of her lover's superiority (an idea in a sense foreshadowed in the "Little Sonnet" of *Black Armour* and recurrent in her later work), consolidates her distinction in a form in which she was from the beginning capable. . . . Succeeding poems . . . proceed to broaden her claim to a warmer humanity, a clearer logic, and a greater naturalness than previously evident; even mere technique invites increasing admiration. . . .

Actually, Mrs. Wylie flaunted an individual gift from the first mature volume onward. Initially, she seemed in some respects like a super-sophisticated Blake, though she opened no doors on the chaos he exposed. Unfortunately, manner largely degenerated into mannerism in *Black Armour* and *Trivial Breath,* with intelligence resolving itself into superficial cleverness time and again, so that much of this material suggests unconscious parody of earlier self. Like much shortly succeeding verse which it foreshadows, a great deal of the work has an air of significance which close examination does not justify.

> George Brandon Saul. *Bulletin of the New York Public Library.* November, 1965, pp. 619–20

Judging from one of her poems, she longed to be freed from hardness, liberated from marble: "Sleeping Beauty," published after her death, shows a strong man carving the "living rock" and releasing, not the angel that Michelangelo is said to have set free, but "a lady like a lioness." This is Elinor Wylie, for her friend compared her bronze hair to a lion's mane, and she identifies herself with lions in several poems—"Pity me," "Unfinished Ballad," and "A Proud Lady." The image of herself as sculptor's work recalls her way of comparing her characters to dolls. She admired the miniature in art: at the British Museum her principal reading matter was the labels on the Tanagra figurines (or so she assures the readers of her essay "The Pearl Diver").

> Celeste Turner Wright. *Twentieth Century Literature.* April, 1966, pp. 22–23

[Wylie] is not, after all, inconsistent in her attitude toward the disparity between the desires or aspirations of the individual and the satisfactions and fulfillments that earthly existence offers him; in her deeply romantic view, the world is an inadequate environment for the individual self. The "self" desires rarity, variety, fineness, beauty, delicacy; the world offers commonness, sameness, coarseness, ugliness, and grossness. Under the ordinary conditions of human life, exquisite esthetic distinctions are an impertinence and fine moral distinctions are futile.

Elinor Wylie's poetry at its best recognizes a dimension of the human spirit least accommodated in existence; her art affirms the validity of the desire for quality in human life—fineness, rarity, delicacy, beauty, and variety.

Thomas Alexander Gray. *Elinor Wylie* (New
York: Twayne, 1969), p. 156

[One] hypothesis for the critical neglect shown Wylie's work is that it is not experimental. She was a traditionalist who chose to preserve the conventions of the nineteenth-century lyric and novel. Yet she lived and wrote at a time when formal innovations were being introduced in fiction and verse. . . .

Fifty years have passed since Elinor Wylie's death. It is a reasonable interval after which to attempt a critical assessment of her art and its importance. And there are good reasons for doing so. Of those American poets capable of excellence in the "open song," she was one of the best and most literate. Her themes—which include the sexual antagonisms of one who, "being woman [was] hard beset"—are both enduring and of her time. They shed light on the nature of the lyric and on the concerns of poets of the 1920s. Because her art was fostered by Aesthetic art but respectful of that Romantic art that she thought the greatest expression of human achievement, her work reveals the consistent influence in American letters of other traditions than the metaphysical. Perhaps more significantly, the intellectual and verbal sophistication of her writing testifies to what one admirer, Sinclair Lewis, thought of as America's coming of age," or more particularly, to the fact that urbane Americans might choose to write about important things with accents and assumptions that were cosmopolitan. . . .

In a sense Wylie had two careers, one as a fabulist, the other as a poet. How and what would she have written had she lived beyond her forty-third year? Her unfinished manuscripts in the Wylie Archive—the *April, April,* fragments about Shelley, a romance about Henry VIII's sister Mary, a symbolic tale about the "Moon" and "Starr" sisters of Philadelphia—suggest that in fiction she would have continued to write fantasies. She looked forward to beginning her "witch" novel with an enthusiasm bred, I think, of a precise understanding of her own powers. Her passion for history, her fascination with magic, the surreal, and the occult (a fascination shared by her hero Shelley and her admirer and supporter Yeats) would doubtless have resulted in tales that were more and more austere philosophically and increasingly shrewd in nuance and invention. Her last poems, *Angels and Earthly Creatures,* might suggest that her poetic style had taken new directions.

Judith Farr. *The Life and Art of Elinor
Wylie* (Baton Rouge: Louisiana State
University Press, 1983), pp. 8–9, 210

In Wylie's sequence ["One Person"] the most startling transportation of the love sonnet from the male to the female key occurs with the employment of bold female figures. . . . Allusions to women's experience in Christian myth—Mary's mothering Jesus and Eve's being torn from Adam's rib—amplify bodily events common to women, nursing and birth. The extreme contrast between the initial depiction of love—"content"—and the final assessment of love—"bitter"—reflects the violent disparities between a womanly and manly conception of the beloved. In imagining herself as the holy mother, Mary, the female speaker thereby confers upon her lover Christlike dimensions. In aligning her lover with Adam, she implies that she assumes for him the negative qualities of Eve. Beyond these double transformations—she as Mary and Eve, he as Christ and Adam—another grisly transformation clinches the speaker's rejection of lovers' expectations. She emphasizes how the Garden of Eden myth makes Adam assume the female rather than the male role in procreation. He is the mother, not the father, to Eve. And in the male appropriation of the female the fixation is on the negative. Whereas her mothering centers on the positive qualities associated with suckling—physical protection, "utmost adoration," emotional comfort—his "mothering" emphasizes the violence of child-birth—the "pain" that makes the mother a "skeleton."

Feminist perceptions underlie her acid . . . drill understatement: "I shall not dream you are my child again." The expectations they each have of the other are damagingly opposite: while she exalts him, he degrades her. Their own experiences of loving are damagingly opposite: while she is enabled to nurture him and to imagine herself as the holy mother, he resents his lover and virtually dies. "Dreams" or myths are dangerous. Wylie implies that male inadequacy—his "bitter and excessive pain"—occasions misogynist myths about women. In recent years we have begun to call attention to how many cultures have tended to imagine women at two extremes, either perfect or sinful, Mary or Eve, angel or witch. As Wylie finds the metaphors to convey the emotional disappointment of heterosexual love, she indirectly provides the same critique: the images imply that the woman lover has helped perpetuate this skewed system. If the man's "dream" has damaged her, so has her "dream" or myth of an unequal relationship—the mother of the child—arrogated authority to her unfairly. . . . In the Eve-Mary sonnet the line "I shall not dream you are my child again" straightforwardly states her position as it obliquely exposes the male perspective.

Phyllis M. Jones. Women's Studies. 10, 1984,
pp. 51–52

It is an irony of modern literary history that the characteristic complexity of Elinor Wylie's poetry has been obscured less by neglect than by superficial appreciation. . . . Only recently have feminist critics begun to chart the disturbing undercurrents in Wylie's poetry, surveying the ways in which Wylie "transforms the verse structures that she inherits, precisely to express and to embody a vision of *complex* beauty, of contrary values." Rather than unitary loveliness, it is dialectic that gives structure to Wylie's best work; thus, "no inflation is left without its deflation, no love without its curse, no innocence without its hardness of heart." This deflation, as Phyllis M. Jones has noted, was one of the goals of women Modernists, who challenged the stereotyped perspectives of male amatory poetry. In "Wild Peaches," perhaps her most anthologized poem, Wylie deflates the aggressively self-centered perspective of her male suitor by opposing her own desolated landscape to his landscape of pastoral plenty. In "Wild Peaches" contrasting female and male perspectives structure a dialectic whereby Wylie engages issues that are largely sexual and political. . . .

While the poem may appear to offer a tale celebrating idyllic love, and while it has been read by critics such as Judith Farr as Wylie's defense of the choice of the aesthetic rather than the passional life in its abandonment of "idyllic for Spartan pleasures," what it enacts formally, narratively, and emotively is a story of suppression, constraint, conflict, and violence between the sexes. . . .

Any careful reading of the artful, angry sonnets of "Wild Peaches" must register the political critique the poem makes; for in narrative, imagery, prosody, and rhetorical design, it exposes the patriarchal conventions of courtship that signal women's oppression. But Wylie's poems are only now beginning to receive the readings they merit. Wylie's readers have been distracted too long from performing the most rudimentary metrical count of her measures, and deflected from considering seriously the larger issue of her contribution as a poet. Recent treatments of Wylie, however, have begun through close readings of single poems to engage this issue. As a result of such readings and of the recent work of scholars and critics such as Judith Farr, the awareness of Wylie's stature has grown. . . . This awareness can be enhanced by an understanding of Wylie's critique of the sexual and social structures that constrict women. Wylie's skill in embodying this critique in "Wild Peaches" constitutes further evidence of her importance in defining and resisting the material forces that would suppress and control the feminine voice that she raises and the feminist canon that she joins.

Anna Shannon Elfenbein and Terence Allan
Hoagwood. *Women's Studies*. 15, 1988,
pp. 387–88, 396

XIAO HONG (CHINA) 1912–42

Hsiao Hung (the pen name of Chang Nai-ying) was one of the writers who wrote several books around the people's struggle against Japanese imperialism in Northeast China after the Mukden Incident. The novels *Life and Death, Ma Po-lo,* and *The History of the Hulan River* are among her works as well as some short stories, and some essays published under the pen-name of Chiao Yin.

Life and Death deals with the wretched life of the peasants in a village near Harbin. After the fall of Northeast China the Japanese invaders fall on them, killing and raping. In their flight from the village, which is made under conditions of great hardship, they come to realize that resistance is their only way out. Eventually all of them—kind-hearted and honest people, old women, young widows, an old man known for his "good conscience," and even Erh Li Pan, a peasant who knows little beyond tending his goat—brace themselves and join the war of national defence. In his preface to the book Lu Hsun says:

> This is of course only a series of sketches. Her descriptions of events and scenes are better than her delineations of character. But the description of the northern people's firm resolution in life and their struggle against death are really good and show the author's keen observation and unusual skill in handling her themes.

In *Ma Po-lo* and *The History of the Hulan River,* her later works, there is less vigor in her writing: her fighting spirit gives way to melancholy. This was due partly to her narrow contact with life and partly to unsound pettybourgeois thoughts and feelings which frequently pushed her into an abyss of despondency.

Ting Yi. *A Short History of Modern Chinese Literature* (Port Washington, New York: Kennikat Press, 1959, 1970), pp. 204–5

Looking at the entire corpus of Hsiao Hung's writings, which by one estimate totals in excess of 700,000 words, the works on which her reputation and position as an important modern Chinese author must be based are *The Field of Life and Death* (for its historical impact, if not its literary qualities), *Market Street, Ma Po-lo, Tales of Hulan River,* and two or three short stories. . . . We must conclude that Hsiao Hung's true genius (for in the terms we have put forth, it can be considered nothing less) lay in her ability to re-create the scenes in her own past and depict the lives of the Northeastern Chinese peasants and the natural beauty of their land with great feeling, perception, and clarity. Hers was the talent of the artist who chose words as her medium of expression; her creations, at their best, remain highly moving and absorbing works of art. . . .

It is primarily in the field of fiction that Hsiao Hung has left her mark on contemporary Chinese letters, and she has done so on the strength of but three novels, two of which are considerably shorter than was generally the rule in fiction of this period. On the basis of two of these novels, and to a lesser extent, a handful of short stories, she established herself as one of the foremost portrayers of peasant life in Northeast China. . . .

In any discussion of Hsiao Hung's style, first mention should be made of her effortless and simple, though often poetic, language. With the exception of almost the entirety of *Tales of Hulan River* and a few of the more spectacularly beautiful passages in other writings, this quality may be overlooked on a first reading, primarily because her language is so natural and flowing; but it is at the very core of her success. Her prose is unaffected, almost never convoluted or overly intricate, and distinctively feminine.

The style of writing that Hsiao Hung customarily employs depends less on characterization, psychological investigation, and prolonged drama than on rhetorical beauty and deep authorial involvement. By temperament an autobiographical and personal writer, there is an almost inverse relationship between her degree of detachment and the success of her works. The greater the element of fiction in her stories, the less convincing they become. Nearly every protagonist in her fiction is a woman, and with one or two exceptions, her female characters are her only successful ones. But besides the sex of her protagonists, there are other notable leitmotifs, among which are the high preponderance of members of the servant class, and the often-repeated situation of a child living with only one parent, or on occasion a grandparent. As for mood, there is no question that most of her writings are tragic and deal primarily with the victimization of defenseless or guileless people. Occasionally . . . they suffer because of their own attitudes, but more often it is the landed, the rich, and the military—foreign or native—who are the villains in her fiction. In some of her stories the victimization comes about as a sort of cosmic irony, in that fate holds the cruelest punishments for those who least deserve them, people whose very goodness or courage is the source of their vulnerability. . . .

It is, of course, too early to produce a definitive statement regarding Hsiao Hung's ultimate position in twentieth-century Chinese letters (at any rate such a statement would necessarily be in the realm of value-judgment, and entirely subjective), but despite her limited output and the mediocre quality of some of her writings, three, and perhaps more, of her works may well prove to have qualities that will help them to transcend time and space. As the appeal of so much of what was written in Republican China abates in proportion to its distance from the time of its creation, the apparent enduring qualities of Hsiao Hung's best writings may ultimately establish her as one of the foremost literary talents of her time.

Howard Goldblatt. *Hsiao Hung* (New York: Twayne, 1976), pp. 126, 117, 123–24, 135

Hsiao Hung's first novel was published . . . in December 1935. It has long been heralded by Chinese critics as one of the two earliest and most important examples of anti-Japanese literature (Hsiao Chün's *Village in August* is the other). Yet the anti-Japanese theme is not the dominant one. Rather the novel is a grim and powerful portrait of the lives of peasants in Northeast China. The effect of the work on its contemporary readers was anger, pity, and a sense of outrage, outrage not only against the outside forces that so demeaned and brutalized the villagers, but also against the fatalistic, passive, conservative mentality of the peasants themselves. To readers of our generation, the forceful impact is lessened only slightly by the knowledge that the events portrayed belong to history. Humanity being what it is we can never be assured that such suffering, cruelty, and ignorance are very far away.

The Field of Life and Death is not the story of any particular individual. Many of the characters we find in it are little more than types, and although the spotlight shifts from one individual or family to another, it seldom stops long enough to give much definition. It is the aggregate village that has the starring role, and with the author's skill, it comes alive. . . .

The careful reader of *The Field of Life and Death* and *Tales of Hulan River,* while acknowledging the almost totally disparate nature of the two novels, will find a great many similarities in style, themes, and specifics. The same issues, for the most part, were the author's concern in both works written six years apart. The plight of the peasants, the role of women, the scenic beauty, all these are at the core of Hsiao Hung's literary creations. In almost every case, these themes are most powerfully and vividly drawn, where they are inextricably tied up with Hsiao Hung's personal experiences and observations. In other words, she is at her finest when she is most openly autobiographical, and *Tales of Hulan River* is an autobiographical novel. . . .

Among the most striking features of *Tales of Hulan River* are the simple beauty of Hsiao Hung's rhetorical style and the vivid quality of her descriptions. The Western reader may occasionally find her repetitive passages tedious, her frequent summarizations redundant, and her language too prosaic. Taken as a whole, however, the unadorned and unpretentious style brings to the work highly evocative and intimate qualities. Her genius in capturing detail and nuance (the camera-like quality already apparent in *The Field of Life and Death*) makes this work appeal to the reader's visual as well as verbal sense. It should come as no surprise to the discerning reader that Hsiao Hung was a budding artist in her youth and continued to paint for most of her adult life.

In the final analysis, *Tales of Hulan River* must stand as Hsiao Hung's representative work; it is her most personal and artistic creation and is a lasting testimony to her artistic genius.

Howard Goldblatt. Introduction to Xiao
Hong. *The Field of Life and Death, and
Tales of Hulan River* (Bloomington: Indiana
University Press, 1979),
pp. xx–xxi, xxiii–xxv

Given what we know of Xiao Hong's life and artistic temperament, including the fact that while she was physically ill and caught up in the war with Japan, she wrote one full-length novel and the first two volumes of a planned trilogy, we must conclude that she was by nature a novelist, a writer who required a broad canvas on which to create her most memorable literary works. However, as any student of modern Chinese literature knows, it was far easier and more expedient to write short stories, which could be sold to the many literary journals of the day—keeping the wolf from the door was always an urgent concern of twentieth-century Chinese writers, particularly during the 1930s and 1940s. So for six of Xiao Hong's nine creative years she wrote nothing but short stories, essays, and an occasional poem or short play. Yet she is known primarily as a writer of novels, the first of which *(The Field of Life and Death)* she wrote at the age of twenty-three, the final two of which (three, if Parts I and II of *Ma Bole* are counted separately) were written shortly before her death nearly a decade later.

In thematic terms, Xiao Hong generally deals with the plight of women from the deprived classes; her stories are almost invariably tragic and seldom offer much hope for change. As a woman who felt herself demeaned, abused, and valued primarily as a feminine object by the men with whom she was associated, Xiao Hong was revolutionary in her desire to expose the cruelties in a male-dominated "feudalistic" society. Her stories are extremely touching and evocative, and, we can assume, effective tools in the awakening process that characterized the period during which she lived and wrote. Most of her stories are set in northeast China, although only a few (including the first story in the present anthology, her first work of fiction) were written there. The only notable exceptions are the stories in her volume *A Cry in the Wilderness,* which are set in the Chinese interior. In only three of the nine stories included here do men play the leading role, and one of these—"The Family Outsider"—is a piece of autobiographical fiction. To take this last point further, a large percentage of Xiao Hong's fictional works, which are told in the first-person narrative mode, are more or less autobiographical, the narrator being a secondary character.

Howard Goldblatt. Introduction to Xiao
Hong. *Selected Stories of Xiao Hong*
(Beijing: Panda, 1982), n.p.

In *Hulan River* we discover some of the major recurrent motifs from Lu Xun's fiction and essays. Xiao Hong continues to explore and develop them. The connection between the two writers has been treated several times in biographical terms, but not in terms of the literary influences. After Lu Xun's death, Xiao Hong wrote a mime, *Soul of the Nation,* in which Lu Xun and the personae of his stories appear: it was a sign of her will to keep Xun's ideas alive. This can help us understand her appeal to her former husband, Xiao Jun, when he claimed to have lost interest in the pen and planned to take up the gun in 1938. She said: "Are you gong to fight a guerilla war? You won't be more valuable than a seasoned guerilla fighter. If you should die, at your age, with your experience of life and ability in literature, . . . the loss would not be yours alone. I'm not appealing to you as your wife . . . but thinking of our literary cause." When she was herself compelled to choose between her writing and her lover, the choice, obviously, was her literary cause.

Xiao Hong had extensive plans for her writing, including a second volume of *Tales of Hulan River.* The critics who claim that this work is passive in spirit, a retreat from the first six years of her career, are hardly convincing. The narrator's own struggle against loneliness, the child-bride's insistence on going to her "own home," Uncle You'er's refusal to commit suicide, and Feng's determination to take firm root in the world, all express a strong desire to live and to live a better life. The absence of collective heroism, as found in Xiao Hong's first novel *Fields of Life and Death,* is not the equivalent of pessimism. On the contrary, she has gone beyond the black-and-white dichotomy of that novel to a more complex picture of human relations in which the obstacles to a decent existence must first be identified before they can be fought against. In contrast to the calm of the objective omniscient narrator of the first novel, the passionate involvement of the adult first-person narrator of *Tales of Hulan* is analogous to the diarist of Lu Xun's *Diary of a Madman* in its appeal to action.

The narrator is the central consciousness, the only one aware of the range of experience in the town, where life is economically poor, culturally backward, and in many respects primitive. The majority live miserably, especially women. If a wife is beaten, she accepts it as normal in married relations, supported in this submissiveness by centuries of tradition and local mythology. The narrator challenges the view that customary patterns are just through her tales of rebellion, introducing change into the "unchangeable" world.

Not all women, however, are portrayed as humiliated. There are some who oppress others. They tend to be elder, and they have power, sometimes money as well, e.g., the narrator's grandmother and mother, the mill owner's wife, the child-bride's mother-in-law. The women struggling for survival or for a better life, like the protagonist of Zhang Tianyi's *Back and Breasts (Jibei yu naizi),* have tremendous endurance: severe torture cannot prevent them from seeking freedom. Xiao Hong's treatment of this theme differs from

Zhang's in showing that women must become conscious of their depressed status before they can rebel. It took the loss of a life to enlighten the ideal daughter-in-law and motivate her escape.

> Tsau Shuying. In Anna Gerstlacher, et al.,
> eds. *Woman and Literature in China*
> (Bochum, Germany: Brockmeyer, 1985),
> pp. 330–32

Xiao Hong has been presented as a feminist, which can lead to confusion if the word is understood in the contemporary western sense, and one would be disappointed if one expected to find her as ardent a feminist fighter as Qiu Jin, who devoted her life to undermining male dominance of society. Qiu Jin described explicitly male exploitation and oppression, inciting women to revolt and reject their lot, never losing hope in the crusade that led to her execution.

Whereas Qiu Jin described the situation of women in the traditional family in a way that led to awareness and lucid revolt, Xiao Hong covered the same ground in a more passive way, neither pointing to solutions or even calling for resistance. She is sooner witness of her times, gifted with enormous clarity of vision and realism about the life and events which surrounded her. She observed the peasants in every detail with special regard for women. It is remarkable to see that although she was only twenty-three, she was perfectly aware of the ties between men and women and the wheels of a social system where the female is always the loser. Even if they try to escape from their miserable lot in suicide, drinking (like Wangpo), religion (Jin Zhi finally decides to be a nun but she cannot even succeed in this since the temple has been destroyed by bombs) or patriotic commitment (which means death in the end) the solution remains elusive, the female characters are doomed to fail. In view of this attitude certain reserve is called for when discussing the writer's "feminist" attitudes.

In this China in a period of transition, Xiao Hong does not give us the impression of any change in women's social status; on the contrary, we have the feeling of eternal continuity. Practically none of the feminine characters express anything like a feeling of revolt.

> Simone Cros-Moréa. In Anna Gerstlacher,
> et al., eds. *Woman and Literature in China*
> (Bochum, Germany: Brockmeyer, 1985),
> pp. 342–43

Vague Expectations is a story of a misconception, of futile effort and hopes in vain. It is the story of a woman's longing for love and the security of being loved, a tragic story about a dream that will not come true. It is also an antiwar story in the sense that war leaves a woman without love, comfort, family, the essence of living. Although this particular war is a patriotic war (the story was written in 1939) which Xiao Hong supported, we can see from the way she uses the contrast of "male, patriotic, egotistic" versus "female, unsophisticated, alone" that her message is to show how women suffer from *any* war. (From Xiao Hong's earlier work *Shengsichang*—1934—it is quite obvious how her humanist and pacifist involvement conflicted with the anti-Japanese message of the novel. . . .

What then, is the expression of femininity in *Vague Expectations* that goes beyond the reading experience of, say, Ye Shengtao's *A Life* or Lu Xun's *The New Year's Sacrifice?* Women's tragic fates, their inability to live a life worthy of a human being, are equally well depicted in both stories. The first describes a woman's muteness and dumbness caused by society's cruel rules, the latter a woman driven into insanity and death by the same society. The contrast of the I-narrator's critical self-examination with Xiangling Sao's tragic fate in Lu Xun's story points out his empathy all the more, nevertheless his reflections reveal a certain distance to the woman.

In my opinion, one example of a woman's way of writing in *Vague Expectations* comes into play exactly at this point: It can be found in the way that plot/action, inner monologue and authorial voice alternate throughout the story. Under closer examination, these shifts betray a pattern hidden between the lines, a pattern which shows the author's deep involvement with her protagonist. . . .

Xiao Hong's authorial involvement with the main protagonist of *Vague Expectations* has created a type of psychological insight into a woman's feelings which I think is decidedly a woman's style of writing. Li Ma is more than a typical young maid-servant, she is a study in female behavior. Her description comes from inside, sometimes to such an extent that the reader cannot distinguish between authorial voice and monologue: "By the time she had returned to the bank of the lake with needle and thread, a troop of soldiers was marching down the road on the other side singing as they raised a cloud of dust. *Is Jin Lizhi in that group of soldiers?* The realization that she was on tenterhooks made her feel a little foolish." (The sentence I have underlined here stands in italics in Goldblatt's translation; Xiao Hong uses neither italics nor direct speech in the original version.)

Again it might be argued that a deep authorial involvement is not necessarily a specific phenomenon of woman's writing. Yu Dafu's I-narrators and protagonists for instance confront us with an exceptionally intense search of their soul. The difference, however, lies in the object of their search; what Yu Dafu exposes are often the doubts and reflections of a melancholy soul, whereas Xiao Hong, as shown in the above attempt at an analysis, points out the everyday oppression of a woman by letting her subconscious speak through small gestures.

Feminine writing is also a matter of perception.

Ruth Keen. In Anna Gerstlacher, et al., eds.
Woman and Literature in China (Bochum,
Germany: Brockmeyer, 1985),
pp. 366, 369, 373–74

Market Street [Shangshi jie] is a work that could be (and has been) mistaken for a series of autobiographical essays or for a piece of fiction. It is, however, the story of the author's life during a specific period of time. It is thinly disguised as fiction (as in the use of pseudonyms for the narrator and her lover), and suggests a fictional style, owing to the selection and ordering of materials and the nature of the telling. Yet, given the known "facts" of Xiao Hong's life, including statements by contemporaries who figured prominently, both in her life and in *Market Street,* compelling reasons exist for accepting the work neither as fiction nor as a casual collection of related essays but as a coherent autobiography, a unified and precisely ordered set of motifs from the author's personal experience. It is also representative of women's auto-biography in the main and gives clear and effective expression to Xiao Hong's world view, largely insofar as issues of gender are concerned. It is both feminine and feminist. . . .

Market Street shares several characteristics with women's autobiography: a downplaying of the narrator/protagonist's own achievements, an emphasis on private rather than public roles, a heavy reliance on anecdote (which captures character at its most typical), and a discontinuous narrative style. Simultaneously, these characteristics invest *Market Street* with the literariness of Xiao Hong's novels and short stories. As a work of literature, *Market Street* rivals many of the most compelling creations of this and other periods of Chinese history in terms of its evocative power, universal accessibility, and rhetorical skill. As autobiography, it reveals the life *and* the general world view of a representative Chinese intellectual, a woman living in a male-oriented and male-dominated society in the chaotic period just prior to World War II. It describes a young woman's attempt to come to grips with the realities of her own life, thereby legitimizing her past to understand her present. *Market Street* is, in sum, literary autobiography at its finest.

> Howard Goldblatt, ed. *Market Street: A Chinese Woman in Harbin* (Seattle: University of Washington Press, 1986), pp. x, xvi–xvii

XI XI (CHINA–HONG KONG) n.d.

Chen Ruoxi's understated skill makes some of Xi Xi's stories seem slightly contrived, a common problem with the short story form. When she is good, however, she is very good. "The Cold" is a beautifully written story about an arranged marriage in contemporary Hong Kong, and, interleaved with quotations from classic poetry and cold, water imagery and her prize-winning story "A Girl Like Me," is delicately macabre.

> Frances Wood. *China Quarterly.* 114, 1988, p. 307

Both Xi Xi and Zhong Xiaoyang are obsessed with China, not so much with the China of the Communist regime as with China in a broader sense—the motherland, her historical past, and the Chinese people at large. Although Hong Kong adjoins China geographically, to obtain official permission on two sides of the border in order to visit relatives has been extremely difficult. It was not until the end of the Cultural Revolution in the mid-1970s that the barrier began to be lifted. Both writers reveal a strong spiritual bond with their motherland. Since their brief visits to mainland China, they often write stories with mainland Chinese settings and characters. . . .

In addition to dealing with exotic and Chinese traditional subject matters, both Xi Xi and Zhong Xiaoyang often probe deeply into the psychological realm of their characters. This type of story mainly exposes the motivation and the development of the hero's or the heroine's intense inner feelings. Meanwhile, due to this personal focus, the environments and locales in the stories are often described in a very few words. . . .

Xi Xi . . . has written one short story focusing on the reality of Hong Kong—"Spring View." Both its theme and contents concern Hong Kong. She even employs special devices in arranging the texture of language so as to create a Hong Kong atmosphere. . . .

One of the techniques that Xi Xi often employs in her fiction is the juxtaposition of two perspectives. She often presents two very different, yet equally valid, points of view.

The scope of the novel [*The Hunter Who Whistles to Bust a Bear*] is magnificent. It attempts to cover the whole Chinese empire in the eighteenth century. In describing the process of Wang's downfall, samples of different types of commoners—farmers, day laborers, hunters, and miners—are presented. The lives of Banner soldiers, minority tribes, and jugglers in the market place, are also depicted. By means of presenting the daily activities and the mind of Emperor Qian Long at work, the scope nearly encompasses the whole of Chinese civilization. The affairs of his court and details from his personal and public life include court audience, comments on submitted memorials, art collections, editing of the imperial classics, furniture, food, and vessels for meals, the architecture of the palace and the summer retreat, relationships with officials, speculations on weaponry, taxation, army, and on the problems of the minority tribes as well as his enemy, that is, the Russian troops on the border. The materials are very realistic and all-embracing. However, they are arranged in such a cluttered and massive manner that they sound dull and monotonous. Furthermore, the consciousness of the Emperor, totally in want of feelings, dimensions, and personal touch, is depicted rather like the memory store of a computer. But Xi Xi should definitely be given credit, for no other Chinese fictional writer in classical or modern times has ever attempted to cover such a magnificent scope and meanwhile employ such ingenious and daring techniques.

Ling Chung. In Michael S. Duke, ed.
*Modern Chinese Women Writers: Critical
Appraisals* (Armonk, New York: M. E.
Sharpe, 1989), pp. 218–19, 222, 224, 226

YAMAMOTO, HISAYE (UNITED STATES) 1921–

"High-Heeled Shoes" (1948) is more essay than story, unlike those that followed, but it has the Yamamoto hallmarks:

(1) References to literary materials outside the Japanese-American tradition. This shows her wide reading. In this story, Freud, Ellis, Stekel, Krafft-Ebbing, and Robert Browning are mentioned. In "Epithalamium," she quotes extensively from Gerard Manley Hopkins as well as echoing the Miltonic poem. This strategy lifts her stories into the wider world of European-American culture and adds surprise and new angles of perspective.

(2) References to actual events, place, or people. In this story she names Wakako Yamauchi as the friend who has given her the plants from which the narrator is picking pansies in the story.

(3) Lists, particularly of foods, flowers, and oddments that give sensory appeal as well as substantiating the reality of the story. In "High-heeled Shoes," she is irritated when the phone rings because she fantasizes that it is a salesman and she does not have money to buy from him. She lists what she would have bought by week's end if she only had money.

(4) Soliloquies and imaginary dialogues. Here she has a talk with Gandhi about non-violent responses versus the suffering of women attacked by rapists. Gandhi does not come off well.

The keynote in all of Yamamoto's work is her use of her own mind: she is analytic, meditative, honest, compassionate, and ironic. Whether she uses the first person or a narrator, the final word is usually hers—and it is frequently so open-ended that the reader feels there are stories and meanings as yet unguessed implicit in each tale.

Yamamoto's pervasive love for humanity is found in "The High-heeled Shoes." The protagonist ("I") is confronted with sexual perversions: she receives an obscene telephone call at the story's beginning and this propels her mind into "unlovely, furtive things" about other encounters with men that she and her friends have had. The most startling was the time she caught sight of a pair of legs in black high-heeled shoes sticking out from the open door of a "dusty-blue, middle-aged sedan." As she approached and glanced in, she discovered that the shoes were worn by a naked man reclining on the front seat . . . and she was, "with frantic gestures, being enjoined to linger awhile."

The narrator calls on her reading for some understanding of this frightening experience but concludes: "Reading is reading, talking is talking, thinking is thinking, and living is different."

A similar personal revelation of the sickness of humankind was revealed in "The Wilshire Bus," a 1950 story, which deals with a Japanese-American woman's fear of being identified as Chinese by a drunken bigot. Shocked at finding this weakness in herself, she lost "her saving detachment . . . and she was filled once again in her life with the infuriatingly helpless, insidiously sickening sensation of there being in the world nothing solid she could put her finger on, nothing solid she could come to grips with, nothing solid she could sink her teeth into, nothing solid."

She has written two stories about gamblers: "The Brown House" (1951), and "Las Vegas Charley" (1961).

["The Legend of Miss Sasagawara"] is probably her finest piece of writing and it is still one of the most evocative of all stories of the [concentration] camp experience (as Wakako Yamauchi says, people did not want to talk about that experience). It is possible that the success of the story results from the way she controlled her own emotions as she wrote, for this time she used a filtered intelligence of a girl obviously herself to give the story through random glimpses of Miss Sasagawara. The rest of the other witnesses are unreliable: an ambulance driver, a teenaged boy, a hysterical woman, and people who love gossip for its own sake, not realizing the human anguish behind bizarre actions.

Dorothy Risuko McDonald and Katharine
Newman. *MELUS.* 7:3, 1980, pp. 24–27

The horror of earthquake seldom has been captured successfully in fiction. Perhaps this is because earthquakes are not only unpredictable (as yet), but lack anything like the ominous overture—the thickening skies, the swirling approaching clouds—that sometimes precedes tornadoes and hurricanes. Earthquakes are such abrupt, random events that they are difficult to weave into the order of a story. The obvious solution—to make the earthquake a correlative to the emotional climax of the characters—usually appears contrived and unsatisfying. Among the few works successful in portraying this fact of the Los Angeles landscape is Hisaye Yamamoto's gem-like story, "Yoneko's Earthquake."

Yamamoto recreates the rural surroundings of Los Angeles in the early 1930s, a time when the landscape was "one vast orange grove" broken occasionally by a truck farm such as that operated by Yoneko's parents. It was a fading way of life, as the author knew, writing twenty years later. By the 1950s the towns near Los Angeles, with their feed and seed stores, their Sunkist and Pure Gold packing houses and P.E. lines, were fast losing their agricultural character and becoming indistinguishable suburbs. And, of course, the Japanese, who had played an important role in the development of California agriculture, had lost most of their lands. Yoneko Hosoume, born in 1923, would have spent most of her teens in a resettlement camp. All of this, known alike by reader and author, is unstated in Yamamoto's story. Instead, it is the Long Beach earthquake of 1933 that demonstrates the fragility of the dream of home nourished by Mr. and Mrs. Hosoume.

Charles L. Crow. In David Fine, ed. *Los Angeles in Fiction* (Albuquerque: University of New Mexico Press, 1984), pp. 200–201

Seventeen Syllables represents a range of work—memoir, short story, short-short story—written between 1948 and 1987. Many of these pieces were first published in the Japanese-American journal *Rafu Shimpo* as well as in *Partisan Review, Harper's Bazaar* and *The Kenyon Review.* Yamamoto writes with distilled realism about ordinary people experiencing romance, racism and family responsibilities. Throughout the book she balances on an optimistic, fey wit. . . .

A distinguishing characteristic of Yamamoto's work is her multicultural casting, and this is especially effective in such stories as "The Brown House," "Wilshire Bus," "The Eskimo Connection" and "Reading and Writing." *Seventeen Syllables* is a book not just about Japanese-Americans but also about Chicanos, blacks, Filipinos, Eskimos and whites of various classes. The collection reflects Yamamoto's rich variety of experiences growing up in California and speaking English as a second language, being interned in Arizona during Word War II reporting for the black weekly *Los Angeles Tribune,* becoming active in Catholic Worker projects in the 1950s and then raising a family with her husband, Anthony De Soto.

Valerie Miner. *The Nation.* April 24, 1989, p. 568

Buried plots operate in different manners in Yamamoto's works. Two of her stories, "Seventeen Syllables" (1949) and "Yoneko's Earthquake" (1951), exemplify the varying ways that Yamamoto uses this device. "Yoneko's Earthquake" is deliciously ambiguous, containing hidden, often tragic, secrets. "Seventeen Syllables" begins with a focus on one plot but subtly shifts to disclose another that intertwines with the original action. The buried plots of each story reveal the experiences of Issei women and the troubling legacies they pass on to their daughters. . . .

Although both "Seventeen Syllables" and "Yoneko's Earthquake" end with Issei women surrendering to patriarchal systems, Yamamoto does not depict these choices as weak or simplistic. On the contrary, by layering her stories and developing buried plots, Yamamoto fully explores the tremendous psychological and emotional costs to Issei women who attempt to pursue their desires in a context hostile to their wishes. Unlike Rosie in "Seventeen Syllables," who can only feign understanding of her mother's haiku, readers who dig through to the buried plots of "Seventeen Syllables" and "Yoneko's

Earthquake" will be rewarded with masterful storytelling by an author who has captured the complexities of Japanese American experiences.

Stan Yogi. *Studies in American Fiction.* 17,
1989, pp. 170, 178

The power of this seemingly simple Nisei tale ["Seventeen Syllables"] comes from several interwoven themes. The primary one reveals a cultural strait-jacket in which a male dominates and destroys a gentle woman who is consumed by an urgent need to create and express herself. Moreover, the narrative suggests another possible female tragedy in Rosie's future. Rosie and Jesus's relationship harbors a potential intercultural conflict, for Jesus is not of her ethnic group or station. Rosie's romance recalls her mother's unfortunate love affair with the young Japanese who was above her social position.

The conclusion of the story echoes the cultural chasm between the mother and daughter also, for Tome asks Rosie, "Promise me you will never marry." Tome receives the same glib agreement Rosie used for haiku—the old lie—"Yes, yes, I promise." Ironically, just as Tome barely understands English, Rosie scarcely understands the mother's suffocating plea. Each is a prisoner, isolated in solitary confinement. Tragically, Tome loses her second child also, this time to an alien culture which does not have an artistic spiritual intuitiveness or the same gender restrictions as the Japanese. Rejected by both husband and daughter, Ume Hanazone is destroyed, no more to be a flowering garden.

What is the reader to intuit about the female role in this culture? These women blossom/create and pay the price—intense personal jeopardy or annihilation. The duration of their flowering shrinks to the length of almost a season; confined and compressed, their existences recall a sparse seventeen-syllable ephemeral haiku.

"Seventeen Syllables" remains irrevocably a woman's story. The flavor and anguish which lace it and make it powerful come from the collision of Eastern and Western values. Tome steps outside her place as child bearer, housekeeper, and farmworker when she attempts to gain control and carve an independent artistic territory for herself, and she is smothered. Rosie identifies with her American background and culture. Ironically, even in Japanese class, she entertains her friend by mimicking a series of British and American movie stars. Rosie doesn't understand Tome, nor does she understand her own roots or the Japanese language and culture.

Both the Japanese and American cultures make demands which by themselves can create intense disequilibrium. In close juxtaposition, they seem to destroy the occupants or at best leave them in the middle of the *woods* (Hayashi). Perhaps a letter written by Yamamoto, which Koppleman quotes in her introduction to this story, throws additional light on the power of this tale; Yamamoto speaks of the pain she feels when she thinks of her mother, who could have used a more understanding daughter. Yamamoto goes on to say that "Seventeen Syllables" is her mother's story, even though the details are not true. Although the Japanese and American cultures do not fuse in this tale, art and the artist do, for "Seventeen Syllables" becomes the daughter's symbolic haiku for the mother—the "yes, yes" said finally, packed with all the intuitive meaning and understanding in Zen fashion.

Zenobia Baxter Mistri. Studies in Short
Fiction. 27, 1990, pp. 200–201

Awarded a John Hay Whitney Foundation Opportunity Fellowship in 1949, Yamamoto was one of the first Japanese American writers to gain national recognition after the war, when anti-Japanese sentiment was still rampant. Several of her short stories ("The High-Heeled Shoes," "The Brown House," and "Epithalamium") appeared in Martha Foley's lists of "Distinctive Short Stories," and "Yoneko's Earthquake" was included in *Best American Short Stories: 1952*. In 1986 she received the American Book Award for Lifetime Achievement from the Before Columbus Foundation. *Hot Summer Winds,* a film based on "Seventeen Syllables" and "Yoneko's Earthquake" and directed by Emiko Omori, was first broadcast in May 1991 as part of PBS's *American Playhouse* series.

Because of her extensive reading and her own experience, Yamamoto writes out of both an Anglo-American and a Japanese American literary tradition. Her method of double-telling—conveying two tales in the guise of one—involves an intertextual use of a familiar narrative technique: unreliable point of view. Three of her most haunting stories, "Seventeen Syllables," "Yoneko's Earthquake," and "The Legend of Miss Sasagawara" (henceforth "The Legend") contain manifest and veiled plots. In the first two stories, the overt "action" is narrated from the perspective of a young girl; the covert drama concerns the conflict between the girl's Issei parents. Unreliable narration assumes strategic as well as thematic significance in "The Legend," a story that interrogates rumors and questions societal definitions of insanity. Though undoubtedly influenced by modernist experimentation with limited point of view, Yamamoto tailors the method to the Japanese American context.

Her stories capitalize on the infrequent verbal communication between issei spouses . . . and between Issei parents and Nisei children. . . . Yamamoto parlays cultural precepts into literary gambits and transforms social rituals into a subtle rhetoric. . . .

The use of naive narrators in "Seventeen Syllables" and "Yoneko's Earthquake" alerts us directly to the limited point of view in those two stories. "The Legend" replicates the gripping power of rumors well before it reveals their dubiousness. By constantly shifting our attitudes toward the title character and by giving her the last word via the poem, Yamamoto piques the conscience of any reader too ready to accept tendentious reports and pronounce judgment. The skepticism that she brings to "The Legend," particularly her interrogation of sources, finds insistent echoes in Kingston and Kogawa. . . .

Cultural and sociological considerations form an inalienable part of aesthetic judgments. The interlocking of thematic and strategic silence in Yamamoto's fiction should make us rethink the debate on the distinction between literature and social history, between aesthetics and politics. . . . Because the relationship between life and art is here as elsewhere indirect, these texts demand and deserve meticulous close reading. Only by anchoring them culturally and historically, however, can we fully disclose the author's formally complex design and the layers of emotions embedded in her ellipses.

> King-Kok Cheung. *Articulate Silences:*
> *Hisaye Yamamoto, Maxine Hong Kingston,*
> *Joy Kogawa* (Ithaca, New York: Cornell
> University Press, 1993), pp. 28–29, 32, 70,
> 72–73

YANG JIANG (CHIANG) (CHINA) 1911–

Yang Chiang's dramas appeared as part of the theater boom in Shanghai during and shortly after the war. It was a period of considerable experimentation in theater and of unprecedented popularity with Shanghai audiences, encouraging writers to explore the potentials of drama as never before. Among the achievements that resulted were developments in comedy, and three of Yang Chiang's four known plays contributed substantially to this genre. The comedies are built on familiar dramatic situations, with orphans and picaresque characters seeking their way in the bourgeois life of Shanghai. But the plays are distinguished by an unusual degree of ironic detachment and a subtle eye for the psychology of her characters. These qualities drew the respect of fellow playwrights, while the sheer hilarity of the comic situations won success with audiences. Although a student of *k'unch'ü*, Yang's dramatic style shows strong Western influence, from neo-classical French drama, eighteenth-century comedies of manners, the nineteenth-century well-made play and its successors, the problem plays of writers such as Ibsen and Shaw.

Yang Chiang's one exploration of tragedy is centered on a young woman, Shen Huilien, who is reminiscent of Hedda Gabler, while her husband, Fang Ching-shan, recalls the demon idealists in other Ibsen plays. As quaint as such comparisons might appear, the characters and their situation speak particularly to Chinese society in the 1940s, its aspirations, its manners, its failings. The heroine, driven by a well-articulated contempt for society and a craving for freedom which neither her husband nor the self-effacing lawyer, T'ang Shu-yuan, can fulfill, ultimately destroys herself. Nowhere is the centrality of psychological observation and the tone of ironic detachment more evident than in this work. Yet, while audiences accepted these qualities in her comedies, the demands of tragedy in this vein could not appeal to them. Today, some thirty-five years later, *Windswept Blossoms (Feng hsü)* remains an intriguing, powerful dramatic work and a distinguished contribution to modern Chinese drama.

Edward Gunn. Renditions. 14, 1980, p. 42

Yang Jiang's *Six Chapters from My Life "Downunder"* is a work of remarkable sophistication which, in its subtle, almost allegorical style, stands as powerful testimony to the insanity of the Cultural Revolution. Read carefully, it takes on added significance with implications for the entire revolutionary process. The author has chosen to describe life in a cadre school by recounting relatively insignificant and commonplace events. Unlike the "wounded" *(shanghen)* literature of the post-1977 years the Gang of Four is never mentioned in *"Downunder."*. . . .

To say that Yang Jiang's writing style is low-key and subtle is in itself an understatement. To say that she skirts the major issues or important concerns of the times is to misread the piece entirely. Granted, most of what she has written is extremely personal and, seemingly, of a commonplace nature. In the long run, that plus the occasional but poignant and fitting authorial comment, is what lends the piece such power.

Yang and her husband fared far better than many of their peers; that fact alone probably went a long way in saving the piece from becoming another narrowly focused "j'accuse." Without relating any "horror stories," the author has given us here her keen observation of the more pervasive effects of the Cultural Revolution's policies.

She makes the reader share in the overall sense of disappointment, frustration and skepticism directed at those people—or the system—responsible for what was visited upon her family and her fellow victims. Several themes emerge from her quiet, matter-of-fact narrative. One is the mutual distrust and general incompatibility between China's urban intellectuals (the "stinking old ninths") and the peasants who were their "masters;" this, of course, tends to invalidate the basic principle behind the *xiafang* movement. Another recurrent theme is waste—particularly the waste of human talent. The author frequently alludes to this by describing the useless or counter-productive activities required of young and old alike, but nowhere does the waste of human resources come through as clearly and alarmingly as in the succinctly told sequence involving the death of her son-in-law, Deyi.

There are other important themes in *"Downunder,"* such as the backwardness of the Chinese countryside, the nature of the "campaigns," and the demeanor of the people involved in them.

Howard Goldblatt. Renditions. 16, 1981,
pp. 6–7

After finishing her *Six Chapters from My Life "Downunder,"* Yang Jiang asked me to look over the manuscript. I felt that she should have written one more chapter, which we can, for the moment, call "A Sense of Shame: Participating in Political Campaigns."

One of the important missions of the Studies Division cadre school was to carry on a political campaign, specifically to ferret out "May Sixteenth elements." Thus the more than two years we lived at the cadre school were spent in an atmosphere of criticism and struggle. The rhythm of this political campaign tightened and relaxed in accordance with other needs such as farm-work, the construction of living quarters, and our moves from place to place; but like recurrent malaria, it was a disease that never stopped plaguing our bodies. Records of "Labor" and "Leisure," or of this and that, are but mere adornments to this larger backdrop, minor incidents in a major story.

All of this belongs to the past and the scene has now changed—we can say that many things have come to light. In this political campaign, as in all that preceded it, at least three types of people emerged. If the comrades who suffered under unjust accusations, who were criticized and "struggled against," were to write an account of this campaign, they might title it "A Record of Grievances" or "A Record of Resentment." As to the masses in general, in reminiscing, they might feel constrained to call theirs "A Record of Shame." This sense of shame and remorse could have its roots in their stupid inability to spot trumped-up charges or misjudged cases, which led them blindly to follow the crowd in trampling on decent people. Or perhaps they would be like me, feeling ashamed of their own cowardice, people who lacked the courage to protest that which they believed unjust, but whose most courageous act was "passive" participation in the campaign. The third type of person persisted in serving as flag-wavers, drum-beaters, and "hit-men" in helping to "settle" case after case in the "kangaroo courts" even though they knew full well that things were always messy and tangled-up, never clear-cut. These people should logically have the greatest need to write "A Record of Shame," but quite likely they have no recollection of what they did and feel no remorse over it. They may have forgotten the past precisely because of a sense of shame, or because they are impervious to shame. Shame often aids forgetfulness; incidents that weigh on one's conscience or are disgraceful are never any fun to recall, so they easily slip through our minds and vanish without a trace. Shame also causes a person to recoil and hesitate, thus retarding his chances in a desperate struggle for survival. People with guilty consciences could, because of a momentary retreat from confrontation, place themselves forever in the ranks of stragglers. That is why shame is an emotion that must be eliminated, not nurtured, and why it is not included among the "seven human emotions" listed in the ancient classics. As life in today's society grows increasingly tense, this state of mind is more than useless—it is harmful. So it is best forgotten in the interest of one's physical and mental well-being.

Six Chapters of a Floating Life—a book I never did like—actually only contains four extant chapters, while *Six Chapters from My Life "Downunder"* should theoretically have been seven. In this day and age, where collectors, antiquarians, and scholars combine their talents and interests, the discovery of unwritten or unpublished manuscripts by authors great and small has rapidly developed into a new field of literary endeavor. So who can say that the day will not come when the missing chapters of these two books will surface to fill in the gaps, thereby lessening somewhat the number of defects in the world of man.

> Qian Zhongshu. Foreword to Yang Jiang.
> *Six Chapters from my Life "Downunder"*
> (1980), *Renditions*. 16, 1981, p. 9

As Howard Goldblatt points out in his introduction, Yang Jiang's *Six Chapters* touches on a number of themes such as the distrust and resentment of the peasants for China's urban intellectuals, the tremendous human waste involved in this effort to "remold" the intellectuals, the poverty of the Chinese countryside, and the mutual devotion of this sexagenarian Chinese couple (Yang Jiang's husband being the well known scholar and writer Qian Zhongshu). More important than the "overall sense of disappointment, frustration, and skepticism" that Goldblatt rightly senses in the work, I believe, is the sometimes subtle, sometimes gently ironic, and sometimes open statement of the complete failure and foolishness of this misguided Cultural Revolution effort—and, by implication, of all of those ideological efforts since 1942—to fundamentally transform human nature to make it fit the Maoist communist mold. She not only "reaffirms the endurance of humanity" but also predicts the ultimate victory of universal human nature over any ideological system that is not in conformity with it.

> Michael S. Duke. *Blooming and Contending:*
> *Chinese Literature in the Post-Mao Era*
> (Bloomington: Indiana University Press,
> 1985), p. 85

YEZIERSKA, ANZIA (UNITED STATES) 1880–1970

Miss Yezierska, most newly arrived of our literary immigrants, does not escape touches of sentimentalism quite alien to Knut Hamsun or D. H. Lawrence. Her little book *Hungry Hearts,* is full of tears that sometimes come too quickly, as if she had not learned that the quickest tears dry soonest. She repeats her formula—an immigrant girl longing for escape from bitter conditions—too frequently. When she leaves the East Side neighborhood to which her art is native she never quite has the look of reality. And yet she has struck one or two notes that our literature can never again be without, and she deserves the high credit of being one of the earliest to put those notes into engaging fiction. As a nation we have taken, she cries out, the bodies of our immigrants and used them to make the nation. But what of their souls? What of that radiant aspiration—alas, too often disappointed—which has drawn our immigrants hither from the most cramped and wretched corners of the earth? What of the uprush of affection which many of them, yes, most of them, still experience long after they may be thought to have won the right to disillusionment? These are elements in the national wealth which simply must not be wasted. *Hungry Hearts* is a genuine little horde of that wealth, an evidence of the tongue of flame which flickers beautifully above the slums in which we negligently leave some of our truest lovers.

C.V.D. (Carl Van Doren). *The Nation.*
November 26, 1921, p. 122

A flame—a leaping, scorching, searing flame—that is the impression scarred into the mind by *Salome of the Tenements.* Sonya is young. She loves life. She yearns for the unattainable. One day she starts out in pursuit of it, and the story of that pursuit is the thread of the tale. Really, "Salome" is a misnomer. Sonya Vrunsky might be likened to many classic figures, but never to Salome.

She might, for example, be called the Père Grandet of the tenements as she presses her experience to her bosom, crying: "Mine, mine, mine only and forever!" Or she might be likened to Mr. Bounderby, exploiter and enslaver of men and women. Sonya is the miser and the monopolist—at heart a businesswoman, not a vamp. Besides, the traditional Salome was a cat's-paw in the hands of Herodias, while Sonya is a devouring monster. She describes herself as "a soul consumed with hunger for heights beyond reach," but in seeking to scale those heights she does not hesitate to set her feet on the necks of her fellows, as when she destroys Lipkin's happiness, or begs her costume from Hollins, or lays the trap for Manning, her millionaire future husband, or buys her landlord without paying the agreed price. Here she is not a soul but a combination promoter and confidence woman.

Salome is an unwholesome book. With the possible exception of Hollins it contains but one character that stands out clearly against the heaving background, and that character, Sonya, exhibits a depravity of spirit and an incapacity to live and let live that rivals the degradation of Balzac's most admirable villains. The book is vivid. In places, it is well done. The life of Manning wins no understanding from the novelist, but the pictures of the Ghetto are admirable and the suppressed aspirations of the Russian Jewess burst into flame in the form of Sonya Vrunsky. This time Miss Yezierska has created, not a hungry heart, but a yawning abyss, an ego that does not project a single ray of social understanding.

Scott Nearing. *The Nation.* June 6, 1923,
pp. 674, 676

A certain measure of achievement there is in this new novel [*Bread Givers*] of Mrs. Yezierska's: complete and colorful personalities live in it; strange, sordid scenes from the Ghetto depths are vividly depicted here; and the fierce vitality of the author seethes through its pages. But this unharnessed and little directed vitality is the author's undoing.

Like a canoe in the rapids, the frail bark, creative genius, is dented again and again by rocks that may easily be avoided in a quieter current. And Mrs. Yezierska has heedlessly ignored her light craft and her inadequate equipment and trusted herself to the mercy of the foamiest torrent. For she is unmistakably a writer for whom the much abused phrase, *furor scribendi,* seems to have been coined expressly. In fact, I imagine that a certain fury characterizes all her actions and that writing is but one of the manifestations of her superabundant and sweeping virility.

It is obvious that she shares the passionately egocentric attitude evinced by her heroine, Sara, who considers physical training courses at the University an injustice because she earns her way through college by working in a laundry, who startles the bursar out of his wits by asking for a refund of tuition fees on the grounds that she had "paid to learn, not to fail," and who is always amazed and angered when her sudden, unsolicited overtures of love are rather impatiently rejected by the objects of her fugitive affection. Equally evident is the fact that, like Sara, our author is the victim of a purely personal morality which is governed neither by code nor by logic but by the particular circumstance. Hence, while the actual incidents portrayed are in every sense kaleidoscopic, the spiritual pattern is a labyrinth; and while the individual parts of the story are probably honest transcriptions of experiences, the entire work is not a true representation of Ghetto life. . . .

There is . . . evidence that Mrs. Yezierska was moved to write this novel before she had thoroughly apprehended its problems. She is concerned with "the slice of life" not with life in the round; she plays all her notes *fortissimo* and in a frantic tempo with the inevitable loss of emphasis and shading.

> John J. Smertenko. *Saturday Review of Literature.* October 10, 1925, p. 192

Not too long ago most anthologists of American writing made it a point to include something of Anzia Yezierska, perhaps from *Children of Loneliness* or *How I Found America.* Miss Yezierska was a particularly eloquent spokesman for the immigrant Jews of America, and her account of what America looked like to the eyes of those who came hungering for freedom fell naturally into place as part of the literary record. Her career may be said to have begun with some short stories she wrote while still working in sweatshops and learning the language. (One of them was chosen by Edward J. O'Brien as the best short story of 1919.) Then a few novels, from *Hungry Hearts* in 1920 to *Arrogant Beggar* in 1927—and silence. A hiatus of more than twenty years in the life of a writer who lived for nothing else but to write, who refused a fabulous Hollywood contract, fabulous even by today's standards, with the cry: "I can't sign it away. Writing is everything I am. . . It's my search for a meaning."

It is this experience to which W. H. Auden refers in his introduction to the present volume [*Red Ribbon on a White Horse*] when he writes: "The sudden paralysis or drying up of creative power occurs to artists everywhere, but nowhere perhaps more frequently than in America." The last eight words probably hold the seeds of contention in them, as do others of his remarks. The fact is that his introduction is so generally penetrating and so comprehending of the material it introduces that one reads it again to wonder at how much he has been able to say and to suggest in eight pages. How, for instance, could Miss Yezierska's predicament, or the reason for her artistic paralysis, be better summed up than this, by Mr. Auden: "To have the desires of the poor and be transferred in the twinkling of an eye to a world which can only be real for those who have the desires of the rich is to be plunged into the severest anxiety. The foreshortening of time which is proper to a dream or a fairy story is a nightmare in actual life."

Such was the foreshortening which Miss Yezierska experienced when she received ten thousand dollars and a summons to Hollywood for the movie rights to *Hungry Hearts* and was whisked away out of Hester Street, where she had been subsisting on this same day upon stewed tea leaves prepared over a rusty gas plate. . . .

William Fox offered her a one-hundred-thousand-dollar contract for three years of writing, and she walked away from it, hearing him call after her, "Who do you think you are, Joan of Arc?" She spent the next ten years trying to find out, to see if she could get back again to the wholeness of spirit that had gone into *Hungry Hearts*. But she had been marred already and there were other things to come—obscurity again, the Depression, the WPA project, and a characteristically foreshortened love affair clouded with all the moonstruck romantics of blind adolescence. It is a measure of Miss Yezierska's writing integrity that she has recorded this now, in the clarity of backward-looking, in exactly the terms and tones of that year so hot with uncertainty. Everything else here—the humiliating experience with the Writers' Project, the attempt to rub shoulders with the world of New England, the brief and painful meetings with her father—everything points to the same glad tidings. If the shocks and alarms of American life had once frozen her into silence, she has unfrozen again. She seems to be writing with as much vision and emotional projection as ever before.

Nathan L. Rothman. *Saturday Review of
Literature.* November 4, 1950, pp. 13–14

Anzia Yezierska thought of herself first as a writer and then as an interpreter of the Jewish immigration experience. Her work appears to us today in the opposite posture: valuable as social history and somewhat less important for its place in literature. These stories, collected together, may reverse that image.

Yezierska was a skilled teller of tales. Gifted at the art of distilling the essence of a feeling, she could capture the poignant moment or evoke the

tears of human sorrow. Instinctively, her language and form take onomato-
poeic shape. The pace of a sentence matches the quickening heart beat of a
tense moment. The words all but wail their despair as they catch a moment
of pathos.

Her ability to write in blood, as one critic put it, was both her strength
and her weakness. "She dipped her pen in her heart," they commented. Absence of form in her work—she resisted obeying what she called the textbook
formula for writing—became the written equivalent of the tense and chaotic
lives she saw on the Lower East Side. Yezierska relied on motion—rapid,
evocative, and assertive—to carry her plots from one place to another. Her
plot structures are simple, even crude, designed as vehicles for a heroine's
self-discovery rather than for intrinsically interesting elements. Her characters never so much developed as they emerged: full blown archetypes of a
culture and often fragments of herself. Each novel or tale works through the
aspirations of the main protagonist. Success or failure matter less than self
awareness. And what matters most of all is the recognition, despairing or
hopeful, of the double reality of the immigrant experience. The eyes of the
central figure see the world and interpret it for the reader. The dreams, like
those in these stories, were her dreams, the struggle hers, and hers the success and the disillusionment of these tales. . . .

A Jewish immigrant community throbbed in Yiddish, and Yezierska
worked at reproducing its essence. She never wrote in Yiddish, though her
prose sometimes reads like a direct translation. Jo Ann Boydston has convincingly demonstrated that she could write fine English prose. But she chose
to create a style in which the Yiddish idiom, translated into English, evoked
the cultural context she wanted to recreate. . . .

Yezierska touched something quintessential of the 1920s that transcended the narrow themes of immigrant adjustment with which her stories
superficially dealt. . . .

She could describe her people in language redolent of Yiddish with a
message hearteningly American. Her mission, as she articulated it in her
tales and in her interviews, was to interpret her people to America. She
would, as she says in *America and I,* "build a bridge of understanding between the American-born and myself. Since their life was shut out from such
as me, I began to open my life and the lives of my people to them. And life
draws life. In only writing about the ghetto, I found America."

> Alice Kessler-Harris. Introduction to Anzia
> Yezierska. *The Open Cage: An Anzia
> Yezierska Collection* (New York: Persea,
> 1979), pp. v–viii

Anzia Yezierska's career spanned more than fifty-five years. During that time
she published five full-length works, two volumes of short pieces, as well as
numerous stories, essays, and book reviews. The best of her writing dealt
with two main themes—the plight of the young immigrant Jewish woman and

the problems of the elderly in American society. To both, she brought a prophet's zeal for pointing out injustice at a time when the difficulties were only dimly appreciated.

Her early writings dealt primarily with life of the Jewish immigrants on the Lower East Side of New York. Her skill in capturing a scene and creating a personality in a few vivid strokes was combined with acute perception of the dilemmas that confronted these people. Focusing primarily on women, she showed their struggles gainst poverty and menial labor, their efforts to gain an education, their longing to carve out decent lives for themselves. Aware of the conflicts and confusions they faced, she was able to show both the warmth and supportiveness of the traditional community as well as the obstacles it placed in the path of women. At the same time she was aware of dangers they faced from the American world with its coldness and indifference. Unhappy choices between material success and spiritual values, between filial duty and personal achievement, between ambition and personal integrity are dramatized with passion and insight. Although she found it useful to play the role of the ignorant immigrant girl who was frequently her heroine, it was her education, and particularly her association with John Dewey, that inspired her and gave her the insight to recreate the world of the immigrant. Because she retained her emotional ties to the world of her origins, she was able to assess more accurately the American world to which these immigrants aspired. Often Yezierska's sense of moral indignation or her desire for a happy ending overrode her awareness of the complexities of her material, but at her best, in *Breadgivers* and in *Red Ribbon on a White Horse,* she treated these people and their situation with compassion and understanding.

When Yezierska was more than seventy years old she found a new cause on which to focus—the mistreatment of the elderly. With the same passion and energy that had marked her treatment of immigrant women, she condemned the cruelties of our society. Whether she was dealing with money-grubbing landlords or insensitive academics, she was quick to point up the injuries sustained by their victims.

Carol B. Schoen. Anzia Yezierska (Boston:
Twayne, 1982), pp. 127–28

Bread Givers, by Anzia Yezierska, is a novel about a crucial aspect of immigration: the struggle between fathers of the Old World (in this case a Rabbi), and daughters of the New. But, in the presentation of this conflict, the author explores the unrewarding and stultifying nature of housework and reveals the extent to which a man is dependent on a wife to save money, to live, to hold on to a job, even if he paradoxically tends to devaluate this important function of women. While identifying the problem of women's devaluation in the opposition between the "public" and the "domestic" spheres, Yezierska presents a particular view of imposed housework as a spur to rebellion against male oppression and as the training ground for the battles which women who choose independence have to fight in order to succeed.

Mariolina Salvatori. *MELUS.* 9:4, 1982, p. 47

[Mary] Antin's self-centeredness, her religious skepticism, and her enthusiasm for America resemble Sara Smolinsky's characteristics in Anzia Yezierska's novel *Bread Givers.* Published thirteen years apart, the two works share other elements. Though *Bread Givers* is set primarily on New York's Lower East Side, "shtetl" values dominate as they had in Antin's Polotzk. Moisheh Smolinsky, like Pinchus Antin, is an old-fashioned patriarch, convinced of his wisdom and authority. In contrast to Mr. Antin's secularism, however, Reb Smolinsky justifies his actions according to Orthodox Judaism. Thus, his four daughters and wife exist to serve him, to enable him to study Torah. Their salvation is rooted in his proximity to God. So persuaded is Smolinsky of this heavenly scheme that he arranges his daughter's marriages for his own profit. Predictably, his ill-conceived plans fail: the marriages are disastrous and his one business venture ruins him. . . .

Moved by their father's religious spirit, the daughters are . . . spellbound, "straining not to miss a word," temporarily forgetting their earthly woes. But the mood cannot last in America which values pragmatism, independence, and above all, success. More importantly, from Yezierska's viewpoint, Reb Smolinsky's piety is shallow, a cloak for his selfishness, and a justification for his tyranny. Though the three older daughters agree to his matchmaking, they never forgive him for their bitter lives. Eventually Shenah's patience is also exhausted; her earlier, more muted criticism grows louder. . . .

Paradoxically, it is Shenah's dying wish, "be good to father," which draws Sara back to the Lower East Side, where she is melodramatically reunited with her father.

Evelyn Avery. *Studies in American Jewish
Literature.* 5, 1986, pp. 46–47

Inevitably, in Yezierska's work, whether the narrator speaks in the first person or in the third, the story is divided between the time the character announces her "wild, blind hunger" for her own life, and the time she realizes she is trapped in a "repression" from which hope of release is dim. The strength of this simple repetition is such that it achieves metaphoric status. Yezierska the immigrant, Yezierska the woman, Yezierska the permanently bereft child are all trapped in that "I want to make from myself a person!" voice. They galvanize one another. With each cry, the words cut deeper, the situation feels more urgent. The character begins to sound as though she were born to speak her piece in this place at this time and in no other.

In the 1920s the cry of the immigrant locked out of mainstream life was heard as something startling, painful, significant. The First World War had left the century up for grabs. The idea of the democracy glimmered with new anger and new hope. It echoed the cry of middle-class women conscious enough to claim they were being locked out of their lives. After sixty years of terrible struggle, suffrage had just been won. The idea of the New Woman was still an open wound in American life. Many novels of the time reflect national disturbance over the question of independence for women. Yezierska's immigrant girl, spilling over with her "wild, blind hunger" to live her life, spoke eloquently—on every score—to the moment.

In Yezierska, the writer, the time, and the experience seem profoundly well-met. . . . The immigrant experience is Yezierska's idiom, but the subject is original loss. The bakery against whose window her nose is pressed is not America, it is her own unfrightened self. At the end of *Red Ribbon on a White Horse* Yezierska writes, "With a sudden sense of clarity I realized the battle I thought I was waging against the world had been against myself, against the Jew in me." By which, of course, she means the shamed and fearful self of which she will never be free. . . .

She is an essence of the alienated immigrant, and of the alienating, independent woman. Her situation is so real, so human, so crucial. She is destined to eat herself alive forever. We all see that. And we see also that— she refuses.

That's the thing finally about Yezierska. She is one of the great refuseniks of the world. She refuses to accept life's meanness and littleness. She refuses to accommodate herself to loneliness of the spirit. She refuses to curb emotional ambition. She's an immigrant? She's not a woman? Her hunger is voracious? intrusive? exhausting? *Still* she refuses. And on a big scale. We cannot turn away from her. Obsessing as grandly as the Ancient Mariner, her words continue, even now seventy years after they were written, to grab us by the collar. They shake and demand, compel, and remind. Attention must be paid. "I want to make from myself a person!"

The performance is astonishing.

Vivian Gornick. Introduction to Anzia
Yezierska. *How I Found America: Collected
Stories of Anzia Yezierska* (New York:
Persea, 1991), pp. viii-xii

In *America and I,* Yezierska wrote of her conflicting feelings for this supposed paradise for beleaguered Eastern European Jews: "Where is America? Is there an America? What is this wilderness in which I am lost?". . . For the Jewish immigrant, the New World promised freedom from the racial/religious oppression of European society. This oppression, which ranged from exclusion to pogrom, remained as bitter memories in the hearts of immigrant Jews who believed in the chance for a better life in spite of ghetto life, abject poverty, and Anglo-American prejudice. But as many Jewish immigrant writers have recorded, the price of Americanization was high—the loss of Jewish traditions and the rich cultural life of the *shtetl*. For the Jewish woman immigrant, this conflict of culture took on an added dimension: not only was she forced to deal with the prejudices of the dominant culture but also with the patriarchal traditions of the Ashkenazi Jewish community. In *Bread Givers,* Anzia Yezierska transforms her own paradoxical experiences as an immigrant daughter of America to expose us to the double bind of the Jewish woman, whose freedom from the rigid strictures of traditional Jewish culture left her rootless and thrust her into a hard and prejudiced world which kept her always a stranger. It is through the protagonist's stormy relationship with her Old World father that Yezierska presents the dialectics of mediation for the Jewish woman and gives us special insight into these immigrant daughters for whom the quest for identity entails both gender and cultural considerations.

Gay Wilentz. *MELUS.* 17, 1991, p. 34

YOSANO AKIKO (JAPAN) 1878–1942

When in the last decade of the nineteenth century some of Japan's most illustrious authors turned from romanticism to naturalism, it was Akiko's *Midaregami* which rekindled the dying flame of the romantic. The sensational impact of her book again helped poetry to prosper. Hers was a poetry of protest, of love, of emancipation for women, of the glorification of the flesh. She sympathized with the downtrodden—the lonely prostitute, the woman kept waiting, the isolated traveler. She defended the woman who yielded to the flesh, and she attacked the priests, the dilettantes of morality. She was the first to glorify the female body. Against the critical world of Meiji she defended sexuality, never sullying it, but seeing in it the union of lovers as natural as earlier poets had associated stags and does. While there were moments for her of the ideal, she was too much a student of human nature not to know that man was not to be trusted, that the woman's world was often lonely after the rewards of love, that there were psychological penalties for the seducer and the seduced. Her tanka pictured women at lonely inns, at home, in the fields, in temples and cities. Her imagination encompassed the world of court poetry and the world of Kyoto's streets. She dwelled in the mind of the priest, the courtesan, the dancing girl, the mourner, the kept woman. Her tanka evolved a richly creative scene, one often filled with the tensions of life. . . .

When Akiko uses the word *midaregami* (which we have preferred to translate as "tangled hair"), we ought . . . to visualize those stray wisps of hair out of place as imagery which is both aesthetic and sexually suggestive. Yet it is part of Akiko's contribution to raise *midaregami* one further level and to connect *tangled* hair with the emancipation of women and sexual freedom, with a beauty and sexuality that go beyond the traditional few wisps of disheveled hair, to hair only in sweet disorder. The implications behind

Akiko's use of *tangled hair,* while embodying the usual meanings attached
to the term, at times are those of a complex and intense pattern of great
beauty, sexuality, and even psychological disturbance or madness.

Akiko's personal note of eroticism and self-glorification and of rebellion
and anti-establishment has made *Midaregami* both historic and modern.

Seishi Shinoda and Sanford Goldstein.
Introduction to Yosano Akiko. *Tangled Hair*
(West Lafayette, Indiana: Purdue University
Press 1971), pp. 19, 23

Yosano Akiko is one of the many poets that most Japanese know and very
few non-Japanese do. One reason is probably the difficulty of re-creating the
music of poetry in a foreign language, especially the music of the thirty-one-
syllable traditional tanka, Akiko's preferred form. Another more important
one is Akiko's uncertain position in the canon of modern Japanese literature,
which has kept her work from being treated with the seriousness it deserves.

Until recently, conventional wisdom held that after the age of twenty-
three, when she published *Midaregami* (Tangled hair, 1901), one of the classics of modern Japanese poetry, Akiko wrote almost nothing of permanent
value. This in spite of the fact that she published prodigiously in a variety of
genres for over forty years and her career spanned the Meiji (1868–1912),
Taishō (1912–26), and Shōwa (1926–89) eras. The reasons for this view having
gained such a foothold are worth several pages in themselves, but suffice it
to say that in the past decade a number of writers have challenged it. The
importance of Akiko's achievement is no longer in question and it has begun
to be mapped in detail. Even before this reevaluation began, however, Akiko's
writings were part of the underground canon of many Japanese women,
her work and the example of her life something they held close to their
hearts. . . .

Tangled Hair is one of the central works of Japanese romanticism. It
was also one of the literary sensations of the century. Describing the early
celebrity it brought Akiko, the poet Saitō Mokichi (1882–1953), who some
years later became the leading figure in the world of tanka himself, said:
"Akiko's fame was really extraordinary. There's no other case like hers in
the history of modern tanka. Even if you call us famous now, it's nothing
compared to what she was. Scholars, writers, everyone praised her."

Akiko's poems were praised for the freshness of their language, the boldness of their imagery, and their passion. Even her greatest admirers, however,
noticed the needlessly complex syntax of a good many of them. . . .

Most of those who attacked *Tangled Hair* did so, however, on the basis
of its open appeal to the sensual emotions. The prominent tanka poet Sasaki
Nobutsuna (1872–1963), in his anonymous review in the magazine *Kokoro no
Hana* (Flowers of the heart) in September 1901, had an imaginary reader
vilify the author of *Tangled Hair* as a woman who spewed forth "immoral
words that belong in the mouths of whores and streetwalkers." For Nobut-

suna's imaginary reader, the problem was not obscurity but too much clarity, about topics that had formerly been taboo.

Tangled Hair was published in the last year of the Victorian period, and proper English Victorians would probably have been as shocked by Akiko's poems as were their counterparts on the other side of the earth. But for young people of literary ambition in Japan at the turn of the century, *Tangled Hair* was one of the three works regarded as "holy scripture.". . . At the height of the Russo-Japanese War (1904–1905), she published the modern-style poem *Kimi Shinitamō Koto Nakare* (Beloved, do not die) and two months later what amounted to a poetic manifesto, *Hirakibumi* (Open letter).

Beloved, Do Not Die was addressed to Akiko's younger brother Chūsa-burō, then twenty-seven. Chūsaburō was drafted into the army during the siege of Port Arthur. Fifteen thousand men had been killed or wounded in the first attack, and since the policy was to use soldiers as "human bullets" (*Human Bullets* was in fact the name of a famous novel about the war), Akiko had every reason to expect her brother to be killed. The burden of the poem is contained in the refrain of each of the five stanzas: "Beloved, do not die."

Akiko later claimed that the phrase was simply a roundabout way of expressing her hope for her brother's survival; but the poem echoes in reverse the traditional samurai motto, "I shall not return alive," said by the warrior as he heads for battle. Given the context, to ask a soldier not to die was to ask him not to fight at all. . . .

In *Beloved, Do Not Die,* she had expressed only her hatred of war. But in *Open Letter,* her prose explanation of the poem, she tried to prove that she supported the Russo-Japanese War. . . .

Then she defended herself from the charge that her thoughts were dangerous, saying that the real danger came from the fashion for urging people to die. . . .

The essence of her argument in *Open Letter* was that human emotions, whatever they were, were the only fit subject matter for a poem. Art that serves a political agenda, the sort of "war literature" that Keigetsu promoted, was not art.

At the height of war, when any whisper of doubt was taken as evidence of disloyalty, Akiko insisted bravely on the right to existence of a realm of purely private feeling, a realm in which the individual could express emotions freely and truthfully, without thinking of the consequences this might have for society at large, or of political or intellectual implications. Akiko's refusal to admit that she had written an antiwar poem is part and parcel of her more basic commitment to this realm, and to the individual. At times, it meant that she took positions on public matters that seemed contradictory or ambiguous, as here, when she wrote a poem that could be used as a manifesto for pacifism but angrily denied that she was a pacifist. This characteristic was a basic part of her. . . .

From 1909, Akiko's poetry also showed a change in tone that seemed to reflect a new kind of interest in women and in her own sexuality. Of her ninth tanka collection *Shundeishū* (Spring thaw, 1911), the earliest poems of which were first published in periodicals in 1909, she would later write: "I feel that with this collection I returned to the female. Before it, without conscious intent on my part, my imagination had come to transcend the division of sexes". . . .

The speaker of Akiko's early poems was sometimes a goddess of love, at other times a flagrantly narcissistic twenty year old who believes her beautiful black hair has the power to lure men to their deaths, at still others one who loves so intensely that the everyday world has ceased to exist. All these, and others, existed in a realm of absolutes, truly transcendent. The speaker of the poems in *Spring Thaw* was different, closer to a real woman. Perhaps this is part of what Akiko meant by her phrase "the return to the female." In any case, most of the poems in *Spring Thaw* are more comfortable to be around and at the same time more affecting in a simple way than many of those in *Tangled Hair* and the other earlier collections.

Akiko's support for Japan's first feminist magazine, *Seitō* (Bluestocking), exemplified another aspect of her "return to the female." The most famous of the twelve poems she contributed to its debut issue in 1911 is *Yama no Ugoku Hi* (The day the mountains move).

Janine Beichman. *Japan Quarterly*. 37, 1990,
pp. 37, 205–6, 210, 212, 214,
217–19, 226

Having established herself as a noteworthy and innovative romantic poet before she turned thirty, [Yosano Akiko] continued to publish an extraordinary number of poems throughout the late Meiji and into the Taishō era (1912–26). Her love for her eleven children provided the impetus for a series of poetic works and children's tales such as: *Yatsu no yoru* (1914; Eight nights) and *Uneunekawa* (1915; Meandering river).

In 1912 Yosano went to France, her first experience abroad, . . . and stayed in Europe for about half a year. While the trip partly inspired another one of Yasano's poetry collections, entitled *Natsu yori aki e* (1914; From summer to fall), more importantly it further stimulated Yasano's already burgeoning interest in feminist issues. After returning to Japan, she began to publish social commentaries on a wide range of topics related to women and education, including such collections as *Hito oyobi onna to shite* (1916; As a human being and a woman), *Warera nani o motomuru ka* (1917; What are we seeking?), *Ai, risei oyobi yūki* (1917; Love, reason, and courage), and *Gekidō no naka o yuku* (1919; Walking into the midst of upheaval). To practice what she preached about women's education, she became in 1921 the school superintendent of the Academy of Culture, a school that advocated a liberal educational philosophy.

Among Yosano's extensive publications were fifteen collections of essays and three volumes of critical writings on the art of poetry. She was also an indefatigable translator of some of the major works of classical Japanese literature into modern Japanese, the most noteworthy of which was her unprecedented four-volume translation of the eleventh-century romance *Genji monogatari (The Tale of Genji)* entitled *Shin' yaku Genji monogatari* (1912–13; A modern translation of *The Tale of Genji*). Toward the end of her life, she even renewed her efforts in producing yet another eight-volume translation of the same work called *Shin shin' yaku Genji monogatari* (1938–39; The newest translation of *The Tale of Genji*).

Yosano continued to publish collections of her poetry and essays in the early part of the Shōwa period (1926–89) such as *Kokoro no enkei* (1928; The distant scene in the heart), *Hikaru kumo* (1928; The glistening clouds), and *Man-mō yūki* (1930; Travels in Manchuria and Mongolia). But among her later works, the most notable was probably her collection *Hakuōshū* (1942; A collection of white cherry blossoms). Published posthumously, many of the poems imparted Yosano's feelings of melancholy and loneliness after the death of [her husband] Hiroshi as well as her reflections on her own illness. She died at the age of sixty-three (sixty-five by Japanese count).

The most prolific and well-known of modern Japanese women poets, Yosano has been best remembered for the sensual quality of her poems and their innovative imagery enlivened by a vibrant, imaginative diction. This was especially true of her romantic love poems collected in her most widely read and most thoroughly studied collection, *Midaregami*. Her long poem "Kimi shi ni tamōkoto nakare" (1904; "Heaven Forbid That You Shall Die!" 1951), published in the midst of the Russo-Japanese War and harshly criticized by the contemporary poet Ōmachi Keigetsu (1869–1925) as unpatriotic, has been cherished by some critics after 1945 as one of the most celebrated antiwar poems in prewar Japan, while others have noted its limitations. All her other poetry collections and her writings in other genres are much lesser known and are awaiting scholarly attention both in Japan and abroad.

> Chia-ning Chang. In Steven R. Serafin and Walter D. Glanze, eds. *Encyclopedia of World Literature in the 20th Century* (New York: Continuum, 1993), pp. 648–49

YOUNG, MARGUERITE (UNITED STATES) 1909–95

Marguerite Young (*A Moderate Fable*) . . . is another who does not seem quite to have come into her own. She scatters her powers unduly among modern physical concepts and a semisurrealist technique. Under this virtuosity of surface, however, she appears to be experiencing authentic emotions and making imaginative observations.

> Louise Bogan. *The New Yorker.* October 21, 1944, p. 92

Miss Marguerite Young's *Angel in the Forest*, which she subtitles "A Fairy Tale of Two Utopias," is one of the most interesting books of nonfiction I've come across in some time. It is also a hard one to describe. Miss Young, whose first book of prose this is (she has already, though, had two volumes of verse published), sets out to tell the story of New Harmony, Indiana. New Harmony is largely forgotten now, but during the early part of the last century, as the seat of two short-lived social experiments, one established in 1804 by German Separatists under the leadership of George Rapp and the other founded in 1825 by Robert Owen, the English philanthropist and industrialist, it was very much talked about. It is not quite accurate, however, to say that Miss Young "tells" the story of New Harmony. Her book is more a prolonged brooding upon it and the small bit of social and human history that was enacted there; it is a series of poetic evocations which try to capture some of the mood and emotion of the past. There were times when I felt that Miss Young was attempting to do in prose what might better have been done in poetry, and times when I thought she was attempting to say poetically what might have been better said in straightforward prose, and still other times when, forced to consult the *Encyclopaedia Britannica* and the *Dictionary of American History* to find out just what *did* go on out in New Harmony, that I deeply wished she hadn't been so reluctant to give dates, to sketch in backgrounds, and to do a few more of the dull chores that are fairly essential to a book of historical non-fiction. But there is not a page of her volume that doesn't show signs of a definite talent, and the short chapters about present-day New Harmony, interspersed with those about the New Harmony of the past, struck me as being very good indeed. I can't promise that everyone will be interested, because the book bogs down now and then, but Miss Young is plainly a writer worth keeping your eye on.

Hamilton Basso. *The New Yorker.*
April 7, 1945, p. 83

Marguerite Young's titanic novel [*Miss MacIntosh, My Darling*] has been in slow generation for more than seventeen years. During this period, published sections of it have signaled, like surfaced bubbles, the dynamism of the submerged whole. Now it appears before us on 1,198 pages. What we behold is a mammoth epic, a massive fable, a picaresque journey, a Faustian quest and a work of stunning magnitude and beauty.

Miss MacIntosh, an old, drowned woman, is "reality" to Vera Cartwheel, whose tidal monologue relates her search for that reality. Broken-nosed, bald-headed Miss MacIntosh was a "plainly sensible woman" who spoke in proverbs and axioms to her young charge. She was nursemaid to the voyager-narrator, whose mother languishes in grandiose dreams under opium in a baroque New England seaside house among imaginary guests and companions whom she "dreams." Miss MacIntosh is unadorned, bare-breasted fact; the uncovered pate of reality; illusion stripped of its wig, its false bosom. . . .

Vera Cartwheel's very environment is illusion, delusion, fantasy. She struggles against "dreaming" people, but when she turns from what is illusion she encounters only illusion again. . . . Vera Cartwheel begins a search for her drowned reality which was, in ironic effect, illusion.

The story of the novel is simply this, and it is created by Vera Cartwheel's journey to rediscover "Miss MacIntosh," whose drowning was never certified. . . .

This is the theme and ground of this sweeping, swelling and inexhaustibly breeding fiction, which pulls behind it, on and on, page after page, loads and burdens of images proliferating images; precise catalogings; inventories and enumerations and facts, plants, hats, heraldries, geographies, birds, rivers, cities ancient and modern, kings and dynasties and archeologies. It breaks into conceits, images, metaphors, preciosities, bizarreries. Concrete character detail elaborates into huge metaphors, into musicalizations, rhapsodies, repetitively rolling and resounding and doubling back upon themselves in an oceanic tumult.

The book's mysterious readability is effected through enchantment and hypnosis. Its force is cumulative; its method is amassment, as in the great styles of Joyce or Hermann Broch or Melville or Faulkner, where references and context become muddled through constant and compulsive tormenting of basic obsessive themes.

Rarely does American fiction break out into fullness of song, into the force and vigor of increase, of organic embellishment. . . . In *Miss MacIntosh, My Darling,* we have come upon a strong, deep loudness, a full-throated outcry, a literature of expanse and daring that makes most of our notable male writers look like a motorcycle gang trying to prove a kind of literary masculinity.

What might appear to be ornateness of style for its own sake . . . is Miss Young's method of relentlessly examining the complexities of her characters and themes. Her style is the very theme itself. We must read this major American work as a passionate affirmation of the snares of its own vision; as an obsessive probing of that vision until its obscure interior turns outward and allows itself to be looked at fearlessly, revealing its very terrible nature. . . .

Miss MacIntosh, My Darling, soaring into the universal, has rooted itself in the American reality. . . . The novel is, in this writer's judgment, one of the most arresting literary achievements in our last twenty years. . . . It is a masterwork.

She has been lurking, like one of her own "dreamed" characters in search of themselves, on the edge of American literature and letters for many years, ominous, shadowy, emerging. She has arrived and her arrival must be proclaimed.

William Goyen. *The New York Times.*
September 12, 1965, p. 5

Miss MacIntosh, My Darling is simply a huge, badly written, apparently not edited, undisciplined spilling out of words in a by now conventional and repetitive blend of a Joycean–*On The Road* credo that as long as you can get it on paper or on tape, anything goes. . . .

What is real, What is dream? is a central question. But it is a thing which is lost in a fantastic assemblage of words, characters and situations touching on drug addiction, women suffrage, murder, suicide, pregnancy (real and imagined), schizophrenia, many strange loves, the psychology of gambling, perfectionism, etc. In the end, one is faced with 1,198 pages of unrelieved phantasmagoria. . . .

It is the shrill, strained lyricism of such prose which gives Miss Young's book the quality of highly charged, very emotional, but unworked poetry (she is the author of two books of poetry). Her book exemplifies, it seems to me, the essential problem of the poem—or novel—left unsolved: unsorted elements, complicated movements, insoluble obscurity—all to the detriment of artistic moderation.

J. M. Edelstein. *The New Republic*.
October 2, 1965, pp. 28–29

Miss Young . . . is "poetic" in a bad sense; in love with words, certainly, but given to endless verbal doodling, the infinitely repetitious elaboration of a single idea over dozens of pages at a time. The prodigious length of her book is not the result of an excess of content, the proliferation of characters and events of the usual jumbo-sized fictional saga: quite simply, it is because her principle of composition is never to use one word if fifteen thousand will do instead. Still, one must be as fair as possible. There can be no doubt that Miss Young does have genuine gifts for the creation of fiction and, in particular, for the writing of evocative imagistic prose. . . .

It is, presumably, pointless to attack Miss Young for not providing something she was not interested in providing. The novel offers a "poetic" rather than a dramatic interest, in intention at least, and we must not complain if the handful of characters disappear for hundreds of pages at a time in a dense verbal goulash.

So the novel stands or falls by its language alone. For short stretches Miss Young's prose, as I have indicated, does have a certain lyrical and evocative power. But the stretches are rarely short, and the kind of prose-poetry which works in brief paragraphs—as for instance in Rimbaud's *Illuminations*—becomes intolerable when protracted over an infinity of pages. Nor, for that matter, are Miss Young's images particularly arresting; she relies very heavily on those traditional properties of the brooding northern imagination which occur so often in literary works with a Gothic tinge: ghosts, angels, snow, fog, darkness, stars, mirrors, ice, rain, moons, seagulls, clouds, the sea. Rimbaud and Dylan Thomas got a good deal of mileage out of them and although they can be described as some of the personal archetypes of the human imagination, Miss Young makes very conventional use of them. . . .

As Dr. Johnson remarked of Ossian, "A man might write such stuff forever if he would but abandon his mind to it."

Bernard Bergonzi. *New York Review of Books.* November 27, 1965, pp. 34–35

The book is too big and too leisurely to read or judge in the usual way— a vast city of associations, classical and modern, in which floating spirits interpenetrate and external realities of time and place break down to become a startling myth of the archetypal human life. One recalls for many reasons, the Joycean archetypes, Father, Mother, Son, Daughter, Poet. It is directly to Joyce, I think, that Miss Young is speaking and she is saying No. No to the Aristotelean view of life as a conflict of generation, corruption, and re-creation; no to the Joycean theory of history, and, above all, no to the theory of love as constraint. Like Joyce, Miss Young knows what tales are worth telling—she has carloads of them, as does Joyce—and like Joyce she tells her tale with highly conscious, highly artificial style. The great difference, from which its further differences sprout, is that Miss Young is a thoroughgoing Platonist—a startling thing to encounter in our time. Thus while both boldly seize as their theme "Everything," the word means more (quantitatively) to Joyce than to Miss Young. Joyce offers a metaphysical explanation of the alphabet; Miss Young is not interested in the alphabet as such but only in the fact that spellings, right or wrong, reflect some remove from the Idea. Joyce is interested in particular responsibilities of specific kings and statesmen as well as in the generic idea Kingship (the crown and scepter, hat and cane), and he relates these to the responsibilities of the father, son, and poet. Miss Young leaps at once to Kingship as love, with hats and cane-like objects (also cloaks, capes, robes) functioning as Freudian symbols. Her allusive style alludes always to the same eternal forms in their infinite disguises; her symbols all center in the same idea. And so, whereas the length of *Finnegans Wake* is justified by the density of the book, its analyses of particulars— places, occupations, institutions, rituals—the bloated length of *Miss MacIntosh* is an effect, simply, of system. The manifestations of recurrent embodiments of the Idea might, in one sense, be broken off at any point: they dramatize a vision which is just as clear and possibly even as convincing in the abstract. The book lacks the emotive power of compression in short; but I am not sure the idea admits of compression. If so, Platonism pushed to its limit is not artistically viable. And if this is true, I must nervously report, Platonism is false. . . .

Miss MacIntosh, My Darling presents the world as a glittering ruin, a dream; as death ("for were we not already dead, we who breathed and walked about, our breath like frozen plumes upon the winter air our eyeballs cracking in the cold?"). Miss Young has put the best years of her creative lifetime into this book, and her craftsmanship, even genius, is impressive. But the book is fiction.

John Gardner. *Southern Review.* n.s. 3, 1967, pp. 460–62

Like her apocryphal firefly, Marguerite Young flourishes outside the strictures of the canon, beyond its margins as well. As an experimental writer, who is also a woman—whose style is labyrinthine enough to withstand all but the most tenacious of readers—she is twice removed from "mainstream" American fiction. . . .

All of Young's works, whatever category readers choose for them, are utopian in the sense that each one recognizes the universal struggle for ideality and the impossibility of reaching it. Ensuring that her characters fail, and filling her utopias with losses, Young preserves the interfusion as well as the resulting *con*fusion of their efforts. With each loss, however, comes the dignity—and privilege—of surviving, a partial success, which is the only success that Young recognizes. As her characters and historical figures pursue what ultimately is, and must forever be chimerical, she records failure after failure: jobs bungled, messages confused, appointments forgotten, distances miscalculated. And loss after loss: lost leaders, lost causes, lost lovers, lost paradises, and specifically in *Angel in the Forest*, the abandoned utopian communities of George Rapp and Robert Owen in nineteenth-century America. Loss occurs early in Young's texts. At the start of *Angel in the Forest*, efforts to establish a new moral order are declared unsuccessful, their evocation laden with the "memory of failure"—"cobwebbed and insubstantial" like the dilapidated country ten-cent store that stands precariously where Rapp's "New Jerusalem" once prospered in New Harmony, Indiana. The title character of *Miss MacIntosh, My Darling* walks off into the frigid Atlantic waters, leaving behind a corset, a frazzled red wig, and a pair of glassless spectacles.

Young believes that all attempts—individual or communal—towards harmony and completion must, of necessity, be imperfect and incomplete, falling finally into disharmony and fragmentation. But she refuses to settle for anything *other* than fragmentation. "More complete in their incompletion than if they had been whole," her characters' broken and fleeting visions shatter conventions of Western logic so persistently and so utterly that they become, particularly in *Miss MacIntosh, My Darling*, the routine affairs of each day's work. For Young, nothing is factitious but the cultural-historical practice of declaring authenticity by subjecting phenomena to the constraints of binary logic.

Miriam Fuchs. *Review of Contemporary Fiction*. 9:3, 1989, pp. 166–67

Young's narrative "ends" on page 1198, but projecting an open-ended textuality, it does not "finish." Always in motion, it ends neither with Miss MacIntosh, nor with the handful of characters that have occupied hundreds of pages. It ends instead with the slow-moving, uneducated Esther Longtree, who surfaces when the book is nearly complete. The novel's two-line final paragraph (its very brevity suggesting incompletion) describes Esther's shutting the restaurant to take a lunch break, a closure that promises reopening.

Vera explains: "She would hang a sign in the restaurant window—Owt to luntsch. Bee bak in a whale." Vera avoids the precision of the past tense (she hung a sign) and the confidence implied by the future tense (she will hang a sign) for the indeterminacy of the conditional tense (she "would hang"). Thus, the novel "ends" with an action that has yet to happen and may not happen, capturing the indefinite space between action and inaction. Exploring what a traditional novel would omit, in this instance, a space characterized by uncertainty but also by its potential, Vera's narrative takes place between possibility and fulfillment, between idea and action. . . .

This novel is story within story, dream within dream. Vera pours out her own "story," which is not a traditional quest, but the particles of a rich, liquid narrative. Always contradictory, *Miss MacIntosh* jolts and disrupts, but encircles as well, pouring out its secrets of life and birth and love. In her testament to the infinite potential for creation, Young casts this power in feminine terms of conception and fecundity. Feminine qualities rise to the surface and are stirred back in the text, surfacing again in male characters such as Mr. Spitzer, Young's way of emphasizing that feminine qualities—sympathy, nurturing, patience—are qualities that cross gender lines. Sixteen pages from the end, Mr. Spitzer confesses to Catherine that he is really Peon, who has learned slowly though the years to love her and to be faithful. His timing, as always, is off; Catherine has just died in his arms. One page before the end, Vera declares that she has conceived a child. And Esther Longtree is about to break for lunch.

Miriam Fuchs. In Miriam Fuchs and Ellen J.
Friedman, eds. *Breaking the Sequence:
Women's Experimental Fiction* (Princeton:
Princeton University Press, 1989),
pp. 196–97

Miss MacIntosh, My Darling inspires in the reader a strange vertigo, a kind of sensory and epistemological overload. In the course of Young's long, paratactic sentences, with their slow shifts and hypnotic repetitions, their exfoliations, divergences, and ramifications, any hope of imposing a unified meaning, of clinging to grammatical hierarchies and teleologies of action, is irretrievably lost. The book imposes its own slow but inexorable rhythms upon the reader; it alters the very possibilities of comprehension, because there is simply *too much* to read. And this "too much," this richness and complexity, is a surplus in an absolute, and not merely a quantitative, sense. The chief resources of Young's language are materiality and plurality, resonance and redundancy. Everything is said so many times, in so many different ways, that it becomes impossible to isolate or specify anything which might simply be asserted once and for all. Reiteration becomes a principle of variation and difference. In the blur of echoes and enlargements, any point of origin, any privileged reference, any founding signifier, is erased, or else transformed beyond recognition. The novel reiterates, therefore, the interchangeability of beginning and end, as of all other polarities: "And his night was his day, and his day was his night, for his twilight was his dawn and his dawn was his twilight, and his moon was his sun, and his sun was his moon, and his beginning was his end, and his end was his beginning." The novel resists fixed categories, because it is pleonastic to the point of excess: the empty space of repetition becomes an inexhaustible reservoir of fragments and semblances of meaning.

Steven Shaviro. *Review of Contemporary Fiction.* 9:3, 1989, pp. 191–92

Marguerite Young's masterpiece *Miss MacIntosh, My Darling* is the kind of work I meant when I referred to "a book that is a whole world," one in which (to start at the top) God is a familiar presence—or a familiar absence, since the emphasis is so often on God's limitations or on what God has forgotten, omitted, been careless about, or that which "was never God's way of life." Terrestrial nature and ordinary people, solid reality, the level of middle earth that belongs to the disciplines of geography and agronomy and government, is another layer of that total universe, the level in which Miss MacIntosh herself is rooted. Finally, there is the individual, whose mind is the microcosm of these two larger (if not greater) orders. . . .

But beyond all this—for the thing about Marguerite Young's modernism, at least, if not all modernisms, is that there can be something that is beyond the entire universe that holds everything within it—is narrative. The world is made up of stories, dozens, hundreds of stories. They form a mosaic, a stained-glass window, a patchwork quilt of stories. (All of these being inapt metaphors, because their appeal is to the eye, whereas Marguerite Young's prose is addressed to the mind's eye but the body's ear.) Even among the encyclopedic narratives in our literary history, there are not many that tell you so many stories that the master narrative seems to consist of nothing but other stories. *The Divine Comedy,* maybe, in itself a quest tale, but one whose quest-journey is leading up (literally up) to something—in fact to "the love that moves the sun and the other stars," which is pretty much everything. Young's equally authentic quest concludes with the end of just one more constituent story, with the novel's penultimate sentence a final punch line, the sign in a restaurant window reading "Owt to luntsch. Bee bak in a whale."

Now, Dante's concluding line, one of the most significant in the history of Western writing, leads the reader forward to perfection, which means the end of narrative. Young's conclusion, deliberately unimportant, turns the reader right back into the text, which is to say into the comprehensive heart of narrative. . . .

Not all the narratives that go into making the master narrative of *Miss MacIntosh, My Darling* are women's stories. (Where, for instance, would we or the novel be without Mr. Spitzer?) But it gives women a great deal more than half the text and, with it, implies that their stories matter—if not in the final sense that the love that moves the sun and the other stars may be said to matter. Miss MacIntosh herself would surely point out that that is not, in any event, our affair. Simply, Marguerite Young lets us know, women's stories matter *as stories. . . .*

Although Marguerite Young is like Dante (and Bunyan and the authors of the Bible) in constituting her narrative out of stories, she is like Blake in the essential nature that directs her narrative. That nature is visionary, not as the mystic is, but as the secular revolutionary—the two Young is obsessed with, for instance [Robert Owen and Eugene Debs]—*has* to be. It is only the critic, in fact, who looks for other places in *literature* where this impulse finds expression. For Young, what is important is the embodiment of the vision itself.

> Lillian S. Robinson. In Miriam Fuchs, ed.
> *Marguerite Young, Our Darling: Tributes*
> *and Essays* (Normal, Illinois: Dalkey
> Archive, 1994), pp. 66–67, 69

Through the individual, Young portrays the age, and her approach to the historical research for the biography is similar to her approach to creating a character in her novel. "You have the same thematic relationship to that research—the flood, the ebb, the flow of history. But the river is a dream—imagination. You have the same relationship to it as you do to the unconscious. It takes over, and you can do the same artistic writing. The fact is that all these people, no matter who they were, of which political party or whether they were opposed to utopia or not, all had a *lingua franca* which all understood and which was based upon poetry, like Whitman, Melville, Longfellow, or Lowell—they all spoke in metaphors. It's about myth, the architect of heaven on earth, the earthly paradise, the lost Atlantis, Noah's Ark—it was for many, many socialists. So they have these dream boats, these enchanted birds speaking, savants coming down through all the millennia. So transcendental socialism preceded Marx. And I go into all that." Through the figure of Debs, she encompasses the age, and the voices of all the poets, philosophers, and social reformers whose ideas propelled the settlement of the New World with a vision of the new social order. Young's pluralistic vision is the spirit of the age.

In each of her works, Young's epic imagination broadened its scope and depth. If her poetry led to the writing of historical work, *Angel in the Forest,* then in pursuing the same themes she explored the psychic dimensions of her characters in a work of fiction in the manner of Joyce's *Ulysses* and Proust's *Remembrance of Things Past.* The creation of the archetypes in her fiction contributed to the scope of her biography of Debs in which the life of one individual gives expression to the spirit of his time. Thus, in these different literary genres can be seen the evolution and the shaping of Marguerite Young's epic imagination.

> Charles Ruas. In Miriam Fuchs, ed.
> *Marguerite Young, Our Darling: Tributes*
> *and Essays* (Normal, Illinois: Dalkey
> Archive, 1994), pp. 83–84

In this age of much-needed multicultural explorations, debates, and struggles, one cannot help but ask, as Young's work challenges us to do: Is it actually possible to define accurately a nation's cultural reality? Can we ever "know" our own cultural reality, even when not ignoring the regional discrepancies that make up the diversity of the United States? According to Young, paying close attention to the minute details that shape our cultural identities itself does not necessarily provide us with a grasp of the cultural reality of the American ways of life. Indeed, *Miss MacIntosh, My Darling,* like her other works, helps us to realize that in trying to describe it, reality does resemble, as she has often pointed out, a hawk rather than a tamed canary easily caged in definitions. Hence her lifelong quest for this visible yet eternally elusive bird in flight, America.

> Suzanne Oboler. In Miriam Fuchs, ed.
> *Marguerite Young, Our Darling: Tributes*
> *and Essays* (Normal, Illinois: Dalkey
> Archive, 1994), p. 91

YOURCENAR, MARGUERITE (FRANCE) 1903–87

Critics have been severe with *The New Eurydice;* I am not quite sure why. Did its form—both abstract and delicate—seem out-of-date to some of my colleagues? Was Marguerite Yourcenar the target of one of those pasing fits of bad temper to which the members of my profession occasionally fall victim? I cannot say, but I am astonished at the reception given this fine, serious book, somewhat austere and owing nothing to current fashion—which may be the problem. Many people, when faced with a novel whose form is classical, feel, I suppose, the same kind of remoteness they feel when, in an exhibition, they see a painting that looks severe, noble, and serious, a painting that gives them the impression that the artist worked on it in depth, not simply to please the eye. That is what is called a "museum painting." There are also "museum novels." *The New Eurydice* is admittedly such a novel, and we are fortunate that a few writers are still working to produce "museum novels" when so many other writers only produce "window novels"—novels to put in the bookstore window, novels that will catch the eye of the passer-by for three months and then vanish from sight.

The interest of Yourcenar's book arises not only from her subject and the sincerity of her psychological analysis but also from her narration. Like Jacques Chardonne, whom she sometimes reminds me of, she is even more a moralist than a novelist, and the commentaries she makes about the situations in which her characters find themselves are almost always admirable. These commentaries are the means by which she situates her characters both in life and in the plot.

> Edmond Jaloux. *Nouvelles Littéraires.*
> February 13, 1932, p. 3

[*Memoirs of Hadrian* is] one of those very rare books that suddenly thrusts us high above the level of the current literary offerings; it is a masterly work that demands our esteem and our admiration.

Hadrian writes in his memoirs: "Every time I have seen a man die in the prime of his life, a man whose successes and failures seemed easy for the world to evaluate, I have remembered that at that age I did not yet exist except in my own eyes and in the eyes of a few friends, who must have had doubts about me just as I had doubts about myself." One could almost apply these words to Marguerite Yourcenar as well. Her name was made known by about ten books published during the ten years that preceded World War II. Her short *Alexis, or, Treatise on Useless Combat* showed some of her preoccupations. *Pindar* revealed her fondness for antiquity. She certainly had the esteem of the "happy few," a reputation in a rather narrow circle. After twelve years of silence, we have *Memoirs of Hadrian,* a work of maturity, and now her name must become known to every reader for whom the word "culture" still has a meaning: she has established herself dazzlingly as one of the most important women writers in French literature. . . .

On my copy of *Memoirs of Hadrian,* Yourcenar was kind enough to write this meaningful phrase by Flaubert: "The gods having died and Christ not yet having been born, there was, between Cicero and Marcus Aurelius, a unique moment when man alone existed. . . ." This is indeed the moment that Marguerite Yourcenar captures in this book, and the meditation upon that wisdom is what gives the book its value—the wisdom of solitary man, which is also his serenity. One inevitably thinks of the loud declarations made by the writers and philosophers of today about the death of God and the solitude of man. Recently journalists have been arguing over who was the first and best blasphemer: Sartre, Cocteau, or Thierry Maulnier. Is this not a ridiculous and indecent spectacle? How much more dignified is the attitude of Hadrian (and the intelligence of his era), how much richer in understanding as well, how much more fertile for heart, mind, and action.

Robert Kanters. L'Age nouveau.
February, 1952, pp. 74–75

Conscientious as Miss Yourcenar has been in presenting the externals of the emperor and his realm [in *Memoirs of Hadrian*], such information may after all be obtained on high authority if not as agreeably in unimaginative handbooks. Her highest success is in a field beyond the range of the orthodox historian, a field to which only the imaginative writer can be adequate, but in which he frequently fails, especially if he is dealing with a non-Christian environment. What was the actual ethical and psychological climate in which these people lived and acted? How did a highly intelligent, responsible, and sensitive man regard the relations between his body and soul and between both and the universe in the period just before a sharp dualism between body and soul, between man and eternal reality, became an unquestioned assumption?

It is difficult almost to the point of impossibility to think away two millennia of a different tradition, whether we adhere to that tradition or reject it, difficult to reconstruct Hadrian's relations to his gods, his conscience, his family, his beloved Antinous, his carnal appetites, to Jews and Christians without revealing moral disapproval, however dissembled, or labored or truculent approval. Hadrian must not be made a stick with which to belabor either Christians or pagans, ascetics or libertines. Miss Yourcenar has come as near as can be to assaying Hadrian's position in these central matters in his own and not alien terms; for us, then, the unfamiliar motivations are a new increment of knowledge rather than a confirmation of existing prejudices.

Moses Hadas. *Saturday Review of Literature.* November 27, 1954, p. 12

Marguerite Yourcenar travels in time as well as space, and on the morning I visited her, I left the feverish exhilaration of the streets of the Left Bank to enter a quiet little salon and talk about the sixteenth century, to which I had traveled [in *Signs and Wonders*] just as she had [in *The Work in Black*]. For her admirable book is also a guidebook, with burning landscapes: Münster, where Anabaptists, starved for purity, saw their splendid dream of a just city annihilated; the hearth of the alchemists, whose mysterious apparatus concealed secrets and symbols that are lost today; the hearth of the human body as well, rediscovered both in its most material aspect (the adventure of the first dissections) and as a mystic symbol (those Adamites who suddenly ran naked into the streets of Amsterdam one December, inspired by a sudden impulse of despair).

The fertile disorder of *The Work in Black* (the discoveries, the doubts, the extreme anguish and hope of men who were faced with challenges to the best-established truths) is not unreminiscent of our own era.

Is it a coincidence that Yourcenar's two most interesting protagonists, Hadrian [in *Memoirs of Hadrian*] and Zeno, the doctor-alchemist-philosopher of *The Work in Black,* are both sages and, even before that, witnesses to their times? A witness herself, Yourcenar is far from indifferent to events. It is not that she is uninterested in the present; rather, the past is also present within her.

Françoise Mallet-Joris. *Le nouvelle observateur.* December 2–8, 1968, p. 44

Marguerite Yourcenar was born in 1903. Her novels turn away from the era through which she has lived. She was born in Brussels: her novels either never mention Belgium or only refer to it in terms of the Flanders of the sixteenth century, so different from the Belgium of today. Since 1939, Marguerite Yourcenar has been living in the United States, but that country and that continent, although they have furnished material for her as a translator, have found no place in her novels. After her mother's death, a few days after Marguerite's birth, Yourcenar lived in France, and spent her childhood on a family farm in the north of France, in Paris, and in Provence. Yet that farm, that city, and those parts of France are described by the novelist only in *The New Eurydice*.

For many years the author was a part-time instructor in two American colleges. No protagonist, no character in her work, is a member of the teaching profession. She has devoted her life to literature. Her life as a writer, her difficulties and torments, her joys and sorrows, have left scarcely a trace on her novels. This writer is a woman, and more attention should be given to the role of women in Yourcenar's work, but it is impossible not to observe immediately that all her central characters are men: Hadrian, Alexis, Stanislas [in *The New Eurydice*], and Zeno [in *The Work in Black*].

In short, everything seems to interest Yourcenar except herself; every life except her own; every condition except the one destined to be hers. . . . The greater her distance from her subject—as in *Memoirs of Hadrian*—the more beautiful and important the book.

Jean Blot. *Marguerite Yourcenar* (Paris:
Éditions Seghers, 1971), pp. 9–10

In *Pious Memories* [Yourcenar] tells of her family background and birth. Indeed, one might venture to call this biography intra-uterine, because it ends a week after the author's birth, when her mother Fernande dies of puerperal fever. Yourcenar sets out in quest of this unknown face, using her mother as well as many other ancestors to ask the eternal question: Who am I? She answers the question only indirectly, going as far back into the past as she was able to by a search of her family archives.

What arises from nothingness in this book is the story of an aspect of bourgeois Belgium. Yourcenar's gift for ventriloquism and for a vision of the past are marvelously effective in describing distant great-uncles and cousins who died a hundred years before her birth. They are seen in all their weaknesses and bourgeois self-importance. In this magical writer the trembling of memory takes on a sort of epic grandeur, and we become as interested (the word is weak) in the difficulties of Rémo—one of her uncles—as if he were one of our own relatives suddenly torn from us.

The "pious memories" of the title refer to the naïve portraits of the deceased which are sent to his friends and which, slipped into a prayer book, serve to perpetuate his memory. Each portrait has a few lines underneath it taken from the Gospels or inspired by the departed one: thus, Marguerite's father wrote, among other things, on the "pious memory" of her mother Fernande: "She always tried to do her best." One can imagine the perplexity produced by this cloudy phrase.

Yourcenar's own portrait remains vague; her own motivations remain secret. She will never confess anything—or perhaps she is saving her confessions for another book. Her genealogical tree hides the forest of her private feelings: that is not the least charm of this sublime book. The detailed history that she has drawn up of her family through the centuries serves to mask the historian. . . . But *Pious Memories* is perhaps Marguerite Yourcenar's richest book.

Jean-Didier Wolfromm. *Magazine littéraire.*
June, 1974, p. 36

Marguerite Yourcenar, the first woman elected to the Académie Française, is a French novelist and dramatist. . . . She published her first play in 1921; her most famous novel in the United States is *Memoirs of Hadrian;* she translated Virginia Woolf's *The Waves* in 1937; and, since her election to the "immortals," she is beginning to receive the international critical attention her large body of work deserves. Her career as a twentieth-century writer spans more than half the century.

When I consider her place in literary history, I am amazed that she has received so little attention as a writer responding to the sexual and political crises of the twentieth century. Defining "political" broadly, to include all relations of power, I find that Yourcenar's political analysis of sexuality and modern culture shapes both her characters and her narratives. Here, I would like to explore sexual politics in her 1939 novel, *Coup de Grâce,* which is a confessional narrative set between the two world wars.

Although her preface to the 1981 translation denies any political value in this human document, the mutual bonding of authoritarian and submissive personalities portrayed in the love triangle of Erick, Sophie, and Conrad certainly derives from a political critique of her culture. In the same preface, she implicitly acknowledges the contemporary historical relevance of her 1939 novel, by alluding to Racine's *Bajazet* as "a tragedy of events close to his own time but occurring in what was then the closed world of the Ottoman Empire." Yourcenar's own novel is a tragedy of events relevant to the impending second European war, but occurring two decades earlier, in 1919–20. Although she has refused to accept the concepts of "feminine discourse" or "feminine writing," her narrative nevertheless reveals that language reflects the gender-linked relations of power. . . .

Coup de Grâce calls for a radical revisioning of culturally based gender stereotypes and requires the reader to envision alternatives to passivity when faced with the threat of violence.

Yourcenar has stated that she began writing *Coup de Grâce* in 1938, in response to the September Munich conference, at which Daladier and Chamberlain, the French and British prime ministers, hoping by their submission to gain peace in their time, yielded to Hitler's demand to "repatriate" Germanic peoples dwelling in the Sudetenland of Czechoslovakia. The conference raised questions about nationality, cultural history, and the proper response to the threat of force; *Coup de Grâce* demands consideration of these same three issues. The novel was published in May of 1939, after the failure of the Munich compromise was evident, but before the German invasion of Poland.

Yourcenar's historical fiction interprets the origin of the Nazi movement in the post-World War I *Freikorps* fighting in the Baltic against Bolshevik revolutionaries. The Baltic cross, or Swastika, those soldiers of fortune brought back to Germany symbolizes the continuity between the Baltic terror of 1919 and the threat of 1939. Like the broken string of pearls Erick carried with him as a memento of Sophie, the Baltic cross is a sign of past actions predicting and defining future character. *Coup de Grâce* is a contemporary historical parable, in which the events of 1919 forecast the events of 1939.

In 1939, reviewers failed to connect contemporary politics with the narrative of Yourcenar's historical novel. Edmond Jaloux, reviewing the novel in August 1939, in *Les Nouvelles Littéraires,* defined it as "une histoire vraie," and Jean Charpentier, in the September 1, 1939 issue of *Mercure de France,* noted "la vérité historique," but neither noted that Yourcenar's psychological tragedy might be relevant to France's moral dilemma of choosing submission or resistance to violent force. Her novel portrays individuals facing that dilemma, and the implications for her national culture in 1939 should have been sobering.

> Judith L. Johnston. In Alice Kessler-Harris
> and William McBrien, eds. *Faith of a*
> *(Woman) Writer* (1984; Westport,
> Connecticut: Greenwood Press, 1988),
> pp. 221–22

Marguerite Yourcenar, by the very independence and creativity of her production, is one of the most original writers of the second half of the twentieth century, and throughout the world today, from the United States to Japan, from Finland to Israel, her enthusiasts are legion.

Her literature portrays characters who rebel against arbitrary moral and sexual strictures ("I believe in the nobility of refusal") and underscores male homosexuality and deviance as important themes common to many of these characters, along with a certain sadistic comportment in their relationships with their feminine counterparts. This is why Yourcenar has been accused by critics, if not of advocating misogyny, as least of favoring contempt for women, citing the conspicuous absence of heroines as proof of their conclusions. Not only are such statements unfair, they are also incorrect. Female characters do appear in her fiction and theater and either have an important supporting role (for instance, Thérèse of *La Nouvelle Eurydice* [The new Eurydice], Plotina of *Mémoires d'Hadrien* [Hadrian's memoirs], Martha of *L'Oeuvre au noir* [Work in black], or are essential to the action of the story and the psychology of the participants: these include, for example, Marcella (*Denier du rêve* [Coin in a dream; Coin in nine hands], Sophie *(Le Coup de grâce),* Electra *(Electre),* Anna *(Anna, soror . . .),* and many from *Nouvelles orientales* (Oriental tales) and *Feux* (Fires). What has vexed some of her detractors has been Yourcenar's unwillingness to join the needless discrimination inherent in the category, *women* writers, since she feels that she does not write as a woman and sees no difference between feminine and masculine writing. Rather, she is an author who happens to be a woman and whose works should be judged on their merit alone. That she objects to a new ghettoization has not precluded her from committing her energy and talent to good causes, including equality—but not similarity—of women in personal, political, or professional endeavors, the fight for Indian and black rights (see her preface to *Fleuve profond, sombre rivière*) and against other social and governmental evils.

By demonstrating that the power of myth and the ineluctable course of history are useful sources of inspiration, Yourcenar has achieved her creative goals. Moreover, she has constructed an absurd world in which man's destiny is directed as much by chance *(le hasard)* as by free will. Alexis, Conrad, Hadrian, Zeno, and the others share the undercurrents created by the conflicts between society's demands and their passions. If and how they resolve these intense inner struggles are, of course, in a large measure results of the strength of their personality. Although some flounder in an unsatisfactory limbo, the majority succeed in imposing their own view of the world, whether through conscious *open-eyed* acceptance of their selves or planned deliberate suicide.

Yourcenar's novels, plays, and essays reveal an artistic subtlety that makes evident the universality of her personages as well as their uniqueness, and it is to all these parallel qualities that readers and critics alike have been attracted. Because she has kept aloof of the literary problems and fashions of the post-World War II period, preferring a restrained, well-order classical form of narration to convey her protagonists' emotions and intellectual force, her influence is not immediately noticeable, and yet there seems to be on the part of several contemporary French authors a desire to emulate the coldly fiery style, the eternal drama of "the human adventure," the concerns about a universe on the verge of self-destruction found in her writings. This is especially evident of such new-generation novelists as François Fontaine (*L'Usurpation ou le roman de Marc Aurèle,* 1979), Serge Bramly (*La Danse du loup,* 1982), and Paul Tabet (*Elissa Rhaïs,* 1982). Outside France, the best-known example is Umberto Eco with his *The Name of the Rose* (1980): we find here a narrative technique and an authorial approach and method reminiscent of Yourcenar's great fictional masterpieces.

Pierre L. Horn. *Marguerite Yourcenar*
(Boston: Twayne, 1985), pp. 96–97

There is of course a profoundly nostalgic strain that permeates Yourcenar's writing, and perhaps it is this characteristic that has given rise to conservative interpretations of her work. She both operates, at the level of her marked predilection for historical subject matter, and advocates within her works what might be termed a "nostalgic" return to times gone by. It is in no way, however, to an epoch of totalitarian sociopolitical structures that Yourcenar invites us to revert. The past that she nostalgically evokes is rather one that precedes the world as we have fashioned it. . . .

Examples of nostalgia for what has been lost are abundantly present in Yourcenar's work. It is almost as if this author cannot contemplate a landscape or an object without sliding back down the corridors of time, just as we saw Zeno do in the meditational abyss of *L'oeuvre au noir.* As the textual equation of Greco-Roman craftsmen with Belgian artisans of "deluxe religious bric-a-brac" suggests, when Yourcenar evokes a past upon which has been stamped the imprint of man, it is more often than not to reveal how perennial has been his volition to desecrate the world that gave him life.

One can also challenge the notion of Yourcenar's alleged conservatism, as Chaillot has pointed out, by looking at her choice of protagonists. With the apparent, but only apparent, exception of the emperor Hadrian—responsible, perhaps, singlehandledly for the puzzling assumption of this author's reactionary leanings—nearly all of her most compelling characters are variations on the theme of subversiveness. Nearly all, moreover, are victims of some form of oppression. . . .

Many of Yourcenar's translations, essays, and television documentaries attest to her volition to give a voice—a French voice—to the victimized. . . .

By these lights, one can clearly see that there is nothing in the least bit escapist about the existential or temporal distance that so often seems to stand between Yourcenar and the characters or epochs she depicts in her work. Her resurrection of our cultural past is an integral part of her connection to our present and concern for our future.

Joan E. Howard. *From Violence to Vision:*
Sacrifice in the Works of Marguerite
Yourcenar (Carbondale: Southern Illinois
University Press, 1992), pp. 266, 268, 272–73

Marguerite Yourcenar was conspicuously and understandably reticent about her private life. She lived in Mount Desert Island, Maine (she preferred to call it I'lle des Monts Déserts after Champlain) with the American Grace Frick until Frick's death. She admired Breughel and Bosch and her French father, who helped invent her *nom de plume.* (Yourcenar is a near-anagram for de Crayencour.) Novelist, poet, critic, biographer, translator and dramatist, she is regarded as an exemplary stylist who revives traditional forms, but her subjects are diverse and unconventional, particularly in matters of sexual desire, sexual taboos and sexual preference. Honored for her achievements in 1981 when she was seventy-eight, she became the first woman ever to be elected into the Académie Française even though she'd been an American citizen since 1947 and had warned her future colleagues she'd neither wear the traditional inaugural costume nor brandish the inaugural sword.

She is best known for the widely acclaimed novel *Memoirs of Hadrian* (1951), in which she reconstructs second-century Rome through the resonant voice of its introspective emperor. (She has described her work as having "one foot in scholarship, the other in magic arts.") Most of her protagonists have been male. Yourcenar reputedly remarked once that one cannot write about women; their lives are full of secrets. *Dear Departed* proves her wrong. . . .

Like its French namesake, *Dear Departed* is a *souvenir pieux* in its own right, a series of portraits of Yourcenar's mother and several maternal ancestors, all unknown to her except through scattered documents and occasional reminiscences. Unlike its namesake, it is an unsentimental meditation on how we know the past, if at all, and what it means to us, especially when we attempt to recreate it. . . .

That Fernande [her mother,] finally remains somewhat remote means only that *Dear Departed* is not really her story. It belongs, first and last, to the inventor who, while searching for her family, finds instead a way of expressing all she holds dear. Thus the most commanding portraits are those in which Yourcenar recognizes herself, as she does with the brothers Pirmez; the most poignant descriptions of her mother have less to do with Fernande per se than with Yourcenar's musings about her. In this way *Dear Departed* is immediate, candid, graceful and touching. Marguerite Yourcenar, in seeking her maternal heritage, has found a way to reveal herself.

Brenda Wineapple. *Women's Review of*
Books. 9, March 1992, pp. 12–13

ZAMORA, BERNICE (UNITED STATES) n.d.

Bernice Zamora is a . . . poet capable of singing in praise of "José el revoluci-
onario" (José the Revolutionary), whose "kisses arm as no other weapon,"
and of roundly denouncing the Chicano student activist's exploitation of
woman from his safe hiding place behind the banners and slogans of the
movimiento. In no uncertain terms she decries the Chicano's contradictory
use of political rhetoric ("The gringo [white man] is oppressing you, Babe!")
as he enjoys the benefits of a Ford fellowship, the sexual favors of *gabacha
guisas* (Anglo "chicks") as well as a Chicana lover, and the domestic pleasures
of a wife and five kids. When he demands to define her poetics, pointing out
that she must "write about social reality," she ironically proves that for her
and other Chicana poets, to write of "pájaros, mariposas [birds, butterflies],
and the fragrance / of oppressing perfume I smell somewhere" *is* to write
about social reality, woman's shared reality of being exploited in the name of
the *movimiento.*

Elizabeth J. Ordóñez. In Beth Miller, ed.
*Women in Hispanic Literature: Icons and
Fallen Idols* (Berkeley: University of
California Press, 1983), p. 322

The Chicana poets Bernice Zamora and Lorna Dee Cervantes, seem very
different, at first glance. Zamora is intellectual and academic; her poetry is
openly cultured, with intertextual references from authors like Shakespeare
and Robinson Jeffers. Metaphor and image predominate over anecdote in
her work. . . . Zamora pursued graduate work at Marquette and Stanford
Universities . . . and comes from the rural and conservative culture of
New Mexico.

[In her first book, *Restless Serpents,*] Zamora makes her poetry a space
of encounter between men and women; she seeks a collaboration between
equals instead of sexual separation and subordination. When the ideal does
not succeed, she seizes the power to celebrate a new ritual, that of writing
poetry about and for her people, about everything for Chicanas. In the end,
this ritual is that of the woman alone, isolated from man, the servant of sexual
and social impulses that she tries to dominate through poetry. In the last
poem of her text, "Restless Serpents," the vipers that were hidden, caught
in the image of the vertebral column, were free to impose a more openly
rebellious ceremony in which poetry would give them what they ask: the
devastation of everything.

Juan Bruce-Novoa. *Revista Iberoamericana.* 51, 1985, pp. 565–66, 573

Restless Serpents (1976) is an ambitious work of Chicano poetry that proposes a radical and complex critique of Western male power in social, cultural, psychoanalytical, and literary discourse. Zamora's interest in such a critique derives from her orientations to Third World literature, Third World movements, ethno-feminism, and from her divergent background. . . .

The metaphor of the restless serpent, it appears explicitly in at least two of her poems and implicitly throughout her book, coils and recoils the reader's praxis of transformation. Her work is a bouncing from reference to reference, from intertextual, extratextual, and inter-sexual codes that break through the constraints of "capitalist appropriations," to use Deleuze and Guattari's phrase. The serpents, indeed, are venomous beasts which can only be soothed by desiring machinic verse, "strokes more devastating than devastation arrived." As Bruce-Novoa stresses, "Zamora's poetry like those serpents fascinates: they are inscrutable signs of life and death in beautiful form, capable of demonic possession."

My hypothesis for Chicano poetics is this: Zamora's restless serpents and her sexually charged figures of speech can function as revolutionary investments of desire, capable of exploding the structures of Western male society. Her erotic art, moreover, is a concrete answer to the question of how our divisions and desires can deploy their forces within the social, political, and literary domain. . . .

Throughout *Restless Serpents,* Bernice Zamora wishes to explode our traditional notions of the human sexes. She does this primarily by making our sexual and cultural silences speak through her verse. She also examines the limits of sexuality and desire, which are never static entities. As Marta E. Sánchez has pointed out, Zamora's poems dramatize "what men have not permitted women to say, or what men themselves have not said." Zamora's world, in other words, is a world "within limits / Fixed by a law / which is not ours." Definitions of the Chicano-Chicana subject, as such, are imposed upon us by outsiders: God, government, and the state apparatuses. In our prisonhouse of sexual and erotic codes, we love each other, for "We have in common / the experience of love."

Zamora herself is a product of this highly repressive world. Colorado, her home state, and the rest of the Southwest have been conquered and colonized by Anglo-American males, the Catholic Church (priests), and by traditionally conservative Chicano males. *Restless Serpents,* therefore, necessarily dramatizes a world of violence, sexually-repressed silence, and productive erotic desire.

In the larger *Restless Serpents* frame of reference, Zamora's poem "So Not to Be Mottled" takes as her object of study conventional psychoanalytical discourse and interpretation. Her text is an expansion of two psychoanalytical opposites, the one male-centered and Oedipal in origin (a tale of neurosis); the other, a tale or allegory of an anti-oedipal, ethno-feminist tradition. "So Not to Be Mottled" covers the whole "blotching" and "streaking" of the subject.

Zamora's poem thus can be read as a critique of traditional Freudian sexist interpretation. "So Not to Be Mottled" suggests a negation of psychoanalytical reduction; namely, it's radical rewriting of the whole rich and random multiple realities of concrete everyday experience into the constrained, strategically prelimited terms of the neurotic. What Bernice Zamora denounces in her text is a system of interpretation of the subject in which the data of one's narrative line are impoverished by its rewriting according to the paradigm of another narrative.

Zamora's "So Not to Be Mottled" schizophrenizes rather than neuroticizes. Her ethno-feminist poems in *Restless Serpents,* I am suggesting, are desiring machines; she stores up her treasure so as to create an immediate explosion. Put plainly, the speaker in *Restless Serpents* in general, and in "So Not to Be Mottled" in particular, knows how to scramble the codes of the self, how to cause erotic flows to circulate, and how to transcend conventional schizophrenia. As such, Zamora's poetic ethno-feminist project desires to destroy the illusions of the ego, guilt, law, limits, and Western repression.

In brief, Zamora's reading of psychoanalytical interpretation is anti-interpretive. Its expansion of the Chicana-Chicano subject employs a vision of infinite division of the self. In this regard, Zamora's project suggests a montage of desiring machines, a schizoid exercise dramatizing a rhetoric of fragmentation that extracts from the text its social and revolutionary forces.

José David Saldívar. *Confluencia.* 1:2, 1986,
pp. 13–15

Releasing Serpents . . . is Zamora's first book in eighteen years and ends a self-imposed period of reclusiveness. After the 1976 publication of her now-legendary *Restless Serpents,* Zamora quit participating in the Chicano movement. She dropped out of sight after being active in a number of Flor y Cantos (literary festivals) and refused to edit any more anthologies or make public appearances. In the early 1980s, after a period of ill health and a short exile in Mexico, she returned to California. She never quit writing poetry, though she has purposely left much of her work unpublished. *Releasing Serpents* contains selections from her first book, some previously uncollected work from journals and thirty new poems. Reading twenty years' worth of work in one volume illuminates the process of aging in the poems. For Zamora, this journey has been one woman's struggle to come to terms with a very self-conscious identity within the rapidly evolving events of the Chicano movement. Community and leadership through the chaotic 1960s and 1970s meant a great deal to her. Her poems clearly show the choice of self-preservation—she backed off writing to save her own spirit—was the right one for her. It became the road that now gives her heightened power in her writing. Poems like "The Sovereign," "On Living in Aztlán" and those in the "Recounting the Day" series read like compact memories of the first farmworkers' strike against the grape growers or the 1972 Chicano Moratorium against the Vietnam War. What makes her short, imagistic poems so magnificent is the way she captures decades-old history, then thrusts it forward into the present without hesitation. Zamora's story is fascinating because of the risks she has taken in her writing, only to withdraw as a spokesperson for years. The newer poems cry with excitement, anger, moments of terrifying revelation and a hard-earned wisdom that sets the stage for Chicanos writing after her. Her poetry disturbs the reader in the same manner as the most lethal poems of Gabriela Mistral, Muriel Rukeyser and Linda Hogan. . . .

The poems in *Releasing Serpents* offer different identities for Chicanos to choose from. We can relate with familial and racial conflict, mourn the past or make the decision to break away from our community to grasp the larger world. Zamora does not offer easy choices. The poetic sequences, divided into seven sections in the book, can be read chronologically or at random. Either way, they say survivors from the 1960s are the ones we need to learn from. Their role, which some feel has been spent, is the identity many Chicanos still search for, despite this period of cultural abundance. Some of them fear that our artistic and social gains bring the danger of covering over the ongoing problems of racism, educational weakness, drugs and gang obsession. Poets like Zamora return because it is time to re-evaluate what has happened over the past three decades. By coming back through poetry, Zamora knows how to catch our attention.

Ray Gonzalez. *The Nation.*
January 31, 1994, pp. 131–32

ZARDOYA, CONCHA (SPAIN) 1914–

Zardoya, who spent some three decades in the United States teaching Spanish literature, returned to Spain permanently ten years ago. Well known as a critic and active as a translator (of Walt Whitman, among others), she has also been a steady producer of poetry since the mid-1940s. *Los perplejos hallazgos* joins twenty-three other collections of poetry which evince a broad and varied range of themes and many stylistic variations. An easily recognizable thematic unity characterizes the new collection, which has as its common denominator the poet's reactions to great works, specifically to the paintings and sculptures of famous contemporary artists whose expositions she has visited in Madrid, mostly in 1984 and 1985. By far the longest of the three sections into which the collection is divided is the first, "Homage to Paul Cézanne," which contains thirty-seven compositions of varied metrical forms, from the "Dialogue with Cézanne" in tercets of blank verse to a considerable number of sonnets—a favorite form—and many more in blank-verse quatrains. Zardoya has avoided characteristic Spanish assonance, preferring to rely almost solely on cadence, alliteration, and metaphors (among which prosopopeia predominates).

Other metrics appear in the second section, "Interlude," which includes poems inspired by works of Tàpies, Zóbel, Morandi, and Arp, treated mostly in free verse. The third section, "Homage to Juan Gris," comprises twenty unrhymed compositions, most often in seven-syllable lines. The collection in its entirety represents the lyric transfiguration of Zardoya's intellectual and artistic experiences inspired by the works in question (whose names figure as titles for the corresponding poems). *Los perplejos hallazgos* would make an excellent companion for the lover of poetry and art during future visits to museums of contemporary art.

Janet Pérez. *World Literature Today*. 62,
1988, p. 100

In the six sections of her verse collection [*Altamor*] Concha Zardoya views creation, raising everything to its highest level of love, or *altamor*. The consistent use of assonance reflects the recurrence of the unifying theme, while the lines of varying lengths reflect the diversity of its manifestations. Nature and its eternal cycles, time, destiny, and the city are all part of one creation. Zardoya voices her quest for answers to its mysteries by using rhetorical questions, as she does in other works, while her use of the prefix *tras-,* less here than in other works, underscores her inquiry into something beyond the tangible. "La flor sabe" may be representative of the pervading spirit in the collection. The flower knows even before birth the length of its life and accepts its own cycle without complaining. The human heart does not know such things but continues winding its clock. Zardoya continues her dynamic search, unlimited by orthodox doctrines, and lyrically proposes *altamor* as a possible solution.

James H. Abbott. *World Literature Today*.
62, 1988, p. 104

The concept of counter-exile is most closely approached in the poetry of Concha Zardoya. The first section of *El desterrado ensueño* (Exile fantasy) (1955) follows the shaky steps of a soul anxious to recover its lost homeland. It sleepwalks, reliving from afar beloved landscapes and declaring an equivalency between dream and perception. Memory makes it possible for the fields, gardens, and people of Spain to appear. The eagerness to return makes the poet hear the seductive call of distant cities and glimpse the day when she will climb the mountain once again. The heightened emotion that she feels before her resuscitated landscapes sometimes brings her to an almost mystical state of delirium. But the immateriality of her spiritual voyage and the awareness of the treacherous possibilities of the dream mar her total triumph over the separation. The preponderance in this book of rhetorical questions and sentences divided by disjunctive coordinates lead one to discover the underlying uncertainty, confusion, and dissociation of the poetic "I" of these poems from the exile fantasy. However, the fantasy of return persists. . . .

Psychological exile, comparable to indefinite nostalgia, and ontological exile, intimately bound up with the idea of the Fall, the expulsion from Eden, correspond less to external conditions than to the author's perception of her personal relationship with earthly life and the divine being. . . .

Concha Zardoya is a poet who meets the conditions of psychological exile. To the nostalgia that we commonly expect to find the exiled writer experiencing is added a primordial nostalgia that goes back to earliest childhood. . . .

In Zardoya the expressions of ontological exile are softened by the comforting warmth of hope. The exile is disheartened to see nothing but death and separation around her and writes many poems in which she questions her own existence and the generosity of God, but beneath the suffering and the misery she always catches sight of signs of a better tomorrow.

Catherine G. Bellver. *Cuadernos americanos.* 4:19, 1990, pp. 164–65

ZELDA (ZELDA SHNEÚRSON MISHOWSY) (ISRAEL) 1914–84

Intense religious experience has not been a prominent subject of Israeli authors, although the poet known simply as Zelda . . . has more recently begun to express an ecstatic certainty of God's presence in the constant face of death.

Leon I. Yudkin. In Leonard S. Klein, ed.
Encyclopedia of World Literature in the 20th Century (New York: Frederick Ungar, 1982), p. 466

From 1967, which saw the publication of her first book of poems, until her death in 1984, the modest and soft-spoken woman known to her Hebrew readers simply as "Zelda" received an extraordinary amount of public attention. To a degree that seems almost unbelievable—especially from the perspective of the United States, where fame is rarely bestowed on a contemporary poet—Zelda captured the eye and heart of the Israeli population. She not only gained national recognition during her lifetime, but her critically-lauded six books—*Leisure* (1967), *The Invisible Carmel* (1971), *Be Not Far* (1974), *Surely a Mountain, Surely Fire* (1977), *The Spectacular Difference* (1981), and *Parting from All Distance* (1984)—remained best sellers even beyond her death. . . .

It is likely that Zelda's religious affiliation was at least part of the cause of the popular fascination: it wasn't usual for a Chassidic woman to publish such highly personal and mystical lyrics. Yet it remains a question why these mystical poems maintained the interest of the Israeli readership, the majority of whom do not identify themselves as "religious." Zelda, in contrast, has certainly been viewed as a "religious poet," and it would be fair to say that most readers assume by this a normative orthodox religiosity. Yet, I would argue, this is a very limited characterization. . . .

Reading Zelda's poetry for the first time, one is likely to be struck by the intense and personal relationship between nature and the poems' persona, who feels empathic joy in nature's unions and pain in its separations.

The mystical experience of union, specifically represented as union of the human self with some aspect of nature, is at the core of many of Zelda's poems. Yet often the moment of union is followed by an immediate with-drawal, a pulling away and pulling back into separateness. . . .

In the face of death—as in the face of the mystical moment of union—distinctions are obliterated and language is silenced. Although Zelda petitions for help in confronting this "heavy silence," she is not entirely without her own solutions. She knows what to do when traditional language, traditional imagery fail her: she evokes a world with a "spectacular difference" of its own. Using images of nature that are, in their simplicity, fresh, poignant, and even startling, she breaks through to a distinct and transcendent vision. In the radiant cosmos of her lyrics, nature becomes a transformative power, the source of healing and redemption. And it is perhaps not entirely surprising, in the end, that even readers who disclaim any affiliation with traditional religiosity—including many feminists who reject the hierarchies of patriarchal theology—may find in these lyrics both sensual pleasure and a resource for new spiritual visions.

Marcia Falk. *Religion and Literature.* 23,
1991, pp. 97, 99–100, 103, 107–8

The year 1967 was the year when critics really began to take note of her poems. The critic Chaim Nagid called her work "poetry springing from Kerem Avraham" (the modest Jerusalem neighborhood where she lived), and another, Moshe Dor, said it was "a gift of love from the muse of poetry, given to us without bidding." . . .

Apparently her first literary efforts in the 1940s did not attract the attention of either the leading modern poets or of younger poets, for at that time the free structure of her writing was not common practice. In her unrhymed lines, sometimes longer, sometimes shorter, sometimes lines of changing length, something extremely personal made its way "from ecstatic depths" (in the words of the critic A. Kariv) which was unfamiliar to them; the religious element stood out like a reminder of the "sins of the Diaspora," as did her name, Zelda, which, though she did not like it, she bore with pride. That is also why she decided to sign her poems without a family name, to reach readers without any barriers, without any identifying marks of family connection or origin. She was both too free and too religious, a combination which occasionally found expression in her life. Another element completely lacking in her poetry is what Zelda called "the fireworks of an agile mind." One might say she presented herself to her readers like Lear's daughter Cordelia, without a scrap of disguise, and "her truth was her dower." . . .

In 1967 Meir Wieseltier, a young poet, greeted her first book, *Pnai* (meaning "repose" or "availability") with the following words: "Zelda's poems are possessed by the silent and fascinating spirit of life; life striving towards rich freedom, refusing to relinquish its primordial form." In the same article Wieseltier also wrote: "The degree of self-consciousness within these poems is extremely complex. It is joy in power and accomplishment drawing its power from the sweetness of secrecy." . . .

One of the most important expressions in Zelda's poetry is the concept of the "inner point" which appears in the Lubavich spiritual treatise, the *Tanya*. For her, phrases from hasidic thought, particularly Habad, were as natural as a mother tongue. As she once said, "I was at the fountainhead," and her use of them is not a literary affectation. . . .

Zelda did not identify only with the world's unfortunates. She also felt comradeship with the elements, with the forces of nature as they had been in the Garden of Eden. In "A Single River Flows to the Sea" which she wrote in her youth, she expresses feelings of guilt towards miserable people because of her feeling for the Garden of Eden, a guilt which prevented her from loving and being happy, along with the opposite feeling of guilt, for not permitting her body to be happy.

One cannot read Zelda's poems without placing the same trust in her which she places in us, as though she were writing us a personal letter.

Aza Zwi. Ariel (Jerusalem). 65, 1986,
pp. 58–61, 65, 69

ZHANG JIE (CHINA) 1937–

This collection [*Love Must Not Be Forgotten*] of five stories and a novella offers a fascinating peek at contemporary Chinese culture. Considered by many to be China's foremost woman writer and first feminist novelist, Zhang Jie gives us an after-the-Cultural-Revolution perspective of women's uncertain lives in a changing civilization. The novella *The Ark* concerns three women, former schoolmates now divorced or alone and sharing a flat, who struggle with ex-husbands, petty bureaucrats, and men who use power in corrupt ways. Although many of her characters lead bleak, unsatisfied lives, there's a curiously romantic flavor to the collection, as the women yearn for gentler times while appreciating their new less restrictive roles. Very interesting cross-cultural reading.

Ann H. Fisher. Library Journal. July 1986, p. 112

Leaden Wings was published in China in 1980 and describes the post-Cultural Revolution struggle between industrial reformers and their opponents in and around the Ministry of Heavy Machinery. Zheng Ziyun, a vice-minister, is keen to promote new ideas of "industrial psychology," to improve efficiency and promote production. Parallel to this high-level attempt at modernization, a similar shake-up is described in the Dawn Motor Works where a new manager's financial initiative improves conditions for the workers after he has dismissed the full-time Party secretaries in each workshop. The opponents of these vanguards are caricatured as corrupt, weak and vengeful.

The novel begins with promise as peripheral characters, many of them women, are introduced in a series of deft sketches. Yet, as Delia Davin points out in her Afterword, many of the female characters "shock or disappoint more than they inspire." At best they are worn out by their acceptance of drudgery, at worst, they are scheming and corrupt.

It is said that part of *Leaden Wings'* success in Germany was due to the number of businessmen who bought it, hoping to understand the machinations of politics within Chinese ministries and factories. These personal and political struggles with their multiple roots and their multiple effects are accurately described as are the home lives of the worn-out women. Though it informs, and despite heroic efforts by [translators] Gladys Yang and Delia Davin, *Leaden Wings* remains disappointing as literature.

> Frances Wood. *China Quarterly.* 113, 1988, p. 137

Zhang Jie's stories [*Love Must Not Be Forgotten*] are eloquent in their fury at the lot of women in China today. The heroine of the title story learns from her dead mother's diary that her mother spent a lifetime loving a married man, who returned her feelings but remained with his wife. In *The Ark,* three divorced women share a flat, experiencing frustration and humiliation. They are handicapped socially and professionally because they are single, and yet they find the quality of marriage so demeaning that they cannot imagine finding a second husband. Zhang's stories are sociologically interesting, but her characters are two-dimensional representations of ideas, not real people. The theme of women's unhappiness is resonant, but the author lacks the skill to lift her work from reportage into literature.

> Beth McKillop. *China Quarterly.* 114, 1988,
> p. 308

Widely translated, and here appearing for the first time in English, Zhang's controversial 1981 prize-winning novel [*Heavy Wings*] shows modern Beijing life through its description of the Morning Light Auto Works, the Four Modernizations, production quotas, the Ministry of Heavy Industry, and the Party. Unfamiliar perhaps, but these facts of life take on meaning through the characters: the reporter who loves her work, the devious politician, the loyal workers and their humane supervisor, the lovers, the idle wife. They have the universal concerns about work, gossip, a decent apartment, a good meal, family, and love. Because husbands and wives have different names, and peers use familiar names, the characters are sometimes difficult to keep straight. Still, this is an important work by one of China's best-known writers.

Kitty Chen Dean. *Library Journal.*
September 15, 1989, p. 138

The career women in Zhang Jie's work tend to find themselves forced into non-traditional roles because as victims of circumstance they have never married (Ye Zhiqiu in *Leaden Wings* is too ugly), or are divorced (Zhang Jie's divorcees have all been maltreated by their husbands), or cannot marry the man of their choice (Yu Zhong in *Love Must Not Be Forgotten* and Zeng Lingr in *Emerald*) and thus seem to pursue a career as a kind of compensation. . . .

Zhang Jie's challenges to traditional morality and traditional women's roles tend to be either superficial or weakened by being qualified. . . .

Thus, for example, in *Emerald,* Zhang Jie flaunts traditional morality by sympathetically depicting a single woman who willingly bears an illegitimate child, but the woman weakens the iconoclastic significance of this act by regarding herself as married to the father. She remains faithful to the man for the next twenty years (though they live far apart and have no contact), totally discounting the possibility of ever forming another sexual relationship, rather in the manner of a chaste Confucian widow.

In "Love Must Not Be Forgotten," she presents love between a divorced woman and a married man, another affront to traditional morality, but depicts them controlling their passions for the sake of the innocent wife. The woman in this story also re-enacts the ideal of the Confucian widow by refusing any other relationship till the day she dies, even though she knew their union was impossible and the two never even so much as shook hands.

Similarly, in *The Ark* Zhang Jie presents women who have broken through restrictive behavior patterns demanded by traditional concepts of femininity (that is that women should be submissive, quiet, gentle, unassertive and so on), but depicts them as devaluing their new-found strength and ability to cope with society by regretting their "masculination." Despite the fact that all three women openly recognize that they must strive to strengthen themselves in order to achieve recognition for their work and equality with men, they cling to a traditional ideal of femininity and do not see that self-strengthening must involve a reassessment of their own traditional perceptions of their ideal selves.

The basic conservatism of Zhang Jie's literary images of women is also evident in the attitude she presents in her writings towards divorce. Though she superficially appears to take a liberal attitude to divorce, a closer look at the divorces she presents and those she encourages shows that her expressed support for divorce has the important qualification that it is only acceptable in cases where serious blame can be attributed to one partner. . . .

Throughout her works sex is associated with the abuse and humiliation of women. . . . On the other hand, Zhang Jie presents several love relationships and happy marriages which are almost all very non-sexual in nature. Most resemble guardian-ward relationships in which a considerably older man protects and guides a childish, helpless and adoring wife. Emphasis is given to the non-physical nature of the relationships.

Rosemary A. Roberts. *China Quarterly.* 120,
1989, pp. 805–6, 809

As a forceful feminist critique of Chinese women's status by one of China's foremost female writers, *The Ark* deserves close attention both for its polemic and for its power to persuade. . . .

The women Zhang Jie depicts in *The Ark* are concerned with the problems of being divorced or separated in a culture that remains predominantly family-centered and looks upon divorcees with suspicion or hostility. The other issues they face are very closely related to their social class but are not otherwise particularly culture-bound, since they are common to women everywhere. They worry whether professionalism implies a concomitant loss of femininity; they are concerned about appearance and aging; about younger women and about being alone without the love and support of men. They desire recognition on their own terms, and acknowledgement of their abilities and individuality separate from their relationship with men. They are vulnerable to sexual harassment and objectification, try to find meaning by living through others and have a low self-image. They are conscious of the imbalance of power between men and women and are usually powerless to change their own situation. They have lost their innocence but not their idealism and they want, like Virginia Woolf, a room of their own. . . .

The narrative technique employed by Zhang Jie and the revealed characterizations that form an important part of it play vital roles in underlining, reiterating, and strengthening the argument of *The Ark*. A wealth of corroborative detail, a lack of ambiguity in the language and message, and a powerful consonance of voices all serve to compel assent. While occasionally lacking in subtlety, *The Ark* nevertheless is a straightforward, effective statement on the nature of women's status in modern Chinese society made powerful by Zhang Jie's sustained exercise in technique. She makes sure we travel with her.

Alison Bailey. In Michael S. Duke, ed.
Modern Chinese Women Writers: Critical
Appraisals (Armonk, New York: M. E.
Sharpe, 1989), pp. 96, 98, 108

Among Zhang Jie's works is the controversial and intriguing story "Love Must Not Be Forgotten" (1979). The beginning of the tale is auspicious: a thirty-year-old woman writes that she is the same age as the People's Republic of China. However, "For a republic, thirty is still young. But a girl of thirty is virtually on the shelf." . . .

Zhang Jie's writings, be they novels or short stories, blend politics, love, women, and sickness. Also, like one of her favorite novelists, Virginia Woolf, she is deeply attuned to nature, in a way that is implicit, for example, in Woolf's [The] Waves. Like the English novelist, Zhang is a devotee of mountains and trees, but most particularly of the sea, with which her characters are intimately related. Unlike most Chinese writers, who are captivated by painting, Zhang Jie is under the spell of Western music, especially Italian. She is also drawn to South American literature, the works of Borges in particular.

Although Zhang Jie believes that a human being's development is determined by his or her environment . . . this does not prevent her from probing the psyches of her characters, as Balzac had done in his time. In *Leaden Wings* . . . a socialist-realist novel, Zhang focuses on the psychological problems of thirty or more characters but also on such empirical problems as how best to deal with industrial-modernization programs. She details the daily lives of her protagonists (workers, hairdressers, journalists, government officials, street urchins, while also sounding out their ideas concerning the betterment of their lot and their disappointments, both political and romantic. She shows that despite the elimination of the Gang of Four, chaos is still present in her land, and with it a mood of disenchantment and confusion. Have things changed? Certainly. But not the bureaucratic rule that not only allows but perpetrates the same cruelties as in by-gone days, accounting perhaps for the fact that the young no longer want to enter politics; they no longer have the confidence they once had in Marxism. Idealists, nevertheless, still remain, ready to fight for reform and for improvement in the lives and circumstances of their people.

Bettina L. Knapp. World Literature Today.
65, 1991, pp. 435–36

The novel *Chenzhong de chibang* (Heavy wings, 1981) by Zhang Jie . . . became famous in Germany because it captured the mood and psychology of Chinese bureaucrats, managers, and workers during the first phase of Deng Xiaoping's reforms. German readers came to view the novel as representative of the new literature coming from mainland China in the 1980s. And Zhang Jie has continued to develop as a writer. Stories of hers like "Ta sheng de shenme bing?" (What's wrong with him?), create an ironic mosaic of contemporary society through satire. Since 1985, Zhang Jie has frequently visited the United States, Germany, and other European countries, where her novels and satirical stories have been well received because of her outspoken social protest and moral courage. Her novella *Fangzhou* (The ark, 1981) has also attracted much favorable interest, as a rare Chinese novel with feminist or protofeminist consciousness. Her confession-like openness brought scathing official criticism down on her during the 1983–84 campaign against "spiritual pollution." . . . [A]n early piece by the author, captures only a part of her talent for describing the moods and thoughts of her protagonists, for Zhang Jie . . has been reluctant so far to write much about her own situation.

Helmut Martin and Jeffrey Kinkley. *Modern Chinese Writers: Self-Portrayals* (Armonk, New York: M. E. Sharpe, 1992), p. 118

ZHANG KANGKANG (CHINA) 1950–89

Zhang Kangkang's novella *Aurora Borealis* (1981) is the story of a young woman's inner struggle to free herself from an unwanted engagement and her quest for life's spiritual meaning in an increasingly materialistic society. . . .

Chen Qinqin, the heroine of *Aurora Borealis,* is profoundly alienated from her fiancé and his young friends who are so easily pleased by China's new consumerism; feels lonely, isolated, and depressed in the urban factory environment which compares unfavorably with the comraderie that existed among rusticated youth in the countryside and she wonders why she always feels so despondent and at a loss.

The other side of this melancholy is a deeply felt longing for something more in life that these young protagonists know simply must exist. Chen Qinqin yearns for "something" she cannot describe but knows must exist, is always hoping for something unusual to happen, and longing for something to move her the way the idealistic youth she's read about in novels of the 1950s were stirred by the chance to realize their ideals in practice. She wants another kind of life, one that has more meaning than mere consumer satisfaction or factory routine. In the end she is attracted to the protagonist Zeng Chu and his friends because she shares his belief that the chief question is how to make life more rational and more meaningful and that "only in the midst of our quest for justice and truth will we discover authenticity, goodness and beauty. . . .

The thematic use of natural objects as symbols and metaphors for human thoughts and feelings is most fully developed in Zhang Kangkang's *Aurora Borealis. . . .*

The beautiful and moving ideal divine lights that are rarely seen are a fitting symbol for all of the intangible spiritual values—love, romance, freedom, idealism, the unending human quest for Truth, Goodness, and Beauty, and mankind's desire to live a truly civilized life—that these stories remind us make up the true meaning of human life.

When Qinqin finally goes off to join Zeng Chu and his idealistic young friends who believe in Socrates's motto that "the unexamined life is not worth living," she learns that he too has been fascinated by the aurora borealis and he assures her that, "no matter how disappointed we are, science proves that the northern lights have definitely appeared before. . . . No matter whether you've seen them or not or whether you admit it or not, they always exist. In our lifetime, we may or may not see them; but they will certainly appear sometime." The intangible values that have always made human life worth living do exist and can some day be manifested in the individual's everyday life and work. This is the genuine hope of China's post-Mao younger generation, and its literary expression does not seem to be a formalistic response to the Party leadership's call for stories that end on an optimistic note.

Michael S. Duke. *Blooming and Contending:*
Chinese Literature in the Post-Mao Era
(Bloomington: Indiana University Press,
1985), pp. 187–88, 202, 204–5

Zhang Kangkang was one of the many young writers who emerged onto the Chinese literary stage in the late 1970s, but she is one of the relatively small number to have successfully made the transition from aspiring amateur to established professional with a national reputation in the course of the years that followed. With six novellas (plus a long novel written in the last days of the "Gang of Four"), over two dozen short stories, perhaps twice as many essays of various sorts, and now a new full length novel to her credit, she has made herself, while still in her mid-thirties, as permanent a presence in contemporary Chinese literature as the ever unpredictable nature of public life in China permits.

Zhang is in many ways a "representative writer" in the Chinese sense— representative in character, but exceptional in quality. She has lived through the same pattern of events as many other urban educated Chinese of her generation and has responded in ways similar to theirs. The themes that recur within her earlier work are unlikely to surprise anyone who has read much post-Mao literature: the hardships faced by sent-down youths (Zhang spent a total of eight years in the countryside of Manchuria between the ages of sixteen and twenty-eight), self-interest and abuse of authority by people in power, freedom to love and to choose one's own goals in life, the search for enduring ideals, opposition to mindlessly materialistic personal goals (seen as an undesirable and unnecessary by-product of current policies), remorse for one's own deeds during the Cultural Revolution, and so forth. While she is not an obsessively autobiographical author, it is clear, even on the basis of the limited biographical information available, that Zhang Kangkang draws extensively on her own experiences in her work. This conclusion could presumably be strengthened if we knew more about the details of her life. We might, for example, see more of her own autobiography in some of the romances, courtships, and marriages depicted in her work, but I am not convinced that this would be the most valuable approach to take even were it open to us.

Rather than reading Zhang's works for new details of the sad story of her generation we already know, we might better look in fairly concrete detail at how she has presented this story in her fiction. . . .

Now, the dominant Chinese narrative tradition is one that tends to establish character by rather crude means, such as physical description and omniscient narration of thought. Zhang Kangkang goes beyond this tradition, both in the character she portrays and in the way that this portrayal is accomplished. What do we learn about Lu Qinqin from this section? That she is indecisive, but at the same time capable of, even accustomed to, independent judgment, and sometimes action; that she is idealistic and even impractical, but not solemn; and that she sees herself as a potential victim. . . .

The creation of such a character is hardly likely to strike us as new . . . in itself. What is important about it, and what makes for some of the moments of clumsiness, is that Qinqin is a person whose like, even unsympathetically portrayed, is all but impossible to find in any Chinese fiction that appeared during Zhang Kangkang's lifetime up until just before *Northern Lights* was written. Indeed, some critics faulted the book for creating a character like Qinqin and then failing to criticize her. What is significant about her narrative is not really the use of Qinqin's fantasies; still less is it the cutting back and forth between realistic and mediated material. The significance lies in the character about whom all this centers. Most characters in Chinese fiction written between 1949 and 1979 can be summed up in a sentence or two. It has taken two fairly long paragraphs to give a sketch of Lu Qinqin, and much has been omitted. What *Northern Lights* means is not that people should be less materialistic or that they should give more thought to compatibility before agreeing to marry. . . .

Rather, the whole story means that individual consciousness is vitally important, whether or not it is "correct" or "progressive" or representative of a particular class. This was a strikingly new proposition for China in 1981 and one by no means universally accepted today. That Zhang Kangkang makes it so convincingly, even using means not particularly revolutionary in themselves, is at the heart of her achievement.

> Daniel Bryant. In Michael S. Duke, ed.
> *Modern Chinese Women Writers: Critical*
> *Appraisals* (Armonk, New York: M. E.
> Sharpe, 1989), pp. 112–13, 129–31

New lyric elements are evident as well in Zhang Kangkang's writings. Born in 1950 in Hangzhou (Zhejiang), she volunteered in 1969 to work at Heilongjiang (on the Siberian frontier), where she spent eight years. The background of her first novel, *Demarcation Line* (1975), details her experiences in the open wasteland she came to know so well, its vast sweeping landscape ushering in a disconcerting yet captivating sense of the infinite. In her succeeding works *Aurora Borealis* and *The Right to Love* she focuses on young love and, what is most important to her, on problems facing women in contemporary China. Her short story "White Poppies" (1980), a complex of poetic and political visions, is summed up metaphorically in the introductory note: "I had only seen red or violet poppies, I was completely unaware of the fact that white ones existed." Poignant but never maudlin, Zhang Kangkang conveys feelings by means of profound identification with nature: the snow that appears to the universe, the piercing winds blowing their lugubrious chantings throughout the land, the utter silence and seeming endlessness of it all—these set the stage for the story's mournful happenings. . . .

Less lyrical and more cerebral (but with sensitive dialogue) is Zhang Kangkang's novella *The Wasted Years.* The protagonist, a teacher, is approached by a student whose parents want him to work to support the family. The student, however, is intent upon learning. Rather than merely repeating his lessons by rote, the lad questions and meditates upon writings he has read, such as a volume authored by the teacher which traces the development of capitalism from ancient Greece to Roman times and concludes that such a social system is "impossible for China, India and Russia to develop . . . completely, because capitalism is not only an economic phenomenon but also a cultural one." Although the young man would like to enter the university, he is aware that his written Chinese—he was taken out of school during the Cultural Revolution—is too imperfect to warrant acceptance. His dedication to learning, however, never abates. Nothing, not even his despotic parents, who have never understood his intellectual needs and from whom he runs away, can persuade him to abandon his studies.

Bettina L. Knapp. *World Literature Today.*
65, 1991, pp. 437–38

ZHANG XINXIN (CHINA) 1953–

Modeled on the racy informal interview style of Studs Terkel, this collection [*Chinese Profiles,* also referred to as *Peking Man* or *Beijing Man*] of conversations with an extraordinary range of social types is going to be essential reading for general and specialist readers. By allowing people to speak in their own voices, Zhang and Sang build up a picture of an astonishingly diverse range of attitudes and life histories. Differences between old and young come across particularly powerfully. The subjects range from a former prostitute to a young lorry driver, a leopard hunter in Henan and a reformed juvenile delinquent trying for a place at art school. The tone is plain and unembroidered: ordinary people talking about their lives. *Chinese Profiles* explains more about China than a dozen travel books.

Beth McKillop. *China Quarterly.* 114, 1988,
pp. 308–9

Zhang Xinxin, one of China's most popular writers and theatrical directors, is also a poet—not in verse but in prose, and not involving esoteric ideas far removed from the workaday world. On the contrary, her lyric vein touches upon such questions as pollution, of both the physical and the spiritual kind.

Une folie d'orchidees (An orchid madness) is strange, elusive, and winsome, despite the fact that it begins with the murder of an old man. Why was he doomed? What did the thieves steal? Nothing material, but rather a pot of Nobilis orchids. Was such a theft worth more than twenty years in prison? Were the flowers worth more than a human life? The question is well worth meditating upon, and that is exactly what Zhang Xinxin does in her short but most charming work.

The small city in which the event occurs is neither picturesque nor beautiful. What distinguishes this dust-covered town from others are its many bicycles, which seem to reflect the dreams, desires, and joys of their owners. More important, however, is the populace's fascination with and cultivation of the Nobilis orchid. Clubs have been formed for the purpose of discussing ways of creating new species, appraising their worth, and keeping them healthy. Magazines are published to disseminate information about them. Taxes ranging from fifteen to fifty percent of the sales price have been levied on merchants who sell these special breeds. Should security be offered the owners of such unusual flowers?

Dr. Zhao is a fanatic on the subject of the Nobilis orchid. Whether in the operating room, with patients, or with other physicians, his conversation always revolves around a most prized and sought-after variety, one with black flowers. As with flying saucers, Zhang writes perhaps with tongue in cheek, no one has ever seen such an orchid as yet. Some of Dr. Lu's patients want to put off their operations, even if it is a question of life and death, just to be with their orchids. He receives gifts of these rare flowers from people in all walks of life. At all hours he receives frantic calls summoning him to patients' homes, not because family members are ill but because an orchid is. When he hears that people fall in love with these flowers he wants them uprooted, destroyed. Enough is enough.

What does this allegorical orchid represent that it can so captivate, lure, and allure an entire town? Certainly it could stand for luxury, the niceties of life that Mao's China has had to do without. It also suggests a very dangerous factor: the manner in which a whole society may be manipulated, dominated by a passion. Fortunately, in Zhang Xinxin's most delightful novel it is for the beauty of the Nobilis orchid.

Bettina L. Knapp. World Literature Today.
63, 1989, pp. 364–65

By presenting divorce as acceptable in cases where women find traditional roles too limiting Zhang Xinxin poses a challenge to traditional concepts of sex roles in marriage. The heroine [of "On the Same Horizon"] is depicted as being unable to gain satisfaction from playing a supportive and subordinate role and asserts her right to strive for success of her own. At the same time she suggests a new role for men in marriage by questioning the concept of an ideal husband, but fails as a consequence to challenge traditional concepts of masculinity. . . .

Fear of the stultifying effects of domestic life is the basis of Zhang Xinxin's strongly negative attitude to marriage, and gains full expression in "Dreams of Our Generation," a work which depicts the quagmire of mediocrity that women may sink into if they yield to social pressure to marry in haste, and then center their lives around a traditional domestic role, seeking to gain fulfillment only through supporting a successful husband. It is fear of the vulgarizing effect of preoccupation with domestic trivia that drives the heroine of "On the Same Horizon" to divorce and the actress in "The Last Anchorage" away from love and marriage. But Zhang Xinxin does not present a negative attitude to sex. In her veiled references to sexual relations in "On the Same Horizon" and "The Last Anchorage," she presents sex as something perfectly normal and untraumatic. . . .

Zhang Xinxin . . . never felt much need to depict politically idealistic images, and rarely even indicates whether her characters are Party members or not. Apart from those in her two earliest stories, characters do not espouse socialist ideals, neither do they pursue altruistic goals for the benefit of the whole of society. They strive for personal success and personal fulfillment, placing individual demands over those of the collective, whether the collective be the family, one's professional circle or society as a whole. . . .

Even though one Chinese critic has hailed Zhang Xinxin's works as "an assault wave from the new tide of women's future liberation," it is evident that the young women she presents are still unable to free themselves completely from the restrictions imposed by traditional culture.

Rosemary A. Roberts. China Quarterly. 120, 1989, pp. 807–8, 811, 813

Not long after publishing a rapid succession of highly acclaimed and highly controversial novellas and short stories, Zhang Xinxin, then thirty-one, began to reconsider the options and obligations of the writer in contemporary China. The penetrating explorations of alienation and spiritual ennui that had earned her a reputation as one of China's most promising and most innovative literary talents were no longer tolerated in 1983–84, when the Anti-spiritual Pollution campaign revoked the fragile promise of artistic freedom issued at the Fourth Writers' Congress in 1979. Her "modernist" stories were suddenly subjected to harsh scrutiny by the literary authorities, deemed not promising new departures but inaccurate and misleading representations of socialist reality. Finding herself a target of condemnation rather than praise, Zhang Xinxin pondered the "present aesthetic mentality of Chinese readers" and decided that, for the moment, writing fiction seemed "pointless, really pointless."

For most of a year she was not permitted to publish and, as she remarks archly, she "kept her head down and her mouth shut." But this period of silence, rather than restraining her creative energies, proved enormously productive. She "worked her guts out in secret" and wrote down what she calls, with mock self-deprecation, a "hundred ordinary people's accounts of themselves." While it was a shift in political winds that initially impelled her to "find new approaches to creativity" this ambitious attempt at oral history, *Chinese Profiles* (Beijing ren), ultimately served to expand her literary repertoire and deepen her understanding of human experience, without compromising her artistic integrity. She had, in fact, found a way to corroborate and validate the themes of her fiction.

Her shift from fiction to reportage in 1984 was clearly no simple capitulation. Declaring that "there can be no purely objective record," that even portrait painters "portray not only the sitters but themselves," she continued, in the best of her non-fiction works, *Chinese Profiles* and *Returning Home* (Hui laojia), to express quite consciously her own subjectivity, albeit as journalist rather than novelist. The resulting synthesis of art and life immediately inspired other writers to attempt similar projects as a way of using individual retrospection to assess the experience of the recent past.

Exposing the truth behind official pronouncements about socialist reality had, moreover, been a consistent goal of Zhang Xinxin's literary efforts. After the Fourth Writers' Congress in 1979 had proclaimed a new climate of openness and emancipated thought in the wake of the Cultural Revolution, she was one of the pathbreakers who boldly relied upon declarations that there were no longer any "restricted zones" as authorization to unmask long denied injuries and inequities. Searing explorations of corruption and oppression, of suffering and sacrifice, appeared in a torrent of short stories by young and recently rehabilitated authors. Some of the most daring, alert to the breakdown of traditional order and the inadequacy of conventional forms, departed variously from the expectations of socialist realism to experiment with novel devices like flashback, stream of consciousness, and interior monologue.

Zhang Xinxin was in the forefront of this literary revolution. It was precisely her bold adaptation of "modernist" techniques and her forthright portrayal of disillusionment, estrangement, and alienation that earned her the admiration of readers avid for stories that acknowledged the reality of their own recent experience. But after she was seriously criticized for distortion and falsification, for presenting an "erroneous depiction of human relationships [based on her] incorrect understanding of the spiritual situation of the whole society, Zhang Xinxin sought a less provocative approach." Reportage enabled her to praise China's current economic reforms and mirror the actual circumstances of people in society, while confirming with an indisputable authenticity the bleakness and negativism conveyed previously through her fiction. Just as the interior exploration of her protagonists had revealed the deepest problems in the society, so the investigation of society could illuminate individual and collective states of mind.

Carolyn Wakeman and Yue Daiyon. In
Michael S. Duke, ed. *Modern Chinese
Women Writers: Critical Appraisals*
(Armonk, New York: M. E. Sharpe, 1989),
pp. 196–97

The emphasis here [in *Chinese Lives*] is on the irrelevant idiosyncracies of individual lives. There's the pressurized student whose parents are keen for her to get that "iron rice-bowl"—the security of a university degree. But she's not even passing her entrance exams. The parents stay home every Sunday to watch her study, and apparently make her feel like a sheep forced to walk to the butchers in Beijing, carrying its own meat along the road.

A blind woman recounts the discovery of tumors in her eyes when she was a little girl. Her father had at first scolded her for her poor work at school, but when he realized how ill she was he borrowed enough money to take her on a tour of China before her sight was gone. Over thirty years later she recalls that a stairway at Fan Pagoda in Kaifeng "had golden veins in the wood." Her father died of cancer before paying off the debts for this trip.

To see old China, the China so many died in order to eradicate, one must turn to the story of a woman who was sold as a maid fifty years ago, at the age of thirteen. After her "owner" raped her she escaped to work in a factory but was tricked into becoming a prostitute. Being only fourteen, she was assumed to be a virgin, and beaten up by her first customer and the madam when they discovered their mistake. By the time she was sent to reform school after the revolution, rivaling Simenon in her number of bed-partners (ten-thousand), she was addicted to heroin and suffering from syphilis which no one had bothered to treat. The only healthy thing about her was her cynicism: "It never occurred to me that a communist wouldn't go to a brothel. I thought all cats ate fish."

But for light relief there's the couple who surely had the worst honeymoon on record. With nowhere to stay in Beijing they spend one night out in the cold and then have to sleep in male and female sections of a bathhouse where the lights are left on all night to minimize theft. The bride throws up if she sits on a bus for more than three stops, so they can't get to the Great Wall, and they're fined when she throws up. They spend five hours at a stretch *queueing,* not fucking, a fact which makes both weep. And finally, just before their departure, the bride gets lost at the station. The groom fingers the soggy and now invalid tickets, wonders irritably if she's been kidnapped, and prepares to queue for a refund.

Lucy Ellmann. *New Statesman and Society.*
October 20, 1989, pp. 44–45

Zhang Xinxin's era is a time when Marxist ideology seems to have reached an extreme point in the process of "decomposition." . . . Counterposed to the expression of uncomfortable truths, exploration of new forms, and writing for pure entertainment, are the state's unassailable principles of patriotism, promotion of Chinese forms over "spiritually polluting" Western ones (which echoes older commitments to "national essence" and Mao's "national forms"), and insistence that literature be edifying.

In the minds of some of her countrymen, Zhang Xinxin's writing has clashed with all three of those principles. Her supposed sins against the first two caused her to become a major target of the campaign against "spiritual pollution" of late 1983–early 1984. As Helmut Martin and Carolyn Wakeman first pointed out, that forced Zhang Xinxin at least to reconsider her commitment to subjective fictional social commentary and "Westernized" technique. She abandoned her avant-garde fiction in 1984, undertaking, in succession, a detective novel, an extended subjective account of a trip to rural Shandong, and a journalistic oral-history novel. When the political fog cleared, she went on to explore history, film, and television.

Her new works transgressed against the third principle, that literature must be edifying. Friends who like "the old Zhang Xinxin" were upset to see her change, while cultural conservatives ("leftists") remained concerned about the continuities in her career. One of them was her continued popularity among young adults. Yet Zhang Xinxin's forays into journalism, popular fiction, and the mass media may indeed be interpreted as new expressions of her modernism. Her reportage is not the sacred Party-directed journalism that held sway in the Maoist years and was reborn at the turn of the 1980s, in a less orthodox form, by enlightened Marxist crusaders such as Liu Binyan. Zhang Xinxin is influenced by the "journalistic tape-recorded novel" pioneered by Studs Terkel and Oscar Lewis—if she is not treading a path closer to that of Capote, Mailer, and Doctorow, who have mixed journalism and the novel for more complex intellectual and literary effects.

Have her setbacks, then, made Zhang Xinxin inwardly as iconoclastic as the May Fourth generation? Many creative people of her generation, such as the "misty" or "obscure" poets affiliated with the 1979–1980 journal *Today,* feel the shame, anger, and sense of betrayal by older generations that was prevalent during the 1920s. Yet, Zhang Xinxin seems more amused than shocked by China's remnants of "feudalism." To her, they are part of eternal human nature—not necessarily a congenital disease peculiar to the Chinese. . . .

The creative writer moves one step farther [then the journalist or oral historian] from raw material, sculpting an impression of his or her subject. The result of this tertiary interpretive activity is a character sketch—or a piece of analytical New Journalism. The raw materials are both hard data and the character's own voice, but they are abstracted and transformed by the synthetic powers of the writer. . . .

As in oral history, all narration is in the voice of the deponnent, and probably hardly any words have been invented. But every word is on the page only because it held Zhang Xinxin's attention. . . .

Zhang Xinxin's and Sang Ye's evident fun with language indicates that *Peking Man* is a work of literature. There is arch use of slang, double meanings, and sheer creativity of expression by the folk. Common people who mistakenly assume the intellectual-sounding Zhang and Sang to be representatives of China's official culture even mock the young writers by quoting government slogans "back at them." . . .

The preface to *Peking Man* has a disclaimer to the effect that names were changed to protect the informants, but in truth, Zhang Xinxin the "pure" literary artist has generally quoted her characters' real names, too. One cannot predict whether she will in future prefer more documentary or more fictive forms. Nor can one say for sure whether she will continue to pursue risky subjects such as problems with the current reforms. For all her modernism, Zhang Xinxin seems to think that China has more scores to settle with History than with the West.

> Jeffrey C. Kinkley. In Paul A. Cohen and
> Merle Goldman, eds. *Ideas Across Cultures:*
> *Essays on Chinese Thought in Honor of*
> *Benjamin I. Schwartz* (Cambridge: Harvard
> University Press, 1990), pp. 139–40, 155–56

The less structured a work appears at first sight, the more chance it has of getting through to us. One of the reasons that Zhang Xinxin and Sang Ye's collection of people talking about themselves, *Beijing ren* (Chinese lives), has made so deep an impression on Western Sinologues is their apparent—but carefully created—naturalness. The people telling us about their lives come across as real people, not as characters in a Chinese novel. Closer reading shows how well-crafted these pieces are, and it leaves us wondering how much of the shaping was by the speakers, and how much by the authors. These are the kinds of reactions that skillful writing from our own cultures evokes, engaging us simultaneously with life and with art. Zhang and Sang draw us into their subjects' lives. That is why I hope the book will win many readers in English.

> W. S. F. Jenner. In Howard Goldblatt, ed.
> *Worlds Apart: Recent Chinese Writing and*
> *Its Audiences* (Armonk, New York: M. E.
> Sharpe, 1990), p. 185

In *Chinese Lives* we find a cross-section of mainland Chinese, warts and all, real human beings sharing the strengths and weaknesses and the ideals and prejudices of the rest of mankind. In the past, the Communist regime presented to the outside world a deliberately distorted view of the people of the mainland—the new "socialist," selfless, self-sacrificing individual whose aspirations were directed toward the benefit of the collective. In turn, the mainlanders, aware of the control and surveillance exercised over them, particularly when social contact involved citizens of other countries, did little to disabuse foreigners of this notion, not unreasonably fearing that any manifestation of non-conformity would bring punishment and social ostracism. In this light it is not surprising that some of the people interviewed for this volume expressed the wish that their names not be published.

To those readers whose only previous contact with Chinese people has been through the medium and filter of China International Travel Service and its interpreters, the book provides a valuable antidote. The picture which emerges from these pages may shake fixed views and prejudices about the personality traits of mainland Chinese. If it does it will have served a useful purpose. Here we find a revelation, both unwitting and otherwise, of high awareness of class distinctions ("Hitting the Jackpot"), manifestations of social climbing ("Newly-Weds") and class snobbishness ("Second Try"), national pride bordering on chauvinism ("Cyclist," "The Sea," "Avionics," "Hard-earned Money" and "Fly in a Bottle" as expressed by a nineteen-year-old male believer in communism who declares: "I'm proud of being Chinese. I've got the vote. I'm a citizen. It gets up my nose when Chinese crawl to foreigners"), pragmatism and materialism. ("Streetcorner Ph.D"), male domination ("Whirlpool"), the vulnerability of single women to malicious gossip ("Irreproachable Conduct"), political cynicism and indifference, personal selfishness ("Gold Miners") and family solidarity.

The picture is a realistic and thought-provoking one and a powerful and timely refutation of the view of the Chinese as an amorphous collection of hard-working, selfless, collectively-minded robots. China is a society in transition as these vignettes make us very much aware. It cannot return to the past, no matter how stridently the present discredited and disgraced leadership beats the drum for Chairman Mao (with all the ambiguity and danger involved in promoting a leader who issued such subversive statements as the essence of Marxism is rebellion) and Lei Feng and other "heroes" of pre-Cultural Revolution days.

We read about people who work diligently and successfully for what they perceive to be the interests of the country ("Builder" and "Bridges and Rabbits") and who are aware that the commodity economy threatens to break up established social and economic patterns and relationships—"Traditional values, socialist morality—they all get buried in commercial competition"— and those who muddle along without ambition or desire to improve themselves, so long as they stay out of trouble. In sum, we read about a variegated mixture of individuals whose common cultural traits and identity, as well as distinctive and particular idiosyncrasies make up a fascinating society trying to unshackle itself from the burdens of its past and come to grips with the confusions and challenges of the present.

Keith Forster. *Journal of Contemporary Asia*. 21, 1991, pp. 126–27

Her novel *On the Same Horizon Line* [*Sur la même ligne d'horizon*, 1981] was condemned by the government for contributing to the "spiritual pollution" of the People's Republic. From a literary point of view, *On the Same Horizon Line* suffers from the merits and defects of most first novels. On the positive side are its enthusiasm, sensitivity, and understanding of the pathos involved in the lives of those whose freedom has been circumscribed; its spirit of satire and power of observation are also noteworthy. The naïveté of its characters, unfortunately, detracts from their depth. The plot, however, is intriguing. A husband and wife take turns narrating their subjective views on life, marriage, and careers, alternating chapters as they convey their respective feelings. . . .

So antagonistic are their attitudes toward each other that they decide to divorce. Chance has them meet every now and then, talk, and try to iron out their differences. The insights into contemporary Chinese life are fascinating, as is the author's light-handed charm when alluding to weighty subjects.

Bettina L. Knapp. *World Literature Today*.
65, 1991, pp. 436–37

Zhang Xinxin . . . was sent down to the countryside during the Cultural Revolution instead of receiving a regular high school education, a disillusioning experience that influenced her early short stories. *Zai tongyi dipingxian shang* (On the same horizon, 1981) depicts conflict among married artists striving for self-realization, told from the perspective of the woman; *Fengkuang de junzilan* (Orchid madness, 1983) aims Absurdist satire at the sudden explosion of materialism that has engulfed China since the 1980s. Her fiction was consequently savaged because of its subversive modernist tendencies during the 1983–84 campaign against "spiritual pollution."

Unable to publish throughout 1984 (and denied her diploma at Peking's Central Academy of Drama, although she went on to become a director at the Peking People's Art Theater when the movement was over), Zhang Xinxin in a fit of defiance decided on a new tack. She and a collaborator, the young journalist Sang Ye, toured China to produce a book of oral history in the tradition of Studs Terkel. They called it *Beijingren* (Peking man, 1985, titled *Chinese Lives* in the authorized English translation). The work won them overnight worldwide fame. The chaotic and unidealized images of "real life" in the book were a sharp retort to Zhang Xinxin's critics in the Communist party who wanted China's new authors to continue as propagandists, only now for Deng Xiaoping's reforms instead of Mao Zedong's utopianism. Zhang Xinxin has since then written a good deal for the Chinese television and film industries, even while continuing her avant-garde experiments in fiction.

Helmut Martin and Jeffrey Kinkley, eds.
Modern Chinese Writers: Self Portrayals
(Armonk, New York: M. E. Sharpe, 1992),
p. 136

ZHU LIN (CHINA) 1949–89

In his introduction to a recent anthology of Chinese short fiction from the 1920s, 30s and 40s, C. T. Hsia remarks that "the abiding question is not why people are so ridiculous or stupid . . ., but why people are so unkind and

cruel." Cruelty on a vast scale was an everyday feature of the Cultural Revolution decade and thus it forms the theme of many neo-realist stories. One
in particular, Zhu Lin's "The Web," takes us back into a world of rural China
not so sardonically depicted since Lu Xun's "The New Year's Sacrifice" of
1924. Lu Xun could have easily and sadly recognized the people standing in
their doorways "watching with relish" as the woman they nicknamed
"Toughie" for her ability to endure her husband's many beatings is forced to
parade the streets beating a gong and shouting out that she is a thief, "the
sound of the gong stirring their appetites." He would know them as the same
people who "went away satisfied, exchanging comments" after listening to
Xianglin Sao's tragic story of how her son was eaten by a wolf.

The story rises to a powerful symbolic ending in which the protagonist
dies of sheer exhaustion after watching a spider (the CCP) build a web (life
in the PRC) into which an unsuspecting fly (herself/the Chinese people)
falls. . . .

Despite this easily decoded symbolic ending, the critical theme of the
story is as old as the *Shi jing* poem "Big Rat" and the "Robber Zhih" chapter
of the *Zhuang zi*. The story asks the questions, "what is really stealing?"
and "who are the real thieves?" through a series of incidents in the tragic
life of the protagonist from the 1950s to the 1970s, all taking place after
"liberation." . . .

Zhu Lin's relentless examination of the meaning of the word *tou,* "stealing," leaves little doubt in the reader's mind as to who the real thieves are
and it is to her credit that she does not pretend that the situation has been
changed overnight due to the new Party leadership.

> Michael S. Duke. *Blooming and Contending:*
> *Chinese Literature in the Post-Mao Era*
> (Bloomington: Indiana University Press,
> 1985), pp. 80–82

Zhu Lin is one of the younger generation of authors to emerge since the end
of the Cultural Revolution. Like many of her contemporaries, she began
her literary career on returning to the city following a prolonged period of
rustication. Known in China for her 1979 novel *The Path of Life* [Shenghuo
de lu], she has also written other short and mid-length adult fiction and a
number of stories for children. She is not an author promoted by literary
awards, publication in nationally-circulated journals or translation by Foreign
Languages Press, and is therefore little known outside China. This lack of
official sponsorship may well be due to her bleak portrayal of Chinese society
and its treatment of women, a portrayal which has more in common with
the leftist exposure of the inequities of the Republican period than with the
optimistic mainstream socialist realism which has predominated since 1949.

The anthology *Snake's-pillow* published in 1984, contains ten short stories written between 1979 and 1983. Four of these have been selected [com-
ment here]. The stories are: "Snake's-pillow" (She zhentou hua), "Pear-

blossoms Gleaming on a Poplar-lined Road" (Tangli hua ying baiyang lu, hereafter "Pear-blossoms") "Eyes" (Yanjing), and "The Web" (Wang). In addition to their having in common a tragic female protagonist, the stories present variations on a shared motif of an innocent girl betrayed and violated by a male figure of authority. . . .

Although not all of Zhu Lin's work is as bleak . . . there is, I think, no other contemporary Chinese writer who portrays rural society so hostile to young women (though her view is corroborated in recent works by Western observers). Purity sullied, decency scorned, personal integrity overwhelmed by official concupiscence; all are motifs that recur in the four stories discussed above. All four share the Edenic unromantic triangle of Eve, Adam and Serpent, with Serpent rampant and Eve ineluctably fated to defilement and banishment. But what gives the stories their great, and I suspect enduring, power is not so much their savage theme as their striking imagery: darkness triumphant over light, snake over flower, spider over fly, leering predator over cowering victim, in a world presided over by the lusterless eyes of a blinded god.

Richard King. In Michael S. Duke, ed.
Modern Chinese Women Writers: Critical
Appraisals (Armonk, New York: M. E.
Sharpe, 1989), pp. 153, 167–68

For a combination of reasons both personal and artistic, Zhu Lin finds herself on the periphery of the literary establishment of her native Shanghai. The author of three novels and numerous mid-length and short stories published since 1979, she still has difficulty placing her work in nationally circulated publications and has yet to travel outside China. While a suspicious nature and a diffidence towards authority may well be factors in her limited acceptance, she has also been slow to follow literary fashion, persisting with the revelation of social and political injustice when most of her peers were moving to other themes, and hesitating to experiment with popular innovations like a stream-of-consciousness narration. . . .

The tragic plot, the triangular relationship of a pure woman, a rapacious official and an inadequate protector, and the use of rape as a metaphor for the relations between man and women (or ruler and ruled)—all are features that recur in fiction written by Zhu Lin in the early 1980s. A further aspect of her writing already evident in *The Path of Life* but used with greater sophistication in the short-story collection *Snake's Pillow* is the use of images drawn from nature to symbolize the savagery of human society. . . .

One constant feature of Zhu Lin's work from her earliest fiction is its concern for the awkward position of women in contemporary Chinese village society, a concern which, to judge from the title at least, will be continued in her third novel, titled *Nüxing-ren* (Women are human), and set for release in 1989. Her work has many resonances with the international body of twentieth-century women's writing and should provide worthwhile material for future research by feminist literary scholars. . . .

It seems to me that the best of Zhu Lin's writing stands comparison with better-known women writers like her contemporary Wang Anyi and the older Zhang Jie; its rural setting also offers an interesting contrast to their concentration on urbanites, often of the "intellectual class." A body of reasonable translations might win Zhu Lin some recognition among Western readers, and thus (since that is how things work in China) increase her popularity and standing at home.

> Richard King. *Modern Chinese Literature.*
> 4, 1988, pp. 171–73, 175–76

ZIYADAH, MAYY (LEBANON–EGYPT) 1886–1941

Marie's [Mayy Ziyadah's] first published work was a collection of verses in French, *Fleurs de Rêve* (Dream flowers), which appeared in 1911 under the pseudonym Isis Copia. Later in the same year her first published essay in Arabic appeared in her father's paper. Moved by a lecture on the emancipation of women delivered by Labiba Hashim, founder of the review *Fatat al-Sharq* (The young women of the east) at the Egyptian University, Marie wrote a brief comment scolding women for their own procrastination.

Marie gave credit for her plunge into the storm-tossed millpond of early twentieth century Arabic literature to the inspiration of Malak Hifni Nasif, whose articles on feminism were appearing in Lutfi al-Sayyid's journal, *al-Jarida,* and to al-Sayyid's encouragement. Classicists and modernists were still disputing the leadership of the literary renaissance, arguing between classical Arabic—hallowed for Muslims by the Qurʾan and beloved of non-Muslim Arabs for its richness and dignity—and modern Arabic, closer to the spoken language and more flexible for expressing contemporary ideas. The easy way out for Marie would have been to continue to write in French or English, but the young author wanted to write as an Arab for Arabs, and to draw the attention of her countrymen to social and literary developments at home and abroad. To do this she could use no language but Arabic. From the beginning she signed her essays not with the name Marie, but with the more purely Arab Mayy, formed by taking the first and last letters of the Arabic spelling of Marie. The name, which was suggested by her mother, is often applied to the Muse by Arabian poets.

For a few years she wrote occasional articles in English and French; these appeared principally in the Egyptian review *Sphinx*. In order to improve her Arabic style, she devoted herself to translations from French, English, and German. . . . [In] 1917 Yaʿqub Sarruf, the founder of the long-established *al-Muqtataf,* invited Mayy to write for his review. To the lengthening list of journals to which she was a contributor—*Muqattam, al-Ahram, al-Fajr, al-Zuhur*—she also added *al-Hilal*. With her clear and graceful Arabic, she was also fast becoming one of the most popular speakers in Egypt. Her weekly literary salon, at which increasing numbers of prominent and aspiring men of letters gathered every Tuesday evening, had now been established for about five years.

After World War I, Mayy began to collect her articles and lectures for publication in book form. The first of these volumes, *Bihithat al-Badiya* (The desert inquiress), published in 1920, was a biographical study of Malak Hifni Nasif and included some of Mayy's most significant critical essays. Mrs. Nasif argued for the pedagogical and social necessity of elevating the Muslim woman, but worked toward the goal within the framework of Islam. Mayy compared her approach with that of the more revolutionary Qasim Amin. The great impact which these two champions of women's rights had upon their contemporaries was caused in part by their own vivid and sensitive writings and in part by Mayy's well-constructed and convincing study. . . .

The following year, 1922, she published a collection of her lectures, covering a decade, under the title *Kalimat wa-Isharat* (Words and allusions). The subjects, indicative of the wide scope of her interests, range over feminist problems, literary criticism, social institutions and cultural events. *Sawanih Fatat* (Thoughts of a young woman), prefaced by the praise of Wali al-Din Yakun, followed soon after and marked Mayy's first attempt to cast her ideas into the short story form. In a volume entitled *Al-Musawat* (Equality) she gave her views on social evolution. . . .

A few months later she published a collection of "small poems in prose," *Zulumat wa-Ashi*c*a* (Shadows and sunbeams). This is her most representative poetical work in Arabic and contains some of the most beautiful things to come from her pen. It is written in the free verse form which had recently been introduced into Arabic from the American school by Amin al-Rihani and Jibran Khalil Jibran, under the influence of Walt Whitman. In the first prose poem, a conversation between a child and his soldier-father, she struck out at the destructiveness of militarism. In "Where Is My Country?" she wondered: "Does our love for something make it ours? Despite my immense love for the country of my birth, I feel there like a displaced person, like a refugee who has no homeland." Two other volumes of hers contain articles on art, literature and travel, and on the problem of Arabic linguistic dichotomy, which she hoped would in time be resolved by the spread of education and some simplification of the literary idiom.

Issues of *al-Muqtataf* for 1924 carried biographical articles for Mayy on the Lebanese Christian poetess, Warda al-Yaziji, and on the Egyptian Muslim poetess and essayist, cAʾisha Taymur. . . .

Mayy was a recognized peer among the leaders of modern Arabic literature and unquestionably the most outstanding woman to attain fame in this sphere. One of the few people to win the love and admiration of both the old and the modern schools, she held their respect with her originality and her

humility. Although hailed as a genius, she considered herself, with characteristic modesty, "only one of the amateurs."

Mary Flounders Arnett. *Middle Eastern*
Affairs. 8, 1957, pp. 289–90, 293–94

The purified poetry of the "neoclassical" school maintained the rigid traditional form of a fixed meter, lines of uniform length and the same rhyme
throughout the poem. Under the influence of Western literature and models
from the Bible and Quran young poets began to experiment, searching for
forms which were better suited to the themes of the modern age. One experiment concerned a "poetry-in-prose" form, which owed much to the style of
Walt Whitman. This form was used by the Lebanese Mayy Ziyadah, among
others. Mayy grew up in Palestine and as a young woman moved to Egypt
with her parents. There she earned the title "Princess of Poetry" and her
salon was for a number of years a fixed meeting-point for poets and writers
in the Egyptian capital.

Hilary Kirkpatrick. In Mineke Schipper, ed.
Unheard Words: Women and Literature in
Africa, the Arab World, Asia, the
Caribbean, and Latin America (London:
Allyson and Busby, 1985), pp. 74–75

Mayy Ziyadah was one of the first Arab women to eulogize women colleagues. Such studies can be seen to constitute the foundation of a tradition
of Arab women writers. In the following piece she points out the significance
of correspondence between Arab women writers. . . . Mayy Ziyadah . . . in
1913, five years after her arrival in Cairo, began a weekly salon frequented
by men and women—the literary luminaries of the day. In her biographies
as well as in her Press Club Speech in Cairo in 1928 she praised Warda al-
Yaziji, Aisha al-Taimuriya as well as Bahithat al-Badiya. By invoking these
names she was giving public recognition to foremothers, women with whom
she could link herself in a line that gave weight and substance to what they
and other later women might say. When Ziyadah died in 1941, the recognition
that she had bestowed on women writers was reciprocated by the Egyptian
Feminist Union, which published a commemorative volume remembering and
honoring their literary sister.

Margot Badran and Miriam Cooke. *Opening*
the Gates: A Century of Arab Feminist
Writing (Bloomington: Indiana University
Press, 1990), pp. 234, xxxii

Ziyadah's biographies have been recognized as achieving a sympathetic and
careful treatment of three women's lives; what has not been pointed out is
how those works built upon the demonstrated capacity of women's biography
in the women's press to highlight gender-role shifts in process and also to

suggest an agenda for further change. They activated, in a sense, concerns spelled out more abstractly in other works by Ziyadah. Her studies of women's lives (and her decision to embark on those studies) were motivated by her own situation in the history of Egyptian feminism and marked by her own sense of what was most important and most urgent in the ongoing struggle of Arab women to take control of their own lives, and their own stories. . . .

Much of Ziyadah's writing on women is found in her studies on women writers: here, her literary talents, her polemical orientation as both speaker and writer, and her concern with "the woman question" came together effectively, while biography gave her a filter through which her feminist views could emerge discreetly. Building on the familiarity that her audience might have had with women's biography in the press, Ziyadah's writings on three Arab women writers constituted a new step in writing women's biography and in using it for feminist purposes. These writings also elucidate Ziyadah's process of self-definition as she became a public figure. Supportive of attempts at concrete reform in social services, education, and the legal system, she herself was more concerned with changing public opinion. She saw this as a historical process and her role as echoing, connecting to, and building upon those of earlier women: notably, those whom she chose to study. She focused on women who she believed had been major forces in the rise of women's awareness in the Arab world. Ziyadah's studies elucidate her notion of what a feminist perspective meant both for the women of her time and for those of a generation before.

Ziyadah's works on these women were both a continuation of and a new stage in educated Arab women's reconstruction of their history, at a time when traditional gender roles were being questioned with increasing fierceness and sophistication and organized feminism was newly active. Role models could be sought, constraints and achievements elucidated, and self-identities interrogated in writing women's lives. Biographies of women already flooded the women's press, their conflicting messages suggestive of the struggle to define and control women's identities, roles, lives. Carrying on a venerable tradition in Arabic letters, they took on new resonance. Ziyadah's works joined this tradition and this struggle. They examined how custom and ideology curtail women's lives, generating pain and desire that refuse equally to remain submerged in silence. Emphasizing communication and alienation, they explored the difficulties faced by women treading new paths. Recovering women she saw as foremothers and sisters, Ziyadah further inserted the study of past women's lives into debates over women's futures. At the same time, Ziyadah explored the power of biography as an explanation of self, making explicit a set of implicit bonds between woman biographer and woman subject. By narrativizing other women's lives, perhaps Ziyadah reassured herself of the meaning of her own.

Marilyn Booth. *Journal of Women's History.* 3, 1991, pp. 38–39, 46, 57–58

ACKNOWLEDGMENTS

The following acknowledgments represent an extension of the volumes' respective copyright pages. The editor and publisher are grateful to individuals, literary agencies, periodicals, newspapers, and publishers for permission to include excerpts from copyrighted material. Every effort has been made to trace and acknowledge all copyright owners. If any acknowledgment has been inadvertently omitted, the necessary correction will be made in the next printing.

AARHUS UNIVERSITY PRESS. For excerpts from essays by Kathleen Feeley, SSND, and Helen S. Garson in *Realist of Distance: Flannery O'Connor Revisited,* Karl-Heinz Westarp and Jan Nordby Gretkind, eds.; Morten Kyndrup, *Framing and Fiction: Studies in the Rhetoric of Novel, History and Interpretation* (Dinesen).

AATSEEL OF THE US. For excerpts from articles by Milicia Banjamin, Evelyn Bristol, Vera Kalina-Levine on Guro; Madeline G. Levine on Koziol; George Mihaychuk on Kostenko in *Slavic and East European Journal.*

ACADEMY CHICAGO PUBLISHER. For excerpt from Sheila Rowbotham's Afterword to *Love of Worker Bees* by Alexandra Kollontai.

AFRICA TODAY. For excerpt from article by Odile Cazenove on Sow Fall. From *Africa Today,* vol. 38, no. 3, 1991. Copyright © 1991 by Africa Today Associates. Reprinted by permission of the publisher.

AFRICAN AMERICAN REVIEW. For excerpts from articles by Trudier Harris on Walker, reprinted from *Black American Literature Forum,* Vol. 11, No. 1, Spring, 1977; Sandra L. Richards on Shange, reprinted from *Black American Literature Forum,* Vol. 17, No. 2, Summer, 1983; Cheryl A. Wall on Larsen, reprinted from *Black American Literature Forum,* Vol. 20, numbers 1–2, Spring-Summer, 1986; Robert J. Willis on Hansberry, reprinted from *Black American Literature Forum,* Vol. 8, No. 2, Summer, 1974. Copyright 1974, 1977, 1983, 1986 Indiana State University.

AGENDA MAGAZINE AND EDITIONS CHARITABLE TRUST. For excerpts from articles by Jean MacVean, W. S. Milne on Raine in *Agenda.*

ALPHA ACADEMIC—A DIVISION OF RICHARD SADLER LTD. For excerpt from article by J. C. Whitehouse on Undset in *Journal of European Studies.*

AMERICA. For excerpt from article by Catherine D. Gause on Ashton-Warner. Reprinted with the permission of America Press, Inc., 106 West 56th Street, New York, NY 10019, in the absence of Catherine D. Gause. © 1966 America Press, Inc. All Rights Reserved.

AMERICAN ANTHROPOLOGICAL ASSOCIATION. For excerpt from article by David E. Whisnant on Menchú in *Journal of American Folklore.*

AMERICAN ASSOCIATION FOR THE ADVANCEMENT OF SLAVIC STUDIES. For excerpts from articles by Vera S. Dunhan on Akhmadulina; Birgitta Ingemanson on Kollontai; Michael M. Naydan on Kostenko in *Slavic Review.* Reprinted by permission of the AAASS.

AMERICAN ASSOCIATION OF TEACHERS OF FRENCH. For excerpts from articles by Cecile Lindsay on Cixous; Renee Linkhow on Chedid; Thérèse Marois on Loranger; Trinh T. Minh-ha on Sow Fall; Jane Moss on Boucher; Kitzie McKinney on Schwarz Bart; Valérie Raoul on Dessaules; Karen Smyley Wallace on Schwarz Bart in *French Review.*

AMERICAN ASSOCIATION OF TEACHERS OF GERMAN, INC. For excerpts from articles by Carol B. Bedwell on Aichinger; Bernhardt G. Blumenthal on Lasker-Schüler; Rudolf Kayser on Kolmar; Helga W. Kraft and Barbara Kosta on Novak, Wohmann; Heinz Politzer on Lavant; Albert Scholy on Rinser in *German Quarterly.*

AMERICAN ASSOCIATION OF TEACHERS OF ITALIAN. For excerpts from articles by Valeria Finucci on Morante; Pietro Frassica on Lagorio; Grazia Sumeli Weinberg on Maraini; Carol Lazzaro-Weis on Guiducci, Maraini in *Italica.*

AMERICAN ASSOCIATION OF TEACHERS OF SPANISH AND PORTUGUESE. For excerpts from articles by Gabrièle von Munk Benton on Storni; Albert Brent on Quiroga; Sherman Eoff on Laforet; Ana Paula Ferreira on Gonçalves; Joel Hancock on Poniatowska; Martha Alford Marks on Quiroga; George D. Schade on Queiroz; Sylvia R. Sherno on Fuertes; Janice Giesler Titier on Storni; Benjamin M. Woodbridge on Queiroz in *Hispania.*

THE AMERICAN SCHOLAR. For excerpt from article by Alfred Chester on Sarraute reprinted from *The American Scholar* Vol. 32, No. 3, Summer 1963. Copyright © 1963 the Phi Beta Kappa Society; Carolyn G. Heilbrun on Sayers reprinted from *The American Scholar,* Vol. 37, No. 2, Spring 1968. Copyright © 1968 Carolyn G. Heilbrun. By permission of the publisher.

AMERICAN STUDIES. For excerpt from article by Mark Schorer on Didion.

AMERICAN STUDIES INTERNATIONAL. For excerpt from article by Lynn Cothern on Suckow.

AMS PRESS, INC. For excerpts from essays by Lillie P. Howard on Larsen in *The Harlem Renaissance Re-examined,* Victor A. Kramer, ed.; Robert K. Morris on Manning in *British Novelists Since 1900,* Jack Z. Biles, ed.

ANMA LIBRI. For excerpts from articles by Jean Duffy on Wittig; Marguerite Le Clézio on Hyvrard in *Stanford French Review;* Nancy Harrowitz on Serao; Marilyn Migiel on Deledda in *Stanford Italian Review;* essays by Colette Hall on Cardinal, Leduc in *Women in French Literature,* Michel Guggenheim, ed.

ANTHROPOLOGICAL QUARTERLY—CATHOLIC UNIVERSITY OF AMERICA PRESS. For excerpt from article by László Kürti on Kollontai.

APPALACHIAN JOURNAL. For excerpt from article by Edwin T. Arnold on Mason. Copyright 1985 *Appalachian Journal*/Appalachian State University.

ARIEL: A REVIEW OF INTERNATIONAL ENGLISH LITERATURE. For excerpts from articles by Meena Alexander on Naidu; Louis R. Barbato on Markandaya; S. A. Cowan on Engel; Brian Crow on Mugo; Lorna Down on Edgell; Simon Gikandi on Hodge; Coral Ann Howells on Engel; Louis James on Rhys; Lawrence Jones on Ashton-Warner; Richard F. Patterson on Senior; Abioseh M. Porter on Njau; Ramchandran Sethuraman on Markandaya; Robert Smith on Pym; C. K. Stead on Hulme; Margaret E. Turner on Watson; Robert Rawdon Wilson on Carter. By permission of *Ariel,* The Board of Governors, The University of Calgary.

ARIEL: THE ISRAEL REVIEW OF ARTS AND LETTERS. For excerpt from article by Aza Zwi on Zelda.

ARKANSAS REVIEW. For excerpt from article by Martha A. Wilson and Gwendolyn Sell on Taggard in *Arkansas Quarterly.*

ARTE PÚBLICO PRESS—UNIVERSITY OF HOUSTON. Excerpt from "Growing Up Chicano: Tomás Rivera and Sandra Cisneros" by Erlinda Gonzales-Berry and Tey Diana Robelledo edited by Julián Olivares is reprinted with permission from the publisher of *International Studies in Honor of Tomás Rivera* (Houston: Arte Público Press—University of Houston, 1985). Excerpt from "Estela Portillo: The Dialectic of Oppression and Liberation" by Arthur Ramírez is reprinted with permission from the publisher of *Revista Chicana-Riqueña,* Año VII, Num. 3, Verano (Houston: Arte Público Press—University of Houston, 1980). Excerpt from "Distinct Voices in the Chicano Short Story: Anaya's Outreach, Portillo Trambley's Outcry, Rosaura Sánchez's Outrage" by Sister James David Schiavone is reprinted with permission from the publisher of *The Americas Review,* Vol. 15, No. 2 (Houston: Arte Público Press—University of Houston, Summer 1988). Excerpt from "La Ansiedad de la Influencia en Sandra María Esteves y Marjorie Agosin" by Luz Maria Umpierre edited by Evangelina Virgil Piñón is reprinted with permission from the publisher of *Woman of Her Word: Hispanic Women Write* (Houston: Arte Público Press—University of Houston, 1987).

ASHGATE PUBLISHING LIMITED (AVEBURY). For excerpt from Wendy Rosslyn, *The Prince, the Fool and the Nunnery: Religious Themes in the Early Poetry of Anna Akhmatova.*

ASSOCIATED UNIVERSITY PRESSES. For excerpts from Hazard Adams, *Lady Gregory;* Sarah Barbour, *Nathalie Sarraute and the Feminist Reader;* essays by Joan L. Brown on Martín Gaite, Montero; Andrew Bush on Moix; Margaret E. W. Jones on Medio; Randolph Pope on Rodoreda; Phyllis Zatlin on Quiroga in *Women Writers of Contemporary Spain—Exiles in the Homeland,* Joan L. Brown, ed.; Leonard R. N. Ashley on Hansberry; Katherine H. Burkman on Norman; Barbara Bywaters on Treadwell; Catherine A. Schuler on Fornés in *Modern American Drama: The Female Canon,* June Schlueter, ed.; May Ellen Bieder on Pardo Bazán; Elsa Krieger Gambarini on Parra; Janet Gold on Oreamuno; Bernice L. Hausman on Ocampo; Elizabeth J. Ordóñez on Pardo Bazán; Janet Pérez on Martín Gaite; Harriet S. Turner on Mistral in *In the Feminine Mode: Essays on Hispanic Women Writers,* Noël Valis and Carol Maier, eds.; John Cronin, *Somerville and Ross;* Grace Eckley, *Edna O'Brien;* Donna Gerstenburger, *Iris Murdoch;* Joseph Hynes, *The Art of the Real: Muriel Spark's Novels;* Richard C. Kane, *Iris Murdoch, Muriel Spark, and John Fowles: Didactic Demons in Modern Fiction;* Edwin J. Kenney, Jr., *Elizabeth Bowen;* Nina L. Molinari, *Foucault, Feminism and Power: Reading Esther Tusquets;* Elizabeth J. Ordóñez, *Voices of Their Own: Contemporary Spanish Narratives by Women* (Martín Gaite, Medio, Montero, Quiroga, Soriano); Mary Ann Singleton, *The City and the Veld: The Fiction of Doris Lessing;* Willard Thorp on Gordon in *Bucknell Review;* Carol Wershoven, *The Female Intruder in the Novels of Edith Wharton.*

THE ASSOCIATION FOR CANADIAN STUDIES IN THE UNITED STATES. For excerpts from articles by Armand Chartier on Hébert; Karen Gould and Elaine R. Hopkins on Boucher; Janis L. Palliser on Maillet in *The American Review of Canadian Studies.*

THE ATLANTIC MONTHLY. For excerpts from articles by Phoebe Lou Adams on Duranti; William Barrett on Maraini; Mildred Boie on Rukeyser; Curtis Cate on Sagan; Peter Davison on Swenson; John Hyde Preston on Stein; Charles Rolo on McCarthy, Nin, Rochefort; John Caswell Smith, Jr., on Petry, West; Edward Weeks on Grau; Glenway Wescott on Porter; Frances Woodward on Rawlings.

AUFBAU-VERLAG BERLIN UND WEIMAR. For excerpts from articles by Annemaria Auer on Seghers; René Schwachhofer on Domin in *Neue deutsche Literatur;* essays by Klaus Kandler on Morgner in *DDR—Literatur '83 im Gesprach,* Siegfried Romisch, ed.; Hans-Georg Werner on Wolf in *Erwurbene Tradition: Studien zu Werken der sozialistischen deutschen Literatur,* Gunter Hartung et al., eds.

AUMLA, JOURNAL OF THE AUSTRALASIAN UNIVERSITIES LANGUAGE AND LITERATURE ASSOCIATION. For excerpt from article by Claudia Marquis on Burnett.

DOMINIQUE AURY. For excerpts from articles on Beauvoir, Pozzi in *Nouvelle revue française.*

AUSTRALIAN QUARTERLY. For excerpt from article by Hugh McCrae on Gilmore.

AUSTRALIAN SLAVONIC AND EAST EUROPEAN STUDIES. For excerpt from article by Halyna Koschersky on Kostenko.

AYER COMPANY PUBLISHERS. For Elizabeth Hardwick's Introduction to *Iowa Interiors* by Ruth Suckow. Ayer Company Publishers, Lower Mill Road, North Stratford, NH 03590.

PETRA M. BAGLEY. For excerpt from article on Plessen in *New German Studies.*

BARNES AND NOBLE BOOKS. For excerpts from essays by Shari Benstock on Johnston; Rosemary Jackson on Hill; Harold J. Mooney on Manning in *Twentieth-Century Women Novelists,* Thomas F. Staley, ed.; Diana Bryden, *Christina Stead;* essay by Bernard Harrison on Spark in *The Modern English Novel: The Reader, The Writer, The Work,* Gabriel Josipovici, ed.; Peter Kemp, *Muriel Spark;* Ellen Cronan Rose, *The Novels of Margaret Drabble.*

BEACON PRESS. For excerpt from Tani E. Barlow's Introduction to *I Myself Am A Woman: Selected Writings of Ding Ling.* Copyright © 1989 Beacon Press. Reprinted by permission of Beacon Press.

JANINE BEICHMAN. For excerpts from articles on Yosano in *Japan Quarterly.*

BELFAGOR. For excerpt from article by Olga Lombardi on Aleramo.

JOHN BENJAMINS. For excerpt from Myriam Díaz-Diocaretz, *Translating Poetic Discourse* (Rich).

NINA BERBEROVA. For excerpt from *The Italics Are Mine* (Tsvetayeva).

BILINGUAL PRESS/EDITORIAL BILINGÜE (ARIZONA STATE UNIVERSITY). For excerpts from "Leave-Taking and Retrieving in *The Road to Tamazunchale* and *The Ultraviolet Sky*" by Geneviève Fabre; "Terra Mater and the Emergence of Myth in *Poems* by Alma Villanueva" by Alejandro Morales in *Bilingual Review/Revista Bilingüe;* "Rites without Passage: The Adolescent World of Ana María Moix's *Julia*" by Sara E. Schyfter in *The Analysis of Literary Texts: Current Trends in Methodology,* Randolph D. Pope, ed.

DELYS BIRD. For excerpt from article on Anderson in *Westerly.*

THE BLACK COLLEGIAN. For excerpt from article by Kuumba Kazi-Ferrouillet on Senior in *The Black Collegian.*

BASIL BLACKWELL, LTD. For excerpts from articles by R. C. Andrews on Seghers; Michael C. Eben on Kolmar; Peter Graves on Kirsch; Jan Hilton on Le Fort; Brian Keith-Smith on Aichinger; Werner Milch on Langgässer; J. C. Middleton on Sachs; W. Neuschaffer, Ita O'Boyle on Le Fort; F. W. Pick on Huch; H. M. Waidson on Langgässer, Le Fort, Rinser in *German Life and Letters;* Jean de Bosschère on Sinclair; Geoffrey Bush on Sontag; Hortense Calisher on Stead; David J. Gordon on Gordimer; Thom Gunn on Jennings, Levertov; Maureen Howard on Ty-Casper; Randall Jarrell on Rich; Louis L. Martz on Wakoski; Robert Phelps on Stein; Martin Price on Ashton-Warner; David Thorburn on Beattie; James W. Tuttleton on Wharton; Robert Penn Warren, Eudora Welty on Porter in *Yale Review;* Damian Grant on Plath; Martin Pumphrey, Theodore Roethke on Bogan; Mark Storey on Smith in *Critical Quarterly.*

BLOODAXE BOOKS LTD. For excerpt on Smith from *The Bloodaxe Book of Contemporary Women Poets* by Jeni Couzyn (Bloodaxe Books, 1985).

BORDAS. For excerpt from article on Anna de Noailles by A. Déchamps in *Dictionnaire des Littératures de langue française.* © Bordas, Paris, 1989.

BOUVIER VERLAG. For excerpts from articles by Johannes M. Fischer on Langgässer; Birgit Johann Lermen on Mayröcker in *Wirkendes Wort;* essay by Joan Ryan on O'Brien in *Studies in Anglo-Irish Literature,* Heinz Kosok, ed.

BOWLING GREEN STATE UNIVERSITY PRESS. For excerpt from essay by Barbara Eckstein on Paley in *Politics and the Muse,* Adam Sorkin, ed.

BOYDELL AND BREWER LTD.—TAMESIS BOOKS. For excerpts from Stephen M. Hart, *White Ink: Essays in Twentieth-Century Feminine Fiction in Spain and Latin America* (Martín Gaite, Montero, Peri Rossi, Rodoreda).

GEORGE BRAZILLER, INC. For excerpts from Claude Mauriac, *The New Literature* (Sarraute); Jean-Paul Sartre's Preface to *Portrait of a Man Unknown* by Nathalie Sarraute.

E. J. BRILL (LEIDEN). For excerpts from articles by Miriam Cooke on Samman in *Journal of Arabic Literature;* Salma Khada Jayyusi, *Trends and Movements in Modern Arabic Poetry* (Malā'ika); article by Wendy Larson on Ding Ling in *Journal of Asian and African Studies.*

BROADSIDE PRESS. For excerpt from Don L. Lee's Preface to *Report from Part One* by Gwendolyn Brooks.

CURTIS BROWN (AUST) PTY LTD. For excerpt from essay by David Martin on Franklin in *An Overland Muster,* S. Murray Smith, ed.

PATRICK BUCKRIDGE. For excerpt from essay on Prichard in *Gender, Politics, and Fiction: Twentieth Century Australian Women's Novels,* Carole Ferrier, ed.

GERALD BURNS. For excerpt from article on Wakoski in *Southwest Review.*

BURNS & OATES LTD. For excerpt from Patrick Braybrooke, *Some Catholic Novelists* (Tynan). By permission of Burns & Oates Ltd.

CAMBRIDGE UNIVERSITY PRESS. For excerpt from Joan Bennett, *Virginia Woolf, Her Art as Novelist.*

CAMDEN HOUSE. For excerpt from Donna L. Hoffmeister,*The Theater of Confinement: Language and Survival in the Milieu Theater of Marieluise Fleisser and Xavier Koertz.*

CANADIAN JOURNAL OF AFRICAN STUDIES. For excerpt from article by E. A. Magel on Mugo.

CANADIAN JOURNAL OF IRISH STUDIES. For excerpts from articles by Keala Jane Jewell on Aleramo; Joseph Ronsley on Gregory.

CANADIAN JOURNAL OF ITALIAN STUDIES. For excerpt from article by Anne-Marie O'Healy on Ginzburg.

CANADIAN JOURNAL OF NETHERLANDIC STUDIES. For excerpt from article by Nancy L. Chadburn on Brouwers.

CANADIAN SLAVONIC PAPERS. For excerpt from article by Michael M. Naydan on Kostenko.

CARCANET PRESS LIMITED. For excerpts from essay by Margaret Byers on Jennings in *British Poetry Since 1960: A Critical Survey,* Michael Schmidt and Grevel Lindop, eds.; Elaine Feinstein's Introduction to *Three Russian Poets* (Akhmadulina, Aliger); Val Warner's Foreword to *Collected Poems and Prose* by Charlotte Mew.

CARDINAL PRESS. For excerpts from articles by Joseph Napora, Harold Preece on LeSueur in *We Sing Our Struggle: A Tribute to Us All,* Mary McAnally, ed.

CARIBBEAN QUARTERLY. For excerpt from article by W. I. Carr on Allfrey.

CATHOLIC WORLD. For excerpts from articles by Riley Hughes, Jean Marie Kann, Robert McCown on O'Connor; article on Dark in *Catholic World.* © 1950, 1955, 1959, 1966 *Catholic World*/Paulist Press.

CENTENNIAL REVIEW. For excerpts from articles by Robert Boyers on Plath; Constance A. Brown on Mansfield; Robert J. Butler on Jong; Kerry Driscoll on Levertov; Michael Greer on Forché.

CENTER OF LATIN AMERICAN STUDIES—UNIVERSITY OF KANSAS. For excerpts from articles by Tamara Holzapfel on Gámboro,Vilalta; Catherine Larson on Garro; Virginia Ramos Foster on Gámboro; Carlos Solórzano on Vilalta in *Latin American Theatre Review.*

EDITIONS DU CERF. For excerpt from Georges Hourdin, *Le cas Françoise Sagan.*

ČESKÝ SPISOVATEL. For excerpts from Frantisek Buriánek, *O české literatuře naseko ve'hu* (Pujmanová); Jiří Opelik, *Nenávedéné řemeslo* (Linhartová); A. M. Piša, *Stopami prózy* (Majerová); Bedřich Václavek, *Literárni studie a podobizny* (Pujmanová).

CHASQUI. For excerpts from articles by Carmen Chaves McClendon on Luft; Lucía Guerra-Cunningham on Ferre; M. Patricia Mosier on Gorodischer; Thorpe Running on Pizarnik.

CHICAGO REVIEW. For excerpts from articles by André Levinson, trans. Susan Cook, on Akhmatova; Jim Powell on Loy; Lisa M. Steinman on Miles.

CHICAGO SUN-TIMES. For excerpts from articles by Elizabeth Bullock on Stafford in *Chicago Sun Book Week;* Margaret Atwood on Gordimer in *Chicago Sun-Times Book Week.* Reprinted with permission, *Chicago Sun-Times* © 1995.

CHILDREN'S LITERATURE ASSOCIATION. For excerpts from articles by Celia Catlett Anderson on Potter in *Proceedings of the Seventh Annual Conference of the Children's Literature Association;* Roger L. Bedard on Burnett; Ruth K. MacDonald on Potter; Eva-Marie Metcalf on Lindgren in *Children's Literature Association Quarterly;* essays by William Blackburn on L'Engle; Jackie F. Eastman on Potter in *Touchstones: Reflections on the Best in Children's Literature,* Perry Nodelman, ed. Reprinted with permission of the Children's Literature Association.

CHINA BOOKS & PERIODICALS, INC. For excerpt from Jennifer F. Anderson and Theresa Munford's Introduction to *Chinese Women Writers* (Bing Xin). China Books & Periodicals, Inc., 2929 24th Street, San Francisco, CA 94110. Phone: 415/282-2994, Fax: 415/282-0994, catalog available.

CHOICE: CURRENT REVIEWS FOR ACADEMIC LIBRARIES. For excerpts from articles by M.Butovsky on Hareven; John H. Ferres on Frame; M. G. Levine on Szymborska reprinted from *Choice* Magazine, copyright American Library Association.

ROBERT CHRISMAN. For excerpt from article on Walker in *The Black Scholar*.

THE CHRISTIAN SCIENCE MONITOR. For excerpts from articles by Elizabeth Janeway on Matute; Melvin Maddocks on Didion; H. J. S. on Dark.

CHRISTIANITY AND LITERATURE. For excerpt from "Of Belief and Unbelief: The Novels of Mary Gordon" by Marcia Bundy Seabury.

CÍRCULO: REVISTA DE CULTURA. For excerpts from articles by Rosario Hiriart on Cabrera; Nora de Marval de McNair on Guido; Julio Hernández Miyares on Cabrera.

COACH HOUSE PRESS INC. For excerpt from Constance Rooke, *Fear of the Open Heart: Essays on Contemporary Canadian Writing* (Gallant).

COLBY QUARTERLY. For excerpts from articles by Marcia McClintock Folsom on Jewett; James M. Haule on O'Brien; Laura B. Van Dale on O'Faolain.

EL COLEGIO DE MÉXICO. For excerpts from essays by Debra D. Andrist on Anzaldúa; Laura Cázares H. on Campobello; María Eugenia Gaona on Hoyos; Manuel M. Martín Rodriguez on Cisneros in *Mujer y literatura mexicana y chicana: Culturas en contacto*, Aralia López Gonzales et al., eds.

COLLEGE ENGLISH ASSOCIATION. For excerpt from article by Claire Mattern on Sandoz in *CEA Critic*.

COLLEGE LITERATURE. For excerpts from articles by Adele King on Condé, Warner-Vieyra; Michael Payne on Cooper.

COLLOQUIA GERMANICA. For excerpt from article by Alan Corkhill on Kaschnitz.

COLUMBIA UNIVERSITY PRESS. For excerpts from Michael Awkward, *Inspiring Influence: Tradition, Revision, and Afro-American Women's Novels* (Hurston); essays by Constance Coiner on LeSueur, Olsen in *Left Politics and the Literary Profession*, Leonard J. Davis and M. Bella Mirabella, eds.; Edward M. Gunn, *Unwelcome Muse: Chinese Literature in Shanghai and Peking 1937–1945* (Chang); Peter Hruby, *Daydreams and Nightmares: Czech Communist and Ex-Communist Literature, 1917–1987* (Majerová); Steven G. Kellerman, *The Self-Begetting Novel* (Murdoch); Manfred Krídl, *A Survey of Polish Literature and Culture* (Nalkowska); Karl Malkoff, *Muriel Spark;* George W. Nitchie, *Marianne Moore;* Ruth Z. Temple, *Nathalie Sarraute*. Copyright © 1956, 1968, 1980, 1989, 1990 by Columbia University Press. Reprinted with permission of the publisher.

COMMENTARY. For excerpts from articles by Pearl K. Bell on Piercy; Elizabeth Dalton on Oates; F. W. Dupree on Stein; Joseph Epstein on Beattie; R. W. Flint on Sontag; Roger Owen on Lessing; Norman Podhoretz on McCarthy; Heinz Politzer on Lasker-Schüler; Thomas Rogers on McCarthy; Theodore Solotaroff on Porter.

COMMONWEAL. For excerpts from articles by Maura Boland on Undset; J. G. Brunini on Le Fort; William P. Clancy on McCullers; Nicholas R. Clifford on Yuan-Tsung Chen; Arthur A. Cohen on Ozick; Thomas F. Curley on Roy; Patricia Donegan on Aichinger; Francis Downing on McCullers; Richard M. Elman on Olsen; Frank Getlein on Sarton; James Greene on O'Connor; Marilyn Hacker on Williams; Philip Hartung on Rawlings; Richard Hayes on Bowles, Gordimer, Stafford; R. T. Horchler on Bryher; Jean Holzhauer on Welty; Catharine Hughes on McCullers, Rochefort; Edwin Kennebeck on Renault; Richard Kuczkowski on Sontag; Henry Rago on Garrigue; John Ratté on Weil; Bette Richart on Millay, Moore; John H. Simons on O'Connor; Gerald Weales on Hansberry, Treadwell; Helen C. White on Richardson, Undset.

CONFLUENCIA. For excerpts from articles by Ines Dölz-Blackburn on Parra; José David Saldívar on Zamora.

THE CONTEMPORARY REVIEW. For excerpts from articles by Loina Collard on Webb; Beatrice Erskine on Pardo Bazán; Rosalind Wade on Lessing in *Contemporary Review;* Richard Church on Sackville-West; J. A. T. Lloyd on Stern; Andrew E. Malone on Kaye-Smith; G. W. Stonier on Mitchison in *Fortnightly Review.*

MIRIAM COOKE. For excerpts from *War's Other Voices: Women Writers on the Lebanese Civil War* (Adnan, Nasrallah, Samman).

CORNELL UNIVERSITY PRESS. For excerpts from Martha Noel Evans, *Masks of Tradition: Women and the Politics of Writing in Twentieth-Century France* (Cixous, Leduc).

JUAN DE LA COSTA. For excerpt from essay by Robert A. Parsons on Gámbaro in *Things Done With Words: Speech Acts in Hispanic Drama*, Elias L. Rivers, ed.

THE CROATIAN P.E.N. CENTER. For excerpt from article by Miroslav Vaupotić on Parun in *Contemporary Croatian Literature.*

CROSS CURRENTS. For excerpt from article by Reamy Jansen on Munro.

CUADERNOS AMERICANOS. For excerpts from articles by Catherine G. Bellver on Zardoya; Carlos D. Hamilton on Mistral; Mauricio de la Selva on Castellanos.

CUADERNOS HISPANOAMERICANOS: REVISTA MENSUAL DE CULTURA HISPÁNICA. For excerpts from articles by Etelvina Astrada de Terzaga on Storni; Salvador Bueno on Mistral; J. Castillo Pieche on Laforet; José Manuel Garieu Rey on Somers; F. Luis on Rodoreda; Juan Villegas on Quiroga.

DALHOUSIE FRENCH STUDIES. For excerpts from articles by Nicole Trèves on Chedid; Jennifer Waelti-Walters on Hyvrard.

DALKEY ARCHIVE PRESS. For excerpts from essays by Suzanne Oboler, Charles Ruas in *Marguerite Young, Our Darling: Tributes and Essays,* Miriam Fuchs, ed.

THE C. W. DANIEL COMPANY LTD. For excerpts from Patrick Braybrooke, *Novelists: We Are Seven* (West).

GAUTAM DASGUPTA. For excerpt from essay on Drexler in *American Playwrights: A Critical Survey,* Bonnie G. Marranca and Gautam Dasgupta, eds. © Copyright 1981 Gautam Dasgupta.

DEUTSCHE POST. For excerpts from articles by Karlheinz Schauder on Drewitz.

DEUTSCHE VERLAGS-ANSTALT GMBH. For excerpt from Karl August Horst, *Ina Seidel.*

LE DEVOIR. For excerpt from "Françoise Loranger" by Jean Basile.

JOANNE FEIT DIEHL. For excerpt from essay in *Elizabeth Bishop: Modern Critical Views,* Harold Bloom, ed.

DOVEHOUSE EDITIONS INC. For excerpt from essay by Bice Mortara Garavelli on Corti in *Donna: Women in Italian Culture,* Ada Testaferri, eds.

GERALD DUCKWORTH AND COMPANY LTD. For excerpts from Gladys Mary Coles, *The Flower of Light: A Biography of Mary Webb;* Margot Strickland, *Angela Thirkell: Portrait of a Lady Novelist.*

DUFOUR EDITIONS, INC. For excerpt from essay by Roger Garfitt on O'Faolain in *Two Decades of Irish Writing,* Douglas Dunn, ed.

LANE DUNLOP. For excerpt from article on Tsushima in *Literary Review.*

THE DURHAM UNIVERSITY JOURNAL. For excerpt from article by F. H. Mares on Wright.

DUTCH CROSSING. For excerpt from article by Nancy L. Chadburn on Brouwers.

DUTCH QUARTERLY REVIEW OF ANGLO-AMERICAN LETTERS. For excerpt from article by José Lanters on Johnston.

DUTTON SIGNET, A DIVISION OF PENGUIN BOOKS USA. For excerpts from Percy Lubbock, *Portrait of Edith Wharton.*

ECW PRESS. For excerpts from essays by John F. Hulcoop on Webb; Peter Stevens on Waddington in *Canadian Writers and Their Work,* Robert Lecker, et al., eds.

EDINBURGH UNIVERSITY PRESS. For excerpt from article by Lacy Collison-Morley on Deledda in *Edinburgh Review.*

THE ENGLISH ASSOCIATION. For excerpt from article by Geoffrey Bullough on Sayers in *The Year's Work in English Studies.*

ENGLISH STUDIES IN AFRICA. For excerpts from articles by J. M. Coetzee on Millin; Jean Marquand on Joubert.

ENGLISH STUDIES IN CANADA. For excerpts from articles by Chris Ferns on LeGuin; Francis Zichy on Duncan.

ENITHARMON PRESS. For excerpt from Elizabeth Jennings's Introduction to *Collected Poems* by Ruth Pitter.

L' ESPRIT CRÉATEUR. For excerpt from article by Rosette C. Lamont on Delbo.

ESSAYS IN LITERATURE. For excerpt from article by Marilyn Yalom on Leduc.

ESSAYS IN ARTS AND SCIENCES. For excerpt from article by Douglas Robillard on Jameson.

ESTRENO: CUADERNOS DEL TEATRO ESPAÑOL CONTEMPORÁNEO. For excerpts from articles by Mary Lee Bretz on Espina and Maria José Rague-Arias on Falcón.

ÉTUDES. For excerpt from article by André Blanchet on Sagan first published in *Études,* Assas Éditions, 14 rue d'Assas, 75006 Paris.

ÉTUDES LITTÉRAIRES. For excerpt from "Sémiotique textuelle et histoire littéraire du Québec" by Irène Duranleau in Revue *Etudes littéraires,* Vol. 14, No. 1, avril 1981 (Brossard).

FAR EASTERN ECONOMIC REVIEW. For excerpt from article by Carolyn Watts on Wang Anyi.

THE FEMINIST PRESS AT THE CITY UNIVERSITY OF NEW YORK. For excerpts from Sylvia J. Cook and Anna W. Shannon's Biographical Afterword to *Call Home the Heart* by Fielding Burke; Maryemma Graham's Introduction to *How I Wrote Jubilee and Other Essays on Life and Literature* by Margaret Walker; Elaine Hedges's Afterword to *The Yellow Wallpaper* by Charlotte Perkins Gilman; Florence Howe's Afterword, Jan and Steve MacKinnon's Introduction

844   ACKNOWLEDGMENTS

to *Portraits of Chinese Women in Revolution* by Agnes Smedley; Margaret S. Lacy's Afterwords to *My Mother Gets Married* and *Women and Appletrees* by Moa Martinson; article by Lillian S. Robinson on Woolf in *Women's Studies Quarterly;* Janet Sharistanian's Afterword to *The Unpossessed* by Tess Slesinger.

FEMINIST STUDIES, INC. For excerpts from Electa Arenal, "Two Poets of the Sandinista Struggle," *Feminist Studies* Vol. 7, No. 1 (Spring 1981): 19–27 (Alegría, Belli); Yi-tsi Mei Feuerwerker, "In Quest of the Writer Ding Ling," *Feminist Studies* Vol. 10, No. 1 (Spring 1984): 65–83; Regenia Gagnier, "Feminist Autobiography in the 1980s," *Feminist Studies* Vol. 17, No. 1 (Spring 1991): 135–48 (Anzaldúa, Cisneros); Anne E. Goldman, "'I Made the Ink': (Literary) Production and Reproduction in *Dessa Rose* and *Beloved*," *Feminist Studies* Vol. 16, No. 2 (Summer 1990): 313–30 (Williams); Marina Heung, "Daughter-Text/Mother-Text: Matrilineage in Amy Tan's *Joy Luck Club*," *Feminist Studies* Vol. 19, No. 3 (Fall 1993): 597–616; Ann Rosalind Jones, "Writing the Body: Toward an Understanding of L'Ecriture Feminine," *Feminist Studies* Vol. 7, No. 2 (Summer 1981): 247–63 (Wittig); Susan S. Lanser, "Feminist Criticism, 'The Yellow Wallpaper,' and the Politics of Color in America," *Feminist Studies* Vol. 15, No. 3 (Fall 1989): 415–441(Gilman); Shirley Geok-lin Lim, "Japanese American Women's Life Stories: Maternality in Monica Sone's *Nisei Daughter* and Joy Kogawa's *Obasan*," *Feminist Studies* Vol. 16, No. 2 (Summer 1990): 289–312; Alicia Ostriker, "What Are Patterns For?': Anger and Polarization in Women's Poetry," *Feminist Studies* Vol. 10, No. 3 (Fall 1984): 485–503 (Wakoski); Deborah Rosenfelt, "From the Thirties: Tillie Olsen and the Radical Tradition," *Feminist Studies* Vol. 7, No. 3 (Fall 1981): 371–406; Hélène Vivienne Wenzel, "The Text as Body/Politics: An Appreciation of Monique Wittig's Writings in Context," *Feminist Studies* Vol. 7, No. 2 (Summer 1981) 264–87. All excerpts reprinted by permission of the publisher, Feminist Studies, Inc., c/o Women's Studies Program, University of Maryland, College Park, MD 20742.

CAROLE FERRIER. For excerpt from *Gender, Politics, and Fiction: Twentieth Century Australian Women's Novels* (Devanny).

WILHELM FINK VERLAG GMBH & CO. For excerpt from Olga Matich, *Paradox in the Religious Poetry of Zinaida Gippius.*

FJORD PRESS. For excerpt from Introduction to *Love and Solitude: Selected Poems 1916–1923* by Edith Södergran, translated by Stina Katchadourian (Seattle, WA: Fjord Press, 3rd. edition 1992). Copyright © 1981, 1985, 1992 by Stina Katchadourian. Used by permission.

FORDHAM UNIVERSITY PRESS. For excerpts from Ita O'Boyle, *Gertrud von le Fort: An Introduction to the Prose Works.* Copyright © 1964 by Fordham University Press.

FOUNDATION FOR NATIONAL PROGRESS. For excerpt from article by Arthur I. Blaustein on Erdrich, reprinted with permission from *Mother Jones* magazine, © 1988, Foundation for National Progress.

FRANCOFONIA. For excerpts from articles by Madeleine Cottonet-Hage on Chauvet; Lise Ouellet on Dessaules.

FRANKFURTER ALLGEMEINE ZEITUNG. For excerpts from articles by Marie Luise Kaschnitz, Karl Krolow, Horst Kruger on Ausländer, first printed in *Frankfurter Allgemeine Zeitung.*

FREEDOMWAYS MAGAZINE. For excerpt from article by Ossie Davis on Hansberry.

FRENCH FORUM. For excerpts from articles by Renée A. Kincaid on Delbo; Trinh T. Minh-ha on Cardinal; Jean Snitzer Schoenfeld on Leduc.

FRENCH LITERATURE SERIES, UNIVERSITY OF SOUTH CAROLINA. For excerpts from articles by Helen Bates McDermot on Rochefort in *Autobiography in French Literature*, first published as *French Literature Series* 12, 1985; Elinor S. Miller on Sow Fall in *Irony and Satire in French Literature*, first published as *French Literature Series* 14, 1987.

STUART FRIEBERT. For excerpt from article on Paley in *Field: Contemporary Poetry and Poetics.*

ÉDITIONS GALLIMARD. For excerpts from Henry de Montherlant, *Carnets 1930–44* (Colette). © Éditions Gallimard 1957.

SUSAN GARDNER. For excerpt from article on Nwapa in *Women's Review of Books.*

GARLAND PUBLISHING INC. For excerpts from Katherine Anne Ackley, *The Novels of Barbara Pym;* essays by Marian Arkin on Richardson; Bruce Bennett on Wright; T. G. Bishop on Harwood; Ramesh Chadha on Sahgal; Phyllis Fahri Edelson on Stead; Margery Fee on Hulme; Pierrette Frickey on Rhys; Liew Geok-Leong on Mukherjee; Yasmine Gooneratne on Jhabvala; Ramā Jha on Markandaya; Fawzi Afzhal Khan on Sidhwa; Diana Libert on Desai; Kirsten Holst Peterson on Emecheta; A.P. Riemer on Jolley; Robert L. Ross on Astley; Rowland Smith on Gordimer; J. A. Wainwright on Munro in *International Literature in English: Essays on the Major Writers*, Robert L. Ross, ed.; Judith E. Funston, Donald Pizer, Judith L. Sensibar in *Edith Wharton: New Critical Essays*, Alfred Bendixen and Annette Silversmit, eds.; Amy Vladek Heinrich on Ariyoshi Sawako in *Proceedings of the Xth Congress of the International Comparative Literature Association;* Michael M. Naydan's

Afterword to *Selected Poetry: Wandering of the Heart* by Lina Kostenko; essay by Agnes Whitfield on Roy in *Redefining Autobiography in Twentieth-Century Women's Fiction,* Janice Morgan and Colette T. Hall, eds.

GENRE. For excerpt from article by Elissa Greenwald on Woolf.

DIANA HUME GEORGE. For excerpt from article on Rich in *Women's Review of Books.*

GERMAN STUDIES REVIEW. For excerpt from article by M. Kay Flavell on Courths-Mahler.

GERMANIC NOTES AND REVIEWS. For excerpt from article by Christine Cosentino on Erb.

VAN C. GESSEL. For excerpt from article on Enchi Fumiko in *Japan Quarterly.*

GORDON AND BREACH PUBLISHING GROUP. For excerpts from articles by Rosaria Champagne on Robinson; Anna Shannon Elfenbein and Terence Allen Hoagwood, Phyllis M. Jones on Wylie; Judy Little on Woolf; E. M. Nett on Taylor; Jean Pickering on Brittain; Linda Ray Pratt on LeSueur; Jacqueline Ridgeway on Bogan; Susan M. Squier on Woolf; Michele S. Ware on Rukeyser in *Women's Studies.*

GRADIVA. For excerpt from article by Pietro Frassica on Cederna.

ÉDITIONS BERNARD GRASSET. For excerpt from Yves Berger's Preface to *L'insoumise* by Marie-Claire Blais.

EDITORIAL GREDOS S. A. For excerpt from Graciela Illanes Adaro, *La novelística de Carmen Laforet.*

GREENWOOD PUBLISHING GROUP. For excerpt from Jürgen Rühle, *Literature and Revolution* (Seghers); essay by Iris Zavala-Martinez on Burgos in *The Psychosocial Development of Puerto Rican Women,* Cynthia T. García Coll and Maria de Lourdes Metei, eds.

THE GUARDIAN. For excerpts from articles by Harold Brighouse on Dane; Norman Shrapnel on Brooke-Rose in *The (Manchester) Guardian;* Anne Duchene on Johnson, Spark; Andrew Leslie on Bedford; Norman Shrapnel on Manning, Morante in *The Manchester Guardian Weekly. The Guardian* ©.

EDITORIAL GUAYMURAS S. A. For excerpts from articles by Mario Esquivel on Lynch in *Tragaluz.*

H. E. S. PUBLIKEN. For excerpts from Myriam Díaz-Diocaretz, *The Transforming Power of Language: The Poetry of Adrienne Rich.*

ELIZABETH I. HANSON. For excerpt from *Paula Gunn Allen.*

HARPER'S MAGAZINE. For excerpts from articles by J. B. on White; Roderick Cook on Bowles; Irving Howe on Plath; Alfred Kazin on Oates; Katherine Gauss Parker on Taylor; Paul Pickerel on Laurence; J. S. on Barker; Frances Taliaferro on White; Louis Untermeyer on Lowell; Carl Van Doren on Wylie; James Wolcott on Oates; article on Taylor. Copyright © by *Harper's Magazine.* All rights reserved. Reproduced by special permission.

THE HEARST CORPORATION. For excerpts from articles by Dorothy Parker on Frame; Malcolm Muggeridge on Leduc in *Esquire.*

MAE G. HENDERSON. For excerpt from article on Williams in *Black American Literature Forum.*

ANNE HERZOG. For excerpt from article on Rukeyser in *Women's Review of Books.*

HIERONYMUS VERLAG NEUVIED. For excerpt from essay by Milicia Banjamin on Guro in *Festschrift für Nikola R. Pribić,* Josip Matešić and Erwin Wedel, eds.

THE HISPANIC INSTITUTE OF COLUMBIA UNIVERSITY. For excerpts from Sidonia Carmen Rosenbaum, *Modern Women Poets of Spanish America* (Ibarbourou, Storni); articles by Ana Paula Ferreira on Jorge, Margaret Persin on Fuertes in *Revista Hispánica Moderna.*

HISPANIC JOURNAL. For excerpt from article by Sharon Magnarelli on Vilalta.

HISPANIC REVIEW. For excerpts from articles by Gabriela Ibrieta on Somers, Mary E. Giles on Pardo Bazán in *Hispanic Review.*

NANCY YANES HOFFMAN. For excerpts from article on Sarton in *Southwest Review.*

THE HOLLINS CRITIC. For excerpts from articles by Peter Cooley on Plath; Gale Flynn on Rich; Miriam Fuchs on Barnes; Richard Kostelanetz on Stein; Irving Malin on Ocampo; Henry Taylor on Sarton in *The Hollins Critic.*

HENRY HOLT AND COMPANY, INC. For excerpts from Russell Blankenship, *American Literature* (Lowell); John Gassner, *Theatre at the Crossroads* (Hellman); Randall Jarrell's Introduction to *The Man Who Loved Children* by Christina Stead. Copyright © 1965 by Christina Stead. Reprinted by permission of Henry Holt and Company, Inc.

THE JOHNS HOPKINS UNIVERSITY PRESS. For excerpts from Margaret Bates's Introduction to *Selected Poems of Gabriela Mistral;* essays by Calvin Bedient, Richard Allen Blessing in *Sylvia Plath: New Views on the Poetry,* Gary Lane, ed.; essays by Robert Daniel on Welty; Vivienne Koch on Gordon in *Southern Renascence: The Literature of the Modern South,* Louis D. Rubin, Jr., and Robert D. Jacobs, eds.; Richard Gray, *The Literature of Memory* (McCullers); Robert Siegle, *Suburban Ambush: Downtown Writing and the Fiction of Insurgency* (Acker) (JOURNALS DIVISION). For excerpts from articles by Jacob H. Adler on Hellman in *Educational Theatre Journal;* A. K. Weatherhead on Moore in *English Literary*

History; William M. Burke on Robinson; Leon Edel on Richardson; Robert E. Fleming on Larsen; Keith N. Hall on LeGuin; Rue McCarthy Maclendon on Munro; Ihab Hassan on McCullers; Maxine Sample on Nwapa in *Modern Fiction Studies.*

SUSAN HOSKING. For excerpt from article on Garner in *Overland.*

HOUGHTON MIFFLIN COMPANY. Excerpt from Henry Seidel Canby, *American Memoir* (Lowell). Copyright 1934, 1936, 1947 by Henry Seidel Canby. Copyright © renewed 1975 by Edward T. Canby. Excerpts by S. Foster Damon and D. H. Lawrence from *Amy Lowell: A Chronicle.* Copyright 1935, © renewed 1963 by S. Foster Damon. Excerpt from Lloyd Frankenberg, *Pleasure Dome.* Copyright © 1949 by Lloyd Frankenberg, © renewed 1977 by Loren MacIver. Excerpts from Maxwell Geismar, *The Last of the Provincials.* Copyright 1943, 1947, 1949, © renewed 1975 by Maxwell Geismar (Cather). Excerpt from Maxine Kumin's Foreword to *The Complete Poetical Works of Anne Sexton.* Foreword copyright © 1981 by Maxine Kumin. Excerpt from John Livingston Lowes, *Essays in Appreciation.* Copyright 1936 by John Livingston Lowes, © renewed 1964 by John Wilbur Lowes (Lowell). Excerpt from F. O. Matthiessen, *Sarah Orne Jewett.* Copyright 1929 by Francis Otto Matthiessen. Copyright © renewed 1957 by H. G. Neubrand. Excerpts from Janice S. Robinson, *H. D.: The Life and Work of an American Poet.* Copyright © 1982 by Janice S. Robinson. All excerpts reprinted by permission of Houghton Mifflin Co. All rights reserved.

HUMAN SCIENCES PRESS/PLENUM PUBLISHING CORPORATION. For excerpts from essays by Glenda Hobbs on Arnow; Roger Whitlow on Dunbar-Nelson in *Regionalism and the Female Imagination,* Emily Toth, ed.

THE HUMANA PRESS INC. For excerpt from Nina J. Kossman's Introduction to *In the Inmost Hour of the Soul: Selected Poems of Marina Tsvetayeva.*

THE ILLUSTRATED LONDON NEWS. For excerpt from article by Sir John Squires on West.

INDIAN LITERATURE—SAHITYA AKADEMI (NATIONAL ACADEMY OF LETTERS). For excerpts from articles by Shayam M. Asnani on Sahgal; V. D. Katamble on Rau; Francine E. Krishna on Desai.

INDIANA UNIVERSITY PRESS. For excerpts from articles by Susan Z. Andrade on Nwapa; Mildred Mortimer on Djebar, Sebbar; Clarisse Zimra on Djebar in *Research in African Literatures,* published by Indiana University Press.

INDUSTRIAL AND LABOR RELATIONS REVIEW. For excerpt from article by James A. Hodges on Vorse.

INSTITUT FÜR ANGLISTIK UND AMERIKANISTIK. For excerpt from essays by Shiv K. Kumar on Desai in *The Twofold Voice: Essays in Honor of Ramesh Mohar,* S. N. A. Rizsi, ed.; Erwin A. Storzl on Jennings in *On Poets and Poetry,* James Hogg, ed.

THE INSTITUTE FOR THE TRANSLATION OF HEBREW LITERATURE. For excerpts from articles by Sonia Grober on Kahana-Carmon; David Melamed, Edna Sharoni on Raab in *Modern Hebrew Literature.* Reprinted with the permission of The Institute for the Translation of Hebrew Literature. Translation © copyright by The Institute for the Translation of Hebrew Literature.

INSTITUTE OF EAST ASIAN STUDIES, UNIVERSITY OF CALIFORNIA—BERKELEY. For excerpt from Victoria V. Vernon, *Daughters of the Moon: Wish, Will and Social Constraint in Fiction by Modern Japanese Women* (Hayashi Fumiko, Sata).

INTER-AMERICAN REVIEW OF BIBLIOGRAPHY/REVISTA INTERAMERICANA DE BIBLIOGRAFIA. For excerpt from article by Marjorie Agosin on Allende.

INTERNATIONAL PUBLISHERS CO. For excerpts from I. Dazhina's Introduction to *Alexandra Kollontai: Selected Articles and Speeches;* Christa Wolf, *The Reader and the Writer* (Bachmann).

INTI, REVISTA DE LITERATURA HISPÁNICA. For excerpt from article by Julia Kushigian on Bullrich.

IOWA STATE UNIVERSITY PRESS. For excerpt from Norris W. Yates, *The American Humorist* (Parker).

THE IRISH AMERICAN CULTURAL INSTITUTE. For excerpts from articles by Joseph Connelly on Johnston; Sean McMahon, Rose Quielle, Lotus Snow on O'Brien; Ann Weekes on O'Faolain in *Éire-Ireland.* Copyright—*Éire-Ireland,* a journal of Irish Studies published by the Irish American Cultural Institute of St. Paul, MN. Reprinted by permission of the publisher.

IRISH LITERARY SUPPLEMENT. For excerpts from articles by Louise Barry on O'Brien; Robert Tracy on O'Faolain.

IRISH UNIVERSITY REVIEW. For excerpt from article by Maurice Harmon on Johnston.

JAPADRE EDITORE-L'AQUILA. For excerpt from Antonio Sfamurri, *L'umanesimo cristiano di Simone Weil.*

BARBARA JEFFERIS. For excerpt from article on Jolley in *Overland.*

JOURNAL OF CANADIAN STUDIES/REVUE D'ÉTUDES CANADIENNES. For excerpts from articles by William H. New on Wilson; Roberta Rubenstein on Atwood.

JOURNAL OF CONTEMPORARY ASIA. For excerpt from article by Keith Forster on Zhang Xinxin.

JOURNAL OF INDIAN WRITING IN ENGLISH. For excerpt from article by Jasbir Jain on Mukherjee.

JOURNAL OF NARRATIVE TECHNIQUE. For excerpts from articles by Elizabeth Fifer on Stein; Barbara Garlick on Anderson; K. R. Ireland on Hill.

JOURNAL OF POPULAR CULTURE. For excerpt from article by Phyllis Binler on Burnett.

JOURNAL OF SOUTH ASIAN LITERATURE. For excerpt from article by Ann Lowry Weir on Desai.

JOURNAL OF THE ASSOCIATION OF TEACHERS OF JAPANESE. For excerpts from articles by Brett de Borg on Miyamoto; Yoko McClain on Enchi Fumiko, Nogami.

JOURNAL OF WEST INDIAN LITERATURE. For excerpts from articles by Edward Baugh on Goodison.

KATYDID BOOKS. For excerpts from Edward Seidensticker's Preface, Keiko Tsukimura's Introduction to *I Am Alive: The Tanka Poems of Goto Miyoko, 1898–1978*.

THE KENYON REVIEW. For excerpts from Geoffrey H. Hartman, "Les Belles Dames San Merci" (Garrigue, Sexton); Hilary Corke, "Reflections on a Great Stone Face" (Stein). First published in *The Kenyon Review*. Copyright 1960, 1961 by Kenyon College.

KODANSHA INTERNATIONAL LTD. For excerpt from Makata Ueda, *The Mother of Drama and Other Short Stories: Portrayals of Women in Modern Japanese Fiction* (Hirabayashi Taiko).

ALFRED KRÖNER VERLAG. For excerpts from essays by Fritz Martini, *Deutsche Literaturgeschichte* (Kolmar, Le Fort).

PETER LANG PUBLISHING, INC. For excerpts from essays by Beth Bjorkland on Mayröcker; Donald G. Daviau on Frischmuth; August Obermayer on Ebner in *Major Figures of Contemporary Austrian Literature*, Donald G. Daviau, ed.; Marie-Odile Blum on Frischmuth; Carine Kleiber on Ebner in *Frauenliteratur in Österreich von 1945 bis heute*, Carine Kleiber and Erica Tunner, eds.; Peter Horn on Reinig; Manfred Jurgensen on Struck, Leutenegger; John Milfull on Seghers in *Frauenliteratur: Autorinnen, Perspektiven, und Konzepte*, Manfred Jurgensen, ed.; George Buehler, *The Death of Socialist Realism in the Novels of Christa Wolf*; Carine Kleiber, *Jeannie Ebner: Eine Einfürung*; Sharon Magnarelli, *Reflections/Refractions: Reading Luisa Valenzuela*; Susanne Mayer, *Die Sehnsucht nach den anderen: Eine Studie zum Verhältnis von Subjekt und Gesellschaft in den Autobiographien von Lillian Hellman, Maya Angelou und Maxine Hong Kingston* (Angelou); Susan Canty Quinlan, *The Female Voice in Contemporary Brazilian Narrative* (Luft); Gerhild Bruggermann Rogers, *Das Romanwerk von Ingeborg Drewitz*; Dagmar C. Stern, *Hilde Domin: From Exile to Ideal*.

LATIN AMERICAN LITERARY REVIEW PRESS. For excerpts from Linda Britt's Translator's Introduction to *There Never Was a Once Upon a Time* by Carmen Naranjo; Laura García Moreno on Valenzuela in *Latin American Literary Review*.

PAUL LAUTER. For excerpt from Afterword to Agnes Smedley, *Daughter of Earth*.

LAWRENCE & WISHART LTD. For excerpt from essay by Sonja Ruehl on Hall in *Feminism, Culture, and Politics*, R. Brunt and C. Rowan, eds.

LEPTA (FORMERLY SOVIET LITERATURE). For excerpts from articles by Vladimir Aleksandrov, Diana Tevekelyan on Panova in *Soviet Literature*.

NEAL A. LESTER. For excerpt from article on Shange in *Black American Literature Forum*.

LETRAS PENINSULARES. For excerpts from articles by Mercedes M. de Rodríguez, Shirley Mangini on Chacel.

LETTRES QUÉBÉCOISES. For excerpt from article by Gérald Gaudet on Brossard.

BRONWEN LEVY. For excerpt from essay on Hazzard in *Gender, Politics, and Fiction: Twentieth Century Australian Women's Novels*, Carole Ferrier, ed.

RALPH LEY. For excerpt from article on Fleisser first published in *University of Dayton Review*.

THE LITERARY CRITERION. For excerpts from articles by N. Meena Belliappa on Rau; Prabhu S. Guptara on Avison; Shyamala Venkateswaran on Markandaya.

LITTLE, BROWN AND COMPANY. For excerpts from John Malcolm Brinnin, *The Third Rose* (Stein); Alfred Kazin, *Bright Book of Life* (McCullers).

LONDON MAGAZINE. For excerpts from articles by Maurice L. Cranston on Murdoch; Elaine Feinstein on Jhabvala; Francis Hope on Murdoch; John Mellors on Johnston, Markandaya; James L. Michie on Warner; Helen Moran on Kennedy; Anthony Quinton on Spark; Anne Ridler on Raine; Alan Ross on Maraini, Plath; J. I. M. Stewart on Brooke-Rose; Peter Vansittart on O'Faolain, Renault; D. M. Thomas on Wright; John Wain on West; Milton Waldman on Lee; Hugh Williams on Jellicoe.

LONDON REVIEW OF BOOKS. For excerpts from articles by Penelope Fizgerald on Smith; Alasdair MacIntyre on Murdoch; Sean O'Faolain on Bowen; John Sutherland on Keane.

ANGELO LONGO EDITORE. For excerpts from Natalia Costa-Zalessow, *Scrittrici italiane dal XIII al XX secolo* (Neera).

LOUISIANA STATE UNIVERSITY PRESS. For excerpts from Alfred Appel, *A Season of Dreams: The Fiction of Eudora Welty*; essays by Martha Fodaski Black, Doris Davis, Barbara C. Ewell, Dorothy H. Jacobs in *Kate Chopin Reconsidered: Beyond the Bayou*, Lynda S. Boren and Sara deSaussure Davis, eds.; Dickson D. Bruce, Jr., *Black American Writing from the*

Nadir: Evolution of a Literary Tradition, 1877–1915 (Hopkins); Leonard Casper on O'Connor in *The Shaken Realist*, Melvin J. Friedman and John B. Vickery, eds.; John Cooke, *The Novels of Nadine Gordimer: Private Lives/Public Landscapes;* Judith Farr, *Life and Art of Elinor Wylie;* Alan Warren Friedman, *Multivalence: The Moral Quality of Form in the Modern Novel* (Richardson); Blyden Jackson, *Black Poetry in America* (Brooks); Louise Kertesz, *The Poetic Vision of Muriel Rukeyser;* Virginia M. Kouidis, *Mina Loy: American Modernist Poet;* Carol Shloss, *Flannery O'Connor's Dark Comedies;* Robert Penn Warren's Introduction to *Collected Stories of Caroline Gordon.;* essay by Frank Wood on Le Fort in *Studies in German Literature,* Carl Hammer, ed.; Introduction to *Baby* by Kirsten Thorup.

LOYOLA UNIVERSITY PRESS. For excerpt from Brian Abel Ragan, *A Wreck on the Road to Damascus: Innocence, Guilt and Conversion in Flannery O'Connor.*

MACMILLAN PRESS LTD. For excerpts from essays by Nancy Bailey, Gayle Greene, Lynette Hunter in *Critical Approaches to the Fiction of Margaret Laurence,* Colin Nicholson, ed. © 1990.

MAGAZINE LITTÉRAIRE. For excerpt from article by Jean-Didier Wolfromm on Yourcenar. © *Magazine Littéraire.*

DAR MAHJAR. For excerpt from Mona Mikhail, *Arabic Literature in North Africa: Critical Essays and Annotated Bibliography* (Binnūna).

GROUPE MAME, NOUVELLES ÉDITIONS. For excerpts from Marie-Magdeleine Davy, *Simone Weil;* Geneviève Genneré, *Simone de Beauvoir;* Gérard Mourgue, tr. by Dorothy Nyren Curley, *Françoise Sagan.*

JANE MARCUS. For excerpts from articles on Jackson in *Iowa Review;* Schreiner in *Minnesota Review;* Woolf in *Women's Review of Books;* Preface and Introduction, *The Young Rebecca: Writings of Rebecca West 1911–17.*

BONNIE MARRANCA. For excerpt from essay by Bonnie G. Marranca on Fornés in *American Playwrights: A Critical Survey,* Bonnie G. Marranca and Gautam Dasgupta, eds. © Copyright 1981 Bonnie Marranca.

ABIGAIL ANN MARTIN. For excerpts from *Ruth Suckow* and *Tillie Olsen.*

MCGILL-QUEENS UNIVERSITY PRESS. For excerpts from Misao Dean, *A Different Point of View: Sara Jeanette Duncan;* Karen E. Smythe, *Figuring Grief: Gallant, Munro and the Poetics of Elegy* (Munro); Elizabeth Thompson, *The Pioneer Woman: A Canadian Character Type* (Duncan).

FRANCES MCINHERNY. For excerpt from essay on Harrower in *Gender, Politics, and Fiction: Twentieth Century Australian Women's Novels,* Carole Ferrier, ed.

MELBOURNE SLAVONIC STUDIES. For excerpt from article by Temira Pachmuss on Gippius.

THE EDWIN MELLEN PRESS. For excerpts from essays by Mercè Clarasó on Rodoreda in *Women Writers in Spain and Spanish America,* Catherine Davies, ed.; Judith Drinkwater on Pardo Bazán; Evelyn Fishburn on Storni in *Feminist Readings on Spanish and Latin American Literature,* L. P. Condé and S. M. Hart, eds.; Lorine M. Getz, *Nature and Grace in Flannery O'Connor's Fiction;* Richard E. Morton, *Anne Sexton's Poetry of Redemption: The Chronology of a Pilgrimage.*

MELUS: THE JOURNAL OF THE SOCIETY FOR THE STUDY OF THE MULTI-ETHNIC LITERATURE OF THE UNITED STATES. For excerpts from articles by Elizabeth N. Evasdaughter on Silko; Charlotte Goodman on Arnow; W. Laurence Hogue on Walker; Nancy Lang on Harjo; Dorothy Risako McDonald, Katherine Newman on Yamamoto; Elizabeth J. Ordóñez on Portillo de Trambley; Mariolina Salvatori on Yezierska; James Robert Saunders on Sanchez; Lynette Seator on Cervantes; Alan Wald on Silko; Gay Wilentz on Yezierska.

MERCER UNIVERSITY PRESS. For excerpts from essay by Dennis Lloyd on Giovanni in *Literature of Tennessee,* Ray Willbanks, ed. Reprinted with permission. © 1984 Mercer University Press, 6316 Peake Road, Macon, GA 31210.

MERCURE DE FRANCE. For excerpt from Francis Jammes's Preface to *Sept dialogues de bêtes* by Colette.

MICHIGAN QUARTERLY REVIEW. For excerpts from articles by Janet Sharistanian on Slesinger; Lisa M. Steinman on Dove.

MIDSTREAM: A MONTHLY JEWISH REVEW. For excerpt from article by Cynthia Ozick on Calisher.

MISSISSIPPI QUARTERLY. For excerpts from articles by Robert H. Brinkmeyer, Jr. on Mason; James E. Rocks on Gordon. Copyright 1968, 1988, 1989 Mississippi State University, Mississippi State, Mississippi.

MODERN AUSTRIAN LITERATURE. For excerpts from articles by Karen Achberger on Bachmann; Bernhardt Blumenthal on Goll; Renate Delphendahl on Bachmann; U. Henry Gerlach on Aichinger; Ritta Jo Horsley on Bachmann; Waltraud Mitgutsch on Lavant; August Obermayer on Ebner; Marilyn Scott on Busta.

MODERN DRAMA. For excerpts from articles by Jeanie Forte on Norman; Pierre Gobin on Maillet; Ralph Ley on Fleisser; Joseph Meroll on Churchill; Vivian M. Petraka on Hellman; Martin Price on Jellicoe; Peter L. Podol on Gámbaro; Jenny S. Spencer on Norman; Kathleen Gregory Klein on Terry; Richard Wattenberg on Norman.

MODERN LANGUAGE ASSOCIATION OF AMERICA. For excerpts from Barbara Johnson, *Textual Analysis: Some Readers Reading* (Hurston), reprinted by permission of the Modern Language Association of America; Julia Cluck on Wylie reprinted by permission of the Modern Language Association of America from *PMLA* (1941): 841; Ann E. Hostetler on Larsen reprinted by permission of the Modern Language Association of America from *PMLA* 105 (1990) 35–36. © Modern Language Association of America.

THE MODERN LANGUAGE REVIEW. For excerpts from articles by Leslie Hill on Duras; Ella Geoffrey Kantaris on Traba; Stuart Parker on Keun; J. S. Ryan on Wright.

MONTHLY REVIEW. For excerpt from Dee Garrison's Introduction to *Rebel Pen: The Writings of Mary Heaton Vorse.* © 1985 by Dee Garrison. Reprinted by permission of Monthly Review Foundation.

MOSAIC: A JOURNAL FOR THE INTERDISCIPLINARY STUDY OF LITERATURE. For excerpts from the following: Craig and Diana Barrow's "*The Left Hand of Darkness:* Feminism for Men" originally appeared in a special issue of *Mosaic: A Journal for the Interdisciplinary Study of Literature* Vol. 20, No. 1 (Winter 1987), pp. 83–84 (LeGuin); Stephanie A. Demetrakopolous's "Archetypal Constellations of Feminine Consciousness in Nin's *Diary*" originally appeared in a special issue of *Mosaic—The World of Anaïs Nin,* Evelyn J. Hinz, ed., Vol. 11, No. 2 (Winter 1978), pp. 121–22; Patricia Elliot's "In the Eye of Abjection: Marie Cardinal's *The Words to Say It*" originally appeared in a special issue of *Mosaic—Data and Acta: Aspects of Life-Writing,* Evelyn J. Hinz, ed., Vol. 20, No. 4 (Fall 1987), pp. 71–72; Phyllis Lassner's "The Quiet Revolution: World War II and the English Domestic Novel" originally appeared in a special issue of *Mosaic—Troops v. Tropes: War and Literature,* Evelyn J. Hinz, ed., Vol. 23, No. 3 (Summer 1990), pp. 95–96 (Howard, Taylor); Brent MacLaine's "Photofiction as Family Album: David Galloway, Paul Theroux and Anita Brookner" originally appeared in a special issue of *Mosaic: A Journal for the Interdisciplinary Study of Literature,* Vol. 24, No. 2 (Spring 1991), pp. 145–47; Marthe Rosenfeld's "The Linguistic Aspect of Sexual Conflict: Monique Wittig's *Le corps lesbien*" originally appeared in a special issue of *Mosaic—For Better or Worse: Attitudes Toward Marriage in Literature,* Evelyn J. Hinz, ed., Vol. 17, Nos. 2/3 (Spring 1984), p.240; Jack D. Zipes, "Growing Pains in the Contemporary German Novel— East and West" originally appeared in a special issue of *Mosaic—New Views of The European Novel,* R. G. Collins and Kenneth McRobbie, eds., Vol. 5, No. 2 (Spring 1972), pp. 13–14 (Wolf).

MOUTON DE GRUYTER, A DIVISION OF WALTER DE GRUYTER & CO. For excerpt from Cynthia Haft, *The Theme of the Nazi Concentration Camps in French Literature* (Delbo).

MS. For excerpts from articles by Anne Bernays on Ginzburg; Adrianne Blue on Weldon; Rosellen Brown on Naylor; Vivian Gornick on Hellman; Patricia Hampl on LeSueur; Margo Jefferson on Morrison; Barbara Smith, Gloria Steinem on Walker; Alice Walker on Dangarembga, Emecheta; Brigitte Weeks on Godwin; Sherley Anne Williams on Naylor; Helen Zia on Tan in *Ms.*

ERIKA MUNK. For excerpt from article on Drakulič in *Women's Review of Books.*

JAMES NAREMORE. For excerpt from *The World without a Self: Virginia Woolf and the Novel.*

THE NATION. For excerpts from articles by Julie Abraham on Warner; Mildred Adams on Mistral; Ammiel Alcalay on Adnan; Charles Angoff on Slesinger; Russell Banks on Erdrich; Louise Bogan on Welty; Dorothy Brewster on Goldman; Sterling A. Brown on Hurston; Jerry H. Bryant on Morrison, Walker; B.U. Burke on Lagerlöf; Robert Cantwell on Undset; Brina Caplan on Munro; David Caute on Wolf; Jan Clausen on Herbst, Lorde; Harold Clurman on Bowles, Hansberry; Carolyn Cooke on Acker, Fell; Alice Denham on Weldon; Erwin Edman on Parker; Mary Ellmann on Warner; Clifton Fadiman on Cather, Lehmann; Louis Fischer on Kollontai; Maxwell Geismar on Glasgow, Nin; Hal Gelb on Moraga; Irene Gendzier on Saadawi; Sandra M. Gilbert on Sexton; Ray Gonzalez on Zamora; Gayle Greene on Drabble; Muriel Haynes on Leduc; Richard Howard on Warner; Florence Howe on Lessing; Rolfe Humphries on Millay, Wylie; Randall Jarrell on Pitter, Rukeyser; Denis Johnston on Rukeyser; Frances Keene on Morante; Robert Kiely on McCarthy; Freda Kirchwey on Goldman, Smedley; Stuart Klawans on Ortese; Joseph Wood Krutch on Colette, Hellman, Suckow; John Leonard on Kingston, Morrison; Denise Levertov on Sitwell; Dierdre Levinson on Lessing; Sinclair Lewis on Vorse; Eugene Löhrke on Undset; Pierre Loving on Colette; Charles Lam Markmann on O'Brien; Margaret Marshall on Porter, Valerie Miner on Tan, Wang Anyi, Yamamoto; Marianne Moore on Bishop; Scott Nearing on Yezierska; Feiner Nuhn on Slesinger; Grace Paley on Wolf; Alice Beal Parsons on Undset; Gail Pool on Webb; Philip Rahv on Boyle; Elayne Rapping on Wolf; Philip Blair Rice on Millay, Porter, Rukeyser; Lillian S. Robinson on Atwood; Paul Rosenfeld on Nin; Nicholas Rzevsky on Petrushevskaya; Kirkpatrick Sale on Erdrich; Louis B. Salomon on Rawlings; Stephen Schlesinger on Menchú; Edgar Snow on Buck; George Soule on Vorse; Carol Sternhell on Paley; Catharine R. Stimpson on Atwood; May Swenson on Rukeyser; Gerald Sykes on Boyle; Allen Tate on Porter; Diana Trilling on Petry, Stafford, Welty; William Troy on Stein; Katrina vanden Heuvel on Baranskaya; Carl Van Doren on Yezierska; Mark Van Doren on Bogan, Dinesen, Teasdale, Undset, Wickham; Eliseo Vivas on Espina; Eda Lou Walton on Buck, Lagerlöf; Paul West on Weil; John R. Willingham on Mitford; Edmund Wilson on Millay; Samuel Yellen on Vorse; Morton Dauwen Zabel on Lewis, Richardson; articles on Jackson, Petry, Smith, Suckow and Undset.

NATIONAL COUNCIL OF TEACHERS OF ENGLISH. For excerpts from articles by Kenneth Bernard on Wharton; Barret H. Clark on Hellman; James G. Southworth on Bishop in *College English;* Phyllis Bentley on Buck; Richard C. Carpenter on Boyle; Melvin J. Friedman on O'Connor; Dayton Kohler on McCullers; Mark Van Doren on Parker in *English Journal.*

NATIONAL POETRY FOUNDATION. For excerpts from essays by Mary Bryan, Gayle Gaskill in *May Sarton: Woman and Poet,* Constance Hunting, ed.

NAUKA. For excerpt from T. P. Agaphína, *Istoria polskói literatury* (Nalkowska).

NELSON-HALL. For excerpts from Roger Whitlow, *Black American Literature* (Walker).

NEOPHILOLOGUS. For excerpt from article by Anna Hausdorf on Goll.

NEUE DEUTSCHE LITERATUR. For excerpts from articles by René Schwachhofer on Domin; Annemaria Auer on Seghers.

THE NEW ENGLAND QUARTERLY. For excerpts from articles by Warner Barthoff on Jewett; Alice Bloom on Mason; Alexander M. Buchan on Wharton; Babette May Levy, Eleanor M. Smith on Jewett; Susan Allen Toth on Freeman.

NEW GERMAN STUDIES. For excerpts from articles by Petra M. Bagley on Plessen.

THE NEW LEADER. For excerpts from articles by Pearl K. Bell on Bainbridge; Hope Hale Davis on Warner; Freema Gottlieb on Berberova; Richard Howard on Matute; Stanley Edgar Hyman on Frame; Donald Phelps on Sontag; Paula Meinetz Shapiro on Walker; Stephen Stepanchev on Wakoski.

NEW ORLEANS REVIEW. For excerpt from article by Gloria T. Hall on Dunbar-Nelson.

NEW STATESMAN AND SOCIETY. For excerpts from articles by Richard Aldington on Mansfield in *Nation and Athenæum;* Helen Birch on Fell; Brigid Brophy on Calisher; A. S. Byatt on Johnson; Gerda Charles on Laurence; Judy Cooke on Roberts, Sidhwa; Patricia Craig on West; R. R. Davis on Weldon; Jenny Diski on Minco; D. J. Enright on Spark; Liz Heron on Duranti; Grace Ingoldsby on Tusquets, Weldon; Naomi Lewis on Macaulay; Desmond MacCarthy on Lehmann; W. J. McCormack on Bowen; V. S. Naipaul on O'Brien; Ralph Partridge on Howard; V. S. Pritchett on Wright; Maurice Richardson on Castellanos; Michèle Roberts on Lessing; Dorothea Smartt on Riley; Logan Pearsall Smith on Field; John Spurling on Ty-Casper; Robert Taubman on Brophy, Jameson; Gillian Tindall on Manning; Boyd Tonkin on Voznesenskaya, Williams; William Trevor on Drabble, O'Brien; Rebecca West on Sinclair, Stern; Marianne Wiggins on Sidhwa; Gillian Wilce on Shaikh in *New Statesman;* Brigid Brophy on Ginzburg, Maraini; Elizabeth Bowen on West; Cyril Connolly on Benson; John Davenport on Bedford; Graham Greene on Weil; Pamela Hansford Johnson on Morante; John Mitfoud on Deledda; Raymond Mortimer on Dane; P. H. Newby on Stark; Sean O'Faolain on Thirkell; V. S. Pritchett on Colette, West; Kathleen Raine on Barnes; John Raymond on Bottome, Sayers; Henry Reed on Mitford, Renault; Maurice Richardson on Cespedes; G. W. Stonier on Pitter; Julia Strachey on McCarthy, Panova; John Summerson on Macaulay; Kitty Warnock on Tūqān; Angus Wilson on Welty in *New Statesman and Nation*; Carole Angier on Tan; Melissa Benn on Drakulič; Helen Birch on Fell; Patricia Craig on Somerville and Ross, Weldon; Lucy Ellman on Zhang Xinxin; Harriett Gilbert on Barker; Julia Hobsbawm on Joubert; Kathryn Hughes on Tan; Sara Maitland on White; Amanda Mitchison on Drakulič; Caroline Moorehead on Voznesenskaya; Chris Mowles on Chedid; Ruth Pavey on Tolstaya, Uno; Robert Sheppard on Fell; Diana Souhami on Weldon in *New Statesman and Society.* Reprinted by permission of The Statesman and Nation Publishing Company Ltd.

THE NEW YORK PUBLIC LIBRARY. For excerpt from article by George Brandon Saul on Wylie in *Bulletin of the New York Public Library.*

THE NEW YORK REVIEW OF BOOKS. For excerpts from articles by Hannah Arendt on Sarraute; Eve Auchincloss on Calisher; Bernard Bergonzi on Young; Frederick C. Crews on Stafford; Denis Donoghue on Porter, Stead; Irvin Ehrenpreis on Wharton; Henry Gifford on Tolstaya; Elizabeth Hardwick on Plath; D. A. N. Jones on Blais; Frank Kermode on Colette; Alison Lurie on Jansson, Lessing; Mary McCarthy on Sarraute; Daphne Merkin on Bowles; Jonathan Mirsky on Wang Anyi; Basil T. Paquet on McCarthy; Christopher Ricks on Oates,

Stead; Charles Thomas Samuels on Bowles; Jean Stafford on Chopin; Donald Sutherland, Virgil Thomson on Stein; Rosemary Tonks on Garrigue; Robert A. Towers on Erdrich; Robert Towers on Spark; Gore Vidal on Renault; John Willett on Wolf; Michael Wood on Drexler, Leduc, Paley, Welty. Reprinted with permission from *The New York Revew of Books.* Copyright © 1965–94 Nyrev, Inc.

THE NEW YORK TIMES. For excerpts from articles by Mildred Adams on Matute; Walter Allen on Rhys; A. Alvarez on Rhys; Newton Arvin on West; John Ashbery on Bowles; Brooks Atkinson on Treadwell; Margaret Atwood on Piercy; Carlos Baker on Johnson; Anna Balakian on Nin; Toni Cade Bambara on Brooks; Clive Barnes on Owens; Donald Barr on Jackson, Lee; Millicent Bell on Tyler; Joseph Bennett on Sarton; Sara Blackburn on Morrison, Piercy; Germaine Brée on Sarraute; Harvey Breit on Jackson; Peter Brooks on Leduc; Anatole Broyard on Johnston, Keane; Gertrude Buckman on Calisher; Otis K. Burger on Ginzburg; John Corkin on Treadwell; Hubert Creekmore on Brooks; Robert Gorham Davis on Nin; Benjamin DeMott on Tyler, Sontag; Babette Deutsch on Doolittle (H. D.); James Dickey on Moore; Lore Dickstein on Sarton; Joan Didion on Lessing; Richard Eberhart on Rukeyser; Rose Feld on McCullers; Thomas J. Fleming on Howard; Rene Fulop-Miller on Nin; John Gardner on Oates; Jean Garrigue on Nin; Maxwell Geismar on Boyle; Judith Gies on Godwin; Richard Gilman on Oates; Gail Godwin on Beattie; Caroline Gordon on O'Connor; May Gordon on McCarthy; William Goyen on O'Connor, Sarton; Francine duPlessix Gray on Bowles; Horace Gregory on Bryher; Elizabeth Hardwick on Beauvoir; Ihab Hassan on Jackson; William Hjortsberg on Drexler; Raymond Holder on Sarton; Perry Hutchinson on Sarton; Elizabeth Janeway on Lehmann, Roy, Sagan, Sarton; Johanna Kaplan on Ozick; Frances Keene on Cespedes, Mallet-Joris; Hugh Kenner on Doolittle (H. D.); Walter Kerr on Owens; Robert Kiely on Calisher; John Knowles on Oates; Alfred Kreymborg on Rich; Seymour Krim on Wilson; Louis Kronenberger on Parker; Laurence Lafore on Johnson; Herbert Leibowitz on Stein; John Leonard on Didion, Renault, West; Robert Lowell on Rich; Isabelle Mallet on Thirkell; Fred T. Marsh on McCullers; T. S. Matthews on Bedford; Paolo Milano on Morante; Ellen Moers on McCarthy; Alice S. Morris on Jackson; Frederic Morton on Morante; Howard Moss on Welty; Julian Moynihan on Ozick; Kathleen Nott on Maraini; Joyce Carol Oates on Drabble, Frame; J. D. O'Hara on Oates; Walter O'Hearn on Blais; Ruth Page on Kunewicz; William Peden on Stafford; Virgilia Peterson on Buck, Macaulay; Henri Peyre on Sarraute; Katha Pollitt on Tyler; Dorothy Rabinowitz on Jhabvala; Clayton Riley on Hansberry; Selden Rodman on Castellanos, Garrigue; W. G. Rogers on Buck; Michael Rosenthal on Brophy; Sara Sanborn on Drexler; Mark Schorer on Hellman; Marc Slonim on Ginzburg; R. A. Smith on Smedley; Jane Spence Southron on Sarton; Anne Stevenson on Rukeyser; Paul Theroux on Gordimer; Diana Trilling on West; Robert Towers on Hellman; Laurence van Gelden on Owens; Helen Vendler on Oates; Edith Walton on Bowles, Renault; Eudora Welty on Cather, Dinesen; Alden Whitman on Parker; Frances Winwar on Mitford; Michael Wood on Oates; Stark Young on Treadwell; article on Nalkowska in *The New York Times.* Copyright © 1920/22/23/25/28/29/33/36/38/39/40/41/43/45/47/49/50/51/52/53/54/55/56/57/58/59/60/62/63/64/65/66/67/68/69/70/71/72/73/74/75/76/77/78/79/80/81/82/83/84 by The New York Times Company. Reprinted by permission.

THE NEW YORK TIMES BOOK REVIEW. For excerpts from articles by Robert Alter on Morante; John Ashbery on Bishop; James Atlas on Stead; Margaret Atwood on Thomas; Jacqueline Austin on West; John Banville on Sontag; Richard Burgin on Telles; Beverly Lyon Clark on Sandel; William DuBois on Seghers; Chéri Fein on Ty-Casper; Barbara Finkelstein on Minco; Laura Furman on O'Faolain; Mary Gordon on Keane; Annie Gottlieb on Naylor; William Goyen on Young; Elizabeth Hanson on Uno; Daniel J. Leab on Vorse; Rudolf Walter Leonhardt on Wolf; Julius Lester on Cunard; Perry Link on Ding Ling; Frank MacShane on Silko; Jane Marcus on Brittain; Bharati Mukherjee on Naylor, Saadawi; Nigel Nicholson on Renault; Joyce Carol Oates; Katha Pollitt on Weldon; Francine Prose on Drakulič; Marilyn Sachs on Blume; Ellen Schecter on Tan; Stephen Spender on Sachs; George Stade on Duranti; Lawrence Thornton on Erdrich; Anne Tyler on Brookner; Mel Watkins on Naylor; Fay Weldon on Voznesenskaya; Julia Whedon on O'Faolain; article on Keane in *The New York Times Book Review.* Copyright © 1932/44/65/67/69/70/74/76/77/78/79/82/83/85/86/88/89/92/93/94 by The New York Times Company. Reprinted by permission.

NEW YORK UNIVERSITY PRESS. For excerpts from Margot Arce de Vázquez, *Gabriela Mistral: The Poet and Her Work;* Louis F. Kannenstine, *The Art of Djuna Barnes: Duality and Damnation.*

LIBRAIRIE A. G. NIZET. For excerpts from essays by Mieke Bal, Michel Baude in *Colette, nouvelles approches critiques,* Bernard Bray, ed.

NORTH AMERICAN REVIEW. For excerpts from articles by Herbert S. Gorman on Wylie; Archibald MacLeish on Lowell; Lloyd Morris on Rawlings.

NORTHEASTERN UNIVERSITY PRESS. For excerpt from Guy Rotella, *Reading and Writing Nature: The Poetry of Robert Frost, Wallace Stevens, Marianne Moore, and Elizabeth Bishop* . Copyright 1991 by Guy Rotella. Reprinted with the permission of Northeastern University Press, Boston (Bishop).

NORTHERN ILLINOIS UNIVERSITY PRESS. For excerpt from Ildikó de Papp Carrington, *Controlling the Uncontrollable: The Fiction of Alice Munro.* © 1989 Northern Illinois University Press. Used with permission of Northern Illinois University Press.

NORTHWESTERN UNIVERSITY PRESS. For excerpt from Maurice Merleau-Ponty in *Sense and Non-Sense* (Beauvoir). © 1964.

NOTES ON CONTEMPORARY LITERATURE. For excerpts from articles by Lori Duin Kelly on Naylor; Philip C. Kolin on Terry.

LE NOUVEL OBSERVATEUR. For excerpt from article by Françoise Mallet-Joris on Yourcenar.

NOVEL: A FORUM ON FICTION. For excerpts from articles by Rachel Blau DuPlessis on Woolf in *NOVEL: A Forum on Fiction* Vol. 21, No. 3, Spring 1988; Gayle Greene on Drabble in *NOVEL: A Forum on Fiction* Vol. 22, No. 1, Fall 1988; Carol Siegel on Webb in *NOVEL: A Forum on Fiction* Vol. 24, No. 2, Winter 1991; Susan Spitzer on Drabble in *NOVEL: A Forum on Fiction* Vol. 11, No. 3, Spring 1978. All excerpts copyright NOVEL Corp. © Reprinted with permission.

LA NUOVA ITALIA EDITRICE S.P.A. For excerpts from Anna Nozzoli, *Tabù e coscienza: La condizione femminile nella letteratura italiana del Novecento* (Banti); Luciana Machione Picchone, Natalia Ginzburg.

NYMPHENBURGER. For excerpt from Karl August Horst, *Kritischer Führer durch die deutsche Literatur der Gegenwart* (Busta). © by Nymphenburger in der F. A. Herbig Verlagsbuchhandlung GmbH, München.

EVELYN O'CALLAGHAN. For excerpt from essay on Broadber in *Progressions: West Indian Literature in the 1970s,* Edward Baugh and Mervyn Morris, eds.

PATTY O'CONNELL. For excerpt from article on Richardson in *Women's Review of Books.*

OHIO STATE UNIVERSITY PRESS—JOURNALS DEPARTMENT. For excerpt from article by Helen Muchnic on Akhmatova in *Russian Review.*

OHIO UNIVERSITY PRESS/SWALLOW PRESS. For excerpts from Benjamin Franklin V and Duane Schneider, *Anaïs Nin: An Introduction;* Olga Anastasia Pelensky's Introduction to *Isak Dinesen: Critical Views;* Sharon Spencer, *Collage of Dreams: The Writing of Anaïs Nin;* Helen Trimpi's Introduction to *Poems Old and New 1918–78* by Janet Lewis; Joyce Piell Wexler, *Laura Riding's Pursuit of Truth* (Jackson).

CASA EDITRICE LEO S. OLSCHKI. For excerpts from articles by Madeleine Cottonet-Hage on Chauvet; Lise Ouellet on Dessaules in *Francofonia.*

MARGARET STEWART OMRCANIN. For excerpts from *Ruth Suckow: A Critical Study of Her Fiction.*

OPEN UNIVERSITY PRESS. For excerpt from essay by Stephen Regan on Gallant in *Narrative Strategies in Canadian Literature,* Coral Ann Howells and Lynette Hunter, eds.

ORELL FÜSSLI VERLAG. For excerpt from essay by Wilhelm Duwe on Lasker-Schüler in *Deutsche Dichtung des 20. Jahrhunderts.*

ORGANIZATION OF AMERICAN STATES. For excerpt from article by Marjorie Agosin on Allende in *Inter-American Review of Bibliography/Revista interamericana de bibliografía.*

OXFORD UNIVERSITY PRESS. For excerpts from articles by Beth M. McKillop on Zhang Xinxin, Zhang Jie; Caroline Mason on Wang Anyi; Rosemary A. Roberts on Zhang Jie, Zhang Xinxin; Frances Wood on Chen Jo-Hsi (Ruoxi), Xi Xi, Zhang Jie; article on Ding Ling in *China Quarterly.*

PACIFIC NORTHWEST COUNCIL ON FOREIGN LANGUAGES. For excerpts from articles by Murl Barker on Berberova; Sigrid Mayer on Wohmann in *Selecta.*

PAJARITO PUBLICATIONS. For excerpt from Luis Arturo Ramos, *Angela de Hoyos: A Critical Look/Lo Heroico y Lo Antiheroico en su poesía.*

PANTHEON BOOKS. For excerpts from Simone Petrémont, *Simone Weil: A Life;* essay by Lillian S. Robinson on Woolf in *The Politics of Literature: Dissenting Essays on the Teaching of English,* Louis Kampf and Paul Lauter, eds.

PAPERS ON LANGUAGE AND LITERATURE. For excerpts from articles by Louise Kawada on Jordan; Vasa D. Mihailovich on Akhmatova.

PARNASSUS: POETRY IN REVIEW. For excerpts from articles by Margaret Atwood on Jong; Rosellen Brown on Sarton; Bonnie Costello on Levertov; Judith Gleason on Forché; John Hollander on Bishop; Constance Hunting on Cassian; Rosemary Johnson on Swenson; Kenneth Lincoln on Rose; Shireen Mahdavé on Farrokhzad; Diane Wood Middlebrook, Muriel Rukeyser on Sexton; R. B. Stepto on Angelou, Lorde; Catharine Stimpson, Helen Vendler on Rich; Katharine Washburn on Kaschnitz.

PARTISAN REVIEW. For excerpts from the following articles: Calvin Bedient on Oates first appeared in *Partisan Review*, Vol. 39, No. 1, 1972; Jean Bloch-Michel on Sagan first appeared in *Partisan Review*, Vol. 25, No. 1, 1958; John Malcolm Brinnin on Plath first appeared in *Partisan Review*, Vol. 34, No. 1, 1967; Stephen Donadio on Porter first appeared in *Partisan Review*, Vol. 33, No. 2, 1966; Richard Howard on Rich first appeared in *Partisan Review*, Vol. 38, No. 4, 1971; Frank Jones on Woolf first appeared in *Partisan Review*, Vol. 15, No. 5, 1948; David Kalstone on Bishop first appeared in *Partisan Review*, Vol. 37, No. 2, 1970.

PASSAGEN VERLAG. For excerpt from article by Klaus Hermsdorf on Seghers in *Weimarer Beiträge*.

PENGUIN USA. For excerpt from Percy Lubbock, *Portrait of Edith Wharton*.

THE PENKEVILL PUBLISHING CO. For excerpt from essay by Catherine Broderick on Enchi Fumiko in *Anaïs, Art, and Artists*, Sharon Spencer, ed.

PENN STATE PRESS. For excerpts from articles by Josie P. Campbell on Schwarz Bart in *Comparative Literature Studies*, Vol. 22, No. 3, pp. 397, 405; Yoshiko Enomoto on Nogami in *Comparative Literature Studies*, Vol. 28, No. 3, pp. 257–58; Carol Farley Kessler on Piercy in *Journal of General Education*, Vol. 37, No. 3, pp. 196–97; Laurent Le Sage, *The French New Novel* (Duras, pp. 85–86); Marilyn Yalom, *Maternity, Mortality and the Literature of Madness* (Cardinal pp. 36–37, 47–50, 69; Kingston pp. 96–97, 99–100). Copyright 1962, 1985, 1991 by The Pennsylvania State University. All excerpts reproduced by permission of the publisher.

PERSEA BOOKS. For excerpts from Vivian Gornick's Introduction (copyright © 1991 by Vivian Gornick) to *How I Found America: Collected Stories of Anzia Yezierska*, copyright © 1991 Louise Levitas Henriksen; Alice Kessler-Harris's Introduction (copyright © 1979 by Alice Kessler-Harris) to *The Open Cage: An Anzia Yezierska Collection*, copyright © 1979 by Louise Levitas Henriksen. Reprinted by permission of Persea Books, Inc.

PFEFFERSCHE BUCHHANDLUNG. For excerpt from Ingrid Müller, *Untersuchungen zum Bild der Frau in den Romanen von Hedwig Courths-Mahler*.

JULIE PHILLIPS. For excerpt from article on Valenzuela in *Women's Review of Books*.

PHYLON. For excerpts from articles by George E. Kent, Margaret Walker on Brooks. Copyright 1950, 1976 by Clark Atlanta University, Atlanta, Georgia. Reprinted with permission.

EDITORIAL PLIEGOS. For excerpt from María Jesús Mayans Natal, *Narrativa Feminista Española de Posguerra* (Galvarriato).

PLOUGHSHARES. For excerpt from article by James Carroll on Rodoreda.

PLURAL: REVISTA CULTURAL DE EXCELSIOR. For excerpt from article by Helena Araújo on Somers.

POETRY. For excerpts from articles that first appeared in *Poetry:* Léonie Adams on Bogan, © 1954; John Ashbery on Stein, © 1957; Frederick Bock on Garrigue, © 1965; John Malcolm Brinnin on Rukeyser, © 1943; David Bromwich on Sexton, © 1976; Winifred Bryher on Doolittle (H. D.), Moore, © 1922; John R. Carpenter on Wakoski, © 1972; Hayden Carruth on Rich, © 1967; Sherman Conrad on Sarton, © 1937; Alfred Corn on Swenson, © 1993; Bruce Cutler on Brooks, © 1964; Babette Deutsch on Teasdale, © 1937; Robert Duncan on Doolittle (H. D.), © 1958; Richard Eberhart on Doolittle (H. D.), © 1959; Ford Madox Ford on Bogan, © 1937; Barbara Gibbs on Miles, © 1946; Donald Hall on Rich, © 1956; H. R. Hays on Jackson, © 1939; Richard Howard on Boyle, © 1960; Richard Howard on Rich, © 1963; Josephine Jacobsen on Ridler, © 1957; Stanley Kunitz on Brooks, © 1950; Stanley Kunitz on Miles, © 1956; Philip Legler on Sexton, © 1967; Laurence Lieberman on Garrigue, © 1968; Laurence Lieberman on Rukeyser, © 1969; Marie Luhrs on Parker, © 1927; Harriet Monroe on Moore, Wylie, © 1922; Samuel Moon on Hébert, © 1968; Marianne Moore on Bryher, © 1959; Jessica Nelson North on Taggard, © 1934; Henry Rago on Taggard, © 1947; F. D. Reeve on Waddington, © 1971; Kenneth Rexroth on Levertov, © 1957; Harold Rosenberg on Rukeyser, © 1936; Henry Roskolenko on Garrigue, © 1953; Vernon Shetley on Erdrich, © 1985; Robin Skelton on MacEwan, © 1966; Dave Smith on Swenson, © 1980; William Stafford on Swenson, © 1967; Ruth Stephen on Livesay, © 1945; Mona Van Duyn on Rich, Sexton, © 1970; Mona Van Duyn on Sarton, © 1967; John Wheelwright on Jackson, © 1932; Amos M. Wilder on Brooks, © 1945; Yvor Winters on Moore, © 1925; David Wright on Smith, © 1958; Morton D. Zabel on Wylie, © 1932; S. P. Zitner on Moore, © 1967. All copyrights by the Modern Poetry Association. All excerpts reprinted by permission of the editor of *Poetry*.

POPULAR PRESS—BOWLING GREEN STATE UNIVERSITY. For excerpts from article by Thomas Matchie on Sandoz in *Journal of American Culture;* Patricia Merivale, *Gender Studies: New Directions in Feminist Criticism* (Didion); Patrick D. Morrow, *Katherine Mansfield's Fiction;* essay by Susan Wood on LeGuin in *Voices for the Future: Essays on Major Science Fiction Writers*, Thomas D. Clareson, ed.

THE ESTATE OF LLEWELYN POWYS. For excerpt from *The Verdict of Bridlegoose* (Millay).

854   ACKNOWLEDGMENTS

THE POWYS REVIEW. For excerpt from article by Glen Cavaliero on Warner.
PRENTICE HALL/A DIVISION OF SIMON & SCHUSTER, INC. For excerpts from Arthur Hobson
   Quinn, *American Fiction* (Chopin, Glasgow, Jewett); Claire Sprague's Introduction to *Virginia
   Woolf: A Collection with Critical Essays,* Claire Sprague, ed. © 1971; Robert Penn Warren
   in *Katherine Anne Porter: A Collection of Critical Essays,* Robert Penn Warren, ed. © 1979.
   All excerpts reprinted by permission of Prentice Hall/A Division of Simon & Schuster, Inc.
THE PROGRESSIVE. For excerpt from article by Linda Rocawich on Drakulič. Reprinted by permis-
   sion from *The Progressive,* 409 East Main Street, Madison, WI 53703.
PUBLISHERS WEEKLY. For excerpts from articles by Penny Kaganoff on Acker, Ai Bei, Corti,
   Hareven, Idstrom, Martinson, Ravikovitch, Rose, Shen Rong, Sontag, Stern; Sally Lodge on
   Okamoto Kanoko; John Mutter on Gilroy, Telles; Maria Simson on Rawlings; Sybil Steinberg
   on Collins, L'Engle, Lidman, Loy, Mitchison, Sandel, Sono; Geneviève Stuttaford on Stark.
PURDUE UNIVERSITY AND THE PURDUE RESEARCH FOUNDATION. For excerpts from articles by
   Flavia Brizio on Loy; Laura A. Salseni on Serao in *Romance Languages Annual.* Courtesy
   of Purdue University and the Purdue Research Foundation all rights reserved unless permis-
   sion is granted.
QUADERNI D'ITALIANISTICA. For excerpt from article by Flavia Brizio on Loy.
QUEEN'S QUARTERLY. For excerpt from article by George Woodcock on Webb.
THE RAMSAY HEAD PRESS. For excerpt from Allan Massie, *Muriel Spark.*
RANDOM HOUSE, INC. For excerpts from Willa Cather, *Not Under Forty* (Jewett); Randall Jarrell,
   Poetry and the Age (Moore); Elizabeth Shepley Sergeant, *Fire Under the Andes* (Lowell).
P. MALLIKARJUNA RAO. For excerpt from article on Das in *Kakatiya Journal of English Studies.*
RELIGION & LITERATURE. For excerpts from articles by Mitzi M. Brunsdale on Undset; Marcia
   Falk on Zelda; William J. Scheick on Redmon. Reprint permission granted by *Religion and
   Literature* University of Notre Dame, Notre Dame, IN 46556.
RENASCENCE: ESSAYS ON VALUES IN LITERATURE. For excerpts from articles by John Coates on
   Bowen; John J. Murphy on Roy.
RENDITIONS. For excerpts from articles by John Cayley on Bing Xin; Howard Goldblatt, Edward
   Gunn on Yang Jiang; Qian Zhongshu's Foreword to "Six Chapters from *My Life Downunder*'"
   by Yang Jiang.
ILEANA RENFREW. For excerpt from *La imaginación en la obra de Delmira Agustini.*
REVISTA CANADIENSE DE ESTUDIOS HISPÁNICOS. For excerpts from articles by Carmen M. Del
   Río on Villanueva; Angela Encinar on Rodoreda; Nancy Mandlove on Fuertes; Sharon Keefe
   Ugualde on Atencia.
REVISTA CHILENA DE LITERATURA. For excerpt from article by Lucía Guerra-Cunningham on
   Bombal.
REVISTA IBEROAMERICANA—INSTITUTO INTERNACIONAL DE LITERATURA IBEROAMERICANA. For
   excerpts from articles by Edna Aizenberg on Parra; Laureano Alban on Odio; Maria Luisa
   Bastos on Bombal; Juan Bruce-Novoa on Cervantes, Zamora; Isabel Camara on Pizarnik;
   Frank Dauster on Garro; Angela B. Dellepiane on Guido; Marta Gallo on Ocampo; Dolores
   Koch on Agustini; Francisco Lasarte on Pizarnik; Martha Martínez on Campos; Francine
   Masiello on Parra; José Miguel Oviedo on Garro; Evelyn Picón Garfield on Naranjo; Elena
   Poniatowska on Traba; Alicia Rivero Potter on Campos; Rima de Vallbona on Oreamuno;
   George Yúdice on Alegría.
REVISTA/REVIEW INTERAMERICANA. For excerpts from articles by Efrain Barradas on Vega;
   Margarite Fernández Olmos on Morejón, Poniatowska.
REVUE DES DEUX MONDES. For excerpts from articles by Gérard d'Houville on Duras; Henri
   Clouard on Gennari.
REVUE GÉNÉRALE. For excerpts from articles by Alexis Curvers on Mallet-Joris; Serge Young
   on Duras.
RICE UNIVERSITY STUDIES. For excerpt from article by Jane Chance Nitzsche on Jong.
ROMANCE NOTES. For excerpts from articles by Richard L. Brown on Telles; Rubén García on
   Meireles; Kathleen M. Glenn on Martín Gaite; Darlene J. Sadleir on Meireles.
THE ROMANIC REVIEW. For excerpt from article by Catherine G. Bellver on Tusquets.
ROWMAN & LITTLEFIELD. For excerpts from articles by Elizabeth A. Say on Sayers in *Evidence
   on Her Own Behalf: Women's Narrative as Theological Voice.*
RUTGERS UNIVERSITY PRESS. For excerpts from Germaine Brée, *Women Writers in France: Varia-
   tions on a Theme* (Duras, Noailles); Morgan Y. Himelstein, *Drama Was a Weapon: The Left-
   Wing Theatre in New York 1929–41* (Treadwell); Elaine Marks, *Colette;* Elaine Marks, *Simone
   de Beauvoir: Encounters with Death;* Gerald Monsman, *Olive Schreiner's Fiction: Landscape
   and Power;* essay by Claudia Tate on Hopkins in *Changing Our Own Words: Essays on
   Criticism, Theory, and Writing by Black Women,* Cheryl Wall, ed.

SAGE PUBLICATIONS, INC. For excerpts from articles by Beth E. Jörgenson on Poniatowska; Doris Sommer, George Yúdice, Marc Zimmerman on Menchú in *Latin American Perspectives*. Reprinted by permission of Sage Publications, Inc.

ST. MARTIN'S PRESS, INCORPORATED. For excerpts from essays by Barbara Bowen, Charles Burkhart, Laura L. Doan in *Independent Women: The Function of Gender in the Novels of Barbara Pym*, Janice Rossen, ed., © Janice Rossen; Michael Cotsell, *Barbara Pym*, © Michael Cotsell; essay by Lucy Frost on Baynton in *Who Is She*, Shirley Walker, ed., © Shirley Walker; Clare Hanson and Andrew Gurr, *Katherine Mansfield*, © Clare Hanson and Andrew Gurr; Katherine Joslin, *Edith Wharton*, © Katherine Joslin; Olga Kenyon, *Women Novelists Today*, © Olga Kenyon (Brookner); essay by Paulina Palmer on Carter in *Women Reading Women's Writing*, Sue Roe, ed., © Sue Roe; Ruth Parkin-Gounelas, *Fictions of the Female Self*, © Ruth Parkin-Gounelas (Schreiner); Lev Raphael, *Edith Wharton's Prisoners of Shame*, © Lev Raphael; Lillian S. Robinson's "The Traffic in Women" in *The House of Mirth by Edith Wharton*, Shari Benstock, ed., © Shari Benstock; Sue Roe, *Writing and Gender*, © Sue Roe (Woolf); John Skinner, *The Fictions of Anita Brookner*, © John Skinner; Judy Spronton, *The Women of Muriel Spark*, © Judy Spronton; Oladele Taiwo, *Female Novelists of Modern Africa*, © Oladele Taiwo (Bâ, Head, Njau, Waciuma); Jane Watts, *Black Writers from South Africa: Toward a Discourse of Liberation*, © Jane Watts (Tlali). All excerpts reprinted with permission of St. Martin's Press, Incorporated.

SALMAGUNDI. For excerpts from articles by Robert Boyers on Sexton; Evelyn Toynton on Stafford.

SATURDAY NIGHT. For excerpts from articles by Valerie Miner on Laurence; B. K. Sandwell on Roy.

SCANDINAVIAN REVIEW. For excerpts from articles by Susanna Nied on Christensen; Ralph Slayton on Lindgren. © The American-Scandinavian Foundation. Reprinted by permission.

SCARECROW PRESS, INC. For excerpts from Lucía Fox-Lockert, *Women Novelists in Spain and Spanish America* (Brunet, Bullrich, Guido, Hernández, Medio, Parra, Poniatowska, Soriano, Silva); Ann Z. Mickelson, *Reaching Out: Sensitivity and Order in Recent American Fiction by Women* (Godwin, Jong); Ronald Schwartz, *Spain's New Wave Novelists, 1950–1974: Studies in Spanish Realism* (Matute, Medio, Quiroga).

SCHOCKEN BOOKS, INC. For excerpt from essay by Ezra Spicehandler on Goldberg in *The Modern Hebrew Poem Itself*, Stanley Burnshaw, T. Carti, E. Spicehandler, eds.

BRIGITTE SCHWAB. For excerpts from essays by Rainer Hager on Wohmann; Wolfgang Maier on Reinig in *Schriftsteller der Gegenwart*, Klaus Nonnenmann, ed.

SEAL PRESS. For excerpts from Yukiko Tanaka, *To Live and to Write: Selections from Japanese Women Writers 1913–1938* (Hayashi Fumiko, Hirabayashi Taiko, Miyamoto, Nogami, Okamoto Kanoko, Sata, Uno); Barbara Wilson's Introduction to *Cora Sandel: Selected Short Stories*.

SEMINAR. For excerpt from article by Sandra Frieden on Plessen.

M. E. SHARPE, INC. For excerpts from essays by Alison Bailey on Zhang Jie; Tani E. Barlow on Ding Ling; Daniel Bryant on Zhang Kangkang; Michael S. Duke on Chen Jo-Hsi (Ruoxi); Richard King on Zhu Lin; Wendy Larson on Shen Rong; Ling Chung on Xi Xi; Lucien Miller and Hui-chuan Chang on Chang; Carolyn Wakeman and Yue Daiyun on Zhang Xinxin; Michelle Yeh on Li Ang in *Modern Chinese Women Writers: Critical Appraisals*, Michael S. Duke, ed.; writings by Zhang Jie, Zhang Xinxin in *Modern Chinese Writers: Self-Portrayals*, Helmut Martin and Jeffrey Kinkley, eds.; essays by Howard Goldblatt on Li Ang; W. S. F. Jenner on Zhang Xinxin in *Worlds Apart: Recent Chinese Writing and Its Audiences*, Howard Goldblatt, ed.; Noriko Mizuta Lippitt and Kyoko Iriye Selden's Introduction to *Stories by Contemporary Japanese Women Writers* (Hayashi Fumiko, Hirabayashi Taiko, Ōba Minako); excerpt from essay by Noriko Mizuta Lippit on Miyamoto in *Reality and Fiction in Modern Japanese Literature* reprinted with permission from *Bulletin of Concerned Asian Scholars*, Vol. 10, No. 2, April-June, 1978.

SHENANDOAH. For excerpt from article by William Fleming on Wright. Reprinted from *Shenandoah: The Washington and Lee University Review*, with the permission of the editor.

SIMON AND SCHUSTER, INC. For excerpt from Wayne Andrews's Introduction to *The Best Short Stories of Edith Wharton*, © 1958 Charles Scribner's Sons; Julia Scribner Bigham's Introduction to *The Marjorie Rawlings Reader*, © 1956 Charles Scribner's Sons; Henry James on Wharton in *The Letters of Henry James*, Percy Lubbock, ed., © 1920 Charles Scribner's Sons; Stuart Sherman, *Critical Woodcuts*, © 1926 Charles Scribner's Sons (Glasgow). All excerpts reprinted with permission of Simon & Schuster, Inc.

SMITH COLLEGE STUDIES IN HISTORY. For excerpt from Leona C. Gabel, *From Slavery to the Sorbonne and Beyond: The Life and Writings of Anna Julia Cooper*.

COLIN SMYTHE LIMITED. For excerpts from Lorna Reynolds, *Kate O'Brien: A Literary Portrait.* Copyright © 1987 by Lorna Reynolds. Extract from pp. 128–32 is reprinted here by permission of Colin Smythe Limited, Gerrards Cross, Buckinghamshire, England.

SOUNDINGS. For excerpt from Christopher Irmscher, "Anthropological Roles: The Self and Its Others in T. S. Eliot, William Carlos Williams and Wendy Rose" originally published in *Soundings: An Interdisciplinary Journal,* Vol. 75, No. 4 (Winter 1992): 599–600. Reprinted with permission of the publisher.

SOUTH DAKOTA REVIEW. For excerpt from article by Fritz Oehlschlager on Sandoz.

SOUTHERN HUMANITIES REVIEW. For excerpts from articles by Ashley Brown on Gordon; Gail Regier on Baranskaya; Sidonie A. Smith on Angelou.

SOUTHERN ILLINOIS UNIVERSITY PRESS. For excerpts from essay by Howard Baker on Porter in *Sense and Sensibility in Twentieth-Century Writing,* Brom Weber, ed.; Edward A. Bloom and Lillian D. Bloom, *Willa Cather's Gift of Sympathy;* James Brophy, *Edith Sitwell: The Symbolist Order;* Bernard F. Dick, *The Hellenism of Mary Renault;* essays by Marvin Felheim on McCullers; Paul Schlueter on McCarthy in *Contemporary American Novelists,* Harry T. Moore, ed.; Joan E. Howard, *From Violence to Vision: Sacrifice in the Works of Marguerite Yourcenar;* essay by Charles Alva Hoyt on Spark in *Contemporary British Novelists,* Charles Shapiro, ed.; David Madden, *The Poetic Image in Six Genres* (Oates); essays by Jane Marcus, Judith Lee in *Silence and Power: A Reevaluation of Djuna Barnes,* Mary Lynn Broe, ed.; Marvin Magalaner, *The Fiction of Katherine Mansfield;* Robert Morris, *Continuance and Change: The Contemporary British Novel Sequence* (Manning); Erika Ostrovsky, *A Constant Journey: The Fiction of Monique Wittig;* Temira Pachmuss, *Zinaida Hippius: An Intellectual Profile* (Gippius); Robert Philips, *The Confessional Poets* (Plath); Richard Rees, *Simone Weil: A Sketch for a Portrait;* Paul Schlueter, *The Novels of Doris Lessing;* Darwin T. Turner, *A Minor Chord: Three Afro-American Writers and Their Search for Identity* (Hurston); Darwin T. Turner, *Zora Neale Hurston: The Wandering Minstrel;* Peter Wolfe, *Rebecca West: Artist and Thinker.*

SOUTHERN LITERARY JOURNAL. For excerpts from articles by Robert H. Brinkmeyer, Jr., Sandra Bonilla Durham, Alice E.Wilhelm on Mason; article on McCullers.

SOUTHERN QUARTERLY. For excerpts from articles by Mary Lynn Broe on Hellman; Thadious M. Davis on Walker; Billy J. Harbin, Nancy D. Hargrove, Lisa J. McDonnell on Henley; Leslie White on Mason.

SOUTHWEST REVIEW. For excerpts from articles by Lodwick Hartley on Porter, Charles Tomlinson on Moore.

SPANISH LITERATURE PUBLICATIONS COMPANY. For excerpts from essays by Nancy Mandlove on Castellanos; Carmen Salazar on Garro; Luz Maria Umpierre on Burgos in *In Retrospect: Essays on Latin American Literature (In Memory of Willis Knapp Jones),* Elizabeth L. Rogers and Timothy J. Rogers, eds.

THE SPECTATOR. For excerpts from articles by R. D. Charques on Wilson; E. M. Forster on Sitwell; Desmond Hawkins on Ridler; E. E. Kellett on Sackville-West; Olivia Manning on Warner; Julian Mitchell on Lessing; Iris Murdoch on Weil; William Plomer on Parker; Anthony Powell on Sackville-West; Isabel Quigly on Ginzburg, Stern; Simon Raven on Brophy; V. Sackville-West on Stark; Rachel Annend Taylor on Richardson; Henry Tube on Brooke-Rose; John Wain on Plath; Rex Warner on Stark; Evelyn Waugh on Bedford; Angus Wilson on Compton-Burnett; articles on Mitford, Prichard, Richardson, Stead.

SPEECH COMMUNICATION ASSOCIATION. For excerpts from articles by Sharon Ammen, Harry J. Elam, Jr., on Benmussa; Robert M. Post on Sitwell in *Text and Performance Quarterly;* Madone Miner on Pollock in *Literature in Performance.* Used by permission of the Speech Communication Association.

SPIRIT. For excerpts from articles by Sally Anderson on Oates; Lynda B. Salamon on Plath.

STAND MAGAZINE. For excerpt from article by Terry Eagleton on Jennings.

STANFORD UNIVERSITY PRESS. For excerpts from Beatrice Farnsworth, *Alexandra Kollontai: Socialism, Feminism and the Bolshevik Revolution,* Walter H. Sokel, *The Writer in Extremis* (Lasker-Schüler); Yukiko Tanaka's Introduction to *This Kind of Woman: 10 Stories by Japanese Women, 1960–1976,* Yukiko Tanaka and Elizabeth Hanson, eds. (Ōba Minako).

STATE UNIVERSITY OF NEW YORK PRESS. For excerpts from articles by Esther Fuchs, *Israeli Mythogynies: Women in Contemporary Hebrew Fiction* (Kahana-Carmon).

STERLING PUBLISHERS PRIVATE LIMITED. For excerpts from articles by Hari Mohar Prasad and Chakradha Prasad Siṅgh, *Indian Poetry in English* (Naidu); K. R. Sŕinivasa Iyengar, *Indian Writing in English* (Markandaya, Naidu).

STUDIES IN AMERICAN FICTION. For excerpts from articles by Alisa Johnson on Dunbar-Nelson; Sharon O'Brien on Cather; Stan Yogi on Yamamoto.

STUDIES IN CANADIAN LITERATURE. For excerpts from articles by Misao Dean on Duncan; Robin Potter, Gary Willis on Kogawa.

STUDIES IN LATIN AMERICAN POPULAR CULTURE. For excerpt from article by Albrecht Moreno on Parra.

STUDIES IN SHORT FICTION. For excerpts from Garth Kemerling's review of *The Foreign Legion: Stories and Chronicles* by Clarice Lispector in *Studies in Short Fiction* 29 (1992): 222–23; Zenobia Baxter Mistri, "'Seventeen Syllables': A Symbolic Haiku" in *Studies in Short Fiction* 27 (1990): 197–202 (Yamamoto); Massaud Moisés, "Clarice Lispector: Fiction and Cosmic Vision," in *Studies in Short Fiction* 8 (1971): 268–81; Phillip Parotti, "Nature and Symbol in Estela Portillo's 'The Paris Gown'" in *Studies in Short Fiction* 24 (1987): 417–24 (Portillo de Trambley). Copyright 1971, 1987, 1990, and 1992 by Newberry College.

STUDIES IN THE LITERARY IMAGINATION. For excerpts from articles by Robert O. Evans on Bedford; Philippa Tristram on Compton-Burnett.

STUDIES IN TWENTIETH-CENTURY LITERATURE. For excerpt from article by Biddy Martin on Morgner.

SUMMA PUBLICATIONS, INC. For excerpts from Paula Gilbert Lewis, *The Literary Vision of Gabrielle Roy.*

SVOBODA. For excerpt from article by Svyatoslav Hordyns'kyy on Teliha.

SWALLOW PRESS/OHIO UNIVERSITY PRESS. For excerpts from Benjamin Franklin V and Duane Schneider, *Anaïs Nin: An Introduction;* Olga Anastasia Pelensky's Introduction to *Isak Dinesen: Critical Views;* Sharon Spencer, *Collage of Dreams: The Writing of Anaïs Nin;* Helen Trimpi's Introduction to *Poems Old and New 1918–78* by Janet Lewis; Joyce Piell Wexler, *Laura Riding's Pursuit of Truth* (Jackson).

SWETS PUBLISHING SERVICE/SWETS & ZEITLINGER BV. For excerpts from articles by H. Lüdeke on Wylie; article on Ridler in *English Studies.*

TAMKANG REVIEW. For excerpts from articles by Daisy S. Y. Ng on Li Ang.

ANDREW TAYLOR. For excerpt from essay on Garner in *Aspects of Australian Fiction,* Alan Brissenden, ed.

TEMPLE UNIVERSITY PRESS. For excerpts from Joanne Branton, *Black Women Writing Autobiography: A Tradition within a Tradition* (Hurston); Elliot Butler-Evans, *Race, Gender and Desire: Narrative Strategies in the Fiction of Toni Cade Bambara, Toni Morrison and Alice Walker* (Bambara); essays by Donald C. Goellnicht, Patricia Lin on Kingston in *Reading the Literatures of Asian America,* Shirley Geok-lim Lin and Amy Ling, eds.; Elaine H. Kim, *Asian American Literature: An Introduction to the Writings and Their Social Context* (Kingston). © 1982, 1989, 1992 by Temple University Press. Reprinted by permission of Temple University Press.

LES TEMPS MODERNES. For excerpt from article by Jean-Louis Curtis on Mallet-Joris.

TEXAS TECHNICAL UNIVERSITY PRESS. For excerpt from essay by Elizabeth Fernea on Adnan in *Literature and Anthropology,* Philip A. Dennis and Wendell Ayres, eds.

THAMES & HUDSON LTD. For excerpt from Frederick R. Karl, *A Reader's Guide to the Contemporary English Novel* (Johnson) © 1963 by Thames & Hudson Ltd.

THREE CONTINENTS PRESS, INC. For excerpts from essays by Charlotte H. Bruner on Head in *When the Drumbeat Changes,* Carolyn A. Parker and Stephen H. Arnold, eds.; Mildred P. Mortimer on Djebar in *Contemporary African Literature,* Hal Wylie, et al., eds.

TULSA STUDIES IN WOMEN'S LITERATURE. For excerpts from articles by Christine Froula on Woolf; Donald C. Goellnicht on Kogawa; Joan Kirkby on Robinson; Margaret Lenta on Tlali; Muriel Mellowan on Brittain; Lillian S. Robinson on Gilman first published in *Tulsa Studies in Women's Literature.*

CHARLES E. TUTTLE CO., INC. For excerpts from Armando Martins Janiera, *Japanese and Western Literature: A Comparative Study* (Hayashi Fumiko); Ivan Morris, *Modern Japanese Stories* (Hayashi Fumiko).

MARK TWAIN JOURNAL. For excerpt from article by Ralph J. Michaels on Espina.

UKRAINIAN QUARTERLY. For excerpt from article by Natalia I. Pazuniak on Ukrainka. *Ukrainian Quarterly,* A Journal of Ukrainian & International Affairs Since 1944, 203 Second Avenue, New York, NY 10003. Subscriptions $30/year [1996].

UKRAINIAN REVIEW. For excerpts from articles by Roman V. Kuchar on Ukrainka; Karl Siehs on Kobylyanska.

UNIVERSIDAD VERACRUZANA. For excerpts from article by Emilio Carballido on Hernández in *La Palabra y el Hombre;* essays by Rene Campos, Juan Manuel Marcos and Teresa Mendez Faith, Gabriela Mora on Allende in *Los Libros Tienen Sus Propios Espíritus,* Marcel Coddou, ed.

ÉDITIONS UNIVERSITAIRES (FRIBOURG). For excerpts from Doris Rauenhorst, *Annette Kolb: Ihr Leben und Ihr Werk.*

UNIVERSITÄTSVERLAG DR. NORBERT BROCKMEYER. For excerpts from articles by Ruth Keen, Simone Cros-Moréa, Tsau Shuying on Xiao Hong (Hsiao Hung) in *Woman and Literature in China,* Anna Gerstlacher, et al., eds.
THE UNIVERSITY OF ALABAMA PRESS. For excerpts from articles by Grace Beárse and Lorraine Elena Roses on Vilalta; J. Townsend Shelby on Matute in *Revista de estudios hispánicos;* essays by Martha Cook on Giovanni; Joanne Veal Gabbin on Sanchez in *Southern Women Writers: The New Generation,* Tonette Bond Inge, ed.; Darlene Williams Erickson, *Illusion Is More Precise Than Precision: The Poetry of Marianne Moore.*
UNIVERSITY OF BRITISH COLUMBIA PRESS. For excerpts from Nancy Bailey, Gayle Greene, Lynette Hunter in *Critical Approaches to the Fiction of Margaret Laurence,* Colin Nicholson, ed. (Vancouver: UBC Press 1990); Jan Bartley, *Invocations: The Poetry and Prose of Gwendolyn Macewan* (Vancouver: UBC Press 1983). All excerpts reprinted with permission of the publisher. All rights reserved by the publisher.
UNIVERSITY OF CALIFORNIA PRESS. For excerpts from essays by Fernando Alegría on Mistral; Linda Gould Levine on Matute, Moix; Francine Masiello on Etcheverts, Elizabeth J. Ordóñez on Zamora; Marcia L. Welles on Bombal, Bullrich, Lynch in *Women in Hispanic Literature: Icons and Fallen Idols,* Beth Miller, ed.; Simon Corlinsky, *Marina Cvetaeva* (Tsvetayeva); Richard Drake's Introduction to *A Woman* by Sibilla Aleramo; Fred P. Ellison, *Brazil's New Novel* (Queiroz); essays by Ralph Freedman, Frederick P. W. McDonald in *Virginia Woolf: Revaluation and Continuity,* Ralph Freedman, ed.; James Gindin, *Postwar British Fiction: New Attitudes and Accents* (Lessing, Murdoch); Simon Karlinsky's Introduction to *A Difficult Soul: Zinaida Gippius* by Vladimir Zorin; Mounah A. Khouri and Hamid Algar's Introduction to *An Anthology of Modern Arabic Poetry* (Malā'ika); Kenneth Lincoln, *Native American Renaissance* (Allen); Janice R. MacKinnon and Stephen R. MacKinnon, *Agnes Smedley: The Life and Times of an American Radical;* Ruth Finer Mintz's Introduction to *Modern Hebrew Poetry: A Bilingual Anthology* (Goldberg); Marta Ester Sánchez, *Contemporary Chicana Poetry: A Critical Approach to an Emerging Literature* (Villanueva); Merlin C. Taylor, *Gabriela Mistral's Religious Sensibility.* © 1954, 1962, 1966, 1968, 1971, 1974, 1980, 1983, 1985, 1988 University of California Press.
THE UNIVERSITY OF CHICAGO PRESS. For excerpts from Susan Hardy Aiken, *Isak Dinesen and the Engendering of Narrative* © 1990; Elizabeth Atkins, *Edna St. Vincent Millay and Her Times* © 1936; Elizabeth Dipple, *Iris Murdoch: Work for the Spirit* © 1982; Chester E. Eisinger, *Fiction of the Forties* (Gordon) © 1963; Herbert Marder, *Feminism and Art: A Study of Virginia Woolf* © 1968; Milada Součková, *A Literary Satellite* (Majerová, Pujmanová) © 1970; articles by Monique Y. Crochet on Rochefort; James J. McFadden and Daniel Kiefer on Tynan in *Modern Philology* © 1991; articles by Anita Clair Fellman on Wilder; Elizabeth Fifer on Stein; Christine Froula on Angelou; Annette Kuhn on Cixous; Brenda Silver on Woolf; Namascar Shaktini on Wittig in *Signs: Journal of Women's Culture and Society* © 1979, 1981, 1982, 1986, 1990, 1991.
UNIVERSITY OF HAWAII PRESS. For excerpts from Rebecca L. Copeland, *The Sound of the Wind: The Life and Works of Uno Chiyo;* Laurence P. Kitching and Jute Koṽamees Kitching, *East Meets West: Homage to Edgar C. Knowlton, Jr.* (Under).
UNIVERSITY OF ILLINOIS PRESS. For excerpts from Judith Arcana, *Grace Paley's Life Stories;* essay by Barbara Brothers on Warner in *Old Maids to Radical Spinsters,* Laura Doan, ed.; John F. Callahan, *In the African-American Grain* (Walker); Blanche Gelfant on LeSueur; Nancy Hoffman on Smedley; Sonia Saldívar-Hull on Anzaldúa in *Tradition and the Talents of Women,* Florence Howe, ed.; Diana Hume George, *Oedipus Anne: The Poetry of Anne Sexton;* Richard Giannone, *Flannery O'Connor and the Mystery of Love;* Sydney Janet Kaplan, *The Feminine Consciousness in Modern British Novels* (Sinclair); Elizabeth A. Meese, *(Ex)Tensions: Refiguring Feminist Criticism* (Williams, Menchú); Roberta Rubenstein, *The Novelistic Vision of Doris Lessing;* essays by Monique Wittig on Sarraute in *Three Decades of the French New Novel,* Lois Oppenheim, ed.; Jane E. Zuengler on Mugo in *The Other Tongue: English Across Cultures,* Braj B. Kachru, ed.
UNIVERSITY OF IOWA PRESS. For excerpt from Celeste Goodridge, *Hints and Disguises: Marianne Moore and Her Contemporaries.*
THE UNIVERSITY OF MASSACHUSETTS PRESS. For excerpts reprinted from essays by Norma Alarcón on Castillo; Yamila Azize Várgas on Esteves; Ellen McCracken on Cisneros; Nancy Saporta Sternbach on Moraga in *Breaking Boundaries: Latina Writings and Critical Readings,* Asunción Horno-Delgado, et al., eds. (Amherst: University of Massachusetts Press, 1989), copyright © 1989 by The University of Massachusetts Press; Ursula A. Barnett, *A Vision of Order: A Study of Black South African Literature in English (1914–1980)* (Amherst: University of Massachusetts Press, 1983), copyright © 1983 by Ursula A. Barnett (Dike, Head, Tlali); essays by Fiora A. Bassanese on Guiducci; Giovanna Bellesia on Cederna;

Flavia Brizio on Romano; Rocco Capozzi on Morante; Deborah Heller on Banti; Giovanna Miceli-Jeffries on Manzini; Mark F. Pietralunga on Lagorio; Paola Malpezzi Price on Cialente; Anthony J. Tamburi on Maraini in *Contemporary Women Writers of Italy: A Modern Renaissance*, Santo L. Aricò, ed. (Amherst: University of Massachusetts Press, 1990), copyright © 1990 by The University of Massachusetts Press; Joyce Avrech Berkman, *The Healing Imagination of Olive Schreiner: Beyond South African Colonialism* (Amherst: University of Massachusetts Press, 1989), copyright © 1989 by The University of Massachusetts Press; Lynne Hanley, *Writing War: Fiction, Gender and Memory* (Amherst: University of Massachusetts Press, 1991), copyright © 1991 by The University of Massachusetts Press (Didion); Abdul R. Janmohamed, *Manichean Aesthetics: The Politics of Literature in Colonial Africa* (Amherst: University of Massachusetts Press, 1983), copyright © 1983 by The University of Massachusetts Press (Dinesen).

UNIVERSITY OF MINNESOTA PRESS. For excerpts from Louis Auchincloss, *Pioneers and Caretakers*, © 1965 by the University of Minnesota (Glasgow, McCarthy, McCullers, Porter, Stafford, Wharton); Jean Garrigue, *Marianne Moore*, University of Minnesota Pamphlets on American Writers No. 50, © 1965 by the University of Minnesota; Lawrence Graver, *Carson McCullers*, University of Minnesota Pamphlets on American Writers No. 84, © 1969 by the University of Minnesota; Frederick P. W. McDowell, *Caroline Gordon*, University of Minnesota Pamphlets on American Writers No. 59, © 1966 by the University of Minnesota; Irvin Stock, *Mary McCarthy*, University of Minnesota Pamphlets on American Writers No. 72, © 1968 by the University of Minnesota.

UNIVERSITY OF MISSOURI PRESS. For excerpts from Diana Benete, *Something to Love: Barbara Pym's Novels;* Rodney Stenny Edgecombe, *Vocation and Identity in the Fiction of Muriel Spark;* Sanford Pinsker, *The Uncompromising Fictions of Cynthia Ozick;* Carmelo Virgillo on Mistral in *Woman as Myth and Metaphor in Latin American Literature*, Carmelo Virgillo and Naomi Lindstrom, eds.; Anne M. Wyatt-Brown, *Barbara Pym: A Critical Biography*.

THE UNIVERSITY OF NEBRASKA PRESS. For excerpts from Kari Easton and Yolanda Molina Gavilán's Afterword to *The Delta Function* by Rosa Montero; Laurie Edson's Afterword to *Mother Death* by Jeanne Hyvrard; articles by William Heyen on Bogan; Debra Hulbert on Wakoski; Lee Lemon on Piñon; Josip Novakovich on Drakulič; Kathleene West on Harjo in *Prairie Schooner;* Myra Love on Wolf in *Women in German Yearbook;* excerpt on Morgner in *Daughters of Eve: Women's Writing from the German Democratic Republic*, Nancy Lukens and Dorothy Rosenberg, eds.; Helen Winter Stauffer, *Mari Sandoz: Story Catcher of the Plains;* article by Paul G. Zolbrod on Harjo in *American Indian Quarterly*.

THE UNIVERSITY OF NEW MEXICO PRESS. For excerpts from essay by Charles L. Crow on Yamamoto in *Los Angeles in Fiction*, David Fine, ed.; Joseph Sommers, *After the Storm* (Castellanos).

THE UNIVERSITY OF NORTH CAROLINA PRESS. For excerpts reprinted from essay by Ehrhard Bahr on Sachs in *Exile: The Writer's Experience*, John M. Spalek and Robert F. Bell, eds.; John M. Bradbury, *Renaissance in the South: A Critical History of the Literature, 1920–1960* (Gordon); Barbara Brothers, "British Women Write the Story of the Nazis: A Conspiracy of Silence" in *Rediscovering Forgotten Radicals: British Women Writers, 1889–1939*, Angela Ingram and Daphne Patai, eds. (Bottome); Donald Fowler Brown, *The Catholic Naturalism of Pardo Bazán;* Nancy R. Harrison, *Jean Rhys and the Novel as Women's Text;* Elizabeth A. Meese, *Crossing the Double-Cross: The Practice of Feminist Criticism* (Freeman, Robinson); Thomas R. Nevin, *Simone Weil: Portrait of a Self-Exiled Jew;* Jon Rosenblatt, *Sylvia Plath: The Poetry of Initiation;* Susan R. Van Dyne, *Revising Life: Sylvia Plath's Ariel Poems;* Jean Wyatt, *Reconstructing Desire: The Role of the Unconscious in Women's Reading and Writing* (Robinson); Copyright © 1957, 1963, 1979, 1982, 1986, 1990, 1991, 1993 by The University of North Carolina Press. All excerpts used by permission of the publisher.

UNIVERSITY OF NORTHERN IOWA. For excerpts from articles by Herbert S. Gorman on Wylie; Archibald MacLeish on Lowell; Lloyd Morris on Rawlings in *North American Review*.

UNIVERSITY OF NOTRE DAME PRESS. For excerpts from Walter M. Langford, *The Mexican Novel Comes of Age* (Castellanos); Aleksis Rubulis, *Baltic Literature: A Survey of Finnish, Estonian, Latvian and Lithuanian Literature* (Under). © 1970, 1971 by the University of Notre Dame Press. Reprinted by permission.

UNIVERSITY OF OKLAHOMA PRESS. For excerpts from Marilyn J. Lyde, *Edith Wharton: Convention and Morality in the Work of a Novelist;* B. L. Reid, *Art by Subtraction: A Dissenting Opinion of Gertrude Stein;* Gleb Struve, *Soviet Russian Literature 1917–1950* (Panova); articles by Alexander Aspel on Under; Sigrid Bauschinger on Kaschnitz; Rafael Bosch on Matute; Helene Cantarella on Ginzburg; R. E. on Kaschnitz; Richard Exner on Domin, Kolmar, Langgässer; Zbigniew Folejewski on Dąbrowska; Frances Frenaye on Morante; Jerry Glenn on Ausländer; Elizabeth Greaves on Wohmann; Thomas Hajewski on Kaschnitz, Rinser;

Ronald Hilton on Pardo Bazán; Ivar Ivask on Lasker-Schüler; Emma E. Kahn on Sachs; Daniel S. Keller on Matute; Anthony J. Klančary on Maksimović; Shiv K. Kumar on Markandaya; Teresa de Lauretis on Morante; George R. McMurray on Castellanos; John Michalski on Kolb; Anna Otten on Domin; Aleksis Rannit on Under; K.Bhaskara Rao on Rau; Sidney Rosenfeld on Lasker-Schüler; Robert Schwartz on Lavant; Zina Tilone on Maraini; Rafael Vásquez Zamora on Laforet; Anacleta Candida Vezzetti on Deledda; Ernst Waldinger on Busta, Lavant; Wayne Wonderley on Kaschnitz; George Wythe on Matute in *Books Abroad* (now *World Literature Today*); articles by Hames H. Abbott on Zardoya; Robert Acker on Mayröcker; Karen Alkalay-Gut on Ravikovitch; Jim Armstrong on Stockenstrom; Joachim T. Baer on Koziol; Gabrielle Barfoot on Duranti; Noel Barstand on Rinser; S. Bauschinger on Seghers; Lucille Frackman Becker on Oldenbourg, Sagan; H. Beerman on Roth; Robert L. Berner on Harjo; Gian-Paolo Biasin on Guidacci; Philip Binham on Anhava; Wes Blomster on Wolf; John L. Brown on Pozzi; Charlotte H. Bruner on Dangarembga, Sebbar; Charlotte and David Bruner on Condé; David Bruner on Condé; Maria Luise Caputo-Mayr on Duranti; Joan T. Cain on Montero; Ana C. Cara on Ocampo; Alice-Catherine Carls on Szymborska; Bogdana Carpenter on Szymborska; Victor Carrabino on Constant; Birutè Ciplijauskaitè on Atencia; Ingrid Claréus on Thorup; Susan L. Cocalis on Struck; Miriam Cooke on Abouzeid, Ba'albakkī, Malā'ika, Saadawi; Danielle Chavy Cooper on Constant; Rufus S. Crane on Corti; Kathleen Osgood Dana on Kilpi; Frank Dauster on Campos; Susnigdha Dey on Ocampo; Marguerite Dorian on Blandiana, Cassian; Michael S. Duke on Ai Bei, Wang Anyi; Wendy Dutton on Kincaid; D. Earnshaw on Wakoski; Doris Earnshaw on Erdrich, Swenson; Barbara J. Eckstein on Munro; Svend Birke Espergård on Tafdrup; Hans J. Fabian on Morgenstern; Lee Fahnestock on Prou; Albert M. Forcadas on Rodoreda; Helena Forsis-Scott on Lidman; Scott de Francesco on Brøgger, Thorup; Anne Fried on Idstrom; Bernard Gadd on Edmond; Samba Gadjigo on Sow Fall; Patricia M. Gathercole on Guidacci, Maraini; Van C. Gessel on Enchi Fumiko; Manuela Gieri on Romano; Jerry Glenn on Kirsch; Judith L. Greenberg on Rochefort; Yvonne Guers-Villate on Prou; Prabhu S. Guptara on Yuan-Tsung Chen; Franz W. Haberl on Wohmann; Alamgir Hashmi on Sidhwa; Evelyn J. Hawthorne on Kincaid; Amy Vladek Heinrich on Gotō Miyoko; Barbara Heldt on Lisnyanskaya; Geary Hobson on Harjo; Marjorie L. Hoover on Petrushevskaya; Faith Inguersen on Brøgger; Micaela S. Iovine on Dimitrova; Lanae H. Jackson on Larsen; Mary Ann Klein on Rhys; Bettina L. Knapp on Berberova, Zhang Jie, Zhang Kangkang, Zhang Xinxin; A. Langemo on Brøgger; Charles R. Larson on Shaikh; Renée Lavrier on Schwarz Bart; K. C. Leung on Ding Ling; Ignacio-Javier López on Atencia; Celeste M. Loughman on Ariyoshi Sawako, Sono; Gregory L Lucente on Loy; Jerzy L. Maciuszko on Koziol; A. L. MacLeod on Gilroy; Kathleen M. March on Campos; Bonnie Marshall on Ratushinskaya; Margareta Mattsson on Jansson; Yair Mazor on Ravikovitch; Russell McLeod on Wang Anyi; Seymour Menton on Vega; Mario B. Mignone on Romano; Vasa D. Mikailovich on Maksimović; Marilyn Jeanne Miller on Uno; Jöran Mjöberg on Peri Rossi; Luigi Monga on Corti; Michela Montante on Ginzburg; G. M. Mosek on Ribeiro Tavares; A. S. Newson on Gilroy; Fred J. Nichols on Brouwers; J. O. J. Nwachukisu-Agbada on Onuweme; Nadežda Obradović on Senior, Warner-Vieyra; Anna Olten on Sarraute; Augustus Pallotta on Maraini; Octavio Paz on Bishop; Natalia Pazuniak on Kostenko; Janet Pérez on Zardoya; Rosetta D. Pichardi on Ginzburg; Nancy du Plessis on Sebbar; Mahusudan Prasad on Desai; Tariq Rahman on Sidhwa; William Riggan on Guidacci; Sheila Roberts on Joubert; Sidney Rosenfeld on Novak; D. M. Roskies on Ty-Casper; Sven H. Rossel on Schoultz; B. A. St. Andrews on Mukherjee; Andrew Salkey on Collins, Riley; Ramzi M. Salti on Saadawi; Ivan Sanders on Nemes Nagy; John Scarry on Harjo; E. A. Scatton on Maksimović; Ernestine Schlant on Königsdorf, Leutenegger; George C. Schoolfield on Jansson, Schoultz, Tikkanen; Biljana Šljivić-Simšić on Maksimović; Steven P. Sondrup on Jansson; Irvin Stein on Gonçalves; Brita Stendahl on Ekman; R. Terras on Roth; Rita Terras on Königsdorf, Wohmann; Barend J. Toerien on Joubert, Stockenstrom; Sinikka Tuohimaa on Anhava; Luis Fernando Valente on Ribeiro Tavares; Helize van Vuuren on Stockenstrom; Dov Vardi on Hareven; J. Walt on Oldenbourg; Victoria A. Woodbury on Ratushinskaya, Tolstaya; Rochelle Wright on Ekman; Margaret Ziolkowski on Baranskaya; John Zubizarreta on Farrokhzad.

UNIVERSITY OF PENNSYLVANIA PRESS. For excerpts from Michael J. Hoffman, *The Development of Abstractionism in the Writings of Gertrude Stein;* Daniel Rankin, *Kate Chopin and Her Creole Stories;* Domenico Vittorini, *The Modern Italian Novel* (Deledda).

THE UNIVERSITY OF PITTSBURGH PRESS. For excerpts from Carolyn Forché's Preface reprinted from *Flowers from the Volcano* by Claribel Alegría, translated by Carolyn Forché, by permission of the University of Pittsburgh Press. © 1982 by Claribel Alegría and Carolyn Forché.

UNIVERSITY OF QUEENSLAND. For excerpts from essay by Lucy Frost on Baynton in *Who Is She,* Shirley Walker, ed.; Ric Throssell's Introduction to *Tribute: Selected Stories of Susannah Prichard;* Shirley Walker, *Flame and Shadow: A Study of Judith Wright's Poetry.*

UNIVERSITY OF SOUTH CAROLINA PRESS. For excerpts from Cheryl K. Bove, *Understanding Iris Murdoch;* Lawrence S. Friedman, *Understanding Cynthia Ozick;* Greg Johnson, *Understanding Joyce Carol Oates;* Alice Hall Petry, *Understanding Anne Tyler;* Carl R. Shirley and Paula W. Shirley, *Understanding Chicano Literature* (Castillo, Cervantes, Villanueva).

UNIVERSITY OF TENNESSEE PRESS. For excerpts from essays by Richard K. Barksdale, R.Baxter Miller on Walker in *Black American Poets Between Two Worlds, 1940–1960,* R. Baxter Miller, ed.; Lynette Carpenter on Glasgow, Wendy K. Kolmar on Cisneros in *Haunting the House of Fiction: Feminist Perspectives on Ghost Stories by American Women,* Lynette Carpenter and Wendy K. Kolmar, eds.; Carole Boyce Davies, *Narrating Mothers: Theorizing Maternal Subjectivity* (Williams); Louise A. DeSalvo on Sackville-West, Jane Marcus on Warner, Carolyn Mitchell on Shange in *Women Writers and the City,* Susan Merrill Squier, ed.

UNIVERSITY OF TEXAS CENTER FOR MIDDLE EASTERN STUDIES. For excerpts from Elizabeth Warnock Fernea's Introduction to *The Year of the Elephant: A Moroccon Woman's Journey Toward Independence* by Leila Abouzeid.

UNIVERSITY OF TEXAS PRESS. For excerpts from *Jean Rhys at "World's End": Novels of Colonial and Sexual Exile* by Mary Lou Emery. Copyright © 1990. By permission of the author and the University of Texas Press; essay by James Gindin on Murdoch in *Forms of Modern British Fiction,* Alan Warren Friedman, ed. Copyright © 1975. By permission of the University of Texas Press; *Jean Stafford: The Savage Heart* by Charlotte Margolis Goodman. Copyright © 1990. By permission of the author and the University of Texas Press; essay by Michael Hillman on Farrokhzad, court decision on Ba'albakki cited in *Middle Eastern Muslim Women Speak,* Elizabeth Warnock Fernea and Basima Qattan Bezirgan, eds., Copyright © 1977. By permission of the authors and the University of Texas Press; essay by John K. Knowles on Hernández in *Dramatists in Revolt: The New Latin American Theater,* Leon F. Lyday and George W. Woodyard, eds. Copyright © 1976. By permission of the University of Texas Press; *Voices of Change in the Spanish American Theater,* edited and translated by William J. Oliver, Copyright © 1971. By permission of the author and the University of Texas Press (Gambaro); Elena Poniatowska's Introduction to *Cartucho* and *My Mother's Hands* by Nellie Campobello. Copyright © 1988. By permission of the University of Texas Press; *No Place on Earth* by Louis D. Rubin, Copyright © 1959. By permission of the University of Texas Press (Glasgow); *Grace Paley: Illuminating the Dark Lives* by Jacqueline Taylor. Copyright © 1990. By permission of the author and the University of Texas Press.

UNIVERSITY OF TORONTO, DEPARTMENT OF ITALIAN STUDIES. For excerpt from Ada Testaferri, *Donna: Women in Italian Culture* (Deledda).

UNIVERSITY OF TORONTO PRESS, INC. For excerpts from Constantine H. Andrusyshen and Watson Kirkconnell, *The Ukrainian Poets, 1189–1962* (Teliha); Constantine Bida, *Lesya Ukrainka;* D. G. Jones, *Butterfly on Rock* (Hébert); essay by Stephen Siobie on Webb in *Canadian Canons: Essays in Literary Value,* Robert Lecker, ed.; articles by W. E. Collin on Hébert, Ellen Z. Lambert on Drabble, Hugh MacCallum on Avison, Janet M. Paterson on Villemaire, article on Webb in *University of Toronto Quarterly.*

UNIVERSITY OF WASHINGTON PRESS. For excerpt from Howard Goldblatt's Introduction to *Market Street* by Xiao Hong (Hsiao Hung).

UNIVERSITY OF WATERLOO PRESS. For excerpts from essays by Dennis Cooley, Paul Denham, Jonathan C. Peirce, Lee Thompson in *A Public and Private Voice: Essays on the Life and Work of Dorothy Livesay.*

THE UNIVERSITY OF WISCONSIN PRESS. For excerpts from articles by Elizabeth Abel on Rhys © 1979; Diane Guffin Crowder on Wittig © 1983; Cynthia A. Davis on Morrison © 1982; Marianne De Koven on Stein © 1981; Leslie Dock on Brophy © 1976; Earl E. Fitz on Lispector © 1987; David Hayman and Keith Cohen on Brooke-Rose © 1976; Norman Holland on Doolittle (H. D.) © 1969; Frederick R. Karl on Lessing © 1972; Elgin W. Mellown on Rhys © 1972; Marjorie Perloff on Wakoski © 1975; Lynn Sukenick on Lessing © 1973; Catherine C. Ward on Naylor © 1987; Evan Watkins on Wakoski © 1981; Alan Wilde on Weldon © 1988 in *Contemporary Literature;* articles by Bernhardt Blumenthal on Goll © 1983; Eva-Marie Jung on LeFort © 1950; Egon Menz on Fleisser © 1981; Mary McKittrick on Seidel © 1938 in *Monatshefte;* articles by Joanna Courteau on Queiroz; Rita Herman on Lispector; Helena Kaufman on Jorge in *Luso-Brazilian Review;* essays by Susan Stanford Friedman and Rachel Blau DuPlessis, Eileen Gregory, Elizabeth A. Hirsch, Deborah Kelly Kloepfer, Cassandra Laity, Adelaide Morris, Alicia Ostriker in *Signets: Reading H. D.,* Susan Stanford Friedman and Rachel Blau DuPlessis, eds. © 1991 (Doolittle); article by Theodore Huebner on Seghers in *Modern Language Journal,* © 1966; article by Samuel French Morse on Loy in *Wisconsin Studies in Contemporary Literature* © 1961; Kristine A. Thorsen, "Gertud von Le Fort's Recollections of an Era," pp. 182–85 in *Imperial Germany*, Volker Dürr, Kathy Harms, and Peter Hayes, eds., *Monatshefte* Occasional Volume Number 3. © 1985 The University of Wisconsin Press; Frederick P. W. McDonald, *Ellen Glasgow and the Ironic Art of Fiction* © 1960 The University of Wisconsin Press. All excerpts reprinted by permission of The University of Wisconsin Press.

UNIVERSITY PRESS OF FLORIDA. For excerpt from Charles Moorman, *The Precincts of Felicity: The Augustinian City of the Oxford Christians* (Sayers).

THE UNIVERSITY PRESS OF KENTUCKY. For excerpts from Samuel Chase Coale, *In Hawthorne's Shadow: American Romance from Melville to Mailer* (Oates); essays by Rachel M. Brownstein on Godwin; John W. Mahon on Gordon; Martha M. Vertreace on Bambara in *American Women Writing Fiction: Memory, Identity, Family, Space,* Mickey Pearlman, ed.; essays by Elaine Tuttle Hansen on Piercy; Catherine Rainwater on Redmon in *Contemporary American Women Writers: Narrative Strategies,* Catherine Rainwater and William J. Scheick, eds.

UNIVERSITY PRESS OF MISSISSIPPI. For excerpts from Robert H. Brinkmeyer, Jr., *Three Catholic Writers of the Modern South* (Gordon); Albert J. Devlin, *Eudora Welty's Chronicle: A Story of Mississippi Life;* Elaine Neil Orr, Tillie *Olsen and a Feminist Spiritual Vision;* essay by Robert L. Phillips, Jr. in *Eudora Welty: Critical Essays,* Peggy Whitman Prenshaw, ed.; essay by Reynolds Price in *Eudora Welty: A Form of Thanks,* Louis Dollarhide and Ann J. Abadie, eds.; Mary P. Reichardt, *A Web of Relationship: Women in the Short Stories of Mary Wilkins Freeman;* essay by Carolyn Rhodes on Godwin in *Women Writers of the Contemporary South,* Peggy Whitman Prenshaw, ed.

UNIVERSITY PRESS OF NEW ENGLAND. For excerpts from Mari Michèle Aina Barale, pp. 166–168 from *Daughters and Lovers: The Life and Writings of Mary Webb,* © 1986 by Michèle Aina Barale, Wesleyan University Press by permission of University Press of New England; Blaca Dimitrova, *Because the Sea Is Black,* viii–ix, xi–xiii, Translators' Introduction © 1989 by Niko Boris and Heather McHugh, Wesleyan University Press by permission of University Press of New England; Blanche Gelfant, pp. 73–74, 61, 69–70, 90–91 from *Women Writing in America* © 1984 Trustees of Dartmouth College by permission of University Press of New England (LeSeuer, Olsen, Wilson); Susan Goodman, p. 155 from *Edith Wharton's Women: Friends and Rivals,* © 1990 by Susan Goodman, by permission of University Press of New England; Jean Kennard, pp. 11–12, 17–18 from *Vera Brittain and Winifred Holtby: A Working Partnership* © 1989 Trustees of Dartmouth College by permission of University Press of New England (Brittain, Gilman); essays by Marta Peinato on Lispector, Mary Helen Washington on Brooks, pp. 271–274, 287–289 from *The Voyage In: Fictions of Female Development,* Elizabeth Abel, Marianne Hirsch, Elizabeth Langland, eds., © 1983 Trustees of Dartmouth College by permission of University Press of New England.

UNIVERSITY PRESS OF VIRGINIA. For excerpts from Mara Faulkner, O.S.B., *Protest and Possibility in the Writing of Tillie Olsen;* essay by Louis D. Rubin, Jr. in *Ellen Glasgow: Centennial Essays,* M. Thomas Inge, ed.; Thomas J. Travisano, *Elizabeth Bishop: Her Artistic Development.* Used with permission of the University Press of Virginia.

VALLECCHI. For excerpts from entry on Cederna in *Dizionario della letteratura contemporanea italiana,* Enzo Ronconi, ed.; Francesca Sanvitale's Introduction to *Le idee di una donna e Confessioni letterarie* by Neera.

VANDERBILT UNIVERSITY PRESS. For excerpt from essay by Thom Gunn on Loy in *On Modern Poetry,* Vereen Bell and Laurence Lerner, eds.

VIKAS PUBLISHING HOUSE PVT LTD. For excerpts from essays by K. A. Abbas, Balwant Ganji on Pritam in *Aspects of Indian Literature,* Suresh Kohli, ed.

VIRGINIA QUARTERLY REVIEW. For excerpts from articles by James Branch Cabell on Wylie; Horace Gregory on Sitwell; Peter Harris on Dove; James William Johnson on Porter; Richard Jones on Sitwell; John Hyde Preston on Millay; Louis D. Rubin, Jr. on McCullers; article on McCarthy.

VISOR LIBROS. For excerpt from Mario Benedetti's Introduction to *Suma y Sigue* by Claribel Alegría.

VOIX ET IMAGES: LITTÉRATURE QUÉBÉCOISE. For excerpts from articles by Joseph Bonenfant on Bosco; Anne Élaine Cliche on Villemaire; Gloria Escomel on Bosco; Jean Fisette on Brossard; François Gallays, Jeanne Goldin on Bosco; Suzanne Lamy on Villemaire; Louise Milot on Brossard; Lise Potvin, Lucie Robert, Claude Sabourin on Villemaire.

LIBRAIRIE PHILOSOPHIQUE J. VRIN. For excerpt from Miklos Vetö, *La métaphysique religieuse de Simone Weil.*

DIANE WAKOSKI. For excerpt from article on Levertov in *Women's Review of Books.*

THE GEORGE WASHINGTON UNIVERSITY. For excerpt from article by Lynn Cothern on Suckow in *American Studies International.*

ERIKA J. WATERS. For excerpt from article on Cliff in *Women's Review of Books.*

WAYNE STATE UNIVERSITY PRESS. For excerpts reprinted from Gian-Paolo Biasin's Introduction to *Landscape with Ruins: Selected Poetry of Margherita Guidacci,* © 1992; articles by Sylvia Bryant on Carter; Sarah Gilead on Wilder in *Criticism,* © 1988, 1989; Marilyn Sibley Fries's Introduction, essays by Heidi Gilpin, Karin McPherson, Christine Zahl Romero in *Responses to Christa Wolf,* Marilyn Sibley Fries, ed., © 1989; Evelyn Picón Garfield, *Women's Voices from Latin America,* © 1985 (Campos); Jeanne Heuving, *Omissions Are Not Accidents: Gender in the Art of Marianne Moore,* © 1992. By permission of the Wayne State University Press.

GERALD WEALES. For excerpt from *American Drama Since World War II* (Hellman).

WEBSTER REVIEW. For excerpt from article on Beattie by Barbara Schapiro.

WESTERN AMERICAN LITERATURE. For excerpts from articles by Fred Erisman on Wilder; Fritz Oehlschlager on Suckow; Rosemary Whitaker on Sandoz.

WESTERN WASHINGTON UNIVERSITY. For excerpts from articles by James Ruppert on Silko, Clarisse Zimra on Manicom, Schwarz Bart in *Journal of Ethnic Studies.*

MARIE-ELISE WHEATWIND. For excerpt from article on Moraga in *Women's Review of Books.*

GAY WILENTZ. For excerpts from articles on Naylor, Nwapa, Walker in *Women's Review of Books.*

BRENDA WINEAPPLE. For excerpt from article on Yourcenar in *Women's Review of Books.*

WISSENSCHAFTLICHE VERLAGSGESELLSCHAFT MBH. For excerpt from article by Walter A. Berendsohn on Sachs in *Universitas.*

WOMEN IN TRANSLATION. For excerpt from Yukiko Tanaka's Introduction to *Unmapped Territories: New Women's Fiction from Japan* (Ōba Minako). © 1991 Women in Translation, 3131 Western Avenue, #410, Seattle, WA 98121–1028.

WYDAWNICTWO LITERACKIE. For excerpt from article by Karol W. Zawodziński on Pawlikowska-Jasnorzewska in *Wśród poetów.*

YALE UNIVERSITY PRESS. For excerpts from J. M. Coetzee, *White Writing in South Africa,* © 1988 Yale University Press (Smith); C. T. Hsin, *A History of Modern Chinese Fiction,* © 1971 Yale University Press (Ding Ling); Stanley Kunitz's Foreword to *Gathering the Tribes* by Carolyn Forché, © 1976 Yale University Press; essay by Lynne Layton on Brittain in *Behind the Lines: Gender and the Two World Wars,* Margaret Higgoret et al., eds., © 1987 Yale University Press; E. W. F. Tomlin, *Simone Weil,* © 1954 Yale University Press.

INDEX TO CRITICS

ASCHER, Carole
  Beauvoir (I) 249
ASH, Susan
  Frame (II) 57; Hulme (II)
  380
ASHBERY, John
  Bishop (I) 293; Bowles (I)
  349; Stein (IV) 270
ASHLEY, Leonard R. N.
  Hansberry (II) 265
ASHWORTH, Andrea
  Drakulić (I) 743
ASNANI, Shayam M.
  Sahgal (IV) 2
ASPEL, Alexander
  Under (IV) 457
ASSIBA D'ALMEIDA, Irene
  Bâ (I) 179
ASTRADA DE TERZAGA,
  Etelvina
  Storni (IV) 289
ATACK, Margaret
  Etcherelli (I) 835
ATHENAEUM
  Field and Cooper (II) 24;
  Sinclair (IV) 149
ATKINS, Elizabeth
  Millay (III) 183
ATKINSON, [J.] Brooks
  Treadwell (IV) 392, 393,
  394
ATLAS, James
  Stead (IV) 263
ATWOOD, Margaret
  Avison (I) 166; Beattie (I)
  238; Blais (I) 301, 302;
  Gordimer (II) 199; Jong
  (II) 459; Macewan (III)
  33, 35; Piercy (III) 553;
  Thomas (IV) 362, 363
AUCHINCLOSS, Eve
  Calisher (I) 449
AUCHINCLOSS, Louis
  Glasgow (II) 158; McCar-
  thy (III) 5, 16; Porter
  (III) 596; Stafford (IV)
  249; Wharton (IV) 646
AUFFERMANN, Verena
  Drewitz (I) 748
AUGSBERGER, Eva
  Langgässer (II) 617
AURY, Dominique
  Beauvoir (I) 244; Pozzi
  (III) 611
AUSTIN, A. E.
  Bowen (I) 342
AUSTIN, Jacqueline
  J. West (IV) 628
AVANT, John Alfred
  Oates (III) 394
AVERY, Evelyn
  Yezierska (IV) 784

AWKWARD, Michael
  Hurston (II) 392
AWWAD, Hanan
  al-Sammān (IV) 12
AYALA, Francisco
  Laforet (II) 593
ʿAYYĀD, Shukrī
  Baʿalbakkī (I) 182; al-
  Malāʾika (III) 53
AZASU, Kwakuvi
  Sow Fall (IV) 226
AZCONA CRANWELL,
  Elizabeth
  Gámbaro (II) 95
AZEVEDO FILHO, Leodegário
  A. de
  Meireles (III) 156
AL-ʿAZIZ, Malik ʿAbd
  Tūqān (IV) 423
AZIZE [VARGAS], Yamila
  Esteves (I) 830

B.A.
  Kogawa (II) 535
BABIGIAN, Consuelo B.
  Ibarbourou (II) 399
BACON, Martha
  Sarton (IV) 46
BADAWI, Mustafa
  al-Malāʾika (III) 55
BADR, ʿAbd al-Muhsin Tāhā
  Tūqān (IV) 425
BADRAN, Margot
  El-Saadawi (III) 807; Al-
  Shaykh (IV) 122; Ziya-
  dah (IV) 836
BAER, Joachim T.
  Koziol (II) 580
BAGLEY, Petra M.
  Plessen (III) 582
BAHR, Ehrhard
  Sachs (III) 816
BAILEY, Alison
  Zhang Jie (IV) 818
BAILEY, Nancy [I.]
  Laurence (II) 644; Munro
  (III) 300
BAIN, Dena C.
  Le Guin (II) 685
BAKER, Carlos
  Johnson (II) 443
BAKER, David
  Jordan (II) 469
BAKER, Houston A., Jr.
  Brooks (I) 390; Sanchez
  (IV) 17
BAKER, Howard
  C. Gordon (II) 209; Porter
  (III) 598
BAKERMAN, Jane S.
  Morrison (III) 284

BAL, Mieke
  Colette (I) 575
BALAKIAN, Anna
  Gennari (II) 115; Nin (III)
  357; Sarraute (IV) 33
BALDANZA, Frank
  Nin (III) 355
BALDUS, Alexander
  Kolb (II) 546
BALDWIN, James
  Hansberry (II) 259
BALDWIN, Stanley
  M. Webb (IV) 581
BAMBARA, Toni Cade
  Brooks (I) 390
BANJAMIN, Milicia
  Guró (II) 247
BANKS, Russell
  Erdrich (I) 819
BANVILLE, John
  Sontag (IV) 220
BARAKĀT, Halīm
  Baʿalbakki (I) 183
BARALE, Michèle Aina
  M. Webb (IV) 586
BARANCZAK, Stanislaw
  Ratushinskaya (III) 667
BARBATO, Louis R.
  Markandaya (III) 104
BARBER, David S.
  Rukeyser (III) 799
BARBOUR, Sarah
  Sarraute (IV) 45
BARFOOT, Gabrielle
  Duranti (I) 766
BARKER, Adele
  Tolstaya (IV) 381
BARKER, Murl
  Berberova (I) 284, 285
BARKHAM, John
  Sarraute (IV) 41
BARKSDALE, Richard K.
  M. Walker (IV) 552
BARLOW, Tani E.
  Ding Ling (I) 699, 700
BARNARD, Marjorie
  Franklin (I) 59
BARNES, Clive
  Owens (III) 483, 484, 485
BARNETT, Ursula A.
  Dike (I) 677; Head (II) 298;
  Tlali (IV) 378
BARO, Gene
  Stafford (IV) 248
BARR, Donald
  Jackson (II) 405; Lee (II)
  671
BARRADAS, Efraín
  Vega (IV) 486
BARRETT, Mary
  Rinser (III) 745

BESSAI, Diane
  Pollock (III) 585
BESSER, Gretchen R.
  Sarraute (IV) 42
BEVERLY, John
  Menchú (III) 165
BEVILACQUA, Winifred
  Farrant
  Herbst (II) 333
BEZIRGAN, Basima Qattan
  Ba'albakkī (I) 184
BIAGINI, Enza
  Banti (I) 208
BIASIN, Gian-Paolo
  Guidacci (II) 237, 238
BIDA, Constantine
  Ukrainka (IV) 454
BIEDER, Mary Ellen
  Pardo Bazán (III) 513; Ro-
  dored (III) 765
BIENEK, Horst
  Kaschnitz (II) 487
BIGHAM, Julia Scribner
  Rawlings (III) 676
BIGSBY, C. W. E.
  Glaspell (II) 167; Hans-
  berry (II) 258
BINHAM, Philip
  Anhava (I), 114
BIRBALSINGH, Frank
  Wilson (IV) 684
BIRCH, Helen
  Fell (II) 18, 21; Weldon
  (IV) 614
BIRCHALL, Ian
  Etcherelli (I) 833
BIRD, Delys
  Anderson (I) 100; Franklin
  (II) 61
BISCHOFF, Joan
  Morrison (III) 281
BISHOP, T. G.
  Harwood (II) 282
BITHELL, Jethro
  Kolb (II) 546
BIXLER, Phyllis
  Burnett (I) 432
BJORKLAND, Beth
  Mayröcker (III) 143
BLACK, Martha Fodaski
  Chopin (I) 535
BLACKBURN, Sara
  Drexler (I) 752; Morrison
  (III) 280;
  Piercy (III) 550
BLACKBURN, William
  L'Engle (II) 697
BLACKMUR, R. P.
  H.D. (I) 714
BLACKWELL, Marilyn Johns
  Dinesen (I) 689

BLANCHET, André
  Sagan (III) 822
BLANKENSHIP, Russell
  Lowell (II) 795
BLAUSTEIN, Arthur I.
  Erdrich (I) 819
BLELLOCH, Paola
  Ginzburg (II) 143; Neera
  (III) 349
BLESSING, Richard Allen
  Plath (III) 576
BLIVEN, Naomi
  Sarraute (IV) 32
BLOCH-MICHEL, Jean
  Sagan (III) 824
BLODGETT, E. D.
  Munro (III) 303
BLOMSTER, W[es] V.
  Lavant (II) 651; Sachs (III)
  813; Wolf (IV) 721
BLOOM, Alice
  Mason (III) 124
BLOOM, Edward A.
  Cather (I) 494
BLOOM, Lillian D.
  Cather (I) 494
BLOT, Jean
  Yourcenar (IV) 802
BLUE, Adrianne
  Weldon (IV) 612
BLUM, Lawrence A.
  Weil (IV) 604
BLUM, Marie-Odile
  Frischmuth (II) 72
BLUMENTHAL, Bernhardt
  [G.]
  Goll (II) 183, 184; Lasker-
  Schüler (II) 634
BOCELLI, Arnaldo
  Manzini (III) 88; Morante
  (III) 265
BOCK, Frederick
  Garrigue (II) 105
BOGAN, Louise
  Lewis (II) 742; Miles (III)
  178; Porter (III) 592;
  Swenson (IV) 306; Teas-
  dale (IV) 345; Welty (IV)
  617; Wharton (IV) 644;
  Wylie (IV) 756; Young
  (IV) 790
BOIE, Mildred
  Rukeyser (III) 792
BOLAND, Eavan
  K. O'Brien (III) 423
BOLAND, Maura
  Undset (IV) 472
BOLD, Alan
  Spark (IV) 243
BONADA, Roberto Amigo
  Agustini (I) 27

BONE, Robert [A.]
  Fauset (II) 13; Hurston (II)
  384; N. Larsen (II) 624
BONENFANT, Joseph
  Bosco (I) 325
BOOKMAN, The
  Suckow (IV) 297; Vorse
  (IV) 505
BOOTH, Edward T.
  Deledda (I) 649
BOOTH, Marilyn
  Ziyadah (IV) 837
BOOTH, Philip
  Rukeyser (III) 794
BORIS, Niko
  Dimitrova (I) 680
BOSCH, Rafael
  Matute (III) 131
BOSLEY, Vivien
  Villemaire (IV) 505
BOVE, Cheryl K.
  Murdoch (III) 326
BOWEN, Barbara
  Pym (III) 638
BOWEN, Elizabeth
  H. H. Richardson (III) 728;
  Welty (IV) 620; R. West
  (IV) 631
BOWEN, John
  Lessing (II) 703
BOWEN, Zack
  Lavin (II) 658
BOWERING, George
  Watson (IV) 579
BOWLES, Gloria
  Bogan (I) 318
BOWRA, Maurice
  Sitwell (IV) 159
BOYD, Ernest [A.]
  Deledda (I) 650; Gregory
  (II) 226
BOYERS, Robert
  Plath (III) 568; Sexton (IV)
  115
BOYLE, Kay
  Mansfield (III) 79
BRADBURY, John M.
  C. Gordon (II) 206
BRADBURY, Malcolm
  Spark (IV) 238
BRAININA, B.
  Bagryana (I) 193
BRANDE, Dorothea
  Undset (IV) 465
BRASIL, Assis
  Lispector (II) 765
BRAUDY, Leo
  Sontag (IV) 217
BRAUGHTON, Trev
  Roberts (III) 752
BRAXTON, Joanne
  Hurston (II) 390

BRAYBROOKE, Patrick
Tynan (IV) 448; R. West
(IV) 630
BRÉE, Germaine
Duras (I) 773; Mallet-Joris
(III) 62; Noailles (III)
365; Sarraute (IV) 32
BREGMAN, Lucy
Weil (IV) 603
BREIT, Harvey
Jackson (II) 406
BREITER, Emil
Kunewicz (II) 582
BRENNAN, John P.
Le Guin (II) 682
BRENT, Albert
Quiroga (III) 647
BRETZ, Mary Lee
Espina (I) 827, 828
BREWSTER, Dorothy
Goldman (II) 178
BRIDGMAN, Richard
Stein (IV) 274
BRIGGS, Elizabeth D.
Wilder (IV) 668
BRIGHOUSE, Harold
Dane (I) 628
BRIGHTMAN, Carol
McCarthy (III) 11
BRINKMEYER, Robert H., Jr.
C. Gordon (II) 209; Mason
(III) 125, 127; O'Connor
(III) 443
BRINNIN, John Malcolm
Plath (III) 568; Rukeyser
(III) 793; Stein (IV) 271
BRISSENDEN, R. F.
Harwood (II) 279; Wright
(IV) 746
BRISTOL, Evelyn
Guró (II) 248; Tsvetaeva
(IV) 422
BRITT, Linda
Naranjo (III) 336
BRITTAIN, Vera
Holtby (II) 358
BRIZIO, Flavia
R. Loy (II) 809, 810; Romano (III) 774
BRODERICK, Catherine
Enchi (I) 806
BROE, Mary Lynn
Hellman (II) 320; Plath
(III) 578
BROMFIELD, Louis
Rawlings (III) 676
BROMWICH, David
Sexton (IV) 118
BROOKE, Jocelyn
Bowen (I) 338; Drabble (I)
729

BROOKS, Jerome
Lorde (II) 789
BROOKS, Peter
Leduc (II) 663; Sontag
(IV) 216
BROOKS, Van Wyck
Chopin (I) 532; Jewett (II)
431; Lowell (II) 797; Millay (III) 183
BROPHY, Brigid
Calisher (I) 449; Ginzburg
(II) 136; Maraini (III) 91
BROPHY, James
Sitwell (IV) 163
BROSSARD, Chandler
McCarthy (III) 2
BROTHERS, Barbara
Bottome (I) 329; Warner
(IV) 571
BROWDER, Sally
Norman (III) 374
BROWN, Ashley
C. Gordon (II) 208
BROWN, Catherine Meredith
Stafford (IV) 247; Wilson
(IV) 680
BROWN, Constance A.
Mansfield (III) 84
BROWN, Donald Fowler
Pardo Bazán (III) 511
BROWN, Edward
Panóva (III) 507
BROWN, E. J.
Akhmadulina (I) 49, 56
BROWN, Joan L.
Martín Gaite (III) 116;
Montero (III) 235
BROWN, John L.
Pozzi (III) 612, 613
BROWN, John Mason
Hellman (II) 313
BROWN, Lloyd W.
Aidoo (I) 42; Bennett (I)
271; Emecheta (I) 796;
Nwapa (III) 383
BROWN, Richard L.
Telles (IV) 352
BROWN, Rosellen
Naylor (III) 344; Ozick
(III) 491; Sarton (IV) 50
BROWN, Ruth L.
Sarton (IV) 48
BROWN, Sterling
Hurston (II) 383
BROWNSTEIN, Rachel M.
Godwin (II) 174
BROYARD, Anatole
Johnston (II) 450; Keane
(II) 499
BRUCE, Dickson D.
Hopkins (II) 365

BRUCE-NOVOA, Juan
Cervantes (I) 504; Zamora
(IV) 808
BRUNER, Charlotte [H.]
Condé (I) 592; Dangarembga (I) 629; Head (II) 297;
Sebbar (IV) 94
BRUNER, David K.
Condé (I) 588, 592
BRUNINI, J. G.
Le Fort (II) 673
BRUNSDALE, Mitzi [M.]
Sayers (IV) 69; Undset
(IV) 474
BRUSTEIN, Robert
Treadwell (IV) 399
BRUTUS, Dennis
Gordimer (II) 195
BRYAN, Mary
Sarton (IV) 53
BRYANT, Daniel
Zhang Kangkang (IV) 822
BRYANT, Jerry H.
Morrison (III) 280; A.
Walker (IV) 537
BRYANT, Sylvia
Carter (I) 473
BRYDEN, Diana
Stead (IV) 266
BRYHER, Winifred
H.D. (I) 713; M. Moore
(III) 238
BUCHYNS'KYY, Dmytro
Koroleva (II) 565
BUCKLEY, Vincent
Dark (I) 634; Gilmore (II)
128
BUCKMAN, Gertrude
Calisher (I) 447
BUCKNALL, Barbara J.
Le Guin (II) 686
BUCKRIDGE, Pat
Prichard (III) 619
BUEHLER, George
Wolf (IV) 713
BUENO, Salvador
Mistral (III) 206
BUKOSKY, Anthony
Grau (II) 226
BUKOWSKA, Anna
Kunewicz (II) 587
BULLOCK, Alan
Ginzburg (II) 140, 146
BULLOCK, Elizabeth
Stafford (IV) 246
BULLOUGH, Geoffrey
Sayers (IV) 60
BURCKHART, Charles
Compton-Burnett (I) 583
BURDETT, Osbert
Jameson (II) 410; A.
Meynell (III) 171

DIAMOND, Elin
Benmussa (I) 261, 263;
Churchill
(I) 543; Terry (IV) 358
DÍAZ, Gwendolyn
Lynch (II) 816
DÍAZ, Janet
Matute (III) 134
DÍAZ ARRIETA, Hernán
Brunet (I) 406
DÍAZ DIOCARETZ, Miriam
V. Parra (III) 528; Rich
(III) 713, 714
DiBERNARD, Barbara
Lorde (II) 791
DICK, Bernard F.
Renault (III) 686
DICKEY, James
Miles (III) 177; M. Moore
(III) 242
DICKSTEIN, Lore
Sarton (IV) 52
DIDION, Joan
Lessing (II) 710
DIEHL, Joanne Feit
Bishop (I) 296
DILLON, Millicent
Bowles (I) 351, 352
DIPPLE, Elizabeth
Murdoch (III) 321
DISKO, Jenny
Minco (III) 196
DIXON, Paul B.
Piñon (III) 557
DOAN, Laura L.
Pym (III) 637
DOCK, Leslie
Brophy (I) 396
DÖLZ-BLACKBURN, INES
V. Parra (III) 528, 529
DONADIO, Stephen
Porter (III) 598
DONEGAN, Patricia
Aichinger (I) 34
DONOGHUE, Denis
M. Moore (III) 243; Porter
(III) 596; Raine (III) 657;
Stead (IV) 259
DONOVAN, Josephine
Jewett (II) 434, 436
DORIAN, Marguerite
Blandiana (I) 306; Cassian
(I) 478
DOUBIAGO, Sharon
Forché (II) 40
DOWELL, Bob
O'Connor (III) 439
DOWN, Lorna
Edgell (I) 784
DOWNING, Francis
McCullers (III) 13

DOWNS, Michael D.
Le Guin (II) 682
DOYLE, Paul A.
Buck (I) 415
DRABBLE, Margaret
Bowen (I) 341; Lessing (II)
711
DRAINE, Betsy
Lessing (II) 718
DRAKE, Richard
Aleramo (I) 68
DRAKE, William
Teasdale (IV) 347
DRAKE-BROCKMAN, Henrietta
Prichard (III) 616
DRAY-KHMARA, Mykhaylo
Ukrainka (IV) 452
DREW, Elizabeth
M. Moore (III) 238
DREWITZ, Ingeborg
Ausländer (I) 165
DREWNOWSKI, Tadeusz
Dabrowska (I) 624
DRINKWATER, Judith
Pardo Bazán (III) 514
DRINKWATER, Mary Catherine
Atwood (I) 149
DRISCOLL, Kerry
Levertov (II) 740
DRIVER, Tom F.
Hansberry (II) 254
DRUMMOND DE ANDRADE,
Carlos
Meireles (III) 154
DRUXES, Helga
Leutenegger (II) 732
DUBERMAN, Martin
Hansberry (II) 260
DUBIE, Kathleen
Woolf (IV) 740
DUBOIS, W. E. B.
Fauset (II) 11
Du BOIS, William
Seghers (IV) 95
DUCHENE, Anne
Spark (IV) 234
DUFFY, Jean
Wittig (IV) 696
DUKE, Michael [S.]
Ai Bei (I) 34; Chen Jo-hsi
(I) 527; Wang (IV) 558;
Yang Jiang (IV) 778;
Zhang Kangkang (IV)
821; Zhu Lin (IV) 832
DUNCAN, Cynthia
Garro (II) 112
DUNCAN, Erika
Raine (III) 658
DUNCAN, Robert
H.D. (I) 714

DUNFORD, Judith
Weldon (IV) 615
DUNHAM, Vera
Akhmadulina (I) 47
DUNLEAVY, Janet Egleson
Bowen (I) 346; Lavin (II)
659
DUNLOP, Lane
Tsushima (IV) 409
DUNN, Robert Paul
Sayers (IV) 65
DUNN, T. A.
Markandaya (III) 100
DUNSANY, Lord
Lavin (II) 653
DUPEE, F. W.
Stein (IV) 272
Du PLESSIS, Nancy
Sebbar (IV) 93
DUPLESSIS, Rachel Blau
H.D. (I) 718, 721; Rich
(III) 712; Schreiner (IV)
82; Woolf (IV) 741
DURANLEAU, Irène
Brossard (I) 398
DURHAM, Sandra Bonilla
Mason (III) 128
DURIN, Carole
Ashton-Warner (I) 136
DUROSZ, Wiktoria
Lehmann (II) 694
DUTTON, Wendy
Kincaid (II) 513
DUWE, Wilhelm
Lasker-Schüler (II) 632
DVORNIKOV, Evgeni
Akhmadulina (I) 47

EAGLETON, Terry
Jennings (II) 425
EAKIN, Paul John
Jewett (II) 433
EARNSHAW, D[oris]
Erdrich (I) 822; Swenson
(IV) 313; Wakoski (IV)
532
EASTMAN, Jackie F.
Potter (III) 608
EASTON, Kari
Montero (III) 235
EBEN, Michael C.
Kolmar (II) 561
EBERHART, Richard
H.D. (I) 715; Rukeyser
(III) 794
EBERTHS, Margret
Drewitz (I) 746
ECKLEY, Grace
E. O'Brien (III) 416
ECKLEY, William
Arnow (I) 128

FRASER, G. S.
Jennings (II) 424; Spark
(IV) 235
FRASER, Mary
Deledda (I) 651
FRASSICA, Pietro
Cederna (I) 501; Lagorio
(II) 612
FREDERIKSEN, Elke
Rinser (III) 748
FREEDLEY, George
Sayers (IV) 60
FREEDMAN, John
Szymborska (IV) 316
FREEDMAN, Morris
Ashton-Warner (I) 135
FREEDMAN, Ralph
Woolf (IV) 735
FREEMAN, John
A. Meynell (III) 171
FREMANTLE, Anne
Castellanos (I) 482; Mit-
ford (III) 219
FRENAYE, Frances
Morante (III) 263
FRICKEY, Pierrette
Rhys (III) 703
FRIEBERT, Stuart
Paley (III) 502
FRIED, Anne
Idström (II) 404
FRIEDEN, Sandra
Plessen (III) 581
FRIEDENTHAL, Richard
Huch (II) 375
FRIEDMAN, Alan Warren
D. Richardson (III) 722
FRIEDMAN, Ellen G.
Acker (I) 7
FRIEDMAN, Lawrence S.
Ozick (III) 495
FRIEDMAN, Lenemaja
Jackson (II) 408
FRIEDMAN, Melvin J.
O'Connor (III) 438
FRIEDMAN, Rosemary
Minco (III) 198
FRIEDMAN, Susan [Stanford]
Cunard (I) 619; H.D. (I)
717, 721
FRIES, Marilyn Sibley
Wolf (IV) 716
FRITSCH, Gerhard
Lavant (II) 650
FRITZ, Walter Helmut
Kaschnitz (II) 486
FROST, Laura
Cliff (I) 567
FROST, Lucy
Baynton (I) 229

FROULA, Christine
Angelou (I) 113; Woolf
(IV) 738
FRUCHTER, Norman
Lessing (II) 704
FRYE, Joanne S.
Kingston (II) 519
FUCHS, Esther
Kahana-Carmon (II) 483
FUCHS, Miriam
Barnes (I) 223; Young (IV)
795, 796
FULLER, Roy
M. Moore (III) 245
FULOP-MILLER, Rene
Nin (III) 354
FUNSTON, Judith E.
Wharton (IV) 654
FURMAN, Laura
O'Faolain (III) 454

GABBIN, Joanne Veal
Sanchez (IV) 19
GABEL, Leona C.
Cooper (I) 600
GADD, Bernard
Edmond (I) 788
GADJIGO, Samba
Sow Fall (IV) 232
GADPAILLE, Michelle
Engel (I) 811
GAFFNEY, Carmel
Hulme (II) 378
GAGNIER, Regenia
Anzaldúa (I) 121; Cisneros
(I) 554
GAILLARD, Dawson
Sayers (IV) 68
GALERSTEIN, Carolyn L.
Salisachs (IV) 6
GALEY, Matthieu
Mallet-Joris (III) 64
GALLAYS, François
Bosco (I) 327
GALLO, Marta
V. Ocampo (III) 434
GÁLVEZ LIRA, Gloria
Bombal (I) 323
GAMBARINI, Elsa Krieger
T. Parra (III) 524
GANNE, Gilbert
Leduc (II) 661
GAONA, Maria Eugenia
Hoyos (II) 373
GARAVELLI, Bice Mortara
Corti (I) 603
GARCÍA, Rubén
Meireles (III) 157
GARCÍA-MORENO, LAURA
Valenzuela (IV) 483
GARCIA REY, José Manuel
Somers (IV) 197

GARCIASOL, R. de
Martín Gaite (III) 112
GARDINER, Judith Kegan
Lessing (II) 721; Stead
(IV) 267
GARDNER, John
Oates (III) 401; Young (IV)
794
GARDNER, Susan
Nwapa (III) 390
GARFIELD, Evelyn Picon
Campos (I) 460; Naranjo
(III) 326; Somers (IV)
199; Valenzuela (IV) 480
GARFITT, Roger
O'Faolain (III) 451
GARGANO, James W.
Wharton (IV) 647
GARGI, Balwant
Pritam (III) 622
GARLICK, Barbara
Anderson (I) 108
GARNER, Helen
Jolley (II) 454
GARRIGUE, Jean
M. Moore (III) 242; Nin
(III) 356; White (IV) 657
GARRISON, Dee
Vorse (IV) 514
GARSON, Helen S.
O'Connor (III) 445
GASKILL, Gayle
Sarton (IV) 54
GASPARONI, Gabriella
Prou (III) 626
GASSNER, John
Hellman (II) 314
GATHERCOLE, Patricia M.
Guidacci (II) 236; Maraini
(III) 98
GAUDET, Gérald
Brossard (I) 402
GAUSE, Catharine D.
Ashton-Warner (I) 133
GAYLE, Addison, Jr.
Hurston (II) 386
GAYN, Mark
Smedley (IV) 175
GEERING, R. G.
Stead (IV) 259
GEETHA, P.
Markandaya (III) 103
GEHERIN, David J.
Didion (I) 671
GEIS, Deborah R.
Shange (IV) 129
GEISMAR, Maxwell
Boyle (I) 360; Cather (I)
493; Glasgow (II) 156;
Nin (III) 354
GELB, Hal
Moraga (III) 260

GELFANT, Blanche [E.]
Le Sueur (II) 729; Olsen (III) 470; Paley (III) 498; Wilson (IV) 685
GENDZIER, Irene
El-Saadawi (III) 804
GENÊT
Sagan (III) 826
GENNARI, Geneviève
Beauvoir (I) 245
GENTILE, Kathy Justice
Compton-Burnett (I) 587
GENUIST, Monique
Roy (III) 785
GEOK-LEONG, LIEW
Mukherjee (III) 296
GEORGE, Diana Hume
Rich (III) 716; Sexton (IV) 119
GÉORIS, Michel
Mallet-Joris (III) 63
GERBER, Margy
Erb (I) 815
GERLACH, U. Henry
Aichinger (I) 37
GERSON, Carole
Wiseman (IV) 690
GERSTENBERGER, Donna
Murdoch (III) 317
GESSEL, Van C.
Enchi (I) 808, 809
GETLEIN, Frank
Sarton (IV) 47
GETZ, Lorine M.
O'Connor (III) 444
GHURAYYIB, Rose
al-Malāʔika (III) 54
GIANNONE, Richard
O'Connor (III) 446
GIBBS, Barbara
Miles (III) 174
GIBBS, Robert
Macewan (III) 35
GIDDINGS, Paula
Giovanni (II) 148
GIERI, Manuela
Romano (III) 774
GIES, Judith
Godwin (II) 173
GIFFORD, Henry
M. Moore (III) 244; Tolstaya (IV) 383
GIKANDI, Simon
Hodge (II) 355
GILBERT, Harriett
Barker (I) 217
GILBERT, Sandra
Sexton (IV) 116
GILBERT DE PEREDA, Isabel
Silva (IV) 147
GILEAD, Sarah
Wilder (IV) 670

GILES, Barbara
Edmond (I) 786
GILES, Mary E.
Pardo Bazán (III) 511
GILL, Brendan
Mitford (III) 216; Taylor (IV) 334; J. West (IV) 627
GILLESPIE, Diane
Sinclair (IV) 156
GILLETTE, Jane Brown
Taylor (IV) 340
GILLON, Adam
Kossak (II) 567
GILMAN, Richard
Drexler (I) 750; Fornés (II) 45; Hansberry (II) 256; Mallet-Joris (III) 60; Oates (III) 393
GILPIN, Heidi
Wolf (IV) 719
GINDIN, James
Lessing (II) 701; Murdoch (III) 311, 317
GIOANOLA, Elio
Lagorio (II) 612
GIRARD, René
Beauvoir (I) 246
GLASSMAN, Peter
Beattie (I) 236
GLEASON, Judith
Forché (II) 38
GLENN, Eunice
Welty (IV) 618
GLENN, Jerry
Ausländer (I) 162; Kirsch (II) 529
GLENN, Kathleen M.
Martín Gaite (III) 113; Montero (III) 231
GLICKMAN, Susan
P. Webb (IV) 592
GLOAG, Julian
Tyler (IV) 441
GLOWIŃSKI, Michał
Kunewicz (II) 585
GOBIN, Pierre
Maillet (II) 39
GODWIN, Gail
Beattie (I) 237
GOELLNICHT, Donald C.
Kingston (II) 526; Kogawa (II) 540
GOLD, Janet
Oreamuno (III) 479
GOLDBERG, Isaac
Ibarbourou (II) 397
GOLDBLATT, Howard
Li Ang (II) 749; Xiao Hong (IV) 763, 764, 768; Yang Jiang (IV) 776

GOLDEN, Marita
N. Larsen (II) 629
GOLDIN, Jeanne
Bosco (I) 326
GOLDMAN, Anne E.
Williams (IV) 678
GOLDMAN, Richard Franko
Lispector (II) 764
GOLDMANN, Lucien
Sarraute (IV) 37
GOLDSTEIN, Sanford
Yosano Akiko (IV) 787
GOLDSWORTHY, Kerryn
Astley (I) 142; Jolley (II) 455
GOMEZ, Jewelle L.
Hansberry (II) 264
GOMEZ, Mirta Pernas
Aguirre (I) 26
GOMRINGER, Eugen
Mayröcker (III) 139
GONZALES, Ray
Zamora (IV) 811
GONZÁLES BOIXÓ, Jose Carlos
T. Parra (III) 523
GOODHEART, Eugene
Ozick (III) 489
GOODMAN, Charlotte [Margolis]
Arnow (I) 131; Stafford (IV) 252
GOODMAN, Susan
Wharton (IV) 651
GOODRIDGE, Celeste
M. Moore (III) 250
GOONERATNE, Yasmine
Jhabvala (II) 441
GORDIMER, Nadine
P. Smith (IV) 182
GORDON, Caroline
O'Connor (III) 436, 440
GORDON, David J.
Gordimer (II) 196
GORDON, Ian
Mansfield (III) 80
GORDON, Mary
Keane (II) 500; McCarthy (III) 9
GORMAN, Herbert S.
Wylie (IV) 753
GORNICK, Vivian
Didion (I) 670, 673; Hellman (III) 317; Yezierska (IV) 785
GOSCILO, Helena
Petrushevskaya (III) 541; Tolstaya (IV) 386
GOTTFRIED, Martin
Jellicoe (II) 422
GOTTLIEB, Annie
Naylor (III) 340

HALL, Colette
Cardinal (I) 470; Leduc (II) 669
HALL, Donald
Rich (III) 707
HALL, James
Bowen (I) 340; Murdoch (III) 315
HALL, Keith
Le Guin (II) 689
HALL, K. Graehme
Sarton (IV) 57
HALL, Vernon
Mallet-Joris (III) 60
HALL, Wayne E.
Somerville and Ross (IV) 207
HALSBAND, Robert
Jackson (II) 405; McCarthy (III) 2
HAMBLEN, Abigail Ann
Suckow (IV) 302
HAMILL, Sam
Jordan (II) 468
HAMILTON, Alice
McCullers (III) 17
HAMILTON, Carlos D.
Mistral (III) 204
HAMPL, Patricia
Le Sueur (II) 722
HANCOCK, Joel
Poniatowska (III) 589
HANLEY, Lynne
Didion (I) 674
HANSCOMBE, Gillian E.
D. Richardson (III) 724
HANSEN, Elaine Tuttle
Drabble (I) 735; Piercy (III) 556
HANSFORD-JOHNSON, Pamela
Compton-Burnett (I) 580; Morante (III) 264
HANSON, Clare
Mansfield (III) 85
HANSON, Elizabeth [S.]
Allen (I) 84; Uno (IV) 478
HARBIN, Billy J.
Henley (II) 329
HARBISON, Sherrill
Undset (IV) 473
HARCOURT, Geraldine
Tsushima (IV) 411
HARDWICK, Elizabeth
Beauvoir (I) 247; Bowen (I) 336; Plath (III) 570; Sontag (IV) 218; Stead (IV) 258; Suckow (IV) 302
HARDY, Barbara
Plath (III) 568
HARDY, John Edward
Porter (III) 599

HARDY, Willene
McCarthy (III) 10
HARESNAPE, Geoffrey
P. Smith (IV) 181
HARGROVE, Nancy D.
Henley (II) 328
HARLEY, Sharon
Cooper (I) 599
HARMON, Claire
Warner (IV) 568
HARMON, Maurice
Johnston (II) 448
HARPER'S
Taylor (IV) 336
HARRIS, Mason
Kogawa (II) 543
HARRIS, Peter
Dove (I) 727
HARRIS, Robert R.
Ozick (III) 492
HARRIS, Trudier
A. Walker (IV) 538
HARRIS, William J.
Giovanni (II) 149
HARRISON, Alice
E. O'Brien (III) 417
HARRISON, Bernard
Spark (IV) 240
HARRISON, Nancy R.
Rhys (III) 702
HARRITY, Richard
Lavin (II) 655
HARROWITZ, Nancy
Serao (IV) 110, 111
HART, Stephen M.
Martín Gaite (III) 118; Montero (III) 237; Peri Rossi (III) 538; Rodoreda (III) 771
HARTER, Evelyn
Boyle (I) 356
HARTMAN, Geoffrey H.
Garrigue (II) 104; Sexton (IV) 112
HARTUNG, Philip
Rawlings (III) 673
HARTUNG, Rudolf
Lavant (II) 649; Seghers (IV) 97
HARWOOD, H. C.
Mansfield (III) 75; M. Webb (IV) 580; R. West (IV) 629
HASHMI, Alamgir
Sidhwa (IV) 137
HASSAN, Ihab
Jackson (II) 407; McCullers (III) 14
HASSELBLATT, Dieter
Kaschnitz (II) 486
HATCH, Ronald B.
Gallant (II) 84

HAULE, James M.
E. O'Brien (III) 421
HAUSDORF, Anna
Goll (II) 185
HAUSMAN, Bernice L.
V. Ocampo (III) 435
HAVIGHURST, Walter
Stafford (IV) 247
HAWKES, John
O'Connor (III) 438
HAWKINS, Desmond
Ridler (III) 739
HAWTHORNE, Evelyn J.
Kincaid (II) 517
HAY, Sara Henderson
Garrigue (II) 104; Millay (III) 185
HAYDAR, Muhammad
al-Sammān (IV) 8
HAYES, Brian P.
Oates (III) 394
HAYES, Richard
Bowles (I) 347; Gordimer (II) 194; Stafford (IV) 247
HAYLES, N. B.
Le Guin (II) 685
HAYMAN, David
Brooke-Rose (I) 377
HAYNES, Muriel
Leduc (II) 662
HAYNES, Roslynn D.
Anderson (I) 105
HAYS, H. R.
Riding (Jackson) (III) 735
HAYWARD, Max
Tsvetaeva (IV) 418
HEANEY, Seamus
S. Smith (IV) 188
HEATH, William
Bowen (I) 339
HEDGES, Elaine
Gilman (II) 120
HEIDT, Barbara
Tsvetaeva (IV) 420
HEILBRUN, Carolyn G.
Sarton (IV) 50; Sayers (IV) 64; Woolf (IV) 736
HEINRICH, Amy Vladek
Ariyoshi (I) 123; Gotō (II) 219
HEITMANN, Annegret
Brøgger (I) 372; Tafdrug (IV) 319; Thorup (IV) 371
HELDT, Barbara
Lisnyanskaya (II) 760
HELLER, Deborah
Banti (I) 211
HEMLEY, Cecil
Sexton (IV) 113

JAMES, Adeola A.
  Nwapa (III) 380; Rhys (III)
  697
JAMES, Caryn
  Slesinger (IV) 172
JAMES, Henry
  Wharton (IV) 643
JAMIE, Kathleen
  Barker (I) 216
JAMIL, Maya
  Jhabvala (II) 437
JAMMES, Francis
  Colette (I) 568
JANDL, Ernst
  Mayröcker (III) 140
JANEWAY, Elizabeth
  Lehmann (II) 692; Matute
  (III) 132; Roy (III) 782;
  Sagan (III) 823; Sarton
  (IV) 47
JANIERA, Armando Martins
  Hayashi (II) 284
JANMOHAMED, Abdul R.
  Dinesen (I) 687
JANSEN, Reamy
  Munro (III) 304
JANUZZI, Marisa
  Valenzuela (IV) 485
JARRELL, Randall
  Bishop (I) 290; M. Moore
  (III) 239; Pitter (III) 559;
  Rich (III) 707; Rukeyser
  (III) 793; Stead (IV) 258
JÄSCHKE, Barbel
  Drewitz (I) 747
JAYYUSI, Salma Khada
  al-Malā'ika (III) 56
J.B.
  White (IV) 660
JEFFARES, A. Norman
  Waddington (IV) 525
JEFFERIS, Barbara
  Jolley (II) 456
JEFFERSON, Margo
  Morrison (III) 281; Ozick
  (III) 493
JEFFREY, David Lyle
  Avison (I) 172
JENA, Seema
  Desai (I) 659
JENNER, W. S. F.
  Zhang Xinxin (IV) 829
JENNINGS, Elizabeth
  Pitter (III) 561
JENNINGS, Regina B.
  Sanchez (IV) 20
JENSEN, Jody
  Brøgger (I) 373
JEROME, Judson
  Rich (III) 708
JEWELL, Keala Jane
  Aleramo (I) 72

JHA, Ramã
  Markandaya (III) 105
JIMÉNEZ, Juan Ramón
  Laforet (II) 594
JIMÉNEZ DE BAEZ, Yvette
  Burgos (I) 420
JOERES, Ruth-Ellen
  Fleisser (II) 29; Kaschnitz
  (II) 491
JOHNSON, Alisa
  Dunbar-Nelson (I) 758
JOHNSON, Barbara
  Hurston (II) 389
JOHNSON, Deborah
  Murdoch (III) 324
JOHNSON, Greg
  Oates (III) 404
JOHNSON, Lemuel A.
  Cliff (I) 565
JOHNSON, Roberta
  Chacel (I) 513; Laforet (II)
  600, 601
JOHNSON, Rosemary
  Swenson (IV) 310
JOHNSON, Sheila
  Morgner (III) 276
JOHNSTON, Denis
  Rukeyser (III) 796
JOHNSTON, Judith L.
  Yourcenar (IV) 804
JONES, Ann Rosalind
  Cixous (I) 559; Wittig (IV)
  692
JONES, Bridget
  Schwarz-Bart (IV) 86
JONES, D. A. N.
  Blais (I) 299
JONES, D. G.
  Hébert (II) 305
JONES, Eldred
  Aidoo (I) 39
JONES, Frank
  Woolf (IV) 727
JONES, Grahame C.
  Poulin (III) 609
JONES, Howard Mumford
  Cather (I) 492; Glasgow
  (II) 155; Porter (III) 593
JONES, Lawrence
  Ashton-Warner (I) 138
JONES, Manina
  Kogawa (II) 543
JONES, Margaret E. W.
  Medio (III) 146, 151; Moix
  (III) 224
JONES, M. William
  Welty (IV) 619
JONES, Phyllis M.
  Wylie (IV) 759
JONES, Richard
  Sitwell (IV) 165

JONES, W. Glyn
  Jansson (II) 414
JÖRGENSEN, Beth E.
  Poniatowska (III) 591
JOSLIN, Katherine
  Wharton (IV) 653
J.R.
  Livesay (II) 776
J.S.
  Barker (I) 215
JUERS, Evelyn
  Wolf (IV) 722
JUHASZ, Suzanne
  Giovanni (II) 147; Lev-
  ertov (II) 735; Plath (III)
  574; Sexton (IV) 117
JUIN, Hubert
  Hébert (II) 307
JUNG, Eva-Maria
  Le Fort (II) 674
JÜRGENSEN, Manfred
  Leutenegger (II) 730;
  Struck (IV) 293

KADIĆ, Ante
  Parun (III) 530
KAFALENOS, Emma
  Brooke-Rose (I) 379
KAGANOFF, Penny
  Acker (I) 10; Ai Bei (I) 33;
  Corti (I) 606; Hareven
  (II) 266; Idström(II) 404;
  Martinson (II) 121;
  Ravikovitch (III) 668;
  Rose (III) 778; Shen (IV)
  134; Sontag (IV) 220;
  Stern (IV) 283
KAHN, Lisa
  Mayröcker (III) 141
KALINA-LEVINE, Vera
  Guró (II) 246
KALSTONE, David
  Bishop (I) 293; Rich (III)
  711
KAMPMANN, Theoderich
  Le Fort (II) 677
KANDLER, Klaus
  Morgner (III) 275
KANE, Richard C.
  Spark (IV) 243
KANG, Younghill
  Buck (I) 413
KANN, Emma E.
  Sachs (III) 811
KANN, Jean Marie
  O'Connor (III) 440
KANNENSTINE, Louis F.
  Barnes (I) 222
KANTARIS, Ella Geoffrey
  Traba (IV) 389
KANTERS, Robert
  Yourcenar (IV) 800

KAPLAN, Carey
Drabble (I) 734
KAPLAN, Johanna
Ozick (III) 489
KAPLAN, Sydney Janet
Mansfield (III) 85; Sinclair
(IV) 154
KAPUR, Vijay Laxmi
Woolf (IV) 734
KARFIK, Vladimir
Linhartová (II) 759
KARL, Frederick R.
Johnson (II) 443; Lessing
(II) 710
KARLINSKY, Simon
Gippius (II) 154; Tsvetaeva
(IV) 416
KASCHNITZ, Marie Luise
Ausländer (I) 161
KATAMBLE, V. D.
Rama Rau (III) 661
KATCHADOURIAN, Stina
Södergran (IV) 194
KATZ, Leon
Stein (IV) 274
KAUFFMANN, Stanley
Chopin (I) 533; Sagan (III)
826
KAUFMAN, Helena
Jorge (II) 472
KAUR, Iqbal
Das (I) 642
KAUVAR, Elaine M.
Ozick (III) 496
KAVAN, Anna
Lehmann (II) 692
KAVENEY, Roz
Roberts (III) 750
KAWADA, Louise
Jordan (II) 467
KAYSER, Rufold
Kolmar (II) 558
KAZI-FERROUILLET, Kuumba
Senior (IV) 105
KAZIN, Alfred
Cather (I) 493; McCullers
(III) 17; Stafford (IV)
246; Weil (IV) 598
KEARNS, Kathleen
Sandel (IV) 22
KEATING, Peter
R. West (IV) 639
KEEFER, Janice Kuylyk
Gallant (II) 89
KEEN, Ruth
Xiao Hong (IV) 767
KEENE, Frances
Cespedes (I) 509; Mallet-
Joris (III) 59; Morante
(III) 263; Sarton (IV) 48
KEITH-SMITH, Brian
Aichinger (I) 39

KELLER, Daniel S.
Matute (III) 131
KELLERMAN, Steven G.
Murdoch (III) 320
KELLETT, E. E.
Sackville-West (III) 818
KELLY, Lori Duin
Naylor (III) 345
KEMERLING, Garth
Lispector (II) 773
KEMP, Peter
Spark (IV) 239
KEMP, Yakini
Brodber (I) 368; Edgell (I)
782; Hodge (II) 353
KENNARD, Jean
Brittain (I) 367; Gilman (II)
124;
Holtby (II) 359
KENNARD, Joseph Spencer
Deledda (I) 649
KENNEBECK, Edwin
Renault (III) 685
KENNEDY, Colleen
Acker (I) 11
KENNEDY, X. J.
M. Moore (III) 240
KENNER, Hugh
H.D. (I) 716; M. Moore
(III) 242
KENNEY, Catherine
Sayers (IV) 70
KENNEY, Edwin J., Jr.
Bowen (I) 343
KENT, George E.
Angelou (I) 109; Brooks (I)
391
KENYON, Olga
Brookner (I) 383
KERMODE, Frank
Colette (I) 574
KERR, Lucille
Poniatowska (III) 590
KERR, Walter
Owens (III) 484; Rama
Rau (III) 660
KERTESZ, Louise
Rukeyser (III) 799
KERTZER, J. M.
Avison (I) 169
KESSLER, Carol Farley
Piercy (III) 554
KESSLER-HARRIS, Alice
Yezierska (IV) 782
KETCHIAN, Sonia
Akhmadulina (I) 51
KEYSER, Elizabeth Lennox
Burnett (I) 435
KEYSSAR, Helene
Churchill (I) 542
KHAN, Fawzia Afzhal
Sidhwa (IV) 141

KHELEMSKI, Iakov
Aliger (I) 75
KHOURI, Mounah A.
al-Malāʾika (III) 55
KIELY, Benedict
K. O'Brien (III) 422
KIELY, Robert
Calisher (I) 451; McCarthy
(III) 4
KIJOWSKI, Andrej
Dabrowska (I) 626
KILMAR, Wendy K.
Cisneros (I) 555
KIM, Elaine H.
Kingston (II) 519
KINCAID, Renée A.
Delbo (I) 644
KING, Adele
Condé (I) 593; Warner-
Vieyra (IV) 575
KING, Bruce
Das (I) 640
KING, Christine
Collins (I) 578
KING, Richard
Zhu Lin (IV) 833, 834
Warner-Vieyra (IV) 575
KINKLEY, Jeffrey [C.]
Zhang Jie (IV) 820; Zhang
Xinxin (IV) 829, 831
KINNEY, Arthur F.
Parker (III) 518
KIRCHWEY, Freda
Goldman (II) 179; Smedley
(IV) 174
KIRKBY, Jane
Robinson (III) 754
KIRKBY, Joan
Baynton (I) 235
KIRKCONNELL, Watson
Teliha (IV) 350
KIRKPATRICK, Gwen
Agustini (I) 31
KIRKPATRICK, Hilary
Adnan (I) 15; Baʿalbakkī (I)
185; al-Malāʾika (III) 57;
Nasrallah (III) 337; Tū-
qān (IV) 425; Ziyadah
(IV) 836
KISSANE, Leedice McAnelly
Suckow (IV) 301
KITCHING, J. Kōvamees
Under (IV) 459
KITCHING, Laurence P.
Under (IV) 459
KIZER, Helen Buller
Lowell (II) 793
KLANČARY, Anthony J.
Maksimović (III) 49
KLAWANS, Stuart
Ortese (III) 481

LANG, Nancy
Harjo (II) 273
LANGBAUM, Robert
Dinesen (I) 686
LANGDALE, E. G.
Jackson (II) 406
LANGE, Victor
McCarthy (III) 3
LANGEMO, A.
Brøgger (I) 371
LANGER, Elinor
Herbst (II) 332
LANGFORD, Walter M.
Castellanos (I) 484
LANGGÄSSER, Elisabeth
Seidel (IV) 101
LANSER, Susan S[niader]
Barnes (I) 224; Gilman (II) 124
LANTERS, José
Johnson (II) 453
LARNAC, Jean
Colette (I) 569
LARSEN, Sven
Christensen (I) 539
LARSON, Catherine
Garro (II) 113
LARSON, Charles
N. Larsen (II) 630; Al-Shaykh (IV) 124
LARSON, Wendy
Ding Ling (I) 701; Shen (IV) 135
LASARTE, Francisco
Pizarnik (III) 562
LASSNER, Phyllis
Howard (II) 369; Macaulay (III) 30; Robinson (III) 755; Taylor (IV) 341
LAUCKNER, Nancy A.
Königsdorf (II) 563
LAURENCE, Margaret
Atwood (I) 152
LAURIER, Renée
Schwartz-Bart (IV) 91
LAUTER, Paul
Smedley (IV) 176
LAWRENCE, D. H.
Deledda (I) 648; Lowell (II) 795
LAWRENCE, Leota
Hodge (II) 351
LAWRENCE, Margaret
Hall (II) 250
LAYTON, Lynne
Brittain (I) 366
LAZAROWICZ, Klaus
Sachs (III) 811
LAZZARO-WEIS, Carol
Guiducci (II) 243; Maraini (III) 95

LEAB, Daniel J.
Vorse (IV) 514
LEBEDOVA, Vira
Kobylyanska (II) 531
LECHLITNER, Ruth
Rukeyser (III) 793
LE CLÉZIO, Marguerite
Hyvrard (II) 393
LEDERER, Katherine
Hellman (II) 318
LEDUC, Violette
Sarraute (IV) 40
LEE, Don L.
Brooks (I) 389
LEE, Hermione
S. Smith (IV) 191; White (IV) 660
LEE, Judith
Barnes (I) 225; Dinesen (I) 688
LEE, Ulysses
M. Walker (IV) 549
LEE-BONANO, Lucy
Alós (I) 98
LEFCOWITZ, Barbara F.
Lessing (II) 713
LEGLER, Philip
Sexton (IV) 115
LEHMANN, John
Sitwell (IV) 160
LEIBOWITZ, Herbert
Stein (IV) 275
LEIDEMANN, Gisela
Mayröcker (III) 140
LEITENBERGER, Ilse
Kaschnitz (II) 486; Kolmar (II) 558; Rinser (III) 746
LEJEUNE, C.-A.
Thirkell (IV) 359
LELAND, Doris
Livesay (II) 776
LEMON, Lee
Piñon (III) 558
LENSING, Leo A.
Keun (II) 506
LENTA, Margaret
Tlali (IV) 380
LEONARD, John
Didion (I) 669; Kingston (II) 522; Morrison (III) 289; Renault (III) 688; R. West (IV) 638
LEONHARDT, Rudolf Walter
Wolf (IV) 705
LERMEN, Birgit Johanna
Mayröcker (III) 142
LE SAGE, Laurent
Duras (I) 770; Mallet-Joris (III) 63
LESEUR, Geta J.
Marshall (III) 108; Shange (IV) 134

LESLIE, Andrew
Bedford (I) 253
LESSING, Doris
Schreiner (IV) 78
LESTER, Julius
Cunard (I) 616; Hansberry (II) 262
LESTER, Neal A.
Shange (IV) 131
LEUNG, K. C.
Ding Ling (I) 701
LEVERTOV, Denise
Sitwell (IV) 162
LEVIANT, Curt
Laurence (II) 640
LEVINE, Linda Gould
Martín Gaite (III) 114; Matute (III) 137; Moix (III) 226, 228; Tusquets (IV) 432
LEVINE, Madeline G.
Koziol (II) 581; Szymborska (IV) 317
LEVINSON, André
Akhmatova (I) 60
LEVINSON, Dierdre
Lessing (II) 718
LEVIS, Larry
Forché (II) 41
LEVITAS, Gloria
Calisher (I) 448
LEVY, Babette May
Jewett (II) 432
LEVY, Bronwen
Hazzard (II) 293
LEWIS, Constance
Compton-Burnett (I) 586
LEWIS, Helena
Triolet (IV) 405
LEWIS, Naomi
Macaulay (III) 26; A. Meynell (III) 172
LEWIS, Paula Gilbert
Roy (III) 790
LEWIS, Sinclair
Vorse (IV) 511; Welty (IV) 618
LEWISOHN, Ludwig
Dane (I) 626; Glaspell (II) 164; Wharton (IV) 643
LEY, Ralph
Fleisser (II) 32, 34
LIBERT, Diana
Desai (I) 660
LIDDELL, Robert
Compton-Burnett (I) 581
LIDOFF, Joan
Stead (IV) 263
LIEBERMAN, Laurence
Garrigue (II) 105; Rukeyser (III) 796

MEYERS, Eunice
  Chacel (I) 513
MICELI-JEFFRIES, Giovanna
  Manzini (III) 89
MICHAELS, Ralph J.
  Espina (I) 825
MICHALSKI, John
  Kolb (II) 547
MICHIE, James
  Warner (IV) 563
MICKELSON, Anne Z.
  Godwin (II) 172; Jong
  (II) 461
MIDDLEBROOK, Diane Wood
  Sexton (IV) 121
MIDDLETON, J. C.
  Sachs (III) 810
MIFOUD, John
  Deledda (I) 650
MIGIEL, Marilyn
  Deledda (I) 643
MIGNONE, Mario B.
  Romano (III) 773
MIHAILOVICH, Vasa D.
  Akhmatova (I) 56; Maksi-
  mović (III) 50
MIHAYCHUK, Goerge
  Kostenko (II) 577
MIKHAIL, Mona
  Bennūna (I) 275
MILANI, Farzaneh
  Farrokhzad (II) 8
MILANO, Paolo
  Morante (III) 262
MILCH, Werner
  Langgässer (II) 614
MILFULL, John
  Seghers (IV) 99
MILLER, Elinor S.
  Sow Fall (IV) 228
MILLER, Jordan Y.
  Hansberry (II) 259
MILLER, Judith Graves
  Sagan (III) 829
MILLER, Lucien
  Chang Ai-ling (I) 517
MILLER, Marilyn Jeanne
  Uno (IV) 476
MILLER, Nina
  Parker (III) 519; Taggard
  (IV) 325
MILLER, R. Baxter
  M. Walker (IV) 553
MILLER, Yvette E.
  Guido (II) 241
MILLS, Ralph J., [Jr.]
  Raine (III) 657; Sexton
  (IV) 114
MILNE, W. A.
  Raine (III) 659
MILOT, Louis
  Brossard (I) 398

MILTON, Edith
  Erdrich (I) 821; Godwin
  (II) 171
MINER, Madonne [M.]
  Morrison (III) 286; Pollock
  (III) 584
MINER, Valerie
  Laurence (II) 641; Tan (IV)
  328; Wang (IV) 560; Ya-
  mamoto (IV) 772
MINH-HA, Trinh T.
  Cardinal (I) 465; Sow Fall
  (IV) 227
MINOR, Anne
  Sarraute (IV) 32
MINTZ, Ruth Finer
  Goldberg (II) 175
MIRSKY, Jonathan
  Wang (IV) 559
MISHLER, William
  Sandel (IV) 24
MISTRI, Zenobia Baxter
  Yamamoto (IV) 774
MITCHAM, Allison
  Roy (III) 789
MITCHELL, Carolyn
  Shange (IV) 128
MITCHELL, Julian
  Lessing (II) 702
MITCHELL, Tony
  Maraini (III) 99
MITCHISON, Amanda
  Drakulić (I) 741
MITGANG, Herbert
  R. West (IV) 637
MITGUTSCH, Waltraud
  Lavant (II) 653
MIYOSHI, Masao
  Tsushima (IV) 410
MIZEJEWSKI, Linda
  Mew (III) 170
MJÖBERG, Jöran
  Peri Rossi (III) 537
MODJESKA, Drusilla
  Dark (I) 636; Devanny (I)
  665; Gilmore (II) 131;
  Prichard (III) 618
MOELLER, Charles
  Weil (IV) 596
MOERS, Ellen
  McCarthy (III) 6
MOHR, Heinrich
  Wolf (IV) 709
MOISÉS, Massaud
  Lispector (II) 767
MOLINA GAVILÁN, Yolanda
  Montero (III) 235
MOLINARI, Nina L.
  Tusquets (IV) 435
MONAS, Sidney
  Panóva (III) 506

MONGA, Luigi
  Corti (I) 605
MONRO, Alida
  Mew (III) 167
MONRO, Harold
  Mew (III) 166; A. Meynell
  (III) 170; Sinclair
  (IV) 153
MONROE, Harriet
  Millay (III) 182; M. Moore
  (III) 237; Wylie (IV) 753
MONSMAN, Gerald
  Schreiner (IV) 84
MONTAGU, Ashley
  Beauvoir (I) 244
MONTANTE, Michela
  Ginzburg (II) 145
MONTHERLANT, Henry de
  Colette (I) 570
MOODY, Jocelyn C.
  Williams (IV) 677
MOON, Samuel
  Atwood (I) 146; Hébert
  (II) 303
MOONEY, Harold J.
  Manning (III) 72
MOORE, Gerald
  Ogot (III) 458
MOORE, Marianne
  Bishop (I) 289; Bryher (I)
  412
MOORE, Patrick
  Bogan (I) 317
MOORE, T. Inglis
  Dark (I) 634
MOOREHEAD, Caroline
  Voznesenskaya (IV) 518
MOORMAN, Charles
  Sayers (IV) 63
MORA, Gabriela
  Allende (I) 87
MORALES, Alejandro
  Villanueva (IV) 494
MORAN, Helen
  Kennedy (II) 502
MORDECAI, Pamela
  Goodison (II) 190
MOREJÓN, Nancy
  Aguirre (I) 24
MORENO, Albrecht
  V. Parra (III) 527
MORIARTY, David J.
  Field and Cooper (II) 27
MORITZEN, Julius
  Lagerlöf (III) 604
MORLEY, Patricia
  Laurence (II) 642
MORPHEUS, G. O.
  Mason (III) 126
MORRIS, Adelaide
  H.D. (I) 722

PACIFICI, Sergio
   Ginzburg (II) 136; Maraini
   (III), 91
PACK, Claus
   Busta (I) 439
PAGE, Ruth
   Kunewicz (II) 583
PALEY, Grace
   Wolf (IV) 723
PALLISER, Janis L
   Maillet (III) 44
PALLOTTA, Augustus
   Maraini (III) 94
PALMER, Paulina
   Carter (I) 472
PAN-AMERICAN Union Bul-
   letin
   Mistral (III) 199
PANAREO, Enzo
   Manzini (III) 89
PANOFSKY, Ruth
   Wiseman (IV) 691
PAQUET, Basil T.
   McCarthy (III) 8
PARAVISINI-GÉBERT,
   Lizabeth
   Capécia (I) 464; Lacrosil
   (II) 592; Manicom (III)
   66
PARENT, Jennifer
   Treadwell (IV) 396
PARINI, Jay
   Rich (III) 712
PARKER, Alice
   Brossard (I) 403
PARKER, Derek
   Sitwell (IV) 161
PARKER, Dorothy
   Frame (II) 49
PARKER, Katherine Gauss
   Taylor (IV) 337
PARKES, Stuart
   Keun (II) 507
PARKIN-GOUNELAS, Ruth
   Schreiner (IV) 83
PARLE, Dennis J.
   Campobello (I) 456
PAROTTI, Phillip
   Portillo de Trambley
   (III) 604
PARRIS, Robert
   Sagan (III) 823
PARSANI, Maria Assunta
   Cespedes (I) 511; Cialente
   (I) 547
PARSONS, Alice Beal
   Undset (IV) 463
PARSONS, Robert A.
   Gámbaro (II) 98
PARTRIDGE, Ralph
   Howard (II) 366

PASQUIER, Marie-Claire
   Benmussa (I) 263
PASTERNAK, Boris
   Tsvetaeva (IV) 414
PATERSON, Janet M.
   Villemaire (IV) 504
PATTEE, Fred Lewis
   Chopin (I) 531
PATTERSON, Yolanda Astarita
   Beauvoir (I) 251
PATTESON, Richard F.
   Senior (IV) 108
PAVEY, Ruth
   Tolstaya (IV) 384; Uno
   (IV) 479
PAYNE, Michael
   Cooper (I) 602
PAZ, Octavio
   Bishop (I) 294
PAZUNIAK, Natalia
   Kostenko (II) 579; Ukrain-
   ka (IV) 455
PEARCE, Donald J.
   Sono (IV) 210
PEDEN, William
   Grau (II) 221; Jackson (II)
   407; Stafford (IV) 248
PEFFER, Nathaniel
   Buck (I) 412
PEIRCE, Jonathan C.
   Livesay (II) 777
PEIXOTO, Marta
   Lispector (II) 769
PELENSKY, Olga Anastasia
   Dinesen (I) 692
PÉREZ, Janet
   Alos (I) 98; Falcón (II) 4;
   Martín Gaite (III) 114;
   Matute (III) 138; Medio
   (III) 150; Moix (III) 230;
   Montero (III) 232; Pardo
   Bazán (III) 512; Quiroga
   (III) 651; Rodoreda (III)
   769; Salisachs (IV) 7; So-
   riano (IV) 223; Zardoya
   (IV) 812
PERLOFF, Marjorie
   Wakoski (IV) 530
PERSIN, Margaret
   Fuertes (II) 78
PESANDO, Frank
   Laurence (II) 640
PETERSEN, Kirsten Holst
   Emecheta (I) 803
PETERSON, Richard
   Lavin (II) 660
PETERSON, Virgilia
   Buck (I) 414; Cespedes (I)
   509; Kunewicz (II) 584;
   Macaulay (III) 27; Sar-
   ton (IV) 48

PETHERICK, Karin
   Boye (I) 354
PETRAKA, Vivian M.
   Hellman (II) 323
PETRÉMONT, Simone
   Weil (IV) 600
PETROV, Pavle
   Bagryana (I) 194
PETRY, Alice Hall
   Tyler (IV) 446
PEYRE, Henri
   Colette (I) 571; Sarraute
   (IV) 33
PEZZINI, Isabella
   Aleramo (I) 70
PFAFF, Françoise
   Sow Fall (IV) 229; Warner-
   Vieyra (IV) 574
PHAF, Ineke
   Condé (I) 589; Schwarz-
   Bart (IV) 86
PHELAN, Peggy
   Shange (IV) 132
PHELPS, Donald
   Sontag (IV) 211
PHELPS, Leland R.
   Kaschnitz (II) 487
PHELPS, Robert
   Stafford (IV) 248; Stein
   (IV) 270
PHILIP, Neil
   Bainbridge (I) 197
PHILIPS, Robert
   Plath (III) 571
PHILLIPS, Elizabeth
   M. Moore (III) 249
PHILLIPS, Julie
   Valenzuela (IV) 486
PHILLIPS, Klaus
   Novak (III) 376
PHILLIPS, Robert
   Weldon (IV) 617
PHILLIPS, Robert L., Jr.
   Welty (IV) 623
PICCHIONE, Luciana
   Marchione
   Ginzburg (II) 137
PICK, F. W.
   Huch (II) 375
PICKENHAYN, Jorge Oscar
   Ibarbourou (IV) 402
PICKERING, Jean
   Brittain (I) 365
PICKREL, Paul
   Laurence (II) 637
PICLARDI, Rosetta D.
   Ginzburg (II) 138
PIERPONT, Claudia Roth
   Barker (I) 218
PIETRALUNGA, Mark F.
   Lagorio (II) 613

PINSKER, Sanford
Ozick (III) 494
PINSKY, Robert
M. Moore (III) 251
PINTO, Mercedes
Ibarbourou (II) 399
PIONTEK, Heinz
Langgässer (II) 616
PIŠA, A. M.
Majerová (III) 45
PIWINSKI, Leon
Nalkowska (III) 330
PIZER, Donald
Wharton (IV) 653
PLOMER, William
Parker (III) 516
PODHORETZ, Norman
McCarthy (III) 2
PODOL, Peter L.
Gámbaro (II) 97
POGGIOLI, Renato
Akhmatova (I) 54; Tsvetae-
va (IV) 413
POHORSKÝ, Miloš
Majerová (III) 46
POLITZER, Heinz
Langgässer (II) 615;
Lasker-Schüler (II) 631;
Lavant (II) 649
POLLARD, Velma
Senior (IV) 105
POLLITT, Katha
Forché (II) 37; Tyler (IV)
442; Weldon (IV) 609
PONIATOWSKA, Elena
Campobello (I) 457;
Castellanos (I) 487; Tra-
ba (IV) 387
POOL, Gail
M. Webb (IV) 585
POPE, Randolph
Rodoreda (III) 770
POPPER, David H.
Smedley (IV) 175
PORTER, Abioseh M.
Njau (III) 362
PORTER, Cathy
Kollontai (II) 553
PORTER, Dennia
Rhys (III) 696
PORTER, Katherine Anne
Boyle (I) 355; Cather (I)
494; Stein (IV) 270; Wel-
ty (IV) 618
POST, Robert M.
Sitwell (IV) 168
POTRIN, Elizabeth
Laurence (II) 648
POTTER, Alicia Rivero
Campos (I) 461
POTTER, Robin
Kogawa (II) 543

POTVIN, Lise
Villemaire (IV) 502
POWELL, Anthony
Sackville-West (III) 819
POWELL, Dilys
Sitwell (IV) 157
POWELL, Violet
Kennedy (II) 503
POWER, Jim
M. Loy (II) 807
POWYS, J. D.
D. Richardson (III) 718
POZZATO, Maria Pia
Aleramo (I) 69
PRASAD, Hari Mohar
Naidu (III) 328
PRASAD, Madhusudan
Desai (I) 659
PRATT, Linda Ray
Le Sueur (II) 726
PREECE, Harold
Le Sueur (II) 724
PRESCOTT, Peter S.
Le Guin (II) 681; Ozick
(III) 489; A. Walker (IV)
540
PRESTON, John Hyde
Millay (III) 182; Stein (IV)
269
PRICE, Martin
Ashton-Warner (I) 133; Jel-
licoe (II) 420
PRICE, Paola Malpezzi
Cialente (I) 547
PRICE, Reynolds
Welty (IV) 623
PRIESTLEY, J. B.
Mitchison (III) 210
PRITCHARD, William H.
McCarthy (III) 7
PRITCHETT, V. S.
Colette (I) 571; Somerville
and Ross (IV) 202; R.
West (IV) 631; Wright
(IV) 748
PROSE, Francine
Drakulić (I) 742
PROTIĆ, Predrag
Parun (III) 531
PRUETTE, Lorine
McCarthy (III) 1
PRUSKA-CARROLL, Mal-
gorzata
Kossak (II) 569;
Pawlikowska-Jasnor-
zewska (III) 535
PRYSE, Marjorie
Petry (III) 547
PUGH, Edwin
M. Webb (IV) 580
PUMPHREY, Martin
S. Smith (IV) 192

PUNTER, David
Carter (I) 471
PURCELL, Patricia
Hébert (II) 303
PUTZEL, Steven
Watson (IV) 578
PYLE, Marian S.
L'Engle (II) 698

QUACH, Gìanna
Buck (I) 416
QUIELLO, Rose
K. O'Brien (III) 428
QUIGLEY, Ellen
Thomas (IV) 365
QUIGLEY, Isabel
Ginzburg (II) 135; Johnson
444; Stern (IV) 282
QUINLAN, Susan Canty
Luft (II) 815
QUINN, Arthur H[obson]
Chopin (I) 532; Glasgow
(II) 155; Jewett (II) 431
QUINN, Kerker
Rukeyser (III) 791
QUINTON, Anthony
Spark (IV) 233

RABAN, Jonathan
Murdoch (III) 316; Spark
(IV) 238
RABASSA, Gregory
Lispector (II) 762;
Meireles (III) 156
RABINOWITZ, Dorothy
Jhabvala (II) 438
RABINOWITZ, Paula
Smedley (IV) 179
RADDATZ, Fritz J.
Seghers (IV) 98
RADFORD, Jean
Hall (II) 252; D. Richard-
son (III) 725
RAGAN, Brian Abel
O'Connor (III) 447
RAGO, Henry
Garrigue (II) 103; Stafford
(IV) 246; Taggard (IV)
324
RAGUE-ARÍAS, Maria-José
Falcón (II) 1
AL-RĀHIB, HANI
al-Sammān (IV) 9
RAHMAN, Anisur
Das (II) 638
RAHMAN, Tariq
Sidhwa (IV) 138
RAHV, Philip
Boyle (I) 357
RAINE, Kathleen
Barnes (I) 221; Ridler (III)
739

RAINWATER, Catherine
  Erdrich (I) 822; Hazzard
  (II) 289; Redmon (III)
  679, 680
RAMCHAND, Kenneth
  Allfrey (I) 92
RAMÍREZ, Arthur
  Portillo del Trambley (III)
  602
RAMOS, Luis Arturo
  Hoyos (II) 370
RAMOS FOSTER, Virginia
  Gámbaro (II) 95
RANG, Bernhard
  Langgässer (II) 616
RANKIN, Daniel
  Chopin (I) 531
RANNIT, Aleksis
  Under (IV) 456, 461
RAO, B. Ramachandra
  Desai (I) 654
RAO, K. Bhaskara
  Rama Rau (III) 661
RAO, P. Mallikarjuna
  Das (I) 641
RAOUL, Valérie
  Dessaulles (I) 662
RAPHAEL, Lev
  Wharton (IV) 653
RAPPING, Elayne
  Wolf (IV) 715
RATNER, Rochelle
  Rose (III) 776; Wakoski
  (IV) 533
RATTÉ, John
  Weil (IV) 598
RAUENHORST, Doris
  Kolb (II) 547
RAVEN, Simon
  Brophy (I) 395
RAVENSCROFT, Arthur
  Head (II) 295
RAVITS, Martha
  Robinson (III) 755
RAYMOND, John
  Bottome (I) 328; Sayers
  (IV) 62
R.E.
  Kaschnitz (II) 488
REAGAN, Stephen
  Gallant (II) 90
REAY, C. J.
  Aidoo (I) 40
RECK, Rima Drell
  Mallet-Joris (III) 60
REDDING, Saunders
  Hansberry (II) 257
REDEKOP, Margaret
  Munro (III) 307
REDMOND, James
  Norman (III) 373

REED, Henry
  Mitford (III) 215; Renault
  (III) 684
REED, J. D.
  Blume (I) 308
REED, Mary Jane
  Hill (II) 345
REES, Richard
  Weil (IV) 597, 600
REEVE, F. D.
  Waddington (IV) 525
REGAN, Robert
  Wakoski (IV) 527
REGIER, Gail
  Baranskaya (I) 214
REICHARDT, Mary P.
  Freeman (II) 71
REICH-RANICKI, Marcel
  Rinser (III) 745; Wohmann
  (IV) 701
REID, B. L.
  Stein (IV) 271
REID, Margaret A.
  Ogot (III) 459
REID, Martine
  Hyvrard (II) 396
REINIG, Christa
  Domin (I) 710
RENNERT, Maggie
  Drexler (I) 750
RENNISON, Lucinda
  Roth (III) 779
REXROTH, Kenneth
  Levertov (II) 733; M.
  Moore (III) 245; Weil
  (IV) 598
REYNOLDS, Lorna
  Lavin (II) 656; K. O'Brien
  (III) 427
REYNOLDS, William
  Sayers (IV) 66
RHODES, Carolyn
  Godwin (II) 174
RHODES, H. Winston
  Ashton-Warner (I) 134
RICCIARDELLI, M.
  Ortese (III) 481
RICE, Philip Blair
  Millay (III) 183; Porter
  (III) 593; Rukeyser (III)
  791
RICHARDS, Sandra L.
  Shange (IV) 127
RICHARDSON, Maurice
  Castellanos (I) 481;
  Cespedes (I) 509
RICHART, Bette
  Millay (III) 185; M. Moore
  (III) 239
RICHTER, Harvena
  Woolf (IV) 730

RICKS, Christopher
  Oates (III) 393; Stead (IV)
  261
RICOU, Laurie
  Thomas (IV) 367
RIDGEWAY, Jacqueline
  Bogan (I) 316
RIDLER, Anne
  Raine (III) 656
RIEMER, A. P.
  Jolley (II) 458
RIGGAN, William
  Guidacci (II) 236
RIGNEY, Barbara [Hill]
  Arnow (I) 130; Atwood (I)
  158
RISUKO, Dorothy
  Yamamoto (IV) 771
ROBBE-GRILLET, Alain
  Sarraute (IV) 35
ROBERT, Lucie
  Villemaire (IV) 501
ROBERTS, Brian
  Lehmann (II) 691
ROBERTS, David
  Stafford (IV) 252
ROBERTS, Michèle
  Lessing (II) 720
ROBERTS, R. E.
  Macaulay (III) 24
ROBERTS, Rosemary A.
  Zhang Jie (IV) 818; Zhang
  Xinxin (IV) 825
ROBERTS, Sheila
  Joubert (II) 476; P. Smith
  (IV) 182
ROBERTSON, Robert T.
  Frame (II) 52
ROBILLARD, Douglas
  Jameson (II) 412
ROBINSON, Hilary
  Somerville and Ross
  (IV) 208
ROBINSON, Jean Hardy
  Gennari (II) 118
ROBINSON, Lillian S.
  Atwood (I) 160; Gilman
  (II) 127; O. Moore (III)
  255; Olsen (III) 474;
  Wharton (IV) 655; Woolf
  (IV) 731, 743; Young
  (IV) 798
ROCAWICH, Linda
  Drakulić (I) 740
ROCKS, James E.
  C. Gordon (II) 207
RODGERS, Carolyn M.
  A. Walker (IV) 534
RODKER, John
  M. Loy (II) 800

RODMAN, Selden
  Castellanos (I) 481; Gar-
    rigue (II) 103
RODRIGUEZ, Fermin
  Alós (I) 99
RODRIGUEZ, Mercedes M. de
  Chacel (I) 515
ROE, Sue
  Woolf (IV) 742
ROETHKE, Theodore
  Bogan (I) 315
ROGERS, Gerhild Brug-
  germann
  Drewitz (I) 749
ROGERS, Katherine M.
  Serao (IV) 112
ROGERS, Michael
  Stark (IV) 255
ROGERS, Thomas
  McCarthy (III) 4
ROGERS, W. G.
  Buck (I) 415; Stein (IV)
    269
ROJAS, Margarita
  Ibarbourou (II) 403
ROLO, Charles [J.]
  Grau (I) 222; McCarthy
    (III) 3; Nin (III) 354;
    Rochefort (III) 757
ROMERO, Christiane Zahl
  Wolf (IV) 717
ROMERO, Lora
  Moraga (III) 261
ROMINES, Ann
  Wilder (IV) 671
RÓNAI, Paulo
  Meireles (III) 153; Queiroz
    (III) 644
RONCONI, Enzo
  Cederna (I) 499
RONSLEY, Joseph
  Gregory (II) 234
ROOKE, Constance
  Gallant (II) 88; Munro (III)
    302
ROSE, Ellen Cronan
  Drabble (I) 732
ROSE, Jacqueline
  Plath (III) 578
ROSE, Paulette
  Franklin (II) 62
ROSENBAUM, Jean
  Piercy (III) 551
ROSENBAUM, Sidonia
  Carmen
  Ibarbourou (II) 400; Storni
    (IV) 287
ROSENBERG, Dorothy
  Morgenstern (III) 272; Mor-
    gner (III) 278
ROSENBERG, Harold
  Rukeyser (III) 791

ROSENBERG, Judith
  Lispector (II) 772
ROSENBERGER, Coleman
  Grau (I) 222; Wilson (IV)
    681
ROSENBLATT, Jon
  Plath (III) 577
ROSENFELD, Alvin
  Sachs (III) 815
ROSENFELD, Isaac
  McCarthy (III) 2; Nin (III)
    353; O'Connor (III) 436
ROSENFELD, Marthe
  Wittig (IV) 696
ROSENFELD, Paul
  Nin (III) 353; Porter (III)
    592
ROSENFELD, Sidney
  Lasker-Schüler (II) 634;
    Novak (III) 380
ROSENFELT, Deborah
  Olsen (III) 468
ROSENSTREICH, Susan L.
  Hébert (II) 309
ROSENTHAL, David H.
  Rodoreda (III) 764
ROSENTHAL, Lucy
  Calisher (I) 451; Plath (III)
    569
ROSENTHAL, Michael
  Brophy (I) 395
ROSENTHAL, M. L.
  Levertov (II) 733; Sexton
    (IV) 113, 114
ROSENWALD, Henry M.
  Huch (II) 376
ROSES, Lorraine Elena
  Vilalta (IV) 491
ROSKIES, D. M.
  Ty-Casper (IV) 439
ROSKOLENKO, Harry
  Garrigue (II) 103
Ross, Alan
  Maraini (III) 92; Plath (III)
    566
Ross, Mary
  Mallet-Joris (III) 59; Roy
    (III) 781
Ross, Robert L.
  Astley (I) 143; Millin (III)
    195
ROSSEL, Sven H[akon]
  Brøgger (I) 374; Chris-
    tensen (I) 540; M.
    Larsen (II) 619; Schoultz
    (IV) 74
ROSSLYN, Weny
  Akhmatova (I) 58
ROTELLA, Guy
  Bishop (I) 295
ROTH, Philip
  E. O'Brien (III) 419

ROTHENBERG, Jerome H.
  Atwood (I) 148
ROTHENSTEIN, William
  Field and Cooper (II) 26
ROTHMAN, Nathan L.
  Boyle (I) 357; Yezierska
    (IV) 781
ROUDIEZ, Leon S.
  Sarraute (IV) 33
ROUSE, Blair
  Glasgow (II) 157
ROWBOTHAM, Sheila
  Kollontai (II) 551
ROWSELL, Mary Dalton
  Compton-Burnett (I) 585
ROYER, Catherine
  Suckow (IV) 297
RUAS, Charles
  Young (IV) 798
RUBENSTEIN, Roberta
  Atwood (I) 154; Lessing
    (II) 716
RUBIN, Louis D., [Jr.]
  Glasgow (II) 157, 159;
    McCullers (III) 19;
    O'Connor (III) 437
RUBIN, Martin
  Millin (III) 192
RUBULIS, Aleksis
  Under (IV) 458
RUDDICK, Lisa
  Stein (IV) 279
RUEHL, Sonja
  Hall (I) 254
RÜHLE, Jürgen
  Seghers (IV) 98
RUIHLEY, Glenn Richard
  Lowell (II) 798
RUKEYSER, Muriel
  Sexton (IV) 116
RUMENS, Carol
  Bainbridge (I) 198; Warner
    (IV) 566
RUNNING, Thorpe
  Pizarnik (III) 563
RUPP, Richard H.
  O'Connor (III) 441
RUPPERT, James [Jim]
  Allen (I) 80; Silko (IV) 144
RUSHDYM, Ashraf H. A.
  Williams (IV) 679
RUSSELL, Delbert W.
  Hébert (II) 308
RUSSELL, Dora Isella
  Ibarbourou (II) 402
RUSTAMJI-KERNS, Rashni
  Mukherjee (III) 294; Rama
    Rao (III) 662
RYAN, Joan
  K. O'Brien (III) 425
RYAN, J. S.
  Wright (IV) 749

SCHOLZ, Albert
Rinser (III) 746
SCHOOLFIELD, George [C.]
Jansson (II) 416, 419;
Schoultz (IV) 72, 75;
Södergran (IV) 196;
Thorup (IV) 374, 376
SCHORER, Mark
Didion (I) 670; Hellman
(II) 316
SCHORETITS, Kasper
Drewitz (I) 745
SCHOTT, Webster
Morrison (III) 284
SCHRADE, Arlene O.
Naranjo (III) 335
SCHÜCKING, Levin Ludwig
Huch (II) 373
SCHULER, Catherine A.
Fornés (II) 48
SCHWACHHOFER, René
Domin (I) 709
SCHWARTZ, Ronald
Matute (III) 136; Medio
(III) 146; Quiroga (III)
649
SCHWARZ, Robert
Lavant (II) 651
SCHWEDHELM, Karl
Sachs (III) 811
SCHYFTER, Sara E.
Moix (III) 225
SCOBIE, Stephen
P. Webb (IV) 593
SCOTT, Ann
Schreiner (IV) 81
SCOTT, Bonnie Kime
R. West (IV) 642
SCOTT, Marilyn
Busta (I) 441, 442
SCOTT-JAMES, R. A.
Pitter (III) 560; Raine (III)
655; D. Richardson (III)
718; S. Smith (IV) 184
SCOTT-JAMES, Violet
Holtby (II) 357
SCOTT-KILVERT, Ian
Manning (III) 71
SEABROOK, W. B.
N. Larsen (II) 622
SEABURY, Marcia Bundy
M. Gordon (II) 214
SEATOR, Lynette
Cervantes (I) 503
SECONDARI, John H.
Cespedes (I) 510
SEDGWICK, Eve Kosofsky
Miles (III) 179
SEELYE, John
Piercy (III) 549
SEIDENSTICKER, Edward
Gotō (II) 218

SEIDLER, Victor J.
Weil (IV) 604
SELDEN, Kyoko Iriye
Hayashi (II) 284; Hirabay-
ashi (II) 348; Ōba (III)
407
SELVA, Mauricio de la
Castellanos (I) 480
SEMRAU, Eberhard
Seghers (IV) 97
SÉNART, Philippe
Duras (I) 770
SENSIBAR, Judith L.
Wharton (IV) 655
S.E.R.
Waddington (IV) 523
SERGEANT, Elizabeth
Shepley
Lowell (II) 794
SERGEANT, Howard
S. Smith (IV) 185
SERKE, Jürgen
Ausländer (I) 164
SERVODIDIO, Mirella [d'Am-
brosio]
Tusquets (IV) 430, 431
SETHURAMAN, Ramchandran
Markandaya (III) 105
SETTERWALL, Monica
Lagerlöf (II) 609
SEXTON, Anne
Plath (III) 567
SEYLAZ, Jean-Luc
Duras (I) 771
SFAMURRI, Antonio
Weil (IV) 599
SHACKFORD, Martha H.
Jewett (II) 429
SHAHANE, Vasant A.
Jhabvala (II) 440
SHAHANI, Ranjee G.
Pitter (III) 559
SHAKTINI, Namascar
Wittig (IV) 694
SHANKS, Edward
Mansfield (III) 76; V.
Meynell (III) 173; Stern
(IV) 281
SHANNON, Anna W.
Burke (I) 428
SHAPIRO, Charles
Oates (III) 398
SHAPIRO, Paula Meinetz
A. Walker (IV) 535
SHARISTANIAN, Janet
Slesinger (IV) 172
SHARONI, Edna
Raab (III) 654
SHAVIRO, Steven
Young (IV) 797
SHELBY, J. Townsend
Matute (III) 136

SHEPARD, Brooks
P. Smith (IV) 180
SHEPHERD, Wilfred
M. Webb (IV) 583
SHEPPARD, Robert
Fell (II) 18
SHERIDAN, Susan
Stead (IV) 266
SHERMA, R. S.
Desai (I) 655
SHERMAN, Stuart
Glasgow (II) 155
SHERNO, Sylvia
Fuertes (II) 79, 80, 81
SHETLEY, Vernon
Erdrich (I) 818
SHEVCHUK, Hryhoryy
Teliha (IV) 349
SHINODA, Seishi
Yosano Akiko (IV) 787
SHIRLEY, Carl R.
Castillo (I) 489; Cervantes
(I) 508; Villanueva (IV)
498
SHIRLEY, Paula W.
Castillo (I) 489; Cervantes
(I) 508; Villanueva (IV)
498
SHIVERS, Alfred S.
J. West (IV) 628
SHOHET, Linda
Roy (III) 788
SHOPTAW, John
Dove (I) 728
SHORTT, Barbara
Hareven (II) 267
SHRAPNEL, Norman
Brooke-Rose (I) 375; Man-
ning (III) 69; Morante
(III) 263
SHULMAN, Alix Kates
Goldman (II) 180
SHUYING, Tsau
Xiao Hong (IV) 766
SIEGEL, Carol
M. Webb (IV) 587
SIEGLE, Robert
Acker (I) 6, 9
SIEHS, Karl
Kobylyanska (II) 532
SIEVERS, W. David
Treadwell (IV) 395
SILVA, Clara
Agustini (I) 28
SILVER, Brenda
Woolf (IV) 744
SIMON, John
Dike (I) 676; Henley (II)
326
SIMONS, John H.
O'Connor (III) 435

TRUESDALE, C. W.
  Silko (IV) 146
TSANEVA, Milena
  Bagryana (I) 192
TSUKIMURA, Reiko
  Gotō (II) 218
TSURATA, Kinya
  Hayashi (II) 285
TUBE, Henry
  Brooke-Rose (I) 376
TUCKER, Martin
  Murdoch (III) 313; Schreiner (IV) 78
TUOHIMAA, Sinikka
  Anhava (I) 113
TURCOTTE, Gerry
  K. Walker (IV) 548
TUREČEK, Otto
  Benešová (I) 259
TURK, Nadia
  Djébar (I) 708
TURNER, Darwin
  Hurston (II) 385
TURNER, Harriet
  Mistral (III) 210
TURNER, Margaret E.
  Watson (IV) 578
TUTTLETON, James W.
  Wharton (IV) 647
TYLER, Anne
  Brookner (I) 381; Paley (III) 501
TYNAN, Katharine
  Macaulay (III) 22
TYNAN, Kenneth
  Hansberry (II) 254

UEDA, Makata
  Hirabayashi (II) 348
UGUALDE, Sharon Keefe
  Atencia (I) 145
ULLMAN, Leslie
  Harjo (II) 270
UMEH, Marie Linton
  Emecheta (I) 801
UMPIERRE, Luz Maria
  Burgos (I) 421; Esteves (I) 828; Ferre (II) 22; Fuertes (II) 75
UNIVERSITY of Toronto Quarterly
  P. Webb (IV) 591
UNKNOWN
  Thorup (IV) 370
UNRUE, Darlene Harbour
  Porter (III) 600
UNTERMEYER, Louis
  Lowell (II) 796; Rukeyser (III) 792; Teasdale (IV) 343; Wickham (IV) 665

UPDIKE, John
  Jong (II) 459; Stead (IV) 262
URBANO, Victoria
  Naranjo (III) 333
URGO, Joseph R.
  Burke (I) 431
URQUHART, Fred
  Manning (III) 68

VÁCLAVEK, Bedřich
  Majerová (III) 45; Pujmanová (III) 628
VALDES-CRUZ, Rosa
  Cabrera (I) 445
VALENTE, Luis Fernando
  Ribeiro Tavares (III) 705
VALERA, Juan
  Pardo Bazán (III) 510
VALLBONA, Rima [R.] de
  Odio (III) 448; Oreamuno (III) 478
VALLIS, Val
  Wright (IV) 750
VAN DALE, Laura B.
  O'Faolain (III) 457
VANDE KIEFT, Ruth M.
  O'Connor (III) 441
VANDEN HEUVEL, Katrina
  Baranskaya (I) 213
VAN DOREN, Carl
  Jewett (II) 431; Wylie (IV) 755; Yezierska (IV) 779
VAN DOREN, Mark
  Bogan (I) 313; Dinesen (I) 684; Parker (III) 516; Teasdale (IV) 344; Undset (IV) 467; Wickham (IV) 666
VAN DUYN, Mona
  Atwood (I) 147; Rich (III) 709; Sarton (IV) 49; Sexton (IV) 115
VAN DYKE, Annette
  Allen (I) 82
VAN DYNE, Susan R.
  Plath (III) 579
VAN GELDER, Lawrence
  Owens (III) 486
VANSITTART, Peter
  O'Faolain (III) 451; Renault (III) 688
VAN VUUREN, Helize
  Stockenström (IV) 286
VARDI, Dov
  Hareven (II) 266
VARGAS, Yamila Azize
  Esteves (I) 830
VÁSQUEZ ZAMORA, Rafael
  Laforet (II) 597
VAUPOTIĆ, Miroslav
  Parun (III) 531

VENDLER, Helen
  Bishop (I) 294; Oates (III) 397; Rich (III) 710; Sexton (IV) 119
VENKATESWARAN, Shyamala
  Markandaya (III) 101
VENSKE, Regula
  Plessen (III) 581
VERNON, Victoria V.
  Hayashi (II) 288; Sata (IV) 60
VERTREACE, Martha M.
  Bambara (I) 206
VETÖ, Miklos
  Weil (IV) 599
VEZZETTI, Anacleta Candida
  Deledda (I) 651
VICKERY, Olga W.
  Stafford (IV) 248
VIDAL, Gore
  McCullers (III) 14; Renault (III) 687
VIERECK, Peter
  Tsvetaeva (IV) 415
VILARIÑO, Idea
  Silva (IV) 147
VILLA PASTUR, J.
  Laforet (II) 596
VILLEGAS, Juan
  Quiroga (III) 648
VILLEGAS, Maruja González
  Ibarbourou (II) 401
VIRGILLO, C.
  Mistral (III) 209
VIRGINIA Quarterly Review
  McCarthy (III) 7
VITALE, Ida
  Ibarbourou (II) 401
VITIER, Cintio
  Aguirre (I) 22
VITTORINI, Domenico
  Deledda (I) 651
VIVAS, Eliseo
  Espina (I) 824
VON HERIK, Judith
  Weil (IV) 602
VON LUHE, Irmela
  Bachmann (I) 188
VORSE, Mary Heaton
  Herbst (II) 330

WADDINGTON, Miriam
  Blais (I) 301
WADE, Michael
  Gordimer (II) 198
WADE, Rosalind
  Lessing (II) 714
WAELTI-WALTERS, Jennifer
  Hyvrard (II) 394
WAGENKNECHT, Edward
  Cather (I) 499